THE ENCYCLOPEDIA OF

Sexual Behavior

THE ENCYCLOPEDIA OF

EDITED BY

ALBERT ELLIS AND ALBERT ABARBANEL

Sexual Behavior

JASON ARONSON, INC. • BOOK PUBLISHERS • NEW YORK

Contributors

ALBERT BRANDT ABARBANEL, PH.D. Psychotherapist, Marriage Counselor, New York City. Formerly Graduate Assistant, Universities of Marburg and Würzburg. Assistant, International Congress for Sexual Reform (Berlin); World League for Sexual Reform (Copenhagen); Research Associate, Institute for Sexual Science (Berlin, Dr. Magnus Hirschfeld); Lecturer, Volkshochschule (Frankfurt am Main); Professor of Philosophy and Social Science, Dana College, University of Newark; Lecturer, New Jersey School of Social Work, Hunter College, Queens College. Author: Many published monographs and articles in the field of sexology, psychology, philosophy, and sociology; *Der Wille zur Arbeit*, 1930. Co-author: *An Assault on Civilization*,[1] 1935; *What Every Woman Should Know About Marriage*, 1950.

CLIFFORD ALLEN, M.D., M.R.C.P., D.P.M. Honorary Consultant Psychiatrist to the Seamen's Hospitals, London; Consultant Neuro-Psychiatrist to the Ministry of Pensions, London. Author: *Modern Discoveries in Medical Psychology*, 1949; *Sexual Perversions and Abnormalities*, 1951; *Homosexuality*, 1958; *The Problem of Homosexuality*, 1958; *A Textbook of Psychosexual Abnormalities*, 1962; *Les Déviations Sexuelles*, 1963; Contributions to *Encyclopaedia Britannica*, 1962.

CARLTON BEALS, M.A. Authority on Latin America. Author: *Mexican Maze*, 1931; *American South*, 1937; *Lands of the Dawning Morrow*, 1947; *House in Mexico*, 1958; *Eagles of the Andes*, 1963; *Latin America: World in Revolution*, 1963.

HUGO G. BEIGEL, PH.D. Private practice in counseling personal and sexological problems. Formerly Associate Professor of Psychology, Long Island University. Author: "Romantic Love,"[2] 1951; *Encyclopedia of Sex Education*, 1952; "Sex and Human Beauty," 1954; "Body Height in Mate Selection," 1954; "Evaluation of Intelligence in the Heterosexual Relationship," 1957; *Sex from A to Z*, 1961; *Advances in Sex Research* (Editor), 1963.

1 Italic type denotes book title.
2 Quotations indicate articles.

HARRY BENJAMIN, M.D. Private practice specializing in geriatrics and sexology, New York City and San Francisco. Formerly Consulting Endocrinologist to the College of the City of New York. Author: "Prostitution and Venereal Disease," 1935; "The Sex Problem in the Armed Forces," 1943; "Prostitution Reassessed," 1951; "An Objective Examination of Prostitution," 1954; "Transsexualism and Transvestism," 1954.

JESSIE BERNARD, PH.D. Professor of Sociology, Pennsylvania State University. Author: *American Family Behavior*, 1942; *American Community Behavior*, 1949; *Remarriage*, 1956; *Social Problems at Midcentury*, 1957; (with Buchanan and Smith) *Dating, Mating, and Marriage*, 1958; "The Adjustments of Married Mates," *Handbook on Marriage and the Family*, 1964; *Academic Women*, 1964.

CYRIL BIBBY, M.A., M.Sc., PH.D., F.L.S., F.R.S.A. Principal, Kingston upon Hull College of Education. Formerly Secretary of the Family Relations Group. Author: Many books on biology and education and *Sex Education, a Guide for Parents, Teachers and Youth Leaders*, 1944; *How Life is Handed On*, 1946.

SAUL BLAU, M.D. Assistant Clinical Professor in Dermatology and Syphilology, New York University Medical Center. Author: "Dermabrasion," 1954; "Erythroplasia," 1955; "Syphilis," 1958.

EWALD BOHM, PH.D. Private practice of clinical psychology, Copenhagen, Denmark; Vice-President, International Society of Rorschach and other Projective Techniques. Author: (with Magnus Hirschfeld) *Sexualerziehung*, 1930; *Lehrbuch der Rorschach Psychodiagnostik*, 1957; *A Textbook in Rorschach Test Diagnosis*, 1958; *Psychodiagnostisches Vademecum*, 1960.

RALPH P. BRIDGMAN, B.D., M.A. Formerly Chief Marriage Counselor, Family Court Center, Toledo, Ohio. Formerly Executive Director, National Council of Parent Education; Acting Chairman of Family Life Department, Merrill-Palmer School. Author: "Parent Education," 1934; "Family Counsel," 1935; "The Home and Family Relations," 1939; "Marital Discord, Divorce and Reconciliation," 1958.

v

DANIEL G. BROWN, PH.D. Clinical Psychologist, United States Air Force Hospital, 815th Medical Group (SAC), Forbes Air Force Base, Kansas. Formerly Associate Professor of Psychology, United States Air Force Academy. Author: "Sex-Role Preference in Young Children," 1956; "The Development of Sex-Role Inversion and Homosexuality," 1957; "Masculinity-Femininity Development in Children," 1957; "Sex-Role Development in a Changing Culture," 1958; "Homosexuality and Family Dynamics," 1963.

FRANK S. CAPRIO, M.D. Psychiatrist in private practice, Washington, D.C. Consultant to the Department of Correction, Washington, D.C.; Consultant to the U.S. Post Office in matters of obscenity; Honorary Fellow of American Medical Authors. Author: *Sexual Deviations*, 1951; *The Power of Sex*, 1952; *The Sexually Adequate Male*, 1952; *The Sexually Adequate Female*, 1953; *Marital Infidelity*, 1953; *Female Homosexuality*, 1954; *Variations in Sexual Behavior*, 1955; *Sex and Love*, 1958; *The Modern Woman's Guide to Sexual Maturity*, 1959.

LEO P. CHALL, M.A. Instructor at Brooklyn College; Editor of *Sociological Abstracts;* President, Sociological Abstracts, Inc. Author: "The Reception of the Kinsey Report in the Periodicals of the United States, 1947–1949," 1955; "Determinants of Human Sexual Behavior: An Attempt at Descriptive Integration," 1963.

EUSTACE CHESSER, L.R.C.P., L.R.C.S. (Edinburgh), L.R.F.P.S. (Glasgow). Honorary Secretary, Society for Sex Education and Guidance; member: Medico-Legal Council, Abortion Law Reform Association, Royal Medico-Psychological Society, Association for Advancement of Psychotherapy, British Executive Committee International Union of Family Organizations, Society for Study of Addiction, International Committee for Sexual Equality, Amsterdam Medical Council Research Direction, Research Council into Marriage and Human Relationships. Author: *Love Without Fear*, 1941; *Successful Living*, 1950; *How to Make a Success of Your Marriage*, 1954; *Sexual, Marital and Family Relationships of the English Woman*, 1956; *Live and Let Live*, 1958; *An Outline of Human Relationships*, 1960; *Women and Love*, 1963.

LEMON CLARK, M.D. Private practice of obstetrics and gynecology, Fayetteville, Arkansas; Correspondence Editor for *Sexology* Magazine. Formerly Instructor in Social Science at Cornell and Colgate Universities and a Minister of the Universalist Church. Author: *Sex Education*, 1928; *Emotional Adjustment in Marriage*, 1937; *Sex and You*, 1949.

ALPHONSE H. CLEMENS, PH.D. Associate Professor of Sociology and Director of the Marriage Counseling Center, Catholic University of America; Consultant to Family Life Bureau of the National Catholic Welfare Conference; Consultant to the Bulletin of the Guild of Catholic Psychiatrists. Author: *Marriage and Family Relationships* (Editor), 1950; *Marriage Education and Counseling* (Editor), 1951; *Survey of the Cana Movement in the United States*, 1953; *Marriage and the Family: An Integrated Approach for Catholics*, 1955; *Marriage Counseling Inventory*, 1959; *Marriage Counseling: A Catholic Approach*, 1960.

WILLIAM GRAHAM COLE, PH.D. President of Lake Forest College. Author: *Sex in Christianity and Psychoanalysis*, 1955; *Sex and Love in the Bible*, 1959.

ROBERT C. COOK. President, Population Reference Bureau; Editor, *Population Bulletin*. Author: *Human Fertility: The Modern Dilemma*, 1951.

GEORGE W. CORNER, JR., M.D. Assistant Professor of Obstetrics, Johns Hopkins University; private practice of gynecology and obstetrics, Baltimore; Special Consultant on cerebral palsy, National Institute of Mental Health. Author: Many papers on obstetrics and gynecology and menstruation, including: "The Dating of Ovulation and Other Ovarian Crises by Histological Examination," 1950; "Torsion of the Human Pregnant Uterus," 1956; and "Endocrine Factors in the Etiology of Spontaneous Abortion," 1959.

DONALD WEBSTER CORY. Author: *The Homosexual in America*, 1951. Editor: *Twenty-one Variations on a Theme*, 1953; *Homosexuality: A Cross-Cultural Approach*, 1959; co-author, *The Homosexual and His Society*, 1963.

ALEC CRAIG. Author: *Sex and Revolution*, 1934; *The Banned Books of England*, 1937; *Above All Liberties*, 1942; *The Banned Books of England and Other Countries*, 1962; *Suppressed Books*, 1963.

BENGT DANIELSSON, PH.D. Associate in Anthropology, Bernice P. Bishop Museum, Honolulu. Author: Several travel books; *Love in the South Seas*, 1956; *Work and Life on Raroia*, 1957.

KINGSLEY DAVIS, PH.D. Professor of Sociology, University of California; Director, International Population and Urban Research; Past President, American Sociological Association; Past President, Population Association of America; Chairman, Section K, American Association for the Advancement of Science. Author: *Human Society*, 1949; *Population of India and Pakistan*, 1951; *The World's Metropolitan Areas*, 1959.

LESTER W. DEARBORN, B.S. Counseling Psychologist certified by Massachusetts Psychological Association, Director, Marriage Counseling Service, Boston Y.M.C.A., Lecturer, Northeastern University. Author: "Some Psychophysical Phenomena Conditioning Marital Adjustment," 1946; "Preparation of the Marriage Counselor," 1946; "Masturbation," 1947; "Extramarital Relations," 1947; "Problem of Masturbation," 1952.

EDWARD DENGROVE, M.D. Private Practice of Neuropsychiatry, West Allenhurst, N.J.; Consultant in Psychiatry and Neurology at the Monmouth Medical

Center and the Point Pleasant Hospital. Author: "War Weariness," 1945; "Psychosomatic Aspects of Dermographia and Pruritus," 1947; "Why Patients Discontinue Treatment in Mental Hygiene Clinics," 1950; "The Psychiatrist," 1957; "Self-Administering Eye Dropper and Irrigator," 1959; "A New Letter-Association Technique," 1962; "Sexual Disorder in Post-concussional and Post-traumatic States," 1963.

SIDNEY DITZION, PH.D. Assistant Librarian and Lecturer in Education, The City College of New York. Author: *Arsenals of a Democratic Culture*, 1947; *Marriage, Morals and Sex in America*, 1953.

WINSTON EHRMANN, PH.D. Professor of Sociology, University of Colorado. Author: Many articles on sex, marriage, and family research; *Premarital Dating Behavior*, 1959.

ALBERT ELLIS, PH.D. Private practice of psychotherapy and marriage counseling, New York City. Formerly Chief Psychologist, New Jersey State Diagnostic Center and New Jersey Department of Institutions and Agencies. Editor: (with A. P. Pillay) *Sex, Society and the Individual*, 1953; *Sex Life of the American Woman and the Kinsey Report*, 1954. Author: Many scientific papers and several books and monographs; *The Folklore of Sex*, 1951; *The American Sexual Tragedy*, 1954; (with Ralph Brancale) *The Psychology of Sex Offenders*, 1956; *How to Live with a Neurotic*, 1957; *Sex Without Guilt*, 1958; *The Art and Science of Love*, 1960 (with Robert A. Harper); *Creative Marriage*, 1961; (with Robert Harper) *A Guide to Rational Living*, 1961; *Reason and Emotion in Psychotherapy*, 1962; *If This Be Sexual Heresy . . .* , 1963; *Sex and the Single Man*, 1963; *The Intelligent Woman's Guide to Manhunting*, 1963; (with Edward Sagarin) *Nymphomania: A Study of the Oversexed Woman*, 1964.

IRVING C. FISCHER, M.D., F.A.C.S. Assistant Clinical Professor, Obstetrics and Gynecology, New York Medical College; Staff Member, Mount Sinai, Metropolitan, Flower Fifth Avenue, and Polyclinic Hospitals, New York City. Author: Many illustrations of the male and female reproductive organs, sperm production and migration, and ovulation and fertilization, in numerous textbooks on obstetrics and gynecology.

JOSEPH K. FOLSOM, PH.D. Late Professor of Sociology, Vassar College; Lecturer in Sociology, Boston University. Author: *Youth, Family, and Education*, 1941; *The Family and Democratic Society*, 1943; "Steps in Love and Courtship," 1955; "Kinsey's Challenge to Ethics and Religion," 1955.

CLELLAN S. FORD, PH.D. Professor of Anthropology, Yale University; President, Human Relations Area Files, Inc. Author: *Smoke from their Fires*, 1941; *A Comparative Study of Human Reproduction*, 1945; (with G. P. Murdock and others) *Outline of Cultural Materials*, 1950; (with Frank A. Beach) *Patterns of Sexual Behavior*, 1951.

E. FRANKLIN FRAZIER, PH.D. Professor of Sociology, Howard University; Lecturer in the School of Advanced International Studies, Johns Hopkins University. Author: *The Negro Family in Chicago*, 1931; *The Negro Family in the United States*, 1939; *The Negro in the United States*, 1949; *Bourgeoisie Noire*, 1955; *Race and Culture Contacts in the Modern World*, 1957.

ROBERT M. FRUMKIN, M.A. Associate Professor of Sociology and Anthropology, State University of New York, Oswego; Research Editor, *Journal of Human Relations*. Formerly Social Research Analyst, Ohio State Department of Mental Hygiene and Correction. Author: "Child Supervision and Mental Disorders," 1953; *The Measurement of Marriage Adjustment*, 1954; "Occupation and Major Mental Disorders," 1955; *The Meaning of Sociology*, 1956; "Social Psychology," 1957; "Social Science and Social Progress," 1958; "American Arete and Teacher Education," 1959; "Attitudes of American College Students toward Civil Liberties," 1960; "Ideological Aspects of Crime," 1961; *Social Problems, Pathology, and Philosophy: Selected Essays and Studies*, 1962; "Sex, Familiarity, and Dogmatism as Factors in Painting Preferences," 1963.

SAMUEL GLASNER, D.D., ED.D. Rabbi; Director of One-Day Religious Schools and Teacher Training, Board of Jewish Education, Baltimore, Md.

JAY GLUCK, M.A. Fellow, University of Tehran; Visiting Professor in American Culture, Wakayama National University, Wakayama, Japan; Roving Editor and member of the editorial board of direction, *France-Asie/ASIA*. Author: *Sex Rites in Japanese Agriculture Today*, 1961; *Iro and Ero*; *The Color of Erotica in Japanese Art and Literature*, 1961; *Calligraphy, Minaret and Other Sex Symbols in Iran*, 1961.

DAVID GOODMAN, ED.D. Syndicated columnist in 45 newspapers: "Marriage, Children, and You." Marriage Counselor, Teaneck, New Jersey. Author: *A Parents' Guide to the Emotional Needs of Children*, 1959.

HILDA M. GOODWIN, M.S.W., D.S.W. Assistant Professor in Family Study in Psychiatry, School of Medicine, University of Pennsylvania; Chief Supervisor of Counseling and Training, Marriage Council of Philadelphia. Author: (with Emily H. Mudd) "Marriage Counseling," 1958.

VERNON W. GRANT, PH.D. Chief Psychologist, Summit County Mental Hygiene Clinic, Akron, Ohio; private practice of psychological counseling. Author: "A Fetish Theory of Amorous Fixation," 1949; "Preface to a Psychology of Sexual Attachment," 1951; *Psychology of Sexual Emotion*, 1957; *This Is Mental Illness*, 1963.

RENÉ GUYON, LL.D. Legislative Adviser, formerly Judge and Public Prosecutor, Thai Government, Bangkok, Thailand. Author: *The Ethics of Sexual Acts* (7 vols.), 1929–1938; *Essais Matérialistes* (3 vols.); "The Child and Sexual Activities," 1952.

HENRY GUZE, PH.D. Adjunct Associate Professor of Psychology, Graduate School, Long Island University; private practice of psychopathology. Author: "Bodily and Behavioral Manifestations of the Menstrual Cycle," 1952; "Relationships of Estrogens and Androgens to Certain Aspects of Sexual Behavior," 1952; "Effects of Pre-Weaning Nursing Deprivation on the Later Maternal, Hoarding and Sexual Behavior in the Rat," 1955; "Sexual Normality and Sexual Health: A Critical Appraisal," 1964.

TORE HAKANSSON, M.A. Technical Assistance Expert, United Nations; Producer of films on primitive dance, arts, and crafts; field work in South Asia.

WILFRED D. HAMBLY, D.Sc. Late Curator of African Ethnology, Chicago Natural History Museum; member, Wellcome Archaeological Expedition to Ethiopia; Leader, Rawsom-Field Museum Expedition to Angola and Nigeria. Author: *Source Book for African Anthropology; Ethnology of the Ovimbundu of Angola; Culture Areas of Nigeria.*

FRANCES R. HARPER, ED.D. Department of Guidance, Arlington (Va.) Public Schools. Co-author: *Exploring Your Community*, 1954; "An Evaluative Study of a Large Class in the Psychology of Family Relations," 1957; "Are Educators Afraid of Sex?" 1957.

ROBERT A. HARPER, PH.D. Private practice of psychotherapy and marriage counseling, Washington, D.C.; Past President American Academy of Psychotherapists; Past President American Association of Marriage Counselors. Author: *Marriage*, 1949; (with John F. Cuber and William F. Kenkel) *Problems of American Society*, 1956; *Psychoanalysis and Psychotherapy: 36 Systems*, 1959; (with Albert Ellis) *Creative Marriage*, 1961 and *A Guide to Rational Living*, 1961.

BRIAN M. HEALD, M.A. Medical editor and non-fiction editor of a New York publishing house. Graduate of Cambridge University and formerly high school teacher in the adult education field in the United States and England.

L. CLOVIS HIRNING, M.D. Private practice of psychiatry in White Plains and Katonah, New York; Consulting Psychiatrist—Guidance Department, Teachers College, Columbia University; Board of Cooperative Educational Services, Schools of Northern Westchester; Neurological Consultant, Grasslands Hospital; Associate, William Alanson White Institute for Psychology, Psychiatry, and Psychoanalysis. Author: "Genital Exhibitionism, an Interpretive Study," 1947; "The Sex Offender in Custody," 1947; "Functions of a School Psychiatrist," 1958.

VIRGINIA E. JOHNSON. Research Associate, Sex Research Project, Department of Obstetrics and Gynecology, Washington University School of Medicine, St. Louis, Mo. Co-author: *The Human Female: Anatomy of Sexual Response*, 1960.

TRYGVE JOHNSTAD, CAND. PSYCHOL. Guest Lecturer at the University of Oslo. Formerly Management Consultant to the Norwegian State Railways and the Norwegian Steelworks.

G. LOMBARD KELLY, M.D. President (retired), Medical College of Georgia; private practice of medicine, specializing in sexual problems, Augusta, Georgia. Author: *Sexual Feeling in Men and Women*, 1938; *Sex Manual*, 1945; *So You Think You're Impotent!* 1957; *A Doctor Discusses Menopause*, 1959.

FRANK KINGDON, D.D., LL.D. Radio commentator and newspaper columnist; Member faculty the New School for Social Research, New York City. Formerly Professor of Philosophy and President, University of Newark. Author: *Humane Religion*, 1930; *When Half-Gods Go*, 1933; *Jacob's Ladder*, 1943; *John Cotton Dana*, 1940; *That Man in the White House*, 1944; *Architects of the Republic*, 1950.

LESTER A. KIRKENDALL, PH.D. Professor of Family Life, School of Home Economics, Oregon State University. Author: *Sex Adjustments of Young Men*, 1940; *Understanding Sex*, 1947; *Dating Days*, 1949; *Sex Education as Human Relations*, 1950; *Understanding the Other Sex*, 1955; *Too Young to Marry?* 1956; *Premarital Intercourse and Interpersonal Relationships*, 1961.

SAMUEL Z. KLAUSNER, PH.D. Research Associate, Bureau of Applied Social Research; Lecturer, Departments of Religion and Sociology, Columbia University. Author: *The New Hebrew Man*, 1955; *Immigrant Absorption and Social Tension in Israel*, 1955; *Psychiatry and Religion*, 1964.

SOPHIA J. KLEEGMAN, M.D. Clinical Professor of Obstetrics and Gynecology, New York University School of Medicine; Visiting Staff, Obstetrics and Gynecology, Bellevue and University Hospitals; Director, Infertility Clinic, Bellevue Hospital; Medical Consultant Eastern League Planned Parenthood Association. Author: Many articles and addresses on gynecological and medical subjects, including "Office Treatment of Pathologic Cervix," 1940; "Diagnosis and Treatment of Infertility in Women," 1952; "Frigidity in Women," 1959.

KRONHAUSEN, EBERHARD W., PH.D., and KRONHAUSEN, PHYLLIS C., PH.D. Specialists in psychology and family life education, Anaheim, California. Authors: "Family Milieu Therapy, the Non-Institutional Treatment of Severe Emotional Disturbances" (1957); "The Therapeutic Family—The Family's Role in Emotional Disturbance and Rehabilitation" (1959); *Pornography and the Law* (1959); *Sex Histories of American College Men* (1960).

HERBERT S. KUPPERMAN, M.D. Associate Professor of Medicine, New York University Medical School; Chief of the Endocrinology Department of the Fertility Service, Margaret Sanger Research Bureau, New York City; Endocrinologist, Bronx Veterans Hospital; Chief, Endocrinology Section, Clara Maass Memorial Hospital, Newark, N. J. Author: "A Two and Six-

Hour Pregnancy Test," 1943; "The Sexual Cycle and Reproduction in the Golden Hamster," 1944; "The Relationship Between Sex Hormones and Experimentally Induced Tumors in Rats," 1947; "Endocrine Therapy in Gynecological Disorders," 1953; "Induction of Ovulation in the Human," 1958; "New Concepts in the Evaluation of Intersex and Infertility," 1958; *Human Endocrinology*, 1963.

HANS LEHFELDT, M.D. Chief of the Contraceptive Clinic, New York University-Bellevue Medical Center and Assistant Clinical Professor in Obstetrics and Gynecology, New York University College of Medicine; Senior Clinical Assistant, Lenox Hill Hospital Out-Patient Department; private practice of obstetrics and gynecology, New York City. Author of many articles on fertility and contraception; *Das Buch der Ehe (The Marriage Book)*, 1930.

HEDWIG LESER, M.A. Former Translator, Institute for Sex Research, Indiana University. Formerly Assistant Professor of German, Indiana University. Author: (with B. J. Vos) *Concise German Grammar*, 1941.

MAXIMILIAN LE WITTER, M.D. Former Assistant Physician, Geriatric Clinic, Metropolitan Hospital and Bird S. Cole Hospital, New York City. Formerly Senior Clinical Assistant, Endocrinological Department of Gynecology, Mount Sinai Hospital, New York City.

ALEXANDER LOWEN, J.S.D., M.D. Executive Director, The Institute for Bioenergetic Analysis, New York City. Author: *The Physical Dynamics of Character Structure*, 1958.

DUNCAN MACDOUGALD, JR., B.A. Philologist and sexologist, Kitzbuehel, Capri. Author of many articles and contributor on sexology to professional journals and encyclopedias, including "The Languages and Press of Africa," 1944, and "Phallic Foods," 1952.

DAVID R. MACE, PH.D. Executive Director, American Association of Marriage Counselors. Formerly Associate Professor of Family Study, Department of Psychiatry, School of Medicine, University of Pennsylvania; and Staff Consultant, Marriage Council of Philadelphia. Author: *Marriage: The Art of Lasting Love*, 1952; *Hebrew Marriage*, 1953; *Success in Marriage*, 1958; *Marriage East and West*, 1960; *The Soviet Family*, 1963.

JOHN S. MACLEOD, PH.D. Associate Professor of Physiology, Cornell University Medical College. Author: Many papers on fertility and infertility, including "The Kinetics of Spermatogenesis as Revealed by Changes in the Ejaculation," 1952, and a series of six papers on "The Male Factor in Fertility and Infertility," 1950–1953.

WILLIAM H. MASTERS, M.D. Associate Professor of Obstetrics and Gynecology, Washington University School of Medicine. Author: Many papers on gyne-

cology, endocrinology, and geriatrics, including "Gonadotrophin Titer in the Adult Human Male: The Effect of Ejaculation," 1952; "The Sexual Response Cycle of the Human Female: I. Gross Anatomic Considerations. II. Vaginal Lubrication," 1959, 1960.

JOHN MONEY, PH.D. Associate Professor of Medical Psychology and Pediatrics, Johns Hopkins University; full-time psychoendocrine research sponsored by the United States Public Health Service, formerly by Josiah Macy, Jr. Foundation. Co-recipient, 1956 Hofheimer Research Award, American Psychiatric Association. Author: Many papers on hermaphroditism and other endocrine disorders; *The Psychologic Study of Man*, 1957.

EMILY H. MUDD, M.S.W., PH.D., D.Sc. Vice-Chairman, Governor's Advisory Council on Alcohol, Pennsylvania State Department of Health; Professor of Family Study in Psychiatry, School of Medicine, University of Pennsylvania; Director, Division of Family Study, University of Pennsylvania; Director, Marriage Council of Philadelphia, Inc. Author: *The Practice of Marriage Counseling*, 1951; "Psychiatry and Marital Problems," 1955; "Knowns and Unknowns in Marriage Counseling Research," 1957; (edited with Aron Krich) *Man and Wife, A Source Book of Family Attitudes, Sexual Behavior, and Marriage Counseling*, 1957; (edited with Abraham Stone, Maurice J. Karpf, and Janet F. Nelson) *Marriage Counseling: A Casebook*, 1958.

RUTH L. MUNROE, PH.D. Late Clinical Psychologist; Visiting Professor, Graduate Division, College of the City of New York. Author: *Schools of Psychoanalytic Thought*, 1955; co-author: *Happy Family*, 1938.

GOTTFRIED NEUMANN, M.D., F.A.C.S. Late Assistant Professor of Gynecology and Obstetrics, and Chief of the Sterility Clinic, N.Y.U.-Bellevue Medical Center. Author: (with Hans Lehfeldt) "The Crystallization Phenomenon of the Cervical Mucus as Pregnancy Test," 1953; (with Hans Lehfeldt) "Le Phenomene de Cristallisation de la Claire Cervicale, Mode le Diagnostic de la Grossesse," 1956; "Cineradiography of Female Pelvic Organs" (a medical motion picture and an article, with Hans Lehfeldt and R. W. Carlin), 1956.

ALWIN NIKOLAIS. Associate Director, Henry Street Playhouse, New York City; Choreographer and Director of the Nikolais Dance Company and the Playhouse Dance Company. Author: Several articles in *Dance, Art,* and *Theatre* Magazines. Choreographer: *Kaleidoscope; Prism; The Bewitched; Cantos; Allegory*.

M. F. NIMKOFF, PH.D. Professor of Sociology, The Florida State University. Former Editor, *Marriage and Family Living*. Author: (with W. F. Ogburn) *Marriage and the Family*, 1947; *Technology and the Changing Family*, 1955.

HARRIET F. PILPEL, B.A., M.A., LL.B. Senior Partner, Greenbaum, Wolff and Ernst, New York City. Author: Many articles on marriage and family law in professional and lay publications; (with Theodora Zavin) *Your Marriage and The Law*, 1952; *Tax Aspects of Copyright Property*, 1953; *Rights and Writers*, 1960; *A Copyright Guide*, 1960.

WARDELL B. POMEROY, PH.D. Private Practice Psychotherapy, New York City. Co-author: *Sexual Behavior in the Human Male*, 1948; *Sexual Behavior in the Human Female*, 1953; *Pregnancy, Birth and Abortion*, 1958.

WILLIAM R. REEVY, PH.D. Associate Professor of Psychology, Texas Technological College. Author: "Female Masturbation and Marital Happiness Prediction," 1959; "Premarital Petting Behavior and Marital Happiness Prediction," 1959; "Vestured Genital Apposition and Coitus," 1959.

IRA L. REISS, PH.D. Associate Professor of Sociology and Anthropology, State University of Iowa; Chairman-Elect of the Research Division of the National Council on Family Relations; Board of Editors of *Marriage and Family Living*. Author: *Premarital Sexual Standards in America*, 1960; "Personal Values and the Scientific Study of Sex," 1963; "Sociological Studies of Sexual Standards," 1963.

OSCAR RIDDLE, PH.D., LL.D., D.H.C. Retired. Formerly Instructor, the University of Chicago; Research Staff, Carnegie Institution of Washington; Department of Genetics, Cold Spring Harbor, New York. Author: "Sex Control and Known Correlations in Pigeons," 1916; "Birds Without Gonads," 1925; "The Preparation, Identification and Assay of Prolactin," 1933; "The Role of Hormones in the Initiation of Maternal Behavior in Rats," 1942; *Endocrines and Constitution in Doves and Pigeons*, 1947; "Prolactin or Progesterone in Parental Behavior," 1963.

MURRAY RUSSELL, M.D. Assistant Clinical Professor of Urology, College of Medical Evangelists; Consulting Urologist to City of Hope, Duarte, California; Member of the Urological Department, Orange County General Hospital. Author: "Studies in General Biology of Sperm," 1951; "Can Male Infertility Be Prevented?" 1954; chapter on "Male Infertility" in the textbook, *Urological Practice* (Barnes and Hadley), 1956; "Preventative Aspects of Male Infertility," 1957.

EDWARD SAGARIN. Instructor in Sociology, Pratt Institute. Author: Numerous papers on perfumery, olfaction, and cosmetics; *The Science and Art of Perfumery*, 1945; *Cosmetics: Science and Technology*, 1957; *The Anatomy of Dirty Words*, 1962; (Translator) *Incest*, by Emile Durkheim, 1963; (with Albert Ellis) *Nymphomania*, 1964.

J. P. SCOTT, PH.D. Senior Staff Scientist and formerly Chairman, Division of Behavior Studies, Roscoe B. Jackson Memorial Laboratory, Bar Harbor, Maine.

Author: Many papers on embryology and physiological genetics, sociobiology, and the social behavior of animals; *Animal Behavior*, 1958; *Aggression*, 1958.

HANS SELYE, M.D., PH.D., D.Sc. Professor and Director of the Institute of Experimental Medicine and Surgery at the Université de Montreal, Canada. Author of many scientific papers and numerous books, including *Encyclopedia of Endocrinology*, 1947; *Textbook of Endocrinology*, 1949; *On the Experimental Morphology of the Adrenal Gland*, 1950; *The Story of the Adaptation Syndrome*, 1952; *The Stress of Life*, 1956; *The Chemical Prevention of Cardiac Necroses*, 1958; *Symbolic Shorthand System for Physiology and Medicine*, 1960; *The Pluricausal Cardiopathies*, 1961; *Calciphylaxis*, 1962; *From Dream to Discovery*, 1964.

GEORGENE SEWARD, PH.D. Professor of Psychology and Director, Clinical Training Program the University of Southern California; Consultant in Clinical and Counseling Psychology, United States Veterans Administration. Author: *Sex and the Social Order*, 1946; *Psychotherapy and Culture Conflicts*, 1956. Editor: *Clinical Studies in Culture Conflict*, 1958; *Current Psychological Issues*, 1958.

JELAL M. SHAH, O.B.E., F.R.C.S., F.C.P.S., F.I.C.S. (HON.), F.I.C.A. Honorary Consultant in Venereology, Pakistan Navy; Colonel, Indian Medical Service (retired); Secretary and Registrar, Pakistan Medical Council, Karachi. Formerly, Dean and Lecturer in Venereal Diseases, Grant Medical College, Bombay University; Surgical Specialist, Third Indian Division, Egyptian Expeditionary Force. Author: "Treatment of Venereal Diseases," 1933; "Sexual Impotence in the Male; Two Ominous Signs," 1956; "Role of Haemotherapy in Sexual Impotence," 1957; *Fertility and Sterility*, 1962.

ROBERT VEIT SHERWIN, LL.B. Practicing attorney, New York City, specializing in the fields of Sex and the Law and Domestic Relations; Administrative Director, the Society for the Scientific Study of Sex. Author: *Sex and the Statutory Law*, 1949; "Female Sex Crimes," 1954; "Sodomy: a Medico-Legal Enigma," 1953.

BORIS SHUB, LL.B. Information Specialist, Latin American Information Committee. Formerly Program Policy Adviser of Radio Liberty, American Committee for Liberation. Formerly Political Adviser of Radio RIAS, Berlin. Author: *The Choice*, 1950; *Since Stalin: A Photo History of Our Time*, 1951.

PITIRIM A. SOROKIN, PH.D. Director, Harvard University Research Center in Creative Altruism, Winchester, Mass.; Emeritus Professor of Harvard University; President of American Sociological Association; President of the International Society for Comparative Study of Civilizations. Author: Many articles and books, including *Altruistic Love*, 1950; *Explorations in Altruistic Love and Behavior*, 1950; *The*

Ways and Power of Love, 1954; *Forms and Techniques of Altruistic and Spiritual Growth,* 1954.

WALTER R. STOKES, LL.B., M.D. Psychiatrist, specializing in problems of marriage and family life, retired, Washington, D.C.; Occasional lecturer, George Washington University Postgraduate School of Medicine. Author: *Modern Pattern for Marriage,* 1948. Contributing author: *Readings in Marriage Counseling* (edited by Clark E. Vincent), 1957; *Marriage Counseling: A Casebook* (edited by Mudd, Karpf, Stone, and Nelson), 1958; *Married Love in Today's World,* 1962; *Advances in Sex Research,* edited by Hugo Beigel, 1963.

ABRAHAM STONE, M.D. Late Medical Director of the Marriage Consultation Center of the Community Church, New York City; Director of the Margaret Sanger Research Bureau; Faculty Member of the New School for Social Research and the New York University College of Medicine. Author: (with Norman Himes) *Planned Parenthood,* 1948; (with Hannah Stone) *A Marriage Manual,* 1952; (with Lena Levine) *The Premarital Consultation,* 1956.

CLARA THOMPSON, M.D. Late Executive Director, William Alanson White Institute of Psychiatry, Psychoanalysis and Psychology, New York City. Author: "Some Effects of the Derogatory Attitude Toward Female Sexuality," 1950; *Psychoanalysis: Evolution and Development,* 1950; (co-editor) *Outline of Psychoanalysis,* 1955.

CONRAD VAN EMDE BOAS, M.D. Psychiatrist-sexologist and psychoanalyst in private practice, Amsterdam, Holland; Formerly Director of the Amsterdam Birth Control and Sexological Clinic; President of the Dutch Association for Group Psychotherapy; President for the Region of Europe, Near East, and Africa of the International Planned Parenthood Federation. Author: *Shakespeare's Sonnets and Their Connection with the Double-Travesti-Plays,* 1951; *Encyclopedia of Sexological Knowledge* (editor of Dutch edition), 1952; *Abortus Provocatus,* 1952; *The Periodical Infertility of Women and Its Importance for Child-Spacing,* 1957.

FRED W. VOGET, PH.D. Professor of Anthropology, University of Toronto. Author: "Acculturation .at Caughnawaga: A Note on the Native-Modified Group," 1951; "The American Indian in Transition: Reformation and Accommodation," 1956; "Man and Culture: an essay in changing Anthropological Interpretation," 1960.

VICTOR H. WALLACE, M.D., F.R.C.S. Private practice of sexological medicine, Melbourne, Australia. Formerly Lecturer on Sex, Marriage, and the Family

at the Adult Education Council. Author: Many articles on sexological subjects; *Women and Children First: An Outline of a Population Policy for Australia,* 1946; *Paths to Peace: A Study of War, Its Causes and Prevention* (editor), 1957.

GEORGE B. WILBUR, M.D. Private practice of psychoanalysis, South Dennis, Mass. Formerly editor of the *American Imago.*

ROBERT ANTON WILSON, M.S. Editor, *General Semantics Newsletter,* New York City; Associate Editor, *The Realist.* Formerly editor of *Verbal Level.* Author: *Joyce and Tao,* 1959; *To the End of Sanity,* 1959; *Sex Education for the Modern Liberal Adult,* 1959.

ROBERT F. WINCH, PH.D. Professor of Sociology, Northwestern University; Associate Editor of *Sociometry.* Author: *The Modern Family,* 1952; (edited, with Robert McGinnis) *Selected Studies in Marriage and the Family,* 1953; *Mate-Selection,* 1958; *La Scelta del Compagno,* 1961; *Identification and Its Familial Determinants,* 1962.

ROBERT WOOD. Graduate of St. John's College, London. Tutor in Adult Education, Extra-Mural Departments of Oxford and Southampton Universities. Formerly Editor of the *Journal of Sex Education.* Author: *The Role of Pleasure in the Good Life,* 1946; *Art and Psychotherapy,* 1951; "Psychology of Sex Behavior," 1951; "Recent Trends in Sexological Literature," 1952; "The Female Sex Drive," 1958.

WU LIEN-TEH, M.A., M.D., MAST. PUBL.H., HON. LL.D., SC.D., D.LITT. Private practice of medicine, Ipoh, Malaya. Formerly plague and health expert, League of Nations; Inspector General of the National Quarantine Service of China; Physician Extraordinary to Successive Presidents of China. Author: *Treatise on Pneumonic Plague,* 1926; *Handbook of Plague,* 1932; (with K. C. Wong) *History of Chinese Medicine,* 1936; *Plague Fighter: Autobiography of a Modern Chinese Physician,* 1958.

KIMBALL YOUNG, PH.D. Professor of Sociology, Northwestern University. Author: *Sociology: A Study of Society and Culture,* 1949; *Personality and Problems of Adjustment,* 1952; *Isn't One Wife Enough?,* 1954; *Social Psychology,* 1956.

THEODORA ZAVIN, LL.B. Private practice of law, New York City, Assistant Vice President, Broadcast Music Inc. Author: many articles on the law: (with Harriet F. Pilpel) *Your Marriage and the Law,* 1952.

HELENE ZWERDLING, M.A. Assistant to the Director, Special Projects Division, American Committee for Liberation, New York City.

Contents

Contents

Foreword

I am amazed, as this 1973 edition of The Encyclopedia of Sexual Behavior goes to press, at the book's continued popularity and the almost unanimous favorable critical comment which it keeps amassing. Little did Dr. Abarbanel (now, alas, deceased) and I realize, when we first planned the work, how the sex revolution would finally catch up to us: rather than, as encyclopedists, we somehow managed to chronicle and overtake it. But the almost impossible dream that we and many of its leading contributors fantasized might occur, in many respects actually has transpired; and the entire field of sex, both written and declaimed, has now surpassed some of our most liberal predictions and predilections.

But the encyclopedia remarkably holds up. Its chief contributors are an outstanding crew. If anything, they have become even more distinguished with age. One of these days, those of them who are still around, together with some of the newer authorities in the field who have recently arisen, deserve to be given the space to bring forth an impressively New and Enlarged encyclopedia for the almost-approaching twenty-first century. That, if I can find time to get around to it, I shall one of these forthcoming years arrange. In the meantime, I am proud of this healthy, sexy offspring. Hundreds of qualified endorsers still cite it as an indispensable work in its field. I not so modestly concur.

The Encyclopedia of Sexual Behavior, which has been more than three years in process, was compiled because no true encyclopedia of sex has ever been published anywhere and the few volumes in English which have called themselves encyclopedias—the most notable of which was the 1936 *Encyclopedia Sexualis,* edited by Victor Robinson—have been nothing of the sort or have turned out to be inadequate in many important respects. These works not only were much too brief, including spotty or no coverage on many significant topics, but the authorship of their articles was distinctly limited in authoritative specialization, first-hand scholarship, and international representation.

The editors of this encyclopedia have taken great care to be able to guarantee that the present volume is truly worthy of its name. It was specially planned so that its coverage would be comprehensive, authoritative, inclusive of wide-ranging viewpoints, and truly international. In addition to its extensive and intensive treatment of the major aspects of the biology, physiology, and anatomy of sex, it also covers the major facets of the emotional, psychological, sociological, legal, anthropological, geographical, and historical aspects of sexuality—including the related fields of love, marriage, and the family. Every one of the articles in the encyclopedia is original and up-to-date in every respect. Its many authors are outstanding individuals in their own areas and include leading spokesmen from scientific, professional, literary, and artistic fields.

We also thought it better, instead of including scores of fragmentary articles on highly specialized and often insignificant topics, to concentrate upon a hundred or so major articles which would comprehensively cover the most important topics. In consequence, this book is almost as much of an anthology as an encyclopedia and can be used as a source of general reading as well as a book of reference. Exactly how many readers will read it from cover to cover we have no way of knowing—but we expect and hope they will not be few.

In spite of the best-laid plans of the editors and publisher, the *Encyclopedia* suffered inevitable mishaps during its period of gestation. Some contributors who accepted invitations to write articles died before they completed their assignments; a few others never found time to start or finish their pieces. The contributors, on the whole, however, were unusually cooperative, prompt, and courteous, considering that all are exceptionally busy people. Four contributors were fatally stricken after they submitted their papers but before the book was published; one of these (Dr. Clara Thompson) apparently knew of her impending death and she most generously finished her contribution before the end. To all the contributors to the work and to others who were helpful in suggesting authors, the editors must offer their most profound gratitude.

The original plan was that *The Encyclopedia of Sexual Behavior* would consist of three major parts: (1) authoritative articles on all the major aspects of sex, love, and marriage that could reasonably be included in a work of this size; (2) a biographical dictionary of the leading sexologists, erotic writers, and other contributors to sexual knowledge; and (3) a comprehensive dictionary of sexual terms.

The wealth and scope of the main body of the book proved, in the end, so comprehensive that it was thought best to present all of the research and writing by the contributors themselves, as fully and completely as they wished, and to do this it was found necessary to dispense with addenda from the editors.

Here, then is the encyclopedia that has emerged after scores of months of planning, corresponding, re-writing, editing, and proof correcting.

ALBERT ELLIS, PH.D.

Analytical Guide to the Contents of This Book

THE following headings represent an attempt to characterize the key concepts or approaches that can be subsumed under the general theme of *Sexual Behavior*. The headings have been abbreviated to single words (in most cases) in order to provide the most flexible organization for this halfway house between a table of contents and an index. As a result, the separate articles in the encyclopedia listed under each heading bear—we hope—valid relations to the heading, but not necessarily to each other.

The absence of an article from all of these lists does not, of course, imply its relative unimportance, but only its *sui generis* character. Nor does the list of articles under any one head exhaust the sources of material on that topic; an arbitrary—and necessarily subjective—threshold level of importance and/or length of discussion has had to be established as a criterion of inclusion; the index will provide many secondary sources. An example of this is the absence, except in certain special cases, of the many national and geographical articles. Although for the comparative study of many topics they provide extremely useful information, they tend, necessarily, to be too brief in their discussion of any one topic for inclusion in this analytical guide to the contents of the book.

THE EDITORS

HISTORY OF MORALS

America, Moral Evolution in, 82 · Ancient Civilizations, Sex Life in, 119 · Art and Sex, 161 · Attitudes towards Sex, Modern, 186 · Autoerotism, 204 · Clothing and Nudism, 268 · English and American Sex Customs, Early, 350 · Europe, Sex Life in, 373 · Freedom, Sexual, 439 · Prostitution, 869 · Protestantism and Sex, 883.

HOMOSEXUALITY

Adolescent Sexuality, 52 · Homosexuality, 485 · Laws on Sex Crimes, 620 · Perversions, Sexual, 802 · Sex Offenders, The Psychology of, 949 · Sex Reform Movement, 956 · Transvestism and Sex-Role Inversion, 1012.

LAW

Abortion, 35 · Artificial Insemination, 180 · Censorship of Sexual Literature, 235 · Clothing and Nudism, 268 · Divorce, 338 · Europe, Sex Life in, 373 · Homosexuality, 485 · Illegitimacy, 503 · Laws on Marriage and Family, 614 · Laws on Sex Crimes, 620 · Marriage, 663 · Marriage Conciliation, 672 · Perversions, Sexual, 802 · Prostitution, 869 · Race and Sex, 897 · Sex Offenders, The Psychology of, 949 · Sex Reform Movement, 956 · Sterilization, 1005.

LOVE

Aphrodisiacs and Anaphrodisiacs, 145 · Courtship and Mate-Selection, 301 · Demography and the Nature of the Sex Drive, 333 · Family, Sexual and Affectional Functions of, 392 · Jealousy, 567 · Love, Altruistic, 641 · Love, Sexual, 646 · Loving, The Art of, 657 · Movement and Feeling in Sex, 739.

MARRIAGE

Family, Sexual and Affectional Functions of, 392 · Courtship and Mate-Selection, 301 · Extramarital Sex Relations, 384 · Loving, The Art of, 657 · *See also* articles under Marriage.

MASTURBATION

Abstinence, 44 · Adolescent Sexuality, 52 · Autoerotism, 204 · Child Sexuality, 258 · Coitus, 284 · Impotence, 515 · Loving, The Art of, 657 · Petting, 812.

NATURE OF SEX

Advances in Modern Sex Research, A Survey of, 25 · Animal Sexuality, 132 · Attitudes towards Sex, Modern, 186 · Demography and the Nature of the Sex Drive, 333 · Love, Sexual, 646 · Nature of Sex, 757 · Sex Differences, 931 · Sex Drive, 939 · Transvestism and Sex-Role Inversion, 1012.

PERVERSIONS

Coitus, 284 · Fetishism, 435 · Guilt and Conflict in Relation to Sex, 466 · Homosexuality, 485 · Laws on Sex Crimes, 620 · Perversions, Sexual, 802 · Pornography, The Psychology of, 848 · Sex Offenders, The Psychology of, 949 · Standards of Sexual Behavior, 996 · Transvestism and Sex-Role Inversion, 1012.

PORNOGRAPHY

Art and Sex, 161 · Censorship of Sexual Literature, 235 · Clothing and Nudism, 268 · Far East, Sex in the Art of the, 412 · Language and Sex, 585 · Literature and Sex, 631 · Pornography, The Psychology of, 848.

PREGNANCY

Abortion, 35 · Artificial Insemination, 180 · Contraception, 293 · Illegitimacy, 503 · Menopause, 718 · Reproduction, Human, 903.

THE ENCYCLOPEDIA OF

Sexual Behavior

Advances in
Modern Sex Research,
A Survey of

KARL MANNHEIM once said that nothing is more stimulating than the realization that our social life is full of phantasies. Few areas of human behavior have a better claim to be so described than sexual behavior. Sex has been glorified in temples and driven out of cloisters; praised poetically and condemned morally; depicted pornographically and studied scientifically. Each generation has rediscovered its pleasures, pains, mysteries, tragedies, and controversiality.

Indeed, a history of the development of ideas on sexuality deserves the same attention and study given to the natural and technical sciences. The best that can be done here is to trace broadly the manner in which sexual behavior has been researched by social and behavioral scientists, and the methods used to accumulate knowledge about it.

The Meaning of "Sexual Behavior"

It must be made clear that the present discussion does not intend to describe, even superficially, the philosophical assumptions and the resultant technology developed in the last fifty years to study the phenomenon of sex. Instead, it will concentrate on one aspect of the phenomenon of "sexual behavior." By sexual behavior we mean the actions of human beings to accomplish sexual union between the male and the female. It is apparent that this "behavior" can be seen from a variety of vantage points, dimensions, or levels of analysis. To accomplish "union of the male and female," the means for

such accomplishment must be on hand. There must be male and female organs, motivation for union, and standards of time, of place, of person, and finally, of purpose. The "union of male and female" may be viewed anatomically or physiologically. The focus of inquiry may be placed on the chemical structures and interrelations that maintain the state of activity necessary for the various mechanisms to take place, leading to the pertinent "reactions" in the sphere of sex: stimulus, excitation, erection, stimulation, ejaculation, "orgasm" for the male —excitation, lubrication, stimulation, "orgasm" for the female. The endocrinological geography of the human body enters into the phenomenon of "sexual behavior" but can be taken for granted when the purpose is the study of the psychological processes of sexual attraction, and may even more safely be ignored when the object of study is the sociocultural context of "sexual behavior."

The "essence" of sexual behavior is what is known under the term "sexual drive," or at other times known as "sexual instinct"—representable only through a synthesis or translatability of the identified (or as yet to be identified) mechanisms conceptually contained within the visible human activity: "sexual behavior." An identified "sexual drive" may have several ways of manifesting itself, depending upon the context or range of available channels of manifestation. For example, autoerotic, homosexual, heterosexual, and sodomistic acts have the same consequences on the physiologic level: tension reduction.

But do these acts have the same psychological consequences? Are the consequences evaluated in the same way socially? In reference to these questions, theoreticians (systematizers and interpreters of observations and accumulated empirical data) and researchers (technicians securing the observations, and organizers of the observations into "meaningful" sequences and wholes) may diverge widely. The divergence is most likely due to the theoretic assumption that the human being is stimulated from the inside—the internal stimulations being channeled and structured into particular ways of gratification by *external* stimulations and constraints. We seldom ask whether autoerotic, homosexual, heterosexual, or sodomistic "sexual behavior" is *subjectively* gratifying to the behaving individual or individuals. The emphasis is usually on the dysfunctional ("abnormal") consequences to the individual of such behavior.

The Three Levels of Analysis

This indirectly leads to the identification of what is spoken of as "normal sexual behavior" on the psycho-social level. Actually, a clear distinction must be made between three levels of analysis (each, of course, containing further sub-levels of analysis): the physiologic, the psychologic, and the sociologic, the last being referred to of late as "socio-cultural." When "sexual behavior" is studied on any one of these levels separately, it has the distinct advantage of not involving any mechanisms existent on the other levels.

Thus, it is possible to have a controversy about the endocrinological *vs.* the psychological bases of homosexuality. A school of thought orienting itself primarily on the physiology of "sexual behavior" will view (and has empirical experimental data to prove it) homosexuality as the "behavioral" equivalent of a different endocrinological pattern—and the researchers emphasizing and remaining on the psychological level (drawing data and inferences from the interaction of the individual with other individuals in the socialization process) will place the origins of homosexuality in the pattern of "interactions" or "social relations" of the individual. Are these two theoretic orientations

contradictory, or are they accounting for the same phenomena on two different levels of analysis? If the latter is true, there is need for a conceptual structure that will translate the endocrinological (physiological) pattern into the psychological level, thus reaching a conceptual theory analogous to the head-and-tail notion of a coin. Without the head, a coin is not a coin; neither is a coin one without a tail. Only the presence of both makes a coin. The endocrinology of sex is part of the psychology of sex, and *vice versa.* The problem is to specify how they are related, how endocrinological structures are translatable into psychological perceptions, feeling-tones, and ultimately into verbalizations and actions.

The three levels of analysis mentioned above must continue the process of delving ever more microscopically into the structure and mechanisms of their analytically separate phenomena. This segmentation of research, frequently spoken of as compartmentalization, must go on, if the complement of analysis—synthesis—is to be achieved. To be sure, the advantage of segmented research is that it creates clarity of conceptualization, leads to analytic insights, and unfolds the existence of unsuspected phenomena. The disadvantage frequently is that such segmented research (specification of levels of analysis) inhibits the synthesizing of the various levels of analysis into broad monistic theories that intellectually grasp "sexual behavior" in its totality.

This discussion of "research in sexual behavior" does not focus on the total realm of "sexual behavior." The attempt is made to describe the precursors of a particular research orientation and technology which arose in the area of the social, or what is also known as the behavioral sciences. Here the first problem is that of taxonomy. It is necessary to know: *what* behavior, *with* whom, under *what conditions,* and *how* much or *how* frequently is the behavior observable. The subjective gratifications are ruled out of this taxonomy, though it is assumed that the gratifications, their types and differentials, depend upon the person with whom the behavior takes place, and the time and place of its occurrence. Certainly endocrinological, anatomic, physiologic, and to some extent psychologic levels of conceptualization are omitted from consideration. This is scientifically legitimate.

We, therefore, will present here one small aspect of "sexual behavior" on a distinct analytic level—the social-psychological. We will show how Kinsey reconceptualized previous work in this area and what has and can be learned through this method. We hope that this does not lead the reader to interpret that nothing else is left to research in the sphere of "sexual behavior." The reader is referred to other articles in this Encyclopedia for discussion of the problems and findings of research in the phenomenon of sex in all its ramifications. By connecting the findings resulting from the various levels of analysis and conceptualization as well as the various content areas, the reader can secure a view of "research in sexual behavior" never before glimpsed through the covers of one work. It is in this spirit that we begin our description with the early history of the study of "sexual behavior" by social thinkers and analysts of the past.

Early History of the Study of Sexual Behavior

During the eighteenth and nineteenth centuries, as a result of the Enlightenment, the study of human sexual behavior separated itself from a discussion of morality. This period was characterized by an extensive utopian literature on marriage, morals, and sex education.

With the spread of evolutionary theory in biology (during the late nineteenth century), the evolutionary framework, coupled with the notion that man's reason and not divine revelation leads toward man's understanding of himself and thus toward self-mastery, created a milieu in which moral and theological explanations were further displaced by new conceptions of what constitutes human behavior or action. These new conceptions became intellectual grids onto which sexual behavior was placed. Sexual behavior came gradually to be viewed more as a manifestation of human needs *as they are,* and less *as they ought to be.*

Works on sexual behavior published during the nineteenth century were characterized by a historicocultural orientation. Social origins of sexuality, control of sexuality, ideas of sexuality, and the resultant ideologies were the major points of discussion. The writers debated contemporary ways and (1) wished to improve the existent sexual *status quo* by making it more moral, (2) assumed that the *status quo* was the highest state of man's development, or (3) utopianly suggested new patterns of behavior and ethical principles.

From this intellectual situation wherein sexual behavior was viewed in a historicocultural, ethico-utopian framework, several physicians published books that gradually changed the perception of sexuality in the Western world. These physicians were interested in the psychological aspects of sexual behavior and used materials (and points of view) from sociology and anthropology to reinforce their psychological orientations. The significant new direction was that they viewed sexual behavior from a concrete-clinical framework, thereby observing what people actually do at close range. They often rationalized what they observed through an ideal notion of what "ought to be." Nevertheless, they saw sexual behavior in its individual context through relatively unbiased eyes.

Of the greatest influence was the seven-volume work of Havelock Ellis, *Studies in the Psychology of Sex* (1897-1928). Ellis secured his material from published case histories in the medical and psychiatric literature and from correspondence carried on with his patients and those who heard of his work and wished to contribute their introspective and phenomenological experiences. In order to understand sexual behavior in the context of psychological interaction, yet be true to the evolutionary framework, Ellis applied biological categories of analysis to psychological phenomena. He used psychological processes as the cornerstones upon which to analyze his concrete-clinical cases. Thus he organized his material and discussed it in this order: the evolution of sexual modesty, sexual inversion, analysis of the sexual impulse, sexual selection in man, erotic symbolism, and finally, sex in relation to society. His reanalysis and reconceptualization led him to develop the notion of "compensatory unlikeness" between the male and female, which became the principle through which he interpreted sexual behavior and phenomena.

The two decades from 1890 to 1910 were especially productive. Books by physicians multiplied. Richard Krafft-Ebing, using his clinical practice as a base of observation, published *Psychopathia Sexualis* (1902) and delimited the range of (pathological) sexual behavior with its etiology and prognosis. August Forel, in *The Sexual Question* (1906), not only detailed the anatomy and physiology of reproduction, but also described the variety of sexual behavior upon which he heaped moral evaluations. At the same time he tried to persuade his readers to accept sexual education in childhood and adolescence, lest poor sex education—or its absence—lead to pathologies, perversions, and degeneration. Magnus Hirschfeld in 1899 began the publication of a *Journal of the Intermediate Sex Stages*, became interested in homosexuality, and founded an Institute for Sex Research. Others such as Iwan Bloch (1903) and A. Moll (1893) proceeded in similar directions and gave the psychiatric, psychological, sociological, and ethical observations a more coherent and new meaning.

This period of research (1890-1910) combined the historicocultural with the concrete-clinical orientations. Statements on sexual behavior were based on a mixture of evaluation and observation. The writers did not fully separate the function of research from the function of evaluating the results of the research. The consequence was that they frequently were not aware of the way in which research and evaluation, if joined together, prevented them from seeing what there was to see and distorted what they saw in the direction of what they expected to see. Their purpose was mainly ameliorative and not fully scientific.

It was with Sigmund Freud that the concrete-clinical method received an added ingredient—logical analysis—which led him to the realization that the nature of sexuality is such that it can permeate every sphere of the actions of human beings, that sexual behavior is the result of the interaction between generations, and that the human sexual drive has a chameleonlike quality. He developed a new set of categories which, when placed into logical relation to each other, produced theories of sexuality capable of being tested in particular concrete-clinical cases. The resultant under-

standing was used as a therapeutic technique.

The complexity of the Freudian theory was such that it did not encourage coupling his "analytic" concepts with a "survey" method on large populations. It was restricted in application to a particular case reaching the psychoanalyst, psychiatrist, or clinical psychologist. Freud's theory (a precisely spelled-out relationship between concepts) gave the psychotherapist a technique to "observe" the behavior of his patient (by telling him what to listen for), and thus guide the patient's process of adjustment, which psychotherapy eventuates. The understanding of the meaning and place of sexual behavior in a personality (suffering light or severe psychopathology) was now possible, but what constitutes "normal" sexual dynamics and behavior still observationally eluded the student of sexuality.

The Quantitative-Empirical Study of Sexual Behavior

The rise of behaviorism in the 1920's added a new dimension of observation. Although the broad assumptions of behaviorism were rejected, the method—studying specific units of behavior, relating them, and considering these units in a context empty of purposes, values, and ethical norms—was accepted. The formulations of operationism in the natural sciences were added and used on social and behavioral phenomena, with the result that techniques of observation capable of being verified through repetition and checked through analysis became available.

Researchers began to specify the language and operations used, depended upon uniformities in their method of gathering data, and desired to build theories of sexuality based on facts secured through empirical observation (induction) rather than through analytic observation (deduction). Specifying and operationalizing observations made it possible to quantify qualitative data that were descriptive of groups of people, thus facilitating the observations of *patterns* of behavior. Present-day thinking and research in sexual behavior has this framework in mind.

Within this framework—securing facts through operationalized specifications of the type of data to be gathered—appeared studies by Exner (1915), Peck and Wells (1923, 1925), Hamilton (1929), Bromley and Britten (1938), Peterson (1938), and many others. It produced specific factual data. It also created new problems.

To illustrate both the type of data gathered and the problems that arose, a table is presented listing findings of the incidence of premarital coitus as found by the major empirical studies done between 1915 and 1947. This table is reproduced in a modified form from Winston Ehrmann's *Premarital Dating Behavior* (1959), one of the best quantitative-empirical studies on dating behavior known to the writer.

TABLE 1. INCIDENCE FIGURES ON PREMARITAL COITUS OF MALES REPORTED FROM 1915 TO 1947

INVESTIGATOR	DATE	SIZE AND TYPE OF SAMPLE	PERCENT-AGE INCIDENCE
Exner	1915	518, college	36
Peck and Wells	1923	180, college	35
Peck and Wells	1925	230, college	37
Hamilton	1929	100, college	54
Bromley and Britten	1938	470, college	51
Peterson	1938	122, college	55
Terman	1938	760, college and high school	61
Porterfield and Salley	1946	285, college	32
Finger	1947	111, college	45
Hohman and Schaffner	1947	1,000, college	68

As the table is inspected, it becomes apparent that the data present a range of coital incidence from 36 to 68 per cent, based on samples ranging from 100 to 1,000 people. When the studies are inspected more closely, it becomes apparent that, although each investigator specified the behavior he was studying, the phrasing of questions and the context in which they appeared were unique to each study. Thus, it is difficult to compare the results or to learn precisely what the incidence of premarital coitus "really" is.

We have learned subsequently that the inconsistent results also stem from the fact that a greater number of characteristics than were understood in these early studies affect sexual behavior (e.g., age, sex, socioeconomic status, attitudes toward sex, religion, life-history experiences, relationship to parents, educational achievement, occupation, position in work group or institution). Thus, further specification and control of a variety of variables were necessary if we were to learn with precision the range and breadth of a specifically defined aspect of sexual behavior.

The inconsistent findings, vague conceptualizations, and poor control of variables of early empirical studies induced Kinsey to undertake his large study based on interviews of 6,300 males and 5,300 females. His percentage figures on premarital coitus again differ from the ones reported earlier. His finding that incidence differs among different groups, by age, and by social-educational characteristics of the groups helped to explain some of the earlier inconsistencies. Among college-educated males, for example, Kinsey found that frequency of premarital coitus increases as age increases—44 per cent among those aged 20, 64 per cent among those aged 25, and 68 per cent among those aged 30.

Within the empirical-quantitative method, actual figures of behavior vary because of the different ways in which data are secured, the different times at which studies are made (1930 as compared to 1950, for example), and differences in conceptualization, sampling variability, and the like. As in the other behavioral sciences, precision is the ideal that can seldom be reached. Despite some inconsistencies in results, the empirical-quantitative method of investigating sexuality has made it possible to describe within a limited range the "actual" sexual behavior of a given population. To fully appreciate the complexities of the empirical-quantitative method, an examination of some of the major processes and difficulties will now be presented.

The Empirical Method

The empirical method is based on observation, summarizing these observations in quantitative terms, manipulating the resultant quantities, and inferring from the "descriptive" categories the geography of the behavior. When "analytic" categories are used and placed into relational statements, it is possible to construct an empirical theory of behavior.

A necessity of empirical observation, whether it is used on economic, political, esthetic, or moral phenomena, is that it delimit, separate, and isolate certain phenomena (human action) from others. Behavior is segmented when the observer defines the scope of the phenomenon to be studied and ignores all other kinds of behavior. He ignores not in the sense that other kinds of behavior are not important or meaningful to the observed behavior, but in the sense that he limits himself to something empirically manageable. Experience has taught that observational justice cannot be done to the phenomenon under study if *all* that is *relevant* and *all* that is *meaningful* to the phenomenon under study is observed. Thus, empirical research is always a compromise between the kinds of data a scientist needs to study a phenomenon and the minimum information necessary to make the study methodologically scientific and socially and culturally meaningful.

When studying sexual behavior, the compromises (between what is to be observed, the way it is to be observed, and the conceptual language through which it is to be observed) are enormously complex because of the social and cultural context surrounding sexual behavior. Although a scientist may make reasonable compromises, he is frequently criticized for doing so. The compromises resulting in the behavioral scientist's *specifications* of phenomena (see Kinsey, who conceptually chose to observe "outlets," i.e., orgasms) are frequently used to question the validity and reliability of his results. Margaret Mead (1948), for example, has argued that the use of the concept "outlet" suggests that Kinsey's "treatment of sex reduced it to the category of a simple act of elimination" and thus has little psychological meaning. This criticism is interesting but not valid since it substitutes Mead's connotation for the term "outlet" for the referent Kinsey specified. It betrays a humanistic attitude toward empirical research rather than an understanding of it.

Let us view operations of the empirical method in greater detail through the work of the Kinsey group. The process of logical conceptualization can be described as follows: First there is the phenomenon of sexual excita-

tion resulting in orgasm. (Note that any notion of the ethical propriety of sexual excitation is not entertained, nor can it be within the empirical framework.) Then there is the distinction as to the singularity or partnership wherein the phenomenon occurs: masturbation, homosexuality, heterosexuality, animal contact. For heterosexual contact, the question is with whom? and under what conditions? Further specification is needed by using a social category, "marriage," to differentiate the conditions under which behavior occurs. We have: premarital, marital, nonmarital, extramarital. A further analytic distinction is: In what way is orgasm reached?—oral contact, manual contact, genital contact, anal contact, etc. These categories are then to be related to twelve basic factors which are social attributes and quasi-variables.

After conceptualization is completed the data-gathering phase begins. The Kinsey data (or observations) were secured by asking people over 500 questions in a face-to-face situation. Among these questions were the twelve above-mentioned factors: (1) sex, (2) race-cultural group, (3) marital status, (4) age, (5) age at adolescence, (6) educational level, (7) occupational class of subject, (8) occupational class of parent, (9) rural-urban background, (10) religious group, (11) religious adherence, and (12) geographic origin.

The variety of sexual behavior that was found to exist by the Kinsey group was grouped under the twelve factors. Such findings (e.g., incidence of premarital outlets among urban as compared to rural respondents) are presented in charts, graphs, and tables, and the discussion illuminates the "meaning" of the findings, i.e., the findings are placed into a social context. The over-all result is knowledge of how people behave sexually. The process of description ends with this, and the process of analysis proceeds. Not only is it possible to learn what people do, but it is possible to learn about qualitative differences among their actions. To learn this, the data are "manipulated," that is, they are combined, separated, and recombined. The adding or subtracting of additional data leads to the discerning of patterns of behavior. It is not sufficient merely to describe existent behavior through singular phenomena; it is necessary to learn the *patterns* of actions. The constant manipulating of the data is performed to identify "qualitatively" different, socially meaningful sexual behavior patterns, not in the sense of socially acceptable, but in the sense that a person's behavior is meaningful to him.

Concretely, the manipulation of data to secure patterns can be shown in the following example. The Kinsey group found homosexual behavior among boys aged 8–10 (inspecting each other's genitalia, entering into mutual sexual play, or jointly masturbating) and among adult males (setting up permanent or impermanent relationships). The duration and frequency of these acts were noted separately. Suppose, through the manipulation of the data, it is found that some boys continue mutual masturbation into adolescence and, as age increases, embellish their masturbatory activities with additional types of homosexual contact, such as oral and anal activity. And suppose other boys indulge in mutual masturbation that declines in their adolescence as their contact with girls increases and heterosexual petting and other activities lead to orgasm. The quantitative change of behavior into these two different directions, that is, the different combination of particular sexual acts, leads to the identification of two patterns. These different patterns based on quantitative data are perceived as different qualitative behavior and are labeled differently. Kinsey's group identified these different qualitative homosexual patterns by different points on their scale of homosexuality/heterosexuality.

We have presented the empirical approach to the study of sexual behavior by using examples from the work of Kinsey, and by indicating the types of data the method can produce, some of the observational techniques developed, and the statistical manipulations used.

Techniques of Observation in Sexual Behavior

If empirical observation in the area of sexual behavior were to be confined to visual observation, no data, at least in the Western world, would be available. Direct visual observation is difficult to achieve, except in specific experi-

mental situations, to which sexual behavior does not readily lend itself. Visual observation of sexual responses has been used only by physicians to learn of the changes in brain waves under coitus as recorded by an encephalograph or by experimenters, such as Masters, who have been interested in the physiology of orgasm. Observations of behavior of people in coital situations or in the human situations preliminary to coitus or other sexual activities have been rarely reported in the scientific literature.

To gain information on or about human sexual behavior, behavioral scientists use the same methods used to gain information about political, economic, esthetic, or other human behavior: indirect techniques. The major techniques used are interviews, questionnaires, content analyses, and scales. All of these techniques in the last analysis ask questions and receive answers. The answers a scientist receives are what he terms "observations."

The memory of the person asked is the sieve through which observations are made. This sieve has presented scientists with innumerable problems. Can the memory of a person be trusted even if the person wishes to tell the whole truth? Does a person tell the whole truth even if he wants to? Is there interference from unconscious sources, especially when it concerns such emotionally charged materials and experiences as sexual behavior? These questions are enormously important, but they are not unique to the field of sexual behavior. The problem exists also when autobiographies are consulted or when historical records and documents are perused. It is questionable whether a statesman in his memoirs presents the whole story, or whether he is cognizant of his "public duty" or "the image of himself" that he desires to present to future generations. The limiting condition that prevails in the behavioral sciences generally is that we can work only with the *given* and constantly attempt to assess its veracity. The methodological researches of sociologists and psychologists have created a variety of techniques whereby the veracity of responses to questions can be assessed and improved. The interested reader is referred to the technical literature on this question by Hyman (1954, 1955), Lazarsfeld and Rosenberg (1955), Kahn and Cannell (1957), and others.

Interviews and Questionnaires

Questions may be asked in a face-to-face situation by a trained interviewer and recorded by him. Or a respondent may receive a questionnaire through the impersonal channel of the mails and answer it in solitude. It is also possible to distribute questionnaires to a group of people who are assembled for that purpose and who complete them in one sitting.

Whether the questionnaire or interview method is used depends upon the assessment of the scientist as to which of the techniques will produce the most accurate data relative to his research problem, and what compromise will facilitate maximum results. Such factors as the availability of funds and of time, and the substantive purpose of the research, are decisive as to the observational technique to be used.

Both the interview and the questionnaire contain an organized sequence of questions so that the subject has a variety of response alternatives. In the interview situation there are, theoretically, unlimited alternatives. The interviewer may pursue a point as far as the interviewee is willing to go and the study permits. In the questionnaire there are limitations to these alternatives, and once a questionnaire is completed by a respondent, a point of no return has been reached. Thus, the interview is more flexible than the questionnaire, but in terms of substantive data, Albert Ellis (1948) found that when studying love and family relations of college girls, either method seems to be satisfactory.

The interview is frequently used as an exploratory tool, searching for relationships or dimensions of experience. The questionnaire is most frequently used when a large sample of respondents is to be surveyed to learn the extent to which a relationship is general or unique, whether it appears often or infrequently.

Content Analysis

The interview and questionnaire are not the only tools of observation available to behavioral scientists. Each time we read a novel, a letter, an article, or a book we observe the thoughts and ideas of other people. The age-old technique of assessing what the written piece of communication contains has in recent times been made more systematic and precise through the technique of content analysis.

When content analysis is used in a systematic, quantitative, and objective manner, it is possible to learn the precise content and the attitudinal direction of the content, i.e., whether the content is communicated with a favorable, noncommittal, or unfavorable tone. Content analysis can ascertain with precision the ideas and ideologies to which readers are exposed by the mass-communications media and specifically can answer questions of "who says what to whom."

Thus, Albert Ellis (1951, 1954) content-analyzed mass-media magazines to learn what types of sexual information is communicated and with what attitudes particular sexual behavior patterns are presented. Chall (1955) analyzed the reviews and articles on the Kinsey report that had appeared in magazines during 1948-1949 to learn whether representatives of intellectual disciplines reacted in the same way to the report and found, for instance, that biologists were most favorable to the report and humanists and literati least favorable.

Scales

Since people have some predispositions about sexual behavior, and predispositions to actions involve feelings as well as thoughts, the assessment of a person's attitude toward sexual behavior frequently becomes important in a research situation.

Behavioral scientists have developed attitude scales to learn not only whether a particular attitude is present or not, but also the strength and intensity of an attitude. Scaling techniques rank behavior on some criterion of "least" to "most." An important example is the Podell and Perkins (1957) Scale of Sexual Experience, which reveals the existence of "a cumulative sequence wherein a person who has participated in a 'more advanced' behavior may be assumed to have experienced the 'less advanced' behaviors." Their scale of sexual behavior is such that a "male who has had oral contact with a female breast has also engaged in lip kissing, deep (tongue) kissing and manual stimulation of the female breast." Such scales make it possible to learn of the distribution of sexual experience in a population and its correlates. Those interested in the complex methodology and technique of scale construction are directed to the large technical literature on the subject as reviewed by Torgerson (1958) and others.

Conclusion

We have briefly described the development of the study of sexual behavior during the nineteenth and twentieth centuries. Early studies produced theories of sexual behavior emphasizing the dire consequences of negative deviations (e.g., masturbation, non-Biblical experimentation, etc.), and the unlimited possibilities of happiness of positive deviation (e.g., a new social order of free love, the coitus reservatus of the Oneida community's fame, the trial marriage advocated by Judge Lindsey, etc.). Some of the theories that were constructed in the past were grandiose in nature, encompassing all manner of sexual phenomena and leaving the essential knowledge of "what people actually do" outside their area of concern.

The empirical-quantitative method, in contrast to the grand theory of a Havelock Ellis, a Sigmund Freud, the Vaertings, or of William I. Thomas, seems dull, plodding, and unimaginative. But this method has produced tremendous advances in studying sexual phenomena by two approaches: conceptually and methodologically. Conceptually, it has created a language describing sexual behavior that is relatively free of "normative" encumbrances and connotations. It perceives sexual behavior as based less on human values traditionally defined and more on frequency and functionality. Methodologically, it has created the research tools and techniques and the logic of procedure whereby the attitudes, opinions, and feelings of large plural populations have been ascertained within a controllable margin of error.

Lest the huge amount of data secured through the empirical-quantitative method drown us in an embarrassment of riches, it is necessary to put some of these data to the test of a theory or to use them as a basis for the construction of a theory. As a ship needs a lighthouse to gain entrance to a harbor, so empirical studies need theory to guide their explorations. There is no need for an immutable or an aprioristic theory, but there is a need for a theory that is flexible to the exigencies of the subject matter and that firmly rests on the observation of "common," and not merely the "unusual," sexual phenomena. The empirical-quantitative method can lead to conceptualizing specific knowledge about what sexuality means to people. The past and some current orientations that have emphasized what the absence of sexuality (or the presence of distorted sexuality) means to a given person have neglected the construction of a much-needed theory by which sexuality can be viewed as a form of "normal sociability," and not merely as behavior through which the malsocialization of the child manifests itself.

References

Berelson, Bernard, *Content Analysis in Communication Research.* Glencoe, Ill.: The Free Press, 1952.

Bloch, Iwan, *Beitraege zur Aetiologie der Psychopathia Sexualis.* Dresden: H. R. Dohrn Verlag, 1903.

Bloch, Iwan, *The Sexual Life of Our Time.* London: Rebman, 1908.

Bromley, Dorothy D., and Britten, Florence H., *Youth and Sex: A Study of 1,300 College Students.* New York: Harper & Brothers, 1938.

Chall, Leo P., "The Reception of the Kinsey Report in the Periodicals of the United States: 1947-1949." In Jerome Himelhoch and Sylvia F. Fava (eds.), *Sexual Behavior in American Society.* New York: W. W. Norton & Co., Inc., 1955.

Ditzion, Sidney, *Marriage, Morals and Sex in America.* New York: Bookman Associates, Inc., 1953.

Ehrmann, Winston, *Premarital Dating Behavior.* New York: Henry Holt & Co., Inc., 1959.

Ellis, Albert, "Questionnaire *Versus* Interview Methods in the Study of Human Love Relationships. II. Uncategorized Responses." *Am. Sociol. Rev. 13;* 61-65, 1948.

Ellis, Albert, *The American Sexual Tragedy.* New York: Twayne Pub., 1954.

Ellis, Albert, *The Folklore of Sex.* New York: Charles Boni, 1951; New York: Grove Press, 1961.

Ellis, Havelock, *Studies in the Psychology of Sex.* New York: Random House, 1936.

Exner, M. J., *Problems and Principles of Sex Education. A Study of 948 College Men.* New York: Association Press, 1915.

Finger, F. W., "Sex Beliefs and Practices Among Male College Students." *J. Abnorm. Soc. Psychol. 42;* 57-67, 1947.

Freud, Sigmund, *Three Essays on the Theory of Sexuality.* London: Image Pub. Co., 1905, 1949.

Gebhard, Paul H., Pomeroy, Wardell B., Martin, Clyde E., and Christensen, Cornelia V., *Pregnancy, Birth and Abortion.* New York: Harper & Brothers, 1958.

Hamilton, G. V., *A Research in Marriage.* New York: Boni, 1929.

Hirschfeld, Magnus, *Sexual Anomalies and Perversions.* New York: Emerson Books, Inc., 1944.

Homan, Leslie B., and Schaffner, Bertram, "The Sex Lives of Unmarried Men." *Am. J. Sociol. 52;* 501-507, 1947.

Hyman, Herbert H., *Interviewing in Social Research.* Chicago: University of Chicago Press, 1954.

Hyman, Herbert H., *Survey Design and Analysis.* Glencoe, Ill.: The Free Press, 1955.

Kahn, Robert L., and Cannell, Charles F., *The Dynamics of Interviewing.* New York: John Wiley & Sons, Inc., 1957.

Kinsey, Alfred C. *et al., Sexual Behavior in the Human Male.* Philadelphia: W. B. Saunders Co., 1948.

Kinsey, Alfred C. *et al., Sexual Behavior in the Human Female.* Philadelphia: W. B. Saunders Co., 1953.

Lazarsfeld, Paul F., and Rosenberg, Morris (eds.), *The Language of Social Research.* Glencoe, Ill.: The Free Press, 1955.

Lindsey, Ben B., and Evans, Wainwright, *The Companionate Marriage.* New York: Boni and Liveright, 1927.

Mead, Margaret, "An Anthropologist Looks at the Report." In *Problems of Sexual Behavior.* New York: American Social Hygiene Association, 1948.

Moll, Albert, *Die Kontraere Sexualempfindung.* Berlin: Fischer, 1893.

Moll, Albert, *Libido Sexualis.* New York: Ethnological Press, 1933.

Peck, M. W., and Wells, F. L., "On the Psycho-sexuality of College Graduate Men." *Mental Hyg. 7;* 697-714, 1923.

Peck, M. W., and Wells, F. L., "Further Studies in Psycho-sexuality of College Graduate Men." *Mental Hyg. 9;* 502-520, 1925.

Peterson, K. M., "Early Sex Information and Its Influence on Later Sex Concepts." Unpublished M.A. thesis, University of Colorado, 1938.

Podell, Lawrence, and Perkins, John C., "A Guttman Scale for Sexual Experience." *J. Abnorm. Sociol. Psychol. 54;* 420-422, 1957.

Porterfield, Austin L., and Salley, H. Ellison, "Current Folkways of Sexual Behavior." *Am. J. Soc. 52;* 209-216, 1946.

Thomas, W. I., and Znaniecki, F., *The Polish Peasant in Europe and America.* Boston: Gorham, 1918-1920.

Torgerson, Warren S., "Theory and Methods of Scaling." New York: John Wiley & Sons, Inc., 1958.

Vaerting, Mathilde, and Vaerting, Mathias, *The Dominant Sex.* New York: Doran, 1923.

LEO P. CHALL

Abortion

ABORTION is defined as the termination of an intrauterine pregnancy before the twenty-eighth week of gestation. At 28 weeks, the fetus weighs about 800 grams (1 lb. 13 oz.) and might be viable. Some pediatricians in especially well equipped hospitals succeed in keeping alive infants weighing as little as 500 grams (1 lb. 2 oz.); these clinicians consider 22 weeks as the upper limit for abortion.

About 10 per cent of all pregnancies in the United States terminate in abortion, a staggering number considering that, in 1955, the latest available date, there were four million pregnancies, four hundred thousand of which terminated in abortions.

Abortions may be divided into spontaneous and induced abortions. Laymen call spontaneous abortions "miscarriages" and erroneously associate the word abortion with illegal abortions only. The medical terminology uses both terms interchangeably.

Spontaneous Abortions

These may be caused by:

1. Pathological conditions in the fertilized ovum, due to maternal or paternal causes.

2. The abnormal development of the placenta, producing a faulty implantation of the fetus in the uterus or a decidual hemorrhage (bleeding between the placenta and the lining of the uterus); hydatiform degeneration of the placenta; or premature rupture of the membranes.

3. Congenital malformations due to intrinsic or more frequently to extrinsic factors, producing a temporarily insufficient blood supply to the fetus and effecting a temporary cessation of development.

4. Cord anomalies, such as loops, knots, or prolapse of the cord, that bring about the death of the fetus and cause a subsequent abortion.

Hertig and Sheldon (1943), in their series of observations found that 48.9 per cent of all abortions are due to pathological ova and embryos. Other scientists quote lower figures, such as Javert (1957), who reports only 34.9 per cent of abortions as caused by such anomalies. The figures of Hertig are generally accepted by the profession; therefore all other causes together can only account for the other 50 per cent of spontaneous abortions.

A precise examination of the pathological specimen frequently shows that several causative agents have been involved, and it may be difficult to determine which are primary and which secondary.

Real and Imaginary Extrinsic Causes

There are many real and imaginary extrinsic factors to which spontaneous nonrecurrent abortion is attributed:

1. A displacement or retroplacement of the uterus will rarely cause abortion. Only if the growing retroverted uterus becomes incarcerated in the pelvis and is not freed will an abortion follow. Usually nature solves the problem by spontaneously bringing the growing uterus forward.

2. Temporary endocrine unbalance in some cases is responsible for abortions. Thyroid disfunctions would especially fall into this category.

3. Laparotomies (abdominal operations)

for emergencies during early pregnancy might cause abortions. However, recent investigations have shown that even the removal of the corpus luteum (an endocrine functioning part of the ovary from which the ovum derived) does not necessarily affect the pregnancy. Carefully performed surgery under appropriate medication will usually preserve the fetus.

4. Radiation in sufficient amounts will definitely cause an abortion.

5. Electric shock and lightning may be a cause.

6. Alcohol, except in excess, as well as nicotine, has no effect on pregnancy, although there exists a report claiming that heavy smoking doubles the incidences of premature births.

7. Coitus as a cause of abortion is questionable, although laymen attribute abortions to it more frequently than to any other cause. This superstition goes back to antiquity. Animals supposedly do not permit intercourse during pregnancy. The physiological facts are as follows: Intercourse, and especially orgasm, evoke uterine contractions and engorgement of the endometrium and decidua (lining of the uterus), creating the possibility of a decidual hemorrhage.

The actual relationship between coitus and abortion has so far not been scientifically determined; therefore, some obstetricians advise the avoidance of intercourse during expected menstrual periods, others suggest abstinence for the first four months of pregnancy. Since very few couples follow these instructions, coitus can certainly be only a very limited contributory cause of abortion.

8. Traveling does not cause abortions. Observations of groups who traveled extensively during World War II and the Korean War showed that the abortion rate of wives of soldiers amounted to half of the average rate.

9. External traumas, including falls, seldom cause abortions. The growing fetus is so well protected that a normal embryo, in a reasonably healthy woman, is extremely difficult to dislodge. Usually only direct injuries to the uterus or traumas causing a separation of the placenta will result in an interruption of the pregnancy.

10. Dental care during pregnancy will not cause abortion or affect the fetus, but it is ad-visable to use local anesthesia without epinephrine, as the latter may have a sensitizing effect on the uterus.

11. Modern birth control methods do not produce abortions. The employment of intra-uterine stem pessaries, used frequently in the past, not only resulted in serious infections but could also induce abortions. However, these devices have not been prescribed, in this country at least, for many years.

12. A negative Rh factor does not produce abortions. Rh sensitization plays a part only in late pregnancy.

13. A carefully performed vaginal examination does not cause an abortion.

14. Psychological factors definitely play a contributing part, but it is difficult to prove a direct relationship. Laymen often erroneously relate abortions to psychological trauma when physical causes were in fact responsible.

Classification

Clinically, spontaneous abortions can be classified as threatened, imminent, inevitable, incomplete, complete, and missed. Typical for the various kinds are the following findings:

1. *Threatened abortion*—Bloody vaginal discharge or frank bleeding occur; slight intermittent low abdominal pain may or may not be present; the cervix is closed.

2. *Imminent abortion*—Bleeding and cramping pain increase and the cervix is effaced (the neck of the womb becomes flatter).

3. *Inevitable abortion*—The membranes (bag of water) rupture and the conceptus starts to protrude through the dilated cervix.

4. *Incomplete abortion*—Part of the conceptus, usually the fetus, is expelled, while the placenta and the membranes remain in the uterus; bleeding, which may sometimes be profuse, continues. Administration of iron for anemia, convalescent regimen for one week, and a checkup after three weeks should bring about complete involution (normal state) of the uterus.

5. *Missed abortion*—The fetus dies in the uterus and a considerable period of time may elapse before its delivery. Missed abortion is often psychologically very trying for the patient. Medical induction (estrogen, progesterone, quinine, and oxytoxics) is apparently

valueless in shortening the interval between the diagnosis of intrauterine death and the delivery of the fetus; if the fetus is retained longer than three to four weeks, surgical intervention is indicated, though it may be quite difficult.

Habitual Abortions

Spontaneous abortions can occur either nonrecurrently or repeatedly; three or more abortions consecutively are called "habitual abortions." A single spontaneous abortion is frequently due to temporary factors, to be compared, as trivial as it sounds, to the premature fall of a bad apple. If no obvious cause for one abortion is found, the physician will suggest the patient try again.

According to Hertig, 3.6 to 9.8 per cent of all abortions are habitual. The incidence is only 0.4 per cent of all pregnancies. Habitual abortions are not accidental. In order to avoid them a complete preconceptional investigation of all aspects is mandatory. The procedure should include:

1. A conference with the husband and wife, discussing the problem and the possible results and prognosis; the obstetrical history is obtained at this time.

2. A routine medical examination, including the following:

   a. complete physical and pelvic examination;

   b. blood studies;

   c. basal metabolism, PBI (protein-bound iodine), and other indicated hormone tests (17-ketosteroids, urinary pregnanediol, etc.);

   d. hysterosalpyngogram for the diagnosis of any anatomical abnormalities of the reproductive organs. Uterus septus, uterus bicornis, double uterus, and cervical pathology, including incompetent internal os, retrodisplacement of the uterus, and fibromyomas and their relationship to the endometrium (inner lining of the uterus) are determined by this diagnostic means;

   e. endometrial biopsy;

   f. careful examination of the husband's semen. Correlations between morphological abnormalities of the spermatozoa and certain types of abortions are suggestive; the quality and quantity of spermatozoa are contributing factors, but further clinical studies are necessary before final conclusions can be drawn.

TREATMENT OF HABITUAL ABORTION

Improvement of the general health of the patient is essential. Weight, rest, exercise, etc., must be controlled, local and general infections eliminated, and, if tests indicate the necessity, thyroid and other hormone therapy administered.

Uterine abnormalities may sometimes be corrected surgically, such as the Strassmann operation for double uterus and the Shirodkar operation for fascial repair of incompetent internal os. The latter operation can be performed during pregnancy up to the sixth month.

Myomectomy for extirpation of myomas is rarely indicated since only submucous myomas can influence the nidation (fixation) of the fertilized ovum and the placenta.

Retroflection of the uterus should be corrected, even if it only rarely produces passive congestion. A ring, inserted preconceptionally and removed after the fourth month, is all that is necessary. The suspension operation, so fashionable in the past, is rarely indicated.

Sexual abstinence is stressed by many clinicians, less because they are convinced that intercourse per se causes the abortion than for the psychological impact it may have on the husband, making him a participant in the regimen.

Syphilis, formerly blamed as the main cause for habitual abortion, is rarely responsible, but may be the reason for prematurity and stillbirth and should therefore be treated.

In the past thirty years therapy of habitual abortion has mainly stressed the endocrinological aspects, although hormonal imbalance can be responsible for only a small percentage of the cases. Since half of the abortions are due to defective germ plasm, and all the other above-mentioned factors are also contributory, the overstress of hormone therapy appears questionable.

Widely used for hormone therapy is stilbestrol, a synthetic female sex hormone introduced by Smith and Smith, which stimulates the placental formation of progesterone. The results reported by Smith and Smith were excellent; however, many authors fail to support this view and some investigators have noted only an increase in missed abortions. Recently, several clinicians have claimed success with newer progesterone-like preparations, but only in cases in which laboratory tests showed low pregnanediol levels. Kupperman, by giving patients 1,000 mg. of progesterone a day orally, succeeded in lowering the recurrent abortion rate significantly.

Vitman E was hopefully used at one time; but many clinicians doubt its effectiveness now. Vitamin C and hesperidin are used for correction of capillary permeability.

The long list of varied and apparently successful treatments poses the question to the clinician as to a possible common denominator. Actually, many critical gynecologists agree that it is frequently not the specific treatment that succeeds, but the enthusiastically employed therapeutic regimen; the results may therefore be related to the personality of the therapist and the response of the patient. For this reason, Mann (1956) and many others, including the writer, stress the psychological aspects in their treatment regimen. Frequent visits and unlimited telephone calls are encouraged. All the psychological problems of the patient are discussed. Good medical care, including correction of poor dietary habits, the taking of sufficient amounts of vitamins, and avoidance of undue fatigue, are stressed in addition to the psychological approach.

Induced Abortion

Induced abortion is defined by Gebhard and his associates (1958) as "expulsion or removal of the embryo, preceded by some intentional act by the mother or another person, before it had developed to a point where it could survive."

History

Induced abortion is as old as the recorded history of mankind and its acceptance or repudiation depends on the general social, ethical, and legal views of the particular society under consideration.

The Assyrian Law, about 1500 B.C. punished with death the woman who willfully aborted; Jewish Law penalized abortion according to the rule "thou shall give life for life."

The opinion of the ancient Greeks was divided. Plato recommended abortion and feticide as regular institutions of the Ideal State. Aristotle advised the practice of birth control in order to keep the population within the limits he considered essential for a well-ordered community, and abortion was the logical choice if birth control failed.

Hippocrates, the father of the oath every physician in this country takes, pledging "I will not give to a woman an abortive remedy," expressed the minority opinion of the Pythagoreans.

The Roman Law did not consider the fetus a human being but only a part of the mother; since it had no independent life, it could not be the object of a killing. Abortion was considered property damage and punishable as such.

This approach remained in force until, centuries later, under the influence of Christianity, the evaluation of the fetus as a human being was introduced into the legislation.

The judgment of the Christian Church also varied in the different periods of history. Tertullian, around 200 A.D. (*Apologeticus,* chapter IX) was one of the first to formulate the idea that the fruit in the womb is a human being and that therefore abortion is murder.

The belief that the fruit has a soul at the moment of conception was subsequently submerged and St. Augustine, for instance, differentiated between a "formed" and a "nonformed" fetus and considered that abortion of the latter does not constitute murder. This distinction became embodied into the canon law about the middle of the twelfth century and from then on into the laws of England and the Continent. St. Thomas of Aquinas introduced the principle that life is related to movement and that therefore life does not start at conception, but at the moment of quickening.

The importance of quickening in relation to abortion and the opinion that termination of pregnancy before quickening is no crime, or at least is a lesser crime, became part of the common law in England and influenced some laws in the United States.

The Catholic Church, on the other hand, has settled the question of animation on the grounds that the soul enters the embryo at the moment of conception and that therefore the gravity of the sin of abortion is the same, regardless of the time when it is committed.

Induced abortions may be divided into two categories: (1) therapeutic and (2) illegal or criminal abortion.

The dividing line between the two, as every physician knows, may be very thin, even if the prevailing law in this country is very clear—that an induced abortion is illegal, unless it is necessary to preserve the *life* of the mother.

Therapeutic Abortions

Interruptions of pregnancy on clinical grounds have declined tremendously with the advance of medicine and therapeutics. Most organic conditions are not aggravated by pregnancy, if the disease is properly managed. Tuberculosis is probably the most striking example.

Postpartum advice to women, explaining the hazards of further pregnancies, has decreased the number of cases requiring therapeutic abortions even more. This type of patient has to make the choice between birth control and sterilization or the practice of abstinence.

INDICATIONS

The most common indications for therapeutic abortions are:

1. Hypertensive renal diseases;
2. Serious cardiac conditions, such as rheumatic heart disease, not amenable to surgery;
3. Advanced tuberculosis in the first trimester, if it does not respond to treatment;
4. Malignancies of the breast and of the genitourinary system;
5. Hyperemesis gravidarum (pernicious vomiting of pregnancy), but only if there is hepatic and renal involvement. This is actually a very rare complication;
6. Thyrotoxicosis and diabetes, but only rarely;
7. Mental diseases, particularly schizophrenia, reactive depressions with suicidal tendencies, and certain psychoneuroses.

The following three indications are accepted by many clinicians, although they stretch the definition "danger to the life of the mother":

1. German measles if contracted in the first twelve weeks of pregnancy will cause serious congenital defects in 10 to 20 per cent of the infants.
2. Rh sensitization might present an argument in favor of therapeutic abortion, but our limited knowledge of the subject and our inability to make an exact diagnosis speak against it.
3. Amaurotic familial idiocy.

As can be seen, there has been a tremendous change in the indications for therapeutic abortions. During the period from 1943 to 1947, circulatory diseases, fibromyomas, and mental diseases accounted for 45 per cent of all therapeutic abortions in New York City; 8 per cent of these were performed for psychiatric reasons. In the years 1951 to 1957, mental conditions alone accounted for 46 per cent of the therapeutic abortions.

LEGAL POSITION OF THE MEDICAL PROFESSION

This shift underlines a precarious situation. The obstetrician is under terrific pressures to widen his indications, but while the "preservation of the life of the mother" remains the only legal indication, he is unable to give in and remain within the law; in self-defense, he shifts the burden of the decision to the psychiatrist, who is requested now to make decisions which, strictly speaking, are the prerogatives of the lawmakers.

The legal position of obstetricians has become so difficult that, in order to protect themselves, they have developed rules and regulations for the management of therapeutic abortions that have become continuously stricter.

Most doctors will undertake a therapeutic abortion only after consultation with colleagues in a reputable hospital. Accredited hospitals have specific regulations for such cases, requiring letters from two consultants (certified specialists in their respective fields) recommending the abortion and outlining the reasons for their recommendation. A specially appointed committee consisting of hospital staff members examines the letters and sometimes requests further tests and examinations.

However, even if the physician follows the

above procedure, he may still come into conflict with the law, especially if a fatality occurs. On the other hand, Dr. Milton Helpern, the Chief Medical Examiner of the City of New York, states that he does not know of a single instance where a therapeutic abortion performed in an approved hospital was ever questioned in court.

TECHNIQUES OF THERAPEUTIC ABORTIONS

The techniques of abortion can be divided into medical and surgical. At this point, only legally and professionally accepted and practiced methods are discussed. The unauthorized, dangerous, and often ineffective methods of illegal abortions will be dealt with later.

1. X-ray radiation destroys the embryo, which will be expelled within a few weeks after the exposure to radiation. However, since an unpredictable temporary or permanent damage occurs to the ovaries, most gynecologists and roentgenologists condemn this method.

2. New experiments with so-called antagonists or antimetabolites are being tried out lately in university hospitals. Antimetabolites interfere with the growth of juvenile cells and therefore with the fetus; the best-known of these drugs interferes with folic-acid metabolism. These compounds are very dangerous in uncontrolled use because, if they are not successful in killing the fetus, they will produce development anomalies that result in the birth of an abnormal child at term; an additional danger is that they may affect the bone marrow of the mother.

3. Intrauterine injections of pastes were at one time thought to be a harmless method, but soon serious complications, including fatalities from fat and air emboli, were reported.

4. Laminaria—a seaweed pencil—is widely used in Europe, but not in this country. The laminaria pencil is inserted into the cervical canal, where, on contact with moisture, it swells and gradually dilates the cervical canal. Instrumental evacuation is performed on the following day.

5. Most obstetricians in this country agree that, if a pregnancy must be interrupted, it should be done in the early months of pregnancy by the technique of dilatation of the cervix and curettage; after the third month, hysterotomy (miniature Caesarean section) is the preferred method.

Sterilization together with therapeutic abortion is often indicated; however, it should definitely not become a routine procedure, imposing a punishment on the mother.

RISKS OF THERAPEUTIC ABORTIONS

Even when therapeutic abortions are performed under ideal conditions, not all risk is eliminated. Hemorrhage, injuries, and infections do occur. In the years from 1945 to 1947, of the 3,000 patients on whom therapeutic abortions in New York City were performed, 3.9 per cent died; this figure includes patients who died from the diseases that had constituted indications for the abortion.

Late sequelae of therapeutic abortions include placenta praevia or placenta accreta in subsequent pregnancies, and sterility. The latter is rare if the surgery has been performed properly.

Endocrine disturbances arise more frequently after repeated abortions.

Psychoneuroses follow abortions more frequently than is usually suspected. The major psychological effects are frustration, guilt, fear of retaliation, and resentment or even hostility against the male partner. This fact seems the more important in view of the increasing psychiatric indications for therapeutic abortions.

INCIDENCE OF THERAPEUTIC ABORTIONS

Nelson and Hunter of the Mayo Clinic estimate that 18,000 therapeutic abortions are performed in the United States each year; they consider 1 therapeutic abortion in 250 pregnancies an accepted rate in a private hospital. Interestingly, the Margaret Hague Hospital in Jersey City had only 8 therapeutic abortions in 150,000 deliveries. In the years from 1951 to 1953, there were 3.5 therapeutic abortions per 1,000 deliveries in New York City.

Illegal Abortions

Incidence

The number of illegal abortions performed yearly is difficult to estimate because of the secrecy surrounding this type of procedure and the fact that the estimate depends to some extent on the judgment of the woman—whether she was really pregnant and caused the abortion or merely brought on a delayed period.

The number of illegal abortions in the United States is estimated to range from 200,000 to 1,200,000 per year. Gebhard and his associates from the Kinsey Sex Research Institute (1958) give the following figures: 88 to 95 per cent of all premarital conceptions terminate with induced abortion; 22 per cent of all married women have had at least one induced abortion; 87 per cent of the abortions are undertaken by physicians, while 8 per cent are self-induced.

The majority of cases of illegally induced abortions come to hospitals with the diagnosis of "incomplete spontaneous abortion," and hospital doctors are in most cases either unable or unwilling to ascertain the true facts.

Legal and Moral Conflicts

The enormous number of illegal abortions makes it obvious that all strata of our society are involved and that a deep conflict exists between the legal, moral, and social theories and the *de facto* findings. Many individuals who are publicly against illegal abortions cannot, under the pressure of biologic necessities and economic realties, easily uphold the hypothetical standards involved.

There is little public interest in this country in changing the existing laws regarding termination of pregnancy, although the United States has one of the strictest definitions in the world for lawful abortions.

Our approach to problems involving sex has changed markedly in the rapidly changing world of sputniks and atomic bombs, but our public attitude toward unwed mothers remains the same and the law still stipulates that premarital pregnancies must be carried to term.

Other factors increase the dilemma. The abolition of prostitution has increased the incidence of premarital intercourse; sex education is hampered by lack of trained teachers and by many reactionary P.T.A.'s. Illegal abortion is one of the results of an education that avoids teaching how to prevent conception but encourages a hysterical rejection of premarital pregnancy.

The problem of pregnancy in the married woman can be nearly as urgent as that of the single woman. Large families, housing shortages, the necessity for the wife to contribute to the family income in order to keep up with the excessive standards of living created and advocated by Madison Avenue, the breakdown of family life, and many other factors force thousands of married women daily to seek the only solution they know.

State laws regarding illegal abortions differ. Most states punish the attempt, *i.e.*, the intent to perform an abortion, irrespective of whether or not it was actually performed. In order to punish the attempt to perform abortion, twenty-seven states require proof that the patient was actually pregnant; sixteen other states do not require such proof. The penalties for performing abortions vary greatly and may range from one year to fourteen years imprisonment. Some states provide penalties for the woman who solicits or consents to an abortion. However, no recorded prosecution of abortion under this law is recorded in the United States.

Death of a woman as a result of an abortion attempt is considered in fourteen states as murder, and fourteen other states regard it as manslaughter.

Techniques of Illegal Abortions

The lay person intending to induce abortion usually tries one of the countless abortifacients on the market before resorting to vaginal or intrauterine manipulations. These remedies have been brought down by word of mouth from generation to generation and vary from country to country and from civilization to civilization, although they are basically alike. The large number of abortifacients makes it obvious that a real abortifacient does not exist. There is no oral medication that can terminate an unwanted pregnancy without doing harm to the mother.

Most of these drugs cause an intoxication of the mother and fetus. The fetus, being the less resistant organism, may die first, obviously leaving no margin of safety for the mother. To mention any oral abortifacient means only to warn against all of them. Phosphorus, arsenic, lead, acids, alcohol, apiol, aloe, ergotrate, quinine, and castor oil have all been tried with tragic results or no result at all.

Most women who claim to have aborted by using drugs or herbs were either not pregnant or would have aborted spontaneously anyhow.

Mechanical abortifacients, such as hot baths, steam, hot douches, etc., are equally ineffective. Certain disinfecting tablets have been especially popular. These have caused extensive erosions in the vagina, with severe hemorrhages and kidney damage from absorption, but no abortions.

Mechanical traumas are still erroneously believed to cause abortions. Jumping, stretching, traveling on bad roads, lifting, and even hitting and massaging the abdomen are practiced with poor results.

Insertion of an instrument and rupturing the membranes is a commonly used method, practiced by thousands who are admitted daily to our hospitals as cases of incomplete abortion. Either the patient herself or another person inserts a knitting needle, or similar instrument into the cervix. If the patient is successful, the abortion starts five to twelve days later. Most people are not familiar with the internal female anatomy and much organic injury, in addition to the dangers of infection from unsterile instruments, can result. Perforation of the uterus and of the vagina, peritonitis, parametritis, and fat emboli endanger the lives of these women.

Intrauterine infusions are used with quicker but even more catastrophic results.

Notwithstanding these dangers, the number of fatalities from illegal abortions dropped in New York City from 140 in 1918 to 15 in 1951, obviously due to the discovery of antibiotics.

Solutions to the Problem

The solution to the problem of illegal abortion is not found by denying its existence. However, the multitude of questions that arise concerning any attempt to manage this problem makes an early solution in this country very unlikely.

Positive approaches to this problem have been tried by other countries who faced this issue, and their experiences might provide us with certain ideas on how to solve the situation.

SCANDINAVIAN COUNTRIES

In 1938 Sweden adopted a law permitting therapeutic abortions for medical, humanitarian, and eugenic reasons; in 1946 the law was extended to include the indication of presumptive debility. Eugenic indications are determined by a special Committee of the Royal Medical Board. Therapeutic abortions number 4 to 5 per cent of all live births.

Contrary to expectations, the abortion law has not reduced the rate of illegal abortions.

Denmark passed a law in 1939 that provides a broad interpretation of therapeutic abortion (so-called extended medical indications), including socio-medical indications in addition to the purely medical, ethical, and eugenic indications. A special board, consisting of two physicians and one representative of the Mothers Aid Society decides upon all applications for therapeutic abortions, about two-fifths of which are approved. All therapeutic abortions must be performed in accredited hospitals.

Illegal abortions continue to flourish.

Norway's abortion laws follow Sweden's pattern. Therapeutic abortions are performed for medical reasons, but social and economic factors affecting the health of the mother are also taken into consideration. A pregnancy that represents a threat to the mother's health, even if it is not necessarily a serious threat, suffices as an indication. Psychiatric indications grow in number.

THE SOVIET UNION

The U.S.S.R. legalized abortions in 1920 and this law remained in force until 1936. Reports mentioning the complications resulting from the abortions began to appear in the early thirties; chronic ill health, ectopic pregnancies, and sterility were the complications most frequently mentioned. Articles concerned with the low birth rate and the consequent low rate of population increase made their way into the press at the same time. The question arises as to whether therapeutic abortions were discontinued for medical or for political reasons.

In 1955, therapeutic abortions were legalized again in the U.S.S.R. They must be performed in special hospitals, where the patient remains for three days or longer if she runs a temperature.

The Russians are apparently very much interested in birth control, not, as in Japan, in order to control the population growth, but as a method of reducing abortions.

JAPAN

Japan legalized abortions in 1948. This law was passed as the most promising method of population control. That this method could reach the proportions it has is due to the fact that the Shinto and Buddhist religions are ethically noncommital on the subject of induced abortion, claiming that there is no moral or ethical distinction between fertility limitation before and after conception. Contraception, therapeutic abortions, and sterilization (the latter usually accomplished by Hyams' method of intrauterine electric cauterization, which seals the entrance to the Fallopian tubes) are all used extensively. In 1956, 1,159,-280 legal abortions were performed. Yet one million illegal abortions were supposed to have been performed during the same year.

There are two reasons for the performance of so many illegal operations in the face of legalized abortion. First, some physicians attempt to avoid the payment of income tax, and second, the patient is saved the mortician's fee, for after the third month, the fetus must be turned over to the mortician, whose fee might be higher than the physician's. In the interests of economy for the patient, the physician frequently alters the records.

Although this large number of illegal abortions is done in physicians' offices, the mortality rate has declined considerably, possibly because the dangers accompanying abortion by a physician are smaller than those of home delivery by untrained persons.

The experience of the Scandinavian countries shows that the extension of legal indications has not abolished illegal abortions. The extreme solution of Japan is apparently not acceptable to the occidental mind. The first step must be the creation of an atmosphere where free and frank discussion is possible.

Actually, a part of the problem of induced abortion might be solved by the practice of birth control. At any rate, the future will compel us to take a stand. Population pressures and other social and economic factors may force the Western mind to look for radical changes in its moral and ethical approach to induced abortion.

References

Abortion in the United States. A Conference Sponsored by the Planned Parenthood Federation of America, Inc. New York: Paul B. Hoeber, Inc., 1958.

Donnelly, Joseph P., "Are There Medical Indications for Therapeutic Abortions?" *J. M. Soc. New Jersey* 52; 112-118, 1955.

Eastman, Nicholas J., *Williams Obstetrics* (ed. 2). New York: Appleton-Century-Crofts, Inc., 1950.

Eastman, Nicholas J., "Comments to Article on Therapeutic Abortion." *Obst. & Gynec. Surv. 13;* 4, 509-517, 1958.

Hertig, A. T., and Sheldon, W. H., "Analysis of 1,000 Spontaneous Abortions." *Ann. Surg. 117;* 596, 1943.

Javert, Carl T., *Spontaneous and Habitual Abortion.* New York: McGraw-Hill Book Co., Inc., 1957.

Joel, Charles A., "Role of Semen in Habitual Abortion." *Fertil. & Steril. 6;* 459-464, 1955.

Gebhard, P. H., Pomeroy, W. P., Martin, C. E., and Christenson, C. V., *Pregnancy, Birth and Abortion.* New York: Paul B. Hoeber, Inc., 1958.

Mann, Edward C., "Psychiatric Investigation of Habitual Abortion." *Obst. & Gynec. Surv. 7;* 589-601, 1956.

Shirodkar, V. N., "Surgical Treatment of Habitual Abortion." *Tendences actuelles en gynecologie et obstetrique. Librairie de l'Université,* Geneva: Georg & Cie, S. A., 1955.

Smith, G. V., and Smith, O. W., "Prophylactic Hormone Therapy Relation to Complications of Pregnancy." *Obst. & Gynec. Surv. 4;* 129, 1954.

Taussig, F. J., *Abortion, Spontaneous and Induced.* St. Louis: C. V. Mosby, 1936.

Thiersch, J. B., "Therapeutic Abortion with Folic Acid Antagonist." *Am. J. Obst. & Gynec. 63;* 1219, 1952.

GOTTFRIED NEUMANN,
M.D., F.A.C.S.

Abstinence

SEXUAL abstinence, or continence, is the practice of refraining from sexual activities. Certain religious groups demand lifelong abstinence of their priests, monks, and nuns. Our society, in addition, requires men and women of all ages to abstain from sexual activities unless they are married. Although this is fortified by laws that threaten fornicators, adulterers, homosexuals, and even minor offenders with punishment, it is honored chiefly through the fear that attaches to its secret circumvention. Practically, this moral demand cannot be enforced and the majority of men and women either have sexual experiences before marriage or after marriage has been terminated. The widespread violation suggests that the average human is incapable of permanent or even extended abstinence. Even those who have voluntarily taken the oath of celibacy do not always equate it to complete chastity. From the Catholic clergy has come the argument that "celibacy . . . does not mean chastity" and the statement that many a priest's abstinence "is no more than a painfully maintained pretense" (Robinson, 1930).

The Controversy

These facts notwithstanding, abstinence is presented as a virtue, as an ideal worth striving for, and as beneficial. As a result, many young people go through a period in which they concentrate all their energies on checking the powerful sex drive. If they do not succeed—and few do—they feel shame and guilt and they sometimes fear that they have jeopardized their health or the happiness of a future marriage. The permission to have sexual relations in the marital union does not in all instances resolve the problems that have been created by these feelings. Many girls can comply with the moral restrictions only by convincing themselves of the lowliness and ugliness of all matters sexual. When they later marry, they cannot free themselves of the disgust they had cultivated in order to fortify their chastity. The aversion, however, deprives them of any pleasure, renders them frigid, and makes sex relations a chore that they try to evade.

It is partly because of this that many psychiatrists, physicians, and students of sexology question the soundness of the moral demand. Indeed, many consider prolonged abstinence detrimental to mental and physical health. They point out that consistent suppression of the sex drive leads to emotional imbalance and that continued inactivity of the sex glands and the nerves relating to them diminishes their ability to function, often to the point of atrophy. Satisfying this innate drive by other means than its natural gratification gives rise to psychoneurotic manifestations and often to behavior that is detrimental both to the individuals involved and to society.

The opinions expressed in these two camps are so diametrically opposed that their foundations must be examined if we want to find the truth.

Benefits of Abstinence

Venereal Diseases

The most dramatic appeal for abstinence plays on fears, in particular the fear of venereal diseases. Two of these, syphilis and gonorrhea, were a scourge of mankind for several centuries. Although marriage is no safeguard against them, the danger of infection increases considerably with promiscuous relations, especially intercourse with prostitutes where prostitution is not controlled.

This is an entirely negative benefit, to be sure, but it is worth considering. Stekel (1930) held that it did not justify the many undesirable consequences of abstinence, since the very fear of venereal diseases made spiritual cripples of people. Freud (1924) was of a similar opinion: Just as gastric disorders cannot be combated by dispensing with food, he said, so venereal diseases cannot be done away with by eliminating sex, but only by searching for cures and prophylactics. Obviously, this is the sounder view.

Actually, such cures have been found. In 1951, the proportion of people affected by gonorrhea or syphilis was about three out of one hundred. Yet the fact that only 1 per cent of the white population but 15 per cent of the colored population were infected indicates that further improvement depends largely on education, which in some groups is still defective. The treatment of syphilis in its early stages nowadays takes from one to two weeks and that of gonorrhea from one to several days. Similarly, means have been found to prevent the affliction of the unborn baby if the mother undergoes treatment in the first half of her pregnancy. Strangely enough, the advocates of abstinence were not silenced by this progress, nor did they seem to be happy about it. On the contrary, they reacted like fighters whose weapons had been knocked out of their hands. The spread of this information, they lamented, would result in loosening the sex mores. Such an argument can only mean that health had never been their true concern. Rather, the threat of venereal diseases was merely a pretext to frighten people into the acceptance of the idea of abstinence.

Marriage

Other benefits conveyed by abstinence, according to its advocates, are its favorable effects on the marital union and on character development.

The alleged advantages for marriage, unfortunately, are always couched in such general terms that it is practically impossible to study them objectively. There is supposedly greater beauty in a union that has been entered without previous experience and experimentation, there is greater happiness and greater depth of love. How abstinence brings about these wonderful states is never explained anywhere in the pertinent literature. Surveys show that actually a great number of young men desire their future wives to be inexperienced in sexual matters, but few appreciate unrelenting chastity when it tends to frustrate their own desires. Girls do not speak readily about their ideas concerning their own sex behavior, but quite a few expect their future husbands to be experienced so that they will not be "their guinea pigs" (Beigel, 1954, 1957).

Of course, these are only opinions. Like many popular beliefs, they could be mistaken. Yet sociological studies show that the adjustment most difficult to achieve in marriage is, as a rule, the reconciliation of the sexual wishes and habits of the partners, and that sexual adjustment is made more easily when the mates are sexually experienced. Together, these findings make it quite clear that about two-thirds of all marriages would be less troubled if our society were not so rigidly opposed to premarital sexual experiences, and that the man or the woman who expects relief from cumbersome restrictions through marriage would not so frequently be coupled with a partner who turned out to be prudish, frigid, or impotent. Even if none of these disturbing phenomena were caused by abstinence, they are often the reason why, to persons so afflicted, the partner's strict chastity is especially attractive. Since, in addition, long abstinence may bring about these states, most psychiatrists are agreed that "complete abstinence is not the best preparation for matrimony and that, in fact, in many instances it defeats the ends of marriage" (Freud, 1924). Their objection is particularly applicable if one partner intends to continue abstinence during marriage. Unquestionably, two people similarly inclined in this respect can build as satisfactory a union as any other two; it is the one-sided demand of abstinence in marriage that unfailingly wrecks the union. And it does so irrespective of any rationalization for this neurotic attitude: that intercourse must not take place unless it aims at procreation, or that the attempt to convert the mate to abstinence is based on its spiritual merits.

Character and Personality Development

The beneficial effects of abstinence on character and personality development are no less dubious. If it is true that the development of neuroses is furthered by abstinence when a predisposition is present, and that abstinence brings forth substitute manifestations that are not appreciated in our civilization, then it is difficult to see how it can be considered beneficial. Certainly, neither the chaotic tangle of prudery and envy that snoops with indignation in other people's intimate affairs nor the inclination to see whatever is said and done almost exclusively from an erotic angle—both attitudes typical of sexually unsatisfied people —can be set up as an ideal of good character.

Of course, these are not features that the spokesmen for abstinence like to mention. Rather, they refer to sublimation to support their claims. The term and concept of sublimation are Freudian. Sublimation is a process in which the inhibited libido is deflected toward socially acceptable outlets. It is assumed, for instance, that ethical, esthetic, and scientific interests emerge as a result of the de-sexualization of the aim-inhibited impulses. In apparent conformity with this concept, people are admonished to sublimate their sexual libido instead of indulging it. In this way, they are promised, they will become creators of culturally valued works.

On the surface this sounds plausible, once one accepts the premise. Yet such an oversimplified interpretation misses the mark. It is possible to pick out several great philosophers, scientists, writers, poets, and artists who seem to have led abstinent lives. But by far a greater number of equally illustrious persons are known to have started an active love life early and to have continued it into old age. The correlate, therefore, is not necessarily the cause. Freud himself, the originator of this concept, did not share the belief in abstinence as a creative power. According to his writings, sublimation is not a conscious process. It cannot, therefore, be commanded at will. Secondly, as he explicitly states, only part of the libido is sublimated. The proportion that lends itself to this process is extremely variable. And finally he says,

... It is contended Freud writes that the conflict with this powerful impulse (sex) brings out all the ethical and aesthetic forces in the psychic life and "steels" the character; and *this is undoubtedly true of some specially favored individuals*. ... But in by far the largest number of cases the struggle against one's sensuality consumes the individual's energy at the very time when the young man needs all his powers to establish his place and station in the world. ... In general my impression is that sexual abstinence does not promote the development of energetic, independent men of action, original thinkers or bold innovators and reformers: far more frequently it develops well-behaved weaklings who are subsequently lost in the great multitude. ...

In another passage, Freud warns that "the very attempts at sublimation produce neuroses or disorders" in those "who are trying to be better than their constitution permits them to be."

These observations are borne out by the many cases in which prolonged abstinence has proved injurious. All too frequently it promotes the development of hostile, acrimonious, and malicious character trends, the emergence of hypochondria, hysteria, anxiety, and compulsion neuroses. It is blamed for many instances of frigidity and psychogenic impotence, for sexual aberrations and physical disorders such as chronic prostatitis, premature ejaculation, weak erections, somatogenic impotence, chlorosis, congestion of the ovaries, and so on.

Although no statistics are available as to the frequency of such ill effects, their very existence makes the stand of those who advocate abstinence untenable. Indeed, one can only wonder that people so concerned with these matters do not seem to be aware of this fact. Of course, they are aware of it, but they pay no heed to the discrepancy between medical opinion and their own because the benefits in which they really believe lie on a completely different plane. These benefits have actually nothing to do with health, happiness in marriage, or a harmonious character development. They originate from concepts much older than scientific observation, hygiene, or rationality. These concepts come out of the ancient belief that human destiny can be managed by magic.

The Magic of Abstinence

Anthropologists have often described man's attempts to control nature's inimical forces. In primitive societies, men must refrain from sexual intercourse before they go on a journey or a big hunt, women before they sow crops or brew beer. The period of their abstinence extends from one night to a week or longer. Violation of this rule would cause the undertaking to fail; the hunters would suffer accidents, the crop would be destroyed by drought or floods. Insecure in his existence, primitive man feels that he is surrounded by hostile forces. Any power he usurps is an invasion into the realm of these spirits, any pleasure is snatched from demons or deities. To avert their envious revenge, therefore, he must sacrifice some of his possessions or some of his pleasures. Guilt, too, has its share in this magic outlook: in some of the head-hunting tribes the men must remain sexually abstinent for several days after their raids.

Strange though such ritualized forms of sexual abnegation may appear to a human being in our civilization, they are not entirely alien to our feelings of hope and guilt. Not only do children regenerate such magic thinking, not only do neurotics often regulate their lives in accordance with it, but quite normal people often secretly pledge themselves to forego certain pleasures in order to secure success in a particular enterprise or to avert a feared event.

Such private magic does not always involve the sexual need; often it concerns food or something else one cherishes, but self-denial with regard to sexual activities takes a prominent place among the offerings. This is so partly because sex involves the mystery of procreation and partly because it is the most flexible of the physiological drives. One cannot go for a long time without food, air, drink, or elimination, but the suppression of the sexual desire does not result in death or an immediately traceable illness. Moreover, having the merit of a virtue, abstinence becomes a magnificent cloak beneath which socially unaccepted tendencies, such as homosexuality, or supposedly shameful conditions, such as impotence, can be concealed. To those who, in fear of the opposite sex, of venereal diseases, of pregnancy, or of

sadistic or exhibitionistic tendencies, have had to repress all libidinal urges, it gives not only the feeling of safety but also one of a superior morality that has succeeded in taming the animal in the human. All these ideas, however, are possible only because the primitive magic has, in a modified form, been implemented with our own religions and has thus become part of the cultural tradition of our society.

The sexual magic of the preliterate groups aimed exclusively at the prevention of a dreaded evil. In some of the monotheistic ideologies it took a spiritual turn. The deity was no longer to be bribed by an occasional sacrifice to favor a certain undertaking of material usefulness; rather, self-denial and relinquishment of earthly pleasures was assumed to please the god. The benefit that derived from the renunciation of wealth, comfort, and sexual pleasure lay in the hope of securing a special place in heaven. With the forcible Christianization of the West these ideas infiltrated Europe and gradually became part of all its national cultures and thus eventually also of the American.

The ideal of voluntary poverty was soon given up, but that of chastity remained. Yet this demand, too, encountered difficulties. Lifelong abstinence was not practicable. The early Christian insistence on complete mortification of the flesh had to be modified: sex relations were permitted for married people. That this concession was granted only reluctantly is quite clear from the letter that Paul of Tarsus addressed to the Corinthians. "But if they have not continency," he wrote, "let them marry. It is better to marry than to burn." Even so, later leaders were not sure that married people who made use of the privilege would not have to burn anyway. For centuries they debated the degree of sinfulness of marital love until they finally agreed that, because sex relations are necessary to procreation, they might be tolerated in marriage. Continence, nevertheless, was regarded as more meritorious.

Economic Considerations

The belief that abstinence conveys benefits is a remnant of these concepts. If its advocates allude to the advantages for marriage and personality, they are merely trying to find rational reasons to prop up a preconceived idea. But these obviously weak props could not have lasted so long had they not had additional support. Although few middle-class families would be happy to see their children choose the career of saint, the moral demand for abstinence does not completely lack in appeal. Limited to "the others," and especially to young unmarried people, it is in harmony with the economic interests of those to whom it does not apply. As long as sons and daughters are economically dependent on their families, parents may not always be able to evade the responsibility for children who might result from their offspring's premarital relations. The moral demand is a great help to them. Young people are therefore instilled with it early and thoroughly. Since the mention of materialistic, that is economic, considerations is not in keeping with the spiritual pretenses of our culture, the moral demand is the main bulwark against desires at an age when the sex drive is strong but foresight is scanty and economic conditions do not yet permit marriage or independence.

Economic considerations, however, have also altered the strictness of the original demand. In our time, it is actually uncompromising only with respect to unmarried young females. Circumvention of the taboo by the young male and by unmarried adults is more or less overlooked.

The benefits of abstinence, then, are not of this world. But this does not imply that restraint may not at times be the lesser of two evils. The economic conditions and their concomitants, such as status considerations and reputation, cannot be entirely neglected. Nor can certain physical factors be disregarded. To give birth to offspring before the reproductive apparatus is fully developed is undesirable for both the young mother and her progeny. Continence must often be advised during an illness that taxes the patient's energies. Abstinence during the period of the mate's sickness, during the later stages of pregnancy, and several weeks after delivery is obviously no more than an inconvenience. And hard though it may be to bear, persons infected with a venereal disease must curb their needs so as not to endanger the health of others.

Disadvantages of Abstinence

Sexual abstinence runs counter to human nature and therefore upsets the normal functioning of the organism. Yet, there is obviously a difference whether it is permanent and total or relative and practiced only over a short period. There is no doubt about the many instances in which it has proved to be injurious, but it is more harmful in certain circumstances and less so in others. Since abstinence may become inevitable in some instances, it seems advisable to examine these various circumstances.

To a certain extent even personal evaluation plays a role. The effects of abstinence on the sexual power, for instance, will be feared by those who intend to marry and, some day, to raise a family, but hardly by those who have decided on a life of celibacy. To them the diminution of the sex drive may indeed be desirable because it also brings relief from sexual phantasies and from the fight against temptations.

But whether it is viewed as a threat or as a promise, the ultimate effect depends on many factors. Physical impairment of the inactive nerve centers or eventual cessation of the sexual function depend on the sex, age, and constitution of the individual, on the duration of the continence, and on its completeness or relativity. In young people, abstinence is apt to increase sexual desire and to evoke an abundance of sexual imagery. This may result in inability to concentrate, irritability, insomnia, extreme nervousness, or more serious complications, the extent of the disturbance depending on the individual's drive intensity, temperament, and environment. These conditions may become so distracting to some people that they cannot work; others manage the situation without lasting consequences. Healthy people who live strenuous outdoor lives can apparently abstain for many months without injury to their systems, and even a temporary weakness of the sexual apparatus disappears on resumption of normal sex relations. In mature persons, the restoration to normalcy encounters greater difficulties than in young ones.

Intensity, Totality, and Relativity

The intensity of the sex drive has been mentioned as a decisive factor. To men and women whose libido is weak, abstinence even of long duration will do little or no harm. The average man or woman can abstain for some time without injurious effect; but the stronger the drive, the shorter the period before disturbing symptoms make their appearance.

Of greatest importance, however, is apparently the completeness or relativity of abstinence. Those who advise chastity mean, of course, the denial of any gratification. Nature has provided a self-regulating device. In males, the sexual products are involuntarily emitted during sleep (nocturnal emission) or in strong excitement. Like all natural devices, however, this safety valve is imperfect. Although harmless in itself, it does not suffice to prevent somatic or psychic ill effects. In addition, in people whose aim is suppression of all sexual manifestations, this involuntary process often rouses fears or feelings of guilt. Besides, prolonged dependence on it appears to cause premature ejaculation when normal sex relations are taken up.

Abstinence is relative when substitute outlets are used to satisfy the sexual needs. Among the many possibilities, masturbation is the most frequent. Unless it becomes excessive it is innocuous. It eases the discomfort of prolonged temporary abstinence and seems to prevent serious consequences. It has, however, the disadvantage of too easy availability, and may result in a fixation, in comparison to which normal sex relations appear full of troublesome efforts. For the same reason it may become a kind of narcotic in which all frustrations can be drowned so that no endeavors are made to overcome them by appropriate action. Furthermore, it is seriously frowned upon, especially when practiced by adults. The unsatisfied husband or wife who tries to relieve his urge by masturbating is often looked upon as "abnormal" by the mate. Young people, too, well aware of the taboo, often have the feeling of being marked and thus of being noticeable to others as masturbators. Self-conscious because of their secret "sin," some become extremely shy, feel morally inadequate, and incline toward depressive moods. The real damage is done, of course, not by the self-gratification itself but by the many tales that are spread about the dangers it holds, such as im-

potence, insanity, and weakening of the brain or of the will power. These may cause sufficient fears to result in neurotic symptoms.

Petting that may or may not involve manipulation of the genitals is another frequent substitute outlet. It is the usual method for two people who are physically attracted to each other but cannot permit themselves sex relations. It is condemned, of course, but not beset by irrational dreads.

Disposition and Environment

The foregoing makes it clear that the physical effects of abstinence need not become manifest in all instances; it is equally evident, however, that undesirable psychological results cannot always be avoided.

Disposition seems to be of major significance. People predisposed toward neuroses are more susceptible to the ill effects of sexual frustration than others. Similarly, psychotic symptoms are sometimes precipitated through inner conflicts in persons who are predisposed in this direction. A stunting of the personality in general, the development of peculiarities in character and behavior, and a tendency toward narrow-mindedness and vindictiveness are expected, albeit not inevitable, syndromes.

Again, disposition, environment, and the degree of conscious frustration are variants that may influence the effect of abstinence. Abstinence to which one is coerced, for instance, is more destructive than voluntary abstinence. To the physical discomfort is added a sense of injustice and powerlessness, which fosters deep resentment against those who are considered responsible. This state of mind is particularly detrimental to the marital union. The normally sexed partner can hardly help resenting the denying or impotent partner. Adjustment is possible, of course, if for some reason the union cannot be dissolved, but it will always mar the personalities involved. Besides, since only the thwarted partner searches for substitutes and most of them are forbidden, it is usually the denying partner who dictates what form the adjustment can or must take. In other people, especially the young, resentment often turns into hatred of the parents, defiance of all their rules and teachings, and an enmity towards society and all its values.

People forced to remain abstinent are naturally more likely than volunteer abstainers to seek substitute outlets. Some of these are not sought, however, but obtrude obsessively on the frustrated persons' minds. If abstinence is prolonged, such obsessive thoughts and phantasies may turn into impulsive or compulsive action and bring the perpetrator in conflict with the law. Men of mature age may molest strange women with whom they come into unintended physical contact, as on a crowded subway, for instance. Elderly men sometimes buy the favors of minors or commit the misdemeanor of exhibiting themselves in public. Thirty-two to 35 per cent of all rapes are committed by persons under the age of 21. In prisons, men and women turn to homosexuality, and violent attacks on an unwilling target are no rarity. The armed forces all over the world have found enforced abstinence a formidable problem, endangering discipline and morale. Several nations have made attempts to counteract this, some by licensing prostitution near camps, others by setting up official brothels, and still others by supplying libido-reducing drugs to their soldiers.

Voluntary abstinence is easier to bear; but in a strongly or normally sexed individual even the best motivation is not sufficient to prevent physical disorders or undesirable mental states from developing. Among the latter are neurasthenia, depressions, phobias, anxieties, and neuroses marked by compulsions.

Anything that makes the fight against temptations more difficult worsens the consequences of abstinence. Therefore, nutrition, occupation, and external conditions also become important. Overeating, alcohol, lack of physical or mental work, boredom, and anything that is sexually stimulating increase the libidinal desire and thus aggravate the psychological conflicts. Absorbing and satisfying work, on the other hand (not to be confused with sublimation), makes temporary abstinence at least more bearable.

In most persons, the intensity of the sex drive lessens as they pass the peak of maturity. But the end of the reproductive period means neither for men nor for women the cessation of all desire. If physiological features were the only decisive ones, these people could, nevertheless, go for a long time without sexual contact. There are, however, so many meanings integrated with the sexual function that, at these stages too, forced abstinence frequently either leads to psychological difficulties or speeds up their development.

Women as a group seem to bear temporary abstinence better than men but, as in the latter, it is ultimately always a question of individual constitution and personality. This, the significance of individual differences, is what the advocates of abstinence apparently cannot grasp. They beat their chests and set themselves up as models for emulation, most of them completely unaware of the havoc their proudly flaunted control of sensuality has wrought on their own personalities. For, varied though the consequences of abstinence may be, the gratification of the sexual drive is a necessity for the normally developed human, and the disregard of this necessity over a long period of time is likely to break the life impulses and thus to affect not only happiness and well-being but also physical and mental health.

References

Beigel, Hugo G., "Body Height in Mate Selection." *J. Social Psychol.* 39; 257-268, 1954.

Beigel, Hugo G., "The Evaluation of Intelligence in the Heterosexual Relationship." *J. Social Psychol. 46;* 65-80, 1957.

Blaschko, A., "Sexual Abstinence." In W. J. Robinson (ed.), *Sexual Continence.* New York: Eugenics Pub. Co., 1930.

Drummond, Isabel, *The Sex Paradox.* New York: G. P. Putnam's Sons, 1953.

Ellis, Albert, *Sex Without Guilt.* New York: Lyle Stuart, 1958.

Ellis, Havelock, *Psychology of Sex.* New York: Emerson Books, Inc., 1940.

Eulenburg, P., "Sexual Abstinence and Its Influence on Health." In W. J. Robinson (ed.), *Sexual Continence.* New York: Eugenics Pub. Co., 1930.

Ford, Clellan S., and Beach, Frank A., *Patterns of Sexual Behavior.* New York: Harper & Brothers, 1952.

Freud, Sigmund, " 'Civilized' Sexual Morality and Modern Nervousness." In *Collected Papers,* Vol. II. London: Hogarth Press, 1924.

Guyon, René, *Sexual Freedom.* New York: Alfred A. Knopf, Inc., 1950.

Kinsey, Alfred C., Pomeroy, Wardell B., and Martin, Clyde E., *Sexual Behavior in the Human Male.* Philadelphia: W. B. Saunders Co., 1948.

Kinsey, Alfred C., Pomeroy, Wardell B., Martin, Clyde E., and Gebhard, Paul H., *Sexual Behavior in the*

Human Female. Philadelphia: W. B. Saunders Co., 1953.

Landis, Judson T., "Length of Time Required to Achieve Adjustment in Marriage." *Am. Soc. Rev. 11;* 672-84, 1946.

Reich, Wilhelm, *The Function of the Orgasm*. New York: Orgone Inst. Press, 1948.

Robinson, William J. (ed.), *Sexual Continence*. New York: Eugenics Pub. Co., 1930.

Rutgers, J., *How to Attain and Practice the Ideal Sex Life*. New York: Cadillac, 1940.

Stekel, Wilhelm, "Sexual Abstinence and Health." In W. J. Robinson (ed.), *Sexual Continence*. New York: Eugenics Pub. Co., 1930.

Taylor, W. S., "A Critique of Sublimation in Males." *Genet. Psychol. Monogr. 13;* 1-115, 1933.

Vecki, Victor, "The Dogma of Sexual Abstinence." In W. J. Robinson (ed.), *Sexual Continence*. New York: Eugenics Pub. Co., 1930.

HUGO G. BEIGEL

Adolescent Sexuality

ADOLESCENCE is usually defined as the period of development in human life extending from puberty to maturity. Puberty is denoted, primarily, by certain physical, physiological, and bodily changes. These, to mention a few of those that are the most indicative, are: (1) occurrence of rapid physical growth, as of the spurt in height and weight, (2) accelerated growth of the sex organs, (3) development of secondary sex characteristics, such as the breasts in girls, and appearance of axillary and pubic hair, (4) occurrence of first ejaculation (in boys), and of first menstruation (menarche, in girls).

Sex and sexuality are words given such a multiplicity, divergence, and broadness of meanings that little or no clarity in concept results. For example, apparently the origin of the word *sex* is in Roman Catholic theology (Robinson, 1933). It derives from the Latin word for six, the number of the Sixth Commandment of the Roman Catholic faith—that is, the commandment that prohibits adultery. To the layman, "sexual" usually implies normal adult heterosexual activity, and usually and more specifically, coitus. In the Freudian view all the phenomena of human life related to pleasure-seeking are encompassed. Brown (1940), one of the more orthodox Freudians in this country, indicates that by the concept sexual is signified, "... all the behavior in which human beings come in close physical contact."

The foregoing illustrates, somewhat, the divergence in meanings attached to the word, but by no means the full extent of such variation. With such nonuniformity of meanings, no specific delineation can result. Consequently, one can go far afield in describing sexuality and especially so if one uses such broad concepts as are contained in the Freudian view. As a result, the word needs to be redefined for the sake of clarity and in order to narrow our scope.

Adolescent sexuality can be defined as the state of the human sexual life during the period from puberty to maturity. Included are those conditions of behavior, phantasy, feelings, and attitudes that have as their aim one or any combination of the following: (1) tumescence, (2) erotic stimulation of various parts of the body, (3) erotic arousal and orgasm, and (4) procreation. Practically considered, adolescent sexuality ordinarily deals with the circumstances of the sexual life of the human from the chronological age of approximately 12 to 21, with early adolescence being from 12 to 17, and late adolescence from 17 to 21.

In discussing adolescent sexuality, the emphasis is usually on sexual behavior in the nonmarital state, making the assumption that marriage is not associated with adolescence. This will be the approach here, although it is known that teen-age marriages are increasing and that at the time of the 1940 census about one-sixth of American adolescents were married.

A complete description of the sexual life during this age span would include an account of (1) motoric sexual response, both normal and abnormal, (2) the attitudes and feelings relating to sexual behavior, and (3) the psychological stimuli, antecedent conditions of motoric response and of the mental imagery that is correlated with, stimulates, or substitutes for motoric sexual activity.

The sexual behavior of the adolescent includes specifically sexual motoric responses and proximal sexual motoric responses. The major types of directly sexual motoric activity that occur during adolescence are, *in toto,* equivalent to those of adulthood and are: (1) masturbation, (2) petting, (3) coitus, (4) nocturnal sex dreams, (5) homosexual contacts, and (6) animal contacts. The proximal sexual motoric responses are those behaviors of the adolescent which, although not always manifestly sexual in the sense of the foregoing, nevertheless are closely related to these activities and accomplish for the human much the same aims with respect to the sexual motive.

Knowledge about the directly sexual motoric activity of the adolescent is not yet complete or definitive and what will be described will apply mainly to the United States. However, it might well apply in broad outlines to Western civilization, for, as Udo Undeutsch (1955) has stated, "The unusually high agreement between the data of Kinsey and those obtained in Europe by others, as well as theoretical considerations, point in the following direction: *sexual activity when regarded within larger populations represents an area of human behavior which shows the largest conceivable uniformity.* Consequently the differences among population groups—especially the occidental—are in all respects unusually small" (italics the author's). Sexual behavior of the adolescent needs further study, as too little research of a controlled nature has been done with the adolescent. And what studies have been done have certainly not been representative of the population as a whole. Until the publication of the Kinsey reports, most knowledge of adolescent sexuality derived from clinical studies (usually of small numbers of delinquents). With the publication of the Kinsey reports and other studies, such as those done by Ramsey, we are in a better position to make reasonable statements about adolescent sexuality. Now we can give a rather general picture of the incidence (accumulative and active) of different types of motoric sexual response of all age ranges, including adolescence.

Kinsey (1953) has called attention to the fact that some thirty-one American studies and some sixteen foreign studies have been done that are statistical in type and serve as the best factual basis for statements about motoric sexual response. Since the publication of the Kinsey reports a few persons have been conducting small-scale studies, statistical in type, that are applicable to the period of adolescence (particularly the late period). The principal investigators are Ehrmann, Kirkendall, and the present author. In the studies of all of these persons the sampling has been small and has related principally to middle-class college students. For these and other reasons the investigations in no way compete with the Kinsey reports. Although these studies have diverse motivations, a few of the findings by these scientists tend to confirm some of the general notions put forth by the Kinsey studies.

Most of the statistical studies that serve as our best evidence for statements about motoric sexual behavior have been either questionnaire or interview studies and, of late, there has been some tendency for the better-known authorities to claim greater validity for the interview technique in the study of sexual behavior (Kinsey, Ramsey, Kirkendall). The first two researchers base their claims mainly on the fact that they have noted a trend for interview studies to show greater total incidence of sexual behaviors of the various types than has been found through the questionnaire studies.

The validity of studies of sexual behavior rests, in the final analysis, upon the ability, desire, and veracity of the informants in telling about their sexual behavior. Some cautions, then, must be adhered to in taking any general statements about sexual behavior as truth, for reports about sexual behavior are subject to certain degrees of inaccuracy. This impreciseness is due mainly to the inability of persons to state the exact facts, even if they are highly motivated to do so. This inability may arise from faulty memory, blocking of memory, or distortions of memory. The truthfulness of reports might also be reasonably questioned on the basis of motives, for persons may be motivated to overestimate or underestimate their sexual performance, being influenced to do so because of various personal, sociocultural, and other motives. Further, there is great difficulty in obtaining adequate, representative samples of persons of any particular group as, for example, a sample typical of upper upper-class adolescents. Some special groups resist the scientific study of sex, and often, then, the researcher confines himself to the use of volunteers. An exception to the foregoing might be where incarcerated groups, such as delinquents, are studied. Since volunteers are most often the subjects of study, it is possible that some distortion in reports results. The evidence (slight in amount) is contradictory on this point, but a few pieces of evidence are suggestive of the fact that little or no error in report is introduced by "volunteer bias."

Taking these cautions into account and being ready to revise our conclusions if in the future more representative and more valid studies provide us with a different picture of the scope and incidence of sexual behavior, we can proceed within the limits of our present knowledge to describe the patterns that seemingly exist today.

Sexual Motoric Behavior

Male Masturbation

Albert Moll (1912), a physician-sexologist who wrote in German during the early part of the century, was willing to give the benefit of doubt to some human males. Berger, as reported by Havelock Ellis in his *Studies in the Psychology of Sex,* concluded that "99 per cent of young men and women masturbate occasionally, while the hundredth conceals the truth." Berger's opinion was upheld by that of Cohn (H. Ellis, 1936), and Moll stated that "the only point in dispute is whether there are any exceptions." Wilhelm Stekel (1950), psychoanalyst and student of Freud, maintained that every human male has had this experience. The evidence from statistical studies, although not confirming these opinions, tends in this direction. The following summary taken from Ramsey (1943) is suggestive of the possible truthfulness of their surmise.

"Data concerning the masturbatory experience of mature males have been reported as follows:"

SOURCE	PERCENTAGE REPORTING MASTURBATION
Dickinson and Beam* (1932)	100
Kinsey* (unpublished data)	97 (2,300 men and older boys)
Hamilton* (1929)	97 (100 men)
Peck and Wells (1923, 1925)	86 (187 college men)
Hughes (1926)	85 (1,029 boys)
Merrill* (1918)	85 (100 boys)
Taylor* (1933)	70 (40 men)
Achilles (1923)	63 (470 men)
Exner (1915)	62 (53 men)
Brockman (1902)	56 (232 older boys and men)
Bromley-Britten (1938)	7 (592 men)

* Personal interview studies.

Studies done on boys of varying ages give an accumulative incidence ranging from approximately 22 to 99 per cent. Many studies done before 1940 report the accumulative incidence before the age of 21 as within the range of approximately 70 to 99 per cent, with some few reporting an incidence of less than 40 per cent. In general the trend is for the later studies to report a greater incidence than the earlier ones. Since there is a tendency for the more recent studies to be more carefully done, the larger figures can be accepted with considerable confidence. We can conclude that by the end of adolescence the accumulative incidence (percentage who have ever masturbated) of masturbation is such that *possibly* every male has masturbated, to the point of orgasm, at least once in his life. For all intents and purposes masturbation can be thought of as almost universal during adolescence. The most extensive study (Kinsey, 1948) gives the incidence as 92 per cent by the age of 20.

For the male sex this behavior reaches its height during later adolescence (age 17-21). This is the period of life when the greatest total proportion (active incidence) of males is actively involved. During this period well over four-fifths (Kinsey, 88 per cent) of the male population masturbates with a frequency of one to four times a week (Kinsey, 1948; Ramsey, 1943), and a mean frequency of about one and a half times a week. The period of highest frequencies of masturbation is just before, however, when among those who masturbate the mean frequency is about two and a half times per week. Most of the males have their first experience after the age of ten, with an estimated 13 to 16 per cent having masturbated before this age.

For a great number of adolescent males this activity precedes slightly or begins with the advent of puberty, after which time the incidence rises markedly. Boys who become pubertal earlier initiate the behavior at an earlier age and maintain a greater frequency of masturbation during the early teens as compared to those whose puberty is delayed. This group (early maturing) is also the group among whom the highest active incidence exists at all ages during adolescence, and by late adolescence nearly 100 per cent have masturbated. During the early teens active incidence is greatest among those of low social level, who attach little value to education. But in later adolescence the active incidence is highest among those of higher social levels, who attribute value to prolonged education. Social level appears to affect the frequency more so than the incidence of masturbation. Kinsey discovered the curious phenomenon that those "destined to go to college"—even if living in an environment of low socioeconomic status—masturbate at all ages during adolescence with greater frequency than those who are destined to stop at the maximum of grade-school or high-school education. He reports the frequency during the period from puberty to age 15 as being, respectively, 1.8, 2.2, and 2.7 times per week for those who will attain grade-school, high-school, and college level, respectively.

With approaching maturity masturbation tends to become less and less a preoccupation of youths of all age levels and social classes. Of course, throughout adolescence there are males who masturbate, and masturbation, considering all individuals together, remains the primary sexual outlet during adolescence. However, by the late teens the incidence of both petting and coitus increases considerably and the frequency of masturbation drops markedly from the period of early adolescence, when about two-thirds of the adolescent's sexual outlet to the point of orgasm is by masturbation. In the late teens the boys of the lower

social classes and those who come from lower educational levels tend to concentrate more and more on coitus. However, those of the higher social levels, who are the more likely to become part of the college group, begin to concentrate on petting as a source of erotic arousal. For all adolescents considered together, however, masturbation still leads all other forms of sexual behavior as a source of orgasm.

Female Masturbation

It appears that a smaller proportion of females as compared to males have had the experience of masturbation during the teens. Few studies deal with the period of adolescence, per se. Usually when the accumulative incidence of masturbation in the female sex is reported, the statistic has been derived from reports of adult women reporting statements in which they recall the facts about their adolescent activity. Such reports of accumulative incidence frequently vary from 9 to 80 per cent, with the majority of the studies giving figures clustering in a range of approximately 30 to 60 per cent. The Kinsey report is almost alone in giving incidence figures derived from any large numbers of adolescents themselves. These are such that it appears that some 12 per cent of girls arrive at puberty (age 12) with the experience, while by late adolescence nearly two-fifths (40 per cent) have had the experience. The figures of other authorities giving data on the proportion of females who arrive at puberty with the experience vary from 12 to 20 per cent.

During any particular year during adolescence smaller proportions of girls as compared to boys have masturbated (total incidence) and are masturbating (active incidence). Kinsey (1953) reports that probably no more than 20 per cent of the female population masturbates at any particular age. He also indicates that, "Many males, projecting their own experience, are inclined to overestimate the incidences and frequencies of masturbation among females." He thus tends to discount the subjective estimates of many early sexologists who frequently wrote without reference to statistical data. Such authorities, to name a few, are Kisch, Stekel, and Haire.

Contrary to the finding with boys, there is no definite trend for girls who reach puberty earlier (or who menstruate earlier) to initiate masturbation at earlier ages or to maintain it at a higher frequency than those who mature late. The young women who are destined to go to college are more accepting of masturbation as a sexual outlet in their late teens as compared to those who will conclude life with the minimum of education. In the early teens, however, the accumulative incidence of masturbation among the various social and educational groups is relatively identical.

In the late teens, especially, girls from the lower social levels and educational backgrounds turn to coitus and away from masturbation as a type of sexual response. Those who will go to college, compared to those who accept other educational levels and are from lower social backgrounds, consider masturbation more desirable than coitus. Consequently, for them, masturbation becomes a major source of sexual stimulation. Particularly is this trend true up to the age of 15 (Kinsey, 1953), when as much as 90 per cent of the total release to orgasm is through masturbation (it is approximately 50 per cent for the grade-school level at this age). This trend for the college-destined girl continues through to maturity for the single girl, and at almost any age or year she achieves more of her outlet in orgasm from masturbation than those girls of lower social level and educational promise. By late adolescence girls of all social levels become more accepting of coitus. However, its incidence is still relatively low among girls of all social levels, even in late adolescence.

As is the case with boys, petting and coitus are the two major activities that tend to displace masturbation, when both accumulative and active incidence are considered. At practically all ages, not only are the incidence and frequency of masturbation for females during adolescence much less than for males, but it is a much more sporadic activity. Among girls greater individual differences in frequency exist and the range of variation is much greater. Some girls report a frequency of masturbation as little as once or twice a year, while others may masturbate as many as ten to twenty times a week. The modal frequency is probably less than once a month.

For all adolescents adherence to a strict religion (devoutness) has a restraining effect upon masturbation, affecting total incidence, active incidence, and frequency. Its restraining effect, in general, appears to be greater upon girls than boys.

The techniques of masturbation, of course, vary somewhat as to sex. But the techniques employed by adolescents are, in the main, no different from those employed by adults. Genital manipulation by hand is the most frequent technique employed by both sexes. Vaginal insertions are sometimes employed by girls. Thigh pressure is a little less frequently used by girls than vaginal insertions. Boys, however, seem to be almost unaware of this technique as a means of inducing orgasm, although it is effective in the male sex also. A few girls rub their vaginal areas against objects such as pillows, bedclothes, covers, edges of chairs, and the like. Similar techniques are infrequently used by boys, who rub their genital organ against bedclothes, pillows, and the inside of mouths of bottles and other holes (Ramsey, 1943).

Petting

As yet there has been, as Ehrmann (1957) points out, little research into petting. But from what evidence we have we can safely say that petting is another motoric sexual behavior that is extremely frequent among adolescents of both sexes. The accumulative incidence of petting during the adolescent period is high. By the end of the period of adolescence the great majority of males and females have engaged in petting and some authorities, such as Ehrmann and A. Ellis, describe its incidence as being universal. Again, as with masturbation, the hypothesized total incidence is 100 per cent. The trend is for later, more extensive studies to report a higher incidence than earlier ones.

The varieties of petting techniques ("... any sort of physical contact which does not involve a union of the genitalia but in which there is a deliberate attempt to effect erotic arousal"—Kinsey, 1948) are numerous in adolescence and are most extensively described by Kinsey, especially on pages 251–259 of the volume on the female. One also can get a good picture of the techniques by reading the studies by Ehrmann (1952) and the author (1959). Of the male sex, very few persons have had a petting experience before puberty. However, a sharp rise occurs in the accumulative incidence of petting at about the age of 13 for both sexes. There is a steady increase into late adolescence in the numbers of persons of both sexes who pet, so that by late adolescence the preponderant majority of adolescents have petted, 88 per cent of the boys and approximately 88 to 91 per cent of the girls by the end of age 20, according to Kinsey (1948, 1953). The highest frequency for the male sex appears to occur after the age of 21. For both sexes late adolescence appears to be the period of highest active incidence, when one-quarter of the girls and one-third of the boys are actively involved to the point of orgasm.

At this period of life over eight-tenths of the girls and nearly all the boys are petting, perhaps not to the point of orgasm but with varying degrees of erotic arousal. The petting of girls is more sporadic than that of boys and estimates as to the frequency of petting among them are much less certain. As in the case of masturbation, there are great individual differences among girls, according to the situation of the particular girl and what time span in her life is being considered. For example, a specific girl may pet three or four times in one evening with several or more partners, and again the same girl in another time period may not pet for weeks or months.

In some subgroups of the adolescent population nearly all of the adolescents have petted. This is particularly true of those who have experienced their adolescence since about 1930 and certainly those of present generations; and also for those adolescents who are of higher social levels and who appear destined to go to college. For this group of male adolescents the accumulative incidence by late adolescence is at least 94 per cent and its active incidence

and frequency become such that it begins to compete with masturbation as a source of sexual arousal. For boys of lower social levels, however, by late adolescence coitus rather than petting competes strongly with masturbation and becomes the preferred source of erotic arousal. Its accumulative incidence in this group nears 100 per cent and its frequency and active incidence are such that approximately seven-tenths (85 per cent of the grade-school level is active) of the outlet in orgasm is being provided by coitus. In the college group, where active incidence nears two-fifths after the age of 20, the proportion of outlet in orgasm by means of coitus is near 20 per cent.

For the female adolescent, there is not as definite a relation between educational level or social level and petting experience, in terms of report of accumulative incidence. The incidence of petting at almost any particular age is almost as great among those who are destined to go to college as among those whose parents come from a laboring class.

For both sexes there is little or no relation between onset of puberty and incidence of petting. Many girls and boys have been pubertal for a few years before they start to pet. However, there is a relation between religious upbringing and the accumulative incidence of petting, although for girls the relation appears to be slight at any age and particularly during the years of early adolescence (before 15), when the difference between the devout and inactive is slight. There is one exception, and that is where petting to orgasm is concerned. Here devoutness affects the activity, petting to the point of orgasm being more frequent among the girls who are religiously inactive. The accumulative incidences and frequencies of premarital petting among the devout and inactive groups are not great where male youth are concerned and especially is this so at late adolescence.

From what studies have been done, some rather clear historical trends are evident with respect to petting. Adolescents today are petting at an earlier age and the accumulative incidence and frequency of petting among today's adolescents are greater than was true of the past (Terman, 1938; Kinsey). Truly, petting can be called a phenomenon of present-day youth, as almost all of today's youth is experiencing it. Its total incidence and its frequency have increased in present-day generations. Also, there is some evidence, as Kinsey has suggested, that today's youth is elaborating the techniques of petting. For these reasons it is a sexual activity that has received much attention and in all probability it merits further study. Present-day adolescents have learned to employ petting as an end in itself, and for many adolescents it is the method of achieving heterosexual orgasm or heterosexual satisfaction in a sociosexual context where, frequently, coitus can be avoided.

Kinsey has spoken much about petting as serving as a substitute for coitus. There is evidence that more elaborate techniques of petting have been and are being generated by present-day adolescents (Reevy, 1959a) to serve as substitutes for coitus. Vestured genital apposition and coitus is one of these techniques. This is a petting technique that seems to be more frequent than, for example, genital apposition, cunnilinctus, etc. The author has given statistical evidence for the existence of this behavior and defined it as erotically stimulating sexual behavior in which coitus is simulated by the male apposing his clothed genital area to the clothed genital area of the female while in the horizontal position, male usually prone, female supine, both or either moving the body in coital-like movements.

All the techniques that in married life are called the techniques of foreplay and that are possible preludes to coitus are employed by adolescents as petting techniques. These, to mention only a few, are kissing (deep), breast and genital petting, mutual masturbation, cunnilinctus, fellatio, and genital apposition. Of these kissing, breast and genital petting, and mutual masturbation are the most prevalent. As Kinsey (1953), Ehrmann (1952), Podell and Perkins (1957), and the author (1959a) have indicated, these behaviors find a hierarchical acceptance among adolescents, with kissing being almost universal and the incidence of such behaviors as fellatio and cunnilinctus being quite low.

Premarital Coitus

Considering both sexes together and without reference to any other factor, such as age, social level, or religious upbringing, coitus (premarital) is one of the major motoric sexual activities of adolescence. The accumulative incidence as well as the active incidence of coitus in the male sex is high. The late teens is the period of the highest active incidence for the male sex, when almost three-fourths are involved (Kinsey, 1948; Ramsey, 1943). The accumulative incidence of premarital intercourse during adolescence reported in other studies varies from 2 to 60 per cent, with many clustering in a range of 40 to 60 per cent.

Some people are very surprised to learn that single adult males are less active in heterosexual coitus than the older teenager, whose mean frequency of intercourse (according to Kinsey) is about one and one-third times a week, and even less active than the early teenager (less than 15), whose frequency is about twice a week. At any age the highest active incidence of premarital intercourse is among those boys who come from (or are destined for) the lowest educational and social level. At about age 15 those with potentiality for the least education have experienced considerable intercourse and the active incidence in this group is about one-half, while among those who are destined for college-level education the incidence is approximately 10 per cent. At age 21, or near the end of adolescence, the respective incidence figures are approximately eight-tenths (85 per cent) and four-tenths to one-half. For the population of adolescents (male) taken as a whole, the accumulative incidence figures rise steadily with age.

Of all the sexual behaviors so far considered, none is more influenced than coitus by cultural influences, such as those reflected particularly in social level and social-class upbringing. Social level is a factor affecting incidence of coitus so markedly that by late adolescence almost all of the boys of the lower social levels but not nearly so many of the higher social classes have experienced intercourse. Approximately one-half of the college-destined, three-fourths of those who have reached the high-

deliberate attempt to effect erotic arousal"—Kinsey, 1948) are numerous in adolescence and are most extensively described by Kinsey, especially on pages 251–259 of the volume on the female. One also can get a good picture of the techniques by reading the studies by Ehrmann (1952) and the author (1959). Of the male sex, very few persons have had a petting experience before puberty. However, a sharp rise occurs in the accumulative incidence of petting at about the age of 13 for both sexes. There is a steady increase into late adolescence in the numbers of persons of both sexes who pet, so that by late adolescence the preponderant majority of adolescents have petted, 88 per cent of the boys and approximately 88 to 91 per cent of the girls by the end of age 20, according to Kinsey (1948, 1953). The highest frequency for the male sex appears to occur after the age of 21. For both sexes late adolescence appears to be the period of highest active incidence, when one-quarter of the girls and one-third of the boys are actively involved to the point of orgasm.

At this period of life over eight-tenths of the girls and nearly all the boys are petting, perhaps not to the point of orgasm but with varying degrees of erotic arousal. The petting of girls is more sporadic than that of boys and estimates as to the frequency of petting among them are much less certain. As in the case of masturbation, there are great individual differences among girls, according to the situation of the particular girl and what time span in her life is being considered. For example, a specific girl may pet three or four times in one evening with several or more partners, and again the same girl in another time period may not pet for weeks or months.

In some subgroups of the adolescent population nearly all of the adolescents have petted. This is particularly true of those who have experienced their adolescence since about 1930 and certainly those of present generations; and also for those adolescents who are of higher social levels and who appear destined to go to college. For this group of male adolescents the accumulative incidence by late adolescence is at least 94 per cent and its active incidence and frequency become such that it begins to compete with masturbation as a source of sexual arousal. For boys of lower social levels, however, by late adolescence coitus rather than petting competes strongly with masturbation and becomes the preferred source of erotic arousal. Its accumulative incidence in this group nears 100 per cent and its frequency and active incidence are such that approximately seven-tenths (85 per cent of the grade-school level is active) of the outlet in orgasm is being provided by coitus. In the college group, where active incidence nears two-fifths after the age of 20, the proportion of outlet in orgasm by means of coitus is near 20 per cent.

For the female adolescent, there is not as definite a relation between educational level or social level and petting experience, in terms of report of accumulative incidence. The incidence of petting at almost any particular age is almost as great among those who are destined to go to college as among those whose parents come from a laboring class.

For both sexes there is little or no relation between onset of puberty and incidence of petting. Many girls and boys have been pubertal for a few years before they start to pet. However, there is a relation between religious upbringing and the accumulative incidence of petting, although for girls the relation appears to be slight at any age and particularly during the years of early adolescence (before 15), when the difference between the devout and inactive is slight. There is one exception, and that is where petting to orgasm is concerned. Here devoutness affects the activity, petting to the point of orgasm being more frequent among the girls who are religiously inactive. The accumulative incidences and frequencies of premarital petting among the devout and inactive groups are not great where male youth are concerned and especially is this so at late adolescence.

From what studies have been done, some rather clear historical trends are evident with respect to petting. Adolescents today are petting at an earlier age and the accumulative incidence and frequency of petting among today's adolescents are greater than was true of the past (Terman, 1938; Kinsey). Truly, petting can be called a phenomenon of present-day youth, as almost all of today's youth is experiencing it. Its total incidence and its frequency have increased in present-day generations. Also, there is some evidence, as Kinsey has suggested, that today's youth is elaborating the techniques of petting. For these reasons it is a sexual activity that has received much attention and in all probability it merits further study. Present-day adolescents have learned to employ petting as an end in itself, and for many adolescents it is the method of achieving heterosexual orgasm or heterosexual satisfaction in a sociosexual context where, frequently, coitus can be avoided.

Kinsey has spoken much about petting as serving as a substitute for coitus. There is evidence that more elaborate techniques of petting have been and are being generated by present-day adolescents (Reevy, 1959a) to serve as substitutes for coitus. Vestured genital apposition and coitus is one of these techniques. This is a petting technique that seems to be more frequent than, for example, genital apposition, cunnilinctus, etc. The author has given statistical evidence for the existence of this behavior and defined it as erotically stimulating sexual behavior in which coitus is simulated by the male apposing his clothed genital area to the clothed genital area of the female while in the horizontal position, male usually prone, female supine, both or either moving the body in coital-like movements.

All the techniques that in married life are called the techniques of foreplay and that are possible preludes to coitus are employed by adolescents as petting techniques. These, to mention only a few, are kissing (deep), breast and genital petting, mutual masturbation, cunnilinctus, fellatio, and genital apposition. Of these kissing, breast and genital petting, and mutual masturbation are the most prevalent. As Kinsey (1953), Ehrmann (1952), Podell and Perkins (1957), and the author (1959a) have indicated, these behaviors find a hierarchical acceptance among adolescents, with kissing being almost universal and the incidence of such behaviors as fellatio and cunnilinctus being quite low.

Premarital Coitus

Considering both sexes together and without reference to any other factor, such as age, social level, or religious upbringing, coitus (premarital) is one of the major motoric sexual activities of adolescence. The accumulative incidence as well as the active incidence of coitus in the male sex is high. The late teens is the period of the highest active incidence for the male sex, when almost three-fourths are involved (Kinsey, 1948; Ramsey, 1943). The accumulative incidence of premarital intercourse during adolescence reported in other studies varies from 2 to 60 per cent, with many clustering in a range of 40 to 60 per cent.

Some people are very surprised to learn that single adult males are less active in heterosexual coitus than the older teenager, whose mean frequency of intercourse (according to Kinsey) is about one and one-third times a week, and even less active than the early teenager (less than 15), whose frequency is about twice a week. At any age the highest active incidence of premarital intercourse is among those boys who come from (or are destined for) the lowest educational and social level. At about age 15 those with potentiality for the least education have experienced considerable intercourse and the active incidence in this group is about one-half, while among those who are destined for college-level education the incidence is approximately 10 per cent. At age 21, or near the end of adolescence, the respective incidence figures are approximately eight-tenths (85 per cent) and four-tenths to one-half. For the population of adolescents (male) taken as a whole, the accumulative incidence figures rise steadily with age.

Of all the sexual behaviors so far considered, none is more influenced than coitus by cultural influences, such as those reflected particularly in social level and social-class upbringing. Social level is a factor affecting incidence of coitus so markedly that by late adolescence almost all of the boys of the lower social levels but not nearly so many of the higher social classes have experienced intercourse. Approximately one-half of the college-destined, three-fourths of those who have reached the high-school level, and eight-tenths of those who have stopped at the grade-school level have experienced heterosexual coitus by the end of adolescence.

Somewhere in the neighborhood of one-third (range of one-tenth to three-tenths, according to Ehrmann, 1957) of the female population has experienced premarital coitus by the end of adolescence. Accumulative incidence as reported in other studies varies from 7 to 87 per cent, with the majority of them reporting an incidence clustering in the range between 30 and 40 per cent. In the mid-teens a greater proportion of girls from the lower social levels has had intercourse as compared to girls from higher social backgrounds, but the differences are not marked and certainly not as great as in the case of boys. Toward the end of adolescence the gap between the social classes, where the female is concerned, becomes less wide, and after 21 or thereabouts there is virtually no difference. In the instance of the male adolescent the accumulative incidence of coitus takes an upswing at about the age of 13, just as in the case of masturbation, while the accumulative incidence in the female grows *gradually* over the period of the adolescent years within a much narrower range. Generally, perhaps twice as many boys as girls have experienced premarital coitus by age 21.

In the male, early puberty is related to greater active incidence in coitus at an earlier age, but in the female the relationship, if it does exist, is slight. Here again we see a trend that was found in both sexes relating to masturbation.

As in the instance of masturbation, religious background is a factor relating to total incidence of premarital intercourse. Also, its active incidence and frequency are found to be less in both sexes among the devout of all major creeds.

For the female adolescent, particularly, premarital intercourse tends to be a sporadic affair. For her it is relatively rare in frequency (under age 20, once in five weeks, over 20, once in three weeks), and rare in another sense. Most premarital intercourse for adolescent girls appears to be experienced with a limited number of partners of about their own age.

Many adolescent girls who have histories of premarital coitus will have one contact with as many as five weeks intervening before there is another. And the majority (over one-half) have intercourse with one person who later may become their spouse. The great majority have intercourse with fewer than five persons.

For the female sex, taking all adolescents and the entire period of adolescence into account, masturbation remains the primary activity throughout, with premarital petting and premarital coitus having about equal status during late adolescence (17-21). As maturity is approached coitus gains considerable ascendancy over petting. For the male sex masturbation is the major sexual activity during early adolescence, with coitus being second in order. At late adolescence coitus becomes the activity of major importance and masturbation is relegated to second place. In terms of outlet to orgasm, petting, for the male sex considered totally, in no way competes with either of the foregoing at any age.

Adults have always been curious about where petting and coitus take place. Today it is much the same as it was in the day of Havelock Ellis. He maintained that the majority of girls lose their virginity in the homes of their parents. Most of the petting, according to Kinsey (the author has confirmatory data), probably occurs in the girl's home, in the male's home, in the automobile, and in rented rooms or other rooms where the girl lives. Likewise, a great proportion of premarital coitus takes place in the female's home, in other domiciles, or in cars. Apparently the patterns of sexual motoric behavior of adolescents are developed before young people leave home (as for example, to go to college) and these patterns develop under their parents' "watchful eyes." Fears that their offspring will behave in markedly different ways sexually, once they leave home, are largely irrational.

Nocturnal Emissions and Nocturnal Dreams

When judged against the yardstick of their importance in contributing to orgastic release, neither nocturnal emissions nor their counterpart in the female, nocturnal dreams, are really important. Kinsey estimates that nocturnal emissions contribute about one-twelfth of the total sexual release in orgasm in the early twenties for the male and nocturnal dreams never any more than 2 per cent for the female. Total incidence for the male is 78 per cent by age 21 and less than 10 per cent for the female. The peak of occurrence of nocturnal emissions in the male is in the late teens, but for the female the peak in the incidence of nocturnal dreams does not take place until after adolescence. As to numbers of persons who experience these activities, Kinsey tells us that in the late teens approximately 70 per cent of the males are having orgasms in dreams while probably less than 10 per cent of the females are.

For both sexes there is practically no relation between socioeconomic level (as exemplified by father's occupation) and the onset of nocturnal dreams. For the female sex there is little or no relationship between the beginning of puberty and the occurrence of nocturnal dreams. But for the male nocturnal emissions tend to occur a year or two after the beginning of adolescence. The educational level a girl will finally achieve has little bearing upon the commencement of nocturnal dreams. But in the male there is a definite, positive relationship between the educational level that will be attained and the occurrence of nocturnal emissions. Before the age of 15, 70 per cent of the college-destined boys are already experiencing nocturnal emissions, compared with 25 per cent of the boys who will conclude life with only the lower levels of education. Near the end of adolescence 91 per cent of the college-level boys and 56 per cent of the boys of lower educational levels are having nocturnal dreams. By the end of adolescence the accumulative (total) incidence of nocturnal dreams is nearly 80 per cent for the male population at large; and 67.5, 80.8, and 94.5 per cent for the grade-school, high-school, and college levels, respectively (Kinsey, 1948).

Homosexual Activity, Animal Contacts

Relatively few adolescents of either sex are involved in actual or "true" homosexual activity. Homosexual relationships of a rather permanent type in which the liaisons approach or resemble the relationship of a heterosexual type in degree of attachment or involvement are relatively rare. Also, animal contacts are uncommon in this period of life. Of course, some adolescents at any age are involved in such activities sporadically and for brief periods of time. By the end of adolescence about 20 per cent of the male adolescents have had an active homosexual erotic contact of such a type as to induce orgasm, while about 3 per cent of the girls have experienced the like. Approximately three times as many girls have had homosexual contacts of a relatively uninvolved, fleeting, social variety than have had homosexual contacts of such a degree of involvement as to induce orgasm. About two-fifths of the boys (by late adolescence) have had occasional casual homosexual experiences.

Though homosexual contacts during adolescence are of social significance, and though there are severe social, legal, and moral strictures against them, they in no way compete with petting, masturbation, coitus, or nocturnal sex dreams as a sexual activity of youth.

Animal contacts for both sexes are extremely rare during adolescence, both in accumulative incidence and in frequency. Probably less than 2 per cent of the total population of female adolescents and no more than 6 to 8 per cent of the males have had this experience. However, adolescence is the period of the most frequent animal contact for the male and female sex. The frequency of animal contacts among the males is practically nil in urban areas but is considerably higher on farms, where as many as 40 to 50 per cent (Kinsey, 1948) of the farm boys have been in such proximity with animals. Among girls, the contacts seem to be confined to household pets, mostly dogs, touching of the animal's genitalia being one of the more frequent sexual responses made by girls. For the male, masturbation of the dog is a frequent type of conjunction with the animal.

When adolescent sexuality is considered *in toto*, these activities are relatively unimportant because of their low incidence in the total population and because of the infrequency of the specific acts in the histories of those persons who have had any experiences of this type. However, these activities are socially significant, undoubtedly, because of the social and moral indignation and psychological turmoil that is aroused when persons are identified as having been involved in such behaviors. Further, most of the states have laws that prohibit such sexual contact and in some cases the penalties are most severe. From this standpoint they receive more attention than is warranted.

Proximal Sexual Activity

A second class of adolescent motoric sexual behavior is that of the proximal sexual motoric type. There exists a class of sexual behavior not always considered as falling in the domain of sexuality, either by the layman or even by many scientists. Therefore this class of activity needs to be defined.

Adolescents take part in many behaviors that are linked with the sexual motive and its aims as previously indicated. These are actions that may (1) stimulate, (2) be antecedent conditions for, (3) substitute for, or (4) be disguises for directly sexual motoric activity. These activities are termed proximal sexual by the author because they are *near to* or closely resemble the directly sexual motoric responses previously discussed in that they are motoric, related to the sexual motive, and have the same or nearly the same aims. These activities often serve the same functions as adolescent sexual phantasies, which can also (1) stimulate, (2) be antecedent conditions to, (3) substitute for, or (4) act as disguises for the directly sexual motoric responses.

Many adolescents of both sexes are attracted to rock and roll dancing. A number of adolescent girls spend time outfitting themselves with tight brassieres, tight sweaters, panty girdles, or special brassieres (to illustrate, ones with holes in the middle so that the bare nipples may jut into the cloth of a tight sweater). Further, they wear tight jeans, toreador pants, or underclothing that may rub the genital regions or, in a highly sexually conscious culture such as ours, draw attention to the buttocks, genital regions, or other parts of the female anatomy. Many adolescent girls strut about when wearing this singular apparel in front of or in places where adolescent boys may view them. Some adolescent girls purchase and wear special, "fancy" panties, which may be highly colored, lacy, crocheted elegantly, or cut in unique ways. These may be worn when they look forward to a special, somewhat premeditated petting session with a certain boy or when the aim is less specific than this, as for example when they are "just going to be downtown."

Adolescent boys outfit themselves in special wardrobes and garb, too. The wearing of particular cuts of trousers, of singular cuts and types of jackets, of certain styles of haircuts (as "ducks' asses"), of long chains, of especial brogue shoes, and the like is behavior that has a sexual significance. Also, they indulge in particular bodily movements, mannerisms, or lingo with which to flirt and to quip with the girls.

Little is known of the true sexual significance of these behaviors as virtually no empirical statistical research has been done in this area. Kinsey, in Chapter 16 of *Sexual Behavior in the Human Female*, presents some data about behaviors of a type related to that under discussion. He indicates that certain patterns of behavior are acquired that lead an individual to react positively or negatively to various classes and types of stimuli. More so than those *actions* discussed by Kinsey, the proximal sexual behaviors appear to be responses that occur in a social situation that has some potentiality for becoming a sociosexual setting. These responses have an effect of stimulating sexual phantasy, sexual emotions or feelings, or directly sexual motoric activity in a second person or one's self.

Taking girls as an example, the wearing of tight sweaters that accent the breasts, or of individually fitted skirts that accent the region of the mons veneris in such a way, for example, as to outline a V shape near the sexual regions, may serve a variety of purposes or aims depending on the individual psychological make-up and preferences for action of the particular girl. It should be pointed out that the girl may be unaware of, or not clearly aware of, the motive for some of these choices.

For one young girl such conduct may be a way of arousing the young boy to further heterosexual responses. The result may be that a boy will interact with her, stimulate her, and bring about direct physical sexual response. For another it may serve as a means of achieving some sexual satisfaction without provoking too-advanced petting or coitus on the part of the male, both being sexual activities of a directly motoric sexual type which may be taboo for her. The sexual satisfaction for this girl may come by way of a complicated process, one example of which (though there might be many others) could be the following. The proximal sexual activity that she initiates has several effects, some upon her and some upon the male. Her sexual phantasies, emotions, and other classes of sexual responses are stimulated, as are the sexual phantasies, emotions, and sexual approach behavior of the male. The reacting human is an integrated complex of phantasy, feeling, and sensorimotor potential for response.

Although one girl may become conditioned to respond erotically with orgasm only if there is actual physical stimulation of the erogenous zones, the girl just being discussed may respond sexually only if a more complicated series of events (reactions) takes place in a chainlike manner. She dresses in a sexually provoking manner. This elicits sexual phantasies, feelings, and some partial sexual responses in her, and perhaps partial tumescence which she would perhaps call, introspectively, a "warm feeling." The male viewing her responds in like manner, perhaps with sexual phantasies and partial erection. He may begin to pet her if the sociosexual setting is environmentally and culturally appropriate. The combination of all these responses in either or both is perhaps enough to bring about (in some instances) sexual orgasm on the part of one or both. The latter response would sometimes, and in some cases, serve the aim of ultimate sexual release without the girl having to think of herself consciously as seriously violating the mores and without having actually been involved in heavy petting, or coitus, which she may fear or wish to avoid. Analogous behavior on the part of the male can achieve the same or similar ends for him.

Feelings and Attitudes
Toward Motoric Sexual Behavior

In view of the fact that masturbation is for male adolescents the major source of sexual outlet during early adolescence (estimate of active incidence 92 per cent by late adolescence), with approximately three-fourths having initiated the activity during early adolescence, we can assume that masturbation is not causing untold conflict in the general male population, at least not enough to stop it. There appears to be a considerable change in the attitude of present-day adolescents toward this behavior from that of adolescents (particularly male) of previous generations. Also, there seems to have evolved a change in the socio-cultural attitude toward the behavior, as well as a change in the attitudes of many professionals, such as educators and physicians.

From what little statistical evidence we have, it appears that in the 1900's, 1920's, and as late as the 1930's the great proportion of male adolescents believed that masturbation had deleterious effects. In studies done before 1940 the majority of boys gave evidence of being concerned over the possible harmful physical and mental effects of masturbation. In one study done by Pullias (1937), 82 per cent of male adolescents thought its effects were noxious and as many as 16 per cent thought insanity could be the direct result. This is not entirely surprising, for these adolescents and their parents were brought up on literature, purporting to be "scientific," that supported such beliefs. As Kinsey (1948) and Ramsey (1950) point out, the *Handbook for Boy Scouts*, all editions from 1911–1945, and many pamphlets (some written by physicians, sexologists, etc.) wrote explicitly about such effects—usually without presenting empirical evidence.

Today, however, psychiatrists, psychologists, and physicians rarely make statements stressing the harmful physical or mental effects of masturbation. The attitudes of many of these professionals are so "enlightened" that theologians and clergymen voice considerable annoyance at them for not stressing moral effects. As a direct result of the changes in attitudes among many professionals who work directly with sexual problems, fewer adolescents are taught that physical and mental deterioration result from masturbation. Although it is reasonable to assume that fewer adolescents have masturbatory guilt, many still have fears and

worries that masturbation will produce physical and mental harm.

Kinsey points out that the adolescents of the higher social levels (among whom masturbation is the more frequent) are better able to rationalize their feelings on the basis of the facts that today's scientific literature has provided them. Since they are often taught that no deleterious effects result therefrom, they feel freer to masturbate and perhaps are *driven* toward this outlet as they apparently have strong social taboos against intercourse. Adolescents of lower social levels, who have strong taboos against masturbation and who consider it somewhat perverted and unnatural, rationalize their greater coital activity on the basis that this is more "natural." These boys are more likely to believe that masturbation will cause physical harm, wear one out, or "drive one crazy." Girls of lower social levels also consider coitus more natural than masturbation and tend to give up the masturbatory activity of early adolescence.

Generally, however, in the female sex, where much smaller proportions report having masturbated, there still remain rather strong attitudes that masturbation is a despicable habit. Several persons who have attempted to study extensively this behavior in the adolescent female have learned that it is a behavioral act about which these adolescents are the most reticent, and that they experience the most discomfort when verbalizing or writing about it. In a questionnaire study done by Wolman (1951) in Israel, many female adolescents left the questions about masturbation unanswered, although they answered questions about premarital intercourse, petting, etc. In a study done by the author, many girls of late adolescent age gave evidence of the fact that they were uncomfortable while talking about masturbation. They talked more freely about all the other types of sexual behavior. Of those who had experienced masturbation, a majority reported that they had felt "unworthy" because of their masturbatory activity. A near majority admitted to having felt guilty about this behavior. Considerable proportions of these adolescents believed that the girl who masturbated excessively could be distinguished from the girl who did not masturbate. They were of the opinion that such a person could be identified by certain covert, revelatory behaviors. This belief may have been a projection of their own guilt feelings about this behavior.

Petting has not only considerable behavioral acceptance, but also considerable attitudinal and emotional approval among youth. Very few adolescents of either sex believe that kissing (light petting) should be delayed until marriage. Over 90 per cent of both sexes believe that kissing is an appropriate activity in the very early stages of dating (Drucker, Christensen, and Remmers, 1952). Petting is an almost universal activity during adolescence and considerable numbers of male and female adolescents express the attitude that heavy petting need not be delayed until marriage. About one-third of the females and two-thirds of the males are of this view. However, the proportion of adolescents actually involved in heavy petting is greater than that allowing it as an acceptable activity. It would seem that, because of the discrepancy between those (total incidence) involved in petting and those who express the foregoing attitude, considerable numbers are in conflict about the behavior. Girls who pet (and who may still be in conflict about the behavior) apparently are motivated to pet in order to (1) please the boy, (2) attain or retain popularity, (3) avoid censure by the peer group, and (4) find acceptance through sexual behavior for felt insecurity of various orders.

The conflict over differences between attitudes and behavior becomes more clear when premarital intercourse is considered. Here the double standard with respect to sexual activity, which is patent in our society in adult life, becomes more clear among youth. And youth echoes the attitudes of adults. Considerably greater proportions of young women than of men believe in the concept of premarital virginity, and the majority cleave to the conservative standards. The female adolescent is a little more demanding of premarital virginity for the female than for the male. When those adolescents who are having intercourse before marriage are questioned about their attitudes on this point, almost all of those whose activity is with the person they expect to marry say that the sexual intercourse is serving as a bond to strengthen their emotional relationship (Burgess and Wallin, 1953). Several studies indicate this trend.

When, however, one looks more closely at the nature of the relationship between the coital partners, things are different. According to an authority (Kirkendall, 1958) who is studying this particular aspect of sexual behavior intensively (*i.e.*, the effect of premarital intercourse upon human interaction), premarital intercourse in the majority of cases adversely affects the relationship between the persons involved. In his analysis, in this culture, since premarital intercourse is taboo, many young people have difficulty in honestly expressing their feelings and motives with regard to having intercourse with each other. Often young girls, to use the language of Reisman (1954), are "other directed" and, as in the case of petting, involved in order to please the date, in order to gain and maintain popularity, or because of fears of various kinds, such as fear of being ostracized by some group or of not being accepted for felt inadequacies in other areas.

Young men, especially those of the lower class, are more accepting of premarital intercourse, behaviorally and attitudinally. And many young men may exert considerable pressure upon girls for sexual intercourse. The motives for such behavior are frequently (1) desire to prove manhood, (2) pursuit of the hypothecated drive, "needed sexual release," *i.e.*, fulfilling of the belief that the male has a need to expulse or get rid of semen, and (3) pursuit of the belief that boys are more sexual than girls, with the consequent attempt to live up to the "level of aspiration" held up to boys by peers, societal propaganda, and the like. The young men, if of a middle or high social class, show a tendency to fulfill these motives by having intercourse with girls of a lower socioeconomic status than their own and are likely to stop at petting with girls of their own social class. This attitude and behavior on their part have given rise to the theory that in our culture the youthful male is sexually exploitative, seeking to "force" sexual relations with girls lower than himself in social status and having a relationship of sexual dalliance with them (Kirkpatrick and Kanin, 1957; Hollingshead,

1949). Recently, this theory has been criticized as a false explanation of the facts and another theorist has advanced the notion that girls of a lower social class may be making themselves more available to men of a higher social class in order to take a chance on bidding themselves up socially.

Whether adolescents are any more sexually exploitative than adults is not certain, but in the main, in this instance as in many others relating to sexual behavior, they reflect, in their general attitudes, the mores of the adult culture. They are aware of a double standard of sexual morality and act on the assumptions involved.

Adolescents share with adults much the same attitudes toward homosexuality, contacts with animals, and other infrequent and socially condemned behavior. There is almost wholesale condemnation of these activities and the efforts of such special groups as scientific investigators, educators, sexologists, etc., have not been very successful in educating the public toward a more rational, scientific, less moralizing approach toward these behaviors, which are now viewed as social problems, as oddities or activities for social condemnation and censure.

Sexual Phantasies and Conditions Antecedent to Motoric Sexual Behavior

As members of both sexes become pubertal their interests become more heterosexual and there is an increase in erotic feeling. Also there is an increase in phantasies with sexual content. Stone and Barker (1937, 1939) found that girls of advanced sexual maturation, although of the same chronological age as girls not so advanced, had different interests from the latter. The more sexually mature girls were more interested in personal adornment, in boys, and in responses, "indicating heterosexual interests." Male adolescents of more advanced maturity—as evidenced by the increased output of androgens—were more likely to be interested in dancing, dating, and other sociosexual activities, as Sollenberger (1940) indicated.

These changes in interests from preadolescence to adolescence have often been attributed to the increased hormonal activity that occurs with the onset of puberty. Irrespective as to the cause, the evidence is clear that, with puberty, for both boys and girls in our culture, a change in attitude toward the members of the other sex results and an increased interest in dancing, dating, and other sociosexual activities eventuates.

It is clear that in the foregoing environmental contexts the opportunities for the types of sexual responses that we have already discussed can arise. Not only does increased interest in the other sex seem to be correlated with increased hormonal activity occurring at puberty, but there is also at this time increased erotic feeling and an increase in sexual daydreams of various types. Various activities and behaviors are phantasied: kissing, viewing the sexual organs of the opposite sex, and sexual intercourse are frequent types of sexual phantasies. Girls to a lesser degree than boys phantasize viewing the sexual organs of the other sex. The tendency of the male to voyeurism is so well known that Kinsey (1953) makes the statement that "There are probably very few heterosexual males who would not take advantage of the opportunity to observe a nude female." The incidence of "peeping" in the male population during adolescence is not well known from statistical studies of random samples but, among cases seen in juvenile courts, heterosexual intercourse, homosexual activity, and fellation appear to be more frequent charges against boys than "peeping," and in the order given (Markey, 1950). Since voyeurism is admitted to by the great majority of adult males, it is reasonable to assume that it is very frequent among adolescent males. That voyeurism is probably frequent among boys is supported by the evidence presented by Ramsey (1943), who found that female nudity was the most potent stimulus to erotic feeling for boys during the years of mid-adolescence.

Conversation involving sex, pictures in which nudity or sex acts are depicted, and daydreaming about sex were the stimuli (in the order mentioned) most potent in producing erotic response. Probably about one-fifth of the female sex and two-fifths of the male sex have phantasized intercourse, the phantasy of most direct sexual content, before the beginning of adolescence. Although exact statistics are lacking, phantasies of kissing, hugging, and petting (heterosexual and homosexual) are much more frequent. In a study done by the author, a majority of the female adolescents of college status (mean age 20.5 years) phantasized men doing sexual acts with women, approximately 16 per cent daydreamed about girls having sexual contacts with other girls, and less than 10 per cent daydreamed about masturbation.

In the Ramsey study, literature was one of the stimuli least provocative of erotic feeling and in the author's study less than a quarter of the girls of the late adolescent period had read books that they would call obscene.

Adolescent boys seem to be most responsive, in terms of erotic feeling, tumescence, and erection, to stimuli such as viewing of female nudity (total or specifically of the genital organs), obscene pictures, and motion pictures. Sex conversations, the viewing of burlesques, and dancing are also stimuli to which they are reactive. Literature, music, and similar abstract stimuli are not very evocative.

The viewing of nudity of the opposite sex (total or genital), of obscene pictures of the opposite sex, and of burlesques is probably not as stimulating erotically to girls as to boys. Girls may be less interested in these stimuli than boys. Or they may have learned to disclaim interest in them in certain social contexts, as for example when in the company of other persons, especially male. Again, as is often the case with premarital intercourse, whatever exhibitionism and showing of genitalia girls partake in with boys may be due to the desire to cooperate with the male in order to accede to his wishes. However, boys, especially in preadolescence, are very interested in viewing the sexual parts of girls and during this age this is a frequent heterosexual activity on their part. Exhibitionistic sex play is the second most frequently occurring behavior of a heterosexual type and young girls are often willing to show their sexual organs to boys or be involved in other exhibitionistic sex activities.

Stimuli more frequently provoking to girls are phantasies of sexual behavior with boys, phantasies of and during masturbation, and reading romantic literature and viewing romantic motion pictures.

The reasons for these differences in responsiveness on the part of boys and girls are not known exactly, but the following are frequent speculations: (1) Boys differ from girls in innate sex drive and/or libido; (2) the sensory capacity to stimulation of boys differs from that of girls; and (3) the sociosexual acculturation of males and females is different.

General Theoretical Explanation of Adolescent Sexuality

It cannot be denied that with the beginning of adolescence there is a marked increase in sexual responsivity and sexual motoric behavior. A frequent and usually undisputed explanation of this fact is that the upsurge in sexual activity is, at base, physiological. The usual explanations, to quote only a few, are the following:

Willoughby (1937), in his review, *Sexuality in the Second Decade,* concludes that "the necessary motive [presumably for increased sexuality] is present in the changes in hormonal balance probably initiated by the involution of the thymus . . . an increase [in hormonal balance] would account satisfactorily for the increasing numbers of individuals manifesting any normal type of sex behavior as the decade progresses."

Kimble (1956) voices a view typical of American psychologists:

The physiological and anatomical considerations important to the understanding of sexual activity parallel those treated in the cases of hunger and thirst. As in the case of hunger and thirst, local stimulation plays an important role in sexual behavior. . . .

As everyone knows, the physiology of sexual behavior is largely hormonal. Indirectly sexual behavior is controlled by the anterior portion of the pituitary gland. . . .

There is little doubt that physiology plays an important role in the increase in sexual activity that takes place during adolescence, in contrast to the period of preadolescence, as the researches of Sollenberger (1940), Stone and Barker (1937, 1939), and others suggest. We have seen how, shortly after the age of 12, sexual behaviors such as masturbation, petting, and premarital intercourse generally increase greatly in accumulative and active incidence, with many persons having their first experiences of various types during adolescence. Such facts, coupled with the evidence that the increase in these activities is correlated with increased hormonal activity at adolescence, suggest that an important and perhaps the original stimulus to this *increased* sexual activity is physiological in type.

The theory of Freud that sexuality is latent from childhood until puberty lends support to the notion of the physiological basis of sexual activity during adolescence. Under the influence of physiological changes occurring during adolescence, sexuality can no longer, according to the Freudian view, remain latent. Mead, Devereux, Malinowski, and others have shown that, without much question, no true latency period exists and that what is found, if one studies sexual behavior closely, is that at all ages of life and in all environments sexuality is universal and ubiquitous. There are always some persons at any age in all places on earth who are doing something that is sexual.

As puberty arrives something happens to make sexual behavior more nearly omnipresent. Undoubtedly, the basic stimulus for increased sexuality at this age is hormonal. But although these physiological changes are necessary, they are not the only factors in sexual response. Even at as late an age as adolescence only very limited types of sexual responses would be evident in the absence of learning. At adolescence, although sex hormones may be at the base of the sex drive, the drive would be largely undifferentiated as to aim if sexual activity did not become psychosexual. The activity of the youngster becomes psychosexual when the initial sexual drive or interest becomes conditioned through learning (cultural, institutional, or individual and idiosyncratic) toward some specific object, goal, or activity.

For example, if a young adolescent couple, both of whom are physiologically and neurally capable of tumescence or erotic arousal or orgasm, learns through dating, perhaps through physical exploration and manipulation, that sexual release or orgasm can be pleasurable to both, this activity may be repeated. Sexual response (but not drive) may be "latent" (but not in the Freudian sense) before adolescence when the cultural framework exerts such pressures (or when the individuals cannot find ways around these barriers) that all responses that might be labeled as sexual are prevented.

Of course, no such *absolute* repression ever exists before or during adolescence and *some* sexual responses of *some* type will be made and conditioning of *some* type will result. Influences exist in any culture (the word environment could be substituted) that will modify the sexual response in some way. When these outside influences are spoken of, taught, or enforced through the institutional body called the church, we speak of religious influence. Thus, for example, a church may teach that masturbation is a sin. If it does, the devout of that church may modify their masturbatory behavior completely or to such an extent that the masturbation may be so truncated, as Taylor (1933) has shown, as to appear not to be masturbation at all. For example, an adolescent boy may sleep on his stomach and when only slightly awake rub his genital organ against the bed clothes without touching his penis and without being fully aware of what is happening.

If by transmission through cultural mores or folkways specific sex practices are recommended or condemned, we speak of cultural influences. Thus, one culture may teach or indoctrinate youth in the specific practice of masturbation while another may condemn the practice through various means, such as the mother threatening the child who masturbates or the culture teaching invidiously that a person who masturbates "is not mature."

In like vein, outside influences of all sorts affect specific sexual responses or behavior. What is taught in sex education courses and how sex is treated in the press and in magazines available to youth are such environmental factors.

The major outside influences that have a relation to adolescent sexual behavior are religion; general sociocultural influences, such as rural-urban upbringing and the socioeconomic level of the family; more specific sociocultural influences, such as the teachings, practices, and mores specific to gangs, peer groups, and certain cultural-ethnic mores; and, finally, general and specific sexual teachings. All these influences can be grouped together as environmental influences and appear to have a major effect upon the specific sexual patterns of groups as well as individuals.

Another class of influences upon the adolescent are the truly psychological—which in a large degree are specific, individual, and often *accidental;* that is, factors in the life of this particular individual. For example, the seduction of a boy by a housemaid might be an individual factor influencing his future sexual response and sexual proclivities and preferences.

A final class of influence is the philosophical, which for most adolescents is very remote from the world of everyday reality and action and response. A youth highly developed intellectually may believe in the "good life," have rationalized that masturbation and homosexuality, for example, are sexual behaviors that interfere with the goal of a "good life," and so avoid these behaviors. Another youth highly developed intellectually may not accept the premise of the hereafter, may not accept masturbation as evil, and may not avoid this behavior.

References

Ausubel, David P., *Theories and Problems of Adolescent Development.* New York: Grune & Stratton, Inc., 1954.

Brown, J. F., and Menninger, Karl A., *The Psychodynamics of Abnormal Behavior.* New York: McGraw-Hill Book Co., 1940.

Burgess, Ernest W., and Wallin, Paul, *Engagement and Marriage.* Philadelphia: J. B. Lippincott Co., 1953.

Butterfield, Oliver M., *Love Problems of Adolescence.* New York: Emerson Books, Inc., 1939.

Drucker, A. J., Christensen, H. T., and Remmers, H. H., "Some Background Factors in Socio-Sexual Modernism." *Marr. Fam. Living 14;* 334-337, 1952.

Ehrmann, Winston W., "Student Cooperation in a Study of Dating Behavior." *Marr. Fam. Living 14;* 323-326, 1952.

Ehrmann, Winston W., "Social Class and Premarital Coitus Among Male and Female College Students." In Jerome Himmelhoch and Sylvia Fava (eds.), *Sexual Behavior in American Society.* New York: W. W. Norton & Co., Inc., 1955.

Ehrmann, Winston W., "Some Knowns and Unknowns in Research into Human Sex Behavior." *Marr. Fam. Living 19;* 16-22, 1957.

Ellis, Albert, *The Folklore of Sex.* New York: Charles Boni, 1951.

Ellis, Albert, *Sex Without Guilt*. New York: Lyle Stuart, 1958.

Ellis, Havelock, *Studies in the Psychology of Sex*. New York: Random House, 1936.

Ford, Clellan S., and Beach, Frank A., *Patterns of Sexual Behavior*. New York: Harper & Brothers, 1951.

Hollingshead, August B., *Elmtown's Youth*. New York: John Wiley & Sons, Inc., 1949.

Kimble, Gregory A., *Principles of General Psychology*. New York: The Ronald Press Co., 1956.

Kinsey, Alfred C., Pomeroy, Wardell B., and Martin, Clyde E., *Sexual Behavior in the Human Male*. Philadelphia: W. B. Saunders Co., 1948.

Kinsey, Alfred C., Pomeroy, Wardell B., Martin, Clyde E., and Gebhard, Paul H., *Sexual Behavior in the Human Female*. Philadelphia: W. B. Saunders Co., 1953.

Kirkendall, Lester A., "Sex Problems of Adolescents." *Marr. Hyg. 1;* 205-208, 1948.

Kirkendall, Lester A., *Premarital Intercourse and Interpersonal Relationships*. New York: The Julian Press, 1961.

Kirkpatrick, Clifford, and Kanin, Eugene, "Male Sex Aggression on a University Campus." *Am. Sociol. Rev. 22;* 52-58, 1957.

Markey, Oscar B., "A Study of Aggressive Sex Misbehavior in Adolescents Brought to Juvenile Court." *Am. J. Orthopsychiat. 20;* 719-731, 1950.

Moll, Albert, *The Sexual Life of the Child*. New York: The Macmillan Co., 1912.

Podell, Lawrence, and Perkins, John C., "A Guttman Scale for Sexual Experience—A Methodological Note." *J. Abnorm. & Social Psychol. 54;* 420-422, 1957.

Pullias, E. V., "Masturbation as a Mental Hygiene Problem—A Study of the Beliefs of Seventy-five Young Men." *J. Abnorm. & Social Psychol. 32;* 216-222, 1937.

Ramsey, Glenn V., "The Sexual Development of Boys." *Am. J. Psychol. 56;* 217-233, 1943.

Ramsey, Glenn V., *Factors in the Sex Life of 291 Boys*. Madison, N. J.: printed by the author, 1950.

Reevy, William R., "Premarital Petting Behavior and Marital Happiness Prediction." *Marr. Fam. Living 21;* 349-355, 1959.

Reevy, William R., *Vestured Genital Apposition and Coitus*. In Beigel, Hugo (ed.), *Advances in Sex Research*. New York: Hoeber Medical Division of Harper & Row, 1963.

Reevy, William R., "Female Masturbation and Marital Happiness Prediction." In press.

Riesman, David, *et al.*, *The Lonely Crowd*. New York. Doubleday Anchor Books, 1954.

Robinson, William J., *Medical and Sex Dictionary*. New York: Eugenics Pub. Co., 1933.

Seward, Georgene H., *Sex and the Social Order*. New York: McGraw-Hill Book Co., 1946.

Sollenberger, R. T., "Some Relationship between the Urinary Excretion of Male Hormone by Maturing Boys and Their Expressed Interests and Attitudes." *J. Psychol. 9;* 179-189, 1940.

Stekel, Wilhelm, *Autoerotism*. New York: Liveright, 1950.

Stone, Calvin P., and Barker, R. G., "Aspects of Personality and Intelligence in Postmenarcheal and Premenarcheal Girls of the Same Chronological Ages." *J. Comp. & Physiol. Psychol. 23;* 439-455, 1937.

Stone, Calvin P., and Barker, R. G., "The Attitudes and Interests of Premenarcheal and Postmenarcheal Girls." *J. Genet. Psychol. 54;* 27-71, 1939.

Taylor, W. S., "A Critique of Sublimation in Males." *Genet. Psychol. Monogr. 13;* 1-115, 1933.

Terman, Lewis M., *et al.*, *Psychological Factors in Marital Happiness*. New York: McGraw-Hill Book Co., 1938.

Undeutsch, Udo, "Comparative Incidence of Premarital Coitus in Scandinavia, Germany, and the United States." In Jerome Himmelhoch and Sylvia Fava (eds.), *Sexual Behavior in American Society*. New York: W. W. Norton & Co., Inc., 1955.

Willoughby, Raymond R., *Sexuality in the Second Decade*. Washington: Monograph of the Society for Research in Child Development, 1937.

Wolman, Benjamin, "Sexual Development in Israeli Adolescents." *Am. J. Psychotherapy 5;* 551-559, 1951.

WILLIAM R. REEVY

Africans, The Sex Life of

SINCE Africa has an area of about twelve million square miles (about four times the size of the United States of America), we can do no more than consider representative samples of its many cultures. The population is estimated at 170 million, mostly Negro, but with millions of Arabs and Berbers in the North and a strong Hamitic element in the East.

The most satisfactory method of describing the sex life of Africans, when brevity is necessary, is by considering (1) a typical sex cycle from conception, through pregnancy, to birth; (2) puberty, with the physical changes, initiation into the tribe, and marriage; (3) normal relationships of husband and wife, and marital maladjustment and divorce; and (4) irregular practices that involve deviations from the usual moral codes.

From Conception to Birth

Negro tribes often do not seem to have a clear idea of the act of fertilization, although, unlike Malinowski's Trobriand Islanders, they do recognize paternity, and generally say that the husband puts something into the woman and it grows.

Children are desired by all tribes, but barrenness, although creating domestic dissatisfaction, is not necessarily a cause for divorce. The husband merely takes a young girl as second wife, but the first spouse keeps her position as chief wife, and she may be distinguished by a special headdress or an ornament. Sterility of the husband is sometimes suspected, and this also calls for a second marriage. Impotence of the husband, however, may cause divorce. If evil magic is suspected as the cause of barren-

ness, a medicine man will apply protective paint to the wife's face, or he may give her a charm to wear. A favorite talisman is the small sea shell known as a cowrie. This shell has a deep cleft and is thought to resemble the vulva.

Abortions are sometimes induced by pressure, but taking herbal concoctions is a more common method. The practice is generally under severe reprobation. Miscarriages from natural causes occur, and the mortality of infants during the first three years of life has been estimated at 50 per cent. But the birth rate is high and, although the exact statistics are not known, the total African population is increasing.

Under a system of legal polygamy and early marriages the social problem of illegitimate births is of little importance. Infanticide has been practiced in time of famine and by hunters on the march, and no doubt deformed children and those with supernumerary fingers or toes were destroyed. Albinos were sometimes allowed to live, and became respected as having some magical power. A regional survey of the attitude toward twins clearly indicates that many different customs prevail. The mother and both infants might be killed, or they might all escape death because the medicine man performed a purification ceremony. Twins might be so welcome that if one died a wooden doll was "nursed" by the mother so that the surviving twin might not suffer from loneliness.

Pregnancy is a condition fraught with many dangers, both physical and spiritual. Negro religion involves a system of ancestor worship, and during pregnancy the spirit of some deceased relative is thought to enter the womb. There is reincarnation. Many taboos are observed, especially with regard to food; thus, flesh of the owl will give the baby large round eyes, and meat from a hare causes harelip. Magical methods are sometimes used to produce offspring of the desired sex. For example, a woman who has borne only boys will contact a woman whose children are all girls. A change of sex is supposedly brought about by an exchange of gifts, the mother of boys receiving a field basket and a hoe, which are symbols of female interest. In return for these, the mother of the girls receives a bow and some arrow points, symbols of manhood.

A system of couvade, whereby the father goes to bed during delivery of the child, is known in Africa but is very rare; however, during a pregnancy the husband has to take special care of himself, for accidents to him might affect the unborn child. Difficulties in delivery are sometimes combated by opening wide all boxes and vessels, and in anticipation of trouble a pregnant woman usually drinks some concoction supplied by the medicine man. Normally the delivery takes place at home with midwives in attendance, but births while a woman is at work in the fields are not unusual. A difficult delivery, such as the birth of twins, is often thought to result from some act of unfaithfulness on the part of the wife, and the midwives exhort her to confess the name of her seducer. Sometimes the names of the parents are changed at the birth of the first child.

The custom of the husband and wife refraining from sexual intercourse during pregnancy and throughout the long period of lactation is common among the Negroes of Africa. But here, again, the medicine man offers his services with rituals and potions that permit sexual relations without harm to the unborn child, or to the infant of a nursing mother. Infant betrothal is fairly common, and the arrangement made by parents is ratified by an exchange of gifts, which are returned if the agreement is not fulfilled. Frequently such infant betrothals are repudiated by the children when they mature.

Puberty and Tribal Initiation

At an early age boys and girls become separated in their play interests. Girls work in the field with their mothers and their play is largely an imitation of tasks relegated to women. Boys make blunt wooden arrows, and at an early age are expert in catching and shooting small game such as birds and small rodents. Before initiation, perhaps in the early teens, boy and girl friendships exist, along with nocturnal visits, which are supposed to be innocent of sexual intercourse. I noticed in Angola that the age range of boys at initiation seemed to be a wide one, probably due to the fact that ceremonies are held only once in three or four years. The boys seemed to vary in age from 12 to 16 years.

When boys are ready to be initiated into the tribe they are assembled in an enclosure in a secluded part of the woods. Tribal elders are in charge, and in some instances each boy has an initiated youth as a personal guardian. The objects of initiation are twofold, mental and physical. A boy must learn respect and obedience toward elders, and he has to be well schooled in tribal laws, especially with regard to permissible marriages, for taboos exist regarding marriage with some, but not all, cousins. Where totems and clans are part of the social organization marriage is forbidden between members of the same clan or totem.

Boys are made to endure hardships in the form of exposure to cold, long, fatiguing days in hunting and fishing, and corporal punishment for minor offenses. Running between two lines of elders who are armed with sticks is a common test of endurance. I saw among the Fulani of west Africa a special type of flogging ceremony in which each of two boys, at the time of their initiation, gave and suffered severe blows on the ribs. The beatings were delivered with a thick stick and in the presence of a crowd of girls who applauded loudly when each boy in turn showed no sign of pain. Circumcision of boys is usual during initiation, and the camp is not disbanded until the last boy is healed. By this time every boy is a capable hunter and fisherman and is qualified to provide food for himself and his family.

Fiber costumes and masks that have been made during the period of seclusion are worn at a final ceremony attended by all villagers, who celebrate the occasion by drinking beer and dancing. At this time each boy receives a new name. This is his adult name and any future use of his juvenile name would be an insult. The novice is now prepared for marriage.

The time for initiation of girls is indicated by swelling of the breasts and the menarche. This is a period attended by many evil possibilities, and many taboos have to be observed. Diet is restricted and the girl perhaps has a separate hut or a part of the living room shut off by mats. Cleansing ceremonies of a magical nature are performed at the end of the menstrual period. In the Mohammedan states of north Africa and among some west African Negro tribes, girls begin a fattening period at puberty. To attain this mark of beauty they may be in seclusion for a few months or even for years, according to the wealth of the parents. If scarification is a tribal custom, certain patterns will be cut on the abdomen, or the scars may be made by applying a hot stick. When the period of menstrual seclusion is ended the girl will resume normal family life, and once more she is able to follow such occupations as weaving or making pottery. But for all her life the menstrual period will involve certain taboos.

When in the initiation camp the girls receive instruction in domestic and sexual matters from several old women, but young females do not suffer the hardships imposed on boys. During residence in camp girls may suffer excision of the clitoris or more severe operations on the genitalia. These rites may cause "infibulation," a sewing up of the vagina so as to make sexual relations impossible, although the orifice is not entirely closed. Before marriage a surgical operation has to be performed.

Authentic accounts from many parts of Negro Africa are not in agreement with regard to the value set on chastity before marriage. The Ovimbundu tribe of Portuguese West Africa are typical of people who at least in time past have demanded chastity, and if a bride was not a virgin she would be sent to her mother with a hole bored in her skirt. The parents would have to refund part of the payment or presents given to them by the groom. The evidence points to regard for virginity among the eastern and southern Bantu Negroes, but to a laxity and disregard for virginity in Bantu tribes of the Congo region.

Marriage

The boys and girls who have completed initiation rites are now men and women who are free to marry, and soon they enter into a state of legal sexual union with the primary object of founding a home and a family. In Negro Africa marriage is a serious legal contract, binding on husband and wife. A brief courtship follows the initiation ceremonies; then a relative of the youth makes an indirect approach to the parents of the girl. Presents are offered, and these vary with the social status of the boy's parents; the gifts may be no more than a blanket and a coil of tobacco. The bride brings with her a dowry, possibly cattle, the marriage contract being ratified by the exchange of gifts.

The husband may have to reside with his wife's people, at least for a time until their first child is born (matrilocal condition). On the other hand, the young bride may be expected to reside with her husband's people. Consummation of the marriage is sometimes delayed for three days or more, while elderly women who have borne children and led happy married lives live in the new home. The duty of these elders is to make new fire by the friction method, to bless the home, and to initiate the new wife in domestic work.

Marital troubles may arise from many causes: impotence of the husband, barrenness of the wife, female frigidity, the wife's incompetence in home or garden. A wife, as well as a husband, may have claims to divorce, but perhaps the most usual cause is infidelity of the wife. Attempts at reconciliation are made by parents, but if a divorce is decided upon the parting ceremony is performed by a village chief. There are rules respecting the rights of a woman to take with her the very young children and some domestic utensils. Adultery is severely punished if the social status of the seduced female is higher than that of her seducer. A man who seduces the wife of a chief is likely to suffer death or castration. With commoners the retribution is less severe; a wife might be beaten by her husband, and her seducer be forced to pay a fine to the aggrieved husband. The idea of sin because a divine command has been broken does not seem to exist.

But ancestral spirits are thought by some tribes to be deeply offended by adultery, and they may inflict calamity on the community.

A contradiction seems to exist in the fact that, whereas adultery is condemned, wife-lending as a form of hospitality is condoned. There are, however, certain reservations in this practice. The man so favored should belong to the husband's age group, and the wife-lending custom must not transgress any local laws forbidding sexual intercourse between certain cousins or members of the same clan or totem.

A wife's duties do not end with the death of her husband. She may have to remain in the hut with the corpse for several days, loudly voicing her grief. Her period of mourning may last for a year or more; then with due purification ceremonies she can remarry provided gifts and propitiatory rites are offered to the ghost of the deceased.

Polygamy

Polygamy has two forms, polygyny, the marrying of more than one wife, and polyandry, the marrying of more than one husband. An extreme form of polygyny was at one time practiced in Dahomey, Ashanti, and in other regions of west Africa. A ruler might have several hundred legal wives and, although he could not possibly have had regular intercourse with all, the women were severely punished for adultery. These plural marriages seemed to be political in their import, for a ruler who secured the persons of many of his leading subordinates felt some security, and his possession of the women encouraged allegiance from their male relatives. In small polygynous families with two to six wives, each wife has her own hut and kitchen within the household compound, and the husband must follow the custom of a one- or two-night cycle.

Polyandry is not common in Africa, but in the northeast of the continent, among the Banyankole and kindred tribes, the system arises from poverty. A man asks one or more of his brothers to join him in the necessary gifts for procuring a wife. She is the legal wife of all who contributed to the dowry and lives with each brother in turn. When pregnant the wife remains with the eldest brother until her child is born. All offspring are recognized as the children of the eldest brother. Concubinage is a term usually restricted to describe the women of a Mohammedan household. In addition to legal wives there are women of the harem (concubines) to whom the male owner has access. In Dahomey a peculiar rite of a woman marrying a woman exists. One form of this custom, which has no connection with lesbianism, is the purchase of a young woman by a woman who becomes her "husband." This purchaser lends the purchased woman to one or more men on payment. The custom has no connection with commercial prostitution, although the men have to make a payment. The point seems to be that children belong to the woman who made the purchase, and these children, by marriage and earning ability, become a profitable possession.

Irregular Sexual Relations

Beyond doubt the general establishment of marriage and the founding of a family is fundamental in the social structure of Africa, but many sexual aberrations occur, as they do in all social groups, ancient and modern. These deviations should not be overemphasized.

Rape is usually punishable as a crime, as it is a violation of property, which calls for payment of a heavy fine. The tendency is toward severe corporal punishment for sexual violence, but as a rule the relatives of the offender muster their resources and save the culprit from retributive violence. Payment of a fine to the injured party is fundamental in Negro law and relates to theft, sex crimes, and personal injury.

There is evidence that solitary and mutual masturbation are practiced among boys, and mention is made of public disapproval of the act after the boys can no longer be regarded as young children.

In Negro society, unaffected by foreign influence, there is no need for commercial sexual relationships. But prostitutes thrive when men are nomadic, as in the Sahara; the Tuareg (Hamitic) and their Negro servants travel from one oasis to another, and in these resting places prostitutes are a part of the social life. In most large towns, where there is an itinerant population, prostitutes live in colonies. Venereal diseases are known and feared. Certain customs may give the impression of a general laxity of morals, but, regarded more closely, the practices are evidently a necessary part of the military system. In the Masai military organization, which demands the services of all males for many years, each warrior has a girl companion with whom he lives during temporary relief from military duties. When the period of service is ended the warriors marry their girl companions.

Details respecting homosexuality are rarely given but this perversion does exist, and I think that the words of my interpreter in Angola are a fair summary of the public reaction. He said of homosexuality, "There are men who want men, and women who want women. The people think this very bad. A woman has been known to make something that helps her to act like a man. There are men who dress as women, [transvestites]; they place palm oil on their hair and join the women to pound corn on the rocks. One man of this kind was laughed at and beaten by his father and brothers, but he would not given up his female dress or feminine habits."

The word *incest* has both a narrow and a very broad application in African Negro society. The limited application of the term is with reference to an illicit sexual relation between brother and sister, father and daughter, mother and son. My interpreter said that people guilty of such incest might be killed, or they "would have to go so far away that no tribesmen would ever see them again." A male sometimes calls his mother's sister's daughters his sisters, and it would be incestuous to marry them; nor may he commit incest by marrying his father's brother's daughters. This is but one aspect of the cross-cousin system of permissive and forbidden marriages, but it serves to illustrate a broader connotation of the word incest. A still wider meaning exists in the application of the idea of incest to coitus between members of the same clan or totem.

Conclusion

A survey of the sex life of African Negroes from birth through adolescence and married life reveals a well-coordinated social arrangement. After allowing for many local differences,

certain general principles become clear. Each person is trained in such a way as to cooperate in the functioning of his social group. Many African ideas and ideals differ from those of western nations, but a system is evident.

Perhaps the greatest difference between the African concept of sex and our own is the lack of a religious backing among Africans. Throughout Negro Africa there is a concept of a supreme being and creator; but he issues no commands relating to sexual morality. And although under such names as Suku or Nzambi he has unlimited power, he does not offer rewards or threaten punishments. The system is concerned with crimes and not with sins. The breaches of law are offenses against individuals and social groups, not against God. The disrupting force of the impact of western cultures is a modern problem for the study of sociologists and anthropologists.

References

Bryk, F., *Voodoo Eros*. New York: Falstaff, 1933.

Bryk, F., *Dark Rapture*. New York: Juno, 1944.

Delafosse, Maurice, *Haut-Sénégal Niger, Soudan Française*. 3 vols. Paris, 1912.

Edwardes, Allen, and Hasters, R.E.I., *The Cradle of Erotica*, New York: Julian Press, 1962.

Ellis, Albert, *The Origins and the Development of the Incest Taboo*. New York: Lyle Stuart, 1963.

Fallers, A. Lloyd, *Bantu Bureaucracy*. Cambridge, England: W. Heffer & Sons, 1956.

Gluckman, Max, *Custom and Conflict in Africa*. Glencoe, Ill.: Free Press, 1955.

Gunther, John, *Inside Africa*. New York: Harper & Brothers, 1955.

Hambly, Wilfrid D., *Ethnology of the Ovimbundu of Angola*. Chicago Field Museum, 1934.

Hambly, Wilfrid D., *Source Book of African Anthropology*. 2 vols. Chicago Natural History Museum, 1937. (Contains a large bibliography that covers this article.)

Hambly, Wilfrid D., *Bibliography of African Anthropology. A Supplement to the Source Book*. Chicago Natural History Museum, 1952.

Herskovits, Melville J., *Dahomey, an Ancient West African Kingdom*. 2 vols. New York, 1938.

Junod, H. A., *The Life of a South African Tribe*. 2 vols. Neuchatel, 1912.

Meakin, B., *The Moors*. London, 1902.

Meek, C. K., *Northern Tribes of Nigeria*. 2 vols. Oxford, England, 1925.

Meek, C. K., *A Sudanese Kingdom*. London, 1931.

Rattray, R. S., *Ashanti Law and Constitution*. Oxford, England, 1929.

Rattray, R. S., *Tribes of Ashanti Hinterland.* 2 vols. London and New York, 1932.

Ross, Sylvia Leith, *African Women.* London: Faber and Faber, 1938.

Schapera, I., *The Khoisan People of South Africa.* London, 1930.

Seligman, C. G., and Seligman, B. Z., *The Kababish, a Sudan Arab Tribe.* Cambridge: Harvard African Studies, 1918. Vol. 2, pp. 106-184.

Rodd, F. Rennell, *People of the Veil.* London, 1926.

Roscoe, John, *The Baganda.* London, 1911.

Roscoe, John, *The Banyankole.* London, 1923.

Seligman, C. G., and Seligman, B. Z., *Pagan Tribes of the Nilotic Sudan.* London, 1932.

Talbot, P. A., *In the Shadow of the Bush.* London, 1912.

Talbot, P. A., *The People of Southern Nigeria.* Oxford, 1926.

WILFRID DYSON HAMBLY

Aging and Sex

IN THE middle forties, if not sooner, a man begins to be alarmed by the slightest change in his sexual power. He is haunted by the fear of the loss of manhood. The average woman, even at an earlier age, dreads the approach of the menopause. To her mind, it seems the coming end of her sex appeal and function, with the loss of all the psychological and realistic value her womanhood has meant to her.

This anxiety in both sexes is without scientific reason—born of superstitions and old wives' tales. Middle age normally brings a leveling off but not an erasure of all physical capacities, including sexual power.

Two Functions of Sex Mechanism

Fears for libido and potency arise because the nature of the sex mechanism is not generally understood. It has two distinct functions: (1) propagation, Nature's method to preserve the human species; and (2) stimulation of the whole organism, especially the brain and nervous system.

Waning of the reproductive potential in no way affects the stimulation function. The sex glands continue to produce hormones—androgen in the male, estrogen in the female. A man may become infertile and even impotent and a woman sterile without weakening libido. Furthermore, it is not unusual for the procreative process as well as the sex drive to remain effective in men through the later years, sometimes into the eighties and beyond. In this respect they differ definitely from women, who become infertile with the menopause, although retaining hormonal activity and libido.

The failure to appreciate this distinction between the two functions of the sexual system makes for confusion and helps foment anxiety. Anxiety, in turn, can hurry both men and women into senility with consequent loss of sexual power and physical fitness. On sex and old age, Dr. Th. H. Van de Velde (1928), noted authority on marital happiness, says: "Moderate and suitable use of the sexual function— which is possible up to a very great age—keeps the entire organism completely vigorous and efficient."

Growing Old Versus Aging

How old is "old"? There are no figures available or even possible because there are too many variations in physique and personality that have nothing to do with the calendar. Age is not chronological—a mistaken idea that has caused much mischief and misery—but physio-psychological. Alarming changes in body and mind come primarily not from advanced age but from earlier physical impairment and emotional disorders, often neglected.

Another important distinction—in addition to that between the two functions of the sexual system—is generally overlooked. There is a wide difference between "growing old" and "aging." To grow old is inevitable; it is a process of maturing and is progressive despite a natural slowdown. To age, however, is pathological and therefore regressive. It is often the result of an unwise mode of living, the abuse and neglect for years of the most marvelous machine known to man—the human body. "Growing old" really starts with puberty. In fact, geriatrics (science of old age) may well be said to begin where pediatrics (science of young age) ends.

Good Health

Given the right heredity, hormonal pattern, and nutrition, sexual power is no more weakened in man or woman by the advancing years than other bodily functions. The ancient Greeks and Romans stressed as their goal a "sound mind in a sound body." There is still no better way, centuries later, to assure sound sexual function and defy passing time.

In the Bible, the natural life span is given as "three score years and ten." Almost three thousand years later, this has finally nearly become the average length. However, thanks to the progress of medicine and hygiene, there are many favorable exceptions. Some individuals live into the eighties and even up to 100 years. And longevity sometimes brings long-lasting sexual competence.

Those who "grow old" rather than "age" respond with reduced strength to *all* emotional stimuli. Their sexual responsiveness is not an isolated reaction. Flagging sensitivity seems to be a subconscious mechanism of defense in a weakened organism. The sexual excitement of younger years could prove a threat to heart and brain.

Statistics can be deceiving. However, there is no doubt that there has been a striking increase in life expectancy in the United States. The life span during the Roman Empire was 23 years. In this country it rose in 1900 to 47, in 1940 to 63, and in 1960 it will go up to 75 years. Here is the challenge: to attack the pathological process of aging, to prevent it, and to revitalize connective tissue, nerve centers, and the endocrine system. It is far more important to add life to years than years to life.

Modern science shows the way. Man—and that means woman, too—must lead a well-balanced life from youth on so that the later years will find him physically and emotionally ready and fit to cope with decreased energies. Then his sexual power will take care of itself.

Dr. Kaare Rodalel of Lankenau Hospital, Philadelphia, has pointed out that "what a man is able to do at seventy depends on what he did at twenty." This does not mean that a man's sexual potential or virility at seventy will be as strong as it was at age twenty. However, if a human being could be protected from the wear and the stress of life per se, his sexual capacity at sixty might well be little impaired.

Change of Life

In the middle years there does come a change for both man and woman. This may consist of a simple slowdown with scarcely any disagreeable symptoms or debilitating ills if the earlier years have not taken their toll in strain and anxiety. From the beginning of the human race the menopause or "change of life" has been considered solely woman's portion. However, in recent years it has been thought by some authorities but denied by others that the male, too, passes through a climacteric. In any event, he also may be beset by unfamiliar physical and psychological disturbances.

Dr. Ernest Boas, eminent authority on geriatrics, says: "Men do not experience an abrupt climacteric as do women. . . . With the years they undergo a gradual reduction of sexual vigor and potency. Sexual capacity does not depend alone on a normal hormonal state—psychogenic factors are of great importance—and men often find that they are as old as they think they are."

Anxiety and Impaired Sexual Function

The extent and degree of waning sex energy in middle age vary in both sexes with the state of mind and physical fitness, and the so-called "change of life" tends to intensify existing body disorders. More often than not a woman's mental and emotional disturbance over her climacteric does more harm than the process itself. Anxiety has been proved to be the prime danger to the well-being of a man or woman during this period. Its destructive power is still not fully realized by the layman.

It becomes more and more obvious that psychological attitudes, especially in the male, determine his sexual capacity more than any other factor. Dr. Milton I. Sapirstein in his book, *Emotional Security*, points out that recent animal experiments indicate that the male sex performance employs the entire nervous system. "Small cerebral lesions will make the male animal impotent. But relatively massive nervous lesions in the female will not interfere with her sexual performance. . . ."

Dr. Sapirstein explains further that when any animal feels threatened, there is a suppression of the sex desire. Naturally, then, when a person is under anxiety for any cause his virility will be afflicted.

Fears—of the loss of virility and libido, rejection by the other sex, shelving by society as outworn, forced retirement—all do a great damage. A man can worry himself into impotence and a woman into frigidity. What Nature deals out to both sexes is kindness compared to what they often do to themselves.

Physical Changes at Middle Age

What actually happens in middle age? The female reproductive organs no longer produce ova after a woman's menopause; the older male may or may not cease to produce fertile spermatozoa. There is general agreement that gonadal (sex gland) failure is the only endocrinal alteration in old age. (The so-called pituitary-adrenal axis, the physiological promoter of sexual power and effectiveness, responds with average expectancy years after the climacteric. The thyroid gland seems to have an age-time curve of reduced capacity. The parathyroids are resistant to the change of age.) As for the sex glands, in the male the secretion of androgen hormones falls from 55 I.U. per twenty-four hours at the age of 30 to about 8 units at the age of 80. In the aging woman estrogen secretion falls sharply at the age of 40 and continues to drop throughout life to less than 7 units each twenty-four hours.

Sexual Activity and Aging

Sexual desire, even in its impaired state, is quite beneficial to an aging person. As long as it functions, interest in life persists. Kinsey reports that "even in the most advanced ages there is no sudden elimination of any large group of individuals from the sexually active. This seems astounding for it is quite to the contrary to the general conception of the aging process of sex." In their volume on the female, the Kinsey researchers describe the difference between male and female in sex desires and capacities. They have found that women retain their sex potential longer than men. According to Dr. Karl M. Bowman (1959), "it poses a

difficult problem to solve, especially for women, about half of whom are widows by age sixty-five or married to husbands with less sexual capacity than their wives." It seems that the role of the sexes is sometimes reversed in later life. Women, freed from the fear of pregnancy and from hampering precautions, often have a "second blooming" just when men are slowing down.

Yet a recent study reported by Dr. Gustave Newman, Duke Medical School psychiatrist, at the twelfth annual meeting of the Gerontological Society, pointed out that more than seven out of ten healthy married couples over 60 are sexually active, some into their late eighties. The age at which couples over 60 stop having sexual relations varies widely. Usually they stop because either the husband or the wife develops ill health. Couples who were asked to compare their sexual virility in old age with that of their youth reported a drop in desire with increasing age, those with the strongest urges in youth retaining greater sexual drive and virility in old age.

There is often the problem of ignorance even at advanced age. Dr. Irving C. Fischer of Mt. Sinai Hospital in New York City says: "Proper instruction in the sex act is always in order, regardless of the patient's apparent sophistication and education." Dr. Fischer has found such patients are often naïve about the "facts of life" and "too ashamed to talk about their sex habits," but they must be encouraged to do so.

Impotence and Behavior Changes

Is impotence a stigma of senescence? And what is "impotence"? The simplest definition is the inability to perform the sexual act. The mechanism of sexual activities has a wide range of expression in the human species. One can be impotent but still sexually desirous. As long as there is interest in sexual play there is hope of restoring sexual performance.

Since libido continues and is sometimes intensified long after impotence has manifested itself, ungratified desires in a maladjusted, aged man may lead to overimpulsive and immodest behavior. Disorders of behavior may develop, which differ little from those found at other years. A sudden flare-up of homosexual or other deviated tendencies may occur as a result of severe emotional disturbance or mental incapacity due to toxic or arteriosclerotic changes in the brain. Such disorders may be treated by a cooperative approach of the endocrinologist, nutrition specialist, and psychotherapist.

Nutrition

Modern science is now certain that nothing is so important to total vitality, which includes virility, as proper nutrition. All authorities on aging stress the right diet for physical and sexual strength and health. Dr. T. Brailsford Robertson, eminent English nutritionist, says (1923): "The quality of food in its chemical aspects exercises a great influence on the endocrine glands—especially on the adrenal cortex and the sex glands." The standard balanced diet for the theoretical average man is not sufficient for the aging man or woman. As the years add up, the aim must be maximum essential nourishment with minimum digestive labor.

Dr. Morton Biskind (1947) attributes impaired libido and potency in the male directly to nutritional deficiency. He believes waning desire and virility begin long before the trophic capacities of the gonads (sex glands) are exhausted. Faulty nutrition leads to impaired liver function, which in turn induces secondary changes—alteration of the estrogen-androgen (female and male hormones) balance. To maintain this equilibrium is the most essential step in correcting disorders of sexual power. Out of our own experience we agree with Dr. Biskind that our main concern should be to correct liver disfunction by proper nutritional and endocrine hormone treatment.

Dr. Tom Spies (1957) and associates believe that geriatric problems, whether physical or mental, correspond largely to tissue changes which need not become "irreversible" if proper assistance is given the patient's ability to mobilize nutritional substances to relieve or retard tissue damage. Prolonged subclinical depletion of essential nutritional elements leads to deterioration of the tissues and premature aging in the body with resulting loss of libido. Supplemental therapy in the form of vitamins, minerals, and hormones, with psychiatric treatment where necessary, can do much to relieve both the physical and psychological symptoms as well as to extend, as Dr. Spies terms it, "the prime of life."

Dr. Alexis Carrel (1928) found factors in the blood responsible for youth and aging, substances still mysterious and unknown. However, he was certain improved nutrition restores glandular balance, reduces body toxins, and avoids the exhausting effects of stress.

What is the proper diet in the middle or later years? Experts agree, first of all, on an increase of protein which supplies the amino acids, the body-building blocks. Proteins have been considered the key to life since the ancient Greeks. Today amino acids are beginning to be used as medicines. Two of them are known to be effective for sex support. Dr. Charles S. Davidson of the Harvard Medical School and Boston City Hospital says: "Eating more protein may retard the withering effects of old age."

The customary diet does not provide sufficient protein for building muscle and tissues, as the chemistry in the aging body is changed with the decreased functioning of certain glands. More beefsteak and other meats can supply the necessary replacements in body protein content. This does not mean that the meat-and-potatoes man is on the right track. He must add fresh fruits, salads, and properly cooked vegetables for vitamins, along with minerals and trace elements to help sustain healthy nervous tissue and lessen fatigue, depression, and listlessness. A liberal use of Vitamin A is recommended for the aging, especially for the health of the liver.

Recent experiments have shown that a lack of Vitamin B leads to the degeneration of the sex glands. One of the factors of the Vitamin B complex is para-amino-benzoic acid, which for some people acts as a sexual stimulant. More important is the over-all action of the entire B complex that helps to stabilize the nervous system.

The benefits of Vitamin B are enhanced by the action of Vitamin E, the antisterility or potency vitamin. The two work together and are necessary to each other. A deficiency in Vitamin E may cause a degeneration of the sperm-forming tissues of the testicles. In both sexes Vitamin E is used by the pituitary, the "master gland," which controls the sex glands.

Both Vitamins B and E are richly supplied by whole wheat cereal and bread. A good portion of wheat germ may fulfill the daily requirement. Other excellent sources of Vitamin

B are liver, brewer's yeast, milk, oatmeal, peas, beans, peanuts, and lean pork. The effectiveness of both Vitamins B and E is increased by a high protein diet. However it must not be too high for that creates imbalance. Vitamin C builds resistance. With Vitamin A it fights infection, shock, allergies, and poisons.

As for minerals, the American diet is woefully lacking in calcium. Dr. C. Ward Crampton, in the Merck report of 1948, calls calcium one of the secrets of youth prolongation. It plays a vital role in heart, brain, nerve, and blood action. In the aging, blood poor in calcium robs the bones and teeth for its needs. Emotional people are great calcium wasters. Sexual excitement can cause a large quantity of calcium excretion in a short time. The best source of calcium is milk and dairy products. Bone meal supplies it as a food supplement.

Essentials, too, for those in the upper age brackets are iron, phosphorus, manganese, cobalt, iron, and other trace minerals. They are found in kale, turnip, and dandelion greens, soybeans, eggs, milk, cheese, molasses, almonds, spring salads, and canned sardines. Steak provides iron and sulphur, together with protein. In Canada, lack of cobalt in the soil was found to induce infertility in the sheep. Sexual vigor needs a certain amount of phosphorus, which is plentiful in fish, particularly sea food. Sunflower seeds supply protein and all the vitamins and minerals.

A reduced intake of animal fats is urged as the years pass. Such foods produce excess cholesterol in the blood—a condition associated with high blood pressure, heart disease, and nephritis. Carbohydrates, too, should be consumed less. They supplant essential nutrients and add unwanted calories. An experiment with animals fed a low carbohydrate diet from birth showed that they lived to an age corresponding in a human being to 100 and 150 years and remained fertile. Overweight, a threat to the aging, results chiefly from excessive consumption of starches and sweets. Lean men live longer, remain youthful, active, and *vital*. At 60, the basic caloric requirement diminishes 35 per cent from that required at the age of 30.

Fortunately, the most needed elements in an adequate, balanced diet are found in the commonest and cheapest foods. All the leading nutritionists join in warning against drastic reducing diets and food fads. They insist that there is no wholesale prescription to be used blindly at 60 (or at any other age). Each individual's needs must be decided by medical examinations and numerous geriatric tests. A short fast may benefit the sex mechanism but prolonged hunger is harmful.

Aphrodisiacs

A belief in magic foods and drugs to stimulate sexuality—a delusion as old as the human race—has been exploded by modern science. There is no magic outside the magic of the sex drive itself. What is good for the whole organism is good for the libido and virility. The popular medical writer and educator, Dr. Herman Bundesen, maintains that sex potency is inseparable from "total vitality" and from a properly cared-for and nourished body.

History reveals how credulous and eager to believe in magic men have been through the ages in their pursuit of potency. The Romans had great faith in lampreys, eel-like fish. Irish peasants praised potatoes, their staple food. (Havelock Ellis has pointed out what a fallacy this was; potatoes are known to be below average in sexualizing activity.) Tomatoes were once called "love apples." At various times there was belief in onions, asparagus—perhaps for their phallic shape or because they were expensive when first introduced—clams, oysters, caviar, eggs, and a host of other foods. Recently it has been steak, rare or raw.

There is some ground for favoring fish, which are rich in phosphorus and iron, as well as caviar, truffles, and eggs, which also provide iron. They nourish the sexual mechanism but are hardly aphrodisiacs.

Some have sought stimulation in drugs like morphine, but these dull libido and weaken potency in addicts. Tobacco in moderation does no harm. The man or woman who likes a glass of wine or beer is sometimes said to preserve sexual power longer than the abstainer. However, the beer must be properly brewed and the wine—or gin or whiskey—properly blended and aged so as not to be poisoned in hasty manufacture. Liquor, wisely used, may sometimes enhance libido.

Aside from the important indirect effect on sexual activity from nourishing foods, there is, of course, the psychological stimulation to be gained from a sensuous atmosphere and setting, a compatible partner, or a well-chosen meal with appropriate drinks. All the senses play a prime part in enriching desire and vigor.

Conversely, a scene that is an affront to the sensibilities—signs of neglect in the man or woman, irritability, discord, petty bickering, and annoying actions—are inhibiting factors. Many a man who thinks he has become impotent and a woman who fears she is frigid owe their disability to impossible conditions. Experts also emphasize the importance of a psychic bond between two sexual partners in marriage.

As men have eagerly sought magic foods so they have pursued aphrodisiacs. Practically none of the many praised at one time or another has real value. Modern science recognizes only two: catharides ("Spanish fly"—a South European beetle—reduced to powder) and Yohimbine from the bark of a South African tree. They are both powerful, dangerous drugs that inflame the gastro-urinary tract, producing violent effects, and may cause death. Science today wants no part of artificial excitement. It is perilous to interfere with Nature, especially in sex matters. It seems that the search for an effective aphrodisiac finally focuses on such prosaic items as fish, dried peas, and beans.

"Rejuvenation"

Sensational claims for methods of rejuvenation have also been found to be wishful thinking. In the 1920's, the European scientists Voronoff, Steinach, and others tried to lead men to the "fountain of youth" on the operating table. Voronoff experimented in transplanting the sex glands of monkeys in senile men. The Steinach operation was intended to stimulate sex secretions. There was temporary improvement but the "rejuvenated" men, encouraged to marry younger women, died rapidly. The strain was too great for their aged bodies. Those that survived became more worn out and decrepit after a few months.

However, it must be acknowledged that those who pioneered in attempts to rejuvenate the aging—Brown-Sequard, Steinach, Voronoff, and Bogomolets, to mention the best known—laid the foundation for modern treatment in endocrinology, nutrition, and psychotherapy. For

all their pioneering efforts, means have not yet been found for transplanting tissues other than our own or those of an identical twin which will take root and last in our bodies.

Any product or therapy that promises to increase, restore, or heighten the capacity for sexual relations is sure to find many takers. Fortunately, today we are protected by the federal government and by our own growing knowledge of medicine against dangerous or fraudulent products, but there was a time when the public fell prey to a host of gadgets, pills, lotions, systems of physical culture, and even medical therapies promising to restore or increase virility. Medical literature describes the most unbelievable contraptions subscribed to by gullible people to raise their potency.

So-called gland products and "hermetically sealed" combinations of gland tablets, phony radioactive water that exploited the discovery of radium by Madame Curie, fake X-ray lamps to "tone up" metabolism, and radiation and gland combinations reaped fortunes for manufacturers. During the 1920's purveyors of many of these products took advantage of sensational rejuvenation claims of gland experts.

Recently, a secret formula of Prof. Anna Aslan of Bucharest, Romania, has been published that purports to restore youth and virility. The drug, H3, is known to contain procaine, a local anesthetic. In a lecture to members of the British Geriatric Society, cases were demonstrated, as for instance the alleged remarkable improvement in a 113-year-old man and in a woman of 73. In both cases white hair turned black, and vigor allegedly was restored. In other cases, old age sufferers from heart and rheumatic disease were said to be regenerated. The medical profession, however, although interested in these experiments, is skeptical until more and better controlled trials are made. The same may be said about the Niehans cellular-change therapy, which has recently been advocated in Europe as especially effective.

Some worried men have gone to physical instructors, who make claims for specific exercises to energize waning virility. Too much is not to be expected. The value of such efforts lies mainly in the benefits to the general health that result when an interest in body-building distracts the individual from anxiety and hopelessness. Virility has nothing to do with muscles. Of supreme importance are steady nerves and vigorous circulation. All-around exercise is the best means of improving both the blood and the nervous system. It increases the intake of oxygen—the greatest nerve food and stabilizer. Swimming is one of the preferred exercises for physical weakness. Incidentally, extreme muscle culture may be emasculating. Some of the "Tarzans" are impotent.

Virility cannot be strengthened or regained by magic pills, massage, lamps, special gymnastics, or gadgets. It cannot be too strongly emphasized that there is no road back through the years except that of general physical and mental improvement under the guidance of a competent physician.

A fierce attempt to preserve his libido and potency is and has always been the angry protest of an aging man in the face of destiny. It is no wonder that, from biblical times to the modern era of endocrinology, scientists have been trying to preserve the sex capacities of their fellow men as long as possible.

In our time it is actually difficult to be a man in the truest sense of the word, especially when handicapped by age. Up to the twentieth century women were largely frigid and expected no sex gratification. Now there has been a shift from almost complete inhibition in woman to the high standards of performance set by the marriage manuals. This tends to create great anxiety in many aging males who feel inadequate when they fall short of these standards. It has been found that the impotent male is often a frightened man.

Science is constantly reporting and physicians applying new revelations in the field of geriatrics. With sensational advances in prolonging life and youth and restoring sexual powers, some day the problem of transplants and other methods of rejuvenation will be solved.

For the present there is real hope for aging men and women fearful of becoming "unsexed." A clinician, equipped with thorough laboratory tests, knowledge of nutrition, and the psychological approach, can often deal effectively with sexual decline and supply new vigor and joy to the later years of life.

References

Benjamin, Harry, "Impotence and Aging." *Sexology* Nov., 1959.

Benjamin, Harry, "Problems of Old Age and Their Treatment." *J. Dent. Med.* July, 1951.

Benjamin, Harry, "The Nature of Old Age." *Senior Cit.* 1958.

Biskind, Morton S., "The Relation of Nutritional Deficiencies to Impaired Libido and Potency in the Male." *J. Gerontol.* Oct., 1947.

Biskind, Morton S., "The Technic of Nutritional Therapy." *Am. J. Diges. Dis. 20;* 61, 1953.

Biskind, Morton S., and Falk, H. C., "Nutritional Therapy of Infertility in the Male." *J. Clin. Endocrinol. 3;* 148, March, 1943.

Blumenthal, "Aging Processes in the Endocrine Glands of Mice." *J. Gerontol.* July, 1955.

Boas, Ernst Philip, *Treatment of the Patient Past Fifty.* Chicago: Year Book Pub., 1947.

Bowman, Karl M., and Engle, Bernice, "Some Current Trends in Problems of the Aged." *Geriatrics.* March, 1959.

Carrel, Alexis, *Man the Unknown.* New York, London: Harper & Brothers, 1935.

Carrel, Alexis, "The Mechanism of Senescence." *New York Acad. Med. Graduate Fortnight. Problems of Aging and Old Age. 4;* 1928.

Castro, J. D., *Geography of Hunger.* London: Gollancz Ltd., 1952.

Crampton, C. Ward, "Selective Nutrition for the Aging." *The Merck Report.* April, 1948.

Kemper, Werner, *Die Störungen der Liebesfähigkeit beim Weibe.* Stuttgart: Thieme Verlag, 1943.

Kinsey, A. C. *et al., Sexual Behavior in the Human Male.* Philadelphia: W. B. Saunders Co., 1948.

Lewin, S. A., and Gilmore, John, *Sex After Forty.* Medical Research Press, 1952.

Pillay, A. P., "The Role of Vitamin A in Infertility." *Indiana Med. Gaz. 75;* 91, 1950.

Robertson, Thorburn B., *The Chemical Basis of Growth and Senescence.* Philadelphia, London: J. B. Lippincott Co., 1923.

Robertson, Thorburn B., *The External Inheritance of Man.* Adelaide: Hassell Press, 1926.

Rubin, Isadore, "The Search for Rejuvenation." *Sexology,* April, 1959.

Sapirstein, Milton I., *Emotional Security.* New York: Crown Press, 1948.

Van de Velde, Theodore H., *Ideal Marriage, Its Physiology and Technique* (translated by Stella Brown). London: W. Heinemann, 1928.

Van de Velde, Theodore H., *Fertility and Sterility in Marriage, Their Voluntary Promotion and Limitation* (translated by Stella Brown). New York: Random House, 1948.

MAXIMILIAN LE WITTER AND ALBERT ABARBANEL

America, Moral Evolution In

A COMPLETE treatment of sex in America should start with—or before—the days of the first settlers and proceed up to the present. But inasmuch as the colonial period and the current "Kinsey" decade are treated elsewhere in this volume, the time span herein treated will extend from pre-Revolutionary years to the middle of the twentieth century.

American ideas and behavior are both involved in studies of sex ethics and sex practices. The materials on behavior are largely inferential because meaningful observation and reporting are available only for recent times. Moreover, ideas set forth in print must predominate because reading has been a chief means for receiving newly formulated approaches to the subject. Furthermore, printed matter is available to research, whereas unrecorded behavior is not.

Up to the early part of the nineteenth century, the churches and the courts (those of New England in particular) were perennially engaged in the religious and legal regulation of sexual behavior. The ample publicity given such activities kept matters pertaining to sex under public discussion. When these means of social enforcement lost their control value, the legal apparatus was, for the most part, laid aside, and religious sanctions were translated into community pressures. From then until the second quarter of the twentieth century, America's sex history was one of reticence, except in those instances where new ideas evoked thunderous rejection from conservative quarters.

Ministers, missionaries, and moralists of every generation have decried the immoralities of their time, but we have no way of translating their laments into specific behavior patterns. Also, from time to time, travelers, observers, and welfare agencies have provided knowledgeable accounts of extensive urban prostitution, and recollections and memoirs of older and wiser men have occasionally mentioned the prevalence of premarital and extramarital sex contact in an earlier generation. Much of America's sex conduct, however, must be inferred from the writings of bolder minds. Most frequently, the subject dealt with by such writers has been the modification of marriage institutions so as to improve the sexual relationship —or to bring it closer to actual behavioral tendencies. Some have gone as far as to suggest the abolition of marriage because, they said, this institution perverted the goals of sex harmony. In more cases than not, ideas were promoted not as sex psychology (or its pre-modern equivalent) *per se*, but as part of larger political, social, or philosophical reform movements. Practically every reform program contained a platform on woman's right to individuality and equality. This was in recognition that the female sex role was at a disadvantage under the *status quo* as compared with that of the male.

The Age of Reason (1750–1825)

From the middle of the eighteenth century until well after the Revolution the dominant theme of "sex" literature was the achievement of marital happiness by basing the choice of mates on an initial sexual attraction rather than on social or financial convenience. Mutual respect and understanding would perpetuate the satisfactions of an originally happy choice. The less compromising rationalists, such as Ben Franklin and Tom Paine, applied the prostitution label to mercenary marriages, but representatives of English and American middle-class thinking confined themselves to a vague insistence on catering (with due regard for parental advice) to the wishes of the individual.

Much of the relevant pamphlet and magazine literature essayed marriage counseling in a generalized and moralistic vein. Here and there one finds an astute observation that departed from the category of glittering generalities. The Reverend Enos Hitchcock noted that the relationship of parents to each other, along with an atmosphere of secure affection in the household, had much to do with children's subsequent success in marriage. The humorists repeated—half in jest—age-old advice to young men against marrying intellectual, high-bred, and markedly beautiful women. Superannuated virgins and termagants were also on the blacklist. Benjamin Franklin came closest to discussing sex liberties in marriage when he cautioned against their abuse. Consistent with his counsel of moderation in all things, he spoke of the commonly (sic) known paradox of indecent relationships between husband and wife. Such abuses, he thought, would dull or destroy the subtle joys of married life.

Other themes touched upon in this period were the status of women in the family and in society, and the outrages committed by libertines upon hapless females. It was commonly agreed that, were victimized women to speak out in self-justification, they would only condemn themselves in the public eye. Still rare and radical, though not unknown, were writers who called for a redefinition of standards of sexual morality, or for a redefinition of the current concept of chastity.

A highly articulate call for the single standard arrived with the importation in the 1790's and early 1800's of Mary Wollstonecraft's *Vindication of the Rights of Women*. One of the worst forms of sexual inequality, this brilliant English feminist pointed out, was the double standard of virtue. Regardless of the sacrifices a woman might make to preserve her reputation, one minor slip would lose it for her; and

her society, especially the female part of it, would never let her regain respectability. There was no such thing as a fractional diminution of public esteem. Men, on the other hand, could preserve their virtue while wallowing in a mire of assorted vices. The evil was compounded when a woman found herself in the once-slipped situation: cast from society, without resources or vocation, only one means of livelihood, woman's oldest, remained.

Mary Wollstonecraft affirmed her belief in conventional marriage; that is, the marriage of social and intellectual equals entered into by mutual desire. William Godwin, that superrationalist and individualist who would later marry Miss Wollstonecraft (their daughter Mary was a famous author and the wife of the poet Percy Bysshe Shelley), rejected the marriage institution completely. He found it an obstruction to social justice, a restraint upon the free expression of human affection, and a drawback to full development of the personality. Godwins' ideas probably became notorious: a long list of vices were imputed to this couple by clerical and lay protectors of morality. The segment of their thinking that dealt with woman's equal role was carried to readers by America's first novelist, Charles Brockden Brown.

That Americans did not need to be incited to violate accepted sex mores is clear from the urgings of certain nineteenth-century clergymen that the church abandon its shyness and speak out against prevalent sex activities outside of marriage. Moreover, it seemed to conservative religionists that writers, playwrights, composers, painters, and sculptors were all too frequently enlisted in the job of seducing weak minds to sin. Their task was not difficult, said the Congregational minister Timothy Dwight as he argued against lenient divorce laws. It was "well known to every observer of human nature, that a prominent part of this nature is *the love of novelty and variety, in all its pursuits.*"

Few at the time defended divorce, but many promoted marriage for patriotic reasons. In Europe the Reverend Thomas R. Malthus, basing his conclusions on Benjamin Franklin's estimate of the New World rate of population increase, was gloomy about the prospect of population outrunning the food supply. In America, Parson Weems spoke for many when he said " 'tis population *alone,* that can save our bacon...."

Marry, and raise up soldiers, might and main,
Then laugh ye may, at England, France, and Spain.

The Free Inquirers and Associationists (1825–1850)

While patriots promoted marriage and propagation for the national welfare, there were always individualists as well as socialists arguing the cause of the individual and presenting the antimarriage point of view. The prime innovators were still Englishmen. In the nineteenth century, however, a few migrated to America to try out their ideas.

Robert Owen arrived in the United States in 1825 to experiment with his brand of community socialism. But his reform program carried more with it. Owen's "Declaration of Mental Independence," delivered (significantly) on the fourth of July, 1826, attacked what he termed a trinity of evils: "... Private, or individual Property—absurd and irrational systems of religion—and Marriage, founded on individual property combined with some of these irrational systems of religion." The plan was for a community committee to take over the registrations and dissolutions of marriage. The new marriage arrangements would correct the difficulties of the old with reference to insincerity of the parties, extraneous considerations in the choice of mates, incompatibility, etc., etc. Owen's community of New Harmony actually decided to follow the family relations laws of the state of Indiana. However, it continued to harbor antimarriage theorists, feminists, divorce-law reformers, and birth-control advocates.

Robert Dale Owen, son of the founder, and Frances Wright, a Scottish freethinker, led the campaigns for reform. Miss Wright was the more effective speaker and carried the causes of women's rights and free thought to the lecture platform. Owen was mightier with the pen. Many a column in the *New Harmony Gazette* and in the *Free Enquirer* was devoted to an anthropological exploration of marriage and sex

practices in a variety of societies. The ultimate effect was to demonstrate that there was nothing sacred about European and American expectations of attitude and behavior. Tolerance of the other person's conduct was the lesson to be learned. The test of successful mating, according to Owen and Wright, was the happiness of the partners plus their ability to nurture and educate offspring. The proposed "marriage" contract—to replace the traditional *slave* contract—would be drawn by mutually independent men and women and would provide for the care of children.

The younger Owen, aspiring to be a scientist of human behavior, was interested in sex education and birth control. Hence the *New Harmony Gazette* carried a communication suggesting that the laws of propagation be taught children according to the measure of their comprehension. The plant-to-animal-to-man sequence was recommended. For an audience far less prepared than present-day readers to accept such notions, two important reasons were offered in justification for teaching sex to children: to relieve their anxieties and to give them useful education. Knowledge of the facts of reproduction would persuade the younger generation to guard the physical constitution that would, according to accepted belief in the 1820's and 1830's, eventually be handed on to one's progeny. Sex needed as much attention as hunger and thirst. All three were drives not subject to the will, and "their activity must therefore be directed."

The elder Owen had announced that a world that operated under the guidance of science and education would produce many times its consumption needs. His son, however, having come under the influence of neo-Malthusian thought, was soon convinced that the working class ought to limit family size for economic reasons. Besides, there was risk to health and life for some women to overbreed; there was also the possibility of checking the transmission of hereditary diseases. Birth control would also promote earlier marriages, curb resort to the brothel, and reduce the need for abortion-inducing drugs.

The little book that Robert Dale Owen produced was called *Moral Physiology* (1831). It dealt mostly with the social aspects of birth control, devoting few pages to the description of three methods of contraception (two of which disappeared from later editions because the author had little confidence in them). Owen, as a matter of fact, knew his own limitations and was probably glad to see Dr. Charles Knowlton's more "physiological" *Fruits of Philosophy* come off the press in 1832. *Moral Physiology* had an estimated circulation of some 60,000 copies by 1874. A tenth edition appeared in Boston in 1881. Owen was subjected to sporadic charges of immorality but the law never challenged him. Knowlton was fined and jailed. Nevertheless, *Fruits of Philosophy; or the Private Companion of Young Married People* went into ten editions as well as numerous reprint editions in France, Holland, and England. The English edition (1876) sold over 300,000 copies in three years.

The utopians of New Harmony felt they were sponsoring woman's liberation when they fought for a freer sex morality, for more rational marriage and divorce laws, and for birth control. The associationists at Brook Farm and in other communities of the 1840's were more conservative in their goals for the advancement of women. They proposed a combined household in which community kitchens and dining rooms would free women for richer family, social, and vocational lives.

The associationists had to reply to charges of immorality partly because their shallow-minded accusers equated community kitchens with community wives, and partly because a few philosophically inclined members became interested in Swedenborgianism and Fourierism. It was Henry James, Senior, who translated and published anonymously Victor Hennequin's *Love in the Phalanstery,* a Fourierist plan for harmonizing sexual relations. James admitted his authorship later and explained his position: Society recognized sex only in marriage, and hence drove many an unwilling party into a relationship he would not otherwise have entered. If the science of human relationships could find a more satisfactory system of outlet for human expression, more power to it! James, a fundamentally conservative person, eventually withdrew to a more traditional position.

Dr. Marx Edgeworth Lazarus, a Fourierist with a strong Swedenborg component, brought together his somewhat superficial knowledge of the natural and social sciences to prove that a true permanent union of souls and/or bodies in marriage was impossible. His *Love Versus Marriage* (1852), addressed "To all true lovers. To the modest and the brave of either sex . . . ," came to the conclusion that everyone's private inclinations were his best guide in the sexual realm.

Freedom in Anarchy

Freedom from regulation by law and social custom was the objective of many social reformers. Much of the talk about the achievement of "passional harmony" on earth and in heaven, an achievement that required the revision or abolition of current sex ethics, covered up one general wish. This was the wish that both men and women be permitted, if they chose, to have more than one sex partner in a lifetime. These urgings for reform clearly wanted to render law and religion more consonant with the reality of sex practices.

The American anarchist call for "individual sovereignty" in law, economics, and sex pursued this line of thought during the second half of the nineteenth century. Stephen Pearl Andrews, who had debated the matter with Horace Greeley and Henry James, Senior, in the pages of Greeley's *Tribune,* proved to his own satisfaction that "free love" was the only true love. If society did not encroach on the sovereignty of the individual, and if the individual did not encroach on the welfare of others, the mutual adjustment of two people would take place without outside interference. "Free love" was still in its doctrinal form in the nineteenth century. Those who did not understand it, or who were not psychologically prepared for it, were advised not to try it. For the time being, free-love advocates gratefully accepted liberalized divorce laws or any other relaxation of social control over marriage. The ultimate goal expressed on the masthead of *The Word,* an anarchist periodical, was "Free Land, Free Labor and Free Love."

The high point of Ezra Hervey Heywood's (editor of *The Word*) campaign for sexual freedom came with his publication in 1876 of *Cupid's Yokes or, the Binding Forces of Con-*

jugal Life. This book, described as "an essay to consider some moral and physiological phases of Love and Marriage, wherein is asserted the natural right and necessity of Sexual Self-Government," brought its author repeated obscenity prosecutions under the Comstock Law of 1873. *Cupid's Yokes* contained many contradictory qualities. Its language was often crass and provocatively candid; at other times it was quite delicate, as when it defined the sex drive as "this mingled sense of esteem, benevolence and passional attraction called Love, [which] is so generally diffused that most people know life to be incomplete until the calls of affection are met in a healthy, happy, and prosperous association with persons of the opposite sex." Again, the book drew on some of the most respected scientific knowledge of its time, as well as on some highly dubious pseudo science.

The free-love forces organized on regional, national, and tactical lines. But always they carried forward the movement in behalf of women's emancipation from an enslaved social and sexual condition; always the leaders called for the building of a science of morals and marriage. At the "Social Freedom" convention of 1875, one participator, Lois Waisbrooker, remarked about the necessity of a "standard of nature and science" as distinct from the existing standard of authority. "To this end," she said, "personal experiences are in order; every person must not only be permitted but induced to come forward and give his or her personal experiences; and in this free enquiry those who are as chaste as ice should have no precedence over those whose fires are irrepressible." The following year marked the meeting of a Sexual Science Association in Boston.

Lacking foundation funds and scientists with twentieth-century knowledge wherewith to make large-scale studies, the sex scientists resorted to the publicizing of dramatic—or shocking—case histories. The freedom clique that specialized in this device was led from Valley Falls, Kansas, by Moses Harmon, an anarchist in spirit though not in name. Its organ, *Lucifer,* started publication in 1880. The abolition of sexual outrages committed by husbands against their subordinate wives was a central purpose of this group. However, Harmon also belabored a eugenic obsession to the effect that the per-

sonalities of offspring were deeply affected by the circumstances surrounding conception. Although he did not realize it, Harmon was considering heredity in the broad social sense, including the quality of parental relationships in general. The anarchist free-love ideology was carried forward in the twentieth century by Emma Goldman, who placed added emphasis on birth control as a measure for woman's social and personal emancipation.

Almost every social reform movement in American history carried a sexual component. The feminists, although mainly devoted to economic, political, and legal aspects of sexual democracy, harbored elements devoted to marriage reform and to the achievement of more satisfying sexual alliances for women. The socialist and communist movements, against the property relationship in marriage, extended their thinking to include the broader sexual problem. Clearly, sex was on the mind of America at all times but found public expression only from the pens and mouths of the most daring citizens.

Sex and the Sects

The influence of major religious bodies has been to discourage exploration and experimentation. This has not been true of several minor sects of the communistic variety. The maverick psychologist, Theodore Schroeder, writing in the early decades of the twentieth century, theorized that many a religious movement—religion itself, in fact—had been born under the stress of erotic excitement and/or denial. He illustrated his hypothesis, which he called the erotogenesis of religion, by delving into the early history of sects that practiced celibacy or polygamy. For example, he pointed out that Mother Anne Lee, the founder of American Shakerism (1774), could never resolve her religious, social, and sex motivations. Marriage had failed to banish her fear of impulses from which she wanted to be protected; it had failed to divest her of her guilt or sin complex. This personality pattern, Schroeder said, generally resulted in prudery or exhibitionism. The Shakers exhibited their celibate practices to the world, and their communities benefited economically from a stable population. The Rappites, who had owned New Harmony before Robert Owen bought it from them, gained an economic advantage by allowing married couples to live as man and wife for one year in seven. This would prevent the expense of more than one complete dependent in any one family at any one time.

Where some sects resolved their troublesome sex drives by "nonogamy," others evolved a system of polygamy. Each fused a religious with a sex rationale and, at the same time, strove for the economic benefits of communitarian structure. To Schroeder, Mormon history revealed that during religious revivals of the early nineteenth century the Mormon leader, Joseph Smith, had practiced adultery before developing a theological justification for polygamy. Moreover, during revival meetings, the parties most subject to "deliriums" were the younger folk whose emotional disturbances could best be ascribed to sex repression during adolescence. Contemporary observers (during the eighteenth and nineteenth centuries) of youthful participants in revivals attest that sexual excitement was generously stirred up along with religious excitement.

In the case of John Humphrey Noyes, inventor of "complex marriage" at Oneida, New York, early sexual disappointments and the stimulus of evangelical revivals are indicated, but it is impossible to say that the religion and sex ethics of his Perfectionism evolved from personal circumstances. What is more certain is that Noyes forced his preference for sexual pluralism into the mold of simple Bible communism. The idea of socialized mating seemed to fit with the re-establishment of heavenly love on earth. The thought was that a man should not embrace one woman exclusively any more than he should hold fast to private property. All men in the community should ideally be potential husbands of all women; and all children the pride and joy of all the adults. The Oneidists worked out a committee system for marriage *pro tem*, and for separation if and when desired. Noyes attempted to solve the population problem by advocating the practice of male continence, implying coitus without ejaculation. He also experimented with stirpiculture, a community-controlled eugenics program.

Sex Science

The influence of such religious and political practice, experimentation, thought, and writing on prevailing behavior was probably small despite fairly widespread controversy in print. The public mind was doubtless enlarged, or feelings confirmed, by the treatises and manuals of doctors and others who backed their words with the prestige of science. As far back as the 1830's, Dr. Knowlton's *Fruits of Philosophy* had consoled readers with the thought that sexual desire, within reason, was just another normal body appetite and had to be honored as such.

Health and diet reformers, such as Dr. William Alcott (cousin to Bronson Alcott) and Sylvester Graham, advised extreme moderation in sexual exercise. Accordingly, they counseled avoidance of "stimulating" foods such as meat and condiments. Sex education in the home and physiological education in the schools also promised a wholesome outcome.

The phrenologists, popularly patronized for psychological counsel and therapy a century ago, concentrated more on the "amative propensity" than on any other of their patients' behavior problems. Among the most popular of their little volumes, the income from which supplemented fees for feeling and massaging cranial bumps, was *Fowler on Matrimony; or Phrenology Applied to the Selection of Suitable Companions.* Another much-read book was *Amativeness: or, Evils and Remedies of Excessive and Perverted Sexuality, including Warning and Advice to the Married and Single.*

The hydrotherapists of the 1840's and 1850's did their share by advising cold wet sheets, baths, douches, and marriage reform. Nearer to modern interests were the water-cure doctors, who did not limit themselves to narrow hydrotherapy. Dr. Russell Thatcher Trall paid much attention to gynecological and sexual problems. His *Hydropathic Encyclopedia* advised on the merits of the "safe period" for women who wanted parenthood to be a voluntary matter. His *Sexual Physiology* (1866) discoursed on sponges, plugs, douches, and drugs as means to prevent conception. Other physicians of the post-Civil War era wrote pieces on social hygiene and women's problems but few were as informative as Trall.

The tenor of contemporary medical reporting indicated a public need for breaking through secrecy on the subject of sex. The prevalence of abortions was an important stimulus to convince physicians of such a need. Dr. Edward Bliss Foote and his son carried the work of informing the public to the beginning of the twentieth century. Their home encyclopedias of health (*Plain Home Talk about the Human System—The Habits of Men and Women—The Causes and Prevention of Disease*—and *Our Sexual Relations and Social Natures*) were best-sellers and brought handsome profits; but much of this income was consumed by court costs and fines resulting from prosecution under the federal obscenity law.

The Twentieth Century

Publishers did a lively business in the first decade of the twentieth century keeping older popularizations in print and adding a few new ones. Some of the more advanced scientific works of R. von Krafft-Ebing, Havelock Ellis, and Auguste Henri Forel were imported or republished here, but these books were generally sold only to physicians. Sigmund Freud and Carl Jung visited America in 1909 to lecture on the sexual roots of behavior and on the conflict between sex and society. American society was not ready to hear, however, and quickly suppressed any disagreeable notions it might have absorbed from the visiting Viennese.

In the five-year period before World War I many sound, inexpensive books were sold to an eager audience. Margaret Sanger offered *What Every Girl Should Know* and *What Every Mother Should Know.* Winfield Scott Hall wrote many family instruction pamphlets and the book, *Biology, Physiology, and Sociology of Reproduction.* Dr. William J. Robinson published in his sex education series *Sex Knowledge for Men; Sex Knowledge for Women and Girls;* and *Woman, Her Sex and Home Life.* A more formal treatment of the subject was published in 1916: it was *Sex Education* by Maurice Alpheus Bigelow of Teachers College, Columbia University.

Much literary, sociological, and psychological publishing and discussion on the perennial war of the sexes ensued during the war years and after. But it would seem that the greater interest lay in techniques of love wherewith to expunge the antagonism. In this genre were Walter Franklin Robie's *Rational Sex Ethics* (1916) and *The Art of Love* (1921), Marie Stopes' *Married Love* (1918), and Harland William Long's *Sane Sex Life and Sane Sex Living* (1919). These works, sold quietly at first and later placed prominently on bookstore counters, furnished a large population of readers both confirmation of their patterns of love-making and suggestions for experimentation. The 1930's brought expensive translations from the Dutch of Theodore Hendrick Van de Velde as well as the reasonably priced and justly popular *Marriage Manual* by Hannah and Abraham Stone. These and large numbers of less widely known manuals were read and discussed and translated into experience. Their major effect was to add a measure of confidence to relationships in which secrecy, productive of fear and diffidence, had formerly prevailed. Subsequent writings on marriage and sex were to succeed by promising to bring freedom from fear. These works were to flourish after psychoanalysis became the layman's property. Ideas of fear, guilt, and repression, when better understood, were more readily accepted.

The past thirty-five years have been notable for a rapidly expanding candor in discussions of sexuality and sex information, vast progress in psychological counsèling towards the resolution of sex-oriented personality problems, and an increased body of sexologic knowledge. Private, social, and religious censorship are still strong, but government censorship has relaxed. Novel (and unpopular) ideas such as companionate marriage have been subjects for public debate. Marriage and sex education have achieved a firm hold in the colleges and are gaining acceptance in the secondary schools. A few advanced communities are employing appropriate sex instruction films in the elementary grades. The former reliance on parental instruction may return when educational agencies will have produced a generation of parents capable of educating their children in sex.

Much of the materials for education have come out of studies on human sexual behavior in which modern psychology, psychiatry, biology, and sociology are participating. Throughout the history of our scientific and pragmatic-minded people there have been expressions of a desire for such studies. The speed with which change in this field of endeavor can occur is illustrated by the contrasting fates of two studies, the second begun barely more than a decade after the first. In 1930 Professors De Graff and Meyer at the University of Missouri were visited with severe academic penalties for preparing and administering a questionnaire whose purpose it was to collect data toward devising a system of sex ethics. When Dr. Kinsey and his associates began their use of the questionnaire technique, both the University of Indiana and the Rockefeller Foundation supported their efforts.

The years following the publication of the Kinsey studies have witnessed an acceleration of behavioral manifestations reported and generalized by researchers at the Institute for Sex Research. Modes of sexual union not necessarily related to marriage and procreation have approximated institutionalization on a modest scale. An increasingly public interchange of communications on sexual questions, the stronger assertion of "rights" by an enlarged young sector of the population, an affluence or economic security that supports the assertion of independence from the surrogate generation, and significantly improved means of birth control—these and subsidiary factors are moving sexual behavior toward the objectives of American marriage critics of the past century and a half. The companionate marriage, generally rejected when Judge Ben Lindsey proposed a legal mechanism for it, has been adopted by substantial numbers without legal sanction. Protagonists of the newer morality see expanding horizons for the further liberation of women, for the rationalization of the marriage institution, and for the extrication of sex life from secrecy and suppression.

References

Calhoun, Arthur W., *A Social History of the American Family from Colonial Times to the Present*. New York: Barnes & Noble, Inc., 1945. (Original three-volume edition, 1917–1919.)

Dingwall, Eric John, *The American Woman, an Historical Study*. New York: Rinehart & Co., Inc., 1957.

Ditzion, Sidney, *Marriage, Morals and Sex in America*. New York: Bookman Associates, Inc., 1953.

Ellis, Albert, *The American Sexual Tragedy*. New York: Twayne Publishers, 1954.

Ellis, Albert, *The Folklore of Sex*. New York: Boni, 1951.

Folsom, Joseph Kirk, *The Family and Democratic Society*. New York: John Wiley & Sons, Inc., 1945.

Lerner, Max, *America as a Civilization*. New York: Simon and Schuster, Inc., 1957 (chapter 8, sections 5-6, and chapter 9, sections 6-7).

Mead, Margaret, *Male and Female*. New York: William Morrow & Co., Inc., 1949.

Oberholtzer, Emil, *Delinquent Saints; Disciplinary Action in the Early Congregational Churches of Massachusetts*. New York: Columbia University Press, 1956.

Sinclair, Andrew, *The Emancipation of the American Woman*. New York: Harper, 1965. (Originally published as *The Better Half*.)

Sorokin, Pitirim, *The American Sex Revolution*. Boston: Porter Sargent, Pub., 1956.

SIDNEY DITZION

American Indians, Sex Life of the

A full treatment and understanding of sexual behavior among American Indian peoples is hampered by four important limitations. In the first place, the diversity of cultures in the New World in combination with striking differences in their complexity do not allow the easy drawing of conclusions that have continental validity. Second, the uneven treatment of sex matters in travel, missionary, and ethnographic reports complicates our understanding the problems not only of behavioral motivation but also of institutionalized sex beliefs and practices. Third, the observation and description of sexual behaviors vary in point of time, some of our records appearing at the beginnings of contact with the West, but many appearing much later, after centuries of change. Fourth, the ramifications of sexual behavior for any people are such that a summary report of sex outside its cultural contexts is certain to oversimplify our understanding of the meaning and significance of sexual activity in the life of a particular people.

In the face of these limiting conditions the possibility for a thoroughgoing inventory and analysis of American Indian sex beliefs and practices is rather slim. However, it is possible to show something of the diversity and range of sexual behavior and belief and to indicate how this basic physiological datum affected Indian interpretations of the world, influenced the social order, and penetrated their daily lives.

Sex and the World View

Like other peoples of the world, American Indians and Eskimos perceive and emphasize the basic dichotomy and physiological differences of the sexes. Indian myths of creation and later transformations offer some distinctive evidences of their interpretations of the role of sex in the universe and in the life of mankind.

Myths of Creation

The creation myths of American Indians generally show deities distinguished by sex. The world of spirit as well as of man is bisexual, and although in daily life they are familiar with hermaphrodites and cross-sex behavior, and may formalize it as transvestism, still American Indians tend to identify the spiritual personalities of their pantheons as males or females. However, they do not stereotype maleness and femaleness. Male figures may be more active, the conquerors of monsters and the transformers of the world, while females engage in domestic activity and care for children, but both sexes may be sexually aggressive and may commit acts of violence.

Creator gods tend to be male, even when a female deity is described as "grandmother" of the gods (Iroquois). It is the grandson, Taronhaiwagon, and not the progenitrix, who creates and animates. Taronhaiwagon is the sky god who looks down upon men with sympathetic and benevolent eyes and supplies the vital generative and regenerative forces for the Earth-Mother and her children. In centers of cultural advancement, such as the valley of Mexico, Yucatan, and the Andean highlands, the creator figures were addressed as "lord, the father," among other titles. Some creator gods, as among Zuni, give the appearance of a primeval ambi-sexuality, since all that is initially created, including maleness and femaleness, is generated by and from this always-existing figure. Yet the common tendency is to attribute maleness to the Creator, as do these very same Zuni, who consider Awonawilona the "Maker and Container of All, the All-father Father." In South America outside the Andes the supreme creators are also addressed as males, very often as "father" or euphemistically as "The Old One" (Yahgan). Female supreme beings occur in a few scattered instances (Cagaba, Yaruro, Chamacoco) in association with matrilineal descent and matrilocal residence patterns. Generally speaking, however, female deities are not of great importance among either the North American or South American hunter-collectors and hunter-horticulturists. The earth commonly may be associated with a "mother" and with female productivity, but it is only among the advanced horticulturists in Central America that earth emerges as a goddess and mother-of-fertility and assumes a prominent place in popular belief and ritual practice.

In their accounts of the primeval creation, Indian and Eskimo alike seem to have a miraculous rather than a sexual generative process in mind. The eastern Eskimo account of the origin of whales and other sea life tells of their being formed from the finger joints of Sedna, the Goddess of the Sea. Deceived by a fulmar spirit who had married her on the promise of a life of ease, Sedna and her father flee the fulmars who attempt to swamp the boat in revenge for the slaying of the deceitful lover. In his terror Sedna's father casts her from the boat, and as she grasps the edge he cuts off her fingers joint by joint; these, falling in the water, turn into whales, fish, etc.

The Hopi Indians people primeval time with two female and two male beings, White-Shell-Woman, Spider Woman, Sun, and Moon. White-Shell-Woman sends Moon for Sun. From the scale-skin rubbed from different parts of her body, White-Shell-Woman creates birds for Sun. The latter in turn creates the deer, antelope, and other animals, and after forming the earth Sun turns it over to White-Shell-Woman. The fabrication of woman is accomplished in the cooperative presence of Sun, who voices impatience at the delay in finishing the human. Now White-Shell-Woman finds the creation of a lone woman "not good" and immediately sets to work to produce a male, also from her skin.

The near-by Navaho begin with First World, an island of dark or red earth floating in a sea of mist. Black Cloud and White Cloud, symbols of femaleness and of maleness, meet in the East and there and at that time the First Man and the first perfect ear of seed corn are formed.

Accounts of these primeval creations seem most matter of fact and sexless despite the apparently miraculous events that take place. Supernatural figures of either sex enter and leave the mythic dramas without any compelling necessity on the part of the narrators to account for their existence. At the dawn of life power is simply rampant and unstabilized when compared with today. Generation and vigorous growth are frequent occurrences, as when Dew Boy makes corn grow for the people of Oraibi (Hopi) in a single day. When the Zuni, during the time of emergence from Earth's four-storied womb, cross a river, the babies on the backs of the women turn into snakes, and those not held tightly by their fearful mothers escape to become water spirits associated with clouds and rain-bringing ceremonies. The Aztecs relate that in the time of Quetzalcoatl corn grew to such size that it was all a person could do to carry a single ear. Gourds measured several feet in length and cotton grew in all colors.

Myths of Sex

Neither the first spirit-beings nor the first men and women are wholly familiar with sex, and they often give the impression that proper attitudes and behaviors have yet to come. Spontaneous passion, violence, avoidance, and fear may be expressed in individual events, all of which, however, seem directed to an explanatory purpose. The Piro of the Upper Amazon relate how Tsla, both hero-trickster and Creator, was born of a mother married to three brothers, tiger-spirits. When she choked while attempting to swallow lice during a wifely delousing operation, they all pounced on her and tore her to pieces. Before all was gone the tigress mother-in-law snatched the uterus and placed it in a tree. From this severed member Tsla and three brothers were born to avenge their mother's death and to perform many feats, including the molding of Indians from red clay and of whites from white clay.

Sex and pregnancy are not portrayed as pleasurable, natural, or necessary for the spirits and people of the primeval days. The natural aspects of sex commonly give way in face of the miraculous, as the Menomini myth of Manabozo's birth illustrates. The first old woman cautions her daughter that she must face only to the south when digging "potatoes." No mention is made of sex or conception by the old woman and the forgetful girl suddenly finds herself turned around and around by a powerful rush of wind out of the north. The old lady threatens her daughter and warns her that she is being punished for disobedience. Later, in childbed, the daughter gives birth successfully to Manabozo and Little Wolf, but the third "child," a flint rock, cuts her and she dies. Disobedience to the injunctions of the old woman leads always to pregnancy and death, yet the daughter's fate, a consequence of her unwitting dereliction, is softened by the child she produces, for Manabozo is to be the instructor of mankind, sent from on high by the Master of Life.

In the Southwest a common event in the formative period of the earth and of man portrays the separation of the sexes, sometimes attributed to scheming Coyote (Navaho), at other times to the presumption of the women, who assert they do not need husbands to be married (Hopi). Generally, women are depicted as more lascivious and unstable in character than the men, symbolized by their lack of fertility, since they are unable to grow as full crops as the men. In their passion women use rocks, feathers, and cacti and give birth to monsters, such as the Great Stone that kills men. The men in their turn satisfy their passion with mountain sheep, mountain lions, and an-

telope, all of which die in the process, and the men are finally struck down by lightning (Navaho). Events such as these are part of the "emergence theme" in the Southwest, which stresses "wickedness" and strife before people learned what to do and eventually established themselves on the present earth. Yet it is like other Indian treatments of the primeval and formative eras since it features miraculous births, generations, transformations, violence, and sexual passion, all of which are cast within a matter-of-fact explanatory framework.

Myths of Animal-Spouses

Lovers and spouses who may be animal-beings belong to the formative period of earth and of man and illustrate the basic qualities of those times. Basic Indian attitudes toward non-human spouses also emerge. Generally speaking, it is considered reprehensible or adulterous for women to have animal-spouses. A common North American story of Bear-Woman describes her as transformed into a ferocious killer of humans when accused of having a bear-lover, or when she learns that her father and brothers have killed her animal husband. The story may turn into a magic flight with the brothers and younger sister ascending into the heavens to become the Dipper. In a Quinault version the father kills the dog-husband, but the puppies that are born (four male and one female) later are "fixed" in a human shape instead of being subject to a day-night transformation as their dog-father had been. They excel in hunting and ultimately are accepted as leaders by those who had abandoned the mother and her dog-babies.

Snakes sometimes figure as adulterers, and when the husband catches the pair *in flagrante*, he may kill the snake and serve up its genitals to his wife, or kill both of them, cutting off her head and sometimes serving her flesh to the children. The explicit phallic symbolism of the snake may account for the violence attributed to the wronged husband, but the killing and eating of an adulterous woman in North America occurs in contexts other than the snake-paramour. The South American Indian treatment of the animal-lover theme is much the same, with the young mother learning the identity of her husband when her baby changes into a deer, bird, reptile, or tiger, or when her husband suddenly bares his teeth and sets out to devour her. When wives or sisters are abducted by animals or sea-beings, husbands and brothers are portrayed in pursuit and finally as rescuing them, sometimes with the assistance of other animals (Northwest Coast).

If women who establish relations with animal-beings or other mythical personages are depicted as punished, devoured, or unhappily awaiting a rescuer, men who consort with animal-maidens or spouses are more often described as abandoned husbands. An Eskimo tale has geese-women surprised in their bath and trapped by the hunter, who holds their bird-skin clothes. He releases all but one, whom he marries and by whom he has two sons. One day while the hunter is away the goose-wife finds some wings and takes flight with her sons. The husband pursues and spears her, despite her effort to escape by feigning death. With this act the family is broken up, for it is stated simply that the sons go away together. In a Plains version a man takes advantage of a buffalo cow mired in the mud. She bears a child and lives with the man, assuming a human shape. However, her husband breaks an injunction not to strike at her with fire and so she and her child rejoin the buffalo herd. In pursuit, the husband is forced by the chief of the buffaloes to pick his child out from the herd. The test is repeated ritually four times, and each time the husband is aided by the buffalo child, who furnishes cues to his identity. In this way the human husband and his buffalo spouse and child are reunited. For the most part, however, animal- or bird-wives are usually easily offended and leave their human husbands, and in the pursuit that follows the family with the children rather than the sexual attraction of the spouse seems to be the important motive for the chase.

In South America the husband does not seem to fare any better than the wife in the animal- or demon-spouse encounters. Death is a frequent consequence when lured by ghosts or sirens who dwell within the dark forest. The advanced horticulturists of Nuclear America also describe these encounters as fateful. In Yucatan today men in the forest guard themselves against the long-haired siren who dwells in the ceiba tree, for she will lure them to their deaths.

Myths of Incest

Acts of incest by spirit-beings and people of the mythic past have also contributed to the formation of the world as men know it. The Eskimos explain the separation of sun and moon as due to the incestuous passion of a brother for a sister, accomplished when sex play occurred with the "lights out." Suspicious, the sister traps the passionate suitor with soot marks from her blackened hands, and in the anger of discovery she cuts off her breasts and offers them for her brother to eat. This act, however, only inflames his passion and he continues in pursuit. Both rush out into the darkness with torches, the brother tripping and extinguishing his light. The pursuit still continues in the heavens, the sister with her lighted torch being the sun, the brother the moon.

Tribes in central and northern California tell of a girl overwhelmed by passion for a younger brother who is kept hidden from her. At her insistence he comes forth and she chooses him to accompany her. This he consents to do, but at night, suspecting her intent, he puts a log in his place and takes flight. Upon awakening, the sister's unnatural desire is now accompanied by homicidal anger and she seeks to kill the whole family, who escape by ascending into the sky in a basket. However, against the instructions of the boy, the mother looks back and the basket falls to earth into the fire prepared by the vengeful sister. Miraculously the boy bounces into the air and escapes, to return later with his children to kill his sister. This he is able to accomplish only by discovering her point of vulnerability, the sole of her foot, into which he drives an arrow (Shasta).

In North America tales of incest seldom include father-in-law and daughter-in-law, mother-in-law and son-in-law, or parent and child, but the Plains Indians, in their lovable transforming trickster, Old-Man-Coyote, possess a source of a wide range of sexual anecdotes that include father-daughter and mother-in-law and son-in-law relations. The tone of these tales is generally humorous, but at the same time the ridicule and public humiliation heaped upon Old-Man-Coyote make the copying of his behavior a perilous act. In the Northern Plains, too, a hunter's penis suddenly begins to talk and will not be silenced until it has been handled by his mother-in-law. Since the mother-in-law—son-in-law taboo commonly prohibited all but the most discreet social interaction and indirect communication, this tale is especially interesting. However, its limited distribution does not permit any blanket explanation of the mother-in-law—son-in-law taboo as based on a repression-projection mechanism.

Sexual desire for a son-in-law occurs in a few recorded tales, and here also lust leads to unrestrained violence, the older woman sometimes drowning her daughter by an act of deception. In some instances the older woman may be unrelated and apparently covets the beauty of both the girl and her youthful husband. She may dress in the skin of her victim, but eventually she is discovered, and with her disguise removed the hateful old woman is revealed. In a Wichita version the husband and chief removes the disguise by singing four "medicine" songs and then directs that the old woman be killed. Later he hears singing that comes from the middle of a river and there he finds his wife, for the old woman had tossed her into the stream. After the camp has been purified with appropriate ritual the wife returns to live with her husband.

Myths of the Sex Act

Although American Indians express the theme of inevitable hate, violence, and destruction when a person is overwhelmed by lust, they seldom describe forced intercourse or rape. The female sex partner never protests when confronted with sexual desire, but males are described as slipping away and avoiding the desire-ridden girl who calls upon them. When rape intrudes it comes in the form of an accusation by a rejected woman. As recorded in the tales, the sex act is not the focus for extended description—there is no heightening of sexual tension in anticipation such as occurs in the romantic literature of the West. Lust simply and suddenly appears and is immediately gratified with the cooperation of the partner.

The general lack of attention to the sex act itself in the Indian literature makes it difficult to infer much about attitudes, fears, and anticipated pleasures in the act-situation. Besides utilizing the sex act to offer explanations as to how some portions of the universe are shaped as they are, the usual Indian intent seems directed to the meanings and consequences of interpersonal relations. The lover who is deceived into disfiguring his face and then is laughed at and rejected by a haughty "princess" of the Northwest Coast, ultimately gains a revenge in which she, too, out of magically induced passion, disfigures herself. The hero, restored and made to look even handsomer by supernatural beings, rejects her and allows his companion to possess her. The princess, in her effort to erase the facial scars, journeys to the spirit land also, but her character does not change, and the spirits, in their fury at her hauteur, destroy her (Tsimshian). Another common theme is the poor, often dirty and ugly, youth who is rejected by his bride. Later he transforms himself and proves to be a handsome "supernatural" being in disguise.

Oedipal situations are hinted in the slaying of nephews or sons by a "jealous" uncle or father, but, as in a Kodiak version, it is not the slaying of his brothers or the implied sexual aggression that moves the Eagle-Boy to vengeance, but the denial of food to loved parents. After dropping his uncle into the sea, the hero induces his parents to accompany him to Eagle-land, where they now live. In like manner the testing of sons-in-law by the father of the bride can be interpreted as instances of sexual jealousy, but the tales do not make this explicit in the least. The test rather seems designed to bring out the "supernatural" powers of the suitor, who may convert the father-in-law by saving him from a perilous death.

The tale of the vagina knifed with teeth offers a striking exception to the usual treatment of the sex act since more description of the act itself is provided and a castration theme is baldly stated. The tale has a considerable distribution north of Mexico and usually portrays a hero outwitting a siren or an old woman and her daughter by substituting wood or stone for his penis. The women monsters usually die in the process and the Navaho make it clear that with this feat Elder Brother forestalled the subsequent appearance of such women among mankind. In the South American Chaco, the Toba and Mataco tell how women let themselves down from the sky with the aid of a rope. They intended to steal food from men, who were in animal form at the time. When their rope was cut by a bird, the women were forced to remain, but men were able to have intercourse with them only after the culture hero, Carancho, broke their vaginal teeth.

Formal Expression and Control of Sex: Sex and Ceremonial

In a broad cultural point of view American Indians quite evidently were concerned with the generation and growth of life. Both in myth and in rite the little-understood but powerfully desired forces that germinate and sustain life were given preferential treatment. However, American Indians do not seem to have dramatized the procreative act itself to any great extent nor to have accorded feigned intercourse and sexual license a prominent part in fertility ceremonies. Their deities were not represented with enlarged genitalia and neither *enceinte* goddesses nor monumental phalli and vulva were enshrined along the trails.

The advanced cultures of Nuclear America provide more than usual evidence of a "fertility consciousness." From the early cultures in the Valley of Mexico many pottery female figurines have been recovered, but the treatment is not overtly sexual. By the time of the Mexican invasion of Yucatan (tenth to thirteenth centuries) the fertility cult may have included dramatization of intercourse, license, and homosexual behavior, for the Maya refer to the conquering Itza as the "unrestrained lewd ones of day . . . /and/ night, the rogues of the world." Possibly a phallic cult may have been introduced to the Maya from the Vera Cruz area about the time of the Mexican invasions.

Excavation in Central America occasionally turns up pottery models of the male organ, but it is on the North Coast of Peru from the Mochica (up to 1000 A.D.) that clay genitalia appear in quantity. The Mochica also possessed a feline god who propagated humans physically and maintained fertility, his organ at the mo-

ment of coitus being bathed with a special fluid by two assisting bird deities. The depositing of sexual pieces and pottery on which sexual scenes are depicted, including masturbation, fellation, cunnilinctus, pederasty, and unusual sexual postures, as funerary furniture may reflect a popular and ritual concern with sex and fertility. Some of the pieces evidently were intended as ribald humor, but others portray a physical destruction of the "pervert." It is quite probable that the male homosexuality prevalent in the coastal areas of Peru and Ecuador at the time of the Conquest was ceremonialized, representing a fertility complex comparable to that of the Mochica.

In comparison with African and Hindu cultures, obvious sexual symbols seem weakly represented in the ceremonial ritual and art of the American Indians. Sexual symbolism commonly was masked, as in the ritual drinking of fermented maguey juice to signify impregnation (Papago) or in the Pueblo ceremonial races where men kicked sticks and women hoops. Indian ceremonialism handled the fertility theme guardedly and with restraint. Commonly the conditions desirable for germination and growth were pressed into the ritual and symbolized, such as clouds, wind, rain, and creatures associated with water as frogs and snakes. Occasionally, as among the Hopi, cylinders and circlets that symbolized the male and female generative powers were taken to a spring by a procession of boys and girls and there smeared with fertile mud and then cast upon four ground paintings as they returned. But to all intents and purposes germination was a mystic act—the intervention of a supernaturalistic power activated by the sacred words and pleasing actions of purified ritualists to the accompaniment of symbolized desire.

Whether facing the issue of germination or growth, American Indians took their cues primarily from the heavens and the plants or from the strength-bringing act of eating. Their instruments for growth consisted of water or fermented drink dropped from pottery vessels, or the tears of children to be sacrificed (Aztec) or of tethered black dogs or llamas (Inca), who evoked the pity of the rain gods through their crying. From the Mexican Aztec to the Andean Inca the gods, as men, were nourished with vegetable food and with the blood and meat of animals, birds, and humans. It was not the germinal and growth processes but the product that symbolized fertility, the first fruits—the full-bodied green corn. Sacrificial victims might be fattened to symbolize a full stomach and a healthy growing body, but not to signify a body pregnant or sexually virile (Skidi Pawnee). The cannibalism of the northwest Amazon tribes such as the Witoto and Cubeo included the eating of the victim's penis by the chief's wife or the warrior's wife. The Cubeo warrior customarily dried the penis and scrotum and performed a dance in which the victim's genitalia covered his own. Eating the penis was supposed to make the woman fertile. For the most part, however, the torture and cannibalistic complexes of the Americas did not include the victim's genitalia as a fertility trait. Rather, the genitalia were burned and otherwise mutilated by the women to humiliate the victim.

Ritual cleanliness also contributed to the general muting of sex in religious ceremonial. Sexual continence was considered essential to the preparation for and participation in ritualized activities and often extended to hunting and war ventures. In their ceremonials Plains Indians selected chaste women for special roles, but religious chastity was institutionalized only in Nuclear America, and even there it was not a universal condition for priest or priestess. Ceremonial continence and not celibacy was the Indian view.

In addition to the basic Indian conception that divided the sexes according to their respective generative roles, ideas about menstruation also influenced the separation of sexes in ceremonials. Women were considered unclean and potentially dangerous to men who worked with the supernatural powers that activated and sustained the world and the individual. Generally the menstruant was barred from public ceremonial and prayers described the ritual purity of the participants as resting in part on the exclusion of the "unclean" woman.

Ceremonial License

Sexual license within a ceremonial context was not a notable feature of Indian behavior. In the hunter-collector and hunter-horticultural societies the predominant association of men with supernatural powers and the special procedures for purification tended to separate and restrain the sexes throughout the ritual performances. Men organized themselves at times into secret fraternities that denied knowledge and participation to women.

The Yahgan of Tierra del Fuego concluded their puberty rites for boys and girls with a mock battle between men and women, and followed this with a feast. Like their neighbors the Alacaluf and Ona, the Yahgan possessed a ceremony that carried the individual beyond the puberty initiation, which was restricted to initiates and involved terrorization of the women. Chaco tribes held religious dances in which a young boy and girl impersonated deities to promote rain, abundance, and protection from disease. Although the "wife" appeared naked, there is no hint of license during or after the dances. Naked Mbaya boys would surround a girl smeared with charcoal and clothed with branches and try to strip her while other girls fended them off. When finally caught by the boys, the girl was taken to the river and the charcoal washed from her face. More often in the ceremonial context, the intrusion of naked sex took the shape of bald humor, as when Zuni men appeared with gourds to simulate phalli and the women drove them back with a bombardment of filth.

The ceremonial drinking bouts so prevalent among South American hunter-horticulturists seldom resulted in sex behavior. Young women commonly were *not* allowed to participate and in some cases no woman whose husband was a party to the bout was allowed to witness the drinking. The usual role of the woman was that of caretaker for the incapacitated and preventer of violence. Drumming and dancing were an integral part of the "bout" and the boasting of the men usually raised resentment and anger but not sexual passion. Similar behavior is reported from North American Indians following the introduction of liquor. The stuporous condition usually attained in these drinking festivities did not favor the arousal and release of sexual energy.

Sexual license was not a usual ritual accompaniment to American Indian fertility ceremonies or puberty rites. Sexual license did occur during the puberty rites of the Californian Yuki, Shasta, and Maidu. However, when fertility and license were combined, it generally occurred among advanced horticulturists in whose cultures premarital and extramarital controls also appear more severe than among the simple hunters and horticulturists. Despite the references of the padres to lascivious dancing and obscene behavior in Mexico, there is no firm evidence of fertility orgies. More often normal restrictions and surveillance were relaxed, stimulating momentary "affairs." Among the Hopi, for example, on the day of the Snake Dance and for three days thereafter a woman might snatch from a man any possession he happened to be carrying. Both married and unmarried women engaged in this sport in the daytime, but as the game continued after dark the married withdrew, leaving youths free to encourage pursuit to a secluded spot by exhibiting some attractive object before a young woman. Ceremonial prostitution for one night is reported for priestesses of the medicine bundles among the Zuni, but there is no evidence that prostitution was expected of priestesses dedicated to cult gods in Nuclear America.

Although fertility may not have furnished the usual context for sexual license among American Indian groups, social festivities of one kind or another did set the stage. Among the Iroquois, belief in a necessity to actualize personal dreams in the interests of individual health and public safety was associated with desire fulfillment of various kinds, including sex. In the Andacwander rite extramarital sexual intercourse was sanctioned so long as it stemmed from a dream. The Eskimo custom of "putting out the lights" and engaging in promiscuous sex play and intercourse took place during a festive social mood. Special situations such as the personal vow of the Plains warrior to become a Crazy-Dao-Wishing-To-Die also invited sexual favors. During the Sun Dance some tribes of the Northern Plains had the pledger's wife submit to the man's ceremonial grandfather (Arapaho, southern Cheyenne), but the Oglala and Arapaho alone seem to have permitted full license at one stage in the performance. During moments of sexual relaxation and even license there is no evidence that a formal contravention of incest prohibitions was enjoined or allowed.

Sex Education

Formal instruction in the practical arts of sex is not in evidence among American Indian societies. Knowledge of intercourse might begin in childhood with observation of parents, whose concealment in the limited quarters never was complete. Information passed on by older youths and occasional adults expanded this knowledge, but usually the coital art was learned firsthand from some person of the opposite sex who was older. When formal instruction that may connect with sex occurred, it usually was associated with transition ceremonies that marked passage from child to young adult. These ceremonies were multifunctional, designed as much to establish favorable relations with the supernatural powers that aid in growth and health and protect the individual and group as to provide moral instruction. The initiation practices also served to induce conformity and respect for adult authority and to signal a change to a status that involved more social responsibility and participation in adult activities in accordance with custom (Ona, Yahgan, Inca, Hopi, Zuni).

Owing to the tendency to bring sex into a magicoreligious configuration, much of the sexual content taught included ritual taboos on foods and avoidances of the opposite sex, besides the appropriate behavior and work for one's own sex. Ingalik men learned that they must take care that no menstruating woman walked over any of their tools or even the castoff products, as wood shavings, for fear of losing their skill at manipulating tools and selecting trees. A woman in her turn had to learn that she must wait awhile before walking to where her husband had left the catch of fish, for if she were to tread on his fresh footsteps, his luck in hunting and fishing would no longer hold.

As with many tribal peoples, American Indians made use of behavioral patterns that dramatized the status-linkage of the interacting individuals. The emotional tone of these patterns tended to be either reserved or expressive, enjoining avoidance or access behaviors. Brother-sister avoidance was widespread in the Americas, generally induced in childhood by a feeling of shame-respect. Proper behavior usually dictated physical separation and restricted communication. When riding in a canoe the Yahgan insisted that brother and sister sit apart, and Arapaho brothers and sisters acted in the best tradition when they did not remain together in the same group and when they exchanged information through a messenger. When talking to her brother an Arapaho girl was supposed to keep her eyes on the ground.

The joining of families in marriage commonly called for restrained relations among the in-laws, and frequently sons-in-law and mothers-in-law followed a pattern of total avoidance. Sexual references were barred in any respect relationship.

The presence of varied behaviors that not only enunciated differences between the sexes but separated them physically and emotionally indicates that American Indians generally conditioned the individual to a wide range of situational restraints with respect to the other sex. The magicoreligious interpretation of menstruation added but another dimension to the restraint configuration, based in this instance on shame and fear.

A contrary behavior can be found in the "joking" relationship that permitted and enjoined liberties, both humorous and sexual. Usually a joking relationship linked those who were potential spouses and sexual allusions, physical contact, and erotic caresses were quite in order. A Hopi youth expected his father's sister and her husband to wrestle him and to joke about his sexual intentions with respect to his aunt. His "grandfather" did not hesitate to include threats of castration in his humor.

Some societies provided practical opportunities for widening individual sex experience prior to marriage. Bororo youths commonly brought their sweethearts to the men's house, and the usually severe Aztec allowed youths in the telpuchcalli school, largely dedicated to training in arms, to have mistresses. On the other hand, the age-grading and segregation of boys and girls was used by Sherente and Apinayé adults to strengthen their control over youthful sex activity since chastity was the rule. Among the Mataco and other southern Chaco tribes, widespread love-making by the young people followed their social dancing. In a limited number of tribes the puberty ceremonies provided immediate opportunity for sexual intercourse. The Sae had the menstruant at the end of her confinement give a basket of food to the man she liked best and he had intercourse with her. Since marriage usually followed shortly after the puberty ceremonies, the issue of absolute restraint was never a serious problem.

Much of the sex instruction seems to have been carried on informally and to have consisted of admonitions and positive suggestions prompted by immediate recognition of need. If children were surprised in sexual experimentation, as two girls lying together, they might be advised to find some boys (Ingalik). Girls seem to have been given many warnings "to keep away from boys," and mothers as well as other relatives would implement the warning with surveillance, according to how permissive the sexual definition happened to be. Older people sometimes told didactic myths or lectured preadolescent children on what was appropriate, but there is no evidence to indicate that sessions of this kind were devoted especially to sexual matters.

American Indians were not inclined to discuss the physiological changes that would appear, except where menstrual taboos were highly developed and required immediate sequestering and ceremony. In such instances mothers would warn daughters to let them know at the first sign. Individual cases of fear and shame at the discovery of menstruation have been recorded, and this may have been a not uncommon experience, for free and easy exchange of information between mother and daughter and parents and children generally was not an ideal to which Indians addressed themselves. The "shame" that covered menstruation did not make it a fit subject of conversation. The thought system that accepted "like as producing like" also inhibited free discussion of sex. For example, the Arapaho were very guarded in talking about birth and related matters for fear pregnancy would follow in some relative.

Training in modesty seems to have intensified around puberty, when adult clothing was donned and puberty ceremonies or other social recognition defined a new status for the individual. Clothing probably implemented modesty in most areas since exposure of the genitals in public usually evoked a feeling of shame. However, in a number of areas nudity or near nudity was the rule. In the Amazon-Orinoco regions both men and women frequently wore but token clothing, such as a penis sheath or a pubic piece. Until adolescence both sexes commonly went naked. In North America male nudity was frequent in California, the Northwest Coast, and the adjacent Plateau and Basin areas. Female nudity never was so widespread as male. Outside the areas where tailored or sewn skin and textile clothing is found, women were not inclined to clothe the breasts.

Childhood and Premarital Sexuality

Most American Indian societies were rather permissive in their attitudes toward childhood and premarital sexuality, especially with respect to males. The extension of considerable latitude to the male apparently reflects a common recognition of more and frequent sexual experimentation for maturing males in comparison with females, in conjunction with the belief that males played a more active role in the whole sexual configuration. A double standard for the sexes generally prevailed.

Fingering or stroking the genitals to pacify the infant was not a common practice, although blowing or stroking to induce urination occurred among the Nootka and Ingalik. Caingang mothers are said to have fingered the male genitals to stimulate sexuality. Over much of North America access to the infant's genitals was denied by use of the cradleboard or pouch. The frequent binding of arms likewise did not allow the nursing infant access to the mother's breast, although toddlers and even children of 4 and 5 could grasp the breast since weaning in the sense of full denial was deferred. It is hard to say to what extent mothers enjoyed the prolonged nursing and tactile contacts with the child. Tepoztlán mothers denied any special satisfaction from nursing, and they were not inclined to permit fingering of the breast because it was not a "toy." Teton Dakota women reported that a teething infant would bite the nipple and they in turn would give the baby's head a thump, sending him into a rage that was quieted by the nipple.

During childhood the naked condition of the children, the half-concealed sexual intimacies of parents, and the activities of animals provided ample opportunities for children to observe the workings of sex. Preadolescent gangs of boys served as a special source for sexual knowledge and experimentation. Such a group of Tenetehara boys would attempt to lure young girls into the bush, where they would attempt intercourse and other sex play.

Masturbation undoubtedly constituted a part of male experimentation since special inquiry usually elicits admission of the activity. As with other sexual behavior, the extent to which autoeroticism was practiced varied regionally and even tribally, Chiricahua Apache contrasting their restraint with Comanche self-stimulation. Group masturbation occurred occasionally. Crow youths as well as preadolescents played a game of "genitals" in which they attempted to touch a sleeping girl or woman, sometimes following with group masturbation. Kwakiutl boys of 5 and 6 would lie together and finger each other's genitals. Masturbation by females apparently was much less prevalent than among males.

The attitude toward masturbation in the young child more often involved amusement than alarm. Few peoples exhibited the extreme of indifference found in Pilagá mothers, who simply ignored the efforts of prepubescent sons to masturbate against their bodies. Neither are there many who follow the Tepoztecans in scolding and beating 5-year-olds who momentarily finger their genitals, although it is possible that the severity and restraint common to contemporary Mexican groups may owe something to a basic pre-Conquest attitude and practice.

Most sex experimentation took place away from immediate adult view and probably involved spontaneous as well as deliberate behavior. Sexual contests of one kind or another were conducted by Crow gangs. The erect penis would be measured against that of another claimant to determine the larger and they would divide according to clans and bet on champions who would attach a line to the penis and then drag a stone as far as possible. Like the Mohave, Crow youths would bet on ejaculation distance. A large penis was prized and preadolescents would pull on the pubic hair to stimulate growth and sometimes they would put an irritating plant juice on the penis to make it swell.

Most males probably had some experience with homosexuality during childhood and adolescence. It might have been mutual masturbation or anal entry, an older boy using a younger for the latter purpose. Adult use of children for homosexual practice was severely condemned, although institutionalized homosexuality as a stage in sexual growth may have occurred among the prehistoric Mochica and historic peoples of Ecuador as well as Caribbean groups, who maintained bachelor houses. Inquiry about female homosexuality prior to marriage usually reveals occasional cases; it appears never to have been so frequent or acceptable as among males.

Children who demonstrated a marked preference for the work, games, and habits of the opposite sex were watched closely in their development but no effort was made to force them into their natural sex pattern. The emergent transvestite was an amusing oddity for the most part, but to the Navaho he was a respected symbol of wealth soon to accrue to the family. The hermaphrodite likewise excited interest but was allowed to develop unhindered since Indians generally regarded sex deviation as a response to an inner nature or "call." Transvestism for a male was considered more acceptable than for a female.

Bestiality seems to have been a rarity in developmental experience except where youth gangs and domesticated animals coexisted. Hopi youths sometimes were directed to bestiality presumably to divert them and to preserve the chastity of maidens. The Plains youths experimented with colts and were known to use a freshly slain animal for sexual purposes.

Both boys and girls seem to have graduated to heterosexual contacts at an early age. Societal recognition of this fact is afforded by the brother-sister respect-avoidance behavior commonly initiated between the ages of 7 and 10. Chaco boys chased girls and openly tried to touch the vulva, and if a girl were caught they might attempt intromission. Kwakiutl boys of 6 or 7 would build little shelters in the forest and play house with girls of comparable age,

lying with them in imitation of adult copulation. Play imitative of domestic life seems to have provided initial sexual contacts in many societies.

During childhood heterosexual relations were varied but predominantly genital. Girls would masturbate boys and themselves solicit digital play and intromission. Crow boys of 8 and 9 were invited by pubescent and sometimes older girls to urinate in lieu of ejaculation. Fellation and anal entry apparently were infrequent.

In most instances puberty marked an immediate transition to married life for girls, automatically terminating their premarital experimentation. Owing to later maturation, boys were a year or two older at marriage than girls and, where war or other special social experience was required, marriage for males might not take place until 18 or 20 years. In meeting the problem of the natural discontinuity in sexual maturation and a prolonged social development, Indian societies usually provided institutionalized opportunities for intercourse, countenanced surreptitious relations, increased surveillance of unmarried girls, and in a few instances imposed chastity on both sexes.

Societies that maintained a young men's house commonly allowed the youths to possess sweethearts or assigned wantons for their pleasure, as among the Yucatecan Maya and Aztecs. Pawnee nephews customarily were provided with a tipi situated next to a maternal uncle and were allowed access to the latter's wife. In the Great Basin a younger brother might share the wife of an older brother in a temporary polyandrous union, while in the Plains an older brother was expected to extend wife hospitality to a younger brother. Widows, both old and young, were frequent sex targets for the unmarried youth. Where parental surveillance occurred, the technique of assignation by a go-between was common. Stealthy access to a girl within the residence also seems to be associated with strict surveillance and deferred marriage for youths (Kwakiutl, Chiricahua Apache). Even girls sequestered at menstruation were visited occasionally by adolescent youths despite the taboos imposed and fear of damage to the penis.

The rather widespread practice of occupying

the unmarried girl in domestic work and in watching her closely at social dances is suggestive of furtive sexual attacks by youths. In the Plains the unguarded girl who strayed too far from camp or who was out after dark might find herself assaulted by a number of youths.

There is some reason for believing that relative tolerance of premarital relations may be associated with a theory of conception that required repeated and continuous intercourse over a period of days (Tenetehara). On the other hand, strict control over premarital relations for both sexes commonly occurs in association with ceremonial transitions that bring the novices into contact with the creative and mystic powers in the universe (Yahgan, Sherente, Zuni). However, neither of these explanation comprehends all the social, economic, and ideological factors necessary to account for premarital latitude or strictness.

Attitude toward Sex, Love, and the Married State

Although American Indians generally accepted sex as a natural reality in their lives, their orientation toward it was a composite of attitudes deriving from special situations. Nowhere can one detect a blanket condemnation of sex underwritten by a feeling of guilt, but customs antecedent to marriage frequently reinforced the youthful shyness with a feeling of shame.

The sex-shame configuration helps to explain the widespread practice of arranged marriages and a general absence of courtship patterns that would bring the husband and wife into a partial intimacy prior to marriage. The married state was more a practical and social arrangement that must be negotiated between families, the proper activity of the parents and other relatives. Although elopement might be tolerated in individual cases, it never was a worthy alternative and people usually validated the union with traditional exchanges of food and goods between the families. More often love grounded in physical attraction crumbled before the demands of the social order or, equally probably, it may never have existed in the romantic Western form. Mothers, fathers, elder brothers, paternal aunts, or maternal uncles, singly and in conjunction with others, traditionally picked out the proper industrious spouse, or at the very least they agreed to the boy's selection and made the arrangements. Girls usually exercised their selection through rejection, but were never wholly free of the persuasive pressures from kinfolk.

Although the attitude toward sexual experimentation, both autoerotic and heterosexual, generally was permissive and tolerant, unrestrained sexuality was not valued. The wanton was socially devalued. On the other hand, a life in chastity was not admired. Continence and restraint were framed by ceremonial requirements or by practical needs, such as ensuring a continuous flow of milk and the good health of the infant. Dedication to chastity was possible within the religious system of Nuclear America and apparently was highly prized. Some Dakota families in the Plains boasted socially of lifelong virgins and distributed goods to honor them. For the most part, however, the married state was considered a natural life state, and the Aztec and Inca alike are said to have forced the marriage of bachelors.

Incest and Selection of Spouses

Incest prohibitions in American Indian societies covered the usual in-family relations between parents and children and between brothers and sisters. Inca marriage of brother to sister or half-sister was the only exception to the rule and here dynastic and social factors prevailed and restricted the practice to the upper class and royalty. Marriage to first cousins was both widely forbidden and permitted.

The presence of unilinear kin groups is often associated with a classification of first and more distant cousins into a sibling (parallel cousin) and a nonsibling (cross-cousin) status. The patrilinear Cubeo custom had male cross-cousins (father's sister's sons and mother's brother's sons) exchanging sisters as spouses, while the matrilinear Haida preferred marriage with a father's sister's daughter except when inheritance dictated union with a mother's brother's daughter. Others not only included parallel cousins in the sibling incest definition but also forbade marriage with one of the cross-cousins, as the Sherente, who would not sanction unions with a mother's brother's daughter. Marriage with a stepdaughter was sanctioned widely in western North America, but societies that barred it were equally numerous. If the absence of occurrence can be accepted as evidence of prohibition, marriage to a niece was rarely countenanced. In some societies it was advantageous to marry a sister's daughter since a man remained in the kin settlement and avoided obligations (Tupinamba, Barama River Carib, Jivaro). When polygyny was widespread, inheritance of the widows by the older son commonly occurred, and it is noteworthy that his own mother was always denied him (Macushi, Araucanians).

Evidence that would allow an assessment of what happened to those who committed incest is scanty. In times of dire illness the Ojibwa were known to confess secret acts of this kind in the hope of escaping death. Among the Chiricahua Apache, eloping first cousins might be killed. It would seem, however, that cases were rare and that when they occurred they drew nothing more than severe public censure. Only the advanced horticulturists considered incest such a heinous offense and ritual sin that agonizing death must follow.

Courtship and Marriage

If courtship is taken to mean a stage preliminary to marriage in which lovers establish a common acceptance and agreement following traditional practices, American Indian societies did not operate under a courtship pattern. Marriage involved families more often than individuals, and arrangements usually fell to the parents. A man's behavior was designed more to secure the approval of the parents than of the girl, since gifts were presented to the bride's parents, sometimes including game hunted by the prospective groom, or the groom performed some useful work and demonstrated his industriousness to his in-laws.

The common Indian view placed experience in living above beauty and romantic attraction. For daily living a man needed a woman who could prepare food, make and mend clothes, and who showed by her industry that she was

a homemaker and not a gossip or a loose woman. In turn, a "good" boy must be a hard worker and known to be restrained and kind in his relations with women.

The widespread acceptance of arranged marriages argues for a rejection-anxiety among men, since the initiative was usually placed in the hands of the youth's family. Ingalik mothers chose for their sons spouses who were industrious and who had passed through the menstrual rite, while Iroquois matrons frequently married their sons to an older, experienced widow. In most societies, however, the husband tended to be older than the wife by a few years. Friendly relations between families and individuals sometimes resulted in child betrothal, an arrangement apparently more common where matrilinear descent and matrilocal residence favored intervention of women relatives in the choice of spouses for their descendants.

The contemporary Tarascans provide an exception to the pattern of arranged marriage since lovers will conspire to have the bride "stolen" during the walk home from Sunday church despite the risk of pursuit and a beating at the hands of the irate father and his supporters. However, everything must later proceed as if the marriage had been negotiated, and intercourse prior to the ceremony will be indulged in only upon permission from the godfather of the bride. Elopement and capture are also frequent among the Eskimo, but economic need of a spouse more than romantic love is said to prompt their action.

Under the system of arranged marriages, initial intimacy did not lead to immediate consummation. An awkward "courting" period of variable length intervened until the girl accepted her spouse. Often the shy resistance of the bride was formalized. A Mocovi bride was expected to cover her head and sulk, rejecting food and other favors offered by her in-laws and taking no notice of her husband. When alone, the husband would test her compliance with a command to stop crying and to bring him some object. In contrast, Tenetehara men were so shy when they moved into the household of their in-laws that the brides after a few days were forced to take the initiative and join the groom in his hammock. Shame and fear of rebuff possibly motivated the behavior of the Tenetehara men. Among the Aztec consummation was deferred for four days while the bride and groom offered food sacrifices and blood drawn from the ears and tongue and fasted.

No tokens of virginity were taken or displayed by American Indian groups. Where for ritual or socioeconomic purposes virginity had value, determination was made beforehand through questioning and observation. In some tribes of the South Colombian highlands a woman deflowered her daughter with her fingers before marriage, while the Conibos of eastern Peru operated on the inebriated and unconscious girl with a bamboo knife and inserted a clay penis fashioned to the size of the husband's organ. No elaborate procedures to adjust a claim for damage in the absence of virginity were developed by American Indians, although a man usually had the right to annul the marriage where chastity was a factor in the bride price.

In the absence of arranged marriages with the accompanying exchanges of goods, the sexual intimacies of an affair ultimately resulted in a union that gained in stability as children were produced. Some highland tribes in southern Colombia permitted a man to feast the parents of eligible girls and to have intercourse with a different girl each day until he found one suitable to his tastes.

Institutionalized intercourse with the bride by a shaman or other officiant was rare, although it has been reported from certain Venezuelan groups (Maracapana, Cumana, Piritu).

The absence of a formal courtship is correlated with a general absence of love songs and a vocabulary of love. Frustrated lovers of both sexes were not inclined to sublimate but resorted to aphrodisiacs or other magical means to force overwhelming passion upon the objects of their desire. Here unconscious projection apparently teamed with the process of like-produces-like to effect emotional release, since the products of local animals noted for their sexual vigor (as the otter on the Northwest Coast and the elk in the Plains) might be sought for the aphrodisiac. Flutes were in use in the Plains to call to a lover but assignations were more often arranged by a go-between or a casual social contact.

The withdrawal of the newlyweds from their immediate families during a honeymoon also is absent. A number of factors undoubtedly are involved, including the customary residence practices, the practical attitude assumed in relation to the married state, and the security requirements of life under the conditions of tribal life.

Adultery and Extramarital Relations

A strict exercise of a sexual monopoly does not seem to have been the usual Indian view. They commonly defined the adulterous relation as illicit intercourse, usually with a married man or woman, but the sexual relations that were permitted either sex under special circumstances hardly allow the application of a narrow definition of adultery to Indian sex practice.

Sexual license within accepted kin relations constituted one extension of nonadulterous behavior. Haida women and men were permitted sexual relations with another who belonged to a spouse's clan, and the most a husband or wife could do was to object softly; jealousy would be out of place here. But beyond these accepted relations a spouse had grounds for divorce. In like manner the Bolivian Siriono extended sexual privileges to the brothers or sisters, real and classificatory, of one's spouse. Adultery was more a matter of neglect than of violating the marriage bond, since the Siriono, as did the Caingang and the southern Chaco tribes, distributed sexual favors freely.

Special obligations to guests, friends, and ceremonial patrons were discharged by an offer of sexual hospitality, usually with a wife's assent (Eskimo, Cumana, Araucay). Or sexual intercourse was permitted if a favor was turned over to the spouse (Crow, Pasto, Eskimo). Some groups, such as the Patangoro and Amani, also permitted wife exchange.

Men away from their spouses on war or hunting expeditions usually were not denied sexual relations unless continence was prescribed to ensure success. Sherente youths on a war raid made use of loose women and the Iroquois permitted hunters a temporary companion when a wife could not accompany them.

The definition of adultery is complicated further by instances such as the Lenca punishing the wife but not the paramour. In contrast, the Maya held the man largely responsible and allowed the husband, after the facts had been verified by the chiefs, to decide whether the paramour should be allowed to live or be killed by throwing a rock at his head. The unfaithful wife, although not punished physically, usually was turned out as a divorced woman. The Gabrielino of southern California allowed a man to turn his own wife over to the seducer and in turn take the wife of the latter for himself.

It is apparent that in their approach to male and female sexuality American Indian societies generally favored the male. In most instances the initiative in extending sexual favors and in taking action when infidelity occurred rested with the male. The tolerance for occasional infidelity among most hunting and hunter-horticultural groups seems to have been generous, the outraged husband doing no more than beating his wife or sending her home. When sanctioned, violent action more often was directed against the offending wife than against the seducer. In the Northern Plains mutilating the nose of an adulterous wife or beating her severely was customary. Punishment by organized rape, in which the husband would turn his wife over to a group of men, sometimes twenty or more, was sometimes carried out in the Plains and the eastern Woodlands. The Amani of western Colombia not only subjected the adulterous wife to organized rape, but starved her to death if she survived this daily treatment. However, in this case the paramour was also slain, and both bodies were left unburied for carrion birds to dispose of.

Among the advanced horticultural groups of Nuclear America marriage carried a religious sanction and adultery was as much a sin as an offense against the person. In the one confession of their lives, the Aztecs included adultery as a sin, and here, as among the Maya and Inca, the state intervened to punish known adulterers with severity. Commoners among the Inca

might be tortured, but when a noblewoman was involved the death penalty was customary.

Retaliatory action in the face of infidelity, temporary separations, and divorce indicates that a feeling of possessiveness and jealousy was present in Indian sexual behavior. The fact that the manifestation of jealousy was hedged by permissive behaviors and implicated in socio-economic rights so complicates the issue that it is not possible to equate jealousy as manifested in the separate societies with any universal configuration. In most societies sexual jealousy tended to be evoked by special situational conditions and was not dependent on a generalized definition of invasion of sexual prerogatives. Jealous anger also tended to be limited to the family, for custom usually muted or diverted the feelings a man might have for a seducer. The Eskimo illustrate this in the public song contests men held when one had induced the wife of another to desert. The winner was determined by his wit and the loser by the public ridicule that followed. The expression of jealousy outside the family was more permissible for women, and when a fight of this kind occurred, men were not inclined to interfere.

Types of Marriage

Like other peoples of the world, most American Indians lived in a state of monogamy. However, polygyny was permitted if not preferred throughout the Americas except where matrilinear descent and matrilocal residence was associated with a horticultural-hunting economy (Iroquois, Cherokee, Hopi, Choroti, Timbíra). In Nuclear America polygyny was confined to the upper classes with virtual harems for the emperor. Paramount chiefs in the Caribbean and adjacent coastal areas also maintained households that included many wives, and the widespread practice of polygyny may explain the equally prevalent homosexuality reported by the Spanish. Both sororal and nonsororal polygyny were practiced, with preference for the former resting on the twin interests of inheritance and harmony. The Tupinamba polygynists usually maintained spouses in different settlements, visiting each in turn.

Social, economic, and political conditions

more often than the simple sex ratio seem to have determined the presence or absence of polygyny in lesser or greater degree. "Exchange marriage," which requires a female in exchange for each one taken as a spouse, is probably a substitute for the passage of consideration or bride-service rather than an exception to social and economic factors (Shoshoni, Patangoro, Amani).

Polyandry occurred sporadically in the Americas, frequently taking the form of a temporary union prior to marriage (Shoshoni). The occurrence of fraternal polyandry among the South American Yaruro and Cawahib implies an institutionalized practice, but polyandrous families were infrequent. The Caingang, described as casual in their regulation of sex, had no more than 14 per cent polyandrous marriages. They also provide the only instance of polygyandrous ("group") marriages, totaling 8 per cent of 308 marriages.

The establishment of households with homosexuals occurred wherever the transvestite was accepted (i.e., everywhere outside Nuclear America). The union usually was a "common law" arrangement, although some were established according to traditional marriage rules. In rare cases the transvestite household was polygynous, but no polyandrous or polygynandrous arrangements have been reported. Marriage with the transvestite was attractive to some because of the economic skills he possessed. In most instances both parties were subjected to frequent ridicule and obscenity.

Coitus

Intercourse usually required a degree of privacy, in darkness or in the seclusion of the bush. Where intercourse with a spouse took place in the daytime, privacy was sought in a thicket or cornfield. Extramarital relations normally occurred away from the dwelling except in those instances when a spouse's approval allowed otherwise or when a "night-crawling" venture was undertaken. Only a few peoples insisted on intercourse taking place in the dwelling at all times (Kwakiutl, Hopi).

Genital manipulation predominated in sexual foreplay, although not to the exclusion of breast and mouth stimulation. Oral stimulation of the female genitals, breasts, thighs, and other body parts apparently did not occur and digital masturbation to arouse the female was not common, some groups objecting to the odor of the female genitalia (Plains). On the whole it would appear as if foreplay was not extended, coitus following almost immediately.

For coitus a woman usually would lie on her back with the man taking position above her and between the outstretched legs. When discretion warranted, partners would lie on the side, facing each other. Intromission occasionally was effected from the rear, both in a prone or in a standing position. In a few societies the woman would squat upon her seated partner, a position said to enhance the pleasure of the female. The Siriono preferred to have the male kneel before his supine partner and draw her legs around his thighs, a position occasionally assumed among the Crow to increase erotic satisfaction in the female. To what extent two or more positions might be assumed in a single connection is not known.

American Indians never developed any standard artificial means for stimulating a female partner or for preventing conception. Generally, women assumed a passive role in the sex act, a posture congruent with the social role usually expected of women. However, the degree of correlation between social-role expectancy and vigorous participation in the sex act is not clear. A generalization from a socially deviant role to the sexual is found among the Piegan, where "manly hearted" women, noted for their sexual vigor, were avoided as mates because of their inclination to dominate husbands. In the Southwest, where women played an important though secondary role in uniting the male and female principles for germinating purposes, Hopi women were known to be active sex partners. Women among the Siriono, Choroti, and Apinayé are said to bite and scratch a partner during orgasm, and in each of these tribes women enjoyed a social status barely inferior to that of the men.

The extent to which women may have reached orgasm in the Indian societies is undocumented. There is no evidence that partners sought to synchronize the orgasms. Crow men tried to stir their partners by deep intromission, but then made no effort to time ejaculation. In view of the premarital sex conditioning to which individuals were subjected in surreptitious encounters, rapid tumescence and ejaculation were probably normal for the male.

The number of successive intromissions attempted apparently was highly variable. Frequency also varied, some peoples reporting intercourse twice a week on the average and some almost daily. Decline in sexual vigor as a person advanced in age is generally admitted, with some cases of people 70 years of age or more effecting intercourse from one to four times a month.

Although passivity is commonly reported for women during the sex act, frigidity is largely undocumented. Passivity or frigidity in a wife was far less disturbing to Tepoztecan males than passion, since the latter raised suspicion of infidelity and heightened insecurity. Situational impotence is occasionally reported, although Tenetehara men may have been subjected to an impotence syndrome with some frequency. Infusions were used to stimulate sexual vigor. The excessive shame and modesty Tenetehara men exhibited is countered by the initiative demonstrated by the women, who, according to myth, first taught men how to copulate.

Although prepubescent sex experience may have proved frustrating to some males and induced an insecurity anxiety occasionally manifest in impotence, these effects probably were erased by early marriage, which allowed unrestricted activity at the peak of physiological vigor. On the other hand, the unwed Araucanian mother might seek to induce impotence in her lover in a bizarre killing of her male infant and roasting of his testicles. Priapism is undocumented, although in the Plains certain individuals always were noted for size of penis and sexual vigor.

Sex and the Life Cycle

American Indian societies considered procreation a necessary requirement for full adult status and role. The burden of fertility fell more heavily on woman than on man, and a husband could always expect sympathetic acceptance of a divorce based on a wife's sterility. Tests for male sterility must have been rare, although

the Arapaho allowed a grandfather to have intercourse with a granddaughter to prove the fault was not hers.

Conception, as birth, was never entirely free of supernaturalistic practices despite the universal belief in the procreative contributions of both sexes. Among the Aymara and Tenetehara, vigorous and continuous intercourse was considered essential to conception but the belief does not seem to have been widespread. Efforts to influence or anticipate the sex of the child were common, and usually made use of some tool, toy, or other item used in the daily life of either sex. Although males were generally valued socially more than females, a decided preference for male children is not in evidence. Any child seems to have been welcome.

Pregnancy taboos usually associated special foods and actions with the health and character of the infant and these more often applied to the mother than to the father. There were no restrictions on sexual intercourse during pregnancy and activity continued to near the time of delivery or when intercourse proved difficult.

The birth of the child was usually followed by restrictions on a husband's sexual contacts with his wife. The time for return to normal sexual relations varied, sometimes following recurrence of menstruation but more often determined by the time of weaning. Weaning might occur at the time of teething, but more often a child would be 2 or 3 years old before the breast was fully denied. Common belief connected renewed intercourse before weaning with spoiling of the milk and weakening of the infant. During the postpartum restriction on sexual relations husbands were not held to strict continence. Where complete weaning was deferred for two or three years, a renewal of relations before this time probably occurred, and apparently without special precautions such as coitus interruptus.

Contraception was unknown. Unwanted pregnancies were simply aborted, usually by mechanical pressure upon the abdomen by pummeling, binding, or pressing against a wooden object. Some use of infusions is reported. Most American Indians treated abortion and infanticide as an individual responsibility, a tolerable way for an unwed mother to avoid humiliation or for a wife to forestall desertion by her husband. However, there was considerable variation in the social acceptance of the practice. Abortion was thoroughly accepted and frequently practiced in most of South America outside the Andean horticulturists. Guaicuru women might abort until they were 25 to 30 years of age, and aborting the first-born was standard practice in the Chaco and in eastern Brazil, with a view to ensuring later and easier births. The Flathead term for abortion is the same as for murder, but feticide occurred nevertheless. The most consistent and severe condemnation of abortion and infanticide, as for adultery, occurred among the organized societies of Nuclear America.

Childhood in American Indian societies involved the inculcation of appropriate conceptions of one's own self, according to sex, and proper attitudes toward the opposite sex. It was a time for educating the individual to the status relationships that permitted sexual and other intimacies in contrast to those that forbade them. Practical instruction in sex was avoided and, where social control was deemed essential to divert and regulate sexual experimentation, fearsome warnings were employed together with the simple device of isolating and supervising the female.

As secondary sexual characteristics appeared to signalize the change in individual life potential, American Indian societies reacted differently. For some puberty meant no more than a change in dress, new responsibilities and activities, or it required special rites of transition to protect the individual and to continue his growth, while for others it called for public ceremonial to announce the new social status attained by the individual. Complex cultural factors seem to be instrumental in determining the differential treatment of the individual at puberty.

Among North American hunter-collectors and hunter-horticulturists, public recognition of puberty with individual or group ceremonial was confined largely to the area west of the Rockies and north of the Pueblo area up to the Eskimo. Public ceremonial applied more often to the girl than to the boy. It appears that the physiological changes manifested by a girl at puberty were viewed as critical for the indi-

vidual's total development and immediately relevant to the welfare of the community. Personal character was determined by actions that symbolized desirable qualities, especially industry, in the adult. Thus, adolescent girls in their confinement at the menarche were kept busy, often carrying water and bringing in wood. The ill-contained and ill-disposed power for procreation and growth developing in the individual required that a girl cover her eyes and look at the ground, for if she were to glance abroad a man's hunting and other luck would be damaged and plant growth would not thrive. Those who controlled supernatural powers, especially the shamans and mature men, must dance and sing over the menstruant, for in this way the incipient power could be controlled and used for the benefit of all. "Mission" Indians such as the Luiseno of southern California added a new note to this general complex in constructing a warm sand-pit bed for the girls, who were guarded and fed by older women. The care accorded the girls at this time included rehearsals of practices usually employed at childbirth. Certain moral admonitions also were given by the shaman.

Seclusion of women at initial and subsequent menstruations was also common in South America. Men avoided them for fear of loss of powers, and often they were denied foods supplied by men or used by the community as a staple. In parts of Venezuela and Colombia it was customary for women to be secluded in a special, often circular, hut at first and subsequent menstruations (Popayense, Moguex, Paez). Along the Venezuelan coast south to the Orinoco the Carib-speaking tribes kept the hut darkened and required fasting of the menstruant. Seclusion for two years might occur at the menarche, the time apparently varying with the status of the girl's family. Some groups, like the Goajiro, kept the menstruant in a hammock within a darkened room until her hair, which had been cut, grew to neck length. While secluded she was taught how to weave and sew and to make hammocks. Generally, she was guarded by several relatives, for men with an eye to matrimony were privileged to look in. The Ona and Yahgan of Tierra del Fuego isolated the girl at first menstruation under the direction of an older woman, who admonished her with moral counsel. Commonly in the Chaco lowlands, Choroti, Mataco, Ashluslay, and Lengua girls were confined to a special hut and restrained from eating meat foods while older women danced and pummeled the earth throughout the night with special staffs adorned with rattles or other noisemakers. Shamans usually participated, and dances by men and occasionally by young men and boys might be included.

Where social status set the tone for family distinctions, seclusion of the girl at the menarche might be prolonged to ensure her chastity and marriageability. On the Northwest Coast the girl was confined to the dwelling behind a screen for upwards of a year while her father readied property to distribute to the opposite moiety in order that she would enter society with a good name. This feast at nubility finds an interesting parallel among the horse-raiding warrior Mbaya and Toba of South America where, besides the slaughter and distribution of horses, a chief tried also to include a scalp to enhance his daughter's status.

In contrast with the peoples of simpler economies, the advanced horticulturists in Nuclear America, including the American Southwest, gave little formal recognition to menstruation at puberty or later. A Hopi girl usually went to the home of a paternal aunt, where she remained behind a curtain and ground corn. She had to retrain from eating meat and salt and used a forked stick to scratch her head. When the flow had ceased, the aunt washed her head and the girl returned home.

Throughout North America north of Mexico, recognition of male puberty was submerged in the search for a supernatural power (guardian spirit) that would implement and guarantee skill in hunting, warring, prophesying, gambling, etc. (Eskimo and Southwest excepted). The venture was framed as an ordeal and a test of the individual, since fasting, endurance, and exposure to the elements without creature comforts was common. In the Southeast fasting, purifying emetics, scarification, and other ordeals were frequently tied to the transition to adult status, later confirmed by a warrior action. West Alaskan Eskimo and adjacent Indian groups, as well as central Californians, accepted pubescent youths into men's houses, where they were instructed in adult skills, but only the latter had special ceremonials to bring the adolescent into contact with supernaturals, as in the Kuksu and "ghost" cults.

Where the individualized guardian-spirit quest was recognizably weak or lacking in the presence of social recognition of puberty, group ceremonials that included instruction tended to be the rule. Moreover, the ceremonials usually concerned the adolescent boys, although a number of instances where girls were included also occurred (Yahgan, Alacaluf, Pomo, Patwin, Hopi, Zuni).

Ordeals of one kind or another were always present in group ceremonials more or less correlated with sexual maturation. Yahgan and Alacaluf novices had to remain quiet, sitting cross-legged, while learning moral precepts and instruction in the arts. North of the Amazon youths were subjected to whippings, scarifications, and the stings of ants and wasps (Taulipans, Aparani). The Inca, Hopi, and Zuni also included a ceremonial whipping in their initiatory rites. Most of these actions seem to have been designed to purify the individual, promote health and character, and contribute a lucky quality to his life. Completion of the ceremonial cycle was usually symbolized by the donning of adult clothing or special ornament, and by the assumption of new responsibilities, including marriage which might follow soon.

Puberty rites must be viewed within the total socialization process. Sex intruded obliquely, for control of the emergent procreative powers and practical and moral instruction in adult skills and responsibilities were more evident than any focus on sex. Molding of the genitalia by circumcision and clitoridectomy did not constitute a part of the puberty cycle. Circumcision has been reported for the prehistoric Mochica, Sumo, Saliva, Achagua, and possibly Diaguita, but the operation seems to have been performed in infancy. Circumcision was apparently confined to northern South America, although a few circumcised individuals were observed among the Algonquian Machapunga (Southeast) in Colonial times.

The sexual life of the individual in Indian societies synchronized well with the peak of sexual vigor, since marriage followed shortly after puberty and was seldom deferred after 20 years for men. The prevalent naturalistic attitude toward sex placed no blanket injunction upon its expression but confined restraint to specific relationships and ceremonial circumstances. Arranged marriages may have had muted romantic love but tied spouses to a larger kin group that facilitated retention of widows and widowers within the family line and provided them with spouses, often through the operation of the levirate and sororate. The linking of sex to kinship and hospitality obligations extended relations outside the conjugal family with public approval and mitigated feelings of guilt and sexual jealousy that might otherwise attend extramarital relations. Sexual expression was denied to none. The male transvestite might be ridiculed for his efforts to simulate menstruation and childbirth, but his deviant expression was accepted as an alternative.

Sexual activity was apparently valued throughout life, although diminishing in frequency with age. Women after the menopause were relieved of the menstrual and ceremonial restriction to which they had been subject. However, social definitions of role never permitted women formal equality with men, who retained control over procreation and growth through their capacity to influence and direct the supernatural in appropriate ritual.

References

Alexander, H. B. (ed.), *Mythology of All Races.* Vol. X, *North American;* Vol. XI, *Latin American.* Boston: Marshall Jones Co., 1916, 1920.

Dennis, W., *The Hopi Child.* New York: Appleton-Century-Crofts, Inc., 1940.

Devereux, G., *A Study of Abortion in Primitive Societies.* New York: Julian Press, Inc., 1955.

Driver, H. E., "Girls' Puberty Rites in Western North America." In *Anthropological Records.* Berkeley, Calif.: University of California Press, Vol. VI, 21-90, 1941.

Dyk, W., *Son of Old Man Hat.* New York: Harcourt, Brace & Co., 1938.

Erikson, E. H., "Observation on Sioux Education." *J. Psychol.* 7; 101-156, 1939.

Erikson, E. H., "Observations on the Yurok: Childhood and World Image." In *University of California Publications in American Archaeology and Ethnology.* Berkeley, Calif.: University of California Press, Vol. 35, No. 10, 1943.

Ford, C. S., *Smoke from Their Fires, the Life of a Kwakiutl Chief.* New Haven: Yale University Press, 1951.

Ford, C. S., and Beach, F. A., *Patterns of Sexual Behavior.* New York: Harper & Brothers, 1953.

Henry, J., *Jungle People.* New York: J. J. Augustin, Inc., 1941.

Henry, J., "The Social Function of Child Sexuality in Pilagá Indian Culture." In P. Hoch and J. Zubin (eds.), *Psychosexual Development in Health and Disease.* New York: Grune & Stratton, Inc., 1949.

Holmberg, A., *Nomads of the Long Bow. The Sirono of Eastern Bolivia.* Washington: Smithsonian Institution of Social Anthropology, Publication No. 10, 1950.

Kroeber, A. L., *Handbook of the Indians of California.* Washington: Bureau of American Ethnology, Bulletin 78, 1925.

Landes, R., *The Ojibwa Woman.* New York: Columbia University Press, 1938.

Leighton, D., and Kluckhohn, C., *Children of the People.* Cambridge, Mass.: Harvard University Press, 1947.

Lewis, O., *Life in a Mexican Village: Tepoztlán Restudied.* Urbana: University of Illinois Press, 1951.

Opler, M., *An Apache Life Way.* Chicago: University of Chicago Press, 1941.

Ray, V. F., "Plateau." In *Anthropological Records.* Berkeley, Calif.: University of California Press, Vol. VIII, 99-257, 1941.

Simmons, L., *Sun Chief, the Autobiography of a Hopi Indian.* New Haven: Yale University Press, 1942.

Steward, J. H. (ed.), *Handbook of South American Indians.* Washington: Smithsonian Institution, Bureau of American Ethnology, Bulletin 143, Vols. 1-5, 1946.

Steward, J. H., and Faron, L. C., *Native Peoples of South America.* New York: McGraw-Hill Book Co., 1959.

Thompson, Stith, *Tales of the North American Indians.* Cambridge, Mass.: Harvard University Press, 1929.

FRED W. VOGET

Anatomy and Physiology of Sex

ANATOMY and physiology constitute the most natural defining characteristics of sex. The word "anatomy" comes from the Greek and means literally a cutting apart. Anatomy is divisible into gross anatomy, embryology, histology, and various subdivisions of these areas. Thus, a true anatomical description should include developmental data (embryology) and also microscopic data (histology). As will be shown later, both of these subdivisions are of extreme importance in the basic understanding of sexual differentiation.

Physiology, too, is a word that comes from the Greek (*physis*, nature; *logos*, a study). Physiology took on the specific meaning of "the study of bodily function" in the work of Fernel (1497–1558). The relationship of structure to function is a basic problem in the biological sciences and is pertinent also to the study of the behaving organism.

Perhaps it is appropriate to begin this article with consideration of the development of sexual differences. These differences, which are laid down in the genetics of the offspring, are manifest later in the sexual differentiation of males and females.

Sex Differences

Throughout life, male and female organisms display a demonstrable cellular distinctness. This finding was first reported by Barr and his co-workers (1958) for the nerve cell of the cat, and has been extended to the human being. Barr, in describing his finding, said, "In the female a body about 1 millimicron in diameter appears as a small satellite to the large nucleolus in all types of nerve cells examined. In the male, a nucleolar satellite is seldom seen distinctly. There is evidence that male nerve cells contain a nucleolar satellite so small that it lies at the limits of resolution with standard optical equipment."

The human data have been productive in the same direction, and Kupperman (1958) has gone so far as to assume that "males" with bodily cells showing the female pattern (and vice versa) cannot beget offspring.

The nucleolar satellite, which looks like a drumstick, is regarded as the extra X of the female reproductive cells. However, those who possess it may develop to look like males, whereas those without it may look like females. This suggests that the gross appearance of the person depends greatly on factors other than nuclear sex.

Embryology

Patten (1946) points out that if an individual is going to be a male, the cords of potential sex cells become more distinctly delimited from the intervening embryonic connective tissue. These cords may then be regarded properly as testis cords. Concurrently, the developing ovary (female gonad) is much less conspicuous in terms of the connective tissue under its covering of germinal epithelium.

By the sixteenth week, the testis becomes more rounded and more characteristically gonadal. Its connection to the mesonephros (primitive kidney) is reduced to a mesentery-like attachment. The mesenchymal concentration around the mesonephric duct develops into the ductus deferens.

An anastomosing network of cells in the form of cords is involved in the meshwork of duct formations that will ultimately become the adult rete testis (*rete,* a net).

The development of the ovary is quite distinct from that of the male gonads. Finally, some of the germ cells present in the mesenchymal stroma exceed others in size and develop into primary ovarian follicles. By the time a fetus enters the world, the follicles resemble closely the younger follicles of the adult ovary. These young follicles may form a small antrum, according to Patten, probably as a result of maternal gonad-stimulating hormones affecting the fetus (*antron,* a cavity).

It is important to remember that one pair of the embryonic genital ducts is potentially male and the other potentially female. In the male, there is a shrinking away and ultimate disappearance of the female genital ducts. This takes place at about the sixth or seventh week. The female system is such that there are major changes at about the twelfth week. The male characteristics shrink away and largely disappear and the female characteristics elaborate into the internal genitalia.

The male ducts are actually appropriated from the primitive kidney, the mesonephros. Some of the tubules become connected with the gonad that is developing and the duct of the mesonephros is used as a discharge passage for the sex cells.

The forerunners of specific sexual development are the Wolffian ducts and the Müllerian ducts for the male and female, respectively.

If one were to simplify the above, it could be said that in both male and female a similar pair of sex glands appears, as well as two pairs of genital tubes. In the male, under proper genetic and endocrine action, the glands become testes which, in turn, stimulate the male tubes while the female tubes shrink away. A reverse condition occurs in the female, where the ovaries act upon the female tubes with a shrinking of the male tubes.

In the male at this time, the testes, still present in the abdominal cavity, attach to the tubes and begin a descent. The prostate gland forms, as does the scrotal sac. The male organ, the penis, develops. It is at about the third month of life that the external organs become distinguishable as male and female. The genital tubercle, the major external projection in the male, becomes the terminal aspect of the penis; in the female it remains as the clitoris.

Internally, the female ducts, which have receded, in the male remain as a vestigial female organ. To the sides and slightly behind the penis are two raised areas known as the urethral folds. These close over the urethral groove to form a tube, thus lengthening the male urethra (or urinary outlet). This occurs at the end of the third month. It is to be noted that the orifice of the male urogenital system is moved to the distal end of the penis from its original position at the base. The line of closure of the urethral groove remains as a deeply pigmented line on the underside of the penis and is known as the penile raphé. A similar scarlike vestige is the scrotal raphé. The prepuce develops over the glans penis as a potential skin fold.

In the female, the urethral folds remain separate and form the labia minora (inner lips). Two other swellings, the labioscrotal folds, fuse in the male to form the scrotum (the external sac that envelops the testes). In the female they form the outer lips, or labia majora.

Anatomy

The term "gonad" refers to a seed. It is a function of the gonads (sex glands) to produce the sexual seed. However, as glands they are also involved in the hormonal interplay of the body. It is necessary to recognize that the anatomy and physiology of sex involve much more than reproduction alone. This is clear when it is understood that sex anatomy is a central aspect of the total developing personality and that the cultural organization forms around the sex role of the individual.

Male

The male gonads are the testes, and these and the ovaries, the female glands, arise embryologically from the same tissue and are formed at the same site. The testes descend through the inguinal canal and enter the scrotal sac, where they remain during the life of the person. This descent takes place before birth at about the sixth or the seventh month. The testes, two in number, are oval bodies, somewhat flattened in shape and measuring one to one and a half inches in length. It is said by Dickinson (1949), after Testut and Jacob, that the testicle-epididymis oval hangs between the thighs at an angle of 45 degrees. The scrotum, or containing sac, is sensitive, as is the penis, to changes in temperature, and it may be high or low under various conditions. Usually the left testis is a little lower than the right and is said to be heavier, but evidence to prove this is lacking.

Apparently when the testis is undescended (a condition known as cryptorchidism), the heat of the abdominal cavity destroys the sperm. Dickinson points out that heat tolerable to the hand can, in a half-hour, arrest sperm manufacture for weeks.

Each testis can be examined grossly to get a three-dimensional view and under the microscope for detail. A large number of coiled tubules that produce the male sex cells is a major component of the testis. These empty into the larger tubules of the epididymis, which are present in a caplike mass lying upon the back and upper part of each testis. These efferent ducts are here connected with the tube that forms the remainder of the epididymis. If uncoiled this tube would stretch some twenty feet. The tail of the epididymis is connected to the testis only by connective tissue, and becomes the vas deferens (ductus deferens).

The tubules of the testis, or the seminiferous tubules, produce the male cells, and between them lie the cells of Leydig, which are involved in the production of the male hormone, testosterone. This endocrine secretion is an androgen, and all male hormones are grouped under this term (andro, man). Testosterone is the effective male principle, and as a hormone it is secreted by a ductless gland into the blood stream and produces widespread alterations of a masculine kind.

The ductus deferens (or vas deferens) passes upward over the brim of the pelvis and emerges in the lower part of the abdomen. Here, a little canal connects each duct to a saclike structure,

the seminal vesicle. This tube is two inches long in situ, but unravels to six inches or more. It is disputed as to whether sperm storage can occur herein; although it has been said that live sperm can be found in an ejaculate two weeks after the vas has been tied in sterilization. The seminal vesicles lie between the bladder and the rectum and they secrete a material that seems to add to the motility of the sperm.

The terminal portion of each ductus deferens, where it joins the seminal vesicle, is known as an ejaculatory duct. It is a fine tube, lies almost entirely within the prostate, and opens into the prostatic part of the urethra. The ejaculatory duct is closed under ordinary circumstances, but during the peak of sexual excitement it opens, allowing semen to pass through.

The prostate is a firm, globular mass that surrounds the urethra, or urinary outlet. It is located behind the second portion of the rectum at the bladder neck, and can be palpated rectally. It has the size and shape of a horse chestnut. The prostate reaches adult size in the third decade and increases slightly, under normal circumstances, during the fifth and sixth decades. Ordinarily this increase is followed by a recession thereafter to lesser size.

In rutting animals the gland is influenced by seasonal changes. One must be cautious about estimations of prostatic size. The prostate is about one and a half inches at the base and has a normal weight of 20 grams. However, according to Mainland (1945), this is an arbitrary figure. It is made up of various tissues. A tubuloalveolar structure characterizes the prostate. The folliclelike tubules are each equipped with excretory ducts, which open into the prostatic urethra. Smooth-muscle cells and elastic-tissue fibers compose the musculoconnective aspect of the gland. It is the smooth-muscle fibers that empty the tubules during contraction. The nerve fibers of the prostate arise in the hypogastric plexus and in the third and fourth sacral nerves. In the female, a small amount of tissue that is connected to the urethra corresponds to the prostate of the male. Lowsley (1942) points out that as late as 1889 the entire subject of prostatic anatomy was in a state of confusion.

At the time of ejaculation there is a release of fluids from the seminal vesicles and prostate, and of sperm from each epididymis. The external secretion that is produced, together with the secretions of the other male genital glands, forms the seminal fluid. Each ejaculate that is carried through the penis contains some 120,000,000 sperm cells and a little less than a teaspoonful of fluid.

Cowper's glands, also known as the bulbourethral glands, are two lobular membranous bodies located behind and lateral to the membranous portion of the urethra. They are each about the size of a pea, and correspond embryologically to the glands of Bartholin in the female. Under sexual excitation these structures release a slippery substance that lubricates the glans penis. It was claimed among early moralistic writers that this substance resulted from lascivious thinking. Dickinson indicates that Cowper's secretion makes the urethra alkaline, so that the sperm are in a favorable milieu during their passage. Although some writers have attributed a mucoid secretion to Cowper's glands, it is possible that the glands of Littré, which are located along the urethra, may be responsible for mucus secretion during sexual excitement.

Mann (1954) has elaborated on the more recent data regarding the chemical nature of the accessory secretions in the male. Citric acid, prostatic phosphatase, fructose, and phosphorylcholine, among others, have been discovered and identified. It is significant that the prostatic secretion contains a fibrinolysin so potent that 2 ml. of prostatic fluid can liquefy 100 ml. of clotted human blood in 18 hours at 37° C. Obviously, previous doubt with reference to the function of the accessory fluids must be re-evaluated. Seminal plasma contains secretions that are involved in the process of semen coagulation and liquefaction. It was suggested by several investigators that a pharmacodynamic influence may be exerted by the seminal plasma upon some parts of the female reproductive tract. As yet this has been demonstrated only with isolated strips of tissue of the uterus or the attached tubes.

The penis varies in length at different times. Numerical studies presented by Dickinson show the flaccid penis to be 10 cm. (4 inches) in length, 3 cm. (1⅛ inches) in diameter, and 8.5 cm. (3⅜ inches) in circumference. During erection it is 15.5 cm. (6 inches) long, 4 cm. (1⅝ inches) broad, and 11 cm. (4⅜ inches) around. There are considerable individual differences. Dickinson points out that the size of the penis is less constantly related to general body size than that of other organs of the body. It is presumably rare, except in pathology, to find exceptionally small penes.

The penis is composed of the glans (head), the shaft (middle portion), and the root, which consists of the attachment of the penis to the front and sides of the pubic arch. In the flaccid condition it is cylindrical in form, but during erection it takes the shape of a triangular prism. Ordinarily, it hangs loosely downward, but when erect it points upward and toward the abdominal wall.

Three longitudinal cylindrical masses composed of erectile tissue form the penis. They are the corpora cavernosa penis and the corpus cavernosum urethrae (sometimes called the corpus spongiosum). The first two lie on top and the third lies below the other two and is pierced by the urethra. Connective tissue and skin bind these together somewhat in the form of a bundle.

Each corpus cavernosum penis is attached to the descending ramus (arm) of the pubis. The corpus cavernosum urethrae is extended backward to the urethral bulb, and in the front it expands into the tip of the organ, the glans penis, which is conelike and smooth. The fold of skin that surrounds the glans is called the prepuce. The word "glans" is from the Latin word meaning acorn.

Each of the three extensions of the penis (backward) is covered by a small muscle. The bulbocavernosus muscle lies over the urethral bulb, while the ischiocavernosus muscles lie over the other two parts. The role of the first muscle is, by contraction, to cause urine and seminal fluid to be expelled from the urethra. The second muscles prevent the blood from returning from the veins of the penis. In this way the penis can be maintained erect during sexual excitement. The change between the flaccid and rigid state of the penis is of particular interest.

Since the male urethra is a common channel for the transportation of both urine and seminal fluid, it shall be briefly described. It originates at the internal sphincter of the bladder, pierces the prostate near its anterior surface, and follows the ventral surface of the penis to the glans. En route, it goes through the two layers of the triangular ligament. It is eight to nine inches long and is divided into posterior and anterior portions. The posterior portion contains the membranous and prostatic parts of the urethra, the anterior portion contains the bulbous and penile parts. The course of the urethra is downward from the bladder for three-quarters of an inch, and then downward and forward to the bulbous area. It then passes in an upward and forward direction to the peno-scrotal junction. Finally, it lies in a downward direction when the penis is flaccid.

(It is important to make note of a little body on the floor of the prostatic urethra, the veru-montanum. This lies between the prostatic ducts. It is composed of erectile tissue, blood vessels, muscle, and nerve. This tiny mound, some few decades ago, was regarded as a key to male sexual problems. It was, in fact, believed essential for erection—which it is not.)

The male germ cells develop in the seminiferous tubules, where they are being formed constantly. The process is known as maturation. It begins with a cell, the spermatogonium. This cell eventually becomes the sperm, after going through a developmental process. In a similar manner the ovum of the female develops from an oogonium to a primary oocyte, a secondary oocyte, and then to an ovum (egg cell). It is beyond the scope of this article to go into the details of the intricate process of the development of the germ cells. However, it is to be noted that when sperms or eggs are formed, it is in such a manner that the two genes of each pair present in the parent become separated. Thus, only one gene of a given pair goes from a parent to an offspring. The word gene means "to produce" or "be produced." The genes within the chromosomes (Greek *chroma*, color; *soma*, body) are involved in the heredity of the individual.

The differentiation of the male and female fetus has been discussed. The genital characteristics of the mature male have been described. The mature female becomes the site in which the fertilized ovum develops into the fore-runner of the eventual newborn.

Female

The female sex glands are the ovaries. Two in number, they lie deep in the pelvic cavity, one on either side of the uterus, or womb. The ovaries weigh two or three grams and are spherical in form. They are about one inch in length, and are supported from above by a fold of peritoneum (a thin, glistening membrane that lines the abdominal cavity and continues on to the pelvic contents). This fold of peritoneum is called the suspensory ligament.

In the ovaries are developed the Graafian follicles (named after Regner de Graaf, 1641–1673). A follicle is a little bag or a pod. At birth these follicles are often referred to as primordial follicles. In the newborn girl, it is estimated that there are some 400,000, but these diminish with age and, after the menopause, vanish totally. Each primordial follicle consists of an oocyte that is surrounded by a single layer of epithelial cells. In time the oocyte becomes the mature ovum, this process beginning at puberty. Presumably one follicle ripens each month, usually midway between two menstrual periods. Menstruation is the uterine bleeding and expulsion of the unfertilized egg that marks the onset of pubescence. It is to be noted that the expulsion of ova does not necessarily occur at the menarche (first menstrual period). There is thus some evidence for a period of adolescent infertility.

The ovum is carried down into the Fallopian tubes to the uterus. These tubes, named after Gabriello Fallopio (1523–1562), a great Italian anatomist, are connected to the upper sides of the pear-shaped womb. They run sideward and are in the front in the free borders of the broad ligament. Some four inches in length, they arch upward and backward over the ovary, forming a funnel-shaped structure with fingerlike processes, some of which are attached to the ovary.

Immediately after the ovum is released (ovulation), a red spot (blood) marks the follicle. This gives way rapidly to a yellow substance, the corpus luteum. If pregnancy does not occur, the corpus luteum is replaced by a white, fibrous structure, the corpus albicans, or corpus fibrosum.

The ovaries also produce two hormones,

estrin and progestin (estrogen and progesterone).

The trumpet-shaped Fallopian tubes are presumed to play a role in directing the ovum in its course. However, there are cases on record where the ovum has entered a Fallopian tube on the opposite side of the body (following surgical removal of one Fallopian tube and the opposite ovary).

The inner aspect of the Fallopian tubes is made of tissue that has many hairlike processes. These may act by directing the ovum toward the womb. The openings from the Fallopian tubes into the womb are minute. It is thus clear that total patency of the tubes is necessary for impregnation to occur. Rubin demonstrated in 1919 that oxygen passed into the uterus would then pass through the tubes and into the abdominal area.

The uterus is a pear-shaped organ about three inches in length. The larger or upper portion is the body and the lower part is the cervix (neck). The uterus is flattened in a front-back direction. Normally, it lies tilted forward with the neck pointed toward the rectum. It meets the vagina at an angle of 90 degrees. The uterus lies above and behind the urinary bladder. The walls are very thick and the central cavity of the uterus is triangular in shape and small. Several ligaments hold the organ in place, two broad ligaments and two round ligaments. The walls of the uterus consist of an inner mucosal layer, a middle muscular layer, and an outer serous coat. The muscular layer is the major part of the uterus and is made up of smooth muscle.

The vagina (sheath or scabbard) is a tube that passes from the external opening to the cervix of the uterus. It lies between the bladder, the urethra, and the rectum. It is about three inches long and varies in size and shape with change of position. When a woman is standing its direction is backward and upward in such a way as to form the approximation of a right angle with the uterus. The front and back walls of the vaginal canal are collapsed or in contact with each other when a woman is standing or prone.

The vaginal walls are lined with a mucous membrane, containing transverse folds. In addition to the mucosa, the walls consist of a muscular layer and an outer fibrous coat. The posterior wall of the vagina is actually two to three inches longer than the anterior wall and a long cervical lip is formed in the back. A shorter lip is formed in the front. The result is a circular depression around the cervix, which thus extends into the vagina. This circular recess around the cervix is divided into four parts, the anterior, posterior, and two lateral fornices (arches or vaults). The posterior aspect of the depression is known as the cul-de-sac (bottom of a bag) of Douglas. This is a pouch that lies between the anterior wall of the rectum and the posterior wall of the uterus. Because it forms a relatively thin bridge between the external vaginal area and the intra-abdominal contents it has taken on significance in recent years: By piercing this area and introducing an instrument known as a culdoscope, it is possible to visualize directly the ovaries and the related field.

The obvious functions of the vagina are to accommodate coital intromission of the penis, to permit discharge of the menstrual fluid, and to serve as the birth canal during normal delivery.

The female external genitals are referred to as the vulva or, more rarely, as the pudendum (that of which one should be ashamed). The most superficial of these is the mons pubis, known also as the mons veneris. The mons pubis is in front of the pubic symphysis (grown-together bone) and becomes covered with hair after puberty. The hair pattern assumes the shape of an inverted triangle in the female and the sides of the triangle are delimited by the groin. Considerable variability in the hair distribution occurs.

The labia majora (major lips) are two large folds that meet in the midline of the body below the pubic arch. When a woman is in standing posture, the labia cover most of the other external genitals. They extend backward, gradually become less thick, and disappear in the region of the perineum. The perineum contains all those structures between the vulva and the anus in the female (between the scrotum and the anus in the male). Anatomists make clear that the perineum extends in a vertical plane; however, there is some dispute as to what it contains.

When the labia majora are separated, the remainder of the external female sex organs become visible. Inside the major lips lie the labia minora (minor lips). They form an angle that includes an area known as the vestibule. The vaginal opening is in this area. At the front apex of the minor lips and above the urinary opening lies the clitoris. This is the homologue of the penis in the male and shows, under stimulation, the same characteristic of erection. It is covered by a fold of skin, the prepuce, and the tip is called the glans.

The vaginal orifice is partially closed, before initial sexual intercourse, by a thin membrane, the hymen. Rarely, the vaginal orifice may remain closed even during pregnancy. The hymen is a tissue that may take several possible forms. Sometimes it completely covers the opening, preventing egress of the menstrual material. Sometimes it consists of a fold of tissue that is perforated by several openings (hymen cribriforms) or divided by an anteroposterior septum (hymen biseptus). Usually it is perforated by a single opening of varying outline.

Skene's glands lie just inside and in the back of the female urethra, a separate tube that extends from the bladder downward and forward behind the symphysis pubis.

The glands of Bartholin, known also as the greater vestibular glands, are located one on each side of the vaginal opening at the base of the labia majora. They secrete a mucous fluid that acts as a lubricant during intercourse.

Physiology

The physiology of sex and reproduction is intimately bound up with endocrinology and neurology.

Removal of the testes before puberty inhibits the normal course of male development, just as removal of the ovaries at this time inhibits female development. The effect in both cases is to intrude upon the growth of secondary sexual characteristics.

Male

In the case of the removal of testes in the male, the effect is a juvenile-appearing, but often very tall and physically feminine, person.

Such prepubertal castrates are called eunuchs. It is important to remember that the sex glands are in constant interplay with the pituitary gland, as well as with stimuli from the external environment. The other glands of the endocrine system also play a major role. The male sex hormones have effects other than those of a primarily sexual nature. They increase nitrogen retention, as well as retention of phosphorus, potassium, sodium, sulfur, and other elements that play a role in tissue formation. In addition, these sex hormones, especially testosterone propionate, stimulate muscular development.

The male pituitary secretes two hormones that act on the testis. These are the follicle-stimulating hormone (FSH) and the interstitial cell-stimulating hormone (ICSH). FSH seems to act on the seminiferous tubules, while ICSH acts on the interstitial cells of Leydig. The ICSH has a reciprocal relationship with testosterone; thus, one may speculate as to whether there is any aspect of rhythm in the male sexual drive, as well as in sperm production. This has not been established.

Androgens have widespread anatomical and physiological effects. Hair growth, voice characteristics, skin quality, and body form are all under the influence of androgens.

Female

Female sexual physiology is more involved than that of the male. Of particular importance is the distinct periodicity of ovulation and menstruation.

Removal of the ovaries produces alterations in the total organism, the degree of change depending upon the age of the female at the time of removal. If removal is before puberty, the secondary sexual characteristics fail to develop. If removal is after puberty, the characteristics that are distinctly female regress to some extent.

Estrin (also referred to as estrogen) is secreted by the maturing follicle and seems to be the major female sex hormone. There are three gonadotrophic hormones known at the present time. They are the FSH (follicle-stimulating) hormone, the luteinizing hormone, and the luteotrophic hormone. These are secreted by the pituitary. There is also a placental hormone, which has some of the properties of the foregoing hormones. This is referred to as the APL substance, i.e., anterior pituitarylike hormone. Since the placenta develops during pregnancy, the APL appears only at that time. (The placenta is the afterbirth and is attached to the wall of the uterus during pregnancy.)

FSH is carried from the pituitary to the ovaries by way of the blood stream and is involved in the growth and activity of the Graafian follicles. Large quantities of FSH administered to a female stimulate the ripening and expulsion of many ova at one time.

As a concomitant function FSH also increases the production of estrin. When the level of estrin rises, FSH is inhibited, and vice versa, a reciprocal characteristic of the endocrine system.

The corpus luteum, the body left after the rupture of the follicle, secretes progesterone. The maintenance of the corpus luteum seems significant for the pregnant uterus, and LH, or the luteinizing hormone, appears to act in a manner that fulfills this function.

Luteotropic hormone (called also lactogenic hormone, or prolactin) is necessary for the secretory activity of the breasts and may also have a function in the maintenance of the corpus luteum during later stages of pregnancy.

The human female shows a cycle as do females of other species notably old-world monkeys and primates above this level.

When the uterine arteries are subjected for two to six days to anoxemia, dehydration, and ischemia (local anemia), an inflow of blood under pressure brings about menstrual bleeding (Phelps, 1959). In other words, circulatory deprivation is the immediate cause of the menstrual flow. The local mechanism is the constriction of the spiral arteries in the womb. Markee believed that the cause of the stasis that weakens the vessel wall may be the shrinking, buckling, and coiling of the arteries. A special substance, as yet unknown, may initiate the vasoconstriction of the arteries. The arterial coiling, however, does not cause the breakdown of tissue that produces the menstrual flow. It is a concurrent phenomenon.

Hormones from the ovaries appear to control the changes in the wall (endometrium) of the womb. The preovulatory phase seems to be a response to estrogen. Estrogenic hormones

stimulate the pituitary gland to secrete luteinizing hormone, which brings about ovulation. The appearance of the corpus luteum is accompanied by an output of progesterone (progestin). There is also an increase in estrogen (estrin). At this time, the postovulatory phase, there is a secretory or progestational stage of the cycle. Gonadotropins from the pituitary are inhibited, and finally there is a fall in estrogen and progesterone secretion. According to Corner, this fall is the cause of menstruation.

At the time of ovulation, estrogen is very high in the blood. As the corpus luteum secretes progesterone, the estrogen level decreases. These two hormones together seem to cause thickening of the mucosa of the womb. If the ovum is not fertilized, the corpus luteum degenerates and the hormonal level in the blood drops. This, as noted above, seems to be the critical period for the breakdown in the uterine wall.

Reynolds (1952) proposes the following hypothesis with reference to the menstrual mechanism:

1. When there is no fertilized ovum, the growth-promoting action of the ovarian hormones is withdrawn.

2. There is then a thinning of the endometrium. This occurs if coiled arterioles are present. The tissue breakdown, and the stasis before it, give rise in the endometrium to a substance that acts as a powerful constrictor of vessels.

3. If there are no coiled arterioles, there is still an accumulation of fluid in the tissue. When the growth stimulus of the ovarian hormone is removed, the tissue shows a diminished vascularity. Tissue fluid is retained and lymphatic drainage is not equal to the burden it must handle. This may account for the menstrual breakdown.

The beginning of menstruation is at puberty (anywhere from 11 to 17 years of age). Menarche is the term that signifies the onset of bleeding. The cycle is repeated about every 28 to 30 days, with some variability.

The onset and maintenance of bleeding is often referred to as the destructive phase. It is a period that lasts from three to seven days with an average of four or five. For the entire phase, the amount of blood is about a cupful (125 ml.). The discharge consists of debris sloughed off from the uterine wall, as well as of blood. Both fibrinogen and thrombin, involved in blood clotting, are not present in menstrual blood. As a result, this blood does not ordinarily clot.

Following the flow, the uterine wall is very thin. This is a period of growth and it is stimulated by the follicular hormone, estrin. This phase lasts about 13 days and is followed by ovulation. The latter occurs at about the fourteenth day and the corpus luteum develops at this time. The control of the corpus luteum seems to be under LH.

How the cycle is regulated is still not totally clear. It is known that, at the end of the flow, estrin concentration is low in the blood. Thus, FSH secretion is increased. This causes maturation of a Graafian follicle and the production of estrin which, in turn, inhibits FSH. Ovulation occurs and the corpus luteum then forms. Progestin concentration is, at this time, low. LH, therefore, is secreted liberally by the pituitary. The corpus luteum then produces progestin. When the progestin level is high, LH is inhibited, the corpus luteum breaks down, estrin and progestin vanish, and the cycle is reinstated.

Of course, much more is involved, and the area is open for considerable research. One may speculate about the role the menstrual cycle plays in behavior, and vice versa. What is the role of the nervous system? How does the cycle differentiate male from female? The questions are intricate and thought-provoking.

References

Barr, Murray L., Bertram, Lee Fraser, and Lindsay, Hugh A., "The Morphology of the Nerve Cell Nucleus, According to Sex." *Anat. Rec. 107;* 283-297, 1958.

Dickinson, Robert Latou, *Human Sex Anatomy.* Baltimore: The Williams & Wilkins Co., 1949.

Kupperman, Herbert S., "Chromatin Sex Determination: III. Endocrinologic Implications and Clinical Value of Chromatin Sex Determination." *Trans. New York Acad. Sci.* (Series II.) *20;* 505-576, 1958.

Lowsley, Oswald Swinney, "The Prostate Gland." In Oswald Swinney Lowsley (ed.), *The Sexual Glands of the Male.* New York: Oxford University Press, 1942.

Mainland, Donald, *Anatomy.* New York: Paul B. Hoeber, Inc., 1945.

Mann, T., *The Biochemistry of Semen.* London: Methuen & Co., 1954.

Marshall, Clyde, *An Introduction to Human Anatomy.* Philadelphia: W. B. Saunders Co., 1941.

Masters, W. H., and Johnson, V. E., "The Human Female: Anatomy of Sexual Response. *Minn. Med. 43;* 31-36, 1960.

Patten, Bradley M., *Human Embryology.* Philadelphia: The Blakiston Co., 1946.

Phelps, Doris, "Menstruation." In J. T. Velardo (ed.), *Essentials of Human Reproduction.* New York: Oxford University Press, 1959.

Potter, Edith L., *Fundamentals of Human Reproduction.* New York: McGraw-Hill Book Co., 1948.

Reynolds, S. R. M., *Physiological Bases of Gynecology and Obstetrics.* Springfield: Charles C Thomas, 1952.

Scheinfeld, Amram, *Women and Men.* New York: Harcourt, Brace & Co., 1944.

Uhlenhuth, Edward, *Problems in the Anatomy of the Pelvis.* Philadelphia: J. B. Lippincott Co., 1953.

HENRY GUZE

Ancient Civilizations, Sex Life in

Greece

GENERALIZATIONS about a culture are difficult to make and apt to be misleading. There are always exceptions, and what is true at one period or in one region is not necessarily true of another. The sexual ideas of the Greeks were, by and large, in harmony with their ideas about life in general. The good life was an art, to be achieved by striking a balance between body and mind. As Aldous Huxley once remarked, there were many gods in the Greek Pantheon, and none was to be cheated and none overpaid. Thus, Greek civilization included appreciation of bodily beauty and of intellectual excellence.

Out of this general philosophy of life the main patterns of Greek sexual behavior emerged. These were marked by reason, balance, the avoidance of excess, and the absence for the most part of mystical and ascetic ideas. Abstention and mortification were, of course, known to the Greeks, but they were occasional practices associated with magical beliefs and the rites of mourning. The Greeks had no special word for chastity, and the Church Fathers writing in Greek were obliged to use the word *agneia,* a general term employed to describe "the rites of mourning."

The fusion of body and mind so highly esteemed by the Greeks found expression in the term *kalokagathia,* meaning a harmonious and symmetrical development of body and soul. Two tendencies in Greek life helped to further a sane and healthy approach to sexuality. One was the emphasis on beauty. This led to the idealization of the naked body and to its glorification in the plastic arts. The second factor was the robust sexuality they ascribed to the gods. What the gods themselves enjoyed was not likely to be despised or shunned by men. Such a background was not propitious to carrying on a war against the body in the interests of the soul. Natural impulses were accepted as good, and the Greeks set out to refine and harmonize them. The foundation of their attitude was provided by a religious veneration of the powers of generation.

In a short survey it is possible to select only a few important features in the Greek view of life as it affected the sexual code. In the first place it must be noted that women were accorded a high position in Greek civilization. This was the natural outcome of a bisexual view of the individual, which regarded every person as in a sense "double-sexed." Life itself was viewed from this androgynous perspective, and this found religious expression in the worship of Hermaphroditus at Cyprus. This god was conceived as bearded, with male sexual organs, but clothed in the dress of a woman.

Women in Greek society were divided roughly into wife and mother on the one hand and courtesan on the other. Both were appropriately honored in their proper spheres. Maternity was highly esteemed in marriage, and the woman ruled over the kingdom of the home and children. Her behavior was expected to be sober and seemly, and, as Hans Licht (1925) pointed out, it is not without significance that there are no words in Greek for "flirt," "gallantry," or "coquetry." The life of the Greek wife and mother may have been dull and narrow when judged by modern standards, but it was greatly honored, and we have no reason to think that Greek women rebelled against it.

Greek marriage was monogamous, and took place after a short betrothal. Virginity was expected of the wife before marriage, as was fidelity afterwards. Divorce laws were simple, and a husband could obtain a divorce for a number of reasons, including adultery, incompatibility of temperament, and childlessness. Sometimes an irate husband killed his wife's lover, sometimes he accepted the situation. The Greek wife was no patient Griselda, however, and sometimes obtained complete ascendency over her husband.

In spite of the fact that a few radical thinkers advocated the same sexual code for men and women, the weight of opinion supported the double standard. The polyerotic tendencies of the male were recognized and accepted, as were his bisexual needs.

Greek marriage took various forms. In some cases the woman was purchased by the husband from her father or guardian, her consent in such cases being unnecessary. In order to make the bride more attractive the father provided a dowry as an added incentive. Marriage was considered a public institution, and the view that it was a private concern involving free individual choice was alien to Greek thought. There seems to have been no legislation against polygamy, but the practice appears to have been regarded as "unhellenic." The early Greeks were sexually polygynous but maritally monogamic, and they would seem to have been averse to marriage; celibacy rather than polygamy was the real problem. Although the Greeks are occasionally spoken of as having had more than one legal wife, these female associates were usually described as "concubines." The wife does not seem to have objected to the existence of concubines as long as they were not accorded equal rank with herself.

Although beauty and love were both idealized and ardently pursued, Greek marriage had little to do either with sexual relations or with love. The wife was regarded as a friend, a housekeeper, a mother of lawful children—but not as a sexual companion. Chastity and fidelity in wives were regarded as family obligations rather than as qualities in an ideal. Seclusion was the remedy for polyandrous impulses, but as Robert Briffault (1927) pointed out, "the concept of such a virtue as chastity regarded as a moral merit, and applicable to both sexes was unthought of by the Greeks." Greek marriage, being a mere matter of fact, could easily be dissolved by divorce. In early times only the husband could sue for divorce, but later this freedom was accorded to the woman as well.

The rules governing men did not preclude extramarital sexual relations as long as these did not involve the wife of another man. In actual practice Greek men sought companionship and sexual stimulation with the hetaerae. These must not be confused with ordinary prostitutes, for they were quite distinct from the girls in the brothels and even from those girls of higher class and more cultivation who sold their favors. The word *hetaera* means "life-partner" or "friend." The hetaerae were socially acceptable and influential, and their high level of education made them suitable companions for some of the most brilliant philosophers, poets, and statesmen. They lived in fine houses, and their activities featured prominently in Greek literature. In great cities such as Corinth they could be found in large numbers. According to Licht, there were one thousand Hetaerae attached to the Great Temple of Venus in that city. Among the courtesans to attain lasting fame were Phryne and Lais.

A sensuality, for the most part subtle and refined, lay at the core of Greek life. The pleasures of the senses were not under a ban, and some philosophers, Aristippus for instance, considered pleasure as the highest good. The right to sensual enjoyment was claimed as an essential part of the earthly happiness of man. This sensuality was associated with intellectual activity, not divorced from it, and the two, in a state of fruitful interaction, created a culture that will be admired until the end of time. Although the concubine died out at the end of the Heroic Age, and heavy fines were imposed for the seduction of a married woman or a girl of good character, Greek public opinion did not blame a man who sought relaxation in the arms of a courtesan, or in the small talk of a beautiful boy.

As the Greeks recognized and accepted the bisexual nature of man, quite logically they catered to this element in the male by the institution of paiderastia. The word is derived from *pais,* "a young man," and *eran,* "to love." It would be a grave mistake to imagine that this had any affinity with what we call pedophilia, the sexual love of children. Sexual relations with children were punished in Ancient Greece. In Greek culture the "boy" was in reality a young man, and the relationship moved predominantly on an ideal level. The relationship was a spiritual and sensual affection of an older man for a younger one, usually unaccompanied by overt sexual acts. After a boy had reached puberty such a relationship was regarded as an essential part of his emotional and educational experience. The Greek ideal of beauty was male, and every man sought to establish a relationship with a youth, to whom he was both counselor and guide. The man was called the "inspirer" and the youth the "listener." To fail to achieve some such relationship was regarded as a disgrace. It was a love relationship, but the performance of sexual acts was, at least in theory, forbidden.

Drama, poetry, and religion were permeated by erotic feeling, and homoerotic emotion was the most important aspect. According to Licht and Hopfner (1948), this did not center around a few isolated acts in the margins of Greek life. Rather, it was all-pervasive and gives the key to Greek culture. We must distinguish between paiderastia, the love of adolescent males, which was highly idealized and was the outcome of a rich fusion of esthetic, mental, and sensuous factors, and the phenomena of male prostitution. In the former case the relationship was, to use Freudian terminology, "aim-inhibited." The male was the focus of intellectual life and esthetic appreciation. Most authorities are somewhat evasive on the physical content of these complex and ambiguous relationships, but the emotion of the lover, the intense physical appreciation, drinking together, nakedness, kisses, and embraces could hardly have failed, in many cases at least, to have been accompanied by more overtly sexual acts. The cau-

tious Licht speaks of the "sensual" love of the Greeks for "boys," and refers to them as "sexual companions." In the case of male prostitution, however, the sexual element was overt, direct, and commercialized. As distinct from the more serious vocabulary of idealized homoerotic love, a comic and satirical vocabulary has been collected by M. H. E. Meier (1930) that leaves no doubt that side by side with the more idealized forms of love there existed a very extensive homoerotic *ars amandi.* Paiderastia was a nonvenal relationship, and if a boy gave himself for money he was despised for so doing. Male prostitution was, however, accepted by the Greeks, and in some temples both boys and girls were available. Some of the poets complained about the avarice of these young men. There were also houses of accommodation and brothels.

In the legislation of Solon (c. 635-560 B.C.) the love of boys was accepted, minors were protected, regulations were enacted against boys who engaged in prostitution, and slaves were forbidden to have sexual relations with free-born boys. The great majority of male prostitutes were not, however, Athenians, and so the law did not apply to them. Solon was himself homosexual.

With regard to homosexual practices among women, little material survives. The focus of attention in Greek life remained obstinately on the male. Women engaging in homoerotic activities were usually called "tribads," from *tribas,* meaning "to rub." The word "tribas" was used to describe women who engaged either in masturbation or in sex relations with other women. This practice came to be associated especially with the island of Lesbos, and the poet, Sappho (born c. 612 B.C.) became the patron saint of the cult. No doubt such activities were widespread, and references to them are found in the *Dialogues* of Lucian, the writings of Plutarch, and, of course, in the extant fragments of Sappho's poetry. In the life of this High Priestess of this form of love and in her circle of girls we have the nearest approach to the male institution of paiderastia. There seems no reason to suppose that these tendencies were in any way regarded by the public as vicious. It is interesting to note that Sappho calls upon Aphrodite to befriend her. That the Greeks accepted and were familiar with female homosexuality is attested by the frequent portrayal of the artificial phallus, or "olisbos." These, as was well known, were employed extensively in homosexual relations as well as in autoerotic activities.

Nakedness played a considerable part in Greek life. The Greeks understood both the erotic use of clothing and ornament and the uses of nakedness. In the archaic period, apparently under the influence of oriental ideas, nakedness was less usual than it became later, but it never became a common habit adopted promiscuously. On certain occasions the Greeks were accustomed to public exhibitions of nakedness. Such occasions included the Spartan wrestling matches between boys and girls, activities carried on in the gymnasia, beauty contests, and performances of the dancers from Thessaly and Crete, who danced naked at the great feasts given by the rich. The naked human body became the norm of all plastic art, and as time went on the Greeks came to feel that, on certain occasions, covering of the entire body was to be deprecated. Such covering was out of harmony with their general philosophy of life. Thus, athletes began to appear quite naked, and any cover for the sexual organs was discarded. Far from regarding the phallus as a low or shameful organ to be concealed, it was revered as a holy organ of generation, and representations of it were carried triumphantly in processions on certain occasions. Representations of the female sex organs were also accorded reverence and displayed on similar occasions. It is significant that these parts were called *aidon,* or *aidoion,* meaning "that which inspires holy awe." Cerinthus was truly representative of Greek thought when he made his famous statement to the effect that man should not be ashamed to name what God had not been ashamed to create. The Greeks, it should be noted, accepted the body as a whole and, as Rattray Taylor (1953) says, "they distributed their sexuality and were as interested in bosom and buttocks as in genitals."

Thus, in Ancient Greece we find a rich, varied, and refined erotic life and an absence of sexual repression in the Freudian sense of the word. Direction and control were consciously exercised on a rational basis. Masturbation, for instance, was accepted and looked upon not as a vice but as a safety valve. It was despised only when it occurred among adult men who, it was considered, should be able to engage in sexual relations with a partner. Many observers of Greek culture, including Licht, have noted the absence of sexual "perversions" in the true sense of the word. Although such relatively harmless deviations as exhibitionism, scopophilia, and bestiality, or zoophilia, are mentioned they seem to have existed on the margins of Greek erotic life. Of much more importance is the fact that no references exist in Greek literature to the abnormal phenomena of sadomasochism. It would seem that Classical Greek institutions were well designed for a full and healthy erotic life.

Rome

The differences between the Greek and the Roman worlds were profound, and these differences found expression in the sexual conventions of the Roman people. Roman marriage, for instance, differed greatly from Greek marriage. In early times there appear to have been three forms of marriage. According to the first form, if a man and a woman had lived together for a year they were considered to be legally married, and their children could inherit property. This form, based upon one year's uninterrupted cohabitation, was called *usus.* It became the commonest form of marriage in later times and was used to emancipate the wife from the authority of the husband. It was plebeian in character and involved something in the nature of an equal partnership.

Another form of marriage was called the *confarreatio.* This was the old aristocratic form and the most solemn and ceremonious. In early times it was incapable of being dissolved. Ten witnesses were required and the ritual was elaborate, Jupiter being invoked and sacrificial acts performed. An important feature in this form of marriage lay in the fact that the guardianship of the woman passed from the father to the husband. It was the form of marriage required by patrician status, and Briffault calls the contract "a deed of transfer." From the father the husband acquired the power of life and death over the wife, but in actual fact the position of the married woman even under this patriarchal form of marriage seems to have been better than that of many other patriarchal societies. Kiefer (1934) tells us that until 445 B.C., full legal marriage was the monoply of the aristocracy, available for patricians in marrying one another. Only later was the ban on mixed marriages lifted.

A third form of marriage was called *coemptio*. This was probably a cheap edition of *confarreatio* devised for the common people. Its effects came to be similar as time went on. Five Roman citizens were required as witnesses, and it differed from *usus* in being recognized as legal from the start. In common with *usus*, however, it did not at first involve a transfer of ownership. It would seem that at certain periods in Roman history all three forms of marriage could be accompanied by what was called the *manus, i.e.*, the woman passing into the power of the husband (*in manum*), but in the case of the authoritarian *confarreatio* this appears to have been invariable. With increasing emancipation women tended to avoid the *manus*. When "ownership" remained in theory with the father and the woman married and went to live with her husband, she became to all intents and purposes free. In later periods in Roman history the Roman woman enjoyed a considerable amount of dignity, freedom, and privilege, and she was not excluded from social life as was the Greek woman.

With the decay of the older aristocratic patterns of life the rituals of marriage became simpler. Few of the older rites survived except the Bridal Procession and the Nuptial Dinner. Legal proof of marriage was provided by the deed of transfer of the bride's dowry. In spite of changes, however, Roman marriage seems to have retained its basic characteristics. It was regarded not as a predominantly sexual institution, but rather as a social and economic arrangement. Roman marriage was monogamic, and fidelity was required from the wife. The patrician code punished the wife's adultery severely, because such conduct invalidated the legitimate inheritance of property. The Roman wife was trusted and given a considerable amount of personal freedom. Her exemplars and the guardians of her code were the Vestal

Virgins. The influence of Vesta on the Roman matrons was, however, not always decisive. Livy tells us that in the year 285 B.C. a temple to Venus was erected out of the proceeds of fines imposed on Roman matrons for adultery. The virtues of Lucrece were evidently not ubiquitous in Roman life. It must be remembered that only a few Romans availed themselves of that form of marriage that was both monogamous and for life.

Among the Roman aristocracy virginity of the bride was esteemed. This esteem, however, was based on practical considerations. The loss of virginity before marriage was regarded as a bad augury for marital fidelity, thus diminishing girl's chance of marriage. There was no admiration for virginity as such. The sexual code for both men and women was eminently practical and secular, and no ascetic, mystical, or religious notions seem to have been involved.

Before the consummation of the marriage it was the custom to instruct the bride in her marital duties. The marriage bed was prepared, and an important feature of the nuptial ritual was the ceremonial loosening of the bride's girdle by the bridegroom. Sometimes the bride sat on the phallus of the fertility god Mutunus Tutunus. It may have been the custom for the bride to have been deflorated by the husband's friends. In any case, the sexual act between the married pair was supervised by a number of deities whose names suggest their specialized functions. Virginiensis helped the husband to undo the girdle of the bride. Subigus and Prema were concerned with bedding the bride and ensuring her submissiveness to the sexual demands of her husband, and Pertunda came to help the husband in the sexual consummation.

It is said that for 500 years after the foundation of Rome there was no instance of divorce, and no legal process by which it could be obtained. The first recorded case was brought by a husband on the grounds of his wife's barrenness. In later Roman law a divorce action could be brought by the husband on the grounds of his wife's adultery and also for other misdemeanors, as, for instance, drunkenness or perverse or disgusting conduct. Under the old system of *confarreatio,* which was indissoluble, the wife might be punished by death for certain offenses. Later penalties inflicted on the adulteress included banishment or death.

There was in Rome a double standard of sexual behavior, and the man was accorded much greater sexual freedom than the woman. Both the unmarried man and the husband were free to lead their own sexual lives. They could consort freely with slaves or prostitutes as long as they abstained from seducing the wives of other men. Concubinage was not regarded as shameful, but it was impossible to have a concubine and a wife at the same time. On the whole, men seem to have been averse to marriage, and this disinclination appears to have worried the Roman authorities.

It was Horace who spoke of the *laudator temporis acti*, the critic of the present and the idealizer of the past. We find this tendency at work in some Roman writers who, for polemic reasons, tended to glorify the austere purity of the past and to bewail the decadence of the times in which they lived. Much of this appears, however, to have been without solid historical foundation. The customs of all societies undergo change. The increase of wealth, the emancipation of women, and the spread of leisure led, no doubt, to increasingly sophisticated sexual patterns, but the simple past imagined by some writers probably never existed.

Prostitution was both widespread and socially accepted in Roman society. Even in early times there was the instance of a prostitute who later married a wealthy Etruscan. She was openly described on a eulogistic inscription as *nobilissima meretrix* ("a most noble prostitute"). Although virginity may have been an economic and social asset to a patrician girl, Roman girls of the poorer class were at liberty to cohabit with anyone, freely or for money, and a girl was not despised for so doing. Even in cases where public approval was withheld, the need for prostitution was recognized. Among representatives of this latter attitude were Seneca and Cicero. Horace recommended it, and expressed the opinion that "young men when their veins are full of gross lust should drop into a brothel rather than grind some husband's private mill." On the whole, brothels were encouraged but, as Havelock Ellis (1936) said, "the Roman entered them with covered

head and face concealed in his cloak." The better class of Roman courtesan never achieved the refinement or the cultural and social rank and influence attained by the Greek hetaerae, and she was never allowed to imitate the habits and costumes of Roman matrons. Probably the rankest region of the Roman sexual underworld was that portrayed by Gaius Petronius, adviser on pleasure to Nero, in the fragment of his great novel *Satyricon*. It gives a wonderful picture of the twilight of the Roman Empire, with its brothels and taverns, its baths and banquets, its pimps, prostitutes, and catamites.

On the whole, a distinction was drawn between free sexual relationships and the venality of professional prostitution; and the woman who took money for her sexual favors tended to be despised. The professional prostitute was forced to enroll her name on the lists of the Aediles. Brothels abounded, and free-lance prostitutes plied their trade in dim corners of the city. The Roman prostitute might be a slave, a free woman, or a free-living aristocrat. The latter occasionally inscribed her name on the lists in order to enjoy the freedom and anonymity of the prostitute's life.

Severe circles no doubt disapproved of these casual and irregular relationships, but the Romans by and large regarded everything pertaining to sex as purely natural. All the sexually free women, from the mistresses of the poets to the unknown girls who lingered in the shadows of the city, were handmaids of the Mysteries of Venus and Cupid. Among the poets' mistresses, the Lesbia of Catullus has been immortalized. Many sexually free girls, such as actresses, flute-players, and dancers, were not ranked as professional prostitutes.

Homosexuality was also accepted by the matter-of-fact Romans as a natural and inevitable part of man's sexual life. Homosexual practices are associated with the names of many emperors and other Roman notabilities. Julius Caesar was ironically called "The husband of all women, and the wife of all men," and Augustus, Tiberius, Domitian, Hadrian, Trajan, and many others were at least bisexual in their tastes. The love of Hadrian for Antinoüs is perhaps the most famous homosexual idyll in Roman history. A vivid picture of homoerotic life among students and wandering bohemians is given in the *Satyricon,* to which reference has already been made.

According to Havelock Ellis, Heliogabalus, "the most homosexual of all the company," seems to have been a true invert of the feminine type; he dressed as a woman and was devoted to the men he loved. It should be noted that homosexuality in Rome, although accepted and widespread, bore no resemblance either in its character or its influence to the highly idealized and all-pervasive paiderastia of Ancient Greece.

There was, of course, a close connection in Roman culture between sex and religion. The powers of generation were regarded as sacred, and the emblem of the phallus was revered, carried in processions, drawn on walls, and reproduced endlessly in the plastic arts. The name of one ancient god, Mutunus Tutunus, may have been derived from the word *mentula,* the male organ. This god, as we have already seen, played an important part in marriage rites, the bride offering her virginity to it. Juno was the guardian of woman's sexual functions.

As time went on, sexual life became more refined in its expression, and more extensive in its ramifications. The cults of Venus and Priapus developed. The former was the guardian not only of marriage, but also of harlots and, later, of male prostitutes as well. Priapus (called "the god of gardens") was a giant phallus connected with a human face. It was associated with fertility and general fecundity and was thus inimical to homosexual rites. The festivals of this god were both crude and licentious. It must be remembered that the phallus in Roman thought was considered to be endowed with magical potency; paradoxically enough, this was the emblem worshipped by the pure Vestals.

In conclusion, it may be said that Roman sexuality expressed itself in more direct and brutal ways than were customary in Greek life. Both cultures connected sex with religion, and both regarded sexual phenomena as a natural part of life. The crudeness of Roman sexuality manifested itself in the coarseness of the old erotic glossaries and in the public and private orgiastic activities that accompanied the decline of Roman civilization. In Rome, homosexuality was culturally unimportant, and Roman sexuality, unlike that of the Greeks, tended to become more and more sadistic. It may be noted that the lower grade prostitutes tended to lodge near the Circus Maximus in order to cater to men whose sexual desires had been inflamed by the spectacle of combat in the arena.

On its highest level, however, Roman sexuality achieved great refinement and subtlety. The sophisticated virtuosity of Roman sexual life found its final and finest monument in the poetry of Catullus and in the *Ars Amoris* of Ovid.

The Hebrews

Hebrew culture was a thoroughgoing theocracy, the laws governing human behavior being regarded as given by God Himself. The family was patriarchal in structure, the father having originally the power of life and death over the children. The wife had little freedom and the husband much. He could take concubines, associate with prostitutes, or divorce his wife. This patriarchal family was polygamous, and the number of wives varied, largely according to the wealth of the particular patriarch, Jewish kings tending to have extensive harems. Opinions differed concerning the ideal number of wives, some authorities recommending four, other Talmudic doctors allowing as many as the man could afford to support. It was only in later times that polygamy decayed and monogamic marriage became the rule.

Westermarck (1922) considers that the right of the husband to divorce his wife must be considered as central in Jewish thought, and although the rabbis introduced various restrictions as time went on, this right was never abolished. At first it applied to the man only, the woman being unable to divorce her husband for any cause. Later the woman could sue for divorce, and the court could compel her husband to give her a bill of divorce, the legal fiction being that he did this of his own free will. Whereas originally the husband could divorce his wife at pleasure and without cause, the woman had to prove notorious depravity, and not merely simple adultery. Later, divorce might be withheld from the husband on compassionate grounds as, for instance, in cases where the wife was insane.

Among the sexual outlets outside marriage, prostitution played a very important part. This prostitution may be roughly divided into two categories, sacred and secular. Hebrew prostitution must be considered in the wider context of oriental prostitution in general. In cases where it was most closely connected with religion, the prostitute was the Temple priestess herself. Among the Canaanites, both male and female prostitutes served in the temples. At other times the prostitute was a "secular" and not a "sacred" person. She would practice prostitution for a short time and devote the profits to the sanctuary. Epstein (1948) says that this kind of prostitution was sometimes borrowed by the Hebrews and introduced into the Temple of the Lord.

The Book of Samuel tells us that the priestly sons of Eli lay "with the women that assembled at the door of the tabernacle of the congregation." This, however, was exceptional and was denounced by their father, the High Priest. We find sacred prostitution referred to again in the fourteenth chapter of the First Book of Kings, in the account of Solomon's son, Rehoboam, who, influenced by his foreign mother, introduced the practice into the Temple at Jerusalem. Another outbreak occurred under Manasseh.

Both male and female prostitution of this type were brought to an end by Deuteronomic legislation under Josiah, who lived c. 640 B.C. Other types of prostitution were associated with street harlots who gave their fees to the Temple treasury. This was also condemned by the new code. Orgiastic rites, including prostitution, although not associated with Jewish worship, flourished at High Places (local sanctuaries built on hills) and under trees, in connection with the religious rites of the immediate neighbors of the Hebrews. No doubt many of the latter were drawn, at least occasionally, to these rites because of their licentious nature. It is very important to remember that many of the sexual prohibitions of the Hebrews were imposed, not primarily to outlaw the sexual acts as such, but rather because

of their intimate association with the worship of strange gods.

Prostitution completely unconnected with religion was a feature of the life of the Hebrews, as it was of other ancient peoples. The whole subject, however, is somewhat complex. In ancient times it would appear that a woman called a *zonah* was a kind of concubine, standing midway between a wife and a prostitute. The degree of approval or disapproval meted out to the prostitute depended to some extent on whether she was a Hebrew girl or a strange woman, the legal code being extremely severe to the former. The Hebrew moralists expressed their disapproval of prostitution in general, and their attitude finds expression in the Book of Proverbs. Levitical law prohibited parents from giving their children into harlotry.

Two important clues to the understanding of the Hebrew sexual code are to be found in the fear of idolatry and the command to procreate. To some extent at least this colored their attitude toward virginity, adultery, masturbation, prostitution, and homosexuality. All these practices militated against religious purity and obedience. He who does not engage in procreation is like one who sheds blood, runs a Jewish proverb.

Although the early attitude to sex was, by and large, affirmative and robust, there were factors present that encouraged a sex-negating and ascetic attitude. In the mythology of the Fall the focal points are the phallic serpent and the temptation to sexual love. Side by side with this we must put the injunction to increase and multiply, and so the use of the sexual functions for this purpose became part of religious obedience. Asceticism became more powerful after the return from the Captivity. This expressed itself in a number of different ways; for example, in the reversal of the Rabbinical antipathy to celibacy, the glorification of barrenness, and the beliefs that pleasure as such is wicked and that sexual pleasure is the most wicked of all. According to Josephus, among the sect called the Essenes pleasure was denounced, continence praised, and wedlock avoided. This attitude led to the segregation of the sexes and the strict supervision of children.

According to Epstein, sexual contact between an unmarried man and woman, unpremeditated and unaccompanied by money, was not considered as harlotry and was not prohibited in the Bible, which forbade only the seduction of a virgin and rape, these being offenses under law. It was later that such contacts were condemned and described as harlotry. Additional restrictions embodied public disapproval of extramarital activities of this kind.

The Hebrews attached a high value to virginity in the bride, and the deception of the bridegroom in this matter was a serious offense. Much importance was attached to what were called "the tokens of viriginity." These Mosaic tokens probably took the form of a bloodstained cloth. In Deuteronomy it is stated that if a man discovers that his bride is not a virgin, and if the tokens of virginity cannot be found and displayed to the Elders, she may be stoned to death.

The menstruating woman was regarded as unclean and required a ritual bath to be cleansed from her impurity. A woman was also regarded as unclean after childbirth. According to Deuteronomic legislation, a sexually mutilated male was excluded from the congregation of the Lord. Deuteronomy, Chapter 23, lays down the rule that "He that is wounded in the stones, or hath his privy member cut off" shall not enter into the congregation. A bastard was also excluded.

At an early period ideas of humiliation and shame came to be attached to nakedness. In the Creation story, as Epstein points out, we are told that both Adam and Eve were naked and were not ashamed. This state ended when they tasted of the Tree of Knowledge, after which they made themselves aprons. All through the early history of the Hebrews their attitude stands in sharp contrast to that of the Greeks. The wife caught in an act of infidelity was publicly stripped by her husband as the final act of humiliation, and in the late period the Hellenizing Jew who participated in the naked exercises of the gymnasium was regarded as an apostate. To uncover the nakedness of somebody was usually associated with sexual approach, and this is the usual phrase employed in Leviticus in connection with persons who,

because of consanguinity, must not be sexually approached. It was forbidden to recite holy formularies or to pray while naked or in the presence of a naked person. When prayer had to be recited during an immersion it was recommended that the water should be stirred up by the feet so that the body should not be seen below the surface. Nothing was more obnoxious to God than public nakedness, and the exposure of the woman's body was even more heinous than a similar display on the part of the male. Uncovering the nakedness usually meant displaying the genitals and was almost akin to sexual intercourse, and therefore, where a parent or relative was concerned, to incest. Ham, it will be remembered, was cursed for seeing the genitals of his father when the latter was drunk.

In harmony with their procreational view of sex, Hebrew teaching strongly deprecated masturbation. Although not specifically condemned in the Canonical Scriptures, it was condemned in Rabbinical teaching. It was a waste of nature and so an offense against God. It was regarded as a "sin," and a "capital crime." All kinds of advice were given in order to avert the unwitting or deliberate waste of semen. For example, it was necessary to avoid touching the genitals and to shun sexually stimulating situations and erotic daydreams. One rabbi, quoted by Epstein, contended that adultery included "lewdness by means of the hand as well." It must be remembered that the "sin" of Onan was not masturbation but coitus interruptus, and its use to describe masturbation is a solecism. Onan disobeyed the laws of God by refusing to raise up seed to his brother by his widow.

In Old Testament time "unnatural sins" were thought to defile the land, which belonged to the Lord. Among these sins was homosexual intercourse. Male homosexual practices were expressly forbidden in Leviticus: "Thou shalt not lie with mankind as with womankind: it is an abomination" (Lev. 18); "There shall be no Sodomite of the Sons of Israel" (Deut. 23). It should be noted that "sodomy" is the correct term for male homosexuality in the Old Testament; bestiality, which is often used as an equivalent term, is quite distinct. Among the prohibitions of the early, simple code of sex morality were rape and seduction, prostitution, buggery, wearing the attire of the opposite sex, attacking the genitals of her male opponent by a quarreling woman, copulation between male and male, and a father's (and probably also a mother's) nakedness in the presence of sons. Sodomy, it would seem, was considered a very serious offense from early times. The stories of Sodom and Gomorrah reflect the belief that it was preferable that an innocent girl be given over to licentious strangers than that these homosexual acts be carried out.

Sodomitical practices came under a double ban: they were sterile on the one hand, and heathen in origin and implication on the other. Probably the Hebrew regarded them as of Canaanite origin. Although the practice was strongly deprecated, neither the Covenant nor the Deuteronomic codes enacted specific legislation against it. Leviticus, however, made it into a capital crime: "If a man lie with a male as one lieth with a woman both of them have committed an abomination; they shall surely be put to death, their blood shall be upon them," (Lev. 20).

Bestiality, which meant copulation with an animal, was closely linked with male homosexuality in the Hebrew mind. The Levitical code condemned to death men or women guilty of this practice. Again, these activities were thought to be Canaanite abominations. The attitude towards homosexuality seems to have been more severe during later periods. It was not only made a capital crime, but the penalties were applied to gentiles as well as to Jews. Taylor (1953) considers that an increasing homosexual anxiety is shown by the prohibition of the father exposing his nakedness before his sons. No such prohibition was thought necessary in the case of his daughters.

Thus we see that sacred sodomy in the form of the Temple prostitute was an imported Canaanite practice introduced into Judea at the time of the early kings. Temple sodomy remained until the reformation of Josiah, and its condemnation at this period was based, not primarily on its assessment as a sexual crime, but rather because of its reputation as an idolatrous practice. It is interesting to note that sodomy with a boy under the age of 9 years

and 1 day was not considered as a sexual crime at all, and not consequently punished by death, but only by public flagellation. The rationale for this lay in the fact that until after this age the child did not become a sexual being. Epstein says that when the death penalty was imposed for adult sodomy it usually took the form of stoning.

It should be noted that a lighter view was taken of homosexual practices among women. There is no legislation in the Old Testament against it, but it was regarded with disapproval as an immoral and heathenish practice. A woman guilty of it was considered unfit to marry a priest. A final Halakah, or ordinance, condemned the act and imposed disciplinary penalties.

Thus, we find in Hebrew culture a simple and primitive moral code gradually becoming more detailed and extensive. The tendency was, by and large, towards asceticism and rigorism, but throughout Hebrew history the outlook remained consistently theocratic, the whole complex network of rules and regulations being subsumed under the concept of "The Law of The Lord."

India

The vastness and complexity of Indian life make generalizations more than usually hazardous. Tribal customs have differed widely from locality to locality and from age to age. On the one hand we find asceticism in its most extreme forms and on the other the apotheosis of eroticism. In spite of this, the dichotomy between sex and religion, so painfully evident in our own civilization, was absent. Sexual abstention was not regarded as good in itself but as a means of obtaining magical power; chastity to avert the envy of the gods was also practiced by priests and holy men. Briffault notes that the aspirant to holiness might hang a heavy stone on his sexual organs in order to mortify the flesh or he might vow to deflower a thousand virgins. By and large it would seem true to say that the religious traditions of India, instead of putting a ban on sexual activity or limiting it severely, have tended to use sexuality for religious purposes. As Havelock Ellis has said, "the sexual act has often had a religious significance in India, and the minutest details of the sexual life and its variations are discussed in Indian erotic treatises in a spirit of gravity, while nowhere else have the anatomical and physiological sexual characteristics been studied with such minute and adoring reverence."

It would appear that among the aboriginal tribes of India marriage was both monogamous and endogamous. Prenuptial sexual acts were lightly regarded so long as they took place within the tribe. The penalty of excommunication was inflicted, however, if such conduct involved a member of another tribe. Occasionally some more primitive tribe will be found to be polygamous. In some tribes child marriage seemed to be the rule, whereas in others marriage took place only in adulthood. Occasionally a ritual of marriage by capture was enacted, and in some parts of India polyandry and group marriages have been found. The Hindus, in common with the Hebrews, attached enormous importance to offspring, and Westermarck thinks that the polygyny of the ancient Hindus was due to the fear of dying childless.

Many important aspects of Hindu religious mythology are closely connected with the sexual functions. Hinduism is not, therefore, an asexual or an antisexual religion. Siva, a member of the Hindu trinity, is associated with generation, and his symbol is the lingam, (phallus); an associated symbol is the yoni (vulva). The hermaphroditic conception of the God is familiar in India, and finds expression in the story where Siva divides himself into male and female. He is often portrayed with a single eye in the middle of his forehead, symbolizing the fusion of the male and female generative principles.

It thus follows that the cult of the lingam is very important. An eighteenth-century traveler reported finding in a grotto a hermaphroditic statue of enormous height, representing man and woman in a single body. One half of the face, one arm, and one foot belonged to the male, while the other half of the body was female. The lingam was not, however, represented in the statue. Dulaure says that representations of the trinity often took the form of a pedestal (Brahma), an urn (Vishnu), and a column rising from the urn (Siva). Not far

from Pondicherry there is a tower consecrated to the lingam and surrounded by colossal stone phalli. Miniature lingams were also commonly used as amulets. The priests of Siva, surrounded by sexual emblems of all kinds, were expected to remain abstinent and sexually unaroused. Among other duties, they decorated the lingam with flowers. It was also their function to initiate the dancing girls into the cult of Siva in the temple of the God, where these girls later served as priestesses and prostitutes.

The phenomena of puberty were widely held to be the result of intercourse with the Moon God. This was sometimes accomplished by means of the girl's "Marriage to the God," which might involve defloration by the lingam of the image. In other cases she embraced a sacred tree representing the God. Sterile women sometimes brought the lingam of the image into contact with their sexual organs or prostituted themselves in the temple to remedy their condition.

Many taboos surrounded the woman and girl in Indian culture. Menstruation was regarded as unclean and dangerous, and the woman was isolated for three days. Elaborate precautions were also taken after childbirth.

Sacred festivals, especially those connected with agriculture, were the occasions for the performance of sexual rites. Briffault describes the *Holi* festival, in honor of the Goddess Vesanti, as "the Saturnalia of India." During this festival many taboos, such as those on incest, were temporarily suspended, and a great deal of license was permitted for both girls and boys. Phallic emblems were carried, and *tableaux vivants* representing the loves of the God were enacted on chariots and stages.

Meyer (1930) points out in his work on the sexual life of ancient India that the ancient Indian epics are full of contradictions. In the Indian soul there coexist burning sensuality and stark renunciation of the world. Although children are ardently desired, the birth of a daughter is often regarded as a calamity. Idealistic views are expounded on virginity, and fidelity in marriage is extolled. The seduction of a virgin or a married woman is deprecated. On the other hand, the sexual nature of woman is emphasized, and the woman in love is credited with the initiative. Caste is very important in sexual relations, and the laws of Manu decree that if a maiden has relations with a man of higher caste she shall go unpunished, but that if her lover belongs to a lower caste she shall be shut up in her house until she comes to her senses. The general pattern laid down in the epics is that the girl should live in chastity and obedience to her parents and receive her husband at their hands.

Many different types of marriage are mentioned, including marriage by capture, marriage by stealing, marriage by purchase, and marriage in which the bride is freely given to the bridegroom by the father. The Brahman may take his spouse from the three higher castes only. If a man has three wives who are not Brahmans and then marries a Brahman woman, she automatically becomes the head wife. The philosophy of marriage depends, as Meyer says, on the general philosophy of life. The Brahman maxim is "give," and this leads to marriage without bride-price, whereas the warrior's maxim is "take," which favors marriage by capture. In some cases the girl has no freedom of choice or only a restricted one. In others she seeks until she finds the man picked out by her heart. Age also is important in marriage. The younger members of the family must wait until the older members marry.

Polygamy in Aryan India, Meyer says, "is as old as the hills, and does not give the slightest offense in the Brahmanic system, although since Vedic times one wife is the usual and obvious arrangement." Polyandry, on the other hand, is utterly repugnant to Indian feelings, only two cases being found in epic literature. However, there seem to be traces of a very early polyandry and "free-love," where the women followed their own inclinations and jealousy was unknown. This belongs, however, to a legendary period.

Great emphasis is laid in Indian culture on the pleasures of sex, and the frustration of such pleasure both for animals and for man was felt to be particularly inhuman. These pleasures were projected into the next world in the conception of a Utopia, where the favored man could have sexual intercourse with thousands of women of extreme beauty and in the flower of their youth. Sexual enjoyment removes the ills of the soul, and the myths of Siva and his wife picture them prolonging the sexual act almost to infinity. In all sexual activity woman is an ardent participant. Without the pleasures of love the woman pines, and much attention is devoted to aphrodisiacs and erotic techniques.

The didactic parts of the epics, according to Meyer, present sensuality as something unclean and enjoin an orthodoxy of peno-vaginal intercourse, condemning deviations such as oral-genital contacts. Homosexuality and bestiality are also regarded as great offenses. Masturbation and all forms of "self-pollution" and even involuntary emissions of semen are much frowned upon.

The evaluation of extramarital coitus depended very largely on the status of the woman. Connection with a harlot or a slave woman did not constitute adultery unless they were the concubines of another man.

In Indian culture the prostitute was often distinguished, wealthy, and influential. In some parts of India every first-born female was dedicated to the tribal god and served for some time as a temple prostitute. "The Hindu has always sung the praises of the public woman as the very type and embodiment of perfect womanhood," according to Meyer. She usually wore a distinctive dress of red. Although as a class she was not highly esteemed, she was the necessary companion of the warrior during military campaigns, and she was often the ornament not merely of the camp but of civil life too. She was often well-versed in speech and skilled in dancing and song, as well as in the arts of love. It was probably because of the prevalence and influence of these women that the didactic parts of the epics fulminate against them.

Side by side with the praise of woman in Indian literature are passages deeply misogynic in tone. Woman is so voluptuous, we are told, that she will seize upon any available male to satisfy her desires. Failing that, women will fall upon one another. Reference is made in this connection to the use of the artificial phallus.

The Hindus in general held homosexuality in abhorrence. However, houses of male prostitution with effeminate male prostitutes dressed as women have been described by travelers. Richard Burton spoke of the brothels for eunuchs and boys in Karachi. In Afghanistan such practices were more acceptable, and Burton described effeminate boys with kohled eyes, rouged cheeks, long tresses, and hennaed nails accompanying the caravans and riding luxuriously in camel panniers.

Female homosexuality seems to have been more common. The Hindustani language has five different words for a tribad. Such relationships took many forms, including the aforementioned use of the olisbos. Havelock Ellis, quoting a personal communication, says that the Hindustani poets treated Lesbianism fully and crudely in a number of poems. In one of these the woman sings the praise of the artificial phallus and its superiority over the male lover.

The interest shown in the arts of love in India is borne out by the fact that there are no less than seven treatises on the subject in classical literature, the best known of these in the occidental world being the *Kama Sutra* and the *Anunga Runga*. The former is a very comprehensive treatise that deals with marriage, courtship, embracing, kissing, and coital techniques. Oral and manual stimulation are also discussed, as are coital acts involving more than two people. Homosexuality in both men and women is dealt with, and a good deal is said about the activities of eunuchs, some of whom are described as dressing as females and engaging in sexual activities with their male clients during shampooing operations.

In these treatises love is regarded not only as a refined and subtle art, but one that must be cultivated by both sexes. Woman's part in sexual activities is regarded as both active and important, and her lover is regarded as having failed unless she too achieves complete satisfaction.

Finally, it must be noted that the teaching and general permissiveness of the love manuals come into collision with some of the more ascetic precepts of epic and law, and a certain amount of sophistry must be employed in order to reconcile the claims of Eros with the injunctions of the more austere moralists and teachers.

References

Briffault, Robert, *The Mothers*. New York: The Macmillan Co., 1927.

Burton, Richard F., "Terminal Essay." In Vol. X of *The Arabian Nights*. London: privately printed for the Burton Club, no date indicated.

Ellis, Havelock. *Studies in the Psychology of Sex*. New York: Random House, 1936.

Epstein, Louis M., *Sex Laws and Customs of Judaism*. New York: Bloch Publishing Co., Inc., 1948.

Goldberg, B. Z., *The Sacred Fire*. New York: Liveright, 1930.

Hopfner, T., *Das Sexuelleben der Griechen und Romer*. Prague, 1948.

Kiefer, Otto, *Sexual Life in Ancient Rome*. London: Routledge, 1934.

Licht, Hans, *Liebe und Ehe in Griechenland*. Berlin: Paul Aretz, 1925.

Meier, M. H. E., *L'amour Grec*. Paris: Stendhal et Cie., 1930.

Meyer, Johann Jakob, *Sexual Life in Ancient India*. London: Routledge, 1930.

Nefzawi, *The Perfumed Garden*. London and Benares: The Kama Shastra Society, 1886.

Ovid, *De Arte Amandi. Amorum. Remedia Amoris*.

Petronius, *The Satyricon*. London: Spearman & Calder, 1953.

Sappho, *Texte et traduction*. Paris: Alphonse Lemerre, 1909.

Schmidt, K., *Das Kamasutram*. Berlin: Barsdorf, 1907.

Schmidt, K., *Liebe und Ehe in Indien*. Berlin: Barsdorf, 1904.

Symons, John Addington, *Studies in Sexual Inversion*. London: privately printed, no date indicated.

Taylor, G. Rattray, *Sex in History*. London: Thames & Hudson, 1953.

Vatsyayana, *The Kama Sutra*. Paris: Librairie Astra, no date indicated.

Westermarck, Edward, *History of Human Marriage*. New York: The Macmillan Co., 1922.

ROBERT WOOD

Animal Sexuality

SEXUAL behavior is one of the most basic and important types of social behavior, being directly associated with the process of reproduction. The most essential part of the process is, of course, the union of egg and sperm, in which the sperm moves toward and makes connection with the egg. Many animals that live in the sea simply liberate their reproductive products into the water and show no real sexual behavior. For land-living animals, however, and also for actively moving aquatic ones, the sex cells must be brought into close proximity by the behavior of the parents. Sexual behavior occurs in the one-celled animals, as in the conjugation of paramecia. It also occurs in all the higher groups of multicellular animals, although not necessarily in every species. There are only three major phyla in which sexual behavior does not occur: the sponges, coelenterates, and echinoderms. All of them are predominantly marine animals that are either completely immobile as adults or are sluggish in their movements (see Table 1).

The Functions of Sexual Behavior

The primary function of sexual behavior is to make fertilization possible, and this is the essential part of sexual reproduction. Although budding and other forms of asexual reproduction occur in many lower animals, sexual reproduction is the general rule, probably because it permits much more rapid genetic changes. Animals that have sexual reproduction evolve much more rapidly than those that do not, and, perhaps because of this, have developed a remarkable variety of sexual behavior. In many higher animals such behavior is not only varied

and elaborate but has taken on a secondary function not directly related to reproduction, that of social coherence and coordination.

Sexual Behavior of Invertebrates

Among one-celled animals, the conjugation of paramecia is perhaps the best example of sexual behavior. There is no differentiation of the sexes, and these actively swimming ciliates usually reproduce by simple division. Under certain conditions, however, two paramecia will come together, join their oral surfaces, and swim around while they exchange nuclei in a manner similar to the union of the sex cells in the higher animals. Once this is done, the pair divide into four small animals which swim around independently and reproduce asexually as before. Other kinds of protozoans, particularly sporozoans such as the malaria parasite, produce eggs and sperm, but there is no sexual behavior of the parent cells.

Thus in the one-celled animals we can see the beginnings of sexual behavior: the origin of special behavior designed to bring about the union of two nuclei, and the development of two kinds of cells to carry these nuclei, one small and mobile, plus the other large and full of nourishment for the combined pair. A large number of invertebrate animals show no more sexual behavior than that of the two kinds of sex cells. For animals living in water under crowded conditions, the sex cells can easily travel the distance necessary to bring about fertilization. As stated above, three whole phyla show no sex behavior, and the same thing is true of many mollusks, such as clams and oysters. As well as living in the water, all these

TABLE 1. THE OCCURRENCE OF SEXUAL BEHAVIOR IN THE ANIMAL KINGDOM

PHYLUM	NO SEXUAL BEHAVIOR	DIFFERENTIATED SEXUAL BEHAVIOR COMMON	FUNCTIONAL HERMAPHRODITISM COMMON	ASEXUAL AS WELL AS SEXUAL REPRODUCTION COMMON
Protozoa (one-celled animals)				x
Porifera (sponges)	x			
Coelenterata (corals and jellyfishes)	x			x
Echinodermata (starfish, sea urchins)	x			
Platyhelminthes (flatworms)			x	x
Nemathelminthes (roundworms)		x		
Annelida (segmented worms)			x	
Arthropoda (crustaceans, insects, spiders)		x		
Mollusca (snails, bivalves, squids)		x	x	
Chordata (especially vertebrates)		x		

animals are highly inactive. The more active invertebrates are likely to show sexual behavior.

For land-living animals sexual behavior is a necessity, since the sex cells cannot survive drying. Fresh water is also a poor environment for the sex cells, because of currents and the lack of a balanced solution of salt. Land-living animals and almost all active fresh-water animals therefore show some sexual behavior.

Hermaphroditism

The evolution of sexual behavior may take one of two directions. The first is toward hermaphroditism, with the development of both male and female organs in the same animal. Most of the flatworms are hermaphroditic, with well-developed male and female organs in every individual. In the free-living turbellarian flatworms, two individuals come together and mutually exchange sperms through penis-like organs. In the case of tapeworms, either cross-fertilization or self-fertilization of the eggs can occur. Many of the annelid worms are hermaphroditic. In earthworms, two individuals come together, lying side by side, both exchanging eggs and sperm, which are left inside a common cocoon. Among mollusks many snails are her-

maphroditic. In these slow-moving animals sexual behavior is not usually elaborate, the pair simply coming alongside into a position that permits the insertion of the penis. Since there is a common genital opening for the penis and vagina, only one of the pair can act as the male at a time. The Roman, or edible, snail has in addition to the penis a sharp dart used to stimulate the other animal before coitus. Some mollusks, such as the European oyster, are protandrous hermaphrodites, *i.e.*, the same individual can be at first a male and later on a female, but there is no sexual behavior in these bivalves. In some other animals hermaphroditism occurs as an anomaly of development, without any function being possible. This is the case in vertebrates, except for one species of fish, *Serranelus subligarius*, which is a functional hermaphrodite. A pair may reverse the sex roles while mating, but there is always one that acts as a male and one as a female.

Differentiation of Behavior

The more general evolutionary tendency in the higher animals is toward differentiation of sex behavior, males becoming more active and females more passive. The lesser activity of the female is often associated with the production of eggs, which tend to be heavy and bulky.

The details of sexual behavior are enormously varied and often appear bizarre to human eyes. Among the squids and octopuses, the males have a special arm that is used to transfer sperm to the female. The sperms are enclosed in little cases, the male inserting these spermatophores into the mantle of the female with his arm. In the chambered Nautilus, the female retains her hold on this arm, which then breaks off. Spiders also have a special appendage for the transfer of sperm. In this case, the end of the pedipalp is used as a syringe to suck up the sperm and transfer it to the female. Before this can be done, the male has to discharge the sperm into a special web that he weaves for the purpose. The female does not have to be present for the discharging process to occur. The males of many species of spiders have elaborate courtship dances, which apparently excite the female. In some of them the female occasionally eats the male, either because she is approached before being receptive, or because the male lingers too long after mating. This cannibalism apparently has no sexual significance, being the accidental result of a carnivorous existence. In crayfish and lobsters, mating behavior is much more like that of vertebrates. The male seizes the female with his claws, holding her on her back so that sperm can be carried into her body by means of a pair of abdominal appendages on the male, which serve the purpose of a penis.

Insects show an enormous variety of sexual behavior. Male grasshoppers and crickets produce their typical sounds which attract the female, after which copulation takes place. In moths it is the females that attract the male by odor, and the males are able to detect this at long distances with their feathery antennae. The mating dances of May flies are familiar to anyone who lives near a fresh-water pond or lake. In insects, mating usually takes place but once in the life history, sperms being retained in the female for long periods.

Reduction of Sex Behavior

A few invertebrates have evolved toward the elimination or reduction of sexual behav-

ior. In one species of roundworms, the male is a parasite that lives in the vagina of the female. Males are parasitic also in the marine annelid worm *Bonellia*, living within the body of the female. In some insects such as aphids the eggs normally develop without fertilization and males are produced only at certain seasons of the year, permitting sexual behavior every few generations. In ants, bees, and wasps the eggs can either be laid fertilized and become females, or unfertilized and become males. In the parasitic wasp *Nemeritis* there are no males and no sexual behavior. However, the mainstream of evolution is toward the development of separate sexes with two distinct types of behavior, and the reduction of sexual behavior is the exception rather than the rule.

Sexual Behavior of Vertebrates

Although vertebrates often live in the water, all of them are relatively large and actively moving animals that have of necessity evolved some type of sexual behavior. The examples given below will give some idea of the variety of sexual behavior that is possible among them.

Fish

In the mouth-breeding fish of the family Cichlidae, the eggs are picked up in the mouth of one of the parents and carried around until they hatch. Sexual behavior itself is much like that in other fish. In the African mouthbreeder, *Tilapia macrocephala,* the male and female first go through a pattern of courtship for several days. They approach, nod their heads, and spread out their gill covers, which exposes sexual markings. One member of the pair may stop and quiver for an instant. They also slap each other with their tails and occasionally may pursue and nip each other. Finally, the female begins to build the nest, scooping up gravel in her mouth. The pair swims over the nest; the female quivers and deposits the eggs, and the male deposits the sperm an instant later. After a minute the male picks up the eggs in his mouth. Here they hatch and develop until they are sufficiently mature to survive by themselves. Once having left the mouth, parental care ceases, and the young are eaten if caught. In other mouthbreeders the sex roles are reversed, the male building the nest and the female carrying the eggs.

Amphibians

Among amphibians, frogs show some of the most complex sexual behavior. The male chorus frog, *Pseudacris nigritus,* produces a loud call during the mating season in the spring of the year. Females approach the noisy male, who seizes one of them from the rear by hooking his forelimbs under her armpits. The pair stays in amplexus while the female moves to deeper water, where she lays her eggs. The contractions of her body stimulate the male to ejaculate the sperm, so that the eggs are fertilized as they are laid.

In salamanders with internal fertilization the pattern of sex behavior is quite different. Males of the genus *Ambystoma* precede the females to the breeding pond. When a female appears, a male twists and writhes around her as he rubs his nose against her tail and works forward on the body. This eventually stimulates the female to pick up with her cloacal lips the sperm case, or spermatophore, deposited by the male. In the axolotl the female picks up the sperm case with her hind feet and inserts it.

Reptiles

Among reptiles, the turtles have always excited popular curiosity as to how mating can take place between mates so completely covered by armor plate. Actually, sexual behavior is quite simple in most species. In the desert tortoise (*Gopherus*) the male approaches the female, nodding his head, and the female replies in kind. He then nips her forelegs and head until she draws them into her shell. Finally, he mounts the female from the rear, grunting, stamping his feet, and clicking his forefeet on her shell. He then inserts the penis into her cloaca and mating is complete.

Among snakes, the male in the mating season approaches the female. The two raise their heads and coil their bodies around each other, rubbing their heads and necks and waving their heads. Finally the posterior portions of the bodies intertwine, bringing the cloacas together so that coitus is achieved. Sex behavior is thus

preceded by a period of tactile stimulation. In lizards, the courtship is likely to be visual instead of tactile. The males are usually brilliantly colored and display these markings prior to actual mating. In *Sceloporus* a typical part of the display behavior is a "push up," in which the male rapidly raises and lowers his head. Finally the male grasps the female by the skin of the neck with his teeth, clasping her with his legs and twisting his tail beneath hers to bring the two cloacas together, and inserts one hemipenis.

Sexual behavior in alligators is quite similar to that in lizards except that in the preliminary stages the males roar in the swamps. A female is attracted by the call, after which the pair swim around, with the male rubbing his throat across the snout of the female and roaring again.

Sexual behavior in reptiles has evolved in two different directions: one in which preliminary stimulation is largely a matter of visual display, and the other in which stimulation is largely tactile. This perhaps points to the kinds of greater specialization of sexual behavior that are typical respectively of birds and mammals.

Birds

Among many birds sexual behavior is part of a relationship between a pair that lasts throughout the breeding season. Herring gulls nest in large colonies on small islands. Pair formation begins when a female approaches a male, walking around him and finally making tossing movements with her head. This stimulates the male to regurgitate food, which the female devours. The pair eventually selects a nest area, which they guard as a territory. Sexual behavior takes place once or twice a day. Both birds toss their heads for several minutes as if begging for food. Finally the male stretches his neck, jumps into the air, and mounts the female. Coition is achieved by bringing the two cloacas together.

Display behavior in courtship can be much more elaborate. In the sage grouse the male develops a special nuptial plumage. During the breeding season the males gather together on special breeding grounds. Early in the morning the males go through the display behavior over and over for hours. The male spreads his tail like a fan, throws his head back, and with a sort of pumping motion inflates the air sacs of the throat, which appear as two bright red spots in the midst of a cloak of white feathers streaming down from the neck. He then releases the air with a sort of plopping noise. Eventually the females arrive. When a female draws near a dominant male she crouches, the male mounts, and coition takes place within a few seconds. Some display behavior is usually a part of the courtship of song birds but is not so obvious in these small and rapidly flying birds. The display behavior may function to organize behavior between males as well as to stimulate the females.

A good deal of research has been done with stuffed specimens to determine what it is that stimulates the male. In turkeys the entire pattern of display and mounting can be stimulated merely by the stuffed head of a female. In Brewer's blackbird the female mates with her head and tail raised. Males mate with a dummy posed in a similar atttiude if either the head or tail is removed, but not both.

In general, the sexual behavior of birds emphasizes preliminary courtship, with much visual display of plumage and considerable movement. The actual contact in coition is very brief. This may be the result of their having feathers, which effectively prevent extensive tactile stimulation. Such is not the case with mammals.

Mammals

It is hard to observe sexual behavior under natural conditions in mammals, and the most detailed studies have been done with laboratory animals. However, some observations have been made, and the following examples are chiefly those of animals observed mating in the wild.

During the autumn breeding season a male moose joins a cow and her calf, staying with her from ten days to two weeks. The male makes a wallow by rolling and pawing on the ground, and chases other males away from it. He urinates in it, paws the ground, and rolls in the wallow. Eventually he approaches the female, sniffs her hind quarters, and then throws his head back, extending the neck and curling the upper lip. This posture is a characteristic

part of the sexual behavior of male hoofed animals, being common in domestic cattle, sheep, and goats. The moose then shoulders the female toward the wallow, mounts her, and stays mounted for approximately three minutes. The wallow apparently plays a part in mating behavior, which always takes place nearby.

Elephant seals breed on islands off the coast of California. Each adult male is surrounded by females. After giving birth to her young the female is receptive to any male, the external sign being an enlarged vulva. The male approaches the female without display or courtship, coming up to her from the rear and pinning her down by throwing his body on top of hers. He then maneuvers her body so that her vulva is close to the penis and, lying partly over and partly to one side, makes a number of pelvic thrusts. The female arches her back to bring the vulva into position, and copulation may last three to seven minutes. Once the penis is inserted pelvic thrusts cease.

In the above two mammals sexual behavior is confined to a brief season. Seasonal breeding is characteristic of most mammals in temperate zones but there are others, presumably of tropical origin, in which breeding takes place through the year. In the domestic guinea pig estrus cycles take place every 16 days or so unless pregnancy interferes. A male approaches any female, investigating her with his nose, particularly around the vaginal opening. If not receptive, she will squat or move away. If she is receptive the male becomes excited, walking around her with a rolling gait and making rumbling noises. He eventually mounts and makes several pelvic thrusts. He may mount more than once before ejaculation takes place, after which he relaxes and becomes difficult to excite for some time. The ejaculated material forms a hard plug within the vagina, which probably interferes with further sexual activity. During any one cycle the female is in heat for only a few hours.

The sexual behavior of primates also shows regular cycles that take place throughout the year, unless the female becomes pregnant. There is a prolonged period of receptivity. Any cycle in which fertilization does not take place is followed by menstruation, a phenomenon that does not take place in any other group of mammals. Many primate females exhibit a swelling of the sexual skin. In the female chimpanzee an area of bright pink skin six or eight inches in diameter projects around the vagina. In sexual behavior she "presents," crouching so that her enormously enlarged vulva is directed toward the male. He mounts, and after many pelvic thrusts ejaculation is achieved. The bright colors of male baboons are probably also connected with sexual stimulation. Primates are unusual among mammals in that visual stimulation, as well as tactile stimulation, appears to be important. In a majority of other mammals the male is stimulated chiefly by odor and touch. There are relatively few mammals in which there is a prolonged preliminary courtship, although the male is frequently attracted to the female before she is receptive.

The Relationship of Fertilization to Sexual Behavior

All animals have some mechanism that ensures that sexual behavior actually leads to the fertilization of the eggs. One of these is the storing of long-lived sperm in the body of the female. In honeybees sexual behavior takes place only once in the life of the female, who may live for two or three years. The queen bee stores the sperm within her body and releases it to fertilize the eggs, which develop into the workers and future queen. Males are produced only when needed, by unfertilized eggs. A similar phenomenon exists in bats, which mate in the autumn, store the sperm throughout the season of hibernation, and produce the eggs to be fertilized in the spring. However, it is far more common for both eggs and sperm to be fragile and short-lived. In most mammals the sperms die after a few hours in the female. The sperms of fresh-water fishes live for only a few minutes.

A second device is to ensure fertilization through the behavior of the female. In a large number of mammals there is a definite period of sexual receptivity that precedes or is closely related to the time of ovulation. For example, the female guinea pig comes into heat about eight hours before ovulation takes place, ensuring that sexual behavior and hence a supply

of fresh sperm will be available at the time the eggs are produced.

A less common device is the control of ovulation by the sexual behavior of the male. In rabbits the eggs are produced by the female twelve hours after copulation has taken place. The domestic cat shows a similar phenomenon. In the latter, the penis of the male is covered with small barbs, and the pain of coitus stimulates the pituitary gland, which in turn releases the hormones that cause ovulation. The phenomenon can be experimentally duplicated by painful stimulation with a glass rod.

Still another method of ensuring fertilization is frequent sexual behavior during the season or time when the eggs are produced. In birds the eggs must be fertilized before the shell is added, and since the eggs are normally laid at the rate of one a day, sperms must be available over extended periods. The birds have solved the problem by repeated mating rather than by the retention of long-lived sperm, and long associations between males and females during the mating season are characteristic of these animals. Somewhat the same situation exists in primates, in which the females typically have long periods of receptivity but produce only one egg at each period. In normal groups of howling monkeys and baboons, the receptive females go from male to male, leaving each one as he becomes satiated. This ensures that a supply of fresh sperm will be available at the time of ovulation. At the same time, prolonged sexual behavior affects more than the process of fertilization, playing an important part in the social organization of the species.

Sexual Behavior and Social Organization

The role of sexual behavior in the social life of a species can vary from none at all, as in many of the lower invertebrates, to a large one, as in many of the higher mammals. Its importance is related to the heredity of the species and to the hereditary mechanisms that produce the differentiation of sexual form and behavior. We are accustomed to think of social organization in the higher animals as being related to three biological types, males, females, and young, with appropriate differences in sexual and other forms of social behavior. In the social insects this differentiation is carried still further. In ants, bees, and wasps, fertilized eggs can either become the sterile female workers who form the majority of the colony, or the fertile queens. Only the males and the queens ordinarily show sexual behavior. Thus, there are three types of adults instead of two as in the vertebrates.

Insects

The patterns of sex behavior in insects are quite distinct between the sexes, without overlap. Occasionally a developing egg may, by accident to the normal division of chromosomes, produce a gynandromorph. This is an individual in which part of the body is male and part female. When the head is one sex and the rest of the body another, the behavior corresponds to the head rather than to the part of the body that contains the sex organs.

In termites there may be several different hereditary types or castes of individuals, ranging from soldiers and workers to the reproductive castes, which show sexual behavior. In general, the importance of sexual behavior to social organization is very slight in the social insects.

Vertebrates

Quite a different situation obtains in the vertebrates, where the two sexes are more alike. Male- and female-producing eggs differ in only one chromosome. The reproductive organs of both sexes develop from the same primitive embryonic organs, and the corresponding parts are exaggerated or diminished to produce the final differences. Likewise, both sexes possess the potentiality for producing the pattern of behavior characteristic of either the male or the female. The usual differences in emphasis of behavior are produced in part by differences in hormones and in part by differences in the anatomy of the sex organs, and are never as sharply differentiated as they are in insects. In many species of mammals the females show the behavior of mounting and pelvic thrusts, in reaction either to other females in estrus or to males in the early part of courtship and sexual behavior.

Many of the vertebrates show seasonal sexual behavior, and in most cases the behavior of the male extends over a longer period than that of the female. As shown above, the females of many mammals have only a short period of estrus, or heat.

BIRDS

A short period of estrus or receptivity is characteristic of animals that do not have a prolonged association between males and females. The contrary is true when mates are associated for long periods. In most of the perching birds the males and females form definite pairs that occupy the same nest during the breeding season. The male usually takes some part in the rearing of the young. Sexual behavior includes a long period of courtship prior to actual mating, and this in part has the function of coordinating the endocrine systems and hence the sexual and parental behavior of the two birds. Sexual behavior is an important part of the pairing bond, which may last several seasons.

Sexual behavior plays a somewhat different role in the gallinaceous birds, to which our domestic chickens are related. In these birds one male typically mates with several females, and the females have the entire care of the young. In the grouse family, sexual behavior is organized around mating grounds, sexual contacts are brief, and the females raise the young apart from the males.

MAMMALS

A similar variety of sexual behavior exists in mammals, some of which have brief contacts and others quite prolonged ones. In the herd animals such as cattle and sheep, a female will normally show one short estrus period during the mating season. Sexual behavior is accomplished without elaborate courtship. The male simply approaches the female, investigates her with his nose, and attempts to mount. If she is receptive, copulation and ejaculation take place within a few seconds. This may be repeated frequently during the estrus period, depending on how many females are present. A similar type of behavior takes place in the elephant seal. These animals come into estrus for a short time immediately after the young are born. A single male mates briefly with each female as

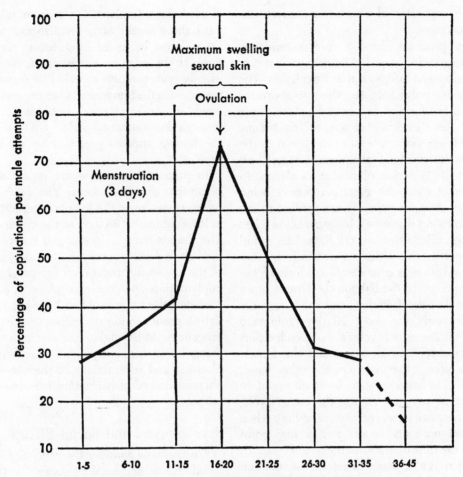

FIG. 1. Sexual receptivity in the female chimpanzee. Copulation occurs at all points in the cycle, which is normally 35 days in length. (After Elder and Yerkes, *Anat. Rec. 67;* 119-143, 1936, by permission Wister Institute Press.)

she is receptive. There is no other sexual behavior throughout the year, nor do the males and females show any close relationship to each other.

This may be contrasted with the sexual behavior of the wolf, which is similar to that of its descendant, the domestic dog. Mating begins in January and February, and may continue until March. The first sign of estrus in the female is a slight amount of bleeding from the vagina. Along with this, and possibly produced by it, the female deposits a substance with her urine that is highly exciting to males. Males will react to the scent of either the urine or the female herself. Under normal conditions, the mated pair of wolves have lived together throughout the year and during this part of the sexual cycle there is a great deal of courtship behavior. Both

animals may rear on their hind legs, throwing the forelegs around each other's necks with the head to one side and the tongue extended. They also exhibit a playful attitude, crouching on the front legs but keeping the hips high, and then darting rapidly away. This results in long periods of running and chasing. During this part of the cycle the female will not permit the male to mount. Full receptivity appears at about the time the bleeding ceases and may last for two or three weeks. The entire cycle may last as long as six weeks, during which the male and female are constantly with each other. Sexual behavior takes place many times during the receptive period. Ovulation occurs approximately 72 hours before the end of the receptive period in the dog and probably also in the wolf. In the latter there is normally only one cycle per year, regardless of whether or not fertilization takes place.

Many primates show a similar tendency toward extended sexual behavior, with receptivity measured in days rather than hours. The females are polyestrus, i.e., the cycles are repeated if fertilization does not take place. Some species show evidence of a breeding season. In the rhesus monkey most of the births in the Cayo Santiago colony take place in March and April, with the peak of mating occurring in July and August, the gestation period being 168 days. As more primates are studied in the field it is found that sexual behavior plays a less important role in their overall lives than would be expected from observations made in captivity, and there is considerable difference between species. In the baboon the female has a menstrual cycle of 35 days, but she is sexually receptive only for about 10 days following ovulation. The estrus cycles are suspended during pregnancy and lactation, and the female will not accept the male. On the other hand, captive chimpanzees have been observed to copulate at any time during the estrus cycle, showing a peak of receptivity at the time when ovulation normally occurs and a low point around the time of menstruation (see Figure 1). Thus there is a tendency to extend the function of sexual behavior far beyond that of fertilization.

Internal Development of the Young

Sexual behavior in mammals is tied up with the process of internal development of the young. Not only must sexual behavior be correlated with ovulation, it must also be secondarily related to the preparation of the uterus for the implantation of the egg and the nourishment of the developing embryo. The primitive estrus cycle in mammals is probably a short one, similar to that which takes place in most rodents. Hormones stimulate both the growth of the lining of the uterus and sexual behavior. At the appropriate time other hormones stimulate ovulation. The uterus is maintained for a brief time, but if the embryo is not implanted its lining regresses and the whole cycle starts over again. In an animal like the dog the period of estrus activity, and consequently of hormonal activity, is extended over several weeks instead of a few days. Implantation does not take place until three weeks after fertilization, and the uterus must be maintained during all of this time. If the eggs do not implant, the female usually goes through a period of pseudopregnancy, with the hormones behaving just as they would in a true pregnancy until about halfway through the pregnancy period. Up to this point the female appears pregnant by all external signs.

In primates the cycles are repeated if implantation does not occur. The intervals between cycles are quite long compared to those in lower animals (35 days in the chimpanzee). The maintenance of prolonged receptivity in the female results in considerable development of the uterus in preparation for pregnancy. If implantation does not take place, the female primate solves this problem by what is essentially a pseudochildbirth, rather than a pseudopregnancy. At the end of each cycle the uterine lining is shed, accompanied by considerable bleeding and contractions of the uterus. This phenomenon of menstruation is found only in primates.

Psychological and Social Effects

We may now consider the psychological and social effects of sexual behavior. In the first place, sexual behavior causes animals to come together, having a cohesive effect upon pairs and groups of individuals. In many of the lower animals the sole effect is the formation of temporary sexual aggregations during the breeding season. If sexual behavior is extended over a long period of time, as it is in many of the higher vertebrates, it may become a much more important cohesive force. Even in the herd animals, where the period of sexual receptivity in the female may only last a day or so, the association between males and females may last several weeks, probably because the behavior of the males is much less limited in time.

In addition, sexual behavior would be expected to have strong secondary psychological effects. In the majority of animals, sexual behavior appears to be rewarding. There are only a few possible exceptions, such as female cats. This means that repeated sexual behavior in an animal capable of advanced types of learning will lead to a very strong secondary motivation toward sexual behavior, and that this will be associated with the individual or individuals with whom it takes place. In short, the biologically attractive effect of sexual behavior will be enhanced and made more specific by psychological processes. There is considerable evidence that this actually takes place in many birds and mammals, that sexual behavior is an important part of the cohesion of social groups, and that some modification of it may even affect the cohesiveness of male groups. Male mountain sheep outside the breeding season sometimes exhibit minor aspects of the pattern of sexual behavior between themselves.

Thus, sexual behavior has evolved in two main directions in the higher animals. One is toward the insurance of fertilization. This tends to restrict or minimize sexual activity, the extreme cases occurring in the social insects, where mating takes place only once in the life of the female and fertilization is thereafter controlled by her physiology. The other direction is toward the use of sexual behavior as a cohesive social force. Both these tendencies exist among vertebrates, sometimes within the same species. There may be a very short period of sexual behavior in the female, ensuring fertilization, and a much longer period of sexual activity in the male, producing social attraction. Even in primates, in which the sexual activity of both sexes is prolonged, there is a higher degree of activity in the male.

The evolution of the social function of sexual behavior has gone further in primates and especially in man than in any other group of mammals, bringing with it certain dangers as well as positive effects. The extension of sexual behavior over a long period compared to the brief time in which the ovum is fresh and in good condition increases the risk of abnormal and defective development. Furthermore, the long-continued high degree of sexual motivation is conducive to maladaptive behavior of various sorts.

Abnormal Sexual Behavior in Animals

We shall here consider certain types of behavior that do not produce the most effective degree of adaptation, particularly maladaptive behavior that arises from functional causes rather than from organic injuries and deficiencies.

The experimental work on abnormal behavior in animals indicates that three conditions are conducive to the development of maladaptive behavior. One is a *high degree* of *excitement* or *motivation*. A second is the *inability* of the animal *to escape* from the source of excitement, because of confinement or other reasons. A third is the *inability to adapt* to the situation, that is, to respond effectively to stimulation. In the case of sexual behavior, motivation can be extremely high, arising as it does from a combination of internal physiological causes, external stimulation, and learned motivation. There are many situations that prevent escape, and in any case the animal cannot escape his own internal stimulation. Finally, there are many situations that prevent sexual behavior. The important thing to remember is that all three conditions must be present in order to produce maladaptive behavior. Furthermore, the response of animals to such situations can be affected by hereditary differences, the primary one of which is the difference in the male and female physiology of sexual behavior.

Response to an Inappropriate Object (Displacement)

Normally, sexual behavior takes place between two individuals of the same species and of opposite sex, but the behavior of animals may depart from this in many different ways. The most extreme deviation is toward inanimate objects. Most of the reported cases have been produced experimentally by the use of models that to some extent resemble the other sex. Most male birds can be induced to respond to stuffed skins, even under wild conditions, provided the posture is appropriate. The most extreme case is that of the male turkey, which will respond to nothing more than the stuffed head of a female.

Self-stimulation appears frequently in male mammals, but occurs most often in primates, which use their hands for the purpose. A curious example is the antler-rubbing of certain members of the deer family. The red deer and moose rub their antlers on trees during the rutting season, and this action is accompanied by erection and extrusion of the penis. Male elk in zoos sometimes dig their antlers into the ground with the same effect. Whether this is true self-stimulation or part of the general pattern of courtship behavior is still in question.

Sexual reactions to members of the same sex are quite common, particularly in captivity where animals of one sex are confined together. In the herd animals males frequently mount each other, especially the young ones, but there is rarely any complete sexual behavior. Two male sheep placed on one side of a fence with a female in estrus on the other responded by exhibiting courtship behavior toward each other. Females of many species, including dogs and rats as well as the herd animals, will mount each other and even make thrusting movements when in estrus. A female in heat may receive this kind of behavior without protest, but a male that is mounted usually reacts aggressively. Beach has recorded a few cases where male rats have accepted a passive sexual role. In general, this type of behavior is extremely common wherever sexually active animals of the same sex are confined together.

Another type of inappropriate response is sexual behavior of an immature animal toward an adult. Male lambs will sometimes respond to a female adult in certain circumstances, such as giving birth to a lamb, and puppies may respond to their mothers in estrus. However, the adults usually reject the advances of the young males, which in any case do not lead to complete sexual behavior. The reverse situation, in which adults respond to young animals, is very uncommon, probably because in most species the young do not have the necessary stimulating properties.

A final type of inappropriate object is the female or male of another species. This sort of behavior is closely associated with early social experience. Animals that are removed from their own species at birth or hatching and raised by another variety tend to transfer social reactions to the adopted species. This is one of the striking effects of imprinting in birds, and it occurs to a somewhat lesser extent in mammals. A young puppy was taken from the mother at the age of four weeks and reared to the age of

several months without direct contact with other dogs, but having contact with people and a male cat. Like most other pet dogs, it made sexual responses to people, but these were immediately discouraged by punishment. As a puppy it played with the cat and made attempts to mount it. Later, when the dog was an adult, a male kitten was brought into the home and the dog responded to it by licking and nosing it. Instead of mounting, the dog would stand over the kitten. When the kitten became mature the dog began licking its posterior. The cat now responded by assuming the position normally taken by a female in coitus. Both animals appeared to obtain some sexual satisfaction. However, the same dog also responded normally to a female dog in estrus.

Many species that normally do not interbreed will mate if placed in close contact in captivity. Lions will mate with tigers in zoos, producing living offspring. Sheep and goats will mate, but the embryos die before birth. This sort of complete sexual behavior between species is of course dependent upon similar anatomy and patterns of sexual behavior.

In summary, sexual responses to inappropriate objects or individuals largely result from two circumstances. One is the lack of opportunity for mating with a member of the opposite sex of the same species. Abnormal sexual behavior is almost inevitable if an animal is subjected to this condition for long periods. The second circumstance is early experience, which can be particularly conducive to mating with members of a different species. Many birds raised by hand appear to be unable to readjust to their own species, but mammals apparently respond to either their own or the adopted species. The vast majority of cases of abnormal sexual behavior occur under conditions of high stimulation and captivity, which fits the theoretical predictions given above.

Substitution of Inappropriate Behavior in Response to Sexual Stimulation

This has not been widely observed among animals but it does occur. For example, in litters of terrier dogs the males are usually larger than the females and become dominant over them. However, an occasional female becomes dominant over a male. The usual pattern of behavior associated with dominance is for the dominant animal to growl at the subordinate, approaching from the side and placing its forefeet on the back of the latter. The subordinate animal will usually stand still or, if unusually frightened, will roll on its back, extending its legs and exposing its teeth, usually growling and yelping at the same time. When a dominant female is approached by a subordinate male who attempts to mount from the rear, she responds to his touch as to an attempt at domination, turning around and driving him off. In short, she responds to sexual stimulation with aggressive behavior and this prevents any further sexual behavior. The same female, however, may be dominated by a strange male and mating will proceed normally.

The same sort of thing occurs in flocks of chickens. The more dominant members of a flock of hens will crouch less often to receive a male than the more subordinate ones. If young cockerels grow up with adult females, the females attack them when they make sexual advances, thus preventing any sort of sex behavior.

In both these cases there is no indication that the animals receive any sort of sexual satisfaction from the aggressive behavior. Rather, these are cases in which certain aspects of the patterns of sexual and agonistic behavior are closely similar, and learned responses interfere with normal behavior.

Repression and distortion of sexual behavior. Sexual behavior of mammals can be drastically altered by certain kinds of early experience. A puppy which is punished for playful sexual behavior in early life will as an adult guard females but will not attempt to mate with them. Male puppies reared in complete visual isolation from other animals frequently show defects in later attempts to copulate. One of the most striking effects of rearing in isolation from species mates is seen in the rhesus monkey, where mating becomes almost completely impossible even with experienced members of the opposite sex. This in part is the result of the complicated sexual posture of rhesus monkeys, in which the male must stand on the ankles of the female. The capacity to perform complete

sexual behavior is normally developed through playful contacts with other monkeys in early life.

Substitution of Sexual Behavior for Other Types of Social Adaptation

Among captive chimpanzees it is quite common for subordinate males and females to assume a sexual posture in response to threats by a dominant male. This usually has the effect of stopping the male from dealing out punishment. Where a competitive situation exists, the female will sometimes offer herself to a male so that she can divert his attention and obtain a piece of food. In some cases it looks as if the female is using sexual behavior as a tool for obtaining other advantages. Conversely, a male may cajole and caress a female in order to take food away from her without actually getting into a fight. However, such uses of sex behavior seem to occur chiefly in primates, where sex behavior is unusually highly developed as a part of social organization.

Conclusion

Sexual behavior is associated with the process of bisexual reproduction in animals. One of the most important functions of the latter is to make possible rapid evolutionary change. In keeping with this, sexual behavior has evolved throughout the animal kingdom into an enormous variety of methods by which sperms and eggs may be brought together. Sexual behavior may involve many different sorts of motor organs and a large variety of sensory experience. In the vertebrates sexual stimulation may be chiefly visual, as it is in many fishes and birds, or it may emphasize contact and odor as it does in most mammals. The varieties of sexual experiences that are possible for human beings are far exceeded by those found in the animal kingdom as a whole.

Sexual behavior has two important functions: ensuring fertilization and social cohesion. The latter is a secondary one that seems to have evolved independently in many species of birds and mammals but reaches its height in the primates. In other social animals, particularly the social insects, the function of social cohesion through sex is minimized.

In those species showing prolonged sexual behavior with an important social function, the problem of malfunctioning sexual behavior is important. It is also in the highly social animals that sexual behavior can be most readily altered by early experience.

In general, the sexual behavior of the invertebrates and lower vertebrates seems to be organized largely by heredity. The restrictions of sexual behavior that prevent sterile sexual activity are based on hereditary control and physiology. In the highly social animals more and more of these restrictions are imposed by social environment and social training. In the higher social vertebrates experience plays a large part in the development of sexual behavior: through the sexual play of immature animals, and the rewarding effect of successful sexual behavior of adults. Most animals are able to mate successfully at maturity without further training, but among chimpanzees held in captivity immature animals apparently have to learn sexual behavior from experienced animals of the other sex. Thus there is a tendency, even in this very fundamental form of behavior, to evolve toward greater modification through experience. This is in addition to the other major tendency in the evolution of sexual behavior, toward the development of social functions other than reproduction.

References

Aronson, L. R., "Reproductive and Parental Behavior." In M. E. Brown (ed.), *The Physiology of Fishes: Vol. 2. Behavior.* New York: Academic Press, Inc., 1957.

Beach, Frank A., (ed.), *Sex and Behavior.* New York: Wiley, 1965.

Berrill, N. J., *Sex and the Nature of Things.* New York: Pocket Books, Inc., 1955. A popular account.

DeVore, I., (ed.), *Primate Behavior.* New York: Holt, Rinehart and Winston, 1965.

Elder, J. H., and Yerkes, R. M., "The Sexual Cycle of the Chimpanzee." *Anat. Rec. 67;* 119-143, 1936.

Etkin, W., "Social Behavior and the Evolution of Man's Mental Faculties." *Am. Nat. 88;* 129-142, 1954.

Evans, L. T., *Courtship and Territorial Behavior of Lower Vertebrates.* Mimeographed.

Ford, C. S., and Beach, Frank A., *Patterns of Sexual Behavior.* New York: Harper & Brothers, Inc., 1951.

Gertsch, W. J., *American Spiders.* New York: D. Van Nostrand Co., Inc., 1949.

Milne, Lorus J., and Milne, Margery J., *The Mating Instinct.* Boston: Little, Brown & Co., 1954. A popular account.

Schrier, A. M., Harlow, H. F., and Stollnitz, F., *Behavior of Nonhuman Primates.* New York: Academic Press, 1965.

Scott, J. P., *Animal Behavior.* Chicago: University of Chicago Press, 1958.

Tinbergen, N., *Social Behavior in Animals.* London: Methuen & Co., 1953.

Young, W. C. (ed.), *Genetic, Psychological and Hormonal Factors in the Establishment and Maintenance of Patterns of Sexual Behavior in Mammals.* Lawrence, Kan.: mimeographed by the author, 1954.

J. P. SCOTT

Aphrodisiacs
and Anaphrodisiacs

Aphrodisiacs

IN THE strangely folklored realm of sexual behavior the subject of aphrodisiacs is unquestionably the most folkloristic. Practically everyone has heard of them, but almost no one knows anything definite about them. Furthermore, it is inordinately difficult, even for the professionally interested, to procure any scientific information concerning them. Today, in our civilization, few people take them seriously, and with the exception of the usual and rarely funny "jokes" about oysters, hardly anyone gives aphrodisiacs a second thought. Erotic stimulants, however, have throughout history played a significant role in the majority of the world's cultures.

An indication of the bizarre lengths to which man has gone in order to devise means of artificially stimulating sexual desire may be gained from the following list: baths, salves, smells, parts of animals, blood (especially menstrual blood), powders, pills, creams, oils, narcotics (opium, hashish, marijuana, etc.), ether, electrotherapy, tattooing, erotic pictures, pornographic literature, "dirty" records (not only records with obscene lyrics, but also recordings that reproduce the sounds, vocal and mechanical, such as the rattling noise of bedsprings and even sometimes scatological details), music, mechanical contraptions (fornicating machines, self-satisfiers, pressure pumps for the male organ), "dames de voyages" (rubber women), "phallic foods" (foods fashioned in the form of the male and female organs), "cabi-nets particuliers," erotic cookbooks, household articles in sexual forms (lamps, drinking cups, etc.), instruments for flagellation and other forms of torture, various forms of contraceptives (shaped like hands, little men, etc.), amulets, charms, and so forth.

First, it should be pointed out that there has been an extraordinary amount of nonsense written about aphrodisiacs. The subject is infinitely complicated and subtle, and very few writers have taken into consideration all the many psychological and physiological factors involved. The literature that deals with the subject is out of date, impressionistic, and unscientific. Strange to report, almost no work on this topic deals with the biochemical, or physiological, aspect, which is, as will be seen, of utmost importance in establishing the validity of the whole concept of erotic stimulants.

Although there has been little written about aphrodisiacs from a scientific point of view, many famous writers have referred to them. Undated medical papyri, probably from the Middle Kingdom (2200–1700 B.C.) of Egypt, give recipes for preparing "erotic potions." The Greeks wrote extensively on the subject, the oldest known passage being, probably, the one in the *Medea* of Euripides (431 B.C.). There are likewise countless allusions to aphrodisiac foods by the greatest names in Latin, Sanskrit, Arabic, Persian, Chinese, and English literature. One of the chief, and largely unsuspected, characteristics of Elizabethan drama is the interest shown in aphrodisiacs. Shakespeare: "Let the sky rain potatoes, hail kissing comfits [bon-

145

bons, sweetbreads]; and snow eringoes [a plant of the genus *Eryngium*, specifically, *Eryngium maritimum*, the European sea holly whose roots were, hopefully, candied as a sweetmeat]; let a tempest of provocation come"; Drayton: "The skirrat [sic] [usually "skirret"—another of the *Apiaceae*, a plant resembling celery, formerly cultivated in Europe for the sweet taste of its roots], which, some say, stirs the blood"; Beaumont and Fletcher: "Will your ladyship have a potato-pie? 'tis a stirring good dish for an old lady after a long lent. . . ." The newly imported potato was considered, oddly enough, to be an especially effective erotic stimulant.

Before discussing the principal kinds of aphrodisiacs, it might be advisable to consider the various ways in which sexual desire can be induced. These include: (1) *local,* primarily, stimulation of the sex organs; secondarily, stimulation of other erogenous zones of the body; (2) *physical,* as in massage and baths in which the skin and muscles are stimulated; (3) *automatic,* the physiological reaction that takes place as a result of artificial stimulation of the gastrourinal tract: an increased supply of blood which causes a swelling of the organs (hyperemia); and (4) *psychophysiological,* as, for example, the libidinal cravings that are supposed to be awakened by erotic "literature" or pictures. In addition, there is still another much more important method (from a scientific point of view) and that is the treatment of hormone deficiency by means of injections.

It should be noted that the term "aphrodisiac," as used in this article, refers to some food, liquid, or drug taken into the body; as such it excludes voyeurism, fetishism, masochism, sadism, and other external forms of sexual stimulation.

The Dominant Role Played by Food in the History of Aphrodisiacs

Of all types of aphrodisiacs, food is the best known. It is obvious that if any food is to have erotic effects, it must do so almost exclusively in a biochemical fashion. In other words, the specific food must contain chemical elements that react physiologically upon the human body.

At this point it is appropriate to point out that there is a much more profound interrela-

tionship between food and eating and sexual desire and expression than is generally realized —even among specialists. Indeed, a number of observers in different fields, including naturalists, neurologists, anthropologists, and physicians as well as psychiatrists, have expressed the opinion that this relationship between the two functions is a physiological and neurological correspondence that might well be interpreted as a psychosymbolic identity.

Thus, the German naturalist, Bölsche (1906):

In this sense eating was the earliest prerequisite of love. With the firstlings of life, there was no opposition between eating and love, eating was a purely logical condition of love.

But then came sexual love, and with it the fusing of life with life, cell with cell, egg-cell with sperm-cell, nucleus with nucleus, chromosome with chromosome, hereditary capital with hereditary capital. From this fusion there arose a heightened growth, a richer, more-sided possession. Thus sexual love with its union was to a certain extent, really a sort of higher eating.

According to the brain specialist, Berry (1928):

Between these two great dominating factors of life, hunger and sex, there is a very close neurological analogy. In both there are hollow viscera capable of varying degrees of distension, though in the one case it is the full viscus which stimulates the neurons, and in the other the empty viscus. These varying degrees of distension constantly arouse enteroceptive impulses which pass through the autonomic nervous system to the central nervous system. In both instances these primary impulses become commingled in the cerebral cortex with the appropriate secondary enteroceptive ones, and it follows that in both cases the desire for food or sex may be aroused by either the primary or the secondary impulse.

In the words of the British anthropologist, Crawley (1927):

Biologically, the sexual impulse is a development from the nutritive, and the primary close connection of the two functions is continued in thought, subconscious and physiological, and appears sometime above the threshold of consciousness. We find further that many human conceptions are not only based on the connection but express it clearly. One of the most obvious links between the two is the kiss, and much popular thought and language preserves similar conceptions.

Or, as Fielding (1929) expresses it:

As the nerves approach the surface of the body, of which they are the medium for sensation, they split up into a network of subdivisions. It is a significant physiological fact that one kind of nerve structures, called *Krause's end-bulbs,* which are unusually large and sensitive, are found principally in the clitoris, penis and lips.

Furthermore, the German nutritionist, Balzli (1931):

The sensual internal surface areas of the sex organs, correspond to the taste-buds of the mouth.

In connection with this last statement, mention should be made of still another physiological correspondence between the function of the oral and sex organs; namely, between the precoital distillation that takes place in the genitalia (Cowper's glands in the male, and Bartholin's glands in the female) and the increased salivation that is brought about by active sexual desire.

And finally, Coriat (1921):

The perpetual driving force of human emotions and conduct comes from the great region of the unconscious. This creative force presents itself in two aspects, the problem of self-preservation or the nutritional libido, and the problem of the perpetuation of the race, or the sexual libido. It seems, however, according to Freud, that instead of there being two libido streams, there is *only one.* For the pleasure derived from satisfying hunger is at the bottom sexual, possibly because of the close interlocking or practical identity of the two cravings.

In addition to the deep-seated neurological and physiological connection between eating and sexual expression, there also exists a number of basic physical analogies between various forms of foods and both the male and female genitalia. In other words, not only does eating equal intercourse, but also food equals penis, vulva. Although little known even to specialists, the making and eating of phallic foods (the representation of certain foods, usually bread, cakes, and other pastries, in the form of sexual organs) is a custom that has been practiced for centuries in many civilizations throughout the world as a significant religious rite. Typical

examples of this food-as-sex symbolism are the early Greek (Sicilian) *mylloi,* the famous sesame and honey cakes mentioned by Athenaeus, which were fashioned after the vulva and carried around in the Thesmophoria rituals; the "priapic and venereal breads," the *coliphia* and *siligone,* described by Lacroix, that were sold in Roman bakeries by servantmaid-prostitutes; the ktenic dishes of medieval France, "*cibi quos cunnos saccaratos appellant,*" as recorded by Höfler (1912); and the modern *phalloi* of bread, which were blessed by priests and carried in the "Thorn Festivals" of certain rural areas in Italy (Elderkin, 1924).

There are, however, no foods that have elements possessing significant and definite effects upon the complicated genital structure of the male and female body. For example, let us examine the chemical analysis of two of the most famous of all—the oyster and the truffle. The oyster is made up, principally, of water (76–89 per cent), carbohydrates (3.7–9.6 per cent), mineral salts (ash 0.9–3.0 per cent), glycogen (0.4–9.5 per cent), proteins (8–11 per cent), and fat (1.2–2.5 per cent). Also usually present are such inorganic constituents as potassium, calcium, and sodium, but only in negligible quantities. Thus, the oyster is composed entirely of elements that do not and cannot affect genital functions. As for the truffle, it is even less "sexy," as it consists of, according to the *Larousse gastronomique,* "water 76.83%, salts 1.57%, albumen 7.62%, fat 0.49% and carbohydrates 13.49%."

At this point an obvious question arises: If foods are generally incapable of inducing sexual impulses, how is it that man has, since the dawn of creation, in every corner of the globe, attributed aphrodisiac powers to many kinds of foods? To best understand this paradoxical situation, we must go back many centuries. In those ancient days one of the most famous concepts was the "doctrine of signatures." This not only "explained" the causes of many sicknesses, but also endowed plants and vegetables with attributes that they did not possess.

The "doctrine of signatures" is the thesis that there exists some resemblance between the external character of a disease and the curative agent. Thus, scarlet fever should be treated with a red cloth. This visual identification, as it were, was carried over into the realm of sex; if a root or leaf or fruit of a plant, vegetable, or tree looked like either the male or female sexual organs, it was assumed that it should possess sexual powers. An interesting example of such reasoning is the word "vanilla." This originally meant "vagina," being derived from the Spanish *vaina* (pod or sheath) plus *alla*, the diminutive ending, from the Latin *vagina* (pod, sheath, vagina). It was given this name because some ancient Roman shrewdly recognized the similarity of the vanilla root to the vaginal canal.

Another example of confused thinking on the part of the ancients is the power attributed to the mandrake, a very famous "aphrodisiac" in the erotic tradition of Europe. This plant is first mentioned in Genesis 30:14–16 in the incident where Leah utilizes the root to "lie with" Jacob. The political writer Machiavelli was so impressed by the mandrake that he wrote a comedy, *Mandragola,* in its honor, and many other great authors have hymned its praises. But, as is always the case, all the enthusiasm about the "wonder-working" efficacy of the plant was in vain, for it has no aphrodisiac effects whatever. Ironically enough, it is actually an anodyne and an antispasmodic. However, it does have the singular quality of resembling both the male and female sex organs.

Not only has this identification been visual; it has been olfactory as well. In the words of one important source, Norman Haire (1940): "Vegetable juices, the smell of which was more or less reminiscent of seminal fluid or of vaginal secretions . . . were credited with aphrodisiac properties and used as such by the people. It was the same with animals; particularly intense vitality, an abnormally long or violent period of heat, or a peculiar odor, caused certain animals to be appreciated for the stimulating qualities of their genital organs."

If the oyster contains no chemical elements that could affect the genitourinary system, there still arises the question of how it ever attained such a reputation as an erotic stimulant. Again the answer seems to lie in the visual identification between the oyster and the *pudendum muliebris;* in other words, in the resemblance that is noted not only in its shape but also in the mucous nature of its texture.

The "Psychology" of the Psychophysiological Effects of Aphrodisiacs

In spite of the fact that it is virtually impossible for food per se to produce erotic effects on the human, does this mean that the entire concept of food-as-aphrodisiacs has no validity? Although the purely physiological after-effects of food are practically nonexistent, foods definitely can and do have erotic reactions in a *psychophysiological* manner. Here, indeed, is perhaps the most fundamental and certainly the subtlest point of the whole subject. Strangely, and significantly enough, because of the complexity of physical love, this aspect of the interrelationship between food and sex is almost completely ignored in the literature.

To best understand how certain dishes can arouse sexual desire, it is necessary to consider the very important role played by their taste, and this includes their texture and their pleasant smell. For example, a "fruit Zabaglione": This is made of slices of pears and strawberries soaked in Cointreau and rum and drenched in a fragrant sauce of beaten egg yolks, confectioner's sugar, cloves, and cinnamon. More than half the persons who have eaten this dessert as served by the author have commented that it was a very "sexy" dish. This "sexy" quality becomes apparent at the first taste, indeed, perhaps at the first sight of it, long before any aphrodisiac could act physiologically. The dessert is smooth, rich, and creamy in texture—qualities we subconsciously equate with sexuality. In addition, its redolence (cloves, cinnamon, liqueur) is "exotic," another quality we tend, however vicariously, to identify with sexual concepts.

In this connection it is interesting to note how few writers on the subject have commented upon the erotic aspects of the pleasing smell of foods—particularly heavily spiced dishes. For centuries perfumes have rightly been regarded as one of the fundamental sexual lures, so it is obvious that "perfumed" food can also at least suggest the amorous. It should be noted here that the psychophysiological aspects of any "aphrodisiac" food are relative and vary from culture to culture and also from individual to individual. Thus, a certain taste or odor that has aphrodisiac connotations in one culture or to one individual might appear as an anaphrodisiac in another culture or to another individual.

It goes without saying that highly nutritive foods that are rich in vitamin content, especially vitamin E, the "antisterility agent," are also important as sexual stimulants; for a well-fed body naturally includes "well-nourished" sexual organs capable of vigorous and continuous expression. When a person is suffering from hunger, his or her sexual desires are diminished in what appears to be a direct ratio to the need for food intake. In other words, hungry or undernourished persons cannot expect to have the rich, full sex life of people whose appetite is completely satisfied by what they eat and who have no "oral" longings.

A most important but little commented-upon aspect of the aphrodisiac quality of foods is the feeling of sensuous, and sensual, satisfaction after the meal is over. When one has eaten a carefully prepared, subtly seasoned meal, together with wine, in an *ambiance* enhanced by soft music and glowing candles, one experiences a delightful glow—not only of the senses, but also of the body—a feeling that can hardly be present after one has consumed a typical American meal of meat loaf, boiled potatoes, and watery beans in a boarding house or diner. Eating a meal of fine food is an exciting and rewarding experience for the different senses of seeing, smelling, and tasting. And these visual-sensory, olfactory-sensory, savor-sensory reactions do tend to predetermine an erotic response pattern. In such a condition of euphoria, it is only natural for the body and mind to be well prepared for the ultimate physical and emotional expression—love-making. As Dr. Hans Balzli writes, "After a perfect meal we are more susceptible to the ecstasy of love than at any other time. . . ."

If any proof is needed of the erotic efficiency of the "esthetic" aspects of food, we only have to turn to a very significant institution devised by the French, surely some of the most sensitive connoisseurs of the relationship between *la cuisine* and *l'amour*: the famous *cabinets particuliers,* also known as *chambres separées.* These were luxuriously furnished private dining quarters, which graced many of the most famous Paris restaurants around the turn of the cen-

tury. In them the pleasures of the kitchen and boudoir probably reached their subtlest and most perfect expression, as both the food and the settings were fastidiously harmonized to produce the maximum degustation of the various sensations involved.

No discussion of aphrodisiacs would be complete without including alcohol, which is of course the most famous of all erotic stimulants. The influence of alcohol upon the human organism is both physiological and psychological. A considerable quantity of alcohol acts as a narcotic or paralyzing agent upon all parts of the brain, apparently in a downward direction, first affecting cortical functions, then the lower areas, and finally the medulla oblongata. Physiologically, it dilates the blood vessels, not only of the skin—which causes a feeling of warmth or glow—but also eventually of the sex organs. Accordingly, this cerebral-physiological-genital alcoholization, as it were, tends to remove "moral" blocks and brings on a light-hearted, often reckless and sexually responsive, state of mind.

The Paucity of Modern Scientific Aphrodisiacs

Of all the many "aphrodisiacs," there are only two that modern science even recognizes as having any stimulating effect, from a physiological point of view, upon the genitalia. These are cantharides, the famous "Spanish Fly" of an unconscionable number of "jokes," and yohimbine. The Chinese plant ginseng (*Panax ginseng*) and musk, a viscid substance drawn from a sac under the skin of the abdomen of the male musk deer, are also supposed to possess magic powers, but neither is officially recognized in pharmacopoeias as a sexual stimulant.

For centuries the cantharis (*Cantharis vesicatoria* or *Lytta vesicatoria*), which is a beautiful sheen-covered beetle found in the southern part of Europe, has been used as an aphrodisiac. The beetles are anesthetized, dried, then heated until they disintegrate into a fine powder. This powder contains a chemical principle known as cantharidin, with an analysis of carbon 10, hydrogen 12, oxygen 4. Taking cantharides internally results in acute irritation of the gastrointestinal system and inflammation of the gastrourinary tract, specifically the mucous membrane of the urethra, with accompanying dilatation of the blood vesels, all of which effects a kind of stimulation to the genital organs. The results of this urethal "excitement" can be sexual in nature, even leading to priapism (unnatural, often continued erection of the male organ usually without sexual desire) or to premature menstruation. However, it must be stated that the folklore reputation of "Spanish Fly" is much more widespread than its scientific validity warrants. As a matter of fact, despite their extensive use in the past, cantharides are vanishing from present-day medicine as an effective sexual stimulant because of the inherent dangers in their use (*see* Craven and Polak, 1954; Nichols and Teare, 1954).

Possibly the best-known modern "aphrodisiac" is yohimbine, a crystalline substance, alkaloid in nature, (carbon 21, hydrogen 26, nitrogen 2, oxygen 3. It is derived from the bark of the yohimbé tree (*Pausinystalia yohimbe*), native to central Africa, where it has long been used by the aborigines to increase sexual powers. Whereas cantharides have been variously employed as vesicants (to raise blisters), as diuretics (to increase urine), and to treat such diseases as pleurisy, neuritis, and meningitis, yohimbine's uses have been principally stimulative in nature, being given to combat sexual neurasthenia (neurotic condition of apathy or weakness) by inducing an increase in the excitability of the lower centers of the spinal cord or through the hyperemia (superabundance of blood) that it produces in the genital organs. Actually, however, both cantharides and yohimbine are now regarded as old fashioned and have been replaced by treatment through hormones, principally testosterone for the male and estrogen for the female.

Erotica Exotica

In addition to the traditional use of internal aphrodisiacs, man has devised other methods to "increase venery," as, for example, the *ampallang* that has been noted in Borneo, the Celebes, and the Philippines. Travelers in those regions have reported that an operation is performed on grown males in which a horizontal perforation is made in the end of the organ. This is done with a bamboo punch; then a dove feather smeared with oil is inserted into the opening and kept in place until the incision heals, after which an *ampallang* is used. The *ampallang* itself is a matchlike piece of copper, silver, gold, or ivory, some two inches long, with little heads, like nailheads, at each end. It is inserted into the perforation in the penis before coitus in order to stimulate the vaginal canal and thus increase erotic sensations. Dyak women are said to indicate the length of *ampallang* they would prefer either by opening their mouths to the desired size, or by leaving on the table a cigarette that they have smoked down to the desired size.

The *guesquel* of the Indians of Patagonia is composed of the stiff hairs of a mule's mane attached to a thread, forming a kind of comb. This comb is attached round the end of the penis, roughly like a wreath, with the ends of the hairs sticking up. Although the *guesquel* causes the woman some pain, indeed slight bleeding, on first use, the female Patagonians gradually become used to it. The effects of this instrument are so extreme, according to one traveler, that the women "foam at the mouth and have such a paroxysmal orgasm that they lie around stupefied and exhausted after intercourse."

Another "aphrodisiac" reported from South East Asia are "tickling stones." An incision is made in the epidermis of the penis and little stones inserted underneath. The operation usually takes place in a stream, in order to allow the flowing water to act as a healing agent for the lacerated organ. According to ethnological accounts, the wealthy refuse to use any globules that are not made of gold or silver.

Even more originality is shown in the variation of this erotic theme by the inhabitants of a section of Burma. Although the operating procedure was the same, the music-loving Burmese preferred to use tiny bells. As many as a dozen of these little bells were inserted under the skin, thus making the organ rough and swollen and providing more pleasure for the women. An Italian traveler in this area in the fifteenth century described the gay musical tinkling of these bells which he heard as Burmese men sauntered along the streets.

Another erotic stimulator is the "Assistant," a

kind of penis pressure-pump that has been sold in certain European countries. According to its prospectus: "This apparatus [a glass tube to which is attached a bulb or small pump] is an invention of supreme importance. Through direct stimulation of the metabolism of the sex organs a continuous invigoration of the sex nerves is effected, without creating any irritating or injurious after-effects. Its manipulation is simple and comfortable. The chief success of the apparatus lies in the fact that it affects both the deep-seated sex organs and the prostate, muscles, nerves and seminal ducts at the same time. Through strong stimulation resulting from increased flow of blood and subsequent nourishment of the sex organs, weakness disappears in a surprisingly short time."

Also to be noted are the products of enterprising French rubber companies—*dames de voyage,* also called *ventre(s) de la femme,* rubber women "traveling companions" who bring *douce consolation de l'amour.* Such elastic females can be blown up, so read the advertisements, to practically any size and shape desired. In addition, they are guaranteed to be authentic copies of the female body, exact in every minute detail.

Nor should the famous "dildo" or "self-satisfier," whose names in several languages are significant, be omitted. The English term "dildo" apparently comes either from the Italian *diletto,* which means "delight," or from the "low" expression, "diddle." In Italy it is known as *passatiempo,* literally, "pass (the) time." In French it is called *godemiche* from the Latin, "enjoy myself," *bientateur,* literally, "do-gooder," and *consolateur.* The Germans give it the typically Teutonic appellation of *Phallusphantom,* "phantom penis." This instrument is one of the oldest of all recorded excitants, being noted in ancient Egypt, Babylon, in Greece, and subsequently in Rome. It has also been mentioned in the Bible, Ezekiel 28:17: "Take thy ornaments of the gold and silver I have given thee and make masculine images thereof and practice harlotry with them."

Many materials have been used in the manufacture of these objects: in England, glass; in Bali, wax; in ancient Greece, bronze; in West Africa, hard clay; and in Italy, rubber. In China

they are made of resin, whose color resembles that of human flesh. In Canton and Tientsin women used to hawk them on the streets with illustrated instructions. The manufacture of these artificial stimulants reached its height in France with the construction of an instrument that was filled with milk and, after an appropriate number of movements, exploded into bits.

Perhaps the best known among Japanese artificial stimulants is the *watama* or *ben-wa,* of the East. This consists of two small metal balls, one of which is empty, the other of which, called "the little man," contains still a third smaller and heavier ball of quicksilver. The Japanese woman inserts the empty ball deep into the vaginal canal, as close to the cervix as possible, then places the heavier one in position. With every movement of the pelvis the little spheres vibrate, producing a continuous tickling sensation. According to one commentator, "Japanese women like to swing themselves in hammocks or rocking chairs, so as to keep the balls in motion, and enjoy to the utmost the resulting intense sexual excitement."

Anaphrodisiacs

Just as the subject of aphrodisiacs is almost exclusively folkloristic, so the so-called anaphrodisiacs are equally intangible. Even the Institute for Sex Research in Bloomington, Indiana, which certainly has one of the largest and best catalogued sex libraries in the world, does not have a rubric for anaphrodisiacs.

The older literature is completely impressionistic. The ancient Greeks are said to have used cold water and sponge baths. Plato and Aristotle thought that going barefoot would reduce the libido. The Romans practiced infibulation to curb desire, and fibulae were also known in India. A number of preparations have been employed for this same purpose, such as digitalis, menthol, salicylic acid, quinine, and potassium bromide. Sodium bicarbonate is said to have been widely used in prisons.

In an attempt to obtain information on this subject, the author wrote to a number of penal and military institutions and also to the most prominent pharmaceutical houses. The information received in answer was negative. The most famous anaphrodisiac is, of course, saltpeter, and it too belongs in the realm of folk mythology, although, oddly enough, it does not appear in the *Standard Dictionary of Folklore, Mythology and Legend* (New York, 1949–1950). Saltpeter, or potassium nitrate (KNO_3), is pharmacologically known as a diuretic, which would appear to be the only logical reason this otherwise completely neutral chemical has acquired a reputation as an anaphrodisiac.

Summary

In spite of the fact that we of the Western world, and indeed elsewhere, treat aphrodisiacs casually, almost jocosely, a study of the erotic proclivities of the human race reveals that this subject has interested mankind, from the time of the earliest civilizations, to a far greater degree than is imagined, by either the layman or professional.

Of all "aphrodisiacs," food is by far the best-known throughout the world, and the majority of the world's great cultures and smaller ethnic groups have developed an extensive "aphrodisiac" folklore, based at least 99 per cent *not* on scientific data but rather on wishful thinking.

Accordingly, it is evident that there are no traditional "aphrodisiacs" that can bring about erotic biochemical and/or physiological results. Thus it may only be concluded that the eons-old theory of aphrodisiacs-anaphrodisiacs as taken into the body is fundamentally nothing but a folk-myth, or, like Mercutio's dreams, ". . . the children of an idle brain, Begot of nothing but vain fantasy, Which is as thin of substance as the air."

References

Of the works listed below, only *Liebesmittel* and the author's article in the *Encyclopaedia Britannica* treat the subject from a scientific point of view.

Athenaeus, *The Deipnosophists*. (Translated by Charles Burton Gulick.) 6 vols. London: William Heinemann, Ltd.; New York: G. P. Putnam's Sons, 1927, Vol. 6, pp. 492-493.

Balzli, Hans, *Gastrophie: Ein Brevier für Gaumen und Geist*. Stuttgart: Hädecke, 1931, p. 34.

Bernstoff, H. von, Kuno, H. A., Lothar, Rudolf, and Scheuer, O. F., *Der Geschmack*. Wien: Verlag für Kulturforschwung, 1932.

Berry, Richard J. A., *Brain and Mind*. New York: The Macmillan Co., 1928, p. 481.

Bölsche, Wilhelm, *Das Liebesleben in der Natur*. 3 vols. Jena: Eugen Diedrichs, 1906-07, Vol. 1, p. 357.

Coriat, Isidore H., "Sex and Hunger." *Psychoanalyt. Rev. 8;* 375, 1921.

Craven, J. D., and Polak, A., "Cantharides Poisoning." *Brit. M. J.* 1386-1388, Dec. 11, 1954.

Crawley, Alfred Ernest, *The Mystic Rose*. 2 vols. New York: Boni & Liveright, 1927, Vol. 1, p. 182.

Elderkin, G. W., *Kantharos, Studies in Dionysiac and Kindred Cults*. Princeton: Princeton University Press, 1924, p. 172.

Ellis, Havelock, *Studies in the Psychology of Sex*. 4 vols. New York: Random House, 1936, Vol. 3, chap. 3.

Fielding, William J., "The Art of Love." In V. F. Calverton and S. D. Schmalhausen, *Sex in Civilization*. New York: The Macmillan Co., 1929, p. 648.

Haire, Norman, *Encyclopedia of Sexual Knowledge*. New York: Eugenics Publishing Co., 1940, pp. 355-386.

Hirschfeld, Magnus, and Lennert, Richard, *Liebesmittel*. Berlin: Man Verlag, 1930, pp. 65-107.

Höfler, M., Gebildbrote aus galloromanischer Zeit, *Arch. f. Anthro. 15;* 243-252, 1912.

Hopfner, Theodor, *Das Sexualleben der Griechen und Römer*. Prague: J. G. Calve, 1938, pp. 272-294.

Lacroix, Paul (Pierre Dufour), *History of Prostitution*. 3 vols. Chicago: Pascal Covici, 1926, Vol. 1, p. 235.

Lehmann, Friedrich R., *Kulturgeschichte und Rezepte der Liebesmittel*. Heidenheim: E. Hoffman, 1955.

Licht, Hans, *Sexual Life in Ancient Greece*. New York: George Routledge & Sons, Ltd., 1934, pp. 513-515.

MacDougald, Duncan, Jr., "Aphrodisiac." In *Encyclopaedia Britannica*. Chicago: University of Chicago Press, 1955.

MacDougald, Duncan, Jr., "Involuntary Regressive Hetero-sexual Phallic Feeding." *Internat. J. Sexology 5;* 165-167, 1952.

Scott, George R., *Encyclopedia of Sex*. London: T. W. Laurie, Ltd., 1939, pp. 22-23.

Stern, Bernhard, *Medizin, Aberglaube und Geschlechtsleben in der Türkei*. 2 vols. Berlin: Hermann Barsdorf Verlag, 1903, Vol. 2, pp. 251-258.

Principally for the sake of completeness the following names of "aphrodisiac" cookbooks are appended.

de Baudricourt, Sire, *Le manuel culinaire aphrodisiaque*. Paris: Édition Photographique, 1903.

de Behac, Achille, *Novissimo manuale di cucina francese*. Napoli: Societa Edizione Partenopea, 1907. (This is an adapted version of Baudricourt's book.)

Bey, Pilaff (pseudonym), *Venus in the Kitchen* (ed. Norman Douglas). London: William Heinemann, Ltd. 1952.

Curnonsky (Maurice Edmond Saillant), *La table et l'amour*. Paris: La Clef d'Or, 1950.

Heartman, Charles F., *Cuisine de l'amour*. New Orleans: Gourmet's Company, 1942. (This is another version of Baudricourt's book.)

Rompini, Omero, *La cucina dell' amore*. Catania: F. Guaitolini, 1926. (This is another edition of Baudricourt's book.)

Vatelle, Alcibiades and Yolande, *Grammaire de gastronomie sentimentale*. Toulon: Éditions Provencia, 1951.

Walton, A. H., *Love Recipes Old and New*. London: Torchstream Books, 1956.

Walton, A. H., *Aphodisiacs*. Westport, Conn.: Associated Booksellers, 1958. American edtion of above title.

DUNCAN MACDOUGALD, JR.

Art and Dance, Sex in Primitive

Definitions

FOR the purpose of this article "primitive" art includes all art produced outside what we call civilized societies. Primitive art is representational, conventional, and intended to be understood by the audience for which the artist creates. He decorates houses and equipment and he composes ceremonies concerned with birth, puberty rites, marriage, ancestors, hunting, harvestings, the seasons, and war. The primitive artist is really a craftsman. He is well integrated with the community in which he works. Whereas in our civilization the artist is a specialist and an outsider, a rebel against the conventions of his society, in the primitive community art is a necessity, not merely a form of entertainment.

Herbert Read (1957) observes that the term "esthetic" covers two very different psychological processes, one tending to an emphasis on *vitality,* the other to an emphasis on the balance and harmony of *beauty.* He concludes that vitality rather than beauty is the dominant esthetic quality in tribal art.

Following Freud, we would use the term *libido* instead of vitality and would suggest that the clearest distinction between the art and dance of "primitive" society and that of "civilized" society can be obtained when these forms of creativity are seen in relation to sexual energy (libido), its repression and sublimation.

Definitions, elaboration, and examples will follow these basic statements:

1. Art in civilized society is a result of a *repressive sublimation of the libido.* It produces an esthetic effect only at a high cost in pain, discontent, and isolation. It is accepted by the majority of the members of the society as a form of entertainment and as a commercial product. Therefore:

Repressive sublimation of libido="civilized" art + Thanatos (death instinct).

2. Art in primitive societies is a result of *nonrepressive sublimation of the libido.* It produces an esthetic effect that is both gratifying and vital and is a useful social phenomenon, leading to participation of the artist-craftsman with the fellow members of his community in the use of his work—generally in dancing, rituals, and feasts. It is not an object for trade. Therefore:

Nonrepressive sublimation of libido="primitive" art + Eros (life instinct).

Art

One of the simplest illustrations of sex in primitive art are the figurines used in the puberty rites in Tanganyika. They are made of clay, and are rarely more than three to four feet high. According to Cory (1956), "When a lesson [in sex practice] was to be given a figurine was put in front of the novices, a song in some way connected with it was sung and finally an explanation of the purpose of the figurine and, if necessary, of the song was given by the instructor or the maker of the figurine. The figurines were prepared either by men or women who were appointed as overseers or instructors of the novices."

Cory describes a dance that took place

among the Nguu on the day on which the boys of the village were circumcised: A figurine in the shape of a phallus combined with various parts of the female sex organ was placed in the center and everybody danced around it. The sculpture conveyed to the natives the impression of an aggressive animal, a symbol of sexual urge.

Another figure called Kandi was kept in the boys' initiation huts. It represented a woman, and if one of the boys had an erection he was told to lie on top of the figurine, while the other boys sang: "To sleep with the Kandi is very pleasant."

In the same tribe the initiation rites for girls included a dance around an image of a phallus with sticks radiating from the top like sun-rays—symbols of virility and generative power.

Another figure depicts two banana stems, one bent down with a heavy bunch of bananas, the other standing straight. The instruction song describes how the penis droops down like a cluster of bananas—but nobody need fear, because a clever woman knows how to bring about another erection.

Elwin (1947) describes carvings on doors, marriage litters, and musical instruments among the tribes of Central India as vigorous and realistic. One of the Juang dancing songs begins: "The clitoris is the vagina's ornament." Elwin also relates how carvings are made on the wooden pieces used as headrests in the dormitories where several boys and girls sleep together. These carvings depict the breasts or the vagina. According to Elwin "phallic symbols are very common. In nearly every 'ghotul' [dormitory] there is somewhere a representation of the vagina, often about two feet from the ground on a central pillar. The boys say that these carvings are very useful as an approach to girls. It may be that the vagina on the central pillar is a relic of a custom now forgotten of initiating smaller boys by pressing them against it."

A colossal example of sex in primitive art are the megalithic representations of the male and female organs in Dimapur, on the India-Burma border. Here in the fifteenth century a tribe called Kacharis erected a group of fertility symbols—about 30 realistic phalli carved in stone, some 20 feet high, and about 20 colossal forked stones representing the vagina. These monuments were erected during fertility rites. Even today the Naga tribes in the same region use phalli and forked posts, although theirs are carved from wood.

Types of Artistic Expression

Sex and sexual functions in primitive art are expressed by naturalism, distortion, symbolism, or abstraction. Naturalism is least common and of less psychological interest. In "civilized" art emotions and experiences are intellectualized and verbalized, whereas in primitive art they express themselves directly in form, in esthetic creativity. There is no need for verbal explanation, and the artist-craftsman and his audience communicate directly, "heart to heart," through form, color, movement, and dance, not through logic and ideologies. Leenhardt (1950) writes in this connection:

We are so accustomed to submitting our thought to the exigencies of the laws of the mind that aesthetics have been relegated to a separate department, where they remain the affair of initiates. Oceanians, on the contrary, ignoring sharply divided thought, employ aesthetics to express any general idea, or representation which they do not know how to express in words. They grasp the form of things before analysing them, and with that, they have sufficient knowledge. They can communicate, with the sensation provoked by these forms, before being able to communicate in words. Their thought has a certain harmony and is already in tune with the aesthetic idea long before it can order itself on logical lines.

The Uli figure from New Ireland is an example of distortion and superimposition. It is a carved figure with large phalli and female breasts expressing an excessive power of fecundity. In Hawaii and New Zealand creative energy is represented by the tiki, which is reproduced in phallic or fetal form.

Symbolism can be direct, as when the form of a vulva or a pair of breasts represents a woman, or indirect, as in figures from the Sepic River region in New Guinea with exaggerated, long noses, indicating virility.

Geometrical patterns are often abstract representations of the sex organs, as when the vulva is indicated by the angular lozenge shape. A great many abstract decorations are actually stylized sex symbols and are fully understood as such by the tribe that uses them. Boas

(1927) believed that abstract designs in primitive art were products of emotion. The repetitions and design led the eye and the unconscious into a kind of dance. This liking for design is relative to what Herbert Read describes as haptic sensation, the kinesthetic experience of form in sculpture. Rubbing and oiling of carvings and phallic images is common in many ceremonies.

To consider another form of primitive art, paleolithic cave paintings have been given a new meaning by Bettelheim (1954):

> Many authors have commented on the fact that the paintings are so commonly located in nearly inaccessible places. In reading their reports I was most impressed by the tortuous paths leading to the places of the pictures. . . . The long, narrow slippery corridors, often crossed by waterfalls, and the chimneys that must be negotiated to reach the pictures. . . . All this suggests to me the possibility that an effort was made to reproduce the setting in which procreation takes place. If so, the crawling through narrow, wet channels might have represented, on entering, gaining access to the secret place of procreation; on leaving, the process of birth might have been symbolically re-enacted. The paintings, therefore, were executed at places that may have been viewed as representing the womb where animals came into existence. It is possible, then, that early man created a new symbol and painted animals in a place which to him represented a womb, so that the real animal might be induced to do likewise. . . . Levy . . . sees a definite and close connection between the pictures, the rituals of early man, and birth, death and rebirth. . . . Among modern preliterate people, Levy stressed the importance of ritual enactment of traveling a long, winding path, and the importance of those experiences that can be had only in caves. . . . Levy leaves little doubt that these caves represent the mother by whom the initiates are born again.

Types and styles of expression must also be studied in a biological context. Konrad Lorenz and modern ethology have introduced the study of *innate release mechanisms* and *imprinting* as well as the concept of *social releasers* or signals. These biological functions are determinants of perception and behaviour not only in animals but also in man. Colours, forms and sounds act as signals. We can look at primitive art as a form of social releasers or *signstimuli*, which release certain instinctive behaviour in other individuals of the same species—mainly concerned with sexuality as far as humans are concerned. The image as signstimuli is not a naturalistic representation or an imitation, but a presentation of certain aspects—usually in simple shapes—of biological forms. These shapes of signstimuli can have different meanings in different tribes or cultures, depending on *minimum* images necessary for the release of the corresponding innate behaviour patterns. This is specifically evident in the presentation of sex organs and sexual functions in primitive art, where the most elementary forms are enough to indicate and initiate the biological and physiological processes.

Dance

Havelock Ellis writes: "The most usual method of attaining tumescence, a method found among the most various kind of animals is some form of dance. It is everywhere the instinctive object of the male to assure by his activity in display, his energy or skill or beauty, both his own passion and the passion of the female. Throughout nature sexual conjugation only takes place after much expenditure of energy."

Elwin describes how the Gond youths in Central India begin the evening in their ghotul (dormitory) with vigorous dances and games that are frankly provocative of the sexual emotion. It must be noted that it is not only the chelik (boys) who by the energy of their display excite the motiari (girls); in one of the dances the girls bend forward, each holding a stick in her hand to represent a penis, and dance with jerky movements of the buttocks that closely simulate the motions of the sex act. As they dance they sing:

> Little little prawn hairs
> Very long horn,
> Where has he gone?

The little prawn hairs are the pubic hairs and the long horn is the penis.

Nowhere is the quality of vitality and dynamism stronger than in the primitive dance. Its purpose, like that of primitive art, is to further increase life and fertility. Gods and heroes, spirits and ancestors, fetishes and mana (spirit forces) are all represented in primitive art, but the dance is "the mother of the arts." Sachs (1952) writes: "On no occasion in the life of primitive peoples could the dance be dispensed with." The purpose of all dance is to produce ecstasy, to release the individual from the too rigid shackles of the ego, to obtain pleasure, and to promote growth.

Glover (1956) states the Freudian view of art thus:

The influence on psychic development of earlier forms of sensory experience i.e. of unmodified sound stimuli of smell, taste and touch; the variations in muscular tension; and above all the recording of different quantities and qualities of rhythmic stimulation, through whichever sensory channel these may operate, have already been harnessed in the interests of psychic expression long before speaking, drawing and writing are available as mental instruments. Naturally therefore the arts of music, miming, dancing and the like retain a connection with primitive instinctual expression which is more direct than later artistic forms. . . . Anthropological studies of primitive art demonstrate convincingly the animistic and magical incentives to creative activity. . . . All works of art must represent sublimations of primitive instincts.

According to the Freudian view, the sexual instincts are regarded as infantile "polymorphous perverse" and as related to erotogenic zones—oral, anal, cutaneous, muscular, and (infantile) genital—first loosely organized and later under genital supremacy. From this Freudian view primitive dance may be seen as a reactivation of all erotogenic zones, a return of pregenital polymorphous sexuality, so that the whole body becomes resexualized on a conscious level.

This Freudian concept of "polymorphous perverse" and "pregenital" behavior of the child may be seriously questioned, since there is no evidence that what Freud called oral and anal "sexuality" is actually anything but cutaneous sensation, or sensuality, which is only mildly, and by no means integrally, related to genital tumescence and orgasm. Moreover, the entire concept of "polymorphous perversion" is a highly questionable construct that largely seems to stem from Judeo-Christian prejudices which highly tout procreative sex behavior and roundly condemn all non-procreative orgasms as "abnormal" or "perverse." Freud, in other words, was almost certainly a victim of unscientific, Judeo-Christian biases when he labeled all kinds of extragenital activity as perverse; and it may well be that many primitive peoples, who do not share the Jewish and Christian prejudices regarding the procreative function of human sexuality (and some of whom do not even fully realize that procreation originates in penile-vaginal coitus), quite *un*perversely encourage sensuous as well as sexual activities, and thereby bring into their sexual participations a much wider, and in many ways emotionally healthier, range of behavior than do many more civilized peoples. Instead of saying, therefore, that the primitive dance may be seen as a return to pregenital polymorphous perverse sexuality, we could just as well say that civilized, and especially Judeo-Christian, sex life may be seen as a neurotic retreat from the potentially wide range of normal sexuality.

According to Sachs, "human fertility dances are drawn from two different phases of sexual intercourse: the mating and the wooing, and the act itself. Often the boundary is extended so that moments of sexual intercourse are brought into the dance and combined artistically with it." Puberty dances aim at the increase of sexual power, which will assure healthy descendants. Sachs writes: "The means of achieving this power are only secondarily instruction and circumcision; they are primarily the dance—to generate power, to prepare and transfer it to the maiden." Dances at the initiation of girls often are "a training in the rhythmic movement of the belly and the posterior."

Quoting Koch-Grunberg, Sachs describes a fertility dance of the Cobéna of Brazil: "The dancers have large phalli made of bast with testicles of red cones—which they hold close to their bodies with both hands. Stamping with the right foot and singing, they dance—with the upper part of their bodies bent forwards. Suddenly they jump wildly along with violent coitus motions and loud groans. . . . Thus they carry the fertility into every corner of the houses. . . . They jump among the women— they knock the phalli one against another."

Herskovits (1938) describes an initiation ceremony in Dahomey in West Africa, the rite of Legba. Legba is the son of the sky goddess and associated with fate. His representative is a girl in a straw hat and a purple raffia skirt.

The large drum sounded, the Legba danced toward the drums. When she reached the drummer, she put her hand under the raffia skirt [which it was explained represented pubic hair] and brought out a wooden phallus the colour of Negro skin. This was apparently attached in such a way that it would remain in the horizontal position of the erect male organ and, as she danced, now beyond the drums toward a large tree where many women were sitting, she made motions of masturbation, first running her curved right hand backwards over the phallus, then her left in which may have been a handkerchief. When she reached the tree where the women were seated—Legba approached one of them, placed the wooden phallus against her side and proceeded with a highly realistic miming of sexual intercourse.

The Marind-anim tribe in Dutch New Guinea has initiation dances in which the men wear headdresses of colored feathers, denoting virility. According to Leenhardt, in former times "women are killed when the show is over to insure the fertility of gardens. Neighboring tribes insist upon the union of a young couple who are transfixed with spears while in the act of embracing, their sacrifice bringing with it the fertility they symbolise."

Devereaux has obtained an account of dance and homosexuality among the Mohave Indians:

The boys who become alyha [male transvestites taking the role of the woman in sexual intercourse] were initiated fairly early. . . . If the boy acted in the expected fashion during the ceremony he was considered an initiated homosexual. . . . The singer drew a circle in the center. . . . The boy was led by two women . . . into the centre of the circle. If the boy showed willingness to remain standing in the circle, exposed to the public eye, it was almost certain that he would go through with the ceremony. The singer, hidden behind the crowd, began singing the songs. As soon as the sound reached the boy he began to dance as women do. Gradually the singer approached the dancer. The dance-steps do not change, except insofar as the boy plays a pantomime in accordance with the text of the songs. Were the boy unwilling to become a homosexual officially, he would refuse to dance. As it is, the song goes right to his heart and he will dance with much intensity. He cannot help it. After the fourth song he is proclaimed a homosexual. The same women who led him into the circle take him down to the Colorado River. After a bath he receives his skirt. He is then led back to the dance ground, dressed as a woman.

Art and Nature

Referring to fertility as the basic cult and to the creation of pregnant female figures of the Venus of Willendorf type, Bettelheim says that for both primitive and paleolithic men reproductive rites were the most important ceremonies. Initiation ceremonies are clearly related to increase rites and concerned with the organs of the opposite sex. Bettelheim refers to Groddeck and emphasizes that penis-envy in girls and castration-anxiety in boys are secondary to the "vagina-envy" of boys and their desire to have breasts, become pregnant, and have children. Margaret Mead (1935) suggests that in initiation ceremonies men try to take over the functions of women.

The death and rebirth ceremonies, combined with circumcision and scarification, are still performed in primitive societies, as in Liberia and Australia. In the Poro societies in Liberia carved masks are used and replicas are given to the initiated boys which, according to Elisofon, "they conceal about their bodies and care for through life, seeking their aid in need."

The Poro deity, a crocodile spirit, swallows the boys, who are then supposed to live in the belly during the initiation period. They are circumcised, and the foreskins are sent to the girl's society where they are cooked and eaten. The clitoridi and labia minora removed from the girls are given to the boys for the same purpose. Bettelheim writes: "As is often the case in oral incorporation, it is difficult to decide which desire is stronger, the hostile desire to take away from the other sex, or the envious desire to possess the incorporated parts."

Another form of primitive art is *scarification*, and in the Poro society these ritual marks are related to death and rebirth phantasies. The scars are supposed to be made by the crocodile spirit, which may also be a representation of the vagina dentata. The fear and mystery about menstruation and childbirth and the vagina-envy are conquered in the symbolic death and rebirth, and the scarification marks on face and body are therefore worn like a certificate of victory over the fear and envy of women.

Margaret Mead (1935) describes the "mysterious half-realized figures in red and yellow on big pieces of bark" used to decorate the men's houses among the Arapesh of New Guinea, and she describes the initiation: ". . . the ritual segregation of man and woman, during which time the novice . . . is incised, eats a sacrificial meal of the blood of the older men and is shown . . . remarkable objects that he has never seen before, such as masks and other carvings and representations." Mead concludes that the cult assumes that boys can become men only by ritualizing birth and taking over, symbolically and collectively, the functions that women perform individually and naturally.

Mead also reports another interesting relation between art and birth. The Mundugumor, a Sepic River tribe, considers men and women who are born with the umbilical cord twisted around their throats as destined to become artists:

> Males so born . . . continue the fine, tight tradition of Mundugumor art, the high-relief carving on the tall wooden shields, the low-relief stylized animal representation on the spears, the intricate painted designs on the great triangles of bark that are raised at the yam-feasts. They it is who can carve the wooden figures that fit into the ends of the sacred flutes, embodiment of the crocodile spirits of the river. Men and women born to arts and crafts need not practice them unless they wish, but no one who lacks the mark of his calling can hope to become more than the clumsiest apprentice.

Sublimation in Primitive and Civilized Societies

The few samples from the world-wide treasure house of primitive art that have been described above, should demonstrate clearly enough the close relation between sex and primitive art and dance. It is now possible to return to the formulas presented at the beginning of this article and show how the acknowledgement and acceptance of sex in a primitive society makes nonrepressive sublimation possible.

According to Freud, the price for civilization is repression (unconscious and conscious) and sublimation (repressive modification) of the instincts. This creates an increasing amount of unhappiness, culminating in a death instinct (Thanatos). A new term introduced by Mar-

cuse (1955), *surplus-repression*, refers to the additional repressive controls "over and above those indispensable for civilized human association. . . . For example the modifications and deflections of instinctual energy necessitated by the perpertuation of the monogamic-patriarchal family, or by a hierarchichal division of labour, or by public control of the individual's private existence, are instances of surplus-repression pertaining to institutions of a particular reality principle."

In our civilization, with an economic competitiveness as "performance principle," libidinous gratification is held to a part-time basis. Even this gratification is taken care of by the entertainment industry. The surplus-repression becomes internalized, libido becomes concentrated in one part of the body (genital supremacy) while the rest is designed for toil. Marcuse writes: "Destructiveness seems to be more directly satisfied in civilization than libido. . . . The sexual relations themselves become much more closely assimilated with social relations, sexual liberty is harmonized with profitable conformity." Artistic work, while opposed to civilization is at the same time bound to it by increasing instinctual repression. The rebellion becomes harder and more desperate, the mental casualities increase while "joy in the making" libidinal creativity becomes a tragic necessity; The shadow of Thanatos is cast over the art forms of our civilization. It becomes "beauty dancing to the tune of death" (Hans Sachs).

We can thus talk about *repressive sublimation* as a form of sublimation that "operates on a *preconditioned instinctual structure*, which includes the functional and temporal restraints of sexuality, its channeling into monogamic reproduction and the desexualization of most of the body" (Marcuse).

"Primitive" art and its companion, the dance, present, as we have seen, another mode of sublimation. Dancing eroticizes the whole body and promotes group cohesion as well. In primitive society sex is accepted as beautiful, clean, and essential; gratification is more important than possessive monogamic unions (marital relations being governed not by instinctual needs but by social pressures). The senses are involved in erotic stimulation (Sinnlichkeit), which overflows and excites other bodies in the dancing. The repression in primitive societies is mainly concerned with finding ritual ways of reconciling the male-female-child components of each individual member into a fearless, joyful unity in the individual and the group.

Against repressive sublimation Marcuse presents the conception of a civilization evolving from, and sustained by, free libidinal relations. He assumes a "genitofugal libido" trend in the development of culture—in other words, "an inherent trend in the libido itself toward cultural expression, without external repressive modification. And this cultural trend in the libido seems to be . . . away from genital supremacy toward its erotization of the entire organism."

Repressive sublimation implies desexualization, whereas in nonrepressive sublimation the instincts are "gratified in activities and relations that are not sexual in the sense of 'organized' genital sexuality and yet are libidinal and erotic. Where repressive sublimation prevails and determines the culture, non-repressive sublimation must manifest itself in contradiction to the entire sphere of social usefulness. Viewed from this sphere, it is the negation of all accepted productivity and performance."

Marcuse concludes that

. . . libido can take the road of self sublimation only as a social phenomenon . . . under conditions which relate associated individuals to each other in the cultivation of the environment for their developing needs and faculties. Reactivation of polymorphous and narcissistic sexuality ceases to be a threat and can itself lead to culture building if socially useful work is at the same time the transparent satisfaction of an individual need. In primitive society this organization of work may be immediate and natural.

Thus we find that the primitive artist-craftsman in his own community achieves vitality and integration of his work through nonrepressive sublimation of libido. Eros is the god of primitive art and dance. The attraction these art forms have for us lies in the fact that they represent something that is forbidden and repressed in our civilization. The joy, freedom, and vitality of Eros challenges the struggle, guilt, and competition under Thanatos' rule.

References

Adam, L., *Primitive Art*. London, 1954.

Bettelheim, B., *Symbolic Wounds*. Glencoe, Ill.: The Free Press, 1954.

Boas, F., *Primitive Art*. New York: Dover, 1955.

Cory, H., *African Figurines*. New York: Grove, 1956.

Devereux, G., "Institutionalized Homosexuality of the Mohave Indians." *Human Biol. 9;* 498-527, 1937.

Elisofon, E., *The Sculpture of Africa*. New York: Praeger, 1958.

Elwin, V., *The Muria and Their Ghotul*. London: Oxford University Press, 1947.

Freud, S., *Basic Writings*. New York: Modern Library, 1938.

Glover, E., *Freud or Jung*. New York: Meridian, 1956.

Hays, H. R., *From Ape to Angel*. New York: Knopf, 1958.

Herskovits, M., *Dahomey*. New York, 1938.

Leenhardt, M., *Arts of the Oceanic Peoples*. London, 1950.

Marcuse, H., *Eros and Civilization*. Boston: Beacon, 1956.

Mead, M., *Sex and Temperament*. New York: William Morrow & Co., Inc., 1935.

Mead, M., *Male and Female*. New York: William Morrow & Co., Inc., 1949.

Mead, M., and Calas, N., *Primitive Heritage*. New York: Random House, 1953.

Read, H., *Icon and Idea*. Cambridge: Harvard, 1955.

Sachs, C., *World History of the Dance*. New York: Norton, 1957.

TORE HAKANSSON

Art and Sex

THE word *art* may be used broadly or narrowly; and in the present article it will be used largely in its narrower sense: pictorial art. What are some of the most important connections between human sexuality and artistic representation as depicted in drawing, painting, and sculpture? What may be said about sex and the artist? These are the main questions this article will attempt to answer.

Sex and Art History

The use of sexual motifs in drawing, painting, and sculpture goes back to the earliest days of human history. Primitive art was, and in many sections of the world still is, replete with sexual and reproductive motifs. Primitive peoples, in their pictures and statues, often tended to exaggerate the loins, rumps, breasts, and sex parts of their figures—probably because, as Dell (1930) points out, these parts of the body were of pronounced and often magical importance to them. Much can be said about the place of sex in primitive art; but since this topic is covered by another article in this *Encyclopedia*, it is merely mentioned here.

In civilized times, the ancient Sumerians, Egyptians, and Chinese produced many notable artistic works; but the full flowering of sexual representations in art is usually acknowledged to have started in Ancient Greece. The earliest Greek art known to us was not highly sexualized; but after 500 B.C. Greek artists began to portray the human body for the sake of giving pleasure in its own right rather than for other and less sensual motives; and pictorial and sculptural art became art in the fullest sense when this esthetic revolution occurred

(Wall, 1932). The Greeks became obsessed with the dream of ideal beauty, and, as Garland (1957) points out, "with the development of Greek art the sculptor creates a type of beauty which has never been excelled: for centuries the measurements and features of the antique Kore and classic Venus are accepted as perfection and ensuing civilizations have created nothing more exquisite than these lovely goddesses, unselfconscious in their nakedness." This is not a universally accepted dictum, but would appear to contain some truth.

The Greeks were also noted for their direct erotic representations in art, and graphic reproductions of the sexual act were numerous and met with little opposition or censorship. Every coital activity the ancients could imagine was portrayed and modeled on their walls, ceilings, vases, and other *objets d'art* (Bloch, 1934; Guyon, 1934; Northcote, 1916). It must not be thought, however, that the famous orgiastic representations (such as those found in the Pompeii excavations) were ubiquitous in the ancient Greek and Roman worlds. There is reason to believe that they were often done on special assignment of certain members of the nobility and that they were no more typical of ancient art as a whole than modern pornography is typical of today's art. The idealization of physical beauty (in terms of shapes, lines, and volumes) rather than the depiction of naked sensuality was the pronounced theme of Greek and, to a much lesser degree, of Roman art.

During the Middle Ages, largely owing to the suppressive influence of the Catholic Church, sensuous and erotic art suffered a severe setback; and from the Byzantine world to England

161

and the North countries fully clothed and highly asexualized representations became the rule. Then, although still kept under wraps to some degree by ecclesiastical restrictions and conventions, the nudes of the Renaissance began to take the center of the pictorial stage; and masters such as Correggio, Botticelli, Titian, and Tintoretto began to display their highly sensuous paintings, with nudes and semi-draped figures. Rembrandt, Rubens, and many other artists continued this tradition into the seventeenth century; and even during the period of the Restoration nudity in art was perfectly acceptable to courtiers, although their own clothing showed a stricter sense of modesty (Markun, 1930).

At the same time that the sensual movement in art was in progress, a coexterminous "earthy" rather than erotic core of pictorial and sculptural art was coming into existence. Artists such as Brueghel and Bosch, though not specializing in nudes, frankly depicted the sex proclivities of some of their subjects; and what has been called "erotic realism" as distinguished from "hard core pornography" (Kronhausen and Kronhausen, 1959) had some of its lustiest beginnings. It may also be noted that some medieval works of art included a grotesque element that was at least quasi-erotic. Thus, the grotesque and "satanic" figures of some of the gothic church sculpture contained an element of "fascination of the evil" which may be considered an interesting subheading under the general classification of "sexual" art.

During the eighteenth century, the erotic content of Western art became even more pronounced in many respects. Masters such as Watteau and Boucher continued to portray sensuous nudes; and in England arose a school of artists who specialized in the erotic, and often in the pornographic. Leading the list of artists who often painted erotic subject matter was the great painter and engraver, William Hogarth; and following him were such minor masters as James Gillray (who specialized in works on flagellation), Thomas Rowlandson, and George Cruikshank (illustrator of a famous edition of the pornographic novel, *Fanny Hill*).

The movement toward the erotization of art continued in the nineteenth century. Degas, Renoir, Toulouse-Lautrec, and Goya were among the outstanding Continental artists whose portrayals of the female form were both reverent and exciting; Gainsborough and Reynolds in England also did some interesting nudes; and a mystic-satanic sexual element was added to painting by Felician Rops and by the pre-Raphaelites, Dante Gabriel Rossetti and Edward Burne-Jones. Mystic voluptuousness, together with overtones and undertones of sexual perversity, were also depicted by Aubrey Beardsley, one of the most famous sexual illustrators of all time.

Late nineteenth-century and twentieth-century Impressionism, Cubism, Dadaism, Surrealism, and other movements in modern art, culminating in the considerable vogue for abstract, nonrepresentational, and nonobjective art, which has many followers today, to some extent reduced the direct depiction of eroticism that had been reborn in Renaissance art. But not entirely. Shapes, colors, and textures, to the eye of the sophisticated viewer of contemporary art, can be unusually erotically stimulating. Wilfred Scawen Blunt attended the 1910 Post-Impressionist exhibition in Paris and saw in the paintings there only "that gross puerility which scrawls indecencies on the wall of a privy" (Markun, 1930, p. 337). And Pitirim Sorokin, one of the guardians of sexual traditionalism of our day, insists that surrealistic pictures and sculptures of today are overloaded with voluptuous scenes and figures and with depictions of procreation and fertility. If sexuality is not rendered visually in modern art, he contends, it is often explicit in the name given by the artist to his design or contraption. "The general trend in our pictures, photographs, sculpture, and other visual arts," he concludes "has been toward a more naked, more sensuous representation of the human body" (Sorokin, 1956, pp. 26–27).

Contemporary art, moreover, is far from being completely nonrepresentational. Artists are still producing male and female representations of the human body that are at times sensual, sexual, or even intensely romantic. And one of the outstanding twentieth-century painters, Jules Pascin, went even further than the nineteenth-century master of nude portraiture, Renoir, in his rendering of pulsating flesh and gave a most realistic, earthy view of female sexuality. As Pascin's biographer, Brodzky (1946), has noted: "Pascin worshipped women, as did Renoir, unashamed."

It is often assumed that there is some kind of a significant and integral relationship of sex to art and between sex and the artist; but exactly what these relationships are has been the subject for considerable unresolved debate. We shall now consider some of the most important theories relating sex to art and try to assess their validity.

Beauty and Art

It is sometimes held that all artistic productions, particularly paintings and sculpture, arise from human concepts of beauty; and that these, in turn, stem from ideas of what is sexually beautiful or exciting. If this is so, then art originates in sexuality and is a major product of the libido. Thus, Freud (1930, 1938), whose views on sexual sublimation and art we shall later discuss in detail, believed that the perception of beauty is at bottom a sensual process and that it becomes esthetic in quality when the sensual aim is inhibited.

The notion that art stems from appreciation of beauty, which in turn originates in sexual desire, has been partly endorsed by several authorities but has also been partly denounced (de Beauvoir, 1953; Bloch, 1908). As Garland (1957) notes in her study of female beauty, art is usually in advance of nature and again and again artists conceive of new types of women which later generations then endorse. Art, Flugel (1945) insists, in a sense achieves a deeper insight into reality than does the mere perception of physical beauty, inasmuch as it abstracts from the uninteresting and irrelevant details of reality more effectually than perception does. Art therefore presents us a sort of quintessence of the aspect of reality that is relevant to the artist's theme and purpose; and if the artist merely followed his biologically inculcated feelings about what is beautiful (or sexually desirable), art in this sense could hardly exist.

André Gide (1949) is even more vociferous on this point: "As the convinced Mohammedan cries 'God is god,' I should like to shout: 'Art is art.' Reality is always there, not to dominate it, but on the other hand, to serve it." Beigel (1952) also holds that though ideas of physical beauty influence art, these ideas themselves, especially ideas of what is beautiful in the female body, are greatly influenced by the concept of esthetic beauty in art.

In regard to beauty and art, then, it would seem wiser to take a middle rather than any extreme road. Sex desires would appear to have *some* influence on evaluations of human beauty; and these evaluations to *some* extent are important artistic considerations. But by the same token, artistic judgments, which depend on many biological and cultural factors of non-sexual origin and which tend to change considerably from one era to another, also importantly affect sexual desire and notions of beauty.

It is most unlikely, then, that the concept of what is beautiful is related entirely to sex. It is partly based on the way in which we perceive things (which itself is both sexually and non-sexually motivated) and the form and proportions of the things themselves. The concept of beauty is intimately related to existing perceptions of time, spatial relations, proportion, texture, and other aspects of external reality as well as to our personal and culturally influenced interpretations of these modes of existence. Sex plays a distinct part in our notions of what is beautiful; but this part hardly equals the whole of those notions.

Sex desire undoubtedly plays an important role in human ideals of personal beauty, particularly of female beauty. Schopenhauer (1898) hotly contended that sex is practically the only influential factor in inducing a male to admire the female form. "It is only," he said, "the man whose intellect is clouded by his sexual impulses that could give the name of the *fair sex* to that under-sized, narrow-shouldered, broad-hipped, and short-legged race; for the whole beauty of the sex is bound up with this impulse. Instead of calling them beautiful, there would be more warrant for describing women as the unesthetic sex." H. L. Mencken (1919) echoed this view; and Havelock Ellis (1936) also presented evidence that women are universally admired by men because they satisfy the male's sensual and sexual impulses.

Nonetheless, a cursory glance at the changing styles in female beauty in the last several decades in the United States would indicate that biological impulses often take a secondary or subsidiary place to social-esthetic standards in the evaluation of feminine beauty. Even in the case of sex attraction, we may still note that our sex "instincts" importantly prejudice our notions of beauty, but at the same time our esthetic ideas significantly influence these very "instincts."

Nudity and Art

It is sometimes held that artists frequently portray nude figures, particularly those of the female, because they are consciously or unconsciously interested, by reason of their basic sexual proclivities, in such figures. Thus, Guyon (1934, p. 310) states that "the truth is that nudity in art delights us because we find, to our surprise, that the flesh is here presented to us without obstacle or hindrance, recalling to our mind pleasant memories and possibilities." Therefore, he contends, the nude is *not* really chaste, as many artists and critics have held that it is; and when it is supposedly used for esthetic effect, its employment actually has sexual undertones.

Other writers on art differ with this sexualized interpretation of nudity. De Beauvoir (1953) feels that the nude is chaste; and Northcote (1916) holds that "the nude in any given production is not necessarily erotic." Nudity, Wall (1932) insists, is in itself sexual or asexual, decent or indecent, depending on one's attitude toward it—and that attitude tends to be very different at one time and place from what it is at another.

Kinsey and his associates (1953) found some evidence that artistic portrayals of nude figures often do stem from sexual motives. In a study that is still continuing they reported that if professional artists are given a series of nudes drawn by other artists they can predict quite accurately whether the draughtsmen are heterosexually or homosexually inclined. The Kinsey research team has also found that although 54 per cent of their male subjects have been aroused by seeing photographs, drawings, or paintings of nudes only 12 per cent of females have been similarly aroused. As would be expected under these circumstances, it has also been found that although female artists frequently produce highly romantic drawings and paintings, they rarely excel in pornographic works of art. By the same token, Dingwall (1957) notes that, as might very well be expected, sex-obsessed countries such as the United States produce better erotic art of the pin-up variety than do other countries. A. Ellis (1960a) also reports that just because nudity in the United States is officially and socially enjoined, it tends to be the more enjoyed. Contemporary mass media are increasingly full of "artistic" nudes that obviously appeal to masculine lasciviousness.

A good case can certainly be made, therefore, for the theory that both artists and their public are sexually motivated when they find "esthetic" satisfaction in the depiction of the nude female form. Artists are, after all, human beings with human desires; and the nude form obviously has connotations, at least to those of the Western world, of sensual activities and delights. To believe that a fine painter or sculptor of female nudes has no sexual interest in or excitement about his work is to be rather naïve. At the same time, it would be equally naïve to assume that graphic portrayals of the nude form are executed *only* because of the conscious or unconscious sexual urges of the artist. The nude body has the kind of form, coloring, and texture that would give it esthetic value even were its representors and their audiences completely sexless. It is these additional nonsexual aspects of nudity that give it such a widespread esthetic appeal.

Sexual Sublimation and Art

Sigmund Freud has been responsible for the most widely discussed and debated theory of sex and art of all time—the theory that art essentially springs from the individual's repressed unconscious thoughts and wishes and is largely a sublimation of his aim-inhibited sex drives. In his *Introductory Lectures on Psychoanalysis* (1920), Freud noted that the artist is constitutionally endowed with a powerful capacity for sublimation as well as with a certain flexibility in the repression determining his inner conflicts.

In the fourth volume of his *Collected Papers* (1925) he stated this hypothesis in more detail:

The artist is originally a man who turns from reality because he cannot come to terms with the demand for the renunciation of instinctual satisfaction as it is first made, and who then in phantasy-life allows full play to his erotic and ambitious wishes. But he finds a way of return from this world of phantasy back to reality. With his special gifts he molds his phantasies into a new kind of reality, and men concede them a justification as valuable reflections of actual life.

In his consideration of an actual artist, Leonardo da Vinci, Freud (1947) held that this painter's genius resulted from "his particular tendency to repress his impulses and, second, his extraordinary ability to sublimate the primitive impulses."

This psychoanalytical theory of sexual sublimation and art was not entirely original with Freud, since several poets and novelists had outlined similar views previously, and Otto Weininger (1906), a contemporary of Freud, independently arrived at the view that art is a sublimation of Eros and that all genius stems from essentially erotic motives, with the artist's love being directed toward the universe and eternal values instead of toward members of the other sex (Klein, 1949). But Freud's version of the sublimation theory quickly won out over all similar views, and it soon had scores of adherents. Ella Sharpe (1950, p. 126) dogmatically stated that "sublimation and civilization are mutually inclusive terms." Lionel Goitein (1948) claimed that "art is possibly the only area for a conflict-ridden humanity to use today, a sublimation for repressed bewilderment and frustrated desire." Emil Gutheil (1951) pointed out that there is a close connection between the daydream and a work of art. And Ernest Jones (1951), in his analysis of the work of Andrea del Sarto, insisted that this artist never fulfilled himself and did not reach the heights as an artist because he shared a domestic existence with his wife, Lucrezia, thus preventing himself from truly sublimating his repressed sex drives.

The Freudian theory that art originates in sexual sublimation has so completely swept the field of psychology, literature, and esthetics that many non-Freudians have vociferously endorsed it—sometimes in enthusiastic ways of which Freud himself might not have completely approved. The noted gynecologist and sexologist, Robert L. Dickinson (1932), held that sexual desire could easily be diverted into what he called the Third Direction, which included work, amusement, asceticism, illness, art, etc. The academic psychologist, Herbert S. Langfeld (1950), thought that art was an escape to a world of so-called unreality, where the artist could have full power over his environment; and that it was in this world of his own making that he solved his inner problems. The social historian, J. D. Unwin (1934), upheld the extreme view that civilization depends almost entirely on sexual repression and that where people are sexually free their culture never matures or deteriorates.

Several correlates to the Freudian position on sex and art may be particularly noted. The first of these is that the main source of artistic productivity is the artist's unconscious mind (Groddeck, 1951; Neumann, 1959). In its most general form, this theory again predates Freud and his followers; but classical psychoanalysis not only posits an unconscious from which artistic productions are drawn, but also the individual's coping with, defending himself against, and finally mastering his unconscious thoughts and feelings—particularly his unconscious sex and aggressive urges. As Bychowski (1947, p. 56) states, "In a really great artist the mastery of technique is but an expression of the mastery of the unconscious material achieved by the ego."

The second correlate of the Freudian theory of art and sex sublimation is that the material the artist dredges up from his unconscious mind and employs in his work is largely repressed material—it has once been conscious and has been censored and squelched by the ego (or superego) because the artist is ashamed of or frightened by it. Artistic work, Marcuse (1955) points out, although opposed to civilization is at the same time bound to it by increasing instinctual repression. And just as we have repressed childish ways of thinking, Weiss (1947) insists, we have also repressed childish ways of perceiving and representing; and it is these latter repressions which are somehow employed by the artist (and which remain unavailable to nonartistic individuals).

A third corollary of the Freudian position on art and sex is that not merely repressed sex drives are necessary for artistic creativeness, but repressed feelings of love and hate as well. As might well be expected, the classical psychoanalysts place Oedipal strivings, and the conflicts to which these strivings lead, at the core of their theory of art. According to Schneider (1954), the artist achieves his power to identify with his characters and his themes from his early identifications with and subsequent transference relations with his parents. Or, in Ella Sharpe's more concrete exposition (1950, p. 135): "Art is a sublimation rooted in the primal identification with the parents. That identification is a magical incorporation of the parents, a psychical happening which runs parallel to what has been for long ages repressed, i.e., actual cannibalism. The artist externalizes his incorporation of the hostile parent into a work of art. He thus makes, controls his power over his introjected image or images."

Because of the Oedipal foundations of art—as Kris (1952), Schneider (1954), and Tarachow (1949) indicate—the artist must fundamentally be a communicating, social person. By conquering his Oedipal conflicts he learns to love himself and his work and to want to communicate productively with others.

A fourth concomitant of the Freudian view of art and sex sublimation is that an economy of psychic energy is involved in artistic creativity. According to Freud (1947), the energy that might be used for artistic production is usually bound by sexual repression; but if the artist is endowed with a certain flexibility of repression this energy can be freed for the work of artistic transformation from the unconscious to the conscious. The artist thus knows how to find his way back to reality from the world of private phantasy.

Joseph Weiss (1947) has gone beyond Freud himself in this connection and has claimed that just as wit, according to classical psychoanalysis, is the economy of expenditure of psychic energy in inhibition, formal esthetic pleasure is the economy of expenditure of psychic energy in perception. In Weiss' own words (1947, pp. 396-397): "When the perception of a picture causes a comparison with a more economic treatment of the same material, psychic energy

is not saved but wasted, and a disagreeable feeling is produced. Thus if two colors are too similar, they can be perceived easily neither as one color nor as two separate colors. The resulting increase in psychic work causes displeasure and we say the colors clash."

A final correlate of the Freudian theory of art and sex sublimation that we shall consider here is the view that art and neurosis are integrally intertwined and that only out of dealing with his own underlying anxiety and guilt can the artist be creative. A feeling of calm, Sachs (1942) states, is a prerequisite to the creation or appreciation of beauty; but calm is only achieved by one's overcoming one's basic hostility and anxiety. The artist, moreover, never really conquers his underlying neurosis, but keeps producing his work as a continual defense against his still-existing disturbance. In Tarachow's words (1949, pp. 224-225): "The artistic creation of beauty is also a relief, but from the intolerable tension of the fear and aggression of others. . . . A motive in the creation of beauty is anxiety produced by a feared and hated object with whom the artist must become reconciled." Ella Sharpe (1950, p. 127) concurs: "Art rises to its supreme height only when it performs a service—first for the artist and unconsciously for ourselves—that it did in ancient times. That service is a magical reassurance." Lee (1947) agrees that an artistic work represents an atonement for the artist's destructive rage against objects and also a means of self-therapy for his neurotic depression, the depression being a requisite for artistic creation.

Otto Rank (1932, 1950) gave considerable thought to the relationship of art and neurosis and took a somewhat more optimistic view of the artist's ability to resolve his own fundamental disturbance through his creative efforts. Like the Freudians, Rank felt that the forming of unconscious phantasy is essential to artistic creation; and that in his phantasy the artist attempts to solve his own deepest problems. The neurotic and the artist thus have a fundamental point in common—they have both committed themselves to the pain of separation from the herd, from unreflective incorporation of the views of their parents and of society. But the artist, through his work, is able to achieve integration of his isolated will by establishing a creative relationship to others. Schneider (1954) also takes a more optimistic view of art and neurosis and holds that art does not directly stem from emotional disturbance, even though some neurotic artists may get secondary (rather than primary) gains from being disturbed.

Critique of the Freudian
View of Sublimation and Art

Although there is much to be said in favor of certain aspects of the classical psychoanalytical theory of sex sublimation and art, the one-sided formulations of this theory that are often given fail to do justice to the immensely wide ranging elements of artistic creativity and, at best, give but partial answers to the questions of why some individuals are artists and why they create what they do. Specific limitations of the Freudian position include the following:

1. That the artist must in some manner tap his unconscious mental processes if he is to produce and communicate to others works of lasting values is almost certainly true. But the "unconscious mind" that he thereby taps is hardly a mysterious entity in its own right. It consists, rather, of the total sum of the individual's experiences, attitudes, beliefs, and memories which, by an act of conscious introspection, he is able to dig into, reactivate, and recombine in an almost infinite number of new ways. All his artistic concepts, as Locke, Hume, and other philosophers have shown for several centuries, merely consist of re-experiences and recombinations of some of his original, if now mainly forgotten, precepts. It is true that he is almost totally unaware (or unconscious) of exactly *how* he reactivates and recombines his past experiences (just as most of us are unaware of exactly *how* we solve a mathematical or a chess problem, although obviously the solution does not really come to us—as it sometimes appears to come—by magic).

2. Granting that art depends largely on creative processes that involve our past experiences, many of which we no longer consciously remember and whose recollection and recombination into art forms are only vaguely understood by us, there is little evidence that the artist's use of his "unconscious" thoughts and feelings invariably implies his coping with, defending himself against, and finally mastering his instinctual urges. This is not to say that *some* artists do not have sexual or aggressive feelings that they are ashamed to admit, that they unconsciously repress, and that consequently impel or compel them to work out these feelings in artistic productions, as a kind of expiation of or defense against these repressed feelings. But to believe that because *some* artists are thus unconsciously driven to creativity *all* artists *must* be so driven is to make one of the commonest errors of logical thinking and to set up a hypothesis for which there are as yet no confirmatory data. One of the most unscientific aspects of orthodox psychoanalysis is the conclusion by its devotees that because A and B, who have been treated for some neurotic symptom, display X complex, every other human being who has the same symptom must also show evidence of X complex. Similarly, presenting evidence that artists A and B were impelled to create because of their defenses against their own unconscious sex or aggressive urges scarcely proves that all creative artists have similar repressed urges.

3. Assuming, again, that unconscious thoughts and feelings play a vitally important role in virtually all artistic creations, there are no scientific data whatever to support the Freudian assumption that these unconscious experiences are dynamically *repressed*. Occasionally, when a person is thoroughly ashamed of his ideas or phantasies, he may dynamically refuse to admit that they exist; and as a result of this kind of repression, he may later be driven to express these unconscious feelings in artistic forms. There is much more reason to believe, however, first that most of our experiences of which we are at any moment unaware consist of fairly neutrally toned thoughts and feelings which we would not hesitate to reawaken to consciousness; and second that the unconscious experiences that artists generally employ in their productions are notably in this class of quite *un*repressed ideas and emotions. Freud believed that the artist (for some mysterious reasons which he never could explain) is the type of individual who somehow is flexible about his repressions and is able to dredge up his repressed unconscious ideas and

use them effectively in his work. It would seem to be far simpler and wiser to assume, instead, that either (a) the artist is the kind of person who is less self-blaming than others and therefore likely to do less repressing; or (b) he is an individual whose "talent" or "genius" (by which may well be meant his unusually well organized brain and central nervous system) enable him in the first place to have more vital life experiences than the nonartist or the inferior artist and in the second place to dig into his unrepressed store of these experiences.

4. The Freudian notion that art is intimately related to Oedipal relationships or to repressed feelings of love and hatred for one's parents (which are ultimately transferred to other significant figures in one's life) probably has a grain—but *only* a grain—of truth in it. For great artists (as we shall note in more detail below) almost invariably love their work and to some degree love (or at least seek the approval of) the audiences to which they present this work. And behind all feelings of loving, vital absorption, and desire for the approval of others it is quite likely that there are *some* remnants of early attitudes and ideas which were learned in one's early family romance. To believe, however, that *all* emotions of love and absorption as well as those of aversion and hatred stem from a boy's originally lusting after his mother and resenting and being guilty about his resentment of his father's intrusion is to make one more of those overgeneralizations for which orthodox Freudians are unfortunately famous. Again: assuming that an artist's loves and hates significantly influence and affect his productions, there is no evidence that his *repressed* feelings of affection and hostility are much more important than his open and avowed feelings.

5. If the Freudian theory of art and sex sublimation were true, one would expect artists to be unusually inhibited individuals who lived ascetically in their garrets, had little or no sex-love affairs, and consequently felt compelled to compensate by throwing themselves into their work. But most of the great artists of all time, as we shall indicate in a later section of this article, were reasonably happily married or engaged in distinctly more than their share of heterosexual or homosexual activities. What repressed instinctual sex-love urges they were artistically "sublimating" is, in the light of these circumstances, difficult to imagine.

6. The Freudian notion that psychic energy is involved in artistic creativity and that formal esthetic pleasure stems from an economy in the expenditure of this energy is particularly hard to take in the light of twentieth-century discoveries in physics and neuroanatomy. Freud's application of nineteenth-century mechanics to the psychic working of the human organism and his "explanations" of human thinking and feeling in terms of his own hypothesized system of libido economy have been much criticized by numerous modern critics of psychoanalysis; and there seems to exist little or no empirical evidence to support his highly imaginative sex-economy theorizings (A. Ellis, 1950; Eysenck, 1953). The mere fact that a host of psychoanalysts, such as Kris (1952), Reik (1945), and Weiss (1947), have heartily endorsed Freud's notion that artistic creativity depends on the economics of the expenditure of libidinous energy by no means adds any validity to these highly theoretical constructs.

7. The view that art and neurosis are integrally related would seem, at first blush, to have some validity, since it is obvious that most great artists have been more or less emotionally disturbed and many of them have even been psychotic (Phillips, 1957). The facts would also seem to indicate that supersensitive and emotionally aberrated individuals (for example, fixed homosexuals) are frequently more interested in art than less sensitive and aberrated persons appear to be. These facts, however, seem largely to be accounted for by several understandable reasons: (a) Great artists are generally unconventional and their very unconventionality is often misinterpreted as severe disturbance. (b) Noted artists are investigated more carefully by their biographers than are hacks or nonartists; therefore we tend to *know* about their aberrations and to remain unaware of how disturbed were their less great contemporaries. Many outstanding artists who live regular and undistinguished lives are rarely written or talked about; while the more erratic ones, such as Gauguin and Van Gogh, are endlessly biographized. (c) We have no way of

knowing how many thousands of highly talented individuals never became fine artists precisely because they were so disturbed that they never actually produced any works of note. (d) Severely disturbed individuals, who have no creative talents themselves, frequently become interested in art because they are interested in being "cultured" or "superior" persons, and thereby winning a derivative kind of social approval.

What little clinical evidence is available tends to indicate that the more severely disturbed an individual is, the less he tends to actualize whatever artistic potential he may possess (A. Ellis, 1959). Moreover, since great art almost invariably involves a considerable amount of mental integration, concentrated drive, and persistent work on the part of the artist, it may seriously be doubted if most outstanding artists were *severely* neurotic or psychotic when they were at the height of their productivity. The Freudian and Rankian hypotheses that the artist "works through" his disturbances in his artistic creations, and helps therapize himself thereby, may have some validity. But it may just as logically be hypothesized that the truly great artist is somewhat less disturbed in most instances than the lesser artist and that that is why his potential talent is more likely to be effectively actualized. It may also be hypothesized that in the case of the inordinately talented artist his genius is so outstanding that, neurotic or not, he finally produces outstanding works and that in understanding him, we might better focus on his genius than on his reasonably irrelevant emotional aberrations.

A Multifactor Theory of Art and Sex

The main objection to the Freudian theory of art and sexuality is not that it is entirely mistaken, and certainly not that it adds nothing to our understanding of the creative and the sexual processes, but that it is at the same time too restricted and overgeneralized. In attempting to account for the "deeper" and more complex aspects of the influence of human sex drives on artistic production, it undervalues some of the simpler and more significant factors

involved in sex and art. A wider ranging and more objective theory of the place of sexuality in art would include some of the following factors.

It should first be noted that man appears to be essentially and inherently a creative animal. Even when he is not particularly intelligent or educated, he tends to restructure his environment in terms not only of utility but also of esthetics. The more intelligent and culturally educated he is, the more artistic, in terms of both productivity and audience participation, he tends to be. Art, therefore, may be conceived as a *normal* aspect of human living; and the question may well be asked, "Why does a human being *not* use his creative potential in some way?" rather than "What makes this or that individual artistic?" To be human, and especially to be a highly intelligent human being, to some degree *means* that one will tend to be inventive, problem-solving, and artistically creative. The mystery, if there is a mystery about esthetic productiveness, is why so few individuals in our society actually do invent and create. And one of the fairly obvious answers to this mystery is that we raise our people to be so nauseatingly approval-seeking and terrified of failure that most of them do not *dare* take the risk of committing their creative potential to actual artistic production.

The second point to be noted in trying to arrive at a wide-ranging theory of art and sex is that art is essentially a form of *work* and that no artist produces anything who does not, at some point in the game, push himself into *action*. Arts such as drawing, painting, and particularly sculpture require physical effort along with mental exertion; and unless the artist is willing, quite consistently, to buckle down to the necessary tasks and chores involved in his activity (including the often boring tasks of mixing paints, stretching canvases, etc.), he simply is not going to accomplish anything in his chosen field. Fortunately, however, all animals to some extent *like* to move, to act, to work; and the artist normally becomes thoroughly absorbed, in a pleasant way, in his activities once he manages to overcome his initial inertia and to get these activities under way. Because he learns, by experience, that it is pleasurable to work in an absorbed, intense manner, he has an incentive to keep going back to his artistic activity, even when he is not too unhappy in a more restful state.

If, as just posited, the creative urge is innate in most men, and if art is a form of activity, which itself is also a normal part of human living, it is not difficult to see that there must inevitably be *some* connection between sex and art. For the human sex drives are certainly to some degree inborn and intrinsic and they are one of the most highly motivating forces (from both an innate and socially learned standpoint) in driving men and women to intense and sustained activity. To accept this fact does not mean that we have to go the whole Freudian or Jungian way and identify life itself as an essentially libidinous or erotic force. Activity-impulsion is probably the most generalized form of aliveness; and sex-impulsion is merely one, albeit a major, form of activitization. But it is hard to conceive of living, behaving, or activity-impulsion without *any* measure of sexuality—especially since, in the human species, reproduction of the race is entirely dependent on sexual processes.

The argument then logically proceeds: If art depends on inborn (as well as culturally acquired) activity-impulsions, and if human behaving and reproducing to some degree depend on inborn (as well as environmentally learned) sexual-impulsions, it would indeed be odd if there were no reasonably direct relationships between art and sex. Or, to state the matter a little differently, under these circumstances it would be remarkable if the main or only influence of sex drives on artistic creativity was, as the Freudians state or imply, the result of such highly indirect factors as sexual sublimation, repression, defenses against anxiety and hostility, reaction formation, and various other kinds of psychic circumlocutions. As Harry B. Lee, himself a psychoanalyst but one who takes a somewhat non-Freudian view of sex and art, has rather poetically stated (1953, p. 283): "Creation and recreation are inventive activities born of spiritual necessity, and they are something more than chance iridescences upon the surface of a daydream."

If we turn from Freudian hypotheses and give a little thought to the possibility of *direct* influences of human sexuality on artistic production, we may soon come up with the following hypotheses:

1. Sexual desire is a highly activating and motivating force behind many pursuits. It spurs people to achieve fame and fortune, in many instances, in order that they may be more attractive to members of the other sex; and it is quite likely that art is one of the main fields in which this sexually impelled fame and fortune is sought.

2. Sexual urges frequently encourage individuals to enter certain professions—as when the physician studies medicine in order that he may be able to undress women or the actor enters the theatrical field because of the attractive women he may encounter there. Certainly, therefore, some artists must be drawn to their work because of their interest in nude models or (as we noted previously in this article) their sensuous pleasure in depicting the nude form.

It has been hypothesized by Rhoda Winter Russell (personal communication) that many painters have highly enjoyable, positive experiences with members of the other sex; and that in their artistic productions they not only create the sexualized forms of the persons with whom they have had pleasant contact but also *re*create the sex pleasures they have had with these individuals. This hypothesis, that direct sex gratification may lead to an urge to recreate images of itself, seems to make good sense and would partially help to explain why many artists are drawn to depict nudes or other sexualized representations in their work—and why some of them may even be drawn to art itself as an enjoyable form of life activity.

3. Karl Groos (as quoted by Forel, 1922), notes that since the object of art is to excite the sensibilities, it is obvious that it will utilize the domain that is richest in emotional sensations—the sexual domain. Drawing, painting, and sculpture in particular are forms of art which require that the sentiments of the observer be attracted and heightened almost instantaneously, whereas certain other art forms (such as literature) must ultimately, but not immediately, strike an emotional cord in the members of the artist's audience. It is therefore to be expected that the graphic and sculptural arts will make particular use of sexual themes.

4. Although sexual orgasm is normally reached, in the final analysis, by means of friction and the sense of touch, sexual arousal in most societies, including our own, is largely mediated by the sense of sight. Art, which appeals particularly to this sense of sight, may consequently again be expected to be more sexualized in many respects than certain other forms of creative expression.

5. Autoerotic impulses, as Havelock Ellis (1936) pointed out, frequently are not directly gratified, but drive the individual into some form of restlessness and nonsexual activity; and it is impossible to say what of the finest elements in art, in morals, in civilization generally may not really be rooted in autoerotism. Ellis quotes Nietzsche in this connection: "Without a certain overheating of the sexual system, we could not have a Raphael."

6. There may well be, as Marcuse (1955) indicates, an inherent trend in the libido itself toward cultural expression, without external repressive modification. Although the Freudian theories of art springing from an economy of energy may well be questioned, as we noted above, there may still be truth in the notion that life is basically an energy-expending process and that sex energy is a most important part of and significantly motivating force behind living. If so, such sex energy could both directly and indirectly contribute to artistic creation.

7. At the bottom of artistic production is sensory input and output. The artist almost hungrily draws sensations from his environment; and, albeit in an often abstract and highly intellectualized form, he communicates them back to his viewers—who, in turn, receive their first impression of the artist's product from their senses. "If man expresses his grasp of the world by his senses," states Erich Fromm (1955, p. 347), "he creates art and ritual, he creates song, dance, drama, painting, sculpture." If this is true, then sex and art are two major ways by which man expresses his grasp of the world by his senses—since, in addition to its use of the sense of sight, which we emphasized a few paragraphs back, sex is indubitably a highly sensualized activity. Artists notably draw upon sensations; and it is quite likely that their sensuousness will lap over into sexual expressiveness. Whether consciously or unconsciously, their art will tend to carry pure tones or overtones of sexuality for themselves and their viewers.

8. In some instances, the artist will very deliberately and consciously employ his art form for the expression of his sex impulses. Thus, a writer may become sexually aroused by his own fictional scenes; and a painter may get an erection while painting a real or an imagined nude. Also, instead of unconsciously repressing his sex urges and sublimating them in his work, an artist may consciously suppress his unsatisfiable desires and throw himself into diverting artistic activity that helps keep him from plaguing himself with lustful thoughts.

In many ways there may be a direct or semi-direct influence of human sexuality on the artist and of artistic creation on sexual desire and fulfillment. The concept of what is artistically beautiful most probably does not depend entirely on sexual craving; but part, and perhaps quite a large part, of this concept does seem to stem from obvious or covert sexual drives.

As for the more indirect aspects of sex and art, particularly those involved with the psychoanalytical theories of sex sublimation, these too would appear to have *some* validity—in spite of the usual orthodox Freudian attempts to overemphasize their importance. In fact, in the case of any given artist, there is no reason why the sexual sources of his creative work cannot be significantly fourfold: (a) He may have conscious sex desires which he deliberately fulfills to some extent in his art—e.g., by painting exciting nudes, sculpting erotic tableaux, etc. (b) He may have unconscious but unrepressed sex urges, which supply him with considerable artistic raw material (such as sensuous images or predilections for sexualized forms) that he incorporates into either representational or more abstract art forms. (c) He may have conscious sex urges which he consciously suppresses by absorbing himself in his art work and which help give this work either a highly sexualized or a studiously asexualized tone. (d) He may have conscious sex (or aggressive) feelings of which he is quite ashamed, which he then unconsciously represses, and to prevent these repressed impulses from returning to consciousness he may set up compensatory or other neurotic defenses which drive him to produce works of art and sometimes to produce them in a specifically sexualized manner.

Only by taking into account several major factors such as those just outlined is it possible for us to account for the full scope of the relationship between sex and art. And when this full scope is accurately perceived, it indeed appears almost universal. For all that—and let this caveat be duly emphasized—art is far from being entirely sexualized in either its origin or its execution. As Herbert Read (1947) correctly indicates, art forms have their basis in the laws and organizations of inorganic as well as of living things, in the processes of biological growth and function as well as in the mathematical and mechanical properties of matter. Art is the representation, science the exploration, of the fundamental structure and processes within and around us.

The Sexual Psychology of Artists

As briefly noted in our discussion of sex sublimation and art, most outstanding artists have hardly been noted for their sexual abstinence or reticence. Craven (1931, 1940) informs us that Titian had at least one mistress; Rembrandt lived in concubinage with Hendrickje Stoeffels; El Greco was a man of many loves; Van Gogh was a constant frequenter of brothels; Gauguin frequented brothels and also lived with a mistress; Modigliani was promiscuous; Matisse had an illegitimate daughter; Picasso lived with various women; Turner was a man of strong sexual impulses who had four illegitimate children; and so on and so forth. Brodzky (1946) tells us that Jules Pascin, one of the outstanding painters of nudes, was highly promiscuous and that "a loose life . . . was as food for him."

When not reveling in heterosexual activities, some of the most renowned artists, including Leonardo, Cellini, Michelangelo, Raphael, and Blake, are suspected of having had homosexual or at least homoamative relations during a large part of their lives. Although the stereotype of the bohemian artist who lives in a garret and is sexually promiscuous is probably largely false—since many quite talented and great artists marry conventionally at a reasonably

early age and remain sexually faithful to their mates for the rest of their lives—it still can probably be found that renowed artists tend to be less conventional in their approaches to sex and to life than are men of equal genius in other fields (such as engineering or research). Quite possibly, this may partly be because the artist usually is a free lancer, who is not directly dependent on a single employer for his financial security, and that therefore he allows himself more freedom in his sexual behavior. But there may also be something about the artistic temperament itself that finds it undesirable or difficult to conform to bourgeois sexual morality.

There is a widespread belief that an unusually high proportion of artists and individuals who are interested in art are homosexually inclined. As far as great artists themselves are concerned, this belief does not appear to hold much water, since the great majority seem to have been distinctly heterosexual and some of those who are suspected of being homosexual (such as Leonardo) are placed in this category on only the flimsiest of evidence. In what seems to be the only study of homosexuality and general creativity that has been done to date, a study by the present author (1959), the data clearly showed that the more homosexual an individual is, the less creative—in terms of originality and inventiveness—he tends to be. Dr. Daniel Schneider, a practicing psychoanalyst as well as an authority on art, has also found (1954, p. 300) that "the great homosexual artist is the exception that proves all the rules." The notion of the homosexual's being highly artistically creative is a myth that has largely been fostered by prejudiced observers, such as Edward Carpenter (1914), Havelock Ellis (1936), and John Addington Symonds (1883), who were themselves homosexual or who (as in Ellis' case) were intimately involved by marital or other emotional ties with homosexuals.

There is much more valid evidence that proportionately more homosexuals than heterosexually interested individuals are artistically and esthetically inclined in terms of audience participation. Just as females in our society tend to attend the ballet, dramatic productions, and musical concerts, whereas males frequently are more interested in the more "manly" sports, so do male homosexuals frequently become esthetically inclined. Part of this participation by homosexuals in artistic interests may be compensatory; part may be imitative and derivative; part may stem from withdrawal from "masculine" interests; and part may be otherwise correlated to homosexual neurosis. Art interest, however, should not be confused with artistic creativity; and there is some reason to suspect that fixed homosexuality takes away from rather than adds to artistic solidity and that those relatively few great artists who have been exclusively homosexual have fought their way to the top of their profession in spite of rather than because of their emotional aberration.

Up until and including the present day, sex differences in artistic creativity have been quite pronounced. Although numerous females attend art school and show considerable talent, and although some of them become outstanding illustrators, relatively few achieve high rank among the truly great artists of their day. Havelock Ellis, after an exhaustive study of sex differences, reported that "there can be no doubt whatever that if we leave out of consideration the interpretive arts, the artistic impulse is vastly more spontaneous, more pronounced, and more widely spread among men than among women" (1929, p. 374). Ludovici (1932, p. 44) concurred: "We find chiefly the names of men in all the records of human greatness." And even Simone de Beauvoir (1953), after pointing out that women have had a unique role in the cultural and intellectual life of Western civilization, was forced to conclude that "however important this collective role of the intellectual woman may have been, the individual contributions have been in general of less value."

Why women have turned out to be less impressive in the field of creative art has often been a matter for debate. Havelock Ellis (1929) believed that although the sexual sphere is more massive in women it is less energetic in its manifestations; and that consequently the female's creativity suffers. Virginia Woolf (1930) held that biology has little to do with the artistic inadequacy of women; rather, she contended, the need for true independence and a room of her own constitute the female's worst handicaps in competing artistically with the male. Simone de Beauvoir (1953) insisted that art and thought have their living springs in action and that because woman has not been engaged in action to any considerable degree, she does not make the most of her artistic potentialities. Other authors feel that the female's main creative outlet is childbearing and child-rearing; and that because she is biosocially focused on this kind of creativity, her contributions to art tend to be relatively secondary, imitative, and usually second-rate.

The mystery of why women are, on the whole, considerably less artistically creative than men is enhanced by two noteworthy exceptions to the general rule. In the first place, in certain esthetic fields, such as the writing of fiction, women are often outstanding creators—e.g., Jane Austen, the Brontë sisters, Virginia Woolf, Katherine Mansfield, Katherine Anne Porter, Elizabeth Bowen, etc. In the second place, women are frequently unusually gifted as performing or interpretive artists, in such fields as dancing, singing, acting, and the playing of musical instruments. Why, then, do they fail, in almost all instances, as outstanding painters, sculptors, and composers?

In addition to the reasons posited two paragraphs back, it may be hypothesized that women, for biological and social reasons, are far more interested in concrete human relations than they are in abstract artistic processes; and that the graphic arts and music, in particular, require for their highest forms of composition a vital absorption in abstract ideas rather than more concrete feelings. None of the foregoing theories of why artistic creativity is lower in the female than in the male, however, have any conclusive data in their support; and the issue remains still scientifically unresolved.

The Diagnosis of Sexual Disturbances from Artistic Productions

During the last two decades art and sex have become associated in a manner that hardly existed before World War II: namely, the psychological diagnosis of individuals with sex (or nonsexual) disturbances through the interpretation of their paintings, drawings, or sculpture. Several psychologists and psychotherapists, including Buck (1949), Hammer (1958), Mach-over (1948), and Naumberg (1950), have published treatises purporting to show that emotionally disturbed, and particularly sexually disturbed, individuals will project their personality problems into their artistic productions and that if these productions are carefully analyzed these individuals may be accurately diagnosed. Thus, drawings and paintings have been employed in revealing the problems of homosexuals, sadomasochists, fetishists, exhibitionists, and other kinds of potential or actual sex offenders.

Evidence presented by the above named authors, as well as many studies by others, would tend to indicate that although artistic productions may be of some use in the clinical diagnosis of sexual and nonsexual disturbances, no foolproof method of diagnosis or prognosis yet exists in this connection and predictive results are spotty, inconsistent, and inconclusive. By far the best method of evaluating an individual's general or sexual disturbances would still seem to be a face to face clinical interview; and projective methods of personality assessment, including the use of artistic productions, are of comparative minor value and low validity (A. Ellis, 1953).

Pornography and Art

Pornography is a term that was originally used to describe prostitutes and their trade but has in recent years been employed to describe literature or art that has been created with the deliberate intention of arousing sexual desire. It is often confused with erotic realism. Thus, some of the descriptions in James Joyce's *Ulysses* or some of the vitally alive nudes of Renoir or Pascin may arouse the most lascivious thoughts in certain readers or viewers; but this does not seem to have been the conscious intent of the creators of these descriptions or portrayals. As Forel (1922) points out, Greek art was enormously concerned with the nude female figure; but most of this art was far from being pornographic or "obscene," since the intention of the artist was to idealize the female form rather than to arouse sexual thoughts and fancies.

The field of art and sex is unusually compli-

cated because the word *sex* has multiple meanings when used in relation to art. Following the suggestions of Brian Heald (personal communication), we shall attempt to break down the term *sex* so that it becomes denotatively clearer when used in the phrase "sex and art." We may thus distinguish among three reasonably clear-cut meanings:

1. *Sex-depicting but nonerotic art.* A considerable number of works of painting and sculpture depict or involve sexual content but do so in a nondynamic or nonarousing way. The majority of the better known examples of Greek nudes, for example, are sexual, in that they depict the feminine form, but they are not erotic, in that they do not arouse the sex impulses of the average viewer. Some Greek nudes, however, such as the Venus Callipyge, are erotic or desire-arousing to members of our society because they emphasize sexual features (in this case, the buttocks) which our mores do not (yet) accept or approve. The Callipygian Venus, therefore, tends to become associated in the mind of today's Western viewer not with nudity but with undressing—which to him is ordinarily tabooed and sex-arousing.

By the same token, Rodin's famous piece of sculpture, *The Kiss,* is sex-depicting (because it deals with sex-love processes) but not particularly, to most viewers, erotic or sex-arousing (because it is relatively objectively descriptive or self-contained rather than dynamically excitative). *The Kiss* may also be deemed to be on the borderline of the two categories of sex depiction and sex arousal because (a) a sizeable minority of viewers may become sexually aroused by it and (b) an even larger number of viewers may become amatively or emotionally (rather than sexually) aroused by its glorification of young love.

2. *Sex-arousing or erotic but nonpornographic art.* A great many works of art not only depict sexual content but do so in a dynamic or arousing manner. Thus, Manet's *Dejeuner sur l'herbe* shows a nude in the company of several young Frenchmen and depicts the girl and her companions so that the average viewer's phantasies tend to move out from the time and place of the painting and to use it as a jumping-off point for his personal sex imaginings. Similarly, the depiction of pubic hair in

a drawing or painting tends to make this work erotic or sex-arousing because, in the same sense as Manet's picture, it draws the attention of the viewer to the "realities" of the situation. The "peep-show" aspect of semi-nudity is erotic because it expresses the dynamism of undressing rather than the *state* of nudity.

Between the objective sex-depicting and the subjective sex-arousing work of art there is often a fine line; and this line changes drastically from community to community and from time to time. Thus, the notorious copulating nudes that were fairly common on public buildings in ancient Greece and India are apt to be sexually-arousing to a much greater extent for us than for their nudity-accustomed and more objective creators. And even for us, if we continue to see many of them and to be accustomed to their nudity, they soon lose most of their erotic or sex-arousing quality. In general, however, there is a considerable body of art that is sex-depicting in an objective way and a body that is sex-arousing in a personal or subjective way. The former will normally be less likely to be banned or bowdlerized than the latter.

3. *Sex-arousing or erotic and pornographic art.* Sex-arousing art may be created by an artist who has little idea of the potential arousability of his work or who wishes to stimulate his viewers esthetically or emotionally and who employs deliberately sex-arousing themes to effect this end. In this case, we refer to his work as being "erotic realism." On the other hand, sex-arousing art may be created by an artist who is fully conscious of what he is doing and who wishes dynamically, concretely, and against some of the mores (or assumed mores) of his day to stimulate the naked sexuality of his viewers. Thus, if Rodin's male in *The Kiss* had his hand on the female's buttocks or genitals his statue would be violently erotic but not necessarily pornographic; while if the female had been having active intercourse with the male or had been another male the statue would be pornographic. Again, the statues of coital figures on Indian temples are erotic, but not pornographic; but the depiction of the same acts in terms of contemporary photography would (in 99 per cent of imaginable cases) be pornographic and not erotic.

It is necessary, again, to distinguish between the motives of the creator and those of the viewer. In the case of the Indian temple statues, for most of the tourists who see them the figures are unquestionably pornographic, but from the standpoint of their creators it would not be logical (except with careful qualification) to call them pornographic art.

If these three categories of sex-depicting, sex-arousing, and pornographic art are valid, it would appear that pornography can normally only exist where sexual mores are to a degree prohibitive and where pornographic productions can therefore be mores-destroying. The laughter at sex acts and depictions—as shown in the tendencies of many primitive peoples to enjoy lascivious stories and in those of the Chinese and Japanese to enjoy their "pillow book" art—is not necessarily pornographic; but where the mores are quite antisexual, it almost necessarily is. In a perfectly mature and permissive society pornography probably cannot exist.

Clear-cut instances of sex-depicting and sex-arousing art are known from ancient times. Primitive peoples have created much sculpture and pottery that portrays sexual and erotic themes. Cicero and Pliny mention *libidines*—highly erotic pictures and bas reliefs used to adorn Roman villas of Pompeii; and many of these have been unearthed in modern excavations of ancient cities (Northcote, 1916). Erotic as well as pornographic playing cards were fairly prevalent in fifteenth-century England and were quite in vogue in the nineteenth century (Bloch, 1934). As noted previously in this article, an entire school of enormously talented erotic (and sometimes pornographic) artists arose in Western Europe in the eighteenth and nineteenth centuries. Edward Fuch's monumental three-volume work on the erotic element in caricature (1909-1912) shows that some of the most renowned artists have deliberately drawn and painted sexually arousing pictures. Bloch (1908) lists, among the great names in art who have created paintings that have frequently been called "obscene," Rembrandt, Watteau, Fragonard, Pascin, and Beardsley.

Can there be great erotic art? There almost certainly can, even though most sex-arousing representations are so focused on some of the more limited aspects of their content that they tend to ignore some of the main elements of composition, organization, and style that are necessary for the existence of truly fine art. But some of the deliberately sex-arousing Japanese drawings—which we would undoubtedly label as being pornographic, though the Japanese themselves would often take a different position—are works of rare beauty and craftsmanship; and when viewed by a cultured person they are likely to appeal to him primarily as works of art and only secondarily as erotica.

Many nonerotic works, ironically enough, have been endowed with a highly stimulating character because of attempts to censor them. Thus, as Havelock Ellis (1936), Forel (1922), and other authorities have pointed out, putting fig leaves on paintings or statues often excites the viewers, by drawing attention to what they conceal, far more than a display of simple nudity would.

Nonetheless, censorship of art representations has been rife from at least the days of early Christianity. Christian opposition to nudity in any form made it a sin, well into the Middle Ages, to use even a naked boy as a model (Stanley, 1955). During the Renaissance, Savonarola preached mightily against nudity in art and burned many pictures portraying delights of the flesh. During the Counter-Reformation, after the Medici popes had passed on, fig leaves were supplied for nude statues in the Vatican, and Michelangelo's "Last Judgment" was made respectable by the addition of painted drawers (Markun, 1930).

In eighteenth-century America, a plaster cast of Venus de Medici could not be publicly shown in Philadelphia; and Vanderlyn's "Ariadne" was looked upon with disfavor. In nineteenth-century America, when Horatio Greenough painted a group of "Chanting Cherubs" for J. Fenimore Cooper, the naked babies aroused great moral indignation. A half-draped statue of George Washington also was looked upon unfavorably. In the 1870's and 1880's, Markun (1930, p. 560) tells us, "it was rather a daring person, even in New York high society, who ventured to hang a nude in his drawing room."

In Victorian England, Watts was called upon to explain in public why he could not have clothed his Psyche and the young girl of his famous Mammon work. William Etty and others continued to paint nudes; but Etty's scheme of decoration for a garden house in Buckingham Palace was rejected because of its "immodesty."

Censorship of so-called obscene paintings and sculptural representations continued into the early part of the twentieth century; and, of course, it still persists, except that there has been considerable liberalization in the "so-calling." In the early 1900's John S. Sumner of the Society for the Suppression of Vice prosecuted the art dealer who displayed the nude painting, "September Morn"; and the French playwright, Paul Bourget, was shocked to discover, when he was visiting America, that the people of Boston refused to permit the forms of two naked children carved by the American sculptor August Saint-Gaudens to appear on the façade of their public library. Trousers were also put on antique statues in Baltimore and Philadelphia (Dingwall, 1957).

It has only been during the last half of the twentieth century that the realistic portrayal of nudity in art has truly begun to come into its own and to remain essentially unfettered by censorship. "September Morn" is now found to be entirely innocuous by the viewing public; and many of our widely circularized periodicals have become exceptionally unsqueamish about publishing full-length, completely bare-bosomed pictures of appetizing young females (Ellis, 1960a). For the moment, at least, censorship of pictures that combine art and sexual themes is well on the decline. To use the distinctions made at the beginning of this section, we may say that both sex-depicting and sex-arousing paintings and sculpture are both widely accepted in Western society today; but the banning of outright pornography is still very much with us.

Art and Sex Education

Sex education is normally carried on in a rather hesitant fashion in Western society; and when it is given it usually consists of written words or spoken lectures. Art, when it is employed at all in this kind of sex teaching, is used for the photographlike illustrations of the sex and reproductive organs that many of the marriage manuals contain.

Other societies, however, are more imaginative and wide-ranging in their use of art for sex education. For centuries, the Japanese "pillow books," which consist of sex manuals illustrated in the most concrete ways, have been given to married couples for use on their wedding nights and subsequent occasions. In New Guinea, Mantegazza (1935) informs us, erotic scenes showing the mingling of men with gods, with the genitals of the portrayed individuals purposely enlarged, are employed to educate young people in sexual pursuits. Recumbent wooden figures four feet long which can be made to move and simulate intercourse are also employed.

In China, as in Japan, illustrated sex picture books have been used for centuries. In Italy, during the Renaissance, Augusto and Annibale Carraci made a series of so-called "figures," showing positions of intercourse, which were sometimes used for sex education. And in the twentieth century the famous gynecologist and artist, Robert L. Dickinson, published his *Human Sex Anatomy* (1933), which was probably the first modern book of repute that contained illustrations of sex positions. In the early editions of this work, these illustrations were published separately, since the publisher was not certain that they would be allowed to circulate through the mails. In later editions, the illustrations were published as an integral part of the book.

Havelock Ellis (1936) believed that art could be very useful in the sex education of children. "Children," he wrote, "cannot be too early familiarized with the representations of the nude in ancient sculpture and in the paintings of the old masters of the Italian school. . . . Early familiarity with nudity in art is at the same time an aid to the attainment of a proper attitude towards purity in nature."

In regard to the use of art in the sex education of adults, most modern writers are still too squeamish to explore the possibilities of the use of erotic art to arouse sex partners who may normally have difficulties in becoming aroused or in achieving orgasm. Some material on this subject, however, is contained in the present author's *Art and Science of Love* (1960b).

Conclusion

Human sexuality is an exceptionally important facet of life. As such, it would be most unusual if it did not play an important role in and have a significant amount of influence over artistic creativity in general and the production of painting, drawing, and sculpture in particular. Although the classical Freudian theory of art and its origins in sex sublimation seems to be both too narrow and too over-generally applied, there does appear to be some measure of truth in it. It would be more accurate, however, to point out that sexuality seeps into art directly *and* indirectly, consciously *and* unconsciously; and there would seem to be no special or unique way in which it affects artists or the viewers of their creative productions. Also to the point: unless the word *sexual* is indiscriminately employed to cover virtually all of life's energizing forces, it would appear that artistic endeavor is significantly nonsexual as well as sexual and that any theory that would truly explain why artists create and why members of their audience find their works immensely satisfying must take into account multifactor hypotheses that cannot be condensed into any pat formula. Art is art and sex is sex; and never the twain shall completely merge.

(The author wishes to thank Tore Hakansson, Leon Kroll, and Rhoda Winter Russell for their helpful criticism on the original manuscript of this article, but to implicate them in no way for the final views expressed in the article.)

References

Beigel, Hugo, *Encyclopedia of Sex Education.* New York: John Day, 1952.

Bloch, Iwan, *The Sexual Life of Our Time.* New York and London: Rebman, 1908.

Bloch, Iwan, *Ethnological and Cultural Studies of the Sex Life in England Illustrated as Revealed in its Erotic and Obscene Literature and Art.* New York: Falstaff Press, 1934.

Brodzky, Horace, *Pascin.* London: Nicholson & Watson, 1946.

Buck, John N., *The House-Tree-Person Manual.* Brandon, Vermont: Journal of Clinical Psychology, 1949. *Psychoanalyt. Rev. 34;* 32-57, 1947.

Bychowski, Gustav, "The Rebirth of a Woman: A Psychoanalytic Study of Artistic Expression and Sublimation."

Carpenter, Edward, *Intermediate Types.* New York: Kennerley, 1914.

Craven, Thomas, *Men of Art.* New York: Simon and Schuster, Inc., 1931.

Craven, Thomas, *Modern Art.* New York: Simon and Schuster, Inc., 1940.

de Beauvoir, Simone, *The Second Sex.* New York: Alfred A. Knopf, Inc., 1953.

Dell, Floyd, *Love in the Machine Age.* New York: Farrar and Rinehart, 1930.

Dickinson, Robert L., *Human Sex Anatomy.* Baltimore: The Williams & Wilkins Co., 1933.

Dickinson, Robert L., and Beam, Lura, *A Thousand Marriages.* Baltimore: The Williams & Wilkins Co., 1932.

Dingwall, Eric J., *The American Woman.* New York: Rinehart & Co., 1957.

Ellis, Albert, *An Introduction to the Principles of Scientific Psychoanalysis.* Provincetown: Journal Press, 1950.

Ellis, Albert, "Review of the House-Tree-Person Test." In Buros, O.K., *The Fourth Mental Measurements Yearbook.* Highland Park, N.J.: The Gryphon Press, 1953.

Ellis, Albert, "Homosexuality and Creativity." *J. Clin. Psychol. 15;* 376-379, 1959.

Ellis, Albert, *The Folklore of Sex.* New York: Grove Press, 1960a.

Ellis, Albert, *The Art and Science of Love.* New York: Lyle Stuart, 1960b.

Ellis, Havelock, *Man and Woman.* Boston: Houghton Mifflin Co., 1929.

Ellis, Havelock, *Studies in the Psychology of Sex.* New York: Random House, 1936.

Eysenck, H. J., *Uses and Abuses of Psychology.* London: Penguin Books, 1953.

Flugel, J. C., *Man, Morals and Society.* New York: International Universities Press, 1945.

Forel, August, *The Sexual Question.* New York: Physicians and Surgeons Book Co., 1922.

Freud, Sigmund, *A General Introduction to Psychoanalysis.* New York: Liveright, 1920.

Freud, Sigmund, *Collected Papers,* Vol. IV. London: Hogarth Press, 1925.

Freud, Sigmund, *Civilization and Its Discontents.* London: Hogarth Press, 1930.

Freud, Sigmund, *Basic Writings.* New York: Modern Library, 1938.

Freud, Sigmund, *Leonardo da Vinci.* New York: Random House, 1947.

Fromm, Erich, *The Sane Society.* New York: Rinehart & Co., 1955.

Fuchs, E., *Illustrierte Sittengeschichte vom Mittelalter bis zur Gegenwart.* Munchen: Albert Langen, 1909-1912.

Garland, Madge, *The Changing Face of Beauty.* New York: M. Barrows & Co., Inc., 1957.

Gide, André, *Journals,* Vol. I. New York: Alfred A. Knopf, Inc., 1949.

Goitein, Lionel, *Art and the Unconscious.* New York: United Book Guild, 1948.

Groddeck, Georg, *The Unknown Self.* New York: Funk & Wagnalls Co., 1951.

Gutheil, Emil, *Handbook of Dream Analysis.* New York: Liveright, 1951.

Guyon, René, *The Ethics of Sexual Acts.* New York: Alfred A. Knopf, Inc., 1934.

Hammer, Emanuel F. (ed.), *The Clinical Application of Projective Drawings.* Springfield, Ill.: Charles C Thomas, 1958.

Jones, Ernest, *Essays in Applied Psychoanalysis,* Vol. I. London: Hogarth Press, 1951.

Kinsey, Alfred C. *et al., Sexual Behavior in the Human Female.* Philadelphia: W. B. Saunders Co., 1953.

Klein, Viola, *The Feminine Character.* New York: International Universities Press, 1949.

Kris, Ernst, *Psychoanalytic Explorations in Art.* New York: International Universities Press, 1952.

Kronhausen, Eberhard, and Kronhausen, Phyllis, *Pornography and the Law.* New York: Ballantine Books, Inc., 1959.

Langfeld, Herbert S., "Feeling and Emotion in Art." In Reymert, M. L. (ed.), *Feelings and Emotions.* New York: McGraw-Hill Book Co., 1950.

Lee, Harry B., "A Theory Concerning Free Creation in the Inventive Arts." *Psychiatry 3;* 229-294, 1940.

Lee, Harry B., "On the Aesthetic States of Mind." *Psychiatry 10;* 281-304, 1947.

Lee, Harry B., Review of Ernst Kris, *Psychoanalytic Explorations in Art. Psychoanalyt. Quart. 22;* 280-284, 1953.

Lewandowski, Herbert, *Ferne Länder-fremde Sitten.* Stuttgart: E. Gunther Verlag, 1958.

Ludovici, Anthony M., *Man: an Indictment.* New York: E. P. Dutton & Co., 1932.

Machover, Karen, *Personality Projection in the Drawing of the Human Figure.* Springfield, Ill.: Charles C Thomas, 1948.

Mantegazza, Paolo, *Sexual Relations of Mankind.* New York: Eugenics Pub. Co., 1935.

Marcuse, Herbert, *Eros and Civilization.* Boston: Beacon Press, Inc., 1955.

Markun, Leo, *Mrs. Grundy.* New York: D. Appleton & Co., 1930.

Mencken, H. L., *Prejudices: First Series.* New York: Alfred A. Knopf, Inc., 1919.

Natkin, Marcel, *Photography of the Nude.* London: Fountain Press, 1937.

Naumberg, Margaret, *Schizophrenic Art: Its Meaning in Psychotherapy.* New York: Grune & Stratton, 1950.

Neumann, Erich, *Art and the Creative Unconscious.* New York: Pantheon Books, Inc., 1959.

Newton, Eric, *The Meaning of Beauty.* New York: The Macmillan Co., 1950.

Northcote, M. A., *Christianity and Sex Problems.* Philadelphia: F. A. Davis Co., 1916.

Phillips, William (ed.), *Art and Psychoanalysis.* New York: Criterion Books, Inc., 1957.

Rank, Otto, *Art and the Artist.* New York: Alfred A. Knopf, Inc., 1932.

Rank, Otto, *Will Therapy and Truth and Reality.* New York: Alfred A. Knopf, Inc., 1950.

Read, Herbert, *Education Through Art*. New York: The Macmillan Co., 1947.

Reik, Theodor, *Listening With the Third Ear*. New York: Farrar, Straus and Cudahy, 1945.

Rosenberg, Bernard, and Fliegel, Norris, *The Vanguard Artist*. Chicago: Quadrangle Books, 1965.

Sachs, H., *The Creative Unconscious*. Cambridge, Mass.: Sci-Art Press, 1942.

Schneider, Daniel E., *Psychoanalysis and the Artist*. New York: International Universities Press, 1954.

Schopenhauer, Arthur, Essays. New York: Willey Book Co., 1898.

Sharpe, Ella F., *Collected Papers on Psychoanalysis*. London: Hogarth Press, 1950.

Skinner, B. F., *Science and Human Behavior*. New York: The Macmillan Co., 1953.

Sorokin, Pitirim, *The American Sex Revolution*. Boston: Porter Sargent, Pub., 1956.

Sparrow, W. S. (ed.), *Women Painters of the World*. London: Hodder & Stoughton, 1905.

Stanley, Louis, *The Beauty of Woman*. London: W. H. Allen, 1955.

Symonds, J. A., *A Problem in Greek Ethics*. London: Privately printed, 1883.

Tarachow, Sidney, "Remarks on the Comic Process and Beauty." *Psychoanalyt. Quart. 18;* 215-226, 1949.

Unwin, J. D., *Sex and Culture*. London: Oxford University Press, 1934.

Wall, O. A., *Sex and Sex Worship*. St. Louis: C. V. Mosby Co., 1932.

Weininger, Otto, *Sex and Character* New York: G. P. Putnam's Sons, 1906.

Weiss, Joseph, "A Psychological Theory of Formal Beauty." *Psychoanalyt. Quart. 16;* 391-400, 1947.

Woolf, Virginia, *A Room of One's Own*. Boston: Houghton Mifflin Co., 1930.

ALBERT ELLIS

Artificial Insemination

ARTIFICIAL insemination (A.I.) is a method of treating infertility and may be regarded as an alternative to adoption. More than 100 years ago Marion Sims described A.I. as follows: "For conception, semen with living spermatozoa should be deposited in the vagina at the proper time."

A.I. is a method of achieving conception by mechanical means instead of by sexual intercourse. It is sometimes referred to as artificial fertilization; but since the procedure does not produce fertility, the term is misleading. The popular and lay press reference to the products of A.I. as "test tube babies," however striking the term, is equally misleading; in none of the many variations of the A.I. technique does the seminal fluid ever get into a test tube, and A.I. babies develop and grow in the mother's uterus in the same manner as all other babies.

We distinguish between A.I. with husband's sperm (A.I.H.) or homologous insemination, and A.I. with donor's sperm (A.I.D.) or heterologous insemination.

History

There is indication that cross-pollination of plants was known to the ancient Assyrians and Cretans. The first mention of artificial insemination is found in the Babylonian Talmud (sixth century A.D.). A Talmudic student, so the story runs, submits to his rabbi-teacher the hypothetical case of a woman who became pregnant after bathing in water that, unknown to her, had contained seminal fluid. The rabbi ruled that the woman was innocent; no intercourse had taken place, and insemination was to be considered accidental. Reference to A.I.D. in animals is found in an Arabic tale dating back to 1322, which describes how hostile Arabic tribes secretly inseminated their enemies' stock of thoroughbred mares with sperm from inferior stallions.

Around 1549, Bartolomeo Eustachio (1524-1574), consulted by a physician's wife because of infertility, gave this advice: after intercourse, the husband should insert his finger into the vagina and move the semen toward the uterus. This was done, and the woman conceived.

The first scientific paper on artificial insemination in dogs was published in 1780 by Lazzaro Spallanzani, a professor at the University of Pavia. He was quite aware that the method could be used for humans, but he limited his experiments to animals because of religious inhibitions.

Several years later, the British anatomist and surgeon John Hunter was consulted by a man suffering from hypospadias: he was unable to ejaculate semen into his wife's vagina. After Hunter had injected the husband's sperm into the posterior part of the vagina with a syringe, the woman conceived.

In 1866, Marion Sims did a series of fifty-five intra-uterine inseminations with husbands' sperm. In his only successful case, the woman conceived after the tenth A.I.H. but aborted in the fourth month. Sims attributed 50 per cent of his failures to faulty technique; he estimated his rate of success as about 1:27.

In 1907 the Russian physiologist Iwanoff published a book on A.I. in animals; ever since, the method has been widely used for breeding horses, cattle, and other species. Using A.I., one thoroughbred can sire many mares, and the danger of injury during the mating act is avoided. The semen can be refrigerated and shipped.

Abroad, A.I.H. became increasingly popular after Döderlein (1912) and Fraenkel (1914) recommended the method. Fraenkel was probably the first to advocate systematic timing to make A.I. coincide with ovulation.

In the United States, Robert L. Dickinson practiced A.I.D. from 1890. Some 10,000 A.I. pregnancies (two-thirds of them A.I.H.) were surveyed in 1941; this figure rose to an estimated 20,000 in 1950, 50,000 in 1955, and 100,000 in 1958. A report of the Departmental Committee on Human Artificial Insemination, presented to the British Parliament in July 1960, estimates that a total of "over 10,000 children were born in the United States as a result of A.I.D. alone."

Technique

A.I. is a simple procedure, usually done in the doctor's office. No strict aseptic precautions are necessary, except for intra-uterine insemination.

The patient is placed on a gynecological examining table; the cervical os is exposed by insertion of a unlubricated bivalve speculum into the vagina. The specimen (husband's or donor's) is then injected by means of a dry glass syringe. The semen is spread around the uterine cervix (*paracervical* insemination); sometimes a few additional drops of sperm are injected into the lower end of the cervical canal (*endocervical* insemination); in an infrequently used technique a curved cannula is attached to the syringe (*intra-uterine* insemination). For the record, we also mention *intratubal* insemination: in this variant, which we condemn as dangerous, intra-uterine insemination is followed by tubal insufflation.

After insemination the patient is left on the tilted table, shoulders lowered and pelvis elevated, for 20 to 30 minutes, sometimes up to one hour.

In a variation of the paracervical method a contraceptive device (diaphragm or plastic cervical cap) is used to establish prolonged and intimate contact between cervix and sperm. With this method the patient can leave the ex-

amining table immediately after insemination. In the cervical cap technique, the cap is filled with sperm and then inserted in the usual manner. There also exists a plastic cervical cap with attached plastic tubing; once the cap is *in situ,* sperm can be injected via the tubing into the paracervical region from outside the vagina. With this tubing, the husband may himself perform A.I. Experience with this new method is still limited; it seems to facilitate multiple insemination without necessitating frequent visits to the doctor's office.

Timing

The life span of human spermatozoa in the female reproductive organs is not accurately known; it is short, presumably between 14 and 36 hours. Likewise, the life span of the human egg is supposed to be very short, presumably between 2 and 24 hours. Therefore, successful A.I. is largely dependent on good timing: the closer it coincides with ovulation, the better the chances of success.

As yet, unfortunately, we have no reliable method to determine the exact period of ovulation. There are subjective signs, such as *Mittelschmerz* (low abdominal pain at the right or left side) and a special type of discharge, both occurring at the time of ovulation, but these signs are noticed only by a certain percentage of women. A fair indication can be obtained by keeping a temperature chart; around ovulation time the temperature will dip, followed by a slight rise. A number of laboratory tests have been designed to pinpoint the date of ovulation, among them Farris' rat test, Papanicolaou's vaginal smear, the crystallization test, and the *Spinnbarkeit* phenomenon of the cervical mucus—all too complicated or too unreliable for practical use.

Indications for A.I.H.

Indications for A.I.H. are:

1. Physical conditions prohibiting vaginal intercourse, such as paraplegia or hypospadias of the husband. We know of some isolated cases of fertile males who, instead of ejaculating sem-

inal fluid through the penis, had a reflux of sperm into the bladder. A.I.H. with sperm recovered from the husband's urine was successful. We also have a single case report on successful A.I.H. in azoospermia caused by postgonorrhoic obliteration of the spermatic ducts; in that case an emulsion of tissue excised from the husband's testicle was used for insemination.

Another indication for A.I.H. is hostility of the cervical mucus to sperm; to overcome this reaction, sperm is injected into the uterine cavity (Kleegman, 1966).

2. Psychological conditions, such as impotence, require psychotherapy. If the condition is refractory to such treatment, marital stability is endangered and A.I.H. is therefore contraindicated.

Indications for A.I.D.

Male sterility due to complete absence of live spermatozoa is an absolute indication, clinical sterility (poor sperm count, for instance) a relative indication for A.I.D.

Genetic reasons, such as serious hereditary disease in the husband's family or past history of an erythroblastic baby, may make A.I.D. advisable. The latter condition is due to Rh incompatibility in the parents (Rh negative-sensitized mother and Rh positive father), and a donor with Rh negative blood must be used.

Physician's Responsibility

Although the physical indications for A.I.D. are relatively easy to define, the psychological and sociological factors to be considered require a great deal of thorough probing. The indications for A.I.D. cannot be evaluated from the medical point of view alone. The physician, who has to make the decision, must have intuition and tact, psychological insight, and experience in marriage counseling. He must make sure that the husband and wife applying for A.I.D. are both mature, well-balanced persons; that they have a stable marriage; and that the desire for a child is equally strong in both part-

ners. If one partner seems hesitant, the physician should rule against A.I.D.

It is widely recognized nowadays that it is best to leave the handling of adoptions to an agency, even though the physician might seem the logical person to be entrusted with such a task. A.I.D. is an even more involved procedure and necessitates a more difficult adjustment for husband and wife. A.I.D. is often called "semi-adoption," because only one marital partner, the husband, is "adopting" the child conceived by A.I.D. Incidentally, indications for A.I.D. and adoption are similar in many respects. However, there is no equivalent to the adoption agency, and it is the physician who by necessity must make all the important decisions connected with A.I.D. Most physicians who have accepted the method know the extent of their responsibilities; the ethical standards by which they should be guided are probably best expressed in the writings of Guttmacher (1958) and Kleegman (1954 and 1963).

Selection of the Donor

Adding to the physician's responsibilities is the selection of the donor. A donor must be free of venereal disease, his hereditary background must be free of lethal genes, he should be of the same race and religion as the prospective parents, and his physical characteristics should resemble as nearly as possible the husband's. He must have a high degree of fertility, preferably be a father himself. If the prospective mother is Rh negative, the donor must also be Rh negative. Complete anonymity between donor and prospective parents is imperative. An amendment to the Sanitary Code of the City of New York, in 1947, imposed certain restrictions on the use of donors. Donors are most frequently selected among medical students, interns, or residents of hospitals.

The current price for semen is about $20.00. The specimen should be produced one hour or two prior to insemination; for this reason one specimen can usually not be used for more than one woman.

The practice of mixing donor and husband sperm seems to make little sense; legally, it could not be used to disprove adultery; psychologically, more will be achieved by suggesting sexual intercourse to the marital partners on the days of insemination. The various legal problems of A.I. have been discussed by Weinberger (1960) and Bergerman (1963). Besides adultery, they include legitimacy and the financial support of children resulting from A.I.D.

Results

The rate of success in artificial insemination is difficult to appraise statistically. Although the procedure has been performed in thousands of instances, few physicians have personal experience exceeding 100 individual cases, and even fewer have published their case material. Some of the publications cannot be properly evaluated, because they do not differentiate between A.I.H. and A.I.D. Such specification is important because the rate of success is incomparably lower with A.I.H. Physicians use widely varying techniques in performing A.I. and have different methods of interpreting results. Obviously, a series in which women were inseminated three to five times per cycle and throughout an entire year cannot be compared with a series in which the patients were inseminated once per cycle and for three months only.

It can be said with certainty that A.I.H. has a very low rate of success. In the largest A.I.H. series published, only 7 out of 132 women (5.3 per cent) conceived, whereas A.I.D. succeeds in 80 per cent. Kleegman reports that 33 per cent of her cases conceived after one insemination, and that 78 per cent were inseminated during three and 92 per cent during six cycles. In a series of 112 A.I.D. inseminations, Murphy and Sorrano (1966) reported that conception was achieved with one single insemination in 68 per cent of the women, while 32 per cent required an average of 7.3 inseminations.

Research Projects

Experience with the following techniques is still limited:

Frozen Semen

Use of frozen semen in animal husbandry is common practice and produces excellent results. Human insemination with frozen specimen is still in the experimental stage. More than two dozen normal children have been produced with nitrogen-frozen spermatozoa (Sherman, 1964), but fear of fetal abnormalities or genetic changes is still prevalent among physicians. A.I. with frozen semen would present a number of advantages: it would reduce waste of seminal fluid to a minimum; it would reduce the cost and increase the availability of sperm; and it might open new fields for the procreation of outstanding men whose semen may be preserved for equally outstanding women. Geneticists and philosophers are pondering these possibilities (Muller, 1963, Kline 1963). Human ova banks comparable to sperm banks may be possible in the future (Medical World News, 1965). Human ova appear morphologically unaltered and fertilizable after frozen storage. For *in vitro* fertilization the ovum was placed in serum and kept at body temperature. Future applications might include a type of artificial insemination applicable in infertility due to obstructed Fallopian tubes. Frozen ova could also be used with frozen sperm for breeding a superior animal in the uterus of a (third) foster animal.

Mixture of Sperm with Penicillin

This technique is supposed to lengthen the span of survival of seminal fluid in the cervical mucus, and also to remove the danger of infection. The latter claim seems unsustainable as penicillin is not effective against all types of infection. Moreover, an increasing number of people have become allergic to penicillin, making its addition potentially dangerous.

Mixture of Husband's Sperm with Donor's Seminal Plasma

When the husband's sperm count is low or the motility of his sperm poor, the sperm is mixed with a donor's seminal fluid from which the spermatozoa have been removed (Rozin, 1958). In this way it is attempted to carry out A.I.H. Pregnancies are on record with this method; but as donor spermatozoa might easily slip into the mixture, it might be difficult to prove that conception really was achieved with the husband's sperm. However, this is a method which might prove acceptable to orthodox Jews who reject A.I.D. (Jakobovits, 1962).

Sex Regulation Through A.I.

It has been claimed that A.I., with either husband's or donor's sperm, produces more male than female babies. Statistical data are as yet too meager to support this theory.

A.I. was used successfully for sex regulation in rabbits; it was achieved by electrophoretic separation of rabbit sperm and consequent insemination. Human semen can also be separated electrophoretically, but the potential danger of damage to the sperm and resulting genetic changes makes the method unpracticable.

Medical and Religious Attitudes

Even though the practice of A.I. is spreading, general acceptance by the medical profession is still lacking. In 1945 the French Société de Gynécologie et d'Obstétrique almost unanimously condemned A.I. as an adventure full of medical, moral, and legal dangers. In the same year, Titus, an outstanding American obstetrician, condemned it as distasteful and unwise. A German textbook on forensic medicine, published in 1957, declared that inability of the husband to perform intercourse made A.I.H. permissible, while it condemned A.I.D. outright. The Great Commission on Penal Law of the German Federal Republic recommended that its new criminal code should prohibit A.I.D. but permit A.I.H. (see Report of the British Royal Commission, 1960).

In order to protect themselves as well as their patients, many physicians obtain written consent from husband and wife before starting A.I. The wife may be sued for adultery after insemination with donor's sperm and, theoretically, even the doctor who performed A.I.D. is subject to prosecution.

Some physicians refuse to deliver their patients after they have performed A.I.D. successfully; knowing that the patient's husband is not the progenitor of the baby, they are afraid that their signature on the birth certificate may bring on legal complications. However, this signature merely certifies the date and hour of birth and that the physician was in attendance.

In 1958, the American Medical Association issued the following statement:

When the physician uses semen from a donor other than the husband, there is a possibility that legal complications may arise. Certainly the physician assumes a certain degree of responsibility as to the suitability of the donor.

More and more physicians nowadays have the confidence to assume such responsibility.

A.I.D. is an effective cure for certain types of sterility; nevertheless, as far as we know, the method is not being used by any of the sterility clinics. In 1947, Guttmacher, Haman, and MacLeod sent a questionnaire to the members of the American Society for the Study of Sterility. Of the 71 members who replied, 7 had an ambivalent attitude, 12 were against, and 52 in favor of A.I.D. On June 4, 1955, the Society passed the following resolution:

If it is in harmony with the beliefs of the couple and the doctor, donor artificial insemination is a completely ethical, moral and desirable form of medical therapy. Conditions under which donor artificial insemination is acceptable include: 1) Urgent desire of the couple to have such therapy applied to the solution of their infertility problem. 2) Careful selection by the physician of a biologically and genetically satisfactory donor. 3) The opinion of the physician after thorough study that the couple will make desirable parents.

When Pope Pius XII addressed physicians at the Second World Congress on Fertility and Sterility in 1956, he made clear that the Catholic Church objects to both A.I.H. and A.I.D. Collection of sperm specimen, be it by masturbation, withdrawal, or in a condom, is immoral according to Catholic law. The only method that gained the official epithet of "probably licit," spermatozoa collected by use of a perforated condom during marital intercourse, is equally condemned by most Catholic moralists. The only Church-approved technique is the insertion of a cervical "spoon" after intercourse, to help passage of the sperm into the cervix. This method, called "assisted insemination," is reminiscent of Eustachio's device and is not very effective.

Only the Catholic Church rejects both A.I.H. and A.I.D. The latter is also condemned by other denominations, such as the Swedish Church and the Church of England (the latter's attitude was reaffirmed at the 1958 Lambeth Conference). Most Protestant Churches of America have not taken an official stand on the subject, leaving the decision up to the individual. Rabbi Jakobovits (1962), presenting the orthodox Jewish point of view, stated that "A.I.D. is unanimously and utterly condemned," A.I.D. is considered "plain adultery" and the children so produced are "Mamzerimm" (illegitimate). However, Halbrecht, reporting on 270 cases of A.I.D. in Israel, says that even religious patients accepted the procedure readily.

References

American Medical Association, "Statement on Artificial Insemination." *J.A.M.A. 166;* 646-647, 1958.

Bergerman, Milton M., "Legal Problems of Artificial Inseminations." In Hugo J. Beigel (ed.), *Advances in Sex Research*. New York: Hoeber, Medical Division Harper & Row, 1963.

Bunge, R. G., "Further Observations on Freezing Human Spermatozoa." *J. of Urology 83;* 192, 1960.

Bunge, R. G., and Sherman, J. K., "Frozen Human Semen." *Fertil. & Steril. 5;* 193, 1954.

Döderlein, A., "Ueber künstliche Befruchtung." *München. med. Wchnschr. 59;* 1081-1084, 1912.

Fraenkel, Ludwig, "Normale und pathologische Sexualphysiologie des Weibes." In W. Liepmann, *Kurzgefasstes Handbuch der gesamten Frauenheilkunde*. Leipzig: F. C. W. Vogel, 1914.

Guttmacher, Alan F., "Artificial Insemination." In Joe V. Meigs and Somers H. Sturgis, *Progress in Gynecology*, Vol. II. New York: Grune & Stratton, 1950.

Guttmacher, Alan F., "Test-tube Paternity." *The Nation 269-272,* 1958.

Halbrecht, I., "Artificial Insemination." *Proc. First World Congr. Fertil. & Steril.* New York, 1953.

Jakobovits, Immanuel, *Jewish Medical Ethics*. New York: Bloch Publishing Co., 1962.

Kleegman, Sophia J., "Diagnosis and Treatment of Infertility in Women." *M. Clin. North America 35;* 817-846, 1951.

Kleegman, Sophia J., "Practical and Ethical Aspects of Artificial Insemination." In Hugo J. Beigel (ed.), *Advances in Sex Research*. New York: Hoeber, Medical Division Harper & Row, 1963.

Kleegman, Sophia J., "Therapeutic Donor Insemination." *Fertil. & Steril. 5;* 7-30, 1954.

Kleegman, Sophia J., and Kaufman, Sherwin A., *Infertility in Women*. Philadelphia: F. A. Davis Co., 1966.

Kline, Calvin W., "The Potential Significance of Sperm Banks." In Hugo J. Beigel (ed.), *Advances in Sex Research*. New York: Hoeber, Medical Division Harper & Row, 1963.

Lehfeldt, Hans, "Indications for Child Adoption." *Proc. First World Congr. Fertil. & Steril.* New York, 1953.

Medical World News (editorial), 6; 34, 1965.

Muller, Hermann J., "Significance of Artificial Insemination in Relation to Practical Genetics in Man." In Hugo J. Beigel (ed.), *Advances in Sex Research*. New York: Hoeber, Medical Division Harper & Row, 1963.

Murphy, D. P., and Sorrano, E. F., "Donor Insemination." *Fertil. & Steril. 17;* 273, 1966.

Pommerenke, W. T., "Artificial Insemination: Genetic and Legal Implications." *Obst. & Gynec. 9;* 189-197, 1957.

Pope Pius XII, "Address to Second World Congress on Fertility and Sterility." *Internat. J. Fertil. 2;* 1-10, 1957.

Portnoy, Louis, and Saltman, Jules, *Fertility in Marriage*. New York: Signet Books, New American Library, 1951.

Report of the Departmental Committee on Human Artificial Insemination. London: Her Majesty's Stationery Office, 1960.

Rozin, S., "The Role of Seminal Plasma in Motility of Spermatozoa." *Acta Med. Oriental. 17;* 24, 1958.

Seymour, Frances I., and Koerner, Alfred, "Artificial Insemination: Present Status in the United States as Shown by a Recent Survey." *J.A.M.A. 116;* 2747-2749, 1941.

Sherman, J. K., et al, in *J.A.M.A. 188;* 39, 1964.

Sherman, J. K., "Research on Frozen Human Semen: Past, Present and Future." *Fertil. & Steril. 15;* 485, 1964.

Sims, Marion J., *Clinical Notes on Uterine Surgery*. New York: William Wood & Co., 1866.

Stone, Hannah M., and Stone, Abraham, *A Marriage Manual: A Practical Guide Book to Sex and Marriage*. New York: Simon and Schuster, Inc., 1952.

Warner, Marie Pichel, "Artificial Donor Inseminations, an Analysis of 100 Cases." *Human Fertil. 13;* 37-40, 1948.

HANS LEHFELDT

Attitudes toward Sex, Modern

SEXUAL attitudes, like other attitudes, generally derive from unspoken and often unconscious premises. Creative thought, which is always articulate and precise, results from frustration: a man sees that a problem must be solved and he creates new thoughts in solving it. But the overwhelming preponderance of human "thought" is not of this purposive, articulate, and creative kind. Most of what we consider our mental activity consists of subarticulate, half-conscious semantic reflexes—reactions to key words as the situation invokes these words in our minds.

The Judeo-Christian Sexual Dogma

For example, our mental reaction to sex—our so-called "philosophy" of sex—is, in most cases, a set of neuropsychological reactions to a few very simple "poetic metaphors." The particular metaphor that has had the strongest influence on Occidental civilization and that underlies traditional Judeo-Christian sexual dogma is that sex is "dirty." Sexuality is a kind of besmirching of oneself. Sexual activity is filthy. Sexual functions are like excremental functions—foul, disgusting, embarrassing, not "nice," etc.

We speak of this as a *simple poetic metaphor* because it can be analyzed as a literary critic analyzes a line of verse. A metaphor is the implicit identification of two different factors. Simile says, "The ship is like a plow." Metaphor, less obvious and therefore more effective, insinuates the identification without stating it

openly: "The ship *plows* the waves." When an identification is not put forth as an explicit proposition we are less likely to challenge it. When we are told that the ship is like a plow, we are apt to ask, "When? how? in what way?" When we are told that the ship plows the waves, we agree at once that, in some respects, the ship *is* like a plow. This identification is all the more effective because we are not aware that we are making it.

Judeo-Christian theology has consistently spoken and written of sex in metaphorical terms as a species of dirtiness. The identification of sexuality and dirtiness has been "built into" the psychological and neurological reactions of countless millions of people subliminally—without their being completely aware of the "poetic" or pre-logical nature of the identification.

When Romantic poets associate sexuality with budding flowers, growing grass, sprouting shrubs, and so on, they are creating an identification that points toward the opposite kind of reaction. Here we get the equation "sexuality equals springtime," in contrast to the Judeo-Christian "sexuality equals dirtiness." Both equations are effective psychologically because they are poetic and imperfectly articulated.

Modern attitudes toward sex are far from consistent or unanimous. Indeed, we can say of twentieth-century sexual philosophy what historian Crane Brinton (1959) said of twentieth-century philosophy in general, that the chief characteristic of modern thought is "multanimity," a word coined to signify the opposite of unanimity. However, behind the sharply contrasting attitudes of modern sexual philosophers one common tendency can be observed—the tendency to reject the Judeo-Christian identification of sexuality and dirtiness.

This metaphorical identification deserves to be more closely scrutinized before attempting to understand the various forms of rebellion against it. According to *Webster's New Twentieth Century Dictionary* (*Unabridged*), *dirt* signifies 1. "Any foul or filthy substance; excrement; earth; mud; mire; dust; whatever, adhering to anything, renders it foul or unclean. 2. Meanness, sordidness. 3. In placer mining, earth, sand, and gravel, before the gold has been washed out ... *v.t.*, To make foul or filthy; to soil; to bedaub; to pollute; to defile." According to a popular epigram, "Dirt is matter in the wrong place." Dirt is that which must be washed off an object before it is sanitary or edible. Dirt is the part of the ore that the placer miner throws away. Dirt is that which, adhering to an object, makes the object less useful or desirable. Any crime or antisocial behavior sounds worse when the word "dirty" is placed in front of it: a "dirty thief," a "dirty murderer," even a "dirty liar" are worse than an ordinary thief, murderer, and liar.

Traditionally connected with the concept of "dirtiness" has been the concept of "obscenity." Etymologically, this word has been traced back to "that which is not represented on the stage," that which is kept *off scene* (Watts, 1958). The traditional view, therefore, makes sex not only repugnant but also mysterious, arcane, *hidden*. Judeo-Christian morality, in short, regards sex much as a civilized man regards drug addiction. It is something to be avoided or, if it cannot be avoided, it must be engaged in furtively. As Alan Watts (1958) remarked, the traditional Occidental attitude toward sex is not so much antagonistic as "squeamish." Squeamishness is characterized not by the open antagonism of a logical position but by the ill-defined negative feelings that result from internalizing an unpleasant metaphor.

Modern attitudes toward sex, then, are "multanimous" rather than unanimous because they are in opposition to a fundamentally cloudy alternative. The orthodox Christian and the orthodox Jew have "squeamish" feelings about sexual functions, but not even their best theologians—not even Saint Paul—have demonstrated *logically* that "sex is dirty." They have demonstrated all sorts of negative things about sex (most of which we now know to be inaccurate) but they have always communicated the concept that "sex is dirty" subliminally rather than logically. The modernist has difficulty, therefore, defining precisely what he is against, and the leading proponents of modern attitudes toward sex differ sharply among themselves according to how clearly they understand that what they are rebelling against is semantic-poetic feelings rather than logical ideas.

Modern and Traditional Sexual Thought

Supporters of traditional attitudes toward sex tend to resent and denigrate all sexual activity not directly connected with conception. The degree of resentment and denigration has varied with epoch and place, but, in general, fornication has been considered bad, masturbation worse, and homosexuality still worse.

Although modern thinkers tend toward multanimity rather than unanimity, in general their tolerance for nonreproductive sexual activities is inversely proportional to the degree of Judeo-Christian contempt for these activities. In other words, fornication has largely come out from under the cloud; masturbation (within sharply defined limits) is no longer considered so contemptible; and homosexuality is still largely under the cloud, as is animal intercourse.

Fornication has almost always found easier forgiveness than other so-called sexual "sins"—and this fact has been little understood or commented upon. Once we are aware of it, however, the reason is not hard to find. Fornication is the sexual "offense" most often performed by ordinary adults, and it does not differ in physical details from the reproductive marital intercourse grudgingly permitted by the Judeo-Christian code. Indeed, the distinction between the love-making of an unmarried couple and the love-making of a married couple is purely metaphysical and social-theological—i.e., purely *verbal*—and cannot be demonstrated to the senses. Given this physical factor, and the ubiquity of the act, defenses of fornication had naturally been made long before "modernism" arose. Troubadour poetry, the songs of the *minnesingers*, the cult of Romantic Love, and, indeed, most of the lyrical art of Judeo-Christian culture have long carried this argumentative burden. The proposition that "Fornication is not a 'sin' if it is accompanied by Love" has been a strong minority conviction for 700 years at least, in spite of the clergy.

Adultery, like fornication, has been accepted in song and poetry for centuries; but, unlike fornication, it collides sharply with property instincts, so that it has not had quite the respectability in literature that fornication has had.

Masturbation is not as commonly practiced among adults as it is among adolescents. Also, it obviously differs physically from the "acceptable" marital intercourse allowed by the clergy. For these reasons it has not inspired poems, operas, and songs in its defense, and has had to wait for the rationalistic twentieth century to bring it out from under a cloud.

Homosexuality differs from marital intercourse in obvious physical details, but since it has been practiced most often among artistic and cultured circles it has been defended off and on through the centuries. However, it has never been able to win wide popular acceptance.

Intercourse with animals, which is practiced almost exclusively in rural communities, has never been defended until Dr. Kinsey (1948) pointed out that it is not harmful or likely to become compulsive.

The Evolution of Modern Thought

Thus, we can see that when modern thinkers began to question the traditional Judeo-Christian sexual code they had behind them a kind of minority tradition. It is no accident, then, that in our time, the orthodox opposition to fornication has been most widely challenged, whereas the orthodox opposition to intercourse with animals has been less widely challenged. "Dirtiness" can be removed from a sexual act only gradually, because the way in which the association with dirtiness was first made was not a logical one. A modern rationalist can more

successfully defend the goodness, harmlessness, or rightness of a kind of sexual behavior if this kind of behavior has been defended earlier by poets, dramatists, and musicians.

The rebellion against the doctrine that "sex is dirty" has grown slowly. Havelock Ellis and Richard Krafft-Ebing introduced scientific objectivity into the study of human sexual behavior, but their influence was, initially, confined largely to doctors of medicine and psychiatry. It was Sigmund Freud who struck the first real blow for modernism, and he seems to have done it somewhat accidentally. Freud's published conclusion (1900) that many—perhaps all—neurotic symptoms result from the sexual upbringing characteristic of Judeo-Christian culture electrified the world. It was not long before people were asking if we had to continue to pay the price in neuroses for the blessings of this civilization. Freud himself (1922) thought that we did have to pay that price, but could alleviate the situation slightly. Others were more radical. Wilhelm Reich (1951) called for a "sexual revolution" that would free man from the age-old taboos and usher in an age of sexual rationality.

Meanwhile, from another direction, aid and comfort arrived for the more radical. Studies of anthropology and comparative religion had shed a great deal of light on how the Judeo-Christian taboos had arisen out of savage ignorance. Sir James Frazer (1892-1914) popularized this subject in a twelve-volume work that made mythology and primitive religion as well known as Darwin had made human evolution. Benedict (1946), Mead (1948), and others helped to make these discoveries known to ever-wider audiences. By the mid-twentieth century, it was generally known that every society has taboos that seem utterly irrational to an outsider, and that the Judeo-Christian taboos on sexuality can be accounted for by the same prelogical thought processes that gave birth, for example, to the Orphic taboo on eating beans. Shame or fear over the act of masturbating seems, in the light of such anthropological knowledge, as irrational as shame or fear over eating beans.

At the same time, a change began to take place in literature, which had been extremely puritanical and evasive during the nineteenth century. One of the causes of the revival of sexual realism in literature was, almost certainly, the example of the psychoanalysts, anthropologists, and other scientific writers. A scientific work cannot be as evasive as the puritan temperament would wish it to be. Freud and Frazer, and their followers, had to discuss sexual matters in specific detail. Literary men, struggling to reveal the truths of human life in terms of their imaginative dramas, could not read such scientific texts without wishing they themselves had the same freedom. Sexual frankness was also necessary to the crusading medical men who led the fight against venereal disease and to the writers who defended planned parenthood. All of this led writers such as D. H. Lawrence, James Joyce, and Ernest Hemingway to present sexual material in their novels with the same frankness that could be found in a scientific treatise. Thus there developed an atmosphere in which sexual matters could be discussed. Sex, no longer completely "off scene," was no longer completely "obscene," either.

In spite of all this, the pressure of orthodoxy is still great. Modern sexual attitudes, in practice, are an uneasy blend of reason and unreason, science and superstition, knowledge and mythology. According to Albert Ellis (1958), the Child Study Association of America, consisting largely of trained psychiatric social workers, wrote in a recent publication that, when parents discover that a child is masturbating, they should "ally themselves with the child's own conscience in this matter and while assuring him that the practice will not harm him, also help him to find ways to grow out of it." On the surface an enlightened, modern viewpoint, this statement contains within itself all the contradictions of our multanimous culture.

To "help" a child "to find ways to grow out of" masturbation sounds better than to frighten him half to death with threats of blindness, as Taylor (1955) tells us was done in the Victorian Age. But the assumption that the child *must* be "helped to grow out of it," as if it were a harmful thing, reveals a partial emotional hangover of Victorian standards since, as Kinsey (1948), Ellis (1958), and others have pointed out, masturbation is not harmful.

However, D. H. Lawrence (1930) writes a poetic and impassioned defense of the right of unmarried adults to fornicate; in the midst of

it he has a diatribe, several pages long, on the evils of masturbation. In the course of this diatribe, Lawrence refers to masturbation as "self-abuse" and even repeats the old, exploded myth that once the habit is formed masturbation "goes on and on, on into old age, in spite of marriage or love affairs or anything else."

Similarly, Theodoor Van de Velde, one of the most liberal and enlightened authors in the "marriage-manual" field, writes (1947) an eloquent, even lyrical, defense of the "genital kiss," as he calls it. But he is careful to add that "carried to orgasm," this becomes a "perversion." On the other hand, Hannah and Abraham Stone (1952) advise that there is "nothing perverse or degrading . . . in any sex practice which is undertaken for the purpose of promoting a more harmonious sexual adjustment between a husband and wife in marriage," and seem to be recommending cunnilinctus and/or fellatio to the point of orgasm. (Why it should be stopped before orgasm Van de Velde does not make clear.) Albert Ellis (1954) is not afraid to recommend cunnilinctus and/or fellation to climax, but he mentions the penalties that can (theoretically) be invoked in various American states, even when these acts are performed between two fully consenting and legally married adults. Connecticut threatens 30 years for mouth-genital contacts; Georgia goes further and threatens life imprisonment at hard labor; Ohio has a 1-to-20-year term.

The same contradictions appear wherever we look. D. H. Lawrence (1930) urged that, for sex to fully escape from the cloud of "dirtiness," we should be able to "give it its own phallic language, and use the obscene words" in love-making. Thirty years later, however, Lipton (1959) writes that the use of these words during love-making is considered "degenerate" and "middle class" by the young Bohemians of today. The same young Bohemians often use obscene words for shock effect in their poetry.

Idealism and
Realism in Sexual Thinking

The wide conflicts of opinion among modernists can, of course, be traced to one or two basic conflicts in primary assumptions. In other words, it is possible to see most of the conflicts we have been discussing as manifestations of a few simple philosophical predispositions. In general, modern sexual thinkers can be divided into the (more or less) idealistic and the (more or less) realistic. The idealists, such as D. H. Lawrence and Wilhelm Reich, tend to be pre-occupied with the life-importance of "the perfect sex-love relationship," and their thinking largely revolves around making such relationships possible for greater numbers of people. The realists, such as Alfred Kinsey and Albert Ellis, tend to accept mankind unconditionally as it is, and their thinking is concerned with helping the individual to accept his own sexual pattern regardless of how "imperfect" it may be.

These remarks, of course, are oversimplified. Nonetheless, there is considerable truth in them. Consider, for example, the matter of premature ejaculation. This very widespread problem makes it extremely difficult for many couples to achieve the simultaneous climax about which the Stones (1952) and other popular authors of marriage manuals write so glowingly. To a Reichian, and to most orthodox Freudians, it is a grave psychological illness of the male and should be cured whenever possible. This is, fundamentally, an idealistic position. Dr. Kinsey, representing realism, counsels that men and women accept themselves as they are; he says (1948) that it is "unrealistic" for wives to expect their husbands always to restrain themselves long enough to achieve simultaneous climax. He urges wives to be more tolerant and husbands to feel less guilty.

The same distinction between idealists and realists can be seen when we examine the matter of frigidity in women. Dr. Edmund Bergler, representing orthodox Freudian idealism, writes (1951): "Under frigidity we understand the incapacity of woman to have a *vaginal orgasm during intercourse*. It is of no matter whether the woman is aroused during coitus or remains cold, whether excitement is weak or strong, whether it breaks off at the beginning or end, slowly or suddenly, whether it is dissipated in preliminary acts, or has been lacking from the beginning. The *sole criterion* of frigidity is absence of vaginal orgasm" (author's italics). On the other hand, Albert Ellis says equally forcefully (1954): "After carefully reviewing the recent literature on this subject and interviewing scores of sexually normal and disturbed

women, I was forced to conclude that the so-called vaginal orgasm is largely a myth."

Like many disputes that seem to be over matters of fact, this is at least partially a matter of values. Dr. Bergler thinks that any woman who cannot achieve "vaginal orgasm," and is, therefore, "frigid," needs psychotherapy in order to become normal. Dr. Ellis thinks that if a woman is achieving any kind of orgasmic satisfaction in sex, she is achieving what is natural for her. In other words, Dr. Bergler represents the idealistic longing for the "perfect love-sex relationship" and Dr. Ellis represents the realistic acceptance of whatever love-sex relationship is possible for the specific individual.

The same conflict underlies the majority of discussions about homosexuality. Dr. Lindner (1956) and others who speak of homosexuality as a "way of life" seem to be concerned with helping the individual homosexual to find such happiness as is open to him or her; Dr. Bergler (1959) and others who speak of homosexuality as a "disease" are, of course, interested in curing it—again, in the interest of "the perfect love-sex relationship." Dr. Ellis (1960) takes an in-between, liberal-realist position and holds that occasional homosexual activity may be normal but that exclusive or obsessive-compulsive homosexuality is the result of an emotional disturbance and can be treated and cured by psychotherapy.

It begins to be obvious that all those we have been calling the idealists are following in the tradition of the cult of Romantic Love introduced to the Western world by the medieval troubadours, whereas those we have been calling realists are representatives of the ethical relativism that has been introduced by cultural anthropology. Perhaps the terms "realist" and "idealist" are too simplified, and we certainly do not intend to have them taken as judgmental; they are meant to serve as brief descriptive labels, and no more. But there is probably food for thought in the fact that the idealists are in some respects closer in spirit to earlier rebels against Judeo-Christian orthodoxy than are the realists. Taylor (1955) has pointed out that most historic rebellions against Judeo-Christian sexual teaching have deliberately taken inspiration from the early Mediterranean fertility cults. The pagan conception of the "holiness" of certain types of sexuality has repeatedly been resurrected as an alternative to Judeo-Christian asceticism. We should not be surprised to see a disguised form of this old pagan ideology appearing as one branch of the modern sexual revolution.

Indeed, among certain of the extreme Bohemians of the so-called "Beat Generation," sexuality has become associated with religious ideas from outside Judeo-Christian culture. Kerouac (1958) describes Tibetan *yabyum* (ritualized coitus) among the California "Beat" mystics. Mailer (1959) has described the entire "Beat" movement as a search for "perfect orgasm," with decidedly religious (non-Judeo-Christian) overtones.

Among the "Beats," however, this search for the perfect love-sex relationship is less orthodox than elsewhere. They believe, for example, that it is as likely to be found in homosexual as in heterosexual relations. McReynolds (1959) quotes a "Beat" girl as saying "that if you liked someone very much you ought to sleep with him or her at least once, because sex helped bring you closer to the person." McReynolds adds that he does not believe this attitude is really an attempt to turn life into "one long orgy"; rather, he thinks, it is an attempt to make real and concrete the "universal love" many earlier Romantic movements have conceived only abstractly.

The "Beats," further, are largely free of the sexual intolerance of most intellectuals. Lipton (1959) emphasizes the amicable relations between heterosexual and homosexual "Beats" and the fact that neither group tries to "convert" the other. There is, instead, a general feeling that each person has a right to seek truth and express love according to the laws of his or her own nature. It is for this reason that "Beats" tend to be unfrightened also of psychoses or criminality. Much of the best literature produced by "Beat" writers deals with friends who were psychotic, criminal, addicted to drugs, or in some other way socially "undesirable." The jazz musician, Charlie Parker, was all of these, and remains a leading "Beat" hero; Lipton (1959) quotes a poem by a "Beat" writer that describes Parker's psychotic episodes with almost clinical lack of emotion and claims that one should neither pity nor condemn, because,

through these experiences, Parker was able to reach the special kind of awareness his music demanded.

The "Beat" philosophy of sex, in short, is like all other aspects of "Beat" philosophy, centered on the individual's achieving his full potential in awareness and the expression of love. No other values are higher than these to a "Beat." Therefore, the only question to be asked about any sexual experience is: does it add to one's awareness or one's expression of love? All other questions of abstract morality or social normalcy are, to a "Beat," irrelevant.

But the "Beat" search for self-fulfillment is only one of the many different present-day approaches to sex. The "Beats" are most interesting because they combine the "idealistic" search for the "perfect" love-sex relationship with the "realistic" acceptance of relativity. Equally important, however, are several vastly different attitudes. In addition to such representative "realists" and "idealists" as we have already discussed, there are unclassifiable thinkers such as Alan Watts (1958), who tries to synthesize modern scientific positivism with ancient Oriental mysticism and, in so doing, has created a philosophy of sex that can be described as more relativistic than the relativists and yet at the same time more perfectionist than the perfectionists. Watts believes, and argues plausibly, that the "perfect love-sex experience" will only come to those who do not seek it, and that to abolish completely the Judeo-Christian squeamishness about sex we will have to abandon also the way of thinking that considers Man apart from nature.

Equally noteworthy are the theories of Ian Suttie (1935), who argues that there is a "taboo on tenderness" in our civilization even more pervasive than the taboos on sexuality, and that we have to become less afraid of selfless love before we can thoroughly cleanse our sexual attitudes of lingering Judeo-Christian denigration. Ashley Montagu (1955) has reiterated psychiatrist Suttie's ideas, with the different emphasis of a physical anthropologist, and has added to them a faint patina of well-concealed puritanism.

In conclusion, it is worth noting that in all the conflicting attitudes of modern thinkers toward sex, one overriding theme is evident. That theme is not, as defenders of orthodoxy often charge, a simple reversion to infantile self-indulgence. On the contrary, we can observe—both in "realists" such as Alfred Kinsey and Albert Ellis, and in "idealists" such as Wilhelm Reich and Edmund Bergler—a deep scientific humanism that demands more of Man than Judeo-Christian orthodoxy ever did, because it respects him more. To believe that Man is capable, through reason, of solving his sexual problems is to have more faith in him than those who believe that his "fallen" state gives him an inborn tendency toward "sin." The self-denial and self-torture of the orthodox is not more "responsible" than the attempt of a modern man to make sex a satisfactory and beautiful experience for himself and his partner. It might even be said that the orthodox person, refusing to attempt to make of sex a wholesome and decent part of life and ruthlessly "denying" himself, is less responsible, more infantile, than the modern. The medieval saint who went off into the desert to punish his flesh looks suspiciously like the four-year-old child who bangs his head against the wall because his parents won't give him what he wants.

Indeed, perhaps the orthodox teaching that "sex is dirty" has no more complex an origin than the fox's pronouncement that the grapes he could not have were sour. Except for masturbation and intercourse with animals, sexual relations always involve more than one person, and, hence, require a certain amount of reciprocity, tolerance, maturity, and responsibility. Those who enter such relations with a decent respect for themselves and their partners are undoubtedly less "self-indulgent" than those who back away in repugnance. The repugnance is very often a mask for a lazy and cowardly refusal to accept participation in ordinary human life with its mixed joys and sorrows. Although the traditionalist will accuse modernists of irresponsible hedonism, the truth may be that he really fears the adult responsibility of modernism.

References

Benedict, Ruth, *Patterns of Culture.* New York: New American Library, 1946.

Bergler, Edmund, *Homosexuality: Disease or Way of Life?* New York: Hill and Wang, 1959.

Bergler, Edmund, *Neurotic Counterfeit-Sex.* New York: Grune & Stratton, 1951.

Brinton, Crane, *A History of Western Morals.* New York: George Braziller, 1959.

Ellis, Albert, *The American Sexual Tragedy.* New York: Twayne Pub., 1954.

Ellis, Albert, *Sex Without Guilt.* New York: Lyle Stuart, 1958.

Ellis, Albert, *The Art and Science of Love.* New York: Lyle Stuart, 1960.

Frazer, Sir James. *The Golden Bough.* 12 vols. London, 1892-1914 (new edition in one vol., New York: Criterion, 1959).

Freud, Sigmund, *The Interpretation of Dreams* (1900) in *The Basic Writings of Sigmund Freud.* New York: Modern Library, 1938.

Freud, Sigmund, *Civilization and Its Discontents.* London: Hogarth, 1922.

Kerouac, Jack, *The Dharma Bums.* New York: Vanguard, 1958.

Kinsey, Alfred C. *et al.*, *Sexual Behavior in the Human Male.* Philadelphia: W. B. Saunders Co., 1948.

Lawrence, D. H., "Pornography and Obscenity" (1930) and "A Propos of Lady Chatterley's Lover" (1930), both in *Sex, Literature and Censorship.* New York: Compass, 1959.

Lindner, Robert, *Must You Comform?* New York: Rinehart & Co., 1956.

Lipton, Lawrence, *The Holy Barbarians.* New York: Messner, 1959.

Mailer, Norman, *The White Negro.* San Francisco: City Lights, 1959.

McReynolds, David, "Hipsters Unleashed." *Liberation,* June, 1959.

Mead, Margaret, *Sex and Temperament in Three Primitive Societies.* New York: New American Library, 1948.

Montagu, Ashley, *The Direction of Human Development.* New York: Harper & Brothers, 1955.

Reich, Wilhelm, *The Sexual Revolution.* New York: Orgone Institute Press, 1951.

Stone, Abraham, and Stone, Hannah, *Marriage Manual.* New York: Simon and Schuster, 1952.

Suttie, Ian, *The Origins of Love and Hate.* New York: Julian, 1952 (first edition, England, 1935).

Taylor, G. Rattray, *Sex in History.* New York: Vanguard, 1955.

Van de Velde, Theodoor, *Ideal Marriage.* New York: Random House, 1947.

Watts, Alan, *Nature, Man and Woman.* New York: Pantheon, 1958.

ROBERT ANTON WILSON

Australia and New Zealand, Sex Life in

MUCH factual knowledge concerning the sexual life of a people, particularly in relation to their reproductive activities, can be obtained from government statistics. This source of information has been used in the writing of this article. No systematic survey of the more intimate aspects of sexual life in all its manifestations has yet been made in Australia and New Zealand. To obtain a reasonably clear picture of sex life in this part of the world, I have consulted anthropologists, psychiatrists, psychoanalysts, police officials, educators, social workers, legal experts, and others whose work is associated with aspects of the sex life of the people.

It should be understood that this article represents collective opinion. It may be objected that this method of investigation is based upon individual impressions only, and not upon strict scientific analysis. Yet, this method is the only one by which it is possible to obtain what may be regarded as a realistic picture of the situation. In fact, the value of any investigation of a sociological nature is increased if its findings are checked against totally different sources of information.

Basically, the pattern of sexual behavior in Australia and New Zealand is the same as in other countries of Western culture, but the fact that primitive native tribes are still found in New Guinea and in some parts of Australia presents us with interesting variations. It seems that, among the more highly civilized Western nations, sexual behavior is remarkably similar, but conventional attitudes toward this behavior vary considerably, with the result that stereotypes have been created and are regarded as being truly characteristic of particular peoples.

Australian Aborigines

Some of the stone age people who still inhabit parts of this continent carry out certain rites which were originally preventive medicine measures, but which, with the passing of time, came to be regarded as initiation ceremonies, the purpose of which was to enable the male adolescent to qualify as a full-fledged member of the tribe.

The operation of circumcision is performed shortly before or at the time of puberty. Morrison has pointed out that this operation was originally performed for exactly the same reasons which gave rise to the custom among the Jews and the Mohammedans, and he considers that it may have arisen *de novo* among the Australian Aborigines. The need for the operation of circumcision arises in dry, dusty regions where there is a scarcity of water. Under these conditions inflammation under the foreskin may repeatedly occur, owing to local irritation and infection, which may readily take place owing to the absence of facilities for cleanliness. The balanitis may result in adhesions being formed between the glans penis and the foreskin. Obviously, the best way to avoid this is to remove the foreskin before trouble arises. In time, the emphasis is shifted so that what was originally a preventive medicine measure becomes quite a social occasion.

Prolonged contact with the white man has caused some tribal customs to be modified or even discontinued, but in earlier days the ceremonies associated with circumcision included dancing on two successive evenings, as well as a lending and an interchange of women. The lending of a woman was an expression of good fellowship. On ceremonial occasions it was done in recognition of past kindness or in anticipation of future favors. The lending and interchange of women was, however, of a purely temporary nature and was confined to those who may lawfully have marital intercourse.

When the boy has completely recovered from the operation of circumcision, another operation is performed on the penis. It is known to social anthropologists as subincision and is an extraordinary procedure. A long incision is made on the under surface of the penis, usually extending from the external urethral opening back to the scrotum. The whole of the penile urethra is thus laid open. The operation is done with a sharp stone knife and it is surprising that no serious complications occur.

The white man has put forward many theories concerning the origin of this operation. It has been suggested that subincision is done for the purpose of preventing conception so as to regulate population growth in accordance with the available food supply. As a matter of fact, the operation has little effect upon fertility, for sexual intercourse takes place in such a position that most of the semen enters the vagina. The number of children in an aboriginal family is usually not more than four. In all tribes practicing subincision every youth, without exception, has the operation performed, so we may exclude fertilization by an intact male.

Morrison gives the most logical and almost certainly the correct explanation of the origin of the operation of subincision. He points out that circumcision is often followed by such complications as meatal ulceration, especially when there is an absence of hygiene and when hot, dry, dusty conditions prevail. Irritation and infection affect the exposed meatus. There is usually a succession of these episodes, with formation of scar tissue and narrowing of the meatal opening, so that there is interference with micturition. The obvious treatment is to

open up the urethra, so that urination is free. The operation usually has to be repeated. Therefore, to prevent this meatal inflammation and subsequent urination difficulties, the urethra is thoroughly opened up at one operation. Subincision is therefore primarily a preventive medicine measure but, like the operation of circumcision, it acquires social significance.

The numbers in the tribe are kept down by infanticide, which the Arunta natives have no hesitation in carrying out as soon as an unwanted child is born. The newly arrived babe is killed if the mother already has an infant to nourish and carry about. It is of interest to note that the aborigines recognize no direct causal relationship between childbirth and sexual intercourse, although they consider that coitus prepares the way. They believe that the totem centers are inhabited by children in spirit form and that only under certain conditions do they enter the uterus.

When an aboriginal woman is about to give birth to a child a shallow hole is made in the ground and she sits in a squatting position over it, her thighs widely separated. Another woman, who squats behind her and supports her, massages the abdomen of the gravid woman, the squeezing and pressure being carried out from the rib-margins down to the hips. Eventually, the baby is expelled into the shallow hole prepared for it and the umbilical cord is cut with a stone knife. For the delivery of a child this attitude has the advantage that it allows the muscles commonly used in expulsion to be used most effectively in assisting the force of the uterine contractions.

The aboriginal women have their own secret ceremonies, of which magical love charms are a feature. There is little reference to the development of the breasts, to menstruation, or to childbirth. In their songs the emphasis is on amorous desires, the securing of lovers, and the various ways of retaining the devotion of a husband. These songs are full of phallic symbolism and make numerous references to coitus. Other songs refer to simple magic and to aboriginal mythology.

Among the primitive Australian natives, marriage and divorce are not the highly complicated procedures which they are in modern civilized society. Long ago group marriage was the rule. This did not differ greatly from absolute promiscuity. At a later stage father-daughter marriages became taboo, and then the ban was extended to brother-sister marriages. In simple manner an aborigine might take unto himself a wife in accordance with the custom of his people but, in some tribes, he might be liable to lose her and abandon his claim if a stronger man admired her and wanted her for his own. This amounts to divorce by right of conquest.

Among the tribes of Northeastern Australia there is a strongly held belief in the contraceptive action of some plants, when their juices are taken by mouth. According to aboriginal belief the plant juices protect a woman's body against the entry of a spirit-child.

The aboriginal woman's claim to social status and prestige is marriage and the bearing of children. Social standing is not won by marriage alone. To gain complete status a woman must have at least three children. She is then regarded as having qualified to be present at the rituals held when a girl reaches puberty. She is also entitled to be present at cases of childbirth.

These brief comments on the sex life of an interesting stone age people do not apply equally to all the tribes scattered over the continent, but they are true of the majority. For those aborigines in close contact with the white man in pastoral work there is a strong tendency for some of the old customs to die out.

New Guinea

The natives of New Guinea are made up of many different tribes with remarkable differences in mode of life, language, and customs. Among the Motu people parents do not mind if their daughters have premarital relations, but they expect them to be faithful to their husbands after marriage. Prostitution is frowned upon. Coitus takes place out of doors in daylight, which is presumably why the pudenda of all the women are ornamented with tattooing.

In the Trobriand Islands the people are sexually uninhibited. There is probably greater sexual freedom at all ages among them than there is anywhere else in the world. Even before the children are really able to have coitus, genital manipulation and other forms of sexual amusement form part of play. Boys and girls have sexual intercourse at a very early age. The adults regard it as natural and see no reason to interfere or to scold the children. Adolescent boys and girls continue to have many sexual experiences before they settle down and accept responsibilities, after which their amorous adventures are not so numerous. The taboo of incest operates early in life. Otherwise, the Trobriand Islanders act sexually in accordance with their natural desires.

On one island of the New Guinea group, owing either to lack of means to pay the dowry or to a shortage of women, there is a custom by which a number of men form a company to acquire a common wife. It is said to work quite well.

The Maoris

The New Zealand Maoris are a Polynesian people and are thus an entirely different race from any of the native tribes already discussed. According to the Sacred Legends, sexual intercourse was a religious duty and parents were directed to give adequate sex instruction to boys and girls at puberty. Sex experience before marriage was regarded as a necessary preparation for a successful permanent union. However, statements by anthropologists concerning the primitive Maoris do not apply to their descendants today. There has been so much intermarrying with the white population that there are comparatively few full-blooded Maoris left. Furthermore, the old customs have either been greatly modified or are no longer observed, so reference to them would be of historical interest only.

White Population of Australia and New Zealand

Masturbation

At one time the production of an orgasm by manual manipulation or by other friction applied to the genitals was regarded as very injurious and was even referred to by some as a sin. Exaggerated statements were made about the harmful effects of "self-abuse." A study of the literature relating to sex clearly shows that these erroneous views were not confined to Australia. Although masturbation is still condemned by the majority of parents, they are more inclined now to adopt a condoning attitude. During recent years the physician has not had to approach the subject of sex obliquely. If he frankly states that masturbation is a natural activity resulting from a desire for pleasurable sensations and that it will almost certainly be discontinued when other sexual outlets are available, he will be understood. He is then in a position to explain that the real harm is done by the tacit threats and unfounded statements concerning the evil effects of masturbation.

It is realized, of course, that the habit can be overdone and that it can take up so much time and expend so much nervous energy that activities essential to the progress of the girl or boy may be interfered with. Statistics are not available, but the general impression is that masturbation is just as common in girls as it is in boys.

Premarital Sexual Relations

It is impossible to obtain accurate statistical data concerning the incidence of premarital sexual intercourse in any community. However, by studying reliable statistics, by considering one's own experience in the consulting room, and by reading the reports of official investigations it is possible to obtain a reasonably accurate impression of the general situation.

What proportion of children are born out of wedlock? Although the figures vary from year to year, the ratio of ex-nuptial to nuptial births in Australia is about one to twenty-three. In New Zealand the ratio is almost exactly the same. Although the ex-nuptial births include children born to widows and divorced women as well as to young women who have not married, the ratio is high when one considers that contraceptives are readily available and that large numbers of pregnancies are terminated artificially.

How many brides are pregnant when they marry? In Australia, in 1963, the total first births that occurred less than eight months after marriage was 25.49 per cent, and the total first births that occurred eight months after the wedding was 3.19 per cent. The proportion of premature births is exceedingly small in Australia and, since the period of gestation is nine months, it is reasonable to conclude that one

woman in every four is pregnant when she marries. There is a vast trade in contraceptives, but it is impossible to estimate the number of single women who use them and do not become pregnant.

Medical practitioners, especially gynecologists, know that premarital sexual intercourse is the rule rather than the exception, and that the incidence of nuptial virginity rapidly diminishes as age increases. Nevertheless, one must be careful not to make sweeping assertions. During the past thirty years I have been giving instruction in contraception to young women who are about to be married, and quite frequently have encountered an intact hymen.

From time to time some incident causes the curtain to be drawn aside so that one variety of youthful behavior is revealed to the public. One such incident occurred in New Zealand in 1954, when a young girl was reported missing. Detectives uncovered evidence that dismayed the public to such an extent that the New Zealand government appointed a special committee to inquire into the whole problem and suggest remedies. To quote from the report: "The police investigations revealed a shocking degree of immoral conduct which spread into sexual orgies perpetrated in several private homes during the absence of parents, and in several second rate . . . theatres, where familiarity between youths and girls was rife and commonplace."

The available evidence makes it obvious that a very high percentage of young people have sexual intercourse before marriage. This is only to be expected, for it is entirely in harmony with biological urges. There is a conflict here between nature and conventional morality, but the more objectionable aspects of this conflict would be eliminated if all children had the emotional security that is provided by parental love, sympathetic understanding, and watchful care.

Marriage and Divorce

The desire to exercise the reproductive function, as distinct from the urge to obtain sexual gratification, is commonly expressed in marriage. In every country there is some variation in the marriage rate, according to changing economic and social conditions. In 1963 the number of marriages per 1,000 of the mean population was 7.4 in Australia and 7.8 in New Zealand, as compared with 5.4 in the Republic of Ireland and 8.7 in the United States of America and 10 in the Soviet Union. In Australia the average age at marriage of brides and bridegrooms has declined during recent years. The average age of brides during the five-year period 1959-1963 was 24.7 and of bridegrooms 28 years. In New Zealand also, the recent trend is for persons to marry at younger ages, the average relative ages of brides and bridegrooms being almost identical with the corresponding figures for Australia. These statistics include remarriages of widowed and divorced persons. Large numbers of divorced men and women in these southern lands marry again.

Despite its superficial popularity, there is a widespread opinion among the Australian people that marriage in its present form is not the ideal type of relationship between the sexes. There are many who consider that marriage is too binding and permanent, that people rush into marriage without giving mature consideration to all that is involved, and that the high divorce rate and the large proportion of broken homes are evidence that marriage, as at present constituted, has failed. On August 26, 1958, the Minister for Social Services stated that "wife desertion has become an alarming problem in Australia during the past few years . . . . The increase—almost 120 per cent—in the number of deserted wives receiving assistance occurred during the longest period of sustained prosperity the country had enjoyed. It was out of proportion to the increase in the marriage rate and the divorce rate."

In these numerous unsuccessful marriages we have a most difficult problem in human relationships, a problem that becomes much more complicated when there are children. In our world there is little stability either in group relationships or in individual relationships. National groups are experimenting with political systems, and conflict between rival ideologies threatens the peace of the world. In individual relationships humanity is striving, rather unsystematically, to find a satisfactory solution to the problems presented by sexual attraction and the reproduction of the species. We are probably still in the early stages of social evolution, still in search of a condition of society that will ensure the greatest happiness of the greatest number of people.

Church and State have combined to bring about a situation in Australia and New Zealand which is not a happy one. Until recently, the divorce laws were different in every Australian state, and New Zealand presented a further variation. Now, however, there are uniform divorce laws throughout the whole of the Commonwealth of Australia. Making the laws uniform, however, will not necessarily improve the general situation. The laws may not be sufficiently liberal. They may still be antiquated and not show the influence of enlightened understanding resulting from a careful study of the human aspects of sexual relationships and the best interests of the children. Statistics show that, in Australia, in about 36 per cent of divorces there are no children of the marriage, and that the number of marriages dissolved varies inversely as the number of children. It would seem that children have a stabilizing influence on a marriage. The facts appear to indicate that, even though there is deep-seated antagonism and repeatedly expressed hostility between the parents, each decides to take no action because of the children. As a matter of fact, the psychological development of children is more normal and less liable to lead to neurosis when such parents are separated and the children, being with one or the other parent, can live in a peaceful, harmonious atmosphere free of bewildering tension. In the future, it is probable that the State will play a greater part in the rearing of children when the parents are incapable of doing it satisfactorily. Each Australian state now attends to the education of children and arranges for medical examinations, for immunization against disease, and for other matters affecting their welfare.

Many considerations deter people from seeking liberation from the bonds of matrimony. Divorce is expensive and is sometimes associated with undesirable publicity. With a view to increased sales, some newspapers delight in publishing intimate details concerning the private lives of citizens. When there are no children and a marriage has gone irretrievably "on the rocks" it should be possible to obtain a divorce quite simply, by mutual consent, after claims relating to property have been settled by an impartial adjudicator. This seems to be the general opinion of the Australian people, except among certain religious groups.

It is generally recognized here that something should be done about the whole problem of marriage and divorce, but the proposed reforms are not sufficiently radical. In Australia and New Zealand, marriage guidance councils have been formed by church organizations and public-spirited citizens, but they deal with difficulties that arise during marriage rather than with the education of single young men and women concerning the wise choice of a life partner. It is true that some lectures are given on preparation for marriage, but such instruction is not sufficiently comprehensive and in any case it does not reach the masses of the people. As long as the choice of a mate is based upon nothing more than romantic love that is not tempered by good sense and discerning judgment, the high rate of failures will continue. To relieve the situation to some extent marriage should not be as binding and permanent as it is at present. It is not in the best interests of society that the misery of unhappily married couples should be prolonged. That is the writer's impression of the attitude of the community, but, like many other impressions, it cannot be scientifically verified.

Prostitution

Man has a strong biological urge to have sexual intercourse with the female of the species and this urge is not diminished by the artificialities and conventional attitudes of civilized society. Sexual desire is stronger and more insistent in most males than in females, partly because of the continuous formation of spermatozoa and their accumulation in the seminal vesicles, causing reflex actions that reach the psychic level and partly because social mores in most regions endorse aggressive male sexuality and discourage sex activity by unmarried females.

Since the dawn of history men of many different types and of every social level have had premarital and extramarital sexual intercourse. This natural demand by the male for sexual satisfaction is met in different ways, one of which depends upon his willingness to pay for the gratification of his desire.

What is the marital status of the majority of the clients of prostitutes? Totally different sources have agreed in stating that the majority of the clients are married men and that in the brothels the proportion of married men is about 90 per cent. That percentage seems high, but several interesting reasons have been given in support of it. An unmarried man, when he desires sexual intercourse, need not visit prostitutes unless his girl friends fail to satisfy his desires in this respect. Free young men enjoy the excitement of the chase, the dining out, the dancing, and the other preliminaries. Sailors are exceptions. While the ship is in port they usually have insufficient time to woo a girl with gifts and attention until she consents to sexual union. They therefore pay cash to prostitutes for immediate satisfaction. Soldiers on leave for a brief period are in the same category.

The pattern of sex behavior has changed, in this part of the world as elsewhere, since reasonably reliable contraceptive methods have become readily available. Furthermore, the progress of medical science has resulted in the use of antibiotic preparations that cure venereal disease much more quickly than the old forms of treatment, greatly diminishing the incidence of venereal disease. Young men and women therefore feel that they can have sexual intercourse with the risk of conception and of contracting undesirable infections reduced almost to zero. To them, love without fear has become a reality. They are often reckless or careless, of course, and pregnancy may result, but it is essential to point out that single men, when they desire sexual intercourse, usually have it with their girl friends.

It is not suggested that all girls readily agree to have sexual relations when such a proposal is made to them. There are many who resent such advances and steadfastly refuse to surrender themselves until after marriage. They regard chastity as a worth-while ideal. However, the percentage of girls who do have premarital intercourse is undoubtedly very high in certain groups. The general attitude of a girl towards sex varies with her upbringing, temperament, and social environment. What other girls in her group do has a powerful influence in determining her own actions.

The married man presents an entirely different picture in relation to prostitution. His wife may suffer from chronic ill-health; she may take little or no interest in sex, or if she does she may no longer stimulate or satisfy him. It has been said that variety is the spice of life. At some time almost every man is interested in more than one woman. After the birth of several children the entrance to the vagina may be greatly overstretched and relaxed. When this condition is present the vaginal musculature does not stimulate the man much or help to maintain his erection. A man thus finds a nulliparous girl in her early twenties more exciting and satisfying. Furthermore, the married man must maintain respectability and seek sexual satisfaction where there is no publicity. The prostitute can satisfy this requirement. As Bertrand Russell says, "the man who has been with her can return to his wife, his family and his church, with unimpaired dignity." Finally, there is a very simple reason why more married men than single men go with prostitutes; there are more of them.

A prostitute has been defined as "a woman who sells her sexual favors for cash, as her only or principal source of livelihood." Prostitutes do a flourishing business in our big cities. The general pattern is probably the same in Australia and New Zealand as elsewhere in the world. Many prostitutes frequent hotel lounges, many have regular "beats" in public places, some stop cars in their competition for clients, while others are in houses that are so well known that the women do not have to go in search of business. Taxi drivers know the various houses.

During the war prostitutes practiced in caravans near military camps. "Call girls" are available in our big cities. In Australia, where living standards are high, prostitutes earn large incomes, especially when they are young and keep themselves attractive enough to appeal to their well-to-do clientele. Those in the highest income groups earn more per week than does the Prime Minister of Australia, but for physiological reasons this rate of earn-

ing does not continue for the whole month. Furthermore, it is not maintained over a long period of time.

It might be thought that all these women who earn a great deal of money create a "happy hunting ground" for the income tax department, but such is not the case as they are too elusive. The earnings of prostitutes are taxable as "Income from Personal Exertion" but, in the absence of records, the taxation officials can do little except watch assets in the form of traceable investments, as they do with other citizens.

The professional prostitutes work in association with "bludgers" (a colloquial term used to denote a man who lives on the earnings of prostitution), and in a brothel the girls are employed by a madame. They are allowed to keep only a percentage of their earnings. It is claimed that there must be a business manager, and there are so many social parasites making money out of this profession that the prostitutes themselves are often inadequately paid.

Although procurers operate in public dance halls, coffee lounges, and elsewhere, obtaining recruits by paying special attention to likely girls, as yet there is in Australia and New Zealand no highly organized white-slave traffic such as exists in older countries. Nevertheless, the police are concerned about the activities of people who, with the growth of our population, are procuring girls in the large cities and taking them to country towns where professional prostitution has not been developed and organized on a commercial basis.

A distinction is often made between the amateur and the professional prostitute. The distinction is not based on ethical or psychological grounds, but economic, and this should be remembered by those who make proposals for social reform. A similar distinction is made in the world of sports, where the professional has made some particular game his specialty and his main or only means of livelihood, whereas the amateur, although he is very fond of the game and plays it frequently with various people, does not rely upon it as a means of earning a living. In prostitution, as in the sporting world, many amateurs turn professional. The amateur prostitute may bestow her favors upon selected males for pleasure, but she usually expects something in return. But the so-called amateur is not a prostitute in the legal or social sense of the word.

Can prostitution be abolished? The answer is definitely "No," because this ancient profession satisfies a distinct human need. There seems to be a biological urge for man to seek variety in his sexual relations. Moreover, there are complex psychological factors that predispose some women towards sexual promiscuity. Many of the girls start at quite an early age and social workers tell me that it is generally futile to try to rehabilitate them after the age of 18 years. Nevertheless, although it is quite impossible to influence the activities of the so-called amateurs, professional prostitutes would be greatly reduced in numbers by changing the social structure so that the commercial exploitation of women would be eliminated and the profit motive removed from this intensely acquisitive society of ours. The professional prostitute seeks sexual intercourse for money, not for physical gratification. The procurers, the madames, and the bludgers are all after money. They flourish today and will continue until society is radically changed.

Comprehensive and detailed laws relating to prostitution have been passed in every Australian state and in New Zealand, but the great extent to which prostitution is a part of the sexual life of the community in the big cities is proof that the laws are not enforced effectively. However, some examples of these laws should be given, as an indication of professed government policy.

In most Australian states the law regarding soliciting for the purposes of prostitution states that "any common prostitute who importunes any person being in or on any public place or within the view or hearing of any other person therein or thereon, or for the purposes of prostitution solicits or accosts any person being or passing in or on any public place shall be liable . . . ." The penalty is a fine that varies greatly in different states, or it may be a term of imprisonment from one to six months. For living on the earnings of prostitution Australian states have a provision: "Any male person who knowingly lives wholly or in part on the earnings of prostitution or in any public place solic-

its for an immoral purpose shall be liable . . . ." The penalty is a fine or imprisonment for six months to two years. With regard to the keeping of brothels, we read: "No person occupying or keeping premises shall harbor prostitutes." The penalty is a fine or up to two years in jail. The law relating to procuring states: "Any person who procures a girl or woman under the age of 21 years who is not a common prostitute of known and immoral character to have unlawful carnal connection with a man either in the State or elsewhere shall be liable . . . ." For this offense the penalty is not a fine, but a prison term from two to ten years. One cannot help feeling that the whole treatment of professional prostitution in Australia is superficial and totally inadequate.

Since it is impossible to abolish prostitution it would be in the public interest to regulate it so that society is adversely affected as little as possible. We should balance the advantages against any possible disadvantages. Furthermore, if prostitution is legalized and controlled reasonably well, the administering authority should ensure that the girls are frequently and thoroughly examined for signs of venereal disease, that they take all possible precautions to avoid such infection, that they get a fair deal, that they are not financially exploited by social parasites and that they are free at all times to change their occupation should they so desire.

In one Australian state prostitution has become a political question. In April 1967 it was reported that "the Young Liberals of Western Australia are calling for licensed brothels to combat mass rape and venereal disease." It is a difficult and complicated social problem to which there is no easy solution. However, attitudes towards sex are changing and probably it will soon be generally realized that it is better to deal with the problem of prostitution constructively rather than by resort to repressive legislation.

Sexual Deviations

In Australia and New Zealand homosexuality is regarded as a definite antisocial abnormality. The existing laws are not concerned with the concepts of homosexuality as a biological fact or as a neurosis curable by psychoanalysis. Offenses of this character are starkly and clearly defined, as the following section shows: "Buggery and bestiality: Any person who has carnal knowledge of any person against the order of nature, or has carnal knowledge of an animal, or permits a male person to have carnal knowledge of him or her against the order of nature is liable . . . ." In three of the six Australian states the penalty is imprisonment for fourteen years. In Victoria "if the other party is under fourteen years of age or if the offence is committed with violence the penalty is imprisonment for twenty years." Up till 1949 the penalty in Victoria was death.

Homosexual relations between males receive greater attention than homosexuality among females and are regarded more seriously by our lawmakers. According to psychiatrists and the police, there is much homosexuality in Australia, but it is impossible to quote any statistics. The Lesbian, or female homosexual, is just as common as her male counterpart, but her activities in this field do not constitute an offense. There are all degrees of homosexuality, with varying proportions of psychic and physical components. Homosexual relations are liable to develop wherever groups of one sex are segregated for long periods.

There is probably much undetected homosexuality. Family physicians and psychiatrists are generally not consulted for this deviation because most homosexuals are content to remain as they are. The true homosexual rarely seeks treatment, but bisexual individuals do because of the heterosexual component.

Exhibitionism is the most common sexual offense in Australia and New Zealand. It is a frequent occurrence on our bathing beaches and also commonly takes place when a man finds himself alone with one or more women passengers in a compartment of a suburban train. Exhibitionists are prosecuted under an indecent exposure clause that is common to all states: "Any person who without lawful excuse wilfully exposes his person in the view of any person in any public place shall be liable . . . ." The penalty differs in each state, being either a moderate to a heavy fine or imprisonment for from six months to three years.

Nudist clubs have been formed in various parts of Australia and New Zealand, but there are no records of complaints concerning exhibitionism by members. Although the emphasis is on healthy outdoor sports and the beneficial effects of sunlight on the nude human body, there is nevertheless a sexual component in nudism, just as there is a sexual element in most dances, in many theatrical performances, in much of our advertising, and in the motion picture industry.

Voyeurism seems to be as common in Australia as in other parts of the world. The "peeper" is prosecuted under the general offense of being unlawfully on the premises. The penalty varies in different states. It may be a heavy fine or imprisonment for a period that ranges from six months to two years.

Transvestism, or eonism, is identification with the other sex, particularly with regard to dress. In most states it is not an offense unless dressing as one of the opposite sex is used to deceive people and facilitate some illegal activity. However, in Tasmania it is punishable: "No person shall, being a male person, be found in any public place between sunset and sunrise dressed in female apparel." It is not stated whether a female impersonator on the stage would be exempt from this law.

In general, sexual deviations indicate a failure to reach full psychological development. Deviations from the normal are exceedingly common, but accurate statistics regarding their incidence cannot be given.

Pornographic Literature and Obscene Photographs

Censorship in Australia is by no means liberal. The censors consider that they are the guardians of public morality and they tend to take a narrow view of the subject. The control of obscenity is exercised by the Commonwealth government through the Customs Department and by the states by prosecutions. According to the Police Offences Act, books, newspapers, magazines, pictures, photographs, statues, or records may be classified as obscene when they tend to deprave or corrupt any person, notwithstanding that persons in other classes or age groups may not be similarly affected. The act makes provision for entering premises to search for obscene articles and for their destruction in the event of a court holding them to be obscene. Works of recognized literary or artistic merit and bona fide medical books are exempt unless publication was not justified in the circumstances.

What is pornographic and what is obscene is largely a matter of opinion, as there is no agreement on a clear legal definition, and is usually determined by the particular magistrate before whom the case is heard.

Sex Education

Discussions with educators and psychiatrists revealed the general consensus that sex education is a part of our sex life. It is necessary to distinguish clearly between sex instruction and sex education. Sex instruction relates mainly to a knowledge of the anatomy and physiology of the male and female sex organs. Sex education includes this and a great deal more. It comprises not only the biological aspects of sex but also ethical considerations that are essential to the formation of character. Sex education should relate sex to the whole of life and particularly to human happiness.

What should be the scope of sex education? The position in Australia and New Zealand can best be understood by answering this question with reference to the three stages at which such education should be given; namely, in infancy and early childhood, at puberty and during adolescence, and finally, throughout adult life. Most parents in Australia give their children inadequate sex education. Usually it is too little and too late. By the time the parent decides to speak to the child about sex the youngster has picked up, possibly from crude sources, much more information than the parent realizes.

When children first ask questions about sex they should be answered simply and truthfully by the parents. Parents should speak casually and without embarrassment, so that, as the child develops, sex will occupy its proper place in his mind. If natural curiosity does not prompt children to ask questions, parents should explain the elementary facts at an early age, using language that can be readily under-

stood. Unfortunately, many parents in Australia are handicapped because they do not know the anatomical names of sexual structures. Some parents have false notions of modesty or they regard sex as shameful. Somehow, this seems to be linked with religion. Whatever the origin of this attitude may be, the result is that parents shirk a duty that they have to a child.

Sex education at school should be part of a course of lectures on elementary physiology. It is now generally agreed that the education of youth should include a knowledge of the functions of the human body and the simple rules of hygiene. The reproductive system cannot logically be excluded. The instruction should be given by the school medical officer, with the aid of charts and specially prepared films. These latter present the subject in such an objective manner and with such a sense of responsibility that the child gains essential knowledge without any undesirable associations.

One survey on sex education in the three most populous Australian states revealed that "the Education departments have not issued any direction forbidding such instruction nor, on the other hand, have they encouraged teachers or given them positive assistance in imparting information on this question." The special committee appointed by the New Zealand government reported as follows: "The school is not the proper place for fully instructing children about sex, although it may be a convenient place in which mothers and daughters together, fathers and sons together, or parents together, may listen to addresses or see appropriate films. This would help to break down some of the barriers of self-consciousness."

The sex education of adolescents and adults may be undertaken in several ways. In Australia excellent courses of lectures are arranged in each state by the adult education councils or similar bodies. Unfortunately, only a minute fraction of the population receives advanced sexual education in this way.

At university level there should be a systematic course of lectures on the anatomy, physiology, and psychology of sex, with emphasis on the ethical aspects of sexual relations. Law students should be instructed in the appropriate aspects of psychology, a knowledge of which would enable them in later life to deal more understandingly with the legal aspects of sex relationships, quite apart from the treatment of sex offenders. Medical students should be taught a much wider range of sexual subjects than they are at present, for medical practitioners should be thoroughly familiar with the techniques of contraception, be able to treat disorders of the sexual function, and be able to practice marriage counseling with sympathetic understanding.

The general opinion among the specialists here is that there is probably more hypocrisy, deceit, and dishonesty in relation to sex than there is about anything else in our lives. The welfare of society and the survival of a soundly based morality are best assured by strengthening the family unit. This is done by promoting marital adjustment, by strengthening family loyalties, by passing legislation that protects the family economically, and by strengthening the social cohesion between all members of the domestic group. This will be facilitated by adequate education from early childhood on all matters pertaining to sex, marriage, and the family.

References

Danielson, Bengt, *Love in the South Seas*. London: Allen and Unwin, 1954.

Malinowski, Bronislaw, *The Sexual Life of Savages in North-Western Melanesia*. London: Routledge, 1948.

Mead, Margaret, *From the South Seas*. New York: William Morrow & Co., Inc., 1948.

Morrison, J., "The Origins of the Practices of Circumcision and Subincision among the Australian Aborigines." *The Medical Journal of Australia*, 1967.

The New Zealand Official Year Book, 1966.

Report of the Special Committee on Moral Delinquency in Children and Adolescents. New Zealand Government Publication, 1954.

Rout, Ettie A., *Maori Symbolism*. London: Kegan Paul, 1926.

Russell, Bertrand, *Marriage and Morals*. London: Allen and Unwin, 1930.

Spencer, Baldwin, and Gillen, F. J., *The Arunta: A Study of a Stone Age People*. London: The Macmillan Co., 1927.

United Nations *Demographic Year Book, 1963.*

Wallace, Victor H., *Women and Children First: An Outline of a Population Policy for Australia*. London: Oxford University Press, 1946.

Year Book of the Commonwealth of Australia, 1965.

VICTOR H. WALLACE

Autoerotism

AUTOEROTISM in its broadest sense is a term referring to the phenomenon of spontaneous sexual emotion engendered without any external stimulus involving another person. Autoerotism is extensive and covers a wide field. It may refer to the incidence of sexual orgasm during sleep or the recognition of sexual feelings during the ecstasy of a religious ceremony or the observation of certain objects of art. It would be impossible in such a work as this to go into any exhaustive consideration of autoerotism, so this article will be confined to a subdivision of the subject, masturbation. This form of activity is more easily observed and has been more carefully studied than any other aspect of the autoerotic field. It is also true that the term "autoerotism" has, in the minds of a great many, been so identified with the subject of masturbation that the terms have become in effect synonymous. It is quite apparent in many of our modern writings on the subject that authors appear to believe that the term "autoerotic" is more polite and less objectionable than "masturbation," so they substitute the one for the other.

Masturbation

"Masturbation" is here defined as any form of deliberate self-manipulation of, or application of pressure on, the sexual organs for pleasure and for the release of tension. Many contemporary writers extend the use of the term to include the use of one's hands on the genitals of another. This also is described by the term "mutual masturbation."

In order to understand the present-day emphasis on discarding the superstitions of the past we must take a glance at history and scan the evolution of concepts that have brought us to the present-day need for a re-evaluation of facts and a re-education of those who have been conditioned by misinformation.

History

No other form of sexual activity has been more frequently discussed, more roundly condemned, and more universally practiced than masturbation. Since in the past it has been condemned by most of the leaders in the fields of medicine, education, and religion, it is reasonable to inquire into the background of the impressions that led to these conclusions and thus to disprove the belief that the old ideas and taboos must have sprung from some observable consequences.

Religious leaders who looked upon masturbation as a sin sought Biblical authority for their contention by the simple device of labeling masturbation as onanism. Onan's withdrawal before emission has been wrongly identified with masturbation. As group survival was of foremost importance in the early tribal days, the elders naturally considered it a sin to waste sperm by any nonprocreative practice. Onan's act was punishable not because of the spill of semen but rather because of his refusal to obey the law of the tribe and have children by his brother's widow. When we turn to the Bible and consider the detailed regulations of sex life, especially under the laws of Moses, it is noteworthy that we find nothing there about masturbation.

Sporadic attempts to create a scientific attitude were defeated by the widespread influence of Dr. Tissot. In about the middle of the eighteenth century this French doctor identified the sin of Onan with masturbation and published a book called *Onana*, subtitled *A Treatise on the Diseases Produced by Onanism.* The book is steeped in ignorance and personal bias and would be of little importance if succeeding writers had not accepted Tissot's thesis and ventured into even more detailed descriptions of the evils of "self-abuse." In these writings they did not produce one iota of scientific evidence to substantiate any of their statements, yet their influence has affected the emotional lives of thousands of people up to the present time.

It is obvious that from the medical writings of Hippocrates to those of Brady in 1890, a span of twenty-two centuries, there was a great ignorance of anatomy and little understanding concerning the causation of disease. There was also a general lack of objectivity and an absence of any scientific approach to masturbation.

The modern attitude is not a sudden change, but rather the result of a long struggle to throw off the shackles of ignorance and to view the phenomenon in the light of reason. It has emerged only after knowledge has replaced superstition, facts have taken precedence over conjecture, and understanding and information have replaced bias and prejudice. It is only fair to note that the occasional pioneers of the past who insisted that facts be the background for opinion were, in the light of recent studies, exceptionally wise in their speculations. It is also noteworthy that the superstitions regarding masturbation have not been entirely annihilated, for we find in a few of our modern writings an insistence upon classifying it under the heading of perversions. Whenever modern religious leaders feel under the obligation to discourage masturbation they are not now likely to refer to any horrible consequences but rather to consider it a religious offense. The Roman Catholic Church, for example, deals with it dogmatically and classifies it as a sin. This attitude is also held by some Orthodox groups and by certain fundamentalist Protestant bodies.

Period of Transition

Prevalence and Frequency—Basic Studies

In 1907 Dr. Frederick Sturgis attempted to make a study of the incidence of masturbation without any consideration of its supposed evils or disabling sequelae. His admittedly conservative estimate was that 60 per cent of both sexes masturbated at some time but he held that were the whole truth known the figure would be nearer 90 per cent. The fact that Sturgis could be interested solely in the incidence of the practice and not its supposed moral and physical consequences bears witness to the new light in which the phenomenon was coming to be viewed.

As to the prevalence of masturbation, all of the studies that have been carried on by competent parties under well-credentialed auspices indicate that well over 90 per cent of all males have a history of masturbation. Although these studies vary somewhat in exactness, running anywhere from 90 to 98 per cent for the male, a study made by Kinsey, Pomeroy, and Gebhard of Indiana University (1948), sets the figure at over 94 per cent, and there will be little disagreement with this figure on the part of modern students of the subject. In 1929 Dr. Katharine Davis reported admitted masturbation on the part of 65 per cent of college women. Since for most of them to admit masturbation was a matter of confession, we are justified in adding 10 per cent as a factor of error, since other studies, notably Hamilton's (1929) and the author's unpublished research, indicate that the figure among single women over 25 runs somewhere between 75 and 80 per cent.

In both sexes the frequency of the experience varies greatly, but the average single woman reports masturbating from two to three times a month, usually just before or after her menstrual period, whereas the average single male reports it two or three times a week. Checking this against Hamilton's study, we find that 49 per cent report masturbating three or more times a week, and the Kinsey figures as reported by Glenn Ramsey show 46 per cent of males who report a frequency of from one to six times or more weekly. Finger (1947), Ross (1950), and Giedt (1957) each made a questionnaire study of a college group of males and reported figures that correlated very well with those of the Kinsey study.

It may be safely assumed, therefore, from all the studies to date, that were we to take the histories of men and women who had reached the age of 25 we would find that masturbation has played a part in the lives of over 90 per cent of all males and over 70 per cent of all females, with the frequency running from once or twice a month up to several times a week. No evidence has been presented that the greater frequency is any more productive of harm than the lesser.

Old ideas persist and, as they are passed down from one generation to another, can have a crippling effect on the minds of youth unless they are successfully challenged and defeated by the truth.

The persistence of the idea that masturbation causes insanity has been one of the most vicious in its effect upon the emotional life of our young. Dr. Maurice Levine of the Child Guidance Center of Cincinnati has said in his book *Psychotherapy in Medical Practice* (1942) that the misconception that masturbation causes insanity is not only exceedingly harmful but extraordinarily persistent. He notes that in one child-guidance clinic 75 per cent of the parents of the children who were patients had threatened their children with the dangers of masturbation. He also says that this attitude is prevalent among physicians as well as among parents, and he feels that it is important that they all come to learn that this is a misconception without a vestige of truth.

Every counselor who deals with the sex problems of young people can add to the testimony of the Cincinnati psychiatrist concerning the persistent influence of this old bogey and the damaging effect it has had on the minds of young people—and older ones too, as many older people are still looking for evidences of the breakdown that they are sure is bound to come as a result of their earlier and perhaps their present masturbatory activity. In this lies the crux of the whole matter. Many of the untoward results of masturbation that have been described by these purveyors of misinformation have actually been observed, but these were not the result of masturbation but of the worry

concerning probable consequences. In this, then, one might assume that the simple way to deal with the problem would be to tell the truth. This is the only effective way, but in doing so we must be sure we do not replace one set of fears with another. It is of little use for a counselor to try to relieve a person's fears by admitting the normality of the practice while on the other hand he shows his distaste by the use of such words as, "It isn't nice," "Young people should find better things to do," or "One should give one's attention to more constructive things," etc. All of these statements are vague, they have little meaning, and can just as definitely produce emotional conflicts as did the fear that stemmed from the earlier threats.

Since all of this is generally accepted by professional students of sex, it is a dereliction of responsibility not to bring these facts to the attention of millions of people who could profit by the knowledge. Today we have, on the one hand, a growing group of the well-informed who accept the normality of masturbation for the release of tension and for the emotional and physical satisfactions involved. There is also a growing body of opinion that masturbation for these purposes is not only normal but carries with it positive values, which in many instances make it desirable and beneficial. On the other hand, we still have those who remain devotees of the ideas and dogmas of the past.

If we could divide time into periods and say that in the earlier days all people felt this way about masturbation, that in the next period opinion had changed, and that now there has come to be a more enlightened attitude and an acceptance of the normality of this type of behavior, then everything could be very logically arranged and neatly pigeonholed. But when one studies this subject in any detail, one finds that it is too complicated to permit the arrangement of any neat pattern. During the times that the wrong ideas were being disseminated there were individuals who rose up in protest, and some valid studies were made that should have been recognized.

Censorship

In the earlier days, as well as today, one effective device for the suppression of truth was censorship. In the early 1900's the works of G.

Stanley Hall, Winfield Scott Hall, Sylvanus Stall, and others were being widely proclaimed and disseminated. At the same time, works such as those of Havelock Ellis, one of the outstanding scientific investigators of sex of all time, were being suppressed, as were also statements made by Sir James Paget, an English surgeon and pathologist, who said that there could not possibly be any more harm in masturbation than in the same amount of intercourse. Writings of many others who proclaimed their disagreement with the old ideas were being censored and the authors were criticized for indecency, the indecency lying in the very nature of the study. The desire to know something about sex and its relationship to human functioning was in itself portrayed as inherently indecent by the adherents of the old school. Consequently, these studies were put away in libraries, hidden in dark corners of the archives, available only to a privileged few and forbidden to the general public, who were not aware that most of the information available to them had long since been disproven and outmoded. To a large extent that has continued up to very recently.

Probably the greatest factor in breaking down censorship and in giving widespread circulation to the most extensive, scientific approach to the study of contemporary sex behavior was the publication in 1948 of the Kinsey report. However, there were many people who protested and who would have liked to have had the volumes suppressed.

Causation and Initial Experiences

Infancy and Childhood

In the infant's first half year he discovers his fingers and toes, and in much the same way he discovers his genitals. Because there are pleasure values in manipulation of the organ from the beginning, he may return to these areas for such satisfactions.

Children from the ages of 3 to 6 are apt to be physically affectionate and sociable. In common with their playmates, they will exhibit an interest in each other's bodies and occasionally wish to see and touch them. With all this there may develop an interest in masturbation.

Whenever dual masturbation (mutual mas-

turbation or group masturbation) has occurred it is likely to have taken place between the ages of 6 and 12. Many report that they do not know when they began to masturbate but do know that they have been doing it from a very early age.

When in the past masturbation has been observed in children it has been the habit to blame someone for teaching them; blame has been put on servant girls, playmates, and boarding-school companions. Although these influences have played a part, and will continue to do so, it is evident that the average child does not need to be taught.

Studies made by modern investigators indicate that more frequently than not individuals report a spontaneous indulgence in the habit. In cases wherever they had engaged in group sexual activities in childhood they feel that they had acquired an interest in masturbation prior to such an experience, although in some instances it is evident that the observing of others engaging in such experience or being solicited to do so themselves had the effect of stimulating an interest in the activity. Girls, however, more often report seduction to this habit than do boys.

Adolescence

Although Dr. Kinsey has reported some cases in which a form of orgasm has been observed in a very young child, orgasm as we think of it, particularly in the male where it involves ejaculation, generally happens after the onset of puberty. Masturbation at this period takes on a more meaningful sexual connotation.

The act is apt to be accompanied by phantasy. Dr. G. V. Hamilton (1929) differentiated between infantile and adolescent masturbation on the basis that one is purely for sensual pleasure while the other has a deeper psychic significance. In the latter, phantasies of coitus are used to add realism to the activity.

Adolescence is the period most frequently studied and more information of this age group is available than of the earlier age groups. Most males claim to have started at ages of 12 to 13. Some girls report that the interest came at the onset of menstruation; many report a much later date for the initial experience.

Although masturbation is an adolescent practice in both sexes, all evidence points to the fact that there is a higher percentage among males than among females. However, at the age of 15 there is every indication that at least 50 per cent of girls have masturbated and that the percentage increases as the group gets older, so that there are many more girls masturbating at the age of 19 or 20 than were doing so in their middle teens.

Parental Attitudes and Home Instruction

If masturbation is observed in infancy or childhood, parents should be very careful not to inculcate fear by scolding or punishing the child or by making the incident seem overimportant. To distract the child's attention it would be best to do so on the basis of "Let's do this" rather than "Stop doing that." It would be well for parents to acquaint themselves with some of the contemporary literature on the subject of child-rearing. They will easily find a forthrightness and freedom from the fear-inspiring admonitions that have characterized much of the past literature. A few writers may seem esthetically critical, but the tendency is to deal with masturbation as a fact and as an accepted part of the child's development. In the life of a happy, well-adjusted child masturbation will play a very minor part. The unhappy and withdrawn child may show a preoccupation with masturbation, a condition that should be regarded as a symptom of a deeper problem. In such a case the parent will be well advised to seek the counsel of a child specialist.

Most adolescent masturbation will go unobserved, and the best thing the parents can do to eradicate any possible fear or concern over consequences would be to see that they have in their home some literature dealing frankly with the subject in the light of modern thinking.

Methods

The physical structure of the male does not admit of a great deal of variety in mastubatory practice and it is usually accomplished manually. However, some variations are reported, such as making coital movements against the bedclothes or a pillow, pressing against objects, etc.

In the girl, because her anatomy permits it, there is considerable variation. The use of a finger on the clitoris is the most usual form, and running a close second is what has been referred to as thigh-rubbing, in which the girl presses her thighs together or crosses her legs and squeezes the inner muscles of her thighs, thus bringing pressure on the labia and incidentally on the clitoris. At this she may become quite skillful and able to prolong the experience or bring herself to orgasm at will. Stimulation of the breasts is often an accompaniment of clitoral manipulation, and in some instances is the total experience.

Other methods are reported, such as pulling panties, nightgown, pajamas, the bedsheet, etc., tight between the thighs and making vulvular motions, which excite the clitoris. Instrumental masturbation, by inserting an object in the vagina, is comparatively rarely reported. The objects mentioned are so varied that they can best be classified as some long, round object. Here again, where vaginal masturbation is attempted, the finger is more commonly used.

Many girls who use the thigh-rubbing method report that they stop short of orgasm. This may be because the method is often used as a substitute after admonition by the parent who has observed some digital exploration. A frequent statement of older females is that they remember having been told, "Don't you ever let me catch you touching yourself again." A household term for masturbation is "playing with oneself"; this often develops a concept in the mind of the child that the harm lies in manual contact. The girl can therefore indulge in thigh-rubbing with less consciousness of guilt because she is not "playing with herself."

Masturbation and Orgasm

It is important at this point to discuss the question of orgasm in relation to masturbation and to point out that some of these methods may act as a drawback to marriage adjustment not because of any harm in the behavior itself but because the transition from the satisfactions obtained from a particular form of masturbation to those obtainable from intercourse may be difficult. It is the author's experience that in those females who report that they pass from clitoral stimulation to manipulation of the whole vulva with emphasis upon stimulation of the vaginal orifice very quickly make an adjustment to coitus, and they will often report they had orgasm at the first experience or shortly thereafter. Those who for a number of years have used only the clitoris find it more difficult to make such a transition, but when they have been relieved of guilt feelings and have a cooperative and skillful husband, such an adjustment is probable within the first six months. The girl who masturbates by the thigh-rubbing method has learned to come to orgasm by the closest possible apposition of the thighs. Any position that permits penetration makes such pressure impossible and thus, because of her conditioning, she is prevented from coming to climax during the act.

Those girls who have denied themselves the direct form of masturbation and have used substitute measures, such as various forms of pressure, breast-rubbing, etc., often force themselves to stop just prior to the climax because they have developed a fear of the orgasm, having conceived the idea that the wrong or harm lies in the release itself. In any case, where orgasm has been suppressed the girl may develop a habit of nonresponse and carry this over into her marital relations, later to report that she has little or no satisfaction in coitus and an inability to come to a climax. We can see that in discouraging a form of direct masturbation in children one may be unwittingly encouraging a substitute activity that will later act as a deterrent to achieving orgasm in intercourse. Also, the guilt feeling that caused a girl to withdraw from direct fondling of her own organs may later cause her to resist manual stimulation on the part of the husband in his attempts at precoital excitation.

Total Outlet

A singularly useful term introduced by the Kinsey study was the use of the word "outlet." Heretofore in studies of autoerotism in adolescence it was frequently stated that masturbation was a practice of the adolescent who eventually outgrew the habit. Nothing was said as to what practices were substituted for it, the implications being that, having matured, he saw how childish this practice had been and simply dropped it. In introducing the word "outlet," Kinsey provided a term that is comprehensive enough to give us a view of composite sexual activity. Kinsey and his associates also showed us that the sexual activities of people on different educational and social levels should be differentiated. To make this plain he divided his population into three groups: the lower, middle, and upper educational level. He showed that between the ages of 25 and 30 masturbation provides a little less than half of the total sex outlet of unmarried college-level males. Those on the lower social level accept sexual intercourse at an earlier age as not only desirable but the only normal method of meeting sexual needs; on this level people look on masturbation as a practice of immaturity. The Kinsey study revealed that in all three groups the outlet is about the same; the difference lies only in the method they accept to obtain satisfaction.

Adults

Many adults need re-education to free them of the taboos acquired in childhood. This re-education could serve a twofold purpose: to relieve them of the fear and worry to which they have been subjected and to enable them to be helpful in giving information to the young. Of course, masturbation is no more harmful in adulthood than at any other time of life. Most unmarried adult males have adopted some method of heterosexual gratification, but this is less frequently true with the female, and the statistics gathered as a result of my own counseling practice are in agreement with those of Havelock Ellis, who said, "After adolescence I think there can be no doubt that masturbation is more common in women than in men." He also said, "I have been much impressed by the frequency with which masturbation is occasionally practiced by active, intelligent, and healthy women, who otherwise lead a chaste life. This experience is confirmed by others who are in a position to ascertain facts among normal people." It is this kind of statement, backed by hundreds of similar ones by competent authorities, that I feel should be brought more frequently to the attention of those who would profit by it. The Kinsey study reveals that among women between the ages of 35 to 45, over half of their total outlet is obtained through masturbation.

The Aging

It is to be hoped that those interested in the field of geriatrics will take into consideration the sexual needs of the aging and encourage them to accept masturbation as a perfectly valid outlet when there is a need and other means of gratification are not available. The author recently had a female client of 73, who came because she was worried over the fact that she masturbated two or three times a week. She reported that she had had a very happy marriage, that her husband had died five years before, and that since then she had had to turn to masturbation. She wanted to know if the counselor could recommend some doctor who could give her medicine to prevent this. She was obviously embarrassed to have to admit masturbation and felt there was something wrong with a woman of her age so indulging.

I tried to quiet her fears and told her that I knew of no method of treatment that would be of any use, and that most of the doctors I was acquainted with would not feel that there was any need for treatment. I told her that she should accept autoerotic release as a perfectly proper outlet and not worry about it, especially as she led a very active life, took care of her home, worked outside, had social commitments, and seemed to have adjusted herself to her widowhood very well indeed—provided she could get rid of the notion that in having sex desires and needing an outlet there was something wrong with her.

Dickinson (1933), in reporting on eleven cases of widows between the ages of 60 and 80, mentioned masturbation as a presented problem. Dickinson said, "All practiced masturbation, three by vaginal method, one by the urethra, and others presumably by the vulva method." He found that at this age it was very embarrassing for a woman to admit such a practice, even to herself. The consensus seems to be that sex is a disgrace at such an age, and that when consulting a doctor a woman desires assistance to fight against her "worst self."

With all that has been said about the naturalness and healthfulness of masturbation as an outlet, there are authors who, while they brush aside the use of the extreme and dire warnings of the past, engage in other forms of condemnation, such as: (1) It is evidence of immaturity; (2) It is solitary and therefore unsocial; (3) One cannot possibly get full emotional gratification through masturbation; (4) It will lead to sexual frustration; or (5) It is one cause of impotence or frigidity (although many claim that it may lead to sexual excess). These statements have been listed in this order to conform to a similar listing by Dr. Albert Ellis in his book, *Sex Without Guilt* (1958), where the reader will find a very cogent answer to each of these objections. Also, in my chapter on masturbation in Fishbein's *Successful Marriage* (1947), I show that it is of little use to do away with old taboos if we replace them with other statements of disapproval that cast reflections upon the character of the individual who masturbates.

When the eternal question of "why" is asked by the one who is always seeking causes, we may say that in any act of masturbation the individual is primarily interested in the sensual pleasure, release of tension, and the sedative effect it has on the nervous system.

Man is endowed with two strong appetites, for food and for sex. Individuals vary greatly in the frequency and the amount of satisfaction demanded by these appetites. Certainly the first appetite has to be met on a much more frequent and regular basis than the second. Nevertheless, neither appetite can be completely denied without unhealthy consequences.

Premarital and Postmarital Masturbation

In both the single male and female masturbation is used as a method of release, admitting a differential in frequency. It is practiced by those who have not accepted any other outlet and by those who have accepted heterosexual intercourse or petting to orgasm but who, because of its infrequency, use masturbation as a supplement. Furthermore, single persons turn to masturbation because of the fear of the consequences of heterosexual intimacy such as possible pregnancy, social condemnation, or parental disapproval, fears that are certainly not without foundation, or of being degraded in the eyes of the partner, illustrated by the girl who said, "I believe if I allowed him to go that far he would look down upon me and would not want to marry me," a fairly common attitude.

If the truth were known, it would probably be difficult to find any considerable number of husbands or wives who have not at some time or other masturbated during their married life. In married people masturbation is used to supplement infrequency on the part of the mate, during the absence or illness of the spouse, when the mate is unwilling to have sexual intercourse, when there has been a disagreement or a temporary hostility toward the spouse or a type of conflict that has developed an aversion for any sexual relations, and when there is a considerable disparity of interest or need. As Levy and Munroe say in their book, *The Happy Family* (1952), "Such people are very sensible."

When we take into consideration the problem of the divorced, the widowed, and the single, it does not take much imagination to recognize how necessary it is that the message concerning the harmlessness of this particular outlet be emphasized. Counselors are meeting more and more young people who have not been indoctrinated with the fearsome warnings of the past. We should not, however, be blinded to the fact that in all probability the larger segment of our society is still laboring under false impressions.

A survey of the present-day literature indicates a trend toward a much more enlightened attitude. Although some of it deals with the subject frankly on the basis that masturbation is normal and that there are no untoward consequences other than those caused by worry and fear, the greater part of it deals with it on a sort of compromise basis. It holds that what has been said about its harmlessness is true unless—and then these statements are apt to be qualified by warnings of the dangers of preoccupation with masturbation or of indulging in it to excess. Certainly the average person has little time or inclination to be preoccupied with sex. There are too many other things in this world that individuals are interested in. This brings us to the use of the word excess, which is a loaded term. Excess in anything means "more than enough," or "too much." The fallacy in the use of this term in connection with masturbation lies in the fact that no one knows what excess is. The word itself is meaningless unless we have a norm by which to measure frequency, and we have none. Any student of physical sex knows that there are physiological limitations to a person's capability of indulging to excess; nature takes care of the matter.

Let it be understood that throughout this paper I am talking about the normal behavior of normal people, about you and the people you meet in business and social life, the classroom, or the people you work with, play with, go to church with.

No attempt has been made to deal with compulsive or obsessive behavior or any form of exhibitionism. When, in psychopathology, masturbation is reported as a factor in a syndrome, let us remember it is but a symptom and never the cause.

Kinds of Masturbation

DUAL MASTURBATION—This is masturbation by two individuals, each in the presence of the other.

MUTUAL MASTURBATION—This refers to two individuals, who practice manual masturbation, of each other. Some laymen loosely use the term mutual masturbation to include any act other than penile-vaginal intercourse and would therefore consider fellation and cunnilinctus as masturbatory acts. But this is loose and inaccurate usage.

GROUP MASTURBATION—This is sometimes referred to as club masturbation, in which a group of youngsters are involved, generally of one sex and between the ages of 6 to 12, although instances have been noted among somewhat older groups. It has sometimes been reported as a game, each one masturbating and reporting his sensations. In the case of the somewhat older boys a contest to see which one ejaculates first has been reported.

URETHRAL MASTURBATION—A few cases of this have been reported by the male, in which something is pushed into the urethra. It is, however, more often a female type of masturbation. She has begun early in life to finger the urethra and has conditioned the sphincter muscle to respond to pressure and in some cases to admit the finger. By doing this she has so sensitized the area that for her it has become the primary erogenous zone of the genitals. In some cases objects have been pushed through the urethra and into the bladder; hairpins have been most frequently mentioned. There are a number of illustrations of this in the works of Havelock Ellis, Iwan Bloch (1910), and others.

Psychic masturbation—This is a form of masturbation in which an individual can concentrate so intently on a phantasy that he responds physically, often even to orgasm, without any manipulation of the genitals.

Nocturnal masturbation—This is a form of masturbation that takes place during sleep. This does not refer to the usually reported nocturnal emission of the male but to those instances in which the individual is awakened by jerking movements of the body and discovers that his hands are on his genitals, suddenly becoming aware that he has been "playing with himself" in his sleep. This type has been frequently reported by females.

Anal masturbation—It is evident that in some cases the fingering of the rectum has led to erogenous response and has in many of these situations led to autoerotic satisfaction.

Oral masturbation—This refers to the ability of some females to suck their own nipples, and to the acrobatic ability of some males to apply their mouth to their penises. This latter is also called self-fellation.

Synonyms—Manustupration (manus, the hand; stuprare, to ravish); ipsation (ipse, himself); onanism; self-abuse; colloquial terms: finger frigging, jerking off, and many others.

Phantasy

Research concerning the masturbation phantasies of normal individuals would be very helpful in order to better understand the use of masturbation as a temporary escape mechanism, as well as for the other purposes previously alluded to. It also would be of great help to the pathologist because it is quite evident in many of the works on psychopathology that the phantasies described are taken as evidence of a deep-rooted emotional disturbance. This may or may not be so. Herbert A. Carroll, in his text Mental Hygiene (1951), says, "Since human beings have the ability to make use of language, they can transcend the present in their role-taking. In phantasy they can change the past to some extent and shape the future to a considerable extent. They can pretend for a time that things are not what they seem to be. Phantasy is a normal activity. It is resorted to by well-adjusted persons as a means of rest from the difficult realities of the present and of the past and from concern about the future. Used in moderation, phantasy is a desirable form of temporary escape."

The fact that there are those who use phantasy to excess and develop a mental aberration in which they retire into a dream world as a permanent means of escape should not blind us to the fact that almost all normal people occasionally indulge in eccentric thinking. Maurice Levine (1942) says, "Bizarre thoughts are perfectly normal. . . . The fact is that human beings are capable of, and often do have, a wide variety of unusual thoughts, when they are not psychotic and when they are not abnormal in any real sense. Homosexual ideas, perverse sexual thoughts or impulses, impulses of hatred and of murder, ideas of being dependent and parasitic, ideas of grandeur, and the like, all may occur occasionally in the lives of individuals who are to a sufficient degree normal and healthy."

Phantasies are an integral part of most adult masturbation, especially in the male, and in a considerable number of females. Phantasies can take many forms but they are so much a part of the experience that we can say in this sense that masturbation is psychosomatic in character. The phantasy may be the picturization of a scene of sexual intercourse, imagining one is enjoying coitus with a satisfactory partner of the opposite sex, or it may deal with some type of sexual practice that may be spoken of as a deviation. Sometimes the phantasies take on a story form and are developed into a short-story type of thinking.

Some phantasies that have been written out for me are built quite like a story, and the authors claim that in thinking about them they go into the details of the characters that take part, the place where the experience is located, the expressions that people use in their conversations, and often the manner of dress of those who are the actors. Sometimes phantasy takes on a serial form. A girl would imagine, for instance, that she lives in a certain place where sexual practices are a part of her experience and, using this locale, she will "revisit" the scene the next time she masturbates, and the time after that, adding to her experiences in story book form. Males will also do this, and it is interesting to note how often rationalization is exposed, how much it is needed in order to make the experience realistic. For instance, one young man told about his imagining that he seizes girls and takes them to a location where they may be stripped and otherwise embarrassed and finally raped. Realizing his lack of strength to kidnap a young woman, and aware of the illegal aspects, he went into great detail to work out how he could provide a place where he could smuggle in food and staff it with servants to help him in the experience. In other words, he had to imagine that in some way it could be possible, otherwise the phantasy would lose its value. This kind of rationalization is expressed in many different ways. If it cannot be done, the sense of unrealism diminishes the erotic value of the phantasy. However, there is no more significance in this attitude than in the attitude of persons who do not enjoy the motion picture or TV show of the whodunit or western type if acts performed in the picture appear to them to be unrealistic or impossible, as, for instance, the shooting of 12 shots from a 6-shooter without reloading.

The Unusual and the Exotic

Positions

Positions in masturbation are seemingly important. A professional woman said she can lie on the bed and masturbate but she cannot have an orgasm unless she is standing, so she must stand on her feet before she finally has the climax. Some say they can masturbate more successfully in a standing position, some sitting, others in a reclining position. One girl's method as a child had been to place a towel on the edge of the bathtub and, throwing one leg over the edge, straddle it. She said she was still using this method as her means of release.

One young woman told me that she had learned as a child to reach up to the top of a door, which she had opened, and then straddle the edge of the door and rub up and down on it as her method of masturbation. In her adult life when she was alone in the house she occasionally reverted to this form. It is noteworthy that the carry-over of childhood practices into adulthood is very common.

Havelock Ellis refers to horseback riding, and this author has had a few cases where the girl who is a riding enthusiast has admitted that when she feels sexual she goes riding and often will have had relief before returning.

Instruments

Instrumental masturbation has been mentioned. Artistic and commercial exploitation of this interest has resulted in the manufacture of imitations of the male organ known as dildoes, *godemiches,* or *consolateurs.* In about the middle of the eighteenth century these instruments were sold quite openly in London, and a similar business in France was done on a somewhat more secretive basis. Bloch (1910) mentions a certain woman who did a large-scale business in Leicester Square and at the same time carried on quite a mail-order business. The history of such instruments reveals that they have been employed for the purpose of masturbation in almost all lands, notably in Turkish harems and in the islands of Zanzibar, where at one time they were regarded as an Arab invention. However, Bloch reports that there were representations of such instruments in ancient Babylonian sculpture, some of which was created in the third century before Christ. Reference is made to the manufacture and use of such an instrument in the Bible (Ezekiel 16; 17). Considerable artistry and skill went into the manufacture of these instruments, which seem to have been most popular in the eighteenth century. These dildoes were cleverly constructed so as to enhance realism in a coition phantasy. A student who wishes to explore this question further will find a very complete description in *The Sexual Life of Our Time* by Iwan Bloch.

Another device that seems to have caught the imagination of investigators is the Japanese instrument known as the *rin-no-tama* (sometimes also called a *watama* or *ben-wa*). This consists of two thin-walled hollow balls, generally of leaf brass, about the size of a pigeon's egg; one ball contains a small amount of quicksilver and the other is empty. The empty ball is placed in the vagina and pushed up against the cervix, and the one with the quicksilver is pushed against it. They are both held in the vagina by a cotton tampon. In walking, or by the use of a rocking chair or swing, the woman obtains what has been referred to as "a delightful sensation."

Such instruments have also been designed for use in a lesbian relationship. An illustration of one of these can be found in Dickinson's *Human Sex Anatomy* (1933). This, however, represents a very simple device and is not the complicated and realistic type described by Bloch. Doctors say that the use of a banana or a cucumber or certain root vegetables is occasionally being reported, as was true in the past. Women sometimes ask if it is true that the internal napkin can serve as an instrument for masturbation. In a few instances it can, but it should be noted that the external napkin is much more liable to arouse sexual feelings and sex consciousness than is the internal type, probably because the external type may be placed so as to cause friction of the clitoris.

Infibulation

Devices designed to secure the woman against the possibility of copulation with anyone but her husband are best exemplified in the well-known chastity belt. However, the use of similar devices for the purpose of preventing masturbation is less generally known. Such devices have been strapped on the female with this purpose in mind, and a cagelike device has been likewise applied to the boy. The author

has a picture of such a device, the design of which can best be described as weird. One might think of it more as an instrument of torture. This particular picture was published in a current medical journal under the heading of "Curiosities." It appears to have been designed by a woman nurse and was patented in 1908.

Need for Research

With all that has been said regarding the physical and mental harmlessness of masturbation and with all that has been emphasized regarding the need to spread the truth in order to reduce the fears and worries that lead to psychic conflicts, nevertheless, nowhere has the author suggested that masturbation can be accepted as a replacement for satisfactory heterosexual relationships nor has he found any number of normal individuals who prefer it. Notice here the word "satisfactory." In marriage, what is reported as satisfactory by one partner is often reported not to be so by the other. One partner may find a great satisfaction in rather frequent relationships of the conventional type of experience, indulging in precoital preparation and intromission and finally orgasm; and although the mate may accept this as an occasional performance, he may also find that as a repetitive experience it becomes rather boring and uninteresting because he is interested in deviated methods of expression and in great variation in positions, places, and times. This spouse may turn to masturbation because in phantasy he can enjoy some of the things he finds it impossible to achieve with his mate. Should the mate become aware of this and interpret such behavior as evidence of the spouse's rejection of their marital relationship, what happens to her ego? What happens to the ego of the one who is disappointed because the spouse won't "play the game" according to his rules? In what way does this disappointment affect other interpersonal relationships, such as communication, social life, attitudes toward children, attitudes toward the future? This is but a sampling of the many patterns of marital behavior that may be definitely and directly related to masturbation. I have in mind the case of a young wife who had conflicts with her husband over money matters and a disagreement over some of their social experiences. She was highly sexed and above everything else desired sexual intercourse with her husband, but was able, through masturbation, to maintain an equilibrium in which she could punish her husband by extending the interval between one act of intercourse and the next without correspondingly punishing herself—as she would have been doing if she did not have masturbation as an outlet.

There is obviously a need for more research concerning the relationship of masturbation to many forms of sociosexual deportment in and out of marriage.

References

Adams, Clifford, *Preparing for Marriage*. New York: E. P. Dutton & Co., 1951.

Bloch, Iwan, *The Sexual Life of Our Time*. London: Rebman, Ltd., 1910.

Brady, E. T., "Masturbation." *Virginia M. Month*. Pp. 256-260, 1891–92.

Broudy, H. S., and Freel, E. L., *Psychology for General Education*. New York: Longmans, Green, 1956.

Brown, Fred, and Kempton, Rudolf, *Sex Questions and Answers*. New York: Whittlesey House, 1950.

Caprio, Frank, *Variations in Sexual Behavior*. New York: Citadel Press, 1955.

Carroll, Herbert, *Mental Hygiene*. New York: Prentice-Hall, 1951.

Cavanagh, John R., *Fundamental Marriage Counseling*. Milwaukee: The Bruce Pub. Co., 1957.

Chetwood, Charles, *The Practice of Urology and Syphilology*. New York: William Wood, 1927.

Davis, Katharine, *Factors in the Sex Life of Twenty-two Hundred Women*. New York: Harper & Brothers, 1929.

Dearborn, Lester, "Masturbation." In Morris Fishbein, *Successful Marriage*. New York: Doubleday, 1947.

DeMartino, Manfred F., (ed.), *Sexual Behavior and Personality Characteristics*. New York: Citadel Press, 1963.

Dickinson, R. L., *Human Sex Anatomy*. Baltimore: The Williams and Wilkins Co., 1933.

Dickinson, R. L., and Beam, L., *A Thousand Marriages*. Baltimore: The Williams and Wilkins Co., 1931.

Ellis, Albert, *Sex Without Guilt*. New York: Lyle Stuart, 1958.

Ellis, Havelock, *Studies in the Psychology of Sex*. Vol. 1, *Autoerotism*. Philadelphia: F. A. Davis Co., 1913.

Finger, F. W., "Sex Beliefs and Practices among Male College Students." *J. Abnorm. & Social Psychol. 42;* 57-67, 1947.

Giedt, F. H., "Changes in Sexual Behavior and Attitudes Following Class Study of the Kinsey Report." *J. Social. Psychol. 33;* 131-141, 1951.

Gottlieb, Bernhardt S., *Understanding Your Adolescent*. New York: Rhinehart and Co., 1957.

Gottlieb, Bernhardt S., *What A Girl Should Know About Sex*. New York: Bobbs-Merrill Co., 1961.

Hamilton, G. V., *A Research in Marriage*. New York: Boni, Inc., 1929.

Holy Bible. Genesis 38:4, *et seq.;* Deuteronomy 25:5-9; Ezekiel 16:17.

Kinsey, Alfred, *et al.*, *Sexual Behavior in the Human Female*. Philadelphia: W. B. Saunders Co., 1953.

Kinsey, Alfred, *et al.*, *Sexual Behavior in the Human Male*. Philadelphia: W. B. Saunders Co., 1948.

Leuba, Clarence, *Ethics in Sex Conduct*. New York: Association Press, 1948.

Levine, Maurice, *Psychotherapy in Medical Practice*. New York: The Macmillan Co., 1942.

Levy, John, and Munroe, Ruth, *The Happy Family*. New York: Alfred A. Knopf, Inc., 1952.

Pike, James A., *Teen-Agers and Sex, A Guide for Parents*. New Jersey: Prentice-Hall, 1965.

Ross, Robert T., "Measures of the Sex Behavior of College Males Compared with Kinsey's Results." *J. Abnorm. Soc. Psychol. 45;* 753-755, 1950.

Spock, Benjamin, *Baby and Child Care*. New York: Pocket Books, 1946.

Sturgis, F. R., "The Comparative Prevalence of Masturbation in Males and Females." *Am. J. Dermat. & Genito-Urin. Dis. 11;* 396-400, 1907.

Tissot, S. A. D., *Onana*. New York: Collins and Hannay, 1832 (first French issue prior to 1767).

LESTER W. DEARBORN

Beauty

What Is Beauty?

ERIC NEWTON in his classic book on beauty, *The Meaning of Beauty* (1950), stresses the point that beauty is a thing that causes man pleasure. What is a pleasure to one man need not be and often is not a pleasure to another. According to Newton, then, each person provides his own criteria of pleasure and of beauty.

Any fixed standards of beauty are based on the experiences of persons with a common background who are able to agree on what is beautiful from their point of view. Thus, for example, Marilyn Monroe is considered beautiful by most men in America—she is a standard of America's beautiful women.

To the artist, Newton carefully points out, that which is beautiful is beautiful because it *is*, not because of its function. This writer disagrees with Newton and will provide evidence throughout this article that human beauty is largely judged on function—directly or at least indirectly on *potential* function. Marilyn Monroe is beautiful not only because looking at her gives one pleasure, as one would gain pleasure from looking at a beautiful Greek statue, but also because, in America, we closely associate certain aspects of beauty with sexual aptitude and the pleasure derived from sexual satisfaction. Marilyn Monroe consequently is beautiful to look at not only because of the symmetry of her form but also because of the potential sexual functions suggested by that form.

David Hume (1875) expressed a view, very similar to Newton's, that: "Beauty is not quality in things themselves; it exists merely in the mind which contemplates them; and each mind perceives a different beauty." Hume's view is alluded to in the common saying that in the imagination of every lover the loved one is a person of great beauty.

The ancient Greeks, however, believed, according to Westermarck (1894), that beauty was the cause rather than the result of love. Thus, they conceived of Eros as an extremely handsome young man and Aphrodite as the goddess of beauty as well as of love. That beauty is good per se was well expressed by Robert Browning in *Fra Lippo Lippi* when he said: "If you get simple beauty and nought else,/you get about the best thing God invents."

Many, on the other hand, have pointed out that beauty per se does not necessarily give pleasure, that beauty is not, as Keats put it, "a joy for ever," that beauty is something beyond and more than form. Socrates stressed the fact that "[human] beauty is a short-lived reign." In a similar vein, Sappho, the Greek poetess, stated that "What is beautiful is good and who is good will soon be beautiful." The contemporary actress Eva Gabor emphasized a similar point in this comment: "I believe that women should make themselves as attractive as possible. But they don't need artificial help, because real beauty and so-called sex appeal come from within." Paul Popenoe, renowned family counselor, stated that "The modern girl is too *vogue* on the outside and too *vague* on the inside. That's the glamour girl: pretty as a picture—overexposed and underdeveloped." Washington Irving restated the point in this way: "After all it is the divinity *within* which makes the divinity *without;* and I have been more fascinated by a woman of talent and intelligence, though deficient in personal charms,

216

than I have by the most regular beauty." Stendhal, seemingly fearful of a kind of Pygmalionism, therefore, in his *De l'Amour* expressed the sexological axiom that "It is *passion* which we demand; beauty only furnishes *probabilities.*"

Beauty Culture

In spite of warnings concerning the ephemeral nature of physical beauty, beauty culture, the art of modifying personal appearance in order to render a person more attractive, more beautiful, and more desirable, is, as *Time* magazine recently put it, "The industry without a recession." The American people spent an estimated $4 *billion* on beauty aids and services in 1957. About 95 per cent of all women over the age of twelve now use at least one of the products made by America's beauty industry. But, *Time* added: "To their credit, more and more women are realizing that beauty is more than skin deep. They want healthy, well-formed bodies and new personalities to go with their made-up faces. Thus the growth of the cosmetics industry is being matched by the growth of reducing salons, gyms and their fellow travelers, the charm schools."

Although modern beauty culture is an art, it also has a broad basis in science and technology because it demands knowledge of what the human body is capable of in the way of adaptation and of how much it can endure without harm. It has been repeatedly pointed out that the temptation to use dangerous chemicals and physical agents without medical supervision is ever present. In medieval times, for example, belladonna was used in eye washes; today, dangerous estrogens are being applied as bust developers.

In broader perspective, beauty culture is closely connected with the fields of hygiene and rehabilitation. Thus, the restoration of a normal appearance after illness or injury involves the correction of constitutional disorders by the physician and physiotherapist, the removal of skin blemishes by the dermatologist, the correction of facial and body disfigurements by plastic and orthopedic surgery, and the fitting of dentures and the correction of malocclusion by the dentist. To this list of beauty technologists should be added psychia-

trists, clinical psychologists, psychoanalysts, and counselors who aid the "social-psychologically ugly" in restoring or developing "social-psychological beauty."

Beauty, it seems, is no simple matter. It is, in fact, a complex thing involving every aspect of human nature.

Standards of beauty are, for the most part, culturally rather than biologically determined, each particular culture developing its own special set of values. Yet Finck (1887) and Havelock Ellis (1936), as well as others, point out that there are some universal standards of beauty. Health is almost universally regarded as a prime requisite of beauty. Another universal criterion is youth—beauty and youth often being inextricably related. In the history of beauty culture, cosmetics, grooming, and dress have often been used to make the person appear youthful, and, for that reason, more beautiful.

A distinction should be made at this point, in order to avoid confusion later, between natural and artificial beauty. *Natural* beauty consists of those pleasing aspects of a person based on the biologically and social-psychologically unique characteristics that person possesses, such as naturally lustrous hair, well-formed body parts, and a pleasant smile that comes from within. On the other hand, *artificial* beauty is comprised of those pleasing aspects of a person that are *not* biologically determined or inherent and which are social-psychologically pretentious, such as dentures, "falsies," and a contrived smile.

Modern beauty is a complex admixture of both natural and unnatural beauty, although the beauty industries largely emphasize the latter type of beauty.

We can, then, summarize our attempt to define beauty by saying that it is that elusive phenomenon which some persons have by virture of the fact that they possess qualities, natural and/or artificial, that are highly valued by the particular culture in which they live and sometimes in all or almost all cultures. Beauty is associated with sexual attractiveness, since health and youth are universally linked with both sex and human beauty. But each culture and each person develops particular conceptions of beauty, some of which have as criteria both universal and particular elements, some natural and some unnatural. The rest of this paper will be devoted to clarifying and interpreting the meaning of this point.

Natural Beauty

Beauty in Men

We have defined natural beauty as those pleasing aspects of a person based on the biologically and social-psychologically unique characteristics of that person. In a general way, Westermarck has emphasized the point that "to be really handsome a person must approach the ideal type of his or her sex. The male organism is remarkable for the development of the muscular system, the female for that of fatty elements; and conspicuous muscles are everywhere considered to improve the appearance of a man, rounded forms that of a woman." Thus, among Europeans high-built and broad shoulders are regarded as constituting an ideal of manly beauty. Malinowski (1932) has stated that among the Trobriand Islanders "A slim, straight, tall body is much admired in a man."

Among the English during the late Middle Ages, according to Curry (1916), a man was admired who had "great stature, enormous strength, long sinewy arms, broad square breast and shoulders, together with a small waist and retreating stomach. His legs are long, with thighs thick and strong; and in general appearance he is more like a giant than a mere knight . . . his eyes are generally blue in color, with the fierce, proud glance of a falcon. . . ."

Havelock Ellis believed that most women admire a man's strength rather than his beauty. As he stated in *Studies in the Psychology of Sex*: "All those qualities which the woman desires to see emphasized in the man are the precise opposite of the qualities which the man desires to see emphasized in the woman. The man must be strong, vigorous, energetic, hairy, even rough, to stir the primitive instincts of the woman's nature; the woman who satisfies this man must be smooth, rounded, and gentle . . . the choice of the man by the woman . . . has to be recognized in the shape of a regard for strength and vigor. This is not purely a visual character but a tactile pressure character translated into visual terms."

George Eliot, in her novel *The Mill on the Floss,* anticipated Havelock Ellis' findings by suggesting that "There is something strangely winning to most women in that offer of the firm arm; the help is not wanted physically at the moment, but the sense of help—the presence of strength is outside them and yet theirs—meets a continual want of the imagination."

Strength and health rather than handsome features seem to be the criteria for judging male beauty. With strength and health usually goes a well-developed musculature. Woman demand that men they admire also have good character, that they have courage, integrity, etc. Thus, male beauty, contrary to Eric Newton's concept, is not that which is beautiful because it *is* but because of what it does. Male beauty or handsomeness must be translated into function. How strong is this man? How courageous? In the Western world there is a strong physical-culture movement among men that is manifested in the so-called Mr. America, Mr. Europe, and Mr. Universe contests. These contests include weight-lifting competitions to see who is the strongest, and competitive posing for "physique" and "most muscular" awards. From the photos of recent contest winners found in *Strength and Health* (a physical-fitness magazine) it is quite obvious that these men combine both strength and health—two important requirements for masculine beauty.

But women, as was already pointed out, demand that masculine beauty include more than strength and health, they demand that men have quality, good character, that they are human beings with understanding and dignity.

Consequently, although many women enjoyed looking at the physique of the movie industry's long-time Tarzan, Johnny Weismuller, they often made fun of the boorish character he was forced to portray on the screen. On the other hand, many maidens have swooned for the shadowy figures but scintillating personalities of Frank Sinatra and Gregory Peck.

Beauty in Women

Dr. Anna M. Galbraith, in her book *Personal Hygiene and Physical Training for Women,* indicated that the ideal measurements of the woman are as follows:

Height	5 feet 5 inches
Weight	138 pounds
Bust	34 inches
Waist	29 inches
Hips	40 inches

These measurements differ decidedly from the average measurements of the Miss Americas from 1921 to 1956. They were as follows:

Height	5 feet 6½ inches
Weight	124 pounds
Bust	34½ inches
Waist	24½ inches
Hips	35 inches

Thus, America's Miss Americas were significantly thinner than Dr. Galbraith's ideal healthy woman.

Likewise, the ideal women of the eugenics experts and of the average American are understandably quite different. Cuber (1955) points this out very clearly when he compares geneticist Scheinfeld's views with that of the average American's views on what constitutes a beautiful woman. Eugenically, physical beauty in the classical Greek sense is unimportant, but strong features, high intelligence, seriousness, sturdy figure, ample waist, broad hips, sturdy wrists, strong hands, solid, sturdy limbs and ankles, and good-sized feet are important. Culturally and esthetically, classical Greek beauty is most important, as well as delicate features, the absence of "deep" intellect, vivaciousness, a slim figure, tiny waist, small hips, dainty hands and wrists, slender, soft, tapering limbs, and slim ankles and tiny feet.

According to Chaucer, as cited by Havelock Ellis, the beautiful woman is one endowed "with buttocks broad and breasts round and high"; that is to say, she is a woman equipped to give birth to and nurse children. Good-sized buttocks and breasts, because they represent aptitude for the two essential acts of motherhood—childbirth and lactation—must necessarily, Ellis believed, be regarded as beautiful among all peoples in all stages of cultural development. A comparative approach to conceptions of beauty reveal, however, that Ellis' assumption is not generally supported by the facts.

Havelock Ellis has stated that "a somewhat greater degree of fatness may be regarded as a feminine secondary character. This admiration is specially marked among several of the black peoples of Africa, and here to become a beauty a woman must, by drinking enormous quantities of milk, seek to become very fat."

Finck asks the age-old question: is a perfect man or perfect woman the more beautiful form? His answer is that: "The universality of curvature as a form of beautiful objects throughout nature and art is of importance in helping us to determine the question which is the more beautiful form—an Apollo or a Venus? A Venus, no doubt . . . in Beauty proper—in the roundness and delicacy of contours, in the smoothness of complexion and its subtle gradations of colour, in the symmetrical roundness and lustrous expressiveness of the eyes—the feminine type is pre-eminent."

It was, perhaps, Rubens' ability to capture these aspects of feminine beauty that placed his nudes among the treasured art works in the world. The Ford and Beach study findings (1951) generally agree with Rubens' conception of female beauty, for the majority of societies whose preferences on body build are recorded feel that a plump woman is sexually more attractive than a thin one. They also found that the Chuckchee, Hidatsa, Pukapukans, and Thonga believe that a beautiful woman, in addition to being plump, should be relatively tall and well built. Most of the societies in their sample admired a broad pelvis and wide hips.

BUTTOCKS

With regard to gluteal and hip development, Ellis says: "The special characteristics of the feminine hips and buttocks become conspicuous in walking. . . . The vibratory movement naturally produced by walking and sometimes artificially heightened thus becomes a trait of sexual beauty." Schapera (1940), in his study of the African Kgatla people, found that they prized large, firm buttocks: "The buttocks, especially, have a powerful erotic appeal, and evoke many compliments, while much of the love play before coitus consists in caressing them. Girls with slim backsides are seldom considered attractive; they are disparagingly said to have 'the bodies of boys.'"

BREASTS

The breasts are also very important sources of sexual beauty. According to Reidman (1956), there are four main types of breasts: conic, discoid, hemispheric, and elongated. In Hawaii and New Zealand the small conical breast predominates, while the breasts of the American Indian woman generally are melon-shaped, elongated, and drooping. Chinese women tend to be flat-chested, and the Viennese are noted for their hemispheric type of breast. The tall blond peoples of northern Europe are known best for the discoid or bowl-shaped type of breast in which the base is longer than the sides.

Curry states that in the late Middle Ages beautiful breasts were described as follows: "The breast of a beautiful woman should be rather broad, and as white as snow or as clear as crystal. The breasts must be small, round as a pear or as an apple of paradise, and as soft as silk to the touch. Large breasts and long, hanging breasts are considered ugly."

The Singhalese like firm, conical breasts "like the yellow cocoa-nut." Westermarck tells us that: "The Kafirs and Hottentots are charmed by their women's long and pendant breasts, which, in certain tribes, assume such monstrous dimensions, that the usual way of giving suck, when the child is carried on the back, is by throwing the breast over the shoulder." However, among the Trobriand Islanders, firm, well-developed breasts are admired in women, according to Malinowski.

Ford and Beach, in their comparative study of sexual behavior in 185 societies, found that the Azande and Ganda peoples preferred long and pendulous breasts; that large breasts were admired among the Alorese, Apache, Hopi, Kurtatchi, Lesu, Siriono, Thonga, Trukese, and Wogeo; while the Manus and Masai believed that upright, hemispherical breasts were most beautiful. It would seem that among Americans, large, upright, hemispherical breasts are those most highly prized, at least judging from the figures of reigning Hollywood beauties.

Albert Ellis (1954) rightly points out that the breast cult in our society might be an indication of what Philip Wylie called momism and what many psychotherapists call infantilism: "The modern male's passion for large-breasted women is monotonously played up in hundreds of magazine and newspaper advertisements for brassieres, falsies, sweaters, bust creams, books, exercisers, and scores of other apparatuses and techniques."

THE FACE

The face has generally figured significantly as a focus of erotic interest. Curry states that medieval people regarded lips to be beautiful that were "sweet, gracious, small and laughing, soft and pleasant to kiss, and in color red or ruddy." Malinowski found that among the Trobriand Islanders erotic interest was focused on the head and face and that "The eyes . . . are to the natives gateways of erotic desire; they are also, in themselves, a center of erotic interest. Biting off the eyelashes, the custom of *mitakuku* as it is called, plays an important part in love-making."

THE SKIN

Joyce and Thomas (1942) tell us that many peoples pay particular attention to enhancing the natural beauty of the skin. Thus, Polynesian women keep their skin beautiful by frequent bathing in fresh water, together with subsequent oiling and shampooing; this makes their skin peculiarly soft and supple, with a sheen like that of rich satin. Curry states that during the Middle Ages people admired a skin that rivaled "the finest silk in softness." Schapera noted that to the Kgatla women "the most important thing was to wash the genitals everyday, 'to prevent them from stinking of sweat,' and so putting off possible suitors." Kgatla women also made their skin more soft and attractive by smearing on ointments. And although Kgatla men showed less interest in facial beauty than in bodily proportions they liked women with "refined oval features, shapely ears, large eyes, slender nose, and relatively thin lips."

THE BEAUTY OF PREGNANT WOMEN

There is, Havelock Ellis noted, "the tendency to regard the pregnant woman as the most beautiful . . . since motherhood is the final aim of woman, and a woman reaches her full flowering period in pregnancy, she ought to be most beautiful when pregnant . . . for with the onset of pregnancy metabolism is heightened, the tissues become active, the tone of the skin softer and brighter, the breasts firmer, so that the charm of fullest bloom is increased."

HEALTH AND BEAUTY

In essence, then, female beauty—even more than male beauty—is the result of health. To most peoples of the world deformity and disease, old age and its accompanying defects rob a person of erotic appeal. Finck, in his classic *Romantic Love and Personal Beauty*, stresses the relationship between health and beauty when he says that: "Inasmuch as Personal Beauty is the flower and symbol of perfect Health, it might be shown, by following out this argument, that *ugliness is a sin, and man's first duty the cultivation of beauty*."

According to Schopenhauer, cited in Finck, "The most important attribute of Beauty, in the lover's eye, is youth. . . . Health ranks next in importance. . . . A fine framework or skeleton is the third desideratum. . . . A certain plumpness or fullness of flesh is the next thing considered in sexual selection. . . . Excessive leanness is repulsive, and so is excessive stoutness. . . . Facial beauty ranks last."

THE MEDIEVAL
CONCEPTION OF FEMININE BEAUTY

Curry noted that to Western man during the Middle Ages, "the type of feminine beauty praised by the poets in the catalogues of charm is, without an exception, a blonde, whose hair is golden or like gold wire, eyes sparkling bright and light blue in color, cheeks lily-white or rose-red, white evenly set teeth, long, snow-white arms, and white hands with long slender fingers. Her figure is small, well-rounded, slender and graceful, with a small willowy waist as a prime standard of excellence. The skin is everywhere of dazzling whiteness, rivaling the finest silk in softness; and the lower limbs are well-formed and white as milk, with small white and shapely feet." This description is almost identical with the description given by Cuber of the *modern* American conception of

feminine beauty and with the Miss America ideal.

THE SIRIONO
CONCEPTION OF BEAUTY

The Siriono of Eastern Bolivia have an extremely different conception of feminine beauty, for their conception, in contrast to the medieval and modern American conceptions, is based on the woman's sexual and procreative functions. Holmberg (1946) writes: "Besides being young, a desirable sex partner should also be fat. She should have big hips, good sized but firm breasts, and a deposit of fat on her sexual organs. Fat women are referred to by the men with obvious pride as *eréN ekida* (fat vulva) and are thought to be much more satisfying sexually than thin women, who are summarily dismissed as being *ikaNgi* (bony). In fact, so desirable is corpulence as a sexual trait that I have frequently heard men make up songs about the merits of a fat vulva. . . . In addition to the criteria already mentioned, certain other physical signs of erotic beauty are recognized. A tall person is preferred to a short one; facial features should be regular; eyes should be large. Little attention is paid to the ears, the nose, or the lips, unless they are obviously deformed. Body hair is an undesirable trait and is therefore depilated, although a certain amount of pubic hair is believed to add zest to intercourse. A woman's vulva should be small and fat, while a man's penis should be as large as possible."

THE HINDU CONCEPTION OF BEAUTY

Havelock Ellis cites the Hindu conception of femininity as a subtle combination of the erotic and platonic: "Her face is pleasing as the full moon; her body, well clothed with flesh, is as soft as the Shiras or mustard flower; her skin is fine, tender, and fair as the yellow lotus, never dark colored. Her eyes are bright and beautiful as the orbs of the fawn, well cut, and with reddish corners. Her bosom is hard, full, and high; she has a good neck; her nose is straight and lovely; and three folds or wrinkles cross her middle—about the umbilical region. Her vulva resembles the opening lotus bud, and her love-seed is perfumed like the lily that has newly burst. She walks with flamingo-like gait, and her voice is low and as musical as the note of the Kokila bird."

Space does not permit descriptions of what other peoples regard as the feminine ideal. Interested readers should consult Joyce and Thomas' comprehensive, illustrated work, *Women of All Nations.*

In summary, conceptions of feminine beauty, although culturally determined and subject to considerable differences due to differential evaluations learned in various societies, have much in common. All societies usually conceive of beauty as closely related to *youth* and to *health* and generally to specific secondary sexual characteristics suggestive of woman's maternal role: well-developed breasts, buttocks, and hips. An important generalization concerning male and female beauty is that in most societies the physical beauty of the female receives more explicit attention than does that of the male. The male's physical appearance, as long as he is fairly healthy, is less important to a female than his skills, strength, courage, and prestige.

Artificial Beauty

Artificial Beauty in Men

Men, on the whole, are not as concerned with their own physical beauty as are women for the simple reason that, as a means of sexual attraction, a man's character, if he is physically healthy, is more important to a woman than his musculature and esthetic features. But to men, the physical beauty of a woman is often more significant than her character, or, at least equally so. Thus, in studies by Judson T. Landis (1958) and others, more than 60 per cent of the men said that, all other factors being satisfactory, they would *not* marry a woman decidedly not good looking, whereas only a little more than 20 per cent of the women stated that they would not marry a man decidedly not good looking—a statistically and social-psychologically significant difference.

THE POULAINE AND THE CODPIECE

Although the clothing of women is often used to enhance their sexual attractiveness, the clothing of men, particularly in Western civilization, seems less so designed. The writer knows of only two significant exceptions. During the Middle Ages many men wore a long shoe known as the *poulaine,* which was in the shape of a phallus and for a long time aroused considerable indignation. The other example was the *codpiece,* popular during the Tudor period (about 1550 A.D.). The codpiece was a bulging portion of the trousers containing the genitals, which was embellished by padding in such a way as to simulate a perpetual erection. To attract attention to their codpieces the men would have them made in attractive colors and sometimes decorate them with bright ribbons and even with gold and jewels.

About the only masculine characteristic that the clothes of men emphasize today in the Western world is the breadth of the shoulders, which is done by the use of shoulder pads in suits, jackets, coats, and some sport shirts. Even this emphasis has been lessened in recent fashion.

Of course, "elevator shoes," shoes that give a man extra height, could be considered as enhancing natural beauty, for tall men are generally preferred to shorter ones.

However, it is in the realm of cosmetics and grooming that modern men have most often enhanced natural beauty in an artificial way. Since a good crop of hair is often associated with youth and vigor, the toupee is very popular, particularly among men in the public eye. Only President Eisenhower and Yul Brynner have lent new dignity to bald-headed men in recent years.

Dentures, plastic surgery (especially on nose and ears), and girdles also help to make men look more youthful and sexually attractive.

SOME HAZARDS OF MEN'S CLOTHING

Some male dress habits are said to be responsible for damaging certain aspects of masculinity. Studies on higher apes have shown, for example, that baldness can be experimentally produced by placing tight bands around the neck and forehead, and it is believed that the tendency for men in the Western world to wear tight collars, neckties, and hats increases their chances of becoming bald. The New York

Times has reported that research in Sweden indicates that the wearing of trousers may be more dangerous to future generations than the fallout from atomic and hydrogen bombs. The researchers believe that the excessive heating of the testicles caused by wearing tight shorts, athletic supporters, oversnug swim trunks, and the like has injurious effects upon spermatogenes. They suggest that men should wear skirts, kilts, a toga, or even trousers fitted with a codpiece. If further research confirms the Swedish report, perhaps there will be, in the not too distant future, a revolution in men's clothing.

Primitive peoples have done much more than civilized nations in providing men with artificial beauty. Nicobarese men would not attempt to make sexual advances until they have blackened their teeth, it is reported by Man (1886). Powell (1883), in his study of the men of New Britain, found a similar custom. Weeks (1913) reported that Boloki men, in order to increase their masculinity and attractiveness, chisel the upper incisors to V-shaped points.

Male Eskimos all along the coast of the Mackenzie River a century ago used to perforate the septum of the nose at the time of puberty and insert as an ornament a small piece of ivory about 3 inches long, according to Armstrong (1857).

Among peoples dwelling in the tropical rain forests, men usually wear some sort of pubic covering, a suspensory or supporter. Such conspicuous coverings as those of gleaming shells, bark, gourds, hide, grass, or cloth tend to attract attention to the genital area rather than hide it.

Tattooing is an art of body adornment highly developed in Japan and Polynesia. Among men of the lower classes in American society it serves as symbol of masculinity and toughness. In some cultures, cicatrization, or scarification, is held to be absolutely necessary to manhood. And so important are these scars as symbols of manhood that many men voluntarily repeat the operations to keep the scars large and fresh. Hoebel (1949) reports that among German fraternity students and university men dueling scars are given great honor. These scars are said to have great sex appeal, so much so that a dueling wound that does not fester and leave a noticeable scar is considered useless.

Artificial Beauty in Women

Among the Chinese, small feet are considered a woman's chief attraction and so the feet of girls are pressed from early childhood. Steatopygy, excessive development of fat on the buttocks, is common and admired among the Hottentots. The Baganda like pendulous breasts so much that their young women tie them down in order to hasten the condition.

Among some people the primary sexual parts of the female body are of erotic interest. Havelock Ellis cites reports that certain primitive West Africans elongate the labia and clitoris artificially by pulling them and attaching small weights to them. According to Ford and Beach, elongated labia majora are highly valued among the Dahomeans, Kusaians, Marquesans, Nama, Ponapeans, Thonga, Trukese, and Venda; and a large clitoris is of erotic interest among the Easter Islanders.

Women among the Maori are considered beautiful if they have received certain marks or tattooings, according to Robley (1896). And Seligmann (1910) reports that Koita and Motu girls have the region from the navel to the breasts, extending laterally to the mid-axillary lines, tattooed. Seligmann adds that Tubetube girls tattoo their faces before puberty and after puberty their chest, belly, and other parts.

Robley notes that the Maori believe that women should have full, *blue* lips and that they look upon red lips as a disfigurement. Coon (1949) states that "All primitive peoples known use some kind of body paint, usually made of clay and ochre mixed with fat. Lumps of this have been found in caves in association with Neanderthal man, who lived over 50,000 years ago. It was with 'lipsticks' of this kind that Cro-Magnon men painted animals on the walls of caves in France and Spain."

So it is that women have from the earliest times been concerned about making themselves attractive by using paint and powder, cutting their hair, cramping their chests, crushing their feet, scarring and tattooing and even mutilating their bodies, wearing bustles, corsets, brassieres, having the nose remodeled and teeth straightened, etc., all in order to live up to what they believed was their society's idea of what constituted the type of beauty that attracted men and, perhaps, made other women envious.

Albert Ellis, in his *American Sexual Tragedy*, has analyzed the psychology of dress among American women. He concludes that fashion decrees that American women *must* be dressed "romantically, fashionably, distinctively, extensively, sex-enticingly, and properly." Thus, he goes on, "a girl carefully chooses her dresses and suits so that they make her appear shorter, taller, thinner, fatter, bigger-breasted, smaller-breasted, or something other than she actually is. Fictionalization thus becomes one of the main purposes of clothes selection."

Laver (1938), in this connection, makes a trenchant point concerning women's fashion and sex: "The female body consists of a series of sterilized zones which are exposed by a fashion which is just going out and an erogenous zone, which will be the point of interest for the fashion which is just coming in. This erogenous zone is always shifting, and it is the business of fashion to pursue it, without ever catching it up. It is obvious that if you do catch it up you are immediately arrested for indecent exposure. If you almost catch it up you are celebrated as a leader of fashion."

Concerning clothes of the future, Barnes (1929) has cited this interesting comment: "The world will be more comfortable and more decent when we progress to the point when both men and women can comfortably go to work in bathing-suits—with pockets." Albert Ellis seems to concur: "We expect the average girl not merely to look like a beauty contest winner but to dress like a duchess. This hardly minimizes her life burdens, nor best predisposes her to a non-anxious, emotionally stable existence."

It is only at the beach, on picnics, and at home, in the Western world and in America in particular, that people tend to wear the casual, comfortable clothes that bring out their natural beauty. Natural beauty will not manifest itself in the workaday world until those casual—and incidentally more hygienic—clothes are also worn there. Until that time, women, particu-

larly in the Western world, are likely to augment the pretentiousness and "fictionalization," that Albert Ellis sees in contemporary behavior.

Social-Psychological Aspects of Beauty

The most significant aspects of beauty, as related to sex behavior, are neither natural nor associated with artificial beauty created by cosmetics, grooming, or clothes, but are rather those associated with such social-psychological factors as status, familiarity, and conceptions of goodness.

Curry points out that: "It is a peculiarity of the medieval mind to think of beauty as a characteristic of the good and to look upon ugliness as the distinguishing trait of the evil." It is quite apparent that this idea is still very much with us. From the earliest literature and folklore, heroes and heroines have generally been portrayed as handsome and beautiful persons. Likewise, evil men and women have generally been portrayed as ugly, deformed, diseased persons. Through the centuries Christ, who was supposed to have been the epitome of goodness, has almost always been portrayed as a handsome person. Evil devils and witches have always been portrayed as extremely ugly.

This idea that the good are beautiful and the evil are ugly is essentially a sound one. Thus, even the most perfectly beautiful person, in natural or artificial terms, is often looked upon as ugly if he is evil. And an ugly person who is good gives us the feeling that he is beautiful. We have defined beauty as that certain something that pleases us. Good persons are pleasing and hence beautiful, whereas evil persons do not please us, and are thus ugly. Consequently, Eleanor Roosevelt has been described by people who know her as one of the most beautiful women in the world because of her altruism, her sincerity, and her genuine love of mankind. Abraham Lincoln, homely by standards of physical beauty, was regarded as handsome because of the kind of person he was. Numerous examples of this kind could be given.

Previous familiarity is another significant social-psychological factor in sexual behavior related to beauty. If two females of relatively equal physical beauty are candidates as sexual partners for a particular male, Ford and Beach report that in most societies the male will select the female with whom he is familiar, providing his previous association with her has been a pleasant one. Thus, while the exotic is often the spice of the erotic, the familiar acquaintance is generally preferred to the stranger. Xenophobia rears its ugly head in sexual relations as well as other human relations.

This fact is closely related to status in many societies. Sexual partners are largely determined on the basis of status relationships between potential partners. The incest taboo, relative both to biolological and to affinal relationships, defines a host of ineligible partners. Age, social class, religious affiliation, and many other factors also operate in sexual selection. Higher-status persons often are more sexually attractive than persons of lower status, because what is pleasing is frequently so because it is highly valued. Waller (1937), in his famous article on "the rating and dating complex" in American culture, showed how the most popular, most handsome, or most beautiful persons were sexually the most attractive to college students.

The important relationship between love and beauty has been expressed movingly by Rodin, who said:

I can only grasp the beauty of the soul by the beauty of the body, but some day one will come who will explain what I only catch a glimpse of and will declare how the whole earth is beautiful, and all human beings beautiful. I have never been able to say this in sculpture so well as I wish and as I feel it affirmed within me. For poets Beauty has always been some particular landscape, some particular woman; but it should be all women, all landscapes. A Negro or a Mongol has his beauty, however remote from ours, and it must be the same with their characters. There is no ugliness. When I was young I made that mistake, as others do; I could not undertake a woman's bust unless I thought her pretty, according to my particular idea of beauty; today I should do a bust of any woman, and it would be just as beautiful. And however ugly a woman may look, when she is with her lover she becomes beautiful; there is beauty in her character, in her passions, and beauty exists as soon as character or passion becomes visible, for the body

is a casting on which passions are imprinted. And even without that, there is always the blood that flows in the veins and the air that fills the lungs.

For the average person beauty is what is pleasing esthetically and emotionally to that *particular* person. He is the only judge of what is beautiful to him. However, to the emotionally gifted Rodin there was no particular kind of beauty, no ugliness; to Rodin all nature was beautiful.

From a mental-hygiene point of view Rodin's conception of beauty is a most healthy one, for it removes the invidious and shallow criteria by which beauty and sexual attractiveness are judged in many societies. Beauty without talent and intelligence is an empty kind of human beauty. It is interesting that the more recent candidates for "Miss America" were somewhat *less* beautiful in a physical sense but more talented, more intelligent, and of greater depth than previous contest winners. In the various male beauty contests, Mr. America contests, etc., winners are still selected on the sole basis of strength and physique, paying little attention to other more important characteristics of beauty. America generally has manifested an immature view of beauty.

Summary and Conclusions

Human beauty is most difficult to define and evaluate, since its attributes may be traced to two main sources, both of which may be internally inconsistent and each of which tends to be in conflict with the other. The first and perhaps primary source is biosocial. As indicated by the comparisons cited in this article, although virtually all peoples of the past and present world seem to accept as beautiful those human characteristics which are closely related to youth and health, ideals of beauty differ considerably from culture to culture. And, as might be expected, the vast majority of individuals in any given community are significantly influenced by the socially inculcated ideals of their region: so that both the upper and lower limits of what they accept as being "beautiful" in members of the other sex are appreciably determined by the means of social control and indoctrination to which they are subjected. To a considerable degree, therefore, we may say that human beauty is that elusive phenomenon that some persons have by virtue of the fact that they possess natural or artificially acquired traits that happen to be highly valued by the culture in which they live.

At the same time, there is a distinctly individual and subjective source of beauty that counterpoints the usual culturally imbibed prejudice. Every human being is a biologically unique person—with his or her own particular taste buds, optic nerves, sense of smell, and other physical receptors. And every man or woman (even one who is a member of a set of identical twins) has his or her own set of life experiences, which are enormously influential in determining final tastes and preferences. These biological and experiential uniquenesses interact with and modify the more uniform biosocial influences which are brought to bear on all human beings residing within a given culture; and, in their turn, the culturally imbibed prejudices interact with and modify the more individualized somatic and experiential taste-producing tendencies which all people inherit or acquire.

The net result of these conflicting and interacting influences on what modes of beauty a given person will favor is bound to be somewhat, though never entirely, different in each individual case. Statistically speaking, it may easily be predicted that *most* members of one sex in a certain region will find a certain member of the other sex either beautiful or ugly. But it can rarely be predicted, except on the basis of an intimate personal knowledge of his or her past and present, how *a particular* person will rate the beauty of another male or female.

It would appear from the evidence surveyed in this article that males, in most regions of the world, tend to place too great an emphasis on the more physical or shallow aspects of female beauty. It is quite probable that if these males judged women the same way that women tend to judge male beauty—that is, primarily in terms of strength of character rather than in terms of esthetics—this might be a better and happier world. For such a standard of beauty would help counteract some of the crippling feelings of inferiority that many admirable persons now experience because they see themselves (as others frequently view them) as esthetically ugly. It is unfortunate that many members of both sexes now stand accepted or condemned by a standard of beauty over which they have relatively little control and which almost inevitably foredooms them as they grow chronologically older.

References

"Aesthetics." In *Encyclopaedia Britannica.* Chicago: Encyclopaedia Britannica, Inc., 1953, Vol. I, p. 267.

Armstrong, Alexander, *Personal Narrative of the Discovery of the Northwest Passage.* London, 1857.

Barnes, Harry Elmer, "Sex in Education." In V. F. Calverton and S. D. Schmalhausen (eds.), *Sex in Civilization.* New York: Macaulay, 1929.

"Beauty Culture." In *Encyclopaedia Britannica.* Chicago: Encyclopaedia Britannica, Inc., 1953, Vol. III, p. 281.

Beigel, Hugo G., "Sex and Human Beauty." *J. Aesthet.* 12; 83-92, 1953.

Brophy, J., *The Human Face.* New Jersey: Prentice-Hall, 1946.

Cladel, Judith, *Auguste Rodin.* Paris: 1903.

Coon, Carleton S., *A Reader in General Anthropology.* New York: Henry Holt & Co., 1949.

Cuber, John F., *Sociology* (3rd ed.). New York: Appleton-Century-Crofts, 1955, p. 187.

Curry, Walter C., *The Middle English Ideal of Personal Beauty.* Baltimore: J. H. Furst, 1916.

Ellis, Albert, *The Folklore of Sex.* New York: Boni, 1951.

Ellis, Albert, *The American Sexual Tragedy.* New York: Twayne Pub., 1954.

Ellis, Havelock, *Studies in the Psychology of Sex.* New York: Random House, 1936, Vol. II, Part I, pp. 136-212.

Finck, Henry T., *Romantic Love and Personal Beauty.* New York: The Macmillan Co., 1887, Vol. II.

Flügel, J. C., *The Psychology of Clothes.* London: Hogarth Press, 1950.

Ford, Clellan S., and Beach, Frank A., *Patterns of Sexual Behavior.* New York: Harper & Brothers, 1951.

Frumkin, Robert M., "Visual Aphrodisiacs." *Sexology* 20; 481-483, 1954.

Frumkin, Robert M., "Intimate History of Clothing." *Sexology* 23; 244-250, 1956.

Frumkin, R. M., *Preferences for Traditional and Modern Painting: An Empirical Study.* Columbus, Ohio: Ohio State University, Ph.D. Dissertation, 1961.

"Hazard of Men's Clothing." New York *Times,* December 29, 1957.

Hoebel, Adamson E., *Man in the Primitive World.* New York: McGraw-Hill Book Co., 1949, Chap. 11.

Holmberg, A. R., *The Siriono.* New Haven: unpublished Ph.D. thesis, Yale University, 1946.

Hume, David, *Essays: Moral, Political, and Literary* (ed. by T. H. Green and T. H. Grose). London: 1875, Vol. I.

Joyce, T. Athol, and Thomas, N. W. (eds.), *Women of All Nations*. New York: Metro Publications, 1942.

Landis, Judson T., and Landis, Mary G., *Building a Successful Marriage* (3rd ed.). Englewood Cliffs, N. J.: Prentice-Hall, Inc., 1958, p. 97, Table 6.

Laver, James, *Taste and Fashion*. New York: Dodd, Mead & Co., 1938.

Malinowski, Bronislaw, *The Sexual Life of Savages in Northwestern Melanesia* (3rd ed.). London: Routledge and Kegan Paul, 1932.

Man, E. H., "A Brief Account of the Nicobar Islanders." *J. Roy. Anthrop. Inst.* (London) 15; 441, 1886.

Miss America Pageant. Atlantic City, Miss America Pageant, 1956.

"Modern Living: the Pink Jungle." *Time 71;* 86-90, June 16, 1958.

Newton, Eric, *The Meaning of Beauty*. New York: McGraw-Hill Book Co., 1950.

Powell, Willfred, *Wanderings in a Wild Country*. London: 1883.

"Qualities." In *Encyclopaedia Britannica*. Chicago: Encyclopaedia Britannica, Inc., 1953, Vol. XVIII, p. 812.

Riedman, Sarah R., "The Female Breast." *Sexology* 23; 226-231, 1956.

Robley, H. G., *Moko: Maori Tattooing*. London: 1896.

Seligmann, C. G., *The Melanesians of British New Guinea*. London: 1910.

Schapera, I., *Married Life in an African Tribe*. London: Faber and Faber, 1940.

Simmel, Georg, "Fashion." *Am. J. Sociol.* 62; 541-558, 1957.

Waller, Willard, "The Rating and Dating Complex." *Am. Sociol. Rev. 2;* 727-734, 1937.

Wax, Murray, "Themes in Cosmetics and Grooming." *Am. J. Sociol.* 62; 588-593, 1957.

Weeks, John H., *Among Congo Cannibals*. London: 1913.

Westermarck, Edward A., *The History of Marriage* (2nd ed.). New York: The Macmillan Co., 1894, Chap. XII, pp. 253-277.

ROBERT M. FRUMKIN

Catholicism and Sex

SEX is viewed by Catholicism, as it perceives all things, from a total and integral point of view. Accordingly, sex is seen in its supernatural and natural aspects, and in its psychological and spiritual aspects. Every "error" relating to sex it believes due to a viewpoint less than total and integral—one that tends to take sex out of its full context. This viewpoint of Catholicism is not an arbitrary one; on the contrary, it is predicated upon a set of principles, laws, and facts garnered from theology, philosophy, and from empirical-clinical findings.

Theological Aspects

Dogma

Through its dogma (and derivatives of dogma) as learned from revelation, tradition, and the teachings of the Church, sex appears as one of the phenomena created from the beginning of the human race. Genesis relates that when God created the human race He established two sexes. "Man and woman He created them" implies that sex is not just a physical variance but relates to the total natures of men and women—their "manliness" and "womanliness." This, in turn, implies, along with an essential equality of both sexes, the existence of psychological and physiological differences that serve as means to their respective roles of paternity and maternity. The sexes, as so created, were amongst those creatures which, on the seventh day, God called "good."

Accordingly, the sex act in original integrity was good, noble, dignified; even since the Fall in the Garden of Eden, sex when rightly used has been considered a noble act. It is consid-

ered an act of the virtue of justice because it accords to one's spouse his or her rights of the marriage contract; an act of the virtue of charity since the sex act is an expression and intensification of love and also since it reduces the dangers of incontinency in one's spouse; an act of the virtue of chastity for this virtue consists in the right and proper use of sex; and an act of the virtue of religion (*Summa Theologica,* Vol. III, Supp. q. 41, art. 4) since its proper use redounds to the praise of God and gives birth to worshippers of God, both in this world and in the next.

For this reason, Catholicism's view of sex has nothing in common with the Puritanical attitudes so widespread in our culture at one time. Before the Fall, although naked, Adam and Eve had no sense of shame. This was because their sensual appetites were subject to reason and will, and reason and will were subject to God. The Fall, having impaired this integrity of man's nature, induced a rightful (though limited) sense of shame. Darkened intellects and weakened wills can no longer enjoy autocratic control over the promptings of lower nature. Temptations to sexual irregularity now come unbidden and sometimes remain against one's will; in addition, during the height of passion, lower nature at times overcomes the reign of rationality.

For this reason, Catholicism believes that a rightful sense of shame is proper and should not be abolished through faulty sex education. Such a sense of shame (not, however, the excessive and damaging inhibitions of Puritanism) furnishes a necessary safeguard to chastity. Sex education when given should use those safeguards required to obviate fallen human nature's proneness to sexual temptation. Although a limited number of physical facts are indispensable for adequate sex education, the undue detailing of such facts can serve little purpose except to incite the passions of a weakened human nature. Because of the sensitivity of weakened nature to sexual arousal, dress, movies, literature, television, radio, and similar means of suggestion and communication should be free of anything of an inciting nature.

Catholicism, accordingly, believes that sex education should include the discipline necessary to handle sex correctly. Mature persons do not give a knife to a child without training the child in its proper use. Similarly, sex education given without benefit of moral control and discipline is deemed extremely dangerous. In this, as in other basic rules of life, the parents have the primary responsibility and grave duty. If, for compelling reasons, parents cannot give it, they must assure themselves that their teacher-substitute will educate their children in all the aspects of sex, including its religious and moral discipline.

Before the Fall, the pleasures of sex were keener because man's faculties were more perfect; this pleasurableness, although lessened after the Fall, remains a rightful part of sex experience. Pius XII in this respect said: "The Creator Who in His goodness and wisdom has willed to conserve and propagate the human race through the instrumentality of man and woman by uniting them in marriage has ordained also that in performing this function, husband and wife should experience pleasure and happiness both in body and soul. In seeking and enjoying this pleasure, therefore, couples do nothing wrong. They accept that which the Creator has given them." On the other hand, to strive to intensify the pleasureableness of the sex act simply for the sake of pleasure has been labeled "un-Christian" by the same Pope. He deplored the current trends by pointing out that "This modern cult of pleasure is empty of all spiritual value and unworthy of Christian couples. . . . Banish from your minds the cult of pleasure and do your best to stop the diffusion of literature that thinks it a duty to describe in full detail the intimacy of conjugal life under the pretext of instructing, directing and reassuring." Despite the impairments due

to the Fall of man in the Garden of Eden, sex remains a noble, good, and virtuous act when rightly used in marriage. It is the union of souls and bodies; for those in the state of sanctifying grace, it is the union of two persons who are "temples of the Holy Ghost."

Furthermore, by the procreation of children, sex imitates the love of Christ for His Bride—The Church—whom He fructifies to spiritual offspring in the waters of baptism. Catholicism conceives the possibility of sex being used in three ways: (1) as an animal, fusing male and female on the physical level and impelled by no motive other than sensual thrill; (2) as a human being—in which sex becomes a union of mind, heart, and will as well as of body and effected by the dictate of reason primarily for the purpose of propagating the human species and secondarily for personal development; and (3) as a Christian—in which case the sex act reflects the union of Christ with His Church, safeguards and promotes the spiritual as well as the psychosomatic well-being of spouses, and propagates worshippers of God. Of many possible methods of expanding the human race and ultimately populating heaven, God devised sex. In the present state of nature, no other means of propagation of the human species is available. It is unmistakably oriented toward this purpose which, accordingly, remains primary.

The indulgence of sex before marriage or with another than one's spouse after marriage avoids the proper generative and educative intent placed on the act by the Creator. This does not imply that married partners must have as their primary purpose the procreation of another human being every time they perform the sex act. But it does imply that, procreation being primary, the birth of a child may not be deliberately frustrated by a couple. In addition, sex properly used has equally clear purposes that serve the welfare of the individual rightly employing it—expression and intensification of love, lessening of sex tensions and drive, psychological and physical prosperity, growth in selflessness and of the total personality, and an increase of sanctifying grace in the souls of those already possessing this grace. Furthermore, the union which the sex act is assists two to become one in a unity so profound that St. Paul commented that a man who "loveth his wife, loveth himself." It is this mysterious profundity of the unity of two persons that constitutes one of the reasons for Catholicism's opposition to divorce; as taught by Christ, "Whosoever shall put away his wife . . . and shall marry another, committeth adultery" (Matt. 19:9).

Moral Code

In its moral code, Catholicism applies the regulations made imperative by the nature and purposes of sex as devised by the Divine Plan. Just as all civil governments think it necessary to regulate sex by civil statutes, so the Divine government of the universe implies certain regulations that alone will ensure the proper use of sex. The sex act is a heterosexual union for purposes both supernatural and natural, social and personal. Fallen human nature, through ignorance or malevolence, will not execute in practice this proper use of sex without the guidance and strength of the Divine Plan for sex. The sex perversions that inevitably accompany religious decline attest to this fact.

Having supernatural purposes, sex must ever be used so as to be an act of justice, charity, chastity, and religion. As a natural act, it needs in all instances to conform to the dictates of rationality and to the pattern found in nature (hence the immorality of artificial insemination). The sociality of sex indicates that any solitary use of sex, such as masturbation, is unnatural, and that it is chiefly intended for the preservation of society. Hence, any intentional and artificial blockage of nature's purposes, such as the use of contraceptives, is deemed immoral; any destruction of the generative potential by sterilization (except for reasons of disease), or any direct aborting of a living fetus before birth, are obstructive of nature's clear intention that the sex act be primarily an act of generation. The act of withdrawal vitiates the procreation purpose and is similarly wrong. Catholicism has ever held to the Scriptural account in which Onan was struck dead on the spot for his unnatural prevention of childbirth, which the Bible castigates as "a detestable thing in the sight of the Lord" (Genesis 38:8–10).

The heterosexuality of the sex act indicates that the use of this act between persons of the same sex is opposed to its nature and purposes, and accordingly unethical. On the other hand, Catholicism does not object to family limitation by cooperating with nature through periodic continence known as "rhythm," provided a compelling and justifiable reason is present. Such abstinence from the sex act during the fertile period, even though it has the same purpose as contraceptive use (family limitation), unlike contraceptives does not employ any artificial instrument for blocking nature's intent, and, after setting nature's processes in motion, allows them (without interference of any kind) to work themselves out to their natural termination. Since this is not in any way a stoppage of nature's processes it can be employed when a just reason (such as repeated miscarriages or probable death of the mother) is present. In the absence of a "justifiable reason," the only purpose of periodic continence would be "selfishness" in one form or another —and selfishness is always wrong.

In fact, for the rhythm method to be used without guilt three conditions need to be present: (1) there must be a justifiable reason, as already stated; (2) it must be mutually agreed upon (except when one has a right to refuse), since the marriage contract requires sex rights to be given one's life partner whenever he or she requests such rights reasonably; and (3) the mutually agreed-upon abstinence must not be a proximate occasion of infidelity on the part of one or both spouses. In the same light, partners in marriage may not, in the absence of compelling reasons (as illness), absent themselves from each other for any prolonged length of time except by mutual consent and provided there is no serious danger to infidelity, or solitary sin. Between married partners, however, any actions (kisses, embraces) are deemed proper only so long as they do not lead to an orgasm outside the act of physical union. Such intimacies are rightful expressions of love and preludes to the act of physical union, and without them the ardor of physical love can easily turn into frigidity. Because of the psychosomatic nature of sex it is desirable that physical union be approached affectionately; each partner has a right to the warmth of human intercourse.

Ascetic Doctrines

In its ascetic doctrines Catholicism teaches that, exalted as is the proper use of sex, the sacrifice of sexual love for the purpose of a more intense dedication to God is deemed even more desirable. Virginity or celibacy is even greater than marriage, not in itself or in every instance, but only when it is taken for God's sake. Catholicism in this matter adheres to the Scriptural teaching: "He that is without a wife is solicitous for the things that belong to the Lord: how he may please God. But he that is with a wife is solicitous for the things of the world: how he may please his wife" (I Cor. 7:32–33). The unmarried who are celibate for God's sake in effect renounce marriage and its sex privileges so that the time, energy, and money that would be rightfully demanded by a family can be used, instead, for promoting the kingdom of God. Furthermore, the practice of celibacy serves as a mute but effective refutation to those who think that continence is impossible.

Even for the married, the ascetic counsels of Catholicism urge that couples refrain from attempting to drain the cup of sex pleasure to its last dregs. Pius XII pointed out that "even here couples must know how to restrict themselves within the limits of moderation. As in eating and drinking, so in the sexual act, they must not abandon themselves without restraint to the impulse of the senses." This is one reason why an emphasis upon the techniques of physical stimulation is condemned by Pius XII as hedonistic and capable of serving no other purpose than the intensification of passionate thrills. Further, married couples are advised (but not commanded) on occasion to voluntarily and temporarily abstain in order: (1) to acquire that self-discipline that is required at such times as prior and subsequent to childbirth; (2) to perform penance, especially during certain penitential seasons such as Lent; (3) to devote themselves less distractedly, for a while, to spiritual matters.

In general, Catholicism views sex as one of the noblest acts human beings can perform on the natural level. It implies the high privilege of participating with God in His creative act; it further implies the greatest creativity of which humans are capable on the natural level —that of other human beings who will live eternally to the praise and glory of God.

Philosophical Aspects

Philosophy, the discipline that discovers truths through reason, has traditionally been called "the handmaid of theology." Through reason some of the revealed truths relating to sex can be known, and others can be more fully understood; but many truths not revealed but relevant to orderly living are arrived at through the use of man's intelligence. In this rational sense, Catholicism views sex only in the light of its total context within the nature and purpose of man, as well as the nature and purpose of sex. Philosophy indicates that man was made by God for His purposes, that these purposes are indicated by His will which, in turn, is partly determinable by His laws. All nature, including man and his sexual components, is subject to laws indicating the Divine Plan and known as "natural laws." These rules for sex and human nature, made by their Creator, are obviously intended (as are all rules attached by human inventors to the products of their minds) to indicate uses that are right and proper and most conducive to order and the attainment of rightful purposes.

On the natural level man is a composite of body and soul intimately integrated into a whole, sometimes called "the self" or "the ego." Sex as a part of man's nature colors both his higher nature of intellect and will as well as his lower nature of emotions and bodily instincts. The attitudinal aspects of sex transcend in importance the physical and should dominate the latter. Sexual incitement, adjustment, or frigidity are, accordingly, more a matter of the psychological than of the physiological component.

A rational study of nature further indicates that the chief purpose of sex in the Divine Plan of the universe was to perpetuate the human species. Reason compels the position that sex is intended for the preservation of the race, even as food is intended primarily for preservation of self. Common sense indicates that the pleasure of eating is a concomitant effect, not an end in itself. Similarly, the pleasurableness of sex, although proper, cannot be its chief purpose. The very intensity of the natural pleasure drive in eating and in sexuality points to the transcendent import of the goals of self- or social preservation. Were the pleasure drive less strong, the goal of preservation of self and species would be more in jeopardy. On the other hand, reason assures us that the procreation and education of children is best served by parents who are happy, loving and loved, companionable, and devoted to each other's happiness and welfare. Sexual love, by deepening the unity, the love, and the development of the personalities of husbands and wives, is a potent factor in expanding their parental capacities as educators of their children.

In addition, the inadequacies of the "manliness" of the male and the "womanliness" of the female are complemented by the psychological characteristics of each sex. In this sexual-psychological union husbands and wives find their complement and their completion. This secondary purpose of marital love maintains its importance even when the procreation of children is not possible or even when prudent reasons exist for the practice of periodic continence. To pursue sex exclusively for pleasure is a form of sexual gluttony not unlike the quest for food beyond the requirements of self-preservation or of social intercourse.

Reason clearly indicates that initiating nature's generative processes and subsequently inhibiting these processes from their clear procreative goal is a contravention of nature's (and the Author of nature) intent. This appears more striking, perhaps, were one to compare it to eating and immediately taking a drug that would destroy the digestive system's assimilation of the food. Further, the easy availability of contraceptives encourages extramarital and premarital sexuality. It intensifies an immaturity that induces individuals to enjoy the pleasures of sex without its corresponding responsibilities.

Again, since any living fetus has a soul within it, directly aborting the living fetus is an act of murder of an unborn but living human being who is a composite of soul and body. Reason similarly assures us that no part of the body may be dismembered except to safeguard bodily health; for this reason, sterilization of

generative organs when they are not threatening the health or life of the individual is against nature and an act of unwarranted mutilation.

In contrast to the pan-sexualism of some schools of thought, reason clearly indicates that the sex drive is merely a part of the total sexuality—both psychological and physical—of human beings. On the other hand, sex is nature's deepest secret; only the most degenerate of people dare to expose it by open, public exhibitionism. In both primitive and advanced cultures, the sex act is recognized as a private and secretive act. Again, modesty in dress, etc., is indicated since secrets must not be easily disclosed, especially if they are associated with a function so important to the welfare of the race.

The nature and purpose of sex demand an adult stature by those using it; after having learned the art of self-preservation as a child and youth, human beings assume the mature responsibility of perpetuating the race. This requires an outgoing attitude, a social instinct, cooperation, selflessness, and otherness. Sex, like marriage, is for adults only. It represents man's highest natural creativity in comparison to which any other human creative effort remains inferior. In general, reason confirms theology in the position that the Author of nature has placed regulations for the proper use of sex, even as He has placed clearly observable rules concerning all forms of nature—inorganic, vegetative, animal, and human. The discovery of all of these laws by revelation, by reason, by observation, and by experimentation remains a continuing challenge to men.

Empirical and Clinical Aspects

The quest for knowledge of nature's laws is the preoccupation of the sciences—sacred, natural, and social. It is precisely because natural science can and does uncover more and more of the laws of nature that Catholicism respects it and has implicit confidence in its capacity to serve God, man, and society. Contrary to erroneous beliefs, Catholicism has no fear of empirical-clinical science; it has only respect and encouragement for it. What are feared, however (with a fear based upon compelling evidence), are the unproved hypotheses and inconclusive theories that are so unscientifically heralded as scientific "facts" or "laws." There is not, unfortunately, a single empirical survey relating to sex (including the Kinsey reports) that has given us any conclusive scientific laws. Due to their inadequate methodology, all of them still present nothing more than feeble theories. In many instances the various surveys directly contradict one another.

Physiologically viewed, the sex act is exclusively designed for generative purposes. The ejection of semen, the search by the semen for the ova, the profuse millions of life seeds in one ejaculation, and the entire orientation and functioning of the female reproductive system in response to seminal penetration compel an acceptance of the primacy of generation in the sex act. Catholicism is as eager as the eugenists to discover the truths of heredity, but realizes that until now little has been proved in this field. Pius XII, addressing a group of geneticists, said: "We ourselves urged the furtherance of research in the hope that some day perhaps results might be achieved which one could be sure of, for up to the present nothing definitive has been obtained." Accordingly, Catholicism teaches that the practice of sterilization of defectives is not only unethical but unscientific. Innovations that run counter to historic experience and natural law (such as contraceptives) must, on a rational and scientific basis, be withheld not only because of the above reasons but also in view of any conclusive proof of the harmlessness of such practices to the individual and to society.

In the face of mounting evidence of a scientific nature, such as the incidence of endemetriosis with the use of contraceptives, it seems unscientific to dash ahead presuming such practices to be innocuous. A growing conviction in psychiatric circles that artificial insemination frustrates the couple and leads to depression further indicates the unscientific rashness of engaging in a practice which, in time, may be proved to be extremely harmful. The complete absence of any medical need for abortion, and in the face of the clearly established adverse results of abortion, the advocacy of this practice also is devoid of scientific premises.

The traditional position of Catholicism that the imparting of sex education is a strict duty of parents stands confirmed by the mounting evidence today of the dire results of the failure to do so. The former hyperemphasis upon physiological detail is now, in the light of clinical data and experiences, giving way to an emphasis upon the attitudinal and emotional components of sex. Catholicism's traditional position that sex is more psychological than physical is constantly being reaffirmed by the findings of psychosomatic medicine. In general, conscious of the fact that theological and philosophical truths have never been contradicted by proved scientific laws, Catholicism urges the progress of true and authentic scientific knowledge. It rests secure in the conviction that her teachings will continue to be upheld rather than contraindicated by genuine and conclusive scientific facts.

Summary and Conclusions

Some of the viewpoints of Catholicism in respect to sex may be stated as follows:

1. Sex is a creation of God and has a set of regulations fixed by Him for its proper use.

2. Sex has supernatural and natural, psychological and physiological, components. The supernatural and psychological transcend in importance the natural and the physiological.

3. It is total and integral, permeating the entire nature of human beings. Sexuality refers more to the differentiations—both psychological and physical—of humans. It is not merely an act, much less a mere physical act. On the contrary, sex embraces all that is implied in "manliness" and "womanliness."

4. Its nature can only be understood correctly in the light of the nature of man himself; its purposes understood rightly only in the light of the purposes of man.

5. The chief purpose of sex is social; only secondarily are its purposes oriented to serve individual goals. Catholicism believes that the current tendency to exalt the personal goals of sex is evidence of "rugged individualism" in marriage.

6. The pleasurableness of sex is deemed a proper concomitant of the generative act. To exalt it to a quest for sexual thrills, however, is thought a form of sexual gluttony. Modera-

tion here, as elsewhere, is considered the golden mean.

7. Properly used, the sex act is one of significant supernatural and natural worth and dignity.

8. To sacrifice sex privileges by a celibate life is superior to the use of the generative function if it is undertaken for the purpose of freeing oneself for an even nobler service of God.

9. Any and all forms of artificial or unnatural birth frustration are immoral; forms of family limitation not violating nature's processes are ethical under certain conditions.

10. Sex education is a serious duty for parents. It must, however, be complete and include education of the will and in religious living, or it will defeat its purpose and result in sexual misuse.

11. Because of man's lack of autocratic control over lower nature and his sensitivity to sexual arousal, modesty in dress, posture, movies, literature, television, etc., is imperative.

12. Good sex adjustment is more a matter of attitudinal and emotional than of physical factors. Contrariwise, frigidity is more frequently induced by Puritanical attitudes or an inadequate affectional rapport than by organic causes.

13. Catholicism trusts that empirical-clinical research will hasten its findings regarding sex. Although it fears the pseudoscience of unproved theories so common today, it remains secure in the fact that not a single proved scientific law in any manner contradicts its teachings. On the contrary, it believes that truth in theology can never disagree with truth in science since God who is Infinite Truth is the Author of both sacred and secular sciences.

Nihil obstat:
Francis J. Connell, C.Ss.R.
Censor Deputatus

Imprimatur:
✠ Patrick A. O'Boyle
Archbishop of Washington

The *nihil obstat* and *imprimatur* are official declarations that a book or pamphlet is free of doctrinal or moral error. No implication is contained therein that those who have granted the *nihil obstat* and the *imprimatur* agree with the content, opinions or statements expressed.

July 17, 1959

References

Buckley, Joseph, *Christian Design for Sex* (2 vols.). Chicago: Fides Publishers Assn., 1952.

Cavanagh, John R., *Fundamental Marriage Counseling.* Milwaukee: Bruce Publishing Co., 1956.

Clemens, Alphonse H., *Marriage and the Family: An Integrated Approach for Catholics.* Englewood Cliffs, N. J.: Prentice-Hall, Inc., 1957.

Davis, Henry, *Moral and Pastoral Theology*, Vol. II. London: Sheed and Ward, 1938.

Hildebrand, Dietrich von, *In Defense of Purity.* New York: Sheed and Ward, 1936.

Kelly, Gerald, *Medical-Moral Problems.* St. Louis: Catholic Hospital Association of United States and Canada, 1958.

Leclercq, Jacques, *Marriage and the Family—A Study in Social Philosophy.* New York: Frederick Pustet Co., 1947.

McAuliffe, Michael F., *Catholic Moral Teaching on the Nature and Object of Conjugal Love.* Washington, D. C.: Catholic University of America Press, 1954.

Messenger, E. C., *Two In One Flesh* (2 vols.). Westminster, Md.: The Newman Press, 1948.

O'Donnell, Thomas, *Morals in Medicine.* Westminster, Md.: Newman Book Shop, 1956.

St. Thomas Aquinas, *Summa Theologica* (translated by Fathers of the English Dominican Province). New York: Benziger Brothers Inc., 1920. (Index Vol. III, p. 3907, see Adam, Adultery, Apparel, Coition, Concubinage, Concupiscence, Concupiscible, Continence, Fornication, Frigidity, Generation, Impurity, Incontinency, Infidelity, Intercourse, Lust, Man, Matrimony, Modesty, Nuptials, Passion, Pollution, Prostitution, Rape, Semen, Sex, Sin Original, Sodomy, Temperance, Virginity.)

Sattler, Henry V., *Parents, Children and the Facts of Life.* Paterson, N. J.: St. Anthony Guild Press, 1952.

Thomas, John, *Rhythm.* Westminster, Md.: Newman Book Shop, 1957.

Wayne, T. J., *Morals and Marriage—The Catholic Background to Sex.* New York: Longmans, Green & Co., 1936.

Wilkins, Vincent, *The Image of God in Sex.* New York: Sheed and Ward, 1955.

Woods, Ralph L. (ed.), *The Catholic Concept of Love and Marriage.* New York: J. B. Lippincott Co., 1958.

ALPHONSE H. CLEMENS

Censorship of Sexual Literature

THE tremendous power exercised by the written word has always invited interference by governmental forces. In ancient China the Emperor Chi Huang Ti ordered the destruction of the *Analects* of Confucius, and Ovid was banished from Imperial Rome by Augustus for writing the *Ars Amatoria*. In Western Europe the discovery of printing intensified this pressure in the fifteenth century. The Roman Church, apprehending the threat to her control over thought and belief, set up the *Index Librorum Prohibitorum,* only recently abolished, which listed over four thousand books forbidden to the faithful except by permission of ecclesiastical authority.

England

Countries affected by the Reformation were by no means exempt from the prevailing trend. Henry VIII of England entrusted the control of books to the new Court of Star Chamber, which insisted that they should be read and approved before printing. The detested Star Chamber was abolished by the Long Parliament in 1641; and it was against the enactment of a new system of licensing for publications that Milton wrote his immortal *Areopagitica*. After the Restoration attempts to reintroduce censorship were short-lived, and henceforward governmental control of literature was mainly exercised through the common law of libel by the judges of the King's courts.

Obscene Libel

Four sorts of libel came to be distinguished: defamatory, seditious, blasphemous, and (a late-comer) obscene. In 1708 an attempt to punish one Read for printing *The Fifteen Plagues of a Maidenhead* proved unsuccessful, the judge saying that because the ecclesiastical courts were powerless it did not follow that the civil courts could deal with the case. In 1739, however, after considerable argument the judges of the King's Bench fined the bookseller, Edmund Curll, for printing *Venus in the Cloister or the Nun in her Smock*. This case firmly established a common-law misdemeanor, and it is both amusing and instructive to note how the old indictments for this offense read:

... A.B. being a person of a wicked and depraved mind and disposition, and unlawfully and wickedly devising, contriving, and intending, to vitiate and corrupt the morals of the liege subjects of our Lord the King, to debauch and poison the minds of divers of the liege subjects of our said Lord the King and to raise and create in them lustful desires, and to bring the said liege subjects into a state of wickedness, lewdness, and debauchery ... unlawfully, wickedly, maliciously, scandalously, and wilfully did publish, sell and utter, and cause and procure to be published, sold and uttered, a certain lewd, wicked, bawdy, scandalous, and obscene libel in the form of a book ... in contempt of our said Lord the King and his laws, in violation of common decency, morality and good order, and against the peace of our said Lord the King, his Crown and Dignity.

This quaint phraseology emphasized the public and widespread nature of the offense as originally conceived. In recent times, however, the public element has not been insisted upon by judges, and convictions have been secured in respect of quite private communications, such as indecent letters sent in furtherance of illicit amours. "Publication" in law can mean no more than giving or lending a book, picture, or manuscript to another person. In the notorious case of Montalk (1932), the accused did no more than take the manuscript of a very literary but risqué Christmas card to a printer to get copies to send to his friends; yet he was sentenced to six months' imprisonment and the sentence was upheld by the Court of Criminal Appeal.

By contrast, the mildness of the eighteenth-century attitude was illustrated in 1750 when a young gentleman, John Cleland, pleaded poverty as an excuse when arraigned before the Privy Council for writing *The Memoirs of a Woman of Pleasure*. The President of the Council, the Earl of Granville, granted him a pension of £100 a year on condition that he did not repeat the offense. The book, better known by the name of its heroine, Fanny Hill, is devoted to unvarnished descriptions of love-making and brothel scenes. With the passage of years it has become a sort of best-seller in spite of all attempts at suppression.

The Obscene Publications Act of 1857

The law of obscene libel did not assume any great importance or interfere seriously with literature or science until the nineteenth century when, with the growing literacy of the masses, the authorities became increasingly concerned about a trade in pornography that the existing processes of the law were too clumsy to suppress effectively. After Lord Campbell had been instrumental in passing a bill through Parliament to restrict the sale of poisons, he gave his attention to "a sale of poison more deadly than prussic acid, strychnine or arsenic," as he put it, and the Obscene Publications Act of 1857 was the result.

This Act enabled the magistrates, on information that an obscene book had been sold, to issue a warrant to search the premises concerned. Any allegedly obscene matter found had to be brought into court, and, unless the owner showed cause to the contrary, could be ordered to be destroyed. The Act was not passed until Lord Campbell, who was Chief Justice of the Queen's Bench at the time, had assured the House of Lords that it "was intended to apply exclusively to works written for the single purpose of corrupting the morals of youth and of a nature calculated to shock the common feelings of decency in any well-regulated mind," and that no change would take place in the legal test of obscenity.

The Test of Obscenity

Lord Campbell evidently considered that in law obscenity was equivalent to gross and worthless pornography, but only eleven years later Lord Chief Justice Cockburn put a very different complexion on the matter. In Hicklin's case, which was brought under the 1857 Act, he laid down his famous definition of obscenity as follows:

The test of obscenity is this, whether the tendency of the matter charged as obscenity is to deprave and corrupt those whose minds are open to such immoral influences and into whose hands a publication of this sort may fall.

Since neither the Act of 1857 nor any of the other statutes in which obscenity is mentioned contain any definition of that word, Cockburn's dictum governed the English courts until recently, and it was the test which judges in their summings up directed juries to apply, and which magistrates applied when considering whether any matter was obscene.

The Customs and the Post Office

Besides the Act of 1857, a dozen or so other statutes dealt with obscene publications in a subsidiary way. These Acts give special powers to the customs, postal, and police authorities. The most serious consequences have flowed from the long-standing powers of the customs authorities now embodied in the Customs Consolidation Acts of 1876 and 1952. These enable customs officers to seize any imported matter that they consider obscene. The consignee must be advised and he can challenge the seizure in court but the Customs can insist on summary jurisdiction. If the seizure is not challenged the matter can be destroyed without a court order. The Post Office has similar powers and it is a criminal offense to post obscene matter even under seal or inoffensive covers.

The Law and Serious Literature

This combination of common and statute law, together with a judicial definition of obscenity so elastic that it could be stretched to cover almost anything dealing with sex, constituted a formidable legal weapon. Its use was successful in suppressing open trade in the grosser sorts of pornography, but a business still flourished in a wishy-washy catchpenny variety that was no doubt just as demoralizing. However, the weapon placed in the hands of the authorities by the judges and the legislature was not allowed to lie idle so far as serious literature was concerned. Scientific and educational works, and serious novels, were not immune from its operation. Important and typical cases are noted below.

In 1877 Charles Bradlaugh and Annie Besant were prosecuted for reprinting Charles Knowlton's *The Fruits of Philosophy*, an exposition of early contraceptive methods by an American physician, first published in 1832. The defendants were sentenced to fine and imprisonment but the sentence was set aside on appeal because of a technical flaw in the indictment.

In 1889 Henry Vizetelly, a publisher with advanced ideas, was sent to prison for publishing translations of Zola's novels, in spite of their being bowdlerized.

In 1898 the first installment of Havelock Ellis' *Studies in the Psychology of Sex*, which had just appeared, was attacked by the prosecution of one George Bedborough for selling it. Bedborough escaped punishment by pleading guilty, and for a generation Ellis' great work had to be published abroad. This case is particularly interesting because Ellis had no opportunity to defend his work. It was by no means a rare event for a book to be condemned as obscene because a publisher or bookseller did not choose to defend it, without the author being able to say a word in defense of his creation.

In 1915 the first edition of D. H. Lawrence's *The Rainbow* was ordered to be destroyed. Similarly, the Customs do their best to keep the unexpurgated edition of *Lady Chatterley's Lover* out of England, although it is widely read. Lawrence was deeply hurt when in 1929 a number of his pictures were seized from an exhibition at the Leicester Galleries in London and reproductions in book form destroyed.

In 1922 the Customs made a bonfire on the quay of Folkestone Harbour of 500 copies of James Joyce's *Ulysses*, and it was not until the American case in 1934 (dealt with below) that the book was allowed, without any official recantation, to circulate in England. Alfred Noyes made a minor but zealous contribution to the banning of a great literary work by securing, through the influence of Mr. Justice Darling, the withdrawal of the book from the sale of Lord Birkenhead's library when he died.

In 1928 Radclyffe Hall's *The Well of Loneliness*, a sincere and high-minded novel dealing with female homosexuality, was ordered to be destroyed. The same year the book was cleared of obscenity by the New York Court of Special Sessions. It was republished in England in 1949 without any action being taken by the authorities.

In the Fortune Press case (1934), a holocaust was made of a number of translations, including the *Satyricon* of Petronius, the *Greek Anthology*, and works by Brantôme, Huysmans, and Pierre Louÿs.

In 1935 sex education received a setback by the destruction order against Edward Charles' *The Sexual Impulse*. This book, besides some philosophical speculations and what was at that time very up-to-date information about contraception, treated the technique of sexual intercourse and coital position with gaiety and lightheartedness. This treatment was in marked contrast to the solemnity and gravity in dealing with sex adopted even by such writers as Havelock Ellis, Van de Velde, and Marie Stopes, which lays so many books of sex instruction open to the charge made by Norman Haire that they tell the reader everything about the sexual act except why anyone should want to perform it.

Charles' *con amore* treatment might have been a considerable advance toward a more healthy attitude regarding the physical side of love; but the expert testimony of more than a dozen distinguished scientists, religious leaders, and social workers to the scientific, educational, and social value of the work went for nothing. The magistrate asked one of the witnesses, Mrs. Janet Chance, the founder of a sex-education center: "Have you ever given the book to a member of the working class?" Even the admissibility of expert evidence on the religious, scientific, literary, or artistic value of a work alleged to be obscene was by no means certain. In *The Well of Loneliness* case the magistrate refused to hear such evidence.

In 1940 another frank book of sex instruction was published that included in its scope the sexual abnormalities which often cause unhappiness in married life—*Love without Fear* by Eustace Chesser, a consulting gynecologist. In 1942 after 5,000 copies had been sold, the author and his publishers were prosecuted for obscene libel at the instance of the Director of Public Prosecutions. The case was defended before a jury and an acquittal secured.

The same year a man who ran a commercial mail-order lending library of books of sex instruction at Bodmin was similarly prosecuted. The books concerned included *The Encyclopedia of Sexual Knowledge*, edited by Norman Haire in 1934, and a number of similar publications, all of which had been openly sold for years. To spare his wife the publicity of a protracted trial he pleaded guilty, and a sentence of twelve months' imprisonment was upheld by the Court of Criminal Appeal. Petitions to the Home Secretary eventually secured his release, but only at the time when he would have been freed under the good-conduct rules.

In 1950, in a case supported by the Director of Public Prosecutions against a number of Blackpool booksellers, a dozen or so books of the same sort, including the *Encyclopedia of Sexual Knowledge* and a posthumous summary of the work of Magnus Hirschfeld, were condemned to destruction. The following year the Hirschfeld book was similarly proceeded against at Newcastle, but Dr. Norman Haire appeared as a witness for the defense and the magistrates refused to make an order.

In 1951 destruction orders were obtained against part of the stock of a secondhand bookseller at Poole. Except for two copies of *Lady Chatterley's Lover*, all the books were works of literary interest in French—one so rare that the bench allowed it to be presented to the British Museum library in lieu of destruction.

In the following year there was an interesting case in which a whole consignment of nudist magazines was seized by the Customs at London docks and the seizure was challenged by the importer. The prosecution made it clear that what they objected to were photographs of the human body in which the sexual organs had not been deleted by retouching. The whole consignment, which included periodicals of the Continental nudist movement that were of great interest to British nudists, was ordered to be destroyed by a magistrate at the Guildhall.

The Customs were again to the fore in 1957 when they seized a two-volume edition of the complete works of Jean Genet in French, which the Birmingham Public Library had ordered for their reference department. The Town Clerk and other representatives of the Birmingham Corporation visited the Customs and Excise office in London and were persuaded that it was useless to challenge the seizure in the Courts. The Customs have in the past also excluded *The Tropic of Cancer* and similar works by Henry Miller, *Molloy* by Samuel Beckett, and *Lolita* by Vladimir Nabokov.

The typical cases noted above show that distinguished authorship, long immunity from attack, foreign language, and bibliographical rarity have not shielded serious literature from attacks under the law of obscene libel, and that the operation of the law has been arbitrary and unpredictable. Only the institution of trial by jury appears to be some safeguard to justice, liberty, and common sense.

Indirect Effects of the Law

The effect of this state of the law on sexual literature was by no means limited to the condemnation of the courts. Authors, publishers, printers, booksellers, and librarians performed their various functions under a shadow that was arbitrary in its nature and unpredictable in its incidence; and they became timorous. Some books never reached publication, some were suppressed in bookshops and libraries, and others appeared after excisions and bowdlerizations or were reticent on matters of concern to their readers. When Paul Elek published an integral translation of Zola's *La Terre* in 1954, the suppression of 1888 was almost repeated, he complained in *The Times* of June 18th, because a large number of printers refused to produce the book. In the translation of Jean-Paul Sartre's *Le Mur,* published in 1950, there were considerable omissions. The British Museum library possesses a large number of printed books of great historical and literary interest that are omitted from the General Catalogue, to the great inconvenience of readers and to subscribers to copies of the Catalogue the world over. The transcription of Pepys' *Diary* at Magdalene College, Cambridge, has only been seen in its entirety by a few scholars. Even the best printed version is sprinkled with asterisks, and it remains to be seen whether the expected new edition will be complete. It is perhaps fortunate that Boswell's journals fell into the hands of an American university, where they are being published in their entirety.

Recent Developments

The obscurantist administration of a law intended to deal solely with gross pornography produced no great opposition until recently, when considerable public outcry was caused by a new turn in events. The circumstances were somewhat peculiar. In 1954 two men, Reiter and Carter, were sent to prison for publishing books by "Hank Janson." The defense put in a plea that books just as bad were published by leading houses and circulated by the libraries, and examples were put into court. This evidence was rejected and the Lord Chief Justice said that the books ought to be looked into. As a result, five prosecutions were launched. All the cases were tried by jury with varied results: Werner Laurie Ltd., publishers, and Margot Bland, author of *Julia,* pleaded guilty; Hutchinson Ltd., publishers of *September in Quinze* by Vivian Connell, were convicted; Heinemann Ltd., publishers, and Walter Baxter, author of *The Image and the Search,* were formally acquitted after two juries had disagreed; Secker and Warburg, publishers, and the printers of *The Philanderer* by Stanley Kauffmann were acquitted, as was Arthur Barker for publishing

The Man in Control by Charles McGraw. The five books had no very great literary merit except, perhaps, *The Image and the Search,* which E. M. Forster described in a letter to the publisher as "a serious and beautiful book." *The Philanderer* case was tried by jury at the requirement of the defendants and produced a masterly summing up by Mr. Justice Stable, who explained that the test of obscenity was not to be so applied as to make criminal the publication of literature unsuitable for adolescents and children.

The fact that in these cases the established and reputable publishing trade had been attacked caused an uproar that contrasted sharply with the equanimity with which the public had regarded attacks on pioneer reformers and *avant-garde* writers over the years. During 1954 and the early part of 1955 *The Times* and other influential papers printed correspondence and editorials about the matter, the British Broadcasting Corporation devoted two Third Programme broadcasts to the state of the law, and questions were asked in Parliament. The Society of Authors set up a committee presided over by Sir Alan Herbert to examine the existing law and to recommend reforms, and their findings were sent to the Home Secretary. A private member's bill to amend the law on the lines of the committee's recommendations was introduced into the House of Commons but it never passed beyond the Committee stage. When the 1957-1958 session of Parliament opened, however, a Select Committee of the House of Commons, which had partially examined another bill, was reconstituted to consider generally whether it was desirable to amend and consolidate the law relating to obscene publications.

The indifference of the public to this subject is well illustrated by the fact that this was the first time it had been considered by an official body since the Joint Select Committee on Lotteries and Indecent Advertisements in 1908. The minutes of that committee contain a lot of evidence about the trade in pornography going on at the time, including the struggle between the British police and Charles Carrington, a distributor of erotic books who operated from Paris and included a number of titles of scholarly and literary interest in his lists. No change in the law of obscene libel resulted from the report.

The Obscene Publications Act of 1959

There is little doubt that, when the report of the recent Select Committee appeared, recommending considerable changes in the law regarding obscene publications, the Government would have liked to quietly pigeon-hole it. Pressure in and out of Parliament, however, was too much for them, and after many delays and amendments the Obscene Publications Act, 1959, came into force on August 29, 1959.

The new Act abolishes the common-law offense of publishing an obscene libel and makes it a statutory offense to publish an obscene article, stating that an article shall be deemed obscene if its effect is, "if taken as a whole, such as to tend to deprave and corrupt persons who are likely, having regard to all the relevant circumstances, to read, see or hear the matter contained or embodied in it."

The Act provides that a person publishes an article who "distributes, circulates, sells, lets on hire, gives, or lends it, or who offers it for sale or for letting on hire." This definition of publication seems sufficiently wide to bring private transactions and personal correspondence within the scope of the obscenity law, but whether it could land some future Montalk in gaol is not clear. Besides reading matter and pictures, the definition of "an article" covers sound records and films, the playing and projection of which constitute publication.

Prosecutions may not be commenced more than two years after the commission of the offense. Cases may be tried summarily within twelve months, and consequently the issue of obscenity will frequently, as in the past, be decided by magistrates and not put to a jury.

The Obscene Publications Act, 1857, is repealed but substantially the same provisions as regards seizure and forfeiture are re-enacted, with the notable difference that the police will no longer have to effect an actual purchase before they can obtain a warrant to seize allegedly obscene matter: the issuing magistrate has only to be satisfied that there is reasonable ground for suspecting that obscene articles are kept for publication for gain on any premises, stall, or vehicle. This change follows the argument put before the Select Committee by police witnesses in 1957, who complained of the difficulty of effecting a purchase from wholesale stores holding obscene books. No doubt the requirement that a purchase must be made put an obstacle in the way of pursuing commercial pornography, but it was also a valuable protection for scholarly and private libraries, which in the nature of things often contain books that would be considered obscene if publicly circulated.

It is provided that in any proceedings for the forfeiture of obscene matter the author or maker of any articles seized "or any other person through whose hands they have passed" shall be entitled to appear before the court to show cause why they should not be forfeited. There is no corresponding right for an author or publisher to appear in prosecutions of booksellers, etc., for publishing obscene articles and it looks as if another Havelock Ellis could be branded as a pornographer without any chance of defending himself because a timid defendant pleads "Guilty."

Further, the Act provides that in any proceedings a defense may be set up "that the publication of the article in question is justified as being for the public good on the ground that it is in the interests of science, literature, art or learning, or of other objects of general concern"; and "that the opinions of experts as to the literary, artistic, scientific or other merits of an article may be admitted."

It is noteworthy that the Act does nothing to curtail the powers of the Customs authorities and the Post Office; and there is no provision to ensure uniform administration of the law and no specific protection for scholars and learned institutions.

The most important case under the new Act resulted in the finding by a jury, in 1960, of a verdict of "Not Guilty" in favor of the publishers of an unexpurgated edition of *Lady Chatterley's Lover*.

The Act was strengthened by an amending statute in 1964 which among other changes made it an offense to possess an obscene article for gain.

Horror Comics

At one stage of these recent developments

the reform of the law of obscene libel became mixed up with the related but rather different question of what are known as "horror comics." The comic is a periodical for children, consisting mainly of strip cartoons. Originally these publications were innocent enough and some still are; but of late years a large number have been devoted to horror, crime, and cruelty, giving considerable anxiety to those interested in the welfare of children and adolescents. Eventually the government dealt with this problem by a separate measure—The Children and Young Persons (Harmful Publications) Act, 1955.

Scotland

Scots law is very similar to English as regards obscene publications, except that the Obscene Publications Acts of 1857, 1959, and 1964 did not apply to Scotland. The Customs and Post Office Acts do, however, apply to Scotland. Public opinion north of the border is rather more puritanical than in England. As a result of the prevailing moral atmosphere, prudery has combined with salacity to secure that all editions of *The Merry Muses of Caledonia,* a collection of indecorous drinking songs and bawdy verses left behind by Robert Burns, should be either bowdlerized or corrupted. The bicentenary year of the poet's birthday saw for the first time an integral and scholarly edition of this valuable source, but it has had until recently to be privately published.

The British Commonwealth

The British Commonwealth absorbed the principles of the English law of obscene libel, though codification and special legislation have effected modifications in recent times. Literary censorship boards have been set up in Queensland and Tasmania. Legislation dealing with comics has been passed in Canada, Australia, and New Zealand.

In 1956 an eminent musician who was visiting Sydney to conduct an orchestra was fined as a result of the Customs' discovering a private collection of erotic books, photographs, and films in his luggage.

Eire

Under the influence of the Roman Catholic Church, southern Ireland used its independence to set up the sort of censorship that had been unknown in the United Kingdom for more than two hundred years. Under the Censorship of Publications Act, 1929, as amended in 1946, a censorship board exists that can ban books and bar periodicals on the ground of indecency or obscenity or because they advocate "the unnatural prevention of conception." The *Register of Prohibited Publications* lists hundreds of nonfiction books and novels that circulate freely in Great Britain; and the suspension of the import of a newspaper or magazine published in Great Britain which has offended the code is a no unusual occurrence.

The United States of America

The Law

The American states inherited the English common law of obscene libel, and in 1879 the Cockburn definition of obscenity was accepted by the courts. A number of states enacted statutes strengthening the common law, and even more potent was federal legislation forbidding the importation and interstate transmission of obscene matter, which culminated in the notorious Comstock Act of 1873. This Act made the mailing of contraceptive information an offense. The federal law is now embodied in the U. S. Code Title 18, 1461-1463 and Title 19, 1305.

Comstockery

The Act of 1873 took its name from Anthony Comstock, the secretary of the New York Society for the Suppression of Vice. Before his time the administration of the law had often been oppressive and it numbered Charles Knowlton and Walt Whitman among its victims. But Comstock was a fanatic with a slogan "Morals, not Art or Literature," and the Act of 1873 enabled him to conduct a sort of reign of terror in the publishing world that lasted for forty years. A year before his death in 1915 he indicted Margaret Sanger in respect of articles on contraception that had appeared in her paper, *The Woman Rebel.* Mrs. Sanger left the country but Comstock, by the use of an *agent provocateur,* secured the imprisonment of her husband for selling a pamphlet on birth control.

Comstockery did not die with its parent. In

1918 Mary Ware Dennett was convicted in respect of a pamphlet giving elementary sex instruction, but the conviction was reversed on appeal. The same pamphlet was, however, condemned to destruction by a London magistrate in 1923. In 1929 copies of Voltaire's *Candide* consigned to a Boston bookseller were confiscated. Theodore Dreiser's *The Genius* was suppressed in 1916 and his *An American Tragedy* in 1930. Books by Sinclair Lewis, Upton Sinclair, St. John Ervine, Bertrand Russell, Olive Schreiner, Ernest Hemingway, were among the serious works condemned.

Recent Judgments

The tide turned against Comstockery when Judge Woolsey's exoneration of James Joyce's *Ulysses* was confirmed by the United States Court of Appeals on August 7, 1934. This case appeared to establish that in regard to literary obscenity: (1) the author's intention is relevant; (2) the work's dominant effect and not isolated passages must be considered; (3) in considering the effect of a book, "the reasonable man" and not an abnormal adult or child must be taken as the criterion; and (4) literary or artistic merit should be weighed against incidental obscenity. These rulings apply principally to the federal courts and they have been followed in many state courts, although in others the Cockburn test is still applied.

In 1938 an important step forward was made when, as a result of Dr. Norman E. Himes' contesting a Customs seizure, the United States Circuit Court of Appeals held, in *U.S.* v. *Certain Magazines* (*Marriage Hygiene*), that contraceptive information could enter the United States provided the consignee, even though a layman, was a person qualified to receive it.

Nudism in Modern Life, by Maurice Parmelee, is illustrated by integral reproductions of photographs of nudist activities. In 1934 the District Court of Columbia ordered copies seized by the Customs to be destroyed because of the illustrations. The American Civil Liberties Union assisted in the defense, and on appeal the U.S. Court of Appeals of the District of Columbia cleared the book on May 14, 1940, a majority decision declaring:

The picturization here challenged has been used in the libeled book to accompany an honest, sincere, scientific and educational study and exposition of a sociological phenomenon and is, in our opinion, clearly permitted by present-day concepts of propriety.

In 1949 a most comprehensive and authoritative account of the present state of American law on literary obscenity was given in a case at Philadelphia involving nine books, three of which, *A World I Never Made* by James T. Farrell, *God's Little Acre* by Erskine Caldwell, and *End as a Man* by Calder Willingham, had been cleared by magistrates' courts in 1933, 1937, and 1947, respectively. In his judgment, Judge Bok said that the law did "not penalize anyone who seeks to change the prevailing moral or sexual code" and that "the modern rule is that obscenity is measured by the erotic allurement upon the average modern reader." He held all the books to be not obscene and was upheld on an appeal to the Superior Court of Pennsylvania.

A long struggle between the American Customs and the Institute for Sex Research, founded by Alfred C. Kinsey at Indiana University, was recently concluded. For years the Customs had been seizing material sent to the Institute from abroad. Protracted litigation culminated on October 31, 1957, in a decision by Judge Edmund L. Palmieri of the United States District Court, Southern District of New York, in favor of the Institute. The gist of the decision was that the material, although unquestionably obscene were it in the hands of the general public, was not obscene in the hands of scientists. The Customs did not appeal and announced that they accepted the decision as a basis for their future policy.

The constitutional position in relation to obscenity legislation equally divided the United States Supreme Court in 1948 in the case of Edmund Wilson's *Memoirs of Hecate County*; but in *Roth* v. *United States,* that Court decided on June 14, 1957, that:

(1) obscenity, whatever it may be, is not within the area of protected speech and press under the First Amendment, and

(2) in view of this exclusion the Court would not apply, in connection with a prosecution involving obscenity, the "clear and probable danger" test which would require a causal relationship between the allegedly offending material and anti-social conduct.

The Court, however, made it very plain that the area which can be excluded from Constitutional protection is narrowly limited. The opinion said, in part:

All ideas having even the slightest redeeming social importance—unorthodox ideas, controversial ideas, even ideas hateful to the prevailing climate of opinion—have the full protection of the guarantees, unless excludable because they encroach upon the limited area of more important interests.

The result of a more recent case will be interesting to readers of English literature. The Grove Press of New York published the unexpurgated text of *Lady Chatterley's Lover* from the author's holograph and with the authority of D. H. Lawrence's widow. The book was banned from the mails but on July 21, 1959, Federal Judge Frederick van Pelt Bryan set aside the ban on the ground that the work was not obscene in American law. The judge made it clear that the Postmaster General had no discretion as to what was to be treated as obscene and that his application of the legal standard could always be challenged in the courts in individual cases.

The Gathings Committee

In 1952 the House of Representatives set up a Select Committee on Current Pornographic Materials, under the chairmanship of Mr. E. C. Gathings of Arkansas, to investigate the extent of the obscene book trade and to make recommendations for changes in the law. The Committee devoted most of its attention to cheap books, "cheesecake" magazines, and "horror comics." The report of the Committee recommended minor changes in the federal law—particularly that all transportation of obscene matter should be prohibited and not only transportation through the post—and urged the publishing trade to put its house in order. A minority report complained among other things that the Committee had not adequately distinguished between "what may broadly be classified as obscene and what falls within the realm of free thought and creative expression."

France

There is a common myth among Anglo-Saxons that France is a land of perfect freedom so far as sexual matters are concerned. This is far from true, and certainly not as regards literature. Although a man of letters is treated with greater respect in France than in Britain or America, the French have quite a bad record as far as the suppression of creative literature is concerned; and a law of 1920 forbidding the spreading of contraceptive knowledge is inimicable to the principles of intellectual and moral freedom.

Outrage aux Mœurs

The French equivalent to the English "obscene libel" is "outrage aux bonnes mœurs," which has been a criminal offense since 1819.

During the nineteenth century works that had come from the pens of distinguished authors such as Ronsard, La Fontaine, Voltaire, Rousseau, l'Abbé Prévost, Béranger, and Barbey d'Aurevilly were condemned as an outrage to good morals. In 1857 two masters of the French language, one of prose, the other of verse, stood in the dock. Gustave Flaubert was acquitted as regards *Madame Bovary*: but six poems from *Les Fleurs du Mal* by Baudelaire were condemned and the poet fined. Late reparation was, however, made, for under a new law of September 25, 1946, the Court of Cassation on May 31, 1949, annulled the judgment against Baudelaire. Under this law a Court decision holding a book to be obscene may be reviewed after twenty years at the instance of the author or the publisher, any of their surviving relatives, or the Société des Gens de Lettres de France.

Toward the end of the nineteenth century a more liberal attitude began to prevail in the administration of the law, but there are grounds for suspecting a political motivation in some of the prosecutions. In the present century, periodicals rather than books have been the subject of attack.

Present Law

The current French law governing literary obscenity is contained in the Decret-Loi of July 29, 1939, articles 119–128. It is an offense to publish writing or designs, etc., "contraires aux bonnes mœurs"; the judicial police may seize obscene matter in France or at its frontiers: and the Post Office may refuse to accept obscene matter. There are interesting safeguards as follows:

1. No prosecution may be brought more than three years after the offense has been committed.

2. The Court may donate to a state museum matter that would otherwise be destroyed.

3. In respect of a book a prosecution can only be brought following a decision of a special commission to be set up to advise the Minister of Justice. This commission, called the Commission Consultative de la Famille et de la Natalité Française, was formed by a decree of January 25, 1940.

There is no statutory test of what is contrary to good morals, and the courts are guided by the dicta of judges and jurists who have stressed the essentially mercenary and gross nature of the offense. A conviction can be quashed if the Court gives no reason for finding the work obscene.

In 1947 "comics" and literature distributed to French youth attracted special attention. As a result, a law was passed on July 16, 1949, setting up a special commission to supervise children's publications and forbidding matter favorable to gangsterism, lying, theft, idleness, cowardice, hatred, and debauchery (Loi No. 49-956).

Recent Cases

Recently the French police have again turned their attention to books of interest to the literary world.

The Olympia Press has for some years published in Paris books banned in Britain and the United States and found a ready market among English-speaking tourists. This firm published Henry Miller's *Sexus,* the first volume of his trilogy *The Rosy Crucifixion,* and it was banned in 1950. In 1957 a number of the firm's books were attacked, including Frank Harris' *My Life and Loves.*

A complete edition of the works of de Sade planned to consist of 26 volumes at about 1,000 francs each, was started by Jean-Jacques Pauvert in 1947. In 1954 and 1955, when most of the volumes had been published, the Commission Consultative gave attention to the matter, and the prosecution of four titles followed on December 15, 1956: *La Philosophie dans le Boudoir, La Nouvelle Justine, Juliette,* and *Les 120 Journées de Sodome.* The case was tried

before the XVIIᵉ Chambre Correctionelle de Paris, and Andre Breton and Jean Cocteau were among the witnesses for the defense. The publishers were fined and the books ordered to be destroyed.

The Court rejected a plea that the edition was intended to circulate among only a small circle of intellectuals on the ground that it had been advertised in a nonscientific journal cheek by jowl with admittedly erotic works. On appeal, the sentence in respect of *Juliette* was quashed because the Consultative Commission was not fully attended when it had initiated the prosecution in respect of that book. Fines in respect of the three other books were suspended but the destruction orders were confirmed. The Court ruled that liberty of discussion allowed all philosophical views to be expressed; only the ways of expression would be condemned. It is worthy of note that the printer in this case on establishing his bona fides was discharged.

Other Countries

Belgium and Switzerland have literary obscenity laws that tend to follow the French model. Other European countries have statutory provisions regarding literary obscenity which, generally speaking, appear to be intended to apply only to pornography. In the Soviet Union all publishing and printing is in the hands of public bodies and very little pornography circulates. The postwar Japanese criminal code contains provisions regarding literary obscenity that suggest American inspiration.

Magazines reproducing integral photographs of nudist activities have been cleared of obscenity by legal decisions in Denmark, Norway, Sweden, and Switzerland.

General Conclusions

The present time is a period of great change in sexual morals and this process is reflected in both speculative thought and creative art. An almost worldwide censorship of books dealing with sex is therefore a particularly grave matter. The above survey demonstrates that the existing laws are most unsatisfactory. Generally speaking, they constitute an arbitrary menace to moral reform, sex education, creative writing, and scholarship; and they are a ready weapon to the hand of authoritarians and obscurantists and a constant temptation to abuse by ignorant puritans.

The widespread incidence in time and space of such laws makes it highly improbable that they will be altogether abolished in the foreseeable future. Indeed the existence of a commercial traffic in subliterature of an ethically irresponsible character addressed primarily to children, young people, and morally unstable adults, would seem to call, in the minds of many people, for the attention of the law. Liberty of expression cannot remain unrestricted if it is abused to overthrow the intellectual and moral judgment that alone makes it worth while.

So far as children and adolescents are concerned, the enactment of special legislation of the sort noted above which does not affect adult literature appears to be justified; and it is clear that the problem is by no means confined to sex. One may only question whether the reading of juveniles is not more a matter for the parent, the schoolteacher, and the minister of religion than for the policeman.

The semiliterate and emotionally underdeveloped adults who throng our industrial cities present a more difficult problem. The long-term solution is undoubtedly to have better and franker sex education and a more intelligent code of sexual morals. In the meantime, almost any system designed to protect the intellectual and moral weakling from the commercial exploiter is likely to be open to abuse.

If censorship is felt to be unavoidable—and there is no doubt that in the present circumstances public opinion would not tolerate complete abolition—legislation should confine its operation to cheap and trashy publications of an irresponsible type, and leave alone books that are addressed to the educated reading public and are published in a responsible manner. There would no doubt be borderline cases to give the courts difficulty; but the principle should be, not the complete suppression of any book, but the restriction of publication to a responsible public. It should be recognized that in a life-loving society the erotic book that stimulates to human love may well have its place.

Censorship in any form, however, can never be more than a necessary evil and it should always be regarded as a transient one. Present systems are dangerously open to abuse, and the following safeguards would appear necessary to provide the minimum protection for serious literature in any future where the principles of freedom are recognized:

1. The idea that a book can be obscene *in esse* is wrong. It is the circumstances of publication that create the evil, if any. Consequently, statutes like the Obscene Publications Act, 1959, that provide for the destruction of books are bad. The law should confine itself to punishing irresponsible and antisocial publication, and any destruction allowed should be incidental. Any matter should be offered to the learned libraries before destruction.

2. The law should be restricted to publications of a public nature; private communications and private possession should be outside its scope.

3. The condemnation of a book of scientific, artistic, or educational interest as obscene is not a matter that concerns only the authorities and the defendants. Not only should the author or any other interested person be heard, but the Court (as in divorce cases) should be bound to consider all questions of public policy involved and to obtain expert evidence on the literary, scientific, and sociological issues involved. Trial of such cases should always be by jury.

4. Special protection should be afforded to bona fide books of sex instruction (including those of a popular character) by responsible authors, books that have been openly published for a number of years, classics, works of historical interest, and books treated as serious in the country of their origin. Integral pictures of the nude human body should not be held to be obscene per se.

5. Learned libraries, universities, and other public bodies should be immune from prosecution so long as they confine themselves to their recognized functions; and printers should not be penalized in respect of work done for reputable customers in the ordinary way of trade.

6. Any powers given to the customs, post office, or other administrative bodies should always be exercised in pursuance of a court order.

7. Machinery should be set up to secure uni-

formity in the administration of the law; and the rehabilitation of condemned books should be provided for.

Finally, we must remember that the motivation of sex censorship goes very deeply into human psychology, having its roots in man's ambivalent attitude to sex. Biologically, eroticism is a passing phenomenon: what lures us today repels us tomorrow. Consequently, we are all tempted to be both readers of erotic books and censors of literature. Moral integrity and clear thinking should enable modern communities to resolve the tensions between these two sides of human nature without hurt to the spread of truth, the increase of beauty, and the furtherance of the good life.

References

General Authorities

Blanshard, Paul, *The Right to Read*. Boston: Beacon Press, Inc., 1955.

Censorship Bulletin of the American Book Publishers Council, December, 1955.

Craig, Alec, *The Banned Books of England*. New York: The Macmillan Co., 1937.

Craig, Alec, *Above All Liberties*. New York: W. W. Norton & Co., 1942.

d'Autrec, Lionel, *L'outrage aux mœurs*. Paris, 1929.

Ellis, Albert, *Sex Without Guilt*. New York: Lyle Stuart, 1958.

Ernst, Morris L., and Lindley, Alexander, *The Censor Marches On*. New York, 1940.

Ernst, Morris L., and Seagle, William, *A Study of Obscenity and the Censor*. New York: Doubleday & Co., Inc., 1928.

Haight, Anne L., *Banned Books*. New York: R. R. Bowker Co., 1958.

Scott, George Ryley, *Into Whose Hands*. London: G. G. Swon, 1945.

St. John-Stevas, Norman, *Obscenity and the Law*. New York: The Macmillan Co., 1956.

Reports of Cases

Commonwealth Vs. Gorden et al. An opinion filed March 18, 1949, by the Honorable Curtis Bok. Reprinted from Pennsylvania District and County Reports, Philadelphia, 1950.

Craig, Alec, *Suppressed Books*. New York: World Publishing Co.

Craig, Alec, "Recent Developments in the Law of Obscene Libel." In A. P. Pillay and Albert Ellis (eds.), *Sex, Society and the Individual*. Bombay: *International J. Sexology*, 1953. (This contains a report of the *Love Without Fear* case at the Central Criminal Court, June, 1942.)

Grove Press, Inc. v. Robert K. Christenberry. Opinion dated July 21, 1959 (D.C. S.D.N.Y. Civil 147-87).

"The Hicklin Case." *Law Reports* (Court of Queen's Bench) *3;* 1867-1868, 1937.

Kauffmann, Stanley, *The Philanderer*. London: Penguin, 1943. (This contains Mr. Justice Stable's summing up at the Central Criminal Court, June, 1942.)

L'Affaire Sade. Procès intenté aux éditions Jean-Jacques Pauvert. Paris, 1957.

Parmelee, Maurice, *Nudism in Modern Life*. Mays Landing, N.J.: Sunshine Book Co., 1952. (This contains the decision of the U.S. Court of Appeals for the District of Columbia, May 14, 1940.)

The Queen v. Charles Bradlaugh and Annie Besant. Queen's Bench Division, June 18, 1877. London: Bonner and Forder, no date.

Official Inquiries

Evidence Submitted to the Select Committees on Obscene Publications by the Progress League, Alec Craig, and the Society of Labour Lawyers. London, 1958.

Report and Minutes of Evidence of the Joint Select Committee on Lotteries and Indecent Advertisements. London, 1908.

Reports and Minutes of Evidence of Select Committees of the House of Commons on the Obscene Publications Bill and Obscene Publications. London, 1957, 1958.

Report of Pornographic Materials by the Gathings Committee, 1952. Washington: Government Printing Office, 1952.

ALEC CRAIG

Chastity and Virginity:
The Case For

THE major civilizations have almost invariably expected premarital chastity of women, and often of men also, as part of the social control of sexual expression deemed necessary for cultural stability. Although it has sometimes been difficult to implement this principle, the custodians of the culture have seldom questioned its validity.

In our era there is a growing belief that the insistence on chastity has been based largely on grounds that no longer apply: the appeal to fear has lost much of its power; the discrimination against women has been considerably mitigated. The assumption is that this therefore disposes of the opposition to sexual freedom.

That is a misconception. In our modern world, many arguments can still be advanced in favor of chastity. Kinsey *et al.*, in *Sexual Behavior in the Human Female* (p. 308), list twenty such arguments, and Ellis, in *Sex Without Guilt* (pp. 34–42), lists and discusses seventeen.

The hazards involved in premarital sexual intercourse fall into many categories, most of which are included in the following summary.

Physical Effects

Venereal Disease

Antibiotics promise to bring syphilis and gonorrhea under control, but there can as yet be no guarantee of immunity. Reported new cases in the United States still run about 350,000 annually, and sharp increases have appeared in the 11–19 age group. In addition, there are unreported cases. Damage done by venereal disease before treatment generally cannot be reversed. It is therefore misleading to suggest that the danger of infection can now be ignored.

Pregnancy

Modern contraceptives are efficient, and even better methods may soon be available. Yet Dr. Henry Bowman (1948), of the University of Texas, estimates that premarital pregnancies in the United States today total about a million annually. It has been estimated (Havemann, 1958) from the Kinsey researches that about one in five of all girls who have premarital intercourse becomes pregnant as a result.

The single girl who becomes pregnant must choose between a forced marriage, bearing an illegitimate child, and an induced abortion. The Kinsey Report indicates that the overwhelming majority go to an abortionist. Among women of childbearing age now alive, it is reckoned that one in seven has already had, or will ultimately have, a premarital abortion (Havemann). Can this wanton destruction of incipient human life be regarded as a matter of no consequence? Can young girls who undergo this experience avoid personality damage?

Emotional Effects

Conditioning

If *satisfying*, premarital intercourse sets up the desire for repetition. The boy is encouraged to seek further experience. The girl is awakened to a new need, which she may compulsively seek to satisfy in undesirable associations if her first partner ceases to be available. Either partner may submit to unreasonable conditions in order to maintain the sexual liaison. Once aroused and satisfied, sexual needs become harder to control.

If the experience is *unsatisfying*, feelings of failure and inadequacy generally result, which in a secure marriage would find compensation in other areas of the relationship. A distaste for sex and avoidance of marriage, with acute conflict, may ensue.

Guilt

Since premarital intercourse is against the conventional code, few can seek it without subterfuge. Young people with religious associations (the majority of American youth today) suffer reactions varying from mild uneasiness to agonizing guilt. They may be consumed with remorse at having broken their code, let down their parents, and earned public disapproval. This results in misery to the individual and tension in the relationship. Where one feels guilty and the other does not, the former is likely to feel exploited. These guilt feelings can easily break up a potentially promising partnership.

Anxiety

Frequently there is constant fear of being found out by parents and friends, with ensuing censure. There is also the recurrent fear of pregnancy, amounting to panic when a menstrual period is late. If the relationship becomes strained for other reasons, the girl may suffer a sense of dereliction, knowing that she has nothing left to give in return for continued affection. If maladjustment appears in the sexual area, the distress caused by failure to function, especially in the boy, is likely to exacerbate the situation and lead to serious emotional conflict. There is not the same incentive to seek help about such difficulties as there would be if they appeared in a marriage relationship.

Rejection

This may be strongly felt when one partner criticizes the other's sexual performance, indicating that it compares unfavorably with that experienced in a previous association. The girl may likewise feel deeply hurt when, having yielded herself sexually to "prove her love," she finds that the boy wishes to break off the relationship. The loss of virginity traditionally implies lowered value in the girl, and when it is not compensated by satisfying rewards it may lead to profound disillusionment. Feelings of rejection thus produced may result in patterns of hostility toward the other sex or in the acceptance of an inferior partner because the boy or girl feels acute loss of personal worth.

Trauma

Sex adjustment is often a delicate and complex process, and premarital conditions, especially when charged with anxiety and guilt feelings, are less favorable to success than the emotional security and social approval that accompany marital coitus. Early coital experiences seem to be determinative of later attitudes, and many girls report that their first premarital experience brought pain, disgust, and disillusionment. Often the setting lacks a well-developed relationship and the sense of love and confidence that characterize marriage. In some cases, the partner's approach is crude and hasty. He may even be a sexually deviant personality. Under such conditions emotional shock may result, laying the basis for stubborn psychosexual maladjustment.

Effects on Mate Selection

Overemphasis on the Physical

Sexual harmony has been given increasing importance in our time as a basis for successful marriage. But it is dangerously false to assume that two people able to perform mutually satisfying coitus thereby establish their suitability to be husband and wife. Many young men today are demanding a "sexual compatibility test" before they will agree to marry. It is an illusion to consider that a successful meeting of such a test guarantees either interpersonal, or ultimate sexual, harmony. The girl may rightly ask whether the boy loves her for herself as a person or merely for her body.

Nor need failure to meet such a test be construed as a contraindication to marriage. Many happily married couples need considerable time and effort to achieve physical mutuality, and finally attain it as a result of the growth of emotional and personal harmony. Preoccupation with physical matching is likely to confuse, rather than to assist, good mate selection.

Overemphasis on Personal Gratification

Mature love manifests itself most clearly in consideration and concern for the beloved. When two unmarried people use each other's bodies for pleasure, the altruistic qualities in their sentiments have little opportunity for expression. Personal compatibility is better tested under the acceptance of restraint, and the agreement to postpone pleasure until it is more appropriate, than in circumstances where mutual exploitation would be a sufficient motive. As a test of marital competence, the capacity to develop frustration tolerance together is likely to be more valid than the capacity to enjoy pleasurable experience simultaneously.

Negative Attitudes in the Male

Many men, although gratified by the sexual yielding of an attractive woman, find their respect for her lowered in the process—especially when they are seriously considering marriage. The argument is that if she capitulates to him before marriage, he can never be sure that she will not be unfaithful to him afterwards. Another negative attitude is the lack of motivation to assume the responsibilities of marriage when the male discovers that he can have all the satisfactions he needs without incurring such obligations.

Negative Attitudes in the Female

The girl who feels under pressure to continue premarital coitus when her personal satisfaction is limited is apt to develop hostility. Add to this the strain of anxiety lest she become pregnant, the furtiveness required to conceal what is happening, and impatience if the boy shows any sign of delaying marriage. The cumulative effect of experiences of this kind is to create doubt as to whether the boy can really love her if he goes on making sexual demands. She may be so confused by these emotions that she may be unable to clarify her real feelings about his suitability.

Feeling of Obligation to Marry

Once a pattern of premarital coitus is established, it may be difficult to break off the relationship without seeming to submit the partner to deprivation. Even when in other areas the bonds between the couple are seen to be tenuous, the sexual involvement may be such that they may feel unable to extricate themselves, and may be swept on into marriage, against their best judgment, by a sense of obligation. If no sex relationship had been established, the same degree of commitment would not be felt.

Effects on Subsequent Marriage

Disclosing Premarital Sex Experiences

There is often uncertainty as to whether to "confess" earlier sexual adventures. When these are disclosed, an attitude of hostility, resentment, and disgust may be engendered in the partner. Yet if the secrets are kept, this may create uneasiness lest the facts come unexpectedly to light, or a sense of frustration because there cannot be complete honesty and openness in the relationship. These troubles are avoided if there are no secrets to hide or to confess.

Recrimination

When marriages are under strain, it is common for the partners to express their hostility by seeking to discredit each other. When there has been known premarital intercourse with another partner on the part of one or both, this often becomes a cause of recrimination, increasing the bitterness of the quarrel. Following traditional community attitudes, a record of unchastity is frequently interpreted as indicative of character deficiency.

Unfavorable Comparisons

More critical attitudes to disappointing sexual responses in the marriage partner are likely when the disappointment is based on unfavorable comparison with patterns experienced premaritally with another partner or partners. If no basis of comparison exists, a husband or wife is more likely to be content with the pattern of sexual interaction that naturally emerges in the marriage.

Resentment of the Partner's Premarital Demands

After marriage one partner may regret having been involved by the other in premarital intercourse—especially if a pregnancy resulted

—and may attribute to this circumstance lack of present satisfaction, sexual or otherwise, in the marriage. Undoubtedly negative attitudes, engendered by unsuccessful or anxiety-ridden experiences of premarital intercourse, may contribute substantially to sexual maladjustment in a marriage.

(The question whether premarital intercourse in general helps or hinders later sex adjustment in marriage remains unanswered. The Kinsey finding of a positive correlation between orgasm achieved in premarital experience and good early sex adjustment in marriage has been widely acclaimed as justifying premarital intercourse. This conclusion is based on a misinterpretation, since it does not follow that the relationship between the two sets of data represents cause and effect. Other studies have led to an opposite conclusion. All we can say, in the light of research data so far available, is that the evidence is contradictory.)

Chances of Infidelity

When a marriage is under tension, and the possibility arises that the other partner may be involved in infidelity, a record of premarital intercourse will inevitably make it harder to dispel suspicion. There is an obvious similarity between premarital and extramarital sexual inducements, and a person known to have yielded to the one may be deemed to be correspondingly susceptible to the temptation to yield to the other.

The theory that chastity and fidelity are related finds confirmation in the Kinsey research findings. In the volume on the female, it was found that women who had had premarital intercourse were more than twice as likely (the rate is 29 per cent to 13 per cent) to commit adultery after marriage.

Social Effects

Loss of Prestige

Community attitudes vary and are changing rapidly; but the anxiety aroused by the fear of being found out is generally well founded. Strained relations with parents and relatives usually result when premarital intercourse is discovered. Censure on the part of church, school, or college, and sometimes of business associates, is likely to follow. There may well be damage to reputation and a resultant threat to self-esteem. There is embarrassment at being a focus of controversy and often an object of malicious gossip.

If a premarital pregnancy is involved, these effects are intensified. The girl known to be an unwed mother, or to have procured an abortion, is regarded as being of questionable character and a potential bad influence upon the young and innocent. Knowledge that the bride was already pregnant at marriage casts a discreditable light upon the couple.

Example to Others

Although premarital intercourse may be considered as a private and personal matter, it identifies those concerned with the principle of sexual freedom for all. They may be willing to accept the full implications of this. Generally, however, they are not. Chesser (1956) found that among mothers who had themselves had premarital intercourse, only 15 per cent wished their own daughters to follow their example. The others, presumably, had some reason to question whether their conduct had been desirable.

Some may decide to conceal their own behavior, and in that way avoid influencing community attitudes. But to do so involves inevitably the risk of hypocrisy. When there is community pressure to take sides, these people will clearly be in a difficult position.

Harm to Children

Almost any act of premarital intercourse may result in pregnancy, and a child may be born in consequence. The child of an unwed mother starts life under a shadow. Even if the parents marry, however, a difficult situation exists for them. The fact that the child's birth followed so soon after his parents' marriage will tell its own story, and he may in consequence suffer from shame and a sense of inferior status to that of younger brothers and sisters.

Cultural Effects

Ethical Implications

Human society has had to maintain a delicate balance between freedom and responsibility.

The selfish pursuit of pleasure based on the exploitation of others is not an inevitable consequence of increased sexual opportunity; but the possibilities certainly become greater. Personal integrity may be damaged by the need to practice deception, by the willingness of a boy to put a girl's reputation in jeopardy, to risk an abortion or an ill-born child, in order to gain personal gratification.

A long-standing human tradition has seen youth as the time when invaluable lessons of discipline and self-control have to be learned, and sex as one of the supreme areas in which the attainment of self-mastery may be demonstrated. Asceticism is unpopular in our time; yet in its true meaning, as the exercise of the moral powers in preparation for life's duties and responsibilities, and as a safeguard against the "softness" to which we so easily fall prey, it has peculiar relevance to an age when opportunities for self-indulgence are abundant. The thesis of J. D. Unwin (1934), that all great civilizations have ultimately gone into decline following the slackening of the sexual code, may have more substance than our contemporary mood is ready to admit.

Family Instability

Freedom to select and reject sexual partners at will would seem to establish a pattern likely to carry over from the premarital to the marital period. The positive correlation found by Kinsey between unchastity and adultery appears to confirm this connection. Adultery has long been held to be the prime cause, or at least the most common symptom, of marital dissatisfaction and impending disruption. There is therefore strong presumptive evidence of a chain reaction beginning with premarital sexual freedom and ending in marital and family instability.

It would be unreasonable, of course, to attribute the high incidence of family disruption in our day directly to the widespread abandonment of chastity. The causes of our modern family crises are many and complex. Yet it is difficult to escape the impression that the modern American, brought up amidst a plethora of material goods, and conditioned thereby to discard any worn article for a new one, may similarly have been prepared, by the relatively easy availability of sexual partners in his youth, for the divorcing habits that he practices to excess as compared with his counterpart in other Western countries.

Threat to Child Life

The sexual function is closely linked ethically with its reproductive outcome. If sex is used to improve child life, it is used aright. If it is used to damage child life, it defeats its obvious biological purpose.

Surely, then, the acid test of any standard of sexual behavior is its total effect on the child. If this be true, premarital sexual intercourse as practiced at the present time appears to stand indicted. It is resulting on a wide scale in the production of incipient human beings who are then destroyed by the thousands, and of a further crop of unwanted, ill-begotten infants, the tragic rejection of whom by their natural parents is mercifully mitigated by the adoptive couples who receive them with love and gratitude. At the same time, the security of tens of thousands of children born in wedlock is disturbed by the breakup of their homes, in some cases at least because their parents learned inconstancy in the school of sexual freedom during their premarital years.

Conclusion

The probability seems to be that premarital sexual intercourse will continue, and indeed that its incidence will increase, in the future. This will be a source of satisfaction to those who consider such a trend to be a mark of human progress. There are those, however, who think otherwise; and they can adduce their reasons. The arguments on both sides need to be clearly stated, and the issues weighed. Only thus can we shape responsibly the patterns that will best serve humanity in the momentous new era upon which it is now embarking.

References

Bertocci, Peter A., *The Human Venture in Sex, Love and Marriage*. New York: Association Press, 1949.

Bowman, Henry, *Marriage for Moderns*. New York: McGraw-Hill Book Co., 1948, pp. 225-246.

Chesser, Eustace, *The Sexual, Marital and Family Relationships of the English Woman*. London: Hutchinson, 1956.

Duvall, Sylvanus, *Men, Women, and Morals*. New York: Association Press, 1952.

Ellis, Albert, *Sex Without Guilt*. New York: Lyle Stuart, 1958.

Gebhard, Paul H. et al., *Pregnancy, Birth and Abortion*. New York: Harper & Brothers, 1958.

Havemann, Ernest, "The New Kinsey Report." *McCall's*, March, 1958.

Hiltner, Seward, *Sex Ethics and the Kinsey Reports*. New York: Association Press, 1953.

Kinsey, Alfred C. *et al.*, *Sexual Behavior in the Human Female*. Philadelphia: W. B. Saunders Co., 1953.

Leuba, Clarence, *Ethics in Sex Conduct*. New York: Association Press, 1948.

Unwin, J. D., *Sex and Culture*. London: Humphrey Milford, 1934.

DAVID R. MACE

Chastity and Virginity:
The Case Against

IN CERTAIN Western religions, the ideas of chastity and virginity accord with special ethical rules, which the followers of these religions may or may not observe. It is not those ethical principles that are here expounded. The present article examines chastity and virginity only as they appear to scientific rationalism, independent of all religious ethics.

Chastity

Chastity can be a state of mind or a state of fact. In the first case, it consists of a refusal to practice or take an interest in even the most normal sexual activities. This is for the benefit of a state of purity which recoils with disgust from certain manifestations that are, nonetheless, insistently dictated by nature. The chastity to which Judeo-Christianity attaches such great value is one of the most systematized forms of this abstention, and is based upon various religious considerations. The result of this state of mind may be a total abstention, as supposedly in the celibacy of Catholic priests and nuns, or a partial abstention, as when coitus is allegedly practiced only for the purpose of reproduction (while somewhat hypocritically minimizing the pleasure thereby obtained).

It goes without saying that modern rationalism does not attach to chastity the exceptional value that a superficial, limited, and unscientific ethic arbitrarily sets upon it. Absolute chastity is a form of ignorance, and the rationalist has little sympathy for ignorance of any kind. Even partial chastity constitutes a blind

denial of "the legitimacy of sexual acts," and is nothing more than a vestige of the ancestral taboo that certain religions persist in teaching without producing any scientific or logical reason to justify it.

Thus conceived, chastity, in its obtuse ignorance, can result only in producing an incomplete and wretched type of life; for sexual enjoyment is an important part of life, many people finding it as indispensable as the satisfactions of taste in eating. Our senses exist for a complete realization of life, and we should make use of them. It is no more meritorious to remain chaste than to go for a week without eating (and some people are foolish enough to attempt such a ridiculous and mischievous *tour de force*); actually, chastity and fasting are equally devoid of any scientific or rational morality. Abstentions may be prescribed for reasons of health, but they become incomprehensible when they are dictated, without examination, by purely conventional sentiments. As a result, to have remained chaste for a lifetime is to have been a self-deluded victim living a wasted life.

Therefore, the modern spirit should at least refuse to admire chastity or to praise it, and should see it for what it actually is: a dogmatic childishness. Today we are seeing the revival of an earlier fashion, the glorification of "the strength of the chaste." This is sheer claptrap. When a physical manifestation is natural, one goes against nature by refusing to utilize it and, by this refusal, one certainly does *not* increase one's chances of physical and mental development and strength. The person who does not use drugs or alcohol has more strength and resistance than one who uses them, but that is precisely because these expedients are *not* natural. When a force is natural and one chooses to sterilize it by nonuse, the final result is likely to be a general neurosis. That is why Professor Metchnikoff considered the state of virginity to be "eminently harmful to the species."

What remains, then, to the credit of the chaste? Very little, indeed, if we remember that, contrary to the conventional assumption, *the chaste individual is not a valuable or desirable member of society*. He is nervous, restless, unstable. He begrudges to others the pleasures that he denies to himself, and he is annoyed by the ease and freedom of their lives. Although he is theoretically chaste, his brain is crowded with images that are far from chaste, images of things against which he has declared war. These things may eventually master him, or they may destroy his well-being: enough has already been written about "repression" and its grievous consequences, which sometimes reach the bursting point and explode in one of those sex crimes that we frequently read about in our newspapers.

Virginity

It should be noted that if we do not distinguish between the ideas of chastity and virginity we inevitably become quickly lost in contradictions and confusions: for there are virgin individuals who are not chaste, and chaste individuals who are not, physiologically, virgins. The way to avoid this muddle is to reserve the word *virginity* for a *material fact*: the fact of not having experienced coitus with a partner, a fact that is generally easily verified by an intact hymen in the case of women, although many times the hymen may rupture from other causes. No test of virginity exists for men.

Somewhere in antiquity virginity seems to have been connected with mysterious reasonings that no longer seem very clear to us today, although they may sometimes be explained by sexual taboos, the significance of which I have elucidated in *The Ethics of Sexual Acts*. Thus

were established the Roman Vestals, and the Virgins consecrated to the Sun among the Incas, the violation of the vow of virginity being punished by death. The Greeks also knew women of this type, dedicated to a faithful service of the Divinity. They did not always succeed in being thus faithful, but in that land of Venus there were ways of arranging such things: when the beautiful Polymeda had an "accident," it was attributed to the passion of Hermes, and her honor was easily rehabilitated by a marriage with an influential man, who felt honored to succeed the god as her lover.

Here, again, the Western tradition is indebted to the Israelites. "The Jews," said Dr. J. R. Spinner at the Fourth Sexual Reform Congress, "were the first to attribute an excessive importance to the hymen, and this opinion, which is maintained to the present day, principally in the Ghetto, was also adopted by the Christians." This has had the unfortunate effect of distorting the meaning of the hymen, setting it up as a metaphysical rather than a physiological element. The Occidentals have, in principle, adopted this extraordinary mistake.

But virginity no longer has this importance when we leave the countries that are contaminated by the doctrine of continence. Havelock Ellis (1935) cites the case of the ancient Slavs, according to the geographer Al-Bekri: "If a man marries and finds his wife a virgin, he says to her: 'If you were worth anything, men would have loved you, and you would have chosen one who would have taken away your virginity.' Then he drives her away and renounces her." Ellis adds: "It is a feeling of this kind which, among some peoples, leads a girl to be proud of the presents she has received from her lovers and to preserve them as a dowry for her marriage, knowing that her value will thus be still further heightened." Among the Iranians, says Dr. Binet-Sanglé, virginity was a disgrace after the age of puberty. Many natives of Africa and Brazil refuse to marry a virgin.

Such examples occur repeatedly among all the pro-sexual peoples. They have no prejudice in favor of virginity. At the very least, one can say that they do not trouble themselves about it. Girls have sexual relations as soon as desire incites them, and they know that the disappearance of the hymen does not bring them discredit, or either family or social complications. They consider the abolition of this membrane merely a task that has to be done, just as the ears must be pierced if one wishes to hang pendants there. Experience exists to simplify it, and good sense prevents its being talked about afterwards.

From the strictly physiological viewpoint, the adolescent girl who cultivates her virginity like a flower in a pot seems a very undesirable oddity to the scientific mind. In our day, the girl who does not understand sexual manifestations (or who, hypocritically, pretends not to understand them) is no more a desirable and charming type than a girl who does not know how to read or write. Her ignorance is an inferiority and is nothing to be proud of. The virgin is an absurdity, a sort of monstrosity. That is doubtless why nuns always give the impression of being strange and, even in their best friends, inspire a slight apprehension, a feeling of suspicion or mistrust. It is because the virgin is an incomplete being. She is revealed neither to herself nor to others. One does not know what life will educe from her. One cannot foresee her feminine reactions before the future surprises of existence. Consequently, on the whole, she is a dangerous creature, as many disappointed partners have learned from the shocks and surprises of marriage. Virginity is thus a hindrance to the natural development of life, an obstacle to that most desirable and essential thing, experience.

Contemporary education in the Western world theoretically imposes physical virginity. This indicates a dreadful lack of understanding on the part of our educators, who fearfully close all windows that give a view of the sexual life. Experience proves (as I have personally been able to observe in non-Aryan societies) that a girl who has had the advantage of a complete sexual education that includes practical experience is often, at about 12 or 13 years, *a young woman*, having a clear understanding of sexual manifestations and ready to complete it by that devirgination which will dedicate her sexual autonomy. And note that this policy of rearing the young has a valuable advantage: *it lengthens* life, it restores to existence a number of years that at present are left barren and wasted. The girl who begins to live sexually at 20 years

of age may have her life reduced by a good third.

One ignorance entails a hundred others: flung into life, the virgin is disarmed, irresolute, hesitant. On the other hand, the girl who has shaken off virginal slavery moves forward with sureness, clear-sighted and strong-willed, maneuvering among the dangerous rocks and reefs like a ship steered by an expert hand. A single glance among the opposite sex enables the well-informed man to separate the sexual simpletons from the sexually educated and increasingly his preference and interest go to the educated.

Yet the prejudice in favor of virginity obstinately remains in the foolish antisexual's catalogue of virtues. A man marries a widow or a divorced woman without concerning himself about the nonexistence of her hymen. It is therefore manifest that the hymen is not of decisive importance in respect to the pleasures of possession and the happiness of the marriage. Yet if a girl has not received the official authorization for devirgination, this fact depreciates her in the eyes of certain suitors. The superstition of virginity thus becomes the most grotesque symbol of the doctrines of continence. There is no prejudice that has caused more ridiculous episodes or more regrettable conflicts. There have been men foolish enough to commit suicide the day after their wedding night, because they found open a door they had believed to be closed. This way of evaluating a person is about the most unbelievable of our sexual illogicalities. As a result, when a young girl in the Western world has sacrificed her hymen to a man, she expects him to pay a great price for this "sacrifice." She often infers therefrom a claim upon the entire life of that man, and if she is unsuccessful in enforcing it, she genuinely believes that she has been robbed. One does not realize all the consequences of this nonsense until one observes that it does not exist among non-Western peoples, where the loss of virginity is only a physiological incident, with no influence on the rest of a woman's life or on the opinion that is formed of her.

In reality, virginity is of genuine interest only to those brutes who find their pleasure in breaking down doors. We have repeatedly learned by the confidences of women that the true lover prefers to leave this surgical operation to those less sensitive. For defloration is crude work. It is usually done badly, and causes pain and repugnance. As an erotic ideal, it seems to have found a place in the Mohammedan Paradise, where the women that are there for the choosing are "perpetually virgin"! But the considerate lover detests this proving of a woman's virginity. He hates having to behave like a ruffian, even when he has intelligently discussed the subject of how to get through this experience with a minimum of blundering—since the Western world does not have schools where sexual love is taught as a science and an art.

There is also the possibility of failure. I have noted identical observations in respect to two well-educated men, both possessed of the most ardent intentions. They immediately found themselves disarmed when the virgin partner began to scream that she was being hurt. Their excitement died away, or rather expressed itself by an "extramural" ejaculation, postponing from day to day any complete and decisive fulfillment. And so, with girls of a very unyielding, resistive nature, the affair becomes a torture to both of the partners.

Referring to Professor Metchnikoff, Léon Blum has written in his *Marriage*: "If I understand him rightly, he would like to see girls, solely in the interest of their health and hygiene, get rid of this regrettable partition as soon as possible, and otherwise than by the natural operation." Blum adds: "Cheerfully discarded at an early age, virginity would no longer exert that peculiar constraint which, at the same time, counterfeits modesty, dignity, and a sort of terror." Instead of this "modesty" and this "dignity," which a rational education would have debunked long ago, it would be far better to do away with all the irritating inquisitions and the needless gossip from which we now suffer. This would be a sort of first communion with nature, a not unworthy god, under the sign of erotic possibilities. And that would render a valuable service to all those females who are now destined to become "old maids," and who, useless and miserable, live all their lives without any transports of ecstasy, never daring to let themselves go for fear of breaking a thread.

Some writers declare that defloration makes a deep impression upon a woman, marking her with a sort of stamp. When the sexologist investigates this point, he never finds conclusive answers. The idea may be a lingering holdover from ancient times or from the Middle Ages, when a young girl (often very young) was thrown into the bed of a stranger who, in a few hours, would become her "lord and master," and when she was allowed little chance of comparison with other contacts. In our day of feminine emancipation and of "polygamy" revived under the form of repeated divorce and successive remarriage, young women appear to find the idea ridiculous. Any such profound impress would indeed be destructive of individuality, and it should be avoided at all costs. Defloration by a physician prevents it in the most hygienic manner. Let us remember that the early travelers to the Philippine Islands reported that the natives had officials charged with the defloration of girls before marriage. Remember also the excellent and practical system found in the South Pacific, which abolishes the brutality of defloration by making it unnecessary, replacing it by a gradual and salutary dilatation produced by repeated contacts between little boys and little girls.

The counsel to be given by all rationalistic sexologists is therefore evident, and may be itemized thus:

1. By means of a specific, scientific, and physiological education, enlighten young girls about the trap that is set for them by the apostles of virginity, and about the advantages of doing away with this grotesque claim upon their life.

2. Deny that there is anything valuable or estimable about virginity, or about any of the conditions, professions, or offices that identify themselves with chastity.

3. To be complete, sexual education should indicate the necessity of emancipating the body and mind from the virginal slavery that narrows and impoverishes life and makes it ridiculous.

4. Do not leave the defloration of girls to the uncertainties and brutalities of chance, but advocate the establishment of a liberating and hygienic defloration by experienced technicians.

5. Return to the tradition of the ancient

world that knew nothing of the grotesque burden of carnal sin, which constitutes such a morose prohibition of the best things in life.

References

Arlington, Norman, "Sex in the World of Tomorrow." *Mattachine Rev. 4;* No. 10, 13-19, 1958.

Blum, Léon, *Du mariage.* Paris: Albin Michel, 1909.

Ellis, Albert, *Sex Without Guilt.* New York: Lyle Stuart and Grove Press, 1966.

Ellis, Albert, *Sex and the Single Man.* New York: Lyle Stuart and Dell Publishing Co., 1966.

Ellis, Albert. *If This Be Sexual Heresy.* New York: Lyle Stuart, 1963; New York: Tower Publications, 1966.

Ellis, Havelock, *Studies in the Psychology of Sex.* New York: Random House, 1935.

Ford, Cellan, and Beach, Frank, *Patterns of Sexual Behavior.* New York: Harper & Brothers, 1951.

Geddes, Porter, *An Analysis of the Kinsey Reports.* New York: New American Library, 1948.

Guyon, René, *La légitimité des actes sexuels* (7 vols.). Paris: 1929-1938. English translations: *The Ethics of Sexual Acts.* New York: Alfred A. Knopf, Inc., 1934 (Vol. I); *Sexual Freedom.* New York: Alfred A. Knopf, Inc., 1950 (Vol. II).

Guyon, René, "The Doctrine of Legitimacy and Liberty of Sexual Acts." In A. P. Pillay and Albert Ellis, *Sex, Society and the Individual.* Bombay: *Internat. J. Sexology,* 1953.

Robinson, William J., *Sex, Love and Morality.* New York: Eugenics Publishing Co., 1930.

Young, Wayland, *Eros Denied.* New York: Grove Press, 1964.

RENÉ GUYON

Child Sexuality

FREUD is generally credited with having stimulated scientific interest in the study of childhood sexuality. As Watson (1959) points out, "before Freud, sexual tendencies in infants were almost completely ignored." The publication of his *Three Contributions to the Theory of Sex* marked the beginning of a new period, not only in theories about personality development but ways of viewing many types of child behavior, including the sexual. His views about sexuality in the child, as well as his theories generally, aroused indignation in his day—and still do today. Frequently his views were summarily dismissed as being those of a most unusual man, if not a lewd one. Since his views of sexuality relate most intimately to childhood development, they should now be given.

Freud's Theories

Freud held that the period of childhood personality development is divided into three stages, each of which is dominated by sexual tendencies. These sexual proclivities are in the nature of instinctual, unlearned urges and the goal of each is the hedonistic one of pleasure. Each tendency seeks its inevitable end in its culminating goal, or aim, of sensual gratification. The instinct seeks its goal in an unhampered, direct fashion until the child learns to modify the instinctual aims through learning, cultural experience, and similar forces. More specifically, during each period of childhood, satisfaction is achieved through stimulation of erotogenic zones and consequent achievement of sensual pleasure.

The first erotogenic satisfaction is sought through stimulation of the oral areas (such as the lips and mouth) by means of oral activity, such as sucking. This is followed by a period of erotogenic pleasure in stimulation of anal areas by anal activities, known as the anal period. The final general period of erotic satisfaction is sometimes divided into two subperiods, the phallic and the genital, characterized by securing pleasure through stimulation, first, of the sexual parts of one's own body (phallic) and, finally, of those of another person (genital).

Freud maintained that there was a normal progression through infancy and childhood from oral, anal, to the phallic and genital periods of personality development unless some condition or state interrupted it. For example, a child might suffer a trauma when at the anal level (as for example by the mother's rigidly insisting that he be regular in his bowel movements). Through this urging on the part of the mother the child might become "fixated" at the anal level of satisfaction. Such fixation would have consequences for later personality development. A person so fixated might become penurious in adulthood and treat money (the unconscious equivalent of feces) as invaluable —as something rare beyond reason. This, Freud maintained, would have resulted from his having learned (become fixated) to value feces and anal activity.

Both Freud's personality theory, based on his concept of child sexuality, and his idea that children and infants were sexual, aroused immediate attack, and considerable criticism of his ideas has followed ever since. Although his concept that infants have a sexual life shocked Victorian laymen and, in fact, many scientists, it stimulated enough controversy to cause both his critics and supporters to take a closer look at childhood sexual behavior.

Havelock Ellis, Moll, Preyer, and others were early students of child sexuality. Although Moll (1912) stated that "Freud has not systematically studied the individual manifestations of the sexual life of the child," he nevertheless credited Freud with being among the first to stimulate interest in this area, saying that "Freud rightly insists that even in all, or nearly all, the works on the psychology of the child, this important department is ignored." In this opinion a recent author concurs with Moll. Watson writes, "it was his work that opened up this important area to psychological investigation." However, even to this day, as Watson further notes, definite controlled research on the question of frequency and scope of sexual behavior in children is lacking. A few rather extensive studies on more or less limited aspects of child sexual behavior have been carried out, but a comprehensive organized study remains for the future.

Some of the more useful studies that give us concrete data about infant behavior incidentally illustrate the limited nature of the aspects of sexuality covered and the need for more comprehensive, organized, and controlled research. Some of these studies are those of Halverson (1940) on erections in male infants, of Conn and Kanner (1947) on children's awareness of physical sex differences in the male and female, of Conn (1948) on children's awareness of the origin of babies and of the reactions of children to the discovery of sex differences (1940a), of Hattendorf (1932) on the kinds of sex questions children ask, and of Kinsey (1953) on orgasm in preadolescent children, on preadolescent heterosexual and homosexual play, and on masturbation. Although the studies to be immediately cited are more clinical than the foregoing, nevertheless they are worthy of note. Of particular interest and value are those of Bender (1937, 1941, 1952) and her co-workers on homosexuality in children and of the effects of adult sexual relations with children upon the child's subsequent behavior. All the foregoing studies, even though they are among the best we can draw upon, can be crit-icized from many technical points of view: too few cases, cases not randomly selected, studies not well controlled, etc. In spite of these criticisms they still remain a basic source of factual information about this period of life.

Theories About Child Sexuality

In the Freudian view, which is the broadest of all the views dealing with sexuality, there is posited an impulse which Freud (1938) designates an instinct. This instinct, he indicates, is analogous to the instinct of hunger. "The source of the instinct is an exciting process in an organ, and the immediate aim of the instinct lies in the release of this organic stimulus." He tells us the instinct is present during childhood and that it has an aim. "The sexual aim of the infantile impulse consists in the production of gratification through proper excitation of this or that selcted erogenous zone."

In this manner, the concept of childhood sexuality arises from assuming a sexual instinct present universally in the human species, which instinct has different aims during different periods of childhood development. The instinct seeks needed pleasurable satisfaction. Pleasurable satisfaction is attained by the achievement of particular aims during particular phases of childhood development, since stimulation of particular parts of the body and subsequent organic release of tension is an ultimate aim. For example, during the oral stage of the child's development the sexual instinct seeks oral satisfaction by stimulation of oral parts of the body, bringing about organic stimulation and release when the sexual instinct has achieved its aim. It is in this manner that many types of behavior in the Freudian view become sexual, as, for example, sucking and defecating.

It is for this reason that Freud's concept of sexuality is criticized as pan-sexual and too general. By such a concept of sexuality many types of human behavior, which ordinarily are not viewed as sexual, come to be so conceived. Certainly the layman seldom thinks of sucking or eating as sexual activities. But such activities can be so considered in the Freudian view. As Meyer (1948) points out, "Freud draws in a number of apparently indifferent doings as manifestations of infantile sexuality. Sucking fingers, a toe, the lips or the tongue, at times with rhythmic pulling of the ear or rhythmic frictions, and at times leading to a kind of orgasm and climax in sleep, is (at least in some children) a kind of autoerotism. . . ." And it is entirely true, as Seward (1946) says, that "the Freudian contention that finger sucking is equivalent to masturbation may sound to the layman extreme if not absurd because of the specific sexual eroticism usually connoted by masturbation." For the layman tends to think of sexuality as very directly involving the reproductive organs.

The views of psychologists other than Freud tend to be more in line with the thinking of the layman, for generally they write about the child's curiosity about sexual differences, masturbation, sexual information of the child, and similar topics. Thus, the view of psychologists less pan-sexual than Freud revolves around concepts of sexuality that connote, particularly, tumescence-detumescence, sexual arousal, motoric sexual reactions, and the like. Obviously, no one would apply the idea of procreation to the period of child sexuality, but the ever-recurring ideas of curiosity about sexual processes, of behaviors involving the primary and secondary sexual characters in some way, of tumescence and detumescence, and of arousal are frequently involved. Again, in order to aid in clarity of exposition, to provide a logical outline to follow, and to help to narrow one's scope so as to give precision of meaning, I will redefine the concept of childhood sexuality.

Definition of Child Sexuality

By childhood sexuality is meant the state or condition of the child with respect to the impulse that has as its aim any one or a combination of the following: (1) tumescence-detumescence, (2) erotic stimulation, (3) tension-relaxation in specific erogenous zones, or more totally.

The first aim is accomplished when there is objective, overtly observable evidence that erection is taking place in the genitalia. Of course, evidence of tumescence in male children is much easier to detect than that in the female, but female children have an analogue of male erection, the erection of the clitoris.

The second aim is accomplished when there is evidence that the responsiveness of the child's genitalia results, not from simple mechanical stimulation of the physical parts but when the impulse life of the child has acquired such direction that the child seeks specific classes of stimulation or responds, when such stimuli are present, with partial or complete tumescence, excitement, interest, or attention.

The third aim is accomplished when there is evidence of rigidity or hardness of erectile tissue (not exclusively of the sexual organs), together with subsequent loss of rigidity of the same. It is not strictly necessary that this tension-relaxation be conceived of as orgasm, although Kinsey (1953) makes a point of presenting evidence that orgastic responses have been directly observed in children younger than a year old.

Sexual Curiosity

In all probability the wonderment of the child about matters such as the nature of the difference between the male and female sexual parts, or about the origin of babies, is, as Kanner (1957) indicates, "a universal sign of legitimate inquisitiveness," part and parcel of the child's developing quest for knowledge about the world of reality. This curiosity is not an expression of some innate drive or instinct but is dependent upon specifiable circumstances that either stimulate or hinder the child's quest for knowledge. The child has curiosity about many events in his environment and included together with these is inquisitiveness about objects or events that can be more particularly termed as sexual. If the quest for knowledge is about such matters as wanting to know where babies come from, what part father plays in the birth of the child, why father has a "stick" and mother a "hole," etc., this is sexual curiosity.

Just as with any other type of enlightenment, the breadth of a child's knowledge about sexual matters increases with age. This will occur for most individuals, whether or not attempts are made to "squelch" the child's search, and as

Conn (1948) particularly has shown, "the period of socialization and logical thinking [of the child], as described by Piaget, has been found to correspond to that age interval during which the child begins to discuss sex topics," and "the scope of their sex interests, like the growth of their appetites and heights, increases with the years."

According to Hattendorf (1932), the most frequently posed questions by children of pre-school age related to the wish to know about the origin of babies and the coming of a new baby, and the second most frequently posed question was about physical sex differences. Conn (1940a, 1940b, 1947, 1948) has done a series of studies dealing with various phases of the development of "sex awareness" and gives us basic information concerning the developing sexual curiosity of the child.

The studies of Hattendorf, who inquired of mothers as to what sorts of sexual questions their children asked them, and of Isaacs (1939), who made naturalistic observations of the sexual activities of children, give us some information about the sexual inquisitiveness of children. From these we learn that the pre-school children of both sexes do have questions that are directly sexual, and that the ones most frequently asked are, generally, as already indicated. Other sexual matters about which children frequently are inquisitive are those relating to the process of birth, the role of father in the reproductive process, the nature of growth within the uterus, and coitus.

Conn and Kanner (1947) studied 200 children ranging in age from 4 to 14 years, whom they claim were "in the main the 'average' population of children," and attempted to answer the questions: what do children of varying ages have to say about the differences between boys and girls and when do they become aware

of genitalia as organs having specific sexual functions? They found that three-fourths of the children mentioned differences in wearing apparel and that no children under 5 mentioned this particular point. A greater proportion of the children of each successive age mentioned difference in dress, but after the age of 11 the proportion of children mentioning dress began to decline rapidly as apparently, from this age on, those of the last-mentioned age began to mention genital dissimilarities at once. Conn and Kanner divided their data into two categories: those dealing with personal differences between the sexes and those dealing with inter-personal relationships. They found that the differences between the sexes that caught the attention of the children and which they mentioned spontaneously took the following order:

> Out of 200 children,
> 150 named differences in attire,
> 116 named genital differences
> 93 named tonsorial differences,
> 44 named differences in urination posture,
> 9 made reference to the breasts and nipples

Of the 200 children, 70 per cent spontaneously mentioned genital differences on their first interview. They divided their subjects by various age groups and indicated the percentage of children in each age range who had the experience of noting genital differences between the sexes. These percentages are shown in the table below.

At all ages studied the differences between the genitalia, when noted, centered around the concepts of differences in size, shape, and "protrusion." All the children of the study knew that urination was a function of the genitalia but knowledge of the function of the genitalia in coitus was known to only 23 boys and 6 girls of the group. Of the 167 children under 11 years

	NUMBER OF SUBJECTS IN AGE GROUP		PERCENTAGE SAID TO HAVE EXPERIENCE		NUMBER SPONTANEOUSLY REPORTING EXPERIENCE	
AGE	BOYS	GIRLS	BOYS	GIRLS	BOYS	GIRLS
4–6	23	19	70	63	12	9
7–8	47	25	77	68	all but one girl	
9–10	34	19	65	68	less than 65% of the boys, all the girls	
11–12	21	8	91	50		

of age, 116 had seen the genitals of persons of the other sex and one-third of these children, according to them, were able to recall their attitudes and give accounts of their memories. Conn and Kanner conclude that most children, whether or not they had been informed about genital differences, ". . . responded to the acquired awareness of genital differences with unperturbed acceptance" or else ". . . had no difficulty in accepting the observed differences in a matter of fact manner. . . ." Over 61 different names were used by these 200 children for the genital organs but all designations for the genitals other than "thing," they write, had something secret and forbidden about them.

Conn (1948), in a study of 61 boys and 39 girls, reported on the ideas expressing a child's awareness of the origin of babies. He found that of the 25 children between 4 and 6 years of age, God was most frequently referred to as the source, one-third mentioned the hospital, and only two mentioned the doctor. Since no children of this age gave evidence of understanding the concept of the birth process, none mentioned the mother as having a part in it.

In the age range of 7 to 8, where 22 were studied, about one-half had been informed that doctors bring babies and that they come from hospitals. In about one-third of the cases the children had been introduced to the ideas of seeds, eggs, and the sickness of the mother at the time of the coming of the baby. Conn indicates that the acquisition of such information "causes the child of this age to begin to look to the mother's body as being the source of the baby." "Throughout this entire group [ages 7 to 8] there is an increasing emphasis and curiosity concerning the mother's role in the coming of the baby" and there is some perplexity about just what role the mother plays in the birth process. Some six children believed that the child left the mother by way of the anus and some knew that a male and female "element" was needed to "produce a baby." The children who had this more advanced knowledge were still, however, in a quandary as to just how these male and female factors come together.

The child of 9 to 11, Conn indicates, has heard his playmates, among other persons, express various theories as to the origin of babies,

and although "the average child of this age has been sensitized under various conditions of shame, scornful laughter and punishment to actual or fanciful names of the genital and excretory organs" and is hesitant to repeat these names, nevertheless many notice and talk about the meaning of the enlarged abdomen and talk about the concept of genital contact. The average boy of 10, of the socioeconomic group he studied, Conn tells us "is beginning to discuss and wonder about the nature and purpose of the sex act."

Although the cases at each age level studied by Conn are few, and there is much question about representativeness of sampling and some question about the influence of or presence of pathology in the group studied, some age trends are noted in the above data. As age advances the children go from more fanciful, unrealistic concepts about the birth process to more realistic and factual ones, and apparently by the age of 10 to 11 boys, at least, have approached a correct factual explanation. The average child of 4 to 6 thinks of birth in terms of the concepts of God, while the child approaching puberty sees that both male and female are necessary to the birth process and learns that coitus is involved. Sex differences and intelligence, however, are factors related to this knowledge. Conn found that there was a difference in sex information given and that "boys were told more directly that the mother carried the baby in her body," and so quite naturally observed and talked about the large abdomen more frequently than girls. He noticed some tendency for the more intelligent children to get more "sex information," to recall more of this information, and to pay attention at an earlier age to the mother as the possible source of the baby.

Conn, in general, concludes that children are much less curious about sexual topics than has been assumed or observed by many who apparently fear bombardment with inquiries. A quotation from his study (1940b) will summarize his evaluation of the sexual curiosity of children:

The facts speak for themselves. Parents must learn that they have been frightened by a few vociferous psychologists living in academic seclusion and by a handful of psychiatrists who have been blinded by a priori theorizing into viewing with alarm the future of the child who has not been "completely" sexually enlightened. Children do not ask for such "complete" explanations. The scope of their sexual interests, like the growth of their appetites and heights, increases with the years. The sexual information that they require cannot be administered in one dose any more than can the vitamins they require.

Masturbation

If one accepts the views of psychoanalysts and the concepts deriving from Freud, masturbation is a universal phenomenon in childhood (Stekel, 1950). If sexuality is considered, following Freud, to include "all phenomena of human life related to pleasure seeking," then masturbation can be omnipresent in childhood. If the thesis is held that all stimulation by means of touch is basically sexual, then it is a logical extension of the idea to deduce that masturbation is found in the history of each and every child.

Even if one takes a more restricted view of masturbation, it is a frequently occurring activity of childhood. If one considers as masturbatory activity only those actions of the individual where his own genitalia are touched or stimulated so as to bring about at least partial erection, or some sexual arousal, masturbation is still a commonly occurring behavior. Statements about the total incidence of masturbation during childhood, as in those of Kinsey for example, are most frequently derived from data gathered from the retrospective recollections of adults. Very few direct observations have been made of children actually masturbating.

Some few cases of direct observation have been reported by Kinsey (1953), and to him these prove conclusively that masturbation can be the source of orgasm in very young children. He reports on direct observation by intelligent observers (not necessarily scientists) of some seven preadolescent girls and twenty-seven preadolescent boys under 4 years of age and states that "these data indicate that the capacity to respond to the point of orgasm is certainly present in at least some young children, both female and male."

Kinsey (1953) reports on the total incidence of masturbation, usually with the criterion of the experience of orgasm, and states that in the female sex .3 percent have masturbated to the point of orgasm by the age of 3 and 8 per cent by the age of 10. He maintains that 1 per cent of the female population has masturbated (with or without orgasm) by 3 years of age and 13 per cent by the age of 10. The approximate figure for the male sex is also 13 per cent by age 10. In the female, masturbation is the most frequent source of preadolescent orgasm, and of those females who report preadolescent orgasm, 86 per cent had their first experience through masturbation. Masturbation is much less frequently the initial source of childhood orgasm in the case of boys. Boys may experience their first orgasms by other means, usually as a result of a variety of emotional situations, such as those stimulating fear, and a variety of physical stimuli. These have been reported by Ramsey (1950). Usually these are the same types of emotional and physical stimuli that induce erections in male children. According to Kinsey (1953), no more than 68 per cent of the first orgasms in boys are due to masturbation.

In the female sex, childhood masturbation is most frequently accomplished by some manual manipulation of the genitalia and most frequently stimulation is of the clitoris. The technique next in order of use is that of accomplishing rhythmic movements of the buttocks while the child lies face down, perhaps on a bed. Quite frequently while the child is in such a position the genital organs may be rubbed or pressed against a blanket or some object, as a toy. These techniques of childhood masturbation in the female sex are surprisingly similar to the techniques of adult masturbation. The order of the frequency of their use is, also, quite similar to that found in adulthood, with the exception of vaginal insertions. Masturbating children are not as prone as are adults to use vaginal insertions as a technique of masturbation.

Manual manipulation is, too, the most frequent technique used by male children. Manual masturbation occurs, according to Kanner, most frequently "in bed before going to sleep or after waking" and "with some children, it becomes a regular routine upon retiring."

Inspection of
Sexual Parts and Sexual Play

Much of childhood sexual play appears to be prompted by curiosity about sexual anatomy. Not all the sexual play has the aims of tumescence, sexual arousal, or arousal of the cycle of tension and release, but some of the childhood sexual play can, conceivably, attain such ends. This is especially likely to result if sexual activity or contacts of children is being or has been guided by adults or older children who give the child information helping him to learn to associate the sexual responses with some type of sociosexual context rather than simply mechanical acts. An older boy, for example, might instruct a younger boy in masturbation by telling him how to manipulate his genitalia in a specific manner and indicating that certain accompanying responses and feelings are to be expected, such as an ejaculate, a pleasurable feeling, feeling of warmth, subsequent relaxation after erection, and the like. Ordinarily, however, much of the sexual play of children takes place in a context where, while manual manipulation may result, the erotic implications of the acts might be unrecognized. A game of "Doctor and Nurse," where there might be touching of the genitalia, or simulated coitus, where the genitals touch, can be without erotic implications or arousal.

Most frequently the sexual play of children appears to be with companions of approximately the same age (whether of the same or opposite sex). Some 30 per cent of the female sex, and some 40 per cent of the male sex, have been involved in childhood heterosexual play. For the boys there is a steady increase in the total incidence of childhood sex play until adolescence. For girls there is a trend to become more reticent in such play in the later years of preadolescence, even though they were so involved in the early and later years of childhood. Near adolescence girls who are active in heterosexual play tend to circulate freely among a wide variety of male partners. As Kinsey (1953) states, "with seven boys involved for every girl who is having any heterosexual play near the approach of adolescence, it is obvious that the girls who do accept contacts at that age must be having a variety of male partners."

Where heterosexual play has occurred, in 99 per cent of both boys and girls genital exhibition is involved and most of the heterosexual play starts with this form of behavior. In the case of the children who are involved in any sort of heterosexual play, genital exhibition is the only form of sex play for 40 per cent of the girls and 20 per cent of the boys. Of those children who take part in any form of heterosexual play, about 81.4 per cent of the boys and 52 per cent of the girls proceed to manual manipulation of the genitalia. Usually the manipulation is confined to mere touching and only in a small minority of the cases are the contacts truly masturbatory in type. For most of the girls who are involved in heterosexual play such contacts of all types are confined to a single experience for just a few, and in 67 per cent of the cases they are confined to a time span of one year or less. Only in 11 per cent of the cases of girls where heterosexual play is found was the behavior prolonged through five or more years during childhood.

Very infrequent types of heterosexual play are oral contacts and attempted coitus. Mouth-genital contacts have occurred in 2 per cent of the cases of girls and 8.9 per cent of the cases of boys who have had heterosexual play experience. The recollections of adults are somewhat unreliable sources of information about many types of childhood sexual behavior, and certainly when adults try to recall whether penetration occurred during attempted coitus they cannot recount dependably whether coitus or mere genital apposition resulted. If genital apposition and attempted coitus are not clearly differentiated, then where some type of heterosexual play is reported, in 17 per cent of the cases of girls and 55.3 per cent of the boys there have been attempts at coitus. When the population of male children is considered *in toto*, 22 per cent have made such attempts.

In very few cases of heterosexual play have there been vaginal insertions, probably in no more than 3 per cent of those cases that report some type of heterosexual play. In these cases it has usually been finger insertion.

Homosexual Play

Homosexual play in the female sex is reported for very few children before 3 years of age but there is a steady increase from about 6 per cent at the age of 5 to 33 per cent at adolescence. Approximately 60 per cent of the male sex have had homosexual play in their preadolescent years. For both sexes where any homosexual play has occurred, genital exhibition is by far the greatest in incidence, with approximately 99 per cent of the females and 99.8 per cent of the males reporting it. For one-third of the females this has been the only form of homosexual play.

For both sexes manual manipulation is the sort of homosexual play next in order of incidence and in the records of children with homosexual play, 62 per cent of the girls and 67.4 per cent of the boys report having had some such activity. Mouth-genital contacts were reported by 3 per cent of the females and 16 per cent of the males with homosexual play experience. Vaginal insertions are reported by 18 per cent of the girls, and 17 per cent of the boys admit to anal intercourse. For the girls, just as in the case of heterosexual play, the homosexual play is in the great majority of cases confined to one year of life and often to one or two such experiences. This is true in the instance of 61 per cent of the cases of girls who have had homosexual play during childhood.

Sexual Contacts with Adults

Most of the literature giving information about the incidence and frequency of sexual approaches of adults to children concentrates on the female sex. In all probability this reflects the Western cultural concern with the taboo of virginity as it relates to the female and is also indirectly an expression of the double standard of sexuality. Although there is no rational or factual reason for an increasing concern about this matter of sexual contacts of adults with children, there is still a widely held belief that all such contacts with the child are universally damaging to personality, character, future sexual adjustment, and future marital adjustment. Just as erroneous is the view of the frequency of such occurrences, which is equally exaggerated and irrational.

Kinsey (1953) presents the most extensive evidence and reports that of the 4,441 female subjects studied, 24 per cent had had experience during the period of preadolescence in which adult males had established sexual contacts with them or appeared to be making approaches. This figure of 24 per cent also includes reports of those persons who had had no actual physical contacts but who had *thought* the man might be making an approach of a sexual type. The most frequent type of contact made by the male was that of showing his genital organs, which occurred in 52 per cent of the cases that report contact with adults. In 31 per cent of the cases reporting sexual approaches the adult patted the child but did not manipulate the sex organs, but in 22 per cent of the cases there was such manipulating. Approximately four-fifths of the girls who had had sexual contacts with adults had but one experience in childhood, 15 per cent had less than six experiences, and 5 per cent had nine or more experiences before preadolescence. Where there were repeated experiences these took place most frequently with adult relatives who lived in the same household with the child.

Kinsey (1953) reports that where repetitions did occur these appeared to take place because the child was aggressive in seeking the experience. This report, which may be surprising and even shocking to many adults, is very much like the reported conclusion of Bender and her associates (1937, 1952) from a series of studies on the effects upon children of sexual contacts with adults. She studied "unselected successive admissions" of prepubertal children who were referred to the Psychiatric Division of the Bellevue Hospital because they had had sexual contacts with adults. Bender points out in her studies that the children who were observed frequently exhibited "unusually charming and striking personalities, ability to make personal contact easily, and a tendency to attract attention, especially from adults." She emphasized the fact that, where there was overt sexuality with adults, the child in many instances sought the contact and the pleasure concomitant with this. The following is from page 514 of her 1937 article:

This study seems to indicate that these children undoubtedly do not deserve completely the cloak of innocence with which they have been endowed by moralists, social reformers and legislators. The history of the relationship in our cases usually suggested at least some cooperation of the child in the activity, and in some cases the child assumed an active role in initiating the relationship. This is in agreement wth Abraham's views. It is true that the child often rationalized with excuses of fear of physical harm or the enticement of gifts, but these were obviously secondary reasons. Even in the cases in which physical force may have been applied by the adult, this did not wholly account for the frequent repetition of the practice. In most cases the relationship was not broken until it was discovered by their guardians, and in many the first reprimand did not prevent the development of similar contacts. Furthermore, the emotional placidity of most of the children would seem to indicate that they derived some fundamental satisfaction from the relationship. These children rarely acted as injured parties and often did not show any evidence of guilt, anxiety or shame. Any emotional disturbance they presented could be attributed to external restraint rather than internal guilt. Finally, a most striking feature was that these children were distinguished as unusually charming and attractive in their outward personalities. Thus, it is not remarkable that frequently we considered the possibility that the child might have been the actual seducer rather than the one innocently seduced.

General theory has propounded that children's sex contacts with adults must inevitably lead to dire consequences in adult or later life. The sexual trauma theory indicates that such contact is almost the only progenitor of mental disturbance and abnormality in the emotional life. Usually the psychological effects of adult seduction have always been presumed to be harmful. Nearly all the psychoanalysts have been in agreement on this—as for example Freud, Klein, Abraham. If theory is not presented in the sexual trauma form, at least a detrimental influence upon later personality development is usually hypothesized. On the other hand, Bender (1952), after follow-up studies, concludes that even incestuous encounters need not be as bad as they are usually presumed to be and that "modern psychiatric follow-up studies of a sizeable series of individuals who as children had known these types of sexual experiences have not disclosed any directly adverse effect of the early incidents upon later social adjustments." In her studies the incidents had run the gamut from fondling to sexual intercourse. Her first series was limited to ten girls and four boys, 5 to 12 years of age, who had had a typical sexual experience with

adults, and the second group consisted of fifteen children, 4 to 12 years of age, who were grouped together on the basis of "the child's deep confusion over his sexual identity." In neither group did the results show gross maladjustment in adult life. She summarizes her conclusions as follows:

A summary consideration of the two groups produces two tentative conclusions on the significance of these types of childhood sexual experiences.

Overt sexual behavior of the several kinds described did not necessarily forecast either their retention into adult life or maladjustments specifically rooted in such experience. None of the children in the first group again needed social correction or attention because of sex activities. None of the second group developed, so far as our material could determine, into the typical adult homosexual personality.

References

Bender, Lauretta, and Blau, Abram, "The Reaction of Children to Sexual Relations with Adults." *Am. J. Orthopsychiat.* 7; 500-518, 1937.

Bender, Lauretta, and Paster, Samuel, "Homosexual Trends in Children." *Am. J. Orthopsychiat. 11;* 730-743, 1941.

Bender, Lauretta, and Grugett, Alvin E., Jr. "A Follow-up Report on Children Who Had Atypical Sexual Experience." *Am. J. Orthopsychiat. 22;* 825-837, 1952.

Conn, Jacob H., "Children's Awareness of the Origin of Babies." *J. Child Psychiat. 1;* 140-176, 1948.

Conn, Jacob H., "Children's Reactions to the Discovery of Genital Differences." *Am. J. Orthopsychiat. 10;* 747-754, 1940a.

Conn, Jacob H., "Sexual Curiosity of Children." *Amer. J. Dis. Child. 60;* 1110-1119, 1940b.

Conn, Jacob H., and Kanner, Leo, "Children's Awareness of Sex Differences." *J. Child Psychiat. 1;* 3-57, 1947.

Freud, Sigmund, *Basic Writings.* New York: Random House, 1938.

Halverson, H. M., "Genital and Sphincter Behavior of the Male Infant." *J. Genet. Psychol. 56;* 95-136, 1940.

Hattendorf, K. W., "A Study of the Questions of Young Children Concerning Sex." *J. Social Psychol. 3;* 37-65, 1932.

Isaacs, Susan, *Social Development in Young Children.* New York: Harcourt, Brace & Co., 1939.

Kanner, Leo, *Child Psychiatry.* Springfield, Ill.: Charles C Thomas, 1957.

Kinsey, Alfred C. *et al., Sexual Behavior in the Human Male.* Philadelphia: W. B. Saunders Co., 1948.

Kinsey, Alfred C. *et al.*, *Sexual Behavior in the Human Female*. Philadelphia: W. B. Saunders Co., 1953.

Meyer, Adolph, *The Common Sense Psychiatry of Dr. Adolph Meyer*. New York: McGraw-Hill Book Co., 1948.

Moll, Albert, *The Sexual Life of the Child*. New York: The Macmillan Co., 1912.

Ramsey, Glenn V., *Factors in the Sex Life of 291 Boys*. Madison, N.J.: published by the author, 1950.

Seward, Georgene, *Sex and the Social Order*. New York: McGraw-Hill Book Co., 1946.

Stekel, Wilhelm, *Autoerotism*. New York: Liveright, 1950.

Watson, Robert I., *The Psychology of the Child*. New York: John Wiley & Sons, Inc., 1959.

WILLIAM R. REEVY

Clothing and Nudism

History of Clothing

THE origin of clothing, like that of many other human practices such as burial, domestication of animals, and firemaking, was lost long before the dawn of history. There is scant evidence concerning the nature of the clothing used by our earliest ancestors. If we consider the lower Paleolithic age as the dawn of culture and Neanderthal man as the bearer of that culture, our discussion of the wearing of clothes may very well begin with that period.

Prehistoric Development of Clothing

What can be written about the use of clothing in earliest times must be based upon conjecture and inference, more largely on the former. An example of pure conjecture in this regard is the theory that clothing originated in response to climatic conditions. There is only the roughest kind of relationship and, as we shall see in connection with the discussion of the purely secondary use of clothes as protection, this conjecture has many "bare spots." It is well known that many present-day primitive people use a minimum of clothing even in very rigorous climates. The lack of clothing of the natives of Tierra del Fuego was first cited by Charles Darwin. The climate in this inhospitable land, where snow was observed to melt on the nude bodies of the natives, has been compared to that of the glacial cold of the Mousterian Neanderthaler. However, the cold of the Ice Age was probably a much more relentless cold. LaBarre (1954) believes that man's relative hairlessness and "linearity" of physique point to a tropical adaptation and that this hairless anthropoid was "caught short" by the Ice Age.

However, clothes may have a protective value on a purely magical or symbolic level as well as on a realistic one. There is a feeling of protection that causes the habitual clothes-wearer to feel a lack of it when he is without them. He finds himself "naked to his enemies" and therefore vulnerable. This feeling of vulnerability may have very ancient origins. There is evidence that clothes may have been used as a protection against the entry of malevolent magic and evil spirits into the body. Closely related to this is the psychoanalytic theory that clothes are a symbolic substitute for the mother's protection and love. Flügel (1950) cites Ernest Jones in this connection as showing that the unconscious fear of cold is derived from a fear of separation from the mother. A feeling of a need for clothes would thus be related to a "womb phantasy," *i.e.*, phantasies of an escape to the warm, enveloping, protecting home of the uterus from a cold and inhospitable world.

A little more inferential is Crawford's (1938) suggestion that, because an awl of chipped flint and a semicircular knife, which still survives among leatherworkers, have been found near the remains of Mousterian man, these imply the use of "a kind of covering but little removed from clothing." Crawford uses the intriguing phrase "Ice, the Schoolmaster," the implications of which are obvious. Man undoubtedly had a lot to learn beyond the development of magic in order to survive. However, fortunately man has often done the right thing for the wrong reasons.

The consistent finding of evidence of the use of ocherous clays even in lower Paleolithic times is pertinent to our subject. Authorities agree that the primary functions of clothing were those of decoration and symbolic magical practice, even in regard to protection. It may be inferred that the painting of domestic objects and of bones in the lower Paleolithic era went along with the painting of bodies for decorative and magical purposes, as has been the case among many primitive peoples of recent times.

It is only in upper Paleolithic times and with the ascendancy of Cro-Magnon man that we find definite evidence of the wearing of clothing. Not only do we discover excellent bone and ivory needles with eyes, which are the tools needed for fine and careful sewing and suggest tailored garments, but we find actual though rare representations of clothed figures. On page 34, Volume I, of *A History of Technology* is a picture of an upper Paleolithic carving in ivory of a female figure in tailored clothing resembling that of an Eskimo.

Linton (1955) mentions that a picture has come to light from upper Paleolithic times that shows a man's head and shoulders in profile with the shoulders covered with some sort of brown garment, presumably a fur robe or parka. Commenting on the rarity of representations of clothed human beings compared to nude ones, he suggests that "perhaps, like the pre-missionary Eskimo, they followed the sensible procedure of stripping whenever they came into the warmth of a cave or a house." This statement contains a suggestion of an early juxtaposition of clothing and nudity.

Textile-making and the Development of Sexual Differentiation

The earliest evidence of textile-making and weaving comes from Neolithic sites dating from about 5000 B.C. in Egypt and Iraq. With the development of weaving, long lengths of textile could be fashioned to clothe the human figure in loosely hung garments. With this development, we may see the *Anlagen* of the dichotomy in clothing that has persisted down to the present time and has become associated, at least in the Western world, with sex difference.

The history of sex differences in clothing is also shrouded in the obscurity of history. Flügel points out that, among modern peoples at any rate, some sex distinctions in dress are to be found "both among savages and civilized peoples." As he puts it, "There seems to be no escape from the view that the fundamental purpose of adopting a distinctive dress for the two sexes is to stimulate the sexual instinct." Among primitive and civilized people some sort of distinction is nearly always found. A discussion of sex distinction in the dress of modern (Western) man involves some very interesting historical data into which we make an excursion before discussing more purely psychological considerations.

As far as Western clothes are concerned, three tendencies can be discerned to come down through the ages—the arctic or northern type of dress, the southern type of dress, and a primitive type coexisting, preexisting, and presumably leading into the southern type. There are intermediate forms. The primitive type is still seen among many peoples in various parts of the world.

There is no evidence that the primitive type was a forerunner of the northern type of dress, as it was of the southern or tropical type. This distinction is recognized by several authorities (Lippert, *Kulturgeschichte*, quoted by Frederick Starr, 1895; and C. H. Stratz, *Die Frauenkleidung und ihre natürliche Entwicklung*, cited by J. C. Flügel, 1950) and is important for an understanding of one of the main influences on Western clothing that has come down to the present time.

The northern type of dress was largely of animal materials and was tailored, consisting of a close-fitting jacket and a tight pair of trousers. It was probably to make this type of garment that the upper Paleolithic and Neolithic awls and needles were used. According to theory, clothing began with wrapping the skins of animals that had been killed in the hunt around the hunter or warrior. These warriors with their skin garments appeared generations later at the gates of Rome after fighting the Roman legions in many parts of the world. The exposure of the Roman soldiers to this type of dress was the beginning of the coming together of two types of dress—the northern and the southern.

Another juxtaposition of clothing and nudity with reference to the classical world is exemplified by the Greek word and Greek concept "gymnastic," namely, the practice of physical culture in the nude state and with no sexual significance.

The southern type of dress was made of vegetable fiber and was loose and flowing, consisting usually of two pieces, a loose, wide-sleeved jacket and a loose and flowing skirt or trousers. The most ancient fabrics so far discovered belonged to predynastic Egypt, dating back to 8000 B.C., and seem to have been made of flax. Dress of this type was used in ancient Egypt, by Greeks and Romans, Chinese, Japanese, and Persians. According to theory, these clothes developed out of the ornamental girdles of the neck and waist of a more primitive type of dress that can still be seen in many parts of the world.

Most authorities agree that adornment and the decorative and symbolic function of clothing had priority over the protective function. They also consider that the concealment function, or modesty role, of dress was secondary and subsequent and not involved as an original motive for wearing clothes.

Psychology of Clothing

Any discussion of the psychology of clothing, about which much has been written, must consider a *multiplicity of motivational factors* —traditional, social, economic, physiological, and psychological—that involve many elements such as status, sex, and even protective symbolism to produce a kaleidoscopic picture of dress and of attitudes toward the wearing of clothes. The best discussion of the subject is by Flügel. We can hardly do justice in this article to all the factors involved, or to their interaction. We can consider only the more important aspects as they relate to the mainstream of present-day Western culture and especially to the subject of sex in that culture.

The juxtaposition of clothing and nudity is a relationship that dates from ancient times and subserves many unconscious needs and objectives. It involved various forms of bodily exposure including the opposite of nudity, genital exhibitionism, which will be discussed below.

There seems to be no doubt of the primacy of the adornment theme in dress, nor that this theme was often motivated by the desire to call attention to sex differences, to secondary sexual characteristics, and to sexual prowess—in short, of the fact that dress has subserved the function of sexual arousal, of calling attention to and emphasizing sex—and still does. Even in modern times in Western culture, the chief functions that seem to be subserved by clothes are protection, maintenance of status, and emphasis on sex difference. It is sometimes somewhat easier to recognize this in primitive peoples, among whom trophies and articles of dress are often worn to indicate sex distinction and status. But modern Western fashions, particularly those followed for formal dress, clearly differentiate between males and females and between individuals of higher and lower status.

It is interesting to note that with the conquest of the ancient world by the northern barbarians and the taking over of their type of dress by the Roman males during their military service, a marked accentuation of sex difference in clothes resulted.

A further development occurred at about the same time. A great increase in modesty took place at the collapse of the Greco-Roman civilization. This increase—due probably for the most part to the influence of Christianity with its body-concealing Semitic traditions—was doubtlessly reinforced by the customs and point of view of northern invaders coming from colder climates. In this way the concealment function of clothes was added to that of sex distinction. As Havelock Ellis (1936) expresses it, "One of the greatest sex allurements would be lost and the extreme importance of clothes would disappear at once if the two sexes were to dress alike; such identity of dress, has, however, never come about among any people."

Modesty and Clothing

In this connection a few words need to be said about the modesty-preserving function of dress. If clothing were worn because of instinctive modesty, two or three things, it would seem, should be true concerning it. First, there should be no naked tribes. Yet there are naked tribes even today, and only a few years ago there were many more. Second, if shame were innate, modest dress should be the same the world over; in other words, there should be the same concept of what constitutes modest dress.

This is far from true, as one authority after another emphasizes. There are few points on this subject about which there is such unanimity of opinion, all kinds of variations being alluded to, such as the modesty concerning the Chinese woman's little foot, the buttocks of some of the inhabitants of Central Africa, and the faces and backs of the head of Arab women. These variations in the part of the body emphasized by the demands of modesty in one people with indifference to the part emphasized by other people certainly casts doubt on the concept of an innate sense of shame relative to the modesty function of clothes.

Modesty relative to the genitals and the alluring quality of partial concealment arrived on the scene of the Western world at about the same time as the breakdown of the Greco-Roman civilization and the ascendancy of the Judeo-Christian influence. Christianity upheld a rigorous opposition between body and soul and taught that attention devoted to the body was prejudicial to the salvation of the soul. The Judeo-Christian emphasis on concealment played an important role in the development of a sense of modesty. One of the easiest ways to divert thoughts from the body is to hide it. But the increase in the amount and complication of garments itself provided the possibility of a new outlet for the exhibitionistic urges that were thus repressed. Concealment and display went hand in hand and have been companions ever since. Even ornamental dress worn largely for status and distinction may promote a feeling of shame if inadvertently left off at the wrong time. Furthermore, some authorities point out the vagaries of the sense of shame, such as shame elicited by an inadvertent covering of what is usually revealed or a wearing of otherwise proper garments at the wrong time.

The tradition of physical education in the nude, which was part of the gymnastic (*gymnos* = naked) body culture of Greece and Rome, survived for a time in the custom of nude bathing with the sexes commingling. Medieval bathing establishments became erotic resorts, which resulted in their being frowned upon by the puritans of the medieval Church. Communal nude bathing has survived in central and northern Europe to this day, largely with the sexes segregated. There are stories of communal co-sexual bathing in Scandinavia and in Russia, where it suffers somewhat under the handicap of being considered old-fashioned and not part of the trend of the modern world. In spite of a possible Communist wish to think of it otherwise, in this connection the spread of prudishness followed Christianity and Western capitalism and imperialism around the world.

Linton (1955) discusses, as have many other authorities, the untoward influence of the Christian missionaries in the South Pacific and elsewhere. He mentions the spread of disease caused by the missionaries' insistence that the natives in the South Pacific keep their bodies constantly covered. It seems that bark cloth was well adapted for tropical clothing since it was wind-proof but had no warmth, and it had the advantage of being plentiful and easily made into clothing. "The natives never bothered to clean it or repair it, when it became torn or dirty it was simply thrown away. Since the natives had never learned to wash or mend clothes, it took them a long time to adapt to European garments which were at first worn until they fell to pieces. There was a great decline in cleanliness with resulting skin diseases and other infections."

Modesty and Display

The most significant methods of sex distinctions are those that depend upon the relative importance of the two great motives of modesty and display. Among ourselves at present the female sex is more decorative than the male. Among primitive people (and for many years in Western culture) the opposite was true. With them, as with most mammals and birds, the male is more ornamental than the female. As we shall see, the decorativeness of the present-day female has an interesting history. Certainly, "modesty" has been more frequently seen among women and probably arises in a good many cases out of the various taboos that affect the female sex at certain times, such as at menstruation or childbirth. The factor of concealment of the absence of a penis may also play a role. This is suggested by the complete absence of female genital exhibitionism and by the degree of importance attached to the display of female pubic hair. This latter is felt by many people, including postal authorities who rule on the obscenity of nudist photographs. The peculiar tenacity of women to hide what is not there is an interesting item in this connection. Clinically, the onset of genital modesty in the female often seems to begin with the growth of pubic hair, even before the onset of menstruation. According to classical Freudian psychoanalytic theory, this would suggest the possible reactivation of an infantile penis envy at the time of early puberty and a disinclination to reveal an absence of something that is present in others.

If, as seems the case among many primitive peoples, men are more inclined to decoration—certainly in connection with trophies and ornaments of war, and with hunting and sex prowess—and women are more inclined toward modesty—and if certain traces of these attitudes are still to be found in contemporary Western culture—the question naturally arises as to what influences have brought about so very different a state of affairs at the present day—namely, that women's dress is so much more ornamental than men's.

Flügel offers some interesting theories in this connection. He points out that from the fall of the Roman Empire to the end of the eighteenth century there was little to choose between the decorativeness of the two sexes except perhaps that, whatever style of dress was in vogue, the skirt was always associated with a certain dignity that was lacking in the bifurcated nether garments of men. Thus, the clergy, the judiciary, and scholars have worn robes down to the present day.

Flügel comments that woman's unconscious struggle for monopoly of beauty in dress is an important social movement and, as we shall see later, certain historical events, notably the French Revolution, contributed to woman's final displacement of the male as the more decorative sex.

Man continued to stake all his attractiveness upon his clothing, except for certain definitely aberrant genital exhibitionists whose attempts to reverse this trend are usually singularly unsuccessful. On the other hand, women made use of the double weapon of exposure and decoration. The psychoanalytic reason for this distinction is probably that the displacement of exhibitionism from the body onto clothes went further in man than in woman.

It has been pointed out by psychoanalysts that in women the whole body is sexualized, whereas in men the libido is more definitely concentrated upon the genital zone. Again the evidence supplied by male genital exhibitionists supports this position. The greater importance of scopophilia and visual sexual stimulation in the male, which has been pointed out by Kinsey's studies, would play a role in reinforcing the difference of the sexes in this connection. Men respond much more than women to visual sexual stimuli. The exposure of any part of the female body works more erotically than exposure of any corresponding part of the male. In view of all these considerations, it is not surprising that women should be at once the more modest and the more exhibitionistic sex.

A curious corollary arises out of this, which Flügel discusses. He theorizes that, because woman's sexuality is more diffuse, she can exercise a great deal of unconscious sexual attraction, whereas with man, with his more concentrated sexual organization, the ultimate genital aim of the whole sexual process is nearer to consciousness. He states (1950:109)

. . . in witnessing female exposure, man is often more acutely conscious than woman herself of its sexual intention. Men may therefore (rightly from their own standpoint) accuse women of being immodest, and women (also rightly from their standpoint) may reply either that sexuality was seen where none was present (*i.e.* consciously recognized) or that they—the women—have a more "natural" and "healthy" attitude to the body (*i.e.* that they can enjoy the pleasures of exposure without apprehending any concomitant sexual desire).

Both sexes have some right upon their side in this dispute. On the one hand, the men have a clearer view of the ultimate biological end of all sexuality, including the decorations and exposures of female dress. On the other hand, the women are undoubtedly right in implying that there is a certain reciprocity between genital sexuality and those other "component instincts" (to use again the psychoanalytical term) which are more especially operative in the relatively harmless pleasures of exposure. The women's argument about their own "natural" and "healthy" attitude is very much the same as that used by the supporters of "nude culture," who are never tired of maintaining that nakedness tends powerfully to diminish "sexuality" (*i.e.* the more directly genital impulses of sexuality). The—by now extensive—experience of the

"Friends of Nature" would seem to show that this contention is correct, the chief reason probably being that the increased pleasures of exhibitionism and of skin and muscle erotism have drained off a certain quantity of sexual energy which might otherwise have taken a purely genital channel.

Women have used another defense against the male charge of incitation with immodesty. They reply that men have made them so, and that it is only in response to an insistent male demand that women are induced to expose their persons. This means that women are refusing to accept the part of the guilty temptress that men, in an endeavor to protect their own sex guilt, are ever ready to thrust upon them. As part of their emancipation, women are objecting to playing the traditional role of scapegoat to men's sex guilts and ambivalences.

"Great Masculine Renunciation"

Flügel further speaks of the "Great Masculine Renunciation" in connection with the sudden reduction of male sartorial decorativeness that took place at the end of the eighteenth century. At that time there occurred one of the most extraordinary turns of events in the whole history of clothing and dress—a turn of events under which we are still living. Up to that time there was little to choose between the splendor and decorativeness of men's and women's clothes, whether in style, ornamentation, materials, or colors. Then quite suddenly —a matter of some fifty years or less—Western man abandoned his claim to be considered beautiful. Henceforth he aimed at being useful, strong, and silent.

Flügel discusses the causes of this "Great Masculine Renunciation" in terms of the psychological concomitants of the political and social changes that took place at the end of the eighteenth century in the form of the manifold consequences of the upheaval of the French Revolution. The emphasis on rank and wealth fell away. The brotherhood-of-man ideal of the new social order demanded clothing that expressed the common humanity of all men, which could be accomplished by means of a greater *uniformity* of dress than had obtained under the *ancien régime*.

The respectability of the ideal of work that came about with the rise of the bourgeoisie demanded a greater *simplification* of dress to a general approximation of plebeian standards. The ideals of the Revolution became progressively consolidated, with each passing decade taking over class after class until they became accepted even by the aristocracies. Man's important activities went on in the workshop and office and not in the mansion and drawing room.

The process of the democratization of clothes is still going on. Within our lifetime, following two world wars, it has affected women's as well as men's clothes. Slacks, shorts, blue jeans, and even "fly fronts" have been added to women's armamentarium of clothing as part of their "emancipation" to masculine ideals of work, uniformity, simplicity, utility, duty, silence, and strength. There are no doubt many other factors involved, as we have already pointed out—a multiplicity of motivations all interacting to produce the complex picture of women's present-day clothing.

However, women still cling to decoration and *décolletage*, ornamentation and revelation, concealment and allurement, in their more "social" dress. The wonder, of course, is why the factors that affected men's clothing in the first place did not similarly affect women's costume, and how men have been able to bear the sacrifice (of being nondecorative) that the new order imposed on them. Flügel propounds these questions and professes to have no answers for them. He says, "To answer these questions fully would require a deeper knowledge of certain fundamental psychological and sociological processes than we at present possess."

Two observations may be of some help in this connection. One comes from Kinsey's finding of the prepotency of visual sexual stimuli in males as against females. This interesting and significant distinction may be physiological in origin and may be underlined by the sexual situation that obtains. On the other hand, it is a finding that confirms and generalizes the psychoanalytic observation of the greater degree of scoptophilia in males so well brought out by Fenichel (1945). This can be discerned in part in the expression of the genital exhibitionist formula "I wish to show you what I look for in you." Clinically, scoptophilia and genital exhibitionism are closely related.

Man's scoptophilia and greater dependence on visual sexual stimulation may very well have played important roles in keeping women in the role of the "observed one," with her emphasis on decoration and *décolletage*. Something in her self-esteem is satisfied by this role and it has kept her from following man in the "Great Masculine Renunciation." Powerful sociological and economic forces have acted to keep women in this position. Women may have maintained the tendency to partial concealment and partial display in order more fully to exploit male scoptophilia—to "keep the price up" on their chief commodity. Other more directly economic forces are those that stand to profit from the allure of partial concealment, such as the powerful garment industry and, in more modern times, the potent forces of advertising, movies, and TV, which depend so much on the sex allurement provided by provocative pictures of pretty girls dressed with emphasis on sex by partial concealment.

The second observation is Flügel's emphasis on the phallic character of man's dress as a protection against unconscious fears of castration. Men associate "the choking collar and the clogging coat" as symbols of virility and respectability. Furthermore, there may be guilt attached to the idea of abandoning the traditional male costume, as the stiff coat and stiff tight collar are symbols of moral restraint to keep the ever-restless male on the narrow path of virtue and duty. Thus, the sexual restlessness of the male would be an important source of his need for tight and stiff clothing to help him adhere to the ideal of work and duty set by the "Great Masculine Renunciation."

Transvestism

An interesting phenomenon that relates to phallicism and to the sex difference in dress may be discussed at this point. Transvestism, or eonism as Havelock Ellis called it, does not necessarily coincide with active homosexuality and may be a phenomenon almost entirely related to the field of clothing. According to Flügel, psychoanalytic studies suggest that in transvestism the phallic symbolism of clothes is of great importance. Fenichel suggested that there are two chief stages in the psychological development of the male transvestite: (1) an unconscious refusal to accept the lack of a penis in women, and (2) an unconscious identifica-

tion of the self with the imaginary penis-possessing woman. Clinically, it is found that dressing in female clothing acts as an anxiety-allaying mechanism in many transvestite males.

Less evidence is at hand for the appearance of the same phenomenon in females, as it blends in a continuum with nonclinical and day-to-day appearance in the dress of modern woman. Here sociological evidence may be invoked. As noted above, this tendency may be connected with the increasing democratization of clothes, as well as with individual refusal to accept the lack of a penis and the utilization of the phallic symbolism of male clothing. As a continuation of the democratization of clothes it may also tie in with a tendency to minimize sex allurement and a rebellion against a period when sex differences (in the Victorian era) reached an all-time maximum.

Nudism

The beginnings of the nudist movement also coincide with the rebellion against Victorianism, which became increasingly manifest during the first three decades of the twentieth century. Many factors are undoubtedly involved in the appearance and spread of this interesting development in dress reform.

History

Modern nudism made its appearance as an organized movement in Germany shortly before World War I, stemming from many sources. The mainspring of modern nudism was probably a romantic back-to-nature rebellion against industrialization, with a neo-Grecian emphasis on body culture. Thus, its appearance in a highly industrialized country such as Germany, where a certain amount of romanticism has been a traditional element of the culture, is not surprising. As early as 1905 Richard Ungewitter urged back-to-nature living and a book on nudism by this remarkable man appeared in that year.

However, one aspect of the growth of modern nudism after World War I bears testimony to the probability that in one way at least the nudist movement represents an extension of the democratization of clothes that had been going on for many years, as discussed above. As intimated by Carlyle in *Sartor Resartus,* communal nudism is the ultimate in equalization. This possibility is supported by the welcome given to nudism after World War I as a progressive movement by worker groups, fostered by Socialist governments of many municipalities of Germany. An extreme uniformity and simplicity in dress and nonconformity in the philosophy of clothes accompanied nonconformity in social and political thought.

Another reason that is often given for the spread of nudism in Germany after World War I is that no country suffered quite so severely as did Germany in the lowering of the national physique due to starvation living during that war and immediately thereafter. The German people, especially the youth, were acutely aware of this and, soon after the war was over, bands of *Wandervögel* or hikers (youths and maidens) roamed the countryside, dedicating themselves to a free, natural way of life, traveling light, and bathing in streams unclothed.

Finally, it may also be thought that the prurient prudishness of the times, although not so strong in Germany as it was in Anglo-Saxon countries, was strong enough to produce a counter-agitation for certain reforms in sex mores. Germany was situated at the crossroads of Europe and was, before Hitler, the site of origin of many experiments in social and cultural reform.

Aims

The main aim of the nudist movement was, in addition to the democratization of man, that of dignifying and demystifying the human body and reintegrating the sex organs into the rest of the body. Desexualization, or playing down of genital sex, has been from the beginning one of the major aims of nudism. Nudists never tire of pointing out that the complete and unabashed practice of nudism has this effect. The standards of sex decorum in nudist camps is extremely high. Very few permit the use of alcoholic beverages. Nudists present many statistics showing that there is a greater percentage of sexually normal people among nudists than among the general population. According to these statistics, divorce, sexual misbehavior, sex offenses, and juvenile delin-

quency are much less frequent among nudists than among the population at large.

It can be readily understood, in view of the tremendous influence of the Judeo-Christian tradition and the prevalence of the body taboo, why, even with these lofty aims, nudists have encountered misunderstanding, intolerance, and persecution. Because their aims are so readily misunderstood, they have been exploited by an ever-ready sensation-mongering press, using such terms as "love colony" and "nudity cult." The term "colony" is not in good usage among nudists because the connotation is of a group of people living a life apart from the rest of the community—a kind of naked world. According to the leading exponents of the nudist movement, nothing is further from their aims.

Their aim appears to be in the direction of providing ordinary people who do not have private estates or other such facilities with a chance to have a vacation from clothes and the by-products of industrialization. Nudists point out that occasional social nudity provides a positive incentive for body care because people become more conscious of physical fitness. There is no question that there is in nudism a strong "back to nature" or "naturist" tendency that fits into a philosophy of physical fitness through a utilization of natural means such as sunlight, fresh air, and proper diet. Rejection of overrefined and overcooked and chemicalized foods is often found among nudists, as well as, among some, a promotion of vegetarianism.

The aspirations of nudism seem to fall into three main categories. One is the permissibility of the pleasure and convenience of going nude where nudity is the natural thing to do, as in bathing. Nudists do not believe in dress merely for the purpose of concealment. The second category of nudist aims seems to fall into the area of promotion of physical fitness by the use of natural means, welcoming also the psychological concomitants of the practice. The third category of nudist goals is the promotion of naturalness and the fostering of emotional health in certain areas as a psychological and sociological result of the acceptance of social nudism by those who now and then participate in a nudist experience. This latter aspect of nudism will be discussed at some length below.

Historically, nudist groups with these general aims multiplied all over Germany during the 1920's. However, it was only during the early thirties that the movement spread to Anglo-Saxon countries such as Great Britain and the United States.

The Spread of Nudism

In general, nudism has had more rough going in English-speaking countries than on the continent of Europe. This has been reflected even in the designations used. In Germany the term *Nacktkultur* was superseded by such terms as *Freiekörperkultur, Lichtkultur,* or *Lichtfreunde.* In France such terms as *amis de vivre* and *naturistes* have been popular. In English, with terms such as "free body culture" and "gymnosophy" sounding awkward, the term "nudism" has become generally used by both the exponents of nudism and, with an element of stigmatization, by nonnudists. There is no more euphemistic term in general use in English.

During the latter years of the twenties many Americans, English, and other Europeans visited German nudist camps, notably Klingberg Freilicht Park, the workers' Koch Schule, and a workers' camp or club of the Socialist party, the Freiluftbund. Dozens of nudist groups sprang up all over Germany, most major cities having several clubs.

Anglo-Saxon visitors were surprised to find that nude bathing on the fine white beaches of the North Sea island of Sylt was authorized by the government of Schleswig-Holstein. Even more astonishing to Anglo-Saxon visitors was the fact that two public swimming pools in Berlin, the Stadtbad and the fashionable Lunabad, were turned over at specific hours and days to nudists. For American visitors, such official recognition, indeed authorization, of *Nacktkultur* by municipalities and the state was the most extraordinary feature of the movement in Germany.

The movement spread rapidly during the twenties into many adjacent European countries such as Czechoslovakia, Switzerland, Holland, and Scandinavia, where unorganized nude bathing had been going on for years. Even predominantly Roman Catholic countries such as France and Austria acquired nudist groups under various names.

However, Roman Catholicism has been a leader in upholding the Judeo-Christian tradition of concealment and has in many places actively opposed the spread of nudism, largely through a misunderstanding of its aims, which as a matter of fact include the promotion of propriety of relations between the sexes. As some of its critics have pointed out, there is a kind of puritanism among nudists with their emphasis on propriety, sobriety, minimization of sex, and rejection of obscenity and pruriency, the big difference being in what is considered obscene. The nudists insist that the unclothed human body is not obscene but that only prurient attitudes would tend to make it so. *Honi soit qui mal y pense.* They point out that to them there is something obscene about emphasizing sex by concealment, especially concealment by implication. They would consider obscene putting a brassiere on a little girl as part of her bathing suit, or a nudist magazine that can be sold on newsstands only if the cover lady's nipples are crossed out with pen and ink. This the nudists would insist is obscene.

As will be seen, controversy as to the purity or obscenity of nudism has raged for many years, with the nudists mustering many rational arguments to support their point of view. What the nudists seem to fail to appreciate is that rationality and consistency play only a small role in this matter and that irrationality and unconscious motivation reign supreme. Few people on both sides, including experts writing pontifically on the subject, are free from such motivations or are amenable to reasoning.

Nudism has made slow progress, especially in Roman Catholic and Anglo-Saxon countries. The first English book on nudism was published in Great Britain by Maurice Parmelee in 1927 under the title *Nudity and Modern Life* or *The New Gymnosophy.* An attempt to publish an American edition was discouraged because of rumblings from a United States district prosecutor warning that the publishers would be liable to criminal prosecution. (This was before some liberalizing decisions were made relative to literary "obscenity," such as those concerning James Joyce's *Ulysses.*) The new book had a preface by Havelock Ellis and contained some clear and unmistakable photographs of undressed men and women. It is noteworthy that Dean Inge of St. Paul's, who was consulted about the morality of publishing it, recommended that it be published with the pictures. He not only defended the morality of the book but made pertinent remarks on the conventional standards of modesty. The juxtaposition of a United States attorney and Dean Inge, neither of whom could be called a nudist, indicates pointedly the controversial nature of the whole subject.

Frances and Mason Merrill (1931, 1932), two Americans who visited German nudist camps during the late twenties, and in 1931 brought out the first book on nudism published in the United States that is still an excellent source, quote figures on the number of German nudists as of 1931 ranging from 200,000 to 3,000,000. The latter figure may be considered a little high and the former a little low, depending on whom one considers to be a nudist. Statistics concerning nudists are very difficult to come by, even at the present time, as we shall see below, largely because there is still so much of the esoteric in the practice of nudism, some of which may be entirely informal and *en famille*.

Nudism in the United States

The first American nudist group met on Labor Day, 1929, in New York State under the leadership of Kurt Bartel. The group met later in the year in an indoor gymnasium in New York City and was raided by the police. In contrast to Germany before Hitler, nudism has made rather slow progress in the United States (even though Benjamin Franklin and Henry Thoreau were early apostles of nudism in America), encountering considerable opposition and persecution, and inevitable journalistic ridicule. Journalists have not tired of sensation-mongering on the subject. In view of the role played by journalistic sensationalism in our culture, this is not surprising, although nonetheless handicapping to the spread of nudism as an organized movement.

Because of the ridicule and actual persecution of individuals belonging to nudist organizations, statistics are completely unreliable. Estimations as to the number of nudists in the United States, as of this writing, vary from 15,000 to 200,000. One authority states that there are about 15,000 dues-paying members. How much domestic nudism and informal adult nudism occurs and has been promoted by the very existence of a nudist movement is unknown. This factor can, of course, operate in both directions. Even Kinsey does not help us very much in this connection. He has some statistics in his book on female sexuality concerning the occurrence of nudity in marital coitus. The figures are on decade of birth of the female and educational status. If they mean anything relative to the attitude toward nudity they indicate that there has been a marked rise in nude marital coitus during the first three decades of the twentieth century and a liberalization of the attitude toward nudity during the years of the rise of nudism in the Western world. They also indicate that there is a rough positive correlation between acceptance of nudity and education. The higher the educational level, the more liberal the attitude toward nudity. This ties in with the acceptance of nudism among more educated people, as noted below.

Kinsey says that "it seems reasonable to conclude that the avoidance of nudity during coitus is a perversion of what is, in a biological sense, normal sexuality." Many nudists would not only heartily endorse this point of view but would extend the statement to include the pointed avoidance of nudity in many other life situations among perversions of sexual normality.

Nudism received a distinct setback in Germany with the rise of Hitler. Because of the association of so many nudist groups with other liberal causes, all but a very few nudist parks were closed and official sanction of nudism was withheld. Since the war nudism has come back in Germany, but not with the exuberance of growth that characterized the movement during the twenties and early thirties. On the other hand, nudism has since World War II shown a slow but steady rise in Anglo-Saxon countries, even if judged only by the number of nudist groups and nudist camps. In the August, 1933, issue of *The Nudist,* which is labeled "Official Publication, International Nudist Conference," there were 21 nudist groups in eight states listed in a directory. In November, 1958 there were three "official" nudist magazines and several others of dubious standing. A perusal of the current issues of these magazines in search of something statistical to report revealed that there were 125 groups in 36 states.

There are two national nudist organizations to which the individual nudist groups belong, with some overlapping and some local groups without any affiliation. The splitting of the American Sunbathing Association in 1951 into the parent organization and a smaller, dissident organization, the National Nudist Council, occurred along administrative and organizational, not ideological, lines.

The growth of nudism has been slowed somewhat by the structure and policies of the nudist organizations. It is not easy to try out nudism in a casual and informal manner. Visiting nudist camps is always by recommendation and invitation only. Application for membership must be made in advance and must be supported by evidence of a sincere interest in nudism. Since application is largely by recommendation and nudist membership is largely secret, getting to know an avowed nudist is not an easy matter for most people. To paraphrase a well-known dictum, "Even your best friends won't tell you —that they are nudists."

Many nudist groups are limited to family membership only and do not admit unmarried adults. Single unattached males, particularly, are met with considerable scrutiny and may find many camps closed to them. Such circumspection has handicapped the spread of nudism. Nudists have had to face the dilemma of trying to further their growth while maintaining a certain degree of discretion and secrecy to protect individual members from ridicule and persecution, as well as promulgating rigid rules to maintain respectability. In the main they have considered respectability more important than proselytizing. Respect of confidences and discretion has been particularly important, since so many of the members are in business, in executive positions, and in professions and belong to the middle class. Nudism has not, as it did in Germany, attracted the working classes any more than socialism has.

Laws Relating to Nudism

The growth of nudism in the United States has been accompanied by an uneven but steady liberalization of laws relative to the practice of nudism. In this way the emphasis on privacy, propriety, and sobriety among recognized nudists may have "paid off." There has been a gradual though uneven growth of tolerance reflected by a greater degree of acceptance of the legality of photographs of the nude body. More decisions have been rendered favorable to nudists and more attempts to pass antinudist laws have been defeated in recent years. The one notorious exception was the passing of an antinudist law in New York State as far back as 1935. Apparently the same forces and the same attitudes that led to the pillorying of Bertrand Russell as a corruptor of youth in 1940, accusing him among other things of being an advocate of nudism, succeeded in 1935 in rushing an antinudist law through the New York State Legislature. New York is one of three states that have antinudist laws. An excellent account of the way in which this law was put through the state legislature and the governor induced to sign it can be found in Shaw (1938). In this book other similarly reactionary legal restrictions are also discussed from a nudist point of view. The chapter on "Comstock and the Post Office Ban" is particularly interesting.

The best discussion of post office censorship in relation to nudism appears in a chapter by that title in Huntington (1958), an excellent book that discusses the subject in a comprehensive manner and contains much statistical data not usually obtained elsewhere.

The chief antagonist of bona-fide nudist publications has been the Post Office Department of the United States, one of the main objectives of which in this connection, for more than a quarter of a century, was the prohibition of the oldest nudist publication from the use of the mails on the ground of "obscenity." The postal authorities brought so many actions throughout the years of their struggle against the publishers that there was scarcely a month when one or more cases against nudist books or periodicals were not pending in federal courts. An analysis of the reasons for this outstanding zeal on the part of the postal authorities lies in the realm of clinical investigation beyond the scope of this article. It must be remembered that when the term "postal authorities" is used, as with other governmental agencies, it means individuals who, in matters like this, can hide their prejudices, irrationalities, and unconscious motivations behind the anonymity of a governmental agency. The emotion behind this zeal can be adduced from a résumé in Huntington

(1958: 174-175) of the many actions that finally resulted in a victory for the nudists:

The legal history of nudism would not be complete without reference to the victories before the Supreme Court of the United States. The first of these was in connection with the famous Schweinhaut decision rendered in the District Court where twenty-seven consecutive issues of *Sunshine and Health* and seven consecutive issues of *Sun* magazine were before the Court. These issues had been taken home over the week-end by Judge Schweinhaut and carefully studied. The Post Office was heard in oral argument and brief; the magazine publishers presented their case entirely by printed brief. This favorable decision was appealed by the Post Office Department to the Court of Appeals for the District of Columbia and when the court failed to sustain the appeal, the Post Office sought a Writ of Certiorari by the Supreme Court. The Supreme Court refused to grant the Writ of Certiorari and the Schweinhaut decision became the law of the land, and still stands as a complete vindication of our contention as to the decency of nudist publications. It was this victory before Judge Schweinhaut that led the editor of *Sunshine and Health* to write an article entitled "Rejoicing in Vindication" which appears as chapter 21 in the present volume.

However, the Post Office was not satisfied and immediately picked up later issues of both *Sunshine and Health* and *Sun*. This case went against the publishers through the lower courts and each time was appealed to a higher court, in the last instance being appealed to the Supreme Court, which rendered a decision completely in favor of the publishers. As these two cases now stand, the first victory before Judge Schweinhaut was allowed to stand without being disturbed in any wise by the Supreme Court, and in the latest case the Supreme Court accepted the request for Certiorari and reversed the lower court decisions. These favorable decisions by the United States Supreme Court terminated a twenty-five years' fight with the postal authorities in many municipal, state and federal courts. Their influence will be felt not only in nearly every state of the Union but internationally as well.

Even with these reversals the postal authorities are still not content. In their campaign against pictures with exposed male genitals and female pubic hair they have forced at least one nudist publication to put out two forms of the same edition of the same periodical, one with unretouched photos for acknowledged members of nudist clubs only and one with retouched photos (with the pubic hair smudged out) for general distribution.

Studies on Psychology of Nudism

In spite of (or possibly because of) the fact that nudism is such a controversial subject and because it has been considered outside the pale of serious study, there are relatively few studies of nudism from a psychological or sociological point of view. That this should be so cannot be without significance. That none of the more recent professional psychological publications contains any studies of an unusual social phenomenon of the proportions of the nudist movement indicates the extent to which irrational attitudes and unconscious motivations influence even workers in the fields of psychology, education, and sociology, to say nothing of psychiatry. It appears to be a matter of expressing disapproval by ignoring and pretending not to notice. A few isolated individuals in the fields mentioned, such as the late Professor Howard Crosby Warren, head of the Psychology Department at Princeton, and the late Professor Prescott Lecky of the Columbia Psychology Department, have expressed approval of nudist ideals, but for the most part there has been popular derision or professional silence.

Flügel has a few favorable words to say on the aspirations of social nudism and a great deal more to say on the controversial subject of domestic nudism or nudism *en famille*. In characteristic fairness, Flügel does not hesitate to quote William Reich as one of the leading psychoanalytic opponents of social and domestic nudism.

In July, 1939, a group of psychologists, psychiatrists, educators, and a psychoanalyst accepted an invitation to visit a nudist camp and hold a conference on the psychological, sociological, and educational aspects of social nudism. This material was privately published in photo-offset form. Understandably but unfortunately the authors of the eight papers presented were designated by initials only. The proceedings of this conference, with the authors anonymous, is one of the few professional studies of communal nudism. Some of the words of the psychoanalyst may be of interest here:

On the evidence [I see] here, my expectation would be that nudist camps are more conventional in sexual conduct than are most vacation resorts. I think one effect of social nudism is to battle against what I may call the age-old psychological enemy of modern mankind—the isolation of sex. If you were in psychotherapy, you would see very clearly that at the bottom of most nervous disorders is a very distorted and very painful attitude toward the other sex. In strong language, you can almost say that for many men women are mostly a big vagina with something attached to it, or a big trap in which they can fall and be swallowed. Men are to many women just aggressive penises with something behind. It is unbelievable how few people are really able to conceive of a member of the other sex as another human being. This is where the problem of empathy comes in.

It seems to me that one of the automatic effects of social nudism is that the sexual organs are *reintegrated* in the human body. For most people these organs have taken on such an exaggerated importance that the rest of the body doesn't count any more. So I should imagine that the most important psychological effect of social nudism on the adult should be a very important stimulus to reintegrate the sexual organs so as to make sex more acceptable.

Although there are few studies on social nudism, there is a little more in the literature on the subject of domestic nudism. The reaction of some orthodox Freudian psychoanalysts toward domestic nudism is negative. They have in mind studies, such as those of J. Sadger, "Die Lehre von Geschlechtsverirrungen," quoted by Flügel, indicating that in fetishism the fetish is often a phallic symbol representing the imaginary penis of the mother—the observed absence of which has had much to do with the development of the "castration complex," which is at the bottom of the fetishism. (One would like to have some confirmatory evidence that the incidence of fetishism and other sexual deviations is greater among nudists than among the general population.) The castration anxiety of the young male child would, according to such psychoanalytic opinion, be evoked by the sight of penisless female members of the household. Some psychoanalysts would also be concerned as to the effect the sight of a well-developed adult penis might have on a little boy whose own penis is comparatively small. Certain psychoanalysts would be concerned as to the pathogenesis of certain psychosexual disturbances such as genital exhibitionism arising out of an aggravation of castration anxiety by the simple sight of penisless females and the aggravation of penis envy and its sequelae by the sight of well-developed male genitals by a penisless little girl.

The subject is a controversial one. Some younger psychoanalysts such as Harry Joseph (1954) have come out very positively in popular literature against domestic nudism, or nudism *en famille,* warning parents not only against allowing children to see the parents of the opposite sex nude but against permitting children to see parents of the same sex nude. (Here again one would like to see some confirmatory evidence that the incidence of sex problems is greater among nudists than in the general population.) This extreme view is not shared by many other authors on the subject, including such popular writers on pediatric psychiatry as Benjamin Spock, who emphasizes the "at-ease-ness" of the parents in what they do, regardless of how they handle family nudity, as being of primary importance.

Psychoanalytically oriented nudists reply that attempting to keep from children the knowledge of sex differences by concealment is a naïve and futile gesture and that the emotional emphasis with which this is usually done, viz., going to extraordinary lengths to maintain sexual modesty when revelation would be the simple natural concomitant of a domestic activity, serves only to intensify the castration anxiety and penis envy. "If my parents make such a fuss about this, it must be significant." They would point out that there is ample evidence that parental tensions are passed on to young children in this manner. Furthermore, contend these critics of what they consider a naïve interpretation of psychoanalytic theory, in view of the well-known proclivity of children to phantasize, hiding from them something about which they are bound to have a vague knowledge and a tremendous curiosity is an almost sure way to stimulate a phantasy that is whipped up by castration anxiety and penis envy into something out of all proportion to the importance of the item in question.

Flügel, who is a well-known psychoanalytic authority, takes a more moderate position than some of his colleagues and recognizes that the subject is controversial, containing many uncertainties not to be settled by dogmatic pronouncements. He states (1950:200):

A consideration of the clothing of children might reasonably be held to demand a statement as to the attitude we should adopt towards nakedness in relation to children. Our general principle points clearly to the desirability of perfect frankness in this respect. With regard to children's own nakedness, this will probably be freely admitted in the more enlightened educational circles. But it would seem that in the lower social classes of England an exaggerated sense of shame is often inculcated, and young children (especially girls) will often suffer great embarrassment if they have to undress for medical inspection. The idea is even prevalent that modesty can only be adequately safeguarded by means of a plethora of undergarments (Macaulay).

As regards the question of whether adults (and especially parents) should show themselves naked to children, there is less agreement. In certain more "advanced" circles this is done on principle, but a query as to its advisability has come from a rather unexpected quarter, namely, from the psychoanalysts, who have been much struck with the great effects that appear to be aroused in children by the appearance of the adult genitals (particularly effects connected with the castration complex). It is admitted that the evidence so far available is far from conclusive; nevertheless, Zulliger, in a recent review of the subject says, "My personal and provisional view is that it is better that children should not see their parents naked." In the opinion of the present writer he does not give due weight to the fact that in ordinary households it is in any case difficult to prevent accidental exposures before children. It would seem likely also that such special precautions as might be necessary to ensure that there is no such accident might very likely do more harm than the evil that they were intended to prevent. Altogether it would seem desirable to await further evidence before we agree to such a departure from the general lines of education suggested by psychoanalysis. However, it is undoubtedly true that the castration complex is of the greatest importance and that everything that is reasonably possible should be done to prevent its exaggerated development (to some extent it is probably inevitable). As Zulliger also points out, adults should bear in mind how difficult it is to be unbiased in this matter, and how liable they are to gratify their own exhibitionism under the pretext of bringing up their children "naturally."

Another psychoanalyst (Reich) also argues against "nude education" on the general ground that it logically implies a very different state of public opinion on sex questions than that which now exists. This argument is in a form that would apply to any departure from conventional taste and morals; if itself logically applied, it would abolish all experiments in education that imply such a departure. The true way out of the difficulty surely lies in the direction of teaching the illogicalities and inconsistencies of human institutions as themselves a part of reality. If, for instance, in the present case, it is decided to bring up children to regard nakedness as natural and ethical, this attitude should be supplemented by the information that nakedness is not everywhere looked upon in the same light. The problem here is, it would seem, exactly parallel to, say, that in the case of agnosticism.

An interesting article on nudism entitled "Nudism and Negroes" came out in a popular Negro magazine, *Ebony*, in August, 1951. In this article an interracial trend in American nudism is reported on, as well as are other aspects of social nudism. This author quotes Havelock Ellis as stating, "If mankind wanted to encourage sexual immorality, it could have devised nothing better calculated to that end than to have insisted upon the universal adoption of clothing."

Trends in puritanical America seem to bear out Havelock Ellis' contention. That phenomenon on the American scene, the movie sex queen who thrives by titillation, is nurtured in a soil that is artificially fertilized by the overemphasis on sex brought about in large part by the creators of obscenity laws and the zealots who for political or personal reasons call for their enforcement.

A case in point is the popularization by Anthony Comstock of the picture "September Morn." The little-known story about this picture is told by Harry Reichenbach (1931). The book is unfortunately out of print and difficult to come by but it tells a story that should be more widely known. Reichenbach, one of the first "publicity men," states:

I applied for work at a small art shop that had printed a lithograph of a nude girl standing in a quiet pool. The picture sold at ten cents apiece but nobody would buy it. I could earn my month's rent if I had an idea for disposing of the two thousand copies in stock. It occurred to me to introduce the immodest young maiden to Anthony Comstock, head of the Anti-Vice Society and Arch-angel of virtue. At first he refused to jump at the opportunity to be shocked. I telephoned him several times, protesting against a large display of the picture which I myself had installed in the window of the art shop. Then I arranged for other people to protest and at last I visited him personally. "This picture is an outrage!" I cried. "It's undermining the morals of our city's youth!" I made him come with me and see for himself.

When we arrived in front of the store window, a group of youngsters I had hired especially for this performance at fifty cents apiece, stood pointing at the picture, uttering expressions of unholy glee and making grimaces too sophisticated for their years. Comstock swallowed the scene and almost choked. "Remove that picture!" he fumed, and when the shopkeeper refused, the Anti-Vice Society appealed to the courts. This brought the picture into the newspapers and into fame. Overnight, the lithograph that had been rejected as a brewer's calendar, became a vital national issue. Songs were written about it, actors wise-cracked at it, reformers denounced it, and seven million men and women bought copies of it at a dollar apiece, framed it and hung it on the walls of their homes. The name of the picture was "September Morn." There was no more immorality or suggestiveness to it than sister's photograph as a baby in the family album. This was my first job in New York. It paid me forty-five dollars and enabled me for one more month to sleep on a desk.

The enforcement of obscenity laws often has an opposite effect, such as the skyrocket selling of a book because some benighted community has seen fit to ban it—yet another example of allurement by concealment. Similarly, an artificial shortage of a commodity is created so some smart market operator can make a "killing." And the obscenity zealots such as Anthony Comstock and many a district attorney in the United States are the more or less unwitting dupes of the interaction of such factors. This is also reflected in trends in American advertising. Probably only in a pruriently prudish culture like that in America or Latin America does the purveying of such a divergent variety of products including beer and automobiles depend so much on pictures of pretty girls clothed for provocative concealment and often in "sexy" poses. The effect of this kind of hypocritical prudish-

ness and concealment-for-effect maneuver has far-reaching ramifications, the analysis of which is beyond the scope of this article.

References

Beaglehole, Ernest, *Social Changes in the South Pacific*. London: George Allen & Unwin, 1957.

Crawford, M. D. C., *The Conquest of Culture*. New York: Greenberg Pub., 1938.

Davies, John Langdon, *The Future of Nakedness*. London: Noel Douglas, 1929.

Ellis, Havelock, *Studies in the Psychology of Sex*. New York: Random House, 1936.

Fenichel, Otto, *The Psychoanalytic Theory of Neurosis*. New York: W. W. Norton & Co., 1945.

Flügel, J. C., *The Psychology of Clothes*. In Ernest Jones (ed.), *International Psycho-Analytical Library*. London: Hogarth Press, and the Institute of Psychoanalysis, 1950.

Gay, Jan, *On Going Naked*. New York: Holborn House, 1932.

Hirning, L. Clovis, "Genital Exhibitionism: An Interpretative Study." *J. Clin. Psychopath.* 8; 1-24, 1947.

Huntington, Henry S., *Defense of Nudism*. New York: Robert M. McBride, 1958.

Jensen, Oliver, *The Revolt of American Women*. New York: Harcourt, Brace & Co., 1952.

Joseph, Harry, and Zern, Gordon, *The Emotional Problems of Children*—A Guide to Parents. New York: Crown, 1954.

Kinsey, A. C., Pomeroy, W. D., Martin, C. E., and Gebhard, P. H., *Sexual Behavior in the Human Male*. Philadelphia: W. B. Saunders Co., 1948.

Kinsey, A. C., Pomeroy, W. D., Martin, C. E., and Gebhard, P. H., *Sexual Behavior in the Human Female*. Philadelphia: W. B. Saunders Co., 1953.

LaBarre, Weston, *The Human Animal*. Chicago: University of Chicago Press, 1954.

Linton, Ralph, *The Tree of Culture*. New York: Alfred A. Knopf, Inc., 1955.

Merrill, Frances, and Merrill, Mason, *Among the Nudists*. New York: Alfred A. Knopf, Inc., 1931.

Merrill, Frances, and Merrill, Mason, *Nudism Comes to America*. New York: Alfred A. Knopf, Inc., 1932.

Nipson, Herbert, "Nudism and Negroes." *Ebony Magazine*, August, 1951.

The Nudist Magazine. New York: Outdoor Publishing Co., August, 1933.

Parmelee, Maurice, *The New Gymnosophy*. New York: Frederick H. Hitchcock, 1927.

Psychological Symposium in a Nudist Camp. Privately printed, 1939.

Reich, Wilhelm, "Wohin führt die Nackterziehung?" *Ztschr. f. Psychoanalyt. Padagog.* 3; 44, 1928.

Reichenbach, Harry, *Phantom Fame*. New York: Simon and Schuster, Inc., 1931.

Russell, Bertrand, *Why I Am Not a Christian*. New York: Simon and Schuster, Inc., 1957.

Scott, George R., *The Common Sense of Nudism*. London: T. Werner Laurie, Ltd., 1934.

Shaw, Elton, *The Body Taboo*. Washington, D. C.: Shaw Publishing Co., 1938.

Singer, Holmyard, and Hall, *A History of Technology*. New York: Oxford University Press, 1954.

Solaire Universelle Nudisme, Magazine. Mays Landing, N. J.: Sunshine Pub. Co., Nov.–Dec., 1958.

Starr, Frederick, *Some First Steps in Human Progress*. New York: Chautauqua-Century Press, 1895.

Welby, William, *The Naked Truth*. London: Thorsone Publishers, 1950.

Welby, William, *It's Only Natural. The Philosophy of Nudism*. London: Thorsone Publishers.

L. CLOVIS HIRNING

Coitus

Definition

COITUS, according to English and English's recent *Comprehensive Dictionary of Psychological and Psychoanalytical Terms* (1958), may be defined as "the introduction of the male sex organ into the body of another, generally with orgasm." Coition is the process in general and coitus is the specific act. The words are derived from the Latin, *coitio*, made up of *co-*, together, and *ire*, to go. Technically, therefore, coitus does not consist merely of penile-vaginal copulation, but of any coming together of two sex partners, so that the genitals of one are sufficiently stimulated by the body of the other.

The one main exception to this rule would be sexual excitement and release obtained through one individual's bringing her (or his) partner to climax by manual manipulation of the partner's genitals. Although, in the most technical use of the term, this might be considered a form of hand-genital coitus, in practice it is invariably given the name of masturbation and is not thought of as constituting a form of coitus. On the other hand, the active insertion of a male's penis into his partner's mouth or anus, or even between his partner's thighs, external vulva, breasts, or armpits, is commonly referred to as oral coitus, anal coitus, femoral coitus, etc.

When used without a modifier, the term coitus almost invariably means penile-vaginal copulation; and it is sometimes distinguished, as I have noted in *The Art and Science of Love* (1960a) and several other books (A. Ellis, 1954, 1958, 1960b), from noncoital or extracoital sex relations—by which is meant all other forms of interpersonal sex stimulation other than penile-vaginal intercourse. It would perhaps be more accurate to call these forms of stimulation extravaginal sex relations, since many modes of interhuman contact, such as oral-genital or anal-genital relations, are actually coital (in the strict sense of the term) without being penile-vaginal.

There are surprisingly few respectable synonymns in the English language for penile-vaginal coitus, the main ones being such terms as *sexual intercourse, copulation, sex relations, sexual congress*, and more euphemistic designations, such as *act of love*. Only one of these terms, *copulate*, can be used as an active verb —"I copulate," or "he copulated." And even this word has its limitations, and is generally used in an indirect form. Thus, one does not copulate somebody else but copulates *with* this other person. And one copulates with someone else largely in medical texts rather than in more popular literature—where, until very recently, one invariably had sexual intercourse with or participated in an act of love with one's sex partner. Norman Arlington (1960) has for the past decade tried to revive the old active English verb *swive* and thereby to allow one to say, with respectability, "I would like to swive her," or "I swived him last night." To date, he has had virtually no success in this attempt to reanimate respectable coital terminology.

Attitudes toward Coitus

Attitudes toward coitus, and hence to some extent toward the breadth of coital practices, significantly differ throughout the world and sometimes radically differ from one community (such as Staten Island, New York City) to a neighboring one (such as Manhattan, New York City). They also importantly clash in relation to whether the participant in coitus is male or female. Thus, whereas most peoples of the world, especially Oriental peoples, believe that penile-vaginal copulation as well as various extravaginal forms of coitus are delightful and proper for unmarried and married males, many of these same groups feel that young unmarried females should be almost completely abstinent and that married women should be severely restricted, even in their husband's beds, in their coital practices.

Even regarding male participation in coitus, many existing societies, especially contemporary American society, create and perpetuate hypocritical standards concerning the value of coital relations, with the result that the average person in these communities views coitus as nasty *and* tasty, vicious *and* delicious. Consequently, as I point out in my *Folklore of Sex* (1960b), most modern Americans are completely muddled in their sex views, feelings, and acts, hardly knowing sex "right" from sex "wrong," and engaging in coital acts which they feel they should not perform but which they would feel even more uncomfortable about not performing.

This is particularly true in regard to oral coitus, anal coitus, and other forms of extravaginal copulation. In Western civilization, largely as a result of Judeo-Christian teachings, extravaginal coitus, up to the beginning of the twentieth century, has mainly been looked upon with horror and has been considered, even when it is completely heterosexually oriented, perverted or deviated. Relatively enlightened modern authorities such as Allen (1949) and Karpman (1956) state or imply that sex acts that are entirely nonprocreative are deviated; and Freud (1924-1950; 1938) and his more orthodox followers (Abraham, 1950; Fenichel, 1945) refer to infant sexuality as being "polymorphous perverse" and to oralism and analism in adults as being deviated survivals of or fixations upon so-called pregenital sex instincts.

As a result of the Judeo-Christian condemnation of nonprocreative sex acts, which has somehow survived even in much of the pre-

sumably "scientific" sex and psychological literature, relatively few Westerners feel completely comfortable with nonvaginal forms of intercourse. As Kinsey and his associates (1948, 1953) have shown, the practice of extravaginal sex behavior, particularly under the somewhat toned-down name of *petting*, is an almost universal phenomenon in modern America. But, according to the same source and to considerable clinical evidence, American females admit to the practice of oral-genital relations only about half as often as do American males; and only about 50 per cent of American males admit to engaging in heterosexual oral relations of any sort. The incidences of male and female practices of anal-genital relations, although not at present statistically known, would appear to be considerably lower than those of oral-genital coitus.

On the other hand, extravaginal modes of coitus are frequently looked upon with much more equanimity and delight among peoples of the Orient and the South Seas. The famous Hindu treatise on love, Vatsyayana's *Kama Sutra*, is perhaps the only sex manual ever written that has a special chapter on *auparishtaka*, or mouth congress. It lists and describes in detail eight different forms of oral-genital contact, including "the nominal congress; biting the sides; pressing outside; pressing inside; kissing; rubbing; sucking a mangoe fruit and swallowing up." Although this chapter is largely concerned with oral-genital relations involving two males, it also notes that "the mouth of a woman is clean for kissing and such like things at the time of sexual intercourse. Vatsyayana moreover thinks that in all these things connected with love, "everybody should act according to the custom of his country, and his own inclination." Other sources—such as Burton (1885-1888), Edwardes (1959), and Forberg (1884) —also confirm the acceptability of oral and anal intercourse, both heterosexually and homosexually, among the Moslems of the Near and Far East.

Ford and Beach (1951), in their study of 190 contemporary societies in the world, note that oral-genital relations are in good repute and are widely practiced in five specific cultures—among the Aranda, Ponapeans, Trobriand Islanders, Trukese, and Wogeo. Interestingly enough, these are all Oceanic peoples and the last four are denizens of the South Seas.

It has also been shown that in most parts of the world, and notably in Western countries where extravaginal modes of copulation are officially frowned upon, innumerable prostitutes and houses of prostitution would hardly stay in business if they did not cater to the oral, anal, and other nonvaginal demands of their clients (Benjamin and Ellis, 1954). Published case-history material as well as objective studies of human sex behavior would also tend to indicate that extravaginal coitus, although still in some disrepute especially among the less educated classes of Americans, is far more widely practiced than it might on the surface appear to be (Dickinson and Beam, 1931; Hamilton, 1929; Strakosch, 1934).

Obviously, therefore, although the official and publicized attitudes toward various nonvaginal forms of coitus are frequently highly negative in certain regions of the world, the less publicized desires and actions of the people of these same regions are often considerably more favorable toward these coital variants. And where the term *coitus* is generally assumed to mean penile-vaginal copulation and little or nothing else, it actually subsumes what Brian Heald (personal communication) has aptly called a wide-ranging "coital complex"—which includes many more sex modes and manners than may have been dreamed of in any Horatio's philosophy.

In the final analysis, almost any form of coitus that may be imagined and employed is part of some kind of an interpersonal relationship between the individuals who are coitally engaged. As such, it includes, at the very minimum, all the varied aspects of interhuman sex play, rather than merely the act of penetration itself and its immediate aftermath. It seems rather senseless to follow the convention of making a neat and arbitrary division between sexual foreplay, coitus, and afterplay since these are all parts of a single (if not always too well unified and integrated) act. And just as there can be considerable difference between one act of intromission and another, so can there be wide variation between one sexual approach or aftermath and another. The coital complex, therefore, properly includes the entire sex act, from the first tentative kisses and caresses to the final climax and lying restfully in each other's arms.

Since man is a psychological as well as a physiological being, coitus in the wide-ranging sense also includes what people say to each other before, during, and after intromission; how they feel about each other and their sexual relationship; what place their sex acts have in their general scheme of living; and a host of other interpersonal and intrapersonal factors. The coital complex also involves growth and development: since human sex-love participations, like all other aspects of living, grow, change, improve or deteriorate, and finally come to an end. In more ways than one, then, coitus may take on a temporal and spatial quality and is not likely to remain strictly static or one-dimensional. Certainly, the more emotionally sound and creative a male and female are, the more unrestricted, imaginative, and continually developing are their coital relations likely to be.

The Coital Complex and Sex Deviation

As has been previously noted in this article, many peoples of the world, especially almost all those who have been seriously influenced by Judeo-Christian ideologies, define as deviational or perverted sex behavior human participation in any sex acts that are not strictly penile-vaginal, or that do not at least terminate with "normal" penile-vaginal coitus. According to this way of thinking, oral, anal, heterosexually masturbatory, and other nonvaginal acts are perfectly proper when they are engaged in as forms of sexual foreplay; but when they are carried on up to and including actual orgasm, without any penile-vaginal copulation actually having taken place, they are deviated or perverted acts (Van de Velde, 1926). In an extreme, and somewhat ludicrous, form this doctrine has been even further extended by such writers as D. H. Lawrence (1959) and Bergler (1956), who state or imply that even penile-vaginal copulation, when it does not result in simultaneous mutual orgasm between a male and female partner, is a serious perversion of human sexuality.

Defining nonvaginal methods of coitus as sexual perversions is unscientific and invalid for several reasons, among which may be listed the following:

1. This concept of perversion *is* merely definitional and, as such, cannot very well be supported or invalidated by clinical or experimental evidence.

2. It is largely based on the dogmatic value judgment that the only valid motive for human sex relations is procreation, which may have made sense when the ancient Hebrews first promulgated it several thousand years ago but makes little sense in the overpopulated world of today.

3. If logically reduced to its own inherent absurdity, the procreative standard of sex deviation would imply that penile-vaginal intercourse itself is a perversion when the participants employ any method of contraception, including coitus interruptus or the so-called rhythm method of birth control.

4. Any standard of sexual perversion makes sense only when it presents evidence that the acts it labels as being deviant are in some way abnormal, unnatural, or inimical to mental or physical health. But extravaginal sex relations, except when they are carried on in an exclusive fixated, fetishistic, or obsessive-compulsive manner, are hardly statistically abnormal (since about half the population even in areas where they are banned or disapproved of seem to engage in them); they are in no way, other than by arbitrary definition, unnatural (since humans and other mammals spontaneously discover and practice them without specific teaching); and there is no evidence whatever that they are mentally or physically harmful when they are carried to the point of orgasm. In fact, in the light of the facts that they are less likely to lead to venereal infection and to unwanted pregnancy, that they are more likely (especially in the case of females) to result in satisfying orgasm, and that they can be engaged in under many circumstances (such as in automobiles) where penile-vaginal coitus might be impractical, there is every reason to believe that nonvaginal sex acts are frequently more productive of mental and physical well-being than is so-called normal coitus.

It is true that in many jurisdictions, including many American states and Great Britain, statutes exist that legally proscribe and severely penalize extravaginal relations between unmarried persons or between husbands and wives (Haire, 1952; Kinsey, 1948, 1953; Sherwin, 1949, 1951). But "sexual deviation" and sex crimes are by no means synonymous, and there seems to be no sane reason why most of our existing statutes against "sodomy," which include proscriptions against heterosexual nonvaginal relations, should remain on the books in this age.

It is also true that in some instances extravaginal acts are exclusively employed by sexual deviants—by fixed homosexuals, for example—who, out of dire fear of penile-vaginal copulation or extreme (conscious or unconscious) hostility against females, may rigidly or obsessively-compulsively stick to nonvaginal sexual behavior. By the same token, however, some highly heterosexual individuals fearfully and obsessively-compulsively remain fixated exclusively on one particular position of penile-vaginal copulation (such as the face-to-face, male-surmounting-female position); and there is every reason to believe that, from a psychological standpoint, these sexually compulsive individuals are almost as perverted as are the exclusive participants in nonvaginal acts.

In other words, it is not any given act of human sexuality that constitutes sex perversion but the psychological motive for which and the consequent inflexible or disorganized manner in which the act is performed (Ellis, 1958, 1960a; Guze, 1959).

Frequency of Coitus

It is difficult to obtain accurate figures showing the frequency of coitus in any region, particularly since coitus may refer, as we have seen, to strictly penile-vaginal copulation or it may include various other modes of sex activity. Probably the best figures we have in this connection are those of Kinsey and his associates (1948, 1953), who use the term *total outlet* to describe male or female orgasm received from any source. The Kinsey researchers found that the average American male has a total outlet of about three orgasms a week before marriage, and the average unmarried female who is sexually active has a total outlet of about 0.4 orgasms a week. After marriage, the average American male still has a mean frequency of about three orgasms a week up to the age of 35, and the average married female who is sexually active has a mean frequency of about two orgasms a week up to the age of 35. Since these figures, especially in the case of unmarried individuals, include masturbatory as well as coital outlets, they must be reduced by about one-third to one-half if we are to estimate coital frequencies.

Recent investigations of Kirkendall (1958) indicate that, especially in the case of the male, and very probably in regard to the female as well, frequency of sex outlet by no means necessarily mirrors the underlying capacity of most individuals. Apparently, many human beings have sex capacities far beyond their usual performances; so that there is every reason to believe that a person's average coital frequency depends as much or more on the availablity of suitable and desirable partners as it does on his or her inherent sexual urges.

In connection with frequency, the question of sexual "excess" often arises. When is coitus "excessive"? There can be no general answer to this question. The frequency of penile-vaginal copulation and/or other forms of coitus should normally vary widely according to the physical and psychological make-up of different individuals; and there is exceptionally little danger (as is also true in regard to masturbation) that any person can have coitus to excess.

From a physical standpoint, it is almost impossible for a male to have "excessive" or "weakening" intercourse because he is simply not able to obtain and maintain an erection an "excessive" number of times during any one period. The female may have intercourse more often than she desires; but if she does have it on this "excessive" basis, it seems to do little or no physical harm—unless she goes to unusual extremes, as in the case of some prostitutes who have ten or more clients a day.

The main physical injuries that may result from "excessive" copulation are (1) loss of sleep on the part of those who engage in it for considerable parts of the night, and (2) occasional irritation of one or both partner's genitals from overly powerful or prolonged friction. These disadvantages can normally be compensated for by intelligent attention to sleep schedules and to adequate coital lubrication. In general, coital frequency may be largely a matter of personal choice and should be expected to range, with different couples, all the way from a few dozen to a few hundred copulations a year. Anything within this range is perfectly normal in most instances—as long as the couple concerned thinks that it is.

Usually, frequency of intercourse steadily but slowly decreases with the age of the individual. According to the Kinsey figures, teen-age couples are likely to have coitus about three times a week, 30-year-old couples about twice a week, and 50-year-old couples about once a week. A small percentage of individuals, however, have coital relations five or more times a week until they are well on in years; and another small percentage even during their younger years have it only once every two or three weeks.

Kinds and Positions of Coitus

Coital relations may be classified in several ways. First of all, as noted previously in this article, they may be categorized as to the mode of contact between the partners' bodies. Thus, the male's penis may have coital contact with a female's vagina, external vulva, anus, mouth, thighs, stomach, breasts, armpits. And, if we are to extend the use of the term coitus to the female's interpenetration with the male (rather than just the latter's penile interpenetration with the body of the former) we may say that the female's vagina may engage in coital relations with the male's penis, tongue, hand, elbow, toes, etc.; while her external vulva and clitoris may engage in contact with the male's penis, hand, foot, knee, arm, lips, tongue, etc. To employ the more usual terminology, coital relations may consist of "regular" intercourse, fellation or irrumation, cunnilinctus, anal intercourse, analinctus, femoral intercourse, etc.

Penile-vaginal intercourse may itself be categorized in several ways. Thus, there is full entry of the penis into the vagina; partial entry; coitus interruptus, in which the male withdraws his penis from the vagina before having his orgasm; coitus reservatus, in which the male and female have prolonged intercourse with the male never achieving any climax; Zugassent's discovery, in which neither the male nor the female have a climax in coitus; and various other modes of penile-vaginal congress that may be dreamed of or performed.

Many positions of penile-vaginal copulation have been invented and described in detail in ancient and modern sex manuals (A. Ellis, 1960a; Thornton and Thornton, 1939; Van de Velde, 1926; and Vatsyayana). Theoretically, there are hundreds of different copulative positions that may thus be delineated but, for all practical purposes, there are only about a half-dozen major penile-vaginal coital techniques, which may be briefly described as follows:

Face to Face, Man on Top

The man lies on top of the woman, but not directly on her, supporting the weight of his own body on his hands or elbows. She spreads her legs and flexes her knees or raises her feet, sometimes placing them around her partner's waist or on his shoulders. If necessary, her buttocks may be raised by putting a pillow under them. Variations on this position may include (a) the woman's keeping her legs apart and flat after entry has been achieved; (b) keeping them between the man's knees; (c) putting one of her legs between his legs; (d) bending her thighs back toward her chest; (e) raising one of her legs while keeping the other flat; and (g) wrapping one or both her legs around her partner's.

Some of the chief advantages of the face-to-face, man-on-top position are: It makes for easy entry if the woman's thighs are parted and raised; it allows the male to set the pace and to slow or hasten his own orgasm; it facilitates great intimacy between the two partners; the male can sometimes continue intercourse after he has had an orgasm; it is convenient for couples who enjoy the male's making vigorous pelvic thrusts; and it is a good position for impregnation, since after intercourse the woman can keep her knees raised and prevent the sperm from leaving her vagina.

Some of the chief disadvantages of this position are: It tends to restrict the female's movements and thrusts; it sometimes leads to too deep penetration; it is often too stimulating for

the male and induces him to achieve quick climax; it is not easy for the male to resort to manual friction on the woman's clitoris in this position.

Face to Face, Woman on Top

In this position the male lies on his back and the woman squats over him and guides his penis into her vagina; or she sits down in an astride position on his erect penis and loins; or the husband and wife achieve penetration in some other position and then gently roll around until the woman is on top. Once entry has been effected, the woman can keep squatting, or can sit astride, or straighten out her legs and place them between or outside her partner's. The man can lie prone, or raise himself on his hands or elbows, or raise his knees on the side of or behind his wife.

Advantages of this position include: The woman often has maximum freedom of action; the quick-triggered male, by being relatively passive, can often last longer; the woman can regulate the depth of penetration and prevent any pain or injury to herself; the woman may achieve deep penetration if she desires it; the woman may be greatly aroused by her own pelvic thrusts; the male may easily caress the woman during intercourse.

Disadvantages of this position include: The male's freedom of movement may be impaired; the position is too acrobatic for many women; vaginal-penile penetration may be too deep and uncomfortable; the man's penis may keep slipping out of the vagina as copulation proceeds; the position is a poor one for impregnation.

Face to Face, Side by Side

In this position the partners lie side by side, facing each other. They may both have their lower legs on the bed and the woman's upper leg over both the man's legs; or the woman's lower leg may rest on the man's lower leg and his upper leg may rest between her legs, so that they are interlocked. As Hirsch (1951) points out, the "side" positions are not exactly what their name implies—as the man is often largely on his back and the woman, resting on him, is partly supported on his chest; or else the wife may be largely on her back, supported by a pillow.

Advantages of the face-to-face, side-by-side position are: It is usually restful for both partners; it is particularly helpful when one or both partners is fatigued, ill, invalided, or old; it enables an easily excitable male to regulate his thrusts and last longer in coitus; it gives both partners relative freedom of movement; it enables the female to make sure that penetration is not too deep if she is vaginally sensitive; it is comfortable for coitus that occurs during the last months of a woman's pregnancy.

Disadvantages of this position include: It is not easy for some individuals to achieve entry in the side positions; it is not comfortable for certain individuals; it is not sufficiently exciting for those individuals who require deep pelvic thrusts; in the interlocking position coital movements may be difficult unless the partners put painful pressures on various other parts of their bodies.

Rear Entry, Man's Face to Woman's Back

In the rear entry (or averse) positions, there are several main possibilities: (a) The man may lie on his side behind the woman (she, too, being on her side), with her buttocks somewhat above his penis and her body slightly curved inwardly, her legs bent at her hips. The man enters the woman's vagina between her legs and his scrotum presses against her buttocks. After intromission she may press her thighs together, providing additional friction for the penis and preventing it from slipping out of her vagina. (b) The woman may kneel on her hands and knees, with her head and breast almost on the bed or sofa, with the man kneeling behind her. (c) The woman may lie on her stomach with her pelvis raised and the man lie on top of her. (d) The man may sit on the edge of a bed or chair, and the woman, with her back to him, sit down on his penis and his lap (or on the lower part of his stomach). The man opens his thighs somewhat and leans back while the woman opens her thighs as wide as possible and leans forward.

Advantage of the rear-entry positions include: The male may be able to feel the woman's gluteal region with his legs, scrotum, and pubic areas and this may be stimulating to him and her; the male can easily put his hands around the woman during copulation and play with her breasts or clitoris; the rear-entry position with both partners lying on their sides may be very restful and enable the man to insert his penis only to the degree that he and his partner desire; the female's vagina may be foreshortened, so that penile-vaginal friction is enhanced if she has a wide vagina or her mate a small penis; the position is often advantageous for impregnation or for intercourse during the last stages of pregnancy.

Disadvantages of the rear-entry positions include: Entry is often difficult, especially in the side position; the male's penis may keep falling out of the vagina; the penis does not contact the clitoris during intercourse; lack of face-to-face intimacy is found to be undesirable by some partners.

Sitting Positions

There are several major sitting positions of coitus, including these: (a) The man sits on a chair or on the edge of a bed and the woman sits on his lap, facing him and with her legs astride his. With his legs apart and the female's around his waist, the male can pull her toward and away from him and raise and lower her pelvis, thus effecting copulatory movements. (b) If the chair or bed that the partners are using is suitably high, the man can sit on it while the woman, facing him with her legs somewhat apart, can stand. He can pull her hips back and forth to him, in between his spread thighs. (c) The man can squat between a woman's thighs, while she is lying on her back facing him, with her legs on his hips. He can then make pelvic thrusts or pull her pelvis back and forth. Or the woman can squat between the man's thighs, while he is lying on his back with his legs apart, and she can move her pelvis in a circular fashion, making churning movements around his penis (Haire, 1952; Malinowski, 1929; Robinson, 1936). (d) The man can sit on a bed or chair, while the woman bends over, in a doubled-up position, with her back to him. He can then, using the rear-entry position, pull her pelvis back and forth over his penis.

Some advantages of the sitting positions may be: In the face-to-face sitting position both partners may have maximum freedom of movement with their hands and very close bodily contact may be achieved, with considerable freedom of movement still being maintained; by leaning backward in this position, the woman may also be able to achieve excellent clitoral contact and stimulation during coitus; it is often quite restful and the male can sometimes retard his orgasm by pulling the female to and from himself, rather than by using sharp pelvic thrusts.

Disadvantages of the sitting positions include: Sexual thrusting may not be sufficiently vigorous for either or both partners; penetration may be too deep; impregnation may be impeded; the standing-sitting positions tend to be tiring, especially for the male.

Standing Positions

If the woman has long enough legs or the man sufficiently short ones, both partners may sometimes stand and face each other and thus have intercourse. Or the woman can lie with her legs dangling over the edge of a table or bed while the man stands between her legs. Or the man can stand while the woman, with her arms around his neck, clasps his hips between her thighs.

Some advantages of the standing or standing-lying positions include: They may be varied and exciting at times because they are not routine; they usually leave one or both partners' hands free for caresses; they can be combined with dancing, taking showers together, and similar pursuits.

Major disadvantages of the standing or standing-lying positions are: Entry may be quite difficult and sustained intercourse may become uncomfortable after a while; it is not easy for either of the partners to control his or her orgasm in most of the standing positions; there may not be a sufficient amount of pelvic thrusting and parrying when either or both partners are standing; the positions are unfavorable for impregnation and for intercourse during the last stages of a woman's pregnancy.

In addition to the various positions of penile-vaginal coitus, there are also, of course, many different positions for extravaginal coitus. Such positions are virtually never discussed in detail in any of the popular sex manuals (with the exception of my recent book, *The Art and Science of Love*, 1960). One such position, however, has become both famous and infamous as a symbol of the most licentious form of intersexual behavior—and that, of course, is the notorious *soixante-neuf* or *sixty-nine* position, in which the male and female partners practice fellation and cunnilinctus simultaneously. Other and less publicized extravaginal positions consist largely of variations on the penile-vaginal copulative positions described above.

Modern Trends in Coitus

As previously noted, some of the Mid-Eastern, Far Eastern, and Oceanic peoples of the world have not only been remarkably liberal in regard to coitus, but have also taken an unusually permissive attitude toward many forms of extravaginal coital relations. This has not by any means been the universal rule, since many Eastern cultures are just as prim as we are about limiting their residents to penile-vaginal copulation, and some of these cultures (such as the Trobriand Islanders as described by Malinowski, 1929) even encourage a single, limited form of vaginal-penile congress and look upon all other forms as being at least slightly outrageous. Nonetheless, Western attitudes toward the coital complex have not always been adhered to by more permissive societies.

As we enter the closing phases of the twentieth century, a curious semireversal of the Eastern and Western attitudes toward coitus seems to be taking place. At least among the highly educated, intelligent, and widely read classes of English-speaking society, an unusually liberal attitude toward extravaginal coital relations has been and is still spreading: so that it may be confidently predicted that by the close of the present century an individual in these classes will be considered neurotically inhibited and to some degree sexually deviated if he does not at times spontaneously and joyfully engage in all forms of heterosexual coitus, vaginal as well as nonvaginal.

This new attitude toward the coital complex would appear to be, from a psychological standpoint, exceptionally sound and wholesome. For sexual deviation largely consists of sexual attitudes and behavior that are overly rigid, phobic, fetishistic, and obsessive-compulsive; and sexual health is mainly involved with flexibility, spontaneity, and freedom of preference. A male, moreover, is not a fine lover, and certainly not a better person, just because he is able to perfect a long-lasting and varied technique of penile-vaginal intromission, nor is a woman a desirable bedmate or ultrafeminine just because she is well able to wriggle in copulatory delight. Much more finesse, subtlety, lovingkindness, and general sexual adeptness than this is required to make a truly excellent sexlove partner. And unless coitus is seen as an almost infinitely complex, varied, and wide-ranging series of activities rather than a single, rather monotonous, sadly constricted ritual, maximum sexual joy and emotional health are not ever likely to be achieved.

References

Abraham, Karl, *Collected Papers*. London: Hogarth, 1950.

Allen, Clifford, *The Sexual Perversions and Abnormalities*. London: Oxford University Press, 1949.

Arlington, Norman, *The Modern Courtesan*. In press.

Benjamin, Harry, and Ellis, Albert, "An Objective Examination of Prostitution." *Internat. J. Sexology 8;* 99-105, 1954.

Bergler, Edmund, *Neurotic Counterfeit-Sex*. New York: Grune & Stratton, Inc., 1956.

Burton, Robert, *The Book of the Thousand Nights and a Night*. (17 vols.). London: Burton Club, 1885-1888.

Dickinson, R. L., and Beam, L., *A Thousand Marriages*. Baltimore: The Williams & Wilkins Co., 1931.

Dickinson, R. L., *Human Sex Anatomy*. Baltimore: The Williams & Wilkins Co., 1933.

Edwardes, Allen, *The Jewel in the Lotus*. New York: Julian Press, Inc., 1959.

Ellis, Albert, *The American Sexual Tragedy*. New York: Twayne Pub., 1954.

Ellis, Albert, *The Art and Science of Love*. New York: Lyle Stuart, 1960a.

Ellis, Albert, *The Folklore of Sex*. New York: Grove Press, 1960b.

Ellis, Albert, *The Search for Sexual Enjoyment*. New York: Macfadden-Bartell, 1966.

Ellis, Albert, *Sex Without Guilt*. New York: Lyle Stuart, 1958.

Ellis, Havelock, *Studies in the Psychology of Sex*. New York: Random House, 1936.

English, Horace B., and English, Ava C., *A Comprehensive Dictionary of Psychological and Psychoanalytical Terms*. New York: Longmans, Green & Co., Inc., 1958.

Fenichel, O., *Psychoanalytic Theory of Neurosis*. New York: W. W. Norton & Co., Inc., 1945.

Forberg, F. K., *Manual of Classical Erotology*. Brussels: Carrington, 1884.

Ford, C. S., and Beach, Frank A., *Patterns of Sexual Behavior*. New York: Harper & Brothers, 1951.

Freud, Sigmund, *Basic Writings*. New York: Modern Library, Inc., 1938.

Freud, Sigmund, *Collected Papers*. London: Hogarth, 1924-1950.

Guze, Henry, "What is Sexually Normal?" Paper delivered at the Second Annual Meeting of the Society for the Scientific Study of Sex, Nov. 11, 1959.

Haire, Norman (ed.), *Encyclopedia of Sexual Knowledge*. London: Encyclopedia Press, 1952.

Hamilton, G. V., *A Research in Marriage*. New York: Boni, 1929.

Hirsch, Edwin W., *How to Improve Your Sexual Relations*. Chicago: Zeco, 1951.

Karpman, Benjamin, *The Sexual Offender and His Offenses*. New York: Julian Press, Inc., 1956.

Kinsey, A. C. et al., *Sexual Behavior in the Human Male*. Philadelphia: W. B. Saunders Co., 1948.

Kinsey, A. C. et al., *Sexual Behavior in the Human Female*. Philadelphia: W. B. Saunders Co., 1953.

Kirkendall, Lester, "Toward a Clarification of the Concept of Male Sex Drive." *Marr. Fam. Living 20;* 367-372, 1958.

Lawrence, D. H., *Lady Chatterley's Lover*. New York: Grove Press, 1959.

Malinowski, B., *The Sexual Life of Savages in Northwestern Melanesia*. New York: Halcyon House, 1929.

Robinson, Victor (ed.), *Encyclopedia Sexualis*. New York: Dingwall-Rock, 1936.

Sherwin, Robert V., *Sex and the Statutory Law*. New York: Oceana Pub., 1949.

Sherwin, Robert V., "Sex Expression and the Law. II. Sodomy: a Medico-Legal Enigma." *Internat. J. Sexology 5;* 3-13, 1951.

Strakosch, F. M., *Factors in the Sex Life of 400 Psychopathic Women*. Utica, N.Y.: State Hospitals Press, 1934.

Thornton, Henry, and Thornton, Freda, *How to Achieve Sex Happiness in Marriage*. New York: Vanguard Press, 1939.

Van de Velde, T. H., *Ideal Marriage*. New York: Covici Friede, 1926.

Vatsyayana, *The Kama Sutra*. Paris: Librairie Astra, no date.

ALBERT ELLIS

Contraception

Definition

CONTRACEPTION includes all methods that permit intercourse between fertile partners without producing impregnation. It is a temporary measure permitting the planning of pregnancy or—to use Margaret Sanger's expression—birth control. The definition does not include abstinence or abortion. Sterilization and castration, generally irreversible procedures, also fall into a different category.

The main criteria for a contraceptive are effectiveness, acceptability, and harmlessness.

Effectiveness

To obtain a true statistical picture of contraceptive effectiveness, it is not enough merely to compare the number of accidental pregnancies in a group of couples who use contraceptives with the number of pregnancies in a group of nonusers of the same size. We base our evaluation of various contraceptive methods upon the length of time during which groups of couples were exposed to pregnancy, deducting weeks or months of nonexposure due to separation, illness, or pregnancy. Then the number of accidental pregnancies is prorated to 100 years of exposure. It is established that couples using no contraceptives at all have a pregnancy rate of 60 to 100 per 100 exposure years. If users of a contraceptive, for instance, the diaphragm-jelly method, show a pregnancy rate of 10 per 100 years of exposure, and if the rate for nonusers within the same population group is 100, we assume that 90 out of 100 pregnancies were prevented, and that the preventive method—in our example the diaphragm-jelly method—has an effectiveness of 90 per cent.

Using this formula, devised by Pearl, we are able to compare the effectiveness of the most commonly used methods. Pregnancy rates are at present being calculated by Potter's (1963) life table procedure.

In the past, a distinction was made between patient-failure and method-failure; today we consider every unplanned pregnancy a failure in couples using contraception.

Motivation and Acceptability

The effectiveness of contraceptive methods is highly influenced by motivation. A method may have a high rate of success with couples of strong determination, yet may fail when used by less determined couples. Another cause of failure may be an emotional desire for pregnancy that is not consciously wanted or advisable. Such an ambivalence in one or both marital partners often defeats the effectiveness of contraception (Lehfeldt, 1959).

Another factor influencing the effectiveness of a contraceptive method is its acceptability. If the contraceptive interferes with the sexual enjoyment of either partner, as is often the case with mechanical devices, it will not be widely used, no matter how excellent its safety record is. Contraceptives requiring preparations shortly before the sex act, such as the condom, all chemical devices, and the diaphragm, are

Contraceptives may be classified as

most effective: orals

highly effective: diaphragm or cervical cap, with jelly or cream; condom; IUD; sequentials; coitus interruptus

very effective: aerosol vaginal foams

fairly effective: creams, jellies alone; foam tablets; suppositories; rhythm method (safe period)

very little effective: breast feeding, vaginal douche

293

frequently rejected as disturbing the mood. The diaphragm may be inserted several hours before intercourse whenever there is a possibility of cohabitation, but even so the psychological connection between contraceptive measure and coitus persists. Another cause of nonacceptability is the failure on the part of the female user to learn the technique of some methods. Unusually tense or apprehensive women may find it impossible to insert or remove the diaphragm; others experience the same difficulty with the firm cervical cap. As the cap can be left *in situ* throughout the menstrual cycle, these women may call on their physician for removal and/or insertion. After receiving instructions from the physician, the husband may sometimes be able to give technical assistance with both diaphragm and cap.

The prescribing physician should be thoroughly familiar with *every* contraceptive technique, for he must be flexible in deciding the method best satisfying the needs of each couple. With all psychological insight, the method of his first choice might not work out. Only experience by trial and error will determine which method is best for each individual couple.

Alternative Use and Combination of Methods

Use of contraceptives may be found more acceptable if recommendations are made for the alternative use of various methods. If, for instance, the husband is reluctant to use a condom and the wife finds the diaphragm objectionable, the compromise of alternating male and female contraceptives may solve the problem. Other couples may find alternating mechanical techniques with the rhythm method more acceptable.

If conception occurs in spite of consistent and correct use of a contraceptive method, as happens in young couples with high fertility and with great sexual activity, additional protection becomes necessary. This may be provided by a combination of methods above and beyond the commonly used combinations of mechanical and chemical contraceptives; for instance, condom and diaphragm plus jelly may be recommended; a more expensive, particularly potent, chemical may be substituted for the cream or jelly, in conjunction with a mechanical device; or couples using mechanical-chemical techniques may in addition practice abstinence during the fertile period.

Such accumulative measures represent increasing mechanization of the sex act, depriving it of its natural spontaneity. Consequently, acceptance of these combinations is low; they should not be recommended to other than very fertile, highly motivated couples who are educated and intelligent, or as a last alternative to sterilization.

Methods Used by the Male

The two most common contraceptives are male techniques: coitus interruptus or withdrawal, and coitus condomatus or use of a sheath during intercourse.

Withdrawal

Withdrawal, mentioned in the Bible as Onan's sin, is probably the oldest of all contraceptive measures. It requires neither preparations nor a medical prescription, but it is effective only if used with great exactitude. The sex act must be interrupted before ejaculation takes place, which necessitates strong will power, especially for the man. When successive cohabitations take place, thorough cleansing before re-entry is essential to avoid transfer of sperm adherent to the male organ and to the vaginal opening.

It is said that over the years coitus interruptus may cause serious physical harm, such as prostatic hypertrophy. There is no proof for this claim. In some cases, the method does produce marital maladjustment. Switching to a different contraceptive technique usually cures these ills.

The Indianapolis study (Westoff et al., 1953) of contraceptive effectiveness—a general population study—considered the most comprehensive survey in the field, showed that the withdrawal method has a pregnancy rate of only 10 per 100 years of exposure. A study based on interviews with 3,000 women from all over England established a pregnancy rate of 8 per 100 years of exposure for the withdrawal method.

In spite of certain shortcomings, the withdrawal technique must be credited with a degree of safety comparable to that achieved by some of the approved mechanical methods.

Condom

The condom is the most widely used mechanical method of contraception. Before World War II, one single German concern sold 24 million condoms per year; recent domestic condom sales amount to 4 to 4.8 million gross annually (Tietze, 1960).

Some sort of condom was probably known in antiquity. In the sixteenth century, a device resembling a linen condom was recommended by Fallopius for antisyphilitic protection. Nowadays, cecal condoms, made of animal intestines, are used, but most condoms are made of rubber.

There are a number of safety rules for the condom. Unless the condom is dated and made by a reliable manufacturer it must be tested before use by air insufflation; after use, inflation with water is advisable in order to detect a possible leak. If the condom breaks or slips off during intercourse, an immediate soap-water douche is necessary; as a safeguard in case of a break, contraceptive jelly (not vaseline) may be put inside the condom.

A good rubber condom can be used several times; after each use it is washed and dried (by hand or with a special drying device) and sprinkled with talcum powder.

In spite of its popularity, the condom is often objectionable to men as well as to women because it interferes with the pleasure of the sex act. As our statistics consist mainly of people who reject the condom, it is difficult to compare its acceptability with that of the best female mechanical devices. In safety, the condom equals the records of the diaphragm and the cap.

Methods Used by the Female

Douches

Douching, widely used, is just as widely mistaken for a contraceptive. Actually, it is of value only as an ancillary precaution to other pregnancy-preventing procedures. Reports from the Margaret Sanger Research Bureau (Sobrero and MacLeod, 1962) show that in fertile couples spermatozoa may enter the cervical canal minutes after unprotected intercourse. No douche will dislodge them from there. When a diaphragm is removed prematurely, a cervical cap gets displaced, or a condom breaks or slips off during intercourse, the douche, if applied in time, will immobilize the spermatozoa and remove them mechanically from the vagina.

Douche water of body temperature and ordinary toilet soap or soap powder should be used. The woman should be in supine position, lying on the bed or in the bathtub, elevating the douche bag not higher than the rim of the tub, to control the pressure; too much pressure may drive the water through the uterus and the Fallopian tubes into the peritoneal cavity and cause serious accidents.

Vaginal Diaphragm

The modern diaphragm consists of a spring (flat or spiral) and a rubber membrane. In England and Germany it is called a pessary or cap. In order to avoid confusion we shall define the diaphragm as a contraceptive vaginal device, the pessary as an instrument for support of the vaginal walls, and the cap as a cervical contraceptive.

Casanova is said to have used a lemon half as a vaginal contraceptive, the acidity of the juice providing chemical protection. In 1838 the German physician Wilde invented a contraceptive "pessary" made of resin. The modern diaphragm was invented by the German physician Mensinga. It was first described in 1881 as an "occlusive pessary" and consisted of a hollow rubber hemisphere, the rim of which was extended by a watch spring. Mensinga warned that contact with fat or oil would damage the rubber; he prescribed five different sizes ranging from 67½ to 77½ mm. in diameter. The diaphragm that we use today differs only in minor details from Mensinga's.

More than thirty years elapsed before a limited number of physicians started to put the diaphragm to use. Among them was Aletta Jacobs, who ran the world's first birth control clinic in Holland. There, in 1915, Margaret Sanger became acquainted with the diaphragm method through the Dutch physician Rutgers; this may account for the name "Dutch cap" or

"Dutch pessary" which is still sometimes used for the diaphragm.

The diaphragm must fit correctly. An individual examination is essential for the selection of the right size, which is usually determined by fitting rings. The anatomy must be explained to the patient, preferably on a pelvic model, and she must be carefully instructed in the technique. She should practice insertion and removal at home and return for at least one more visit to have her technique checked by the physician before she starts to use the diaphragm. In rare cases, women need a special instrument to facilitate insertion.

The diaphragm spring attaches itself to the vaginal walls. Between the tightly fitting diaphragm and the vagina, there is always a microscopic space that is sealed by a spermicidal chemical, without which the diaphragm must not be used. This is spread in a thin layer on the inside and outside of the diaphragm; if the woman has sufficient natural lubrication, cream is used—otherwise, jelly. No oily substance should be used as it would damage the caoutchouc. Some physicians recommend the use of additional jelly or cream if cohabitation occurs more than four hours after the diaphragm is inserted; in my opinion this is unnecessary.

The diaphragm should be left *in situ* for 8, but not more than 24 hours; during this time the spermatozoa are immobilized by vaginal secretions and by the spermicidal chemical. If the diaphragm is removed earlier, and only then, a soap-water douche must be applied.

The diaphragm must never be boiled; it is washed with water and soap, dried with a towel, and powdered with talcum. The high quality of the rubber in this country permits use of the diaphragm for one year. Some women wear it longer, but this is not safe because of the deterioration of rubber by age.

In cases of extreme vaginism or pronounced vaginal prolapse, use of the diaphragm is contraindicated.

Cervical Cap

Cervical caps are made of various materials; a widely used variety is of soft rubber, the Prorace cap of Mary Stopes in England. The Dumas and Mizpah caps are similar. Like the vaginal diaphragm, these rubber devices must be removed after 24 hours; they are not safer than the diaphragm and insertion and removal are more difficult. In the past, caps were also made of resin, celluloid, and metals, including gold, silver, and platinum. All these materials have been abandoned; today we use a cap made of lucite, a firm plastic material. This cap can be worn for two years without showing deterioration, and it causes no irritation.

Like the diaphragm, the cap, which is generally manufactured in three different sizes, must be fitted by a physician. Its shape resembles a cone; it has a narrow rim that adheres to the vaginal walls and also facilitates removal. The cap should not fit as tightly as the diaphragm, a small space remaining between cervix and cap. Before insertion, a small quantity of contraceptive cream is filled into the cap.

In contrast to the diaphragm, the cap can safely be left in position throughout the menstrual cycle, but has to be taken out just before menstruation occurs and reinserted after it ends. Women fitted with a cap are protected while it is in place and thus are spared the necessity of introducing contraceptives before each coitus. Because the cap frees the couple from the immediate preparation for contraceptives, it makes it possible to disassociate contraception from the sex act, which is its most important advantage over the diaphragm. We have also found the cap useful in crowded areas, where lack of privacy often creates a problem for the user of a diaphragm.

The cap sometimes develops a disagreeable odor, which can be eliminatd by douching. This symptom can be avoided by removing the cap every few days, a procedure advisable for women who have no difficulties with the technique. Sometimes the male partner feels the cap as disturbing; in such cases, a different contraceptive method should be prescribed. Cervical erosions or deep lacerations are contraindications for the cap.

Chemical Contraceptives

Chemical contraceptives are tablets, jellies, creams, and foams. The chemical must be inserted shortly before intercourse. In dissolving, some tablets develop a foam that covers the cervical os, thereby preventing ascent of the spermatozoa. But tablets dissolve and are effective only in the presence of a sufficient amount of natural vaginal lubrication. They are therefore not too reliable.

Suppositories, as well as jellies or creams, used alone, without mechanical devices, have been recommended as "simplified" contraceptive methods. In the writer's opinion, they are simpler or more convenient only inasmuch as they can be applied without medical instruction. However, the injection of cream or jelly by means of a syringe, or the insertion of a suppository—precoital manipulations associated with chemical contraceptives—present the same psychological problem as the diaphragm.

"Simple Techniques"

Among the "simple" contraceptive techniques, the vaginal aerosol foams enjoy a high degree of acceptance. Clinical experience and laboratory tests (Johnson, Masters and Lewis, 1964) indicate that the foam method is slightly more effective than jelly and cream alone (Table I), but it must be emphasized that it is less effective than the diaphragm and other techniques. Foam is valuable as an *addition* to other contraceptive techniques (diaphragm, cervical cap, condom). At Bellevue Hospital it has been successfully used for IUD wearers during the first three months after insertion, during which expulsion of the device occurs most frequently.

Orals and IUDs

Two new contraceptive techniques have revolutionized sex and marital life: oral contraceptives and intrauterine devices (IUDs). Large groups who, for various reasons, had not previously used birth control have become regular contraceptors, including many underprivileged women and juveniles. There are several reasons for the changed attitude in these groups. In contrast to the older conventional methods (with the exception of the cervical cap), the new techniques do not require special preparation for each individual sex act: contraception and coitus are separated. This makes these methods more acceptable. The IUD, which is specially suited for develop-

ing countries, requires no continued motivation of the wearer after it has been inserted; its manufacture in mass production is inexpensive. Similarly, oral contraceptives, or "pills," have now become inexpensive enough for even poor families. The indigent can obtain the pills in the clinics free of charge or at a minimal cost. According to recent estimates, 7 million women in the U.S., and some 5 million in foreign countries have used pills up to the present.

The pill poses a moral problem relating to the unmarried: does this method, by its convenience, promote promiscuity? There is no evidence that it does. Physicians and sociologists believe that the withholding of contraceptives does not prevent promiscuity. On the other hand, use of these contraceptives has most certainly reduced the number of unplanned pregnancies.

Orals

The basic research in this field was done by John Rock (1956) and Gregory Pincus (1958). Contraceptive pills consist of two synthetic hormones, progesterone and estrogen. They prevent pregnancy by suppression of ovulation. Every month, the woman in the reproductive age group expels an egg (ovum) from her ovary. This event—ovulation—occurs about mid-time between two menstruations. If ovulation is prevented—as it is during pregnancy—no conception can occur. At present, eight such oral contraceptives are commercially available in the United States. All have been approved by the F.D.A. but can be obtained only by prescription. Most physicians prescribe one tablet per day for 20 days, from cycle day 5 to 25. (Cycle day one is the first day of the menstruation.) At Bellevue's contraceptive clinic, pills are prescribed for 25 successive days (from cycle day 5 to 29). By following this routine, the cycle is regulated to a length of 30 days and the woman may expect to have her menstruation on more or less the same calendar day of each month (Lehfeldt 1965).

The effectiveness of oral contraception with this combination method is close to 100 per cent. In virtually every case, when a woman on oral contraception has become pregnant, it has been shown that she had omitted a pill or two.

Side-effects of oral contraception are minor and usually disappear within a few months of medication. The most frequent side-effects are weight gain, nausea, tenderness of the breasts, and breakthrough bleeding. There is no indication whatever that the pills cause cancer. Some physicians even believe that they may prevent cancer. There is also no evidence that the pills cause thrombosis or pulmonary embolism.

A subspecies of the above discussed "combination" pills are the "sequentials." Beginning with cycle day 5, the woman takes 15 pills containing estrogen plus progesterone for 5 more days. While this variety of oral contraception seems to produce slightly less side-effects it is not 100 per cent effective; also, omission of one single pill may be followed by pregnancy.

Intrauterine devices

Until a few years ago, intrauterine contraceptive devices (IUDs) were considered dangerous and were not used by most gynecologists. A few resolute investigators in various parts of the world nevertheless continued to explore the potentialities of this technique. It has been known for centuries that a foreign body in the uterus will prevent pregnancy. The modern version of IUD dates back to Ernst Gräfenberg, a Berlin gynecologist who later practiced in New York City. Gräfenberg's devices were first made of silkworm gut, later of silver, gold, or platinum. When he published his method in the 1920's, it enjoyed only a brief period of popularity (Lehfeldt, 1928). The reasons for the renascence of the intrauterine technique are twofold: present IUDs are made of non reactive material: stainless steel or plastic. Infection occurring in wearers of such devices, while not caused by the devices, was a dangerous complication 30 years ago. Nowadays, such infections are easily brought under control with antibiotic or sulfonamide medication, without even necessitating removal of the IUD.

While there is no question that the IUD is highly effective, its mode of action in the human is still a mystery. The great advantage of the method is that it requires nothing more of the woman than the decision to have the device inserted. One single procedure only is necessary to provide protection for years.

Unfortunately, this method has still a number of shortcomings. It is best suited for women who have already given birth; in the nullipara, the insertion can be extremely difficult and painful, and the effectiveness is lower. Expulsion of the device occurs in a minority of cases. In others, it has to be removed because of bleeding or menstrual pain. Still, it is a highly effective method of contraception as 80 out of 100 inserted women have no problems with this technique. The IUD method, as well as the oral contraceptives, represent great progress in the field of fertility control.

At the time of this writing, about one and a half million women all over the world have been inserted with IUDs. The most extensive study (Tietze, 1966), a statistical evaluation of more than 22,000 insertions by 33 investigators, as well as our own clinical experience (Lehfeldt 1965, 1966) indicate that the large plastic loop invented by Lippes (1965) is the IUD of choice.

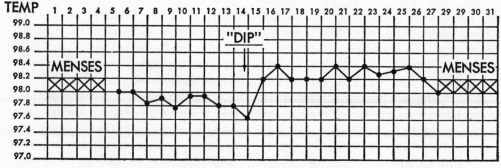

FIG. 1

The Safe Period, or Rhythm Method

The rhythm method restricts intercourse to the period of physiological sterility in the woman's cycle. Conception occurs when an ovum, or egg, is fertilized by a sperm cell. As a rule, the ovary expels only one ovum per cycle, a process known as ovulation; this ovum stays alive not longer than 24 to 48 hours, and there is evidence that the sperm cells also remain fertile for only about 48 hours after entering the uterus and tubes. Hence, conception is possible during only a few days of each cycle; if intercourse is avoided during this fertile period, i.e., during ovulation time, conception should be impossible.

The difficulty with this method is determining the exact date of ovulation. We owe most available data to the thorough research done by Ogino (1932) in Japan and Knaus (1964) in Austria. Independently, both authors discovered that ovulation occurs in midcycle, not around menstruation time, as had been assumed; that, irrespective of the cycle length, the ten days preceding menstruation are infertile and constitute a "safe period"; and that there is another "safe period" at the beginning of the cycle. This part of the "safe period" is very short, however, especially when the cycle is short, as for instance in women who menstruate every twenty-one days. For this reason some clinicians recommend only the ten days preceding menstruation as the "safe period."

But the fact that very few women menstruate with absolute regularity complicates the determination of even these last ten cycle days. The cycle of 50 per cent of women varies in length over ten days and more, according to Ogino. Couples who intend to use the rhythm method therefore need medical advice for exact determination of the safe period. The woman must keep an accurate record of the menstrual cycles for three to six months (for one full year, according to Knaus), *before* applying the rhythm method.

One of the methods by which the physician can determine ovulation time is the temperature record. During an entire cycle the woman writes down her temperature every morning before arising; the chart will show that on one day around midcycle the temperature drops, followed by a rise the next day and several days thereafter (see figure). There is considerable evidence that the time of the temperature dip coincides with ovulation time.

One of the few available clinical investigations of the rhythm method, from the Free Hospital in Brookline, Mass., reports a pregnancy rate of 14 per 100 years of exposure. Tietze and associates (1951), who compiled the data, conclude that "the rhythm method offers a satisfactory degree of protection against unwanted pregnancy to rigorously selected and carefully instructed wives who, with their husbands, are intelligent and strongly motivated. For others and for those to whom pregnancy would be dangerous, the effectiveness of the method is not considered adequate."

In comparing the effectiveness of the rhythm with other contraceptive techniques, we must realize that the exposure time in rhythm couples is curtailed by abstinence during one-third to one-half of each cycle; therefore, 100 years of exposure time in couples using the rhythm is actually not equivalent to the same length of exposure time in users of other contraceptive methods.

"Continence, either periodic or continuous, is the only form of birth control not in itself morally objectionable," says Father Kelly (1958). The rhythm method, the only contraceptive technique permissible for Roman Catholics, is used only rarely by non-Catholics. It might, however, become valuable as an alternative to other techniques, if we learn how to use it more accurately. In its present state of development, the method is being criticized even by Catholics. John Rock (1963), who was instrumental in developing the pill, has urged the Vatican to permit the use of oral contraception as a preventive measure. A prominent lay Catholic, Clare Boothe Luce (1967), has described the rhythm method as "checked-off love and clocked-out continence." According to the GAF (Growth of American Families) study (Ryder and Westoff, 1966), 53 per cent of American Catholics are using some method of contraception other than the safe period. It is to be hoped that the Papal Commission on Marriage and Birth Control will take a progressive attitude in its final dealing with the question of fertility control.

References

Calderone, Mary S., (ed.), *Manual of Contraceptive Practice*. Baltimore: The Williams & Wilkins Co., 1964.

Dickinson, Robert L., and Bryant, Louise S., *Control of Conception*. Baltimore: The Williams & Wilkins Co., 1932.

Fraenkel, Ludwig, *Die Empfaengnisverhuetung* (The Prevention of Conception). Stuttgart: Ferdinand Enke, 1932.

Haire, Norman, *Birth Control Methods*. London: George Allen & Unwin, Ltd., 1938.

Hartman, Carl G., *Time of Ovulation in Women. A Study on the Fertile Period in the Menstrual Cycle*. Baltimore: The Williams & Wilkins Co., 1936.

Himes, Norman E., *A Medical History of Contraception*. New York: Gamut Press, 1963.

Himes, Norman E., and Stone, Abraham, *Practical Birth Control Methods*. New York: Modern Age Books, Inc., 1938.

Hoellein, Emil, *Gegen den Gebaerzwang* (Against Compulsory Birth). Berlin-Charlottenburg: Published by the author, 1928.

Kelly, Gerald, S.J., *Medico-Moral Problems*. St. Louis, Mo.: The Catholic Hospital Association, 1958.

Knaus, Hermann, *Human Procreation and its Natural Regulation*. New York: Ivan Obolensky Inc., 1964.

Lehfeldt, Hans, "Contraceptive Methods Requiring Medical Assistance." Paper read at Sexual Reform Congress of World League for Sexual Reform. London, 1929.

Lehfeldt, Hans, *Das Buch der Ehe* (The Marriage Book). Berlin: Aufklaerungs-Buecherei-Verlag, 1930.

Lehfeldt, Hans, "Intrauterine Contraception: tailed vs. tailless devices." *Livre Jubilaire* for Dr. J. Dalsace. Paris: Masson & Cie., 1966.

Lehfeldt, Hans, "The Firm Cervical Cap." *J. Contraception 2;* 106, 1937; and *J. Sex Educ. 1;* 132-148, 1949.

Lehfeldt, Hans, "The first five years of contraceptive service in a municipal hospital." *Am. J. Ob. & Gyn. 93;* 727, 1965.

Lehfeldt, Hans, *Vortraege und Verhandlungen des Aerztekurses vom 28.-30. Dez. 1928*. (K. Bendix, ed.) Berlin: Selbstverlag, 1929.

Lehfeldt, Hans, "Wilful Exposure to Unwanted Pregnancy (WEUP). Psychological Explanation for Patient Failures in Contraception." Paper read at Sixth International Conference on Planned Parenthood. New Delhi: February, 1959.

Lehfeldt, H., Kulka, E. W. and Liebmann, H. G., "Comparative study of intrauterine contraceptive devices." *Obst. & Gynec. 26;* 679, 1965.

Lippes, J., "Contraception with intrauterine plastic loops." *Am. J. Ob. & Gyn. 93;* 1024, 1965.

Luce, Clare Boothe, *McCall's*, Feb. 1967.

Mears, Eleanor (ed.), *Handbook on Oral Contraception*. Boston: Little, Brown & Co., 1965.

Murphy, John P., and Laux, John D., *The Rhythm Way to Family Happiness*. (rev. ed.) New York: Hawthorn Books, Inc., 1960.

Ogino, K., "Ueber den Konzeptionstermin des Weibes und seine Anwendung in der Praxis (Time of Conception in Women and Its Application in Practice)." *Zentralbl. f. Gynaek. 56;* 721-732, 1932.

Pincus, Gregory et al., "Fertility Control with Oral Medication." *Am. J. Obst. & Gynec. 75;* 1333-1346, 1958.

Pommerenke, W. T., "Phenomena Correlated with Ovulation as Guides to the Appraisal of the So-called 'Safe Period.'" *Proc. Third Internat. Conf. Planned Parenthood.* Bombay: The Family Planning Association of India, 1952.

Potter, R. G., "Additional Measures of Use-Effectiveness of Contraception." *Milbank Mem. Fund Quart. 41;* 400, 1963.

Rock, John, *The Time Has Come. A Catholic doctor's proposal to end the battle over birth control.* New York: Alfred A. Knopf, 1963.

Ryder, Norman B. and Westoff, Charles F., "Use of oral contraception in the United States 1965." *Science 153;* 1199, 1966.

Sanger, Margaret, *My Fight for Birth Control*. New York: Farrar & Rinehart, 1931.

Sanger, Margaret, and Stone, Hannah M. (eds.), *The Practice of Contraception*. Baltimore: The Williams & Wilkins Co., 1931.

Sobrero, A. J. and MacLeod, J., "The immediate post-coital test." *Fertil. & Steril. 13;* 184, 1962.

Stone, Hannah M., and Stone, Abraham, *A Marriage Manual*. New York: Simon and Schuster, Inc., 1952.

Tietze, Christopher, *The Clinical Effectiveness of Contraceptive Methods* (preliminary ed.). New York: National Committee on Maternal Health, 1958.

Tietze, C., *The Condom as a Contraceptive*. New York: Nat. Comm. on Maternal Health, 1960.

Tietze, C., "Contraception with intrauterine devices," 1959-1966. *Am. J. Ob. & Gyn. 96;* 1043, 1966.

Tietze, Christopher, Lehfeldt, Hans, and Liebmann, H. G., "The Effectiveness of the Cervical Cap as a Contraceptive Method." *Am. J. Obst. & Gynec. 66;* 904-908, 1953.

Tietze, Christopher, Poliakoff, Samuel R., and Rock, John, "The Clinical Effectiveness of the Rhythm Method of Contraception." *Fertil. & Steril. 2;* 444-450, 1951.

Westoff, Charles F. et al., "Social and Psychological Factors Affecting Fertility; the Use, Effectiveness, and Acceptability of Methods of Fertility Control." *Milbank Mem. Fund Quart. 31;* (3), 291-357, 1953.

HANS LEHFELDT

Courtship and Mate-Selection

Definitions

COURTSHIP denotes the interaction be- tween a man and a woman characterized by one or both of the following conditions: (a) one or both of the parties may express an *attitude* of love toward the other; (b) one or both may be seeking to bring about a *goal-state* involving the other. The goal-state usually in- volves one or more of the following: (1) estab- lishing oneself in the affections of the other, i.e., causing the other to "fall in love" with ones- self, (2) sex relations with the other, (3) mar- riage to the other. Generally it is assumed that the two persons involved in a courtship are not married, and, *a fortiori,* not married to each other, but advice-givers do sometimes counsel a person to court a spouse. In this case the goal- state would have to involve (1) and/or (2). Occasionally one of the parties to the courtship seeks the goal-state on behalf of a third party, as when John Alden wooed Priscilla in behalf of Captain Miles Standish.

Mate-selection is the process whereby nubile men and women acquire spouses. Mates may be acquired by mutual volition of the prin- cipals, by arrangement, or by capture. Sumner and Keller (1929) remark that in the last case the woman has no customary rights but is wholly "the possession of the captor." Thus they conclude that marriage by capture is "really no marriage at all." *Mutual volition* is the practice familiar in middle-class America whereby the prospective bride and groom choose each other with little or no necessity to obtain permission from their kinsmen or from others. Usually it is assumed that mate-selection

on the basis of mutual volition is premised on a pre-existing mutual love. *Arranged marriage* refers to mate-selection resulting from negotia- tion between the family of the bride and the family of the groom. Frequently such negoti- ations are highly formalized and involve one or two go-betweens and the transfer of prop- erty (dowry or bride-price). It seems probable that arranged marriages have been the custom in most societies throughout history. Tradition- al China and rural Ireland are examples of this procedure. A special form of arranged mar- riage occurs in a patrilineal and patrilocal soci- ety when a family with one or more daughters but no son adopts a son as groom for a daughter.

The word courtship comes from the practice of courtly love in the medieval courts of western Europe. At that time it was generally thought that love between husband and wife was not possible because of the functional nature of the marital relationship. Courtly love was a more or less clandestine relationship be- tween a man and a woman of high rank who were not married to each other.

In American society we use *dating, courtship,* and *engagement* to denote varying degrees of commitment in the premarital social interaction of men and women. Dating implies no commit- ment concerning marriage; engagement implies that both parties have agreed to marry each other. From the above definition of courtship it is seen that there is one sense in which this term may represent an intermediate level since it may imply an intent on the part of one or both parties to make a commitment to marry.

In a society in which mate-selection is based

on mutual love, as in modern America, the dating-courtship-engagement sequence has the functional value of fostering premarital interaction between the sexes and thus of allowing young men and women to find persons within their fields of eligibles (explained below) with whom they are emotionally compatible. Waller (1937) has leveled objection against this line of reasoning, however, on the ground that the selection of partners for dates and the nature of dating activities do not conduce to the sound selection of marriage partners.

The Field of Eligible Spouse Candidates

Let us understand a differentiated society to be a society containing a relatively high number of social strata and specialized occupations. The people of such a society may also be highly diversified with respect to religious affiliation, ethnic background, and extent of formal education. In general it appears that social class, occupation, religious affiliation, etc., are variables that polarize interaction with the result that people interact most with people like themselves with respect to these variables, e.g., that upper-class people tend to associate more with other upper-class people than with people from lower classes, and Baptists tend to associate more with other Baptists than with non-Baptists. Thus it is argued that, to the extent that society is differentiated with respect to these variables, patterns of differential association develop whereby people tend to have associates who resemble themselves with respect to these variables.

Where mate-selection takes place on the basis of mutual volition, one ordinarily selects a mate from one's associates. From the argument of the preceding paragraph it should follow that where mate-selection takes place on the basis of mutual volition, homogamy should prevail, i.e., mates should tend to resemble each other with respect to such variables of social differentiation as social class and religious affiliation. Thus we speak of these variables as functioning to provide each normal, adult, participating member of a society with a field of eligible spouse candidates (eligible because of similarity in such valued social characteristics as social class) or more briefly as a *field of eligibles*.

Enough studies have been done on mate-selection in American society to corroborate the argument in the foregoing paragraph. There is considerable evidence that American marriages are more likely to occur between people who are similar rather than dissimilar with respect to the following social characteristics: *age*, e.g., a young person tends to marry someone who is also young; *race*, e.g., a Negro tends to marry another Negro; *religious affiliation*, e.g., it is probable that a Baptist will marry another Baptist and even more probable that he will marry another Protestant; *ethnic origin*, e.g., an American of Italian extraction is more likely to marry someone also of Italian extraction than of, say, Swedish extraction; *location of previous residence* (also known as *residential propinquity*), e.g., a young man is more likely to marry a girl living within a couple of blocks than one who lives on the opposite side of the country; *socioeconomic status*, e.g., an upper-class person is likely to choose a mate from his own stratum; *extent of formal education*, e.g., a college-trained person is likely to marry someone who has also had some college education; and *previous marital status*, e.g., a man marrying for the first time is more likely to marry a girl who has never been married before than one who has been widowed or divorced. In general, if a person selects a mate outside his or her field of eligibles, the marriage is socially disapproved and is regarded as a *mésalliance*.

Another way of accounting for the tendency toward homogamy is in terms of ethnocentrism (or group-conceit). There seems to be a virtually universal disposition for peoples to dislike and to distrust those who differ from themselves in race, religion, and cultural background. Ethnocentrism is expressed in feelings and gestures of disapproval about a marriage between a member of one's own group and a person from a markedly different group who, therefore, presents markedly different social characteristics.

There is, however, a countervailing force to ethnocentrism and its pressure toward homogamy: the incest taboo. Every society has some form of incest taboo, and related to the incest taboo in each society will be found a prohibition against marriages between people in certain kinship relationships to each other. The prohibited degrees of kinship vary from one society to another and may extend to all known blood relatives. The result of the incest taboo is to foster heterogamy (marriage between people who are unlike). As Linton Freeman has pointed out, every society has some conception of preferential mating that is a resultant of the two conflicting pressures: ethnocentrism and the incest taboo. In any society the field of eligibles is defined by the relative strengths of these two principles.

The general argument to this point has been that within societies and segments of societies there are societal principles that define in general the field of eligibles for every normal, fully participating adult. There remains the question as to how selection goes on *within* the field of eligibles. How does man A happen to get wife X rather than Y or Z when all three women are within his field of eligibles?

The first step in trying to answer this question is to note the kind of selective process: is it a process of mutual volition or one of arranged marriage? If it is the former, then we look at the bride and groom to find an answer to our question. If it is the latter, we look to the parents of the bride and groom, to those who stand *in loco parentis*, or more generally to their respective families. If husband and wife are choosing each other, we should expect that the criteria of selection will be relevant to the expectations these two people have as to what they will get or hope to get out of the marriage. If it is the two families who are choosing, it is reasonable to anticipate a somewhat different set of criteria.

The Theory of Complementary Needs in Mate-Selection

Under some conditions love is defined as the most important criterion for the selection of a mate from the field of eligibles. Winch (1958) has argued that love is likely to be the chief consideration where (a) choice is on the basis of mutual volition, (b) the marital relationship is culturally defined as a rich potential source of emotional gratification, and (c) there are institutionalized provisions for premarital interaction between men and women in order to provide the opportunity for testing out personalities of a variety of potential mates.

In this context love is defined as: the positive emotion experienced by one person (the person loving, or the lover) in an interpersonal relationship in which the second person (the person loved, or the love-object) either (1) satisfies certain important needs of the first or (2) manifests or appears (to the first) to manifest personal attributes (e.g., beauty, skills, or status) highly prized by the first, or both.

Thus love is stated in terms of the needs of the individual, and selection of a love-object is contingent upon the complementariness of the need-patterns of the two individuals, or more formally: In mate-selection each individual seeks within his or her field of eligibles for that person who gives the greatest promise of providing him or her with maximum need-gratification.

At this juncture it is useful to distinguish between an individual's values, interests, and tastes on the one hand and his drives or emotional needs on the other. It is the writer's view that love is most likely to occur between a man and a woman who are (a) in each other's field of eligibles, and (b) who have similar values, interests, and tastes, but (c) whose emotional need-patterns are *complementary* rather than similar.

Point (a) concerning the field of eligibles has already been discussed. As regards (b) it seems clear that similarity provides a basis for the interaction of the couple, whereas difference removes such a basis. Thus, if a man and a woman share an interest in religion or in athletics, attendance at church services or at football games provides them with a basis and a context for interaction.

With respect to certain emotional needs (c), however, Winch has concluded that attraction is based on complementariness rather than on similarity. He has derived this general conclusion from a rather intensive study of twenty-five young married couples. He has hypothesized that there are two kinds of emotional need with respect to which complementary mate-selection takes place: (a) a highly nurturant and a highly receptive person seem attracted to each other; and (b) a highly dominant and a highly submissive person seem mutually attracted.

Arranged Marriage

It appears that mate-selection on the basis of love tends to take place generally where the family, as a societal institution, is weak relative to other societal institutions. More particularly, the relative weakness of the American family is reflected in the fact that other institutions in American society have relatively great capacity to control goals that motivate the individual and thus to control the life organization of the individual. On the other hand, in a society where the family is relatively strong, much of the individual's behavior is dictated by familial considerations. Traditional China was such a society. When a son in a family of the traditional Chinese peasantry obtained a wife, the significance of the event was interpreted as: (a) the son's mother was getting a helper; (b) the young man's family was establishing a friendly relationship with the family of the new daughter-in-law; and (c) the young man's family was being supplied with a means for carrying on the family line. Note that the attractiveness of the young woman in her husband's eyes does not appear in this list of considerations. It is reasonable, therefore, that rather than the son, who was so little involved, the parents and especially the mother should select the daughter-in-law; that the marriage was made in the names of the parents who took a daughter-in-law rather than in the name of a son who took a wife; and that at the time of the wedding the bride and groom might be total strangers to each other. In this setting, as in so many others around the globe and throughout history, the selection of a spouse has been regarded as a matter of too great importance to the families to be left to the discretion of the young man and woman who are inexperienced and whose choice might be influenced by emotion rather than by sound reason.

Summary

Courtship is interaction between a man and a woman which may or may not be oriented to eventual marriage. Mate-selection is a process that may or may not involve the active participation of the prospective marital couple. As a resultant of ethnocentrism and the incest taboo, a field of eligible spouse candidates is defined for each person in any society. If the family as a societal institution is weak, selection of a mate from the field of eligibles is likely to be done by mutual volition; if the family is strong, by arrangement. If selection from the field of eligibles is on the basis of mutual volition, it is likely that love will be the basis of choice. Love has the best chance to flourish as a basis for mate-selection where there is an extensive basis for premarital interaction between the sexes. Such a basis exists when the couple shares a large number of common values, interests, and tastes. It is in this context that courtship will appear as a prelude to marriage. Love is defined in terms of complementary needs. In particular it is hypothesized that nurturance-receptivity and/or assertiveness-submissiveness are dimensions of complementary needs along which marital choices are made.

References

Arensberg, C. M., and Kimball, S. T., *Family and Community in Ireland*. Cambridge: Harvard University press, 1940.

Burgess, Ernest W., and Wallin, Paul, *Engagement and Marriage*. Philadelphia: J. B. Lippincott Co., 1953.

de Rougemont, D., *Love in the Western World*. New York: Doubleday Anchor Books, 1957.

Goodsell, Willystine, *A History of Marriage and the Family*. New York: The Macmillan Co., 1934.

Hsu, F. L. K., "The Family in Modern China." In Ruth Anshen (ed.), *The Family: Its Function and Destiny*. New York: Harper & Brothers, 1949.

Kelly, E. Lowell, "Personality Factors in Assortative Mating." *Psychol. Bull. 37;* 576, 1940.

Kerckhoff, Alan and Davis, Keith E., "Value Concensus and Need Complementarity in Mate Selection." *American Sociological Review; 27,* 295-303, 1962.

LeMasters, E. E., *Modern Courtship and Marriage*. New York: The Macmillan Co., 1957.

Levy, M. J., Jr., *The Family Revolution in Modern China.* Cambridge: Harvard University Press, 1949.

Lowie, R. H., *Primitive Society.* New York: Liveright, 1947.

Merrill, F. E., *Courtship and Marriage.* New York: William Sloane Associates, Inc., 1949.

Popenoe, Paul, "Mate Selection." *Am. Sociol. Rev. 2;* 735-743, 1937.

Richardson, Helen M., "Studies of Mental Resemblance." *Psychol. Bull. 36;* 104-120, 1939.

Sumner, W. G., and Keller, A. G., *The Science of Society,* Vol. 3. New Haven: Yale University Press, 1929.

Waller, W., "The Rating and Mating Complex." *Am. Sociol. Rev. 2;* 727-734, 1937.

Winch, Robert F., "A Re-examination of the Theory of Complementary Needs in Mate Selection." *Journal of Marriage and the Family,* in press.

Winch, R. F., *The Modern Family.* New York: Henry Holt & Co., Inc., 1952.

Winch, R. F., *Mate-Selection: A Study of Complementary Needs.* New York: Harper & Brothers, 1958.

Winch, R. F., and McGinnis, Robert (eds.), *Marriage and the Family.* New York: Henry Holt & Co., Inc., 1953.

Young, Kimball, *Isn't One Wife Enough?* New York: Henry Holt & Co., Inc., 1954.

ROBERT F. WINCH

Culture and Sex

CULTURE and sex is one of the broadest possible topics: since it includes a study of sexual attitudes and behavior in all possible regions, and often of several sub-communities within a given region. There will be no attempt within this present article to cover this subject in anything near its entirety, for several good reasons. First of all, the topic is too big for anything but a summary presentation in a single article of the present size. Secondly, many of the aspects of sex and culture are covered in various other articles in this Encyclopedia, especially those relating to sex in various individual regions and cultures. Thirdly, many of the salient details regarding comparisons of sex behavior in different past and present world cultures have been covered by the writer and Dr. Frank A. Beach in *Patterns of Sexual Behavior* (1951).

Keeping the foregoing limitations in mind, it is still possible to give a summary view of some of the more important aspects of culture and sex. Human sex behavior finds expression within the context of culture, the patterned ways of living that characterize social life. These life-patterns are the heritage from thousands upon thousands of generations of experience in existing and surviving. They represent what the ancestors of each society have learned about how to live and reproduce. It is within this setting that each individual is born and matures and within this atmosphere that his activities take place.

Comparative Cultural Patterns

In order to obtain some view of the relationship between sex and culture it is necessary to move outside the frame of reference provided by American society alone. Unless this is done it will be impossible to find a base line, a concept of human nature divorced from the particular culture patterns that characterize our own people. We might otherwise assume, for instance, that social life everywhere would involve strict monogamy, a ban on childhood sexual activities, a repudiation of homosexuality, and a disapproving attitude toward marriage between first cousins. Through the comparison of a number of societies a quite different picture emerges. Under different social conditions a man may be urged to acquire many wives, children may be expected to imitate their elders in sexual activities, the homosexual may be trained for his part from childhood and become a respected and powerful member of the community, and a man's cross-cousin (his first cousin: the child of either his father's sister or his mother's brother) may be the preferred mate.

This is not to suggest that all is completely relative and that there are no limits set to the behavior of the members of a society save traditional and arbitrary codes and attitudes. On the contrary, a comparative study of the relationship between culture and sex reveals an extraordinary set of uniformities that have been independently learned by those human societies that are surviving today. Human beings are much alike everywhere and human societies have much in common with each other. People everywhere have a common heritage from organic evolution, the same basic urges and emotions, the same capabilities for learning and behaving. Societies have a comparable heritage from societal evolution, the ways of living and surviving that have been learned, modified, and incorporated into their traditional lifeways.

Nor is there the implication that behavior which may be approved in some other society, but not in our own, is to be recommended for an American. The fact that a number of societies find it congenial for their children to cohabit for several years before marriage does not imply that parents in our society could take such an attitude lightheartedly. Our society has a structure and culture that is not congenial to such behavior and all sorts of complications would arise were parents suddenly to modify their moral codes in this or other respects. But it does indicate that there is nothing inherent in people which preordains their adaptability to some forms of behavior. Under some conditions one pattern may be more "natural" than another, which in turn may be more "natural" when conditions change. On the other hand, there do seem to be some forms of behavior that have been generally discovered for one reason or another to be dangerous to group welfare or otherwise unsuitable for adoption.

Incest Prohibitions

For the most part, humans live in family groups, consisting of mother, father, and offspring. There are many societies that permit a man to have more than one wife if he can afford to do so, but in most of these relatively few men actually have several wives for any great length of time. The individual is thus, generally speaking, born as the member of a nuclear family group. He belongs to other groups as well, kin and local, but with respect to sexual activities the family is of primary importance.

The maturing individual in any society learns sooner or later that sexual relations with members of his family are forbidden. The prohibition against primary incest is apparently everywhere a part of the social atmosphere for at least the majority of the population. Intercourse between daughter and father, son and mother, brother and sister is everywhere forbidden. In addition, every society extends the incest prohibition to other relatives. For some the extension is not very broad and may include only secondary relatives, such as one's father's sister or mother's sister. Some forbid sexual relations

between first cousins, as we tend to do. Others extend the incest prohibition much more broadly and may, in effect, exclude as sex partners all but relatively few members of the community.

Incestuous relations do occur in many societies, apparently, but for the majority of the population at least they are always forbidden and detected offenders are usually severely punished. In a few societies, such as the ancient Egyptians, royal families insist upon brother-sister marriage. But examples of this are rare and quite exceptional.

It is clear that the incest prohibition and its extensions are a heritage from learning experience and not the reflection of some inborn revulsion for near relatives. Reported phantasies and dreams in our own and in other societies clearly reveal that erotic attraction between members of the primary family is a common occurrence. Moreover, incestuous relations do occasionally occur and it is very probable that they would occur far more often were there not strong prohibitions against such behavior.

The origins of the prohibition against primary incest are lost in history, but apparently this was a lesson learned very soon after man's appearance as a distinct species. It is not difficult to imagine how the lesson was learned. Young boys and girls are for a long time at the mercy of their parents and a boy competing with his father for the same sex object would not stand much of a chance. A daughter would in similar fashion find it difficult to compete successfully with her mother for the affections of her father. The forbidding of relationships between brother and sister could readily arise as an extension of the controls imposed upon daughter-father and son-mother incest.

Whatever the origins of incest prohibitions may have been, they now characterize all human societies. They serve at least two useful functions. First, they tend to cut down on competition within the family unit, on jealousies that might interfere with the functioning of this most important social group. Second, they insure that mating will take place outside the family, thus widening the circle of people who will band together in cooperative effort and in face of danger. The incest prohibition may or may not have biological adaptive value. Not enough is known about the matter to make a definitive statement. The functional significance of the incest prohibition and its extensions has been carefully analyzed by Murdock and the results of his study have been published (1949) under the title of *Social Structure*.

Bestiality

In addition to the prohibition against incest, primary and extended, societies generally exert controls over potential sex partners in other ways. As in our own society, most peoples either threaten with punishment or ridicule individuals who seek sexual satisfaction through relationships with lower animals. This is not, however, universally the case. Indeed, for a few societies, bestiality is required of growing boys in the conviction that otherwise they will not mature properly. But these are exceptions to a general feeling that sexual relations with lower animals, if not wrong, are at best inadequate and a last resort.

Homosexuality

In our own society social pressures are levied against homosexuality for both men and women. Differentially, more pressure is exerted against male homosexuality and the legal codes of many states carry severe penalties for convicted male homosexuals. This is not the case for females, very few states providing legal penalties for detected homosexual relations between women. But generally speaking, female homosexuality meets with disapproval and social censure in most sections of the United States. Despite these pressures, however, relationships between members of the same sex do occur in our society.

Some other societies share with us prohibitions against homosexuality. Some of these peoples mete out the death penalty to overt homosexuals of either sex. In most of these societies, however, persons who seek sexual satisfaction with members of the same sex are derided and ridiculed rather than physically punished. Pressures against homosexuality are generally brought to bear early in life and continue through childhood and into adolescence.

There are a number of societies that consider homosexual activities of one sort or another both normal and socially acceptable. Under these conditions homosexual behavior, among men in particular, appears to be common and frequent. In some instances all the men and boys in the society engage in anal intercourse and are considered abnormal if they hesitate to do so. In other instances only a few individuals in the society adopt a feminine role and may even by this means achieve a prestige in the community they did not enjoy previously.

The most common form of homosexuality in socially approved form is that of the *berdache* or *transvestite*. The berdache is a male who adopts the feminine role in the society, dressing and acting like a woman and having sexual relations with male partners. Less commonly, women may dress and act like men, seeking to play the male role with female sex partners. Of particular interest is the fact that in societies where homosexuality is not disapproved of such activities do take place and more often than not the individuals exhibiting such behavior indulge in heterosexual relations as well.

Masturbation

In addition to forbidding sexual relations with members of the same sex, American society generally condemns self-stimulation of the genitals. Most adults in our society consider the deliberate excitation of one's own genitals as a perversion on a par with homosexual relations and seek to prevent such activity on the part of their children. Despite these pressures levied against the practice, self-stimulation of the genitals does take place commonly among boys and girls in our society. Apparently, for most children, such activities tend to disappear in adolescence and are replaced by heterosexual relationships.

Generally speaking, most societies look down upon self-stimulation among adults, regarding this as an inferior form of sexual activity. Many societies, however, do not extend this feeling to comparable activities on the part of youngsters. In these societies children of both sexes finger their own genitals early in life. In these same societies other forms of sexual activity are permitted children. Under these conditions heterosexual play tends to replace self-stimulation as they approach puberty. Indeed, in many of these societies the emphasis on the part of the adults is in the direction of encouraging children to play at being man and wife in all respects. They apparently conclude that early practice in sexual relations between young boys and girls is a part of their education for adult life. It will be remembered, however, that in societies where such freedom for children exists there are still the restrictions imposed by the incest prohibition and the local variation of its extensions. Youngsters are in no society permitted complete promiscuity in their sex relations.

Premarital Intercourse and Adultery

In addition to restricting sexual activity in terms of incest, bestiality, homosexuality, and self-stimulation, American society tends to forbid all sexual intercourse except that between a married couple. Premarital intercourse and adultery are both prohibited. Both premarital and extramarital liaisons are, nevertheless, known to be quite frequent in our society, particularly during late adolescence prior to marriage and on the part of married men.

With respect to premarital sexual relations there are many societies that take a much more lenient attitude than we do. For some people adolescents are expected to indulge in sexual intercourse prior to marriage, providing only that they observe the incest regulations. It is interesting to note that under these conditions relatively few pregnancies seem to occur. This may be explained at least in part by the phenomenon of adolescent sterility. Though a girl has passed the menarche she may not yet be ovulating or may be incapable of carrying a fetus to term. In some societies a girl must prove that she is sexually mature and can bear a child before she is permitted to marry.

In other societies a more restrictive attitude toward premarital sex relations prevails. In most of these it is the girl whose activities seem to be of the greatest concern. Generally, a double standard of sex behavior is imposed, placing the greater burden upon the girl. However, there are a few societies where it is the male who is singled out for control and who takes the blame for transgression. In some few societies the restrictions imposed upon adolescents are more severe than in our own. But it appears that the actual control of heterosexual activities prior to marriage is very difficult to achieve in any society, and violations of the prohibition, if it exists, are not uncommon.

With respect to extramarital sex relations, a large number of other societies share much the same attitude as most Americans. For the most part it is the married woman who is particularly forbidden to engage in sex relations with anyone except her husband, but in some the mated man is equally restricted. However, not all societies forbid all extramarital sex relations. For some peoples it is customary for a host to lend his wife to his guest during the latter's visit. In others, men who are related to one another may exchange wives for a period of time. For quite a few societies there are periods of ceremonial license, which may be religious in nature, during which the normal ban on extramarital affairs is lifted.

In connection with the cultural attitude toward extramarital sexual relations it should be noted that a great many societies permit a man to take more than one wife if he can afford to do so. Quite frequently the custom is for a man to take as his secondary wife the younger sister of his first wife, a practice known as sororal polygyny. In such societies extramarital liaisons between siblings-in-law may be permitted even though a man cannot afford to support additional wives. There are a few societies that are polyandrous, i.e., permit a woman to have more than one husband. In such societies it is generally expected that the married woman will have sexual affairs with her husband's brothers.

In broad perspective it appears that though certain extramarital affairs may be permitted and even encouraged they are always fairly well controlled. Even in the case of wife-lending and wife-exchange the husband is always aware of what is happening and his formal permission is obtained. In the case of ceremonial license formal rules apply, specifying just when and where the temporary lapse of normal restrictions will occur. The control over extramarital affairs would seem to have adaptive value in reducing friction between members of the group that might arise out of open and excessive sexual competition. On the other hand, it also appears that a certain amount of extramarital intercourse generally takes place in every society. This in turn may also have some value. Pregnancies may be brought about in this manner among women whose marriage with their husband is for one reason or another a sterile one. Indeed, there are some societies who explicitly make an exception of the general ban on extramarital affairs if a wife fails, after a period of married life, to conceive. She is then permitted to take a lover in hopes that this will bring to the married couple a much-wanted offspring.

Controls Relating to Bereavement, Privacy, and Special Occasions

After the death of a spouse, most societies, including our own, do not think it proper to resume sexual relations for some period of time. A decent interval is expected before either husband or wife in our society remarries. In other societies the period may be only a few days or it may last a matter of years. Usually a widow is expected to abstain from intercourse or to refrain from remarriage for a somewhat longer time than a widower. In some societies other persons in addition to the surviving spouse are affected. These are generally relatives of the deceased and are expected to abstain from sexual activities for a number of days.

Within marriage there are social controls exercised over sexual activities. Generally speaking, it is considered proper in most societies for intercourse to take place between husband and wife in comparative privacy. For some this may mean only within the family, the children not being excluded from observing their parents' sexual activities. For others privacy means the exclusion of the children, and parents either wait until the youngsters are asleep or take other precautions to ensure the desired privacy.

In addition, social controls are generally imposed that govern the occasions when sexual intercourse may take place. It is of interest to note that in some societies the person who is ill is expected to abstain from sexual activities.

In a few cases the relatives of an ill person are likewise expected to be continent during the period of his illness. There are other occasions, too, that may carry with them a social admonition to abstain from intercourse. Many peoples who depend upon hunting or fishing for their livelihood may require the persons involved to be continent. Other activities frequently accompanied by admonitions against sexual relations include preparing for a long journey, gardening, pottery making, canoe building, and engaging in warfare.

Menstruation and Pregnancy

Very widespread is the attitude that a man should not have sexual intercourse with his wife (or any woman) when she is menstruating. Only a very few societies consider the menstruating woman a fit sex partner. Most peoples regard the menstrual discharge as "unclean" and the intimate contact with it which would occur during the sex act something to be strictly avoided. In addition to the ban on intercourse, the menstruating woman may find that she must avoid certain foods, discontinue bathing, or refrain from participating in certain social activities, such as dancing. In other societies the menstruating woman is even more restricted in her activities and may be confined for her period to a special compartment in the dwelling or in a separate hut.

During pregnancy there may be restrictions imposed upon sexual intercourse. Medical men in our society apparently agree that it is not dangerous for a woman to engage in sexual activities during the early part of pregnancy, but urge caution during the later months when vigorous movements and pressure on the abdomen might have unpleasant consequences. In other societies, as well, there seems generally to be a tendency to restrict the sexual activities of the pregnant woman during the later phases of gestation. Only a few peoples encourage coitus up to the point of labor. A few other societies extend the prohibition against sexual intercourse backward in time and forbid coitus from the very beginning of recognized pregnancy.

After childbirth there is a period of five to

six weeks during which the vaginal and cervical tissues are healing. During this period in our society the husband is generally not expected to have intercourse with his wife. For a few societies the period of abstinence is shorter, lasting only a week or two after parturition. But in most the period is as long and in many instances much longer, and for some may be as long as the entire period (two to three years) during which the mother is nursing her child.

The peoples who enforce long periods of abstinence on the mother after parturition apparently do so in the hope of avoiding another pregnancy during lactation. Many of them advance the opinion that should conception take place while the mother is lactating, her milk supply would diminish and the child would have to be prematurely weaned.

Summary

It is clear from the above comparative information that sexual activities are shaped and controlled in every society by traditional and patterned ways of life. Sexual activities are, of course, subjected to different pressures, and some societies are much more lenient than others in their permissiveness toward sexual expression, but all societies have sexual activities under some control, however minimal it may be.

There are very few societies in cross-cultural perspective that take the attitude that all sexual activities should be avoided save those that take place between man and wife in a monogamous marriage. But there are no societies that do not insist upon some extension of the primary incest prohibition, thus delimiting the number of eligible sex partners. And in all societies there are general controls exercised over extramarital relations.

The differential effects of the various ways in which societies control sexual activities on the individuals concerned is not known. This would seem to be an important area for investigation, especially since it is clear that the culture of one's society and its social structure provide the learning conditions of experience for the maturing individual. The kind of person an individual becomes will depend in large measure upon the social pressures that are exerted upon him by his fellow men. Particularly in the case of sexual activities, it would seem, these pressures could be profoundly important in shaping the developing personality. Furthermore, the society in which a person lives provides the conditions for acceptable individual adjustment.

References

Beach, Frank A., *Hormones and Behavior*. New York: Paul B. Hoeber, Inc., 1948.

Davis, Katharine B., *Factors in the Sex Life of 2,200 Women*. New York: Harper & Brothers, 1939.

Devereux, George, "Institutionalized Homosexuality of the Mohave Indians." *Human Biol.* 9; 498-527, 1937.

Dickinson, R. L., and Beam, L., *A Thousand Marriages*. Baltimore: The Williams & Wilkins Co., 1931.

Dubois, Cora, *The People of Alor*. Minneapolis: University of Minnesota Press, 1944.

Ellis, Albert, *The Folklore of Sex*. New York: Grove Press, 1961.

Ellis, Havelock, *Studies in the Psychology of Sex*. New York: Random House, 1936.

Erikson, Erik H., *Childhood and Society*. New York: W. W. Norton & Co., Inc., 1950.

Ford, Clellan S., *A Comparative Study of Human Reproduction*. New Haven: Yale University Press, 1945.

Ford, Clellan S., and Beach, Frank A., *Patterns of Sexual Behavior*. New York: Harper & Brothers, 1951.

Fortune, R. G., *Sorcerers of Dobu*. New York: E. P. Dutton & Co., Inc., 1932.

Gorer, Geoffrey, *Exploring English Character*. New York: Criterion Books, Inc., 1955.

Hamilton, G. V., *A Research in Marriage*. New York: Boni, 1929.

Henry, Jules, *Jungle People*. New York: J. J. Augustin, Inc., 1941.

Kinsey, Alfred C. *et al.*, *Sexual Behavior in the Human Male*. Philadelphia: W. B. Saunders Co., 1948.

Kinsey, Alfred C. *et al.*, *Sexual Behavior in the Human Female*. Philadelphia: W. B. Saunders Co., 1953.

Landis, Carney *et al.*, *Sex in Development*. New York: Paul B. Hoeber, Inc., 1940.

Linton, Ralph, "Marquesan Culture." In A. Kardiner, *The Individual and His Society*. New York: Columbia University Press, 1938.

Malinowski, Bronislaw, *The Sexual Life of Savages in Northwestern Melanesia*. New York: Harcourt, Brace & Co., 1929.

Mead, Margaret, *From the South Seas*. New York: William Morrow & Co., Inc., 1939.

Murdock, George P., *Social Structure*. New York: The Macmillan Co., 1949.

Rivers, W. H. R., *The Todas*. London: The Macmillan Co., 1906.

Schapera, I., *The Khoisan Peoples of South Africa*. London: Routledge, 1930.

Terman, Lewis M., *Psychological Factors in Marital Happiness*. New York: McGraw-Hill Book Co., 1938.

Westermarck, Edward, *The History of Human Marriage*. New York: The Macmillan Co., 1922.

Whiting, John W. M., *Becoming a Kwoma*. New York: Yale University Press, 1941.

Whiting, John W. M., and Child, Irvin L., *Child Training and Personality*. New Haven: Yale University Press, 1953.

CLELLAN S. FORD

Dance, Sexual Dynamics
in Contemporary*

THIS article discusses sex in relation to contemporary dance—by which is not meant all forms of today's dance, but only what is often called "modern" dance. No attempt will be made here to consider sex in relation to popular dance, classical ballet, folk dancing, or other modes of present-day dance.

Historical Background

Dance, as a modern art, was heralded by the American artist Isadora Duncan at the turn of the century, a time when the Western mind was being directed historically and sociologically toward the more primal aspects of the behavior of the individual. Undercurrents of man's basic nature, theretofore submerged beneath traditional veneers of taste and decorum, had begun to break through. New vistas of human background were opening to the arts and sciences, permitting a more reasonable attitude toward this basic nature and paving the way for inquiry into it.

Isadora Duncan's revelation was a matter of natural historical process. The science of psychology was being developed, and, just as the stripping away of man's external behavior patterns characterized this early period, so Isadora's disrobing symbolized the same renascence. She discarded corsets, toe shoes, disguising costume contraptions—all the inhibiting vestments that denied her the freedom to move

* The author wishes to thank Rhoda Winter Russell, Murray Louis, and J. Allison Montague for their comments and editorial assistance with this article.

her body to the dictates of the "soul." John Martin wrote in 1939: "This was a profound overturning, clearing away ages of accumulation of intellectual restraints and yielding the power of motion to the 'inner man,' which is what Isadora meant by the 'soul.'"

Now the dancer was permitted freedoms he had never been allowed before. He was released from costume restraints that had not only inhibited and obstructed his movement but had denied him full representation as common man. This became particularly evident in the 1930's when the male dancer often appeared in a semblance of trousers and shirt, while the female wore skirts rather than the tutu and corset or bodice. They danced in soft shoes, sandals, or were barefoot. Dancers could now appear as more direct representations of man and woman.

They were released also from the physical ritual of preordered movement patterns. The classical gesture, edited and refined, became a cliché, and individual movement style and invention were encouraged. Several movement techniques were evolved during this period from the personal movement styles of new dance artists. Dancers appearing in the company of a particular artist had to be trained in the technique of that artist, although frequently they had studied other techniques as well.

This does not imply the complete lack of individual expression prior to the 1930's. The importance of personality, however, was more greatly stressed in this new period and its significance became of direct concern. This was

313

evident in the highly individual styles of the new dancers and their remarkable variety and invention of movement.

It was inevitable that from these new interests and freedoms would develop a psychological dance drama, a dance eloquent of our sociological time and its psychodynamic concerns. Yet with all the wealth of material occurring between 1920 and 1950, no comprehensive scientific studies were made that referred specifically to the psychodynamic background of the dance. This is particularly regrettable since during this time, now in decline, the nature of the dance made it especially open to such scrutiny.

There was a considerable amount of research into kinetics from a physiological point of view. Only Rudolf Laban (after 1920), however, experimenting mainly in Germany, can be singled out for his scientific study of motion as an art. Shortly after Isadora Duncan began her explorations in dance, Laban started to experiment with a crystal icosahedron as a form surrounding man to which gestures, in the effort to find potential movement balances, were related. He categorized movement qualities and also invented a comprehensive method of movement notation. His research, however, did not carry him extensively into the psychological area.

Following Isadora Duncan's success, modern dance passed through a series of developmental episodes. In America, Ruth St. Denis and Ted Shawn made very substantial contributions to modern dance; and their eclectic teachings helped develop three dancers who thereafter instituted the period of the psychological dance theater: Martha Graham, Doris Humphrey, and Charles Weidman. Mary Wigman of Germany was becoming the leading exponent of modern dance in Europe at this time, and Hanya Holm, who came to America in the early 1930's from Miss Wigman, developed her individual style and was recognized (along with Graham, Humphrey, and Weidman) as one of the four major American dance figures. It is the character of the work of these people and their time that is most generally referred to as modern dance.

The prime concern of the artists at the height of this period (1930–1950) was the revelation of man in his efforts to achieve consonance and to move freely from out of his own dynamic content. Their subjects dealt with the conflicts that arose within man's nature and with their resolution.

This was not a surface storytelling, as had been much of the dance that preceded the 1920's. This was a vertical semantic exploration in which deep-lying turmoils within man's inner being were brought to the surface and given esthetic communicative form through motion. It was the artistic counterpart of the social concerns that were engaging the field of psychology. Although it certainly owed some debt to psychology, dance operated fundamentally out of its own organic stimulations.

Not all the work of these dancers resulted in psychological dance theater. It all had in common, however, a search for motivational sources out of the inner nature of man. The effect of this was felt even in ballet, where the rigid classical structures were broken down and themes of contemporary concern introduced.

Along with the substantial achievements of the artists mentioned above, this new nature of material for dance attracted many practitioners who brought to it pedestrian concepts of art expression, rather than the exalted visions that qualify classical art. This, too, was a logical outcome. Dance now innocently opened a path to self-expression in the cathartic sense. To the uninitiated eye, this took on the guise and sanction of art. Thirst for individual expression led to exhibitions of personal turmoil, and the quest for individual rights and freedom often brought intense orientation to personal and political reasoning as art ends in themselves, rather than as subjects and means toward an esthetic end. This often confused the issues of art. Politics and psychology frequently got the upper hand, causing distortion to the psychodynamic content of art, particularly if one looked upon these efforts as esthetic accomplishments.

Yet dance, in the best sense and exposition of its new nature, inherited the same sexual concerns encountered in psychological exposition. Analytically speaking, the same problems of determining derivations and measuring sexual dynamics that beset the psychology of motivation are evident in the dance.

This dance period lends itself vividly to the examination of sexual content, and in so doing we reaffirm that sex as a subject, as well as inadvertent sexual intrusions and necessary sexual quantities, is incidental to, rather than the basis of, art. It is due to the accrediting of primal motivational power to these secondary sexual factors that much controversy has arisen in efforts by science to explore the arts.

General Basis of Art

To understand the more fundamental basis of dance we need to look first to art principles generally. Dance is an art; its sources and its basic characteristics are common to all art forms. The foundation of dance is art. Human motion is the medium and serves as the means of communicating the artistic idea.

Fundamentally, art is created through motivational energies that are aspects of the basic force activating man. The specific nature of this life energy and its translation into the terms of the psychodynamic nature of man is still a mystery to science. One thinks immediately of the great accomplishments of Sigmund Freud. Still, we find broad disagreement regarding the Freudian theory of this energy in man as a sexually dominated libido. Lack of scientific substantiation to this or any subsequent theory makes a precise definition of the sexual content in the practice of art in its initial arisings impossible. The obvious sexual issues as they occur in a work of art pose no great problem; the difficulties exist mainly in the diverse interpretations of motivations, derivations, symbols, phantasies, so-called sublimations, and other factors, all of which play an active part in the practice of art.

Followers of Freud are inclined to view both the artist and his product as mainly problems in pathology. Jung, on the other hand, ascribes intellectually unfathomable attributes to the artist and his work. He indicates the possibility of the artist attaining a purity from pathological influence at the time of creativity and then achieving a resonance with primordial undercurrents of life.

Freud's point of view would place art in the dominated (if not completely controlled) sexual drive. Jung's view places sexual influence in an incidental position in the artist's acts of creativity and the art product. Neo-Freudian opinion would lie somewhere between these two almost opposing theories. Still other theories put the artist in the sterile confines of the provision of mere entertainment, simple pleasure, and amusement. Actually, there are no comprehensive scientific data in this matter. Findings thus far are more in the nature of circumstantial evidence rather than proof. The jury is hung.

The teacher of art, as well as the artist, is inclined to favor the Jungian theories, viewing the Freudian analysis of art as naïve, insensitive to, and unobservant of the underlying semantics of esthetics. He argues this on the basis of experiences in work and teaching, which reveal aspects that cannot be accounted for in theories ascribing sexual beginnings to all art. These experiences are not documented; the artist's business is, after all, art and not science. Yet the artist alone is endowed with the total vision of art and his vantage point would be the more reasonable one from which to inspect the contents. At the moment, the artist finds unacceptable the interpretation of every cavity as vaginal, every elongation as phallic, and every pulsation as fornication. He points out that it is child's play to make almost every evident thing or event coincidental with sex on the basis of its shape or motion.

The Art Process

A description of the art process, insofar as it is possible to describe, may indicate likely or unlikely areas of sexual influence and their extent. To describe the artist and his function we must necessarily refer to mankind in general as a participating instrument in the universal mechanism. It is then possible to distinguish the artist in his more specialized activity.

We might conceive of man as an intricate and delicate computer capable of receiving sensations and experiences through its sensory organisms. These sensations in turn interact with primal life drives, most of which are common to all mankind, others of which have individual characteristics and intensities. The latter differences derive from genetic sources and are further qualified by relativities of man to time, space, and sociological factors. The result is a world population of two billion individuals, no two of which are alike. Yet, generally speaking, these individual differences are not pathological. We cannot even describe them as variations until we can refer to a single genesis or primal evolutionary form.

Our human computers have an infinite variety of differences. However, these are predominantly matters of variations in degrees and relativities of basic drives and interpretations; there is an underlying stratum of experience that is more or less universally common. The heat of fire, for example, is not disputable although its intensity may have a band of variance in interpretation.

The vital questions are: When, how, and why do sensations and experiences become distorted and out of key to the universal fact? When is the well-being of mankind violated by misinterpretation or malfunction of his experiences? Under what circumstances does the reality of the outside world become distorted and cause man's mental machinery to discolor and erroneously or disproportionately compute the facts of nature?

The general process of education is meant to guide the individual through the morass, indicating known and collected data that hopefully quicken his absorption of worldly fact and bring him to a general par of life and function with his time, space, and capabilities. This process has a high percentage of *ersatz* in it in the academic sense; that is, the knowledge so gained is a distant experience rather than a fundamental one. These *ersatz* experiences begin almost immediately in childhood when the child imitates and mimics his parents. Formal education continues this, in a somewhat different vein, by pursuing a fact apart from its actual happening. History, for example, relates that an event took place; the student was not actually there. He can, therefore, only absorb facts concerning the event through his imagination. Contemporary education is attempting, however, to make the acquiring of knowledge a more fundamental experience through visual aids, field trips, etc.

The artist, on the other hand, operates out of primality of experience. His work emphasizes culture rather than education. This fact of fundamental experience is particularly apparent in the case of an innovator of art, who may serve as catalyst for a new area and invariably sets off a whole school of imitators and reflectors whose congenialities are not fundamental and usually show as such.

The artist's knowledge is necessarily fundamental rather than peripheral, and although he may devise a story or picture out of imagined sources, his basis derives from primal substances. His proximity and congeniality toward the nature of things has the quality of intense experience. His human mechanism must be refined to the highest point of efficiency within the area of his interests and endeavors.

A look at history's art masterpieces, properly interpreted, vividly refutes the idea that man simply displays his sexual, deviative, or neurotic nature in his creativity. It similarly refutes any theory of the artist as creating mere entertainment through pleasurable changing patterns of sight or sound. Nor does the artist illustrate only the external facts of nature. (The latter interpretation is a common fault of a broad segment of people whose perceptions stop at the literal visible level.)

The artist is not unlike the scientist. His exploration of nature and his adjudgment of its content derive from his hypersensitive mental mechanism, an instrument far more delicate and complex than any other known to science. The artist's summation of his experience and knowledge is then translated and reported through his media, whatever it might be: color, sound, motion, or word symbols. He cannot afford to sully this process with inept, circumstantial, or pathological intrusions. His product is adjudged as first, second, or third rate according to the vividness and depth of his revelation.

Science, too, must pass the same scrutiny. However, the two differ in this critical judgment: The artist's result is a revelation of that which is fundamentally felt or in some mysterious way known, but is either unrevealed or relatively unrealized. Science contends with the provable fact of what appeared as mystery theretofore. The results are measurable. The results of art are not.

The artist deals with mysteries not intellectually comprehensible. Yet the facilities that enable an artist to actualize his basic function are exactly the same as those enabling the on-looker to perceive the artistic result. Both abilities have a common bond and affinity with basic generic natural dynamics. Whether or not artistic insights are fully explainable by science is momentarily irrelevant. They are comprehended by man simply because he is himself a product of nature and therefore brings kinship and the faculty of understanding to that heritage. Art recalls and vivifies that fact. Science is obliged to stick to the provable surface.

Looked upon in this light, one cannot reasonably assign dominant pathological attributes to art or the artist anymore than one can to the scientist and his findings. The artist, like the scientist, has his predilections. He tends to favor certain areas and remain relatively unstimulated by others. However, the really great artist is usually described in heroic proportions. The scope, intensity, and skill of interpretation of subject determine him as a small or great talent. Similarly, the art critic tends to be dominated by some areas and is relatively unperceptive or unexcited by others. The consequence of this is that evaluations rarely agree, particularly of contemporary works of art. It would seem unreasonable to expect the scientist, also uniquely schooled and directed, to evaluate and dissect art as a whole. Merely to squeeze and pigeonhole certain aspects of art into existing psychodynamic theories without comprehensive reference to the tenets, intents, and extents of art offers little illumination to the field.

Thus far it has been like the story of the hungry soldier who arrives in a village and proposes to make a soup of stones. Securing the stones and water he suggests that the villagers add various vegetables to aid the flavor. They are hoodwinked into believing that the resulting brew derives from the stones. So, too, with the theories of sex in art; it is more likely that the character of art comes from the vegetables rather than the stones. Although we have soup, we cannot call it stone soup.

In summation, then, it would seem that scientific probings into art content must first accept the initial materials of art as having identity apart from the artist's individual characteristics; that the artist, like the student or mathematician, is fundamentally concerned with things outside himself; that his predilections and abilities qualify his choice and vitality of inspection, perception, and translation; that it is likely that we will find any malfunctioning or overpowering deviative nature within the artist, if allowed to intrude upon his subject, inevitably devaluating his created work to the extent of that intrusion; that the artist is fundamentally an interpretive instrument and the malfunction of that instrument at the time of creativity is as detrimental to the result as it is in any other similar instance; that sexual contents are there by tolerance of subject and media rather than because of pathological domination; that sexual contents are as infinitely varied as subject; and finally that a work of art can be as abounding in sex as a mathematical equation or a Parisian prostitute.

In the final outcome, we may find the artist and scientist one and the same. The nearer the scientist comes to the adjudgment of universal mechanism by means of his own substantiated human instrument, the closer he comes to being an artist. There are evidences in this direction. Some pictorial graphs made to illustrate natural mechanisms have attracted the attention of esthetes. The resemblance of these graphs to modern abstract painting is quite remarkable in the art sense.

The Artist and
His Deviant Background

At this point another question arises. In the eyes of society generally, the artist seems to be of a peculiar and highly deviant nature. There are two observations that may tend to refute certain conclusions made as a result of this.

Aside from the usual claptrap of smudged dungarees, berets, pony tails, and "bohemianism," there are fundamental peculiarities that often distinguish the artist. Primarily he is necessarily concerned with the basic balances of nature, which do not always coincide with the social mores of his time. Isadora Duncan's removal of corset and shoes was considered an act of vulgarity in the eyes of the society of her time. On that basis she was unquestionably a deviate. Today, however, we would hardly ascribe a pathological nature to this act. The artist must necessarily break down barriers, just as the scientist does. The artist employs his more primal instrument toward this end and his behavior must of necessity be affected; otherwise he dulls the very thing that allows him his means of life.

Another aspect of this is the nature of the kind of individual attracted to art as a profession. The Kinsey-Pomeroy report seems to indicate certain sexual predilections by artists reflected in their choice of media. In the case of dance, for example, we may admit obvious narcissistic tendencies. However, it is repeatedly in evidence to the dance instructor that this tendency and any other pathological one must be sublimated to the tenets of art; otherwise there is no art. (There is evidence of high homosexual tendencies among those who choose dance as a profession. It has been the author's experience, however, that when the moment of art arises, the physical mannerisms and qualities of the homosexual completely disappear. This would substantiate theories of art arising from a source more deeply seated than the character of pathology.)

It has also been noted that deviation sharpens the wit and perception in particular areas. In the practice of art, however, this deviant energy and intensity is properly utilized toward the ends of art rather than toward personal catharsis. This is an unmistakable qualification of great art.

It would therefore appear that for whatever reason a flute player enters the profession of flautists, he must ultimately produce music and forego masturbation. His deviation may prejudice him somewhat in regard to choice, facility, and vitality, but in the end he practices art, not sex, and his deviation must be either relegated to nonperceived hideaways or translated into art energy. It is likely that the artist fundamentally practices a transformation or metamorphosis of energy, placing it in the path of art and enhancing rather than causing or interfering with it. Sexual drive may also be conceived in the nature of a catalyst; a substance that allows a thing to take place but loses its dominant identity in the process, or is cast aside as refuse after the metal is extracted. More illuminating results might occur if the concept of art and artists was reversed and the artist regarded as sublimated to art—not art to the artist.

The Artist's Emotions

In the preceding material we have approached vaguely the consideration of the art idea or *noumenom*. It is that mind-stuff made up of thoughts selected and formed, the ultimate conclusion going into a unit that becomes the basis of a particular work of art. *Noumenom* refers to the art idea prior to its appearance in concrete form or communicable character.

We have indicated that the artist's predilections or deviant character may govern his choice of subject and heighten his perception. Insofar as his predilections or deviations are caused by sexual energies, influence must be recognized to that extent. Even in this instance, however, the author has had repeated experiences which indicate that pathological turmoil unresolved within the individual often deters the formation of a *noumenom*.

Here is an example: In an elementary choreography class, students may be asked to formulate an idea for a dance. In many instances the subjects chosen turn out to be ones in which the students are strongly involved emotionally. One particular instance is that in which a young married man chooses to dance about a dream wife who is his ideal companion. The second section of the dance is to deal with a flesh-and-blood wife whose comparison to the dream version leaves something to be desired. The third section concludes the affair. Needless to say, not only is the dance left unfinished, but the portions that are finished show only the most banal surface substance. This particular approach produces similar negative results with all students. Other experiences in which direct emotional energies are used have produced equally negative results. It has been noted again and again that art requires a basis of abstraction, an objective removal from the immediate personal concern of the artist.

Poetic Basis

Sexual influences in the formation of an art *noumenom* are vague and remain scientifically undefined unless one follows the school of thought that attributes sexually characterized energy to all motivation. The formation of an artistic idea is a process no different from the creation of any other idea. It is distinguishable in that it embodies a certain quality that stratifies it in the art area. This quality is often referred to in esthetics as "poetry." However, this is not the poetry of words, but that designation given to certain indefinable and mysterious factors that breathe vitality and beauty into what otherwise would be stillborn, banal, or merely interesting or entertaining. It is that which makes the difference between a wallpaper design and a painting by Van Gogh. It is the difference between spilled paint and a Jackson Pollock. It is the difference between a female basketball player and Galina Ulanova.

Some clue may be found in the manner of use, or implications by the artist, of those yet unsolved intuitions of time and space. Jung again appeases the artist somewhat with his "collective unconscious." Within this concept lies the implication that in the human is a primordial sense of all time and space, an unrealized kinship with a genesis and energy disguising itself in infinitely multitudinous forms and characters. It may be that the artist succeeds in imbuing poetic life into his work when, through his collective unconscious, he is able to judge the right variety and proportion of this time-space essence in relation to his subject and translate it into his medium. His *noumenom* embodies a matter of depth semantics and relativity, an insight into the fundamental nature of the components, a microscopic perception allowing him to equate mathematically and translate involved energies into a balanced finished product.

Perhaps the artist gives back to the world, in translated form, that quantity of energy which was primarily abstracted from it. In the meantime it has transpired through human understanding. We might accredit to the perfect act of love this same union and resonance. And if so, might we not reverse the theory and ascribe sex to art rather than art to sex; or both to the mysterious equation we call love? The artist may agree to a theory of love as the basis of his work, particularly if such a term can be divorced from the negative semantic stigma of sex and sentimental romanticism. In the creation of the art *noumenom*, the artist recognizes the necessity of his vicarious union with his subject. His identity and his intimacy with his materials allow the insight and inspire

the vitality that breathe life into his art work.

We may discover that the mysteries of sexual dynamics await the solutions to the mysteries of time, space, and energy and their relative union with other factors. We may find that art and sex have more in common with these abstractions than with metaphorically erotic fables.

We come now to the artist's media, that material through which his *noumenom* takes communicative characteristic or form. These are his colors, his sound, his written word. In the case of the dancer: the human body.

Dance As a Mechanism of Communication

Dance is essentially nonverbal. It is capable of direct expression in that it need not be translated into any external language or symbol of thought. The state of the living human body is the immediate revelation of man as he exists in that particular instrument. Therefore, his thought or state of being, if allowed consciously or unconsciously to possess his body, will be immediately apparent. Even more, if one conceives thought as energy, it is the human body that is the channel for release of that energy. If it is not allowed to do so, mental indigestion results. This release may be brought about by sublimation or transformation. With the painter this transformation occurs in color; with the writer it is words. In the dancer's case it is not transformed into removed symbols—it is directly enacted.

Dance was the first of the arts, yet it remains today one of the least understood. This is not difficult to understand, for man's greatest enemy, lover, counterpart, and enigma is man himself. An individual confronted with man as a vehicle of art may bring into the picture all his own phobias, predilections, and confusions toward man more directly than he would in encountering a painting or musical composition (although he will do this to some extent here as well). So we come again to a consideration of pathology and art. We find that just as the artist must sublimate his deviant nature to ensure correct adjudgment of his art statement, so also must the onlooker to art. Otherwise he will misinform himself of the art content. This has been one of the major problems in the scientific analysis of art, one of the most notable examples being Freud's analysis of Michelangelo's "Moses."

Metakinesis

In the case of human motion as a medium of expression, communication is accomplished mainly through the metakinetic faculty. This faculty enables the onlooker to experience as his own the sensations of the person or creature being observed. It is this same faculty that translates the inanimate, external world metaphorically to man in terms of himself. In drama the word "empathy" is used somewhat in the same context. The process is readily noted in the functioning of the salivary glands in one person watching another suck a lemon.

However, metakinetically communicated sensations and feelings need to be (or are reflexively) interpreted by the recipient in terms of his own experience and orientation. Perception is often adversely influenced by blind spots, deformation of sensation and emotion, social mores, hypersensitive and insensitive areas, and personal focal forces. These all tend to cause imbalance and misinterpretation.

One complex factor in dance as a medium of art rests in the fact that the dancer's instrument of art is the same as that which he employs for the operation of his personal psychobiological energies apart from art. Unlike the musician, whose instrument is not a part of him, the dancer as a person and instrument are one.

Here occurs one of the most obvious examples refuting the possibility of any direct pathological basis in art. In the case of the dancer it is vividly apparent that this instrument will not operate properly when dominated by psychodynamic characteristics of a deviant source. The instrument becomes unbalanced and out of tune. Even if the dancer's subject happens to be purposely pathological, he must be in tune with the out-of-tune-ness of his subject. He cannot indulge in a personal imbalance at the same time without confusing his interpretation of his subject.

In effect, then, the artist as a person hovers in remote control over the artist as a performer. It is to the performer that he relinquishes not only his body, but his psychodynamic energy as well. The performer and performance are at the moment synthetic, and all substances are brought within the bounds of voluntary manipulation. The dancer becomes the source and life power of a created being who, as a newly evolved integration, temporarily tenants the being.

So we have as the source of power and motivation the art *noumenom*. This then is fed into and permeates the dancer's body. The dancer designs his motion as a vehicle, releasing, translating, and making the art idea visible through his body. If he patterns his actions uncongenially in shape, motion, time, and space, he will frustrate the release of his idea to that extent and consequently make it unintelligible. Choreography is the skill of designing the components of the dance to serve the communication of the *noumenom*.

This does not mean that there is no individual distinction possible in the performance of a dance. On the contrary, it is individual energies that often lend semantic character and give further vitality to the subject, fortifying it with all the possible individual ammunition at hand. Just as we have individual predilections and energies utilized in the positive sense in the formation of the art *noumenom,* so, too, the dancer as an interpretive artist (separate from the choreographer) lends his substance to the dance.

It is unlikely that any performing artist succeeds entirely in impersonal remote control of his material, nor is it known whether or not such success is desirable in terms of art. In any event it is likely that whatever portion of the dancer's habitual identity appears in his created role, it is a voluntary contribution intended to coalesce and substantiate that role. (In motion pictures we have become accustomed to the term "type casting," which implies reliance upon the performer's personal characteristics rather than on his skill in becoming a new entity. In this practice the illusion of a metamorphosis of being is more or less disregarded and the demands upon the performer are relegated to the act of engaging himself in a synthetic situation.)

With this complex potpourri of conscious and unconscious psychodynamic contributions to the art scheme, it is impossible to come to any but broadly general and theoretic conclusions about the sexual character of art and dance. The direct manifestations of sex in the physical nature, posture, and motion of the dancer offer us another area of examination.

Physical Implications of Sex

We may start with the obvious fact of fundamental structural differences between male and female. Bearing this in mind, it would seem impossible for sex to be ignored completely in any form of dance, no matter how innocent of sex the content itself might be. Yet within even the innocence of shape there rests implications of greater or less manliness or womanliness without exploitation of this fact by the individual. There are seemingly endless varieties of human shape brought about by environmental, genetic, sociological, and other backgrounds. The human body acts as housing and instrument for the psychobiological energies of the individual. Inasmuch as its shape and growth and motional facility take into account the needs of the individual, it will vary accordingly as far as it is possible for it to do so.

In addition to normal sexual appearances, the human body may also vary as to deviant characteristics, promoting or discouraging certain physical developments. Obvious examples are those of the small man who promotes his muscular development to enlarge himself. Or the breast-embarrassed female adolescent who with stooped shoulders attempts to hide her new physical developments. These are rather blatant examples of a process which in many subtle ways causes the shaping of the body as a result of even minor pathological and sexually derivative circumstances. Often the turmoil that caused the concern is mastered or eliminated, but the body continues to hold the musculature and development, showing a physical result of that turmoil, though no longer tenanted by its cause.

Certainly the genetic background again brings in sexual aspects through predilections in mating, etc., which date back practically to the primordial jelly. Consider, too, the frequently evident outcome of an individual endowed genetically with a body for which he has insufficient psychodynamic energy.

So the dancer appears in front of his spectator, supposedly a complex mass of sexual and psychodynamic history and presence. Yet again he ignores and refutes these external reasonings. For the artist is a prestidigitator of the first order. The now-you-see-it-now-you-don't technique is one of his major facilities. It is likely that, should the artist not wish you to see his sexuality, you would not see it. It is there, nevertheless, in the simple physical fact, should one's orientation require it or if one subconsciously promotes it.

So is art there. We may miss the one in the effort to pursue the other.

Sex and Motion

Motion may assume a myriad of characters. Our concern here is with those having sexual connotations. To investigate this we shall have to inspect another skill of the human body that the dancer employs and extends toward his own ends.

In describing the body as a malleable housing, reshaping itself to the needs of the individual, we find that the process of motion continues this subservience to the individual's immediate psychobiological needs. The motions are manifest first through concentrating energy in a particular part or parts of the body. This may be a subtle or violent gathering of forces, depending upon the task or thought at hand. This concentration can take on the character of directional grain or path of flow of energy. It may appear to advance, retreat, rise, fall, suspend, lock, etc.

By the relative application of this grain the artist may consciously or unconsciously invite the eye of the onlooker to a certain part of the body, the attention of the onlooker deflecting from other body sections. This does not imply that such an exploitation of a particular part of the body has a specific meaning in itself. Such a gesture or condition is rather like a word in a sentence, as vague by itself in narrative as any isolated verb or noun. Its actual statement is apparent only when surrounded by other body conditions and actions that compose the act into specific meaning. For example, the exploitation of the pelvic area is not essentially a sexual posture; the body must supply surrounding overtones to make it become so. The finger, wrist—or for that matter any other part of the body—may be eloquent of sex when given gestural or qualitative background so directed.

The attitude of the dancer not only toward that body part but also toward the movement itself, or the motivation behind the movement, can add weight to the sexual or nonsexual implications of the movement no matter where it may be taking place in the moving figure.

Deviations from Art Ideal

Deviations and derelictions from esthetic concepts may enlarge or distort the basic sexual contents incidental or integral to art. Within the early period of psychological dance theater (1930–1950), these imbalances were particularly evident due to preference for the subject and the personal exposure physically and psychologically that was allowed.

Remembering that this period was vitally concerned with the pains, sorrows, soul-searching passions, and violences of man—all legitimate art subjects—it is apparent that dancers with sadomasochistic tendencies were well supplied with self-expressional outlets. All the sexual over- and undertones attributable to such a state accompanied the act.

Another area of deviation concerns the masturbatory tendencies in motion; the dancer lusting upon his own action. Here the parasitic attachment to the dance act overpowers the intended expression, leaving in its stead the communication of the parasitic and/or narcissistic act rather than the art idea.

These deviations often make a confusing issue of art dance evaluation. The immediate character and intimate confessions of the performer sometimes produce a compellingly interesting exposé. Such displays in this period were often reviewed as sensitive works of art dealing with "Freudian" subject matter. With strong social focus upon sexual reasoning, critics, dancers, and teachers were sometimes deflected from the abstract and transcendent demands of art and engrossed with case histories.

Proper evaluation of the sexual contents of art can be made only from the broad vantage point of esthetics. Personal idiosyncrasies, the social climate of the moment regarding sexual attitudes and behavior, and psychological sophistication—or lack of it—in the audience play too biased a role in proper evaluation. Esthetics offers a more objective area for appraisal than those less constant areas in which personal prejudices for the various schools of psychology play a part.

Sociological Influences

In considering sociological influences upon the dance we enter a more tangible territory. Society has its effect upon the motion of man and upon the dancer as well. It qualifies the sexual content of the subject material he performs.

Within the contemporary dance period both aspects are vividly apparent. The very birth of contemporary dance through the figure of Isadora Duncan was an outcome of a sociological renascence. The same atmosphere that permitted her release from social restraints allowed the growth of dynamic psychology. It was an intramural affair occurring within the logic of historical time.

As a whole new volume of motion was released to the dancer, variation from the accustomed motional character became more apparent. The effect of the social atmosphere upon an individual's concept of beauty is a strong one. An example is the evolution of concepts that implied the weakness of the female and her dependence upon the strength of the male. Before this century, most interpretations of womanhood illustrated a standard of erotic beauty, evinced through a coy display of weakness and helplessness and the accompanying attitudes of shyness, recession, demureness, etc. What resulted was a manifestation in physical posture and movement which in effect produced the desired erotic expression. The head had a slight tilt; gestures of the arm seemed to terminate at the wrist or knuckle, de-energizing the remaining extremity; the torso had a slight slump, mincing steps in which the feet crossed over the line of travel rather than entering directly upon it—all characterized the female. The male had to hold up his counterpart with the appearance of strength, stiffness of spine, squareness of shoulder, firmness of grip, a straddling of his line of travel to give him a broad base as against the rather tottering one exemplified by the female. Members of both sexes denied their primal endowments of motion to a certain extent, upholding erroneous proportions according to the current criteria of erotic attraction.

All this was reflected in the dance. In romantic ballet it was exemplified by the tilt of the head, the soft unfolding arm, and the delicacy of the wrist and fingers. Ballet further emphasized these erotic concepts in its subject matter and general theatrical treatment.

With the advent of contemporary dance, there came some release from these concepts of male-female beauty and behavior. Out of an extended survey of physical kinetic mechanisms, a more purely functional technique of motion arose. The psychic and physical forces of the human organism and their relationship were more closely observed. This observation was not solely based upon scientific exploration, but rather upon expressional techniques as applied to the contemporary evolvement of art dance.

An example in point is Hanya Holm, who drew on her background in Germany and Switzerland with Mary Wigman, Rudolf Laban, and Dalcroze in the practice of specific balances of kinetic mechanism, the agreement of the psychic and physical content in realizing motion toward given points in space. It involved Jungian principles of the archetype in which the dancer, at least within his technical capacities, strives to reach the epitome of his being and to move out of that context.

In relation to Miss Holm's early work it is interesting to note that one of the major critics deplored its sexless quality. It is difficult to know whether the quality was actually sexless or whether the critic still adhered to mores demanding certain erotic mannerisms as a condition of beauty. Similarly, much of today's more "abstract" dance is also called sexless or "dehuman," a more contemporary word, and receives negative critical response when it projects nonsexually. Is this a reaction to the overt sexual themes of the late 1930's and entire 1940's in that sex is still expected to play a large

part in dance, or has the great stress in our present society on psychoanalytical interpretations become the leading criterion for dance evaluation? Despite critical comments, a growing number of important dancers and choreographers, in both ballet and modern dance, are now developing themes and dance-theater ideas that indicate that sex as a specific, overt adornment of dance is an arbitrary rule rather than a basic esthetic requirement.

International Differences

Within the sociological temper we find great differences of involvement in, and reaction to, modern art dance in the various Western countries. Only Germany and America have produced contemporary dance in any quantity. England, France, and Italy have produced nothing in dance of clear-cut contemporary stamp. What is more, these countries have no great congeniality for modern dance and receive performances of this kind with only mild interest. This seems to have no particular reference, however, to abhorrence of any of the sexual frankness often evident in modern dance. Flourishing ballet companies in these countries, particularly in France, have utilized sex themes with equal frankness. It may be due in part to the abstract language of motion created by modern dance. These countries have, nevertheless, accepted and produced modern art and music, and so their disinclination to accept modern dance seems to stem from a difficulty in accepting human motion in abstract terms.

There exists considerable difference in the evolvement of dance in Germany and America. The German character comes through in metaphysical involvements, whereas the American material is characterized by more outspoken qualities. Although dance in America is by no means free of it, the aspects of self-expression and sentimentality seem more prevalent in German dance.

Sex as an overt subject has not been prominent in German dance. From the point of view of sexual content, American modern dance offers the best study. The very nature of its motional inventiveness and life was born in an era of "sex consciousness." And since art tends to reflect its time, modern dance has had tendencies that were not as prevalent as in ballet, which relied heavily upon tradition.

American Modern Dance

The American modern dancer Martha Graham is unquestionably the greatest artist of the period following Isadora Duncan. In almost her entire later period she has devoted herself to dance subjects that strongly emphasized psychoanalytical involvement. "The soul in search" is a phrase that has almost become a slogan for modern dance. Her "Cave of the Heart," "Herodiade," "Deaths and Entrances," "Dark Meadow," "Errand into the Maze," "Theatre for a Voyage," and "Appalachian Spring" are all examples of this emphasis.

However, Miss Graham's dance figure or heroine is never commonplace. She is the "divine normal" often faced with sexual issues achieving unmistakable heroic conclusion. Hers is a supernatural world. It fulfills classical definition and as such her work stands within the realm of timelessness, transcending the immediate psychoanalytical concern. In this sense, Miss Graham supports Jung's classical concepts of the artist's role as mediator relating the conscious life of man to its archetypes in the "collective conscious." (The word "classical" was used to denote the highest order of merit as early as the second century A.D. It suggests the exemplary creation born out of aristocracy of being, of balance of idea, media, and narrative execution.)

The frank treatment of sex on the concert stage by such a figure as Graham, along with the highbrowism of psychoanalysis, fortified the less heroic segment of dancers who began to color the entire dance field. Reviews of dance concerts, particularly during the 1940's, sounded like social case histories. They were rife with such terms as "fetal," "phallic shapes," "umbilical cords," "fertility rites," "Freudian overtones," etc. Often such psychoanalytically focused interpretations were hung upon dances having no such overt indications. Sex and art seemed for a time almost synonymous and soon more souls were laid bare on the modern dance stage than the public could tolerate in the name of art. Our present scene finds sex virtually missing as a dominant subject and the dance field pursues new images and vehicles as a framework for art.

New Dance Manifestations

Shortly after World War II a new kind of dance began to be evident. Whether or not it should be considered a natural outgrowth and evolvement of the previous concern with psychological dance theater will be a matter for later historical analysis. Although its particular vigor is apparent in the United States, there seem to be similar occurrences in Sweden and Germany.

There is an obvious difference in subject, costume, music, and movement manner. After a few false starts, dance critics have developed a style of reportage to accommodate it, and it enjoys a continually growing audience. Its concern coincides with that of science in its exploration of the nature of energies and their transformation into primary forms. It is as if the artist produces hieroglyphics to illustrate the patterns of energy as it takes on initial character.

In dance one now no longer sees skirts and trousers. Either beautifully colored tights or fantastic costumes are used. Sometimes the human form is made more vivid or totally erased. There is rarely a literal gesture suggestive of pain, joy, fear, or anger. It is remarkably indifferent to the distinction of sex. Whereas the earlier dance revolved around a human characterization, this, if it appears at all now, is incidental rather than dominant. It has been deplored as "dehumanized" and "emotionless" and its level of abstraction is far more in the range of the musical or mathematical rather than the literal level of emotion.

The previous period of dance dealt with strong emotionalism and was dominantly in the hands of the female. This new dance level of abstraction seems to find the male choreographer in control. Where, buried in all this, the sexual deviants lie is as confusing a question as always.

To this new artist the story revolving around the fetal and the phallic, the umbilical cord and the oedipus complex, are as jejune as the arabesque. In some instances Zen Buddhism replaces Freud, and just as art heretofore tolerantly looked upon the self-expressionists, it now bears a new variety in the form of what are known as "beatniks." The "beatnik" has usurped the bohemian. That continuing contingent of human frailty climbs upon the bandwagon, their inadequacies and failures marked again in the guise of art.

Yet, within all this, there is still evidence, as there has been in every period of art, that, whether dancer or flautist, painter or creator of mobiles, the artist stands as a supersensitive mediator between man and the universal mysteries which both science and art continue to probe.

References

Bolitho, William, "Isadora Duncan." In Paul Magriel (ed.), *Chronicles of the American Dance*. New York: Henry Holt & Co., Inc., 1948.

Duncan, Isadora, *My Life*. London: Gollancz, 1924.

Ellis, Havelock, *The Dance of Life*. Boston: Houghton Mifflin Co., 1923.

Freud, Sigmund, *On Creativity and the Unconscious*. New York: Harper & Brothers, 1958.

Horan, Robert, "The Recent Theatre of Martha Graham." In Paul Magriel (ed.), *Chronicles of the American Dance*. New York: Henry Holt & Co., Inc., 1948.

Jacobi, Jolande, *The Psychology of Jung*. New Haven: Yale University Press, 1943.

Laban, Rudolf, *The Mastery of Movement on the Stage*. London: Macdonald & Evans, 1950.

Lawrence, D. H., *Fantasia of the Unconscious*. London: 1922.

Lloyd, Margaret, *The Borzoi Book of Modern Dance*. New York: Alfred A. Knopf, Inc., 1949.

Martin, John, *The Modern Dance*. New York: A. S. Barnes & Co., 1933.

Martin, John, *Introduction to the Dance*. New York: W. W. Norton & Co., Inc., 1939.

Reviews of dance concerts published in *Dance Magazine*, *Dance Observer*, and *Dance News* between the years 1946-1954.

Terry, Walter, *Invitation to Dance*. New York: A. S. Barnes & Co., 1942.

ALWIN NIKOLAIS

Dancing, Social

THE drama of man-woman relationships, with its erotic overtones, is symbolized in social dancing. This does not mean that social dancing has always been a mere excuse for sexual intimacy, as many a religious reformer has protested. Rather, social dancing is an esthetic—and joyous—way for men and women to become closely acquainted—to live rhythmically together for an hour—without becoming more involved with each other than would permit a graceful withdrawal.

He was a poor friend to mankind who first taught that sex per se was evil. The great religious leaders, with one notable exception, never took such a point of view. They condemned any cruelty or deception that a member of one sex might practice upon another, but taught that love itself was good and beautiful. Those, however, who could not succeed at the game of love—because they lacked the inner grace and warmth—felt inferior, and, making a virtue of necessity, declared that their limited way of life was the noble one, the one that God had ordained.

Some moral extremists make even social dancing seem an evil, mainly because it brings the sexes in close proximity, which to them could be only for sensual reasons. Those who connote morality with misery think that nothing good can also be joyous. The poet W. B. Yeats declares that "the good are the merry" and in this simple sentence refutes the gloomy view of the Puritans and the Calvinists who repressed the spirit of youth for generations.

What a man is in his essence, and what a woman is in her essence, is revealed to the partner in the way they dance together. You can sometimes get better acquainted with the total self of a person of the other sex in an hour's dancing together than in an hour's conversation or work together, or in nearly any other social relationship. If a couple have a true inner harmony, he and she become "we." Like lovers in the sexual embrace, each tends to anticipate the move of the other. A loving pair dancing together experience an exquisite felicity of harmony between the sexes, of body-mind rest in motion, because each accommodates spontaneously to the inner feeling of the other.

The popularity of dancing arises from the fact that it permits this rich heterosexual exchange in socially acceptable ways. Male and female make a kind of reconnaissance of each other's physical, mental, and social being, and yet each is free of future commitment. The dancers may later return to the rhythmic attack or withdraw, according to the discoveries each has made of the other. The body, too, communicates, and talks often more wisely than the mind.

Dancing has a particular significance for youth. A valuable part of their education is learning to dance. And each young man or woman reveals his family history, his relationship to his own parents, the quality of the breeding he received at home, the minute he steps upon the dance floor. The shy, repressed child, whose parents failed to show him the love and appreciation that would enable him to feel confidence in himself, moves about with diffidence and restraint. The well-loved and accepted child, free of the inhibition of perfectionist standards, steps forth upon the dance floor with a kind of exuberant enthusiasm, with a poise that shows faith in his ability to please.

"It is the dance that socialized man," said Havelock Ellis (1923). And indeed, as we scan man's social history, we note that those periods were most joyous and creative in which men and women danced freely together without repression or reproval. An ancient Chinese maxim quoted by Ellis in his *Dance of Life* (1923) declares: "One may judge of a king by the state of dancing during his reign."

History of Social Dancing

From man's earliest beginnings he has turned to the dance for the spontaneous release of his emotions. Joy over the harvest was expressed in the harvest dance; heroic rage in the war dance; romantic excitement in the social dance. Anthropologists who read man's early history in the behavior of present-day primitive tribes gather a wealth of information by observing their dances.

Modern civilization began with the Renaissance, its birthplace was in Italy, and in Italy, too, came the renaissance of dancing. France soon followed. In France all forms of dancing were studied and perfected. Folk dances of other nations would be polished in France until they became the graceful steps of the aristocracy.

The *Pavane* and the *Branle* are amongst the earliest of the French dances, and they were especially popular because they included the practice of kissing. The most graceful and sophisticated of the early French dances was the *Minuet*. The splendor and glory of "the great king," Louis XIV, the artificial manners which were typical of his court, and the sensuous and sensual preoccupations which infused all its activities were perfectly illustrated in the Minuet. Other early French dances were the *Gavotte*, the *Cotillion*, the *Lancers*, the *Polka*, the *Quadrille*, and finally, even the *Waltz*, which most people believe to be the product of nineteenth-century Austria.

France may have been the land where the dance was most cultivated as an art, but Spain is the country where dancing is the most natural expression of the feeling of the people. The most famous dances of Spain are the *Bolero*, the *Seguidilla*, and the *Fandango*.

Great Britain was French in culture through much of her history, and her people were therefore devotees of the French dances. There were, however, some purely native dances in England, such as the *Morris Dances*.

But England is the country which showed most strongly how the joyous enthusiasm of the people for dancing might be repressed by a harsh religious doctrine. During the regime of the Puritans, dancing almost entirely disappeared in England. With the Restoration, it became popular again, and in the reign of Queen Anne we had an era of many balls in the grand manner, guided in fact or in spirit by the dandy, Beau Nash.

Of all modern dances, the *Waltz* is undoubtedly the most widely popular. It has had a cosmopolitan history. It originated in Germany, was developed in France, but experienced its full flowering in Austria toward the end of the nineteenth century and the beginning of the twentieth. The whole world responded to it with enthusiasm. The Strauss Waltz is a manifestation of the joyous meeting of the sexes.

Another exhilarating dance is the *Polka*. It originated in Bohemia in a servant girl's fantasy and by the middle of the nineteenth century was the rage of Europe and America. The music of the Polka is exuberant. Those who come under its spell feel an enthusiasm for life —an intensity of joy in man-woman relationships—that shows the full capacity of the dance to release repressed feelings.

The *Barn Dance* and the *Square Dance* are typically American. They started in rural areas as a means of getting neighbors together to help build a barn. They have an especial value in that they induce general participation. Old and young, the clumsy and the adept, join in the gaiety and merriment. The square dance still persists in rural areas and even in some urban centers. The emphasis is social rather than sexual.

The *Polka-Mazurka* is popular in Austria and Hungary. The *Polonaise* and *Mazurka* are Polish dances. The *Sir Roger de Coverley* is an old English dance that is still popular at social gatherings in England and that may be danced even by an elegant crowd at the conclusion of a formal ball.

These are only a few of the great social dances of the modern world. If we could in imagination see each one of them exhibited before us, we would learn much of the social history of the particular peoples who practiced them. They would reveal how the men and women of each country regarded each other, joined with each other in love, romance, or marriage. Some might show the joyous abandonment of a folk free of superstition and glad to enjoy the good earth and each other. Some would express a graceful stateliness, because the people had developed a complex code of intersexual behavior. And finally, in some we would see simple folk who released their energies in rhythmic movements, made all the more joyous because both sexes joined in them. Sex is, directly or indirectly, the prime motivating force in all social dancing.

Modern Dancing

Modern dancing may be said to have begun in the United States in 1912. Previously Americans had imitated European dancing, particularly the *Polka*, the *Viennese Waltz*, and the *Cotillion*.

In 1912, with ragtime and jazz music popular throughout the land, the first jazz dances appeared also. They were the *Turkey Trot, Bunny Hug,* and *Grizzly Bear*. These dances, like the jazz music to which they were danced, seemed to express the nervous, irregular motions of a machine-run civilization. But just because ours is a machine-run civilization pervaded by an almost maddening monotony, our people require the release which these jazz dances allow. The whole country was swept by enthusiasm for jazz dancing. Old and young took part in the so-called "dance craze." After a time the seemingly crude and vulgar steps were brought into a kind of dignity and order by such exponents of popular dancing as the Castles and their protégé, Arthur Murray, who standardized ballroom dancing and sold it as a social necessity all over the country.

The staple dance steps of the present generation are the *Waltz* and the *Fox Trot*, though some of the jitterbug steps, like the *Charleston*, still persist. South American dances, the *Tango*, the *Rhumba,* and the *Conga*, are growing in public favor, especially among the more sophisticated in the larger cities.

Of all modern social dances, the *Fox Trot* is the most popular. The rhythm is simple and is therefore easily and quickly learned. Yet it possesses a combination of possible steps that is varied and interesting. The dancers enjoy an easy proximity, unforced and natural and yet close and satisfying.

Some of the more conservative elements in American society were shocked by the apparent self-abandon of the new dances and spoke of them as a "psychic epidemic," a "dance craze," similar to the dance manias of the Middle Ages. But others contended that the new dances were a normal and natural revolt against Puritanism and Victorianism, and merely showed the need of our people to release their pent-up feelings.

Dr. A. A. Brill, the psychiatrist, who had translated Freud and made him popular in America, was moved to look into this "dance craze" and wrote an interesting paper for the *New York Medical Journal* (April 25, 1914), entitled "The Psychopathology of the New Dances." Before expressing his own opinion on the cause and significance of the "dance craze," Brill reviewed the opinions of certain famous writers, especially Havelock Ellis, on the sexual significance of social dancing. Here is his quotation from "An Analysis of Sexual Impulse" (1921) by Havelock Ellis:

In civilization dancing is not merely an incitement to love, but very often a substitute for the normal gratification of the sexual instinct, procuring something of the pleasure and relief of gratified love. This may be especially seen in young women who will very often expend a prodigious amount of energy in dancing, thus procuring not fatigue but happiness and relief. It is significant that after sexual relations have begun girls generally lose much of their ardor for dancing. Even our modern orthodox dances, it is interesting to note, are of sexual origin. Thus the most popular dance of all, the *Waltz*, represents the romance of love, the seeking and the fleeing, the playful sulking and shunning, and finally, the jubilation of the wedding.

Brill quotes from other observers, too, who maintained that the object of the dance is to produce a state of sexual excitement, particularly in the male.

But for himself, Brill came to a somewhat different conclusion. He declared that the dance craze was not confined to America, but was worldwide and a normal expression of the spirit of the times, and that its sexual emphasis is probably much more in the eyes of the beholders than in the minds—or bodies—of the dancers. He showed that many religious denominations have always objected to any form of dancing. The quotations from Ellis and others might seem to justify this religious objection, but by a questionnaire, Brill brought out the interesting and significant fact that while people get considerable romantic release in dancing and experience some sexual excitement, varying in degree according to the people and the way they dance, dancing is usually a wholesome activity and not an agent for promoting immorality.

To resolve the issue of whether the new dances were more erotic than the old, Dr. Brill sent the following questions to a few hundred enthusiastic dancers:

1. Did you ever become sexually excited while dancing the new dances?
2. Did you ever become sexually excited while watching the new dances?
3. Did you ever experience the same feelings while dancing or watching the old dances?

The answers that were received from 342 persons indicated that the new dances were hardly more prone to produce sexual excitement than the old ones, and that significantly enough the onlookers felt more sexual excitement than the dancers.

From the Freudian point of view, the dance is a wholesome and socially acceptable release of mental and emotional repression, all with a sexual core, as most repression is. Brill, who was, of course, an enthusiastic Freudian, declared:

Our present dancing epidemic is fundamentally due to similar causes. It, too, is a result of repressed emotions and feelings, and judging by the nature of the manifestation it must be concluded that it is sexual repression which has broken through. Puritan prudery and Anglo-Saxon hypocrisy have for centuries acted the part of the ostrich and refused to acknowledge the existence of the sexual impulse. Ignorance was confounded with innocence, and the most important functions of the human body were not only ignored but relentlessly debased. The very thought of sex was considered evil and disgusting.

To a certain extent this also held true of continental Europe, but there it never attained the extreme degree it has in this country and England. It is for this reason that Europe is much slower to take up the new dances. The women are the most eager dancers because they have been carrying the heaviest burden of our system of cultural development. The double standard of morality allows the men some sexual outlet, while feminine virtue is treated as the foolish peasant treated his valuable fur in the market. He was not content to sell it for the high prices offered by the merchants because he thought that he could make more money by tearing out the hairs from the skin and selling them singly.

The continual advance in Anglo-Saxon civilization with its complex economic problems is marked by a steady increase in frigid women and old maids. Sublimation is not only carried to an enormous degree, but the women are also forced to take up academic and other work and compete with men.

Religion, the emotional outlet par excellence for women, has been rapidly disappearing. There are almost as many irreligious women in England and America as men. Decadence of religion means an increase in nervous diseases. These causes have been operating for a long time, and as some adjustment had to take place England gave us the suffragette and America the new dances.

Brill concluded with this strong defense of the dance enthusiasts: "Moderate dancing, old or new style, can only do good and should be encouraged. I absolutely disagree with those who assert that it does harm, that it promotes sexuality, and so on. My own experiences (I do not dance) taught me just the opposite. The new dances offer good exercise and enjoyment to thousands of people, and serve besides as an excellent sublimation."

Among the authorities he quoted was Oskar Scheuer, whose article, "Die Erotik in Tanze," appeared in a German journal entitled *Sexual-probleme,* in January, 1911. This article inclines more toward the erotic emphasis in dancing than Brill's paper does. Scheuer declared that dancing, like singing and personal adornment, is always an erotic lure. He quoted from *Illustrierte Sittengeschichte,* a work by E. Fuchs, who in somewhat poetic language declared that dancing was and is never anything else than a stylized, rhythmically transformed eroticism: wooing, courting, hesitating, promising, fulfilling.

Scheuer illustrates this theme with descriptions of erotic dances in many lands, such as the Hula-Hula in the Polynesian Islands. He refers also to Medieval orgies of dancing and discusses the many moral reformers who cried out against all forms of social dancing as mere sexual manifestations. In conclusion Scheuer says, "Nowadays the dance is neither an orgy nor a phallic representation, but it nevertheless glides pretty often on the border land of forbidden fruit."

Today we are perhaps witnessing a final resolution of the age-old conflict between the advocates of sexual repression and those of sexual liberty, with the believers in sexual sublimation coming somewhere in between. All three are represented in criticisms of modern social dancing.

There are still some, such as Pitirim Sorokin, author of *The American Sex Revolution,* who declare that present-day Americans are sex-obsessed and that our survival as a nation may well depend upon our learning to control our sexual behavior.

Others call for more sexual freedom. The leader of these is Albert Ellis, who in his *Sex Without Guilt* declares that nothing is wrong in any sex act as long as adults who practice it together agree with and accept each other's mode of expression. To this group modern social dancing would be an altogether admirable and happy release of heterosexual feeling, and the more ardent it is the better.

Youth in particular should be allowed its dance freedom. All our outcries against the mad preoccupation of our young people with jazz, "rock 'n' roll," and so on fail to recognize the fact that youth represents the primitive period in the history of the race, that youth is full of physical energy and has a legitimate right to a release of this energy in socially acceptable forms.

A recreation authority, Jack Petrill, author of *After the Whistle Blows,* tells a significant story in *Dance Magazine* (May, 1957), of how a group of rough Detroit boys were socially tamed by being introduced to social dancing.

The time was the Prohibition Era. These youngsters, ranging in age from 15 to 18, were all tough kids who took part in bootlegging liquor from Windsor, Canada, across the river. They spent part of their days at a church playground where Petrill attempted to organize their play. They were a belligerent, cocky group of "wise guys."

Nevertheless, they responded to Petrill's invitation to participate in a social dance to be held in a church house in two weeks. The girls were to come from good Detroit families and would be chaperoned. The boys dressed up for the party and behaved in such a gracious, gentlemanly manner that the girls were delighted and impressed. Petrill says of this incident,

To me it indicated then, as it does now, that social dancing is an essential part of any recreation program. The human being who does not respond to ballroom dancing, or for that matter, dancing in any form is rare indeed.

Dancing, unlike most other recreational pursuits, is a social activity that can include the entire family. It also relieves the tension and monotony which may be built up during the working day.

Important benefits are the introduction to physical contact with the opposite sex—legitimately, it permits the male to put one arm around a lady's waist, while she has one hand in his.

Ballroom dancing requires many graces of etiquette—for instance, how to ask a lady to dance, the proper escort technique both going on and off the dance floor, and expressing appreciation for the dance.

The points impressed in personal appearance are proper hair-grooming, use of deodorants, clean well-pressed clothing, shined shoes, etc.

Dancing teaches the man to be careful of his posture, of how he puts his arm around his partner's waist, of how he holds her hand, an awareness of moving in unison—and watching that he does not step on the lady's toes. All this makes a man more considerate of other people.

For boys aged 14 and 15, dancing with a girl dispels many of the fears of association with the opposite sex. A great initial personality change for the better can occur with this introduction.

Many other writers have written at length of the satisfaction in dancing for the adolescent. Dancing heads the list of forms of recreation for both boys and girls. Research indicates that in the high-school years 60 per cent of the boys and 85 per cent of the girls can dance. At Syracuse University a recent poll shows that 92 per cent of the freshman college girls knew how to dance.

Adolescents enjoy learning intricate dance steps and showing them off to their peers. Another source of satisfaction is "cutting-in." This latter practice has declined because of the tendency of young people to "go steady," and, therefore, to dance with one partner throughout the evening. The adolescent who does not know how to dance loses out, no matter in what community he or she grows up.

Sometimes young people indicate deep-seated sex tendencies by the way they dance. A young psychology student humorously said of a girl with whom he danced at a fraternity party: "Her penis-envy was obvious as soon as she started dancing, for she always insisted on leading."

Many boys for their part show a weak heterosexual approach by their hesitant manner in approaching a girl in leading her off to the dance floor. Then there are the assertive young males who firmly grasp a girl's waist, and definitely lead in all dance steps.

The dance offers a valid therapy for many of the social ills of youth. It is likely that we could take the edge off their persistent rebellious feeling and reduce the amount of loose and perverse sexual behavior by providing in every town, in every neighborhood, an attractive center where young people could meet and freely enjoy dancing.

Sex in Social Dancing

How much of sex one sees in social dancing may very well depend upon the individual beholder. "Beauty," says Emerson, "is what the artist brings to the picture," and many a sociological study is what the sociologist brings to the survey. Those who have written on the subject of social dancing and sex bring into the discussion not only their own ideas and ideals, but obviously their own prejudices. Each is justified in his own way, but who will say that each has the final answer? The noted sexologists Iwan Bloch, Paolo Mantegazza, and Havelock Ellis, and the sociologist Leo Markun all discuss the sex factor in social dancing with point and emphasis.

An interesting work is Leo Markun's *Mrs. Grundy* (1930), an attempt to tell the history of that "tyrannical censor of morals," that "stickler for conventional propriety" whom all good citizens more or less feared however much they might mock at her stupidity and igno-

rance. Markun traces her influence as far back as the Renaissance church zealot Savonarola, who damned all public dancing; through Calvin, the Swiss moral ascetic, who wanted to impose his moral views upon all people, and who preached the wrath to come upon any who would indulge in such earthly pleasures as dancing; through Knox, the Scotch religious reformer whose eloquence on the subject of sin and damnation terrified even the pleasure-loving Mary, Queen of Scots; through the Puritans, who, first in England and then in America, banned all dancing; down through modern Victorianism, which permitted dancing, but only in a prim and restricted way. Even the worldly Byron, iconoclast and libertine, wrote critically of the Waltz as encouraging licentious behavior. In the age of Queen Victoria, Mrs. Grundy herself sat upon the throne.

The Italian Paolo Mantegazza, in *Sexual Relations of Mankind* (1932), pursues the anthropologist's interest in the amatory dances of primitive races in South America, Australia, Africa, and elsewhere. He tells how "the explorer Cook observed in Tahiti a love-dance, called *tinwrodi*, which actually consisted of sexual intercourse set to music! He who kept perfect time with the music was singularly honored and admired." The Eskimos also practiced love dances.

In all these primitive dances the male usually initiates the proceedings. The women are attracted to the most vigorous and valiant dancers. Thus it is that through the dance nature makes her selection of the fittest to survive and propagate the race.

Among the most noted of modern sexologists was the German, Iwan Bloch, heralded at the turn of the century as a great humanitarian and founder of sexual science. Bloch describes with realism the ballrooms and dancing salons of Berlin and Paris of the early twentieth century. "Here," he says, "the dance is not the principal thing—procurement and prostitution are widely diffused" (1937).

The poet of sex, as well as its best philosopher, was Havelock Ellis, to whom all life was a dance, and the dance of love the richest of its many manifestations.

In the third volume of his monumental *Studies in the Psychology of Sex* (1921), devoted to *An Analysis of the Sexual Impulse*, he traces the history of the dance through nature, through primitive man, and into the life of modern civilized society. He describes the love dance of insects and birds, culminating in the love embrace, and expresses his surprise that creatures mentally so undeveloped should nevertheless be able to express their love life in such an endless maze of patterns of sentiment and feeling.

He then describes love dances among the primitive tribes of Australia, the Malay Islands, Africa, and North and South America. He makes these significant points regarding the love dances of primitive people: "The interesting point for us here is that singing and dancing are still regarded as a preliminary to the sexual act. The whole object of courtship, of the mutual approximation and caresses of two persons of the opposite sex is to create the state of sexual tumescence.

"It will be seen that the most usual method of attaining tumescence—a method found among the most various kinds of animals from insects and birds to man—is some form of the dance."

He quotes G. Stanley Hall, author of *Adolescence*, as declaring the famous cakewalk dance of the South to be perhaps the purest expression of this impulse to courtship antics seen in man.

Havelock Ellis carries his analysis of the sexual significance of the social dance down into periods of modern civilization. Always it is a sexual stimulant. However, it may become not only "an incitement to love and a preliminary to courtship, but it is often a substitute for the normal gratification of the sexual instinct, procuring something of the pleasure and relief of gratified love."

As civilization advances, says Ellis, the religious and martial uses of dancing fall away, but it still remains a sexual stimulant. As proof of this he cites a statistical report:

An International Congress of Dancing Masters was held at Barcelona in 1907. In connection with this Congress, Giraudet, president of the International Academy of Dancing Masters, issued an inquiry to 3,000 teachers of dancing throughout the world in order to ascertain the frequency with which dancing led to marriage. Of over one million pupils of dancing, either married or engaged to be married, it was found that in most countries more

than 50 per cent met their conjugal partners at dances.

But it is in *The Dance of Life* (1923) that Ellis portrays the art of dancing as the apotheosis of man's life and love. In the beginning dancing was a religious rite. "A savage," says Ellis, "does not preach his religion—he dances it." But to the agnostic, and yet spiritual, Ellis, "dancing throughout the world has been so essential, so fundamental a part of all vital and undegenerate religion that whenever a new religion appears, a religion of the spirit and not merely an anemic religion of the intellect, we would still have to ask of it the question of the Bantu: 'What do you dance?' "

Ellis goes on to declare that dancing is not only intimately associated with religion; it has an equally intimate association with love. It is as old as love and traces its history through all living creatures who live and love. However gross some of the primitive love dances may have been, there is always behind them the desire to express love in strength and in beauty. "In fact," says Ellis, "dancing has ever been in existence as a spontaneous custom, a social discipline. Thus it is that dancing meets us not only as love, as religion, as art, but also as morals."

References

Bloch, Iwan, *The Sexual Life of Our Time*. New York: Falstaff Press, Inc., 1937.

Brill, A. A., "The Psychopathology of the New Dances." *New York Medical Journal*, April 25, 1914.

Ellis, Albert, *Sex Without Guilt*. New York: Lyle Stuart, 1958.

Ellis, Havelock, *Studies in the Psychology of Sex*. Philadelphia: F. A. Davis Co., 1921.

Ellis, Havelock, *Psychology of Sex*. New York: Emerson Books, Inc., 1946.

Ellis, Havelock, *The Dance of Life*. Cambridge, Mass.: Houghton Mifflin Co., 1923.

Mantegazza, Paolo, *Sexual Relations of Mankind*. New York: Falstaff Press, Inc., 1932.

Markun, Leo, *Mrs. Grundy*. New York: D. Appleton & Co., 1930.

Petrill, Jack, "Dancing in Recreation." *Dance Magazine*, May, 1957.

Scheuer, Oskar, "Die Erotik im Tanze." *Sexualprobleme*, January, 1911.

Sorokin, Pitirim, *The American Sex Revolution*. Boston: Porter Sargent, 1956.

DAVID GOODMAN

Demography and
the Nature of the Sex Drive

TWO ESSENTIAL first steps of any science are the collection of available raw data and the winning of social recognition of its right to call those data scientific. It is therefore not surprising that the writing and publication of the Kinsey reports are milestones in the early history of the very young behavioral science of sexology. Not only are the reports characteristic, in their objectives and methodology, of the early stages of any field of work; they are also partial solutions of one of society's abiding problems of sexual behavior, the relation of theory to practice.

The second point is important. There is no "pure" behavioral science: at their best, these sciences represent the attempts by trained workers to answer the urgent questions asked of them by the societies in which they live. Their projects, their techniques, and the theory that guides them are shaped only partially by the histories of their specialties; the pressures of social need—both positive and negative—are as strong as the laws of formal development.

If this is as true of sexology as it is of the other behavioral sciences, it is probable that sexology will experience, very early in its development, that process of reconsideration of some of its fundamental presuppositions that is usually characteristic of the maturity of a science. With one—perhaps the central one—of these reconsiderations we propose to deal (however tentatively) in this article.

Although one of the first demands we make of any scientist is that he tell us—accurately and objectively—what is going on, we soon follow it with the demand that he explain why it is going on and how it relates to other phenomena. And in areas of interpersonal behavior broader than those covered by Kinsey's concept of total emissions these questions are being asked with increasing vehemence. The whole complex of man's relationships to man—of the Self and the Other, of subject and object—has become the preoccupation of today's thinkers and creators. From Kerouac to Sartre—from the emotional reaction of the Beatniks to the rigorous thought of Heidegger—the problem of man's interaction with his environment (both animate and inanimate), of the escape from his sense of isolation and insecurity, has become almost as important as the problem of his continued existence.

It is obvious that, as the closest and most hypnotic of interpersonal bonds, sexual relations (using the term in its broadest sense) have been and will be brought under this type of scrutiny. But so far that scrutiny has usually been by observers whose special interests are in other fields. Many of the younger writers of today give the impression of being *aficionados* of this form of human relationship, but neither we nor they would number them among the behavioral scientists. The brilliant discussions of Sartre are not those of a sexologist. The application of all aspects of modern thought to the problems of the nature and significance—rather than of the diverse contemporary forms—of sexual behavior has scarcely begun.

The Problems of Demography

One way to approach this unexplored territory is to consider the problems common to all demographic research and faced by Kinsey *et al.* during the formulation of their procedures. A prerequisite to any demographic work is the isolation of a quantifiable—a countable—common factor in the raw complexes of behavior that are observed. We cannot amass statistics unless we can find some constant and observable unit of overt behavior whose appearance in our data can be the trigger to a check mark in our counting tables. Kinsey *et al.* were investigating *The Sexual Behavior of the American Male (Female)*, the various manifestations of the sex drive in our culture. As liberal members of that Judeo-Christian culture, two assumptions became obvious to them: that the one true end of love was genital coitus between the sexes leading to orgasm—preferably mutual; and that deviations from that end were to be expected. The application of demographic techniques within the bounds of those assumptions resulted in a monumental study of the genital activities of contemporary Americans, quantifiable in terms of total emission.

Kinsey *et al.* were fortunate in that this keystone—however weathered—of our sexual ethics is an act that lends itself readily to enumeration. Procreative genital coitus between husband and wife may be the most private of acts but it is still a statistical unit. Were our researchers to have come across a large colony of practitioners of *Karezza* (coitus in which the male does not come to orgasm) or of followers of the masturbatory practices that some native mothers perform on their baby sons their data would have been considerably more confused.

The point should not be regarded lightly. A *drive* is, of course, not an action or a series of actions, but the nature of a drive—or of a researcher's concept of a drive—is displayed by those actions he selects as being the "purest" or "simplest" observable expressions of that drive. Readers familiar with experimental psychology will remember the many ingenious tests that have been devised to reveal expressions of the invisible forces of the human psyche in observable and comparable actions. And the definition and selection of these expressive forms is the task of the experimenter and not of the subject. The fact that the typical American would agree with Kinsey's definition of the active expression of the sex drive does not make

that definition correct. Kinsey, not Kilroy, does the defining.

The Specificity of Drives

A subsidiary problem is the degree of specificity of drives in general. We can note a fairly consistent trend in contemporary psychology to break down drives, instincts, basic needs, and so on into simpler and less specific units. An aspect of this development in psychology is, of course, the discussion of the role assigned to social conditioning. The development of the field theory by Lewin (1936) and its application to the problem of drives by Brown (1936, 1939) has led to some of the most cogent discussions of the nature and role of drives, summed up by the latter in his statement: "Implicit in field theory is the idea that social behavior depends on the biological nature of the individual as an integral part of groups whose characteristics are intimately connected with cultural phenomena" (1936, p. 863).

Recognition of the fact that drives are simple and broad expressions of human and animal biology and that their expressions are shaped by the social environment of the individual points to an important task before researchers into sexual behavior. It is obvious that the socially conditioned manifestations of the sex drive are dangerous guides to a full understanding of its nature (unless we can separate the conditioning from the drive), and it is also obvious that the interaction of drive and social conditioning may have major consequences upon the mental and physical health of the individual, according to the degree to which the conditioning satisfies or distorts the satisfaction of the drive. It would seem probable that the nature of the sex drive—what need it is that drives men and animals to expressions of sexual activity—and the extent to which our contemporary sexual practices and theories satisfy or distort that drive are important objects of research.

No reader of the articles in this encyclopedia needs to be told that sexual practices are infinitely varied and almost totally conditioned by the mores of the relevant culture. And it is important to realize that rebellion against these sexual mores also is directed by them; the lure of forbidden fruit is conditioned by the existing taboos on fruit. For this reason it is logically impossible to count noses—or anything else—in an attempt to establish norms of sexual behavior: unless there exists or existed a society encouraging certain expressions of the sexual drive, those expressions will be comparatively few in number.

The task of a Kinsey outside time and place in formulating an observable common denominator of this infinite variety of sexual expressions is, I believe, impossible. It would take more space than is allowable in this article to prove this; the simplest approach is to give some examples of the negative criteria. The definition of the common expression of the sex drive may not presuppose genital or nongenital activity; orgasmic or nonorgasmic climax; heterosexual or homosexual partners; approximate parity of age or great disparity. There is only one observable common factor: in all cases the sexual relationship is accompanied by more or less acute emotional tension. Unless forced upon the partner—by physical power or custom—the sex act is not an emotionally neutral one. But the emotion that is present is also infinitely variable: from the least romantic to the most; from religious sobriety to conscious and "wicked" violation of moral codes; from the greatest tenderness to hostile rape; from sexual activity as a statement of divine origin to the gay triviality of a "roll in the hay." Mankind has not only expressed the sex drive in every conceivable way, he has accompanied it with every conceivable emotion.

Sexual Emotion and Sex Drive

It may very well be that the second of these two variables—the emotion accompanying or motivating the relationship—provides us with a clue to the nature of the sex drive. An emotion—the conscious inner manifestation of need—is, by definition, a reasonably specific thing. It invites inspection by the superego; it brings with it suggestions of permissible or impermissible action; it is a candidate for socialization. And an emotion—or, indeed, anything that impinges upon the consciousness—is not a drive; it is the conditioned superstructure erected upon a drive.[1] The logical conclusion would seem to be

that if we are to identify the sex drive we must seek it below the level of emotion, regarding all sexual emotions and acts as partial, conditioned results of the operation of the drive within the social animal.

The Criteria of a True Drive

Considering the highly emotional nature of sexual activities, we are left with considerable problems. Perhaps an important criticism of current definitions of the sex drive may help us here. It has been pointed out that two essential criteria of a true drive are that it be universally present and that it be necessary for existence, and critics have remarked on the obvious fact that some individuals apparently do not possess a sex drive and that, whether they possess it or not, some men and women are able, because of conviction or necessity, to do without its satisfaction without important harm to themselves.

Let us then postulate the broadest possible definition of the sex drive and see whether any observable manifestations of it satisfy the conditions of universality and necessity. Let us assume that, within the human (and animal) psyche, there is *a fundamental impulse away from the solitary state.* Interestingly enough, one of the most important developments of experimental psychology has been the identification of precisely such an impulse or drive, in the demonstrated necessity of close physical con-

---

[1] I am here using a definition of emotion best phrased by James (1894, cited by Wenger, Jones, and Jones, 1956): Emotion is the "perception of the exciting fact."

This definition, of course, runs afoul of many schools of psychological thought and their favorite definitions. But the whole trend, mentioned above and a central point in this article, to assign an increasingly important role to social conditioning and to break down drives, instincts, etc., into simpler and broader units of the dynamic aspect of the organism, necessitates an *ad hoc* approach to most definitions at this level.

Apropos of the last point, I should, perhaps, add that in this article I am accepting Hartley and Hartley's formulation, that there are physical states "variously called drives, motives and needs—physical states of imbalance within the organism which impel it to activity" (1952, p. 234) and am placing that statement in the context of Brown's work.

It is obvious that this lack of differentiation between drive, motive, and need will be regarded by some as impossibly crude, and that, when we know more about the biological nature of drives, we will be able to erect a conceptual superstructure upon them. But one cannot build a superstructure until the floors stay still, and as yet they have not done so.

tact and "mothering" or Tender Loving Care for the young of both man and animal. Unless the baby, kitten, infant rat, or similar experimental subject is given the benefit of close and loving physical comfort by a mother or mother surrogate (which does not even have to be animate, so long as there is a tactile similarity between it and the animate), the infant will suffer developmentally, in extreme cases going into that progressive and fatal lassitude and "withering away" which we know as the "marasmus" of the pediatric textbooks.[2]

It is probable that here we do have something that either is or very closely resembles a "pure" expression of a drive. And although it satisfies the broad general definition we have suggested—it is a fundamental impulse away from the solitary state—it is obviously rather far removed from the emotions of a Romeo or Juliet. But an essential part of our hypothesis is that the sex drive lies below the level of any conscious emotion, and we can expect different manifestations of it to be emotionally dissimilar.

We have, then, the high probability that at an early age, when he is experimentally manipulatable, man (and his cousins the animals) requires close, loving, tactile communication with his fellows. And it is a legitimate assumption—although it certainly has not yet been scientifically proved—that this need continues throughout life. Conditioned by appropriate social mores, psychology, and biological equipment, this need may be "perceived" as mother love, romantic love, lust, "love of mankind," and a whole continuum of other emotions. To a certain extent, but not completely, it can be satisfied on a symbolic level, and one form of expression can be transformed into another with varied degrees of freedom.[3]

[2] These experimental results have, of course, been questioned, as any work with important implications should be. The biologic nature, the degree of "essentiality," and the quantitative aspects of these findings are still unsettled. But they have been reported by enough workers, on a sufficient number and variety of experimental subjects, and under a sufficient variety of experimental conditions, for there to be little doubt that —in the broad terms used in this article—*something* is there.

[3] It should be noted that this continuum of emotions extends beyond the range of accepted meanings of the word "love." The "need for love" (usually the "need *to be* loved") in present-day society is, without

The Rhythm of Conjunction

What we have in effect hypothesized is that the organism—of whatever degree of complexity and level of evolution—has in addition to the rhythm of metabolism what we may call the rhythm of conjunction. It is for the biologists to tell us whether the word "whatever" in the preceding sentence is correct; possibly a certain level of organization (and power of locomotion) is required. But certainly, if we use the term "conjunction" with sufficient breadth, it is an observable requirement of animal life. And being organic it is, by definition, a physical thing. Certain expressions of this rhythmic drive may be satisfied symbolically in the man, but sooner or later he is strongly driven to touch. In addition, it would seem apparent that orgasmic touch—coitus—is only one form of that rhythm; that before coitus is physically possible and after it has ceased to be desired, physical communion with the Other is perhaps a necessity for—certainly highly conducive to—emotional (and perhaps physical) health.

This physical communion is apparently centered around a tension state that is definitely lower than that of the climb toward orgasm. A truer satisfaction of the essential tendency expressed by this drive would seem to be provided by that emotion identified as *Agape*, "compassion," "tender loving care," and so on. This, of course, in no way implies an assumption that any of the varieties of sexual expression found in present or past societies are distortions of what we should now call the "sex" drive; it merely denies that the central biological urge that motivates human relationships is necessarily sexual in its character (as we use

a doubt, symptomatic of the ills of our society and its members, and its individual manifestations are frequently neurotic. We must not assume that neurotic manifestations of a particular perception of a drive invalidate the concept of the drive.

One way of expressing our postulate (which may be useful in helping readers to avoid bringing in that much-abused and ambiguous term, "love") is to say that we assume the "gregariousness drive" of the theoreticians to be a socially conditioned manifestation of the same "rhythm of conjunction." What is gregariousness among young men today was a very different thing in, for example, ancient Sparta. Or, to put it another way, the "impulse away from the solitary state" does not refer to bachelordom. It refers to the asocial— the *solitary*—state in all its aspects.

the word *sex*) or coital in its technique. We may guess that the "closest" physical contact is orificial and that an evolutionary development attached the tension-release mechanism of orgasm to those orifices concerned with fertilization in approximately the same way that flowers developed color and scent. It is a natural climax to certain types of animal and human contact but demonstrably not the essence of all contacts.

Some Implications

It is perfectly obvious that we are in the realm of the purely speculative. But it is interesting to note how these speculations interact with many of our current problems and interests. Our dissatisfied preoccupation with coital sex as the sole culturally encouraged expression of intimate physical contact between adults; our oft-repeated expression of the need for more "love" in our relationships and the rather obvious difficulty of giving that love a socially acceptable local habitation and a form; the increasing realization that the tension associated with heterosexual (and homosexual) intimacies is in some obscure way a violation of the essence of the relationship—these and many more of our psychological, philosophical, and ethico-moral problems would seem to relate to the problem of the nature of the sex drive.

It is evident that in this sketch of the problem and suggestion of a hypothesis no firm conclusions have been drawn, except perhaps that the subject merits further investigation. Nor are these thoughts on the inadequacy of demographic research as a defining tool meant to cast reflection on the real value of that work. Among the questions that man is asking of the behavioral scientists, that of the actual forms of his interpersonal practices is a real and important one. But he is also asking other and deeper questions about his relations with his fellows, and these cannot be answered by a statistical abstract of his current sexual behaviors.

References

Ashley, Montagu, M. F., *The Direction of Human Development.* New York: Harper & Brothers, 1955.

Barrett, W., *Irrational Man.* New York: Doubleday, 1958.

Brown, J. F., *Psychology and the Social Order.* New York: McGraw-Hill Book Co., 1936.

——, "Individual, Group, and Social Field." *American Journal of Sociology* 44; 858-867, 1939.

Halmos, P., *Solitude and Privacy.* London: Routledge & Kegan Paul, 1952.

Hartley, E. L., and Hartley, R. E., *Fundamentals of Social Psychology.* New York: Alfred A. Knopf, Inc., 1952.

Himelhoch, J., and Fava, Sylvia F., *Sexual Behavior in American Society.* New York: W. W. Norton & Co., 1955.

James, W., *Psychological Reviews 1;* 516-529, 1894 (cited in Wenger, Jones, and Jones).

Lewin, K., *Principles of Topological Psychology.* New York: McGraw-Hill Book Co., 1936.

May, R., Angel, E., and Ellenberger, H. F. (eds.), *Existence: A New Dimension in Psychiatry and Psychology.* New York: Basic Books, 1958.

Von Urban, R., *Sex Perfection and Marital Happiness.* New York: Dial Press, 1949.

Watts, A. W., *Nature, Man and Woman.* New York: Pantheon Books, 1958.

Wenger, M. A., Jones, F. N., and Jones, M. H., *Physiological Psychology.* New York: Holt, Rinehart and Winston, 1956.

BRIAN M. HEALD

Divorce

DIVORCE is the legal termination of a marriage. It is merely the formal recognition of a severed marital relationship. As such it may have little if anything to do with the actual relationship between the man and woman involved. In most cases—reported to be about two-thirds in one study of young divorced mothers—the "real," that is the sociological and psychological, severance of the relationship has occurred at least six months before the divorce decree is handed down. The divorce itself is usually anticlimactic and of relatively little significance, since the important psychological and sociological effects have begun at the point of separation rather than at divorce. Participants and observers often comment on the "unreality" of the legal proceedings. Friends may not even know the exact time when the divorce has been granted since they, too, recognize that the new status for the marital partners began long before the decree.

Divorces may be absolute or limited. Limited divorce is the same as legal separation: the spouses may not remarry. Sometimes divorces are not final until after a period of time. In all cases, however, the marital relationship as a functioning unit has been legally severed.

Divorce is only one way of dealing with marital unhappiness. It is not necessarily even the most common one. On the basis of a study of Chicago in the 1920's it was estimated that separated but nondivorced persons were at least as numerous as divorced persons and might have been twice as numerous. Analysis of 1940 census data showed the number of separated couples to be 5.4 per cent of the number of married couples living together, a ratio of 1 to 18 or 19. In 1955 the number of men separated or not living with wives was 1,155,000, as compared with 990,000 who were divorced; for women the figure was 2,343,000 and 1,366,000, respectively. In addition to separation as a substitute for divorce are such escapes as: engrossment in work, in sports, in fashion, in social life, in community activities, in travel, in hobbies, in alcohol, in extramarital relationships, or in children.

"Causes" of Divorce

The legal "causes" of divorce give little insight into the true situation; they reflect, rather, the mores of the time. In the period 1887-1906, the "causes" of divorce in the United States were: cruelty, 40.8 per cent, desertion, 29.6 per cent, and adultery, 16.3 per cent. In 1929, these figures were, respectively: 21.8 per cent, 38.9 per cent, and 16.3 per cent. In 1932 it was estimated that only about one-third of all divorces were granted on grounds recognized by law (20 per cent for adultery, 8 per cent for long-time desertion, 2 per cent for drunkenness, and 3 per cent for minor grounds); the remaining divorces were really divorces for incompatibility by mutual consent.

As yet, however, open recognition of incompatibility as grounds for divorce exists only in New Mexico (since 1933) and Alaska (since 1935). Increasingly, divorce is granted on the grounds of voluntary separation of, say, three to five years; this is, in effect, divorce by mutual consent: the couple divorce themselves and then ask the court to ratify their new status. It has been predicted that if this trend continues, all other grounds of divorce may become mere relics.

In most jurisdictions the theory that there must be a contest is still held: One party must enter court with clean hands; the other must be proved guilty of some offense. If there is any agreement on the part of both parties that they want a divorce, they are guilty of collusion. If collusion can be proved, the divorce will not be granted.

There is a strong feeling among professional personnel connected with divorce that these legal assumptions should be reconsidered. For the sake not only of the parties themselves but also of the children, the feeling is that the emphasis should not be on the conflict aspect, in which each party vies with the other in reviling the mate, but rather on the constructive aspects. The concept of the so-called therapeutic divorce is therefore gaining ground. In some jurisdictions—notably Los Angeles, New Jersey, and Ohio—marital counseling is either recommended or mandatory for all couples applying for divorce, although counseling at this stage comes too late for most couples.

The "causes" of divorce may be said to exist in most, although not necessarily in all, marriages. One psychiatrist concluded that "the sources of marital discord are ubiquitous." Situations and conditions and behavior, which at least some courts would consider legal grounds for divorce, occur in a large proportion of marriages: Kinsey found that about half of all married men in his study had engaged in adultery; the kind of behavior that at least some courts would define as cruelty occurs from time to time in many marriages; drinking is a problem in an indeterminately large number of families. In fact, it could be said that "causes" of divorce are almost inevitably a part of the intense relationship of marriage. The enormous upsurge in the divorce rate in Moscow, which quadrupled when liberal laws were passed in 1926 sweeping away institutional props supporting marriage, suggests that "causes" are fairly widespread. Yet, despite the widespread incidence of "causes" or grounds that at least some courts will accept as justifying divorce, most couples do not make use of them. They do not apply for divorce. They select some other way to deal with their difficulties.

Factors Involved in a Decision for Divorce

Whether people will select divorce rather than some other way of dealing with marital unhappiness depends on a number of factors, namely: (1) cultural provisions, (2) social milieu, and (3) personality orientation.

Cultural Provisions

Where there are no legal or customary provisions for divorce, where there are no provisions in the social structure for a divorced person, it is obvious that divorce will not occur. Catholic cultures, for example, accept the doctrine that marriage is a sacrament and hence also the doctrine stated by the Council of Trent in 1563 that marriage is indissoluble for any reason. Functional alternatives to divorce will, to be sure, emerge in such cultures, such as the practice of annulment. In cultures that define marriage as a civil contract rather than a religious sacrament, provision will be made for divorce, although these provisions may be extremely stringent. And even when civil authorities are ready to liberalize divorce, cultural resistance may delay actual implementation for many years. (It was twenty-five years, in fact, from the time in 1912 when a Royal Commission in England recommended that five grounds for divorce, in addition to adultery, be recognized; it was not until 1937 that Parliament extended grounds to include desertion, cruelty, and insanity.)

But legal provisions constitute only one phase of the cultural milieu. In the United States, for example, omitting extremely liberal states (Nevada, Idaho, Arkansas) and illiberal states (New York, District of Columbia, North Carolina, South Carolina, and Louisiana), and omitting the four states with more than one-third Catholic population, an analysis in 1932 found that in the remaining 37 states, where the law was essentially the same and the population predominantly Protestant, great variations in the divorce rate still occurred. Folsom (1943) concluded that whether or not divorce will be resorted to "depends very much upon cultural values which cut across economic, class and religious lines."

If the mores are punitive divorce will not readily be sought. Even if divorce is not punished by social sanctions, it can still be discouraged if no provision is made for the divorced person in the social structure, if living conditions are difficult, if jobs are unavailable, if discrimination is practiced, or if social life is truncated. In the United States cultural forces mitigating against divorce have been receding. Mores have changed. In a large urban community in the 1940's it was found that 70 per cent of a sample of divorced mothers reported no social discrimination because of their divorce. But there still remains a cultural lacuna in that there are few clearly defined institutional guides to postdivorce behavior. As contrasted with bereavement, for example, divorce still results in a socially ambiguous status. Divorced persons can be treated neither as single nor as married and the exact role patterns for the divorced status have not yet been fully institutionalized.

Social Milieu

Even within the same general culture, however, not everyone resorts to divorce as a way of dealing with marital unhappiness. Even if cultural provisions for divorce are adequate, divorce is not likely to be resorted to if the social structure is antipathetic. It has been found that divorce tends to "run in families." If a person's parents have been divorced the chances that his own marriage will also end in divorce are increased. Indeed, it has also been found that a person's chances for divorce increase if his friends or associates have been divorced. There seems to be, in brief, a strong group component in susceptibility to divorce.

This social component reveals itself statistically in a lower incidence of divorce among persons with high degrees of education. At mid-century, for example, the rate of divorce per 1,000 women was 3.4 for those with four or more years of college education, as contrasted with a rate of 4.9 for those with only one to three years of high school. The divorce rate of the college-educated segment of the population tends to be low.

The social component in divorce reveals itself also in the fact that people in certain occupations are relatively vulnerable to divorce. Persons in professional, semiprofessional, proprietary, and managerial occupations tend to have low "divorce-proneness"; service workers tend to have extremely high rates. Among professionals, physicians have a high rate; clergymen, a low one. People exposed by occupations to numerous and unrestricted contacts with members of the other sex tend to be vulnerable.

The social component is seen also in the fact that marriages that end in divorce are less likely to have produced children. Where there are children in divorced families, there are likely to be fewer than in intact families.

Personality Orientation

Even when the cultural and social determinants of a decision to resort to divorce have been invoked, there still remains a personal component in this decision. There are two models of this personal component: one may be called the "divorce-won't-help" model and the other the rational model.

The "divorce-won't-help" school implies that seeking divorce is itself a neurotic symptom and that nothing but psychoanalytic reorientation will solve the problem. Divorce and remarriage will only mean playing the same old tune over on a new instrument. The difficulty resides in the neurotic personality, not in the marital situation. Evidence to support this position can, to be sure, be supplied. It is true that if one analyzes the population of divorced persons at any given time, a disproportionate amount of emotional pathologies is found. Thus, the death rate, the suicide rate, and the illness rate are all higher among divorced persons than they are among either the widowed or the married. That some of this is due to the traumas of separation can be concluded from the fact that widowed persons also show higher rates than married persons. But that some of it is due to the "selection" of certain types of people into the divorced population is also shown by the fact that divorced persons show higher rates than widowed, despite a generally younger average age. Further evidence to support the personal-pathology school of divorce is the fact that the divorce rate among remarried divorced persons is higher than that of first marriages; and the more marriages the higher the divorce rate.

But there is also evidence to support the theory of rational divorce. Of the divorced persons who remarry and remain remarried, a very large proportion are reported as having marriages of at least average success. These persons were unsuccessful in one mating but successful in a later one. Divorce is a rational, nonneurotic course if a marriage is destroying one or both partners; if it is creating a destructive environment for children; if it is impeding the functioning of any of the family in their nonfamilial roles.

Conversely, the decision to reject divorce as a way of dealing with marital problems might be quite abnormal, even pathological. Some women, for example, cling to abusive or alcoholic husbands even when their very lives are endangered thereby; or husbands may reject divorce even when their wives flaunt their contempt and destructive hostility. And people may decide to remain married despite serious maladjustments for quite rational considerations; if the social costs in the form of ostracism or sanctions or loss of position are extremely high, a man or woman might elect to remain in an unsatisfactory union rather than pay the costs of divorce. This would be judged a rational decision by most persons.

In brief, neither remaining married nor seeking divorce can be viewed as always a neurotic or as always a rational course of action. Either course may be selected on rational or neurotic grounds.

Sociological and Psychological Divorce

The sociological and psychological divorce, as distinguished from its legal validation, is a process that takes a varying amount of time. Some couples know soon after marriage that the relationship cannot endure; others come to this realization only slowly after years of effort and desperation. Sometimes one mate sees the inevitability of divorce long before the other; sometimes the divorce even comes as a surprise to one of the partners. It is quite possible that a marriage may have been successful over a period of years and yet end in divorce, since no relationship is static in nature. Indeed, there is some evidence that reported success in marriage does vary with duration, showing a critical phase in the middle years.

The average duration of American marriages that ended in divorce in 1953 was 6.1 years. In one study of young divorced mothers in an urban community, the elapsed time between first serious consideration of the idea of divorce and the final decision actually to go ahead and

seek divorce averaged 4.6 months. It took that long, on the average, for these women to crystallize their decision. We may picture this as a time of great uncertainty and conflict. Should she really go ahead with it? Is this situation partly her fault? Has she brought this unhappy condition upon herself? Is she really worse off than other women? We may conceive this phase as one in which she is torn between conflicting goals, in which she has to weigh alternative values and decide which will yield the higher returns. The situation may be complicated by the fact that she must put up a front to family and friends in case she decides not to seek the divorce. She tries to keep the breach private. For those who reject the idea of divorce, some other alternative is worked out. But for those who finally decide to seek divorce, a period lasting, on the average, some 3.2 months follows in which, presumably, some kind of preparation is made. By now the woman is willing to let the outside world know that the marriage is failing.

These two periods—4.6 months (between first serious consideration and final decision) and 3.2 months (between final decision and actual filing)—cannot, for statistical reasons, be added together to arrive at the total elapsed time from first serious consideration to filing of suit. This time, between first serious consideration and filing of suit, averaged exactly one year for the sample as a whole. The average interval between filing of suit and handing down of decree was 8.3 months. The total time from first serious consideration to final decree averaged two years (23.8 months).

The relative rapidity with which women passed through these phases varied. In marriages in which either the husband or the wife, or both, came from a rural background the elapsed time between first serious consideration of divorce and actual filing was considerably longer than it was in marriages in which the partners were city-bred or from small towns; almost twice as long, in fact, where the wife was from a rural background.

The longer the duration of the marriage, the longer the process of reaching and implementing the decision to file for divorce after the idea was given serious consideration. This was true regardless of the age of the women. For women aged 35 or over who had been married fifteen or more years, it took almost two years after first serious consideration of divorce before suit was actually filed; for women of this age who had been married less than fifteen years, the time was only about half this long. Similar differences were found for younger women also. The more durable the marriage, in brief, as measured in the number of years it has survived, the longer it takes to break it up.

The period between first consideration of divorce and final suit was shorter in the cases (one-fourth) in which the husband was the one who first suggested it (5.4 months) than in the three-fifths of the cases in which the wife was the first (12.9 months) or in the 13 per cent of the cases in which it was a mutual suggestion (18.5 months). The implication is that when the husband suggests the divorce, the final suit is likely to occur with relatively greater speed.

Although it is usually the wife who files suit for divorce, it is reported that the husband is more likely to be the first to desire the divorce. Wives, according to this theory, are manipulated into a position in which they suggest and proceed to divorce by what is called the "strategy of divorce." The husband can, within a pattern of behavior that is acceptable by the outside world, be so obnoxious to his wife that in desperation she seeks relief. Conversely, however, a wife can, without the outside world's knowing about it, also make the husband so miserable by sexual refusal that he becomes reconciled to divorce.

Emotional traumas occur at all stages of the divorcing process. The "curve of trouble," using Goode's (1956) expression, which is already high by the time of the final decision, reaches its maximum at the time of final separation; thereafter it declines so that by the time of the final decree only a small proportion of divorced women reported traumas. A surprisingly large proportion—some 37 per cent, in fact—reported very little incidence of traumas.

The sex life of the divorced woman is complicated by her anomalous position. Since she is experienced, it is sometimes assumed by men that she is approachable. This is true in some instances; Kinsey reports that some women welcome the opportunity to secure a wider variety of sexual experience after divorce. But many do not miss heterosexual contacts; they are content with masturbation or homosexual contacts. Others report missing sociosexual contacts. The median frequencies of sexual outlet are greater for separated, divorced, and widowed women (between 0.4 and 0.9 per week) than for single women (0.3 to 0.5 per week) but less than for still-married women. Most of these result from heterosexual contacts, but the proportion declines with age. Men who are divorced, separated, or widowed continue to have almost as active a sex life as when they were married, and 80 per cent of their postmarital activity is heterosexual in nature.

Although divorces are less common when there are children, still at least a third of a million children are involved in divorce each year. The evil effects of divorce on children have received a great deal of attention. There is evidence, however, that adolescent children in homes in which there is conflict are less well adjusted than are children in homes in which there has been a divorce. One study in St. Paul found that removing the father from the home was often the best way of salvaging the rest of the family.

Most divorced persons, especially the younger ones, remarry. And a large proportion of these remarriages are reported by informants who know them well to be of at least average success.

Summary

The divorce rate in the United States has shown a long-time upward trend, reaching an all-time high in 1946 (17.8 per thousand females). Since that time it has declined and leveled off (9 and 10 per thousand in 1954 and 1955. One marriage in four entered into would end in divorce as of 1955.

It is clear that the future trend cannot be predicted with complete accuracy. But from what we know about divorce in the past the rate may be expected to decline, although it will probably never be as low as it was in the nineteenth or first quarter of the twentieth centuries. The conditions that make divorce a feasible way of dealing with marital difficulties will continue. But increasing numbers of men and women are achieving high-school and even college education and this variable is associated with a low divorce rate. A growing body of research has alerted us to the nature and hazards of modern marriage, and ways of meeting them are in process of developing. The profession of marriage counseling is growing so that its services should be increasingly available to couples needing help. Courses in high schools and colleges are available to prepare young people for marriage, and churches are developing similar programs for those beyond school age.

Even though divorce will continue, the chances are that its traumatic effects will be mollified by institutional structures. It will probably never be possible to eliminate the hurt, the grief, the disillusionment, the self-doubt, the humiliation that accompany any failure in human relations. But a therapeutic approach will minimize them and will use them for rebuilding more successfully.

References

Bergler, Edmund, *Divorce Won't Help*. New York: Harper & Brothers, 1949.

Bernard, Jessie, *Remarriage, A Study of Marriage*. New York: The Dryden Press, 1956.

Cahen, Alfred, *Statistical Analysis of American Divorce*. New York: Columbia University Press, 1932.

Davis, Kingsley, "Divorce Downswing," New York *Times* Magazine, May 8, 1955, p. 67.

Eisenstein, Victor W. (ed.), *Neurotic Interaction in Marriage*. New York: Basic Books, Inc., 1956.

Folsom, Joseph Kirk, *The Family and Democratic Society*. New York: John Wiley & Sons, Inc., 1943.

Geismar, L. L., and Ayres, Beverly, *Families in Trouble*. St. Paul: Greater St. Paul Community Chest and Councils, Inc., 1958.

Glick, Paul C., *American Families, A Demographic Analysis of Census Data on American Families at Mid-Century*. New York: John Wiley & Sons, Inc., 1957.

Goode, William J., *After Divorce*. Glencoe, Ill.: The Free Press, 1956.

Jacobson, Paul, *American Marriage and Divorce*. New York: Rinehart, 1959.

Johnson, Roswell H., "Suppressed, Delayed, Damaging and Avoided Divorces." *Law & Contemp. Prob. 18;* 72-97, 1953.

Kinsey, Alfred C. *et al.*, *Sexual Behavior in the Human Male*. Philadelphia: W. B. Saunders Co., 1948.

Kinsey, Alfred C. *et al.*, *Sexual Behavior in the Human Female*. Philadelphia: W. B. Saunders Co., 1953.

Lichtenberger, James P., *Divorce, a Social Interpretation*. New York: Whittlesey House, 1931.

JESSIE BERNARD

Education in Sex

Definition

FOR clarity of discussion, several arbitrary distinctions will be made at the outset. First, we shall differentiate between "sex education" and "sexual conditioning." The latter term will be employed as the general one to refer to all acquisitions (by whatever method) of covert or overt patterns of sexual behavior. Whenever the individual learns a form of sexual functioning or develops an attitude toward such functioning, he is being sexually conditioned. When such learning is part of an organized program designed to instruct the individual regarding sex attitudes or actions, the term "sex education" is applied. Sex education, then, is a special, organized form of sexual conditioning and is the major concern of this article. Since educational efforts are greatly affected by the other forms of sexual conditioning to which members of a society are subjected, however, we shall have need from time to time to refer to the more generic learning process.

Another type of distinction that is applicable to both sex education and to sexual conditioning is the difference between information-dispensing and attitude-affecting. It is possible, for example, that a child will arrive at the age of 10 in one of our modern societies without having acquired much, if any, specific information on sex of the type often presented in sex education courses: the approved names of the genital organs, the nature and method of conception, the process of gestation, and the way the fetus is nourished in the uterus. It is even possible for a very protected and isolated child to have acquired no unapproved information or

misinformation along such lines. It is utterly impossible, however, that the child will not have had his attitudes toward sex affected in one way or another: by silence, by indications of embarrassment regarding nudity or some bodily functions, by the exchange of knowing looks during certain sex-approaching trends in conversations, by lack of emotional freedom between males and females in his environment, and by countless other attitude-affecting interactions. This is true even if no specific sex information as such has been communicated to the child. Information-dispensing and attitude-affecting are generally not rigidly separated in either sexual conditioning or in official sex education offerings. In the latter, the assumption has often been made (without any scientific support) that "wholesome" sex attitudes will somehow automatically arise in individuals who are exposed to a certain amount of information about reproduction.

A final differentiation, based in part on the distinction we have just discussed, is a form of reconstructive learning. Since much sexual conditioning of the attitude-affecting type has taken place in the individual prior to his exposure to any program of sex education, and since (as we shall discuss later) much of the sexual conditioning in our society (and in most others) is not reality-oriented, a special type of sex education is required to reach rational and realistic sex goals (which we shall also treat below). This special type of sex education, quite in contrast with the information-dispensing programs generally developed, is designed to make possible the changing of basic attitudes, the reconstruction of the individual's fundamental beliefs, feelings, and actions. In

344

order to avoid confusion, we shall refer to this reconstructive learning process by a separate term: "sex therapy."

History

Most efforts at sex education date back no more than four decades. In fact, in most Euro-American civilizations, even informal sexual conditioning was frowned upon by "respectable people" and took place behind the thick shroud of Victorianism. Gradually, however, as social changes attendant upon industrialization, urbanization, democratization (including the partial emancipation of women), and secularization penetrated the Victorian veil, many problems of interpersonal relations, including those of sex, reached the awareness of a minority of citizens in most Western societies. Beginning with the much advertised (although unvalidated) sexual freedom of the "flaming youth" of the 1920's, a few educators, ministers, YMCA and YWCA personnel, and others began to point to the need for youth to have sex education.

What these initial proponents of sex education (and most of their successors) had in mind was to instruct young people so as to bring their sexual behavior in line with the mores of the societies to which they belonged. Stated differently, post-Victorian sex education has been mainly directed toward the re-establishment and reinforcement of Victorian-type sex attitudes. In the United States, at least, alleged befrienders of sex education (which, as we shall note below, has been euphemized and often rendered unidentifiable in "family-life education") have often been at the forefront of efforts to prevent the free dissemination of the best available information on how people actually behave sexually (notably, the Kinsey reports) and the frank and realistic consideration of desirable ways for people to behave sexually.

Goals

Although the desirability of some kind of sex education (in euphemistic terms) has become a generalization to which many have subscribed, an objective evaluation of goals toward which such education should be directed is yet to be effected. So long as discussions of such matters move at a high level of abstraction, peace reigns among parents, educators, and other concerned citizens. All will agree, for example, that a goal of sex education is the instilling of "wholesome" attitudes toward sex. It is also frequently stated that children should be led to understand the "spiritual" as well as the crass biological functions of sex. If, in such discussions among chronological adults, someone rises to question what is meant by "wholesomeness" in sex attitudes and "spirituality" in sex functioning, he is dismissed as a troublemaker.

It seems quite clear to seasoned observers that people in most, if not all, of our Western societies do not want to discuss specific goals of sex education because they know that such discussion will lead to the radical alteration of our sex mores. Many citizens may not be fully aware of the motives for their reluctance, but resistance to the change of customs, especially those that are morally and religiously sanctified, nevertheless underlies this reluctance. Even though sufficient facts are readily available to indicate that a great number of children, adolescents, and adults do not really behave in accordance with official moral precepts regarding sex, most people do not want to face these facts. Perhaps we can say it is mainly *because* it is now widely known that our sex codes do not realistically relate to our sexual behavior that many individuals are *afraid* to examine specific goals for sex education.

We cannot here outline what we would consider to be realistic goals for sex education, for they and the methods designed for their realization would consume many times our allotted space. Certain preliminary fundamentals that need to be faced prior to the development of specific objectives for sex education may be briefly mentioned: (1) Western societies, among others, are in a state of serious and severe confusion on the subject of sex, with beliefs and practices in great incongruence. (2) The major cultural heritage of attitudes about sex is still persistently puritanical, with its twin by-products of the pornographic and the phoney glamorous (the allegedly "spiritual," desexedly romantic). (3) Facts (1) and (2), operating side by side, have produced a truly schizoid cultural condition. For example, the official position of our society is still, puritanically, that masturbation, petting, and premarital coitus are morally wrong—a position generally incorporated unchanged and unchallenged in most courses on sex education. Yet it is widely known that masturbation and petting are almost universal practices among our youth and that premarital coitus is undertaken by a probable majority. (4) To teach as "right" a sex morality that does not function adequately for most people (and to be able to offer no rational support for the morality—simply the irrational contention that "right is right, no matter what people may do or say") increasingly undermines the potentialities for a warm, loving relationship between males and females.

We may summarize by stating that a foremost preliminary goal for sex education is facing the fact, and honestly communicating this fact to our children and adolescents, that we are greatly confused about sexual morality and are now prepared to try to work out rational and realistic goals for sex education by admitting our lack of these goals. Until this is done, sex education will be vapidly impotent at best and destructively schizoid at its increasing worst.

A courageous admission of our current uncertainties and confusions about sex would soon permit us to find the kinds of rational and realistic goals toward which we want to move in sex education, and data from psychological, psychiatric, biological, and ethnological studies make evident the desirability of marked departures from Victorian or puritanical goals.

The trend will be toward a society in which parents and other adults will be eager to guide their children toward full appreciation of sex and the wise enjoyment of it in and out of marriage. They will help young people to achieve a degree of sexual freedom almost undreamed of by anyone in our present societies. Such adults will realize that this greater sexual freedom and appreciation will in turn release warmth and affection in other types of interpersonal relations.

Goals like these, only much more specific and with concrete educational steps toward their fulfillment, will begin to appear once we honestly face our present sexual confusions and resolve to do something about them. It is because such goals are sensed and feared by vested moral interests in our societies that the consideration of a reality-oriented sex education program is so bitterly fought.

European and Asiatic Countries

Of all the countries that have made some effort to educate their people in sexual matters, Sweden seems to have done the most outstanding job of effectively reaching large portions of its people with realistic information about reproduction and contraception, as well as the emotional and social aspects of sex. The Swedish government has made sex education in the schools compulsory. It is not merely education in reproduction, and it is not diluted and concealed as "family-life education."

The Swedish culture probably takes the least moralistic attitude toward premarital sex relations of any of the Euro-American civilizations. This offers some indirect substantiation for our premise that a more realistic recognition of existing sexual behavior is a necessary preliminary to the development of a reality-oriented sex education.

England has undertaken no sex education program as such, but it provides a considerable amount of not overly moralistic sex instruction through the premarital and marital counseling of the National Marriage Guidance Council. Although local groups sponsored by the Council depend upon voluntary enrollment, the percentage of people reached is much greater than by any counseling program offered in the United States.

One important recent liberalizing educational effort in England was the Report of the Committee on Homosexual Offences and Prostitution under the chairmanship of Sir John Wolfenden. This report has not only directed the attention of many English citizens to various realities long ignored on the specific topics of homosexuality and prostitution, but has also apparently aroused thoughtful and spirited discussion and efforts at further investigations about many other long-buried facts of contemporary sexual relationships.

Education regarding contraception has developed in many European and Asiatic countries. Although the urgent importance of population control demands increasing emphasis on this phase of sex education in *all* countries, there is little evidence of effective educational treatment of the emotional and social aspects of sex indirectly deriving from birth control activities. Some interest in a broader program of sex education, however, is discernible in some of the nations (notably Belgium, the Netherlands, India, and Japan) where population control has begun to take strong root.

Reliable information about what is taking place in the way of official or unofficial sex education in Communist countries is difficult to obtain. In general, however, there seems to be a more accepting and realistic attitude toward sexual functioning, but little effort to focus public attention on the development of rational sex values.

United States

Sex education in the United States today has little separate existence. It has been absorbed and largely emasculated by family-life education. It has been generally decided that sex education can be handled by teachers, parents, administrators, and (allegedly) students more effectively by treating it along with other topics related to marriage and family living. In any case, a frank and honest facing of the intimate, practical problems of the sexual aspects of life is rare to the point of nonexistence in American classrooms, from elementary school through college.

As is traditionally the case with American education in its treatment of controversial issues, there is a tendency in this area for school officials and teachers to adjust to the most strongly propagandized and power-centered point of view in the community. American education seems to lack leadership around which liberal and enlightened public attitudes toward sex could begin to form. No support is forthcoming (except in exceedingly rare instances, such as Indiana University, where officials have consistently provided financial and other support for the research activities of the late Alfred C. Kinsey and associates) for educators to examine existing cultural confusions, hypocrisies, prejudices, and myths about the role of sex in human relationships—let alone communicate the fruits of such examinations to their students.

As a result, the only kind of sex education found in American schools and colleges consists almost entirely of a pedantic treatment of the anatomical and physiological aspects of sex, a rehash of the conventional morality, and a quick movement onward to emotionally safer topics, such as budgets and in-laws. This form of sex education is predominantly available in the colleges. A relatively small percentage of high schools provide an even more pallid variety of such education, but rare and progressive indeed is the elementary school that approaches sex even gingerly via the flora and lower orders of fauna.

Early Sexual Conditioning

Even if there should be a sudden birth of courage, wisdom, and realism regarding sex education in the public schools, there would be much destructive work to be undone before constructive work could in most instances begin. By this we mean to make clear that by the time the average child reaches the *first* grade of school, many of his basic attitudes toward sex have been negatively conditioned. It is not only too late to achieve much in the way of fundamental sex education with college and high-school students, it is very late indeed even with elementary-school children.

In a very real sense, the child's sexual conditioning, however realistic or unrealistic, began at birth (or before, in the sense of the pre-established attitudes of his parents), was fairly well fashioned in the first few years of his interactions with parents and siblings, and had its fundamental finishing touches in situations with his preschool playmates and in fortuitous encounters with adults other than his parents.

Whatever else we may wish to credit to Freud, he performed an important reality-facing service for Euro-American culture in calling reluctant scientific attention to the long-repressed fact that sexuality is an attribute of human beings from infancy onward. Sex-love feelings (response to warmth and enjoyment of being fed in their most rudimentary form) start no later in life than when the newborn baby is first held and fed. The practice that still exists in many hospitals of removing the baby from the vicinity of the mother for some time after birth may be considered one of the earliest negative contributions to the child's emotional development and sex-love responsiveness.

Even without such negative assistance from a hospital, many mothers seem unaware or indifferent to the fact that physical contact is essential for the young child's development of a sense of security, which is the basis for his later ability to love. It is still a common practice in our society to keep the baby clothed and isolated from all but the minimum tactile experience during feeding. The antisexual tradition goes so deep with some women that bodily contact with even their own infant is repugnant to them. Even for mothers who make an exception for the very young child, strong restrictive measures regarding the expression of affection are introduced soon after early infancy. In one way or another, antisexual attitudes of the parents are communicated to the child, reinforced by other associates who have been similarly made to feel fear and guilt and anxiety and shame regarding sex-love feelings, and delivered in a closely sealed and difficult-to-sexually-re-educate form at the school's door.

Sex Therapy

In our discussion of sexual conditioning we did not intend to convey the idea that nothing can be done about the sex education of the child. We strongly believe quite the contrary. But our observations indicate that *in many instances under present cultural conditions* there is not much hope of reaching children in a basic attitudinal way with any kind of sex education program other than one that is essentially *reconstructive psychotherapy.* By the time many children reach school age, anxiety has usurped emotional security, deep-seated guilt and hostility have displaced love, and sex attitudes have become tenacious, perverted dynamisms that cannot be altered by a casual, superficial sex education that is linked with

"other interesting things to be learned about life."

In this connection it seems pertinent to note that even relatively liberal writers on the subject of sex education say it is advisable to weave in sex information and attitude formation with other aspects of life. The child in the classroom, they hold, should not have his attention called to sex any more than he has it called to arithmetic, history, or physical education. Such counsel overlooks the most significant reality that we have just noted: namely, the child already has a set of fundamental sex attitudes which, because they are reflective of a confused culture (most particularly confused on sex-love feelings), are bound to need some special remedial work. Remedial work cannot be accomplished in any subject, be it sex or reading, without centering attention on the subject. To try to teach the average child of our society sound sex attitudes in a casual way as a part of a synthesis of life realities would be somewhat comparable to trying to cure a chronic alcoholic by subjecting him to a course on interesting life activities without focusing his attention on problems related to habitual and excessive drinking. "Do not," the common counsel goes, "isolate sex as a subject with special problems. It should be treated as just one of many wonderful facts about life." Alas, as we have already pointed out, sex, in even the most favorable of home environments, has already been isolated, given special negative emphasis, and cast with a personalized problem atmosphere.

Individuals and groups vary, of course, in the quality and quantity of sex therapy they need to develop relatively sound sex attitudes. A growing number of psychologists and psychiatrists, as well as some nonpsychiatric physicians, such as gynecologists, have developed various successful remedial techniques with children, adolescents, and adults. Group psychotherapy has been particularly effective because it encourages people with essentially the same sex-love difficulties to gain encouragement and support in facing and doing something about these problems. Although some therapy groups have been successfully operated under auspices such as the YMCA and YWCA, Planned Parenthood centers, Social Hygiene societies, and various church groups, they usually work most effectively under private sponsorship. There tends to be a "contamination" of a group by conventional sex attitudes as a result of any institutional sponsorship.

Contamination by the current mores is, of course, never completely overcome in the most advantageous of therapeutic circumstances. The leader, as well as the group members, is a product of his society. But if the leader has himself faced and worked through his interpersonal problems in psychotherapy (which is one of many standard requirements for conducting individual or group therapy), he is most likely to be in an emotional position to provide freedom and safety for the members of his group, or for the individual patient, to engage in the painful process of working through their attitudinal distortions. This, along with the special needs for remedial work in sexual beliefs and practices in the average product of our confused society, is another reason why we must think in terms of sex therapy and not merely of sex education.

Some may consider sex therapy a luxury for the limited few rather than any kind of solution to our general cultural need for sex education. Under present circumstances, only a relatively small percentage of people are reached by sex therapy, but the method is no luxury. Thus far, at least, we have developed no more effective, or less expensive, way to reconstruct sexual attitudes and practices to a point where the average individual can function in a happy, loving, outgoing manner.

Meantime, it is quite clear that none of the Western societies has reached the point where it will consider the problems of sex education in the terms of sex therapy. Even if the money and the popular support were suddenly available for such a program for a large portion of the population, personnel (generally trained in psychotherapy and specifically trained in sex therapy) to conduct the groups would be a long time forthcoming. But to speak glibly of sex education in other than reconstructive terms is fatuous. Sooner or later, if we are to make advancement as a civilization, we shall need to turn a great deal of our attention to a therapeutic form of sex education.

References

Baruch, Dorothy, *How to Live with Your Teen-ager.* New York: McGraw-Hill Book Co., 1953.

Chambre, A. C. F., *The Sexual Development of Your Child.* New York: Lyle Stuart, 1958.

Comfort, Alex, *Sexual Behavior in Society.* New York: The Viking Press, Inc., 1950.

Ellis, Albert, *Sex Without Guilt.* New York: Lyle Stuart, 1958.

Harper, Robert A., and Harper, Frances R., "Are Educators Afraid of Sex?" *Marr. & Fam. Living 19;* 240-244, 1957.

Joint Committee on Health Problems, *Sex Education* (series of five pamphlets). Washington and Chicago: National Education Association and American Medical Association, 1955.

Kinsey, A. C. *et al., Sexual Behavior in the Human Male.* Philadelphia: W. B. Saunders Co., 1948.

Kinsey, A. C. *et al., Sexual Behavior in the Human Female.* Philadelphia: W. B. Saunders Co., 1953.

Royal Board of Education in Sweden, *Handbook on Sex Instruction in Swedish Schools.* Stockholm: Royal Board of Education, 1956.

Stokes, Walter R., *Modern Pattern for Marriage.* New York: Rinehart & Co., Inc., 1947.

Stokes, Walter R., *A Pioneering Venture in the Sex Education of Children.* Unpublished manuscript, 1959.

ROBERT A. HARPER

FRANCES R. HARPER

English and American
Sex Customs, Early

TO UNDERSTAND the sex customs of present-day America we must study the sex customs of early England and America. It is therefore the purpose of this article to examine some of the significant sex customs practiced during the Middle Ages, the Renaissance, and the Reformation in England, and during the seventeenth and eighteenth centuries in America.

The Nature of Human Sex Behavior

Human sex behavior, because it is learned, not innate, inborn, or inherited, can never be understood apart from the society that created it. In *all* societies there are rules and regulations governing sexual behavior and concerning the social roles of men and women. Some societies are more severe than others, but all, as Seward (1946) has noted, attempt to and do control sex behavior.

Since sex behavior is human behavior concerned with the social roles of men and women, it includes marital relations; extramarital relations, such as fornication, adultery, promiscuity, prostitution, and its consequences, venereal disease; noncoital sex relations, such as kissing, petting, and masturbation; sex relations involving pregnancy, and hence illegitimacy, birth control, abortion; attitudes toward nudity, sex organs, pornography, sexual intercourse, and sexual lust; sex crimes; incest; perversions; sex rites; sex education; and courtship and dating.

In dealing with the sex customs of early English and American societies, an attempt will be made to discuss most of the above aspects of sexual behavior. Throughout the entire article it should be made clear that in all human behavior there is often a discrepancy in what is the expected, the *ideal* behavior, and what is actually practiced, the *real* behavior. For example, sexual chastity of women prior to marriage is an ideal behavior pattern in most Western societies. However, as far as real sex behavior is concerned, premarital chastity is not maintained by all women. Furthermore, the trend seems to be toward increased premarital sex relations, especially among engaged couples. Human sex behavior, real and ideal, exhibits trends. In general, according to Reiss (1957), the trend is toward greater permissiveness in sex relations and away from exploitative, body-centered types of sex activity to more affectionate, person-centered relations.

In most Western societies throughout recorded history, masculine and feminine roles have been generally well defined and differentiated. That is, they have been very much the same for the majority of classes (particularly for the middle and lower socioeconomic groups): men have been the protectors and breadwinners, women the homemakers.

The significant fact, of course, accounting for the divergence of role expectations is that women bear and nurse the children. They spend up to nine months in a condition that sets certain limits on the kinds of behavior they might engage in, and they usually nurse the infant for varying periods of time with milk created from their own breasts. Because pregnancy and nursing keep women close to the home, a number of domestic functions have become a part of the usual feminine role: child care, cooking, and housekeeping. The homemaker-mother role, it might be said, is the heart or core of the most common feminine role. One could infer that, because the pregnant woman and mother is somewhat handicapped during the period of pregnancy and lactation, the husband has been obliged by necessity to take over what has become the traditional role of the breadwinner and protector. Thus, if men, and not women, had babies, it could be inferred that these almost universal traditional roles would be reversed.

So-called masculine and feminine roles, therefore, depend upon how a particular society interprets the physical differences that exist between men and women. It is conceivable that some day, even in Western society, strong distinctions between traditional masculine and feminine roles will no longer exist. In fact, during recent times the distinctiveness of the roles has become less and less clear so that, in terms of roles, we might be said to be approaching a state of unisexuality—one in which very similar social roles exist for both sexes. Kirkpatrick (1955) presents some evidence that democracy is directly related to the equality of the sexes, whereas tyranny is directly related to the inequality of the sexes.

It will be seen later in this article that during a large part of recorded history women, especially at the middle and lower socioeconomic levels, have been regarded essentially as sexual property and menial servants, and have had a subordinate, second-class status.

Ideological Foundations of the Western Conception of Sex

Conceptions of sex held in Western society can be traced, for the most part, to the early Hebrew and Christian traditions. Among the early Hebrews there was a strong patriarchal pattern of authority in a generally monogamous form of marriage.

The key to the Hebrew attitudes toward sex, marriage, and the family can be found in the Hebrew male's idea of immortality and the biology of conception. In Mace's (1953) words: "It was through his sons that a man lived on, for through them his 'name' was continued, which to the Hebrew meant that his identity was preserved from extinction. The dying of a man's line was to be dreaded above everything else, for it was the quenching of the light of his immortality. Therefore at all costs he must secure sons to himself. If his wife did not give him children, he might resort to almost any expedient to remedy the situation. On this ground polygamy, concubinage, and divorce were excused if not actually commended; and it was on this foundation that the custom of the levirate rested." The high value that Hebrew men placed upon the virginity of the bride is also related to this idea of immortality. Thus, Mace (1953) states that: "To the man, his bride represented the soil in which his seed was to be planted, the means by which he could secure offspring which represented his immortality. It was therefore imperative that her sexuality should be his and his alone; any idea that he was securing 'second-hand goods' would be intolerable to him."

The Hebrews knew nothing about the part played by the ovum in conception. They believed that the male alone possessed the "seed" which, when placed or "planted" in the womb of a woman, became his child. The woman, they believed, gave nothing of herself to the child; she merely provided the "soil" in which the "seed" could grow and develop. So important was the continuance of the line, the man's immortality, that even incest was justifiable in order to preserve it, as in the case of Lot and his daughters.

Because the Hebrew husband had exclusive possession of his wife's sexuality, he could be sure that the sons she gave birth to were his. Adultery, which referred only to the sexual intercourse of a married woman with someone other than her husband, was a heinous crime because it put in jeopardy, in doubt, the immortality of her husband that was imperative to his peace of mind. For a man to die without rightful heirs to carry on his name was the greatest tragedy. In Mace's words again: "The unpardonable crime lies not in her defilement, but in the fact that she has shown that her integrity cannot be relied on. This makes her useless to any man for the chief purpose required of a wife—namely, to give him offspring which are indisputably his own."

However, in marked contrast to the Christian tradition that followed it, the early Hebrews had a very positive, naturalistic attitude toward sexual intercourse between husband and wife, believing that sex was blessed of God and given by Him as a good thing to be enjoyed. And in spite of the fact that the Hebrew husband had exclusive possession of his wife's sexuality, he did not have such possession of her person. She was not his slave. In comradeship with her husband, she ranked as his equal. In her home the Hebrew wife was very much a queen rather than a chattel.

What changed the Hebrew's positive attitude toward sex in marriage? And what led to changes in the high status the Hebrew wife once enjoyed as companion, homemaker, and mother?

The early Christians were of low socioeconomic status and there was a determined effort to destroy them. They were extremely unpopular. They had great hostility for the upper classes and advocated opposite practices. There was a strong Manichaean dualism in their philosophy in which the "spirit" was pitted against the "flesh." Their low regard for sex, marriage, and the family was, in part, attributable to their belief in the Second Coming of Christ and their desire to prepare for the Day of Judgment. Thus, to quote Mace (1953) again, ". . . the early Church viewed sex as vile. It condemned not only fornication, adultery, pederasty, masturbation, and bestiality, but also contraception, abortion, reading of 'lascivious' books, singing 'wanton songs,' dancing 'suggestive' dances, bathing in mixed company, wearing 'improper' clothing, and attending the theater. A sterner code would be hard to envisage. Several of the Church Fathers, notably Origen, actually practiced self-mutilation, becoming eunuchs for the sake of their religion."

In the teachings of Paul, Augustine, and Thomas Aquinas, the dualistic interpretation of sex won out over the Hebrew naturalistic interpretation. These men viewed virginity as the best state of all. None of them saw the really positive aspects of sex in marriage and they only grudgingly conceded that marriage, although it was a lower estate than celibacy, was still honorable. Cole (1955) indicated that the view that sex was evil, a view that persists today, thus had its origin in early Christianity, which rejected Hebrew naturalism with regard to sex in favor of an Oriental-Hellenistic dualism in which things of the "spirit" were regarded as higher than things of the "flesh."

As we shall see later in this article, the Christian dualistic interpretation of sex and the Hebrew idea of immortality combined to form a concept of sex that has persisted with little change throughout the history of England and America. Almost all the sex customs we shall consider can be traced to the above origins.

In summary, the early Hebrews left us with a naturalistic attitude toward sex, a double standard of sex morality, a view that married women were the sexual property of their husbands, an emphasis on the idea that immortality was achieved through the birth of sons whose biological relationship to the father was unquestioned, and great respect for women as companions, homemakers, and mothers. The early Christians, on the other hand, left us with a dualistic conception of sex, sex being regarded as a lower estate than virginity and celibacy, a view that sex was right only in marriage and primarily for procreation, that it was, at best, a necessary evil, and that women were the incarnation of sex and therefore the incarnation of sin.

Early English Sex Customs (ca. A.D. 450–1607)

Early Middle Ages, or Anglo-Saxon Period (ca. A.D. 450–1066)

In the early Middle Ages the sex mores, standards, and behavior of the English were largely controlled by what is known as Anglo-Saxon culture. In that culture everyone belonged to a localized kinship group (a sib) to which he was answerable and which in turn had much responsibility for him.

The purpose of marriage was to produce children who would continue and give strength to the sib. Men enjoyed patriarchal authority and its privileges; women were generally relegated to the status of menial servants. Extramarital and premarital intercourse were forbidden but were nevertheless prevalent. Penalties for such behavior consisted, for the most part, of the offending person, usually the male, paying damages to the injured party or to the guardian or master of the injured party, usually the female. According to the law of King Canute (also spelled Cnut) who ruled from 1017–1035, if it became public that a wife had committed adultery she would have both her ears and nose cut off.

If this law seems harsh, then the customs prevailing during the early Anglo-Saxon period were even more harsh. Says Sanger (1913): "When a couple were detected in the commission of the offense, the woman was compelled to commit suicide, to avoid greater tortures awaiting her if she refused. Her body was then placed on a pile of brushwood and consumed. Nor did her partner in guilt escape punishment; he was usually put to death on the spot where her ashes lay collected." Fortunately, most of these earlier customs were abandoned a short time after the Anglo-Saxons had settled in England.

With the decrease in the penalties for adultery and premarital sex relations, prostitution became popular. Saint Augustine's mission to England in 596 did not help matters. By the ninth century prostitution seems to have been widespread throughout the country. During the reign of King Athelstan (925–940) it was held by some canonists that the clergy had a right to demand one-tenth of the profits earned by prostitutes. An early law that encouraged prostitution provided that if a man seduced the wife of another, he was compelled to procure for him another woman, whom he was to pay for admitting him to her bed. This practice reduced female chastity to a marketable commodity whose loss could be repaid by a small sum of money. Women were thus a form of sexual property to be bought, sold, and insured against trespassing and damages.

The sources of information on sex behavior during this period include many questionable ones, but some documents suggest dominant attitudes and practices. Heterosexual relations seemed to be governed by a strongly authoritarian conception of loyalty, and women were regarded as *sexual property*. When a man vio-

lated the sexual mores his loss, if any, was what he had to pay in damages to the injured parties; it was an *economic loss*. On the other hand, if a woman violated the sexual mores she suffered primarily a *loss of social status*, sometimes also economic loss, and less often physical punishment, injury, or death.

For those women and men who wished to escape unhappy family life and sib relations the increasing number of Christian religious convents and monasteries provided refuge. There was evidently no thought of sex as being a particularly evil or good thing. The double standard of sex morality and the idea of immortality were very much like those of the early Hebrews who, like the early Anglo-Saxons, exacted the more severe penalties on a female committing adultery.

Middle and
Late Middle Ages (1066–1516)

More is known about the sex mores of this predominantly feudalistic period than about the earlier Anglo-Saxon period. Feudalism placed an even greater economic emphasis on family life than did the Anglo-Saxon culture.

The Christian Church had gained in strength and influence. Mates were selected by parents and male dominance continued. The Church evidenced inconsistent ideologies concerning the status of women. As the wife of Adam, woman was the evil instrument of the devil and inferior to man. But as the mother of Christ, she was pure and good and worthy of being placed on a pedestal. Sexual desire in itself was considered by the Church to be sinful and the sexual act excusable *only* if offspring were the possible and desired outcome. Contraception was therefore condemned as an obvious evil. Many authorities feel that the Church's doctrines on sex influenced the masses only superficially, however, and that few were troubled by the conflicting ideas and sentiments. And certainly the Church's doctrines had little effect on the licentious behavior of the royal courts or on the clergy itself. James in 1908 commented that during this period the clergy were the great corrupters of virtue among the lower classes, and were often the most frequent customers of prostitutes.

Of the greatest consequence during this period were, perhaps, the influences of chivalry. The Norman Conquest of 1066 brought to England the sexual folkways and mores, known as chivalry, of the Norman knights and ladies. In chivalry *romantic love* was glorified and regarded as more important than marriage and procreation. It agreed with the Church and feudal ideology that marriage was a duty, an economic transaction in which property could be preserved and transmitted to rightful heirs. But it exalted *love without marriage.* The general position was that love should be a free gift. Marriage extinguished love because it called for sexual union on the basis of duty. Love was regarded not as a duty but as a free choice of action by a free person.

Although chivalry was probably never practiced by more than a small minority of upper-class persons, its influence on literature was great. It gave rise to the ideal of romantic love, a conception that later became an integral part of modern Western sexual behavior. This romantic love involved an extramarital relationship, typically between a knight and the wife of his nobleman host, and was supposed not to involve sexual union, but when the nobleman was away the knight often went astray. Generally speaking, despite its decline, chivalry tended to raise the status of women to some degree.

Aside from the influences of chivalry, few factors changed the status of women from that of the earlier Anglo-Saxon period. The desire for the concentrated transmission of feudal estates to legitimate offspring tended to make chastity a woman's main virtue—that is, for women of privileged birth. But the feudal lord's power over his serfs was exemplified in the *jus primae noctis*—his right to have sexual intercourse with any new bride among his serfs. Women still seemed to be regarded as sexual property, therefore, and sex standards were developed that concerned rights and privileges with reference to that property. Chivalry was for that reason a challenge to feudalism and the treatment of women as chattels. But although the knights treated women of rank with respect and dignity, they often treated women of low rank with scorn and cruelty. Prostitution flourished during this period. In large cities there were official brothels—municipal, state,

or church perquisites. Calhoun (1919) related that strangers of note were supplied prostitutes at municipal expense. In 1161 Henry II legalized houses of prostitution near London, and since that time prostitution has flourished in England.

In summary, the sex customs among the English during the feudal period were based very much on a combination of the early Hebrew and early Christian conceptions of sex. The only addition was one that came from Norman knights, the idea of chivalry and romantic love. This ideal challenged the strong emphasis on the economic basis of marriage and on love as a duty. Instead, chivalry exalted love as something based not on duty but on free choice. This romantic complex, Kolb (1950) contends, is at its best the core of a democratic society and democratic human relationships. Thus, some authorities believe that the ideals fostered by chivalry during the Middle Ages contributed positively to present sex customs.

The Renaissance and Reformation Periods (1516–1607)

The Renaissance was the period in which traditional authoritarian power and orthodox thinking were challenged by Humanist scholars who ushered in a great intellectual awakening. On the continent Erasmus, in his famous book *Praise of Folly* (1511), exerted a tremendous influence on the leaders and thinkers of that era. Among his influential friends in England was Thomas More, whose *Utopia* (1516), a work on an ideal type of democracy, precipitated the English Renaissance.

In Wittenberg, Germany, one year later, Martin Luther, repelled by the tactics of Tetzel, a seller of indulgences, posted his now famous *Ninety-five Theses* on the door of the Castle Church at Wittenberg, an act that precipitated a series of events culminating in the Reformation and the founding of various Protestant churches. England had been influenced by Thomas More, Erasmus, and other leaders of the Renaissance, but their effort was rather to purify the old Church than to form a separate organization.

England's separation from the authority of the Pope in Rome was caused by the Pope's refusal (in 1527) to grant Henry VIII a divorce from his first wife and his queen, Catherine of Aragon. Henry had a violent passion for Anne Boleyn, one of Catherine's maids of honor, and, in order to get her to share his bed—which she allegedly refused to share unless he married her—was intent on getting a divorce from Catherine. Since the Pope was not willing to grant the divorce, Henry took matters into his own hands. He married Anne Boleyn privately in January, 1533, obtaining his divorce through Cranmer, Archbishop of Canterbury, in May, 1533, when Anne Boleyn was manifestly pregnant. This made his second marriage lawful.

In 1535 he declared himself supreme head of the Church of England. Thus, sexologically, Henry's relationship with Anne Boleyn was both adulterous and incestuous. For, on the authority of Bishop Fisher, it was said that Anne was Henry's illegitimate daughter and, as mentioned earlier, Henry had caused Anne's pregnancy *before* their marriage was declared lawful. Therefore, Henry was legally guilty not only of adultery and incest, but also of committing bigamy.

Out of this incestuous, adulterous, and bigamous union of Henry VIII and Anne Boleyn the ingenious Elizabeth, one of England's greatest queens, was born on September 7, 1533, less than five months after Henry's marriage to Anne had been declared lawful. Thus, ironically, Pope Clement VII's refusal to grant Henry VIII a divorce ended in the establishment of the Anglican Church and the beginning of the Reformation in England. Some historians believe that Henry's real reason for wanting to divorce Catherine was not the sexual attractiveness of Anne Boleyn but the fact that Catherine had denied him what among the early Hebrews every husband felt he must have in order to preserve his immortality: a son.

England's Reformation was set in motion by Henry VIII's making himself head of the Anglican Church in 1535, but the full flower of England's Renaissance blossomed during the reign of Henry's daughter Elizabeth, who ruled from 1558 to 1603 in what is often regarded as the Golden Age of English history. During this period the old feudalistic system broke up completely, papal authority was rejected, and great navigators such as Frobisher, Raleigh, and Drake set sail to discover new lands. Elizabeth

was the patroness queen under whom England's literature flourished magnificently with such immortal poets as Edmund Spenser, William Shakespeare, and Ben Jonson leading the field.

There was at this time an outburst of sexuality in the literature that reflected in part the libertarian sexual behavior occurring in private life. Although Elizabeth was often called the "Virgin Queen," most historians agree that she had little right to that title. It is said that she indulged in almost indiscriminate lewdness, and that Essex, Hatton, Leicester, Mountjoy, and numerous others shared her favors, many reporting that Elizabeth had an extremely passionate sexual nature. It is not surprising, therefore, that early English novels and dramas were full of sexual allusions and jests about sexual delinquencies, although much of the literature on love was clearly Platonic. In many ways, as A. Ellis notes in *The Folklore of Sex*, it might be said that sexuality in literature during the Elizabethan period was very much like the outburst of sexuality that occurred in American literature after World War II.

A real understanding of American sexual mores and behavior comes, however, from analyzing Luther's and Calvin's contributions to the Protestant Reformation and from examining that predominantly Calvinistic religious movement called Puritanism.

Both Luther and Calvin believed not that sex was good but that it was an inevitable, necessary evil. They had no appreciation for sex as a means of expressing married love. Reproduction remained for them, as it had for Augustine and Aquinas, the only truly positive purpose of sex. Sexual pleasure *sui generis* was regarded by them as evil and sinful. For them, particularly for Calvin, sexual relations were to be confined to marriage and even in marriage must be restricted. Only marriage could draw the veil over the sin of sex.

The most significant idea in the Calvinistic doctrine, as far as sexual behavior is concerned, was that of *predestination*. As Calvin saw it, God had created man in His likeness and image, and had given him all the blessings of life in the Garden of Eden on condition that he never eat the fruit of a certain tree. But man, tempted by woman, broke the contract, thus disobeyed

God and thereby lost all right not only to the joys of Eden but also to happiness in the world to come. The punishment did not stop there. Not only the original parents but also their children, and their descendants *forever*, being conceived in iniquity and born with the taint of original sin upon them, were in justice outside the pale of God's forgiveness. However, God, in his infinite mercy, sent his Son into the world to suffer in place of those who had been chosen to be saved. By the sacrifice of Christ on the Cross, all those whom God had predestined and foreordained to be saved were freed of the punishment that rightfully should have fallen upon them. Only such persons as God had "elected" to be saved could benefit from the sacrifice of the Son. All the rest of mankind, including unborn infants, were "elected" to be damned. Thus, man's acts could not influence his eternal fate; hence, the whole pressure of his religious interest was to *know* whether or not he was saved or damned.

The anxiety and tension created by not knowing led to a reinterpretation by Théodore de Bèze, first theologian of Calvinism, who stated that good works, although they could not influence salvation, could be interpreted as *signs of grace*. A good tree (one who was saved) could not bear evil fruit. Thereafter, the elect came to be identified with the "righteous," those who did the will of God, and the damned with "sinners," those who failed to obey God's will.

Max Weber (1930) has contended that this Calvinistic philosophy gave rise to and supported the development of modern capitalism, a movement led by the merchant class. The upper classes were licentious and pleasure-loving, characteristics that interfered with hard work and elevating one's economic status; most of all, hedonism interfered with finding out whether they were "righteous" or "sinners." Obviously, since sex was evil (although a necessary evil), those who indulged in sexual and other pleasures were in all probability damned. Likewise, those who obeyed the will of God were in all probability saved. Thus, activity in this world should be directed toward rational mastery of the flesh in the interest of the glory of God, not toward self-indulgence and hedonistic gratification.

Although Luther opposed the usurious tendencies of the bourgeoisie and Zwingli denounced the possession of private property in social life, Calvin justified both the practice of profits and the wisdom of usury, and thus gave religious sanction to commercial pursuits. The Puritans with this Calvinistic ideology became worldly ascetics. Their poetry was chastened, churches bared of ornament and filigree, theaters banned, music subdued, art purified, and marriage became to them a commercial transaction. Maypole processions and horse racing were forbidden. Smoking was regarded as a sinful practice. Gaudiness in dress was outlawed and domestic interiors reached extremes of colorless simplicity. Chastity in word, in thought, and in sex became the supreme virtue. "Money-making" was classified as the most "God-given" occupation. Everywhere there was a denial of things sexual, an avoidance of sex description, and a condemnation of anything suggestive of sex reality. Thus, the Puritans did not shrink from prescribing the death penalty for adultery, which they believed, as did Calvin, to be one of the gravest of all sins. As shall be seen later, in the American colonies the Puritans actually carried out the death penalty for adulterers.

Paralleling and complementing the Puritanism of the merchant classes was the growth in some upper-class quarters of the ideal of Platonic love. Romantic love, stimulated by Elizabethan literature, also became a motivating force in some marriages. Although most marriages were arranged in terms of financial considerations and women continued to be legally subordinate to men, the ideals of chivalry and Platonic love were instrumental in subsequent attempts to raise the status of women. In Platonic love there was neither male domination nor the adoration of women, as represented in chivalry. Instead, Platonic love called for an equalitarian friendship between the sexes based on mutual respect and sincerity. Although it is known that many of the Platonic academies that flourished were much like the medieval courts of love and were centers of sordid sensuality, the ideal of Platonic love had a significant effect on the attitudes of many thoughtful people and was perhaps one of the bases for the strong feminist movements that arose in the eighteenth and nineteenth centuries.

With the general population, however, the double standard of sex morality still persisted. Young men were expected to sow their wild oats and respectable young women were expected to remain chaste. The Puritan ideology characterized the double standard and sex outside of that in marriage and for procreation as for the damned. Male chastity became a novel virtue, but never attained the status of sanctity enforced upon females. In general, Puritan Englishmen were religious fundamentalists, unsociable, independent, patriarchal, and extremely fertile. Their families were among the largest in the world, and both wives and children were harshly treated. (Calvin even prescribed the death penalty for disobedient children.)

In the Renaissance there was a short period of naturalistic sexuality exhibited in sexual behavior, art, literature, and the theater. The Reformation and the rise of Puritanism led to sexual repression and worldly asceticism. Thus, the Puritans, although they rejected papal authority, as did other Protestants, in most matters they supported that authority, especially in regard to sex; that is, sex was considered evil and sinful, although necessary.

Generally speaking, the character of English sex behavior changed very little from the early Middle Ages to the founding of Jamestown in 1607.

In summary, the sexual heritage brought to the American colonies by the English consisted of some of the following characteristics:

1. There was an essentially dualistic conception of sex: sex was regarded as a necessary evil, its primary purpose being procreation.

2. The idea was held that woman was the incarnation of evil because she was "sex"; but she was a necessary evil. She had to be chaste and obedient to her husband. Her primary purpose was to bear children and thus to aid her husband in maintaining and preserving his immortality. To this the Puritans added the idea that the acquisition and preservation of property was good, as it was a means of knowing that one (and one's children) had been saved; in fact, it was the only way God could indicate whether one was saved or damned.

3. Marriage was considered a civil contract, an economic transaction, the purpose of which was the acquisition of wealth and property. The more economically advantageous the transaction, the more sure one was that he was among the saved rather than the damned.

4. Sexual repression was the order of the day and sexual relations outside of marriage were severely punished. Although the Puritans emphasized a single standard of sexual morality, the double standard was maintained by men who had followed the aristocratic mores, especially among the Cavaliers, with whom we shall deal later. Women were always more severely repressed than men.

5. Families were dominated by men and were semipatriarchal in nature, but male dominance was being challenged by the ideals of chivalry and Platonic and romantic love. These challenges to the Manichaean dualistic conception of sex were never a serious threat because Calvinistic Puritanism reaffirmed and strengthened that conception, giving it secular as well as religious support.

Sex Customs in Early America (1607–1800)

This portion of the article will deal with sex customs of the thirteen original English colonies (founded between 1607 and 1733) in North America during the seventeenth and eighteenth centuries.

During the seventeenth century the colonies were largely English as far as the composition of their population was concerned, but in the eighteenth century numerous immigrants came from northwestern and central Europe, primarily German, Dutch, Swedish, French, Scotch, and Irish settlers. By 1775 the Negro population was estimated at 500,000, or one-fifth of the total colonial population.

There were many reasons why immigrants came to settle in North America but the main ones seem to have been religious, political, and economic. During the seventeenth century thousands of Englishmen, particularly Puritans, came to America because of religious persecution. During that century the political situation in England also led to the immigration, particularly to Virginia, of many so-called

Cavaliers. The Cavaliers were the supporters of King Charles I, who had been defeated by the supporters of Parliament, the Roundheads, during the great English Civil War. To Virginia and the South these Cavaliers brought and developed an aristocratic tradition. However, in all of the colonies most of the people were from the middle or lower classes. Besides freemen and Negro slaves, there were also large numbers of indentured servants and criminals who made up the colonial population.

Farming was the chief occupation in all of the colonies. In the North wealthy farmers had the help of indentured servants; in the South slaves worked for a landed aristocracy that developed large plantations.

In general, the New England colonies, as contrasted with southern colonies, were made up of towns and their people were chiefly engaged in trade, commerce, and manufacturing. Farming was for sustenance and raw materials only. In the South, agriculture was the source of wealth and there was little commercial and industrial activity.

New England was predominantly Puritan; the middle colonies contained many different Protestant denominations, except for Maryland, which had a fair number of Catholics from England. In the South the Church of England was dominant.

The New England Colonies

The New England colonies consisted of Massachusetts, Connecticut, Rhode Island, and New Hampshire.

It was in the New England colonies that Calvinism was most severe. Children of Puritan families suffered through the gloomiest religious training. Family prayers were the custom, and the daily reading of the Bible by parents and children was never overlooked in the majority of families. The childhood years of many sensitive children were blackly overshadowed by the doctrines of original sin, predestination and election, and the punishments of a flaming, material hell. Puritans accepted unequivocally the view of the ancient Hebrews, of Paul, and of the early Christian Fathers that women were an inferior order of beings to be held in control by their lawful spouses and masters in order to prevent them from getting

into trouble. Like the early Church Fathers, the Puritans looked at sex as a sin and at women as the cause of original sin, the personification of sin. All adults were expected to marry. Unmarried adults were looked upon with suspicion, and in many communities unmarried men were taxed because they engaged in the selfish luxury of bachelorhood. It was thus expected that everyone live as a member of some household.

Although frontier conditions gave rise to greater independence in mate selection, parental consent was usually needed to undertake courtship. In Connecticut, young people who did not obtain parental permission to begin courtship were punished by fines. Both parents and the community worked together to control mate selection.

In early New England strict rules were laid down concerning the limits within which marriage was permitted. Persons violating these rules were punished by having to wear the capital letter "I" (for incest) sewn on the arm or the back.

To the Puritans, adultery was the most heinous of all sins, and they did not shrink from prescribing the death penalty for it. The records of the Massachusetts Bay Colony show that two persons were executed for adultery in 1644, and a third execution is mentioned by Cotton Mather in his *Magnalia Christi Americana.* No distinction of sex was made in the Puritan laws concerning adultery, both men and women suffering the consequences. However, female offenders were generally more severely treated than male offenders. Plymouth and Rhode Island prescribed a severe flogging rather than the death penalty. In addition to flogging, Plymouth also required the offender to wear a scarlet letter "A" upon the breast until death. Wearing this scarlet letter, graphically portrayed by Hawthorne in *The Scarlet Letter,* became law in Plymouth in 1658 and in Massachusetts in 1794. At Plymouth in 1639 a woman was sentenced to be "whipt at a cart tayle," to wear a badge upon her sleeve, and, if she went without the badge, to be burned in the face with a hot iron. With the prevalence of extreme penalties went some reluctance to convict, but there were still times when chivalry was certainly dead. In 1707, for example, an adulteress was sentenced in Plymouth to stand on the gallows, receive thirty lashes on her naked back, and forever wear the scarlet letter "A". The adulterer in this case was acquitted without any assignment of reason. In another case in Boston an adulteress had to stand in the marketplace and wear a placard reading, "Thus I stand for my adulterous and whorish carriage." Most adulterers were sentenced only to pay fines or to spend a few hours in the pillory, but, as among the ancient Hebrews, the female offender received a severe punishment.

Widows and widowers were always remarrying and were allegedly involved in illicit sexual relations while seeking new marriage partners. As evidenced by church and other official records, premarital fornication was quite common among engaged couples. In Connecticut, unmarried persons guilty of fornication were enjoined to marry, or were fined, or flogged—or suffered all three penalties. Some of the offenders were pilloried and others branded on the cheek. When a young married couple had a child "too soon," they had to make a public confession in church in order to save the infant from eternal perdition.

The unwed mother was often severely treated. Even though it might be known that she had been seduced and deserted she was generally whipped, fined, or imprisoned. Even if the father was identified, he was not punished in most cases, although he might be ordered to help support the child.

Yet in the records of the Groton Church between 1761-1775 the parents of one-third of the baptized children publicly confessed to having had premarital coitus. Thus, it seems that in Puritan times, despite the stern sexual code (perhaps because of it) sexual morality was not appreciably different from the mid-twentieth-century American variety.

Another form of illegitimacy was quite common in New England: this was the miscegenative type that resulted from illicit sex relations among whites, Negroes, and Indians. In 1705, Massachusetts forbade the intermarriage of whites and Negroes, and in 1786 this prohibition was extended to Indians. All such interracial marriages were declared void. Massachusetts kept these racist laws on the books until 1843.

Besides adultery, illegitimacy, and premarital and extramarital relations, sodomy was not uncommon and even buggery had to be dealt with occasionally.

Some authorities believe that it was because the stern Puritan sex mores did not allow for a class of recognized prostitutes that such illicit sex relations were so prevalent. Because the Puritans continually sought to prohibit all sexual activity save for procreation within marriage, their efforts at sex repression, gossip about scandals, numerous public confessions, and sadistic punishments—combined with the fact that they tended to lack other pleasures as well—tended to develop in them an unhealthy, obsessive interest in sex, an interest very much reminiscent of the preoccupation with sex in America today (Ellis, 1951, 1954).

The extreme sexual prudery of the Puritans is shown in the following event recorded by Earle (1960): "It was not prudent for the Puritan husband to be publicly demonstrative. Captain Kemble of Boston sat two hours in the public stocks (1656) for his 'lewd and unseemly behavior' in his kissing his wife 'publicquely' on the Sabbath upon his doorsteps when he had just returned from a voyage of three years."

The Massachusetts colony even had a law that women suspected of witchcraft be stripped and their nude bodies be scrutinized from head to toe by a male "witch-pricker," to see if there was not the devil's mark upon them.

Calhoun, eminent social historian of the American family, stated: "It cannot be doubted that the publicity accorded to cases of sex errancy was an unwholesome influence that tended to augment the evil by creating a kind of social hysteria. Such sensationalism was of the nature of suggestion. Living under terrible repression—environmental and social—the New Englanders found morbid satisfaction in conscience-prying and soul-display. The detailed descriptions of their offences that adulterers gave in church outwent the wildest flights of modern sensationalism as an enrichment of the service and doubtless brought and held a large audience."

Besides being the epitome of sex and sin, women were also very much like breeding animals: Green, a Boston printer, had 30 children, and families with 15 or more children were quite common. Maternal and infant mortality were extremely high. Typical of inscriptions on gravestones was the following: "Here lies——with twenty small children."

Yet, in spite of all the evidence of sexual subordination, there is little evidence that women themselves felt degraded or resentful. And, although marriage was a secularized and serious business, rude merriment occasionally attended New England weddings. Thus, in Marblehead the bridesmaids and groomsmen put the newly married couple to bed. It is also known that the bridal chamber was the scene of drinking and praying. Particularly among the wealthy it was common, it seems, to visit the bridal chamber.

That slavery was the occasion for sexual irregularities was suggested by an earlier statement concerning laws against miscegenation. In 1705 Massachusetts enacted a law condemning Negroes and mulattoes guilty of illicit sexual intercourse with whites to be sold out of the province.

Two unusual sex customs in New England deserve special mention and will be taken up in some detail: smock marriages and bundling.

Smock Marriages

An interesting custom of colonial times was the smock marriage. This practice was carried over from England, where it was believed that if a widow was married in her smock without any clothes or headgear on, the husband would be exempt from paying any of her debts that she had contracted before marriage. Many such marriages took place in the evening to save the bride from embarrassment, especially if she was extremely modest. In one case described by W. C. Prime in *Along New England Roads,* the bride stood inside a closet, wearing not a stitch of clothing, and held out her hand to the groom through a diamond-shaped hole cut in the door. In another case, described in Hall's *History of Eastern Vermont,* a widow stood naked and hidden in a chimney recess behind a curtain while marrying her groom. It is said that many of these marriages took place when the marrying widow wanted to avoid her past debts. Alice M. Earle (1893) indicated that although smock marriages were generally confined to the New England colonies, they were also known to have taken place in the middle

colony of Pennsylvania. A Mr. Hahn, traveling in Pennsylvania around 1748, reports that a bridegroom went to meet his widow bride on the highroad and announced in the presence of several reliable witnesses that the clothing he brought his bride and considerably threw over her immodestly clad body was only lent for the wedding festivity.

Bundling

The custom of bundling—of male and female lying together in bed, fully or partly dressed, with or without a board separating them, and usually covered with a blanket to keep warm—was practiced among courting or engaged couples as well as with traveling strangers as a show of hospitality. It was confined largely to the poorer classes, who generally lived in one-room houses and who, during cold weather and especially in the evenings, wanted to conserve firewood and candlelight.

There seem to have been several origins for this custom. Bundling is believed to have been common in England, Scotland, Holland, and Scandinavia and was brought to the colonies primarily by the Puritans and the Dutch. Among the Dutch it was called *queesting;* along the Massachusetts coast it was called *tarrying.* Because bundling often took place in the presence of parents, sexual intimacy was restrained. The custom was generally governed, it is said, by a kind of "honor system" so that violation of the sex mores was uncommon. In many cases, however, it is known that there was little restraint, and much of the illegitimacy of the times was attributed to this practice. Bundling was most common in the Connecticut valley, and was also fairly prevalent in Pennsylvania, New York, and other New England colonies.

That economy was the main purpose of bundling is illustrated by this popular verse of the times:

> Since in bed a man and maid,
> May bundle and be chaste,
> It does no good to burn out wood,
> It is a needless waste.

As mentioned earlier, to the abuses of this practice has been attributed much of the illegitimacy of the times, especially following the French and Indian War (1763), when returning veterans, habituated in camp and army life to vice and recklessness, stripped bundling of its alleged innocence. Yet despite the disrepute into which this practice came, mothers with daughters circulated this poem:

> The country girls in clusters swarm,
> And fly and buzz, like angry bees,
> And vow they'll bundle when they please.
> Some mothers too, will plead their cause,
> And give their daughters great applause,
> And tell them, 'tis no sin or shame,
> For we, your mothers, once did the same.

Judging from the following verse found in a 1785 almanac, bundling evidently helped some girls to win a potential marriage mate:

> But last of all, up speaks romp Moll
> And pleads to be excused,
> For how can she e'er married be
> If bundling be refused.

Some Puritan clergy defended this practice as being innocent, virtuous, and prudent, and said that it was attended by much more chastity than was the method of sitting on the sofa.

Because bundling was essentially an economic expedient, its decline is attributed largely to improved material conditions: larger and more efficiently heated homes, improved social conditions, and less difficult living conditions. Although bundling was a matter of court record as late as 1845, Stiles (1871) notes that it was generally abandoned about 1800.

The Middle Colonies

Of the thirteen English American colonies, New York, Pennsylvania, New Jersey, Delaware, and Maryland constituted the so-called middle colonies. Unlike the New England and southern colonies, the middle colonies were not almost exclusively English and homogeneous but were extremely heterogeneous. Accordingly, besides English immigrants, New York contained large numbers of Dutch and German settlers. In New Jersey, in addition to the English, there were Dutch, Swedish, Scotch, Irish, French, and German settlers. Pennsylvania was a cosmopolitan colony that included Dutch, Swedish, Scotch, Welsh, Swiss, Irish, and many Germans, in addition to the English. In fact, by 1775, Pennsylvania had about 100,000 Germans, one-third of that colony's population. Delaware had, in addition to Eng-

lish settlers, many Swedish and Dutch immigrants. Lord Baltimore attempted to make Maryland a refuge for English Catholics but persecution of Catholics had led to the establishment of the Church of England. Of the middle colonies, Maryland was least heterogeneous, being predominantly English.

Since the population of the middle colonies was so heterogeneous, the sex customs that prevailed also varied. In contrast to New England life, life in Dutch-dominated New York was very placid. Although the Dutch colonists had strict regulations concerning sexual behavior and severe sentences for adultery, sexual transgressions were never treated with the wrath that characterized New England's treatment of sex offenders. The Dutch had no death penalty for adultery, nor did they require adulterers to wear the scarlet letter "A." Women and children enjoyed a high status, an advantage not frequently found in the other colonies.

Bundling, or *queesting* as it was called among the Dutch, was quite common among young Dutch men and women, who would spend the night sleeping together at inns. They were said to have had great restraint and Dutch females were alleged to have reported that Dutch young men would never think of acting improperly during queesting time. In New York, consequently, the Dutch exerted a conservative, wholesome moral influence.

Although the Quakers in Pennsylvania contributed attitudes of great tolerance, miscegenation was often the occasion for the infliction of the severest penalties. Negroes were castrated in Pennsylvania for *attempting* rape of a white woman, and a Pennsylvania law of 1700 provided the death penalty to Negroes for buggery and for rape of a white woman. Illicit sexual intercourse of the lower-class whites —particularly indentured servants—often took place with Negroes, and many of these white female servants gave birth to mulatto bastards. Even Benjamin Franklin was openly accused of having colored mistresses.

Woolston (1921) stated that among the "Pennsylvania Dutch" (Germans from the Palatinate), premarital intercourse was an accepted custom.

In New Jersey in 1682, however, a man and woman who had indulged in premarital intercourse were ordered whipped on their naked bodies, the man to receive thirty lashes and the woman thirty-five lashes. The man was kept in jail one day and ordered to pay costs.

The Delaware assembly during the eighteenth century made sodomy, buggery, and rape capital offenses. For the killing of bastards it fixed the death penalty without benefit of clergy. Woolston said that, like the "Pennsylvania Dutch," it was a custom among the Delaware Swedes to engage in premarital sexual intercourse.

Like the southern colonies, plantation life dominated the life of Maryland. It was a custom in Maryland to use Negro males as "stallions" to increase the slave population. Polygamy, rape, and sodomy were capital offenses in Maryland. The death penalty was also often imposed for killing bastard children.

Because of their unusual composition, the middle colonies, compared to the other colonies, had a wide variety of sexual behavior, behavior which, as in all societies, reflected the values that each particular group held dear and wanted to perpetuate.

The Southern Colonies

The southern colonies, composed of Virginia, North and South Carolina, and Georgia, were made up largely of English settlers. Scotch and Irish were also to be found, particularly in Virginia and the Carolinas, and numerous French settled in South Carolina. Portuguese Jews were to be found in South Carolina and Georgia. And Georgia was a kind of melting pot for Scotch, Germans, Swiss, Italian Protestants, and Portuguese Jewish immigrants.

Plantation life predominated in these colonies, as did English culture. The "Southern Chivalry" we hear so much about was developed by the aristocratically aspiring Cavaliers but was not general among the common people. There was a definite double standard of sex morality in which promiscuity was condoned only on the part of husbands. Although courtesy, protection, and service were rendered to women of the aristocracy, they were rarely shown to servants, poor whites, and Negro women.

Premarital chastity and fidelity were thus expected of aristocratic white women but upper-class white men freely and quite casually exploited Negro women. It was reported that sexual relations among white men of high position and Negro slaves took place quite openly. It was known that several southern governors openly kept Negro mistresses and numerous southern gentlemen acknowledged their illegitimate children from such unions. Yet it is reported that although most of these white male-Negro female sex relationships were not enduring, some of them were genuine, lasting mutual attractions—a kind of concubinage. In fact, some white wives were so jealous of their husbands' love for particular Negresses that they sold them to distant plantation owners without their husbands' knowledge so that they could not be found and bought back. Frazier (1951) claims that all classes of whites were involved in such relations with Negro women.

Negro family life was highly unstable because slaves were usually bought and sold without the slightest consideration for family ties. It is known that where there was a shortage of Negro women, Negro men were set up as "stallions" to increase the slave production. And since mulatto slaves brought a high price on the slave market, some white masters urged their Negro slaves to have sex relations with their white indentured servants in order to increase their mulatto slave population.

Throughout the southern colonies the religious tenets of the Church of England were dominant. Generally, only marriages performed by the Church of England clergy were recognized.

The Englishmen who first came to Virginia were primarily fortune hunters; they were not family men like the New Englanders. Later on, men were encouraged to marry, settle down, and develop the land. Most of these settlers were of humble origin and there were also many indentured servants and criminals. Women were domestic and subordinate. The "ducking stool" was often used to curb gossiping women. A landed aristocracy stimulated by the Cavaliers made familism strong in the South.

Because maternal and infant mortality was high as a result of excessive childbearing, many men married as much as four or more times. Widows were eagerly sought by men—for their sexual experience and economic advantage—

and illicit sexual relations were apparently quite common among widowers and widows. But since a double standard of sexual morality existed, women received whippings more often than men. Punishments for sexual offenders were much less severe than those meted out in Puritan New England.

Miscegenation was quite common between whites, Negroes, and Indians, and many laws were enacted to prevent and punish such sex unions. Attempted rape of a white woman by a Negro male was punished by castration.

In the South, generally speaking, as Frumkin (1956a) has shown, sex morals were largely based on economic questions and were so regarded by legal authorities.

Summary

Most of the differences in the various regional colonies were related to the contrasts between village and plantation life and between Puritan and Cavalier attitudes toward sex and other behavior. Families were viewed as agencies for the regulation of sex, and the primary purpose of sex was essentially procreation. The sexual ethics of the ancient Hebrews and the early Church Fathers persisted in supporting male dominance, premarital chastity, marital fidelity on the part of the wife in particular, filial piety; and the dualistic conception of sex as an evil, an evil made obligatory by the necessity of reproduction for survival. The naturalistic attitude toward sex manifested during the Elizabethan period in England never found expression in the American colonies, except, perhaps, to some extent on the part of Cavaliers in the southern colonies. Women were regarded as inferior beings, as breeding animals and sexual property. It seems that the Calvinistic Puritans indelibly marked the American character with what Briffault called an eternal Christian sexophobia.

General Summary and Conclusions

Sexual behavior, like all human behavior, primarily learned and symbolic in nature is rooted in ever changing historical-social situations. Therefore it is necessary in order to understand early English and American sex customs, to seek their social origins in the his-

tory of the ancient Hebrews and early Church Fathers. For it was their social situation, teachings, and beliefs that formed the basis for most of these sex customs.

Generally speaking, the character of early English and American sex behavior remained quite consistent from the early Middle Ages (*ca.* 450) to the election of Jefferson to the presidency of the United States in 1800. Only during the English Renaissance—the Elizabethan Age—was the character of sex behavior essentially different, essentially free from the Manichaean dualism that had continually dominated and still dominates Western sexual ideology and behavior. For the 1,350 years covered in this article, except for the relatively short duration of the Elizabethan Age, early English and American sex customs were characterized by some of the following features:

1. Sex was regarded as a necessary evil, its only justification being procreation and the maintenance of male immortality.

2. Woman was the incarnation of evil because she was "sex." She was necessary as the "soil" in which the male "seeds" grew, and her main function was essentially that of a breeding animal.

3. Marriage was a civil contract, a business whose purpose, as perpetuated by the Calvinistic Puritans, was to acquire wealth and property in order to determine whether one was among the saved or the damned.

4. Sexual repression was the everlasting order of the era. Except for procreation, sex activity interfered with mammonistic money-making that helped one, in the view of Calvinistic predestinationism, to find out if one were damned or saved. Women were always more repressed than men, for the double standard in favor of men generally prevailed. Thus, punishments for female sexual offenders were consistently more severe than for male offenders.

5. Families were dominated by men and were generally patriarchal or semipatriarchal in nature. During the late Middle Ages, the Reformation, and the Renaissance the ideals of chivalry and of Platonic and romantic love challenged this dominance.

6. But the dualistic conception of sex—the idea that sex was evil, that women were sexual property, and that sex must be repressed—was

reaffirmed and strengthened by the Calvinistic Puritanism that dominated the English American colonies during the seventeenth and eighteenth centuries and still finds expression in America today.

Christian sexophobia is not a simple matter. It is a complex phenomenon that has had a long development and can only be understood by examining the main historical trends of Western civilization. In recent decades this sexophobia has been re-examined in the light of anthropological, psychoanalytical, social psychological, and other behavioral science viewpoints, and has been seriously challenged by such brilliant authorities on the nature of human nature as Sigmund Freud, Havelock Ellis, Bertrand Russell, Margaret Mead, Alfred Kinsey, Albert Ellis, and others. This challenge has grown in strength but has not yet been able to uproot the deeply ingrained dualistic conception of sex that converted the Hebrews' naturalistic attitude into the Calvinistic Puritan antisexual attitudes. These attitudes have gained new impetus in recent times not through the new religious bodies resulting from the Reformation but rather from the ever increasing vigor of the Church that Luther revolted against more than four centuries ago. What is in store as far as man's future sexual behavior is concerned is a matter that only time can answer. However, there are signs everywhere that sex is beginning to be viewed and acted upon in a perspective more consistent with our present knowledge and understanding of the nature of human nature.

References

Abrams, A., *English Life and Manners in the Later Middle Ages.* New York: E. P. Dutton & Co., Inc., 1913.

Beowulf, A metrical translation into modern English by J. R. C. Hall. Cambridge: Harvard University Press, 1926.

Calhoun, Arthur W., *A Social History of the American Family* (Vol. I). Cleveland: A. H. Clark Co., 1919.

Calverton, V. F., and Schmalhausen, S. D. (eds.), *Sex in Civilization.* Garden City, N.Y.: Macaulay, 1929.

Chaucer, Geoffrey, *Canterbury Tales.* Numerous editions.

Cole, William G., *Sex in Christianity and Psychoanalysis.* New York: Oxford University Press, 1955.

Davis, Kingsley, "Jealousy and Sexual Property." *Social Forces 14;* 395-405, 1936.

Davis, William S., *Life in Elizabethan Days.* New York: Harper & Brothers, 1930.

"Deans Will Act on Question of Parietal Dormitory Hours." *Reserve Tribune* (Western Reserve University), *63;* 1, March 24, 1967.

Earle, Alice M., *Customs and Fashions in Old New England.* New York: Charles Scribner's Sons, 1893.

Earle, Alice M., *Colonial Dames and Goodwives.* Boston: Houghton Mifflin Co., 1895.

Ellis, Albert, *The Folklore of Sex.* New York: Charles Boni, 1951.

Ellis, Albert, *The American Sexual Tragedy.* New York: Twayne, 1954.

Frazier, E. Franklin, *The Negro Family in the United States* (rev. ed.). New York: The Dryden Press, 1951.

Frumkin, Robert M., "Early American Sex Customs." *Sexology 22;* 354-361, 1956.

Frumkin, Robert M., *The Meaning of Sociology* (ed. 2). Buffalo: University of Buffalo Bookstore, 1956a.

Frumkin, Robert M., *The Patient as a Human Being.* Buffalo: University of Buffalo Bookstore, 1956b.

Frumkin, Robert M., "Authoritarian Sexual Jealousy and American Ideology." *J. Fam. Welfare 4;* 1-7, 1957.

Genesis, 19:30-38.

Goodsell, Willystine, *A History of Marriage and the Family* (rev. ed.). New York: The Macmillan Co., 1939.

Hawthorne, Nathaniel, *The Scarlet Letter.* Numerous editions.

Hodgkin, R. H., *A History of the Anglo-Saxons* (2 vols.). Oxford: The Clarendon Press, 1935.

Howard, George E., *A History of Matrimonial Institutions* (3 vols.). Chicago: University of Chicago Press, 1904.

"In Baltimore Program: 'Active' Girls Given Birth Control Pills." *Cleveland Plain Dealer 126;* 1, April 19, 1967.

Irving, Washington, *Knickerbocker's History of New York* (2 vols.). New York: G. P. Putnam's Sons, 1894.

James, B. B., *Women in England.* Philadelphia: G. Barrie & Sons, 1908.

James, M., "Puritanism." In E. R. A. Seligman and A. Johnson (eds.), *Encyclopedia of the Social Sciences* (Vol. XIII). New York: The Macmillan Co., 1934.

Kirkpatrick, Clifford, *The Family.* New York: The Ronald Press Co., 1955.

Kolb, Wilson, "Family Sociology, Marriage Education, and the Romantic Complex." *Social Forces 29;* 65-72, 1950.

Leuba, Clarence, *The Natural Man.* New York: Doubleday & Co., Inc., 1954.

Leuba, Clarence, *The Sexual Nature of Man and Its Management.* New York: Doubleday & Co., Inc., 1954.

Lindesmith, Alfred R., and Strauss, Anselm L., *Social Psychology* (rev. ed.). New York: The Dryden Press, 1956.

Mace, David R., *Hebrew Marriage*. New York: Philosophical Library, Inc., 1953.

Mannheim, Karl (translated by L. Wirth and E. A. Shils), *Ideology and Utopia*. New York: Harcourt, Brace & Co., 1936.

Margold, Charles W., *Sex Freedom and Social Control*. Chicago: University of Chicago Press, 1926.

May, Geoffrey, *Social Control and Sex Expression*. London: George Allen & Unwin, 1930.

May, Geoffrey, "Prostitution." In E. R. A. Seligman and A. Johnson (eds.), *Encyclopedia of the Social Sciences* (Vol. XII). New York: The Macmillan Co., 1934.

Mead, Margaret, *Sex and Temperament*. New York: William Morrow & Co., Inc., 1935.

Murdock, George P., *Social Structure*. New York: The Macmillan Co., 1949.

Page, Thomas N., *Social Life in Old Virginia*. New York: Charles Scribner's Sons, 1898.

Partridge, Eric, *Shakespeare's Bawdy*. London: Routledge, 1947.

Prestage, Edgar (ed.), *Chivalry*. New York: Alfred A. Knopf, Inc., 1928.

Queen, Stuart A., and Adams, John B., *The Family in Various Cultures*. Philadelphia: J. B. Lippincott Co., 1952.

Reiss, Ira L., "The Treatment of Premarital Coitus in 'Marriage and the Family' Texts." *Social Problems 4;* 334-338, 1957.

Sanger, William W., *The History of Prostitution*. New York: Medical Publishers Co., 1913.

Seward, Georgene H., *Sex and the Social Order*. New York: McGraw-Hill Book Co., 1946.

Stiles, Henry R., *Bundling*. Albany: Knickerbocker Publishing Co., 1871.

Thorpe, B. (ed.), *Ancient Laws and Institutes of England* (Vol. I). London: Commissioner on the Public Records of the Kingdom, 1840.

Turner, E. R., *History of Slavery in Pennsylvania*. Baltimore, 1911.

Weber, Max (translated by Talcott Parsons), *The Protestant Ethic and the Spirit of Capitalism*. New York: Charles Scribner's Sons, 1930.

Woolston, Howard B., *Prostitution in the United States* (Vol. I). New York: Century Co., 1921.

Zimmerman, Carle C., *Family and Civilization*. New York: Harper & Brothers, 1947.

ROBERT M. FRUMKIN

Eugenics

THE word "eugenics" was coined by Sir Francis Galton in 1890 as "the study of forces under social control which enhance or impair the inborn qualities of future generations."

That inborn qualities could be greatly modified by artificial selection was appreciated by ancient civilizations, which developed breeds of livestock by the application of rule-of-thumb methods of selective mating.

History

The idea that human beings differ in their hereditary endowment is also very old. Without attempting a review that would be mainly of antiquarian interest, a few references to Greek writings may not be out of place. In the sixth century B.C., Theognis took a pessimistic view of then current human mating practices:

With kine and horses, Kurnus, we proceed
By reasonable rules, and choose a breed
For profit and increase, at any price,
Of a sound stock without defect or vice.
But in the daily matches that we make
The price is everything; for money's sake,
Men marry; women are in marriage given.
The churl or ruffian, that in wealth has thriven,
May match his offspring with the proudest race.
Thus everything is mixed, noble and base.
If, then, in outward manner, form and mind,
You find us a degraded, motley kind,
Wonder no more, my friend; the cause is plain,
And to lament the consequence is vain.

Among the Spartans, mate selection was practiced, and the age at which marriage took place was regulated to assure procreation at the time of life when it was believed the production of fine progeny was most likely. Exposure of weak or defective infants to the elements was practiced by the Greeks and by many other peoples throughout history. In *The Republic,* Plato set forth a comprehensive code of eugenics that has become almost a horrible example of what an abstract philosophical approach can lead to.

Although different mating systems—endogamic or exogamic—have affected the genetic constitutions of human populations throughout history, their eugenic effects have been mainly accidental or incidental. The exact knowledge of the genetic process on which a rational eugenic policy might be based has existed for less than half a century. Until the key had been found to the riddle of heredity, man's penchant for theorizing had little practical value, and these ancient writings have now only an historical interest. Not until the latter half of the nineteenth century did factual bases for manipulating the "inborn qualities of future generations" begin to be developed. The publication of Darwin's *Origin of Species* in 1859 marked a turning point in biological science and provided the intellectual environment for experimental work on the phenomenon of evolution.

Darwin envisioned evolution as an interaction among the variable factors inherent in all organisms exposed to the rigors of survival. Those organisms better adapted to a particular environment tended to survive and to perpetuate their kind. The less well adapted variants failed to survive or to reproduce. This selective "sieve by veto" of the environment, operating over hundreds or thousands of generations, resulted in the emergence of strains of organisms showing remarkable adaptation to most varied environments. Darwin was puzzled by the nature of the variability of organisms that he saw as an essential factor in the evolution process. His speculations as to how and why variability occurred have proved in the light of much experimental hindsight to have been mainly erroneous.

The key that unlocked the mystery of variability and heredity was provided by Abbot Gregor Mendel in 1865. His experiments with peas, conducted in a monastery garden in what is now Czechoslovakia, formed the basis for the modern science of genetics. Mendel's pioneering was so revolutionary that thirty-five years elapsed before biological concepts had reached a point in development where his discoveries could be understood and evaluated. The science of genetics actually began with the rediscovery of Mendel's paper in 1900, rather than in 1865.

During this interval a cousin of Charles Darwin, Sir Francis Galton, had become convinced that heredity was a prime factor in determining the quality of human beings. Basing his studies on Darwin's evolution concept, Galton attacked the problem of heredity and environment—of nature *vs.* nurture—statistically. Between 1869 and 1883, he published three books supporting his view that nature—the inborn qualities of a human being—was a major component in the development of the gifted individual. In *Hereditary Genius, English Men of Science: Their Nature and Nurture,* and *Inquiries into Human Faculty* Galton reported his statistical analyses of the background of gifted individuals. He also pioneered in pointing out the value of studying identical twins as a means of learning more about the nature-nurture problem.

Galton's work broke new ground in analyzing factors that contribute to the development of human intelligence and personality. His studies convinced him that heredity played an essential part in the development of individuals of unusual competence, and this became the motivation of his later years, leading to his founding of the eugenics movement. Toward the end of his life he wrote (1908):

I take eugenics very seriously, feeling that its principles ought to become one of the dominant motives in a civilized nation, much as if they were one of its religious tenets. . . . Individuals appear to me as partial detachments from the infinite ocean of Being, and this world as a stage on which evolution takes place, principally hitherto by means of natural selection, which achieves the good of the whole with scant regard to that of the individual.

Man is gifted with pity and other kindly feelings; he has also the power of preventing many kinds of suffering. I conceive it to fall well within his province to replace Natural Selection by other processes that are more merciful and not less effective.

Galton devoted the later years of his life to promoting an acceptance of his view on eugenics and, through his influence, the Eugenics Education Society was founded in London in 1908. He bequeathed his fortune at his death to the University of London for the establishment of the Galton Laboratory.

Recent Advances

The past half-century has seen a very rapid advance in the science of genetics, adding to the effectiveness of animal-breeding techniques. The problem of nurture *vs.* nature has been experimentally studied, and in its original form it has been found to be meaningless in the sense that no blanket answer can be given. It is an approach useful only in terms of specific heredity and specific environment. For example, blood groups and eye color are very little affected by environment, whereas body weight and intelligence are considerably more labile.

That many important physical characteristics of human beings are largely determined by genetic differences can no longer be questioned. Pedigree studies of many characteristics, both normal and pathological, are to be found in the literature. These heredity-determined differences range from trivial characteristics such as a blaze of white hair or a minor variation in ear form to profound physical or mental defects: sickle-cell anemia, sex-linked muscular dystrophy, color blindness, specific forms of mental defect, and the like.

The question of the extent to which mental, emotional, and personality differences are due to heredity is still under exploration.

Frederick Osborn (1951) surveyed the psychological and genetic studies on the interaction of heredity and environment made over the previous twenty-five years, and concluded:

1. Variations in capacity for developing intelligence tend to follow family lines. Similarity of hereditary factors accounts for a substantial part of the known similarity in intelligence between parents and children.

2. Individual differences in intelligence are in part due to individual differences in inherited capacity. When the environment of two unrelated individuals is similar, differences in heredity probably play the major part in making the individuals different. When their environments differ and their heredity is somewhat similar, the environment is probably the major cause of their differences.

3. There is no evidence on hereditary factors as a cause of differences in the average intelligence of racial or regional groups in this country. Known differences in their environment are probably sufficient to account for present differences in the average intelligence of racial and regional groups.

4. Hereditary factors appear to account for a part of the average differences in intelligence between the skilled groups and the unskilled occupational groups....

In order to obtain a proportionate increase in the number of persons at the upper levels of intelligence, it would be necessary to raise the level of hereditary capacity for intelligence.

That evaluation holds today. Although our picture of the genetic mechanism has changed, Galton's appraisal of the importance of inborn qualities in the emergence of high intellectual endowment has ample support. Granting that the expression of inborn endowment of man can be considerably modified, the evidence indicates that the inborn component remains paramount: it sets the limits.

Now, whether these limits are achieved depends on the nature and effectiveness of environmental stimuli. "Wooden legs are not inherited, but wooden heads are," Dr. E. G. Conklin remarked many years ago. The observation still holds.

Even before Osborn, a group of distinguished geneticists subscribed to a statement that explicitly spelled out the tremendous improvement in the human breed that might be made in a very few generations if the enhancement of the inborn qualities of future generations of mankind were purely a genetic exercise:

. . . The intrinsic genetic characteristics of any generation can be better than those of the preceding generation only as a result of some kind of *selection,* i.e., by those persons of the preceding generation who had a better genetic equipment having produced more offspring, on the whole, than the rest, either through conscious choice, or as an automatic result of the way in which they lived. Under modern civilized conditions such selection is far less likely to be automatic than under primitive conditions, hence some kind of conscious guidance of selection is called for. To make this possible, however, the population must first appreciate the force of the above principles, and the social value which a wisely guided selection would have.

. . . conscious selection requires, in addition, an agreed direction or directions for selection to take, and these directions cannot be social ones, that is, for the good of mankind at large, unless social motives predominate in society. This in turn implies its socialized organization. The most important objectives, from a social point of view, are the improvement of those genetic characteristics which make (a) for health, (b) for the complex called intelligence and (c) for those temperamental qualities which favour fellow-feeling and social behaviour rather than those (today most esteemed by many) which make for personal "success," as success is usually understood at present.

A more widespread understanding of biological principles will bring with it the realization that much more than the prevention of genetic deterioration is to be sought for and that the raising of the level of the average of the population nearly to that of the highest now existing in isolated individuals, in regard to physical well-being, intelligence and temperamental qualities, is an achievement that would—so far as purely genetic considerations are concerned—be physically possible within a comparatively small number of generations. Thus everyone might look upon "genius," combined of course with stability, as his birthright. And, as the course of evolution shows, this would represent no final stage at all, but only an earnest of still further progress in the future.

Mutations and the Human Gene Pool

The years that have elapsed since the "Geneticists' Manifesto" was written have seen remarkable developments in genetic theory. Some of these give a heightened urgency to the need for developing means to conserve the adaptive efficiency of the gene pool of the human species. In his presidential address before the Society for the Study of Human Genetics in 1950, Dr. H. J. Muller explored the proposition that the lack of selection against nonadaptive genes means an inevitable deterioration of the human species. The principle is illustrated by the loss of organs and even organ systems in parasitic species. It is now clear that this deterioration is not due to a Lamarckian response to the nonuse of the organs, but rather to the buildup of nonadaptive mutations in organs no longer having survival value for the species, and thus no longer exposed to effective selection.

The reason for this is to be found in the nature of the mutation process, which has been intensively studied in many organisms during the past thirty years. It is now established that mutations occur spontaneously at all loci, the rate of occurrence varying with the locus. These mutations are conceived of as being biochemical changes in a highly complex system, which is integrated and timed to trigger developmental and/or metabolic sequences. Defects such as albinism or diabetes are due to the absence of gene-controlled enzymes essential to pigment synthesis or to carbohydrate metabolism.

The development of organic adaptation is thus seen to consist of a process of scanning and screening the mutative changes that are constantly appearing in any species, the vast majority of which are deleterious.

The scanning process consists of sexual reproduction, which includes meiosis (crossing-over) and the formation of gametes, showing all possible combinations of parental genes, and the random recombination of these gametes at fertilization. A wide array of genotypic combinations from heterozygous parents is displayed in the progeny, to be screened by the test of survival. Under natural conditions this consists mainly of the ability of the organism to live and to reproduce.

The Problem of the Future

Until very recently, it would appear that the scanning-screening process has applied to the human species in much the same manner as it has applied to all other organisms. But Dr. Muller estimates that in order to maintain the present level of morbid mutations in the human gene pool, some 20 per cent of the population would have to suffer selective elimination through death or nonreproduction. Since in the advanced industrial countries today less than 5 per cent of the population fails to reach the age of 25—the mid-period of reproductivity —it is apparent that a buildup in mutations is occurring. Muller concludes that today "nothing like the equilibrium quota is eliminated by death before the age of reproduction." Nor, it might be added, by nonreproduction.

The rate at which this deterioration in the human gene pool is occurring is not definitely established, for adequate statistics do not exist in any country to permit a direct estimate of the existing load of morbid mutations. Over a short period of time it is a matter of no great consequence, for the buildup will unquestionably be slow. In the long run, however, the effects may be profound.

Muller foresees that the elimination of adaptive selection will eventually result in the biological disintegration of the human species:

Our descendants' natural biological organization would in fact have disintegrated and have been replaced by complete disorder. Their only connections with mankind would then be the historical one that we ourselves after all had been their ancestors and sponsors, and the fact that their once human material was still used for the purpose of converting it artificially into some semblance of man. However, it would in the end be far easier and more sensible to manufacture a complete man de novo, out of appropriately chosen raw materials, than to try to refashion into human form those pitiful relics which remain.

As matters stand today, it appears that the current patterns of survival and fertility are not calculated to enhance the inborn qualities of the human species, either physically or psychologically, but rather are increasing the proportion of morbid genes in the gene pool of the modern industrial nations. The almost universal existence of birth rates that favor the reproduction of the less intelligent offers no prospect for upgrading the inborn intelligence factors of future generations, and the need to substitute some form of humane and voluntary selection for the stern selective forces of the past is the crucial eugenic dilemma. To hope that entire gene systems can be made over through some form of microgenetic magic is about as realistic at the present time as proposing to solve the population problem by resorting to space travel.

Accomplishments and Hypotheses

How this eugenic miracle is to be brought about remains an enigma, and the eugenics movement has not made much progress in coming to grips with this problem. In the early years of the eugenics movement in England, it was naively assumed that the "divinely ordained" social classes into which the English population had traditionally been divided provided a ready-made criterion of eugenic excellence. To enhance the inborn quality of future generations nothing more would be needed than to encourage the breeding of the aristocrats and to check the breeding of the plebeians. In the United States, in a society lacking hereditary classes, the early eugenists could turn to no such convenient criterion of inborn excellence. This difficulty was met by the equally questionable assumption that race provided the necessary criterion. The eugenic salvation of mankind was given into the hands of the Great Blond Nordic. This theme developed an interesting variation in the delimitation of "problem families" (the Jukes, the Kallikaks, and the Nams). It was hoped that their elimination through compulsory sterilization would pretty much solve the eugenic problem.

The adoption by Adolf Hitler of a program of "race purification" based on superficial and perverted derivatives from the naive concepts of the early eugenic enthusiasts understandably engendered opposition to any program of eugenic reform. Yet the problem remains.

The Scandinavian countries, with relatively homogeneous and stable populations, have made considerable progress in locating in their populations some strains that have a high frequency of human hereditary disease. Programs of voluntary sterilization with adequate legal safeguards have made some impact in reducing hereditary defect. But these are trivial in terms of the over-all problem of enhancing the inborn qualities of the human population.

Since its establishment in 1921, the American Eugenics Society has undergone some changes of outlook and policy. Over the past ten years it has evolved the policy that it is possible to build into the culture a pattern of living which, without conscious volition on the part of the individual, will automatically assure a eugenic distribution of births. In a "Program of Positive Eugenics" published by the Society in 1953, it was stated:

> . . . there are strong grounds for believing that the same means could be used to improve both the social and genetic inheritance. There is no divergence between the qualities desirable in a good social inheritance and the inherent capacities of a good genetic inheritance. The home conditions which are best suited to child development depend among other things on affection, intelligence, patience, honesty, loyalty and respect for the individual. . . . It seems almost certain that a distribution of births which would improve the social inheritance along these lines could be developed in such a way that at the same time it would tend to improve the genetic inheritance.

This has evolved into a "Eugenic Hypothesis" that the criterion for eugenic excellence is the "healthy family." "Health now includes almost all aspects of human well-being" and these aspects are held to be related. "Health, like liberty, is indivisible." This "healthy-family" complex is assumed to be transmitted in families more or less as a unit. The postulate therefore is that, once reproduction has become a matter of voluntary choice, the healthier families will desire to have the larger number of children and the unhealthy families will automatically desire to have the smaller number of children.

All that is necessary, according to this view, to start on the road to a eugenic millennium is a social situation in which parenthood is voluntary. The enhancement of the inborn qualities of the human breed will follow almost automatically.

That eugenic progress can be assured without the need for the individual to make choices except those that are assumed to be virtually automatic by reason of being a member of a "healthy family" or an "unhealthy family" appears to err on the side of naiveté. Furthermore, the assumption that all members of "healthy families" carry an equally favorable genetic endowment is untenable in view of the extreme heterozygosity of the human species. Finally, and the most serious objection to the

"Eugenic Hypothesis," the existence of a genetic complex that can be defined as a "healthy family" runs counter to all genetic experience. A basic tenet of genetics is that the units that transmit heredity are discrete and independently inherited. Nor can the phenomenon of linkage, which tends to transmit genes located on the same chromosome as a unit, be adduced to support this concept. And crossing-over means that in populations—as distinct from pedigrees—the unfavorable alleles are as likely to be linked as are the favorable alleles of the "healthy family" genes.

Only when relatively pure genetic strains of human beings exist can the "healthy family" act as an adequate selective criterion. Such strains are not to be found today; and human mating patterns do not provide much basis for expecting them to appear. The effective selection envisioned by Dr. Mueller and the signers of the "Geneticists' Manifesto" cannot be achieved by the application of the "Eugenic Hypothesis."

It is unfortunate that the publication of the "Eugenic Hypothesis" produced so little comment or discussion. The writer proposed an alternative hypothesis, hoping it might stimulate further exploration of what appears to be the central problem of eugenic motivation. This took the view that an effective eugenic program must necessarily be based on the individual rather than the family as the unit of selection. Its effectiveness would therefore depend upon highly motivated individual decisions: the motivation would have to be strong enough to result in individual decisions *not to have progeny* where the genetic prognosis was unfavorable.

It was postulated that a basis exists for developing such a compelling motivation: the overwhelming desire felt by virtually all women to bear perfect children, without physical or mental defect. Obstetricians testify that this desire is so deep-seated and overwhelming that the first question a woman asks about her newborn child is not "Is it a boy or girl?" but "Is the baby *perfect*?"

During the years since Galton, very little progress has been made in developing, identifying, and utilizing those forces under social control that might be called on to produce a eugenic society. Until the effective "motivational pressure points" that will promote sound eugenic decisions are identified and applied to bring about a selective pattern of births, eugenics will remain a paper discipline.

The crux of the eugenic dilemma lies in how to manipulate these "forces under social control" in order to assure a selectively favorable pattern of births. That social and economic factors influence fertility cannot be questioned. For example, in the United States over two-thirds of the female population between the ages of 20 and 24 is married, as compared to less than a fifth in Ireland. If the one Irish woman in five who marries during the years of maximum fertility had a better-than-average inborn endowment, the genetic quality of the Irish people would be rapidly enhanced. If the reverse were true, eugenic deterioration could be very rapid. No evidence exists that provides an answer to which—if either—of these situations exists in Ireland.

In the United States, on the other hand, where a situation approaching pangamy exists, any possibility of rapid enhancement of inborn qualities seems much less likely. Pangamy may be democratic, but it can hardly be selective. When virtually every woman produces approximately her quota of children, effective birth selection does not exist.

Neither in England nor in the United States —or in any other country, for that matter—does there exist a climate of opinion extensive enough and strongly enough motivated to form the basis for an effective program. The steps which are being taken to develop such a climate of opinion are pathetically inadequate to produce any measurable effect.

In a population enjoying a very high degree of genetic enlightenment, the urge toward perfection could be a compelling and effective eugenic motivation. This is not the case today, anywhere on earth. Were it possible to identify in the heterozygote a majority of the existing lethal and morbid genes, a major revolution in attitudes toward reproduction might be brought about. Much progress in identifying heterozygotes has been made in recent years; and such a possibility may be realized before very long.

However, until more is learned, the mandate to perfection—which appears to be deeply built into our species—could be strong enough, if properly directed, to motivate a voluntary with-holding from reproduction on the part of those so unfortunate as to carry an unfavorable genetic heritage. Great numbers of women have foregone reproduction for far less compelling reasons.

Since eugenics deals with human conception, with birth and death, it is the center of one of the most highly charged areas of emotional stress in human experience and action. Eugenic progress will continue to be an extraordinarily complex and difficult field of human endeavor, but it remains a challenge that cannot indefinitely be evaded.

References

Blacker, C. P., *Eugenics: Galton and After*. London: Duckworth, 1952.

Blacker, C. P., "Family Planning and Eugenics Movements in the Mid-twentieth Century." *Eugen. Rev.* 47; 4, 1957.

Cook, Robert C., "Eugenic Hypothesis B." *Eugen. Quart. 2*; Nos. 3 and 4, 1955.

Darlington, C. D., "The Major Policies of the American Eugenics Society." *Eugen. News, 38*; No. 2, 1953.

Darlington, C. D., "The Control of Evolution in Man." *Eugen. Rev. 50*; 3, 1958.

"Differentiation in Current Mating and Fertility Trends" (Symposium). *Eugen. Quart. 6*; No. 2, 1959.

Galton, Francis, *Memories of My Life*. New York: E. P. Dutton & Co., Inc., 1908.

Holmes, S. J., *Human Genetics and Its Social Import*. New York: McGraw-Hill Book Co., 1936.

Lorimer, Frank, and Osborn, Frederick, *Dynamics of Population; Social and Biological Significance of Changing Birth Rates in the United States*. New York: The Macmillan Co., 1934.

Muller, H. J., "Our Load of Mutations." *Am. J. Human Genet. 2*; 111, 1950.

Osborn, Frederick, *Preface to Eugenics* (rev. ed.). New York: Harper & Brothers, 1951.

Roberts, J. A. Fraser, *An Introduction to Medical Genetics*. London: Oxford University Press, 1959.

Stern, Curt, *Principles of Human Genetics*. San Francisco: W. H. Freeman & Co., 1950.

Woodworth, R. S., "Heredity and Environment: A Critical Survey of Recently Published Material on Twins and Foster Children." *Social Science Research Council Bull.* No. 47, 1941.

ROBERT C. COOK

Europe, Sex Life in

ON THE globe Europe is the narrow north-western cape of the immense Eurasian continent, bathed by the Polar Sea, the Atlantic, and the Mediterranean. It may seem hard to realize that in this small part of the world so many different people should dwell, each with his own culture and thus his own sex life.

That is why the title of this article, suggesting a more or less uniform sex life in Europe, is somewhat misleading. This, however, is unavoidable; a different title such as "European Sex Life," would be even more misleading. For Europe, with its twenty-six national states—not counting the smaller countries as such—has never been a political-cultural unit, even during the Roman Empire or the Holy Roman Empire.

In these twenty-six national states the populations regard themselves as nations, clearly different from their neighbors, each with a language, history, and culture of its own, as well as its own sexual culture, habits, and customs. This number of twenty-six does not, however, reflect the reality. In a country such as Britain there are Scotchmen, English, and Welshmen; in Belgium, Flemish and Walloons; in Switzerland, French, German, Italian-Swiss, and Rhaeto-Romans; and in a country such as Jugoslavia, Serbians, Slovenes, Croatians, Bosnians, Macedonians, etc., who can all be considered separate nations, in so far as their sex life is concerned.

During the almost two centuries since the French Revolution, national cultural differences have increased rather than decreased, in spite of closer contacts between peoples. Two world wars with their resulting enormous migrations and modern techniques of mass communication may have acted as important counterweights, although their leveling effect has nevertheless remained very limited. Our first conclusion, therefore, must be that there is no more or less uniform European sex life, and there never has been one.

Hellas and Judea

At the cradle of the national and subnational cultures of Europe stood Hellas and Judea. All present-day European peoples have inherited —via Rome, or via Rome and Byzantium—essential elements from these two important Mediterranean civilizations. As far as our sexual attitudes are concerned we have, unfortunately, to admit that the Judean element—as understood and passed on by the early Christians— proved to be strongly dominant. Greek culture accepted love in all its forms—including that of lust—quite naturally as a source of happiness. Each was free to seek his own satisfaction as long as he did not interfere with the rights of others.

As Pierre Louÿs (1932) has noted:
"Love, with all its consequences, was, for the ancient Greeks, the sentiment most virtuous and most fecund in grandeurs. They did not attach to it those ideas of shamelessness and immodesty which Israelite tradition, along with the Christian doctrine, has handed down to us."

For the Greeks sexuality was "a condition, mysterious but necessary and creative, of intellectual development." Louÿs says they lived for the time when "human nudity"—the most perfect form, since we believe in the image of God, which we can know or even conceive— could reveal itself through the features of a sacred courtesan before the twenty thousand pilgrims upon the strands of Eleusis; where the most sensual love—the divine love whence we are born—was without stain, without shame and without sin."

But this ancient culture perished when decadent imperial Rome was defeated, first politically by the Barbarians, and then in the areas of religion and culture by young, ascetic, and militant Christianity. When the latter triumphed and soon after became the state religion of the remnants of the old empire, the struggle started between ascetic Judea and life-assenting Hellas—a struggle that has never ended and that gives to each European culture its special color and shade, according to the relative influence of these antithetic elements.

Under the influence of the new theocracy, whose asceticism was only equaled by their proselytism, a new attitude evolved comparatively quickly that rejected the body since it was the source of lust. This went so far that St. Augustine expresses regret in his *Confessions* that the necessary function of eating should be accompanied by lust. A new, rigidly ascetic code of morals, which regarded as sinful every sensually pleasing act not directly concerned with the maintenance or procreation of life, spread during the following centuries over all the newly formed national states of Europe.

During these first centuries of the new Europe, this drastic curtailment of legitimate bodily satisfaction could be enforced only by the imposition of severe penalties for transgressions—penalties that helped to change the structure of the superego of Medieval man. The feudal, hierarchic society in which he lived made him dependent, not only in deed but in thought and feeling as well, on his direct and indirect superiors: the secular and, even more important, the clerical authorities. He believed in their image of the world, in their image of the hereafter, in their heaven and hell, and their conception of what was sinful and what was permitted. In the terms of dynamic psychology, he internalized their prohibitions, the nonverbal as well as the verbal ones.

Thus a new human type originated, with different "impulses" and with a different "conscience." The "new" prohibitions created new guilt feelings and new anxieties with regard to impulses, inclinations, and wishes that had been perfectly acceptable in earlier cultural periods when they could be acted out freely. "Lust of the body" became the "sin of the flesh." One single sexual outlet remained permitted: coitus in marriage that had been sanctified by the Church. And this in fact only because mankind would become extinct if all devoted themselves to the highest ideal of complete chastity.

"Mortal Sins"

Every use of the sexual functions not directed toward this primary goal was called an abuse, an unnatural and capital sin. It was easy enough for adroit moral theologians after "establishing" by a priori axioms that the sexual impulse was in reality the impulse to procreate, to prove by impeccable syllogisms that all other sexual acts stood outside the divine law of nature, were therefore unnatural and "mortal" sins. "Mortal" indeed, because the conqueror writes not only the history but the morals as well, and the laws by which they are maintained. During the long following period of European history, canonical laws largely determined the secular ones, and as far as sexual offenses were concerned the two codes were usually identical: what was a mortal sin for the Church became a capital offense to the secular arm. This category included more or less without differentiation every sexual offense: premarital sexual intercourse, adultery, masturbation, and homosexuality.

To St. Paul, homosexuality, because of its prominence in the Near-Eastern, Hellenic, and Hellenistic religious practices of antiquity, was primarily a religious sin and a part of every form of heresy. Under his influence, therefore, the fight against homosexuality was started first and with the greatest vehemence, for here the antiheathen attitude and the morals of the new rulers reinforced each other. That is why in Europe homosexual love was tabooed much earlier, much more intensely, and much more efficiently than other "prohibited expressions" of sex life; a taboo that has continued to our own days.

In this historical process an important part was played by the inconsistency by which official commandments and prohibitions were implemented in different places and periods for the different layers of population. Notwithstanding all their efforts, clerical and secular rulers never succeeded in entirely stopping premarital sexual intercourse, concubinage, adultery, prostitution, and masturbation. This was partly due to the fact that from the early Middle Ages until the explosion of Victorian morality, the formally severe laws relating to heterosexual practices were administered with varying degrees of laxity by secular and even by clerical authorities.

The reason for this was that, regardless of official prohibition, leaders and respected members of society of pre-Reformation Europe not only tolerated but openly indulged in premarital and extramarital sexual relations. Wanton priests and monks contributed no less than sovereigns and cardinals to the fact that heterosexual prohibitions became much less a part of instinctive belief than those concerning homosexuality. Pressure on different heterosexual outlets was therefore much less strong, much less venomous, and above all much less constant. For such a pressure has to work intensively and uninterruptedly for some generations if it is to change human structure fundamentally.

The Reformation

With the victory of the Reformation and the rise to power of the bourgeois class in northwestern Europe, this informal element of permissiveness disappeared, particularly in the Germanic states, where the historical influence of Roman culture had been slight and short-lived, or totally lacking. From then on a clear differentiation began in the cultural development of the European peoples. The Protestant peoples in the northwest, the Romanic in the southwest (which after the victory of the Counter-Reformation remained Catholic), the equally Catholic population in southern Germany and the Habsburg countries, and finally the Slavonic people of the Balkans and Eastern Europe under strong Byzantine influence, were touched in an unequal measure by antisexual tendencies. These spread more and more during the following centuries, but their fatal effects were tempered by the amount of Hellenic, Roman, and Byzantine inheritance that had remained alive in the different peoples.

Here again we meet the already-mentioned dialectical processes. The severer imposition of external restraints by accepted authority results, after some generations, in a change of the superego, which becomes more severe and more rigid and thus increases the emotional importance of social conformity. Henceforth, in direct connection with the life standards of the young bourgeois society, sexuality is identified both consciously and unconsciously with procreation. From now on every sexual expression not directly aiming at procreation is rejected as "antinatural" and sinful, on the basis of ethics and philosophy as well as religion. The scientific fiction is born that there is no sexuality in children, that it announces itself as if by magic during puberty, in the form of an irresistible attraction that is possible only between males and females, whose expression and goal is solely the continuation of the species.

An attempted renaissance of Hellenic culture and attitudes, including those toward sex, arose in Italy, but its role outside that country remained very limited, the antisexual tendencies of the Reformation being too strong for it. In the eighteenth century a development began in England and Holland that was to reach its culminating point in the following two centuries: the sexual morals of the bourgeoisie began to affect the working class, whose mental and emotional structure became adapted to that of the ruling class. This further spreading of ascetic morals to new layers of population, who had so far remained more or less immune against it, was once more challenged by the life-assenting wave of the Rococo. The Rococo has been regarded as merely the "après nous le déluge" attitude of the doomed feudal class, but it would seem wrong to see in it only the negative elements; its positive elements should be recognized—not least because of its efforts to create for the first time after the early Renaissance a refined erotic culture, of which Casanova will always remain the incarnation.

This counterwave of the Rococo was broken by the French Revolution. Another movement, launched in the same century and stimulated by this very revolution, did far better. Far into the eighteenth century canonical law exercised, as mentioned before, a great influence on the criminal law in different European countries, especially as far as moral offenses were concerned. Thus, in most countries a great uniformity prevailed in this field. In the course of this century, however, the changed distribution of power between sovereigns, nobility, church, and bourgeois strengthened the tendency for separation of church and state. The influence of rationalistic bourgeois philosophers added to the endeavors to base the punishment of sexual offenses on new principles of retaliation.

Under the canonical law of the Middle Ages, moral offenses were punishable as such. The new legal philosophy, however, required that punishment for "crimes," including so-called immoral sexual acts, be decided only by the extent to which the rights or interests of others were violated by them. The Napoleonic Code, in which these principles were originally embodied, no longer punished all sorts of sexual acts, however heinous they had formerly been regarded. This reformation applied even to coitus with animals and with humans of the same sex—the "sodomy" of the old laws—which had been punishable nearly everywhere with the death penalty. As the Napoleonic Code was only applied in the Romanic countries and in the Netherlands, there has prevailed for one and a half centuries in this respect a great divergence between this group of countries and all the others, where the influence of the old canonical law with respect to the penalty for homosexuality and other sexual offenses was still at least partially in force.

In spite of the more liberal—or better, more humanistic—tendencies in legislation, the suppression of sexuality still continued during the nineteenth century. It reached its culminating point in the Victorian era, where puritanism and its inseparable companion hypocrisy reached new heights, to influence almost all elements of the population. But in a typical dialectical process, counterforces developed, leading during our century toward a new wave of sexual emancipation. The most striking example of this dialectic is perhaps the development of psychoanalysis, which could originate only during a period and in a place where sexual suppression had grown so far that hysteria had become the fashionable disease of the well-to-do class. This wave of sexual emancipation by which our time is characterized is the result not of a new science or a new ideology, but of the tremendous changes in the social field, which took place mostly under the influence of two world wars and affected particularly the role of women. A coincidental industrialization and urbanization of great parts of Europe dislodged old patriarchal family relationships and narrowed the bases on which marriages were built. The erotic aspects of marriage therefore became much more important than at any time since the fall of Hellas. Possibly the most decisive element in this revolution was the collapse of unquestioning acceptance of the dogma of unity of sexuality and procreation.

Contemporary Europe

Modern European man has developed a new attitude with regard to procreation, a "preventive attitude" that renders it impossible to accept the consequences of unrestricted fertility. This attitude—certainly a phenomenon of sociological origin—which has become an inevitable accompaniment of the attainment of a certain cultural and material level of civilization, has led to the modern movement for conscious family planning. Love has emancipated itself from procreation.

We have already drawn attention to the great differences between the present-day European nations with regard to sex life. We can now specify these differences a little further by stating, that they are the result of a number of historical factors, especially of the degree to which Hellenic-Roman-Byzantine culture, early Christian ascetic morals, the Renaissance, Reformation and Counter-Reformation, the Rococo movement, the French Revolution, and finally the nineteenth-century industrial and the twentieth-century sexual revolutions made themselves felt during the shaping of a country's ethos.

In addition, the effect of the sexual revolution of our century has varied from country to country. Even contemporary developments are uniform in neither speed nor direction, as has been proved by the regressions of the thirties in Nazi Germany and Stalinist Russia. Nevertheless, it is undeniable that in great parts of Europe, noticeably in the Scandinavian countries, especially in Sweden, new sexual morals are evolving—in a gradualistic rather than revolutionary manner—that differ essentially from the hypocritical double standard of nineteenth-century Europe. During this development a new sociological phenomenon has made its appearance: ideological movements, such as the World League for Sex-Reform, developed by men and women who desired to direct and lead this development on the basis of their philosophy of life and their scientific views.

Sex Reform Movements

Some sociologically naive supporters of this movement believed in sex reform from the top. They formulated elaborate programs without realizing that written or unwritten moral codes of the community cannot be altered by decree. Others, more realistically, understood that their task had to be limited to a systematic effort to direct and hasten the historical tendencies of development as much as possible. For this purpose they cooperated in many cases with local progressive and radical political groups.

During the twenties this movement for sex reform reached its culmination in central Europe, where men such as Forel and Hirschfeld were the leading figures. By means of the spoken and written word, war was waged against obsolete bourgeois morals. These new morals, born during a period of social and political emancipation of women, were based on two principles: complete equality of rights for both sexes and the liberation of sexual love from the single objective of procreation. Although continuing—especially after the failure of radical reform efforts in Soviet Russia—to regard lasting monogamous marriage as the highest ideal, the new sexual code includes a more realistic attitude toward premarital and extramarital relations. To achieve this, however, proper sex information for women as well as for men is needed. This ought to begin in early childhood, in order to prevent the fatal loss of the ability to give or receive love that was characteristic of nineteenth- and early twentieth-century man. In addition, more attention should be paid to the art of sexual love, as a preventive measure against today's endemic female lack of orgastic ability.

In spite of the high value these reformers attach to a normal, heterosexual, and durable love relationship, they demand that both society and the individual understand and tolerate all other expressions of human sexuality: the immature, the neurotic, and even the perverse. These should be considered not as punishable offenses but—so long as the rights of fellow men and of the community are not violated—as objects for pedagogic and psychotherapeutic efforts. Lastly, the reformers advocate birth control in the sense of planned parenthood. Criminal abortion ought to be fought, not by inhuman laws, but by reducing the number of unwanted pregnancies to a minimum by legalizing abortion in a number of clearly and sharply defined indications: medical, medicosocial, eugenic, and humanistic.

The World League for Sex-Reform

All specific proposals put forward by the different national leagues and the World League for Sex-Reform can be brought back to these principles, as is shown by the program drafted in 1928 by the League. Steiner (1935) listed the following items from that platform:

1. Political, economic and sexual equality of rights of men and women.
2. The liberation of marriage (and especially divorce) from the present Church and State tyranny.
3. Birth control, so that procreation may be undertaken only deliberately and with a due sense of responsibility.
4. Race betterment by the application of the knowledge of eugenics.
5. Protection of the unmarried mother and the illegitimate child.
6. A rational attitude toward sexually abnormal persons, and especially toward homosexuals, both male and female.
7. Prevention of prostitution and venereal disease.
8. Disturbances of the sexual impulse to be regarded as more or less pathological phenomena and not, as in the past, merely as crimes, vices, or sins.
9. Only those sexual acts to be considered criminal which infringe the sexual rights of another person. Sexual acts between responsible adults, undertaken by mutual consent, to be regarded as the private concern of those adults.
10. Systematic sexual education and enlightenment.

The World League, which during the years 1928–1932 organized almost annual conferences with a demonstrative ideological and at the same time scientific character, found for some of its claims natural allies in progressive women's movements and national neo-Malthusian ideology, especially after the split between socialists and orthodox Malthusians at the Liège conference in 1902. In central Europe neo-Malthusianism had even developed into mass movements for sexual reform.

Counter-Reactions to Sexual Reforms

The movement had its natural adversaries, however, who were to prove considerably more powerful than its political friends amongst the liberals, left-wing socialists, and—until about 1930—the Communists in eastern and central Europe. These adversaries—the ultranationalists, clericals, and Catholics as well as orthodox Protestants, Fascists, Nazis and, after 1936, Communists—were spurred to their counteroffensive by the great response of the population to the movement for sex reform. In France, under the pressure of right-wing chauvinists, a law was passed in 1920 against birth control, with increased penalties for abortion. Belgium and Fascist Italy soon followed suit. On December 31, 1930, the Vatican issued the encyclical letter *Casti Connubii,* in which Pope Pius XI once more with the greatest emphasis stressed the old doctrine of the primarily procreative purpose of sex. The opposition of the Roman Catholic Church to the sex-reforming aims of the World League was thereby established. This fact has had profound effects on government policies in all European countries where Roman Catholic political parties are of importance.

The heaviest blow against the movement for sexual reform, however, fell in 1933, when the Nazis seized power in Germany, which was then the center of the movement. The burning of Magnus Hirschfeld's archives of the Institute for Sexological Science was more than a symbol; it was the beginning of a systematic destruction—first in Germany itself, then in Austria (1938), Czechoslovakia and Poland (1939), Denmark, Norway, and Holland (1940), and shortly after in the whole of occupied Europe—of everything that had been built up during decades by scientific ideological and practical sociomedical work. Only Sweden escaped this catastrophe and became, thus, the one European country during those dark years

where a progressive evolution could take place and be reflected in legislation. Here Elise Ottensen-Jensen founded in 1933 the *Riksførbundet för Sexuell Upplysning,* which acquired not only a growing mass support but increasing political influence as well.

After the liberation of Europe in 1944–1945, a revival of the movement for sex reform did *not* occur; there were other and more direct concerns. When at last problems of sexuality became apposite, the political conditions for a revival of the movement proved to be lacking nearly everywhere, primarily because of the enormously increased Catholic influence on government affairs in France, Italy, Belgium, Western Germany, Austria, and the Netherlands. At the same time, the Stalinist antisexual policies were slavishly followed in the "peoples' democracies," until the beginning of the "thaw" in 1955–1956. Only in the three liberated Scandinavian countries, Denmark, Norway, and Finland, was a progressive trend evidenced, and there important reforms following the Swedish pattern have recently been enacted. Thus, the "sexual revolution" of the twenties, seemingly on the point of victory, has been held up almost everywhere.

Future Sex Reforms

But social evolution does progress and certainly in the near future the necessary conditions will exist for the interrupted revival of the movement for sex reform. Many symptoms indicate that this revival is not far off. The Soviet Union and the peoples' democracies returned shortly after Stalin's death to a more liberal sexual policy, and the same applied to Jugoslavia. In France, Belgium, and Italy as well, efforts are observed, although perhaps only timid ones, to revive the movement for sex reform and birth control. These two efforts are at present united nearly everywhere in Europe under one movement for planned parenthood and sex education. In the Netherlands, where a right-wing clerical cabinet had pushed through new punitive measures against contraception, abortion, and homosexuality as early as 1911, and in 1927 had taken the legal status from the Neo-Malthusian League, the socialist minister of justice (in a coalition cabinet composed mainly of right-wing socialists and Catholics) in 1958 was forced to re-establish this status by the pressure of public opinion. The strongest impulse for this revival of sex reform may be expected to come from the leaders of Protestant churches, who have, nearly everywhere in Europe, broken their old common front with Roman Catholic moral-theologians in regard to the controversial subjects of love and marriage, and who now voice new and progressive ideas.

Since 1959, an evolution has been in progress in Europe in respect to the attitudes of the worldly and spiritual leaders and of the medical world towards the problems of family planning, abortion and homosexuality. In various countries (France, the Netherlands), new bills are being drafted or introduced in Parliament to remove restrictions on family planning. In Britain, the proposed amendments of the legislation pertaining to homosexuality and abortion are in an advanced stage. These developments could not have taken place were it not for a great change in the attitude of both the leaders of the principal Protestant denominations and the higher and lower Roman Catholic hierarchy. These favorable developments do not as yet include such issues as A.I. D. and the surgical transformation of transexism.

Historical Tables

The most important events of the sex history of Europe during the last century can be found in Table 1, and facts concerning legislation are in Tables 2 through 6. These serve to illustrate better than an elaborate argument the struggle that was so courageously fought by the "lost generation." They also prove that this struggle was not completely in vain.

TABLE 1. EVENTS OF THE SEX HISTORY OF EUROPE*

1798	Malthus: *Essay on the Principle of Population*
1829	Discovery of the human ovule (Von Baer)
1838	Dr. Wilde invents the cervical cap
1842–45	Formulation of a (false) safe-period theory (Pouchet, Bischoff, Raciborski)
1859	Darwin: *Origin of Species*
1861	Bachofen: *Mother Right*
1865	Mendel: *Laws of Genetics* (rediscovered 1900)
1868	Avrard formulates a better safe-period theory
1869	Term "homosexuality" coined by Benkert
1877	Bradlaugh-Besant trial. Foundation of the British Malthusian League
1879	Bebel: *Woman and Socialism*
	Neisser discovers gonococcus
	International Medical Congress in Amsterdam discusses birth control techniques
1881	Foundation of the Dutch Malthusian League
1883	Mensinga cervical cap invented
1886	Krafft-Ebing: *Psychopathia Sexualis*
1890	Aletta Jacobs starts the first birth-control center (Amsterdam)
1895	Freud and Breuer: *Studies on Hysteria*
	Carpenter: *Homogenic Love*
	Oscar Wilde case
1896	First (German) edition of Havelock Ellis
1897	Scientific Humanitarian Committee founded in Berlin (Hirschfeld)
	Battle against German antisexual statute, §175 starts

1900	Freud: *Interpretation of Dreams*
	First International Malthusian Congress (Paris)
	Foundation of International Neo-Malthusian League
	Dr. Rutgers (Rotterdam) starts training of laywomen as "birth-control nurses"
	Medical split in Dutch Neo-Malthusian League, Aletta Jacobs and others withdraw
	Jahurbuch für Sexuelle Zwischenstufen (Annual for Sexual Intermediate Types) founded
1904	Forel: *Sexual Problems*
1905	Second International Neo-Malthusian Congress (Liège)
	Suffragettes start terrorism
	Conflict between Malthusians and Socialists
	Freud: *Three Contributions to Sexual Theory*
	Schaudinn-Hoffman detect *Spirochaeta pallida*
1907	Limited franchise for women in Norway
1907–09	Eulenburg case in Germany
1910	Ehrlich and Hatta invent Salvarsan
1911	New laws in the Netherlands against contraception, abortion, and homosexuality
1913	Proposals for legalization of abortion in Norway
	Universal franchise in Norway
	Zeitschrift für Sexualwissenschaft (Journal of Sexology) founded (published until 1932)

* Partly quoted from Max Hodann.

TABLE 1. EVENTS OF THE SEX HISTORY OF EUROPE—Cont'd.

1915	Stella Browne advocates legalization of abortion for Great Britain
	Theory of intersexuality (Goldschmidt)
1917	Russian Revolution — Alexandra Kollontay, Commissar for Maternity and Child Welfare, starts "sexual revolution"
	Malaria therapy of syphilitic paresis (Wagner-Jauregg)
1918	Universal franchise for women in the Netherlands
	Limited franchise for women in Great Britain
1919	Abortion legalization bill in Bâle defeated
	Institute of Sexual Science and first sex consultation center founded (Hirschfeld, Berlin)
1920	Soviet Russia legalizes abortion
	Leftist action against statute §218 in Germany
	Law against birth control in France
	Increased penalties for abortion
1921	First International Congress for Sexual Reform (Berlin)
	First British birth control clinic (Marie Stopes)
1922	First sex-consultation center founded in Vienna
1923	First lay association for sex reform and birth control founded in central Europe
1923	New divorce law in England
1924	Heiser abortion trial in Germany
	Birth control clinics founded in Scandinavia
1925	Laws against birth control in Italy
1926	Birth control centers in U.S.S.R.
	Van de Velde: Ideal Marriage
1927	Malinowski: Sexual Life of Savages
	Draft of new abortion bill submitted to German Reichstag
	Discussions against abortion in Russia
	Birth-Control Information Center and Investigation Committee founded (London)
	Reich: The Function of the Orgasm
	Hirschfeld: Geschlechtskunde
	Victor Marguérite: Ton corps est à toi
	Dutch Government rescinds legal status of Dutch Neo-Malthusian League
1928	Universal franchise for women in Britain
	Knaus and Ogino formulate an improved version of Avrard's theory of the safe period
	World League for Sexual Reform (W.L.-S.R.) founded (Copenhagen)
	Scandinavian countries start sex consultation and education
1929	Danish castration law for criminals
	Third W.L.S.R. Congress (London)
	Fleming discovers penicillin
1930	Seventh and last International Neo-Malthusian Congress (Zürich)

	Lambeth Conference accepts birth control
	Encyclical Casti Connubii
	Fourth W.L.S.R. Congress (Vienna)
1931	Aletta Jacobshuis founds first fully equipped sexological clinic (Amsterdam)
1932	Fifth and last W.L.S.R. Congress (Brünn)
	Medical and humanitarian indications for abortion accepted in Poland
1933	Latvia legalizes abortion (on medical, eugenic and social grounds)
	Swedish Sex Education Society founded (Elise Ottensen-Jensen)
	Nazis destroy the Institute of Sexual Science (Berlin)
	Nazis close all German sex consultation centers and birth-control clinics
	Compulsory sterilization in Germany
1934	Iceland legalizes medical and social indications for abortion
	Massacre of homosexuals in Germany
	New laws against homosexuality in Russia
	Leunbach abortion trial in Denmark
1935	Death of Hirschfeld
	Dissolution of World League for Sexual Reform
	Latvia rescinds social indications for abortion
	U.S.S.R. rescinds social indications for abortion
	W. Reich: Sexualität u. Kulturkampf
	Domagh discovers bacteriocidal qualities of sulfonamides
1938	Alec Bourne abortion case (London)
	Sweden legalizes medical abortion
1938–41	Nazis suppress birth control and sexual reform in occupied countries (Austria, Czechoslovakia, Poland, Denmark, Norway, Netherlands, etc.)
1939	Home Office Report on Abortion (England)
1944	Legal equality for homosexuals in Sweden
1944/45	Penicillin introduced for venereal disease therapy
1945	Sweden: Sex education in school obligatory
1946	Sociomedical indications for abortion legalized in Sweden
	Meeting in Stockholm of planned parenthood leaders
	First postwar conference on planned parenthood
1947	Dutch New Malthusian League transformed into Dutch League for Sexual Reform
1948	Second International Conference on Population and World Resources (Cheltenham)
1949	Pius XII rejects all forms of artificial insemination (reaffirmed: 1951, 1956)
1951	Foundation of International Committee for Sexual Equality (Amsterdam)

TABLE 1. EVENTS OF THE SEX HISTORY OF EUROPE—*Cont'd.*

1952	Dutch Reformed Church endorses family planning
1953	Fourth International Conference on Population and World Resources (Stockholm)
	International Planned Parenthood Federation founded
1954	Revival of planned parenthood movement in Italy
1955/56	Legal abortion and family planning re-established in U.S.S.R., Czechoslovakia, Poland, and Jugoslavia
1956	Revival of family planning in France
1957	First Regional Conference on Planned Parenthood (Berlin), first international meeting in Germany since 1933
	Wolfenden report on homosexuality and prostitution (Great Britain)
	Dutch Reformed Church rejects artificial insemination by donor
1957/58	Revival of planned parenthood in Belgium
1958	Lambeth conference endorses birth control
	Dutch Society for Sexual Reform regains legal status

TABLE 2. BIRTH CONTROL AND CONTRACEPTION

	ILLEGAL	ALLOWED (WITH PRESCRIPTION)	FREE (RESTRICTIONS ON SALE AND PURCHASE)	FREE	FREE, EXCEPT FOR RESTRICTIONS
Belgium	+				
Germany	Bayern, Westfalen Rh. Phaltz		other parts		
Italy	+				
Jugoslavia		+			
France		+			
Austria		+			
Hungary		+			
Denmark			+		
Finland			+		
Netherlands			+		
Sweden			+		
U.S.S.R.			+		
Czechoslovakia				+	
Wales					+
England					+
Norway					+
Switzerland					+

TABLE 3. ARTIFICIAL INSEMINATION

	CIVIL LAW	CRIMINAL LAW
England	cause for divorce: child may be considered illegitimate	equated with adultery in some cases
France	cause for divorce or judicial separation: husband may repudiate child (because of his impotence or absence, or if birth is concealed); child may be claimed by unmarried donor	punishable for married woman, if husband sues her; for unmarried woman: if A.I. takes place in manner conflicting with the Droit Criminel (performed in public; immoral sexual behavior)
Germany	cause for divorce: charge for damage; illegitimacy of child, if husband repudiates and if it is impossible that it is the husband's	A.I.D. without consent of husband: act of violence, outrage, bodily harm; doctor may be disciplined; doctor is punishable if he treats a woman he knows to be without means of support
Switzerland	husband and heirs can dispute legitimacy of the child	husband punishable as accessory if he submits his wife to A.I.D. against her will, if woman dies or if her health is impaired after pregnancy and delivery
Netherlands	if husband did not give consent to A.I.D., he can dispute legitimacy of the child; may be "excess" (judicial separation); doctor may be sued	art. 284, 1. Wb.-Str.r.: as for attendant factors (in public)

There is no legal status for artificial insemination (A.I.) in England, France, Germany, Netherlands, Scandinavia, and Switzerland.

TABLE 4.   HOMOSEXUAL OFFENSES

	ENGLAND, WALES	SCOTLAND	AUSTRIA	DENMARK	BELGIUM	FRANCE	GERMANY	GREECE	ITALY	NETHERLANDS	NORWAY	SPAIN	SWEDEN
Sodomy	impris. max. life	impris. max. life			under 16 impris. max. 15 y.; 16–21 other cases, max. 5 y.	impris.				under 21 impris. max. 4 y.; special circumst. max. 6 y.	impris. max. 1 y.; under 14 max. 15 y.; or for life; 14–18 max. 5 y.		impris. max. 6 y.
Attended sodomy	impris. max. 10 y.	impris. max. life											
Indecent assault (male by male)	impris. 6 m.– 10 y. max.	impris. max. 2 y.											
Indecent assault (female by female)	impris. 6 m.– 10 y. max.	impris. 3 m. max.											
Acts of gross indecency (between males)	impris. max. 2 y.	impris. max. 2 y.											
Procuring acts of gross indecency (between males)	impris. max. 3 y.	impris. max. 3 m.											
Attempting to procure acts of gross indecency (between males)	impris. max. 2 y.	impris. max. 3 m.											
Assault with intent to commit sodomy	impris. max. 10 y.	impris. 6 m. or 2 y. max.											
Persistent soliciting or importuning of males by males, for immoral purposes	impris. 6 m. or 2 y. max.	fine £5 max.											
Offenses against bylaws	fine £5 max.	impris. max. 3 m. max.											
Libidinous practices & behavior betw. males			impris. max. 5 y.										
Indecency against nature			impris. max. 10 y.	impris. max. 4 y.									
Indecency with violence, etc.													
Minor acts			impris. 8 d.–6 m.										
Outraging public decency				impris. max. 4 y.	impris. max. 1 y. or fine 500 frs.; under 16, impris. max. 6 y. or fine 1,000 frs.	impris. max. 2 y. or fine 12,000 frs.			impris. max. 3 m.	impris. max. 2 y. or fine f.300. 3 days or f.15 max.	impris. max. 3 m.	impris. max. 6 m., or fine 5,000 pes. public order: impris. max. 30 d. max. or fine 1,000 pes.	
Homosexual acts				impris. under 15 max. 6 y.; force, fear, etc., max. 6 y.; under 18 max. 4 y.; under 21 max. 3 y.		under 21 impris. max. 3 y. or fine 500,000 frs.; under 15 max. 10 y.; with violence, etc.: hard labor	between males; under 14, violence, etc., impris. max. 10 y.; other cases: max. 5 y.			under 21 impris. max. 4 y.; special circumst. max. 6–8 y.			under 15 or parent victim impris. max. 4 y.; under 21 with insane, dependence, etc., impris. max. 2 y.
Unnatural sex intercourse (all forms of indecency)								under 17 for gain, etc., impris. max. 5 y.	violence, impris. max. 10 y.; abuse of authority: max. 10 y.				under 16

TABLE 5. GROUNDS FOR LEGAL ABORTION

	MEDI-CAL	EU-GENIC	MEDI-CO-SOCIAL	LEGAL-HU-MANI-TARIAN	DATE OF LEGIS-LATION
Denmark	+	+	+	+	1939
Finland	+	+		+	1950
Germany, East	+	+	+*		
Iceland	+		+		1934
Jugoslavia	+				
Poland	+	+	+	+	
Norway	†				
Roumania	+	+			
Sweden	+	+	+	+	1938, resp. 1946
Switzerland	+	‡		‡	1942
U.S.S.R.	+	+	+	+	1920–1936, 1955
Czechoslovakia	+	+	+	+	1957

* Rescinded, 1950.

† Norway: No modern legislation, but official statement permits strictly medical abortion.

‡ Switzerland: Different laws in different cantons.

All other European countries have no modern abortion legislation.

References

Bebel, August, *Woman Under Socialism*. New York: New York Labor News Co., 1903, 1917.

Bloch, Iwan, *The Sexual Life of Our Time*. London: Rebman, 1908.

Ellis, Havelock, *Studies in the Psychology of Sex*. New York: Random House, 1936.

Forel, A., *The Sexual Question*. New York: Physicians and Surgeons Book Co., 1906.

Freud, Sigmund, *Basic Writings*. New York: Modern Library, Inc., 1938.

Freud, Sigmund, *Collected Papers*. London: Hogarth, 1925-1950.

Handbook on Sex Instruction in Swedish Schools. Stockholm, 1957.

Himes, Norman E., *Medical History of Contraception*. London, 1926.

Hirschfeld, Magnus, *Die Homosexualität des Mannes und des Weibes*. Berlin: Marcus, 1920.

Hirschfeld, Magnus, *Men and Women*. New York: G. P. Putnam's Sons, 1935.

Hirschfeld, Magnus, *Sexual Pathology*. New York: Emerson Books, Inc., 1940.

Hirschfeld, Magnus, *Sexual Anomalies and Perversions*. London: Aldor, 1944.

Hodann, Max, *Sex Life in Europe*. New York: Julian Press, Inc., 1932.

Krafft-Ebing, R., *Psychopathia Sexualis*. New York: Physicians and Surgeons Book Co., 1922.

Louÿs, Pierre, *Aphrodite*. New York: Illustrated Editions Co., Inc., Copyright 1932.

Papers of the Royal Commission on Population. London, 1949, 1950.

TABLE 6. DIVORCE

	GROUNDS	WAITING TIME
Austria	a, ab, m, im, o, abm	180 days
Belgium	a, v, m, o, mc	10 months
Bulgaria	a, ab, m, im, o, par, mar	6 months
Denmark	a, ab, m, im, o, par, mc	10 months
Finland	a, ab, m, im, par, mar, o, mc, abm	10 months
France	a, m, o, dcp, d	300 days
Great Britain	a, ab, i (5 y.), m, ul	–
Greece	a, m, im, o	365 days
Germany	a, ab, m, b, ul, i (3 y.), dl	10 months
Hungary	a, ab, m, im, abm	10 months
Iceland	a, ab, m, im, o, par, mc	10 months
Italy	–	–
Ireland	–	–
Jugoslavia	a, ab, m, im	9 months
Luxemburg	a, m, im, o, mc	300 days
Netherlands	a, ab, im, m	300 days
Norway	a, ab, m, im, par, mar	10 months
Poland	–	–
Portugal	a, ab, m, im, o, mc	1 year
Roumania	a, m, im, o, mc	10 months
Spain	a, ab, m, im, o, par, mar, mc	301 days
Sweden	a, ab, m, im, o, par, mar, abm	10 months
Switzerland	a, ab, m, o, mar, abm	300 days
U.S.S.R.	mc, pd	–
Czechoslovakia	a, ab, m, im, o, mar, abm	–

Explanation of abbreviations:

a	*adultery*	im	*imprisonment*
ab	*abandonment (malevolent or not)*	m	*maltreatment*
		mar	*mental aberration*
abm	*abuse in marriage*	mc	*mutual consent*
b	*bigamy*	o	*offenses*
d	*dissipation*	par	*physical aberration*
dep	*degrading corporal punishment*	pd	*one party's desire*
		ul	*unnatural lewdness*
dl	*danger of life*	v	*violence*
i	*insanity*		

Report of the Committee on Homosexual Offences and Prostitution. London: Her Majesty's Printing Office, 1959.

Report of the Inter-Departmental Committee on Abortion. London, 1939.

Ryksförbundet för Sexuell Upplysning 1933-1958. Stockholm, 1958.

Steiner, Herbert, "Sexualnot und Sexualreform." *Proc. 4th Cong. World League for Sexual Reform*. Vienna, 1931.

World League for Sex-Reform, *Proc. 2nd Congress*. Copenhagen: Levin and Munkgsgaard, 1929.

CONRAD VAN EMDE BOAS

Extramarital Sex Relations

Definition

LITERALLY applied, the phrase "extramarital sex relations" refers to all sexual interactions that take place outside of marriage. The term is occasionally so used in the literature: that is, to include all interpersonal sexual behavior other than that which occurs between a person and his or her spouse. It is the more usual professional practice, however, to consider sexual relationships between unmarried people under the heading of "premarital sex relations," a procedure to which we adhere in this encyclopedia. Technically, of course, when an unmarried person has sex relations with a married person, this nonmarital interaction may be designated as "premarital" for the unwed individual and as "extramarital" for the one who is married. To avoid the awkwardness and confusion that would result from such linguistic purity, we shall refer to *all nonmarital sexual activity between male and female under circumstances in which one or more of the participants is currently married as extramarital sex relations.* Although the focus of our attention in this article is extramarital coitus, we shall give some brief attention in a later section of the article to the noncoital, nonmarital sex interactions of married persons, termed "extramarital petting." At all other times, "extramarital sex relations," "extramarital coitus," and "adultery" are employed as synonyms.

History

Regulations regarding extramarital coitus and violations of these regulations are certainly deeply buried in man's prehistoric past. In a very realistic sense, the form of sexual activity to which we attach the term "adultery" may be considered antecedent to the institution of marriage. If groups of men had not feared the mate-stealing and mate-deserting activities of their fellow men, the various sets of behavior patterns designated as "marriage" would probably never have been invented and culturally transmitted. Some inferential support for such theorizing derives from studies of infrahuman animals. Especially among the mammals most closely related to man, the primates, males relate to mates they have acquired as property to be defended against the aggressions of other males, and the propensities of both males and females to take advantage of sexual opportunities with others than their mates are readily observable.

Whatever may be the detailed truths of man's prehistory, all known cultures have some limitations set upon extramarital sex relations and some means of enforcing such designated taboos. But definitions of approved and disapproved extramarital coitus and the methods used to elicit conformity to these definitions vary widely from society to society. The outstanding issue involved in most preliterate groups, ancient societies, and even recent civilizations has not been a matter of sexual or characterological morality. Adultery has most often been considered a threat to the economic stability of a society: most specifically, male property rights. Out of primary male concerns about holding on to their mates, secondary interest in the welfare of dependent offspring seems to have been transmitted to males by females.

Some cultures, especially those with a strong

Judeo-Christian tradition, have adopted, but varyingly emphasized, the theoretical principle that adultery is a cardinal sin for either a man or a woman. In practice, however, various official or unofficial exceptions have been made for some males in every past or present society. Study of the historical, anthropological, and sociological data fails to reveal a society that has consistently suppressed and severely punished extramarital sex relations for its males. Many of the societies that take the strongest theoretical positions regarding the undesirability of such relations make unofficial arrangements for actively encouraging, or at least covertly condoning, extramarital coitus for males who proceed with prudence.

For females, the cultural situations have tended to be different. Somewhat better than half of the human societies that have been studied in this regard by social scientists completely prohibit and severely punish sexual relations of a married woman with anyone other than her husband. About one society out of ten rather freely permits extramarital coitus for women, and in the remaining (approximate) 40 per cent of the societies some degree of extramarital relations under special circumstances and/or with particular persons is permitted married women. In an occasional society, for example, it is the custom for a male to lend his wife (or one of his wives) to his guest. In other situations, coitus is permitted, or even required, of a wife with her brother-in-law in a barren marriage, at the time of certain religious ceremonies or celebrations, or as a part of the marriage ceremony.

Most of the distinctions between attitudes toward male and female adultery can be understood in terms of the property conception of women in many societies. For a married man to stray sexually is (at least unofficially) viewed in most societies as his understandable privilege as a free agent. For the married woman to so behave, on the other hand, is the undesirable functioning of a piece of property and a threat to economic stability of the whole society. The dominant males in many societies have also tended to consider the adulterous activities of their wives as signs of weakness not only in property defense, but also in general masculinity and social prestige for the particular

males who have been made cuckolds. Even in the relatively rare societies with rather lenient attitudes toward female extramarital coitus, such activity is not treated as a threat to the security of husbands because it is carried out under their rules and with their benign and generous control.

Even in those societies that most rigorously enforce penalties against such activities on the part of wives and come the closest to practicing their theoretical intolerances of the extramarital sex relations of husbands, the evidence is overwhelming that a great deal of adultery occurs. Biographies, oral and printed legends, diaries, personal confessions, historical documents, ethnological studies, interviews, questionnaires, and police records are some of the sources that contain the ever-recurring theme of married men and women in great quantity and all degrees of quality engaging in coitus with other than their spouses. When literature has adopted the adultery motif from life, it has almost invariably declared the activity very enjoyable in process, but doomed to end in tragedy for the participants. Such facts as are available indicate that in life itself large numbers of adulterers meet with less devastating destinies than do their counterparts in fiction. It seems only fair to state, however, that the joys of adultery in reality seem to fall short at times of their literary depiction.

Incidences and Frequencies

A review of many American and European studies that purport to give some picture of the degrees of extramarital sex activity in at least certain sections of the population of the countries represented leaves the critical reader with no confidence of the reliability and validity of the facts with which he emerges. This is not intended to be a biting criticism of the scientists who have tried to collect data on the subject. Many of these investigators seem to have obtained the best results possible under difficult circumstances, and many of them have been careful to point out factors that contribute to the inadequacy of their statistics, such as the unrepresentative nature of their population samples, concealment of pertinent facts by some subjects, and ineffectiveness of the interviewing or questionnaire techniques to elicit full cooperation of actual and potential subjects. The general results are such, however, that we feel unjustified in quoting any exact figures for incidences or frequencies of extramarital sex relations for any social population or subpopulation.

It is perhaps less misleading to speak of general comparisons of incidence and frequency within a particular population sample. No one, for example, is in a position to offer scientific evidence that Russians practice more or less adultery than Americans. There are, on the other hand, some probably reliable indications that the incidence of adultery is higher among Russian female students than among Russian peasant women and likewise higher among college educated American males over 40 and females over 25 than among less educated American males and females of the same age groups. The value to be gained from such comparative listings is doubtful, however, in light of the fact that we are left with nothing other than speculation regarding their differential etiology and significance.

It is nevertheless worth noting that married women have lower incidences and frequencies of extramarital sex relations than married men in all societies where comparative studies between the sexes have been made. There has been considerable discussion of the extent to which such differences are a reflection of a greater biological proclivity toward sexual variety on the part of males or of more rigid cultural restriction of females. The more widespread and frequent promiscuity of males than females among infrahuman mammals is often cited as inferential support for the biological argument. But the same data may be used to contend that the greater size and strength of anthropoid males creates for them a social dominance that enables them to apply restrictions on their females not dissimilar in crude form from those found in human societies. It is perhaps relevant to the comparative incidence of coitus with other than regular mates among males and females to point out that both human and infrahuman males seem, in general, more quickly responsive to nontactual sexual stimuli than females. At the human level, though, possible biological differences in responsiveness of

the sexes are so obscured by cultural factors that no definitive assertion can be validated.

Even if some biological basis for greater predisposition toward extramarital coitus is somehow and sometime established, it is apparent that females who are given sufficient social opportunity often find that adultery has its attractions. In those countries where considerable progress has been made toward social equality of the sexes, such evidence as exists indicates increased incidences among married women of extramarital sex behavior that approximates the male pattern. Cultural changes that have accompanied the processes of industrialization and urbanization in many Euro-American countries have brought greater freedom of movement for people in general and women in particular. At the same time, there has been an undermining of the enforcement of the Judeo-Christian sex mores and of their patriarchal bias. These and other social changes have been conducive to a rise in the incidences of extramarital coitus generally and among women particularly.

Although the incidences of extramarital sex relations have apparently increased in many societies (and especially among the married females in these populations), there is no evidence of any increase in the frequencies of participation in the activity by either sex. Average frequencies are apt to be misleading even when accurate, for the activity, in accordance with variable opportunity, is in most instances quite sporadic. A married woman, for example, might take advantage of four week-end absences of her husband in the course of a calendar year to engage twenty-four times in extramarital coitus. She then becomes a statistic of a woman who has had extramarital sex relations an average of twice per month during that year: a statistic that gives us little insight into the sexual patterns of this woman.

In males, the frequency of extramarital coitus, like that of other sexual outlets, generally declines with age. For women, however, both the frequency of extramarital sex relations and their percentage of total outlet increase. The accumulative incidence of female adultery likewise increases with age. These facts are probably to some extent causally related. As husbands decline with age in their sexual interest and activity, more of the older wives turn with increasing frequency to extramarital satisfaction. Not only do many older women have their sexual interest and ability unimpaired, but some have their sexual desires intensified when fear of pregnancy has been removed by the passing of the climacteric. There is also some evidence that older women are more skeptical of the validity of the moral taboos against extramarital sex relations that seriously impressed them in their earlier years.

Legal Status

Laws in America and in those European countries that are still strongly influenced by Judeo-Christian moral codes have tended toward the proscription of adultery under all circumstances. In general, however, the penalties exacted are mild and enforcement is rare. Even in instances where there is public admission of adultery in a civil divorce case, criminal prosecution of the confessed adulterer is most unusual. When criminal action is taken, the prosecution and punishment of the adulterer are often used as a means to work off personal or political grudges, as a method of one spouse to obtain property or child-custody advantages over the other spouse, or to further some tangential social cause (such as the reduction of prostitution). Despite the official inclusion of adultery in the criminal code of most nations, the predominant contemporary attitude is to consider the activity a personal concern. It is thought by most people to be a social offense only when it is so indiscreetly pursued that it becomes general knowledge. Even then no legal action is likely unless the adultery, left unpunished, is thought to set a bad moral example for youth or otherwise to encourage wrongdoing.

Contemporary Values: Complexity and Confusion

Adultery is one of the most emotion-loaded subjects with which a student of human behavior can be asked to deal. It is not only a topic about which most people show a high degree of value sensitivity; their positive and negative reactions are often quite inconsistent and inter- twined, variable and blurred. Although officially (and sometimes unofficially), extramarital sex relations are represented as the gravest threat to the very existence of the sacrosanct institutions of marriage and the family, unofficially (and sometimes officially) these same activities are represented as the most romantic, glorious, ecstatic, and self-fulfilling available to an individual of either sex. In case a particular citizen might consider such creative delights worth pursuing, however, he is officially reminded that the inexorable end for the adulterer (in this world or the next) is indescribable misery. Unofficially again, however, room is left for doubt with many persons that *they* would meet with such a fate as a result of *their* adulterous actions—*but*, they are reminded, it was just such heretical doubts as these that lured men and women of the past to their self-destruction.

Not only are complexity and confusion the outstanding characteristics of contemporary value systems related to sex in general and adultery in particular, but there is widespread resentment of any scientific or educational efforts to bring light into the attitudinal darkness. As Kinsey and his associates have ably demonstrated, activities designed to obtain and reveal *facts* about human sexual behavior are reacted to by many citizens as indecent, irreligious, corrupting to the morals, and even downright criminal. It is often viewed as even worse to *reason* about facts that have been obtained on such a tabooed subject as extramarital sex relations: that is, to examine the reality and rationality of existing actions and rules and attitudes. With a full realization of the inadequacy of available facts and of the unattainability of total objectivity in such a labyrinth of values, we do our best in the following paragraphs to look rationally and realistically at adultery. Since positive and negative values are so entangled, it seems artificial to make separate listings of the arguments for and against extramarital sex relations. We try, instead, to consider both sides of matters that have some base in fact and to ignore contentions for which supporting data do not exist. We number our observations for the convenience of reading and reference and not with implications of ordinal significance.

1. Regardless of the particular kinds of sex training administered to individuals in the various cultures and subcultures, a majority of men and women in all societies at some times and under some circumstances find extramarital sex relations interesting, attractive, appealing, and exciting. The factual support for this assertion comes from many reports of direct observations of sexual behavior and of oral and written statements about sexual attitudes. Whether or not an individual *acts* upon his feelings and thoughts of interest and excitement toward an adulterous union depends upon a large number of individual and social factors, some of which we consider below.

2. Historically (but decreasingly so contemporaneously), being a male increased the probability in most societies that any particular individual would act upon his inclination to commit adultery.

3. Although it is possible that human males are, in general, more strongly predisposed toward having a variety of sex partners, the greater leniency accorded the male than the female on the question of marital fidelity in most societies would seem to be largely a consequence of the dominant role of the male in the evolutionary development of social customs. Stated differently, male rulers and rulemakers have been more sensitive to male needs and values than to female needs and values.

4. Although every society has developed values that place some restrictions on extramarital sex activity, even the societies with the most rigid restrictions have recognized the need for accepting some such activity under certain circumstances for at least some of its male members.

5. The most severely punitive attitudes toward adulterers have been associated with religious fanaticism, where supernatural significance has been superstitiously imposed upon the institutions of marriage and the family. Even at the height of official prosecution of adulterers at various periods in various societies, records indicate a considerable unofficial condoning of adulterous behavior for at least privileged elements in the populations concerned.

6. The mildest restrictions on extramarital coitus have been in societies where little or no meaning other than pleasure has been attached to the sexual experience. Such cultures have been rare—a Himalayan group (the Lepchas of Sikkim) and an Australian aboriginal tribe (the Arunta) are two notable examples—but there have been periods in various societies during which attachment of high significance to the sexual act has been less apparent. Western culture in general seems to be experiencing a trend toward more emphasis on the pleasure value of sex.

7. Although rationality does not often seem to be closely related to the development of human customs in general or of sex values in particular, some restraint on extramarital sex relations seems realistically related to survival in a society with a simple technology. In such a society, the family for all practical purposes constitutes the essential social organization upon which the economy of survival rests. Completely unrestrained adulterous liaisons would undoubtedly ruin such a social structure.

8. Modern industrialized, urbanized, economically specialized societies have developed to a point where the institutions of marriage and the family are of much less significance for survival and physical well-being. Adultery has, therefore, ceased to be a serious threat to the economy of these societies.

9. Values, on the other hand, that originated to some degree out of physical necessity are still so deeply rooted in many of the individuals of modern societies and especially in the official cultures of these societies that adultery is still treated at times *as if* it were still a threat to the whole social structure.

10. In addition, new values related to the *psychological welfare* of the individual have been invented and superimposed upon and intertwined with old values associated with pre-existing economic needs (point 8) and continuing superstitions (point 5). Both facts and unproved hypotheses regarding the developing personality of the individual, especially the child, have brought new value emphases on the importance of husband-wife and parent-child interactions. With rare and rather sporadic exceptions (such as those undertaken in Israel and the Soviet Union), contemporary societies

have made no energetic, experimental attempts to develop new social institutions to meet the new psychological values. Nor have these societies, for the most part, attempted any major reconstruction of the marriage and family institutions in ways designed to recognize the departure of old economic values, the nonexistence of supernatural factors, and the development of new personality needs. Instead, as we have pointed out, the general cultural tendencies have consisted mainly of a confused accumulation of undifferentiated old and new values. The current jumble of values concerning adultery is but one product of the general cultural disorder. "Psychological sanctity" of the family, in short, has now joined value forces with persisting "economic sanctity" and "supernatural sanctity" to discourage adultery. But, because of the irrationalities and inconsistencies of these accumulated values and because of counteracting forces that encourage extramarital sex relations, the process of cultural discouragement appears increasingly ineffective.

11. In addition to the widespread appeal of sexual variety (point 1), many of the conditions of living in the contemporary social world contribute to a rising incidence of adultery. Some of these factors follow:

a. Despite the confusing value indoctrination to which they have been subjected (or, perhaps, in a deeper psychological sense, *because* the indoctrination contained so much confusion), a growing number of intelligent and informed citizens are no longer deterred by anxiety or guilt from engaging in extramarital coitus.

b. For even a greater number of individuals, the possibly deterring risks of pregnancy and venereal disease have been largely removed from extramarital sex relations by contemporary methods of contraception and prophylaxis.

c. Risks of detection and resultant social difficulties have been greatly reduced by the ready availability and privacy of present-day transportation to and housing for adulterous activity.

d. Adultery has conscious and unconscious appeal as an antidote for or an escape from many of the problems of modern living. The average citizen is filled with tensions and anxieties that not only stem from his own peculiar difficulties, but are tied in with the general social turmoil (hot and cold wars, threat of an atomic holocaust, growth of thus-far insoluble population and economic problems, confusion and ineptitude of many social institutions, revolutionary changes in the physical and technological environment, and a plethora of other social pathologies). Extramarital sex relations sound to many adults, besieged by difficulties from without and within, like (at least temporarily) a new chance at life: love, adventure, excitement, peace, romance, ego-inflation, increased power, return to youthful delights, conquest, and personal fulfillment hoped for, but not achieved, in marriage. In societies like the contemporary ones, especially with cultural traditions that have persistently glorified the joy-achieving propensities of extramarital sex relations, growing numbers of individuals will surely feel they have little or nothing to lose and quite possibly something to gain by engaging in such relations.

e. Many citizens are currently unhappy with not only life in general, but marriage in particular. Divorces, separations without divorce, plain desertions, and the readily observable unhappiness of couples who remain together give documentation to the generalization that many people find modern marriage an unsatisfactory relationship. This adds to the specific popularity of adultery as a supplement to more generalized flight-from-reality devices, such as motion pictures, radio, television, ataractic drugs, and alcohol. It seems indisputable that many members of contemporary societies find life unbearable without various types of solace. Legal and hortatory sanctions against adultery seem doomed to a fate comparable to that achieved by the American experiment with the prohibition of alcoholic beverages.

12. Although extramarital sexual relations seem often to function as neurotic avoidances of or escapes from life problems in marriage and the family or in other social relationships, there is no evidence for stating that all adulterous activities arise from individual or social pathology. Even where emotional and/or social disturbances appear indisputably the

source of a particular adulterous liaison, there is no support in reality or rationality for a condemnatory and punitive attitude toward the adulterers. Such actions, when pathological, have almost inevitably arisen compulsively out of such conditions as those we have discussed in point 11. Personal and social therapy, not persecution, is the rational and realistic answer to adultery that arises out of personal and social pathology.

13. Adultery is a high-risk undertaking under present social circumstances for a person who is fairly happy in general and who is well satisfied with his marriage in particular. Persistence of the strong cultural tradition that adultery is a marriage-destroying act often makes it so, even though there seems no logical reason why this should be true. Probably only a small percentage of men and women in our society have fully freed themselves of deep-seated anxieties and guilts about extramarital sex relations, and still fewer probably have mates who are similarly free. Where the individual himself is free of anxiety or guilt about the infidelity itself, he may find himself concerned about being dishonest with a mate who would disapprove if she knew. And, even where reciprocal knowledge and approval exist, frequent or long-extended extramarital sexual activities can produce negative effects on marital (and, hence, personal) happiness by draining time, energy, money, affection, and other factors from the marriage relationship.

14. Although such facts as those just discussed make adultery risky for happily married people in present-day society, they offer no support for the moralistic assertion that adultery is universally and intrinsically evil. For unhappily married persons, of whom there are many (see 11, *e*), point 13 has no relevance, and extramarital sex relations offer a convenient temporary (and, in some cases, permanent) route away from marital discord. Secondly, these facts apply for happily married persons under present social circumstances. There is no reason to believe that man, if he wishes, cannot invent ways to reduce or remove the social conditions that make extramarital coitus hazardous for happily married people. Finally, what is risky is not inevitable: there is

some evidence from both clinical and survey sources to show that some happily married persons nicely surmount the hazards and avoid serious marital difficulties.

Extramarital Petting

To a considerable extent extramarital petting may be considered a social compromise, especially popular among Americans of the higher socioeconomic and college-educated groups, between the dullness and drabness with which rigidly monogamous sexual behavior fills many contemporary citizens and the more socially dangerous and morally condemned excitements of extramarital coitus. Approval of conscience and of mate for extramarital petting in various types of social situations (such as automobile rides, drinking parties, dances, and picnics) seems relatively easy to obtain for many contemporaries.

Since premarital petting has become an increasingly important pattern for youth of the higher-educated and upper-class groups, the apparent growth of extramarital petting may be, in part, simply the extension of earlier established sexual habits in a later age period. It is also probable that for many, extramarital petting is not a substitute for, but a prelude to, extramarital coitus. The Kinsey investigators, however, report that approximately one-sixth of a sample of more than 1,000 married females had engaged in extramarital petting without ever having engaged in extramarital coitus.

Additional and more precise data are needed on the extent, functions, and implications of extramarital petting in modern societies. Our tentative judgment is that the apparent trend toward increased extramarital petting may be viewed as a further undermining of the moral position that married people should strictly confine their sex interests and activities to their marital partners. It also seems possible that the future incidence of extramarital coitus will be augmented by recruits from extramarital petters. Although the recent increase in premarital petting apparently brought no comparable rise in the incidence of premarital coitus, various factors differ in the extramarital situation. First, technical virginity and related inhibitions prevent some premaritally petting girls from engaging in premarital coitus. Not only has such a barrier been removed for married women, but positive movement from petting to coitus has been well established in their marital sexual activities. Secondly, and closely related, both women and men often have coitus psychologically conditioned as the natural, mature, and most satisfying form of sexual satisfaction and are less likely (as married adults than as unmarried adolescents) to settle for what they view as the less natural, less mature, and less satisfying experiences of petting. Thirdly, although official taboos are stronger against extramarital than premarital coitus, opportunities for comfortable and undetected and unhurried nonmarital coitus are more plentiful for many married than for many unmarried people.

References

Bernard, W. S., "Student Attitudes on Marriage and the Family." *Am. Sociol. Rev. 3;* 354-361, 1938.

Davis, Katharine B., *Factors in the Sex Life of Twenty-two Hundred Women.* New York: Harper & Brothers, 1929.

Dearborn, Lester W., "Extramarital Relations." In Morris Fishbein and Ruby J. R. Kennedy (eds.), *Modern Marriage and Family Living.* New York: Oxford University Press, 1957.

Duvall, Sylvanus M., *Men, Women, and Morals.* New York: Association Press, 1952.

Ellis, Albert, *The American Sexual Tragedy.* New York: Twayne Pub., 1954.

Ellis, Albert, *Sex Without Guilt.* New York: Lyle Stuart, 1958.

Ford, Cellan S., and Beach, Frank A., *Patterns of Sexual Behavior.* New York: Harper & Brothers, 1951.

Hamilton, G. V., *A Research in Marriage.* New York: Medical Research Press, 1929.

Kinsey, A. C., *et al., Sexual Behavior in the Human Female.* Philadelphia: W. B. Saunders Co., 1953.

Kinsey, A. C., *et al., Sexual Behavior in the Human Male.* Philadelphia: W. B. Saunders Co., 1948.

Kirkendall, Lester A., *Understanding Sex.* Chicago: Science Research Associates, 1947.

Lindner, Robert, "Adultery—Kinds and Consequences." In Albert Ellis (ed.), *Sex Life of the American Woman and the Kinsey Report.* New York: Greenberg Pub., 1954.

Locke, Harvey J., *Predicting Adjustment in Marriage.* New York: Henry Holt & Co., 1951.

Murdock, G. P., "The Social Regulation of Sexual Behavior." In P. H. Hoch and J. Zubin (eds.), *Psychosexual Development in Health and Disease.* New York: Grune & Stratton, Inc., 1949.

Ohlson, W. E., "Adultery: A Review." *Boston U. Law Rev. 17;* 328-368; 533-622, 1937.

Rosenthal, H. C., "Sex Habits of European Women vs. American Women." *Pageant* 52-59, March, 1951.

Zuckerman, S., *The Social Life of Monkeys and Apes.* London: Kegan Paul, 1932.

ROBERT A. HARPER

Family, Sexual
and Affectional Functions of the

Definition

A FAMILY is an enduring social group of individuals whose interrelationships are defined primarily by the process of biological reproduction. In other words, it is a *consanguine* group. The concept excludes casual sex relations, but admits common-law or *de facto* marriages. Since marriage normally leads to, or anticipates, parenthood, the concept of the family includes childless marriages and also the substitutes for biological parenthood, such as adoption or marriage to a person who is already a parent. Family members have many interrelationships other than the defining biological relationship.

Parents with *their* children are called a *nuclear* family. When a group includes three generations, or in other words two generations of married persons, it is called an *extended* family. "Family" implies a group that has a common dwelling or nearby dwellings, or that has continuous, intimate association, readily distinguishing it from other groups and relationships. Consanguine relationships outside such an intimate group are called *kinship*. A group of kinsfolk defined through father-child relationships is called a *patrilineal sib* or *clan*. In our society such persons are identified partly by having a common surname. A group of kinsfolk defined through mother-child relationships is called a *matrilineal sib* or *clan*. In many societies this, rather than the patrilineal, is the prevailing concept, and it determines rights, duties, and marriage choices. Patrilineal and matrilineal clans are *unilateral*. A village or settlement may include mostly the members of a single clan, with their spouses taken from other clans. But often the clan connections are recognized to such a remote degree of kinship that not all members of a clan can live in the same community.

However, many societies, including our own, give fairly equal importance to father and mother kinship; this pattern is called *bilateral*, and a group of kinsfolk defined by actual consanguine nearness rather than a unilateral descent is called a *kindred*. Our society is now patrilineal as regards name only, i.e., it is *patronymic*. In earlier times it had other patrilineal features such as male inheritance of property. In the Spanish division of Euro-American culture, bilaterality is recognized through a person's taking both father's and mother's surname.

A family as defined by the United States Census is two or more persons related by blood, marriage, or adoption and living together in either a household or quasi household. In 1950 the population living in families was 138 million, and the average family consisted of 3.60 persons. The Census defines a household as all who occupy a single dwelling unit, which may be a house or an apartment. The average household consisted of 3.38 persons. Quasi households are hotels, lodging houses with five or more lodgers, labor camps, military barracks, and "institutions." Students are usually accounted as living in their family homes rather than their school or college dormitories. In the

392

United States in 1950 the population, then 151 million, was divided as follows: 145 million lived in households and 6 million in quasi households.

The phrase "the family" is often used not to mean any particular family or kinship group, but in a generic, abstract sense, meaning the sum total of all families, or the whole system of family relationships. In this sense, which will be indicated by capitalization, the Family is considered as one of the several institutions of society, the other principal ones being the State, the Church, the School, and the Economic System. According to Chapin (*Contemporary American Institutions*, p. 412), an institution "consists of segments of individuals' behaviors organized into a system, and not of whole individuals or groups." An institution is a form that endures while its personnel commonly changes. Thus, a family, or family system, differs from other institutions in that it is identified with particular persons and their offspring. Its turnover of personnel is by birth, death, marriage, or divorce, not by other types of joining and resigning, hiring and firing, matriculation and graduation. Thus the Family is more than an institution; it is a natural, precultural social grouping existing also among lower animals, which, strictly speaking, have no institutions. Animals have no marriage ceremonies, but they do have more or less enduring, habit-supported bonds between particular sexual partners and between mother and offspring. Humans symbolize and ceremonialize these relationships in various ways, but the relationships are real and quite distinct from momentary sexual or nurturing contacts.

The above definitions of the family are structural. Like a machine or an organism, a society or any portion thereof may be viewed in three aspects: (1) structure, (2) operation or function, (3) change or development. These aspects cannot be entirely separated in discussion, but they furnish convenient viewpoints for analysis. A *functional* definition of the family would be: that social grouping which nurses, nurtures, and trains the young until they are able to subsist independently. It is now a common practice among American family sociologists to conceptualize the family in terms of development. The family is a continuous flow of human interaction and experience, centered about the reproductive and child-rearing processes, operating within an intimate group that changes slowly as members are born and as they mature, marry, divorce, age, and die.

These events lead to various kinds of separations and also to new connections; units divide and combine, but throughout there is continuity: no beginning and no end. The group into which one is born is called his *family of orientation;* that in which he is a parent is his *family of procreation.* From this point of view, nuclear family units normally pass through these phases or stages: establishment phase, expectant phase, child-bearing phase, families with preschool children, families with school children, families with teenagers, the launching phase, the family in middle years, and aging families. Obviously, these phases overlap and a cycle begins for the younger generation long before the older generation has completed its cycle.

Universal Characteristics of the Family

"A woman with a child, and a man to look after her"; thus Margaret Mead once defined the essence of the family. Among at least all warm-blooded vertebrates there is some more or less durable set of social relationships that we call "family." The nucleus of this is always the bond between the dependent young and the mother. These always remain together. Moreover, this mother-with-inseparable-young continues to be sexually pursued, fed, guarded, bossed, or otherwise habitually treated for some period of time by the identical male or males.

These relationships may be called natural social relations or interactions. They precede mankind and hence culture. They are not, however, "instinctive"; they are acquired by learning in individual experiences. Their uniformities within a given society, or within a species, or even within all mammals or all birds, are due to the common denominators of the environment and of the anatomical structures that must learn to react to this environment, but not to *preformed* nervous pathways. Thus arise such natural habits, misleadingly called "instincts," as heterosexual preference, parental love, sexual rivalry and jealousy, protective behavior, gregariousness, collecting behavior. The occasional variations from the uniform pattern under special conditions, as illustrated by homosexuality, hostility to the young, etc., lend weight to the habit theory.

A natural habit can be prevented from forming, or can be modified, by arranging situations so that a different psychological conditioning takes place. "Natural" does not mean "inevitable," but merely "most probable to develop in the world as it is."

In all known past or present human societies the complex of social relations we call "family" seems to have these characteristics:

1. The great majority *prefer* heterosexual coitus to any other means of sexual satisfaction, although it may not always be the most frequent form of sexual activity.

2. The typical coitus is a repetition of the act with a familiar individual rather than a casual or varietist act; "promiscuity" never applies to most of the people for most of the time.

3. Within a given society there are always certain largely uniform attitudes of sexual avoidance. The tabooed sex objects always include the members of the nuclear family other than the spouse. There are a few exceptions to this minimum definition of incest, especially among upper classes, in a few societies.

4. Males are always the more active, the more combative, and the more effectively possessive in pursuit of sexual satisfaction, although not necessarily desirous or capable of more frequent sexual orgasm. The perpetually smoldering fires of conflict over sexual privileges are held in check by some scheme of rules. In this scheme males generally control females, and the more powerful or capable males control a disproportionate number of females, or the more generally desired females, or both. This inequality of control may express itself in upper-class polygyny with lower-class polyandry, or merely in unequal distribution of sexual privileges, or in specializing women into celibates, wives, prostitutes.

5. Mothers almost always nurse and care for their own babies. Both mother and child find organic satisfactions in this process, which builds up the strongest, most lasting, and most personal of emotional attachments.

6. This mother-child(ren) relationship is al-ways supplemented by an adult male, nearly always the biological father, thus forming a "nuclear family" that is always distinguishable as a unit even in the presence of larger familial or kinship groupings. In a very few societies the maternal uncle or another male performs some or all of the social functions of fatherhood. In civilized societies widows are often left with only financial assistance, whereas in many primitive societies they are taken on by the deceased husband's brother (levirate) or other male as a duty.

7. The nuclear family group performs economic and educational functions, with a division of labor between men and women. Despite great cultural differences, women's occupations are those that require less mobility and can easily be interrupted by the care of children. Thus, woman's natural place is in or near the home. Likewise it is natural that occupations requiring extreme muscular effort, speed, or longer absences from home should be practiced by men.

This natural, universal pattern is modified by numerous variations among the various societies of the world. These variations are commonly said to be cultural. They are culture traits if they are imitated from generation to generation. Some variations, however, are natural adaptations to different environments and conditions, and would recur with each generation without imitation.

Variations of Family Systems

The following three sections present some significant variations of the family system among various societies.

Material and Economic Traits

In 1950, 64 per cent of all United States dwelling units were in single-family detached houses. Despite the earlier development of "flats" and apartment houses in cities, the general trend of American living is toward the single-family house. In 1950, 83 per cent of new, permanent, nonfarm dwelling construction was in single-family houses, in 1956, 97 per cent. In the 1920's and 1930's this proportion was less.

In the Soviet Union also, plans call for a trend to single-family residences. There are great regional and national differences in this variable. Continental cities and New York consist largely of multifamily houses, whereas our western and southern cities, and rural areas everywhere, are more given to separate residences. In London, Philadelphia, and Baltimore many dwellings are considered single family because they have separate ground entrances, even though they are attached to adjacent houses. When Khrushchev in Stalin's days suggested that Russian collective farmers be moved from their many villages of single-family houses to large apartment houses in fewer, centralized "agrarian cities," he met with the cold shoulder and dropped his plan.

Until about 1880 the American farm population (which is only a part of the rural population) was more than half of the total population. From then on it grew very slowly, became stationary, and then declined until in 1956 it was only 13 per cent of the total population. In 1950 our population was 64 per cent urban by the new definition then inaugurated by the census, 21 per cent rural nonfarm, and 15 per cent farm. The average of all households contained 3.38 persons, but the average farm household contained 3.98 persons.

The suburban population is difficult to define, because political units do not correspond very well to ecological communities. It is mostly an urban population but some of it is rural nonfarm. The suburban population is growing much faster than the population of the central cities, and it is largely a population living in single-family houses. In 1950, 64 million of the urban population was in the 168 metropolitan areas; of this, 49 million lived in the central cities and 35 million in suburban areas.

About 55 per cent of occupied dwelling units are now owned by their occupiers, as against about 47 per cent at the beginning of the century. However, 44 per cent of these owned dwellings are mortgaged, as against 32 per cent in 1900. About 85 or more per cent of families have telephones, 96 per cent radios, 81 per cent televisions, and 50 per cent central heating—yet 15 per cent still do not have piped running water. In all these respects American home life has advanced beyond that in most other countries.

Many of the changes in family life are due to the fact that farm families before approximately 1880 were the majority of all families, while now they are only 9 per cent of all families, although containing 13 per cent of the population because of their larger average size. The farm population, although reduced to a much smaller proportion, still feeds most of the rest of the American population.

Farm families are not the only ones that carry on their occupations in or near their homes. Such is also the case with many families who own retail stores and small workshops. However, these also are on the decline, and thus the separation of home from workplace, except for full-time homemakers, has become the pattern of living for the great majority of Americans. This is less true of small-industry countries, even though rather highly urbanized, such as France.

The Roles of the Sexes

The division of labor between the sexes varies greatly. In many societies, especially those of central and eastern Europe, women work extensively in agriculture. They develop the muscular strength and endurance to carry heavy burdens. Nursing babies are sometimes brought to their mothers in the fields, and a few older women who remain in the home sometimes care for children other than their own. The Russians under Communism have developed this economical pattern still further by putting many young children into nurseries under the day care of a relatively few women.

The employment of Russian women as professional engineers, locomotive and tractor operators, railroad and construction laborers, doctors, judges, and at times in field military operations is not communistic, but quite in accord with traditional Russian culture. It takes less muscle to pull the levers that operate a modern locomotive than to scrub clothing on a washboard. Physicians were usually women in Russia before the Revolution; women doctors were even used in the army. There is no natural reason why women should be less fitted than men to practice medicine. The contrasting dim view taken of women doctors in Germany was due to the attitude that professional or high-status occupations, even if sedentary, should belong to men.

The labor-force sex ratio in the United States in 1900 was about 450 males per 100 females;

in 1920 about 400; in 1950–1957 it was about 230. The sex ratio of the total population changed only slightly, from 104.4 in 1900 to 98.4 in 1957. Yet these changes have merely brought the United States to the same pattern that has existed ever since 1900 in Great Britain, which has a labor-force sex ratio of 230-240. In France the ratio has been about 180 throughout the half-century. In the Czarist Russia of 1913 the ratio was about 300, and it became about 115 in 1926 and again in 1950. These very low ratios were due partly to the high war deaths of males and the generally low sex ratios after the two world wars. A more normal figure for Russia would be 130, as it was in 1939 and as is predicted for 1970. (Warren M. Eason in Bergson, *Soviet Economic Growth*, 1953.) A ratio of 130 of course is unusually low, apparently reflecting the Soviet policy of obtaining the most efficient possible use of woman power.

However, Russia is a country of collective farms, and the women who work on them are counted in the occupational statistics. The Russian figures of 1939—before the war withdrew millions of men—showed more women than men employed on farms. By contrast, American census figures show the men occupied in agriculture to be over four times as numerous as the women. If these Russian agricultural women workers were "deflated" to correspond to their proportion in the United States, the Russian labor-force sex ratio of 1939, and presumably of 1970, would stand at about 180 rather than 130. This still reflects a high use of woman power outside the home.

Special significance has been attached to the percentage of married women who are employed outside the home. In the United States this was about 6 per cent in 1900 and was estimated at about 30 per cent for 1955. In France it has been constantly about 20 per cent. In Britain, after a wartime high, it shrank to 18 per cent in 1947.

In the United States and Russia there have been marked changes since 1920 in the way women spend their time. In Russia the major changes have been due to rapid industrialization and farm collectivization. In America the changes have come somewhat more through labor-saving devices in the home, reducing both domestic service and essential homemaking time and encouraging the absorption of women's released time into white-collar occupations outside the home.

Too much has been said about the status of women in *general*. Thus Hobhouse, Wheeler, and Ginsberg find by their tribe-counting method that "the position of women in the simpler societies is not favorable as judged by modern standards." There is, moreover, "no substantial change according to grade or type of culture except that the unfavorable tendency is accentuated in the pastoral state." Woman is inferior in 73 per cent of the agricultural and 87.5 per cent of the pastoral tribes (*The Material Culture and Social Institutions of the Simpler Peoples*, 1930, pp. 170–175). But as Robert Lowie points out: "It should be noted that the treatment of woman is one thing, her legal status another, her opportunities for public activity still another, while the character and extent of her labors belong again to a distinct category" (*Primitive Society*, 1925, p. 186).

There is a definite attitude toward woman that has spread through a number of contiguous peoples in Siberia, indicating probable diffusion. This attitude is that woman is property, but it does not involve her seclusion. A wife can travel quite freely without her husband. In Australia, Melanesia, and New Guinea there is another widespread attitude that stresses the segregation of the sexes. Among advanced societies in the Islamic world and the Near East, we may note the great tendency to seclude and segregate women without unduly harsh treatment. In Russia and Central Europe, by contrast, women perform heavy outdoor labor, are seen frequently in public places and in the fields, and have political equality; but the tradition of wife-beating has only recently been on the wane. Western Europe has been influenced by the ideology of chivalry, which tends to protect woman, as the weaker sex, from heavy manual work, but does not bar her from social or political life.

Relations Between Old and Young

The relation of parents to children varies from extreme authoritarianism to extreme permissiveness; and also, along another independent dimension, from intense, protective love to comparative neglect and indifference.

Lately in American society there has been a shift toward greater permissiveness. This has had bad as well as good results. The serious danger lies not in authority, but in the rejected child—one who is not wanted or not genuinely loved.

Educated people in America have been worried about the Oedipus complex, in which a boy tends to love his mother intensely and to hate his father, who is jealous of this mother-son relationship. This pattern appears to be more frequent in German and central European society. In America, the problem lies rather in the effort to conform to the demands of the peer-group.

German culture, unlike French, English, Russian, Italian, or Spanish, has stressed for many decades the revolt of young men against their fathers and elder-dominated society. This expressed itself in the custom of *Wanderjahr* and the Youth Movement, which later played into the hands of Hitler. Psychologically, Hitler was not the father of Nazi Germany, but the older brother who led a revolt against stuffy oldsters.

When we view the whole range of human societies, we see that the roles to which children are trained vary enormously. Among the Manu of Melanesia the child is taught to be skillful in swimming and climbing, and is imbued with such an extreme respect of property that he even comments upon the possible ownership of a morsel of food seen floating about in the water. On the other hand, he strikes and insults his parents with impunity. In Samoa, although trained to render a decorous respect to elders, he is allowed to run about freely in parties that spy upon adolescent love-making and gather to witness the process of childbirth. Among many peoples, free sex play is tolerated and even encouraged among children. In Samoa, children of about 6 to 12 are made responsible for the supervision of their younger brothers and sisters, and devise various methods to prevent the latter's annoying adults. When adolescence comes, the child is relieved of this responsibility and enters upon a more interesting and less burdensome life.

The aged are treated in very different ways. In primitive Australia, as in civilized China, the old men rule by virtue of their age. In Polynesia, hereditary rank commonly takes priority over age. Among the Plains Indians, Trobrianders, and others, age is a pitied rather than a highly respected status. Among some peoples living in difficult environments, old people are sometimes killed or abandoned on migrations. Modern France certainly makes life easier for old people than modern America. To mention only one facet, a love or sex affair between a young person and a much older person, of either sex, is treated sympathetically by French, but not by American, literature.

Family Structure and the Larger Societal Structure: Kinship

The Family is a part of the larger social structure and it also has a structure of its own. Every individual has a position in the family system; at the same time, he has positions in the other institutions. It is the Family that gives the individual his basic identity, not only through the biological process of birth, but also by naming him and training him through his earliest years. The question "Who am I?" is answered primarily in terms of family relationships. Anthropologist George P. Murdock's book *Social Structure* deals entirely with familial and kinship structure. He says nothing about industry, church, state, or school. This becomes understandable when we note that his materials are drawn from a survey of 250 representative human societies. A representative sample of human beings would be heavily weighted by people from the larger and more advanced societies such as the United States, the Soviet Union, India, and China. A representative sample of human *societies*, on the other hand, is necessarily weighted heavily with small primitive societies. In such societies social structure very largely consists of familial and kinship structure. The other institutions, although present in embryo form in all societies, undergo most of their development in the more advanced societies.

The Family is the one institution that does not become more complex as society becomes complex. It does not follow the general law of evolution, which implies continued differentiation, integration, and hence complexity. It would be too much to say that it follows the reverse trend; it is sufficient to note that some of the most complicated kinship and family systems are found among societies that are "backward" in other respects. For example, one primitive Australian society uses 71 different terms to discriminate different kin-relationships (W. Lloyd Warner, "The Family and Principles of Kinship Structure in Australia." *Am. Sociol. Rev.* 2:46, Feb., 1937). Among the Trobriand Islanders, descent is traced through the mother line, yet the newly formed nuclear family lives in the village of the father. A boy lives with his natural father and mother until puberty, but he owes duties and obedience to his maternal uncle, from whom he inherits his property, rights, and rank, and in whose village he normally goes to live at maturity. His relation to his father is one of affection more than of obedience and discipline, and fathers try to keep their sons with them as long as possible (Bronislaw Malinowski, *The Sexual Life of Savages in Northwestern Melanesia*, 1929). Among the Andaman Islanders, a preliterate and also preagricultural people, married couples frequently exchange their children, so that a child may have several sets of parents and foster parents, all of whom love him, visit him, and feel responsibility for him. These cases may be contrasted with the typical middle-class American nuclear family, which has little interest in its kinsfolk except those who happen to be personally pleasant or useful, and which may be inconvenienced by any strong bonds of obligation or affection outside the nuclear family circle. In both the upper and lower classes in America there is somewhat more interest in, and contact with, kinsfolk than in the climbing, status-seeking middle class.

Kinship structure and nomenclature show no evolutionary trend through history, nor are they greatly influenced by diffusion of patterns from neighboring societies. Rather, they fall into a limited number of types that are distributed over the earth without discernible law and order. The important types as regards the marital relation are described in the article "Marriage."

The modern Euro-American family is nuclear and monogamous. Of Murdock's sample of 192 societies, 47 have normally only this type. Everywhere this is the basic unit, out of which more complex units may or may not be built.

A simple polygamous family (usually polygynous, rarely polyandrous) consists of two or more nuclear families affiliated by having one parent (usually the man) in common. An extended family consists of two or more nuclear families affiliated through the parent-child relationship with or without plural marriage, e.g., by joining the nuclear family of the married adult with that of his parents. In Murdock's sample, 53 societies have polygamous but not extended families, and 92 have some form of extended family.

In some bilateral systems, marriages tend to take place within the local community that is composed of relatively near kindred (*endogamous demes*). In most societies, however, marriage is exogamous with respect to some unit—the community, the near kindred, the matrilineal or the patrilineal clan. Everywhere there is an incest taboo upon marriage of the closest relatives such as brother and sister.

The History of the Family System

There are four explanatory principles of social change that have been promulgated: evolution, diffusion, adaptive functionalism, and cyclical fluctuations. Early sociologists and anthropologists saw the family system as an evolution from promiscuity through polyandry, polygyny, to monogamy; from a mother-centered family to patriarchy; and then to sex equality and democracy. This view was "debunked" by anthropological evidence, which showed no correlation between the form of the family and the general stage of social evolution. Later, the diffusionists and historical anthropologists sought to explain each culture as the result of diffusion or borrowing from other cultures with which it had been in contact. Geographic culture areas, each with its own regional history, became more important than any general, world-wide history of culture. In primitive America at least, evidence showed matrilineal systems to be correlated with more advanced cultures than the patrilineal. The *couvade*, a custom by which the father goes to bed at the birth of a child, was interpreted no longer as a natural stage in world-wide evolution, but as a custom that just happened to arise in one or more places and from them spread to others.

More recently, both the evolutionary and diffusionist principles have been overshadowed by adaptive functionalism, which holds that any social change must be explained as an adaptation to other changes—in society or in other conditions of life. The crucial question becomes, not what historical epoch, nor what geographic location, but what social context. It is seldom possible to learn enough about any of the numerous primitive family systems to explain why it is just what it is, or how it came to be that way. It is also unsound to infer that the present-day primitive societies are a fair representation of the prehistoric phases of civilized societies.

Zimmerman (1947) has found a cyclical sequence of forms in the history of our Euro-American society which, he claims, is more significant than the study of many small and primitive societies. He finds three main types: the trustee family, the domestic family, and the atomistic family. These types are outlined as follows.

In the trustee or large patriarchal family system, property belongs to the family in perpetuity, the living members having its use only during their lifetime. The large extended family or clan is responsible for the acts of all its members; it disciplines them and also protects them from outsiders. The individual, as it were, has his personality delegated to him by the family.

In the domestic family system, property belongs to the living family, primarily to the male head. It can sometimes be sold, and trade becomes prominent. There is still passive solidarity of household members in case of minor law violations, but also a tendency toward individual responsibility. Antagonistic relations sometimes develop between family and state. The notion arises that society consists of compacts made by individual persons. During most of the domestic family period in Europe the Christian Church regulated family life. Very roughly, this type of family corresponds to what some writers have called the small patriarchal type.

In the atomistic or individualistic family system, property belongs largely to the individual; marriage does not necessarily involve property transfer. Children obtain the right to their own income rather early. Legal responsibility is mainly individual, except for certain responsibilities of parents for the acts of their minor children. The person as such is sacred, but he begins to be dominated by the rising power of the State, which in the last analysis controls Family, Church, and all other institutions.

After the extreme atomism, individualism, and disorganization of family patterns in the late Roman Empire, there was a return to the trustee type in the Middle Ages and then a repetition of the ancient sequence. When America was settled the family system had for the most part arrived at the domestic type, but in the Appalachian-Ozark frontier regions there was a return to the trustee type. From these historic cycles Zimmerman predicts that the atomistic family of today is not a final stage, nor a step toward the final "withering away" of the family institutions, but that it will be succeeded by a stronger and more organized family, probably of the domestic type. Zimmerman's theory of family cycles is closely allied to the sociological theories of Le Play and Sorokin. In general, these thinkers hold to a theory of limits: when a social system goes too far toward some extreme, it will inevitably swing back again.

The trustee family of Euro-American society, as displayed in ancient Greece and Rome, the early Middle Ages, and the frontier days in America, was a patriarchal family. It was patrilineal, patrilocal, extended, and strongly dominated by males, normally the oldest male. Indeed, "patriarchal" was the name Zimmerman originally gave to this pattern. Except in some cases (as under Mormonism), it was monogamous, thus differing from the polygynous patriarchal family system of Chinese, Islamic, and ancient Hebrew civilizations.

The patriarchal trustee family was a part of the patriarchal clan—a part sufficiently small and local to permit a common residence or adjacent residences and to maintain control over its members. It becomes more understandable when we note that it really performed many functions now in the hands of Church or State. This also explains the occasional reversion to the trustee family system on frontiers. The private vengeance and feuding of clans in Appalachian America, persisting until about 1900, may be explained by the absence of effective government and police power in that region. Bad roads and limited government budgets made law enforcement difficult. It is natural that the frontier clans and families took the law into their own hands, even though their ancestors had been accustomed to effective civil government in Britain. Having the law in their own hands, they were loath to yield power to police and other government officers who invaded the hills to arrest feudists or to discover illicit whiskey, but eventually they had to.

The domestic type of family is characteristic of most of rural Europe and America of the past few centuries. Within this type some families are nuclear only and some are three-generation extended families. There is male dominance, reflected until lately in the superior legal rights of man and husband. But the clan is less prominent than under the trustee system, and there is much less authority and interference from kinsfolk outside the immediate household. People are governed by State law and Church law according to where they live, not any longer by clan law according to their distant kinship. The reforms of Cleisthenes in Attica, the pacification of the Scottish clans, and the suppression of feuds in eastern Kentucky represented a transition from the trustee to the domestic family system.

Prominent under the domestic type is the *stem-family* pattern, which means that one son in each generation customarily inherits the farm and is responsible for maintaining it as a family property in perpetuity. The daughters marry into another family, the other sons go to the city or move elsewhere, but any brothers and sisters or their children may return to the family farm in case of need. Thus there is always a continuous "stem" of persons on fixed land, from which other persons in each generation "branch out." In many countries the rule for selecting the heir to the land has been primogeniture. But this is not always the case. In Quebec, for example, a middle son in a large family is more likely to become the one who carries down the family stem. In France, Napoleon's laws requiring equal division led to the fragmentation of estates, disturbance of the stem-family pattern, birth control, and a slowdown of population increase. In French Quebec, which adhered to the older system of passing down undivided farms, the population has continued to expand, emigrate, and develop new lands. (This observation implies no judg-ment on what alternatives could or should have been followed.)

Zimmerman's term "atomistic" suggests to some a kind of moral condemnation, but it merely indicates the fact that in this type of family there is more individual freedom and less social control. In the domestic type of family persons are free from clan control, but retain certain obligations to parents and siblings even when adult. In the atomistic type the individual tends to become entirely free from all family control as soon as he becomes adult. American state laws still make persons responsible for support of indigent relatives, but it is increasingly easy to prove "inability," and to cast this burden upon the state. In an atomistic period even the children and adolescents within the nuclear family gain more freedom in practice from parental control. The line between legitimate "correction" and "cruelty to children" subtly moves away from parental power and toward juvenile "rights." Although formerly the husband had the right of "moderate correction" over his wife, wife-beating has been practically outlawed or defined as "cruelty" and thereby in most states is a ground for divorce. The school, the character-building agencies, and the peer-group gain more and more allegiance from the young at the expense of the family.

Clearly, this trend toward atomism or individualism is closely connected with urbanization, as it was in late Greece and late Rome. It can be observed in European peasant families and American rural families that move to the city. Yet in some cultural groups strong family authority has persisted despite urbanization, notably among Catholic peoples in Europe and in America.

Müller-Lyer (1931) divided the history of the family into a tribal or kinship epoch, a familial epoch, and a personal epoch, corresponding roughly to Zimmerman's three types. Müller-Lyer also recognizes that the Middle Ages saw a new kinship or patriarchal epoch, but he treats this as a new beginning among a different people (the Teutons) rather than as a continuation of Roman civilization. He makes his "personal epoch" peculiar to modern times: his late Roman family went into a late familial phase but no further. Müller-Lyer and Zimmerman differ in interpretation of the same facts. Zimmerman sees family history as forever oscillating between limits; Müller-Lyer sees a great unidirectional evolution, sometimes retrogressing here and there, but in world-wide terms moving toward a humane individualism with social control through cooperation of family, church, and school. Müller-Lyer's is in general the philosophy of most family sociologists today. It has been called "progressive individualism" in contrast with Zimmerman's "institutionalism." Its central theme is expressed by the subtitle of Burgess and Locke's *The Family*: *From Institution to Companionship*, and fits in better with the principle of adaptive functionalism than with the other great theories of social change.

We witness today a convergence toward the general pattern of the Euro-American family: monogamous; nuclear; planned and limited in reproduction; residentially separated from other families and from agricultural, manufacturing, and commercial operations; less authoritarian and more equalitarian; more concerned with health, leisure, and companionship. This convergent development has been due to many causes. It is not explained by blind imitation of the West, coercion by the West, or by any law of evolution inherent in the family system as such. The functionalist theory helps toward an explanation, e.g., the family system progressively adapts itself to other changes in society.

First, industrialism calls for rationality (i.e., efficiency) in the use of space and of human skills. Elaborate kinship rules and taboos, the extended family, polygamy, nepotism, and sentimental attachments to persons and places are nuisances under industrialism. In an environment of machines and specialized tools, children are less useful, more dangerous to themselves and others, than where simple manual work is to be done. Competition places under handicap those adults who slow down their working operations in order to train children on the job. The relegation of children to the home and school, and of mothers of small children to tasks that can practically be performed while tending these children, becomes more obviously advantageous. All this is a form of the greater specialization of work that goes with economic development. The rewards of industrialism entail eventually greater leisure, for some persons at least; this new leisure tends to be spent at places, times, and activities quite separate from those of the workaday world with its atmosphere of tension and competition. This is very different from primitive leisure, which consisted in elaborating and ritualizing the daily work itself.

Second, a high valuation upon some sort of equality, justice, or democracy among individuals has emerged in some form in all advanced societies.

Third, modern medical and other sciences, by demonstrating success in the reduction of pain, suffering, unwanted births, and premature deaths, become attractive to perceptive persons everywhere. There is, therefore, a slow, unconscious drift toward those patterns of living that are objectively more efficient in preventing human suffering or in maximizing individual human satisfactions.

The Probable Future of the Family

About 1920 it was widely proclaimed from two very different sources that the Family would adapt itself to these other social changes by disappearing altogether. It was argued that the functions of the Family could all be as well or better performed by other institutions or by individuals acting in unpatterned freedom. One source of this prophecy was the leadership of the new Marxist Russia. Engels, who had elaborated Marxism with some ideas from Lewis Morgan's evolutionary anthropology of "stages," considered the Family a capitalist institution which, like the State, would "wither away." Said the Bolshevik Commissar of Education, Lunacharsky: "Our problem is now to do away with the household and to free women from the care of children." He would not force this development, but he anticipated that people would live more and more in communal houses with children's quarters, and that in time such phrases as "my parents," "our children," would become obsolete, to be replaced by the generic, nonpossessive, concepts of "adults" and "children."

The other source was the American behavioristic psychologists, who from Russia had taken over Pavlov but not Marx, Engels, or Lenin.

Their leader, John B. Watson, declared that the home and the parent-child relation were doomed to disappear. "I would gamble my all, too, that after three months in our nursery no youngster will want to go home even for a week-end" (quoted in Victor F. Calverton and Samuel D. Schmalhausen, eds., *The Newer Generation.* New York: Macaulay, 1930, p. 73).

No such outcome is implied by the philosophy of progressive individualism. It is not even good evolutionism, but rather a doctrinaire projection of certain selected trends of family development to their logical conclusion without regard to the whole picture, a way of thinking rather characteristic of Marxism.

Likewise, the institutionalist cyclical view, although founded upon detailed historical scholarship, has an exaggerated concern with social control and its failures, with the breakdowns of orderly social structures so obvious in late Roman and in modern times. It gives little attention to the other functions of the Family.

Some thirty years have not only failed to reveal any withering away of the Family either in the U.S.S.R. or the United States, but have revealed trends toward making the Family stronger and more important. A careful review of the functions of the Family along with its structural position in society will show the unreasonableness of the Lunacharsky-Watson predictions.

Changing Functions of the Family

The functions of the Family may be outlined as follows:

I. NATURAL-SOCIAL

(pertaining to higher animals and all mankind)

Reproduction
Sexual satisfaction
Feeding and care of helpless young
Love and companionship

II. INSTITUTIONAL

(cultural, purely human, varying greatly among the world's different societies)

Economic production:
  Material goods
  Material services:
    feeding, care of clothing and body, shelter, rest, privacy, transportation

Protection of members
  Against enemies and dangers
  Against want (support, assistance, insurance)
Social control and culture transmission
  Personal identification and status-ascription
  Property control and transmission
  Socialization (basic discipline) of child
  Control of sex behavior
  Other behavior controls over
    children, adolescents, and adults
  Education
    informal and formal
  Religious worship and education
Recreation
Hospitality and friendship

Protection against enemies and dangers, and behavior controls over adults, were largely transferred to the State when the trustee family or clan phase passed away. With the Industrial Revolution the production of material goods was largely transferred from home to factory. Protection of deprived individuals and nuclear families has been transferred from the extended family to voluntary charities, private insurance companies, and more lately to the social-welfare and social-security organs of the State. Religious education and worship have probably declined within the home and many families seek to have this function performed more by the Church. For the remaining functions enumerated above, a very poor case for decline can be made, and indeed much evidence points to an enlargement of some of the functions.

Parsons and Bales (1955) say: "The family has . . . been coming to be more sharply differentiated from other units and agencies of the society, and hence coming to be more specialized in its functions than has been true of the family in our own past and in the other known societies." The Family occupies a position in *series* rather than in *parallel* with other institutions. It is the final convergent channel, the nonbypassable medium through which most of the goods, services, and satisfactions reach the individual as final consumer. This is more fully explained below.

The decline in material production in the home has been offset by a greatly increased production of services by and in the home. For example, bread is now seldom baked in the home, nor meat cured, but food in greater variety is purchased with more careful selection, is prepared and served in a variety of ways with esthetic embellishments and much catering to individual tastes and needs. Cloth is no longer woven at home, but everyone has more clothing and the very selection, purchase, storage, cleaning, and repairing of this clothing takes much labor. The number of person-hours of labor in the home amount constantly to about half of those in paid occupations outside the home. This is indicated by the fact that a fairly constant 40 to 45 per cent of the population are in the labor force and about 21 per cent are full-time homemakers. Several studies show that the average homemaker works at least as many hours per week as does the average worker in "gainful occupations."

From 1890 to 1957, through a period of great social change, the percentage of total population engaged in full-time homemaking has remained at 21 per cent. This represents a balance between countervailing trends. During this period the average household has declined from 4.9 persons to 2.9 persons. This drift toward more and smaller households naturally tends to call for a larger percentage of homemakers in the population. On the other hand, the percentage of women of homemaking age has increased along with the general percentage of adult population. Also, a much larger percentage of these adult women are now in the labor force. Consequently, a considerable percentage of today's families have no full-time homemaker. In 1957 about 30 per cent of all married women and 40 per cent of all mothers of school-age children were in the labor force.

Homemaking work is still there to be done. It is increasingly done as an extra job by wives who work outside, and the evidence is that it is increasingly shared by husbands. Machinery and modern conveniences shorten it to some extent; on the other hand, paid servants have decreased rather than increased. Children and adolescents help, and they are playing an important role through baby-sitting and other brief assignments in homes other than their own. But we do not know whether in sum total of person-hours their contribution has increased or decreased. In general, homemaking is becoming everybody's job. Important in this connection is the do-it-yourself movement, which involves men and all members of the family.

The Family has increased and elaborated its direct services to its own members as final consumers, it is undertaking construction and repair work formerly delegated to outside agencies, and through the ubiquitous family automobile and garage it is heavily involved in the transportation function which, except on farms, was formerly left to the railroads and streetcars.

It has also been commonly alleged that the Family is losing its educational functions. This is a false inference from the undeniable fact that formal school education has vastly increased. The School has merely added functions which in earlier times were less necessary and which society could not afford. Our increased prosperity and standard of living reflect themselves partly in increased schooling. In the Soviet Union, where nurseries for children under 3 and kindergartens for those from 3 to 6 play a large role, these institutions do take much of the time of children and give them a certain basic habit training that would otherwise be left to parents, if performed at all.

But in Russia, as in the United States, the increased activity of schools involves also increased parent education and involvement of parents in the school activities of their children. The Parent-Teacher Associations illustrate this tendency. In Israel, the Kibbutzim with their children's quarters, designed originally to meet economic necessity by freeing more time of parents for agricultural or industrial production, are not an expanding pattern. The tendency is rather, as prosperity increases, for people to leave the Kibbutz and establish individual homes.

As to the recreational or pleasure functions in modern American urban society, the schools, churches, and recreational agencies under both commercial and welfare auspices foster much organized leisure-time activity outside the home, which was not characteristic of frontier, peasant, and earlier American rural societies. Peer-groups based on the school, the welfare agency, or the street corner gang take more and more control over adolescent behavior. All this is offset by other trends: radio, television, the greater recreational and esthetic equipment of the modern home, especially in the suburbs. One leading social worker sees in the suburbs a "renaissance of the family." This comes about through an "increasing need of the family members to rely on their own stability in view of the instability of life around them." An article by Margaret Mead, "The Pattern of Leisure in Contemporary American Culture," says, in abstract, that in the decade 1947–1957 there has been, psychologically, a subtle shift in the balance from "work" and "good works" to "the home": the home is now the center for existence, which in turn justifies working at all.

One can argue that the Family has gained more functions than it has lost, or vice versa, but this all depends upon how one lists and subdivides the "functions"; it is a semantic question. The only reasonably discussable index is a quantitative estimate of the total person-hours of time used in all family operations. When this index is applied there is no evidence for any withering away of the Family.

The Sexual and Affectional Functions of the Family

It is notable that the natural-social functions of the Family, those which pertain more or less to animals as well as men, have shown no attrition.

Despite sporadic ideological glorification of free love and the right to motherhood, despite temporary increases in illegitimacy due to war or other abnormal conditions, the vast majority of births—if not conceptions—take place within marriage. The Kinsey reports (1948, 1953) tell us that approximately 46 per cent of all sexual outlets of American males are obtained through marital coitus, but about 85 per cent of the outlets of the married male population are so obtained. It must not be assumed, however, that the nonmarital outlets consist mainly in illicit coitus. They include a great deal of masturbation and nocturnal emissions, especially before the age of 25.

During the three or four decades of behavior covered by the Kinsey reports, there was no substantial change in the frequency of marital coitus, except possibly an increase among the younger people of the lower educational level. Lower-class males have tended to begin their sexual experience in general at an earlier age and Kinsey attributes this mainly to improved

nutrition. There has been an increase in the proportion of wives who achieve orgasm in marital coitus. There has been an increase in the percentage of women who have premarital and extramarital coitus. However, this increase in the number of women involved does not necessarily mean an increase in the total volume of such nonmarital intercourse, and even if it does it is small compared with the volume of marital intercourse. Much evidence points to an increase since 1920 in America of premarital coitus among couples who later marry, which accounts for a large part of the general increase in premarital coitus. This increase, which to many older persons appears as an alarming evidence of irresponsibility and disregard of moral standards, may rather indicate that we are shifting toward mores that have for a long time been characteristic of northern and central Europe. The norm that expects a girl to be a virgin at marriage seems to have been strict in Victorian England, at least in the upper and middle classes; and it is also very strict among Mediterranean peoples such as Greeks and Italians, and at least in the upper and middle classes of the Hispanic world. The Latin peoples and the Greeks practice considerable separation of the sexes in youth and chaperonage of marriageable girls, in contrast to the freer mingling of the sexes during youth in northern and central Europe and Russia.

A 1955 cross-cultural study of small sample areas showed the following comparison (Christensen, 1955):

	PERCENT OF ALL BIRTHS WHICH ARE ILLEGITIMATE	PERCENT OF MARITAL FIRST BIRTHS WHICH OCCUR WITHIN FIRST SIX MONTHS OF MARRIAGE
Utah County, Utah	.9	9.0
Tippecanoe County, Indiana	2.9	10.0
City of Copenhagen	11.2	31.1
Whole of Denmark	6.6	34.9

In both Utah and Indiana the modal (most frequent) date of first conception is one month after marriage; in Denmark it is five months *before* marriage. It would appear that in rural

Denmark there is greater expectation that a pregnancy will lead to marriage, whereas in Copenhagen this norm is less demanding, so that either irresponsibility or rational judgment, or both, allow the tolerated premarital intercourse to result in more births outside of wedlock.

The Family, of course, never has and probably never will establish an absolute monopoly over sexual intercourse, still less over "total sexual outlet." In a broad historical and anthropological perspective, the Family appears as an institution designed not so much to provide and to contain all sexual satisfaction, as to limit whatever sexual satisfactions it may contain exclusively to the married pair, or to specified kinship relations—in other words, to define and prevent incest. To most peoples in the world and in history it has presumably not seemed that any institution is needed to regulate a satisfaction which is so natural or instinctive and also, unlike food and shelter, so unhampered by shortages of supply. As long as the two sexes are reasonably balanced in numbers, the means exist in proportion to the ends. The function of institutions is rather to control and channelize the sex instinct for the sake of other human instincts or ends.

But with modern rationality less and less is entrusted fully "to nature." We believe, with good reason, that we can improve upon nature. We tend to label all phases of living with words and to assign them to the responsibility of various institutions. By this process of verbalization and rationalization much is obviously gained and it is still to be proved that anything is irretrievably lost, even though Max Weber alluded to the "disenchantment of the world." Whatever attitudes may be taken toward other sexual outlets, sexual satisfaction is coming more and more to be verbally recognized and emphasized as a major function of the marital relationship in the modern American type of family, toward which many other societies are converging.

Indeed, the Judeo-Christian tradition has long recognized the legitimate purposes of marriage as including not only the procreation and education of children, but also the unity of man and wife as persons and as an outlet for sexual desire. Jewish culture regards marriage and procreation as preferable values for all persons.

Christianity offered monastic celibacy as an honorable alternative. This celibacy acquired in some sense a higher value but was never chosen by enough persons to threaten the adequate increase of population. The Catholic Church today recognizes the values of spousal unity and personality development through sex, but, according to Pope Pius XII in 1951, these values are subordinate to procreation; and according to the rules of the Church, in effect they must be paid for by taking a risk of unplanned procreation somewhat greater than would be entailed by the use of modern contraceptive devices. On the other hand, modern Judaism and Protestantism recognize the unifying and personal-development values of sex as legitimate aims even if accompanied by scientific minimization of the risk of conception. Recently, Christian theologians have discovered, or newly emphasized, statements in both the Old and New Testaments that express a more positive and permissive attitude toward sex in marriage than was formerly found by the churches (Bailey, 1952; Hiltner, 1953; Martinson, 1960).

As Martinson shows, the Judeo-Christian model, with all its variations, is only one of three models or value-schemes that are influencing modern marriage. The others are the Romantic model, dating from the twelfth-century troubadours and chivalry, and the Rationalistic model, which arose out of twentieth-century sociology and psychiatry. These models are not based upon religion or traditional authority, but upon feeling and reason respectively. Many persons, of course, are guided wholly by romance or reason and ignore traditional authority. Many others find comfort and reassurance in the cited reinterpretations of religious authority, which tend to bring it more nearly into harmony with the romantic or rationalistic value schemes.

The Romantic as well as the Judeo-Christian scheme tends to imply the pleasures of sex without the explicit and detailed *verbalization* which comes with the rationalistic view. Indeed, a certain reticence would seem to enhance the values of sex in our culture and in many other cultures. The great nineteenth-century literature of Russia, noted for its extremely detailed description of human feelings and behavior and its sympathy for human deviations, is actually very reticent and indirect when it comes to the description of sexual behavior. Most societies which we know tend to throw a veil of privacy about the sexual act and the acts which immediately precede it. Why this should be so widespread a human trait has not yet been adequately explained. Possibly one basic motive is to prevent interference by potential rivals. This does not explain why, both with us and with the Trobriand Islanders, a man's sex relations with his wife are more unmentionable to trusted male associates than are his extramarital adventures.

Rationalism is more than science. It makes full use of available science; but in addition it makes fuller use of familiar, *common-sense* knowledge than does nonrationalism, because it insists that every pertinent detail be made visible, plain, or open to verbal discussion (Ellis, 1962). The rational attitude toward sex holds that if sexual pleasure is inherently desirable, then since ends justify means, whatever increases sexual pleasure, if no harm is done, is desirable. While sex outside of marriage does harm, or creates grave risk of harm, in our type of society, it seems reasonable that within marriage all barriers should be removed, and the way made plain, from excitation to ejaculation. So we have been making sex into an art or skill, and since all arts and skills are communicated and improved with the help of words, it is rational to talk about it freely. We have learned to talk about it in the language not of poetry or of the gutter, but of technology.

In recent years much of such talk has flowed and much print piled up. In general two main purposes are discernible: the negative purpose of preventing illicit or harmful sex behavior, and the positive purpose of increasing the benefits of hygienic marital sex life. In the early part of this century the negative purpose was more prominent; we began to think that syphilis might be easier to prevent if we named it and described it and told people what does not cause it as well as what does. Since 1920 the positive purpose has grown in prominence. It is now possible not only to agree with the Judeo-Christian theme that sex unifies the partners or enriches their love life, but also to admit dis-

creetly in public what everyone knows, that "sex is fun."

A little mathematics applied to the birth rate and the Kinsey report will show that in normal, long-enduring marriages there is about one birth for every thousand acts of marital coitus. One may ask of the remaining 999 acts whether they are merely unsuccessful attempts at procreation or have other purposes. Levy and Munroe (1941), studying happily married couples, observe that the mood and purpose of coitus vary with ease and freedom: close affection, tenderness, solemn passion, a "wholly frivolous" mood, "routine satisfaction of a bodily need" (as well as the several attempts commonly necessary to bring about each desired pregnancy). "Our uninhibited happily married couple will take all these variations and find them good."

All of this talk and print about sex may be called sex education. It may be subdivided in still another way: according to what age, sex, or marital status group it is meant for. Catholic and many other leaders still believe that the sex education of children, at least before puberty, should be carried out by the family. Odette (1945), for example, has a little 32-page brochure of good taste and religious overtones, addressed to parents and advising them how, gradually, delicately, and honestly, to initiate their children to the facts of life. It says nothing about schools, but for older adolescents it advises that parental teaching be supplemented by books from a recommended list.

Around 1920, however, a movement for sex education by the public schools began to develop, on the ground that many parents neglect or badly perform this function, and that it is better for children to get these facts through a universal program, even in advance of their spontaneous curiosity, than that some children should become the victims of ignorance or of "gutter" education. Only a few schools at first dared put this philosophy completely into practice, as for example Winnetka and Bronxville, while the New York City schools were forbidding the teaching of *mammalian* reproduction. One practice was to let parents decide whether their child should join a sex-education class. In general the schools have tried to "integrate" sex materials into various courses through the curriculum rather than to give special lectures known as "sex" (Folsom, 1941). The objectives of school sex education have been mainly to present the essential facts of reproduction, to inculcate "healthy attitudes toward sex," and to discourage all voluntary "sex outlets" before marriage.

These aims of enlightened parents and of schools have been more negative than they have been positive in any specific, concrete sense. The adolescent boy of the past few decades has been learning plenty from school or parents to deter him from premarital coitus, and even learning that masturbation is merely a childish habit and not a cause of insanity. But, if he wanted to know how one performs coitus with a maximum of safety or mutual satisfaction he had to seek other sources—his more sophisticated peers or some adult book outside of his usual range of literature. Supposedly he did not "need" to know these things yet, but in plenty of cases he sought the information anyway, and got it, correctly or incorrectly.

About 1940 a sample of 291 boys, mostly 12–16, white-middle-class-urban, mainly Protestant, revealed that male companions were their primary source of sex information; 55 per cent stated that neither parent had contributed to their sex instruction; and only 15 per cent rated their parents' efforts as fair or adequate (Ramsey, 1943). The topic most often presented by parents was the origin of babies; for this information 31 per cent could primarily thank their parents. Information about intercourse, prostitutes, and contraceptives was obtained, in an overwhelming majority of cases, from companions. Perhaps the best method of concretely positive sex education would be to have books around the house which we pretend we do not want the children to read.

Since the 1920's, however, there has been some thoughtful reaction in various directions against the exceedingly rationalistic philosophy of sex and sex education, even though this was embraced, perhaps, only by the more educated classes. After a period of radical sex education in Russia, the great educator Makarento, in the 1930's, held that when a child asked a sex question the parent might properly answer: "You are too young to understand; when you are older I will tell you." In America we have come

to question the policy of telling facts early before curiosity arises.

Some religious and also some secular thinkers have opposed the rationalistic approach because they fear that the rational arguments for sexual continence and for monogamy are not sufficiently convincing to hold the sex drive of many persons in check; they feel that a suprarational sanction is also necessary. They feel also that a detailed knowledge of the facts of sexual behavior will stimulate such behavior. When the Kinsey reports came out, Margaret Mead (1949) wrote: "The sudden removal of a previously guaranteed reticence has left many young people singularly defenseless in just those areas where their desire to conform was protected by a lack of knowledge of the extent of non-conformity."

In 1956 a leading psychiatrist criticized our current sex education on the ground that it is too coldly factual, presented in a toneless voice, and that in purging sex of disgust and guilt we are also purging it of tenderness and warmth (Martin, 1956). Other thinkers have said some good words for sex humor, holding that laughter rather than tense seriousness may play a helpful role in preparing people for a satisfying sex life.

It would be a mistake to conclude, however, that the rational approach to sex has failed and that we should or shall again go back to hush-hush, indirect allusions, or to entrusting sex to blind "nature." Rather, the philosophy of the 1920's was too narrowly and naively rational and was ignorant of certain areas of scientific evidence. On its more adult level it was heavily influenced by Freudian theory, and insufficiently influenced by sociology and cultural anthropology.

Yet throughout both the "hush-hush" period and the period of sex education we may discern a constant thread of awareness that the major problem is the communication of attitudes and values, rather than of facts. Policies have changed because attitudes and values have changed. Even the concept "healthy attitude toward sex" does not mean the same thing concretely at all times, among all nationalities, among all social classes. It is here suggested, however that a healthy attitude toward sex, in universal human terms, would have these characteristics: (1) lessening inhibition of sex *feeling* by fear and disgust, whatever controls may be necessary over *action*; (2) prevalence of heterosexuality with a minimum of homosexuality and of conditioning to nonhuman objects; (3) separation of sex feeling from anger, violence, and cruelty (in other words, minimum sadism). The thing to be most afraid of in our current erotica is not the things we call "lewd," "lustful," "obscene," "earthy," "vulgar," and "immoral," but those which portray a pretty girl and a revolver in the same picture.

It was Kinsey in 1948 who was made the chief scapegoat by the conservatives, for his allegedly needless and harmful exposure, in the name of science, of man's sexual behavior. Yet it was Kinsey who corrected some of the most harmful errors of the 1920 sexual philosophers and educators. First, Kinsey found that there were universal human and even mammalian differences between males and females in sexuality, and that Victorian culture and prudishness could not be entirely blamed for the relative "frigidity" of women or the desire of women, on the average, for less frequent and less regular intercourse than is the case with men. Other investigators also have found that husbands in general want intercourse more often than their wives (Burgess and Wallin, 1953).

A most important cause of sex differences, Kinsey found, is that genital excitation in the male is much more reactive to psychological stimuli: sights, sounds, nudity, fetishes, imagination, and memories. The female's arousal is more dependent on actual physical contact. The male's greater tendency to promiscuity is not due to the fact that his sexuality is more "physical" and less "mental," as popularly assumed, but to precisely the reverse.

Kinsey also found that highly educated women are more frequently virgin at marriage, and also more likely to achieve orgasm in marital intercourse. Also, in his massive data the evidences of incest and desire for incest, as implied in the Oedipus theme of the Freudians, play a very small and insignificant role. "As a factor in the development of the homosexual, age of onset of adolescence (which probably means the metabolic drive of the individual) may prove to be more significant than the much dis-

cussed Oedipus relation of Freudian philosophy" (Kinsey and others, 1948). Kinsey finds that prolonged intercourse with nudity, preceded by a great deal of petting, is much more characteristic of the educated classes than of the mass of people. He estimates that for "perhaps three-quarters of all males orgasm is reached within two minutes after the initiation of the sexual relation."

In general, Kinsey shows the tremendous importance of basic sex differences, individual differences, age, the different social classes with their different codes of sexual behavior, the process of biological maturation, and the process of psychological conditioning.

In view of all these findings, it now appears that the 1920 adult sex education, which stressed the equal or similar drive of the sexes, Victorian repressions as cause of the frigidity of women, the importance of prolonged foreplay and prolonged intercourse, and the seriousness of failure to achieve simultaneous orgasm and of the failure of a husband to give his wife the same kind and amount of satisfaction as he receives, was somewhat unrealistic. By setting up goals that are not attainable by many persons, and by imputing failure and inferiority to those who did not attain these goals, sex education of the 1920's was setting up a new rigid value system as much as it was releasing people from traditional values; and it was making those who read its literature feel that they must conform to these new values. Many persons became dissatisfied with their marriages, many experimented with or encouraged extramarital relations in the name of mental health or personality development, many got divorced who would have been happy and well adjusted—either under the traditional values or perhaps with more complete information and rational acceptance of the exceedingly varied "facts of life" that Kinsey later provided.

Burgess and Wallin (1953) report that general marital happiness correlates only about +.50 with sexual adjustment and that "there is relatively little association between wives being low on marital success and their having low sexual adjustment scores," and that "wives are less disposed than their husbands to be critical of, or dissatisfied with, their sexual relationship.

The explanation for this may be that women do not expect as much as men from the sexual sphere of marriage."

These conditions can be changed. For example, one physician reported that technical instruction enabled most of her "frigid" women patients to achieve orgasm in marital coitus. But we need to know what is factually normal before we become too compulsive in struggling for what is ideally normal.

We have come also to realize more keenly that we cannot with impunity set up ideals or customs within the individual family, no matter how theoretically desirable, in defiance of the value system of the neighborhood in which we choose to live. Children suffer acutely when their parents' behavior or teachings contradict those of their peer groups. These peer groups cannot be escaped in modern life and their power to inflict punishment and misery upon the nonconformist is greater than the power of the Family, the Church, or even the State. The Oneida and other deviant patterns of sex life might have survived had it not been for the pressures of the larger society, exerted largely upon the younger generation.

One of the most needed areas of research is that of the privacy and secrecy of sexual behavior. In general, rationality and science call for factual truth and more open communication. But what kinds of facts are and should be communicated—to whom and under what conditions? The ethic of honesty conflicts at innumerable points with the ethic of loyalty.

The major achievement of science and rationality in the sexual field is probably permanent and irreversible: we have learned to talk about sex behavior, to study it, and to improve it through talk and study, as we do with all other phases of life. By achieving this verbal recognition, sexual satisfaction *seems* to have become a more important function of marriage than ever before; but it may be merely that we are recognizing an importance which was formerly unverbalized. This recognition may cause extramarital methods of sexual satisfaction to be less frequent or to be more frequent; but it will tend to render them less necessary, less compulsive, less worthy of the sacrifice or risking of all the other values which flow from stable marriage.

For achieving the best possible performance of this sexual function within marriage, the best present wisdom is aptly summarized by Martinson (1960):

Optimum sex expression is a learned rather than a natural accomplishment of the married couple. . . . [BUT:] It is generally agreed today that there are no right techniques for bringing about sex satisfaction, no right bodily position of the partners in relation to each other, no right time of day for love-making, and no right frequency for sex experience. Each is to be determined by the couple in respect to their mutual desires and wishes. But marriage partners are, for the sake of each other and for the sake of the relationship, obligated to make sex as satisfying an experience as possible. Equipped with some knowledge of the facts of life, permissive attitudes, and love and tenderness on the part of both, intimate love-making should become a recurring satisfying communion between husband and wife.

With the separation of the Family from agriculture and industry, the lessened harshness of discipline, and the greater equality of the sexes within and without marriage, the familial function of satisfying *nonerotic* love and companionship needs is also becoming more prominent. Research has shown the greater tendency of the unloved and rejected child to become a psychopath or a delinquent. Research has shown the great need, for emotional health, of young children for a steady, ever-present parent-person, even though this may be other than the biological mother. Adolescents and adults in courtship seek security and permanence of love more than they seek variety of sexual satisfactions.

The feelings of tender love and yearning are not the same thing as the erotic feeling. They are located in different parts of the body and involve different physiological processes. They can be fused—or separated—by the experiences of human learning, both overt and imaginary. Tender love, in its less intense degrees, becomes a warm friendly feeling such as occurs in gregarious behavior. In the Middle Ages, says Halmos, Europeans were given more than now to a warm gregarious fellowship with bodily contact, like animals which huddle together for warmth. Puritanism, the modern nuclear family and its well-equipped home, have brought about a higher valuation of exclusiveness and privacy (Halmos, 1952).

In many primitive and peasant societies there was a diffusion of warm friendly feelings among kinsfolk and friends in the relatively unchanging community environment. People were emotionally attached to the place itself; homesickness reveals such attachment. In modern urban society, with frequent change of residence, the satisfaction of these emotional needs depends more than ever upon marriage and the nuclear family.

Hence arises the paradox of the modern nuclear family. It becomes more intensely the provider of love, yet the extreme valuation of love and its concentration within the family makes the family more vulnerable. Institutionally speaking, there is no loss, because most divorces are followed by remarriages, and more people than before are living at any one time within some marriage, some private home. But the full satisfaction of love needs requires permanence of relationship, with freedom from anxiety, hostility, and regret. This fullness of satisfaction is scarred by divorce and remarriage, and by the divided allegiance of the children of broken marriages. The modern urban family has not lost but gained in its responsibility for the love function, but its performance is marred by many breakdowns and personal traumas. This problem calls not for re-emphasizing the sacredness of the Family *as an institution* (which implies possible changeability of personnel), but for more reverence *for each family* as a natural—and sacred—group.

Whether or not we accept Zimmerman's cyclical theory of family history, or his proposal to strengthen its traditional institutional aspects, we may find hope and meaning in his suggestion that in the future the Family may not merely adapt to other institutions, but other institutions may adapt to it. In line with this possible trend is the current family-life movement, with its efforts to increase education for family life in the schools and churches and to set up family-counseling centers. Social work thinks of itself increasingly as a service to families rather than to categories of individuals. Medicine, psychiatry, and religion are becoming family-minded. Even industry is

catering to family life in ways that would have been surprising in the nineteenth century. The National Council on Family Relations, spearhead of the family-life movement in the United States, was founded by a lawyer, Paul Sayre, who believed that the aim of his profession should be not to arrange divorces but to prevent them.

References

Arensberg, Conrad M., and Kimball, Solon T., *Family and Community in Ireland.* Cambridge: Harvard University Press, 1941.

Bailey, Derrick S., *The Mystery of Love and Marriage.* New York: Harper & Brothers, 1952.

Bossard, James H. S. (ed.), "Toward Family Stability." *Annals. Acad. Polit. & Social Sci.* 272; 1-315, 1950.

Bossard, James H. S., and Boll, Eleanor S., *Family Situations, An Introduction to the Study of Child Behavior.* Philadelphia: University of Pennsylvania Press, 1943.

Burgess, Ernest W., and Locke, Harvey J., *The Family: From Institution to Companionship* (2nd ed.). New York: American Book Co., 1953.

Burgess, Ernest W., and Wallin, Paul, *Engagement and Marriage.* Philadelphia: J. B. Lippincott Co., 1953.

Davis, W. Allison, and Havighurst, Robert J., *Father of the Man: How Your Child Gets His Personality.* Boston: Houghton Mifflin Co., 1947.

Duvall, Evelyn M., *Family Development.* Philadelphia: J. B. Lippincott Co., 1957.

Ellis, Albert, *Reason and Emotion in Psychotherapy.* New York: Lyle Stuart, 1962.

Folsom, Joseph K., *Youth, Family, and Education.* Washington: American Council on Education, 1941.

Folsom, Joseph K., *The Family and Democratic Society.* New York: John Wiley & Sons, 1943.

Folsom, Joseph K., "Family, USSR." In Joseph S. Roucek (ed.), *Slavonic Encyclopedia.* New York: Philosophical Library, 1949.

Glick, Paul C., *American Families.* New York: John Wiley & Sons, 1957.

Goodsell, Willystine, *A History of Marriage and the Family* (rev. ed.). New York: The Macmillan Co., 1934.

Halmos, Paul, *Solitude and Privacy.* London: Routledge, Kegan Paul, 1952.

Hill, Reuben, "Review of Current Research on Marriage and the Family." *Amer. Sociol. Rev. 16*; 694-701, 1951.

Hill, Reuben, Katz, Alvin M., and Simpson, Richard L., "An Inventory of Research in Marriage and Family Behavior: A Statement of Objectives and Progress." *Marr. Fam. Living 19*; 89-92, 1957.

Hiltner, Seward, *Sex Ethics and the Kinsey Reports.* New York: Association Press, 1953.

Kingsbury, Susan M., and Fairchild, Mildred, *Factory, Family, and Women in the Soviet Union*. New York: G. P. Putnam's Sons, 1935.

Kinsey, A. C., Pomeroy, W. B., and Martin, C. E., *Sexual Behavior in the Human Male*. Philadelphia: W. B. Saunders and Co., 1948.

Kinsey, A. C., Pomeroy, W. B., Martin, C. E., and Gebhard, P. H., *Sexual Behavior in the Human Female*. Philadelphia: W. B. Saunders and Co., 1953.

Kirkpatrick, Clifford, *The Family as Process and Institution*. New York: The Ronald Press, 1955.

Kyrk, Hazel, *The Family in the American Economy*. Chicago: University of Chicago Press, 1953.

Levy, John, and Munroe, Ruth, *The Happy Family*. New York: Alfred A. Knopf, Inc., 1941.

Martin, Alexander Reid, "Do We Teach Our Children Too Much About Sex?" *McCalls*, Oct. 1956, 33-40.

Martinson, Floyd M., *Marriage and the American Ideal*. New York: Dodd, Mead & Co., 1960.

Mead, Margaret, *Male and Female*. New York: William Morrow & Co., 1949.

Miner, Horace, *St. Denis, A French-Canadian Parish*. Chicago: University of Chicago Press, 1939.

Müller-Lyer, F., *The Family*. New York: Alfred A. Knopf, Inc., 1931.

Murdock, George P., *Social Structure*. New York: The Macmillan Co., 1945.

Myrdal, Alva, *Nation and Family*. New York: Harper & Brothers, 1941.

Odette, Vincent F., *Comment de dire: Nos Petits et les Mystères de la Vie*. Montreal: La Famille, 1945.

Ogburn, William F., and Nimkoff, Meyer F., *Technology and the Changing Family*. Boston: Houghton Mifflin Co., 1955.

Parsons, Talcott, and Bales, Robert F., *Family, Socialization and Interaction Process*. Glencoe, Ill.: The Free Press, 1955.

Ramsey, Glenn V., "The Sex Information of Younger Boys." *Am. J. Orthopsychiat.* 13; 347-352, 1943.

Zimmerman, Carle C., *Family and Civilization*. New York: Harper & Brothers, 1947.

Sociologie Comparée de la Famille Contemporaine. (Colloques Internationaux due Centre de la Recherche Scientifique.) Paris: Editions du Centre Nationale de la Recherche Scientifique, 1955.

JOSEPH K. FOLSOM

Far East,
Sex in the Art of the

THE ARTIST of the Far East does not base his craftsmanship on the study of the nude, as does his Western colleague, but on the study of the landscape. This landscape is studied not as an organic whole with pertinent detail filled in but rather as a miscellany of discrete objects assembled, at least apparently, by chance. The result is not a panorama in geometric perspective with a centripetal tendency toward one point, but rather a series of scenes connected by a temporal continuity as the viewer strolls visually through these chance-assembled fragments of life continuing off the canvas into reality. When the Far Eastern artist does treat the nude as subject, either singly or in composition, he composes it as a landscape of the human form, in a series of impressions gained during the pauses in a stroll.

Nepal is the westernmost portion of the Far East. Here the Indian and the Chinese treatment of the nude co-exist; they do not blend, but exist separately side by side. The Indian concept of the nude is related to the Grecian school of naturalism, infused with romantic idealism, an idealism realized to such a degree as to give the sculpture at temple complexes such as Karnak the appearance of being thousands of portraits of the one and the same couple in thousands of poses and positions. Chinese art portrays the human figure as naked rather than nude, evincing neither idealism nor naturalism but rather a deromanticized realism which, as we follow the style eastward, becomes harsher and more and more of an outright caricature.

The overlapping of art styles is paralleled by the overlapping of Hinduism and Buddhism, but here in religion there is a blending, resulting in Tantric Buddhism, which has been called "Buddhist Hinduism" and "Saivism (the worship of Siva) in Buddhist garb."

Tantrism

Tantra is a *web* or *warp*, a continuous or uninterrupted series; in religion this becomes *an orderly rite or ritual*, thus implying ritual carried through to its ultimate conclusion; as a web, encompassing all. In its present form, ascribed to the sixth or seventh century A.D., Tantrism has two aspects. It is a systematization of vulgar magical rites, of usages and popular formulas which were practiced in an earlier age and which belong to a type of primitive thought that varies little in the course of centuries. The second aspect is a Buddhist innovation that has developed it into a theurgy, the Vajrayana, a highly developed mysticism.

Both aspects of Tantrism make use of erotic art with both literal and figurative connotations. According to Foucher, the rite of Sadhana prescribes the pattern according to which Tibetan, and possibly Hindu, artists worked. Sadhana is the evocation of a god (or holy spirit) to the place of meditation, through offerings, mental or real, the practice of the virtues of friendship, pity, joy, and indifference, and the fixation of the mind on the essential voidness of all things. Merit (punya) and wisdom (jnyana) thus acquired, the ascetic is ready for the creative rite: the execution of black or white magic, worship, the creation of art, or the continuing of the Sadhana rite into its second phase.

The Nepalese believe that an ordinary person, incapable of performing such an esoteric rite, may partake of it by looking at works of art which portray the necessary offerings and practices. The animal virtues must be appealed to emotionally and physically. Erotic art accomplishes this, distracting the conscious mind, freeing the subconscious to continue its quest for communion.

Art or Pornography?

In the absence of theurgy or a philosophy of art, is this erotica art or is it simply pornography? Among primitive peoples the representation of human and animal figures with obvious or exaggerated genital organs or of the organs alone for religious or magical purposes is common. But there is an equal frequency of use in secular contexts. Among the Bare'e Toradja tribe of the Celebes the breasts and genitalia alone are used as decorative motifs. The natives state they have no significance other than to "delight the eyes"; they have thus a conscious artistic significance. Samoans carve paired, half-moon marriage spoons with nude male and female handles, genitals in excitation. They interlock as in intercourse, now forming a large full-circle spoon, and are used in the marriage rite. They are valued in proportion to their craftsmanship and esthetic qualities; thus also are, consciously, art.

As the culture becomes, in a Western sense, more advanced, the theurgical use of erotica declines, leaving the artistic variety of erotica dominant. Evidence of former theurgical use may remain, as rationalization, serious or otherwise, or as a fragment of legend of no obvious relevance, sometimes bordering on the superstitious. No traditional Chinese family would have considered a house fully furnished without a collection of erotic paintings, not regularly displayed but stored. They are referred to as *pi huo t'i*, fire-prevention maps—further indication that the Chinese artists consider the human body in terms of landscape. Religious association lingers in Nepal where temples are made largely of wood and on many of them, including those not otherwise decorated with Tantric erotica, the exposed ends of wooden structural members such as roof beams, usually bracket-supported rather than tenoned, are decorated with carved and painted representations of the sexual act. Nepalese claim these are charms against lightning and fire.

In Japan, in some shrines whose transverse roof beams are tenoned through the pillars, the protruding ends are carved into phalli. Tiled roofs, except for those on some modern, low-cost structures, incorporate decorative finials that serve as charms against fire and lightning. These are found at both ends of the ridge spine, the highest points on the roof, joined to the ridge pole, or at the corners of the roof at the terminals of the main roof members. Most common motifs are the fish, the stylized "fish" of obvious phallic intent, the mystic lion mask (the name for lion, *shi-shi*, is a homonym for the child's word for urinate), the mask of the evil-repelling *div* (also part of the armor of the Buddhist guardian gods and worn just above the groin), and the peach or sheaf of rice grain, both standard Japanese representations of the female genitals. Many temples and shrines preserve ancient tiles, between three hundred and a thousand years old, showing the peach flanked by or in association with mushrooms or undisguised phalli, and various other representations of pudenda. Shinto shrines of traditional pre-Buddhist architecture indicate the sex of the spirit enshrined within by their *chigi*, scissor-shaped bargeboards set as finials and extending above both ridge ends like V's, much as tent poles extend above a tepee. If the upper end of each board is cut so that the edge is parallel with the ground, the enshrined genius is female; if cut roughly perpendicular to the earth or to its own axis so that it forms a point aimed at the sky, the genius within is male. There are no known hermaphroditic geni, but Yoshida Shrine in Kyoto, which houses, temporarily in seasonal transit, a multitude of spirits, mixes its *chigi* genders. The bottom end of the main pillar, embedded into the earth and under which the human sacrifice or its later substitute was laid, is priapic.

An important source of income for Shinto shrines and some Buddhist temples is the sale of pictorial or calligraphic charms against fire. Shrines associated with fertility rites usually sell representations of the sexual organs. These charms are sealed in paper, not meant to be seen by mortals, and are pasted, never mailed, to the main wooden vertical beam, preferably near the ridgepole or close under the eaves.

Most lightning repellors are male or, in the case of the sexual act and the peach (which symbolizes not merely the vulva, but the pregnant womb near delivery), male-repellent. Lightning is the manifestation of Siva's masculinity. Among the Buddhist priest's ritual paraphernalia is a small wand called variously the mystic lightning bolt of Siva or the vajra. Vajra is also used as a "decent" and mystical synonym for the male member, as the lotus, *padme,* is for the female.

Sadhana Rite

Full communion is the second phase of the Sadhana rite. A predominantly spiritual interpretation is Tantricism of the Right Hand, manifested in Vedantism, Yoga, and Shingon Buddhism; a predominantly carnal interpretation is Tantricism of the Left Hand, practiced by Saivite cults, Mahakalatantra, Tibetan Sakhti, the Boga aspects of Yoga, and the "heretical" offshoot of Shingon, the purely Japanese Tachikawa sect. The Tachikawa sect began in Japan about the time of the Mongol world empire, in the thirteenth century, contemporary with the rise of similar Manichaeo-Christian heresies in Europe, and probably inspired by the exiles who also were responsible for the rise of Zen Buddhism. It is the source of some of Japan's finest erotic art, especially sculpture. It was probably exterminated during the Imperial restoration of the 1860's as part of the suppression of rural Buddhist revolts, although rumors have it still existing in isolated mountain hamlets.

The devotee enters the second phase of the Sadhana rite as his summons to the deity is answered by the appearance of (to use the basic Indian terminology) Kumari, the non-virgin, or the vajrayogini (literally "phallus-yoga practitioner-female"), female divinities. Buddha is traditionally represented to have three bodies or manifestations, but the left-hand school believes it is his third body which is the only true body, the Body of Bliss, the Vajra, "with which the eternal tathagata or Bhagavat embraces eternity" in the body of Sakti. Thus, in order to actualize his attainment, or degree of attainment, of Nirvana, the ascetic must perform rites of sexual union. "Buddhahood abides in the female organ/ Everything is pure to the Pure Man/ Do not fear, you do not sin."

Tachikawa Buddhism further popularized this doctrine by explaining that Nirvana could be attained while incarnate, by advancing through the stage of the Western Paradise of Amitabha, a Buddha of Persian origin (which by their interpretation was almost identical to the Moslem Paradise of the houris), and by obliterating the self into Nirvana when ready. Paradise was earthly existence without restriction, and was manifested mainly in orgies. Whereas conventional asceticism and monasticism attempt the conquest of desires through repression, the Tantrism of the Left Hand abandons the self to desires, either mentally or in reality, so that, once sated, they no longer exist and have thus been conquered.

This parallels various interpretations of the Temptation of Buddha. When it was seen that Gautama Shakyamuni, meditating under the Bodhi tree, was about to attain Buddhahood, Evil manifested itself in the form of the ideal of sensuous womanhood in order to tempt him back to the realm of desires. The conventional Buddhist interpretation has Gautama resist and pass on to become the Buddha. The Tachikawa interpretation is that "everything being pure to the pure man," he becomes the Buddha because he need not resist.

Temptation of Budda

The Temptation of Buddha is a popular subject for Buddhist artists. Tachikawa sculptors show the becoming-Buddha seated in meditation, his face in the ecstacy of perfect communion, while in front of him Mara the temptress is portrayed with a combination of Indian romantic idealism and Japanese reality in caricature that results in the most erotic examples of female beauty. To the casual observer, these figures are merely renditions of the traditional subject. But viewed from any angle other than frontal, as a supplicant before the altar would see it, a priapic Buddha is seen to be in heroic physical communion with Mara. Japanese mask-makers are famous for their ability to carve three or more expressions into a single mask that will alternate with changes in the angle of illumination or view. In these Tachikawa sculptures, Buddha's expression of meditative ecstasy changes to a knowing smile, erotic ecstasy, or any other expression the sculptor may have seen fit to include. A play of light as slight as the flicker of a candle also will give Mara and Buddha the appearance of erotic motion in rhythm with the light change.

In traditional iconography Buddha sits upon a lotus pedestal before a backdrop of a ray-splashed auriole; in Tachikawa art Buddha is a phallus, the lotus a scrotum, and the auriole a vulva with the light rays pubic hair. Other Tachikawa representations include the lotus as a vulva, pictorial representations of the meditative positions applied to sexual concourse, mudras or mystic hand symbols (similar to those used in the Cabbala) with sexual interpretations or new ones with sexual meanings. A Mandala is a picture meant to induce meditation and these of course became natural mediums for Tachikawa erotica, usually in caricature of the traditional, the eightfold path, for example, being indicated by the spread arms and legs of a couple in intercourse.

Shakti and Kanki

These Japanese representations can be considered a vulgarization or practical application of the concept of *shakti* (var. *sakhti*). This takes artistic form in Tibet in representations similar to those of the Tachikawa "temptation of Buddha" sculptures. The Sakhti is the metaphysical force generated by the Absolute and is represented as a divine female who enters into orgiastic embrace with the representation of the divinity which generated her. This symbolism became very popular in Tibet, especially as a subject for painting and sculpture. In Japanese Shingon Buddhism, a right-hand Tantric school, it is known as *Kanki*, the representation as *Kanki-san*. "San" may mean "person" or it may mean "temple." When applied

to a divine sculpture it may thus mean a temple personified. As we shall see, it develops along a different line in Japan in Buddhism and Shinto (both Ryobu and Reformed).

The Jewel is in the Lotus

Om mani padme Om—The Jewel is in the Lotus—is the ultimate truth. The Tachikawa devotee could depart for Nirvana when he felt himself ready. If the lotus is the vulva and the vajra is the phallus, the concourse of the two brought one into the presence of Buddha, or into Buddhahood. The sword is a form of the vajra. (The "swords" of the days of the gods of Japanese mythology were not blades but polished stone priapic sceptres from the second century A.D.). The devotee, seated upon a special lotus platform, went into the Sadhana rite reciting the self-hypnotic magic syllables. When the attending priest beneath the platform believed him at the proper pitch of ecstacy, he thrust a sword up through a slit in the vulvar-lotus, above which sat the devotee, who was thus dispatched directly into Nirvana.

If Tachikawa art is brazen, Shingon art is suggestive in a way that invites meditation. Ganesha, the elephant-headed wisdom deification, is prominent in Shingon art but is always represented as two identical figures in face-to-face embrace, suggestive except that no sex is so much as hinted at for either. Properly illuminated, the figure casts a detailed and naturalistic phallic shadow.

Sculptures were common in Shinto shrines during the period when the syncretic Ryobu Shinto was dominant, or until the purging of Buddhist elements from Shintoism a century ago. Until that time Buddhist and Shinto deities were considered to be avatars of each other. Despite the wealth of its pantheon, Buddhism had few atavars for the variety of erotic and fertility deities of Shinto. The period of this identification as Ryubu Shinto enabled Shintoism to develop a minor iconography which in rural areas survived the purifications and idol-smashing of the 1860's. Paired Ganeshas, called *Kanki-san* in Japanese, are still enshrined in Shinto shrines, *Kanki-gu*, which obviously survived the purge. But in most Kanki-gu, the embracing Ganeshas have been replaced by a large phallus, the folds of the foreskin duplicating the folds of the robes of the Ganeshas, the scrotum often in the shape of two rice bales.

Often the Kanki-gu shrine will be set near a female shrine, usually a cave or a tree whose roots resemble, or at some distant time did resemble, a vagina. In Shirahama, Wakayama prefecture, a Kanki-gu stands outside another shrine set against the cliff face, covering a small natural cave bearing a close resemblance to a vagina, slightly open. Records trace the history of the shrine for twelve centuries, to about the time that the nearby hot springs, Japan's oldest, were discovered.

Hot springs almost always have Kanki-gu or similar pudenda-form deities in association. Springs are curative, sterility is an ill. In North Japan, women attempt to cure their barrenness by bathing, taking into the natural bath a wooden phallus and leaving it there as an offering, so that there is soon little room left for bathers and old phalli must be allowed to overflow and wash away.

The seven lucky gods are a Sinification of several major Shinto deities, having been given their present stylized human forms only three or four centuries ago. These in turn are of great antiquity, probably once being the principal deities of lesser tribes, the deities of the major tribes having become the principal gods of national Shintoism. In rural areas images of these gods, almost always enshrined singly, evidencing their old role as tutelary deities for an area or tribe, are often phallic. Daikoku, the god of prosperity, stands astride two rice bales, his cloak falling so as to give him a phallic silhouette, his hood taking the shape of the head of the penis.

Fertility Deities

Two Neolithic fertility deities who survive today as popular folk heroes noted for their genital development are the Monkey and the Mushroom Girl. In folk literature monkeys and primitive men are often confused; even the present-day pygmy of Africa reportedly believes the chimpanzee to be a type of man. The erotic adventures of Hanuman, the monkey general, are a source of subplots in the literary and pictorial Thai versions of the Ramayana epic, as in the Temple of the Reclining Buddha, Wat Po, in Bangkok. In South China, the monkey general is a guerilla chief who kidnaps maidens. In Japan he is the aboriginal Japanese who, as Saru-ta-hiko, monkey fellow, senior deity of the native clans conquered by the mainlanders or Yamato people, becomes the god of both fertility and the dance. His most common representation is in the form of a coarse doll, occasionally stone or wood but usually clay, cradling in his arms his penis, which is almost as big as his torso. The identical representation in life-sized stone sculpture is found in Javanese temples and the motif is used by Hokusai in his comic pornographic sketches. Clay monkey dolls are sold in folk crafts shops today, but occasionally, because of modern squeamishness, are changed so as to pass a superficial examination as "Monkey mother and child." Folk representations of the three monkeys, See, Speak, and Hear No Evil, often show them as simian phalli with thin wispy arms sprouting from the foreskin roll. In view of this lightness with which the monkey god of fertility is treated, it is difficult to evaluate the priapic tomb figurines of 1,200 to 1,800 years ago that are found in the pre-Buddhist tumuli. The exact significance of these Haniwa, clay figures, usually a human figure above the hips but a cylinder below, has not been established. Figures of animals and houses occasionally have the cylinder bases as well, but are otherwise complete. A few armored warriors have an exaggerated erection extending out from the joint between torso and cylinder. In other pieces, it is not a human in armor but a phallus. An aid to intercourse of later centuries was a tortoiseshell jacket fitting over the penis, with a shell cap for the penis head, which were called "warrior's armor and helmet." These also are valued in proportion to their craftsmanship and esthetic qualities, thus consciously are "art."

At Mohenjo Daro and Harappa (2500–1500 B.C.), in association with the Siva Linga, are found small, coarse terra cotta figurines of a kneeling person, probably female, the significance of which is not yet known. In Wat Po, Bangkok, around the Siva Lingam in the temple courtyard, are many small terra cotta figurines of a kneeling person, obviously female, placed there as offerings by women desiring children. Newer offerings are colorful, clothed in light silk, with human hair on the heads, but the coloring is a water-base gesso which washes off after a few months of weathering, leaving only the almost indestructible terra cotta base form. Japanese phallic shrines, to which is attributed the power to cure barrenness, often receive as offerings small, squat river-stone or ceramic figurines of squatting, oval-faced women. The Japanese add many refinements. The female often carries mushrooms, her face is suggestively vaginal, with puffy cheeks and forehead and a pudgy clitoral nose. The bases of the Thai figurines are unfinished spherical indentations; those of the Japanese may be worked into oversized vaginas, finished in great detail. Finer pieces may be themselves enshrined as objects of veneration, if not of worship, or kept in homes as charms. The degree of artistry and craftsmanship demonstrated in some privately owned figurines ranks them as masterpieces of the potter's art and they are treasured more as such than as religious objects. In some, there may be a man concealed under the figure's garment, engaged in sex play or intercourse. The same treatment is often found in other purely secular china figurines portraying various activities of work and play.

In the Kojiki, an eighth-century publication of older oral tradition, the supreme Sun Goddess hides in a cave, plunging the world into darkness, and is lured out by the Goddess of the Ritual Dance, Ame-no-Uzume, who bares her breasts, lifts her skirts, and performs a parody of her own dance. Marukawa interprets this as being an offering of her genitals, credited with a power to please gods and exorcise evil spirits, in the same way that Pliny suggests that a nude woman will dispel a storm.

The hand gesture imitating the vagina, the "fig," making a fist over the thumb with the thumb tip protruding from between the fore and middle fingers, has the same significance as it has in the West. It is found on both Shinto and Tantric Buddhist fertility-associated images. In Java a large stone sculpture of such a fist is worshipped as a cure of barrenness.

According to the Nihon Shoki, Ame-no-Uzume marries Saru-ta-hiko. In folk tradition the former is often known as Ota-fuku, and the figurines always as Ota-fuku. Saru-ta-hiko is portrayed with a long, phallic nose. At spring rites near Nara and elsewhere, male dancers masked as these two enact rice seeding in the shrine, using phallic implements, Neolithic originals of which have been excavated. Saru-ta-hiko then rapes Ota-fuku, duplicating it symbolically with his nose in her face. Talismanic plaques of the two masks so positioned are sold. Small bronze votive plaques from Luristan, Iran (eleventh to seventh centuries B.C.), portray a fertility goddess in intercourse with a large nose of an "offstage" face.

Many of the masks of Ota-fuku and Saru-ta-hiko in his various *tengu* manifestations are masterpieces of folk art. In the highly developed art of Noh mask carving which evolves out of this folk art, the Ota-fuku loses much of her physical symbolism but the audience continues to associate erotic qualities with her characterization. The erotic character of the *tengu* in Noh is completely lost. However in such proto-Noh forms as Mibu Kyogen his mask and stage characterization attain their highest level of erotic connotation.

The Hachiman temple-shrines of Shinto are better described as proto-Buddhist. Hachiman is the "War God" of Shinto, in actuality the deity of the Scythe and Sword. The associated gods have sculpted human forms, of which some are avatars from Hinduism through Buddhism and others are possibly original. One such is Benzaiten, or Benten, the sole female among the seven lucky gods, sometimes considered an avatar of Kwannon-Avalokatesvara. In Hinayana (Southeast Asian Buddhism) are nude Buddhas such as the Emerald Buddha of Thailand and the Walking Buddhas, on some of which actual clothing is draped as on a human. In Japan the Buddha at Ren-jo temple in Nara has in place of its member a lotus vulva, although the human Gautama was a male and the Absolute is represented as masculine. Metaphysical force, manifest as worldly action, is female. Benzaiten is often naked, to be dressed in cloth. The sculpture of her at Tsurugaoka Kamakura is shown in most books on art in Japan, but in this she wears a breech cloth. A more beautiful piece, also twelfth-thirteenth century and of wood, is at nearby Enoshima and is seated fully naked. "The factual taste of the Kamakura period has bestowed earthly charms on heavenly beings with an obvious relish which would have shocked the over refined sensitivies of . . . patrons" of the earlier epochs, says Paine in *Art and Architecture of Japan*. The Enoshima Benzaiten, is fully bestowed with genitals, depicted in as great detail as in the Ota-fuku figures.

Many other fertility deities not associated with avatars of Buddhism do not take on a human form. They may manifest themselves as a natural object such as a rock, cave, or tree, and they have a gender. Common among such objects of worship are natural phalliform rocks and hillocks, vulvar-form caves, rock outcroppings, and root formations, forked trees, or combinations of these, especially if representing both sexes in proximity. The Japanese landscape seems to abound in such natural phenomena. Near Nagoya is Tagata Shrine, which boasts a small forest full of trees with crotchlike forks and vaginalike roots, and several outcroppings of feminine rock. During the middle of every March at the time of the great spring rites this forest abounds in a peculiar vegetable parasite that resembles pubic hair except under the most exacting scrutiny. Not a mile away is another enshrined glade abounding in natural phalli. The pubic moss is carried home as a charm for crops and personal virility. Portable phallic or vaginal stones, tree knots, vegetables, especially Siamese-twin radishes and carrots joined so as to resemble hips, thighs, and legs, are offered to the shrines by supplicants.

The shrines also sell charms, besides the ubiquitous fire-prevention charms, that vary from sanctified talismans and souvenirs to objects of worship (for family god-shelves) and are enclosed in the plain, white paulownia box which comprises the holy of holies of all Shinto shrines. More usually the box is empty or contains folded paper strips (paper is a homonym for god, or "above") sometimes inscribed with a religious saying. Objects of worship may be a vagina or phallus, either sculpted of fired ceramic or carved of wood. Other charms include sake wine cups shaped like vaginas or a vaginal cup with a phallic straw; phallic cigarette holders; ordinary wine cups with an in-

complete magnifying lens in the bottom, which is optically completed by the addition of a clear liquid, thus revealing a colored miniature of a vagina or a penis or of intercourse; seated dolls (sometimes Ota-fuku), fully clothed but which when upturned reveal heroic or caricatured genitals; genital chopstick rests; teacups decorated with semisacred carnal scenes; or nonfunctional representation of pudenda, either singly or combined. One interesting combination is a foreshortened penis which when turned over is seen to be joined to its scrotum in such a way as to form a vagina. Most of these objects are in a serio-comic vein. As in Greece at the Orphic rite of Liknophoria, the Eleusinian mysteries, and marriages, sacred cakes (sacra) in phallic or vaginal shape are also sold.

In the Far East, especially in Japan, the dividing line between the sacred and the profane has rarely been very clear. Some antique glazed ceramic phalli, purportedly intended as objects of worship in household shrines, are actually phallic clay bottles meant to be filled with warm water and used as instruments of masturbation. Thousands of these charms have been bought to use as conversation pieces at stag meetings or romantic rendezvous. Some of these, made as "pop-outs" in otherwise innocent-looking objects such as cigarette holders or ordinary key chain charms, may be given as a Valentine-type of gift by girls of traditional families who would consider it immoral to be seen speaking to the male recipient without a chaperone.

The use of these erotic charms as key chain fobs is of course a modern adaptation. An older adaptation was for use as medicine box fobs or tobacco pouch fobs, known as *Netsuke*. During the Tokugawa period the carving of these *netsuke,* in wood, bone, and ivory, reached its highest artistic development. Erotic subjects were popular similar to both the charms and the ceramic figurines. The challenge of the medium invited greater imagination and the artists rose to the challenge, creating numerous masterpieces of miniature sculpture.

Most shrines have treasure picture scrolls, few dating back more than three centuries but of undoubtedly more ancient tradition and executed in the Yamato-e style. These may portray some event in the mythology or history of the shrine or illustrate its main rite or festive procession. Most of them are comical or satirical, even when done by artists noted for serious work. All these shrines have at least one annual festival that includes one or more elements such as a procession of the objects worshipped or treasured (where male and female shrines adjoin, they will hold a wedding procession), perhaps carried by men costumed in sexual symbols or dummy organs (as in Rome until stopped by the Council of Tours in 1396); a ritual dance or play that is often lewd; a tug-of-war at two giant ropes of obvious gender joined in intercourse; a scramble of naked youths for a magic phallic wand; midwinter naked bathing; a female buttocks-pinching melee in the dark; and (in parts of Kyushu on rare occasions) a "ritual" of real rape. Such festivals are widespread, numbering in the hundreds. Shrine scrolls draw on these for subject matter.

Erotic Paintings and Prints

Buddhist pilgrims returning home from Kyoto three hundred years ago passed Otsu. Here an artist of the Kano school, circa 1630, mass-produced delightful little paintings on coarse paper that illustrated Buddhist deities, stories, and parables. They were usually of a satiric, humorous burlesque, or risqué nature: A man walking a dog on a leash, his fist upraised, his kimono gathered up, baring his legs so that the cloth gathers in two gigantic lumps before his groin and his upraised arm appears to be the erection to match the gargantuan testes, with a splotch of red formed by his sash-knot to suggest where he has just been; a courtesan, or perhaps a fox in human female form, standing coyly so that the folds of her multilayered kimono drape to form a gigantic vulva; etc. These Otsu-e, pictures from Otsu, became a tradition and were reproduced for several generations.

This was a period of great peace and prosperity during which plebeian art, the Ukiyo-e or Floating World pictures, attained mass circulation through assembly-line production of woodblock printing. The woodblock print was later "discovered" as a great art form by the West, having been looked down upon in its homeland as intended only for the ignorant masses and therefore beneath the attention of the connoisseur. It is probable that this was because the pictures treasured in the West were considered secondary by the natives, who preferred, and treasured, the same artists' magnificent erotic prints. These prints have been completely overlooked, except for passing mention, by Western art authorities.

The Floating World erotica, whether paintings or prints, have a double heritage: the Chinese "Fire Prevention Maps" and the folk-religion fertility charms and mementos. The Japanese institutionalized the Chinese tradition, as they have so many others. As Western art students must draw the nude as a drill, the Far Eastern art students drew erotica, not as an exercise in anatomy but as an exercise in composition and suggestion. Most Chinese erotica were painted by students or tyros, which may account for their coarseness and lack of esthetic qualities. The Chinese themselves admit this and it is probably the only art form in which the Chinese recognize Japanese superiority.

The great incentive to the development of erotic painting, such as of the Ukiyo-e school, was the discovery of Western art as introduced into Japan by the Portuguese in the mid-sixteenth century. Chinese artists subordinated the human figure to nature, but the Japanese from earliest times were fascinated by humanity as a subject for painting. Tradition-bound Japanese painters forced their works to remain within the bounds of the adopted Chinese tradition. Japanese artists excelled in Buddhist formal religious portraits. The Yamato-e horizontal scrolls of the eighth through fourteenth centuries dealt with mankind on a scale unknown in China, but it was mankind in the mass and as an integral part of the landscape. European copperplate etchings inspired the Japanese to adapt the older native religious woodblock print technique to secular art. They soon excelled in this technique and developed multicolor printing. Geometric perspective also fascinated the Japanese. The Portuguese brought in their own erotica and pornography, which was both copied and adapted upon, wedded with the Fire Prevention sketches and tempered with native wit and love of exaggeration.

The Japanese never developed an esthetic appreciation of the nude but under Western influence they did discover anatomy. Western medicine and the science of anatomy appeared at the same time. To the Chinese the nude was immoral, and the development of medicine in China suffered accordingly. The Chinese never saw a nude person—even few long-married Chinese men have. Unclothed peasants were unknown and only subhuman aborigines and monkeys bared the body. The Japanese masses, on the other hand, were apathetic to clothing until the present century, and felt that nothing natural could be immoral. Culturally, the rural Japanese is more Polynesian than Chinese, and has the Pacific Islander's respect for an able (as opposed to an esthetically pleasing) body. Nude bathing, working in the seminude (and sometimes complete nude), gave the artist many opportunities to observe the naked form. The upper classes, however, were prisoners of Chinese tradition. Erotic art, rather naturally, was a plebeian development.

Japanese print artists experimented with the problems of geometric perspective, combining it with their traditional perspective of impression, which was born of their fixation for arrangement. They developed a trick to draw attention to a noncentripetal character by placing him slightly out of geometric perspective —a trick of contortion. Nowhere else has geometric perspective posed more fascinating challenges than in erotica, with the problems of portraying simultaneously all of the areas of erotic interest of a female body in intercourse with a male. Similar seemingly impossible problems in design were repeatedly attacked and often completely solved by the adaptation of geometric perspective.

All the woodblock artists created erotica except two: Sharaku, a mysterious artist who was known for only ten months in 1794 and then disappeared into obscurity as suddenly as he had appeared from it, and Hiroshige (d. 1858), who was noted for his landscapes and who never successfully dealt with people as a subject matter beyond their being objects in his landscapes. They catered to the same audiences as did the newly rising Kabuki and Bunraku puppet theaters and the gay red-light "play areas," which were all also the principal subjects of their prints. The production of erotic art was a major source of income even to the name artists, and to some it was their main source. To most Oriental connoisseurs, and to some Western ones, the greatest masterpieces of the Ukiyo-e woodblock prints are to be found among the erotica.

Sex Censorship

The government imposed limits on their work, as it did on the theater, for its "immorality." The government was becoming almost a caricature of the Confucian superbureaucracy. Editions of prints were seized and destroyed and artists and publishers fined. However, portions of the prints, with the actual carnal areas expurgated, were published. The discovery of the individual proved a new medium for the traditional art of arrangement with its perspective of impression, wherein scholars had been shown as serene, warriors as fierce, rulers as benign by their bearing and a shorthand rendition of facial expressions. Artists soon mastered the portray of full facial expressions and body attitudes (as opposed to the old posturings). Prints of a woman's face and shoulders were censored although she was fully clothed, as her facial expression showed that she was obviously engaged in intercourse and it was so masterfully executed as to be considered excessively stimulating and therefore immoral.

The erotic picture often served an educational purpose—in China to teach the upperclass male the techniques of approaching his bride, whose mother had briefed her well, and in Japan to show the well-protected city or upper-class bride (the peasant was not likely to be inexperienced) how to keep her husband satisfied so that he would not lead them to the financial ruin of addiction to the "gay quarters" and the geisha. These bride books are a dying, but not yet dead, tradition. They explain the mechanics of intercourse, its preliminaries and positions, and sometimes they provide primitive hygienic information, although the scientific advances of the past century have been ignored.

References

Braun, Waldo, and Braun, Alicia, "The Kansai Chronicler." Tokyo: *The Asahi Evening News,* Feb. 1, 1958, p. 5.

Buckley, E., *Phallicism in Japan.* Chicago, 1898.

Casals, U. A., *A Discursive Essay on Phallicism, Phallic Symbolism and Related Manifestations in Japan.* Kobe: Manuscript (6 carbons privately circulated), 1952.

Empson, William, "The Nude." Peking: *Tyro 2; 5,* 1948.

Fanti, Silvio, "They Prefer Sex to Invention." Tokyo: *Orient Digest 12; 26,* March, 1955.

Gluck, Jay, "Rape Me, It's an Old Japanese Custom." Tokyo: *Orient Digest 3;* 1954.

Gluck, Jay, "Ribbing the Gods in Rural Japan." Delhi: *Thought 11; 38,* Sept. 19, 1959, pp. 15, 16.

Gluck, Jay, and Gluck, Sumi, "Springtime in Japan." Tokyo: *The Japan Times,* Spring Tourist Supplement, 6th Edition, March, 1960, pp. 3-7.

Kanda, T., *Notes on Ancient Stone Implements of Japan.* Tokyo, 1884.

Kato, Genchi, "A Study of the Development of Religious Ideas Among the Japanese People as Illustrated by Japanese Phallicism." Tokyo: *Transactions of the Asiatic Society of Japan,* 1924.

Kidder, J. Edward, *Japan Before Buddhism.* London: Thames & Hudson, 1959.

Kinsey, Alfred, Private Collection of Japanese Erotica, unpublished.

Marukawa, Hitoo, "Sexual Observances as a Religious Rite in Japan." *Tenri Journal of Religion 2;* 5-17, December, 1959.

Miki, Fumio, *Haniwa.* Tokyo: Dai-Nippon, 1958 (plates 40, 49, 53).

Mizuhara, G., "A Study of the Tachikawa School as a Heretical Religion." Kyoto, 1937.

Munro, Neil Gordon, *Prehistoric Japan.* Yokohama, 1911.

Nishioka, H., *History of Phallicism in Japan.* Tokyo: Myogi Pub. Co., 1958.

Waddell, L. A., *Buddhism of Tibet.* London, 1895, p. 152.

Welken, G. A., *Verspreide Geshriften.* Hague, 1912.

"Yukai," from *The Precious Mirror* (Hokyosho), translated and quoted in Ryusaku Tsunoda, Wm. Theodore de Bary, Donald Keene, Eds., *Sources of the Japanese Tradition, Sex & Buddhahood.* New York: Columbia Univ. Press, 1958.

JAY GLUCK

Femininity

Definition

A PRECISE definition of femininity, applicable to all human females, is impossible. Even the term "female" is not always easily defined, for there are freaks of nature in whom the reproductive organs of the two sexes are mixed. One finds people with both testes and ovaries or, more frequently, with the reproductive organs of one sex and the external genitalia of the other. However, these hermaphrodites are relatively infrequent, and in general one can define a female of the mammalian species as a being who, at some time at least, has had ovaries, a uterus, a vagina, mammae, and the appropriate accompanying endocrine system. However, what is feminine is subject to wide variation. Every culture has its stereotype of femininity, and there may be wide variations from culture to culture. A Japanese woman, for example, has quite different characteristics from a Samoan or American woman.

Our first consideration is, are there any characteristics of woman's nature that are anatomically based and, therefore, common to all womankind, or is a woman, apart from her sexual organs, just like a man, as some of the ardent suffragettes of the early part of this century maintained? The answer is that woman's anatomy and physiology leave marks on her character that cannot easily be eradicated, but that there are, in addition, many culturally induced traits that vary not only from culture to culture, but from time to time in the same culture.

The Anatomical and Physiological Bases of Femininity

From puberty on, the female usually tends to be smaller and to have less powerful skeletal muscles than the male (although anthropologists tell us that, as civilized man depends more and more on machines to do his heavy physical labor, and as women become more and more athletic, there is a tendency for the two sexes to become more and more alike in skeletal musculature). Nevertheless, in general the distinction still holds, and this undoubtedly contributes to the fact that woman looks to man for physical protection in times of danger and tends to use other than physical methods in competing with or fighting with men. The day that the younger brother knocks his older sister down in a scuffle is a warning to her that her days of physical prowess are over. There are tomboys, of course, who continue to hold their own far into adolescence, but they are the exceptions. Women are not weaker than men in general, but their particular areas of physical strength are different from those of men, and this difference leaves its mark on their characters.

The other important area of anatomical and physiological difference is that of sex itself, and all that immediately relates to it. To a great extent, sex dictates the body structure. The feminine form in most societies has wide hips and narrow shoulders. The breasts are more developed than in the male. There is no beard, and the pubic hair is distributed in the form of an inverted triangle, whereas in the male the pubic hair usually extends upward in a point to the navel. However, there are individual exceptions to each of these—there are women with boyish builds, little breast tissue, masculine hair distribution, and more or less facial hair growth. Such females may still be feminine in personality (unless being built differently from the average has socially conditioned them), and quite capable of carrying on their biological functions. In the United States, the boyish build has at times been the fashionable figure, although facial hair has never been popular.

From puberty to the menopause, a rhythmical ovarian and uterine activity, called the menstrual cycle, occurs in the female. When this cycle is normal it does not interfere with her daily activities and, in all areas except that of sexual interest and activity, may have no effect on her life pattern or character. However, since it differs radically from the male physiological picture, it has acquired a significance in every culture as a symbol of differentiation between males and females. In the animal species, the estrous cycle determines the female's availability for sexual activity—that is, the female will accept the male only when she is "in season." This is not true of the human female. Although many women report waves of increased sexual interest at the time of ovulation and premenstrually, this does not seem to be true of all women. Furthermore, many women continue to have sexual desires after the menopause—when no ovulation is acting as a stimulant. One explanation for this constant receptivity to sexual excitation in women is that the human, with his capacity to remember and recreate—and create feelings through phantasy—can produce stimuli apart from those of biological need. Nevertheless, in general the female is not as continuously receptive to or desirous for sexual activity as the male (although in our civilization not every male is either—again we have difficulty in basing a description on a purely physiological basis).

Nobody will deny that pregnancy, childbirth, lactation, and nursing cause women to play a role in life that is definitely different from that of men. Whatever her other interests, if a woman gives birth to a child her way of life is altered, temporarily at least. The experience has a profound effect on her nature, and it is an experience that no man can have. However, this natural response of peace in creation, of mothering tenderness for the newborn, can be extensively altered by social attitudes. For example, the illegitimate or unwanted child can cause a pregnancy to be filled with bitterness and despair. A narcissistic overvaluation of beautiful breasts can lead a woman to abhor or forego nursing.

Another important difference between males and females is the nature of the sexual experience. Although coitus is a mutual act, the experience of the two people is different; one gives and one receives—or gives differently. This difference will be discussed further.

We can sum up the characteristics of femininity as: a body musculature weaker than the male's, a sex life based on periodic rhythms, an accepting attitude towards pregnancy, a nurturing, responsible attitude towards the newborn child, and a receptive attitude towards the male in periods of sexual excitation. Each of these facts influences the personality of the woman, and when she can react to them in a positive, constructive way we have an individual representing basic femininity.

Cultural Influences on Femininity

In no culture is the picture of femininity simple and clear cut. There have been societies in which women wielded the power and later, for many centuries, societies in which men had the power. Today, men still have it, although there is a tendency to share it more and more with women. These differences in cultures have left their mark on the concept of femininity.

In the early matriarchies, the whole culture was feminine—that is, it centered around child-rearing, homemaking, and food-getting. The women tilled the fields and discovered and cultivated the edible vegetables and herbs. Men had little responsibility. They brought food from the hunt and they helped with the heavy work at certain times, but for the most part, they were free to wander. Being feminine meant being strong, courageous, hard working, and responsible. What power there was in organized society rested in the women.

Men began to dominate when, with the domestication of animals, movable personal property was acquired. A man's success was measured by his personal wealth and he began to acquire women for a price—so many cows, goats, or sheep. Although women still had a dignified role and work to do that was respected, their position began to be considered inferior to that of men. This became more and more the case as they had less and less responsibilities, and eventually they became chiefly the pets or toys of men. In the age of chivalry, woman's helplessness was glorified and she became correspondingly useless and degraded at the same time that she was put on a pedestal.

For centuries, it was not considered worth educating women, except in some light amusement, such as harp playing, where it was more important that she display her beautiful arms and hands than that she play well. Women had no legal rights without the consent of the husband. Since to be feminine meant being weak, helpless, inferior, and the property of the male, women cultivated this femininity. They fainted on the slightest provocation. Headaches and general indisposition were the accepted accompaniments of menstruation. Pregnancy was something to be ashamed of; a pregnant woman was too embarrassed to appear in public. Sex was something in which a "good" woman had no interest. In short, everything that was truly feminine as we know it was belittled or denied.

It is no wonder that women with spirit and intelligence resented their status, and that they had, as Freud discovered, penis envy. Femininity was a mark of inferiority and, as women began to rebel against their fate, they naturally assumed that equality lay in the direction of being as much like men as possible. They fought for equal education, equal voting rights, the opportunity to work at so-called men's jobs. During World War I, when their services were in demand, they won a great part of this battle and went a step further, demanding equal sexual freedom. In the 1920's, there was a tendency to deny femininity in our society because it was still considered a sign of weakness and inferiority. A woman was proud of having a mind like a man, of being able to do anything a man could do, and so forth. To be a flapper, bob one's hair, smoke, drink, wear slacks, and conceal breasts was being a modern woman.

The extreme reaction of this period has abated, but the woman of today is different from the woman of pre-World War I. She still smokes and drinks. She often wears her hair short, but usually it is attractively arranged. She still wears slacks on occasion. She has achieved equality of education and has made much progress towards equal work opportunities. But some of the rebellion against being a woman has disappeared, and she is more willing to consider and make adjustments to her physiological differences. For example, work situations based on women's needs are being created. Considerations of pregnancy and the early days of care for the small child are a part of her work plans as a matter of course. The concept of femininity of the age of chivalry does not apply today. Women are strong and self-respecting. Although their position in society is still in a state of rapid change and the feeling of self-respect and acceptance of being a woman is not universal, even in the United States, much has been accomplished toward a new ideal of femininity.

What Is Femininity?

Femininity is created out of a combination of physical and cultural factors. There have been many cases of the femininity of female children being submerged when the parents were disappointed in their sex. When the desire for a boy is strong, boyish characteristics are often cultivated in the girl child. On the other hand, many mothers have an opposite attitude toward girl children. One mother, who also had two sons, told the author that in spite of herself she found herself being more protective of the daughter. She was less willing to have her take physical risks, she was more concerned when she got into fights with other children. Many say their daughters are neater and more docile than their sons, but it is impossible to say how much of this is due to different training and how much is innate.

The attitude of the father and mother tends to be different toward the child of the other sex; the father is less likely to be ambitious for his daughter's career unless he has tried to have her take the place of a son. The mother is more likely to identify with the girl child and to enjoy teaching her the ways of the home. It has been said that girls are more teachable than boys in the early years, possibly because of the greater motor restlessness of male children. This may be a part of their natural endowment, but it is also possible that mothers are more permissive with their male children and less insistent on their obedience. Whatever the cultural and family situation, by the time the child has reached the age of 6, the foundation of his sex personality has been laid.

There is no doubt that at puberty the distinction between the sexes becomes much more apparent, both physically and characterologically, and that a significant part of this change stems from the appearance of the new sex hormones. Also, society develops new attitudes toward adolescent boys and girls and some of these attitudes are not based on anatomy. The physical differences between the sexes at puberty will not be described for they are sufficiently obvious. One point might be mentioned, however, and that is that in general girls mature about two years earlier than boys. A practical result of this is that they suddenly find their former male companions "just kids." This is a confusing experience to a girl and may add temporarily to her difficulties in understanding her new role. What she experiences is a new kind of interest in boys and a need to attract their attention in a new way, which presently becomes clarified as sexual.

From the observation of animals, it is apparent that physiologically motivated female activity is related to attracting the male for sexual purposes. The adolescent girl in every culture has the same drive, but in each culture she is taught certain controls and acceptable ways of expressing it. In the Victorian era she expressed it by being modest and shy, possibly exposing her ankle a bit on occasion or casting a discreetly seductive glance. Any more forthright assertion of interest was considered unfeminine and usually repelled the male, who had also been indoctrinated with the cultural standards. The male, of course, did not make a sexual advance toward a woman he respected until they were properly married. If in the heat of passion he did make such an advance and she responded, she immediately lost status and was no longer a respectable woman.

Today the standards are quite different. Sexual intimacy before marriage is very frequent and does not, among many groups, entail any derogation of the woman.

Now women strive to have an orgasm and there is less need to conceal or deny sexual desire, although the complete freedom of the animal in expressing sexual need is still not considered quite womanly in our society. Today's woman is no longer ashamed of being pregnant. She does not have to hide. In fact, she is often proud of her condition. So femininity in these respects has come closer to its physiological basis.

Is woman's place in the home? In some cultures women leave their babies with older children or old women while they work in the fields. In these situations the home is certainly not the only place for the woman. In present-day Western society, is housekeeping an essentially feminine job? One practical reason for considering it so is that, during the years when it is essential to mother small children, being in the home and always available is convenient. But women are not innately fond of housekeeping, and raising small children is not a lifelong occupation. So women are coming to realize that they need more in their lives, other interests, even in many instances gainful occupations, if they are to lead full and satisfying lives; and men are becoming less antagonistic to this. Less frequently do we meet a man whose manhood is threatened by his wife's contributing to the family income. As a result, femininity is no longer inconsistent with many interests and activities outside of the home, nor is it necessary to accept being sheltered, protected, and supported in order to be considered feminine.

Femininity is a changing concept in a changing culture. It need not include a feeling of inferiority, for a woman does not have penis envy unless her life circumstances have made her feel that men are superior. Woman can only fulfill herself by being a woman. In being a woman her role is fully as important as that of a man, although necessarily different. The basic differences between the sexes are physiological; all else is culturally determined and capable of endless change as the culture changes. Care of the young, apart from breast feeding, for example, is not an essentially feminine duty. In some animal species the father does the postnatal "mothering," and in the United States today men often share in the care of the infant without loss of face.

Being feminine includes a desire, or willingness, to be a mother and a desire and capacity to be sexually attractive to the male. Capacity to be attractive does not necessarily mean being beautiful, although conforming to the standards of beauty of the particular culture is an asset. Thus, slender women are desirable in some cultures and fat women are at a premium in others. The ability to be attractive to the male also springs from deep roots in the character and may be observed even in women who are considered plain. A feminine woman today may have many characteristics that were formerly considered masculine. A woman may be educated, have a profession or career, or be active in politics—and still be completely womanly if these activities are not engaged in as a form of rebellion against her sex. She will not work like a man or think like a man but will bring to the task a special female orientation.

Qualities that are inescapably feminine are based on anatomical and physiological facts. It is conceivable that women, basically, have less need to achieve success than men because their creative urge is satisfied physiologically. As the need to procreate diminishes, women will doubtless turn more to the "masculine" creative fields. A woman who became pregnant after several years of active participation in her husband's work told me of a reaction that I think may well be characteristic of this. During her pregnancy her husband was worried about some experimental work he was doing. As usual, he talked over the problem with her. Her former attitude had been one of deep concern and she had actively contributed to the solution. On this occasion, however, she suddenly realized that the problem was of little importance to her. She thought, "I am busy at something much more important. Why all this fuss? Supposing it doesn't work out. He'll find some other solution." Since, today, a woman is not continuously pregnant, this blissful state of creation by the simple method of sitting and waiting can no longer completely satisfy her. She is beginning to feel the need to create in other spheres.

Another aspect of woman's physiology that influences her character is that in the sex act she plays a receptive role. She does not have to participate beyond permitting coitus, although normally she gives much more than that. The male on the other hand must achieve and maintain an erection and, in our present sex-enlightened era, he must also be concerned with satisfying the woman. This conceivably puts a greater emphasis on achievement in the male's life than in the female's. The female on the other hand has a great need to be accepted unconditionally, i.e., without proving her worth.

Also, possibly she finds deception more acceptable than does the male, as she can appear to participate in the sex act when actually she may not be sexually aroused. However, this situation may also involve nonphysiological factors: deception for manipulative purposes is the weapon of the underdog, and to the extent that woman has been treated as an inferior, she has learned to get what she wants by indirect methods. It is probable that as equality of status is more firmly established women will become more direct, and forthrightness will be included as an aspect of femininity.

Conclusion

Femininity is a quality greatly dependent on cultural attitudes. What was unfeminine in 1900 is not necessarily unfeminine today. What is acceptable female behavior in the United States may be all wrong in Japan. Certain anatomical and physiological differences from the male should furnish a basis for true femininity, but these may be frustrated or exploited by the culture in such a way as to distort their impact on the character. The desire to be a man (penis envy) is not part of a normal woman's life. It appears when the cultural attitude is one of derogation of women or when the individual's personal life experience has made her feel that being a woman is a calamity. In recent years many traits formerly considered masculine have been included in the feminine picture, and as the need for large families diminishes, women will be driven to seek self-expression more and more in ways hitherto considered masculine. So the femininity of the future may be quite different from that of today.

References

Abraham, Karl, *Selected Papers of Karl Abraham, M.D.* London: Hogarth Press, 1942, Ch. 22.

Benedek, Therese, *Psychosexual Functions in Women.* New York: The Ronald Press Co., 1952.

Briffault, Robert, *The Mothers.* New York: The Macmillan Co., 1931.

Deutsch, Helene, *Psychology of Women* (Vol. I). New York: Grune & Stratton, Inc., 1944.

Deutsch, Helene, *Psychology of Women* (Vol. II). New York: Grune & Stratton, Inc., 1945.

Fliess, Robert (ed.), *The Psychoanalytic Reader* (Sect.

II). New York: International Universities Press, 1948.

Ford, Clellan S., and Beach, Frank, *Patterns of Sexual Behavior*. New York: Harper & Brothers, 1951.

Freud, Sigmund, *New Introductory Lectures on Psychoanalysis*. New York: W. W. Norton & Co., Inc., 1933, Ch. 5.

Freud, Sigmund, *Collected Papers* (Vol. V). London: Hogarth Press, 1950, Chs. 17 and 24.

Friedan, Betty, *The Feminine Mystique*. New York: W. W. Norton & Co., Inc., 1963.

Fromm, Erich, "Sex and Character." *Psychiatry 6;* 21-31, 1943.

Kinsey, A. C. *et al.*, *Sexual Behavior in the Human Female*. Philadelphia: W. B. Saunders Co., 1953.

Komarovsky, Mirra, *Women in the Modern World*. Boston: Little, Brown & Co., 1953.

Landes, Ruth, *The City of Women*. New York: The Macmillan Co., 1947.

Mead, Margaret, *Male and Female*. New York: William Morrow & Co., Inc., 1949.

Thompson, Clara, "The Role of Women in This Culture." *Psychiatry 4;* 1-8, 1941.

Thompson, Clara, " 'Penis Envy' in Women." *Psychiatry 6;* 123-125, 1943.

Thompson, Clara, "Some Effects of the Derogatory Attitude Towards Female Sexuality." *Psychiatry 13;* 349-354, 1950.

Thompson, Clara, "Towards a Psychology of Women." *Pastoral Psychol. 4;* 29-38, 1953.

CLARA THOMPSON

Fertility in Men

Male Sterility

Definition

ABSOLUTE male sterility in the otherwise normal individual may be defined as that deficiency of the male reproductive tract which is manifested by a complete absence of spermatozoa in the ejaculate. This condition may be caused by (1) a congenital failure of development of the germinal epithelium, (2) a failure of existing germinal epithelium to develop spermatozoa to maturity, (3) obstruction of the ducts through which the spermatozoa pass from the testes to the urethra, or (4) a failure of development of all or part of the duct system in the presence of normal spermatogenesis. Male sterility is not to be confused, as it often is, with impotence. The potential fertility of the impotent individual may be high; he lacks only the ability to deliver the spermatozoa to the female reproductive tract by normal intercourse.

What Is Normal Male Fertility?

This question does not allow a facile answer. Theoretically, since only one spermatozoon is required to fertilize the ovum, the presence of a single active sperm cell in the ejaculate would connote a fertile male, but it is all too obvious that millions of active spermatozoa must be deposited in the female genital tract to ensure that one will reach the vicinity of the ovum and thereafter produce conception. Conversely, hundreds of millions of spermatozoa may be present in the ejaculate but if a certain percentage of them do not possess a degree of motile activity, the chances of conception are remote. The assessment of male fertility, therefore, resolves itself around an analysis of the cellular components of the ejaculate to determine (1) if enough spermatozoa are present and (2) if a sufficient number of these spermatozoa possess a degree of motile activity to facilitate their journey through the uterus and Fallopian tubes to the ovum. A third criterion is concerned with the morphology or structure of these cells, but this factor is so closely bound with the motility of the spermatozoa that for all practical purposes they can be considered together.

In males between the ages of 20 and 45 years, the average ejaculate volume after three days of continence is about 3.50 cc. The mean sperm count will range between 90 and 110 million cells/cc., and of this number, approximately 60 per cent will show progressive motile activity of a degree considered adequate. These characteristics of semen quality are predicated upon a period of continence of three days, but will vary considerably according to the period of continence. Since the average marital frequency of intercourse in this age group is about twice weekly, the figures above may be considered as representative of the semen quality likely to produce conception in an average married population. But there is a very wide range of sperm counts in a normal population of men, that is, in men whose wives have become pregnant and produced normal children. The sperm count in such a population may vary from 5 to 500 million/cc., but the great majority lie in the range between 20 million and 100 million/cc. The essential difference in the frequency distributions of sperm counts in fertile and infertile populations lies in the range under 20 million/cc. Certain authorities in the field have taken these figures to mean that sperm counts between 20 and 30 million/cc. may be considered as the lower end of the normal range consonant with fertility.

There is, however, sound reason to believe that the male fertility potential does not increase above a certain sperm count level but rather is more directly related to the motile activity of the cells. The question is where to fix, in terms of the sperm count, the minimal level under which an individual may be considered infertile. The answer to this question in the human is fraught with so many complexities that to attempt to supply the answer in any individual case of marital infertility is impossible. Conceptions have occurred under the most extraordinary conditions of poor semen quality and have failed to occur under apparently ideal physical conditions in both partners. The psychosomatic aspects of human infertility are most important, but the problem is so very complex that it cannot be brought into sound statistical focus. But if large enough populations are studied, certain imponderables can be reduced to a minimum and allow us to draw conclusions that will hold reasonably true if applied to large populations and not to individual cases.

The latest findings are that the sperm count per se is not the most important factor in human male fertility, but that the motility and morphology of the sperm population in the ejaculate have greater significance. After three days of continence the sperm count should be at least 20 million/cc., at least 40 per cent of the total sperm population should show vigorous forward progression, and at least 60 per cent of the cells should be normal in structure. The chemical nature of the ejaculate and its volume will be considered under a separate heading, but it should be said that the volume should be at least 2.0 cc. It is seldom that good motile activity is found in the presence of many cells of poor structure (morphology). Indeed, this writer believes that poor sperm morphology in itself is seldom the major cause in male infertility.

The Nature of the Ejaculate

The human seminal fluid—and, indeed, the seminal fluid of most species—is a complex medium. Its primary function would seem to be to act as the carrier of the spermatozoa from the male to the female reproductive tract, but its chemical complexity suggests that it contributes some factor or factors to the economy of the spermatozoa. The secretions that comprise the ejaculate are derived from the testes, the ducts of the epididymis and the vasa, the seminal vesicles and the prostate, and, in small part, from the bulbo-urethral glands. The major volume is contributed by the seminal vesicles and it is this secretion that supplies the simple sugar, fructose, which is so essential in initiating and maintaining the motile activity

of the spermatozoa. So far as can be determined at present, the very high concentrations of citric acid, vitamin C (ascorbic acid), and other chemical substances (including many enzymes) found in the ejaculate do not impose their influence upon the spermatozoa. The buffering (antiacid) properties of the fluid in the form of bicarbonate and phosphate may well protect the spermatozoa for a time against the high vaginal acidity. Similarly, the volume of the ejaculate may be important in the transport of the spermatozoa after ejaculation from the posterior fornix of the vagina into the cervical canal of the uterus. A low ejaculate volume could hinder this transfer and an unduly high volume may cause such dilution of the spermatozoa that the appropriate number cannot reach the relatively safe zone of the uterus before the hostility of the vaginal environment kills off the cells.

Complete absence of external ejaculation in the presence of orgasm and normal erection is, although uncommon, frequent enough to warrant mention. The condition is seen frequently in the diabetic male. Normal ejaculation may be present in the early stages of the disease, but the diminution in its volume becomes progressive even though the diabetes is controlled. The failure would appear to be partial loss of function of the smooth muscle of the reproductive tract and may be part of the neurogenic disturbance that is so common in diabetes.

Failure of external ejaculation in the presence of otherwise normal sexual functioning is seen, too, in the condition known as retrograde ejaculation, in which the semen is forced back into the bladder instead of outwards in its normal urethral pathway. The anatomical failure in this case would appear to lie in the smooth muscle of the internal sphincter of the bladder, the closure of which normally prevents the entrance of semen into the bladder. Dramatic results (pregnancies) in such cases have been produced by removing the spermatozoa from urine produced after orgasm and depositing it in the cervical canal at the appropriate time in the menstrual cycle.

Causes of Male Infertility

1. Complete *absence of spermatozoa production* in the otherwise normal individual is rare.

The testicular biopsy picture will show seminiferous tubules that contain supporting cells but none of the cells of the germinal line. The male hormone-producing cells usually are normal in appearance and these individuals do not show any signs of hormone deficiency. The reason for this defect is obscure, but failure of the primitive germinal cells to migrate into the developing testes at an early state of embryonic development is a possible cause. There is no treatment for this condition.

2. Germinal epithelium may be present but *lacking the terminal states of its developing spermatozoa*. This condition is known as "maturation arrest." The cause is unknown and hormone therapy fails to correct it.

3. Prior to the appearance of the antibiotics, *obstruction of the ducts carrying spermatozoa* from the testes to the urethra was a common cause of male sterility. In particular, gonorrheal infections, which were slow in responding to treatment, produced inflammatory conditions in the duct which, in turn, led to the formation of scar tissue and ultimate occlusion of the narrow ducts. If these occlusions did not involve the entire epididymis and if the occlusion of the ductus deferens (the duct leading from the epididymis to the urethra) was at a point in the duct that would allow the patent portion to be brought over to the epididymis, surgery could be attempted. This procedure involves severing the duct above the obstruction and joining the open end by anastomosis to the duct of the epididymis. Normal spermatogenesis usually is not affected by gonorrheal infections nor does an ensuing obstruction inhibit the normal production of spermatozoa. The success rate in the surgical approach to this problem varies according to the claims of the operators, but it is by no means 100 per cent. Since the advent of penicillin, gonorrheal obstruction of the ducts is seldom encountered and the incidence of infections other than gonorrheal producing sterility is not high.

4. *Congenital absence of part of the duct system* as a cause of male sterility is more common than was once supposed since it can be determined only by exploratory surgery. This condition is due to a failure in the embryonic development of the ducts and may involve a mere fragment of the duct system. If spermatogenesis is normal and the gap in the duct is at a point where uniting of the patent ends is feasible, the same surgery as that used for obstruction may be attempted.

5. *Failure of descent of the testes* (cryptorchism) prior to puberty may be a cause of future sterility. The testes should be in the scrotum at birth. Either one or both may not be, but subsequent, spontaneous descent usually occurs during the years of infancy and before the years when the first indications of spermatogenesis are seen. Normal spermatogenesis cannot proceed at body temperature. The temperature of the scrotum is 1° to 2° C. below that of the body and it is this small differential that allows normal development of the spermatozoa. During the years prior to puberty (birth to 8 years of age) the cells of the germinal epithelium are undifferentiated and apparently not affected by temperatures that, at a later age, would inhibit spermatogenesis. Unilateral failure of descent is much more common than bilateral and the usual position of the affected testicle is the groin (inguinal canal). In this instance, and if the cryptorchid testis does not descend spontaneously, the descended testicle may later possess enough normal activity to ensure normal fertility. However, there is certain evidence to suggest that the failure of descent, whether unilateral or bilateral, is due to inherent testicular deficiencies and that the descended testicle in the unilateral cases may also be deficient. In any event, if only for cosmetic reasons, an attempt should be made to "bring down" the undescended organ.

If the testes do not descend spontaneously before the age of 7 or 8, it is mandatory, if future fertility is to be ensured, that they be brought down either by surgery or by hormone therapy. There is still some dispute as to whether therapeutic measures should not be taken at an earlier age, but certainly they should be taken before age 10. Hormone therapy (chorionic gonadotropins) first should be attempted, but only for a short time inasmuch as excessive administration of the only hormone effective in such cases may induce precocious puberty. If hormone therapy fails, then surgery is necessary, if the testis or testes are in a position where surgery can have any hope of success. If the testes are not in the scrotum by age 14 at the latest, irreversible damage to the germinal epithelium is almost inevitable.

6. *Permanent damage to the germinal epithelium results from x-irradiation.* This has often occurred when physicians have failed to protect the genital region while performing fluoroscopy, or when the testes of a patient have not been fully protected during irradiation of the pelvic region. Isolated cases are on record of permanent sterility being produced in males of known fertility after direct irradiation of the scrotum for fungus infections. This type of therapy for a minor disease in so sensitive a region is inexcusable. However, if the number of roentgens applied in such cases is low enough, regeneration of the germinal epithelium may occur even after prolonged periods of azoospermia in the ejaculate, as evidenced by the reappearance of adequate numbers of active spermatozoa therein. One would have to question in such cases whether or not irreversible damage had been inflicted upon the genetic components of the spermatozoa.

7. Temporary sterility in the adult male may be induced by *relatively minor diseases* such as chicken pox and even by streptococcal and other infections which may otherwise not incapacitate the individual. Debilitating illnesses of any kind are notoriously prone to cause disturbances in spermatogenesis. The temporary sterility in these cases usually does not appear for several weeks after the onset of the infection or the illness and may overlap their terminations by several weeks or months. Semen examinations, therefore, that are performed within weeks after such disturbances should, if the results are poor, be interpreted with care. Recovery of normal spermatogenesis usually occurs.

8. *Mumps in the adult male* may be a dangerous disease if only for the possibility that the testes may be involved. Mumps in the prepubertal male seldom involves the testicles or, if it does, does not produce permanent damage thereto. In the adult male it may induce swelling of the testes although, oddly enough, usually only one testicle is involved (unilateral mumps orchitis). Atrophy of the affected testicle and cessation of all germinal activity usually ensues after the swelling subsides. If the other testicle is not involved and normal spermatogenesis was present in it prior to the mumps, the potential fertility of the individual usually is not affected. Bilateral mumps orchitis is rare. When a complete absence of spermatozoa, or a relative sparsity of cells, is found in the ejaculate after mumps orchitis, in the absence of a semen examination prior to the disease, it is not always safe to attribute the sterility or infertility to the mumps. The individual concerned may have always had a poor fertility potential.

Male Infertility

For reasons already stated, the definition of this state must always be controversial. Two individuals, the male and the female, always are concerned in any given infertility problem. If active spermatozoa, however small the number, are present in the ejaculate of a male capable of having normal intercourse, the possibility of conception must always be present. The female partner may have passed all the known tests for potential fertility, but it is by no means certain that the *known* tests for the female cover all the defects that may be present in the wife. Therefore, when our statistics tell us that conception is not likely to occur when the sperm count in the ejaculate is below a certain level, even though the spermatozoa present may show normal structure and activity, they are based on the assumption that the female partner has, by test, been given a clean bill. But standards (such as they are) have been set up by various authorities for the normal range of human male fertility. To say that the authorities agree on these standards would be an exaggeration. There are those who will insist that sperm counts below 60 million/cc., regardless of the other qualities of the semen, are not likely to produce conception, and others who would feel more comfortable in an optimistic prognosis if the sperm count were well above that level. More liberal thought in the field would allow a 40 million/cc. count level, provided that the spermatozoa met other requirements in structure and activity.

Unfortunately, most of the standards promulgated are based upon studies of infertile populations and on the semen quality found in men who sought medical help because they *had* an infertility problem. They do not consider the possibility that the semen of many men who have fathered one or several children in a marital union and who had no need at any time to submit their semen for examination, may show defects that usually are associated with infertility. The writer and his associates have taken the most liberal stand in this matter after a study of the semen of a large number of men of proven fertility and of those who had an infertility problem. Earlier in this article, we indicated that counts below 20 million/cc. seemed to be below the danger level emerging from these studies. The most liberal standards suggested to date are those that have emerged from the above statistical analysis. These standards demand that the sperm count be above 20 million/cc., that at least 40 per cent of these cells be active with a normal degree of forward progression, and that at least 60 per cent of the cells display normal structure. These standards suggest further that less emphasis be placed upon the sperm count and more upon the motile activity of the cells. If this point of view is accepted, then we must also accept the fact that from 5 to 10 per cent of our American adult male population will fall into the infertile category. If the more conservative standards are used, a much higher percentage would have to be considered as infertile. We should add, perhaps, that the same essential data have been derived from studies in every country in which sound records have been kept. We feel that it would be more reasonable to accept the liberal standards. It does not seem logical to suppose that nearly 30 per cent of the adult males (otherwise normal) in any population selected at random would be infertile and this would be true if the high sperm count levels were accepted as the minimal levels of normal fertility and if only the sperm count was used as the criterion.

If, in the presence of an adequate sperm count, poor sperm motility is accepted as another reason for infertility (as it must), then to the infertile group with low counts must be added another significant percentage of men whose fertility is questionable only because of poor sperm motility.

Reasons for Male Infertility

The maturation of the spermatozoa in the human testicle is detected first at about age 10 and appears to be initiated by a secretion from the anterior lobe of the pituitary known as the follicle-stimulating (FSH) hormone. The same hormone in the female stimulates the growth and certain stages of development of the ovum. The secretion of this hormone in the female is cyclic. It appears to be constant in amount in the male, and is responsible not only for initiation of spermatogenesis at puberty but for its maintenance thereafter in the adult. Is inadequacy of this hormone responsible for the infertility due to impaired spermatogenesis? There is no sound evidence that this is so. Indeed, the excretion of the hormone in the urine may be elevated under certain conditions of germ cell deficiency. This would suggest that (1) there was a failure to utilize the hormone by the testicular tissue, or (2) there was increased secretion by the pituitary. Administration of the FSH hormone to individuals with low sperm counts has not met with success and there are suggestions that this approach may actually produce depression of the count. It should be stated, however, that the only pituitary hormone containing FSH available for general use is extracted from the pituitaries of animals (sheep, bulls, etc.) and probably is destroyed rapidly in the human.

Generally speaking, the causes of oligospermia are unknown. The men concerned usually are normal individuals without obvious physical or endocrine deficiencies. Nutritional deficiency is seldom apparent. Activity of the thyroid has often been considered as one of the possibilities, but thyroid therapy, even its empirical use in individuals with normal thyroid activity, has not been an effective approach. There are certain possibilities that are not susceptible to easy proof. The first is that a rather steady percentage of the male population is born with a deficiency of the germinal epithelium which does not allow the testicle to respond in appropriate fashion to the hormones of the pituitary or to any known therapy after the oligospermia has been detected. The second is that the childhood diseases such as measles, chicken pox, and whooping cough may, in some individuals, affect the undifferentiated germinal epithelium so that spermatogenesis, when initiated at the proper time, is subnormal. The truth is that we just do not know why oligospermia should be so common.

A less frequent but still common cause of

male infertility is concerned not with numbers of spermatozoa, but with their motile activity. Complete absence of motile activity (necrospermia) in the total population of spermatozoa in the ejaculate is rare. Its cause is unknown and in most cases it is not associated with obvious structural defects in the cells. Inherent defects in the chemical components of the cells is probably the answer. Much more common, however, are the semen specimens that contain adequate numbers of spermatozoa of which too few show motile activity of good quality, i.e., the forward progression of which is too sluggish. The reason for the defect again is difficult to assess, but in many cases is apparently not due to an inherent deficiency in the chemistry of the cells since an improvement in sperm motility can be obtained by certain therapeutic approaches.

Certain facts about sperm transport and its timing from the testicles to the exterior of the body must be understood. It is estimated that from the time the cells leave the testicle, nearly three weeks elapse before they appear in the ejaculate. In the interval, they must traverse the long duct system of the epididymis and the ductus deferens, and during this three-week span they must depend upon the cells lining the ducts for their sustenance since they are not in immediate contact with the blood circulation. The cells lining the ducts are in immediate contact with the circulation and are functionally dependent on the male sex hormone, testosterone. It is thought that the failure of motile activity of the spermatozoa may be related to a diminution in function of the duct epithelium cells.

Therapy

The only therapy for male sterility, the surgical approach where occlusion of the ducts is involved, already has been discussed. There is no known treatment for deficient or absent germinal epithelium. The treatment of relative male infertility, generally speaking, is most disappointing. When all the tests for physical well-being have been performed and any obvious defects such as anemia or dietary deficiencies have been corrected, there is little the internist can do to elevate a low sperm count, particularly when the count is very low (1–10 million/

cc.). In recent years, the "testosterone rebound" approach has been suggested. The rationale of this therapy is that if enough testosterone is given to a male, the sperm count may be depressed to zero. This effect is mediated via the anterior lobe of the pituitary and its secretion of the hormone (FSH) necessary for spermatogenesis. High blood levels of testosterone inhibit this secretion and, as a result, spermatogenesis. Recovery will take place when exogenous testosterone is withdrawn, and it is claimed that the recovery is accompanied by a marked increase over the original number of spermatozoa in the ejaculate. The results of this treatment, however, appear to be equivocal. After years of intensive testing, the results in general are not encouraging. We already have indicated that other hormone therapy has failed.

The use of small amounts of testosterone may be beneficial where poor sperm motility is the factor in infertility. The rationale of this approach lies in the assumption of the possibility, mentioned above, that a failure of the cells of the duct system may not provide the appropriate sustenance for the spermatozoa and that stimulating the duct cells by elevating the blood level of testosterone may in turn restore normal motility to the cells. The approach has been used in the writer's laboratory and encouraging results are being obtained. Thyroid therapy in this condition has not been as effective as might have been supposed.

However, in recent years, a marked advance in the therapy of male infertility as well as a better understanding of the etiology of this problem, has occurred as a result of the discovery that there is a relationship between the presence of varicocele and poor semen quality. Varicocele is a circulatory disturbance, almost invariably found in the left testis, which manifests itself in an engorgement and varicosity of the veins leaving the testis, particularly those leading into the left internal spermatic vein. The varicosity apparently results from the failure of the blood returning from the testes to flow off into the renal vein. Indeed, it has been demonstrated that blood actually may flow backwards from the left renal vein.

This disturbance occurs in perhaps 10 per cent of all adult males and may not be noticed as physical discomfort by the individual. Its presence does not necessarily cause a disturbance in testicular function but often does. It have been suggested by British workers who originally discovered the infertility connotations of varicocele, that this circulatory disturbance produces an elevation of temperature in the whole scrotum. If this were true, the bilateral effect (on both testes) of a unilateral anomaly would be rationalized. American workers, by direct measurement of scrotal and testicular temperatures have not been able to confirm this theory. Rather do they believe that the retrograde flow of blood in the left internal spermatic vein so often found in the presence of varicocele may induce a disturbance in the blood chemistry of the veins serving the left testis which in turn is transmitted to the right testis by veins which connect the two.

Whatever the reason for the disturbance, high ligation of the left internal spermatic vein at a point close to the inguinal ring produces a degree of recovery of spermatogenesis in a surprisingly large number of the affected individuals. Indeed, this approach is the first positive one of importance to have appeared in the therapy of male infertility. The pregnancy rate in hitherto sterile couples following this operation approaches 40 per cent.

One other approach should be mentioned as a possibility where none other can be expected to work. Oligospermia usually, if not always, is enumerated as the number of cells per unit volume of fluid (count/cc.). If the ejaculate volume is high (above 5.0 cc.), the count per cubic centimeter may be low, but the total count may be reasonably good if not high. For example, ejaculate volumes of 10 cc. after normal periods of continence are not uncommon. The sperm count may be only 10 million/cc. but the total sperm count in such cases would be 100 million. No matter what the total sperm count is, however, high ejaculate volumes never seem to produce conception easily. When this problem is encountered, advantage can be taken of the fact that the bulk of the spermatozoa appear in the first part of the ejaculate. The patient is instructed to produce a semen specimen in such fashion that the first portion of the ejaculate, preferably the first one-third, is caught in a sterile container. The remainder can be discarded. In this manner, the sperma-tozoa are concentrated physiologically and can be used for homologous insemination at the appropriate times in the cycle. Since only very low volumes of semen are required for insemination directly into the cervix, this approach can be used in the oligospermic individual whose ejaculate volume is within normal range. If the average sperm count is 10 m./cc. in the complete specimen (say of 3.0 cc. volume), it can be increased to nearly 25 m./cc. in the first part of the split ejaculate.

References

Bayle, H., and Gouygov, C., *La stérilité masculine.* Paris: Association Française d'Urologie, 1953.

Buxton, C. Lee, and Southam, Anna L., *Human Infertility.* New York: Paul B. Hoeber, Inc., 1958.

Charny, C. W., "Effect of Varicocele on Fertility." *Fertil. & Steril. 13;* 47, 1962.

Hotchkiss, Robert S., *Fertility in Men.* Philadelphia: J. B. Lippincott Co., 1944.

MacLeod, J., "Seminal Cytology in the Presence of Varicocele." *Fertil. & Steril. 16;* 735, 1965.

MacLeod, J., "The Male Factor in Fertility and Infertility; an Analysis of Ejaculate Volume in 800 Fertile Men and in 600 Men in Infertile Marriage." *Fertil. & Steril. 1;* 347, 1950.

MacLeod, J., and Gold, R. Z., "The Male Factor in Fertility and Infertility. II. Spermatozoon Count in 1,000 Men of Known Fertility and in 1,000 Cases of Infertile Marriage." *J. Urol. 66;* 436, 1951.

MacLeod, J., and Gold, R. Z., "The Male Factor in Fertility and Infertility. III. An Analysis of Motile Activity in the Spermatozoa of 1,000 Fertile Men in Infertile Marriage." *Fertil. & Steril. 2;* 187, 1951.

MacLeod, J., and Gold, R. Z., "The Male Factor in Fertility and Infertility. IV. Sperm Morphology in Fertile and Infertile Marriage." *Fertil. & Steril. 2;* 394, 1951.

MacLeod, J., and Gold, R. Z., "The Male Factor in Fertility and Infertility. V. Effect of Continence on Semen Quality." *Fertil. & Steril. 3;* 297, 1952.

MacLeod, J., and Gold, R. Z., "The Male Factor in Fertility and Infertility. VI. Semen Quality and Certain Other Factors in Relation to Ease of Conception." *Fertil. & Steril. 4;* 10, 1953.

Mann, T., *The Biochemistry of Semen and of the Male Reproductive Tract.* New York; John Wiley & Sons, Inc., 1964.

Meaker, S. R., *Human Sterility.* Baltimore: The Williams & Wilkins Co., 1958.

Scott, L. S., and Young, D., "Varicocele." *Fertil. & Steril. 13;* 325, 1962.

JOHN MACLEOD

Fetishism

Definition

FETISHISM is a psychosexual aberration or complex in which the person's sex impulse or libido becomes attached to or *fixated* to something that constitutes a *sexual symbol* of the love-object. By "fixated" is meant the sexual interest is centered entirely on some inanimate object or "fetish."

The term was coined by Binet (1888), who introduced the concept of this particular sexual deviation to science. The word is derived from the Portuguese *fetico*, meaning charmed, a term originally stemming from the Latin *facere*, to make. It conveys the idea of something artificially made. Eulemburg proposed the use of the phrase "sexual symbolism" but it was never permanently adopted. Havelock Ellis preferred the term "erotic symbolism."

Types of Fetishists

The fetishist may be erotically attracted to a woman's shoe, stocking, glove, handkerchief, corset, undergarment, ornament, hair, or other material or wearing apparel. Thus we have shoe-fetishists, glove-fetishists, fur-fetishists, silk-fetishists, velvet-fetishists, lingerie-fetishists, rubber-fetishists, leather-fetishists, or hair-fetishists. Fetishism may involve hair-snipping or stealing women's clothing. The act of stealing the garment produces great erotic satisfaction. According to Karpman (1954), some fetishists may even commit burglary, theft, or assault to secure the object. Because of this fact fetishism has forensic importance. Fetishists are very often aggressive and antisocial.

Psychodynamics

Fetishism occurs almost exclusively in men. Psychoanalysts classify this peculiar sexual phenomenon as a highly symbolic form of *psychic masturbation*.

Sadomasochism and Exhibitionism

We speak of fetishists as "symbolists." Fetishism is a form of sexual regression, a retreat from adult sexuality, what Stekel (1940) referred to as psychosexual infantilism. Many fetishists harbor the delusion of being sexually impotent with women, even though they have never made an attempt at coitus. Their aberration assumes the nature of an obsession. It is compulsive in nature and is associated with sadomasochistic features. To illustrate, one fetishist expressed the following sadomasochistic fantasy:

"I would imagine having women that I knew and liked as captives in my fortress and making their position so desirable that they liked being there and being my mistress. But the dreams and phantasies that aroused me most were those wherein some persons who had been mean and quarrelsome to me were my captives and I would build them up only to humiliate them and then to satisfy my sexual desires."

Fetishism is akin to exhibitionism insofar as it is motivated by a compulsive impulse that the offender cannot control because of his lack of understanding of the psychodynamic factors involved.

A young married man, aged 26, was referred for a psychiatric examination because he got into difficulty with the law: he was a fetishist and had been arrested for stealing ladies' panties from clotheslines.

During his early adolescence, at the period of sexual awakening, he had become fascinated by panties that his sister had carelessly left about in her bedroom. He had become sexually stimulated whenever he entertained phantasies of what women looked like clad in panties, and had finally developed the idea of acquiring ladies' panties by stealing them from clotheslines. The stolen panties played a role in his masturbatory activities. The court recommended psychiatric treatment, which led to his rehabilitation.

A strange epidemic occurred several years ago that gave the newspapers material of an unusual nature. Young high-school girls who wore their hair in pigtails, a fad at that time, were surprised by having one of the braids clipped off while riding in a trolley or bus. The offender or "braid-cutter" was undoubtedly a hair-fetishist. The police immediately set out to apprehend the "mystery man," but he was never found. The incidents aroused curiosity and wonderment as to what would make an individual go around clipping girls' hair. The offender probably used the lock of hair as a masturbation stimulus, and the cutting of the hair (sadism) represented what psychoanalysts call "symbolic castration."

Incest Wish

In many cases of fetishism there exists an unconscious incest wish. The incestuous striving is directed at some symbol or representative of the person toward whom the wish is directed. In a case of hair-fetishism reported in *Sexual Deviations* (1951), a book that I coauthored, the patient's mother and sister had black hair, which was the symbol chosen to represent the love-object. The patient's incestuous attachment to his mother and to his sister could not be attained in reality, so he chose a symbol of them, their hair, and used it in his autoerotic phantasies. His primordial attachment was to his mother, and his incestuous fixation to his mother remained hidden at the root of the sexual impulse, as was shown by his description of the beauty of his mother's hair when he was a child. According to Stekel, fe-

tishism has been found in every case to have had its origin in early life, and it is rare for the child to seek a direct genital symbol before puberty. In this particular case, the patient became aware through analysis that when he was 12 years old the hair of his sister had had a definite stimulating effect on his autoerotic life.

Thus we see that the object in many instances may be associated with an incestuous phantasy and may represent the hair, glove, shoe, or undergarment of the mother or sister. Stekel tells us that "because of his obsession with the object for which he has so strong a sexual attraction the fetishist very often becomes a collector of these objects, or of representations of them." He refers to such a collection as the "harem cult," inferring that each additional object represents in phantasy a substitute symbol for another woman (a mother- or sister-surrogate).

Further enlightenment regarding the psychology of the compulsive fetishist is shed by Dr. John Oliven (1955), who writes, "his need is usually for possession; he is an inexhaustible collector of 'his' kind of fetish; and he may keep books punctiliously about the date and the origin of his acquisitions. Periodically, he looks at, fondles, manipulates, smells, or kisses his objects, and this may suffice to gratify him. Some have spontaneous ejaculations during this activity; others 'use' the objects to produce masturbatory orgasm."

The object thus becomes for the fetish-lover an emotional short circuit, leading to erotic stimulation and satisfaction.

Psychic Impotence

Fetishism is closely related to psychic impotence. For most fetishists, the contact with the fetish or object is a *conditio sine qua non* for the satisfactory performance of the coital act.

Franz Alexander sums up this phenomenon psychoanalytically by saying that "It has always a phallic connotation and denies the absence of the penis in the woman." This theory is also shared by Fenichel (1945) and other psychoanalysts, who explain fetishism on the basis of the fetishist's refusal to acknowledge that a woman has a penis. Stekel adds that it always develops into a depreciation of the female regardless of the causes. According to Freudian symbolism, the shoe, foot, hand, or any other elongated object represent penis symbols. Fur is a symbolic substitute for pubic hair.

Karpman expresses the opinion that there is no fetishism in women because "the feminine experience of world and love is more bound to a concrete, personal level," adding that "males have active visual imagery, while masturbating; women do not."

Fetishism is often confused with partialism. In partialism, the individual is erotically attracted to a certain part of a woman's body. The sexual fixation may involve such parts of the female anatomy as the breasts, buttocks, thighs, legs, ankles, feet, or hands. Some observers regard partialism as a type of body-fetishism.

Combined Forms

It is not uncommon for the compulsive fetishist to indulge in other types of sexual aberrations such as exhibitionism, homosexuality, voyeurism, transvestism, coprolalia, etc. Various combinations coexist in the same individual.

One particular fetishist would cut out pictures of women from magazines, and would masturbate while looking at them. He also would call up strange women on the telephone and use obscene language, masturbating while he was talking. He described his activities as follows:

I would lay these pictures out on the floor nearby and masturbate while talking to these women while at the same time looking at the pictures of the women. As I reached a climax I would use an obscene word, phrase or ask a question of great personal intimacy. In several of these calls I would introduce myself with a fictitious name, inform the women that I was a total stranger to them, and then tell them a lurid story of being a war casualty whose need of sexual stimulation was great and who was deprived of normal outlets due to convalescence. In several cases of phoning, I was sharply rebuffed, threatened with police action or smartly told off. When a woman quarreled with me over my use of obscene language, I seemed to enjoy it most and would sometimes pretend to be overawed and apologetic to them, in the meantime I would masturbate up to the point of climax and then would inject a filthy remark. . . .

Throughout the summer, window peeping was my main source of sexual satisfaction. For a short while I had stolen women's underthings from clotheslines such as brassieres, slips and silk stockings and would then use them to stimulate my sexual desires by rubbing them against my body and then masturbating.

An editor of a magazine brought to my attention the case of a restaurant owner who had collected, over many years, hands made of marble, wood, ivory, stone, metal, crystal, and ceramics and ranging in size from miniature to oversize. In addition, he had collected plaques, paintings, drawings, and sketches of hands. The editor asked me to evaluate this unusual hobby in terms of the psychological motivation. Since the hands were actually inanimate objects insofar as they were reproductions of human hands, the phenomenon came under the category of fetishism rather than partialism.

In speculating about the psychology of this particular case of hand-fetishism, we have to take into consideration the various associations connected with hands. An individual may have been deeply impressed as a child by the hands of his mother, sister, or friend. The impression may have become a fixation or obsession and the person may find himself in adult life making hands the central theme of what appears to be an innocent hobby.

Or the hands may be associated with some past sexual experience that the person cannot forget. Psychoanalysts would say in this case that the hands had become *genitalized*. The individual would therefore find anything in connection with hands highly erotic.

If the hand-fetishism involves the hands of both sexes, we might conclude that the person's erotic attraction to hands is bisexual in origin.

Distinction from Hobby Collections

The urge to collect certain objects is not abnormal by itself, nor does every collector's item have to have a sexual meaning. There are stamp collectors, women who collect teacups or spoons, men who collect first editions, and others who buy and collect valuable paintings. Their motivations are not necessarily erotic.

Nevertheless, one can speculate as to what

would make a person go to so much trouble to acquire a particular object to add to his collection. For one thing, a collector is somewhat of a *narcissist*. He enjoys the vanity of knowing he has something that most other people do not have. He derives a vicarious thrill from seeking something "new" or "different." His hobby may be an outlet of some kind for an inner frustration, and he harbors a certain amount of exhibitionism (nonsexual) insofar as his collection attracts the attention of his friends.

All these and many other psychological factors enter into the phenomenon of hobby collections. In other words, there is a normal type of fetishism that exists among normal persons.

By the same token, one must also realize that there are kinds of fetishism and types of fetishists that come under a different category. If an individual boasts of an extensive collection of pictures of nude women and is sexually inadequate, the psychiatrist is justified in assuming that he is suffering from some type of sexual neurosis. The same applies to pornography.

The man who collects guns may be normal or neurotic. According to Freudian psychoanalysts, a gun is a phallic symbol. Hence it would follow from their point of view that a bachelor who collects guns and was never too interested in women and marriage might be suffering from some form of neurosis.

Psychoanalytical interpretations and speculations regarding anything are justified so long as one is cautious about making sweeping generalizations and allows for exceptions to which the theory may not necessarily apply. Thus, we might say that although it is true that every collector is not necessarily a fetishist, the compulsive fetishist is often a collector.

Causes of Fetishism

Binet was one of the first to conclude that fetishism is caused by some association of an object with the first awakening of the *vita-sexualis*. His conclusion was that "in the life of every fetishist there may be assumed to have been some event which determined the association of lustful feeling with the single impression."

Thus fetishism has its roots in childhood. It can be traced to some "accidental" experience during childhood or adolescence when the individual became sexually aroused by contact with some object belonging to or associated with his mother, sister, aunt, grandmother, or some other woman. It is somewhat like a conditioned reflex.

It develops as a result of psychosexual immaturity, a fixation of the libido at some early stage of development. In most cases, the patients are able to recall associations in childhood of an early sexual arousal with specific experiences that brought into a sexual focus a particular object (their mother's or sister's shoe, glove, or undergarment).

Treatment

Every case of fetishism must be studied and treated on the basis of the particular factors involved.

Since fetishism is a neurosis it can be eliminated with proper treatment. Disclosing the original experience of the episode that channeled the libido does not by itself necessarily effect a cure. If the condition has persisted for a long time, it may require intensive psychotherapy and re-education.

References

Binet, A., *Études de Psychologie Expérimentale*. Paris, 1888.

Caprio, Frank S., "Hand Fetishism." *Sexology* 24; 578–583, April, 1958.

Caprio, Frank S., *Variations in Sexual Behavior*. New York: Citadel Press, 1955.

Ellis, Albert, *Sex Without Guilt*. New York: Lyle Stuart, 1958.

Fenichel, Otto, *The Psychoanalytic Theory of Neurosis*. New York: W. W. Norton, 1945.

Karpman, Benjamin, *The Sexual Offender and His Offenses*. New York: Julian Press, Inc., 1954.

Kinsey, A. C., *et al.*, *Sexual Behavior in the Human Male*. Philadelphia: W. B. Saunders Co., 1948.

London, Louis S., and Caprio, Frank S., *Sexual Deviations*. Washington: Linacre Press, 1951.

Oliven, John F., *Sexual Hygiene and Pathology*. Philadelphia: J. B. Lippincott Co., 1955.

Stekel, Wilhelm, *Sexual Aberrations*. New York: Liveright Pub. Corp., 1940.

von Krafft-Ebing, R., *Psychopathia Sexualis*. New York: Physicians and Surgeons Book Co., 1934.

FRANK S. CAPRIO

Freedom, Sexual

THE most distinctive characteristic of man as compared to nonhuman animals is that man's behavior is essentially learned, it is not innate or biologically determined. Thus, man's behavior is a social psychological phenomenon. And so is his sexual behavior. Furthermore, according to such authorities as Leuba, as well as Ford and Beach, it is suggested that, *without* specific sexual experiences, man outside of culture—that is, so-called feral or natural man—or the extreme social isolate does not generally engage in sexual behavior upon reaching puberty. There is no sexual instinct in man. And since man's sexual behavior is symbolic, since it is social, learned, it is *always* shaped in a particular cultural milieu and oriented by the values of the society maintaining that milieu. The nature of sexual behavior in man, like *all* his truly human behavior, *varies* with his culture, with reference to the society in which he is socialized and in which he becomes a human, social being.

When, consequently, sexual freedom is discussed, it must be qualified with reference to the behavior of specific groups of men (societies) with specific patterns of behavior (cultures). Only in this way can sexual freedom (or, as a matter of fact, any behavior of man) be dealt with objectively and with understanding.

A Definition of Sexual Freedom

Freedom in popular usage is a term of little scientific precision. From the modern behavioral scientist's point of view, there is, in reality, no such thing as *freedom* as the word is generally used in everyday language. That is, the idea that every person has an ability, freedom, to act in accordance with his own inner conviction, independent of the situation-process in which he is operating, is a fiction. The idea of free will, a concept closely related to the idea of freedom, must also be rejected. It too is fictitious. Man in culture and in society, *Homo socius,* social man, as compared to *Homo sapiens,* natural or feral man, is never free, nor does he have a free will. His behavior is *always* anchored and shaped by his culture and society. There is no such thing as sexual freedom, popularly defined, there are only *limited alternatives of action,* of behavior, open to the individual in regard to sex relations. These limited alternatives are generally explicitly defined in the ideology of the group or groups in which an individual has membership and/or with which he identifies. Thus, all freedom, including sexual freedom, merely represents the social-psychologically based choice a person has among several alternatives of culturally defined actions. There is, then, sexual freedom in this limited sense only where man has the right to select and does select any one of several behavior alternatives with reference to sexual values and goals.

Perhaps the following illustration will clarify matters. In American culture two married persons not strongly identified with or not affiliated with a particular traditional church group have some of these alternatives, with regard to family planning and sex relations: (1) they may practice planned parenthood using mechanical and chemical means of contraception, an action consistent with the value orientations of Methodists, Reformed Jews, Scientific Humanists, the upper classes, and with most college graduates, but inconsistent with Roman Catholics, Orthodox Jews, the lower classes, and those persons with a limited formal education; (2) they may practice the rhythm method of planned parenthood, an action acceptable to Roman Catholics under special circumstances, unacceptable to most college graduates and liberal Protestants and Jews; (3) they may practice complete abstinence except when children are desired, a view unacceptable to almost all groups; (4) they may practice *coitus interruptus,* unacceptable to Roman Catholics and Orthodox Jews on religious grounds and to Reformed Jews, Methodists, and Scientific Humanists on secular grounds, but commonly used among the poorly educated, the lower classes of society, regardless of religious affiliation.

Theoretically, an independent married couple has at least these alternatives in regard to family planning and sex relations. But, in reality, is any couple really free to select any of the alternatives? Generally speaking, no. A couple having a liberal college education is likely to be strongly in favor of planned parenthood using the best available methods. Couples with little formal education are likely to reject or even be unaware of the significance of the best planned-parenthood techniques. The specific backgrounds of a particular couple always work toward setting limits on alternatives of action by circumscribing choice within a circle of value orientations.

If then we define freedom as the right and ability of the individual to make a choice among a limited number of alternatives of action in regard to a particular value or goal, we might define *sexual freedom* as *the right and ability of the individual to make a choice among a limited number of alternatives of action in regard to sexual values or goals.* A society which permits the individual a relatively large number of constructive alternatives in sexual behavior is said to be one that is *prosexual;* one that rigidly adheres to few constructive alternatives or rejects all but one is said to be *antisexual.* In examining the idea of sexual freedom it will be seen that there is a kind of continuum of sexual freedom, ranging from strongly antisexual to strongly prosexual societies.

Sexual Freedom in Cross-Cultural and Trans-Temporal Perspective

The most extensive cross-cultural studies of sex behavior have been done by Ford and Beach, and by Murdock. The former studied 185 societies, the latter 250. Both depended much for their data on the Yale's Cross-Cultural Survey, now called the Human Relations Area Files, Inc. Seward has accomplished almost as much, perhaps, in an intensive study of a few contrasting societies, depending heavily on the works of Kardiner, Malinowski, and Mead for comparative analyses. Using the materials available on nonliterate and literate societies past and present, an attempt will be made to construct a continuum of sexual freedom in terms of prosexual and antisexual behavior patterns in 12 different societies. Figure 1 illustrates the continuum.

The Shakers
(The United Society of Believers)

The Shakers founded numerous communities in America during the latter part of the eighteenth century and the beginning of the nineteenth century. The community at Mount Lebanon (New Lebanon), New York, is the oldest and largest Shaker community and is

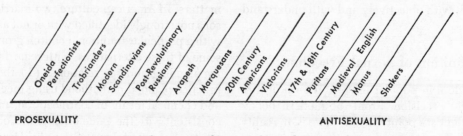

PROSEXUALITY   ANTISEXUALITY

FIG. 1. A Continuum of Prosexuality and Antisexuality

recognized as the central executive of all the Shaker communities. Ann Lee, born at Manchester, England, in 1736, was the founder of the Shaker movement. She believed that in Christ's second appearance, which was imminent, he would appear in a woman's form and that she was that woman. Ann Lee regarded the sexual relationship as the most sinful of all human relationships. Therefore, she demanded chastity of all permanent residents of the Shaker communities. There was no marriage (nonogamy); the two sexes occupied separate parts of houses, and when married couples joined the community, they regarded each other as brothers and sisters and never again engaged in sex relations. During the second quarter of the nineteenth century there were about 6,000 Shakers in America scattered in more than 25 communities. Today, there are less than 500 members. Historically, the Shakers represent, perhaps, one of the most antisexual societies known to the world. According to Ditzion, the view of sex expressed in Shakerism is closely related to the personal experiences of Ann Lee, whose husband ran away with another woman after fathering four children who died in early infancy and childhood. To Ann Lee, therefore, the most vile feature of life on earth was sex. As a self-ordained prophetess, she endeavored, along with her followers, to expiate this original sin for all mankind.

The Manus

According to Margaret Mead, the Manus (a nonliterate people) of New Guinea regard sex as a necessary evil, as inherently shameful and unpleasant. Frigidity and painful sex relations are experienced by most Manus women, who regard sex as a humiliating experience. Manus culture is unique in the sense that there is no word for love in its language, no romantic stories, songs, or dances. As Mead points out, the Manus are "a puritan society, rigidly subduing its sex life to meet supernaturally enforced demands which are closely tied up with its property standards." In this sense the Manus are very much like certain segments of American society, particularly the status-striving upper middle class. It is also interesting that among the Manus, kissing is unknown, and

breast stimulation and similar forms of love play in sex relations are generally lacking. Tenderness and playfulness are dissociated from sex relations. To the Manus, sex is sin.

The Medieval English

Feudalism placed a great emphasis on Medieval English family life. The Christian Church, with its antisexual attitudes and policies, had gained in strength and influence. As the wife of Adam, woman was the instrument of the devil and inferior to man. Sexual desire in itself was regarded as sinful and sexual intercourse excusable *only* if offspring were the desired outcome. The feudal lord's power over his serfs was exemplified in the practice of *jus primae noctis*—his right to have coitus with any new bride among his serfs. Women were generally regarded as sexual property and sex practices were developed which concerned rights and privileges with reference to that property. The emergence of Chivalry was the only hopeful light in this dark period, the only challenge to feudalism and the treatment of women as chattels. But while knights treated women of rank with respect and dignity, they often treated women of low rank with scorn and cruelty.

This does not mean that the Medieval English were wholly antisexual in their practical social mores. Orthodox church teaching was not always followed to the letter; and the practice of *jus primae noctis* itself was neither ecclesiastically upheld nor was it, in spite of its undesirable aspects, entirely antisexual. In fact, some of the sex customs of medieval days, like those of some of the more modern oriental peoples, were prosexual just because they were anti-equalitarian: since when males subjugate females, they frequently do so to their own sex advantage. In the broadest usage of the term, this still results in antisexualism, since females constitute approximately one-half the human species, and neglect of their sexual urges and full consent to participation is hardly conducive of fully enjoyed sex relations. But in a narrower sense, it cannot be said that anti-equalitarians are necessarily thoroughly prudish; and in this sense there was much that was prosexual about Medieval English attitudes—

at least, below the surface of the church-influenced laws of the day.

New England Puritans

Perhaps, aside from the Shakers, no historical people, after medieval times, has been as antisexual as were the New England Puritans. The childhood years of the Puritans were overshadowed by Calvinistic doctrines of original sin, predestination, and election, and the punishments of a flaming, material hell. Puritans accepted unequivocally the view of the ancient Hebrews, of Paul, and the early Church Fathers that women were an inferior order of beings, to be held in control by their lawful spouses and masters. Like the early Church Fathers, the Puritans looked at women as the cause of original sin, the personification of sex as sin. To them adultery was the most heinous of all sins and they did not shrink from prescribing and carrying out the death penalty for violators. The records of the Massachusetts Bay Colony show that in 1644 two persons were executed for committing adultery, and a third execution is mentioned in Cotton Mather's *Magnalia Christi*. While Plymouth and Rhode Island did not prescribe the death penalty, they did call for a severe flogging for adulterers. In addition, Plymouth also required the offender to wear a scarlet letter A upon the breast until death. Wearing the scarlet A for adultery became law in Plymouth in 1658 and in Massachusetts in 1794. The meaning of adultery in Puritan New England was described by Nathaniel Hawthorne in his *The Scarlet Letter*.

So antisexual were the Puritans that unwed mothers, even those seduced and deserted, were often whipped, fined, and imprisoned. Very much like the Manus, the Puritans frowned on any public demonstration of tenderness and affection between man and wife.

Besides being the epitome of sex and sin, women were also very much like breeding animals. Green, a Boston printer, had thirty children. Families with fifteen or more children were quite common. Both infant and maternal mortality were extremely high.

The Victorians

In the nineteenth century, Western culture suffered under the yoke of Victorian repression, which had more than a superficial resemblance to Shaker, Manus, Medieval English, and Puritan sex values. Sex was regarded as a sin. There was a kind of cult of idealized feminine purity supported by masochistic tendencies. Sex had to be concealed at all costs. The taboos of the day extended to what a virtuous woman might see or hear as well as do. A gentleman would call a leg a "limb" and he would ask a "clean" woman for permission to smoke in her presence. The stage and the novel were desexualized. In all social classes the age at marriage was later than today, for people tried to keep "untainted" by sex as long as possible. Even in marriage sex was restrained. A virtuous wife was not supposed to show or even suggest that she enjoyed sex relations. Love play was regarded as "unnecessary" sex and "beastly." Russell Lynes notes that it was fashionable for the Victorian lady never to smoke because only sinful actresses did that, never to cross her knees, never to go out unchaperoned in the evening even when in a crowd, never to use lip rouge, and always to sit with the base of her spine against the back of the chair, since only "sinful sirens" slouched. While many Victorian habits of behavior have vanished from our present way of life, many still persist. It is still commonplace for many husbands to interpret their wives' aggressiveness in sex relations as unladylike. Likewise, many American women feel guilty and sinful if they enjoy or desire sex relations.

Twentieth Century Americans

According to Ford and Beach (1951), American attitudes toward sex are somewhat unique in that, although they are fairly representative of those existing in modern industrialized society, they consist of an unusual combination of Puritan mores inextricably accompanied by considerable sexual stimulation. Theoretically, modern America is one of the few societies that recognizes only one form of sexual partnership —that of one man "legally" married to one woman. Multiple sex partnerships as well as premarital and extramarital liaisons are socially and often legally forbidden. In the Ford and Beach sample of 185 societies only 16 per cent similarly restricted sex relations to single partnerships.

On the side of actual American sex practice, however, Kinsey's data suggest that, in spite of our Puritan-Victorian attitudes, approximately 50 per cent of our women and 85 per cent of our men have engaged in premarital intercourse; and that about 25 per cent of American wives and 50 per cent of American husbands have had extramarital coitus. As Albert Ellis has shown in his *Folklore of Sex* and *The American Sexual Tragedy*, American sex attitudes and behavior reveal numerous conflicting elements. On one hand, our mass media continually bombard us with sexually stimulating materials; on the other hand, our consciences are filled with Puritan-Victorian promises of hell and eternal damnation if we engage in the great, though necessary, sin of sex. Like the Manus people, Americans seem to place economic values above sexual ones. Unlike the Marquesans, Americans overeat as a compensation for frustrations and anxieties related to sex hunger. The Marquesans do the reverse, that is, they use sex as a compensation for frustrations and anxieties related to food hunger (see below). In line with the Calvinistic conception of predestination, Americans consider it safer and wiser to suppress sex and accumulate material possessions so that they may find out if they are damned or saved for the life after death. It seems strange to many that in our democratically oriented society we are so undemocratic, so authoritarian, and sometimes so inhuman in our sex attitudes and practices. There are very few authoritative voices that have spoken for sex sanity in our country, with the exception of such courageous persons as the late Alfred Kinsey, Walter Stokes, and Albert Ellis. As the Harpers (1956) recently pointed out, even those persons especially trained as family-life educators are often so afraid of sex that they do little but perpetuate those very attitudes that make American society fundamentally antisexual.

The Marquesans

It is suggested by Seward that the Marquesans (a nonliterate people), somewhat like some lower-class Americans, have resorted to sex as a means of compensating for their frustrations, particularly those concerning food hunger and starvation. The overvaluation of sex occurs at all stages of development in Marquesan society. Thus, for example, masturbation is used by adults as a pacifier for infants. There are systematic efforts to elongate the labia, thereby increasing female sexual attractiveness. Regular coitus is begun *before* puberty by boys and girls, and sexual play is a favorite form of activity. The Marquesans are also known for their extensive love play before coitus. Men are adept at stimulating a woman's breasts and genitalia with the lips and tongue. Exclusive sexual possession is socially disapproved. Sexual jealousy is considered to be in poor taste. Because there is a shortage of women, every woman attempts to become a skilled artist in sex relations in order to get and keep the best men for husbands. Consequently, Marquesan society is neurotically prosexual, using sex activity as a means of compensating for the food hunger frustrations and anxieties, according to Kardiner. Americans are neurotically antisexual, overeating as a means of compensating for sexual frustrations and anxieties.

The Arapesh

In contrast to the Manus and Marquesans, the nonliterate Arapesh have an extremely mature and healthy conception of sex. The Arapesh women and men are betrothed in childhood. At that time the girl goes to live among her husband-to-be's family and after long years of living together like brother and sister, sex relations occur as a natural outgrowth of their growing affection for each other. While there is no specific interest in erotic satisfaction, sex relations are accompanied by and are an outgrowth of mutual affection. Sex to Arapesh men and women is always an expression of affection that enhances the processes of growth around which their world revolves, according to Margaret Mead. The Arapesh are a cooperative, friendly, and peaceful people.

Post-Revolutionary Russians

According to Seward, post-Revolutionary Russia had an extremely wholesome, prosexual orientation of values. Sex was not regarded as either sacred or profane but as a natural thing that was an intrinsic part of the individual's life from early childhood. Not shrouded in mystery, not continually the focus of morality, sex was not the center of neurotic anxiety nor an expression of a need for security. Instead sex was freed, to become a constructive force uniting men and women. There was but a single standard of sex morality, both men and women having complete freedom in sex relations as long as there was no violation of the dignity of the individual. Birth control was legal and its practice was encouraged. Without it, sexual freedom would have been impossible. As in the modern Scandinavian countries, children born out of wedlock enjoyed the same social privileges and legal rights as did those born of wedded parents. Marriage and divorce laws were relaxed. Abortions were legal and free or inexpensive. But in 1936, as Hindus pointed out, the Soviet Union began to reverse its former policies relative to sexual behavior. Individual responsibility in sex relations was called bourgeois and against Soviet ethics. Abortions were outlawed except in matters of life or death. Birth control was frowned upon and literature on the subject vanished. Divorce was no longer free and easy. Marriage registration became compulsory. Women who gave birth to eight or more children were made heroines. Everything was now geared to increasing the population.

Today, according to Geiger and Inkeles, the attitudes the Russians hold toward sexual relations are generally characterized by considerable reticence about the open discussion of sexuality and a rather puritanical attitude toward showing interest in sexual matters. The double standard again prevails, as in pre-Revolutionary Russia, and wives are expected to take a passive role in sexual relations. In fact, oddly enough, sex in the Soviet Union nowadays is reminiscent of the bourgeois sex attitudes the post-Revolutionary Russians so strongly denounced.

Modern Scandinavians

Svalastoga has recently stated that "Coitus before marriage now may safely be considered the rule and chastity the exception in Scandinavia. The taking up of a going-steady relation frequently marks the beginning of regular sex relations." For those persons going steady and particularly for those who are engaged, "a certain amount of recognition of rights of privacy and sexual intercourse may be granted."

Approximately one-half of the first births come *before* nine months of marriage and almost 10 per cent of the births are out of wedlock. Because premarital coitus is not connected with casual daters but rather with persons going steady or engaged, paternity, unlike that in America, is never difficult to establish and a child born of the union is *not* in jeopardy. Also, unlike America, Scandinavian countries have taken steps to guarantee equal freedom in the sex act for male and female—to enforce a single, prosexual standard of sex morality. Thus, financial protection is provided for the woman and her child if premarital and extramarital relationships result in pregnancy, and both mother and child are granted equal status with women having children in wedlock.

Effective contraception and moral acceptance of its use is considered to be a deterrent to abortion. Generally speaking, the Scandinavians are prosexual on a mature level. Their society does not have a sex-centered morality. Rather it is a morality based on a respect for human dignity in all human relations, of which sex is but one small part. There is a tolerance for prostitution in the sense that it does not come within the province of the law as long as it is practiced *without* public disorder, spread of contagious disease, or profit to a third party. Male homosexuals in Scandinavia are organized in an association which has its head office in Copenhagen. There seems to be relatively little overemphasis on or dread of sex in Scandinavia, as there is in America.

The Trobrianders

Perhaps few existing societies have been as constructively prosexual as the nonliterate Trobrianders, made famous by the writings of Malinowski.

Among the Trobrianders, children become acquainted with sex at a very early age by witnessing their parents in sexual intercourse and by imitating with their playmates their parents' sex behavior. The art of love is gradually developed from the sexual games and play of Trobriand children into the passionate liaisons and partnerships of adolescence and adulthood. Adolescent couples find privacy in premarital coitus in the so-called *bachelor's houses*. Sexual experimentation precedes rather than follows marriage.

Sex for pleasure alone after marriage is regarded as childish. In marriage sex is a means of expressing affection and companionship, an attitude similar to that of the Arapesh. But at certain seasons the Trobriand people gather together to play games involving the erotic features of body contact, rhythm, singing, and, at times, outright sexual license.

Because of the Trobrianders' use of sex as recreation after marriage, due to their custom of sexual experimentation before marriage and their positive attitudes toward sexual expression, the Trobriand society is one of the few free from sexual perversions. In general, the Trobrianders are great lovers, who devote a considerable period of time to precoital activities (oral and manual stimulation of the genitalia and breasts, kissing, etc.), to variations in coital position (they are not, as most Americans, fetishistically attached to the coital position in which the woman is supine with the man above and facing her), and to expressing sex in song, dance, and story. While Americans suffer from a society that is both sex-stimulating and sex-repressing, Trobrianders achieve much happiness in a society in which sex serves as an expression of affection and companionship and as a form of pleasureful play and recreation.

Oneida Perfectionists

Most students of sexual freedom agree that the Oneida Community, led by John Humphrey Noyes, was one of the most daring and rational sex experiments in the history of mankind. According to Ditzion, Noyes believed that "a choice of motherhood had to be added to a free choice of wifehood to make a reality of sex equality. The thought was that a man should not embrace one woman exclusively any more than he should hold on to private property. All men in the community should ideally be potential husbands of all women; and all children the pride and joy of all adults." Thus, the Perfectionists had no marriage ceremonies nor permanent ties between couples. This kind of marriage Noyes called *complex marriage*. The community assumed all responsibility for the support and education of children.

When children were wanted by a couple, the community decided if they were eugenically fit to reproduce themselves. If longevity and health are evidence of success in this revolutionary type of parenthood and reproduction, the Noyesian Perfectionists at Oneida were most successful, and according to reliable reports, one of the healthiest communities this nation has ever had.

Sex to the Perfectionists was both an art and a science that could be learned. Young adolescent males and females were taught sexual skills by adult members of the community. Women who had passed the menopause would teach young males the art of "male continence" (*coitus reservatus*), the ability of withholding ejaculation indefinitely, a practice which Noyes made widely known by the distribution of his pamphlet entitled *Male Continence* (1872). (This method of birth control was later revived by the teachings of Madame Karezza.) Likewise young females were taught the art and science of sex by skilled "continent" men in the community. But sex to the Perfectionists was not, as many laymen believe, a neurotic means of compensation; it was a constructive force handled in a way that liberated these people for vigorous living in all aspects of life.

Economic security and pleasant living conditions were accepted as basic necessities. Outside labor was hired for work—particularly household chores—considered to be mere drudgery. There was no asceticism in this community. Both children and adults enjoyed a program of amusement and recreation reminiscent of Brook Farm, which included plays, concerts, games, sports, lectures, and readings. When Noyes was asked what relation there is between religion and sex, he answered: "The next thing a man wants, after he has found salvation of his soul, is to find his Eve and his Paradise." John Humphrey Noyes found that Paradise at Oneida—until Puritan-Victorian groups outside Oneida forced Noyes to abandon his Paradise and to end what Holbrook has called "The Perfect Society." No men since then have founded a New Oneida.

Individual Views of Sex Freedom

William McDougall

Calverton and Schmalhausen (1929) have hopefully called the late distinguished psychologist and social philosopher William McDougall "the last of the mid-Victorians," for his views on sex were more prudish than those of almost any distinguished recent scholar. Thus, McDougall stated that "Promiscuous mauling and pawing [his terms for petting and necking] are not only extremely undignified and in the worst possible taste; they are fatal to happiness." He also believed that sex was unnecessary for "strong men," and that if a man did not marry he should remain as chaste as a Shaker under all circumstances. In keeping with these views he applauded every rigid law against homosexuality and sex deviation. But, perhaps, his most authoritarian view concerned the place of jealousy in marriage. McDougall was of the opinion that "Jealousy is the grand preservative of family life and marital faithfulness. . . . Jealousy is the inseparable companion of love and its intensity is a pure gauge of love's strength." He believed that it was indecent for young married women to attend dances—particularly dances in which partners were changed frequently—with their husbands, as it might lead to adultery.

Pitirim Sorokin

Today's outstanding sexual conservative in America is Pitirim Sorokin, who has been the first professor and chairman of the Sociology Department at Harvard University and who is presently the director of the Harvard Research Center in Creative Altruism. In many of his writings, and particularly in his book, *The American Sexual Revolution* (1956), Sorokin has roundly condemned "loose behavior and false values" and has almost hysterically warned that American civilization is threatened by the possibility of complete sex anarchy. Using a historical approach, and emphasizing the now generally discredited views of J. D. Unwin (1934) on sex and culture, Sorokin has contended that any kind of premarital or extramarital relations are intrinsically harmful to human well-being and that there should be a return to ultra-Victorian sex attitudes and practices.

Dorothy A. Mohler

Although not so distinguished a pedagogue as McDougall or Sorokin, Professor Mohler is a social scientist who presents the view that, in essence, *only* penile-vaginal coital orgasm is normal sex behavior and noncoital orgasm is fundamentally unnatural, perverted, and even sinful. Furthermore, she continues, such penile-vaginal coitus must *only* take place in marriage and primarily for procreation. Sexual satisfaction is *always* a secondary matter.

David R. Mace

Dr. Mace is one of many outstanding marriage counselors and family-life educators who is quite entrenched in Christian sex-centered morality. He contends that sex is so complex a topic we can provide no final answers and he opposes sex behavior outside of marriage as being inconsistent with Christian ethics.

Alex Comfort

One current authority seems to have a consistent attitude to the problem of premarital sexual intercourse—Alex Comfort. He suggests that *premarital petting, up to and including orgasm,* is the intelligent and logical substitute for the premarital penile-vaginal coitus which parents and protectors of public morals fear will lead to numerous unwed mothers, illegitimate children, abortions, venereal disease, and general human depravity. Since, according to Kinsey and others, *any* kind of orgasm prior to marriage generally leads to a more satisfactory sexual adjustment in marriage, Comfort's suggestion seems a reasonable answer to one of the most controversial issues of the day.

Havelock Ellis

One of the most distinguished champions of greater sexual freedom in the first half of the 20th century was undoubtedly Havelock Ellis (1922). Concerning sexual freedom he had this to say: "It is not until a child is born or conceived that the community has any right to interest itself in the sexual acts of its members. The sexual act is of no more concern to the community than any other private physiological act. It is an impertinence, if not an outrage, to seek to inquire into it. But the birth of a child is a social act. Not what goes into the womb, but what comes out of it concerns society. The community is invited to receive a new citizen. It is entitled to demand that that citizen shall be worthy of a place in its midst and that he shall be properly introduced by a responsible father and a responsible mother. 'The whole of sexual morality,' as Ellen Key has said, 'revolves around the child.'"

If we interpret Ellis liberally, he seems to be saying that sex behavior should involve a greater degree of individual responsibility and need not be the concern of the community until and unless a child is conceived as a result of the sexual union. But such individual responsibility cannot be, in any society, independent of the social responsibilities an individual act implies.

Alfred Kinsey

Landis (1956) has recently summed up the late Kinsey's contributions in relation to greater sexual freedom: "Dr. Kinsey of recent years has crusaded for a more rational approach to the control of sex deviant behavior. His studies show that most sex offenders in prison are there for sex acts which he considers not to be in any way socially damaging. He would confine social concern to sex acts which are socially damaging, namely sex acts that involve an adult and a child, sex acts that involve compulsion of one party, and sex acts involving incestuous relations. Most male sex offenders are in prison for homosexuality or other acts which Kinsey considers normal forms of mammalian behavior; although they violate rigorous taboos, he believes they are not in any rational sense socially damaging. . . . Kinsey, in fact, makes a strong case for the biological desirability of premarital sex experience, holding that long abstinence, restraint, and avoidance of physical contacts and emotional responses before marriage may well lead to the building of inhibitions which damage the capacity of the organism to respond sexually in marriage. Petting to orgasm, intercourse to orgasm, or even masturbation to orgasm, he believes help prepare the organism to react physiologically."

Walter R. Stokes

Dr. Stokes (1953) is a courageous psychiatrist, physician, and marriage counselor who states publicly that he strongly believes that the best sexual development is possible through premarital sex experiences under emotionally favorable conditions. Stokes also believes that in women there is a relationship between sex response and the development of the vaginal musculature which can be aided by premarital coitus. In his practice he has found that almost invariably those very chaste young men who reach marriage without any sort of overt sex experience, including masturbation, have turned out to be completely impotent to a degree requiring extensive psychiatric treatment. He rejects the idea that sex is beautiful only in marriage.

Albert Ellis

Few scholars, scientists, clinicians, or laymen in recent years have contributed so much to promoting a sane view of sexual freedom and morality as has Albert Ellis (1954, 1958a, 1958b). In his *The American Sexual Tragedy* and *Sex without Guilt*, Albert Ellis asks for sex sanity not based on subjective, biased mystic beliefs but on the basis of scientific clinical evidence. In November, 1958, *Pageant* magazine published an article by Ellis entitled "10 Indiscreet Proposals," in which he asked Americans to live up to their democratic ideals and not support *sexual fascism*—the double standard of morality, treating women like second-class citizens, and intolerance of any sex behavior except penile-vaginal coitus in marriage.

Dr. Ellis maintains that American women are in large part responsible for the creation of homosexuality. Masturbation, he states, is not self-abuse but rather one of man's best friends and has done more good for civilized living than innumerable sermonizings to the contrary. He also advocates premarital sexual relations for adult, bright, well-informed, and reasonably well-adjusted unmarried adults. His is one of very few refreshing voices in a world full of warnings of sin and damnation for those desiring to express rather than suppress love and affection.

Recent Trends in
Sex Behavior around the World

In spite of the inhibitory attitudes persisting today with regard to sex, there are signs everywhere that in the real behavior of persons, as opposed to their stated Puritan-Victorian ideals, people are putting into practice some of the scientifically valid proposals of Kinsey, Stokes, Comfort, and Albert Ellis. In the United States the traditional sex code has been weakening. Thus in the Davis study in 1923, only 70 persons out of 1,000 married women (7 per cent) had premarital coitus. But in Burgess and Wallin's recent study of 666 married women (1953), 306 (46 per cent) had had premarital sexual relations, and, furthermore, 275 (90 percent) of those women *said that it had strengthened their relationship.* In general, Reiss (1957) has indicated there is a trend toward greater permissiveness in sex relations, toward less exploitative, body-centered types of sex activity, toward more affectionate, person-centered relations.

The "International Issue on the Family," an entire issue on family life in more than sixteen countries and geographical areas throughout the world appearing in the November, 1954, issue of *Marriage and Family Living,* suggested that the increased permissiveness of sex attitudes and behavior is due in large part to the spread of democratic Western ideology, particularly with relation to the status of women. Fascistic and feudalistic countries are likely to have strong antisexual double standards of sex morality, whereas more democratic countries are more likely to have a single, prosexual standard. The Scandinavian countries seem to have the most progressive sex standards among the civilized nations. Early post-Revolutionary Russia for a time had a sane sex morality but this was engulfed by Communistic imperialistic ambitions in the late thirties.

What happens to sex relations in the future is always related to what happens to human relations in general. In a peaceful, democratic world, a sane sex morality is more likely to prevail than in a brink-of-war or fighting world.

Summary and Conclusions

Human sexual behavior is learned. It is learned in the context of particular cultural values supported by particular societies. Sex behavior in human beings can never be free in the sense that freedom is popularly defined. Scientifically, freedom in man's behavior is always related to his ability to make a choice among limited alternatives. In this sense, some societies, as we have seen, are freer than others but *all* societies control the sexual behavior of their members.

Those societies which have permissive attitudes toward sex and allow numerous alternatives in regard to sexual behavior we call prosexual. The Oneida Perfectionists, the Trobrianders, and modern Scandinavians can thus be said to have been or to be prosexual. On the other hand, we also have societies which have extremely repressive and restrictive attitudes toward sex. Such societies can be said to be antisexual. Shaker society reached the nadir in antisexuality, very closely followed by the Manus, Medieval English, Puritans, Victorians, and some segments of the modern American population.

Various individuals have also expressed antisexual and prosexual views. The late Professor William McDougall was so antisexual that recent sexologists have called him "the last of the mid-Victorians." At the zenith of prosexuality stands the contemporary psychotherapist and author, Albert Ellis.

Despite a powerful remaining element of fascistic ideology, there seems to be, generally speaking, a strong, persistent democratic trend toward more rational sexual behavior both in the free world and certain areas behind the iron curtain. Even though since 1936 there has been a strong antisexual trend in the Communist world, some of the gains, particularly relative to the status of women, have persisted. What is needed now are a few thousand Walter Stokeses and Albert Ellises in private clinical practice and particularly in our schools and colleges.

References

Anthony, R., *The Housewife's Handbook on Selective Promiscuity.* New York: Documentary Books, 1962.

Bassett, M., *A New Sex Ethics and Marriage Structure.* New York: Philosophical Library, 1961.

Burgess, E. W., and Wallin, P., *Engagement and Marriage.* Philadelphia: J. B. Lippincott Co., 1953.

Calhoun, A. W., *A Social History of the American Family.* Cleveland: A. H. Clark Co., 1919, Vol. I.

Calverton, V. F., and Schmalhausen, S. D. (eds.), *Sex in Civilization.* Garden City, N.Y.: Macauley, 1929.

Comfort, A., *Sexual Behavior in Society.* New York: The Viking Press, Inc., 1950.

Crouch, B. C., *Absolute Fidelity and Marital Success.* Fulton, N. Y.: mimeographed, 1963.

Davis, K. B., *Factors in the Sex Life of 2200 Women.* New York: Harper & Brothers, 1929.

"Deans Will Act on Question of Parietal Dormitory Hours." *Reserve Tribune* (Western Reserve University), *63;* 1, March 24, 1967.

Ditzion, S., *Marriage, Morals and Sex.* New York: Bookman Associates, Inc., 1953.

Ellis, A., *The American Sexual Tragedy.* New York: Twayne Pub., 1954.

Ellis, A., *Sex without Guilt.* New York: Lyle Stuart, 1958a.

Ellis, A., "10 Indiscreet Proposals." *Pageant.* November, 1958b.

Ellis, H., *Sex in Relation to Society* (3rd ed.). Vol. VI in *Studies in the Psychology of Sex.* Philadelphia: F. A. Davis Co., 1922.

Ford, C. S., and Beach, F. A., *Patterns of Sexual Behavior.* New York: Harper & Brothers, 1951.

Friedan, B., *The Feminine Mystique.* New York: Norton, 1963.

Frumkin, R. M., *Social Problems, Pathology, and Philosophy: Selected Essays and Studies.* Oswego, N. Y.: Frontiers Press, 1962.

Geiger, K., and Inkeles, A., "The Family in the U.S.S.R." *Marr. & Fam. Living 16;* 397-404, 1954.

Harper, R. A., and Harper, F. R., "Are Educators Afraid of Sex?" *Humanist 16;* 122-127, 1956.

Himelhoch, J., and Fava, S. F. (eds.), *Sexual Behavior in American Society.* New York: W. W. Norton Co., 1955.

Hindus, M., "The Family in Russia." In Anshen, R. A. (ed.), *The Family.* New York: Harper & Brothers, 1949.

Holbrook, S. H., *Dreamers of the American Dream.* Garden City, N.Y.: Doubleday, 1957.

"In Baltimore Program: 'Active' Girls Given Birth Control Pills." *Cleveland Plain Dealer, 126;* 1, April 19, 1967.

International issue on the family. *Marriage and Family Living 16;* 291-404, 1954.

Kardiner, A., *The Individual and His Society.* New York: Columbia University Press, 1939.

Kinsey, A. C. *et al., Sexual Behavior in the Human Female.* Philadelphia: W. B. Saunders Co., 1953.

Kinsey, A. C. *et al., Sexual Behavior in the Human Male.* Philadelphia: W. B. Saunders Co., 1948.

Landis, P. H., *Social Control* (rev. ed.). Philadelphia: J. B. Lippincott Co., 1956.

Leuba, C., *The Natural Man.* Garden City, N.Y.: Doubleday, 1954.

Leuba, C., *The Sexual Nature of Man.* Garden City, N.Y.: Doubleday, 1954.

Lynes, R., "Is There a Lady in the House?" *Look 22;* 19-21, July 22, 1958.

Mace, D. R., "Discussion: Premarital Sexual Behavior." *Marr. & Fam. Living 15;* 239-242, 1953.

Malinowski, B., *Sexual Life of Savages in Northwestern Melanesia* (3rd ed.). London: Routledge, 1932, 2 vols.

Marcus, S., *The Other Victorians.* New York: Basic Books, 1966.

Mead, M., *Male and Female.* New York: William Morrow & Co., Inc., 1949.

Mohler, D. A., "Letter." *Marr. & Fam. Living 15;* 253, 1953.

Murdock, G. P., *Social Structure.* New York: The Macmillan Co., 1949.

Reiss, I. L., "The Treatment of Premarital Coitus in 'Marriage and the Family' Texts." *Social Problems 4;* 334-338, 1957.

Seward, G. H., *Sex and the Social Order.* New York: McGraw-Hill Book Co., 1946.

Sorokin, P., *The American Sex Revolution.* Boston: Porter Sargent Pub., 1956.

Stokes, W. H., "Discussion: Premarital Sexual Behavior." *Marr. & Fam. Living 15;* 235-239, 1953.

Svalastoga, K., "The Family in Scandinavia." *Marr. & Fam. Living 16;* 374-380, 1954.

Unwin, J. D., *Sex and Culture.* London: Oxford University Press, 1934.

Yarus, J. A. M., "The Victorian Era and Sexual Behavior." Cleveland: unpublished paper, 1967.

ROBERT M. FRUMKIN

Frigidity

Definition

FRIGIDITY is a term that has, unfortunately, been used to cover a multiplicity of sexual disorders and disabilities. It has been applied to women who are anesthetic, indifferent, incompetent, and inorgasmic. Included among females who have been labeled frigid have been those who are not easily stimulated; who have pain or displeasure in intercourse; who are unable to reach a climax; or who have little or no satisfaction even when they do attain a sex peak (A. Ellis, 1952; Oliven, 1955).

Most of the sexologists of an earlier day, including the orthodox Freudians, tended to consider a woman frigid, no matter how high her sex desire or how climactic her performance, if she did not achieve full sex release "vaginally"—that is, during coitus (Bergler, 1956; Hitschmann and Bergler, 1949; Stekel, 1926). Most contemporary authorities give the term frigidity a considerably narrower connotation and do not include under its heading females who are able to achieve a satisfactory climax through clitoral or other noncoital means (A. Ellis, 1954, 1958; Hirsch, 1957; Kelly, 1953; Kinsey *et al.*, 1953).

Causes of Frigidity

The main factors that result in a woman's being difficult to arouse or satisfy sexually may be summarized under three major rubrics: organic causes, relationship causes, and psychological causes.

Organic Causes

Although sexual insensitivity and incapacity usually have no organic basis, they sometimes do. Physical reasons for frigidity may include innate or constitutional lack of sexual responsiveness; inborn defects of or injuries to the sex organs; infection or inflammation of the clitoris, cervix, ovaries, or other accessory organs; serious nutritional lacks; lesions or defects of the central nervous system; circulatory defects; irritations or pathological conditions of parts of the body located near the sex organs; general organic ailments or diseases, such as diabetes, heart disorder, anemia, or leukemia; fatigue and low vitality; overindulgence in alcohol or drugs; and normal aging processes.

Two organic causes of frigidity may be singled out for special comment. It has recently been shown (Kupperman, 1959) that the male sex hormone, androgen, plays an enormously important role in the sexual activation of both males and females; and that if a female is low or deficient in the secretion of androgen she may well be sexually anesthetic. Treatment of such females with proper doses of sex hormones may effect dramatic changes in their sexual proclivities.

It has also recently been pointed out by Kleegman (1959) that a very large proportion of women who suffer from dyspareunia (painful intercourse) and are consequently frigid actually have small and correctible lesions of the external genital tract which may easily go undetected in a routine gynecological examination. If these lesions are found and surgically or medically treated, frigidity may completely clear up in these cases.

Therefore, although virtually all authorities agree that most cases of female sex inadequacy result from psychological rather than physical factors, the latter should by no means be overlooked. Whenever frigidity is in evidence a complete medical and gynecological examination should first be made before it is assumed that the disturbance is of nonorganic origin.

Relationship Causes

Relationship causes of frigidity arise from the fact that human sex proclivities are frequently disorganized and unfulfilled when one partner in a sex, love, or marital relationship becomes disturbed about her own or her mate's attitudes or actions (Caprio, 1953; Knight, 1943; Stekel, 1926). Thus, a woman may be sexually inhibited because she does not love her husband or feels that he does not sufficiently care for her; because she consciously resents him for things he has or has not done; because she is not physically attracted to him; because his sexual technique or capacity is, in her eyes, deficient or insufficient; because she thinks that his sex demands on her are too great; or for a host of similar reasons concerned with her personal and sexual relationship with her husband. In such a case, a woman may be said to be relatively or maritally rather than absolutely frigid, inasmuch as she may be theoretically capable of a high state of arousal and satisfaction with someone else than her spouse or may be quite unfrigid with her spouse, providing that some of the conditions of their relationship improve.

Psychological Causes

Aside from relationship difficulties between mates, a number of other psychological reasons may exist for a particular woman to become sexually indifferent or inadequate (A. Ellis, 1955, 1960; H. Ellis, 1936; Oliven, 1955; Terman, 1938). Thus, she may have been raised to have severe feelings of shame or guilt about all sex relations, including marital intercourse. She may fear her mate's disapproval or her own lack of self-control if she fully lets herself go sexually. She may be consciously or unconsciously afraid to become a mother and hence find sex relations irritating. She may fear sexual disease or injury. She may have homosexual or fetishistic tendencies that block her interests in heterosexual relations under all or certain circumstances. She may have a deep-seated attachment to her father or some other male relative, which arouses guilt reactions and inhibits her releasing herself sexually with her husband or lover. She may have masochistic or self-punitive tendencies that interfere with her allowing herself full satisfaction. She may be so childish and narcissistic that cooperating with another human being, even for her own pleasure, may be beyond her ken. Or she may be so generally disturbed—that is, severely neurotic or psychotic—that she is incapable of focusing adequately on sexual stimuli and coordinating her physical movements sufficiently well to achieve full sexual arousal and climax.

It has been customary for past and present authorities, such as Bergler (1956), Freud (1924-1950, 1938), and Knight (1943), to stress the importance of an overpowering sense of guilt as a causative factor in frigidity. The present writer as well (*The American Sexual Tragedy* and *Sex Without Guilt*) has presented considerable evidence to the effect that women in our society are often warped by the antisexual attitudes with which we indoctrinate them from birth; and that consequently they are inordinately guilty about letting themselves go and fully enjoying themselves sexually. Varying degrees of frigidity in their sexual behavior result.

Sex Shame

Be that as it may, another phenomenon has come to exist in contemporary society that is different from and in many ways even more pernicious than the sexual guilt that was so prevalent in previous days. This phenomenon is that of intense shame—which overlaps with guilt in some significant respects but which is also somewhat different. Whereas, when he feels guilty, an individual believes that he has acted wrongly or wickedly in the eyes of some God, fate, or social value system, when he feels ashamed or inadequate, he is more likely to believe that he has acted ineptly or weakly in his own eyes and in those of the people with whom he has immediate contact. As Piers and Singer (1953) and several other psychological and sociological thinkers have recently pointed out, shame and its concomitant feelings of inadequacy (as distinguished from guilt and its concomitant feelings of sinfulness) are likely to be particularly enhanced in a society, such as our own, that stresses success rather than goodness, achievement rather than sainthood.

As a result of our having so many millions of shame-inculcated individuals in this country, I and my colleagues have recently been seeing, in our psychotherapy and marriage counseling practices, one woman after another who, in spite of her having had rather adequate sex education, is distinctly frigid. These sexually inadequate women are often highly "sophisticated" individuals who do not feel that sex is wicked and who have little or no sense of guilt about engaging in premarital or marital relations. Indeed, they almost universally want very much to experience orgasm and will do anything in their power to help themselves experience it. Whereas, in previous years, it was frequently the husbands who would come to complain to the psychotherapist or marriage counselor that their wives were not too interested in sex relations, today it is just as likely to be the wives who complain that they want greater satisfaction than they are receiving.

Ironically, one of the major reasons these women are not achieving full gratification is that they are so overdetermined to achieve it. Because of their culturally inculcated need for success, they are so ashamed if they do not reach the greatest heights of expressive sexuality that they are rarely doing what they should be doing to attain orgasm and are, instead, tragically sabotaging their own desires. That is to say, instead of focusing clearly on the real problem at hand—which, baldly stated, is "How can I think of something sufficiently sexually exciting and how can I concentrate on movements that are stimulating enough to bring on my orgasm?"—these women are focusing on quite a different problem—namely "Oh, what an idiot and an incompetent person I am for not being able to have an orgasm without any difficulty."

Stated differently: women who are sexually anesthetic or nonorgasmic are often obsessed with the notion of *how* rather than *what* they are doing when they are having sex relations. Sex desire and fulfillment are largely mediated through the central nervous system and the cerebral cortex; and in order for arousal and satisfaction to be maximal there must be a concerted focusing, by the individual who would achieve orgasm, on specific sexual ideation. If, instead of concentrating on sexually arousing stimuli, a woman keeps telling herself, over and over, that it would be terrible if she did not

have an orgasm; that this would prove that she was worthless and inferior; that she simply must be able to get as many orgasms as her best girl friend; that when she gets a climax, bells should ring and lights should flash; and so on—if this is the kind of nonsense that a female sex partner keeps repeating to herself, it can only be expected that she will rarely if ever achieve a high degree of excitement and fruition.

Another form that sex shame currently takes in our society is equally inhibiting—that is, when it acts as a block against varied coital and noncoital technique. We may note that today fewer and fewer college-educated and middle-class females are desisting from trying various coital positions or types of noncoital sex play which once were erroneously called "perversions." Having little sex guilt, in the old-fashioned sense, they do not deem these aspects of sex wicked.

At the same time, however, literally millions of women are employing noncoital sex methods only as "preliminary" or "love play" techniques and are not using them, when necessary, up to and including the achievement of orgasm. Their reasons for so restricting themselves are again bound up with shame: that is, they feel that they "should" be able to achieve an orgasm through "natural" coital means and should not require digital manipulation of the clitoris, oral-genital relations, or other techniques of coming to climax. If they do require such methods—as innumerable women do and always, probably, shall—they feel that there is something "wrong" with them and that they are sexually "inferior" or "incompetent." This feeling, of course, is perfectly illogical and is almost entirely a consequence of their arbitrary notions of what is "shameful." To compound the problem here, many of the husbands of these women also believe that they are "inferior" when they cannot give their wives an orgasm with their penises but have to resort to noncoital methods.

In increasing numbers of instances, then, it would seem to be shame rather than guilt that produces frigidity today. Worrying and catastrophizing about the possibility of lack of fulfillment actually brings on that very lack. As soon as a woman tends to believe that she *must* be sexually competent and begins to tell herself how frightful it would be if she did *not* achieve a tremendous state of desire and climax, her very exaggeration of the *necessity* of her being sexually successful will frequently prevent her success. Any time an individual believes that she *must* succeed in some endeavor, rather than that it would be *preferable* if she did, disaster in that endeavor is likely to befall. This is particularly true of women who feel that they have to succeed at achieving orgasm and that it is catastrophic if they do not.

By the same token, whenever a woman convinces herself that she must achieve sexual arousal and satisfaction in a particular manner —such as in certain coital positions, or within a few minutes after intercourse has begun, or in the same manner that most other women presumably achieve gratification—she is setting herself on the road to failure. The first and main law of psychology is that of individual difference; and in the sexual as well as non-sexual areas of life each woman tends to be significantly different, in many respects, from every other woman and to require specialized modes of physical and psychical participation which are experimentally and open-mindedly tailored for her own requirements. Any notion she may have, therefore, that she should or must be satisfied the way *others* are satisfied will probably doom her to sexual inadequacy.

IGNORANCE

Another common psychological block to sex satisfaction that is frequently ignored in the psychiatric literature (and especially the Freudian literature) is that of simple ignorance. Millions of civilized (and primitive) women, because they have never received any incisive knowledge of the psychology and physiology of sexual response, seem to be completely ignorant of the fact that sexual arousal and satisfaction are not a function of proper physical stimulation alone but are largely a cerebral function—a result of what the individual *thinks* and *imagines* while she is engaging in sex relations. They do not realize that women, in particular, often have to *focus persistently* on sex-love objects and relations while their bodies are being adequately stimulated. When they fail to do so, and focus instead on nonsexual objects and concepts while they are

engaging in sex acts, they frequently set up insuperable psychological blocks to satisfaction. If the facts of frigidity were fully known, it might well be found that guilt and shame, although important factors in creating frigidity in many instances, are often less important than a woman's failing, out of sheer lack of sex knowledge and proper training, to try to focus on stimulating things and events when she is having sex relations.

The Treatment of Frigidity

The treatment of frigidity may be subdivided into two main forms; self-treatment and medical or psychological treatment. Both forms should be tried simultaneously, since self-treatment will frequently be ineffective without competent medical or psychological supervision.

Self-Therapy

The first part of self-therapy of frigidity consists of arousing sufficiently strong desire in those instances where this kind of arousal is difficult (A. Ellis, 1960). Pointers that may be helpful in this respect include the following:

1. The woman who is not easily arousable should engage in sex relations at a time best suited for excitability: for example, when she is relaxed, well rested, not pressed for time, and away from troubling circumstances.

2. The woman's partner should make overtures at a time when the mates have been getting along excellently together and when there is a minimum of strain and hostility between them.

3. Kindness, consideration, and love by the mate is likely to be more effective than any rough kind of treatment.

4. Special care should be taken to locate and adequately to stimulate the special erogenous zones of the woman after these have been experimentally explored and determined.

5. Intercourse itself, even though at first not too stimulating, may lead to arousal in some instances.

6. Periods of rest in between arousal attempts may sometimes be desirable.

7. The application of ointments or hand lotions (such as camphor-menthol ointment or

K-Y jelly) to the woman's external genitals may sometimes be advisable. Saliva is sometimes an adequate and easily available lubrication material.

8. Considerable direct genital stimulation by the male partner's fingers, or tongue, or penis, particularly in apposition to the female's clitoris, may be required before any intravaginal penetration is attempted.

9. Mild intake of stimulants (such as alcohol) may be employed.

10. Focusing by the woman on sexually exciting things and incidents is particularly important. She should literally practice thinking of various things that excite her and should, if necessary, keep forcing herself to think of these things as she is having sex relations. Stories, pictures, past sex participations, thoughts of future pleasures—anything and everything that excites the woman mentally—may be used to keep her mind focusing on arousing subjects and events.

Assuming that a woman with a tendency toward sexual anesthesia has achieved sufficient arousal, there are several techniques that she and her mate may employ to help her attain full climax:

1. If the woman is found to have special areas of sex sensation, such as the clitoris or the upper wall of the vagina, her partner should exert steady, consistent, rhythmic pressure on these areas until she approaches or reaches climax.

2. In certain instances, special kinds of strokings—such as intermittent, irregular ones or very forceful massage—of the woman's sensitive parts will be desirable.

3. Verbal or attitudinal expressions by the woman's partner—such as protestations of love—may sometimes be helpful in bringing her to fulfillment.

4. Deep, forceful penile-vaginal penetration, which can best be obtained in certain coital positions (such as the position where the woman surmounts and sits astride the male) may sometimes be preferable.

5. Multiple physical contact is desirable in many instances, such as the male's kissing or caressing his wife's breasts or caressing her clitoris while they are having coitus.

6. A variety of noncoital stimulations and coital positions is often necessary, since a relatively low-sexed woman may today become bored with the same tactic that yesterday was terribly exciting. Varietism in sex play is often more desirable for the female than for the male, since the latter tends to have an orgasm more easily and quickly in most instances.

7. Undue emphasis on the achievement of simultaneous climax should particularly be avoided when a woman has difficulty obtaining an orgasm, as she will otherwise become so concerned about obtaining it *at the right time* that she will probably not obtain it at all. Orgasm, however and whenever achieved, should be the goal of any woman who has difficulty coming to climax. Whether she obtains her orgasm exactly at the same moment as her mate obtains his is relatively unimportant—unless she erroneously *thinks* that this is important.

8. There is no law against a woman's stimulating herself at the same time that her husband is also endeavoring to help her to climax. Self-stimulation is often the most effective method for a female who has difficulty achieving orgasm.

9. As emphasized earlier, females who do not easily achieve orgasm should practice focusing on maximally exciting things and ideas and try to prevent themselves from being distracted by nonsexual and nonloving thoughts.

Medical or Psychological Treatment

If consistent use of all or some of the foregoing techniques fails to help a woman become fully aroused or to achieve orgasmic release, it should be assumed that she may well have a medical or psychological problem and that she should seek professional help. On the physical side, she should preferably be examined by an experienced gynecologist and should also receive a complete medical examination. Treatment, on the basis of such an examination, should be prescribed by the physician and closely followed. It may consist of administration of hormones or vitamins, use of other medication, minor surgery, or other medical measures indicated in individual cases.

On the psychological side, the frigid woman (and usually her husband as well) should see a recognized psychologist, psychiatrist, psychiatric caseworker, or marriage counselor.

Treatment will usually consist of the therapist's discovering what set of blocking or inhibiting ideas the woman has, how these ideas originated, how they have been sustained, and what can be done to challenge and contradict them and replace them by realistic, rational ideas. Although prolonged, depth-centered psychotherapy is sometimes indicated, a competent and active therapist can frequently get to the root of a woman's psychological sex problems in a relatively short length of time and show her how to overcome these problems.

As a very brief case in point, I recently saw a 25-year-old wife who had never achieved an orgasm with her husband and was ready to divorce him because of her shame about her own and his sexual ineptness. Without even attempting to uncover any of her so-called deeply unconscious feelings of guilt, hostility, or anxiety, I quickly and forcefully explained to this woman how she was forestalling her own orgasms by telling herself, almost constantly, how horrible she was, how she could never get an orgasm, how she could not be successfully married to anyone, etc. I insisted, in session after session, that she could focus on sexually exciting stimuli and that she could bring herself to have fully satisfying climaxes.

My patient at first resisted these suggestions; but after eight sessions of fairly repetitive psychotherapy, I began to convince her of the truth of my statements. She began to focus more and more on sexually arousing stimuli and for the first time in her life started, some of the time, to achieve climax. On one occasion, she tried mutual oral-genital relations with her husband and found that she was extremely aroused by this method but that it was so exciting that she could not focus adequately on her own climax. When her husband was independently practicing cunnilinctus, however, she was able to focus on her own genital sensations and soon was having strong orgasms.

After some practice, this patient was able to focus on her own climax during coitus as well as during extracoital sex relations. She was recently in to see me and reported that, after her husband had been away on a business trip for a few days, they spent almost the entire night having sex relations in many different positions and ways—with complete satisfaction.

Summary

Sexual inadequacy or incompetency on the part of a female may result from organic, relationship, or psychological causes; and in most instances seems to arise from irrational, guilt- and shame-invoking ideas which have been inculcated in the frigid woman early in her life and which she has been unconsciously reiterating to herself for many years. Usually, frigidity can be considerably lessened or overcome if the afflicted woman accepts her own sex participation as a fine and valuable act of living and practices focusing on sexually exciting stimuli.

When self-therapy does not work, the frigid woman should have a complete gynecological examination and should obtain psychological help. In most instances, a highly active, directive, rational psychotherapist can help her get to the core of her problem in fairly rapid order and forcefully to see, understand, and challenge and contradict her own irrational notions that underlie her sexual disability (A. Ellis, 1958b). There are very few cases in which frigidity cannot be largely or completely ameliorated, when medically and psychologically attacked in a forthright manner.

References

Adams, Clifford, An Informal Preliminary Report on Some Factors Relating to Sexual Responsiveness of Certain College Wives. University Park, Pa.: author, 1953.

Berg, Louis, and Street, Robert, Sex: Methods and Manners. New York: Robert M. McBride Co., Inc., 1953.

Bergler, Edmund, Neurotic Counterfeit-Sex. New York: Grune & Stratton, Inc., 1956.

Burgess, Ernest W., and Wallin, Paul, Engagement and Marriage. Philadelphia: J. B. Lippincott Co., 1953.

Caprio, Frank S., The Sexually Adequate Female. New York: Citadel Press, 1953.

Clark, LeMon, "Female Sex Sensation." Sexology 25; 208-212, 1958.

Davis, Katherine B., Factors in the Sex Life of 2,200 Women. New York: Harper & Brothers, 1929.

Dickinson, Robert L., and Beam, Lura, A Thousand Marriages. Baltimore: The Williams and Wilkins Co., 1931.

Ellis, Albert, "Applications of Clinical Psychology to Sexual Disorders." In L. E. Abt and D. Brower (eds.), *Progress in Clinical Psychology*. New York: Grune & Stratton, Inc., 1952.

Ellis, Albert, *The American Sexual Tragedy*. New York: Twayne Publishers, 1954.

Ellis, Albert, *The Art and Science of Love*. New York: Lyle Stuart, 1960.

Ellis, Albert, and Harper, Robert A., *Creative Marriage*. New York: Lyle Stuart. Reprinted as *The Marriage Bed*. New York: Tower Publications, 1966.

Ellis, Albert, "Guilt, Shame and Frigidity." *Quart. Rev. Obst. & Gynec.* Oct., 1959.

Ellis, Albert, and Sagarin, Edward, *Nymphomania: A Study of the Oversexed Woman*. New York: Gilbert Press, 1964; New York: Macfadden-Bartell, 1965.

Ellis, Albert, "Rational Psychotherapy." *J. Gen Psychol.* 59; 35-49, 1958b.

Ellis, Albert, *Reason and Emotion in Psychotherapy*. New York: Lyle Stuart, 1962.

Ellis, Albert, *Suppressed: Seven Key Essays Publishers Dared Not Print*. Chicago: New Classics House, 1965.

Ellis, Albert, *Sex Without Guilt*. New York: Lyle Stuart, 1958a.

Ellis, Havelock, *Studies in the Psychology of Sex*. New York: Random House, 1936.

Ford, Clellan S., and Beach, Frank A., *Patterns of Sexual Behavior*. New York: Harper & Brothers, 1951.

Freud, Sigmund, *Basic Writings*. New York: Modern Library, Inc., 1938.

Freud, Sigmund, *Collected Papers*. London: Hogarth, 1924-1950.

Hamilton, G. V., *A Research in Marriage*. New York: Boni, 1929.

Hirsch, Edwin W., *Modern Sex Life*. New York: New American Library, 1957.

Hitschmann, E., and Bergler, E., "Frigidity in Women—Restatement and Renewed Experiences." *Psychoanal. Rev. 36*; 45-53, 1949.

Kegel, A. H., "Sexual Functions of the Pubococcygeus Muscle." *West. J. Surg. 60*; 541-542, 1952.

Kelly, G. Lombard, *Sex Manual*. Augusta, Ga.: Southern Medical Supply Co., 1953.

Kinsey, A. C., *et al.*, *Sexual Behavior in the Human Female*. Philadelphia: W. B. Saunders Co., 1953.

Kleegman, Sophia J., "Frigidity." *Quart. Rev. Obst. & Gynec.* Oct., 1959.

Knight, Robert, "Functional Disturbances in the Sexual Life of Women." *Bull. Menninger Clin. 7*; 25-35, 1943.

Kupperman, Herbert S., "Frigidity: Endocrinological Aspects." *Quart. Rev. Obst. & Gynec.* Oct., 1959.

Masters, William H., and Johnson, Virginia E., *Human Sexual Response*. Boston: Little, Brown & Co., 1966.

Oliven, John F., *Sexual Hygiene and Pathology*. Philadelphia: J. B. Lippincott Co., 1955.

Piers, Gerhart, and Singer, Milton B., *Shame and Guilt*. Springfield, Ill.: Charles C Thomas, 1953.

Pillay, A. P., and Ellis, Albert (eds.), *Sex, Society and the Individual*. Bombay: Internat. J. Sexology, 1953.

Shuttleworth, Frank, "A Biosocial and Developmental Theory of Male and Female Sexuality." *Marr. & Fam. Living 21*; 163-170, 1959.

Stekel, Wilhelm, *Frigidity in Women*. New York: Liveright, 1926.

Terman, Lewis M., "Correlates of Orgasm Adequacy in a Group of 556 Wives." *J. Psychol. 32*; 115-172, 1951.

Terman, Lewis M., *Psychological Factors in Marital Unhappiness*. New York: McGraw-Hill Book Co., 1938.

Van de Velde, Th., *Ideal Marriage*. New York: Covici Friede, 1926.

Woodside, Moya, "Orgasm Capacity Among 200 English Working Class Wives." *Internat. J. Sexol. 1*; 133-137, 1948.

Wright, Helena, "A Contribution to the Orgasm Problem in Women." *Internat. J. Sexol. 3*; 8-12, 1949.

ALBERT ELLIS

Great Britain,
Sex in

Historical Survey

SOCIAL attitudes to sex in Great Britain have shown great fluctuations since the Reformation, when the State took over powers that had previously been held by the Church. The immediate result of the change was to impose more drastic penalties. Thus, in 1533 an act was passed that introduced the death penalty for sodomy. Later, under the Commonwealth, a law was added that made "incest, adultery, and fornication" capital offenses, but it did not survive the Puritan regime.

For a period morals became more relaxed, only to be tightened again with the rise of the middle class in the mid-eighteenth century. A continental visitor wrote in 1700 that "the women of this country are much given to sensuality, to carnal inclinations, to gambling, to drink, and to idleness." (*Londres et l'Angleterre,* J. E. Zetzner, Strasbourg.) This may be compared with the advice given by Dr. J. Gregory in a widely read book, *A Father's Legacy to his Daughters,* published in 1774, in which he urges women to be shy, blushing, and genteel. They must show no interest in sex, and preferably be ignorant of its existence unless married; then they must submit to their husbands without giving any sign of pleasure. Mary Shelley could write in 1811 that "Coarseness is completely out of fashion." And the cult of delicacy was carried to such extravagant lengths that in a scientific work, *The Functions and Disorders of the Reproductive Organs*

(1857), Dr. W. Acton roundly stated that it was a "vile aspersion" to say that women were even capable of sexual feeling.

The swing of the pendulum had less effect on the laboring classes and was rather slow to be felt in the upper classes until Queen Victoria came to the throne. The author of the play in which the redoubtable Mrs. Grundy appeared died as early as 1838, but the character he created became subsequently a symbol of Victorian prudery. In its heyday the very legs of pianos were draped with crinolines. It was thought indelicate to offer a leg of chicken to a lady at the dinner table. One did not speak of breasts, but of "necks"; or, at the most daring, "bosoms." Artificial aids were used by women to make them look flat-chested until about 1860 when evening *décolletés* once more became low.

Yet all through this period of false modesty prostitution was rampant in England, homosexuality defied the savage penalties of the law, and the immorality of the very poor was notorious. The fact that divorce was available only to the rich—since it required a special Act of Parliament—is no proof of the absence of adultery among those who could not obtain legal redress. Its existence was merely concealed.

Nor was the taboo on mentioning sex in polite society any evidence of a lack of interest. Although Bradlaugh was indicted for defiantly publishing a book on birth control, there was a vast underground traffic in pornography. As might be expected, the repressive atmosphere gave rise to unsavory phantasies and a spate of books dealing with perversions.

Why the standards of one age are rigorous and of another lax is a matter for speculation. The significant change that took place in the twentieth century was hastened by World War I but not entirely caused by it. The main factors were the spread of education, the demand for sex equality, and the decline of churchgoing. The war, of course, opened up new opportunities for women to enter what had been masculine preserves, and this proved to be an irreversible process.

The seeds were sown in the nineteenth century thanks to the energy of a few ardent reformers. Divorce law ceased to be administered by the ecclesiastical courts in 1857 and the way was then open—though by no means easy to follow—for subsequent modifications. The Married Women's Property Act profoundly changed the status of women, and the granting of the right to vote, after a bitter campaign, set a seal upon their legal independence.

The repercussions of the emancipation of women on sexual morality were indirect. Perhaps the most decisive factor was the fact that this emancipation was paralleled by improvement of contraceptive techniques. A woman who had economic as well as legal independence and to whom the fear of pregnancy was no longer the great deterrent, naturally looked upon sex relationships differently from her Victorian predecessors.

The decade following World War I was undoubtedly marked by a sexual freedom that would have been unthinkable for the middle classes in the nineteenth century. A new outlook on sex was shaped by the literature of the period, which included popularizations of psychoanalysis and cheap books on birth control. On a more serious level there were the writings of D. H. Lawrence (some of which were banned), Bertrand Russell, and others.

No doubt the new freedom was often abused and the theories of Freudian psychology travestied, but the old taboos had been lifted and nothing could be quite the same again. Sex education was increasingly seen as a necessary preparation for life. The last barriers went down when it was introduced into school curriculums.

Divorce was made easier in 1937, and after World War II, a Royal Commission was appointed to inquire into still further reforms. A Departmental Committee on Prostitution and Homosexuality published a remarkably outspoken report in 1957. Although no action has as yet been taken on homosexuality, the fact that it was possible to discuss even homosexuality on radio and television shows how far public opinion in Great Britain has moved since the times of Mrs. Grundy.

Some think it has moved too far, others not far enough. In 1935 Canon Bickersteth wrote in *The Times*: "The increase in adultery and the breaking of the marriage laws are greater dangers to national safety than bombing from the air."

There is no way of establishing the prevalence of adultery either now or in the period when divorce was a privilege for the few. Obviously we cannot gain the information from statistics of divorce alone. The following analysis of different aspects of sexual behavior suggests that the most striking change has been within social classes, and that adultery is no longer so restricted to prostitution. More "broken homes" do not necessarily mean less happy homes. Statistics show that marriage was never so popular in Britain as today.

Marriage and Divorce

The Royal Commission on Marriage and Divorce (1956) failed to agree on any radical changes in the law. One of its conclusions was that "matrimony is not so secure as it was fifty years ago." If this is merely taken to mean that today there are more divorces the statement is obviously correct, but it does not give the whole picture. In the Victorian age the marriage rate was declining. Between 1911 and 1954, however, the proportion of married women has risen by one-third. Only 13 per cent of women today are spinsters, and that is fewer than at any time since 1881, when the population was only 60 per cent its present size.

Against much loose talk about the collapse of family life there is the testimony of a report issued by the Church of England Moral Welfare Council in 1958, which stated categorically: "Far from disintegrating, the modern family is in some ways in a stronger position than it has been in any period in our history of which we have any knowledge."

More people in Britain are getting married than ever before and the average marriage lasts longer. Yet it is also true that more people are getting divorced. The reason for this apparent paradox is that marriages tend to take place at an earlier age, owing to the improved economic situation, and that there are fewer broken homes caused by death, thanks to the progress of medicine.

It is sometimes forgotten that divorce is not the sole cause of broken homes. The tragedy of the loss of the breadwinner—doubly serious when large families were the rule—is not only less common today, but is softened, when it occurs, by various forms of state aid.

The increase in divorce cannot be taken by itself as an index of a decline in moral standards because changes in the law have made divorce available to a far greater number of people.

When it became possible in 1857 to dissolve a marriage by judicial decree the theory was that divorce was relief granted to an injured party. At first a husband could obtain a divorce on the ground of his wife's adultery, but the wife had to prove desertion or cruelty as well as adultery in order to divorce her husband. This anomaly was abolished in 1925 and there were no further important changes until 1937.

It then became possible to obtain a divorce on grounds of desertion or cruelty without adultery. Another innovation was that no divorce in England and Wales (although not in Scotland) could ordinarily be obtained during the first three years of marriage. Also divorce could be granted on grounds of insanity even though no matrimonial offense had been committed.

These provisions opened the door to many more applications, but there was still the barrier that cases had to be heard in the High Court, and poor people could not afford to take advantage of the new Act. The provision of free legal aid in 1950 removed the last obstacle.

The divorce statistics reflect these changes. Before 1914 the number of annual petitions was below 1,000. They reached 5,000 in 1935, 10,000 in 1942, and rose to 47,041 in 1947. Since then they have fallen and would appear to be stabilized at about 30,000. The Registrar General has estimated that approximately 7 per cent of marriages end in divorce.

The postwar statistics show some interesting trends, although a great deal of vital information has yet to be analyzed. There has been a rise of 16 per cent in the petitions based on cruelty, for example, but it is more likely that the definition of cruelty has been broadened than that there is any increase in sadism. More than 40 per cent of all divorces are granted on grounds of desertion and insanity, the latter constituting only a small proportion. In these cases the marriage must have lasted at least three years and divorce is therefore legal recognition of an established situation.

It is still the case that only the injured party can petition for divorce. Thus, there are many couples living apart but legally tied because the injured party refuses to take any action. A Private Member's Bill to remedy this state of affairs was given a second reading in the House of Commons in 1950, but withdrawn on the promise that a Royal Commission would be set up. The Royal Commission, however, failed to agree to the proposal that if the parties had been separated for seven years there was sufficient ground to dissolve the marriage.

Two new grounds were recommended: first, if a wife accepted artificial insemination by a donor without the husband's consent; second, if one party had been detained for at least five years as a mental defective of dangerous or violent propensities.

Although the Report of the Royal Commission was shelved, the fairly even division of opinion on the main issues probably reflects the split mind of the public on these matters. Meanwhile, among the curious anomalies that remain is the law that permits marriage with a deceased wife's sister (or deceased husband's brother), but not with a divorced wife's sister or divorced husband's brother.

The views of the Church of England, as expressed by the Archbishop of Canterbury and reaffirmed at the Lambeth Conference by 300 bishops, are uncompromisingly in favor of regarding marriage as indissoluble. A few individual clergy, however, have taken an independent line in opposition.

Divorce in Britain today no longer carries the old social stigma, but it is still a barrier in court circles. The abdication of Edward VIII and the more recent episode of Princess Margaret and Group Captain Townsend show that it is not tolerated in the Royal Family. Divorced persons cannot enter the Queen's Lawn at Ascot, but in politics they need no longer fear ruin. The example of Sir Anthony Eden shows that to obtain a divorce and remarry is no bar even for a Prime Minister.

Family Planning

Birth control was an unmentionable subject in Victorian times. Malthus had provoked bitter controversy by his prediction that population must tend to outstrip the food supply, but the only remedy he proposed was late marriage and abstinence. Those who advocated other measures were called neo-Malthusians.

For selling an old American pamphlet called *Fruits of Philosophy* by Dr. Knowlton, a Bristol publisher was sent to prison in 1876. It was reissued by Charles Bradlaugh and Mrs. Besant and they, too, were convicted at the Old Bailey and sentenced to imprisonment. The judgment was reversed on appeal and from that time birth-control propaganda was tolerated.

After World War I matters were carried further by Dr. Marie Stopes, who not only wrote popular books on birth control, but opened a clinic in London. Her campaign met with strong opposition from Roman Catholics, but it was obvious that it could not be halted.

A further step was taken with the formation of the Family Planning Association in 1930. By stressing the positive as well as the negative side of birth control, the Association gained the support of many people who had hitherto remained aloof. The Association provided services to help infertile couples as well as those who wished to restrict the size of their families. Clinics have been started all over the country.

Books giving advice on birth control are on open sale and contraceptives can be bought without the slightest difficulty. One result has been a great change in the family life of women as compared with their situation in the last century.

In the 1890's the average wife spent fifteen years in pregnancy or nursing. Whereas the average working-class family had seven or more children, today only 2 per cent attain such a size. In the first thirty years of the present century the average number of children of working-class families has dropped from over six to two and one-half.

Other factors have entered into the general improvement in health, both of mothers and children, but smaller families have undoubtedly made an important contribution. A woman aged 20 in 1900 had an expectation of life of 46 years; today, she can expect to live 55 years and only 7 per cent of the time will be spent on maternal duties (Richard Titmuss, *Essays on the Welfare State*, 1958).

Indeed, women who reach the age of 60 now live four years longer than men, on the average —i.e., until the age of 76. The revolutionary consequences are seen in the labor market. More and more wives and husbands have jobs and can therefore afford better living conditions than formerly. Although fewer babies are born, more survive, and the population seems in no danger of declining.

The attitude of the Protestant churches has undergone a steady change toward the use of contraceptives. Early in the century two Lambeth Conferences condemned birth control. In 1930 there was a cautious modification of this attitude, but in 1958 the Lambeth Conference declared roundly that there was nothing Christian in allowing children to die as a result of pestilence and malnutrition. Married couples should not be selfish, but should make the welfare of children for which they are responsible the primary consideration.

By dropping the older view that the sole object of sexual intercourse must be procreation, the Church of England expressed the view of the majority of the public. The Non-Conformist churches are in agreement with Anglicans on this subject.

Abortion

Where Anglicans and Roman Catholics take a common stand is in their opposition to legalizing abortion. It has been estimated that there are about 200,000 abortions each year and that the majority are performed by unqualified persons at great risk to the mother's life. There has been a strong agitation to end this dangerous situation. In 1953 an attempt was made to introduce a Parliamentary bill rectifying an obsolete law, but the Government refused to support it.

As things are at present a doctor acts entirely on his own responsibility. If he can prove that the life or health of the woman would be seriously jeopardized by allowing pregnancy to continue, he may terminate it. This concession was won by two judgments before the war. Dr. Aleck Bourne, an eminent gynecologist, deliberately performed an abortion on the victim of an atrocious rape and informed the police. He was tried at the Old Bailey, but the jury refused to convict.

This case and the decision in Rex v. Bergman and Ferguson (1939) established the right to make serious danger to life or health a justifiable reason for therapeutic abortion. But as there has been no statutory change in the law every individual case has to be treated on its merits. Many doctors feel that it is unfair to place the onus upon them of convincing a jury of laymen that there would have been damage to physical or mental health if they had not intervened. There is a not unnatural reluctance on the part of the medical profession to incur the risk of a criminal prosecution.

Prostitution

The sight of streetwalkers in certain areas of London aroused periodical protests in Parliament and the press until 1959, when it was decided to implement the recommendations of a Departmental Committee and make street solicitation an offense punishable by imprisonment. There is no evidence, however, that prostitution in England has increased since Victorian times. On the contrary, there is reason to believe that the professional prostitute has lost ground to the amateur or "good-time girl."

In 1839 the police estimated that there were about 7,000 prostitutes in London, rising to a peak figure of between 8,000 and 10,000 in the next decade. As the adult male population of London was then well under a million this works out to about one prostitute for every hundred males. Allowance must be made for males who were old or ill in assessing the proportion of customers.

It is unlikely that anything like this ratio of prostitutes to able-bodied males exists in London today. Admittedly the record of annual convictions shows a rise from 995 in 1930 to 11,878 in 1955, but this is a somewhat misleading figure since the same women may be convicted many times in a year. In 1953, for example, 6,829 arrests were made in the West End Central Division, but only 808 individual prostitutes were involved. Some of these were arrested twenty times or more.

A more interesting clue is provided by estimates of the male clients. The average number of customers a London prostitute receives in a week is thought to be between twenty and twenty-five, although we cannot know how many of these are "regulars." In relation to the size of the population, the extent of commercial vice is not large. What has increased is the number of casual pickups and the practice known as "kerb-crawling."

Prostitution itself is not a crime. The term "common prostitute" has not been given a statutory definition, but is taken to mean "a woman who offers her body for acts of lewdness for payment." In practice any woman convicted of importuning came automatically under this category. The immediate effect of the Street Offences Act of 1959 was to clear the streets and drive prostitution underground. Strip-tease nightclubs and the call-girl system promptly came into operation.

For a man to live on a prostitute's earnings is a serious offense punishable by imprisonment. The same is true of keeping a brothel or allowing premises to be used for immoral purposes. On the other hand, the law can be evaded by letting flats or rooms to individual prostitutes. Provided they ply their trade singly the landlord is not responsible.

Sensational stories of white-slave traffickers and organized gangs forcing unwilling girls into prostitution may be discounted. Most prostitutes have deliberately chosen their way of life. In the top grade they can earn big money, although they have to pay excessively high rents to unscrupulous landlords. In the lower grade they operate in public parks, taxis, and cheap hotels.

The Wolfenden Report, published in 1957, recommended progressively heavier penalties for solicitation. For the first offense the maximum fine should be £10 instead of £2; for the second offense £25; and for the third or subsequent offenses three months' imprisonment. At the same time it was proposed to close loopholes in the law affecting landlords. These changes succeeded in their objective, which was to drive the prostitutes off the streets rather than to eradicate the evil. It was frankly admitted that surreptitious prostitution would continue to flourish and that the public concern was mainly over the visible and obvious presence of the streetwalker.

One criticism of the changes was that they would leave the field wide open to the amateur. Certainly no study of sex life in Britain would be complete without reference to a type of girl who does not indulge in formal solicitation, but who hangs around army camps and is to be met in dance halls and public houses. She may or may not require cash payment for her favors, and she is not necessarily indiscriminate. But her promiscuity makes her a formidable competitor to the professional prostitute.

There is no possibility of computing the number of amateurs and the only records in which they appear relate to venereal disease. These prove conclusively that although the discovery of antibiotics has reduced the extent of disease, the amateur is more likely to be a carrier of infection than the professional.

Thus, the figures for known cases of female gonorrhea contracted in the United Kingdom in 1956 were as shown in Table 1.

Homosexuality

According to English law, male homosexuality is a crime, but female homosexuality is not. There are two main classes of offense, apart from assault: sodomy and gross indecency. Sodomy is a felony, which means that anyone who knows it has been committed must inform the police. If the offense has been committed with a minor the maximum penalty is imprisonment for life; otherwise imprisonment for ten years. Gross indecency became a criminal offense in 1885 and covers private acts between consenting adults.

The most contentious feaure of the Wolfenden Report was the proposal to bring English law into line with the law of those countries where acts performed in private between freely consenting adults are no longer punishable. Representative committees of the Anglican and Roman Catholic Churches supported the proposal. Public opinion polls suggested that the nation was almost evenly divided, a slight majority opposing the recommendation. In these circumstances, despite a strong agitation for reform, the Government deferred any action.

There are, of course, subsidiary offenses concerning procuration, importuning, and the keeping of homosexual brothels. The distinction between sodomy and gross indecency is preserved even in cases of blackmail. There are heavier penalties for extorting money by threat of exposure where sodomy is involved.

Judged by the number of prosecutions, there would appear superficially to have been a great increase in homosexuality during the present century, but all the figures really prove is the greater zeal of the police in bringing cases to court. The annual average of arrests between

TABLE 1.	PORTS	INLAND CITIES	LONDON	QUIET AREAS	TOTAL
Total number of cases	446	199	466	42	1,153
Cases in which information is available	408	124	452	39	1,023
Cases due to prostitutes	89	8	114	4	215
Cases not due to prostitutes	319	116	338	35	808
Percentage of cases due to prostitutes	*21.8*	*6.5*	*25.2*	*10.3*	*21.0*

1900 and 1909 was 13 per million males; between 1920 and 1924 it rose to 32; and in the period 1950–1952 the figure reached 107. Statistics published by the Home Office for 1952–1953 show an eightfold increase over the decade 1930–1940 for acts of indecency.

The scale of prosecutions for many types of sex offenses depends to some extent on the personal predilections of the Home Secretary. If he decides to "clean up" the clubs or crusade against pornographic books or proceed more energetically against homosexuals, the police act accordingly. This explains the apparent lull, followed by a spate of prosecutions, in all these fields.

In any event, only a small proportion of homosexuals are detected. The majority even of these are not guilty of offenses against minors, as is popularly believed. Another fallacy is the belief that most of them are sodomists.

Naturally, little is known of the great bulk of homosexuals whose activities take place behind closed doors. We can only guess at the number of exclusive homosexuals. They do not usually betray themselves, as is mistakenly supposed, by peculiarities of speech and dress.

Kinsey estimated that in the United States about 4 per cent of the white males are exclusively homosexual. Over a third of the 4,000 American men interviewed admitted some adult homosexual experience. There seems no reason to expect the percentage in Britain to be less, especially as the segregation of sexes in schools and the older universities may even strengthen homosexual tendencies. On this basis it is probable that there are at least a million exclusive homosexuals in Britain.

A more understanding attitude toward the problem is gaining ground, thanks largely to the influence of leading churchmen and the spread of psychological knowledge. Although the facilities for psychiatric treatment are still meager, the results give ground for a more hopeful outlook than was possible not many years ago.

For example, nearly half the cases selected for therapeutic treatment in prisons in 1954 benefited, although they were not completely cured. Satisfactory results have also been obtained from treatment of outpatients referred by the courts to clinics.

Psychotherapy, including group therapy, is increasingly preferred to physical methods. In prisons the use of estrogens is forbidden in England and Wales, although not in Scotland. Castration, even with the consent of the offender, is totally forbidden and few people advocate it.

The Law on Obscenity

The degree of freedom allowed to periodicals and books dealing with sex has fluctuated since Elizabethan times. In this field also the relevant fact is not the letter of the law, but the manner in which it is applied. The amount of frankness tolerated is a barometer registering the climate of opinion.

Some of Shakespeare's plays contain such outspoken passages that an unexpurgated edition is still a rarity. The same is true of translations of the classics—e.g., Aristophanes and Petronius—the franker passages of which are usually left in the original language.

The eighteenth century was remarkably uninhibited in this respect and a blind eye was turned on many books that were unquestionably pornographic. But in 1824 it became an offense to expose obscene books and prints in public. The Obscene Publications Act of 1857 remained law for over a century. It gave the police power to seize and destroy stocks of such publications after a complaint had been laid at a magistrate's court. The author, publisher, and bookseller were liable to a criminal charge.

There is no formal censorship of books in Britain, although plays have to be passed by the Lord Chamberlain. Those responsible for the publication of books and periodicals issue them at their own risk and any private citizen has the right to lay information on which the authorities may act. Not only is this the same situation as that regarding libel, but the wording of the charge is similar. An obscene publication is called, oddly enough, an obscene *libel*.

The definition of an obscene publication given by Lord Chief Justice Campbell was a work "written with the single purpose of corrupting the morals of youth and of a nature calculated to shock the feeling of decency in any well-regulated mind." However, the qualifications were removed eleven years later by the ruling of Lord Chief Justice Cockburn. It was only necessary to convince a jury that any mind, well-regulated or not, could be "corrupted" by reading such a book. This could be interpreted in such a way as to ban many literary classics and even scientific works. For books recently banned see *Censorship of Sexual Literature*.

The demand for a change in the law was brought to a head in 1954 when several prominent publishing houses were prosecuted. One of the proposals was that expert evidence on the literary or scientific merits of the work complained of should be admitted. There was no such provision under the 1857 Act. Another sought to limit the power of the Customs authorities and Post Office who had hitherto been allowed to destroy books without a court order. The Obscene Publications Act of 1959 explicitly stated one of its objects to be "to provide for the protection of literature." Accordingly, it was made a good defense to call experts to pronounce upon the cultural merits of the disputed book. There is undeniably a much greater freedom of expression than was tolerated thirty or forty years ago. Novelists write frankly about sex, and even homosexuality and prostitution are acceptable themes. Isolated actions may be taken but a book that is seized in Blackpool may be sold freely in Brighton. The national sales are only stopped when a full-scale prosecution is initiated on grounds of obscene libel, and this is a rarity.

Changing Morals

The broad picture of sex life in modern Britain contrasts with that of preceding centuries. An indication of the changes of attitude that have taken place is given in *The Chesser Report*, which is based on questionnaires completed by 6,000 married and single women approached by their general practitioners. Altogether, 1,500 doctors cooperated in this social survey.

A steady increase in premarital sexual relationships is shown during the present century. Women born before 1904 came to sexual maturity during or right after World War I. For both married and single women the proportion in this group who had intercourse be-

fore marriage was one-fifth. This proportion rose to one-third in the group born before 1914. The trend continued upward among married women born in the following two decades.

The incidence of petting has also risen among both married and single women during the past fifty years and it is significantly higher among younger women. No doubt in many cases the liberties permitted were restricted to the future husband, but clearly twentieth-century women no longer accept the passive role assigned to them by Victorian standards.

The great majority of those who declared that they were happily married stated that they found intercourse enjoyable. Whereas this is not surprising today, such a fact would not have been admitted a hundred years ago.

The influence of social class upon sexual attitude cannot be ignored in such an analysis. Thus, women in the higher social groups appear to derive more satisfaction from intercourse and to indulge in premarital relationships at a later age than those of the working class. All classes make considerable use of birth control, but measures are more often taken by the woman only at the higher social level.

The real revolution in the attitude toward sex has been among the middle classes—among whom, 150 years ago, the prudery that infected English manners began. In the very lowest stratum, as among the very rich, morality has always tended to be lax. In modern Britain, however, extreme poverty has almost disappeared, and there is no longer a sharp income distinction between the manual and the white-collar worker. Inevitably, they tend to adopt the same standards.

Those who lament that morals are declining usually mean that Britain has departed from the standards of the nineteenth century. It is fair to point out that Victorian family life involved frequent pregnancies and a high death rate, great severity in bringing up children, and unhealthy repression. The status of women was inferior and their chastity was upheld by tolerating prostitution on a wide scale. The marriage bonds were often fetters from which there could be no escape.

Life in Britain nowadays is freer and franker. The sexes mingle with a lack of restriction that would have been inconceivable to their grandparents. They marry early and they plan their families. Sex instruction is widespread and there are various organizations—birth-control clinics and marriage-guidance councils—to which all who need advice can turn. Such is the progress that has been made.

References

Abortion: Report of the Interdepartmental Committee. London: His Majesty's Stationery Office, 1939.

Artificial Human Insemination: Report of a Conference Held in London under the Auspices of the Public Morality Council. London: His Majesty's Stationery Office, 1947.

Bibby, Cyril, *Sex Education.* London, 1948.

Bloch, Iwan, *Sexual Life in England, Past and Present.* London, 1938.

Board of Education, *Sex Education in Schools and Youth Organizations.* Educational Pamphlet No. 119. London: His Majesty's Stationery Office, 1943.

Chesser, Eustace, in collaboration with Joan Maizels, Leonard Jones, and Brian Emmet, *The Sexual, Marital and Family Relationships of the English Woman.* London, 1956.

Cole, Margaret, *Marriage: Past and Present.* London, 1939.

Comfort, Alex, *Sexual Behavior in Society.* London, 1950.

Craig, Alec, *The Banned Books of England.* London, 1937.

Ellis, Havelock, *Studies in the Psychology of Sex.* London, 1948, New York: 1936.

Evidence for the Department Committee of Inquiry, Association for Moral and Social Hygiene. London, 1955.

Gorer, Geoffrey, *Exploring English Character.* London, 1955.

Laird, Sydney M., *Venereal Disease in Britain.* London, 1943.

London County Council, *Some Notes on Sex Education.* London, 1949.

Mace, David R., *Marriage Counseling.* London, 1948.

Pollard, Robert S. W., *The Problem of Divorce.* London, 1958.

Population: Report of the Royal Commission. London: His Majesty's Stationery Office, 1949.

Report of the Archbishop's Commission on AID. London, 1949.

Report of the Departmental Committee on Homosexual Offences and Prostitution (Wolfenden Report). London: Her Majesty's Stationery Office, 1957.

Report of the Royal Commission on Marriage and Divorce. London: Her Majesty's Stationery Office, 1956.

Rolph, C. H., *Women of the Streets.* London, 1955.

Scott, George R., *A History of Prostitution from Antiquity to the Present Day.* London, 1952.

Slater, E., and Woodside, M., *Patterns of Marriage.* London, 1951.

Sterilization: Report of the Departmental Committee. London: His Majesty's Stationery Office, 1934.

Taylor, G. R., *The Angel Makers.* London, 1958.

West, D. J., *Homosexuality.* London, 1953.

Westermarck, Edward, *A Short History of Marriage.* London, 1926.

Williams, Glanville, *The Sanctity of Life and the Criminal Law.* London, 1958.

EUSTACE CHESSER

Guilt and Conflict
in Relation to Sex

Outline of the Problem
and Definition of Terms

IT IS important to observe that "sex guilt and conflict" is here used in reference to arbitrary, unrealistic, irrational interpretations of sex, not to the kinds of conflict about sex roles and behavior that might *reasonably* arise as a result of contacts between peoples of diverse cultures or persons from different segments of the same culture. Obviously, it is often difficult to be sure precisely what is rational and what irrational in culturally conditioned patterns of sex behavior, but the distinction is nevertheless one that should be attempted, since rational concepts (which accord with our best understanding of natural law) offer some prospect of universal understanding and acceptance, while irrational ones (at variance with natural law) lead to confusion and can never attain universal understanding and general acceptance.

A considerable number of scientific observations, notably those of Beach (1947, 1949, and 1950) and Yerkes (1939), on the sex behavior of animals, have indicated that for subhuman species the sex drive tends to assert itself in a manner that is relatively sure and predictable. That is to say, the sex urge is expressed in the behavior of the subhuman organism in a constant and foreseeable way, thus giving it the character of a true instinct.

Among humans, however, manifestations of the sex drive follow no such automatic behavior formula. It does not appear likely that the sex urge of man is weaker or less uniformly present than in his biological relatives. Rather, it would seem that man's more complex central nervous system, with its functional creation of cultural organization and ritualization, induces in him much distortion and conflict in his perception and evaluation of his sex feelings. Classical examples are seen in the Hebraic doctrine of sex as original sin and in the Christian corollary that the crucifixion of Christ was a necessary and divinely ordered atonement for man's original sin (sex).

In the modern cultures of Western Europe and America it has been traditional to impress upon children a frightened awareness of all sex feelings and manifestations. Our children have been (and generally still are) indoctrinated with the cultural illusion that the self-respecting and worthy child either possesses no sex feelings or recognizes them as basically evil, deserving only to be repressed with an intense sense of shame. Equally taboo is an interest in the excremental functions and any display of resentment against parental authority. Likewise, it is our custom to impress upon children that any form of self-love or pleasure-seeking through the satisfaction of inner needs is a selfish act; that the only truly sound motivation lies in serving others, accepting their motives as one's own, denying the self. Concerted effort to train children according to these irrational concepts form so flagrant a denial of the basic nature of children that it cannot fail to induce in them painful feelings of guilt and a great loss in sense of self-worth, whatever may appear superficially in their behavior.

The guilty child is a fearful one. He is filled

with feelings of hatred against forces with which he cannot cope. His capacity for love of a real, confident, spontaneous sort is hampered or lost. As he grows up he is therefore impelled to react to life through rigid use of the fearful, defensive attitudes and devices by which he learned to conceal his guilt-linked feelings of early childhood. His faith is not in his primitive appetites and drives but rather in the avoidance of them or in his ability to express them in a devious or disguised manner. So, in his social functioning he is in effect a frightened hypocrite, mistrustful of himself and of his fellows and frantically devoted to maintaining an illusion of social acceptability by practicing the unloving rituals of defense that were forced upon him during his formative years.

In very broad terms, this is the picture of our common neurosis. From it emerges a great volume and variety of psychosexual disturbances. Among these are sexual impotence, frigidity, sexual deviations, pornography, sadomasochism, unreal ideas of romanticism and glamour, and the generally unhappy state of most contemporary marriages. In still broader terms of total personality adjustment, the irrational guilt factor is the principal contributor to neurosis, psychosis, alcoholism, psychosomatic illness, delinquency, and criminal behavior.

When contemplating any definition of guilt it is important to discriminate between guilt that is conscious and guilt that is unconscious but active in stimulating compulsive defenses against its conscious acknowledgment. Conscious guilt, such as over masturbation, may be very disturbing. But the most damaging guilt is often altogether unconscious, as in the more severe cases of sexual impotence or frigidity or as manifested through phobias or sexual deviations. Whatever the type and nature of sex guilt, it serves to make its victim feel isolated from his fellows and mistrustful of them. Warm, loving enjoyment of sex is possible only when men and women approach each other with a high degree of confidence in themselves and in each other. Feelings of guilt make the affectionate and satisfying enjoyment of sex impossible or impose a damaging handicap.

One of the by-products of sexual guilt is the inhibition of realistic sex experience and the substitution of unreal, unworkable phantasies about the nature of romance and sex. All human beings who attain emotional maturity must come to recognize the folly of excessive idealization of a love-object and must accept the sometimes painful phenomenon of ambivalence in the sexual relationship. That is, they come to realize that the most loving and sexually compatible men and women at times have hostile feelings toward each other. Through experience they acquire an ability to see episodes of hostility in realistic perspective and develop social skill in handling them. To view marriage adjustment in an aura of sentimental idealization that denies the universal problem of emotional ambivalence is to defeat empathic communication about areas of difference or disagreement in marriage. Empathic communication depends upon a respectful awareness (not necessarily with sympathy) of another person's actual feelings and attitudes. Such communication is indispensable to an ongoing and successful marriage and it can be attained neither when severe feelings of guilty defensiveness are present nor when the shattering of silly romantic ideals has created an acute state of panic and anger.

In the present-day stage of our cultural evolution we generally fail to realize how essential to emotional maturity it is to face in an open and courageous manner all ambivalent or conflicting emotional situations of life: dependent versus independent impulses; enjoyment of primitive appetites versus social restraint; good versus evil; and love against hate. These are areas of emotional experience in which our mystical and authoritarian heritage often serves us poorly. The philosophy of authoritarian righteousness insists upon many irrational solutions that inevitably create confusion, hate, and guilt. A humanistic and democratic approach, on the contrary, makes for realistic and successful adjustment of ambivalent emotions, greatly reduces feelings of guilt, and facilitates mutual trust and affection.

Clinical Manifestations of Sex Guilt and Conflict

Serious degrees of unconscious guilt about sex emotions produce a large array of disturbances in sexual behavior. Chief among these are a compulsive interest in the pornographic; sadomasochism (linkage of sex assertiveness with cruel aggression and the degradation of a sex victim); the sex deviations, such as compulsive homosexuality, fetishism, partialism, transvestism, voyeurism, and exhibitionism; many cases of frigidity and impotence; and a wide range of neurotic and psychotic compulsive personality disturbances that may include any of the above-mentioned kinds of sexual behavior.

It is of critical importance to bear in mind that the specific sexual disorders listed above never exist as isolated personality characteristics but are invariably associated with more or less ramified instability in the general personality structure. That is, they are prominent (but not exclusive) evidences of a neurosis or psychosis in which many other functions of personality are impaired. Awareness of this is of the utmost significance in formulating any conceptions related to prognosis, therapy, or prevention.

No adequate appreciation of disturbances in sex behavior stemming from unconscious guilt is possible without a vivid awareness that this kind of sex behavior is rigidly compulsive in nature, altogether lacking the comfortable adaptability of guiltless sex expression. This quality of compulsive rigidity is clearly apparent in the frankly puritanical repudiation of sex. It is not so superficially obvious in sex deviations or in pornographic ritualism but will nevertheless be discovered upon close scrutiny.

Therapy of Disorders Arising from Sex Guilt and Conflict

Against compulsively rigid types of sexual behavior, springing as they do from unconscious feelings of guilt, superficial methods of re-education and persuasion are disappointingly ineffective. Indeed, persistent use of such therapy is likely to serve no purpose but to stimulate a sense of failure and to produce further loss of self-esteem. This is not to say that, in case of doubt about whether a certain sex behavior is truly compulsive, the therapist should not first test the possibilities of re-education and common sense. But when such an approach is ineffective it should be abandoned with reasonable promptness and deeper-level therapy, aimed at reaching the unconscious,

should be initiated. This is a task for the psychiatrically trained therapist and should not be undertaken by others. Psychiatric training and experience are essential to a sharp grasp of the dynamics of unconsciously motivated behavior and to the recognition of certain serious risks associated with therapy, such as the hazard of precipitating a psychosis or suicide.

Since the early days of Freudian psychiatry it has been recognized that the compulsive behavior produced by feelings of unconscious guilt constitutes a defense against consciously acknowledging repressed feelings. Compulsive behavior nearly always has its roots in early childhood, when it was adopted as an expedient to reduce unbearable anxiety. In its inception it was, however unrealistic, the best defense that could be contrived to meet a terrifying threat.

The particular form of a defense reaction against sex is often seemingly unrelated to sex, as when fear of masturbation finds expression as a compulsion to wash the hands with excessive frequency, upon a rationalized basis of fear of dirt and infection. In other instances the sexual theme is retained but is converted into a form that seems less dangerous, as when genital interest is converted into erotic devotion to a fetishistic object. In any event, the purpose of morbid sex ritualism is to reduce, or seem to reduce, the fears aroused in a child by external (cultural, moral) threats to the open expression of his sexual feelings.

Ideally, it would seem that a child should receive adult approval of his basic sexual emotions and interests and should enjoy the benefit of affectionate adult guidance in their social expression. Instead, he is all too likely, in our culture, to acquire a powerfully negative cathexis (hostile feeling) about his sex urge so that he must appear to deny it altogether or to express it only in some furtive or disguised way. In so doing he is adopting a neurosis, which is in effect the complete or partial denial of an innate behavior drive.

In a provocative recent paper the Russells (1957) have pointed out that a true biological instinct produces a characteristically rigid, set pattern of behavior. They believe this sheds considerable light upon the rigidity of neurotic compulsive behavior, because such behavior is the product of an innate drive turned against itself by ego forces and under the constant lash of unresolved childhood terror. Certain it is that neurotic mechanisms are reactions initiated to reduce severe, unbearable childhood anxiety and that, once firmly established, they are not easily given up or readily modifiable. It is a tragic fact that although they served a useful purpose in reducing childhood anxiety they operate in adult life to defeat full, comfortable sex expression and to hamper warmth and trust in all social relationships.

In a broad sense, deep-level psychotherapy aims at bringing about abreaction (living over again) of traumatic, repressed childhood experiences, attitudes, and imaginings. Since these often involve painful feelings of guilt it is not easy to bring them into consciousness. Also, it does not follow automatically that insight into repressed sources of guilt at once dramatically dissipates neurotic defense reactions. But it is an indispensable step in that direction. Once the iron grip of compulsive behavior is relaxed there still remains the inescapable task of developing ego strength through the process of reality testing (the adaptation of guilt-freed feelings to the world of reality). Accomplishment of this takes considerable time, just as the healthy emotional growth of childhood demands time and actual experience with life. One might accurately say that after the arresting grip of neurotic compulsion is broken the patient still faces the assignment of resuming the emotional development that was interrupted in his childhood and of acquiring the ego strength that is possible only through appropriate realistic experience with life itself. A vital factor in the achievement of all this is the transference phenomenon, which is essentially the development by the patient of feelings of trust and affection toward the therapist, replacing the feelings of mistrust or extreme ambivalence that were felt toward persons important to him in childhood. Through the medium of positive transference the therapist should, like an ideal parent, supply much-needed reorientation, guidance, and support, but he cannot provide life experiences or magically grant the ego strength that can be attained only through personally directed living. However, the therapist's role, both in freeing his

patient from compulsive, guilt-dictated motives and in providing him with a new set of values, is altogether necessary in making it possible for the patient to face life with the realism and sound self-awareness so essential to constructive social adaptation.

It needs to be stressed that most of man's cultures, including our own, operate in such a way as to fill children with unnecessary feelings of guilt and thus to undermine their self-image and ego strength. They are encouraged to seek relief by dependence upon the rigid demands of the culture for social conformity. So in the mass picture, individual neurosis finds expression through such means as racial intolerance, religious bigotry, chauvinistic nationalism, and puritanical sex mores.

Up to the present day man's culture does not reflect a very good appreciation of the real strengths and fine qualities of human nature; indeed, it seems frequently devoted to denying them. Some awareness of this appears to have been dawning slowly upon mankind during the past century. With our growing insights to aid us, new and improved cultural developments seem probable, perhaps coming at an astonishingly rapid rate, once our rigid attachment to guilt-saturated myths can be generally abandoned and replaced by a realistic appraisal of human nature.

Before leaving the subject of the application of psychotherapy to sex guilt manifestations it seems appropriate to give some estimate of how successful, by present standards, such therapy is likely to be. It cannot be too strongly emphasized that in no event is therapy likely to be successful unless the patient is deeply serious in recognizing that he has an emotional illness and is determined to cooperate in treatment. Half-hearted dabbling with therapy or entry into it under coercion is almost certain to fail. On this account there is little therapeutic success when sex deviates or alcoholics enter therapy by court order or under heavy family pressure. Compulsive homosexuality and sexual exhibitionism have, in general, responded poorly to psychotherapy but this is not always so; some striking successes have been recorded.

Neuroses in which impotence or frigidity are prominent symptoms generally respond well to deep-level therapy but there may be exceptions where the underlying pathology is particularly deep-rooted and complicated.

It is important to underline the observation that the therapeutic outlook regarding any special disturbance in sex behavior must take into account the entire pattern of the neurosis, the whole personality of the patient. Thus, a symptom such as frigidity may be part of a mild neurosis in one patient and part of a very severe one in another. The therapeutic prognosis will vary accordingly.

Avoidance of Sex Guilt and Conflict

Whatever we may still have to learn about human personality structure and development (and assuredly there is much both to learn and to correct), a few things are already fairly clear and available to guide parents and educators.

At the top of this list should be placed our recent awareness that treatment of children that causes them to feel guilty serves to destroy affection and trust; paralyzes honest interpersonal communication; creates a miserable self-image; leads to neurotic defensiveness; and in general impairs or destroys the ability to achieve affectionate and cooperative relationships with others. To state the matter in positive terms, it is becoming apparent that sound, constructive social motivation and behavior is fully attainable only by human beings whose ego structure contains a warm, comfortable self-image. This is not possible so long as we force children to believe that certain of their biological characteristics are thoroughly "bad" and unacceptable. I refer to such things as the urges of excrementation and sex and the universal tendency of children to resent frustration and angry domination. These are the three "master sins" of our culture, things of which the "good" child must be deeply ashamed in order to deserve the "respect and affection" of adults. This price for "respect and affection" is too high; indeed, it is irrational and impossible. A child cannot know the real meaning of love upon such terms. In bald truth he is simply being terrified into sharing the common neurosis of his culture, and so great are his fears that he can have no adequate conception of himself as a loving and lovable person.

Dimly we are beginning to realize that the emotionally mature, stable, loving personality is not richly attainable by our children unless we, as adults, can contrive a culture in which their complete biological natures can be understood and accepted by us with respect and affection. This is not to suggest that children do not need adult guidance. Rather, it is to emphasize that they should have a kind of adult leadership founded upon a respectful and empathic awareness of all their emotional needs, instead of the traditional adult attitude of scorn and hatred toward their innate qualities.

As we pass the middle of this century we are able to witness some remarkable evidences of favorable changes in adult attitudes toward children, such as demand feeding of infants; increased gentleness and patience in bowel and bladder training; acceptance of thumb-sucking; improved understanding and management of bed-wetting and stammering; more accepting attitudes about masturbation; the beginnings of realistic sex education at home and in schools; allowance of greater and more realistic sex freedom for children and young people; educational preparation for marriage and family life; and more widespread and tolerant understanding of the phenomena of sex deviation and other forms of sex-linked neurotic behavior.

It is comforting to observe that the new role of parents and educators in seeking to minimize feelings of guilt in children is likely to prove a far happier task than that of their ancestors, who were painfully forced by their culture and their own neurotic compulsions to treat children meanly and to foment hostility in them. The new role of parents and educators is likely to be attended by much more spontaneous affection and mutual trust on both sides than was possible under the traditional procedure. The net gain in human happiness and in wiser management of our society seems to have favorable possibilities beyond present imagination and would seem to be our principal hope in the human struggle to win the emotional maturity that is our sorest need and can well become the happiest of all our achievements.

References

Baruch, Dorothy, *How to Live with Your Teen-ager.* New York: McGraw-Hill Book Co., 1953.

Baruch, Dorothy, *New Ways in Discipline.* New York: McGraw-Hill Book Co., 1949.

Beach, F. A., "A Cross-species Survey of Mammalian Sexual Behavior." In Pitti Hoch and J. Zubin (eds.), *Psychosexual Development in Health and Disease.* New York: Grune & Stratton, Inc., 1949.

Beach, F. A., "A Review of Physiological and Psychological Studies of Sexual Behavior in Mammals." *Physiol. Rev. 27;* 240-307, 1947.

Beach, F. A., *Sexual Behavior in Animals and Men.* Springfield, Ill.: Charles C Thomas, 1950.

Bergler, Edmund, *The Basic Neurosis.* New York: Grune & Stratton, Inc., 1949.

Briffault, R., *The Mothers.* New York: The Macmillan Co., 1927.

Briffault, R., *Sin and Sex.* New York: Macaulay, 1931.

Comfort, Alex, *Sexual Behavior in Society.* New York: The Viking Press, Inc., 1950.

Ellis, Albert, *The American Sexual Tragedy.* New York: Twayne Publishers, 1954.

Ellis, Albert, *Sex Without Guilt.* New York: Lyle Stuart, 1958.

Fromm, Erich, *Man for Himself.* New York: Rinehart & Co., Inc., 1947.

Guyon, René, *The Ethics of Sexual Acts.* New York: Alfred A. Knopf, Inc., 1934.

Huxley, Julian, "Knowledge, Morality and Destiny." *Psychiatry 14;* 129-151, 1951.

Kardiner, Abram, *Sex and Morality.* Indianapolis: The Bobbs-Merrill Co., 1954.

Kinsey, A. C. *et al., Sexual Behavior in the Human Female.* Philadelphia: W. B. Saunders Co., 1953.

Kinsey, A. C. *et al., Sexual Behavior in the Human Male.* Philadelphia: W. B. Saunders Co., 1948.

LaBarre, Weston, *The Human Animal.* Chicago: University of Chicago Press, 1956.

Malinowski, B., *The Sexual Life of Savages in Northwestern Melanesia.* New York: Halcyon House, 1929.

Mead, Margaret, *From the South Seas.* New York: William Morrow & Co., Inc., 1939.

Reich, Wilhelm, *The Sexual Revolution.* New York: Orgone Institute Press, 1945.

Russell, Claire, and Russell, W. M. S., "An Approach to Human Ethology." *Behavioral Sci. 2;* 169-200, 1957.

Schur, Edward M., (ed.), *The Family and the Sexual Revolution.* Bloomington, Ind.: Indiana University Press, 1964.

Stokes, Walter, *Married Love in Today's World.* New York: The Citadel Press, 1962.

Stokes, Walter, "Our Changing Sex Ethics." *Marriage and Family Living 24;* 269-272, 1962.

Wolbarst, A. C., *Generations of Adam.* New York: Stokes, 1932.

Yerkes, R. M., "Sexual Behavior in the Chimpanzee." *Human Biol. 11;* 78-111, 1939.

WALTER R. STOKES

Hermaphroditism

Definition

FROM classical times until the present century the definition of hermaphroditism was simple: a hermaphrodite was a person who possessed elements of the sexual anatomy of both sexes. Hermaphroditus, in the statues and murals of antiquity, was represented as having normal masculine genitals and female breasts and hips. In the sixteenth century, Ambroise Paré, famed French surgeon, described four varieties of hermaphrodites, each having ambiguous looking, malformed external genitals. By the nineteenth century it was known that people with apparently normal genitals could be hermaphrodites, their ambisexuality concealed. Surgeons found cases of "normal" men with a uterus and Fallopian tubes herniated into the scrotum with the testes; and cases of "normal" women with testis and vas deferens in each groin and a total lack of internal female organs. In 1873 Klebs codified the knowledge of his day in a threefold classification: male and female pseudohermaphrodites with two testes or two ovaries, respectively; and true hermaphrodites with both ovarian and testicular tissue in the gonads—separately or as a pair.

In 1949 a simple anatomical definition of hermaphroditism became anachronistic. Barr and his associates in Ontario demonstrated that cells from a female mammal possessed in the nucleus a small mass of chromatin not present in male cells. By this method of nuclear sexing, a correct diagnosis of sex could be made consistently in normal individuals of many mammalian species, including man, by microscopic examination of skin biopsy material, mucosal scrapings, or blood films. The recognition of the sex-chromatin body has provided a new and very helpful criterion for the correct diagnosis and understanding of sex anomalies, and has initiated a revision of the concept of hermaphroditism.

Sex-Chromatin Body*

The origin of the sex-chromatin body has aroused much speculation. Probably it represents one of the two X chromosomes coiled and visible in the resting state. Until recently, it was considered that when the nuclear sex pattern was female (or chromatin-positive) the sex chromosome constitution was XX, and that when the nuclear sex pattern was male (or chromatin-negative) the sex chromosome constitution was XY. And so, when certain apparently normal females who failed to mature owing to congenital lack of gonads were found to have male nuclear sex, the incongruity was explained on the basis of animal experiments as a form of sex reversal in which a genetic male with the XY chromosome constitution had developed embryonically into a morphological female. Similarly, certain sterile hypogonadal men who had female nuclear sex were assumed to have an XX chromosome constitution, and thus to be examples of embryonic sex reversal

---

* The following two paragraphs, embodying among other things unpublished findings from his own work, were written by Dr. M. A. Ferguson-Smith of Glasgow.

in the opposite direction.

Studies on the chromosomal constitution of these individuals show that this concept of sex reversal is untenable. The fundamental defect in these two conditions appears to be an abnormality of cell division occurring during the formation of sperms or eggs and leading to an alteration in the normal number of 46 chromosomes in the fertilized egg. In the case of the sterile man with female nuclear sex, an extra chromosome can be demonstrated and the sex chromosome constitution is XXY. In the woman with congenital absence of gonads and male nuclear sex, there is a deficiency of one chromosome, and this is believed to be one of the X chromosomes, giving a sex chromosome constitution of XO. Excepting those cases with abnormalities in genotype (which are seldom accompanied by visible clinical features of hermaphroditism), and with the possible exception of certain cases of true hermaphroditism at present under study, the normal sex chromosome constitution, which is the genetic or zygotic sex, may be inferred from the nuclear sex.

Today a hermaphrodite must be defined as a person in whom at least one of five physical variables of sex is contradictory of the remainder. These are: (1) nuclear sex; (2) gonadal sex; (3) hormonal sex and pubertal virilization or feminization; (4) internal accessory reproductive structures; and (5) external genital morphology. To illustrate, it is possible for a baby to be born completely female on all counts except the fifth, the external genitals being incompletely masculinized, although sufficiently so to cause the child to be declared a boy and reared as such.

It is impossible to predict, from the appearance of the external genitals alone, what the internal reproductive organs of a hermaphrodite may be, or what the gonads and sex-chromatin pattern may be. Ambiguous looking external genitals are encountered in some varieties of hermaphroditism in which the external genitalia remain incompletely differentiated as either male or female. Ambiguous external genitalia are always unfinished genitalia. It is embryologically impossible for a hermaphrodite to possess two full sets of external organs, one male and one female.

Syntactical confusion easily arises in the gender terminology of hermaphroditism. In this article, boy and girl, man and woman, he and she, will always refer to the sex in which a person is living or being reared. Male and female will refer, as adjectives, to specific nouns or noun phrases (e.g., male gonads), unless the context makes it clearly and unequivocally otherwise. Standing alone to qualify the noun hermaphroditism, the adjectives male and female refer to gonadal structure. The prefix "pseudo-" in the term pseudohermaphrodite is obsolete in an age of sex-chromosome determinations.

Causes and Varieties of Hermaphroditism

Hermaphroditism is an anomaly of embryonic and fetal sexual differentiation. Postnatal contradictions in virilization or feminization are not defined as hermaphroditism.

The stages of sexual differentiation in the normal course of events show both ovary and testis differentiate from the same gonadal anlage. Likewise, the external genitalia of male and female are homologous and differentiate from the same anlagen. The internal reproductive structures, by contrast, do not differentiate from the same anlagen. In this respect the embryo is initially hermaphroditic, possessing both wolffian ducts of the male and müllerian ducts of the female. Subsequently, one set of ducts proliferates while the other atrophies.

It is known from the experiments of Jost (1953) in France that mammalian sexual differentiation as a female takes precedence over sexual differentiation as a male. Jost succeeded in the highly delicate task of castrating rabbit embryos in utero without destroying their viability. He found that male embryos castrated on the twenty-first uterine day developed anatomically as females, just as did their sisters. Only three days later, castration was no longer effective in suppressing male differentiation. Remarkably enough, unilateral castration of a male on the twenty-first day produced feminine differentiation on the castrated side only.

The human counterpart of Jost's rabbits is found in the condition formerly known as ovarian agenesis (Turner's syndrome), now known as gonadal aplasia in girls with an XO or mosaic chromosome pattern. Wilkins (1965) has marshaled evidence to demonstrate also that in cases of incomplete gonadal aplasia (testicular hypoplasia) there is some degree of masculinization of an otherwise feminine genital tract, the degree of masculinization being dependent on the amount of rudimentary or hypoplastic gonadal (testicular) tissue present. All gradations of phallic size may be found, from a clitoris-like organ to one of penile proportions with an uncovered gutter instead of a urethral tube (hypospadias).

A word in parenthesis about hypospadias: Any misplacement of the urinary orifice away from the tip of the penis is called hypospadias. It is not necessary to suspect internal signs of hermaphroditism, except perhaps an anomalous sex-chromatin pattern, when hypospadias is very mild and the testes are fully descended. But when the urethral tube and orifice are severely malformed, especially if the testes are poorly descended, a full work-up for other signs of hermaphroditism is absolutely in order.

Not all examples of hermaphroditism in genetic males can be accounted for on a graduated scale of embryonic gonadal deficit. Two other varieties of male hermaphroditism need to be accounted for, their etiology being very imperfectly understood at the present time.

First, there are those male hermaphrodites with male sex-chromatin pattern who have a well-developed uterus and tubes coexistent with testes that, instead of being aplastic or vestigial, are well-differentiated and of good size. Nor do they have extremely feminized external genitals. The penis and scrotum may be normally formed, although some degree of hypospadias is more likely. Usually these patients virilize at puberty.

Second, there are sex-chromatin males with fully formed, although sterile, testes in the groins, male internal organs, and perfectly formed female external organs. Since the testes produce estrogen at puberty these people with the syndrome of feminizing testes are completely simulant females except for their amenorrhea and sterility. The anomaly runs in families, probably through a sex-limited, dominant gene, so that the quota of normal male offspring is not filled. It appears in successive generations, namely among the aunts and nieces of patients. The chromosome constitution is XY.

The variety of hermaphroditism in which ovarian and testicular tissues are found coexistent is known as true hermaphroditism. Each gonad may be an ovotestis, or there may be a testicle on one side and an ovary on the other. There may also be two ovaries and two testes. Cases have been reported of oogenesis and spermatogenesis in the same person. Contrary to popular myth, the external anatomy does not permit equal versatility in the coital role of both the sexes. The appearance of the external genitals ranges from near-female to normal male. There are many possible permutations and combinations of male and female elements internally. The chromatin pattern may be male or female, irrespective of what other sexual structures prevail. The cause of true hermaphroditism has not been elucidated.

A form of hermaphroditism, less rare today than formerly, is found in females with normal reproductive ovaries, the only anomaly being external: a large, penile-looking clitoris and partial or complete labioscrotal fusion. It has long been known that this form of hermaphroditism could be produced by an excess of androgen in the pregnant mother's blood stream. Recently it has been discovered that the modern treatment of threatened abortion with progestinic hormone may produce the condition. In a few women progestin, metabolizing into androgen, crosses the placenta and masculinizes the external genitalia of a female fetus.

There has been rapid advance in the last 20 years, associated particularly with the name of Lawson Wilkins, in understanding the etiology of the most common variety of female hermaphroditism, the female andrenogenital syndrome. This condition, of fetal onset, is caused by hyperplasia of the adrenal cortex with a concomitant excess of androgen in the adrenocortical hormones, measurable as excess 17-ketosteroids in the urine. The condition is transmitted as a recessive gene. Only when both parents carry the recessive gene does the condition appear in the children, the chances being one in four for each pregnancy. Males with the condition are morphologically normal at birth but their subsequent growth and puberty are precocious. Females with the condition, although morphologically female internally, have external genitals that look ambiguous at birth. In rare instances the external genitals are so completely masculinized that the baby looks like a male with an empty scrotum.

The continuing excess of adrenal androgen produces accelerated growth and precocious, virilizing puberty. Untreated, the patients grow up with all the secondary sexual morphology of a male. Cortisone substitution therapy corrects the hormonal anomaly. Virilism can be completely prevented when treatment is begun in infancy and continued indefinitely.

A recently identified variety of abnormality is like the Turner's syndrome in that the reproductive organs are usually not ambiguous but simply contradictory of the sex-chromatin pattern (Klinefelter's syndrome). Individuals in this category are male on all counts except that they have a female sex-chromatin pattern and are sterile. The testicular tubules are hyalinized. Body morphology may tend to be eunuchoid. The penis, although in most cases normally formed, may be hypospadiac. In some instances duct tissue of the breasts proliferates to produce a moderate gynecomastia. Cytogenic research has revealed that the female-type sex-chromatin mass in the cells of these men represents an anomalous XXY (or even XXXY) chromosome constitution, instead of the normal XX (female) or XY (male).

The Newborn:
Criteria of Sex Assignment

In the nineteenth and early twentieth century gonadal sex was regarded as true sex, and the microscope was, almost tyrannously, the final arbiter. With the advent in the past decade of sex-chromatin and sex-chromosomal determinations, a few people have been tempted to identify true sex with chromosomal sex and to decide a hermaphrodite's sex of assignment accordingly. Such a decision would be manifestly absurd in the case of men with Klinefelter's syndrome, for they are men in every respect except the chromosome pattern. It would also be an absurd decision in the case of women with the syndrome of testicular feminization who are women in every respect save their infertility and lack of menstruation, despite their gonadal architecture and XY sex-chromosome status. Likewise, in the case of Turner's syndrome these girls, also of apparent male sex-chromatin (XO chromosome) status, became women in every respect save their gonadal aplasia and infertility once their hormonal deficit is corrected by substitution therapy.

In actual fact, in cases like the foregoing, no one has been so absurd as to use the sex-chromatin pattern as the criterion of true sex and to assign or reassign the sex of these patients accordingly. These people, it must be remembered, have normal-looking external genitals, even though genital morphology and sex-chromatin pattern are mutually contradictory. Consequently, there is no indecision about their sex at birth. The evidence of the external genitals is taken at face value and no one—doctors, parents, or the patients themselves—ever has reason to doubt the validity or appropriateness of the decision.

In the case of those varieties of hermaphroditism in which, unlike the foregoing three varieties, the external genitals look ambiguous, the sex of assignment must be deliberated and decided upon at the time of birth. Subsequently there may be controversy about sex reassignment. The age of the patient makes a world of difference so far as psychological sex is concerned. The principles of sex assignment are, therefore, quite different for the newborn than for older children. What follows in this section *applies only to the newborn.*

In those varieties of hermaphroditism where the genitals look ambiguous, it is a cardinal rule when assigning the sex of a newborn infant that the genitals should not defy surgical reconstruction in agreement with the sex of assignment. Eventually the external genitals and the haircut must agree—which is not to say that the external genital appearance alone is the ultimate arbiter, but simply that primary importance is given to the adaptability of the genital anatomy to surgical reconstruction, for male or female function.

In some cases it proves necessary and wise to disregard chromosomal and gonadal sex, and to make the decision about sex of assignment on the basis of genital morphology alone. Such a decision is almost never required in the case of female hermaphroditism, but quite commonly it is required in male hermaphroditism, especially if the testes are hypoplastic. Here one finds sex-chromatin males with hypoplastic and malformed testes, but the penis is hypospadiac and so small and clitoris-like in proportions that it can never be surgically repaired into a functional penis. It would be a psychological disaster to rear such a baby as a boy. Reared as a girl, the patient can in infancy be surgically feminized in external genital appearance. Later, feminizing puberty can be induced hormonally and an artificial vagina can be constructed. In girls with the penutest type of male hermaphroditism with a uterus well-developed, menstruation can be induced hormonally, with cyclic therapy, since the uterus is well developed.

Decisions concerning the sex of assignment in the newborn with true hermaphroditism are similar to those for male hermaphroditism. Since by definition testicular and ovarian tissue are both present, there is no controversy regarding congruity between gonads and genital morphology, whether the genitals be predominantly male or female. The sex-chromatin pattern, however, may be incongruous and may need to be disregarded in deciding sex of rearing.

In female hermaphroditism it so happens that the uterus is always well differentiated, and the vaginal orifice, even though it may open internally into the urethra, can be brought down surgically into the normal position. Thus, once the diagnosis has been established, there is little problem in deciding the sex of assignment of newborn female hermaphrodites. The only exception might be one of those very rare adrenogenital cases in which the clitoris has become a normal looking penis and the labia majora have fused to become an empty scrotum; but such a case would not be recognized as one of hermaphroditism at birth unless there were other reasons to suspect the adrenogenital syndrome.

Babies with progestin-induced hermaphroditism need no treatment other than surgical repair of the genitals, which can often be completed once and for all in early infancy. They grow up and reproduce as normal females. Babies of the adrenogenital variety also require corrective surgery—clitoridectomy and vaginoplasty, the latter perhaps needing postponement until teen age. Above all, however, adrenogenital patients need corrective hormonal therapy with cortisone. Without this therapy they virilize excessively and precociously, and develop none of the female secondary sexual characteristics. Cortisone therapy must be regulated and continued throughout life.

Older than Newborn: Sex Assignment and Gender-Role Imprinting

It has been implied in the preceding section that psychological development as a male or female does not depend automatically, mechanically, or instinctively on the nuclear sex (sex-chromosome pattern), nor on the gonadal structure. Money and his associates have studied over a hundred cases of hermaphroditism in order to find out what becomes of gender orientation, outlook, or role when one or more of the five physical variables of sex is contradictory of assigned sex. Gender role is defined as all those things that a person says or does to disclose himself or herself as having the status of boy or man, girl or woman, respectively. It includes, but is not restricted to, sexuality in the sense of eroticism. It has been found that gender role usually becomes established, following birth, in accordance with the sex of assignment and rearing. Exceptions are rare. Gender role ordinarily agrees with sex of assignment despite contradictions among the other five variables of sex, namely, nuclear sex, gonadal structure, hormonal function, internal reproductive organs, and external genital morphology.

Establishment of a child's gender role appears to get well under way around the time that he commences to have a command of language, namely between 18 months and 2 years of age. In normal 2-year-olds one observes an intense amount of impersonation of, and identification with, the parent of the same sex. By the time of the fourth birthday, the gender role is firmly established in most children. Henceforth it will be fixed—so irreversible and indelible that mankind for generations has assumed that human sexual outlook as male or female must be exclusively inborn. Of course, it is possible for an individual to establish an ambiguous gender role, just as it is possible for him to become bilingual, and in some individuals a defective or erroneous gender role may become imprinted. The majority of human beings, however, become imprinted with a gender role and orientation congruous with their genital equipment and reproductive capacities.

The concept of imprinting is a new one in sexual theory, as it is in psychological theory in general. Imprinting is a kind of learning that requires a highly specific perceptual stimulus, without which it cannot take place and in the presence of which it cannot fail to take place, provided the nervous system is intact and functional. The stimulus can be varied, but only within the boundaries of specifiable perceptual dimensions. Imprinting takes place readily at critical periods of the life history, which differ for species and type of imprint, after which it will not take place at all or only imperfectly. Once an imprint takes place, it is indelible, if not for life then for a particular epoch in the life history. An excellent presentation of imprinting theory and experiment in birds, fish, and mammals can be found in C. H. Schiller (ed.), 1957.

In the management of hermaphroditism, it often happens that a provisional or inadequate diagnosis is made at birth and is later found to need revision. Then arises the thorny question of whether or not to make a reassignment of sex. In such a case, the degree to which the gender role has become fixed and ineradicable is the all-important consideration. Individual maturation rates differ, so that there are no fixed chronological boundaries in the establishment of gender role. Rather, there are time zones. Each case requires individual evaluation

of the extent to which gender role has been fixed.

Under the age of about 18 months, an infant's sex may be reassigned with the expectation that he will adapt readily to the change and subsequently will be unable to recall it. At this early age, it is the understanding and attitude of the parents that is of paramount importance. Unless all ambiguities regarding the sex of their child are correctly resolved in their own minds, there will be a grave danger that they will insidiously communicate their own uncertainty and equivocation to their growing child. Relatives and neighbors, especially juveniles, present a problem, but not an insuperable one.

After the age of 18 months it is too late to make a reassignment of sex with impunity, and for the most part a change should be avoided. A calculated risk is sometimes justified, however, notably in the case of children whose external genitals totally contradict their assigned sex. Psychiatric supervision and follow-up should never be omitted. Another exception, also very rare, when a reassignment of sex is justified is in the case of an older child whose gender role has been established contrary to the assigned sex, the child himself desiring a change. Overt requests for sex reassignment are more likely to be made by teen-aged than juvenile hermaphrodites. Such requests are usually the culmination of efforts to resolve ambivalence and doubt and are deserving of serious consideration.

Some people have argued in favor of arbitrarily imposing a sex reassignment on older children if, with proper surgical and hormonal treatment, they will be enabled later in life to be fertile and have children, instead of being infertile in the sex of original assignment. This fertility argument actually can be applied only to female hermaphroditism, since congenital infertility is the rule in all other varieties of hermaphroditism. The argument breaks down insofar as being fertile is not the same as being reproductive. Patients who are arbitrarily forced into a reassignment of sex retain the gender role that was already established and henceforth act and feel like homosexuals and do not reproduce. Thus, a hyperadrenocortical female hermaphrodite who has been reared for years as a boy retains the sexual inclinations and desires of a male, irrespective of being forced into surgical feminization and the assumption of life as a female.

Management of Hermaphroditism

I: Diagnosis and Sex Assignment

When a sexual ambiguity is recognized at the time of delivery, it is advisable to tell the parents that they have a baby who is *sexually unfinished* and that various tests will have to be performed before the baby can be declared a boy or a girl. In this way the parents can curtail announcements of the birth and avoid the embarrassment of having to make public a second, contradictory announcement.

It is desirable to arrive at a speedy decision about the sex of assignment and rearing. Even more important than speed is thorough conclusiveness and finality. All debate should be disposed of so the subject need never be opened again. It is in the best interest of the child that henceforth everyone agree about his being a boy, or her being a girl. The sex of assignment will be decided on the basis of anatomical and physiological findings. Psychological findings require consideration only in the older children, not in the newborn.

Whatever the age of the patient, the usual work-up commences with a complete physical examination, particular attention being given to genital morphology. Next follows the simple procedure of obtaining a buccal smear from which a slide is prepared, along with a control from a normal female, for sex-chromatin determination. This process requires a half day, and is more practicable than an actual chromosome count, which is still a time-consuming procedure.

If the sex chromatin is female, determination of urinary 17-ketosteroid output per twenty-four hours will be necessary. A twenty-four-hour urine specimen is obtained from untoilet-trained infants by harnessing them in a special urine-collecting crib. Elevated 17-ketosteroid output, accompanied as early as the age of 2 by clinical signs of precocious growth and virilism, differentiates female hyperadrenal hermaphrodites from nonadrenal female hermaphrodites

and from either true hermaphrodites with a female chromatin pattern or males with Klinefelter's syndrome.

Nonadrenal female hermaphrodites can often be differentiated from true hermaphrodites by the mother's clinical history of treatment with progestin while pregnant with the patient. In doubtful cases, exploratory laparotomy and gonadal biopsy may be needed. Gonadal biopsy alone confirms a diagnosis of true hermaphroditism. The chromosome count is typically XX, the same as in female hermaphroditism.

When the buccal smear yields a male chromatin pattern, there are no hormonal determinations, such as the 17-ketosteroid test for female hyperadrenal hermaphroditism, that are specific for a differential diagnosis. However, urinary follicle-stimulating hormone (FSH) is elevated after the expected age of puberty in gonadal aplasia and Klinefelter patients.

After the finding of a male sex-chromatin pattern, the remainder of the differential diagnosis will depend on the findings from the physical examination and, when needed, those from radiographic studies, surgical exploration, and gonadal biopsy. The syndromes of gonadal aplasia and testicular feminization can both be diagnosed without surgical exploration.

Three other categories of male-chromatin hermaphroditism remain: the testicular hypoplastic type, the type with penis + uterus + testes, and a subcategory of true hermaphroditism. The latter can be differentiated from the former pair only by gonadal biopsy, usually requiring surgical exploration, since by definition both ovarian and testicular tissue are present in true hermaphroditism. This differentiation is so often of academic interest only, and not of pragmatic significance, that it has been common practice not to push to the limits of differential diagnosis. Pragmatically, it is much more important, especially when the patient is being reared as a girl, to establish whether the müllerian organs are present and well developed, which will be the case in the one male type and in most cases of true hermaphroditism. Radiographic evidence may be sufficient, but exploratory surgery is generally more conclusive.

No single one of the foregoing differential

diagnostic procedures, taken alone, will give the answer as to what the sex of assignment and rearing should be. The combined findings of these procedures, however, will be sufficient to decide the sex of assignment of the newborn and very young infants for whom, because of their age, psychological diagnosis of gender role is not pertinent. The foregoing findings will also be sufficient in the case of those hermaphrodites for whom the issue of sex assignment is never debated, namely, those whose external genital organs look entirely male or entirely female. These patients ordinarily are far past infancy, their gender role manifestly declaring itself, when they first come to medical attention. Since they have normal appearing genitals, their concealed hermaphroditism may pass unsuspected for years.

Psychological diagnosis of gender role and orientation comes into prominence after the period of early infancy in cases where the genitals are ambiguous looking and where there is serious questioning regarding the appropriateness of the sex already assigned. Gender role is appraised from information about activities, interests, and behavior reported by parents; from first-hand observation of social activities and play; from psychological tests; and especially from interviews that combine frank, direct inquiry with oblique, indirect inquiry.

II: Psychological Management

After the issue of assigned sex has been settled once and for all, the program of hermaphroditic management becomes threefold: psychological, surgical, and hormonal.

The psychological program has its beginning in the knowledge and understanding given to the parents, and to the older patients themselves, of the nature of hermaphroditism and what can be done for it. Anxieties of parents, and of patients old enough to be aware of their predicament, can be allayed if they understand something of the embryology of hermaphroditism. The average layman does not know about the derivation of male and female external organs from the same embryonic beginnings. The concept of hermaphroditism as a condition of being sexually unfinished has laid

low the specter of a "morphodite" as a half-boy, half-girl freak in the minds of many a hapless parent or patient.

What to tell friends and relatives, including younger siblings, is a problem for parents and older patients. Emotionally neutral medical terms are a great help in this respect. For each case a suitable term or explanatory phrase can be found—hypospadias, for example, or adrenal overactivity—and written down if necessary.

It is wise to be frank with patients, as well as with parents, for they so often overhear or guess what one fondly imagines they are being spared. When the information is properly presented, it is not inevitably harmful for a patient to learn that his sex chromosomes are female or her sex chromosomes are male, but it is imperative that this information be explained and its significance spelled out with almost schoolish instruction. Similarly, with regard to gonadal biopsy findings: if they are discussed, as so often they must be, their precise significance must be explained. It is utterly different for a woman to be told bluntly that she has a testicle than to be told that, under the microscope, an abnormally formed sex gland with a cell structure resembling a testis has been found. The horror of most people on learning of a contradictory sex variable in themselves or their offspring stems from their impulsive assumption that this contradiction will induce perverse desires and homosexuality—that is, falling in love with a person of the same declared sex. That such is not the case needs to be aired in frank discussion.

Insidious self-blame for having produced a deformed child is rather common and is wrapped up with folk superstitions about heredity, the sins of the fathers, and pregnancy accidents. A brief scientific acquaintance with the facts of heredity may be disproportionately valuable in terms of the worry it dispels. Knowledge of how heredity works to cause plural familial incidence of the adrenogenital and testicular feminizing syndromes is absolutely imperative for parents who have produced the condition once, so that they may more confidently decide whether or not to enlarge their family.

Hyperadrenocortical female hermaphroditism is the only type in which the issue of hereditary transmission by the patient occurs, for in adulthood these women can become pregnant, if maintained on cortisone. Delivery usually requires a Caesarian operation. The mother's hyperadrenocorticism does not appear in her offspring unless by an unlucky chance—the odds are about 1:150—the father should happen to be a carrier of the recessive gene for the condition. Nonadrenal female hermaphrodites can reproduce but their condition is not hereditary. In all other types of hermaphroditism, the chances of reproduction are absent or so low that the psychological problem is not heredity but sterility.

When it is certain that a hermaphroditic child will be sterile as an adult, there is no point in euphemizing or hiding this information after the child is old enough to comprehend it. Tact and delicacy are required in disclosing the information, which should always be done in the broader context of a full and proper sex education. The advantage of the disclosure is that all need for deceit and false euphemism is abolished. It is an additional guarantee of psychological health that the child thenceforth construes the expectancies of parenthood, normal in all children's daydreams, accurately in terms of adoptive parenthood.

The sex education of hermaphroditic children should be frank, straightforward, and begun at an early age. It is doubly important that children who have, or who might remember, visible genital ambiguity entertain no confusion about the difference between the sexes. Little girls definitely should know that, whereas little boys have a penis, girls have a baby tunnel. This knowledge is of crucial importance to girls, if they are old enough to comprehend it, prior to clitoral surgery. Otherwise they may misconstrue their surgery as mutilating rather than corrective.

It is not too early for a bright child to know at 3 or 4 years of age that babies grow from a baby egg in a baby nest and come out down a baby tunnel. Later, and as their comprehension matures, they can learn about the swimming race of the sperms—200 million of them, and only one wins!—from the testicles, down

the penis, up the baby tunnel, and into the baby nest to find the egg. Menstruation can be explained as nest-cleaning day. The emotional aspects of love and sex make no sense to children until erotic feeling matures in their own bodies at puberty. It is usually wise to advise a child that talk about where babies come from is one of the private things in life, reserved preferably for mother, daddy, or doctor. If children inappropriately employ sex information, it is primarily because they are not told when to use it.

Be frank with your child in matters sexual, and you keep his confidence. This is the best way to guarantee against the leakage of family secrets into the neighborhood, and against self-exposure in childhood play, which could set the neighborhood gossiping in a most disturbing way.

III: Surgical Management

It is a good idea to outline the anticipated plan of surgical management to parents. They and the doctor may then keep the child informed, if multiple admissions are required and if genital repair cannot be completed early in life. Children prove extraordinarily adaptable to genital anomalies provided that, not left in the dark, they feel a sense of participating in a constructive venture, even though it may be unpleasant and painful. For instance, a boy unable to stand up to urinate owing to an incompletely repaired hypospadias may have his morale completely broken without the social assurance and self-confidence that comes from knowing the what and the why planned for him by his surgeon.

Female genital reconstruction, when needed in cases of female assigned sex, can be commenced as soon after birth as is consistent with surgical safety. The problem of surgical safety arises almost exclusively in those cases of female hyperadrenocortical hermaphroditism complicated by deficiency of the adrenal salt-retaining hormone. Until their salt balance is perfectly regulated, these infants can be suddenly precipitated into an adrenal crisis by any physical stress, including the stress of an operation.

Feminizing surgery almost always involves amputation of an enlarged clitoris. An entire chapter of potential psychological problems is eliminated when clitoridectomy is completed very early in life. An older child should never undergo clitoridectomy without being told beforehand what will be done, and why. Evidence obtained from older hermaphroditic women who have undergone clitoridectomy, and from normal women who have undergone radical vulvectomy, indicates that clitoridectomy does not destroy the capacity for orgasm and erotic pleasure. All these women had a vagina. It is not known what would happen to erotic feelings following clitoridectomy in a hermaphrodite born without the orifice of either a blind vaginal pouch or communicating urogenital sinus from which to reconstruct a functional vagina. A wholly artificial vagina, opened surgically through the perineum in the absence of a natural orifice, does not communicate erotic feeling. It may therefore, be preferable to conserve the enlarged clitoris of these patients lest they be deprived of too much erotically sensitive tissue.

In addition to clitoridectomy, feminizing surgery may require vaginoplasty as well. If the vaginal orifice is near the normal position, the necessary surgical adjustments can often be made in infancy. When there is a major problem of structural rearrangement, however, vaginoplasty should be postponed until early teen age, when the organs are larger and a more perfect result can be obtained. A girl does not need to go through the embarrassment of waiting for marriage before having this operation; she should be allowed to feel free to ask for it at her own convenience without any moral eyebrows being raised.

In some cases of hermaphrodites assigned as females, surgical reconstruction will involve the removal of contradictory internal reproductive structures. Gonadectomy is an insurance not only against hormonal incongruity at puberty, but also against malignancy in abdominally placed and deformed gonads. There is one exception: the gonads found in the inguinal canals of girls with the syndrome of testicular feminization should be preserved, at least until after puberty, in order to avoid the necessity of estrogen replacement therapy. There need be no moral problem about inducing sterility by removing the gonads of male hermaphrodites living as girls and women, for the testes in male hermaphroditism are, virtually without exception, defective and aspermatogenic. There is a causal relationship here: dating back to embryonic life, testicular defect allows other reproductive structures to feminize.

In some cases of hermaphrodites assigned as males, with or without contradictory gonads, it will be necessary to remove contradictory internal organs. The chief problem of masculinizing surgery in hermaphrodites, however, is repair of the hypospadiac penis so that the boy can stand to urinate. In most cases it is not feasible to do the plastic construction of a urethral tube in the penis until the boy is 5 or 6. It may be desirable to wait even longer, until the organ has grown larger so that a better result can be obtained. The first step in plastic repair of the penis is to free the organ of the fibrous tissue that binds it down and prevents it from hanging freely. This stage of surgery can be done in earliest infancy. Around school age more than one operation may be needed, depending on the size of the opening to be closed underneath the penis, before the urethra is constructed. Follow-up admissions may be needed if small fistulas break open, as they sometimes do.

Artificial testes, made of silicone plastic, can be implanted in the empty scrotum of boys who have no testes of their own. This piece of surgical cosmetics corrects a boy's self-perceived image of his own body, as well as the image other people see. This correction gives an immense boost in morale to teen-age boys who, otherwise subject to ridicule whenever they go swimming or shower in public places, may become social isolates. In marriage, normality of appearance and feel are a satisfaction to both husband and wife. Implanted at puberty, when the scrotum is of good size, artificial testes can be left permanently in place.

IV: Hormonal Management

In the period of infancy and childhood, active hormonal intervention is required in only one variety of hermaphroditism, namely, the female hyperadrenocortical. The hormonal problem in these cases is to suppress adrenal androgen output and, for those living as girls and women, to keep it suppressed by cortisone therapy. In some cases it is also necessary to substitute for a deficiency in salt-retaining hormone. The proper hormonal regulation of hyperadrenocortical patients with cortisone requires the technical skill of an expert who is keeping up to date with the constantly changing advances in this new treatment, which originated only in 1950. It is common for patients to be undertreated. Hardly ever does one hear of examples of overtreatment. Cortisone dosage needs to be increased as growth proceeds from infancy to adulthood. A typical oral daily dose of cortisone for a young infant is 25 mg., and for an adult 37.5 or 50 mg. Individual dosage is calibrated on the basis of routine urinary 17-ketosteroid determinations, bone-age changes, and over-all clinical evaluation.

When the body is subject to stress, such as is induced by surgery, injury, or infections and common ailments accompanied by fever, it needs extra cortisone. Ordinarily, the adrenal gland makes extra cortisone itself. In cortisone-deficient patients, however, the extra cortisone must be given as pills or shots. Parents of adrenal hermaphrodites should know that, when the child develops a fever, the cortisone dosage may be safely doubled until the fever subsides. In an emergency, this knowledge can mean the difference between life and death.

Hyperadrenocortical hermaphrodites do not need estrogenic treatment at puberty, since cortisone regulation of adrenal function enables the ovaries to produce female hormone in the normal manner. Infants regulated on cortisone since birth enter puberty at the usual age. Children whose statural growth and bone age galloped ahead before cortisone regulation was established, however, are likely to enter a normal puberty earlier than usual, perhaps even as young as 8 or 9. Properly handled psychologically, this early sexual maturity can be negotiated smoothly and without untoward incident. Physical sexual precocity is not accompanied automatically by emotional and behavioral precocity. These children do not become sexually wild.

Hyperadrenocortical hermaphrodites living as boys are encountered more and more rarely in this era of cortisone treatment. During childhood, their statural growth and precocious virilism can be held in check by cortisone. There is no danger of feminization if the gonads have been removed. These boys virilize at the regular age of puberty if cortisone therapy is augmented with testosterone.

Hyperadrenocortical hermaphroditism is the only variety in which the problem of precocious sexual maturation arises. In all other varieties of hermaphroditism, the problem of hormonal management does not arise until the usual age of puberty. The decision then lies between treatment with estrogen or androgen, to feminize or masculinize, respectively, dependent on the sex of assignment and the gender role established.

Hormonal substitution treatment will in some cases have been preceded by the surgical removal of contradictory gonadal tissue to avoid the possibility of an incongruous puberty. The notable exception to the rule applies to the syndrome of testicular feminization, for the body responses only to the estrogen made by these testes.

Hormonal substitution treatment will be necessary in other cases where the gonads, neither structurally nor functionally contradictory of the assigned sex, do not need to be removed. The necessity for treatment is dictated by defective gonadal function and an insufficiency of gonadal hormone. It so happens that among hermaphrodites it is always testicular function that is defective in this way, ovarian tissue never being so involved except possibly in a rare case of true hermaphroditism. A large proportion of male hermaphrodites living as boys will, therefore, need androgen therapy in order to virilize at puberty. Even so, some will fail.

Hormonal substitution therapy is necessary in cases of congenital gonadal absence (gonadal aplasia). Patients with this condition always live as girls, their only incongruity being the sex-chromatin pattern. They need estrogen therapy in order to mature at puberty. Since they have a uterus, menstruation can be induced by the usual method of simulating nature, namely, cyclic withdrawal of estrogen for one week in every four. Cyclic therapy also effectively induces menstruation in male hermaphroditism, following gonadectomy, if a uterus is present. Menstruation is so strong and valued a symbol of femininity that a girl does not want to be denied the experience if it is biologically possible for her to have it. Even later in life the symbol retains its strength so that very few patients elect against cyclic therapy and in favor of the convenience of no periods.

Psychic Hermaphroditism

There is no standard definition for the term "psychic hermaphroditism." Although its use is questionable, it is used from time to time as a synonym for homosexuality, transvestism, or contrasexism, the compulsion to have the body surgically and hormonally transformed to that of the other sex. The idea is that in these three allied conditions the patient is psychologically of one sex and morphologically of the other, and so is a hermaphrodite. Hermaphroditism, being traditionally a physical condition, the term psychic hermaphoditism implies a physical or constitutional basis for the discrepancy between sexual psychology and morphology. Theoretically and morally, the three disorders become more respectable, to some people, as a result of this implied physical etiology.

In point of fact, there is little or no scientific evidence that so-called psychic hermaphroditism is, causally speaking, in the same category as morphologic hermaphroditism. Homosexuals, transvestites, and contrasexists have typically been found to have no physical anomalies or stigmas that differentiate them from other men, or women, as the case may be. Their sex-chromatin pattern agrees with their genital morphology, and so does their hormonal function. Hormone levels are neither deficient nor incongruous. No amount of hormone medication will change the direction of erotic inclination, even though estrogen will feminize the male body and androgen will virilize the female

body. Androgen may increase erotic desire or leave it unchanged, in either sex, and estrogen may functionally castrate the testes, but in either case masculinity or femininity of sexual desire is left unchanged.

There is a good chance that the phenomena grouped together as psychic hermaphroditism can be explained as imprinting phenomena. Among morphologic hermaphrodites it is known that gender role, including erotic orientation, can be established independently of chromosomes, gonads, hormones, and genital structures, and in direct contradiction of these physical variables. It is perfectly possible, therefore, that a gender role and orientation can be established contradictory of the other sex variables in morphologically normal males and females. In such cases the imprinting is a misprinting, so to speak. Why this misprinting takes place cannot at present be adequately explained. It probably relates to imprecise and incomplete perception and learning, to misconstrued deductions about sex, and to faulty identification with, and impersonation of, the parent of the other sex—all of this dating from infancy and early childhood when gender imprints are laid down and become almost ineradicable.

Forensic Considerations

In modern society hermaphrodites are not the subject of special legislation. Nor are they subject to harsh legal discrimination or imposition. In fact, expositions of jurisprudence have singularly little to say about hermaphroditism. It is mentioned in common law only in very specific contexts. Thus, according to Lord Coke in the sixteenth century, a hermaphrodite may by the common law of England "be either male or female, and it shall succeed according to the kind of sex which doth prevail." Succession to a hereditary title is today the only occasion in which dispute as to the prevailing sex may arise. Hermaphroditism is also recognized by English common law as sufficient cause for annulment of a marriage contract.

In the United States a hermaphrodite may make a formal change of sex and may, with medical evidence, have his birth certificate changed as a matter of routine. A hermaphroditic marriage may be annulled on grounds of sterility, if the spouse was not previously informed. Hermaphroditism has not been, and probably will never need to be, the subject of test cases brought before federal or state courts for judicial decision.

References

Barr, Murray L., "Cytologic Tests of Chromosomal Sex." *Progr. in Gynec. 3;* 131-141, 1957.

Childs, B., Grumbach, M. M., and Van Wyk, J. J., "Virilizing Adrenal Hyperplasia; a Genetic and Hormonal Study." *J. Clin. Investigation 35;* 213-222, 1956.

Ellis, Albert, "The Sexual Psychology of Human Hermaphrodites." *Psychosom. Med. 7;* 108-125, 1945.

Ferguson-Smith, M. A., "Cytogenetics in Man." *Arch. Internal Med. 105;* 627-639, 1960.

Finesinger, Jacob E., Meigs, Joe V., and Sulkowitch, Hirsh W., "Clinical Psychiatric and Psychoanalytic Study of a Case of Male Pseudohermaphroditism." *Am. J. Obst. & Gynec. 44;* 310-317, 1942.

Hampson, Joan G., and Money, John, "Idiopathic Sexual Precocity in the Female." *Psychosom. Med. 17;* 16-35, 1955.

Jones, Howard W., Jr., and Scott, William Wallace, *Hermaphroditism, Genital Anomalies and Related Endocrine Disorders.* Baltimore: The Williams and Wilkins Co., 1958.

Jost, Alfred, "Problems of Fetal Endocrinology: The Gonadal and Hypophyseal Hormones." *Rec. Progr. in Hormone Res. 8;* 379-418, 1953.

Money, John, *Hermaphroditism: An Inquiry into the Nature of a Human Paradox.* Unpublished doctoral thesis, Harvard University Library, 1952.

Money, John, *The Psychologic Study of Man.* Springfield, Ill.: Charles C Thomas, 1957.

Money, John, Hampson, Joan G., and Hampson, John L., "An Examination of Some Basic Sexual Concepts: The Evidence of Human Hermaphroditism." *Bull. Johns Hopkins Hosp. 97;* 301-319, 1955.

Money, John, Hampson, Joan G., and Hampson, John L., "Hermaphroditism: Recommendations Concerning Assignment of Sex, Change of Sex and Psychologic Management." *Bull. Johns Hopkins Hosp. 97;* 284-300, 1955.

Money, John, Hampson, Joan G., and Hampson, John L., "Imprinting and the Establishment of Gender Role." *Arch. Neurol. & Psychiat. 77;* 333-336, 1957.

Money, John, Hampson, Joan G., and Hampson, John L., "Sexual Incongruities and Psychopathology: The Evidence of Human Hermaphroditism." *Bull. Johns Hopkins Hosp. 98;* 43-57, 1956.

Morris, J. McL., "The Syndrome of Testicular Feminization in Male Pseudohermaphrodites." *Am. J. Obst. & Gynec. 65;* 1192-1211, 1953.

von Neugebauer, Franz Ludwig, *Hermaphroditismus beim Menschen.* Leipzig: Klinkhardt, 1908.

Schiller, C. H. (ed.), *Instinctive Behavior.* New York: International Universities Press, 1957.

Stewart, John S. S., Ferguson-Smith, M. A., Lennox, Bernard, and Mack, W. S., "Klinefelter's Syndrome: Genetic Studies." *Lancet* pp. 117-121, July 19, 1958.

Wilkins, Lawson, *The Diagnosis and Treatment of Endocrine Disorders in Childhood and Adolescence* (ed. 3). Springfield, Ill.: Charles C. Thomas, 1965.

Witschi, E., Nelson, W. O., and Segal, S. J., "Genetic, Developmental and Hormonal Aspects of Gonadal Dysgenesis and Sex Inversion in Man." *J. Clin. Endocrinol. 17;* 737-753, 1957.

Young, Hugh H., *Genital Abnormalities, Hermaphroditism and Related Adrenal Diseases.* Baltimore: The Williams and Wilkins Co., 1937.

Young, William C. (ed.), *Sex and Internal Secretions* (3rd ed.). Baltimore: The Williams and Wilkins Co., in press. (See chapters by Burns, Jost, Guhl, Young, Money, and Hampson and Hampson.)

JOHN MONEY

Homosexuality

Definition of Terms

THERE is little doubt that homosexuality is today the most discussed and possibly the most widespread of the deviant forms of human sexual behavior. The word *homosexuality* is applied both to the practice of engaging in a sexual act in which both persons are of the same sex, and to the psychological arousal that motivates a person to desire such act. It is used when the act is participated in by two women or by two men. A few laymen have misunderstood the term to cover oral-genital relations and other noncoital acts between a man and a woman, but such acts do not constitute homosexuality.

The word *homosexual* is both a substantive (i.e., a person is called *a homosexual*) and an adjective (as a *homosexual novel*). As the former, it is applied quite indiscriminately to a man or to a woman, whether the desires and activities are oriented exclusively toward the same sex, or toward both the same and the other sex. In the latter case, the word *homosexual* should not be used. The term *bisexual* has come into common use and will probably remain, despite some confusion with hermaphroditism (a completely different phenomenon) and some efforts to change the word to *ambisexual*.

A few other words and terms are found in the scientific and lay literature, as well as among homosexuals themselves. *Inversion* or *sexual inversion* (the corresponding substantive is *invert*) was at one time preferred by homosexuals and their friends. It was used by Havelock Ellis, and carried an implication of sympathy and friendliness in contrast to the implied hostility in the words *perversion* and *pervert*. Today, the words *inversion* and *invert* are seldom encountered, although a few writers reserve them for a special use: for them, an *invert* is an individual who desires or seeks homosexual relations and at the same time tries to adopt the complete sex role of a member of the other sex.

Lesbianism and *Lesbian* are more widely used words; they denote rather exact descriptions, being synonymous with female homosexuality and the female homosexual, respectively, and they seem to be unique in that they carry a minimum of stigma and are equally acceptable in heterosexual and homosexual circles and in both the professional and lay press. No correspondingly descriptive words, carrying so little implied hostility, seem to be available for the male homosexual.

The slang of almost all languages has developed a rich vocabulary around homosexuality, including terms used by heterosexuals (usually with considerable scorn and ridicule) and by homosexuals (usually rather euphemistically). In the former group, the words are sometimes borrowed from a foreign language or describe the phenomenon as foreign, e.g., *bugger* (from Bulgar), *French* love, *Greek* love, etc. The slang of the English language has such terms as *fairy, pansy, queen,* and *queer*, and it is interesting that these words are difficult to use in their traditional context in ordinary language (particularly *queer*) without bringing homosexuality to mind. Several of these words (as *queen*) are more frequently used to describe the effeminate male homosexual, rather than any male homosexual, but this distinction is by no means universal.

Among homosexuals, the word *gay* is most widely encountered (*he is gay*, or *he goes to a gay bar*), and is applied both to males and females. Despite the extraordinarily frequent usage within homosexual circles, however, this meaning of *gay* is still unknown to millions of adult Americans.

The female homosexual has been called a *dike* or a *butch*, with the latter term reserved for those who display considerable outward manifestations of masculinity. Homosexuals sometimes refer to heterosexuals as *straight*; and to the outward display of obvious homosexuality, particularly when a person flaunts the manifestations of the other sex, as *camping*. A person who practices camping is called a *camp*.

Historical Background

Homosexuality seems to have been known almost from the dawn of civilization. There is an abundance of references in Greek and Roman literature (Petronius, Plato, Virgil, etc.), but it was not until the latter part of the nineteenth century that an effort was made to bring the subject into open discussion. This effort took two main forms. On the one hand, some homosexuals began to speak up on behalf of themselves and their group, while at the same time serious scientific workers wrote several volumes and papers that were devoted, in whole or in part, to the subject. Whitman in America sang in only slightly ambiguous terms of comrades in love and bodies bound together in comradely passion, but took occasion, when pressed for a direct answer to an embarrassing question, to deny the homosexual content of his poetry.

In Germany, Ulrichs wrote a series of pamphlets, under a pseudonym, openly espousing and defending homosexuality. (He called it *Uranism*, and the homosexual an *Urning*, but all efforts to popularize and perpetuate these terms have failed). Ulrichs identified himself with the practice and maintained that the condition was inborn and therefore natural to those who were involved with it. Early European writers on sex (Forel, 1906; Krafft-Ebing, 1922) wrote comments on homosexuality that are still referred to today, although their concepts are

of doubtful current value. In England, Symonds wrote two studies on the subject; Havelock Ellis devoted one large section of his monumental *Studies in the Psychology of Sex* (1936) to it, calling the volume *Sexual Inversion;* Westermarck summarized attitudes and practices among primitive peoples in a section of *The Origin and Development of Moral Ideas;* and Edward Carpenter wrote many books, all adding up to a glorification of homosexual love.

Freud devoted considerable attention to homosexuality, particularly in *Leonardo*, *Three Contributions*, and elsewhere; following Freud, there were almost countless books and articles that reflected his influence to a greater or lesser degree.

During the early years of the twentieth century, considerable propaganda and scholarly studies were published in Germany, largely under the influence of Hirschfeld. The movement to change legal restrictions against and negative public attitudes toward homosexuality gained wide support among German intellectuals.

Among the defenders of homosexuality, particularly in England during the first two decades of this century, Edward Carpenter was a unique figure. As a young man he had met Walt Whitman and was largely under his influence; or perhaps he exercised an influence over the older poet. In a series of books, lectures, pamphlets, and in an organization in which he played a dominant role, Carpenter glorified homosexuality as the truest, firmest, finest, highest form of love. He adapted his concepts of homosexuality to fit into the puritanism of mid-Victorian morality, contending that the bonds of friendship between two males were more profound and faithful and meaningful than could exist under ordinary circumstances between man and woman, and that the physical gratification was secondary, incidental, and (under the most ideal conditions) entirely absent!

Theory of Inborn Homosexuality

Among the pre-Freudian writers there was a general tendency to accept the concept of inborn or congenital homosexuality, although the condition was not believed to be hereditary. Some people described homosexuals in vague terms as constituting a third or intermediate sex, standing somewhere between the complete male and the complete female, and having a mind (or rather, a psychosexual orientation) of one sex in a body of the other. To substantiate this viewpoint, which was shared by Havelock Ellis among others, the early writers cited cases in which people recalled their homosexual yearnings as having occurred at an unusually young age, perhaps at 4 or 5. They further noted the "obvious" inborn physical characteristics of the female that many male homosexuals had.

Hirschfeld and his co-workers, as well as other groups, undertook anatomical measurements of homosexuals in an effort to amass data that would prove the concept of the physiological differences, and thus make out a prima-facie case for inborn homosexuality. (Incidentally, although the present writer does not believe that there are physiological or anatomical differences between homosexuals and heterosexuals, he does believe that, even if there were such differences, they would not in and of themselves be proof of inborn homosexuality, as there are other possible explanations of such alleged divergences.)

The belief in inborn homosexuality, with physical differences (perhaps endocrinological, the adherents postulate) was not completely and unequivocally rejected by Freud, although it would seem to go counter to the entire body of psychoanalytic thought. However, it was repudiated by most of the neo-Freudians (such as Stekel, Adler, and Ferenczi). It is a viewpoint that continues to have adherents among some specialists to this day, but it has been challenged by Allen, A. Ellis, Harper, Cory, Henry, and others who contend that not even the slightest bit of factual evidence has yet been presented to support the belief in inborn or congenital homosexuality.

In order to accommodate their theories to observations of widespread simultaneous homosexual and heterosexual activity (or, as this is now called, bisexuality), and to help combat the general atmosphere of hostility toward homosexuals, many early writers denounced bisexuals as depraved individuals who were seeking lustful pleasures but who were not true inverts, while they defended the latter as living the natural life into which they had been born.

Theories of Genesis

Theories on the psychological genesis of homosexuality are numerous. Freud was one of the first to focus attention on the infantile sexual life of the individual as leading to a distortion of development in a homosexual direction. His theories centered particularly around the relationship of the child to the parents (usually the parent of the other sex). Homosexuality was frequently, according to Freud, a flight from incest, with the child developing strong incestuous desires (Oedipus or Electra complex) toward the parent of the other sex because of overabundance of affection, lack of one parent, identification with one parent, etc. In oversimplified terms, the dynamism of such a development might, according to Freud, follow one of the following paths:

1. In the complete absence of a father, or in the presence of a weak father, or perhaps an alcoholic father who spews forth hatred against the mother, the boy-child falls in love with his mother and seeks to become her lover. In panic-like flight from the specter of incest, he represses this desire most effectively by suppressing entirely his sexual feelings toward all women. With the first strong awakening of sexuality, the path toward women is blocked, and the attraction is diverted toward the other segment of humanity, the males. Freud explained the strong antipathy and overwhelming fear of incest in so young a child by his theory of racial memory, but modern adherents of the Oedipal concept would contend that the child is repulsed, consciously and unconsciously, by the mother, and is made to feel the evil and sin of his desires.

2. In other instances, according to Freud, almost opposite circumstances would lead to homosexuality. The child falls in love *with the parent of the same sex,* and replaces and attempts to oust the parent of the other sex. The boy, suppressing his desires for his father, seeks to be like the woman accepting this father, but

unable to accept the incestuous sin of father-love, seeks the father in other males. Such a boy might be effeminate, might play the femalelike role in the sex act, and would be expected to be attracted to older men. However, the almost universal attraction of homosexuals toward youths might seem to be an argument against this theory.

Some writers have contended that homosexuality is an arrest or fixation of emotional development. They believe that young people go through cycles, and that in adolescence homosexual attraction is a passing phase. For some reason (possibly indoctrination into homosexual practices), some youths do not continue their emotional development and maturation, and remain fixated at this adolescent or homosexual stage. Modern thinkers, skeptical of the theory of cycles, would not entirely reject such a development, but would restate it in terms of a polymorphous pansexuality during the puberty and adolescent years that may find fuller or easier roads to gratification with others of the same sex, and may make an unconscious adjustment to this easier path by the suppression of the needs for heterosexual relations.

A. Ellis, Harper, and a few others have emphasized antisexual puritanism in the home as making a major contribution to homosexual development. A boy develops a repugnance toward and fear of sexuality, which he has been told is vile, dirty, sinful, and a defilement of the purity of womanhood. As awakening sexual drives imperiously demand fulfillment, this boy's feelings are diverted into a channel that can accommodate the puritanism; woman remains pure and *untouchable,* and his own dirty feelings are gratified with other vile males.

This writer has noted the same phenomenon in a home in which the morals have been quite the opposite. A young boy observed his mother in frequent consortment with numerous male lovers; he developed shame over her activities, and a resentment toward all male-female relationships. Sex was a horrid thing for this youthful Puritan, but his desires could be channeled into the currents of homosexuality without interfering with his basic antisexuality.

Numerous other case histories can demonstrate a variety of backgrounds leading to homosexuality. These include fear of the consequences of sex (pregnancy, venereal disease, responsibility of children, etc.), fear of inadequacy (Adler) and of inability to play the role of the male (or female) successfully, and a relinquishment of the struggle.

Probably an eclectic and pluralistic approach would be closest to the truth. If one excludes inborn homosexuality and constitutional predisposition, one may find the fear of inadequacy, flight from incest, overidentification with one parent, misconceptions about sex, search for a method of gratification during adolescence (ease of finding the homosexual approach, with an effort to adjust to this gratification), and antisexual puritanism, with many other contributing factors, all present to a greater or lesser degree in certain individuals, with some factors present in many cases, and others in only a few cases. Probably no single factor alone is present in all instances, and possibly no single factor is exclusively responsible in one individual; but, to a greater or lesser extent, many of the causes outlined above are found, as a thread of continuity, in most instances of exclusive or overwhelming homosexual development.

Effeminate Male and Masculine Female Homosexuals

The homosexual who has developed strong characteristics and manifestations of the other sex is probably in a minority among homosexuals, although the writer, from personal observations, believes that some at least minor signs of effeminacy can be found in almost all male homosexuals. No serious study of the effeminate male has ever been published. Based exclusively on personal observation, the writer believes that effeminized males have no measurable physical characteristics different from those of other homosexuals or of heterosexuals. They have normal beard growths, male pattern of baldness in later years, lack of female bust development, and height and weight distributions that fall within the limits of the statistical norm for the entire male population.

The effeminacy is found in the use of the voice, facial gestures, walk, gait, manner of wearing the hair, and other characteristics, all easy to control, manifested on a conscious or unconscious level when the psychological desire to be effeminate, or to relinquish one's identity as a male, is present.

Some of these people adopt the dress of the other sex (transvestism) and live as a member of the "adopted" sex, even getting married. It has been claimed that many transvestites are not homosexuals; this is difficult to believe, although men in our society may fear transvestism less than they fear homosexuality, and may therefore engage in transvestite practices when they really would unconsciously prefer to be homosexual.

Although the effeminate homosexual has many severe psychological problems (desire to renounce his sex, desire to be punished and ridiculed by the world, etc.), he is often free from any severe problem of concealment, which constitutes one of the greatest hardships on other homosexuals.

Physical Practices

Little has so far been written on the nature of physical homosexual practices. A few isolated passages appear here and there (sometimes in Latin), but Cory (1951) has made one of the few efforts to describe, classify, and explain the nature of these practices and the reasons they are indulged in by different individuals. Most common in male-male relationships are fellation, anal intercourse, mutual masturbation (petting and fondling), single masturbation of one person by another, and interfemoral relations. It is probably significant that some homosexuals show an extremely strong preference for some of these activities; perhaps such preferences may be correlated with the extent of identification with the other sex, the search for pain and humiliation, and the meaning of homosexuality to the particular person. Inasmuch as Kinsey interviewers have gathered data on this subject, it is likely that their forthcoming book, devoted entirely to homosexuality, will reveal information on this potentially important phase of the subject.

Whatever form the physical expression may take, the sexual act is more likely to be frustrating for homosexuals, even for those who reach a climax, than a heterosexual act is for hetero-sexuals. This is because of physical obstacles to a satisfactory relationship (the lack of a biologically complementing fit) and because for many of these people homosexuality is not a search for but a flight from something unknown, something that holds them in constant terror and fear. Their imperious desires for male-male relationships are actually vicarious and substitutive diversions from other desires, and therefore leave unanswered and unresolved the basic needs of the individual. It is for this reason that the astonishingly frequent partner-changing and the short-lived character of homosexual relations must be viewed not as healthy varietism and freedom from puritanical codes of artificial fidelity, but as a revolt against the partner with whom sex has been consummated and as an unending search for an ideal and unobtainable total gratification.

Incidence

The controversial question of the incidence of homosexuality among various peoples, in different countries, at different times, and under a myriad of conditions is obscured, first, by concealment of life histories and the general difficulty of obtaining information from those involved; second, by the problem of classifying those who are completely homosexual, mainly so, partly so, as well as those who may change their pattern from one stage of life to another; and third, by the difficulties that face any student of the demographic distribution of psychological, and particularly of psychosexual, disorders.

Up to the time of Kinsey (1948), the incidence of homosexuality was arrived at by guess and by observations, the latter being made by physicians, police officers, and homosexuals. Some suggested that about one person per thousand was involved in a homosexual life (whether physical practices, desires, or both), while others found the figure as high as five persons per hundred. Many writers ventured to suggest that the females outnumbered the males, while others believed the opposite to be true.

Utilizing his now famous rating scale, in which a person was classified in a group identified by a whole number from 0 to 6 (the former being the completely and exclusively heterosexual, and the latter being the extreme on the homosexual side of the scale, with groups 1 to 5 taking care of the various points on a human continuum), Kinsey found male homosexuality among the white American population to be extremely widespread, and female homosexuality much less so. A few statistics from his findings are as follows: 4 per cent of white males are exclusively homosexual throughout their lives, after the onset of adolescence; 8 per cent are exclusively homosexual for at least three years between the ages of 16 and 55; 10 per cent are more or less exclusively homosexual for such a three-year period; 13 per cent are more homosexual than heterosexual for this three-year period; between 2 and 6 per cent of the unmarried females and less than 1 per cent of the married females in the Kinsey sample were more or less exclusively homosexual between the ages of 20 and 35.

Although the accuracy of the Kinsey studies has been challenged by some, it is generally conceded that Kinsey demonstrated, and all available evidence supports this conclusion, that male homosexuality of an exclusive or an almost exclusive character involves several million white Americans, and probably not a lesser percentage of the American Negro population and of the population of other ethnic groups in most civilized countries of the world. If this is the case, and if homosexuality is a pathological condition, then it is one of the most common psychological disorders known. It is an illness involving more people than heart conditions or cancer, warping the lives of literally millions who are expending great amounts of energy in their efforts to understand themselves, adjust to their guilt, conceal their activities, find gratification, and resolve the many paradoxes and contradictions inherent in their situation.

Lesbianism

Although Lesbian relations, or sex affairs between two women, have been given a great deal of attention in modern literature, such relations are actually much less common than male homosexuality. According to the Kinsey findings, female homosexual behavior is ap-

proximately one-third as prevalent as male, and this is true for both exclusive and partial homosexuality.

An interesting and valuable question to investigate is: Why are females less often homosexual than males? Both the origin of homosexualism and possibilities of preventing its development may well be significantly revealed as we attempt to answer this question. From many years of studying the literature on the subject as well as from employing my personal observations, I would say that some of the main factors contributing to a lesser incidence of female than male sexuality are the following:

1. Male sexual demands, particularly during puberty and adolescence, are often so imperious that they require a search for outlet, almost any outlet; while female sexual demands are usually less imperious and may more easily be suppressed or repressed. Once the male does give in to homosexual behavior during adolescence, he frequently accommodates himself psychologically to this form of outlet and foregoes or suppresses his heterosexual tendencies.

2. Any females who are highly sexed and who do desire frequent outlets can more easily find them with males than can highly sexed males find fulfillment with females in our society. Actually, we make it easier for the young male to enter sex activity with other males than with females; and male homosexuality thus becomes temporarily a road of least resistance. Ironically enough, this easier path may later become the harder one, because of the persecution of homosexuality in our communities. But at the time when the path is first taken it is, or at least seems, an easier one to take.

3. Females who, for neurotic reasons, seek to suppress their heterosexual drives, and especially those who have fears or hatred of males, often develop into frigid or so-called sexless women. Males who are equally afraid of or hostile to heterosexual relations rarely, for biological and social reasons, retreat into asexuality, but instead turn to homosexuality.

In spite of the fact that there are considerably fewer Lesbians than homosexual males, female homosexuality is not uncommon. Some of its main causes are: (a) a strong love for the father and hence identification with a male figure (as indicated in the famous novel, *The Well of Loneliness*); (b) a distinct jealousy by the female of the male's more favored role in our society; (c) a sexual maleducation that teaches females that men are dirty and untouchable and that glorifies women as being more "pure"; (d) intense love for a mother and distaste for a weak or brutal father and consequent assumption of the male role by the daughter, who symbolically becomes her mother's husband.

Lesbianism is not condemned as severely by the heterosexual public as is male homosexuality. This is partly because the female homosexual seldom adopts the extreme mannerisms of members of the other sex, and when she does so her mannerisms may be acceptable as a manifestation of the strong, athletic, career-type woman. This manifestation of other-sex characteristics by male homosexuals—who are often called "fairies" or "pansies"—is one of the main causes of antihomosexualism among heterosexual individuals.

The Lesbian, moreover, often lives a more discreet kind of life than the male homosexual; and often even finds it possible to be heterosexually married and to accept, with some degree of frigidity, sex relations with her husband. Lesbians, again, more frequently than homosexual males form long-lasting and quite "monogamous" attachments with other women. Their sexual life tends to be accompanied by more affection, less promiscuity and varietism, than are the lives of male homosexuals. In this respect, ironically enough, the Lesbian acts in accordance with the biological and cultural factors that make her a woman and the male homosexual acts in accordance with the factors that make him a man. Biology and culture eventually will out—even in those who show extreme sex deviation.

Male and female homosexuals show considerable mutual antagonism (filled as they are with fears and hatred of the other sex), but they are sometimes friendly with one another and on occasion have been able to get together in homosexual groups, such as the Mattachine Society, which include members of both sexes. So far, however, such homosexual groups have included few Lesbians and have mainly consisted of male homosexuals.

Disturbances

The homosexual is beset by many problems. In recent years it has been thought that these problems are exclusively and entirely created by the hostility of society. It is claimed that guilt is thrust upon the individual, he is compelled to feel ashamed, compelled to conceal his true identity, made to seek gratification and fulfillment in out-of-the-way and often distressing places. If he openly expresses his predilections for homosexuality, it is because he is so disturbed that he is seeking further conflict with society and further punishment, scorn, and ridicule from fellow men. If he seeks to conceal his desires, he must balance this concealment and even pretended hostility with a belief in the propriety of his own interests and activities. The paranoia that may be involved in the development of the individual becomes fortified by the realities of persecution and the fear of being discovered, with the concomitant feelings of shame and ruination.

The fears under which the homosexual lives can hardly be overemphasized, and the anxieties that are created by the social organism are probably beyond exaggeration. However, in this writer's opinion this does not negate nor does it explain the anxieties and disturbances inherent in the psychosexual development of the homophile and in his flight from heterosexuality. Briefly summarized, the homosexual is definitely emotionally disturbed, suffering from fear of the other sex, puritanical distortions about sexuality, self-abnegation, feelings of inadequacy, self-destructive drives, and compulsive desires.

These neurotic traits, although not originally produced by society's persecution of the homosexual, become all the more anxiety-producing because of the circumstances under which they are lived out. For example, the compulsivity toward gratification leads to relationships of a difficult and self-destructive nature. The puritanism leads to enhanced guilt because of the nature of the experience, and the greater guilt leads to further search for humiliation, self-contempt, and self-destruction. The unfortunate and unhappy experiences that are unconsciously sought further convince the homosexual that he is a victim of fate, a persecuted and damned individual, thus supporting with some reality his phantasies of paranoia.

Adjustments and Therapy

The general trend among those who do not denounce the homosexual as a sinner has been to close the door on therapy. No less an authority than Freud felt that homosexuality was beyond man's power to change, and that homosexuals should learn to live with themselves and to adjust to the realities of their surrounding (hostile) culture. Freud's famous letter to an American mother no doubt had a great effect in retarding the development of an effective mode of therapy for homosexuals.

The present writer, following Freud and being under certain misapprehensions, misunderstandings, and limited experience, formerly urged but no longer espouses an orientation toward adjustment within the framework of homosexuality, rather than an expenditure of energy in the effort to effectuate a change. This preference for adjustment seems to have been mistakenly chosen by many modern therapists (particularly Freudians, such as Dollard), and is also espoused, for entirely different reasons, by most homosexuals. It is quite natural that homosexuals, searching for an alleviation of the great stigma that attaches to their lives, would wish to convince themselves and the public that therapy is impossible, or almost so. Their belief is that if it were widely felt that homosexuals could be cured if only they would try to be, the hostility of the public would be aggravated, for it would be directed against those homosexuals who, in effect, chose to remain in their condemned mode of life. Whether this thinking has validity is itself open to question, but essentially it is irrelevant in a discussion of therapy.

The aim of therapy is to relieve the hostility toward and fear of relationships, sexual and other, with the other sex, rather than to seek to suppress the homosexual interests. The reasons for this are twofold: (1) to aid the homosexual to get at the root of the problem, and not to attack what is merely a symptom—his problem is not so much that he is attracted to males, but that he is in flight from females; and (2) to assure the homosexual that whatever pleasures and gratifications he is deriving from his present mode of life will not be removed, but if anything will be increased (because pleasures are enhanced without concomitant guilt), and to convince him that these gratifications are going to be complemented and supplemented by an entirely *new* field to be added to the old. That this new form of satisfaction will prove even superior, more gratifying, and more fulfilling does not have to be overemphasized at first, for it will only be looked at with skepticism that can be a cover-up for the fear that the therapist is really trying to wean the patient away from homosexuality. The patient himself, when the fears of the other sex have been removed, and when heterosexual relationships have been established, may realize, in a very successful therapy, that this new form of satisfaction makes the old one obsolete and unnecessary, although not sinful.

A successful therapeutic procedure, therefore, would leave the male patient interested in actively seeking gratification with females as well as still attracted to males—relieved of fear and anxiety in both relationships, but not substituting for his old fears a new set of shibboleths in which the male-male relationship is damned as dirty, vile, and disgusting.

If such an individual continues to obtain gratification from his own sex, he should do so without compulsivity, choosing conditions free from self-destruction; but, over a long period of time, his interests along such lines will probably diminish as he finds that the physical relationship with another male no longer answers the needs within himself.

Such a therapeutic procedure is undoubtedly very difficult, and it is unlikely that it is going to be followed by any large number of homosexuals. For these people, adjustment within the realm of homosexuality seems to be another course of action, likewise difficult, but not quite so difficult as the struggle to change their orientation. More liberal social attitudes should make such adjustments easier but cannot solve the basic inner contradictions inherent in the psyche of the exclusively oriented homosexual.

References

Allen, Clifford, *The Sexual Perversions and Abnormalities: A Study in the Psychology of Paraphilia.* London: Oxford University Press, 1949.

Berg, Charles, and Allen, Clifford, *The Problem of Homosexuality.* New York: Citadel Press, 1958.

Bergler, Edmund, *Homosexuality: Disease or Way of Life?* New York: Hill and Wang, 1956.

Brody, M. W., "An Analysis of the Psychosexual Development of a Female—with Special Reference to Homosexuality." *Psychoanalyt. Rev. 30;* 47-58, 1943.

Carpenter, Edward, *An Unknown People.* London, 1897.

Carpenter, Edward, *Ioläus, an Anthology of Friendship.* Boston: Charles Goodspeed, 1902.

Carpenter, Edward, *The Intermediate Sex.* London: Allen & Unwin, 1930 (reprinted in Cory, 1956).

Cory, Donald Webster, *The Homosexual in America: A Subjective Approach.* New York: Greenberg, 1951; (2nd ed., New York: Castle Books, 1960).

Cory, Donald Webster, "Homosexuality: Active and Passive." *J. Sex Educ. 5;* 19-22, 1952.

Cory, Donald Webster, *Homosexuality: A Cross Cultural Approach.* New York: Julian Press, Inc., 1956.

Ellis, Albert, "The Sexual Psychology of Human Hermaphrodites." *Psychosom. Med. 7;* 108-125, 1945.

Ellis, Albert, "On the Cure of Homosexuality." *Internat. J. Sexology 5;* 135-138, 1952.

Ellis, Albert, "Are Homosexuals Necessarily Neurotic?" *One 3;* No. 4, 8-12, 1955 (reprinted in Cory, 1956).

Ellis, Albert, "The Effectiveness of Psychotherapy with Individuals Who Have Severe Homosexual Problems." *J. Consult. Psychol. 20;* 191-195, 1956.

Ellis, Albert, "A Homosexual Treated with Rational Psychotherapy." *J. Clin. Psychol. 15;* 338-343, 1959.

Ellis, Havelock, *Studies in the Psychology of Sex* (Vol. II: *Sexual Inversion*). New York: Random House, 1936.

Forel, August, *The Sexual Question.* Brooklyn: Physicians and Surgeons Book Co., 1906.

Freud, Sigmund, *Collected Papers.* London: Hogarth, 1924-1950.

Freud, Sigmund, *The Basic Writings of Sigmund Freud.* New York: Modern Library, Inc., 1938.

Glass, S. J., Deuel, H. J., and Wright, C. A., "Sex Hormone Studies in Male Homosexuals." *Endocrinology 26;* 590-594, 1940.

Glass, S. J., and Johnson, R. H., "Limitations and Complications of Organotherapy in Male Homosexuality." *J. Clin. Endocrinol. 11;* 540-544, 1944.

Harper, Robert A., "Psychological Aspects of Homosexuality." Paper delivered at the meeting of the Society for the Scientific Study of Sex, New York, May 22, 1959.

Henry, G. W., *Sex Variants: A Study of Homosexual Patterns.* New York: Paul B. Hoeber, Inc., 1941.

Hirschfeld, Magnus, *Die Homosexualitäte des Mannes und des Weibes.* Berlin: Marcus, 1920.

Hirschfeld, Magnus, *Sexual Anomalies and Perversions: Physical and Psychological Development and Treatment.* London: Francis Aldor, 1944.

Hooker, Evelyn, "The Adjustment of the Male Overt Homosexual." *J. Proj. Tech. 21;* 18-31, 1957.

Kinsey, Alfred C., "Criteria for a Hormonal Explanation of the Homosexual." *J. Clin. Endocrinol. 1;* 424-428, 1941 (reprinted in Cory, 1956).

Kinsey, Alfred C. *et al., Sexual Behavior in the Human Male.* Philadelphia: W. B. Saunders Co., 1948.

Kinsey, Alfred C. *et al., Sexual Behavior in the Human Female.* Philadelphia: W. B. Saunders Co., 1953.

Krafft-Ebing, R., *Psychopathia Sexualis, with Especial Reference to the Antipathic Sexual Instinct.* Brooklyn: Physicians and Surgeons Book Co., 1922.

Mercer, J. D., *They Walk in Shadow.* New York: Comet Press Books, 1959.

Moll, A., *Perversions of the Sex Instinct: A Study of Sexual Inversion Based on Clinical Data and Official Documents.* New York: Julian Press, Inc., 1931.

Rosenzweig, S., and Hoskins, R. G., "A Note on the Ineffectualness of Sex-hormone Medication in a Case of Pronounced Homosexuality." *Psychosom. Med. 3;* 87-89, 1941.

Severinghaus, E. L., and Chornyak, J., "A Study of Homosexual Adult Males." *Psychosom. Med. 7;* 302-305, 1945.

Stekel, Wilhelm, *Bi-sexual Love; the Homosexual Neurosis.* Boston: R. G. Badger, 1922.

West, Donald J., *The Other Man: A Study of the Social, Legal, and Clinical Aspects of Homosexuality.* New York: Whiteside, Inc., Wm. Morrow & Co., 1955.

Westermarck, Edward, "Homosexual Love," from *The Origin and Development of Moral Ideas* (reprinted in Cory, 1956).

Westwood, Gordon, *Society and the Homosexual.* New York: E. P. Dutton & Co., 1953.

Wolfenden Report: *Report of the Committee on Homosexual Offences and Prostitution.* London: Her Majesty's Stationery Office, 1957 (reprinted in Berg and Allen).

DONALD WEBSTER CORY

Hormones, Sex

IN ORDER to elaborate upon the role of sex hormones in the physiology of reproduction and their effect upon sexual function, one must thoroughly understand the interrelationships existing between the glands of internal secretion—particularly those concerned with gonadal function.

Pituitary Gland

The pituitary gland, considered by many to be the dictator of the endocrine system, controls the function and activity of the majority of the dependent endocrine glands in the body, namely, the gonads, the adrenals, and the thyroid. The endocrine glands that are independent of pituitary control—the pancreas and the parathyroids—are beyond the realm of our discussion. However, it may be stated that the level of their secretory activity is dependent upon the relative blood levels of the substances that they control, that is, the level of calcium and phosphorus in the blood affects the rate of secretion of parathormone in much the same manner that insulin release from the pancreas occurs under the influence of hyperglycemia.

The control the pituitary gland has over the endocrine end organs it regulates is not absolute; actually, the gland is a kind of reciprocal homeostatic regulator in that its secretion is inhibited, in part, by the hormone of the end organ it has stimulated to secrete. In other words, the hormones produced by the dependent glands under the influence of pituitary secretion in turn control hypophyseal secretion by inhibition of the particular pituitary tropic hormone responsible for maintaining the functional activity of the end organ and the secretion of its active principle. (The interdepend-

ence between the pituitary gland and the end organs is diagrammatically depicted in Fig. 1.) Here the source of electrical energy, the battery, is akin to the pituitary gland. The battery transmits its electrical impulse (the tropic hormone) by way of the wire to the motor (or end organ).

By speeding up, the motor rotates the governor (homeostatic mechanism), raising the arms (hormone level) to such a degree that the electrical contact is broken. Stimulus from the battery source is thus interrupted until the arms (hormonal level) of the governor (homeostatic level) are depressed, permitting alignment of the electrical contact so that once more the battery (pituitary gland) stimulates the motor (end organ) to rotate, thereby reinitiating the cycle of events. This type of self-regulatory or "feed back" mechanism is necessary in order to prevent excessive production of the hormone produced by the end organs through continued secretion of the tropic hormones from the pituitary gland. Indeed the "feed back" principle is characteristic of most self-regulatory activities. Further discussion of the relationship between the pituitary gland and its dependent end organs will be concerned only with the gonadotropic hormones and their relationship to the function of the ovaries and testes.

Pituitary-Ovarian Interrelationships in the Female— Gonadotropic Hormones

The gonadotropic hormones controlling the secretion and function of the ovaries are three in number (Fig. 2). The primary hormone, responsible for initiating the cyclic sequence of

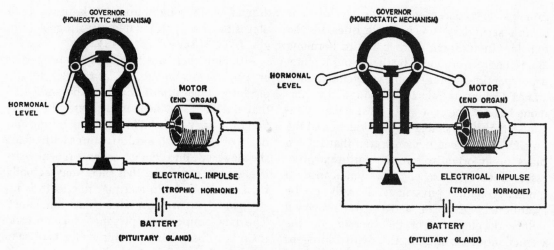

FIG. 1. Diagrammatic presentation of homeostatic mechanism for control of
pituitary hormone secretion

events, is the *follicle-stimulating hormone (FSH)*, which stimulates the ovaries to bring about follicular growth. The development of the primordial follicle to the initial stage prior to the development of the liquor folliculi, or beginning of the Graafian follicle, is, as Hisaw (1947) notes, not under pituitary control. FSH will cause an increase in the size and function of the Graafian follicle, resulting in increased estrogen elaboration.

When follicular growth approaches its pinnacle, a critical level of estrogen is secreted into the blood stream. Estrogen at this level has two effects upon the pituitary gonadotropic hormones. One is to inhibit further FSH hormone secretion and the other is to induce a release of the pituitary *luteinizing hormone (LH)*, whose primary role is to induce ovulation (Bradbury, 1946, Greep and Jones, 1950).

The release of luteinizing hormone may be caused either by a direct effect of estrogen on the pituitary gland itself or indirectly, by stimulation of the hypothalamus with secondary effect upon the pituitary. Donovan and Harris (1955) show that the area of the hypothalamus between the paraventricular and supraoptic nuclei is the one associated with release of LH. The release of the luteinizing hormone in the presence of a properly developed follicle and in the absence of any mechanical blockage in the ovary will result in ovulation.

After the egg has been ejected from the ovary, the wall of the follicle in which it had been contained collapses and this area is then converted into a corpus luteum by cellular hyperplasia of the theca interna cells. The corpus luteum, or yellow body, is made up of large polyhedral cells with pale eosinophilic cytoplasm containing lipid material. These cells are concerned with the secretion of progesterone and estrogen.

At this time, according to Astwood (1941), the third gonadotropic hormone takes over—the *luteotropic hormone*, which is closely related to or may be identical with the lactogenic hormone. The function of this hormone is to maintain the activity and integrity of the corpus luteum.

Progesterone and Estrogen

Progesterone, like estrogen, affects secretion of the gonadotropic hormones of the pituitary gland. This effect is primarily one of inhibition: progesterone inhibits further secretion of luteinizing hormone, thereby preventing supraovulation from taking place.

The sequential secretion of the three gonadotropic hormones occurs in orderly progression as a result of hypothalamic regulation due, in part, to the direct or indirect effect of the ovarian steroids on hypothalamic function, thereby affecting pituitary gonadotropic elaboration.

The steroid hormones produced by the ovaries—estrogen and progesterone—are the principal ones concerned with the development of the secondary sex characteristics in the female. (In addition, there is a third hormone almost entirely produced by the corpus luteum, a polypeptide, water-soluble, proteinlike substance known as relaxin. Although this hormone has not been shown to be specifically involved in the physiology of reproduction in the human, it has been demonstrated that relaxin plays an important role in the parturent processes of the guinea pig. Its significance in human gonadal physiology is still to be established.) Estrogen and progesterone will induce development of the breasts and the vaginal introitus, and together with androgens from the adrenal cortex, growth of pubic and axillary hair. They eventually stimulate the uterus to the extent that menstruation can occur.

Menstruation

Menstruation represents the desquamation or sloughing off of the endometrial lining of the uterus, occurring as a result of a diminution in estrogen and progesterone secretion. Menstruation may be due either to estrogen with-

drawal or to progesterone withdrawal in a uterus previously stimulated by estrogens (Engle, 1935; Hisaw, 1938, 1942).

Although there are no particular properties or physiological activities attributed to the products of menstruation, folklore has indicated that at the time a woman menstruates the secretion from her pores will bring about wilting and death of certain botanical structures with which she may come into contact. In more recent years it has been suggested that there may actually be a menstrual toxin and that this toxin is instrumental in bringing about such an effect. The data to support the presence of a menstrual toxin have been based upon the effects of such agents upon endometrial desquamation and the adverse effect they have upon plant life.

Initiation of menstruation in a young girl, the menarche, confers upon her the full endowment of womanhood in the sense that she is then theoretically capable of reproduction. However, this does not necessarily mean that the young girl has reached the peak of her femininity. Normally, menstruation begins between the ages of 10 and 14 years. Menarche prior to the age of 9 to 10 years is considered to be evidence of premature or precocious sexual

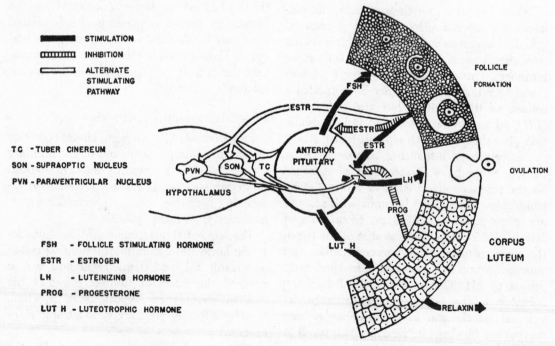

FIG. 2. Diagrammatic presentation of normal ovarian-hypothalamic-pituitary interrelationship

maturation, and menarche after the age of 14 to 15 years may be designated as a manifestation of delayed sexual development. Failure of menstruation to occur at all in the absence of organic pathology, pregnancy, or lactation is an indication of the lack of secretion of estrogen and/or progesterone by the ovaries. This may be due primarily to ovarian failure or secondarily to insufficiency of pituitary FSH secretion. Increased pituitary gonadotropic excretion in the urine may be noted in those individuals with primary ovarian failure inasmuch as the depressing effects the sex steroids would normally have upon gonadotropic hormone secretion or production are no longer present.

Menstruation continues until the climacteric, which in the majority of women occurs between 45 and 55 years of age. The ovary and not the pituitary gland is responsible for the initiation of the climacteric. The life span of the ovary with its production of ova is apparently thirty-thirty-five years, at the end of which time it is no longer capable of responding to pituitary-gonadotropin stimulation, resulting in organ refractoriness and atrophy. The processes through which the menarche is initiated and the climacteric occurs are not well understood. The ability of the ovaries to respond much before the time of the menarche and their failure to respond at the time of the climacteric are problems medical science has still to solve.

Female Libido

The cessation of menstruation does not necessarily represent the initial step in aging or deterioration of the female, and the sexual responsiveness of the female, which is usually initiated with, although it may precede, the menarche, does not cease with the climacteric. As a matter of fact, libido may actually be enhanced at the time of the climacteric in those women in whom a fear of pregnancy may have been responsible for their lack of enthusiasm for sexual contact. Although psychiatrists attest to the concept that libido is supratentorial in origin, endocrinologists feel that hormones play as important a role in establishing satisfactory sexual relationships and in maintaining an adequate libido as they do in any other organ system or systems in the body.

Women who have never known libido and who are frigid because of their social conditioning are candidates for psychiatric therapy and will usually never show an increase in sexual receptivity or in libido when appropriate sex steroid hormones are administered. On the other hand, women who have once experienced libido and have since lost it, and in whom frigidity prevails, or women in whom diminished libido is prevalent, may show an enhanced libidic response after appropriate sex hormone therapy.

Androgens and Libido

Paradoxically, as Kupperman (1951, 1959), Salmon (1941), and Greenblatt, Mortara, and Torpin (1942) have demonstrated, it is the male sex hormone that has been found to be most effective in enhancing libido in the female. The logic for the use of this steroid becomes apparent if we accept the premise that the center of eroticism in the female lies in the area of the clitoris. Since this organ with its rich nerve supply represents the phallic anlage in the female, its response to androgens would be anticipated. Evidence from many clinical reports and observations has established unequivocally the role of androgens in enhancing libido in the female. During the early days of pellet implantation of androgens for fibromyomatas of the uterus many patients treated volunteered the information that, despite the fact that therapy was being employed solely for menstrual aberrations, they had noticed an increase in libido. Similar responses were observed when methyltestosterone was employed for the treatment of dysmenorrhea or when androgens were given in large doses for the suppression or amelioration of neoplastic disease of the breasts. Many of these patients voluntarily offered the information that their libido had been increased even though the initial purpose for administering such steroids had nothing to do with increasing libido. The following therapeutic agents may be employed to enhance libido in the female:

1. *Oral*: Oral ingestion of *methyltestosterone*, 10 mg. twice a day for 15 days, followed by 10 mg. per day thereafter, may produce an adequate response. If this is achieved, the dose may be reduced to 5 mg. per day and eventually

to 5 mg. every other day. Subsequent discontinuation of the steroid will not result, in many patients, in cessation of the desired therapeutic effect observed soon after the initiation of the oral therapy.

2. *Parenteral:* Intramuscular administration of 50 mg. of *testosterone cyclopentylpropionate* or 100 mg. of *testosterone enanthate,* both as oil solution, or 50 mg. of *testosterone phenylacetate* as an aqueous suspension, every 18 to 21 days may also be effective in enhancing libido in properly selected patients.

3. *Topical:* It has been said that topical application to the clitoris of an ointment containing 10 mg. of *testosterone* per gram of vanishing-cream base is effective in increasing libido. Although a potential androgenic effect may be anticipated from such a procedure, the possible response of the clitoris to manual manipulation may in itself be conducive to increasing libido in a properly receptive female. Hence, studies on the topical action of testosterone by clitoral application cannot be objective and interpretation of such investigation must be questioned.

Nymphomania may occasionally be treated successfully with androgens. As paradoxical as this may seem, it can be explained as follows: Those patients exhibiting nymphomania who respond to androgens by a decrease in desire for repeated sexual contacts are probably women who have been attempting these many sexual contacts without deriving sexual gratification owing to failure to achieve an orgasm. The addition of androgens helps them to achieve an orgasm, thereby accomplishing gratification so that an excessive number of sexual contacts is no longer necessary.

Other Sex Steroids and Libido

Although androgens enhance libido in the female, the use of other closely related sex steroids may actually diminish libido. For example, progesterone may result in a decrease in libido of a significant degree. It has been of value in the management of certain nymphomaniacs in whom sexual gratification is accomplished with each contact but who need repeated intercourse. In these individuals progesterone suppositories administered one per day in doses of 25 or 50 mg. have been found to be effective in diminishing libido. This type of medication has also been of particular help in decreasing libidinous desires or erotic dreams in the elderly patients when such episodes are disturbing because of moral or religious beliefs.

However, the use of such progesterone preparations, either vaginally or parenterally, may well induce such a decrease in libido as to be of concern to the patient. The fact that this has not been uniformly seen with "oral progesterone" (Ethisterone) may well be attributed, in part, to the fact that this compound, although correctly labeled generically is really ethinyl testosterone and not progesterone per se. This compound is androgenic and does have arrhenomimetic potentials so that the antilibidinous effects usually attributed to progesteronelike steroids may theoretically be nullified to a significant extent by the androgenic potentials of such preparations.

The role of estrogens in female libido is problematical. Estrogens nevertheless may assume an important role in libido in the aged in that they promote enough mucoid elaboration to cause lubrication of the vaginal introitus, thereby making sexual contact more comfortable. There is no doubt that in the patient with atrophic vaginitis androgens are probably of little therapeutic value in enhancing libido. The combined use of estrogens and androgens in such patients is a logical form of therapy, possibly having a synergic effect on the libido. In patients receiving estrogens in order adequately to regulate the menses by preventing endometrial hyperplasias the addition of cyclic therapy with progesterone would not be expected to adversely affect libido.

Pituitary-Testicular Interrelationships in the Male— Gonadotropic Hormones

Sexual function in the male depends upon similar gonadotropin-gonadal interrelationships as exist in the female, except that there are only two gonadotropic hormones known to be of importance in the physiology of reproduction in the male.

Follicle-stimulating hormone (FSH) is responsible for stimulation of the seminiferous tubules to produce sperm (Fig. 3). This pituitary gonadotropin hormone, peculiarly designated as FSH, is gametogenic in the male, as it is in the female. The second gonadotropic hormone in the male, known as the *interstitial cell-stimulating hormone (ICSH)*, is identical with the LH hormone of the female and stimulates and maintains the function of the Leydig cells. These cells are responsible for the secretion of steroids usually attributed to the testes, the principal and major one being testosterone.

It has been suggested that a second hormone may be produced by the testes, particularly by the Sertoli cells. Its prime purpose is presumably to inhibit gonadotropic secretion. McCullagh (1932) pointed out that this hormone, known as inhibin, unlike testosterone (which is lipid-soluble), is an aqueous-soluble substance that is insoluble in the usual lipid solvents. Since testosterone is a comparatively poor pituitary inhibitor, it has been suggested that inhibin is the hormone which, by virtue of its inhibiting effect upon pituitary gonadotropic secretion, regulates the secretion of the latter and thereby prevents excessive stimulation of the testes by gonadotropin-stimulating hormones. The testes may have an ambivalent potential and are capable of producing both estrogens and androgens simultaneously. Interestingly enough, the stallion—the epitome of maleness in the animal kingdom—excretes more estrogen in its urine, as Zondek (1934) has shown, than any other animal, even more than the pregnant mare.

The source of the estrogen, according to recent data and concepts, is presumably the Leydig cells. This ambivalence of the Leydig cells is no doubt responsible for the production of adolescent gynecomastia in pubescent boys. Beginning stimulation of androgenic activity by the Leydig cells may be simultaneously associated with increased estrogenic output sufficient to induce gynecomastia. There are those, however, who believe in the monovalent concept that the Leydig cells may only secrete androgens. On the other hand, it is thought that these androgenic steroids may be converted during their process of degradation by the body into physiologically active estrogens. Fortunately, although gynecomastia is noted in one-

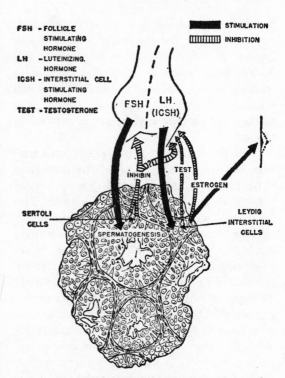

FSH - FOLLICLE
     STIMULATING
     HORMONE
LH - LUTEINIZING.
     HORMONE
ICSH - INTERSTITIAL CELL
     STIMULATING
     HORMONE
TEST - TESTOSTERONE

STIMULATION
INHIBITION

FIG. 3. Diagrammatic presentation of normal testicular-pituitary interrelationship

third of boys going through puberty, only a small percentage are permanently affected.

Male Libido

The use of androgens to enhance libido is more predictable in the female than in the male. The problem in the male, despite its apparent simplicity, is a complex one and many times not as easy to manage as that seen in gynecology. It is not unusual for a male who shows decreased libido with one sexual partner to exhibit a normal or enhanced libido with another. Unlike decreased libido in the female, where we have no significant diagnostic procedures to help differentiate those with endocrine factors from those in whom frigidity is supratentorial, there are two tests to establish the presence of an abnormal hypoendocrine state in the male suspected of having hypogonadism: the determination of 17-ketosteroid level and the extent of urinary gonadotropin (FSH) excretion. If the 17-ketosteroid level is low and the FSH level is high, we then have laboratory evidence to support the concept that the decreased libido is due in all probability to testicular insufficiency or failure. The use of androgens for enhancement of libido in such patients will usually be crowned with success. Those males with a normal 17-ketosteroid and FSH level will invariably show a poor response to androgens, as their defect may well be supratentorial in origin.

Normal sexual function may persist for a considerably longer period of time in the male than in the female. Many males still show spermatogenesis at the age of 70 or 80 years. The presence of viable gametes in a female of this age would be a most unusual phenomenon. As a rule the human female is not capable of reproducing after the age of 60 years. Overt expression of sexual emotions in the young male may appear long before the onset of spermatogenesis, which usually takes place at about the same time that the menarche occurs in the female. Eroticism in the young male may be expressed by erections occurring during urination or after repeated manual manipulation.

Hypogonadism

An important part of male sex endocrinology is the diagnosis and treatment of hypogonadism in the young male. The external position of the male genitalia makes them more subject to comparative study or ridicule by the young male's peers. As a result, the young man with a small phallus and testes may be subject to embarrassment and ridicule by his companions. This may set up a psychological block that later on will make sexual function and activity a difficult problem. Such boys, grown to manhood, may feel inferior to their fellow men and thereby initiate a pattern of aversion to sexual intercourse or a feeling of incompetency with respect to sexual performance.

The appropriate use of gonadotropin hormone and sex-steroid replacement therapy in these boys may alter the personality of such young males from one of inferiority to one of self-confidence. The use of gonadotropins in these patients should be predicated upon either one or all of the following factors: (a) the external genitalia are grossly small for the patient's age and size, (b) urinary 17-ketosteroid excretion is low for his age, (c) the patient

himself is aware of his anatomical limitations.

In such individuals—with or without low 17-ketosteroid level—the administration of gonadotropins will demonstrate to the patient that his genitalia may be stimulated so as to command the respect and admiration of his peers. The use of gonadotropins will not have any adverse effect upon these patients' genitalia and will not promote nor delay epiphyseal closure over and above what would normally occur in a patient of the same chronological age who has adequately developed genitalia.

The usual procedure employed is as follows: in boys below the age of 9 or 10 years, human chorionic gonadotropin (APL-Ayerst) in doses of 500 I.U. three times a week for three weeks, followed by 500 I.U. twice a week for three weeks. Above the age of 9 or 10, we would use 1,000 I.U. in the same schedule. Obviously a small 12-year-old boy might well receive the smaller dose while a large 9-year-old would be given the larger dose. In conjunction with the gonadotropin hormone we also use an anabolic steroid, such as norethandrolone (Nilevar), 10 mg. twice a day for 20 days, followed by the same dose once a day. This steroid enhances the therapeutic response to the injected chorionic gonadotropin. It is important to emphasize that the chorionic gonadotropin may in some boys induce bilateral gynecomastia similar to that occurring during spontaneous puberty. This effect is rarely permanent and does not require discontinuing the recommended dose schedule. It is akin to the gynecomastia in a boy going through normal pubescence. One may note at this time that there is no contraindication to the use of these doses of chorionic gonadotropin in hypogonadal boys. Since the source of the gonadotropin is human pregnant women, sensitization reactions are rarely, if ever, seen. For the same reason, the development of antihormone to the administered gonadotropin would be unlikely.

Hormone Preparations

The physician has a wide choice of preparations that may be used for the treatment of sex-hormone deficiency states in the male and female. The preparations available may be administered orally, intramuscularly, or by pellet implantation. The following compounds are effective and used most widely.

Androgens

ORAL

Methyltestosterone (Oreton M, Metandren, Neo-Hombreol) usually available as a 10-mg. tablet or linguet. We have never been able to demonstrate any significant superiority of the linguet over the tablet and hence we advise our patients to swallow the medication instead of keeping it beneath the tongue.

Fluoxymesterone (Halotestin, Ultandren). This compound is said to be some four to five times as active as methyltestosterone and is available in 2- and 5-mg. tablets.

Testosterone linguets are available for oral use. However, we do not feel that such compounds are as effective as claimed in linguet form and we do not recommend their use.

PARENTERAL

Testosterone propionate in oil is available in concentrations ranging from 25 to 50 mg./cc. The activity of testosterone propionate in this form is rather short-lived, and its use has been supplanted by the longer-acting preparations that follow.

Testosterone cyclopentylpropionate in oil, (Depo-testosterone) available in 50 and 100 mg./cc. This is a well-tolerated steroid, remaining active for two to three weeks after administration. The average dose in the hypogonadal male is 150-200 mg. every two to three weeks.

Testosterone enanthate (Delatestryl) is available in doses of 200 mg./cc. and has the same advantage and duration of activity as testosterone cyclopentylpropionate—although it is only one-half as active.

Testosterone phenylacetate (Perandren phenylacetate) is an aqueous suspension and is available in concentrations of 100 mg./cc. It is well tolerated and the duration of effect is from two to three weeks, its potency being equal to that of testosterone cyclopentylpropionate.

Testosterone in aqueous suspension is also available, but we believe that its use has been supplanted by the other longer-acting preparations listed above.

PELLET IMPLANTATION

Pellets containing 75 mg. of testosterone are available for implantation. The advantage of pellet implantation is that the effect will last from four to six months. Implantation of the pellet with a standard trochar is a simple and quick office procedure. We usually implant seven to nine pellets in males with hypogonadism when it is difficult for the patient to receive injections over two to three weeks.

Estrogenic Compounds

ORAL

There are a number of excellent compounds available on the market and only a few of these are listed below in comparable dose form:

Ethinyl estradiol (Estinyl, Lynoral, Eticylol), .05 mg.

Conjugated estrogens equine (Premarin, Amnestrogen, Conestron), 1.25 mg.

Chlorotrianisene (TACE), 12 mg.

Dienestrol, 0.5 mg.

Hexestrol, 3 mg.

Stilbestrol, .3 mg.

PARENTERAL

Estradiol propionate and *estradiol benzoate* as oil solutions have been available for some time. Because of their relatively short period of action their use has been supplanted by the longer-acting preparations listed below.

Estradiol cyclopentylpropionate (Depo-testradiol), 5 mg./cc. This is an oil solution. Its effect will persist for some two to three weeks.

Estradiol valerate (Delaestrogen), 10 mg./cc. This is also an oil solution and has the same period of effectiveness with its potency being one-half that of estradiol cyclopentylpropionate.

Aqueous suspensions of estrogenic substances, representing biologically active products prepared from the urine of pregnant mares, are available for use. These preparations are prescribed on the basis of international units/cc. of material. Their duration of effect is approximately seven to ten days except for estradiol polyphosphate where 40 mg. as a single injection may last for one to three months.

PELLET IMPLANTATION

In the same manner as testosterone, *25 mg. pellets of estradiol* are available for implantation. Their duration of effect is from six to eight months. Usually three pellets are implanted at one time. They should, however, never be used in a patient unless she has had a total hysterectomy and bilateral ovarectomy.

Progestational Steroids

PARENTERAL

Progesterone is available as an *aqueous suspension,* but because of the marked irritating effect that this form of the steroid has, its clinical use is contraindicated.

Progesterone in oil, available in concentrations of 25 and 50 mg./cc., is usually well tolerated if injected deep into the gluteal muscle with a dry syringe and needle. A single 100-mg. dose is generally used to induce withdrawal bleeding.

17-hydroxysteroid progesterone caproate (Delalutin), 125 mg./cc. in oil solution, has a longer duration of effect than progesterone, but does not appear to be superior to progesterone in inducing secretory changes. In addition—its slow dissipation of effect makes it undesirable for use in patients where a prompt and rapid effect is desired.

ORAL

Norethindrone (Norlutin) and norethynodrel (Enovid). Administration of 10 mg. of either preparation twice a day for seven to ten days will produce an adequate secretory effect with marked stromal accentuation.

Ethisterone, 50 mg. twice a day, will produce an effect comparable to that noted with Norlutin and Enovid except for the excessive stromal effect.

Medroxyprogesterone (Provera), 5 mg. is equivalent to 10 mgm of Norethynodrel.

SUPPOSITORIES

Suppositories of *progesterone,* 50–75 mg. per day for seven days, will give an effect comparable to that noted with the other steroids.

References

Astwood, E. B., "The Regulation of Corpus Luteum Function by Anterior Pituitary Luteotrophin." *Endocrinology* 28; 309-320, 1941.

Bradbury, J. T., "Ovarian Influence on the Response of the Anterior Pituitary to Estrogens." *Endocrinology* 41; 501-513, 1946.

Donovan, B. T., and Harris, G., "Neurohumoral Mechanisms in Reproduction." *Brit. M. Bull.* 11; 93-97, 1955.

Engle, E. T., Smith, P. E., and Shelesnyak, M. C., "The Role of Estrin and Progestin in Experimental Menstruation." *Am. J. Obst. & Gynec.* 29; 787, 1935.

Greenblatt, R. B., Mortara, F., and Torpin, R., "Sexual Libido in the Female." *Am. J. Obst. & Gynec.* 44; 658, 1942.

Greep, R. O., and Jones, I. C., "Steroid Control of Pituitary Function." *Rec. Proc. Hormone Res. J.* 197-254, 1950.

Hisaw, F. L., "The Corpus Luteum Hormone. 1. Experimental Relaxation of the Pubic Ligaments of the Guinea Pig." *Physiol. Zool.* 2; 59-79, 1929.

Hisaw, F. L., "Development of the Graafian Follicle and Ovulation." *Physiol. Rev.* 27; 95-119, 1947.

Hisaw, F. L., and Greep, R. O., "The Inhibition of Uterine Bleeding with Estradiol and Progesterone and Associated Endometrial Modifications." *Endocrinology* 23; 1-14, 1938.

Hisaw, F. L., "The Interaction of the Ovarian Hormones in Experimental Menstruation." *Endocrinology* 30; 301-308, 1942.

Kupperman, H. S., and Epstein, J. A., "Endocrine Therapy of Sterility." *Am. Pract. & Digest. Treat.* 9; 547-563, 1958.

Kupperman, H. S., "Hormonal Aspects of Frigidity." *Rev. Surg. Obst. & Gynec.* 16; 254-257, 1959.

Kupperman, H. S., "Modern Concepts of Endocrine Therapy in Gynecic Disorders." Exhibit at A.M.A. Meeting, 1951.

Kupperman, H. S., "Stress and General Adaptation Syndrome." *J. Dent. Med.* 11; 53-61, 1956.

McCullagh, D. R., "Dual Endocrine Activity of the Testes." *Science* 76; 19-20, 1932.

Salmon, U. J., "Rationale for Androgen Therapy in Gynecology." *J. Clin. Endocrinol.* 1; 162-179, 1941.

Zondek, B., "Oestrogenic Hormone in Stallion's Urine." *Nature* 133; 494, 1934.

HERBERT S. KUPPERMAN

Illegitimacy

Definition

ILLEGITIMACY is the state or quality of being illegitimate. The child who is born out of wedlock is an illegitimate child (bastard, natural child); the mother who has given birth to such a child is an illegitimate mother. The law makes a further distinction between various states of illegitimacy depending on whether 1) the mother could have lawfully married the father at the time of conception; 2) there existed at that time some legal impediment to marriage such as a close family relationship or a racial barrier; 3) the child was conceived by a married woman by a man other than her husband. In the last instance, the child is designated an adulterine or adulterous bastard.

Legal Penalties

Depending on the conditions under which the child was conceived, the unwed mother may be penalized for fornication or, if her youthful age precludes this, treated as a juvenile delinquent. Her child may inherit from her after her death only if she dies without legitimate issue, and the child may not inherit from her relatives or from the putative father. The married illegitimate mother may suffer the penalties some states impose for adultery; her child may be deprived of the right to inherit from either parent, as may the child resulting from an incestuous union. In some regions the law explicitly forbids the acknowledgement of a child born of an adulterous relationship.

The vindictiveness of these laws becomes particularly apparent when they provide—as they do in several jurisdictions—that the illegitimate child's status must be clearly defined upon the birth certificate and that, unless the child is legally adopted, this must not be changed. The powerful objection to any attempts to introduce less punitive legislation, on the other hand, clearly indicates that such laws are not merely forgotten leftovers from more primitive ages, but that they still reflect the sentiments of a great part of the American population. In fact, since in many instances the authorities do not take legal action on their own initiative, some communities try to penalize the offending woman indirectly. Thus, many localities have only recently introduced a provision that denies Aid to Dependent Children grants to unmarried mothers who have more than one illegitimate child.

History

The hostile attitude toward illegitimacy is often defended as a means of preserving the strength and unity of the family. But actually the cohesiveness of the family has been consistently diminished by the State, the Church, and the growing industrialization of countries in Western culture.

Nations in which the family still functions as an economic unit—a function it has long since lost in our civilization—consistently hold attitudes that are favorable to both the illegitimate mother and the illegitimate child. In many of them, children are considered an asset regardless of whether they are born within or without wedlock. In some, girls whose premarital relations had consequences are preferred for marriage; in others, both husband and wife may have lovers but if the wife's extramarital relations result in children, these are the property of the husband.

In its younger days—roughly speaking before the sixteenth century—Western civilization took a much more tolerant view of illegitimacy. Many politically powerful leaders, for instance, bestowed titles, high positions, and responsibilities on their "bastard" sons. In the lowest ranks, illegitimacy was hardly avoidable since farm hands and maids slept in the same room or barn. Like the deplorable living conditions of these people, the consequences of their involuntary cohabitation did not interest either landlords or clergy until, in the wake of Luther's Reformation, the followers of the Protestant sects started thundering against general immorality. They proposed nothing to improve living and working conditions, but where they were in power they imposed severe punishment on sinners. Confronted with the accusation of moral laxity, State and Church in the camp of the Counterreformation naturally would not be outdone. Thus, in Bavaria in 1598 an edict was issued ordering that unwed women who became pregnant were to be fined and publicly exposed in the stocks. After the fourth pregnancy the woman was to be expelled from the country. Other countries followed this example.

But successively promulgated legislation showed that moral indignation was merely a convenient vehicle for economic advantage. The legitimate wives, sons, and daughters were predominantly interested in preventing the "love child" or "natural child" from claiming any part of their inheritance. Various laws, accordingly, make it impossible for parents to leave to the illegitimate child more than half of what the legitimate offspring gets, or to bequeath to him more than to the legitimate one. A related element—resentment of economic responsibility by the community—becomes particularly evident in regions where premarital sex relations are accepted as a part of the courtship. The couple usually marries when the girl becomes pregnant. But when the man refuses to marry her, mother and child are penalized by contempt and social ostracism.

In the course of the nineteenth century these attitudes gradually took a turn for the better. The change began with the sentimentalization of the seduced maiden. The tragedy of infanticide under such circumstances is a frequent motif in Romantic literature. By the middle of the century these ideas also resulted in practical measures. Charitable organizations set up shelters for unmarried mothers. Although from a modern point of view these were nothing to be especially proud of, such shelters eased the plight of the girls to some extent.

During the past three decades several more enlightened countries took additional steps to improve the lot of these women. The goals were: (1) material assistance and hospital care for the impecunious illegitimate mother; (2) education in birth control for the married and the unmarried; (3) elimination of directly or indirectly punitive laws; (4) care and protection of the illegitimate child; (5) educational pressure to influence the attitude of the public; (6) legal means to obtain the father's assistance in the support of the child.

No one country has as yet completely fulfilled this program. The moralistic attitude of those not caught in a similar predicament is especially difficult to change. Several countries, however, have made considerable progress in the indicated directions. In some, the mother has a legal right to preface her name with the title Mrs. instead of Miss; in some, discrimination is counteracted and diminished by governmentally supported counterpropaganda; in some, birth control is not only taught by competent agencies, but apothecaries are compelled to stock and sell contraceptives; in some, termination of pregnancy is allowed on the grounds of social indications. In Sweden, the child takes the father's name if the mother and father were engaged to be married, and he is entitled to inherit from both. If during the child's dependence the father dies, the child has a claim to his estate. A guardian is officially appointed to safeguard the child's rights and interests until he is 18 years old.

Conditions in the United States

In this country many improvements have been introduced. Public and private agencies have been established to advise and shelter the woman in distress, to provide hospital care and legal aid, and to make arrangements for the sustenance of the illegitimate child. In most states, special laws, statutes, or ordinances regulate some or all of their activities. But some states so obviously disapprove of the immoral act that prompted the mother's situation, or are so engrossed in their special interests, that those of both mother and child are not served best. Since social security legislation in 1934, for example, illegitimate mothers are eligible for financial assistance; yet some public welfare departments deny it to the married woman who has an illegitimate child. Although a married woman may be vitally interested in keeping her condition secret from her husband, who admittedly is not the father, some agencies will not accept the child for adoption unless the husband is notified. Some social agencies refuse to serve married women who are illegitimately pregnant, or girls who have become pregnant a second time.

In some southern cities, those who need assistance most urgently—the Negroes—are excluded from otherwise available facilities without being given an adequate equivalent. Some agencies are rigidly religious and provide services only if the clients surrender completely to their control; others turn away those who do not want to discuss their psychological state. Some require the mother to stay in the home as long as six months after delivery although the child is offered for adoption, and some accept the mother only if she consents—long before the birth of the child—to relinquish all rights to her offspring.

Public and semipublic agencies are, naturally, meant in the first place for women who do not have funds of their own and for those who leave their families and home communities in order to remain anonymous. Yet a great number of homes are unwilling to waive or even reduce the cost of their services, and others insist on informing the family or the home community. Some are even said to use the threat of court action because of delinquency, immorality, prostitution, or the like to make the mother comply with their specific demands, as, for instance, to surrender the child.

These and similar practices explain why a considerable number of those who need aid never turn to the agencies meant for them. Indirectly they also contribute to the high mortality rate among illegitimate children, which is four times that of children born in wedlock. By the end of the sixth month of pregnancy, 87 per cent of all married women have seen a doctor; in contrast, the percentage for the unmarried is only 47; among married women, only 4 per cent fail to receive any prenatal care, but the percentage among illegitimate mothers is 23.

The Illegitimate Mother

The number of illegitimate births in the United States, disregarding various possible camouflages, is about 180,000 per year. It constitutes over 4.5 per cent of the yearly birth rate, and is somewhat higher in rural areas than among the urban population. Girls not yet married make up the largest group of illegitimate mothers, married women the smallest. Widows and divorcees stand fairly in the middle between them, although in absolute figures they rank lowest. Among white women, the greater number is above 20 years of age, among Negroes under 20. Since one out of three illegitimate mothers is colored, the majority of the total group is in their teens. Among white girls two out of five illegitimate mothers are teenagers. About 1.3 per cent of all unwed mothers are between 10 and 14 years old.

Class Status

The disproportionately high frequency of illegitimacy among the Negro population has often been cited as proof of racial inferiority. Actually it only demonstrates the influence of socioeconomic status on the rate of illegitimacy. If the population of the United States is divided on the basis of socioeconomic status, 10 per cent of the total fall into the upper stratum, 40 per cent belong in the middle, and 50 per cent in the lower stratum. When this division is applied to the Negro population alone, only 5 per cent rank in the upper, 30 per cent in the middle, and 65 per cent in the lower class. If, on the other hand, white illegitimate mothers are classified by class characteristics such as income and education, an equally disproportionately high rate is found to come from the low socioeconomic group. Although motherhood without the benefit of wedlock occurs on all levels of family background and education, it is heavily concentrated in the families in the lowest income brackets and with relatively little schooling.

These factors are significant in considering the aid given and available to illegitimate mothers. In the United States the agencies entrusted with this task tend to emphasize psychological rehabilitation. The concentration on the "diagnostic approach" inevitably impinges on the funds available for material, legal, and medical help, and hence is justifiable only if the "causes" of illegitimate motherhood can be found in the deviating psychological make-up of the women involved. The above-mentioned combination of economic and educational factors, however, suggests not only different causes but also different remedies.

Causes of Illegitimacy

What have the explorers of causes so far brought to light? There are several theories and each proposes definite characteristics that differentiate the illegitimate mother from other women.

Popular opinion, as presented by the gossiping environment, by sermons, and by magazines designed for popular consumption, is fairly agreed on two qualities: these girls are oversexed and immoral. They are immoral either because they are "born bad" or because they lack religious training. More sophisticated investigators hold that these girls are often mentally defective.

A great number of the girls themselves attribute their predicament to rape, amnesia, knock-out drops, and intoxication.

Among the scientifically oriented, two views dominate the field. The one presents illegitimate motherhood as the outcome of compulsive behavior motivated by unconscious needs and desires; the other attributes it to environmental influences. Let us examine the latter theory first.

Environment

Environmental influences are defined as bad companions, recreational disadvantages, bad home conditions, early sex experiences, mental conflicts, etc. Some forty-five such factors have been enumerated and are, in varying combinations, considered to be causative of, or associated with, "crimes, among them illegitimacy."

Advocates of environmental causation do not believe in inborn badness; rather, they regard frustration and misery as responsible for delinquent behavior. But, basically, delinquency, crime, and illegitimacy appear to them closely related in derivation and consequence. In this respect, they are essentially agreed with that part of public opinion that blames fornication on immorality.

Immorality

Immorality thus becomes an issue worth our attention. Simultaneously it covers another alleged cause, namely oversexedness, which by many is considered one of its generative elements. The immorality hypothesis rests on several observable details. The rate of illegitimacy is consistently rising. It was 87,000 in 1938, 133,200 in 1949, and 176,000 in 1954. Two decades ago, practically all illegitimate mothers were well above 20 years of age, whereas today the majority are in their teens.

The Negro people, as well as the white lower economic classes, have always been accused of moral inferiority in this country, and not only because of their high illegitimacy rate. In both these groups, illegitimate motherhood has never caused the same shock as it has in the middle and upper strata. Not so long ago, a judge refused to authorize county funds for the care of Negroes in boarding homes on the grounds that "Negroes always care for their children." Yet, neither they nor the white lower classes cherish illegitimacy more than other groups. Rather, they have learned to take this undesirable phenomenon in their stride, like so many other disadvantages with which their lives are beset. They do not know what to do about it, just as they do not know what to do about their overabundant legitimate children. Are people in these groups more highly sexed than elsewhere?

Although more unwed mothers belong to the lowest socioeconomic group, the percentage of those who have premarital sex relations is actually smaller in that group than in the middle and upper strata. This fact in itself destroys the myth of low class = low morality. Yet it is not presented here to claim greater virtue for lower-class girls. They marry earlier than those of the two other classes; hence, the period of premarital maturity is shorter for them. Nevertheless, relatively more become pregnant when they have premarital sex relations, and—even though a greater percentage marries during pregnancy—a greater number of these pregnancies result in illegitimate births.

These data invalidate the conclusion that the illegitimate mother is more highly sexed or more inclined toward delinquency or immorality than any other woman who has premarital, extramarital, or postmarital sex relations. Besides, among the laws designed to safeguard morality, none openly threatens illegitimate motherhood with punishment. Often, to be sure, pregnant girls are sent to penal institutions, but even then the penalties are imposed not for the mishap of becoming pregnant or giving birth, but for the "immorality" committed by having premarital sex relations. And there is obviously quite a difference between the causes of illegitimate sex relations and the reasons for preventing their results.

But what about illegitimate sex relations themselves? Terms such as "immorality" or "oversexedness" make sense only if they indicate a deviation from the mores that are followed, if not by all, then at least by a significant majority of the population. Two questions consequently arise: 1) Are illegitimate sex relations indulged in only by a minority within the country? 2) Are American girls more immoral than those in related cultures?

Data on women who have or have had sex relations before marriage give 52 per cent for Australia, 40 per cent for England, and 98 per cent for Denmark. The estimates for Sweden, France, Russia, Germany, and Switzerland lie between the highest and the lowest of these. In the United States the computations vary between 50 and 60 per cent. Among married women, one out of four has or has had extramarital relations with one or more men other than her husband during the duration of the marriage. Among those who are widowed and divorced and separated, three out of four have sex relations.

In the face of these facts, illegitimate sex relations are better classified as part of our mores than as a deviation from them. Whatever stand the banner-bearers of morality and

social adjustment take toward this reality, it is evident that their criteria fail to distinguish between the women who give birth to illegitimate children and the more fortunate ones who escape pregnancy or who know how to terminate it.

Psychological Diagnosis

The psychological approach adopted almost generally by those who professionally deal with illegitimate mothers comes closer to the actual issue in two respects. It has eliminated the terms delinquency and immorality and it tries —although not always successfully—to emphasize only those motives that cause the female to bear the consequences of her illicit sex relations.

Unfortunately, these diagnosticians are so fascinated by the spectacle of unconscious motivation that they consider illegitimate motherhood to be purposive in all instances. Driven by unconscious motives, they contend, the woman predestined to contact a family agency, a maternity home, or a placement center is "seeking pregnancy." She is compelled to do so "because the child will be symbolically the child of her father"; or because she resents his refusal to have a child with her; or because by having a child she dominates the illegitimate mate and thus "gratifies her basic resentment toward him"; or "because she wants to present her submissively loved mother with a child." It appears that these charitable minds can drive out the ghosts of immorality and delinquency only by calling another ghost in, namely neurosis. "The unmarried mother," their credo runs, "is a neurotic individual," and illegitimate motherhood "a symptom of an underlying problem."

Unquestionably, most girls who find themselves pregnant are in a state of panic. It is equally likely that there is a high percentage of neurotics, psychotics, and psychopaths among illegitimate mothers. To assume, however, that in all instances illegitimate motherhood is brought about by "a compelling unhealthy urge to bear a child" presupposes a complete disregard of reality.

The explanation of unconsciously intentional pregnancy has a certain attraction since illegitimate motherhood is relatively rare. According to the findings of the Kinsey report on the sexual behavior of American females, and the most recent publication of the Kinsey Institute, on birth, pregnancy, and abortion, about 40,-000,000 of all American females alive today have had or will have sexual intercourse before marriage. One out of five of these has become or will become pregnant. Of these, 19 per cent marry during their pregnancy and thus escape the stigma of illegitimacy. Of those who do not, 5 per cent have miscarriages, and only 6 out of a hundred give birth to illegitimate children. The rest, 89 per cent, rid themselves of the fetus before it is born. Among the 10,000,000 women who are divorced, widowed, or separated, 7,300,000 have sex relations. Approximately 1,387,000 of them (19 per cent) become pregnant at one time or another, but only 4 per cent, that is, somewhat more than 55,000, become mothers. The figures for married women are less reliable since illegitimacy of the child can be more easily hidden.

Considering, then, the millions who know how to elude the consequence of illegitimate sex relations, it may appear strange that some— to whom birth must be equally undesirable— find no way to avoid it.

Unconscious purposefulness is just not the answer. The difference between those who become illegitimate mothers and those who do not can usually be traced to much simpler causes, which may appear alone or in combination. Some of these are associated with socioeconomic status and/or the ages of those who constitute the majority of illegitimate mothers.

Ignorance

Class status is highly correlated with education. The lower classes are deficient in this respect. The greatest number of women who become pregnant before marriage have ended their education with grammar school. Of those who have had some high-school education, 7 per cent become pregnant by the age of 20, whereas only 3 per cent of the girls who are in college suffer the same mishap at that age.

It is not, of course, the knowledge acquired in schools that accounts for the difference but the higher learning potential, the family background of better education, and the training that allows them to pick up worldly wisdom outside the classroom and to sift it with regard to its value. Those who are handicapped by poorer education are also more credulous and uncritical in their sexual behavior. They trust their luck, they are more likely to credit the most absurd misinformation and to use all kinds of ineffective means to forestall pregnancy.

It is therefore more than likely that ignorance accounts for a great number of unwanted pregnancies. In particular, lack of information on contraception is an important factor. Although approximately 78 per cent of the females who have premarital sex relations use preventive devices of one kind or another, 11 per cent do not use any. The kind of contraception used is also of importance. The man's promise that he will be careful, for instance, is a dubious device, more likely to be trusted by a simple mind than by a sophisticated one. Although what is usually understood by sex education in our era does not, as a rule, include information on contraception in either the upper or the lower strata, the girl who comes from a family with a better education, or who has received a better education, moves in circles where mutually conveyed information is more reliable than that it is in the less-educated groups. She is also more likely to consult a physician or a gynecologist than is the girl of the poorer stratum and hence to get answers to her questions or to pick up relevant suggestions inadvertently.

The dangers inherent in ignorance are aggravated by youthfulness. Girls who come from the families of manual workers and laborers start their sexual activities five to six years earlier than those brought up in white-collar homes. But whatever the class and the family background, an early sexual awakening is not accompanied by commensurate foresight and knowledge. Many of these 13-, 14-, and 15-year-old girls crave to prove themselves adult, to be attractive to men; and even those somewhat older girls are often indiscriminate in their choice and have to trust the partner's knowledge about prevention of pregnancy. They are often merely curious about the secrets of sex. Indeed, some derive a feeling of safety from the fact that they started early: still unable, physically, to become pregnant in the earlier stages of puberty, they feel no need to look for effective contraception until one day, as a result of the gradual maturation of the reproductive apparatus, they find themselves pregnant.

Even among older girls ignorance is not limited to the lowest classes. In some circles the topic of sex is taboo and, in spite of her greater learning, a girl may remain naive in this field. And sometimes it is not even the young person's own ignorance that so endangers her; rather, parental restrictions prevent her from applying her knowledge. She knows about contraceptives, for example, but because of her mother's strictness she does not dare to have one in her possession.

What applies to contraception also applies to abortion. The interruption of pregnancy in a healthy woman is illegal, and doctors who perform such operations do not advertise it. Also, because of the legal risk involved, an abortion is very expensive. Those who have little money quite frequently prefer, therefore, to take all kinds of drugs, only to become aware of their ineffectiveness when it is too late. Although religious convictions do not keep all women from premarital or postmarital intercourse, they do sometimes interfere with the decision to have an abortion. In other instances, girls are too afraid to take this step. Their fear is not surprising since their sources of information and, indeed, even the average newspapers and magazines invariably depict it as an undertaking that results in death, sterility, or irreparable damage. Therefore, for those who cannot obtain reliable information, it is an act to be resorted to only in desperation.

Although most of the pregnant women—married as well as unmarried—nevertheless take that risk, there is obviously a minority that does not find its way through the maze of difficulties. Not knowing to whom to turn, misinformed about the danger involved, rejected by the father of the child, and unable to raise money, they have the baby, without any conscious or unconscious desire for it.

Lack of Intelligence

Although ignorance is not necessarily correlated with low intelligence, among illegitimate mothers the latter is somewhat more frequent than it is in a random sample. With regard to mental defectiveness and illegitimacy, studies

differ too much to say anything definite. But whether the mother is actually feeble-minded or somewhere between mental deficiency and average intelligence, she is handicapped for all the reasons presented under ignorance. She has the additional disadvantage of being more easily seduced by promises of love and marriage. (However, girls of low intelligence are not the only ones who are induced by such promises to surrender to a man's desires or to surrender under unfavorable circumstances—that is to say, when they cannot protect themselves against conception. And there are couples who have intercourse because they plan to marry anyway, but cannot realize their intention because an accident or the man's death makes it impossible.)

Negligence

Carelessness rivals ignorance for first place among the factors causally associated with unwanted pregnancy. The two are frequently combined. In about 11 out of a hundred instances, girls take precautions occasionally, but at other times they take a chance. Their imprudence may result from laziness and poor training or from lack of foresight, and also from passion and from inhibitions about appearing materially concerned in a situation that is supposed to be purely emotional.

What people deplore as bad luck can often be traced to carelessness. Married and divorced women are often overoptimistic. They know that one may have intercourse many times before one conceives, but they know as little as anyone else whether the gamble will turn out in their favor or not. Others are slipshod in inserting and removing contraceptives, or in the care of the perishable material of which they consist. Men often believe themselves to be thrifty rather than rash when they use the same condom over again.

The circumstances responsible for unexpected conception in these instances are not different from those in married life except that a husband is usually more cooperative because he is more vitally concerned in the avoidance of pregnancy than is the infatuated lover or the chance acquaintance to whom the whole affair is only a pleasant adventure.

In premarital, extramarital, and postmarital

sex relations, therefore, negligence and ignorance operate more decisively according to the selection of the sexual partner. The male may be indifferent to the consequences that his carelessness can have for the female. He may promise to take precautions but actually not do so. He may be so impatient as not to allow his partner to make preparations, or he may object to artificial devices because they allegedly diminish his pleasure. Men often feel no responsibility at all toward girls who are known to have promiscuous relations. Many do not exercise the same control with girls of a low class as they do with a girl of their own class, and some prefer such relations for this very reason. Others are tempted to prove their superiority over the opposite sex through deliberate inconsiderateness, or try to allay doubts of their own masculinity by provoking the risk of pregnancy.

Certain personality features constitute a particularly fertile soil for recklessness, carelessness, and indiscriminate choice of the partner. Among them are (1) impulsiveness, (2) an inclination toward overoptimism, and (3) greater-than-average suggestibility. With reference to the sexual situation, these traits may mean that the girl can be relatively easily persuaded to ignore unfavorable circumstances. Further characteristics may be listed, including (4) submissiveness: the woman is easily intimidated by a show of disapproval and confused by peremptory or loud commands, and (5) latent masochistic tendencies: under their influence the girl may consistently be attracted to men of whom consideration either during sex relations or afterwards cannot be expected.

The girl's willingness to yield may pervade the whole personality or be concentrated in the field of sex and affectionate relations. In the latter case, an excessive need for popularity, for being loved and desired, for proving her femininity hinders her in the evaluation of the partner's dependability or urges her to comply with his wishes, perhaps against her better judgment. Unconscious rebellion against overly restrictive and domineering or unloving parents also sometimes produces foolish and stubborn daring.

Intoxication

Pregnant girls frequently assert that they were plied with alcohol until they were drunk, and then were misused. Although this story is not an invention in all instances, it usually distorts some of the facts. There is no doubt about an existing connection between intoxication and pregnancy. Trustworthy studies show that the total consumption of alcohol in comparable regions is highly correlated with the number of births out of wedlock.

The effect of alcohol is to cause an otherwise fairly provident women to become foolhardy, gullible, and negligent. For them, as well as for the inexperienced who lose their inhibitions, the situation is aggravated by the fact that men, even when they are only slightly intoxicated, often become more aggressive and callous about self-control.

Rape

Severe intoxication may so lower some men's power of restraint that they commit rape or incest. Even so, rape is more often an excuse than a cause of illegitimate motherhood. Actually a number of premarital sex relations fall into the category of statutory rape (sexual intercourse with a female under age, irrespective of her consent) but when the illegitimate mother claims rape she always means that she has been violated against her will, by force or under threat of force. The more fanciful allegations include secret administration of drugs in drinks or coffee, a hypodermic injection, and the use of hypnotism. As a rule, such allegations can be easily disposed of, and are withdrawn in the course of close investigations.

Rape does occur, of course—for the year 1956, for example, the FBI reported 20,300 cases—but as a cause for illegitimate motherhood it is a quantitatively insignificant factor. In many instances, the girl may in fact not have explicitly consented to intercourse, but she did not put up any resistance or she had sex relations with the same man before or after the incident. Frequently she delighted in heavy petting, but when she meant to check her partner, he could not be stopped anymore. Girls who associate with the rougher male elements, such as adolescents gathered in delinquent gangs, are well aware that their sexual teasing exposes them to this peril. It is worth mentioning, however, that among delinquent girls (classified so because of other derelictions than the one that brings them to the maternity home) the incidence of motherhood is lower than among nondelinquents. The reason is not higher morality, for most delinquent girls have frequent and often promiscuous sex relations, but the fact that they are more able to take care of themselves.

Incest

Offspring resulting from incestuous relations are *ipso facto* illegitimate since the term incest applies exclusively to sexual contact between people who are legally barred from marriage. Such children cannot be legitimized by the father. Their number is difficult to determine because incest carries a heavy penalty for both parties; and the mother, unless she claims rape, is not likely to reveal the father's name. Incest with or without consequence is a crime largely confined to the lowest economic stratum. In the United States, pregnancy that is the result of rape, or even of incest and rape combined, cannot be legally terminated.

Purposive Pregnancy

In a relatively small percentage of cases, illegitimate pregnancy is intentional or purposive. Motherhood is consciously purposive if readily available means to prevent or to terminate a pregnancy are not utilized. Occasionally, for example, by confronting the putative father with the news of her pregnancy, a girl hopes to force him to marry her. If she has misjudged the strength of her argument—as sometimes happens if there is a wide gap in social status or if a married partner cannot induce his wife to divorce him—she may have to join the ranks of illegitimate mothers. Married women sometimes get into a similar plight. If, for example, the marriage remained childless, she may be so tortured by the suspicion that she is sterile that she tests her ability to conceive in an extramarital relation. Another may so fervently desire a child that she takes the risk, hoping that she can convince her husband of his paternity. If he is not deceived, or is unwilling to recognize the child as his, he has grounds for divorce and the child is considered illegitimate.

Intention and goal are unequivocally admitted by the Bachelor Motherhood League in England. Its members are not content with fighting prejudice against illegitimate motherhood, but insist that every woman who so desires should have the right to become a mother even though, because of the shortage of men, she must remain single.

Unconscious Purposiveness

Unconscious purposiveness as a causative factor indicates needs and desires so compelling that they nullify all overt attempts to prevent illegitimate pregnancy and motherhood. The compulsion is symptomatic of a neurotic state.

Contrary to the assumption that this is the driving force in practically all females who become mothers without the benefit of marriage, it is relatively rare. Unconscious needs do, of course, play as significant a role in sex relations as they do in every form of human behavior but, except in severe neurotics and psychotics, their significance is limited and subordinate to reality considerations. It is probable that unconscious needs are at work in the selection of a sadistic partner, for instance, but for all its undesirable consequences, that makes neither pregnancy nor motherhood intentional. Rivalry with the mother or sister may be the unconscious motive for taking up promiscuous sex relations, but given the proper information, even a promiscuous woman will take effective measures against conception. If, nevertheless, she becomes pregnant, as happens because of negligence, passion, intoxication, impulsiveness, etc., in millions of cases of married and unmarried women, she will, in accordance with the means at her disposal, take steps to escape the predicament.

Among the more frequent neurotic motives that compel a woman to have a child out of wedlock are self-punishment; punishment of the prohibiting parent, usually the mother; and unconquerable craving for affection in girls who feel and always have felt rejected. In such a constellation, forgetfulness, carelessness, and recklessness may unconsciously be put into the service of the crucial need.

Facilities for the Poor

It has been mentioned that the great mass of illegitimate mothers come from impecunious homes. Fewer females with better education and home training, even when they are as frequently involved in illicit sex relations, get pregnant, and if they do, they know how to end this state. Having money, they can also take care of hospital expenses at a place where discretion is guaranteed.

The others who lack sufficient funds have more often to rely on publicly and privately supported facilities. So must middle-class and upper-class girls sometimes, if they cannot turn to their parents for support. Facilities provided for them are—disregarding intermediaries such as the family agency—the maternity home, the boarding home, and the child-placement agency.

Maternity Homes

These organizations are as a rule under the control of the welfare departments of the various states. Most states have established standards for licensing and supervising maternity homes. They are designed to meet the needs of both the mother and the child. The needs involve the skills of the obstetrician, the pediatrician, the nurse, the social worker, and, in some instances, those of the psychologist, the psychiatrist, and the lawyer. Of course, only in the ideal home are all these services available under one roof. Homes that do not have a hospital arrange for obstetrical service in community hospitals. All of them give advisory health supervision before and after delivery and some have arrangements with the local board of education to provide teachers for the girls who are still of school age. Legal aid is required when the child is to be offered for adoption or when support from the father is to be obtained through court action. Most shelters also have nurseries for the care of the babies.

Unfortunately, many unwed mothers cannot afford even the limited aid of the maternity home, since for them the fees are prohibitive. Quite a few shelters refuse to waive or reduce the cost. Others are so keen on recovering their expenses from the fees adopting parents pay that they do not take in anyone who has not committed herself to surrender the child for adoption.

The Boarding Home

Older women and very young girls frequently do not fit into the community life of the maternity shelter since activities there are geared to the majority, which consists of adolescents. If possible, these women and others who are handicapped are placed in private boarding homes. The agency responsible for them selects the homes interested in boarding unwed mothers and makes the necessary arrangements with regard to the different kinds of aid needed. A few agencies provide so-called wage homes. In wage homes, the girls pay for their sustenance with their work. Most agencies, however, consider this one of the least desirable forms of care.

The Child

Once the child is born, the duty of providing for its maintenance rests with the parents. If the father is unknown, the mother is responsible for it. If the father acknowledges the child as his own, either he can make a private agreement regarding its support or he can be forced by court action to contribute to the child's upkeep. In about 10 per cent to 25 per cent of the cases, paternity is established in court. If the putative father denies paternity, blood tests give him a limited chance (55 per cent) to prove that he is falsely accused.

Acknowledgment of paternity per se does not make an illegitimate child legitimate. This change is usually brought about by adoption. Although in approximately two out of ten cases the putative father marries the pregnant girl before she gives birth to their child, marriage after the child is born occurs only in two out of a hundred cases. It is often the hope for such an eventual marriage that causes the mother to keep the child.

Strangely enough, social agencies concerned with advising and counseling unwed mothers consider the girl who wants to keep the child with her, instead of offering it for adoption, as "the least healthy"—that is, the most neurotic. It is impossible to establish to what extent this idea is supported by fact and to what extent it is merely the outgrowth of the general philosophy of these agencies. It has been claimed that some of them actually exert a more or less severe pressure on the mother to give up her child. It is an indisputable fact, of course, that the mother who keeps her child with her is handicapped with regard to occupational work and later marriage. Nonetheless, all comparable agencies in other countries do not share this view. It is possible that underlying the voiced philosophy are not only the stated considerations but also others, among them distrust in the girl's ability to care and plan properly for her child.

Keeping the Baby

When the illegitimate mother keeps the baby, she may actually live with him, or she may place him with relatives. In the latter case, she may or may not keep in contact with the child; she may become known to the child as his mother or she may be presented to him as a visiting aunt.

How many of the mothers actually keep their children cannot be determined with even approximate accuracy. Agencies do keep records of course, but only a fraction of illegitimate mothers use such agencies. Even the records extant do not present the complete picture, because the mother who insists on keeping the child may independently place it for adoption later. To the extent that limited follow-up studies are significant, it appears that about 20 to 29 per cent of the live children live with their mothers, and about 11 per cent are placed with relatives.

For the rest, three possibilities exist: 1) placement for adoption, 2) placement in a foster home, and 3) placement in a public institution.

Adoption

Adoption is a legal act in which the mother relinquishes forever all rights and obligations in respect to her child. Although adoption statutes vary greatly, all states regulate proceedings and requirements. In most of them, the state department of social (public) welfare and/or specially licensed private agencies are entrusted with the task of selecting suitable families for the child. Besides these agencies, however, there flourishes what the official agencies call a "black market" or "gray market," and it appears that many adoptive parents and many mothers prefer what is less derogatorily named "independent placement." Approximately 45 per cent of all adoptions are made independently. The reason seems to be that both parties are spared much red tape and many embarrassing questions. The illegitimate mother in particular appreciates the greater discretion exercised in the unofficial market.

Although adoption is not inexpensive, there are approximately ten times as many applicants as there are children offered for adoption. Nevertheless there are difficulties in placing some of the babies. Among those hard to place are the progeny of the visibly distinguishable minority groups such as Negroes, Japanese, and Mexicans. Only 7 per cent of these children can be placed, although the colored groups make up 15 per cent of the total population and their rate of illegitimacy exceeds the proportional expectations.

Mongolian idiots, hydrocephalics, cretins, etc., are nonadoptable. These children are placed in institutions under the auspices of welfare departments.

The Foster Home

Equally nonadoptable are children whose mothers have not relinquished them legally. The mother may have abandoned the child or she may have been unable to make up her mind. These children are placed either in foster homes or in orphanages and similar institutions. A mother may place her child in a foster home at her own expense. If she discontinues payment, the child becomes a public charge. Similar is the fate of partially blind, deaf, or crippled children. There are, at the present time, about 175,000 children living in foster homes, and 95,000 children in public institutions. But only 5 per cent of these are legally free to be adopted.

Follow-up of Illegitimate Mothers

A few studies inform us about the lot of the illegitimate mother after she has given birth. Although only 2 per cent marry the putative father of the child, about 76 per cent marry within seven years. Younger persons, naturally, have an advantage over older ones, and those who surrendered their children for adoption are more likely to marry than those who kept them. In one out of five cases, the husband never learns about the girl's experience; in four of five he learns about it before marriage. In some instances, the mother after marriage recovers the child from relatives or from a boarding home, and the husband adopts it. The marriages themselves do not seem to differ from any others.

References

Bensing, R. G., "A Comparative Study of American Sex Statutes." *J. Crim. Law & Criminol. 42;* 57-72, 1951.

Block, Babette, "The Unmarried Mother." *Pub. Health Nursing* July, 1951.

Block, Babette, *Foster Family Care for Unmarried Mothers.* Washington: Dept. of Health, Education and Welfare, 1955.

Brasol, Boris, *The Elements of Crime.* New York: Oxford University Press, 1927.

Clark, Lemon, "A Report on the Virginity of American Unmarried Women." *Internat. J. Sexology 4;* 166, 1951.

Clemens, A. H., "Unscientific Aspects of Sex Education." *Marr. & Fam. Living 15;* 10-14, 1953.

Davis, Annie Lee, "Attitudes Toward Minority Groups." *The Child 13;* 6, 1948.

Doob, Leonard W., *Social Psychology.* New York: Henry Holt & Co., 1952.

Fink, Lotte A., "Premarital Sex Experiences of Girls in Sidney." *Internat. J. Sexology 7;* 42, 1954.

French, Thomas M., *The Importance of the First Interview with the Unmarried Mother.* Washington: Dept. of Health, Education and Welfare, 1952.

Gebhard, Paul, *et al., Pregnancy, Birth, and Abortion.* New York: Harper & Brothers, 1958.

Hayman, Marguerite M., *Casework Treatment of the Unmarried Mother.* Washington: Federal Security Agency, Children's Bureau, 1954.

Hutchinson, Dorothy, "How Can We Revise Agency Policies to Better Meet the Needs of Unmarried Mothers and Babies?" *Florence Crittenton Bull. 14;* 3, 1949.

Josselyn, Irene M., *What We Know about the Unmarried Mother.* New York: National Association on Service to Unmarried Parents, 1953.

Kinsey, A. C., *et al., Sexual Behavior in the Human Female.* Philadelphia: W. B. Saunders Co., 1953.

Levy, Dorothy, *A Follow-up Study of Unmarried Mothers.* New York: Family Service Association of America, 1955.

Queener, Llewellyn, *Introduction to Social Psychology.* New York: Wm. Sloane Associates, Inc., 1951.

Schatkin, Sidney, *Disputed Paternity Proceedings.* Albany: M. Bender & Co., Inc., 1958.

Shake, Virginia, *Case Work Services to Unmarried Mothers.* New York: National Association on Unmarried Parents, 1957.

Thompson, William B., "Symposium on Adoption." *West. J. Surg. 62;* 257-283, 1954.

Young, Leontine, *Out of Wedlock.* New York: McGraw-Hill Book Co., 1954.

HUGO G. BEIGEL

Impotence

Definition

THE term *impotence* applies only to men. A man who is unable to have sexual intercourse in the normal manner, with erection and intromission, because of inability to attain or maintain a satisfactory erection, or because of structural deformity, is said to be impotent.

In the type of impotence known as partial, the individual may be able to have a brief erection and may even enter the vagina, but will then have an immediate ejaculation of sperm. This condition is known as premature ejaculation and is divided into two types that will be discussed later.

Nature of Erectile Tissues

The penis in the male and the clitoris in the female (which is the homologue of the former) are both composed chiefly of erectile tissue. Erectile tissue consists essentially of numerous fibrous strands, called trabeculae, that are attached to the undersurface of the thick covering (tunica albuginea) of the organ (penis or clitoris) and stretch from there across the interior of the structure. They form a fine spongelike network whose interspaces communicate freely with one another and contain varying quantities of blood, draining through direct communications with the veins of the penis or clitoris. The size of the erectile organ varies with the amount of blood in these spongelike cavernous spaces. When distended with blood the organ becomes erect.

There is a marked resemblance of the penis to its homologue, the clitoris. Both organs have a body composed of two columns of erectile tissue and known as the corpora cavernosa; a head or glans, which also is composed of erectile tissue; and, passing backward from the head in the penis, a long column of erectile tissue known as the corpus cavernosum of the urethra (since the urethra or passage from the urinary bladder traverses it). This column ends below in an enlargement known as the bulb of the penis. In the female a somewhat separate erectile structure, known as the bulb of the vestibule, lies on each side of the orifice of the vagina.

The corpora cavernosa of both the penis and the clitoris extend backward and downward as legs or crura and are attached to the periosteum of the medial sides of surfaces of the pubic arch. The crura in both sexes are overlaid by the ischiocavernosus muscle and the bulb in each sex is covered by the bulbocavernosus muscle. The ischiocavernosus muscle may assist in erection by pressure on veins from the penis.

In the male the bulbocavernosus muscle covers the bulb of the penis and contracts spasmodically during the sexual climax or orgasm and squirts the semen from the posterior urethra. This contraction is an involuntary reflex act initiated by the orgasm to ensure the passage of spermatozoa into the vagina. (This muscle, used voluntarily, empties the last drops of urine from the urethra.) In the female also the muscle contracts spasmodically during orgasm and in some instances the male partner can feel the tightening around the penis. Voluntary contraction of this muscle, known also as the sphincter vaginae, during sexual intercourse produces a voluptuous sensation greatly appreciated by most male partners.

An examination of medical drawings will

make clear the spongy or cavernous nature of the erectile tissue of the penis. Blood normally flows into and out of the penis or clitoris at about the same rate, but during sexual excitement and at other times, as during the so-called morning erections, the blood flows in at a much faster rate than it flows out. As a result, the spongy tissue spaces are filled, but the surface of the organ is supported by the tough tunica albuginea so that it cannot stretch beyond a certain degree. When this point of maximum distension is reached the organ becomes stiff and the inflow and outflow reach equilibrium. This condition may be of varying duration, from minutes to an hour or longer, depending upon the mood and the capability of the individual. Normally the erection is lost soon after the climax, or orgasm, which in the male causes the ejaculation through the contractions of the bulbocavernosus muscle, and in the female the spasmodic contractions of the sphincter vaginae muscle around the vaginal orifice.

The Anatomy of Erection

Blood enters the erectile tissues of the penis and clitoris through arteries. The only anatomical explanation of the cause of erection this writer has found is made in the following statement from Morris' *Human Anatomy* (1945):

The nerves supplying the penis are the anterior scrotal branches of the ilioinguinal, and the perineal branches and dorsal nerve of the penis from the pudendal. Sympathetic fibers from the third and fourth sacral nerves constitute what are termed the nervi erigentes, since stimulation of them produces erection of the organ. An anatomical provision for the production of this phenomenon has been found in the occurrence of peculiar thickenings of the intima of the arteries of the penis, by which the lumina of the vessels are greatly diminished or even occluded when in a state of moderate contraction, as when the organ is flaccid [soft]. When the arteries are dilated the intimal thickenings become reduced in height and the blood is afforded a free passage into the lacunar spaces of the corpora cavernosa, which thus become engorged.

The penis may be compared with a hollow cylinder, blind at one end and filled with dry sea sponge. If the open end is dipped in water the marked increase in the weight of the cylin-

der will quickly be noticed. This state will continue as long as the water remains in the sponge inside the cylinder. One may simulate the phenomenon to a lesser degree by pouring water into a rubber glove until all the fingers and the thumb stick out like the teats on a cow's full udder.

At the time the patient with partial or complete impotence attempts to have intercourse there is some inhibition to the proper rate of flow of blood into and from the cavernous spaces of the erectile tissues of the penis. At other times, as under the influence of phantasies, in masturbation, or in morning erections, the inflow is faster and the organ becomes erect. In such cases the difficulty is psychogenic and not organic.

The Physiology of Erection

As a preparation for sexual intercourse, the process of erection is initiated by the higher centers of the central nervous system—that is, by centers in the large brain or cerebrum. The impulses travel downward over nerve pathways to the lower segments of the spinal cord, which contains a group of nerve cells usually referred to as the erection center. Passing outward from this center in the spinal cord in its sacral region, nerve fibers extend downward to the erectile tissues of the penis and clitoris. These nerves, which belong to the parasympathetic division of the autonomic nervous system, are called the *nervi erigentes,* or erection nerves, since it is their function to regulate the blood content of the spongy tissues in the erectile organs, thus rendering them turgid and rigid. The penis and clitoris also receive sympathetic nerve fibers by way of the hypogastric and pelvic plexuses, but these fibers have an inhibitory influence and tend to prevent erection.

The Nervous System

It will help the intelligent patient if he comprehends the nature of the human nervous system. It consists of the central portion, made up of the brain and spinal cord; of the peripheral nervous system, which consists of nerves passing from the central nervous system all over the body to muscles, joints, internal organs, skin, and so on; and of the autonomic nervous system, which has control over the involuntary activities of the body, such as circulation, respiration, digestion and absorption, and so on.

An intact *central nervous system* is necessary for the adequate performance of the sexual act. Many cases of organic impotence, which comprise less than ten per cent of all cases of impotence, are due to lesions in the brain and spinal cord, much more often in the latter. The brain and spinal cord must be able to send their impulses and to transmit them in order for the erectile tissues to respond normally. This response means filling with blood and becoming tense and firm. If a motor peripheral nerve is cut or severely damaged it cannot transmit impulses from the brain and/or spinal cord to the muscle it normally supplies. The result is paralysis of the muscle. The principle is the same.

It is also necessary for the *peripheral nervous system* to be intact, for what one sees, hears, smells, or feels may determine one's response to erotic stimuli.

The stimuli and impulses that affect the *autonomic nervous system* are of the utmost importance in carrying out the normal act of coitus. For example, in the act of coitus the *sympathetic division* of the autonomic nervous system has an inhibitory effect. If a man is overcome by grief or seized by fear, he cannot attain an erection. As a matter of fact, fear of failure, fear of detection, fear of causing an unwanted pregnancy, or any other kind of fear may prevent a satisfactory erection.

On the other hand it is the *parasympathetic nervous system* that stimulates the erectile tissues and aids in producing erection. It is inhibition of the parasympathetic function resulting from overactivity of the sympathetic that causes most cases of impotence.

Fortunately, we have drugs that quiet or sedate the sympathetic nerves and drugs that stimulate the parasympathetic, to such an extent that the evil influence of the former is overcome and the salutary influence of the latter is enhanced, thus bringing about erection.

It is thus clear that the act of coitus requires a conscious desire, or libido, which acts on the erection center in the spinal cord and stimulates

it to bring about the phenomenon of circulatory distention of the cavernous or erectile tissues of the copulatory organs. When this occurs in partners with normal organs, proper and mutually satisfactory sexual intercourse is possible.

Erection and ejaculation may occur without conscious sex desire, as in the so-called "wet-dream" or nocturnal emission. Even in such cases it cannot be doubted that the influence of the higher centers (in the brain) is effective in bringing about the sequence of events.

In normal and healthy men only powerful emotions of an inhibitory nature can prevent the smooth-running physiology of erection from accomplishing the desired purpose.

Types of Erection

Cerebral Erection

The normal and usual type of erection occurs spontaneously as a result of sexual excitement. Erotic thoughts can bring it about, but on physical contact it will take place even more quickly. In young men especially it happens and persists for a considerable time during petting or dancing. This is the cerebral type of erection and results largely from impulses passing downward from the higher centers (in the brain, or cerebrum) to the lower centers in the spinal cord and thence over the erection nerves of the parasympathetic nervous system to the erectile tissues. This type of erection may persist into old age, but in middle life or later the speed of the phenomenon is much lessened. In the later decades of life it may become necessary to depend upon the other principal type of erection.

Reflex Erection

This is the tactile or reflex type and requires a varying amount of massage of the penis, preferably by the wife. It may take from two or three to five or ten minutes of slow massage, with the use of a good lubricant. Although the surgical lubricating jellies are very good for this purpose, their composition seems to have recently become somewhat stiffer and hence not so slick. An excellent lubricant for this purpose is Jergens Lotion or Hinds Honey and Almond Cream or any equivalent lotion. If a condom is used surgical jelly is better and should be applied before it is put on.

Some patients complain that massage of the penis in this manner brings on the orgasm and thus dissipates their desire. This is simply a matter of inadequate technique. The massage should be slow and backward and forward over the head of the penis. When the sensation grows too acute the husband uses some signal (such as a slight pinch on his wife's thigh), or asks her to stop for a moment. After the sensation becomes less acute, the wife proceeds again with the massage. Further directions in this regard will be given in the discussion of the medical treatment of psychogenic impotence, although most men will not require any medication in order to achieve a perfectly satisfactory reflex erection. This type of erection is usually much more stable than the very quick cerebral erections of young men, who reach a climax so quickly that the wife is unable to attain orgasm.

The slowness in attaining erection and the need for massage in some older men cannot certainly be explained with our present knowledge of the changes that take place in the blood vessels and tissues of the erectile organs, but it has been surmised that arteriosclerotic changes in the arteries may be at least partly responsible.

Although many men, unaware of the existence of the reflex type of erection, conclude that they are impotent, many others learn in one way or another of the reflex erection and realize that they are not impotent, but merely slow in getting started. They may experiment with themselves by massaging their penes and bring on the erection in this manner while the wife waits. It never seems to occur to them that it is much more satisfactory to have the wife bring it about. Some men learn the technique through conversation with other men.

Possibly old men could attain adequate potency by means of appropriate medication and the technique described above for the reflex erection. Certainly, if a morning erection can occur, the anatomy and physiology of the erectile apparatus are intact and merely require proper treatment, assuming that the male has a good libido. Unfortunate are those cases in which the man has lost all desire, yet has an ardent wife who craves satisfaction. Alleviation of the spouse's desires in instances of this kind will be described in the discussion of the artificial phallus.

Types of Impotence and Their Causes

There are three types of impotence, based on the underlying causes: organic, functional, and psychic (psychogenic).

Organic Impotence

Organic impotence is due to some anatomical defect in the reproductive organs, or in the brain or spinal cord. Because of an extreme condition of hypospadias the penis as such may be absent, represented by what resembles a very large clitoris. The external urinary opening (from the bladder) is underneath the base of the phallus and it is necessary for the individual to squat in order to urinate. In cases of hypospadias in which there is a normal-sized or even a small penis, a urological surgeon can make an artificial channel to the end of the organ. Thereafter the patient can stand and void and can also ejaculate inside the vagina.

The testicles may have been lost by disease or accident or have become incapacitated following febrile diseases such as mumps. If this loss occurs before the individual has attained maturity and reached full sexual development, impotence is the rule. (Loss of the testicles after adulthood during which a full development sexually has been attained will not cause impotence for many years.)

The urethra may have been so injured that it cannot stretch sufficiently to permit normal erection.

Disease of, or accident to, the brain or spinal cord may so affect centers concerned with perception or erection that impotence results.

It is said that the penis is very rarely too large for entrance into a vagina of average size, although enormous hypertrophy has been said to have prevented intercourse in some instances; also deformities or disease of the penis or surrounding structures (as of the scrotum in hydrocele or in elephantiasis) may render intercourse impossible. Neither of these conditions constitutes impotence in the usual sense.

Impotence caused by anatomic malformation or disproportion may be cured if the deformity is not too great. If disease is the underlying cause, its cure may bring about correction of the deficiency.

Functional Impotence

Functional impotence is, as the name implies, caused by some disturbance of the various functions of the generative organs. It may be a nervous disturbance, affecting centers in the brain or spinal cord or interfering with nerve tracts or nerve endings; it may be a circulatory or inflammatory condition, resulting in congestion or erosions in the sex glands or in the urethra; or it may be due to subnormal activity of the male hormone glands.

The time element is very important in coitus. The stages are realization of libido (sex desire), erection, orgasm, and ejaculation. As pointed out elsewhere, the orgasm reflex causes the emission; it is not the ejaculation that causes the orgasm.

One of the principal causes of functional impotence is exhaustion. This may affect the central and peripheral nervous systems as well as the organs of reproduction. The exhaustion may be caused by sexual excess, coitus interruptus (withdrawal before ejaculation), excessive masturbation, gonorrhea, heavy petting at frequent intervals without intercourse, or even by moderate masturbation. It should be emphasized that sexual intercourse begins with kissing and necking and continues with all of the phases of petting. It should continue normally to completed coitus, which is the final phase of intercourse. Frequent congestion of the sex organs and their associated glands without safety-valve orgasms and ejaculations should not be expected to have a salutary effect. It does not.

Psychogenic Impotence

Psychogenic or inhibitory impotence is caused by the effects of impulses from the higher centers (in the cortex of the cerebrum or brain) on the lower centers (in the spinal cord) and through them upon the erectile nerves and the generative organs themselves. Various emotions usually set up the inhibitions. Fear is the most frequent: fear of detection, fear of causing pregnancy, fear of venereal disease, fear that youthful masturbation might cause impotence. Distaste for the partner, great joy over good news, untoward attitude of the woman, and many other disturbing factors may cause temporary psychogenic impotence.

Some men become perturbed because they fail to have proper erection or have premature ejaculation (before entrance) when they attempt to have intercourse (1) with a woman for the first time or first few times; (2) under adverse environmental conditions, as in an automobile, or when fearing detection; (3) or both. Such men are not impotent at all; they are merely unduly excited and require only to get better acquainted with the prospective partner; have proper surroundings or mental repose for the act; or both. Some sensitive men fail after overcoming protracted feminine resistance or when they feel the woman is yielding for their special benefit in spite of moral or other scruples. Too much anticipation often thwarts successful realization. With sympathetic understanding and full assurance of mutual desire and cooperation on the part of the feminine companion, this temporary psychological "impotence" will be overcome.

Here we may say that in the treatment of all organic and functional cases the causes must be found and if possible removed. An extremely thorough examination will have a good psychic effect upon the patient. The power of suggestion alone is often sufficient to cure impotence. The wife of one such young man to whom I had given a good talking came in after a few weeks complaining I had "overtreated" her husband and asked if I would not do something to reduce his potency. Electrical treatments and psychoanalysis have been recommended. Change in environment may prove beneficial.

Premature Ejaculation

In 1946 this author reported earlier experience with the use of a local anesthetic (1 per cent Nupercaine ointment) in the control of what is believed to be one of the most frequent causes of premature ejaculation in sthenic males—supersensitivity of the head of the penis, usually in association with abnormally high sexual tension. The vigorous or sthenic type of male is especially prone to this kind of sexual deficiency, which must be regarded in these individuals as a manifestation of nervous and mental influences arising from a high degree of potency. Premature ejaculation is, therefore, not impotence in the ordinary sense, although erection is lost after untimely orgasm and ejaculation and a practical impotence sets in. In contrast to the sthenic or strong male, the asthenic or weak male, most often past middle age, exhibits premature ejaculation as a result of a low degree of potency, or virtual impotence, caused by sexual hypotonus and insufficient erection.

Definition

This condition has been variously defined. A good practical definition of this sexual deficiency is ejaculation that occurs too soon for satisfactory expression of the mutual love of husband and wife (assuming, of course, that the wife is sexually normal and can reach a climax within a reasonable time). It is impossible to fix an arbitrary time range for the normal; "biological variation" must be allowed for in both partners. But ejaculation occurring prior to entrance or within a very short time thereafter is to be considered premature. In our experience, such a conclusion has provided a basis for practical study with a view toward diagnosis and control.

Etiology

Presumed supersensitivity of the urethra has focused attention on the long-suffering *colliculus seminalis* (old terminology: *verumontanum*) so that it has been bombarded with silver nitrate or other irritants ever since the invention of the cystoscope. As Schapiro (1953) has stated, "an intense controversy has been carried on over the question whether changes in the posterior urethra, at the verumontanum (colliculus seminalis) in particular, are the cause of premature ejaculation."

Actually of far greater significance, however, is the supersensitivity of the head of the penis (glans), where the genital corpuscles are located and the phenomenon of the orgasm attains its highest intensity. As evidenced by the frequency with which satisfactory control of premature ejaculation has been obtained

through the use of Nupercaine ointment applied to the head of the penis, the most common cause of this abnormality in sthenic males must be assumed to be supersensitivity of the nerve endings in the head of the penis rather than supersensitivity of the urethra, particularly of the colliculus seminalis.

Treatment

Treatment of premature ejaculation is, of course, directed toward removal or neutralization of the factor or factors involved in its causation. Circumcision would seem to be indicated in patients with a long foreskin.

A considerable percentage of patients complaining of premature ejaculation will be found to be primarily affected by psychic influences and should have the benefit of expert psychiatric care.

Excessive intercourse or masturbation may eventuate in a tendency to premature ejaculation; rest, sedation, and a return to normal sexual relations have been quite beneficial in such cases.

Although drastic measures seem to be indicated in certain patients, our experience through many years is that the treatment of the great majority of cases of premature ejaculation is a relatively simple matter. It is probable, as our results show, that in the great majority of sufferers from premature ejaculation the prime causative factor is supersensitivity of the head of the penis, in association with excessive sexual excitement and eagerness. Sedation is helpful in restoring composure. As a rule, only the local anesthetic will be required, with a sedative to be added to the treatment in accordance with the needs of the individual patient.

Distinction must be made between the asthenic and sthenic types of patients with the complaint of premature ejaculation. In the asthenic type, premature ejaculation is associated with exhaustion and irritable weakness; sexual hypotonus and erectile insufficiency are also generally involved. As patients of this type are usually men of middle age or older, impotence or semi-impotence must be considered probable. The asthenic type should not be expected to respond favorably to partial anesthesia of the head of the penis; in fact, its use is contraindicated in all patients who do not achieve erection with ease. It would do more harm than good in men requiring massage for reflex erection.

In contrast, the sthenic patient with the complaint of premature ejaculation is younger, under middle age, healthy and vigorous, with no history of neurasthenia, sexual excesses, or sexual weakness. Libido and erection are normal, as are ejaculation and orgasm except for the rapidity of onset. Characteristically, such a patient, after a lengthy period of continence, has so intense a sexual desire that the entire process of coitus is accomplished too quickly to be fully gratifying to either partner. This type of patient may be expected to respond to partial anesthesia of the glans penis, with mild sedation also being necessary in some cases.

NUPERCAINE OINTMENT

The use of 1% Nupercainal was suggested by the present writer as early as 1946; further recommendation has been made by Aycock (1949). The ointment containing 1% Nupercaine has been found to be adequate for the majority of patients of the type just described (it may be obtained at any drugstore without a prescription). However, a minority have required an ointment with a higher percentage of Nupercaine (2.5% or even 5% in some instances).

The patient should be instructed to massage thoroughly into the head of the penis and the groove just behind it a quantity of the ointment about the size of a large pea. The optimal quantity will vary with different individuals and must be determined by trial. He should wait twenty to thirty minutes before beginning coitus (a few patients have reported they have to wait an hour). The time needed for full effect varies with the individual. One patient who stated he required sixty minutes had previously reported failure with the shorter interval.

Control of premature ejaculation through the application of Nupercaine ointment to the head of the penis has been gratifying in the great majority of patients of the sthenic type. Many have expressed enthusiasm concerning the resultant more satisfactory performance of the sexual act, with particular reference to the greater satisfaction derived by the female partners. Retardation of erection does not appear to occur if directions are followed. Application of considerably too much of the ointment and waiting too long may in most cases interfere with erection.

No instances of sensitization have been reported, nor have there been any reports of dermatitis or irritation or loss of sensation, although many patients have used the 5% strength for years, two for over ten years. After confidence in the method is attained sedation may be discontinued.

The writer has dispensed several other local anesthetics to patients for trial, but reports concerning their use have been for the most part negative.

Impotence in Eunuchoid Men

The word eunuch means a male who has been castrated. In olden times such individuals served as chamberlains in palaces or as servants in harems. The word *castrato* (from the Italian) means a male castrated in boyhood in order to retain an unchanged or soprano voice. Such individuals were brought up as choir singers.

Although the term castration now has a wider application, to include removal of the ovaries in women, spaying in female animals, and even the removal of stamens from flowers, the original meaning was the excision of the testicles or male gonads from an individual before the age of puberty. The same procedure is performed on domestic animals as a rule while they are young. A familiar example is the steer or ox, produced by the castration of a bullock.

The human eunuch, if typical, has characteristics similar to those of a steer, as well as of some other castrated animals. Before the advent of potent male hormone preparations such persons went through life untreated. An experienced observer could recognize such an individual at sight. The stature is gaunt, the shoulders square, the facial skin loose and finely wrinkled. There is a full head of hair, and never baldness, and the voice is high pitched. Lack of muscular development is noticeable, with accompanying fatigability. The complexion is usually sallow. A physical examination of the eunuch who develops in such a manner because of lack of the necessary hormones in his system will show that his penis is quite small, his testicles about the size of shelled peanuts, that he has no hair in his armpits and no pubic hair, or very little, and that what there is does not extend up toward the navel as in the typical male escutcheon. The subject rarely if ever shaves. There is, of course, no libido or sexual desire and the individual is both impotent and sterile.

The artificial eunuch, made so by castration in boyhood, would have most of these characteristics, but there would of course be no testicles at all. If male persons are castrated after they are fully grown and sexually mature and have lived normally active sex lives, they will not develop such characteristics, nor will their sexual powers wane for some time, often not for years. To quote from Chapter 21 of this author's *Sex Manual*:

In human castrates the evidence indicates that capacity to participate in sex acts is not held completely in abeyance. In women after the menopause the reproductive function is of course lost, but the sexual function may remain unchanged. One-half of men 25 to 30 years of age when castrated continue to have sexual desire and ability to copulate. Hammond reported seven cases of men castrated between 30 and 51 years of age who continued coitus after operation, one for as long as 17 years. Many other instances could be cited, both for men and women.

Eunuchoidism means having the symptoms of a typical eunuch, such as those produced by castrating a male in boyhood. The "natural" eunuchoid patient who was "born" or developed that way because of hormonal insufficiency (failure of a portion of the anterior lobe of the hypophysis to bring about the development of the sex organs and secondary sexual characteristics) can easily be recognized and successfully treated. There are two qualifications to this statement: (1) the treatment must be started early enough in life, although well after the age of puberty; (2) the individual will always be sterile.

Where the services are available it is wise for such patients to be given thorough endocrine laboratory checkups, in addition, of course, to the routine history and physical examination. Of particular interest is the determination of the 17-ketosteroid output in a twenty-four-hour

collection of urine. The 17-ketosteroid output in twenty-four hours will be quite subnormal in a eunuchoid person before treatment. As treatment continues there will be a rise to normal or even above-normal levels. Eventually there will be subjective and objective changes in the patient and, except for the very small testicles, he will in time develop into an apparently normal sexual adult, and probably get married (if treatment is begun early enough in life).

In successfully treated cases there will be an enlargement of the penis, even beyond normal size; development of pubic hair, eventually in some cases up to the navel; and growth of hair in the armpits and increased hair on the face and body as a whole, so that shaving as often as every other day becomes necessary. Muscular growth and strength replace the former lack of development and fatigability. A definite sex desire sets in, as well as ability to perform coitus in a normal manner, except that there may be little or no ejaculate and that what there is will contain no sperm. The skeletal structures, of course, will remain the same, but the typical eunuchoid appearance may become less marked. Treatment with hypophyseal hormones (gonadotropins) may prove beneficial if given early in patients with pituitary insufficiency. From the viewpoint of the physician this subject is well covered in Greenblatt's *Office Endocrinology* (1952).

For the development of primary and secondary sex characteristics the eunuch depends upon treatment with androgens or male sex hormones, which must be kept up indefinitely. Some preparation of testosterone is generally used, given either by intramuscular injections into the buttocks or by pellet implantation beneath the skin.

The Medical Treatment of Impotence

Although the average layman thinks a doctor can give him a pill or a "shot" for almost anything, this confidence is not deserved when it comes to the treatment of impotence. Each case must be carefully studied and the appropriate treatment decided upon after diagnosis. The age of the man and the type of impotence are important factors in determining the course to be followed.

Impotence may be associated with various physical deficiencies, such as anemia, avitaminosis, hypothyroidism, fatigue, and exhaustion. Before beginning treatment of impotence all possible debilitating conditions should be ruled out. If anemia is present it should be corrected in the usual way. Multiple vitamins with liver extract and an ample supply of vitamin B_{12} are often very helpful. Small doses of a good thyroid preparation may be used if hypothyroidism is present. Rest, of course, is the cure for fatigue or exhaustion. There may be other physical abnormalities that require treatment. Whatever they are they should be eliminated if possible before treatment for impotence itself is instituted.

Having determined that the patient is suffering from impotence in spite of the correction of all physical conditions that might have contributed to it, the next step is to recall the essential factors previously discussed.

In cases of impotence in asthenic men, sedation of the sympathetic nervous system and stimulation of the parasympathetic nervous system should aid in production of erection. The sedative is one of choice on the part of the physician. There are many sedatives to select from. They may be bromides, barbiturates, or alcohol, and if one does not succeed, another may. One caution must be given: either barbiturates or alcohol may be used, but never barbiturates and alcohol together. Triple bromides obtained as effervescent disks in large glass tubes may prove sufficient. The quick-acting barbiturates, such as Nembutal or Seconal, are to be preferred, as they are quickly absorbed and quickly excreted. Half the hypnotic dose of either of these—or even the full dose—may be employed, taken by the patient about a half hour before marital relations. If alcohol is selected as a sedative it may be taken in any form desired by the patient.

At present the drugs of choice for stimulation of the parasympathetic are strychnine and yohimbine. More research needs to be done with both to determine fully their action and the proper dosage.

Max Huhner, in his *Disorders of Sexual Function*, advised 1/20 of a grain of strychnine sulphate in three doses at two-hour intervals. The textbook dose of strychnine sulphate is 1/60 of a grain when taken in broken doses daily. When prescribed for stimulating the erection center in the spinal cord, larger doses are necessary, but they are not taken daily—only a short time before marital relations. This writer has found two doses of 1/20 grain with a two-hour interval usually sufficient, and in many cases one dose of 1/20 grain may be all that is needed. If two doses are taken, one may be just after the evening meal and one fifteen or twenty minutes before coitus, with an interval of two or three hours between doses. The recommended dosage may be taken daily for several days if desired, although it is not likely that the patient will often desire to employ the remedy on consecutive days.

One point must be borne in mind: coated strychnine tablets should never be used, as they will not dissolve promptly in the stomach; the plain white so-called hypodermic tablets, whether of hypodermic quality or not, should be prescribed. The enteric-coated tablets will not dissolve until they reach the intestine and by that time the need for the action of the drug will have long passed.

Hormones

The use of hormones in medicine is to substitute for the lack of a sufficient quantity supplied by the various glands of internal secretion (endocrine glands). The use of insulin in diabetes; of thyroid in hypothyroid states such as myxedema and cretinism; the use of adrenalin in treating shock; the use of estrogens (female sex hormones) in treating hot flushes and other discomforts of the menopause; and the treatment of many disorders by use of the newer hormones, cortisone and ACTH, have been made known to many. This general knowledge has been spread by articles in newspapers and magazines and by acquaintance of relatives or friends who have been treated by this method. It is a method of treatment by substitution: supplying to the body some chemical the body has failed to supply for itself.

Naturally, when male hormones were successfully prepared there was great hope that a panacea for impotence was at hand. Unfortunately, this did not prove to be true. The reason is that most cases of impotence are not caused by a lack of such hormones in the individuals concerned, but are due to psychogenic factors that produce varying degrees of inhibition. In short, substitution treatment is not in order. Greenblatt, in his *Office Endocrinology*, sums up the situation as follows:

In the study of the male factor as a cause of sterility, impotence is not infrequently encountered. Relative or complete sexual impotence may be due to a variety of factors, *not the least of which is of psychogenic origin* [italics added]. Constitutional local inflammatory processes and endocrinologic factors may play important roles. Impotence, when due to testicular deficiency, is amenable to treatment with androgens (male hormones), at times with gonadotropins. Impotence of psychic etiology will not respond to endocrine (substitution) therapy. In fact, androgen therapy may add to the psychic trauma.

We can then understand why the use of testosterone in eunuchoid patients is uniformly successful (except for curing the permanent sterility due to the undeveloped testicles). In these individuals there is a marked deficiency of androgens, such as testosterone, in their circulating blood, and substitution therapy is needed to increase the amount to that required for sexual development. There is a hypophyseal or pituitary failure in such patients and theoretically treatment with potent gonadotropins during the adolescent period of sexual development would bring about normal growth of the reproductive organs, including the testicles. When this period has passed, it is still possible by adequate treatment to bring about a marked development, except in the testicles.

There is a means of testing how much of the androgens are being excreted daily by members of both sexes. Preparatory to the test it is necessary for the patient to collect all the urine voided during a period of twenty-four hours. If the laboratory report shows that the twenty-four-hour output of the substances tested for (17-ketosteroids) is much lower than the average, then it is not unlikely that substitution therapy with male sex hormone will be helpful. If the report shows that the patient is excreting a normal amount of male hormones there is little likelihood that substitution treatment will be of value for impotence.

A small percentage of men can be said to pass through a period of life when, in the middle years or later, they may have nervousness and hot flushes that appear to simulate conditions of the menopause in women. Many of these men may complain of impotence and of feeling depressed and discouraged. However, some of them may be suffering from melancholia without being impotent. The differential diagnosis may be made by asking the patient if he actually is impotent. Some will readily admit that they are. Others will say they have no desire for sexual relations because of the severe depression, but nevertheless insist that if they tried to have intercourse they could do so. It is these patients that have melancholia. They should be referred to a qualified psychiatrist for electroshock or other psychiatric therapy. It is claimed that this will restore nineteen out of twenty to health and good spirits.

In those cases in which it is clear that the patients need substitution treatment, male sex hormones may be administered by mouth, by intramuscular injection, or by pellet implantation. The intramuscular injections (of testosterone propionate, etc.) are usually given into the buttocks, alternating on the two sides in successive treatments. Pellet implantations have the advantage of being needed only once in four to six months, as compared to once or twice weekly when injections are given. They are ideal for patients that come from a distance.

Mechanical Treatment of Impotence

Since man is not so fortunate as some species of lower animals that have bones in their penes, the idea of a penile splint has exercised human ingenuity for many years. Most men are cognizant of the existence of the types of penile splints that have survived commercially in this country. All are very much alike. They consist of a flat metal core covered with rubber and terminating at each end in a rubber ring. Large, medium, and small sizes are usually offered.

On the basis of examination of this type of penile splint and on the strength of its rejection by patients, this writer cannot recommend it. Although such a support might prove to be of some value to an occasional patient who happens to obtain one that fits well, the number of sizes is too small, especially as concerns the length; there is not an adequate support at the base; and the rubber ring is not sufficient.

Fortunately, there is available a well-made penile splint that is manufactured in England. This device is worth many times more than its cost. When precisely fitted—and it must fit accurately—it is a dependable aid which, in the opinion of the author, has no peer. The Coitus Training Apparatus (CTA), manufactured by Down Bros. and Mayer & Phelps Ltd., is sold in the United States on a prescription basis only.* A description of the apparatus and its use is given in a booklet by Joseph Loewenstein, entitled *The Treatment of Impotence, with Special Reference to Mechanotherapy.*† Its use is primarily for the treatment of psychogenic impotence, and is supplemented by psychotherapy. Nevertheless it can be used on the basis of its own value alone, for it will infallibly carry the flaccid penis into the vagina. Dr. Loewenstein cites many cases of men who became readjusted to marital coitus and dispensed with the use of the device. His cases were also treated with psychotherapy.

To put on the apparatus the tiny rubber ring is slipped from the "leg" to which it is not attached and the "legs" spread apart; then the CTA is placed over the penis, shaft underneath, and the head of the penis is pulled forward and upward so that the distal ring can be closed around it by replacing the rubber band on the other "leg." Intromission can now be accomplished. If the ring does not fit snugly, the head of the penis may slip out. Any lubricant used should be added after the distal ring is fastened snugly in place around the completely dry "neck" of the penis. The ring fits so precisely that the portion of skin beneath it remains dry.

A condom may be used with the apparatus. A good quality condom must be used, for when put on outside the apparatus the open end must be pulled around the large proximal metal ring. If the condom is old it will probably tear when this is done.

A man may be impotent while not sterile. If such a man cannot deposit semen at the bottom of the vagina because of failure to gain erection and full penetration, it is possible by use of the device to ejaculate inside the vagina. The distal ring compresses the neck of the penis so tightly that all of the semen does not come out. Before withdrawing, the little rubber ring should be pulled off so the "legs" of the device can open. This will permit the distal ring also to open far enough for the remainder of the semen to pass out of the urethra into the bottom of the vagina and to increase the chances of conception.

Any man can use the apparatus with satisfaction, whether he requires it at all times or not. If one is slow in attaining erection and the time for intercourse is necessarily short, the device is the answer. Sometimes during the use of the device one may find that erection has taken place. It should then be removed by pulling the little rubber band off the "leg" it is not attached to, and intercourse continued without the apparatus.

The writer has dispensed the apparatus successfully in premature ejaculation when the patient has no difficulty in obtaining an erection, but loses it almost immediately on entering the vagina. It may seem strange that a device that fits the soft penis will also fit the erect organ. The little rubber ring around the "legs" stretches and the distal ring accommodates itself around the "neck" of the penis. It will feel tight, of course, but it does not have to be removed. The tendency to ejaculate prematurely will be overcome by the fact that the wearer knows he can stay in the vagina as long as he wants to—or, more important, as long as his wife wants him to. Even if he does ejaculate before she has reached a climax, he can lose his erection and still remain in the vagina until she has attained orgasm.

Penile Prosthesis (Artificial Phallus)

As a practical sexual scientist the author feels that the state of taboo that surrounds the subject of the artificial penis is unwarranted, unjustifiable, and doubtless a relict of the "morals" of the Victorian Age. That there are legitimate medical indications for dispensing suitable devices of this nature is incontestable. These indications will be discussed later.

One of the principal deterrents to the manufacture and supply of artificial phalli to patients who need them is the general belief that such procedures are illegal. Insofar as this writer has been able to determine this is not true when there are definite medical indications and when the dispensing is done by a licensed physician.

What are the medical indications for the dispensing of a prosthesis of this kind to a married man? One very obvious need would be the loss of the penis. Disease and accidents bring about such a loss. Cancer of the penis requires immediate amputation. Other diseases may bring about more or less complete destruction of the organ. The penis may be partly or completely lost after injury. Often the testicles are not injured in such accidents so that a normal libido or sex desire may continue. Of course the husband would not obtain sexual relief for himself by use of a penile prosthesis, but he could have the satisfaction of taking care of the sexual needs of the woman he loved. If the woman were entirely frigid there would naturally be no need on her part, but the majority of women are not frigid.

A second strong indication for the use of an artificial penis, at least temporarily, is that of the premature ejaculator, who may not even succeed in entering the vagina or who has orgasm immediately after intromission. If and when he is cured, the prosthesis may be dispensed with. It is far better that such a husband satisfy his wife by this method than that she should turn against the act or become a nervous wreck from repeated disappointments. Again, it is true that if the wife is completely frigid there would be no need on her part for coitus, but the woman who remains coldly uninterested when approached by a loving husband, even though he cannot remain in the vagina but a very short time without ejaculating and losing his erection, is certainly in the minority.

Even though the writer rejects the claim that any woman who does not have a vaginal orgasm is frigid (the Freudian thesis) and maintains that the vast majority of women depend upon stimulation of the clitoris for satisfaction, there is undeniably a small percentage of women who refer the climactic sensation to the vagina. Such women as a rule derive no pleasure from excitation of the clitoris, and many will not even permit its being massaged. If the husband with a wife of this type cannot remain

in the vagina sufficiently long for her to reach orgasm, she cannot reach it at all—unless by use of a penile prosthesis. She has grown up with the idea that she must have an erect penis in her vagina in order to enjoy sexual intercourse fully and to obtain complete satisfaction. The solution of this problem is to recognize the situation and supply the needed device. In many cases it will save marriages.

Some normal women have two or three orgasms during one act of coitus, or would like to if their husbands continued the act long enough, with or without intermission. With intermission, the husband withdraws and his erection subsides until his wife is ready for her second or third climax. He regains erection when she has rested and continues until she is fully satisfied, reaching his own climax with her when she has the last one. Some highly sexed women can have a half dozen or more orgasms during one continued act of intercourse if the husband's technique will enable him to continue in the vagina the required length of time. In any of these cases of multiple orgasm, which require as a rule protracted intercourse, it may prove impossible for the husband to restrain himself and put off orgasm as long as his wife desires. In such cases the use of a penile prosthesis is the answer.

After a quarter of a century of effort to find a maker of an artificial phallus, success belatedly arrived through a reference obtained from a university school of medicine (department of medical illustration). The material is a soft plastic and the phallus is realistically made. It has a rectangular base with four grommet holes for attachment of tapes for fastening in place. It is available in four sizes. Very favorable comments have been received from physicians who have dispensed it.

*Southern Medical Supply Co., P.O. Box 1168, Augusta, Ga. 30903.
†Now out of print.

References

Aycock, L., "The Medical Management of Premature-Ejaculation." *J. Urol. 62;* 361-362, 1949.
Bergler, E., "Premature Ejaculation." In A. P. Pillay and A. Ellis (eds.), *Sex, Society and the Individual.* Bombay: *Internat. J. Sexology,* 1953.

Caprio, F. S., *The Sexually Adequate Male*. New York: Citadel Press, 1952.

Ellis, Albert, *Sex Without Guilt*. New York: Lyle Stuart, 1958.

Ellis, Albert, *The Art and Science of Love*. New York: Lyle Stuart, 1960.

Greenblatt, R. B., *Office Endocrinology*. Springfield, Ill.: Charles C Thomas, Pub., 1952.

Hirsch, E. W., *The Power to Love*. New York: Citadel Press, 1948.

Hirsch, E. W., "The Role of the Female Partner in Premature Ejaculation." In A. P. Pillay and A. Ellis (eds.), *Sex, Society and the Individual*. Bombay: *Internat. J. Sexology*, 1953.

Kelly, G. L., "Problems of Impotence in Aging Males." *J. Am. Geriatr. Soc. 3;* No. 11, 1955.

Kelly, G. L., *Sex Manual, for Those Married or About to Be*. Augusta, Ga.: Southern Medical Supply Co., 1957.

*Kelly, G. L., *So You Think You're Impotent!* Augusta, Ga.: Southern Medical Supply Co., 1957.

Kinsey, A. C. *et al.*, *Sexual Behavior in the Human Male*. Philadelphia: W. B. Saunders Co., 1948.

Levie, L. H., "Disturbances in Male Potency." In A. P. Pillay and Albert Ellis (eds.), *Sex, Society and the Individual*. Bombay: *Internat. J. Sexology*, 1953.

Loewenstein, J., *The Treatment of Impotence, with Special Reference to Mechanotherapy*. London: Cassell & Co., Ltd., 1947.

Morris, H. *et al.*, *Human Anatomy*. Philadelphia: The Blakiston Co., 1947.

Oliven, J., *Sex Hygiene and Pathology*. Philadelphia: J. B. Lippincott Co., 1955.

Pillay, A. P., "Common Sense Therapy of Male Sex Disorders." In A. P. Pillay and Albert Ellis (eds.), *Sex, Society and the Individual*. Bombay: *Internat. J. Sexology*, 1953.

Podolsky, E., *What You Should Know about Sexual Impotence*. New York: Cadillac Publishing Co., 1953.

Schapiro, B., "Premature Ejaculation, a Review of 1,130 Cases." *J. Urol. 50;* 374-379, 1953.

Stekel, W., *Impotence in the Male*. London: Vision Press, 1952.

Stone, C. T., *Sexual Power*. New York: Grosset & Dunlap, 1950.

Walker, K., and Strauss, E. B., *Sexual Disorders in the Male*. Baltimore: The Williams & Wilkins Co., 1954.

G. LOMBARD KELLY

India and Pakistan, Sex Life in

Glimpses of the Past

IT MAY be useful at the outset to try to catch glimpses of the sex life of the subcontinent of India and Pakistan in the ages past, however distant.

To go back to the era of the Rigveda, the ancient scripture of the Hindus, composed about 2500 B.C., a close study of the original records available leaves no doubt that it was not unusual at the time to separate and seclude women from men. In other words, Purdah (literally a curtain, here meaning one specially designed to screen women from sight of strangers) was in vogue in India even at that early age. Women lived in separate apartments (Patninam), which were strictly private (Guha Karati Tosha), reserved for the exclusive use of females, just as the Sadan Osdas (Baithak Khanas) were the sole preserves of males. In public, women invariably wore cloaks, the married covering themselves further with mantles or shawls. It was unthinkable for a respectable woman to be seen in public insufficiently protected from the gaze of man.

Similarly, in the two great Epics, the Mahabharata and the Ramayana, the main events of which took place in the latter half of the second millennium and in the sixth century B.C. respectively, we come across numerous references, if anything on more elaborate and comprehensive scales, to the privacy, aloofness, isolation, and privileged position enjoined on women.

Manu (800 B.C.) forbade women mixing with men, and Jagnavalka (600 B.C.), some-what relaxing the restrictions, permitted women mixing with men but only with those who were physicians, merchants, or mendicants. Wives of absentee husbands, however, were prohibited from attending sports meetings, marriage ceremonies, and social functions generally.

Incidentally, the common belief that the Purdah system in India was introduced by the Mogul Emperors has no foundation. As we have seen, the practice in some form or other was prevalent in the country some 3,000 years before the first Muslim ruler set foot in the subcontinent.

Apart from the *Mahabharata* and the *Ramayana*, the two outstanding classics of the age, and other standard compositions from widely separated periods in the history of old Indian literature, there were many Sanskrit authors in the first century A.D., who are known to have left treatises on different patterns of physical love and sex knowledge.

In *The Kamasutra*, the monumental work of Vātsāyana, the noted Indian scholar of the second century B.C., we read of at least seven different ways of kissing, eight varieties of touch, eight playful bites, four methods of striking the body with the hands, and eight sounds that may be emitted while so doing.

In the India of *The Kamasutra*, sexual congress was looked upon as not merely a conjugal duty for begetting children but a pleasurable activity for both parties, one from which they could derive the richest experiences of life in attaining the highest spiritual aspirations of mankind, closely linked with the search for the Divine. Religious feeling and sexuality at its loftiest level had a very definite place in the mythology of ancient India.

The Epic Age

In the *Mahabharata* and the *Ramayana,* which still influence the ideology of the devout Hindu, we are provided with most valuable sources of information about the relations of the sexes and the concepts underlying those relations in the India of the period, some 1,500 years ago.

Fundamentally, however, the Epics differ—from the virile, undaunted, passionate tone of the former to the meek, almost timid, deeply religious feelings of the latter.

Broadly speaking, the ancient Hindus were divided into two distinct groups—the licentious and the self-indulgent constituting one category and the renunciators of the flesh and the world the other. It was not unusual for seemingly incorrigible delinquents, proud and boastful of their manly strength and sexual vigor, notorious as ravishers of virgins, suddenly and irrevocably to forsake voluptuousness and promiscuity and assume austere celibacy and strict abstinence from the joys and pleasures of life as atonement for past sins, spending their remaining days in prayers and meditation in preparation for the Great Call—toward incarnation in a different body. According to Hindu theology, it is one's Karma, the sum of a person's actions in one of his successive states of existence, that decides his fate or destiny in the next.

Marriage

Marriage ceremonies, in conformity with the ancient Hindu idea of the sanctity of wedlock between man and woman, were elaborate proceedings, full of rituals. Chastity, the hallmark of virginity, was absolutely and strictly demanded from maidens seeking matrimony. It was a bounden duty of a father or guardian to find not only a husband but a suitable husband for his daughter on her approaching the age of puberty. A father failing to find a worthy husband for his marriageable daughter would be, according to the *Mahabharata,* as guilty as one who had murdered a Brahman—the most atro-

cious sin a Hindu could commit. The laws prescribed under various codes were equally emphatic in their condemnation of erring parents or guardians in this respect: "Each time a [ripe] unwedded maiden has her monthly course, her parents or guardians are guilty of the heinous crime of slaying the embryo." If no suitable husband were found by the father for his daughter for three years after the commencement of her menstruation, she was at liberty to seek a mate for herself, the father remaining forever condemned for his unpardonable failure in a sacred duty.

A girl achieved a new sacramental birth through marriage, just as a Brahman would be born a second time when given the holy cord.

According to the *Mahabharata,* there were eight kinds of marriage. In the first four types, which could be entered only by Brahams, there was no dowry for the bride, since such unions between high-caste couples were supposed to bring their own rewards in the other world.

The other forms of marriage were: (a) the Purchase or Demon marriage; (b) the Love or *Gandharva* marriage; (c) the marriage by Capture (*Rakshasa Vivaha*), which was the prerogative only of the warrior or the conqueror; and (d) the so-called marriage by Stealing (*Paicaca Vivaha*), where the man had come to possess the girl by some dubious or dishonorable means.

Of these eight forms of marriage, two were considered unlawful, the *Paicaca* and the Purchase or Demon types. A *Shudra* (low-caste person) could marry by Purchase or by Stealing, but such marriages were strongly disapproved by the law codes. A man could have intercourse with a *Shudra* woman for pleasure, but decent society did not accept children from such unions as legitimate. A Brahman conceiving a child with a *Shudra* woman had to atone for it in various ways.

If a man had previously married one, two, or three non-Brahman women and then married a Brahman woman as his fourth wife, the Brahman wife took precedence over the other wives and assumed, and was invariably accorded, the status of senior consort.

Two honorable motives governed all marriages and were earnestly prayed and hoped for—the blessings of children, specially of sons, and of true love between the husband and wife. An auspicious time and date of the marriage was determined by the Brahman priests.

Marriages of daughters were costly affairs, often extending the father financially far beyond his means. The birth of a daughter was not particularly hailed in Hindu families, whereas the divine gift of a son was always the occasion for unbounded joy, celebration, and thanksgiving, it being the prerogative of a son to perform the last rites at his father's death.

Incidentally, this aversion to daughters was not by any means unique in ancient India, being also prevalent at times in some other Eastern and Western countries. In Arabia, before the advent of Islam, the Arabs in many cases killed their daughters at birth.

Notwithstanding this general antipathy toward female offspring, the woman, as a devoted mother and wife, held a unique position in Hindu Society; many women played significant roles in the history of ancient India. Even in ordinary day-to-day life, females were invariably treated with deference and courtesy. Sita, Damayanti, Savitri, and other Hindu heroines are honored and revered to this day.

Sex Pleasures

After the ceremonial bath taken on the fourth day of the monthly course, a woman became *Snata Ritusnata* (one that has bathed). A married woman, now considered clean, was thus eligible for, and deserving of, the delights of love (*Suratra*). Females were thought to be more passionate than males. According to a saying of Canakya, "mankind was made old by cares, the warrior by fetters, the woman by a life without coition."

Coitus was said to have been first practiced in the Devapara Age. Previous to that, in the Golden Age, sexual union was unknown. In the Silver Age, children were said to have been begotten by touch. It was only in the *Kate* or Evil Age that coitus came to be considered essential but it had to be regulated. Apart from other restrictions—and there were many—indulgence in coitus by married couples was tabooed in the open or in day time, being permissible only during the night and in strict privacy. It was prohibited at other times be-

cause the morning hours were meant for prayers and midday and the afternoons were intended for attending to one's worldly affairs.

Complete abstinence from sexual contact was enjoined on husband and wife during the first night of the new moon, the night of the full moon, the fourteenth night and the eighth night of each half of the month. These were *Parvan* days, when evil spirits were said to be about, specially in empty and deserted houses, graveyards, near trees and pools of water. These places were considered to be particularly dangerous for indulgence in the sexual act.

Penalties for Improper Unions

Intercourse with a teacher's wife was an abominable and most shameful act. The punishment for one, who "stains the teacher's bed was to seat himself on a glowing iron plate, cut off his own member and go away with uplifted eyes." Sexual union by a man with a woman of a higher caste or by the wife of a Brahman with a low caste man merited severe public punishment.

A man dishonoring a virgin with her consent would be heavily fined and compelled to marry her irrespective of any caste distinction. Deflowering a virgin girl against her will was a most detestable crime, the evildoer being publicly whipped and banished and his property confiscated.

A girl having intercourse with a Brahman went unpunished but if she bestowed a similar favor on a man of a lower caste she would be locked up in her house till she repented and came to her senses. The wives of actors and singers could be visited and copulated with freely and without let or hindrance by all strata of society, no question of rape or adultery arising in such cases.

Homosexuality and sex perversions of any kind were punished severely There were five serious offenses for which no worldly atonement or punishment was laid down for the simple reason that the offenders in such cases automatically became outcasts, unworthy of association with their forefathers, gods, and pious men, being eventually doomed to hell where "they would be roasted, like fish, and would live on matter and blood." These five crimes were: (1) murdering a Brahman; (2) cow slaying; (3) intercourse with another's wife; (4) professing no religion; and (5) living on a woman's earnings.

Adultery

To be guilty of adultery, it was not essential that sexual intercourse should actually occur. Manu, Vajnav, Narada, and Brihaspati have held that various forms of contact or association within the two sexes, without actual sexual intercourse, constituted adultery and would be adequately punished: "He that is together anywhere with the wife of another, as for instance at the junction of streams, at bathing places, in gardens, in forests, or speaks with her, touches her on her clothes, ornaments or body, particularly at unseemly places, or lets himself be touched by her in those parts, sits on a bed with her, takes her hand, hair or hem of her garments, sends a procuress or a letter to her, such a one by this commits adultery."

Forms of Coitus

According to the old Indian teaching, there were eight types of copulation (*Maithuana*): (1) *Samarana* (merely thinking of it); (2) *Kirtana* (speaking of it); (3) *Keli* (dallying with it); (4) *Prekshana* (viewing it); (5) *Guhyabhashna* (secretly conversing); (6) *Samkalpa* (firmly willing to indulge in it); (7) *Adhyavasaya* (resolving to do it); (8) *Kriya-nishpatti* (the actual act). Each one of these eight reactions, thoughts, or deeds constituted *Maithuana* (sexual union).

Influence of Geography and Diet

Geography and diet have had considerable influence on the sex life of the people in India and Pakistan. Considerations of climate, atmospheric humidity, and nourishment cannot easily be overlooked when, to any keen observer of the habits and modes of life of the population, the contrast between the inhabitants of the various provinces becomes only too apparent.

Broadly speaking, in the northern spheres and in the foothills of the Himalayas, where there are extremes of temperature in the summer and winter months and the humidity is comparatively low, most of the people—Muslims, Sikhs, and some castes of Hindus—are meat-eaters and are not only of better physique and stature but are also more virile than those dwelling in the southern and coastal areas, where there are no extremes of temperature and a fairly high humidity. Here, the majority of the population, Hindus, are vegetarians.

Varying Ideals and Codes of Life

It would be convenient to consider sex life in India and Pakistan under six main categories of the population, each with different ideals and codes of life, varying, as we shall see, from the highest to the lowest standards of morals, from the sublime to the degenerate. This may appear an unusual classification for our purpose but the sex life in mystic India and Pakistan bears out such a classification.

The Orthodox Group

To begin with the orthodox and the superstitious (orthodoxy and superstition in this subcontinent seem to go hand in hand with many individuals), sexual union in this circle between husband and wife, to a greater or lesser degree and in some form or another, assumes a religious or semireligious significance, not infrequently associated with silent recitals of hymns and prayers, devotional observance of rites and rituals, and the wearing of talismans and charms on the body.

In this group, particularly among the more dogmatic, there are some who rigidly adhere to the doctrine that sexual contact in wedlock is only permissible specifically for procreation of the species, coitus otherwise being considered vulgar, if not sinful. The extremists among them, bordering on the puritanical, even go to the length of strictly limiting sexual intercourse between married couples to certain prescribed days of the lunar month, which, according to their philosophy of life, are looked upon as of good omen and auspicious for the fulfillment and realization of the one cherished hope and ambition of all who enter holy matrimony: the bestowal by the Almighty in His infinite mercy of the gracious gift of progeny, especially a male offspring.

The birth of a son and heir, which is looked forward to and warmly welcomed by all parents in India and Pakistan, is a particularly joyous occasion for Brahmans, as previously noted. The happy birth is joyfully celebrated by thanksgiving to God and the distribution of alms to the poor in humble acknowledgment of the Divine favor.

Premarital and extramarital relationships rank as the most heinous crimes among these people and are a rarity. However, as will be described later, sexual union outside the marriage bond does occur among some sects of Hindus in certain circumstances. Here it also acquires a religious overtone, being viewed not as an irresponsible, pleasurable indulgence but an earnest and solemn compliance with sacred obligations to the deity.

The "Middle Classes"

The major element of the population, coming from various walks of life and with different standards of education and enlightenment, although not necessarily irreligious or free-thinkers, entertain no particular scruples or restrictions in their sex life. Generally speaking, they are happily married, taking a practical and common-sense view of their matrimonial affairs and enjoying life within the family circle. Premarital and extramarital relationships are not indulged in on any excessive scale by this group, who may be considered to be wedged in, so to speak, between the orthodox and the more promiscuous groups.

Sexual "Delinquents"

A comparatively small number of people, known for their promiscuity, specially among the males, may be said to consist of delinquents from all classes in the subcontinent—from the "smart set" of high society to workers and artisans.

Freedom of social intercourse, dinner parties, dances, late nights, alcohol, and wealth may be determining factors for promiscuity on the part of some among the upper classes. At the same time, illiteracy, neglect of moral training and education from childhood, unhealthy environments, and lack of privacy in their homes (usually single-room tenements) may often have the same effect among some sections of the lower classes. The working class generally have large families, which inevitably leads to

relaxation of parental control. In this unhealthy environment the children easily fall into the hands of sexually undesirable elements.

The men are more involved in sexual irregularities than the women. In fact, one of the greatest assets of the Indo-Pakistan subcontinent is its female population. Apart from their loyal and devoted services to their countries in their own spheres, in many cases they act as effective reformers of their "erring" husbands or male relatives. Instances are not wanting where the worst possible characters have been completely transformed as a result of the tactful handling of their womenfolk.

Lawless Tribes

There are some wild savage tribes, dwelling in or about remote villages and out-of-the-way boroughs, who are in a class by themselves. They are notorious for their frequent indulgence in illicit intercourse and for their criminal tendencies. Their main occupations seem to be kidnapping young girls and boys for immoral purposes and commitment of sex offenses, thefts, dacoities (robbery by an armed band), and murders.

Marriage among these tribes is extremely tenuous, desertions of husbands to elope at the first opportunity with other women being common incidents. The efforts of the authorities to educate these turbulent tribes and to find employment for them may gradually reform them, but it is an uphill task.

Prostitutes

The professional prostitute has had a long and unique record in the subcontinent. Even today, although shorn of the old glitter and pomp associated with the ruling princes and aristocracy of old, she still plays an important role in the social life of some sections of society.

In prepartition days, prostitutes had considerable influence and power at the courts of the rulers. In not a few cases they were the "powers behind the throne," making and unmaking ministries, finding jobs for their favorites, and generally "running the show."

Prostitution largely runs in particular classes or communities. There are even "prostitute families," the females following the profession and the males acting as procurers. As a rule, brothels are located in certain localities of the cities, grouped together, the prostitutes sitting on the balcony after dark under powerful lights. In the Kamatipura district of Bombay they sit in "cages" at night to solicit customers.

It is not unusual for a prostitute to marry and settle down, leading thereafter a normal family life with her husband and children. Many, however, "marry" within the "trade" from the host of procurers attached to different brothels. Female children born to them in "wedlock" are brought up to follow the mother's profession. Sons of these unions, however, have been known to grow up into useful, law-abiding citizens, joining "learned" professions or otherwise earning honest livings. The stigmata of their family backgrounds, however, make it difficult for them to marry girls other than those from prostitutes' families.

Previous to the partition of the subcontinent, some ports, such as Bombay, Madras, Calcutta, and Karachi, had what were called "Welcome Houses." These were maintained by small groups of European women who had previously been in the profession themselves and were now running these institutions as matrons or "Madams." The inmates of these "Welcome Houses" were invariably European girls, although there were occasionally a few fashionable prostitutes from the East.

Visitors to these establishments were mostly foreign European clients, sailors predominating, with only a select set of Orientals from various Asiatic countries. There was no hint of coarseness or vulgarity about these "Welcome Houses"; if anything, they were noted particularly for their almost oppressive atmosphere of decorum.

Most of these "Madams" adopted this occupation as finishing stages to their past careers in various parts of Europe and the East, with the purpose of accumulating money before their final retirement. Having in a few years piled up quite sizeable fortunes, they would go home, to be absorbed into a respectable family life.

Conditions have considerably changed since the partition of India, the banning of prostitution being the declared policies of both India and Pakistan. Prostitution, and with it these "Welcome Houses," is no longer in vogue, openly at any rate, although it has not been entirely eradicated.

An extensive investigation into the sex life of the prostitute in Bombay was conducted some years ago when the introduction of a "Prohibition of Prostitution" bill in the Legislative Assembly was being considered by the Bombay Government. The Police Commissioner of Bombay and the writer of this article spent many weeks investigating all the aspects of the life of professional prostitutes, including the problem of venereal disease, the prevention of which was one of the main objects of the bill. Contrary to popular opinion, the professional prostitute is not the only source of venereal disease.

The investigations in Bombay were confined to the Kamatipura district, where the majority of the brothels were located. We questioned, and the writer examined, practically all the prostitutes and learned that not one of them had less than three visitors nightly and that, without exception, they were infected with venereal disease.

Conditions are improving both in India and Pakistan, not only as regards the extent of prostitution but also in respect to venereal disease, more and more facilities for treatment being made available.

The Hijras

In India and Pakistan there is a community of eunuchs, known as Hijras, who prostitute themselves as passive agents. They wear female clothes, adopt feminine nicknames, and assume girlish manners and gestures.

Many of them have had their genitals removed in childhood or early boyhood. In some cases, the testes are atrophied as a result of being constantly squeezed and pressed during infancy, in order to render the child devoid of any sexual function when he grows up so that he may remain with the fraternity.

The writer of this article has been called upon by the police on numerous past occasions to examine young boys who had been initiated and prepared for their future careers as Hijras in this community. The method used in these cases was the repeated insertion of well-greased graduated wooden or metal cones into the rectum. The anal sphincter of practically all the boys could easily admit three fingers.

Hijras are popular in certain circles as professional singers and dancers, the accompanying musicians being invariably males not belonging to the tribe. Females are strictly taboo in Hijra society, although hermaphrodites, passive agents by inclination and not necessarily "full-blooded" Hijras, are eligible for membership and are frequently seen associated with them and observing their accepted codes of life.

It has been said that homosexuality is comparatively more common among the Muslim population of the subcontinent than among others because of the lack of female companionship due to the seclusion of their womenfolk, who remain behind the purdah (veil). This may or may not be so, but within the professional experience of the writer, judging by the number of extragenital syphilitic chancres, mostly anal, seen by him in hospitals, homosexuality seems to be equally prevalent in all communities in India and Pakistan.

It is only fair to add that this subcontinent, in common with Eastern countries generally, has earned an undeserved notoriety in the West as being the "hotbed" of homosexuality and other sex perversions—"Asiatic vices," as such practices are described by many writers. In point of fact, sexual deviations exist in all countries without exception, and it is hoped that this subcontinent and other countries of Asia will receive more unbiased treatment in this respect at the hands of Western writers and students.

Arranged Marriages

Arranged marriages of their sons and daughters by parents or guardians seem to be the prevailing practice in India and Pakistan. Intermarriages between boys and girls from the same families, or cousin marriages, are by no means uncommon among the Muslims and Parsees. Owing to the purdah (veil) system observed by Muslim women—now gradually being given up, although still rigidly maintained by the more orthodox—it is quite possible for a Muslim

youth and his bride to be complete strangers to each other, meeting for the first time on the marriage night.

It is extraordinary that the majority of the educated and enlightened youth of the subcontinent, who in these days are very vocal and jealous of their rights and independence in various matters affecting their future welfare and happiness, should still meekly submit to this interference with their independence and discretion by their parents or guardians in the all-important sphere of marriage.

There are unfortunately many boys and girls who, although physically unfit for marriage and themselves aware of their handicaps and unsuitability for wedlock, yet submit to a marriage arranged by their parents. Premarital medical examinations of the contracting parties are not in vogue, and, although in some cases the disability might be amenable to minor surgery or professional advice, quite a few marriages prove unhappy, many leading to separation or divorce. Such procedures are not generally welcomed by the elders of the family as they bring dishonor to the ancestral reputation.

With the progress of time and the gradual relaxation of ancient customs and conventions among the present generation, more particularly the educated and traveled sections of the population, there is a growing tendency for individuals to discard the system of arranged marriages. There are numerous examples of boys marrying outside their castes or communities, or even with foreign girls, Eastern as well as Western, and many such unions are proving successful and happy.

Customs, Rituals, and Perversions

The Nuptial Night

It is not at all uncommon for prospective bridegrooms, as a rule young men without any premarital experience and on the friendly advice of elder friends and well-wishers, to visit prostitutes on the eve of their wedding to test their virility. Potency may assert itself, but venereal infection will unhappily often be their wedding gifts to their unfortunate brides. As a matter of fact, to be infected with venereal disease (some openly priding themselves on that account) is often taken as the acme of potency.

The nuptial night may turn out to be a painful and at times tragic hurdle for young inexperienced couples. Consummation of marriage with a virgin girl, in the popular mind of India and Pakistan, is necessarily associated with vaginal bleeding from the ruptured hymen. Among some Muslim communities, if no such evidence is forthcoming on the morrow of the marriage night, the chastity of the bride is doubted and her family is thoroughly disgraced in the eyes of friends and acquaintances.

Deflowering the virgin bride on the night of marriage by a priest, prior to her union with the husband, was by no means a rare ritual among some Hindu sects in the past.

Traditionally with most people, coitus must take place on the first night of marriage; if it does not, the virility of the husband comes under suspicion. On the other hand, if sexual congress does take place and no token of virginity is noticeable in the morning, the bride is considered to have been unchaste.

In many communities in India the events in the bridal chamber are matters of the keenest personal interest and concern to many persons besides the newly married couple themselves, for whom there is hardly any privacy even after their retirement to bed.

At the end of the festivities in celebration of the marriage, late at night, after the guests and members of the family have left, it is customary in some Muslim communities for an elderly lady, not as a rule a relative, to slip in quietly to whisper to the young bride, deliberately within the hearing of the husband, that consummation of marriage must be attempted as soon as possible that night. At the same time, a white handkerchief or a piece of white cloth is handed to the bride and she is told to use it when the expected bleeding occurs. She is assured sympathetically that some pain and hemorrhage are inevitable and that she need not be alarmed, and her adviser promises to look in early in the morning to take away the blood-stained handkerchief.

When the bridal pair are finally allowed by the family and intimate friends to be alone together, and the bedroom door is formally locked from the outside, many relatives, usually elderly women, remain in the adjoining rooms, talking with one another as loudly as possible about the marriage and the expected evidence of the bride's virginity.

From the psychological point of view, the nervous tension experienced by the bridal pair, especially if young and inexperienced (since adequate sex education has not yet been established in India and Pakistan), is very strong, and is heightened by the rule-of-thumb procedures laid down for their guidance and implicit compliance.

For the bride, in not a few instances merely the fear of the expected pain and bleeding can bring about psychic frigidity. Added to this is her fear that there may be no bleeding and that she may be branded by her own family and friends as unchaste and of low character. Examples are not wanting of irate fathers having killed their daughters who had thus failed to prove their virginity.

The position of the bridegroom is no less difficult. If consummation of marriage has not been accomplished or even attempted his potency is suspected. Impotence, to many, carries with it a stigma and the impotent man is degraded not only in his own eyes but in those of his fellows. In the family circle, his lot becomes more and more unbearable until the marriage ends in separation or divorce.

Among the lower strata of society, such a recently wedded youth is usually brought to a doctor by several members of the bride's family, the groom's father or uncle also accompanying them on sufferance, and is literally kicked into the clinic as if he were a criminal.

Sexual debility and impotence in the male are, of course, known in all parts of the world. In this subcontinent, however, mainly because of the system of arranged marriages and the gossip of well-meaning but inquisitive friends, such disabilities are perhaps more likely to be publicized.

These old customs are being rapidly given up with the spread of education, but there are some families who still follow "tradition."

Deva Desis

There is a long-established ritual among some sects of Hindus that is solemnly observed in certain circumstances. In compliance with a vow or oath taken by the parents, usually barren couples, their first-born female child is dedicated to the deity and, upon the approach of puberty, is formally handed over to a temple by her parents, to become a permanent inmate. In the future she is at the disposal of priests or worshippers in the temple, who have sexual intercourse with her as a sacred duty.

Intimacy with Deva Desis, as these girls are called, is devoid of lust or passion and is considered a serious performance of duty, sanctioned by Divine authority and looked upon as a spiritual union with the deity through the hallowed person of the Deva Desi.

A somewhat similar ritual is occasionally observed in the case of sterile couples. The wife is temporarily dedicated to the temple and, as a sacred duty, has sexual intercourse with the priests and worshippers in the hope of being rewarded by the deity with the gift of an offspring.

Since the advent of independence in India in August, 1947, and the adoption of a secular policy for the country, there has been a growing tendency to ban both the dedication to the temple of Deva Desis and married women, and other orthodox sex rituals not in keeping with the advanced public opinion in present-day India.

Phallus Worship

In some Hindu sects sex organs are considered sacred, sexual functions assuming a religious character. The phallus, the lingam, is venerated as symbolic of virility and generative power. Phallus worship (Linga Puja) in Siva temples by disciples of Siva is enjoined on married couples who have not been blessed with children.

Menstruation

Sexual intercourse between husband and wife during menstruation is strictly prohibited in Hinduism and Islam, as it is among the various minority communities living in India and Pakistan.

The menstruating Hindu woman becomes untouchable in the family circle, eating, sleeping, and generally living aloof from all others in the house, even from the husband, until purified by the ceremonial bath at the end of her period. The Muslim woman, when menstruating, also has certain restrictions binding her but not to the extreme degree of her Hindu sister. She must not offer her daily prayers, touch the holy Koran, observe fast in the month of Ramazan, or enter a mosque. There is otherwise little change in her mode of life within and outside the household. Short of sexual intercourse, she is allowed other intimacies with her husband at the time. "A woman in her periods," the rule says, "must bind up her girdle. What lies above is at the disposal of the man."

Among Hindus, sexual contact between married couples is not only prohibited on certain prescribed days of the lunar month but at any solar or lunar eclipse. Fasting Muslim married couples are also prohibited from indulging in sexual intercourse during the month of Ramazan; it is permissible at nighttime, however, when they are not fasting.

Polygamy

Islam sanctions plural marriages under certain specified conditions, and some Muslims in the subcontinent take advantage of it. The custom, however, is gradually dying out, not only for economic reasons but because of the growing opposition to the practice on the part of the progressive elements among the women themselves.

Hindus too, strictly speaking, can marry more than one wife, but in practice they seldom do. Some Maharajas of old, of course, had their senior and junior Maharanees but even these ruling chiefs of preindependence India, now that they have been pensioned off and deprived of their gadis (thrones), can presumably ill-afford such luxuries.

Aphrodisiacs

The craving for aphrodisiacs is very strong among all classes of youth in the subcontinent, even though they may be perfectly normal sexually. The abuse of sex hormones by the more educated and the use of cheap sex stimulants of unknown composition by the illiterate and the poorer classes, given them by practitioners of the indigenous systems of medicine or by quacks, has a deleterious effect on the sex life of these young people. Overindulgence both in sexual stimulation and sexual experiences can be a vicious cycle and may in the long run lead to impotence and disillusionment.

Family Planning

The rapid and marked increase in the populations of India and Pakistan within recent years is of grave concern to both governments. The vigorous implementation of family planning has been adopted as the official policy in the two countries. Despite these efforts, however, and those of the medical profession, private associations and societies, and municipal and other public bodies, to enlighten the people —particularly the masses in the villages—and to provide facilities at nominal cost, the task remains still somewhat undone. The least relaxation could bring catastrophe to the subcontinent.

References

Ahmad, Said, and Ahmad, Maqbool, "A Case Report of a Eunuch with Carcinoma of the Rectum." *Medicus*, Dec., 1957, 101.

Allen, Clifford, *Homosexuality*. London: Staples Press, 1958.

Beadnell, C. M., *The Origin of the Kiss*. London: Watts & Company, 1942.

Hasanat, Abul, *All About Sex, Love, and Happy Marriage*. Calcutta: Sree Kali Press, 1951.

Meyer, Johann Jakob, *Sexual Life in Ancient India*. London: Routledge, Kegan Paul, Ltd., 1953.

Modi, Jaising P., *Medical Jurisprudence and Toxicology*. Bombay: N. M. Tripathi, 1952.

Nefzawi, *The Perfumed Garden*. London and Benares: Kama Shastra Society, 1886.

Thomas, P., *Kama Kalpa*. Bombay: Privately printed, 1957.

Vātsāyana, *The Kamasutra*. Paris: Libraire Astra (no date indicated).

Walker, Kenneth, and Strauss, E. B., *Sexual Disorders in the Male*. London: Cassel, 1954.

JELAL M. SHAH

Infertility in Women, Diagnosis and Treatment of

THE barren marriage is a problem as old as the history of mankind. In widely separated cultures and generations, it has been regarded not as an illness but as a misfortune and disgrace—a curse from some demon or displeased god who needed to be propitiated with prayers, religious rites, and magic potions. The childless woman was the victim of superstition, fear, and prejudice, for through the ages, and until our generation, the onus of barrenness usually fell upon the female.

Awareness of possible male responsibility is evident in the writings of Aristotle, Socrates, and Plato. In most instances, however, sterility in the male was considered only when he was impotent.

It has been within the past few decades that we have come to realize that each mate is equally in need of investigation when the wife cannot become pregnant. However, customs change so slowly that even today the examination of the husband is often inadequate. Sterility is still considered a gynecological problem and it is usually the wife who comes to the physician for help.

Definition

Synonyms of sterility are infertility, barrenness, and inability to conceive. According to the standards of the American Society for the Study of Sterility, a couple is considered infertile when pregnancy has not occurred after a year of coitus without contraception. *Primary sterility* denotes that conception has never occurred. In *secondary sterility* there have been previous pregnancies, but further conception cannot be accomplished. Such a definition makes husband and wife equally responsible.

In recent years sterility has referred to those couples in whom the inability to conceive is apparently irremediable. For most couples the prognosis is not so grim. *Infertility* is the term applied when fertility is potentially possible but is so reduced that pregnancy does not take place or, if pregnancy is initiated, a viable child is not produced.

Diagnostic Studies

Diagnosis must precede treatment. The physician is like a sleuth, searching for every possible factor that might reduce the fertility of either mate. This requires an organized plan of examination of both husband and wife. In 80 per cent of cases it is not one factor or one mate, but a combination of several factors in each that contributes to the infertility. The diagnostic study consists of:

1. Detailed history, including a search for all factors that affect general health and fertility in particular;
2. General physical examination;
3. Gynecological examination;
4. Special tests related to the anatomical (structural) causes of infertility;
5. Endocrine tests related to physiological (functional) causes of infertility;

6. Psychological investigation related to emotional factors that influence fertility.

Enthusiastic cooperation of the couple is obtained more readily if time is spent demonstrating the anatomy of the reproductive system and the highlights of its physiology with pictures and models. Understanding reduces anxiety.

History

A careful history is taken, the husband and wife being interviewed separately. Frankness is encouraged by assurance that confidential information, such as an episode of venereal disease or pregnancy before marriage, will be recorded in code and never divulged.

Family history: Sterility is not inherited, but a low ratio of fertility may be present in the family. Associated infertility in siblings is within the range of coincidence in most cases.

Previous medical history: Following mumps, complications affecting female fertility are rare. Scarlet fever or recurrent tonsillitis may have a damaging effect on the generative organs. The general health during the pre- and adolescent periods influences the development of the reproductive system. Varying degrees of defective or incomplete genital maturity may be caused by some acute systemic infection in early life or by poor health, overwork, malnutrition, anemia, and chronic fatigue before and during adolescence. Venereal diseases may reduce or destroy fertility. History of weight, past and present, and points reached above or below average should be noted.

Previous surgical history: Date, indication, and clinical result of any previous surgical procedure are obtained—especially any that were done for the relief of sterility. Acute appendicitis may seal the tubes. Previous surgery for ectopic pregnancy or tubo-ovarian operations may result in damaged reproductive structures.

It is to the couple's advantage that transcripts of any previous series of tests and treatments, and copies of all operative reports and X-rays, be sent to the physician currently taking care of them.

Menstrual history: We have no direct means of studying the ovum, but the menstrual history is one of the helpful indirect gauges of function. Considerably delayed onset of menstruation, lack of regularity, especially prolonged absence of, or prolonged duration of, menstrual periods indicate disturbed endocrine function. Normal menses with regular rhythm and adequate flow with little or no discomfort are usually associated with a normal endocrine development. Severe pain with periods does not mean reduced fertility. Change in menses after marriage from a regular to an abnormal pattern may indicate either endocrine imbalance due to emotional tensions or acquired disease of the ovaries and/or tubes.

History of diet, habits, and mode of life: All these have a direct bearing on fertility. A comprehensive picture of the couple's general health and vitality will include their hours and type of work and rest, the proportion of time spent in recreational activities and outdoor exercise, the amount of physical and emotional stress and strain to which each is subject, and their habits regarding drugs, alcohol, and tobacco.

Emotional history: What was the emotional climate in which the wife grew up? What was her relationship to her father and mother as a child? What is it now—is she mature or dependent? How did she acquire her sex education? What is her attitude toward her female role, toward sex, toward pregnancy? Has she had any traumatic sex experiences? What is the physician's evaluation of her emotional maturity and stability?

Marital history: The answers to the following questions may elicit clues to the causative or contributory factors in the existing infertilty. Is this the first marriage for both? If not, what is the marital and pregnancy history with any former mate? What is the frequency of intercourse, the history of libido, potency of the husband, depth of penetration? Is intercourse pleasurable, and if not, why? Is the wife a willing and actively participating mate? What is her experience in regard to orgasm? How long have they been involuntarily sterile? Was there a prior period of voluntary sterility? If so, what was their method of contraception? For how long does she remain quietly in bed after intercourse? (It is surprising how often the physician will learn that some women always get up to void or "to wash" immediately after intercourse. Occasionally we are astonished to discover that women, anxious to conceive, invariably douche right after intercourse "to keep clean.")

Physical Examination

Careful general physical examination should precede any tests. Body morphology, fat, and hair distribution are related both to heredity and to endocrine function. The physician wants to know that there is no general health factor that might contraindicate pregnancy and that the woman is in good physical condition for pregnancy.

Gynecological Examination

The gynecological examination may reveal defective or immature development, past or present infection, or chronic pelvic congestion. The last two may cause mechanical interference to sperm migration.

Some women who come for examination only because they cannot become pregnant are found to have an intact hymen. Removal of this, together with instruction in the facts of life, brings a happy result promptly for 90 per cent of these couples.

Retroversion: A common error is to tell a woman that she cannot become pregnant because "her womb is turned." Twenty per cent of retroversions are present from birth (congenital). If such a uterus is of mature development and freely movable and if the postcoital test shows that sperm migrate freely into the uterus, then the retroversion is not causing or contributing to the infertility. An acquired retroversion with accompanying pelvic congestion may reduce fertility. An adherent retroversion is usually accompanied by inflammatory disease of the tubes, which seriously interferes with fertility. When a retroverted uterus can be brought forward, it should be kept in normal position with a supporting pessary.

Fibroids: The presence of small fibroids on the outer wall of the uterus usually does not interfere with fertility. When the fibroids are large, distort the uterus considerably, or especially if they occupy part of the uterine cavity, then they often do interfere with fertility. In the latter cases, their size, number, and location usually warrant surgery per se. When operating for fibroids on a woman who desires children, every attempt is made to remove the individual fibroid nodules (myomectomy), leaving the uterus intact. Such surgery is often followed by successful pregnancies if all other factors are normal.

Anatomical Tests

Postcoital Test (Huhner test): This test is usually done three to eight hours after intercourse and provides microscopic proof as to whether the sperm are able to reach the cervical canal in sufficient numbers, and whether the cervical secretion allows the sperm to travel freely into the uterine cavity. It is planned for the day before, or day of, expected ovulation, at which time the cervical secretion is most favorable for sperm reception and migration. The postcoital findings are dependable only if the test is done around the time of ovulation and if the quantity and quality of the sperm have already been established by detailed examination of the semen.

Tubal patency test (Rubin test): We are greatly indebted to Dr. I. C. Rubin for this simple means of testing whether the tubes are open. The kymographic tracings taken during the test record the contractile ability (peristalsis) of the tubes. Both patency and peristalsis are necessary for fertility. The gas used is carbon dioxide and requires control of the pressure and the volume.

A normal tube has a freely open passageway throughout its length, continuous with the uterine cavity at one end and opening into the abdominal cavity at its free end. The normal tube is free to contract rhythmically. This rhythmic contraction is apparently necessary to bring together the sperm traveling from the uterine end and the ovum, which enters the tube from the abdominal end. Impregnation takes place in the tube.

Normal tubes usually cannot be felt on examination. If they are sufficiently diseased to form pathological masses, then the reason for the infertility is thereby apparent. However, tubes that seem normal on pelvic examination may still have an obstructed lumen, or may be unable to contract rhythmically due to adhesions.

The test should be done three to five days after a period and before ovulation. Gas (only carbon dioxide) is blown through the cervix and, with normal patency, flows freely through the continuous passageway into the abdominal cavity. The machine used should give accurate pressure and volume control of the gas, and an attached kymograph records this passage and the rhythmic contractions.

It is unnecessary to perform this test if there is any contraindication to pregnancy or if the husband is sterile.

This test must *not* be done if:

1. There is any systemic infection, or any infection in the generative tract and appendages;
2. There is uterine bleeding;
3. There is any possibility of pregnancy having already started. The temperature graph will reveal an early unsuspected pregnancy. A study of the basal temperature graph and limiting this test to the preovulatory phase of the cycle will avoid such an error.

Salpingohysterography: This is similar to the Rubin test except that instead of carbon dioxide, the physician injects radio-opaque fluid into the cervix and X-rays are taken. We can thereby visualize the continuous passageway of cervical canal, uterine cavity, tubal luminae, and the spillage of the fluid into the peritoneal cavity if the tubes are patent. If the tubes are closed, we can see the site of closure. Such X-rays will also reveal pathology in the endometrial cavity, such as polyps and small submucous fibroids, as well as unsuspected congenital or other malformations that cannot be felt by examination.

Physiological Tests

These are to evaluate the function of the pituitary, thyroid, adrenals, and ovaries essential to produce a fertile ovum or to maintain it after impregnation.

Basal temperature: Daily recording of basal temperature (morning temperature before arising and before any activity) is a simple means of determining if and when ovulation takes place. In most women ovulation occurs 12 to 14 days before menstruation, regardless of the length of the interval between periods. The temperature before ovulation is 0.6 to 1.0 degrees (Fahrenheit) lower than it is after ovulation. If no period occurs and the basal temperature remains elevated for 18 or more days, we can thereby diagnose pregnancy earlier than with any other test.

Subjective signs of ovulation: Some women have a characteristic ache in the lower abdomen on the day of ovulation ("Mittelschmerz"). Some may notice some scant and brief bleeding. Many women have an increased slippery vaginal discharge that is like raw egg white.

Objective signs of ovulation: The physician can often detect the day of ovulation by characteristic changes in the vaginal and cervical secretions.

Endometrial biopsy: This is a simple office procedure. A few small pieces of the tissue lining the uterine cavity (endometrium) are removed and studied microscopically. This gives us valuable information about ovulation and about the response of the endometrium to the various ovarian hormones necessary for pregnancy.

Psychological Investigation

Psychosomatic gynecology is a relatively new field, but it deserves increasing attention. The emotional state of the woman is a potent factor influencing her endocrine physiology. Emotional conflicts, fears, and tensions—particularly in relation to sex, pregnancy, and to the total husband-wife relationship—may be the major, if not the determining cause of infertility in some women. A neurotic mother-daughter relationship, such as a corroding hostility or an overdependent child and an overprotective-possessive mother, may inhibit mature endocrine function. In some women various tensions may inhibit ovulation for years. In my experience, impotence of the husband (unless he is old) is invariably due to psychological foctors. In many instances this relates back to emotional traumas in his parental relationship. Careful history of all emotional factors is an important part of the diagnostic study.

Starting with the history, and going through each step of the diagnostic study, every factor, small or large, that contributes toward reducing fertility is considered. In most infertile couples, two or more causative factors will be found in each mate.

Prognosis and Therapy

Prognosis depends upon the findings. We are helpless when there is absence or atrophy of the gonads or if the union of a fertile sperm and fertile ovum cannot be effected. Fortunately, only a small percentage of cases falls in this group. When the prognosis is hopeless, it is the physician's responsibility to present the true facts and to help the couple make a healthful emotional adjustment. For the emotionally suitable couple, advice and help in adopting a child is often the indicated therapy.

With the exception of the small number of couples with irremediable sterility, the dire prediction "You cannot become pregnant" should be avoided. Many an "expert" has been proved wrong over and over again. The prognosis is best if the combined fertility is not too low and the etiological factors are remediable.

The plan of therapy should be as well organized as the diagnostic study. No one plan can be prescribed. Each couple must be treated on the basis of the individual findings.

Raising the constitutional level of each mate to the optimum is the first step. General constitutional diseases such as tuberculosis, hyperthyroidism, hypertension, chronic nephritis, or syphilis, constitute a contraindication to pregnancy, and, where possible, these conditions should be treated.

Obesity or malnutrition should be corrected. Alcoholic excesses must be avoided. An infertile couple should be advised to give up smoking. It is impossible to estimate individual susceptibility to the toxins absorbed by smoking, but in general, the increased salivation induced by even moderate smoking, its consequent interference with normal digestive processes, the absorption of the toxins by the buccal and nasal mucous membranes, and the ingestion of various toxic by-products of smoking that usually reach the lungs and stomach will undoubtedly depress the fertility of susceptible individuals.

When the diagnostic study shows insufficient anatomical or physiological abnormality to account for the couple's infertility, further search for emotional tensions may yield the clue. Emotional factors are to be suspected when the husband is of normal fertility and the only abnormal findings in the wife relate to functional disturbances of the menstrual cycle. These disturbances, coupled with an anxious or tense personality, should raise the question of psychogenic tensions being sufficiently strong to interfere with normal endocrine function.

Psychiatric consultation or treatment may be needed prior to or concomitant with physical or endocrine treatment. Pregnancy is no cure for psychosis—or severe neurosis. In fact, if the wife is in a state of depression, presumably because she is not pregnant, no attempt should be made to help initiate pregnancy. Severe neurosis is a contraindication to pregnancy, and referral to a psychotherapist is indicated.

Some women will become pregnant after the first visit because of release of anxiety. Many become pregnant during or immediately after the diagnostic study and before any treatment is initiated. The tests themselves are apparently helpful mechanically and/or emotionally. On the other hand, some women may have their fertility reduced as a result of intensive study and treatment. It is most harmful for a woman to become too involved in daily temperature recordings and in timing intercourse according to the calendar rather than according to natural desire. Joyous and spontaneous sex life is the best treatment for the endocrine glands. Couples should be frank with their physicians and communicate any emotional feelings—whatever they may be.

Endocrine treatment should be instituted after the diagnostic study is completed, and only if and as the various tests indicate the need. Great progress has been made in the development of powerful hormones.

Therapeutic (Artificial) Insemination

This has received a great deal of publicity recently. Its application has a limited field of usefulness, as follows:

Insemination with the husband's semen is indicated when:

1. The only abnormal factor disclosed in the diagnostic study is that abnormal cervical mucus does not allow the sperm to pass through into the uterus.

2. The wife is of apparently good fertility, and the husband's sperm number is very low but with normal vitality and morphology. In

my own experience, intra-uterine insemination of sperm with *poor* vitality and *abnormal* structure resulted in successful pregnancies only occasionally.

3. The husband is impotent and the marriage is stable. Psychiatric consultation should precede this therapy. In this small group, many of the husbands have had considerable psychotherapy without relief of the impotence. Many of these couples have an excellent interpersonal relationship in spite of this sexual disability, and can usually be helped to a better sexual relationship as well, within the framework of his impotence. Enabling such a couple to achieve parenthood is most satisfying provided the physician ascertains that the marriage is stable and the couple suitable as parents.

4. Anatomical anomalies of the wife or husband (congenital or acquired) prevent complete intromission and cervical insemination.

Insemination with donor's semen is indicated when:

1. The husband is sterile, or the sperm is so infertile as to render him clinically sterile.

2. Rh negative–Rh positive incompatibility has already resulted in the birth of an erythroblastotic infant, and the couple request insemination of the wife with the semen of an Rh-negative donor.

3. The husband's family history is so bad genetically that he is unwilling to perpetuate his genes.

4. An abnormal child has already been born to the couple and traced to the husband's genetic strain.

Therapeutic donor insemination can be considered only for couples who are mature, who have a true love of children, and who are entirely *en rapport* as to this form of therapy to cure their barren marriage. It is most important that the marriage be stable and the relationship well rooted. If their religion forbids this therapy, they should be so informed.

With resources available from which to choose donors of superior moral, intellectual, and eugenic background, and with equally careful and experienced selection of suitable couples, this therapy results in superior children who contribute immeasurably to the happiness of the couples and the welfare of the community.

Secondary Sterility

Secondary sterility is the inability on the part of a couple to initiate a pregnancy after having accomplished one or more previous pregnancies. Cervical and tubal pathology are the more common causes of this condition. Even without any intervening constitutional or specific infections, the fertility of either mate may become reduced considerably over a period of several years. The diagnostic study should be as thorough for both husband and wife as it is for primary sterility. Therapy is determined by the findings.

Spontaneous Abortion

Spontaneous abortions terminate 12 to 15 per cent of all pregnancies. A woman who has had three or more consecutive abortions is classified as a habitual aborter. Of these, some abort regularly in the first two months of pregancy. The cause may be defective ovum or sperm wherein the pregnancy can be initiated but cannot be carried through the first trimester. Another cause of early habitual abortion is deficiency of the hormones necessary for the implantation and nurture of the fertilized ovum in the uterus. Occasionally local pathology of the uterus itself will prevent a pregnancy from proceeding. In late habitual abortion, the pregnancy progresses normally and the abortion takes place after four or six months. These abortions later in pregnancy may also be due to an endocrine deficiency or to a defect in the upper cervical opening. Various endocrine tests and special X-ray examination of the uterus and cervix are the diagnostic steps to be taken. Psychogenic factors may be the sole cause or important contributory causes. Diagnosis and treatment of abortion have been improving constantly in recent years.

Prophylactic Treatment

In these days of preventive medicine, we must stress the prophylactic treatment of sterility. Many instances of severe reduction in future fertility must occur in childhood. Undoubtedly some severe infections during childhood may destroy germinal epithelium in the testes. This could account for the healthy adult male who is found to have this destruction on testicular biopsy but with no history to account for it. It might be revealing if physicians palpated testes regularly when examining male children during the course of any severe general infection, at any age.

Teaching parents how to instill wholesome sex attitudes in their children will prevent many of the psychosomatic causes of infertility in both men and women.

Healthy family relationships help toward mature sexual development and will prevent those instances of impotence and frigidity that stem from a traumatic emotional climate during the growing-up years. Healthful habits of eating, sleeping, working, relaxation, and overall living are rooted best in childhood. This includes education of the young in the harmful effects of smoking and excessive drinking.

Innate fertility cannot be estimated accurately. Some couples procreate easily despite the presence in each mate of several factors that are not conducive to fertility. In dealing with an infertile mating, however, we are dealing with a couple whose inherent fertility is obviously reduced. Improving the fertility of each mate to the individual's optimum with therapy based on a careful diagnostic study will give the best results.

References

Buxton, C. L., and Southam, A. L., *Human Infertility.* New York: Paul B. Hoeber, Inc., 1958.

Blinick, G., and Kaufman, S. A., *Modern Office Gynecology.* Philadelphia: Lea & Febiger, 1957.

Cohen, M. R., Stein, I. F., Sr., and Kaye, B. M., "Optimal Time for Therapeutic Insemination." *Fertil. & Steril.* 7; 14, 1956.

Davis, M. E., "Problems of Sterility Today." *Am. Pract. & Digest Treat.* 1; 1, 1946.

Decker, A., and Decker, W., *Practical Office Gynecology.* Philadelphia: F. A. Davis Co., 1956.

Dickinson, R. L., "Ensemble of Ovulation." *J. Contracep.* 3; 219, 1938.

Farris, E., *Human Ovulation and Fertility.* Philadelphia: J. B. Lippincott Co., 1956.

Gepfert, J. R., "Reconstruction of the Oviducts in the Human." *Am. J. Obst. & Gynec.* 45; 1031, 1943.

Goldberger, M. A., "Clinical Evaluation of Hysterography." *J. Mt. Sinai Hosp., New York.* No. 1; 243, 1943.

Greenhill, J. P., *Office Gynecology* (7th ed.). Chicago: Year Book Publishers, Inc., 1959.

Guttmacher, A. F., *Babies by Choice or by Chance.* New York: Doubleday & Co., Inc., 1959.

Holden, F. C., and Sovak, F. W., "Reconstruction of Oviducts—An Improved Technique." *Am. J. Obst. & Gynec.* 24; 684, 1932.

Huhner, M., *Sexual Disorders in the Male and Female Including Sterility and Impotence.* Philadelphia: F. A. Davis Co.

Kaplan, Ira, "The Genetic Implications of Clinical Radiation of Women Suffering from Sterility." *J.A.M.A.* 52; No. 1, 13-16, 1960.

Kleegman, S. J., "Office Treatment of Pathologic Cervix." *Am. J. Surg.* 48; 294, 1940.

Kleegman, S. J., "Diagnosis and Treatment of Infertility in Women." In R. J. Lowrie (ed.), *Gynecology.* Chicago: Charles C Thomas, 1952, Vol. I, Chap. 48; Vol. II, Chap. 70.

Kroger, W. S., and Freed, S. C., *Psychosomatic Gynecology.* Philadelphia: W. B. Saunders Co., 1958.

Mann, E. C., "The Role of Emotional Determinants in Habitual Abortion." *S. Clin. North America.* April, 447, 1957.

Mazer, Charles, and Israel, S. Leon, *Diagnosis and Treatment of Menstrual Disorders and Sterility.* New York: Paul B. Hoeber, Inc., 1959.

Meigs, J. V., "Endometrial Biopsy and the Uterine Index." *Am. J. Obst. & Gynec.* 38; 161, 1931.

Papanicoloau, G. V., "The Sexual Cycle of the Human Female as Revealed by Vaginal Smears." *Am. J. Anat.* 52; 519, 1933.

Portnoy, L., "Artificial Insemination." *Fertil. & Steril.* 7; No. 4, 327, 1956.

Potter, R. G., Jr., "Artificial Insemination by Donors: Analysis of Seven Series." *Fertil. & Steril.* 9; 37, 1958.

Rock, J., "Causes and Relief of Infertility." In J. V. Meigs and S. H. Sturgis (eds.), *Progress in Gynecology* (2nd ed.). New York: Grune & Stratton, Inc., 1950.

Rubin, I. C., *Utero-Tubal Insufflation.* St. Louis: C. V. Mosby Co., 1947.

Schellen, A. M., *Artificial Insemination in the Human.* New York: Elsevier Pub. Co., 1957.

Simmons, Fred, "Diagnostic Techniques and Treatment of the Sterile Couple." In J. V. Meigs and S. H. Sturgis (eds.), *Progress in Gynecology* (2nd ed.). New York: Grune & Stratton, Inc., 1950.

Speck, G., "Phenolsulfonphthalein as a Test for the Determination of Tubal Patency." *Am. J. Obst. & Gynec.* 55; 1048, 1948.

Speck, G., "Determination of Time of Ovulation. *Obst. & Gynec. Surv.* 14; No. 6, Dec., 1959.

Stone, A., and Ward, M. E., "Factors Responsible for Pregnancy in 500 Infertility Cases." *Fertil. & Steril.* 7; No. 1, 1956.

Tompkins, P., "Basal Body Temperature Graphs as an Index to Ovulation." *J. Obst. & Gynaec. Brit. Emp.* 52; 241, 1945.

SOPHIA J. KLEEGMAN

Islam,
Sex Life in*

COMPARED with Europe, the Arab Middle East is a relatively homogeneous culture area. However, within the area dramatic cultural differences are found. Corresponding to these cultural differences, there is a great variation in sex life. Marked differences in sexual attitudes and practices exist among the urban, village, and Bedouin populations as the regions—the Arabian peninsula, the Levant, and the Nile and Tigris-Euphrates valleys—are the homes of various Arab subcultures.

General Description of Sexual Behavior

Sexual Frankness

Many European travelers in the area have felt that the Arab is abnormally concerned with sex. Harrison (1924) reports that the Arabs have an abnormally developed sex appetite and that their whole emotional life revolves about it. Philby (1952), visiting the same area several years later, was impressed by conversations about sex. He remarked upon the frankness and freedom with which men of the

* Appreciation is expressed to the staff of the Human Relations Area Files at Yale University for their assistance in gathering information on sex life among Bedouin tribes and agricultural villages.

The author's research on the sex life of a restricted sector of the urban population was made possible by funds granted by the Ford Foundation. That Foundation is not, however, the author, owner, publisher, or proprietor of this research and is not to be understood as approving by virtue of its grant any of the statements or views expressed therein.

Arabian highlands spoke of their amorous dreams, of how many times they had sex relations each night, and of the slave girls they kept as concubines. Granqvist (1947) felt that the very separation between the sexes was sexually stimulating. In her study of a Palestinian village, she found that the barriers raised between them made the sexes more interesting to each other. To her it appeared that the awakening of sexual feelings among the Arabs had the force of strong natural power. She noted that the girls secretly wished to show their beauty to the young men and bask in their admiring glances but that this was prevented by the strict isolation of the sexes demanded by society. Granqvist (1950) even attributed two-thirds of the pregnancies to the passion of jealousy of women who wanted to show others that they were still going to bed with their husbands and demanded their rights to have intercourse with their husbands.

Sexual passions in the Arab world are often aroused by less blatant means than these direct demands for intercourse. The woman goes about in public almost completely covered and the revelation of small parts of her body becomes infused with erotic significance. Thomas (1932) tells us that the hand has sexual significance and that to grasp a woman's hand is a shameful overture. The wearing of the veil is enjoined in the Quran (XXIV:31): ". . . they should Draw their Veils over/ Their bosoms and not display/ Their beauty. . . ." The breasts are also used erotically. Musi (1928) observed that among the Rwala Bedouins of Saudi

545

Arabia, women raised their dresses so that their breasts showed through when the men went forth to battle as a promise of what awaited the victors and to encourage them to bravery. Philby was puzzled to note that a married woman, while traveling, sat down by a stream to wash and drink and exposed her bust. However, this reflects the differing significance of the breasts of the wed and unwed. The breasts are also revealed in public during nursing and do not have the same erotic meaning. Musil also reports on the sexual significance of hair among the Rwala. He says that long hair and tresses are the chief adornment of women and that every youth wants to marry a girl so adorned. Dickson (1951), observing practices in Kuwait, notes that from the day she marries a woman must religiously keep her person free from hair and that this is done in the public bath either by using zinc and arsenic or by plucking the hairs by hand.

Virginity and Sexual Controls

Yet the Arab culture places severe restrictions on certain forms of sexual expression. The demand that a girl be a virgin at marriage is ubiquitous in the Arab world. Musil remarked that girls are so aware of the severe punishment for losing their virginity that when they meet their lovers they place a saber between them, warning, "I am a maiden. Fear Allah!" The disgrace attendant upon having been compromised is so great that a false accuser of a girl may have his hand cut off by the girl's kinsmen. Granqvist (1935) told of a girl whose reputation was stained and whose parents had to save the situation by quickly getting her married off in a distant place. According to Dickson, pride in virginity is so great in Kuwait that it is considered good form among the Bedouin for the young wife to struggle with her husband to save her virginity. A custom common throughout the Arab Middle East is for a husband, after first cohabitation, to take the bedsheet to the bride's male and female relations and to call out in pride and pleasure, "God whiten your faces. You have indeed kept your daughter pure." In Oman, according to Thomas, an unmarried expectant mother would, on discovery, be murdered by her father or her brother. In South Arabia the girl

would be turned out of the tribe to fend for herself, and her male relations would wreak vengeance on a female relation of the seducer.

Sexual control through castration occurs. Eunuchs were known in earlier days but are quite rare today. The castrating of eunuchs is forbidden to a Muslim, and Coon (1951) says that the Muslims employ Coptic Christians to perform the operation. Although eunuchism as a control on sexual behavior has been known, celibacy is almost unknown in Islam. The *Quran* (S II:223, v.248-9) recommends marriage, saying, "Your wives are a tilth unto you;/ So approach your tilth/ When or how ye will." Bliss (1917), studying the Levant near the turn of the century, found that celibates of either sex were almost unknown except for a few in the more rigid dervish orders.

Although not forbidding sexuality, Islam does set limits upon the times when intercourse is permitted. The *Quran* (S II:187:197) notes that one is not to have intercourse during the days of the fast: "Then complete your fast/ Till the night appears;/ But do not associate with your wives while ye are in retreat/ In the mosques. Those are/ Limits [set by] God."

Prostitution

The isolation of the sexes before marriage is bound to give rise to tensions. These are managed by allowing some limited contact between the sexes. The *Quran* (XXIV:33) does not explicitly forbid prostitution but discourages forcing a girl into prostitution. It says, "But force not your maids/ To prostitution when they desire/ Chastity, in order that ye/ May make a gain/ In the good of this life." There are sharp differences in the role of prostitution in the urban and Bedouin sectors. Worthington (1946) found organized brothels in Lebanon and Syria. The permissive attitude toward prostitution is confirmed by Dickson, who notes that in Kuwait a man may indulge in strange women without disgrace—provided they are "public" and work for hire—but he notes that the Quranic injunction not to let a chaste girl lapse is taken seriously. He further reports that in the larger towns prostitutes live in separate quarters and that they are usually girls without relatives. Were they to have men relatives the girls would probably be killed. These girls are not allowed to roam the streets and accost men but keep male and female servants to procure for them. Dickson as well as others has noted that there is no prostitution among women of the desert. However, the consensus seems to be, as maintained by Bailes (1952), that there are few Arab girls among the prostitutes, not only in the deserts but even in the towns. Most of the girls are imported from Somaliland, Sudan, or Ethiopia. Yet Dickson reports that in Kuwait, during the absence of the husbands who go pearling, there is some amateur prostitution among the divers' wives who practice it because of a need to supplement family income. These women are said to practice noncoital forms of intercourse through fear of having a child.

As might be expected, there is a correlation between prostitution and venereal disease. Sinderson (1947), who gave much attention to the urban population, found venereal disease a problem in the Middle East. On the other hand, Marett (1953) who focused his attention on Saudi Arabia, held that venereal disease does not exist in Saudi Arabia proper because prostitution does not exist. He excepts Bahrein from this generalization and attributes the venereal disease there to the employment of Indian prostitutes.

Homosexuality

Another possible consequence of isolation of the sexes is the prevalence of homosexuality. There is a good deal of discussion about homosexuality among Middle Easterners. Usually it is noted with tolerant jocularity. *The Handbook of Arabia* states that in the Hadhramaut dancing is permitted only among persons of the same sex. This observation applies rather generally throughout the area. It is the opinion of students of the area that this monosexual social life leads to more homosexuality among women than among men, often attributed to the fact that the men have recourse to prostitutes. Campbell (1949) relates how homosexuality may develop among women from precisely the social situation that allows men to be heterosexual. He repeats a tale of an Arab leader who kept some 3,000 women in concubinage. These women were condemned to live unloved and unseen in the vast harem until they kissed and

made love to each other from very sadness of heart. Gulick (1955) was impressed by the homosexual nature of the women's solo wedding dances in Lebanon. He related them to ancient fertility themes, saying that the pelvic movements have the purpose of sexual stimulation. Dickson tells of a form of homosexuality in Kuwait in which widows and sexually starved women have sexual relations with Negresses, who act the part of the men and who tend to become overbearing and jealous tyrants over their protégées. However, he presents no evidence on the frequency of this arrangement.

Middle Eastern folklore is replete with tales of shepherds having intercourse with sheep and of sexual contacts with donkeys. There is no objective evidence on this. Musil claims that animal intercourse is almost unknown among the Rwala, as is homosexuality. The penalty for both is death.

Circumcision

Although an Arab may not marry until he is circumcised, its significance seems to be more related to his membership in the larger group. Male circumcision is, of course, enjoined in the *Quran*. However, in practice, observers have found that among some Bedouins it is exaggerated into an ordeal of bravery. Philby found that, among the Tihama tribes of the Arabian Highlands, deferred circumcision is the general rule and that the ordeal is regarded as a test of personal courage and endurance. He says that circumcision in these tribes involves cutting the skin across the stomach below the navel and thence down to the thighs, after which it is peeled off, leaving the whole area—stomach, pelvis, scrotum, and inner legs—completely uncovered. Philby adds that this ordeal has of late been forbidden by the Wahabbi administration of Saudi Arabia.

There has been some debate among students of the Middle East as to the extent of female circumcision. Granqvist (1947) did not find it practiced in the Palestinian villages she studied. However, Worthington claims it is spreading in the Sudan and attributes this to Muslim influence. He says that it is carried out between the ages of 4 and 10 and assumes two principal forms: the Sunna form in which one or more of the sexual parts is excised, and the Pharaonic form in which infibulation or partial occlusion of the vaginal orifice is performed, in addition to the removal of some parts.

Marriage

As is well known, the *Quran* allows a man to take as many as four wives at a time. Actually, polygyny is not as widespread in the Middle East as it theoretically might be because of the requirement that a man be able to provide for his wives and because the number of men and women is more evenly distributed than it was among the warlike tribes of the Quranic period. The Rwala Bedouins studied by Musil are probably closest to the tribal form that existed in those days. He writes that the Rwala usually have one woman in a tent, less often two or three. The tendency is to remain faithful to a wife until the sixth or seventh month of pregnancy and then to look for another girl.

When marrying, a Rwala man spends seven nights with the new wife but must also devote himself to any previous wives. As far as adultery of the wife is concerned, Twitchell (1953), in discussing adultery in Saudi Arabia, says a girl is liable to be buried to the waist in a pit and stoned to death. However, he points out that adultery is uncommon, attributing this to the fact that a man may have four wives. The United Nations report estimates that not more than 5 per cent of the married men in the region have more than one wife at a time. Granqvist, in her study of a Palestinian village (1935), found that of a total of 199 married men, 13 per cent were polygynous.

Concubinage, as a way of increasing the number of women beyond four, exists wherever slavery is continued. A half-century ago there were still remnants of slavery in the Levant, and Bliss found concubinage with slaves a recognized right of the husband. Today, traces of slavery remain only in the Arabian peninsula. Dickson, in his study of Kuwait towns, found that a bought slave girl is a man's property and that it is not wrong for the master to take her as his concubine.

The Arab family emphasizes the husband-wife relation more than that of the parents with their children. Harrison says that the world of the Saudi Arabian Arab does not revolve about his children. They are a mere incident, although petted and spoiled. A man delights in the physical enjoyment of a new and pretty wife.

The attitude toward intercourse is not that it is a service rendered by the woman to the man but a service that he renders to her. This is reflected in an observation by Musil that, among the Rwala, if a near relation of a woman dies her husband is expected to have intercourse with her for several nights in order to comfort her.

Restrictions Placed upon a Man's Enjoyment of His Wife

Granqvist (1947) lists restrictions imposed upon the man regarding intercourse. She writes that when a man wants to have intercourse with his wife he lifts up her garment and says, "I seek refuge in God from the accursed Satan. In the name of God, the Beneficent, the Merciful." This is said so that Satan will retire and God be present, for it is believed that the woman is exposed to danger if the name of God is omitted. Granqvist (1935) also says that when a man returns from a long journey he must sometimes wait three weeks before he can have intercourse with his wife. However, this is not confirmed by other observers.

A further restriction placed on marital intercourse relates to the notion of menstrual uncleanness. The injunction against intercourse during menstruation is found in the *Quran* (S II:222:247), where it is written, "So keep away from women/ In their courses, and do not/ Approach them until/ They are clean./ But when they have purified themselves,/ Ye may approach them/ In any manner, time or place/Ordained for you by God." Observers have reported that this avoidance during menstruation is adhered to. Khadduri (1955), in discussing Muslim law, explains that a husband may not divorce his wife during her menstrual period since he usually does not have intercourse with her at that time. Thus, his failure to have intercourse at that time would not indicate that an aversion exists. Granqvist (1935) says that in a Palestinian village a man becomes unclean if he sleeps with his wife during her period. Musil observed that among the Rwala men do not touch women for three to five days during their period.

Bailes discusses marital adjustment in relation to frigidity of Arab women. She quotes from a book by Carver, who states that no wives are more abused, embittered, and more obviously frigid than the Arabian wives. Female frigidity, according to Carver, plays an important role in the Arab cultural pattern, making for the world's unhappiest husbands. Although there is a grain of truth in this observation, it appears exaggerated.

Sexual Behavior among the Baghdad Elite

During 1954, the author had occasion to obtain histories of sexual behavior from 101 individuals in Israel. These included sixty histories of Jews who had recently migrated from Baghdad, Iraq. The sample was a fairly homogeneous one. The interviewees were in their twenties and thirties at the time of the research. All had completed secondary school in Baghdad and came from families in the upper economic brackets. Only data on the unmarried are reported here. The data were gathered according to the format used in Kinsey's studies (1948, 1953), with comparable results (see p. 555).

The unit of reporting is the mean number of orgasms per week at each age for each source. (For details of interviewing procedure and definitions of terms, the reader is referred to the article, "Sex Life in Israel" in this book, where comparable data for native-born Israelis are presented.) Since these data concern a restricted sector of an urban community, they cannot, of course, be generalized to apply to rural, Bedouin, or lower-class urban Arabs. However, the patterns of the Baghdad Jews studied probably have a good deal in common with the patterns that would be found among Muslim and Christian urban Arabs of the same educational and economic strata.

Age of Maturity

The average age of first ejaculation for males of the Baghdad-born sample was slightly above that of the American males studied by Kinsey. The Iraqi males report their first ejaculation at a mean of 14.24 years. Those studied by Kinsey report 13.88 years. It also appears that maturity comes a bit later to the Iraqi females. The mean age of first menstrual period was 13.17. The American females interviewed by Kinsey had

a mean age of 13.0. Similarly, the Iraqi females experienced their first orgasm at a mean age of 14.18. Although Kinsey does not report this figure explicitly, American females seem to experience their first orgasm somewhat later.

Total Outlet

The total outlet of the Baghdadi males varies from about three orgasms in two weeks at the time they enter high school to five orgasms in two weeks at graduation (Table 1). This frequency is maintained through the age of 21 and then drops back to two in three weeks by the mid-twenties. This total outlet is slightly lower than that of Kinsey's American sample. American males average about two and a half orgasms a week, or about five in two weeks during the entire period.

The total outlet of Iraqi females is considerably less than that of the males. Upon entering high school the frequency jumps from one orgasm in ten weeks to about three in four weeks, and then drops back to about one in two weeks by graduation. During their early twenties, the Iraqi females again experience about three orgasms in four weeks. This pattern is slightly higher than Kinsey's finding among American females of the same educational and economic status, which is about one orgasm every two or three weeks.

TABLE 1. TOTAL OUTLET

Mean Number of Orgasms Per Week

AGE	IRAQI MALES (BAGHDAD)	IRAQI FEMALES (BAGHDAD)
11	.37	.23
12	.81	.22
13	1.23	.19
14	1.57	.84
15	1.74	.73
16	2.06	.48
17	2.33	.57
18	2.50	.59
19	2.30	.63
20	2.25	.81
21	2.39	.64
22	1.58	.70
23	1.58	.81
24	1.74	—
25	1.29	—
26	1.33	—
27	.93	—
28	1.05	—
29	.70	—
30	.70	—

Masturbation

By the age of 16 about two-thirds of Baghdadi males have tried masturbation and about three-fourths have done so by their early twenties (Table 2). For those actively practicing masturbation the frequencies drop from over three times a week in the pre-high school period to about twice a week during high school and to about once a week in their early twenties. During secondary school masturbation accounts for about half of the weekly orgasms of the entire male population. By the early twenties, only one in three orgasms derives from self-stimulation, and in the mid-twenties only one in four.

Kinsey found that American males had a higher accumulative incidence during most of the period and also a slightly higher frequency. American males who masturbated did so over twice a week at age 15 and about one and a third times each week between 21 and 25. Masturbation also accounted for more of the total outlet for the American males, being four-fifths of the total at age 15 and over half of the total between 21 and 25.

Iraqi females were somewhat slower to begin masturbating than were the males (Table 3).

At age 15 one in four females have begun masturbating and by 18 half have had the experience. By their early twenties about eight out of ten of the females interviewed had masturbated at one time or another. For those active in masturbation, the frequency showed a steady decline from once a week at the time of entering high school to once in two weeks by graduation time. During the early twenties the frequency drops to less than once a month. The importance of masturbation as an outlet varies considerably by age. During early adolescence, about one out of four of all orgasms for the population is achieved through masturbation. By late adolescence the proportion drops to one in ten but rises again to one in four by the early twenties.

The females studied by Kinsey masturbated much less. Only about a third had had the experience by age 20 and not quite half had had it by age 25. Throughout, the frequency was approximately once in two or three weeks. However, the relative importance of masturbation as an outlet for the American females was more significant. At age 15, masturbation accounted for 93 per cent of the orgasms and for about half of the orgasms at age 25.

TABLE 2. MASTURBATION AMONG IRAQI MALES (BAGHDAD)

N	AGE	ACCUMULATIVE INCIDENCE PERCENTAGE	FREQUENCY TOTAL POPULATION	STANDARD DEVIATION	ACTIVE POPULATION PERCENTAGE	FREQUENCY ACTIVE	STANDARD DEVIATION	PERCENTAGE OF TOTAL OUTLET
41	11	9.8	.37	1.27	9.8	3.87	1.93	100.0
41	12	12.2	.42	1.39	12.2	3.90	1.67	51.8
41	13	22.2	.67	1.65	22.0	3.06	2.40	54.4
41	14	29.7	.85	1.81	31.7	2.69	2.36	54.1
41	15	51.2	.97	1.50	48.8	2.04	1.59	55.7
41	16	63.3	1.10	1.88	58.4	1.89	2.15	53.4
41	17	63.3	1.20	2.18	53.7	2.24	2.57	51.5
40	18	62.5	1.10	2.20	52.5	2.10	8.53	44.0
36	19	69.4	.96	1.80	55.6	1.73	2.13	41.7
34	20	67.6	.89	1.93	50.0	1.28	2.45	39.5
33	21	69.7	.90	1.02	57.5	1.57	1.06	37.6
28	22	71.4	.49	.74	53.6	.91	.80	31.0
22	23	72.7	.43	.68	54.5	.29	.77	27.2
21	24	76.2	.38	.66	47.6	.80	.77	21.8
13	25	53.8	.34	.65	30.7	1.09	.76	26.4
10	26	60.0	.37	.49	30.0	1.25	.73	27.8
7	27	71.4	.53	.43	42.8	1.25	.84	56.9
4	28	50.0	.50	.29	—	1.01	.99	47.6
4	29	33.0	.00	—	33.0	.02	.01	—
3	30	33.0	—	—	—	—	—	—

TABLE 3. MASTURBATION AMONG IRAQI FEMALES (BAGHDAD)

N	AGE	ACCUMU-LATIVE INCIDENCE PERCENT-AGE	FREQUENCY TOTAL POPULATION	STANDARD DEVIATION	ACTIVE POPULATION PERCENT-AGE	FREQUENCY ACTIVE	STANDARD DEVIATION	PERCENTAGE OF TOTAL OUTLET
19	11	5.2	.05	.94	5.2	1.00	0.00	21.7
19	12	10.5	.04	.37	10.5	.41	.66	18.2
19	13	10.5	.04	.37	10.5	.41	.66	21.0
19	14	21.0	.21	.55	—	1.02	2.25	25.0
19	15	21.0	.21	.55	—	1.02	2.25	28.7
19	16	26.3	.12	.21	5.3	.58	1.13	25.0
15	17	33.0	.07	.21	26.7	.27	.48	12.3
14	18	50.0	.08	.20	42.9	.20	.06	13.5
13	19	61.5	.08	.17	45.6	.18	.06	12.0
10	20	80.0	.12	.25	50.0	.25	.67	14.8
8	21	75.0	.15	.21	62.5	.25	.09	23.4
6	22	83.3	.16	.17	66.7	.16	.09	22.8
4	23	75.0	.22	1.10	75.0	1.63	.90	27.1

TABLE 4. PETTING TO ORGASM AMONG IRAQI MALES (BAGHDAD)

N	AGE	ACCUMU-LATIVE INCIDENCE PERCENT-AGE	FREQUENCY TOTAL POPULATION	STANDARD DEVIATION	ACTIVE POPULATION PERCENT-AGE	FREQUENCY ACTIVE	STANDARD DEVIATION	PERCENTAGE OF TOTAL OUTLET
41	11	—	—	—	—	—	—	—
41	12	2.4	.35	.22	2.4	14.00	—	43.2
41	13	4.9	.24	.16	2.4	10.00	—	19.5
41	14	7.3	.23	.12	4.9	4.75	3.18	14.6
41	15	17.1	.26	.11	14.6	1.79	2.64	14.9
41	16	22.0	.29	.11	17.1	1.75	2.38	14.1
41	17	29.3	.30	.11	24.4	1.23	2.11	12.8
40	18	30.0	.31	.12	17.5	.80	.25	12.4
36	19	44.4	.36	.12	35.3	1.08	2.03	15.6
34	20	50.0	.40	1.27	32.4	1.26	2.04	17.7
33	21	51.5	.42	.65	36.3	1.16	.74	17.6
28	22	46.4	.20	.51	28.6	.72	.76	12.6
22	23	54.5	.34	.67	27.2	1.25	.74	21.5
21	24	57.1	.35	.65	33.3	1.04	.76	20.1
13	25	53.8	.27	.59	30.7	.89	.84	20.9
10	26	50.0	.10	.08	20.0	.52	.31	7.5
7	27	28.6	.00	—	14.3	.05	.01	—
4	28	25.0	—	—	—	—	—	—
4	29	—	—	—	—	—	—	—
3	30	—	—	—	—	—	—	—

Petting to Orgasm

About one in four of the Baghdadi males achieves orgasm through petting by the conclusion of secondary school, and about one out of two have done so by the age of 20 (Table 4). The failure of the accumulative incidence to increase after this age indicates that males who did not have this experience by the age of 20 or 21 do not tend to be initiated into the practice thereafter. For those active in petting to or-

gasm, the frequency drops from somewhat under twice a week during adolescence to a little over once a week on the average during their early twenties. During the entire period, petting accounts for about 15 per cent of all the orgasms of this male population.

Kinsey's study showed that about the same proportion of American males, a little more than half, had experienced orgasm through petting by their early twenties. However, the American males active in petting use this outlet less frequently, having about one such orgasm in three weeks. At no time does this outlet account for more than 7.5 per cent of their total outlet.

Petting to orgasm is a much less frequent occurrence for Baghdadi females (Table 5). About one in four have had the experience by age 18, and a bit over one in three by their early twenties. Even for those active, the experiences were few and far between. Until age 20, even the females who had the experience at all did

not do so more than once or twice during the year. After this, those active in petting were reaching orgasm through petting on the average of once in three weeks. During adolescence it accounts for an insignificant proportion of their total orgasms and for about 10 per cent during the early twenties.

Although not a frequent occurrence in the sample of American females studied by Kinsey, the American incidence of petting to orgasm is higher than that of the Baghdadi females.

TABLE 5. PETTING TO ORGASM AMONG IRAQI FEMALES (BAGHDAD)

N	AGE	ACCUMULATIVE INCIDENCE PERCENTAGE	FREQUENCY TOTAL POPULATION	STANDARD DEVIATION	ACTIVE POPULATION PERCENTAGE	FREQUENCY ACTIVE	STANDARD DEVIATION	PERCENTAGE OF TOTAL OUTLET
19	11	5.2	.00	—	5.2	.02	.00	—
19	12	5.2	—	—	—	—	—	—
19	13	5.3	—	—	—	—	—	—
19	14	5.3	—	—	—	—	—	—
19	15	5.3	—	—	—	—	—	—
19	16	5.3	—	—	—	—	—	—
15	17	20.0	.01	.00	13.3	.04	.00	.00
14	18	28.6	.00	.00	7.1	—	—	—
13	19	38.5	.03	.23	7.7	—	—	4.6
10	20	20.0	.05	.22	10.0	—	—	6.1
8	21	37.5	.07	.21	25.0	.29	.08	10.9
6	22	50.0	.12	.21	33.3	.37	.03	17.1
4	23	75.0	.44	.71	50.0	.88	.88	54.3

TABLE 6. INTERCOURSE WITH COMPANIONS AMONG IRAQI MALES (BAGHDAD)

N	AGE	ACCUMULATIVE INCIDENCE PERCENTAGE	FREQUENCY TOTAL POPULATION	STANDARD DEVIATION	ACTIVE POPULATION PERCENTAGE	FREQUENCY ACTIVE	STANDARD DEVIATION	PERCENTAGE OF TOTAL OUTLET
41	11	—	—	—	—	—	—	—
41	12	—	—	—	—	—	—	—
41	13	—	—	—	—	—	—	—
41	14	—	—	—	—	—	—	—
41	15	—	—	—	—	—	—	—
41	16	—	—	—	—	—	—	—
41	17	4.9	.05	.31	4.9	1.06	1.32	2.1
40	18	5.0	.10	.63	5.0	2.06	2.73	4.0
36	19	8.3	.13	.68	5.6	2.50	2.12	5.1
34	20	11.8	.03	.17	5.9	.51	.69	1.3
33	21	12.1	.05	.21	6.6	.86	.18	2.9
28	22	14.2	.02	.79	3.4	.75	—	1.2
22	23	18.1	.06	.18	13.6	.45	.33	3.8
21	24	28.6	.15	.46	14.3	.83	.82	8.6
13	25	15.4	.06	.21	15.4	.42	.47	4.6
10	26	20.0	.12	.66	20.0	.62	.27	9.2
7	27	14.3	.07	.21	14.3	.50	.18	5.3
4	28	—	—	—	—	—	—	—
4	29	—	—	—	—	—	—	—
3	30	—	—	—	—	—	—	—

The accumulative incidence reaches 34 per cent by age 25 and those actively engaged during their early twenties were having orgasms from this source on an average of once in three months. This outlet always accounted for less than a fifth of their total orgasms.

Premarital Intercourse with Companions

It is very rare for an Iraqi male to achieve orgasm in intercourse with a female companion during adolescence (Table 6). By the age of 20, slightly less than 12 per cent have had the experience. Even in the ensuing years less than one in five have ever used this outlet. However, for those few who do achieve sexual liaisons with their companions, intercourse takes place relatively frequently. At age 18, the frequency for those active is about twice a week. During the early twenties the frequency varies between three and four times a month. Intercourse with companions accounts for only an insignificant part of the total outlet for the population as a whole.

The comparable males in Kinsey's study had an accumulative incidence of 44 per cent by age 20 and 64 per cent by age 25. Those active were having intercourse with companions about three times a month. At age 20, this outlet accounted for about 9 per cent of all orgasms and for about 19 per cent at age 25.

None of the females in the sample interviewed reported experiencing intercourse with companions during the entire period under study. The females from the same educational group in Kinsey's study show an accumulative incidence of intercourse with companions of about 10 per cent by age 20 and 24 per cent by age 25, with frequencies of about three times a month for the active group.

Intercourse with Prostitutes

Orgasms achieved through intercourse with prostitutes plays an important role with the Iraqi males (Table 7). By age 18, one in three males has had the experience of visiting a prostitute, and by the early twenties three out of four have done so. Those active during high school tend to visit prostitutes about once a week. During the following years the frequency drops to about once in two weeks. Late ado-

lescents on the whole achieve about one in seven or eight of their orgasms through intercourse with prostitutes. After the age of 21, this accounts for a quarter to a third of the total outlet.

The accumulative incidences of intercourse with prostitutes of American males as found by Kinsey is roughly similar to that of the Iraqi males. However, American males seem to begin later. By the age of 18 less than 14 per cent of American males had visited a prostitute and by 25 less than 29 per cent had done so. During late adolescence the active population tends to visit prostitutes about once in five weeks, and during their early twenties the frequency rises to about once in two weeks. During late adolescence, less than 3 per cent of all orgasms of the American sample were achieved with prostitutes, while during their early twenties the relative proportion rose to 3.5 per cent. Thus, it claims a less important place in the total outlet for American males than for Iraqi males.

Spontaneous Orgasms

By early adolescence, three out of four Iraqi males have experienced a spontaneous orgasm without mechanical self-stimulation or social sexual contact (Table 8). Almost all of them have had such orgasms by the close of adolescence. The experience is a recurring one, with almost all of the population experiencing it throughout all of the years. The active frequency tends to decrease with age. Upon entering high school, these males have about one spontaneous orgasm a week. The frequency drops to about one nocturnal emission in two weeks by the early twenties. During most of the period this accounts for about a fourth of their orgasms.

The males in Kinsey's sample had about the same accumulative incidence but had only about one nocturnal emission in three weeks, and these accounted for about a sixth of all their orgasms.

About half of the Iraqi females entering high school have had spontaneous orgasms and about three-fourths experience orgasm from this source before graduation (Table 9). The accumulative incidence rises only a few percentage points by their twenties. During early adolescence about half of the females are ex-

TABLE 7. INTERCOURSE WITH PROSTITUTES AMONG IRAQI MALES (BAGHDAD)

N	AGE	ACCUMU- LATIVE INCIDENCE PERCENT- AGE	FREQUENCY TOTAL POPULATION	STANDARD DEVIATION	ACTIVE POPULATION PERCENT- AGE	FREQUENCY ACTIVE	STANDARD DEVIATION	PERCENTAGE OF TOTAL OUTLET
41	11	–	–	–	–	–	–	–
41	12	–	–	–	–	–	–	–
41	13	–	–	–	–	–	–	–
41	14	2.4	.00	.00	2.4	.05	–	–
41	15	2.4	.00	.00	2.4	.25	–	–
41	16	14.6	.15	.65	14.6	1.05	1.51	7.3
41	17	17.1	.14	.64	14.6	1.02	1.50	27.5
40	18	35.0	.35	.96	35.0	1.01	1.43	14.0
36	19	47.2	.29	.74	47.2	.62	.99	12.6
34	20	61.8	.38	.65	61.8	.61	.74	16.8
33	21	66.7	.56	1.22	66.7	.84	1.43	23.4
28	22	78.6	.45	.65	67.6	.67	.70	28.5
22	23	81.8	.43	.55	72.7	.59	.57	27.2
21	24	76.2	.58	1.05	76.2	.76	1.15	33.3
13	25	61.5	.30	.55	63.8	.56	.65	23.2
10	26	90.0	.41	.31	90.0	.45	.59	30.8
7	27	85.7	.15	.59	85.7	.18	.09	16.1
4	28	75.0	.10	.32	–	.14	.10	9.5
4	29	66.0	.10	.10	66.0	.10	.02	14.3
3	30	100.0	.10	.10	100.0	.10	.02	14.3

TABLE 8. SPONTANEOUS ORGASMS AMONG IRAQI MALES (BAGHDAD)

N	AGE	ACCUMU- LATIVE INCIDENCE PERCENT- AGE	FREQUENCY TOTAL POPULATION	STANDARD DEVIATION	ACTIVE POPULATION PERCENT- AGE	FREQUENCY ACTIVE	STANDARD DEVIATION	PERCENTAGE OF TOTAL OUTLET
41	11	2.4	.00	.00	2.4	.25	–	
41	12	4.9	.05	.31	4.9	1.12	1.23	6.2
41	13	31.7	.32	.77	31.7	1.02	1.11	26.0
41	14	61.0	.49	.84	61.0	.81	.96	31.2
41	15	75.6	.52	.69	75.6	.68	2.29	29.8
41	16	85.4	.52	.76	82.9	.64	.80	25.2
41	17	87.7	.64	.80	85.4	.75	.82	27.4
40	18	90.0	.64	.89	87.5	.74	.92	25.6
36	19	91.7	.57	.66	88.9	.64	.67	24.7
34	20	91.2	.56	.81	88.2	.64	.84	24.8
33	21	96.9	.46	.54	93.9	.49	.55	19.2
28	22	96.4	.42	.49	89.2	.47	.49	26.5
22	23	100.0	.33	.45	90.9	.36	.46	20.8
21	24	90.5	.31	.46	76.2	.40	.50	17.8
13	25	92.3	.33	.52	92.3	.36	.54	25.6
10	26	90.0	.34	.32	90.0	.38	.59	25.6
7	27	85.7	.18	.30	85.7	.21	.22	19.4
4	28	75.0	.45	.66	75.0	.60	.47	42.8
4	29	100.0	.60	.38	100.0	.60	.43	85.7
3	30	100.0	.60	.38	100.0	.60	.43	85.7

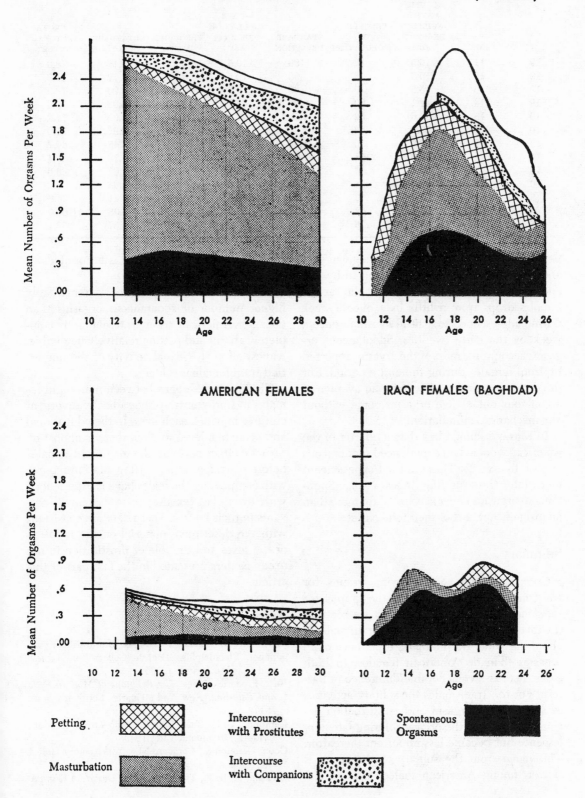

AMERICAN MALES

IRAQI MALES (BAGHDAD)

Mean Number of Orgasms Per Week

2.4
2.1
1.8
1.5
1.2
.9
.6
.3
.00

10 12 14 16 18 20 22 24 26 28 30
Age

10 12 14 16 18 20 22 24 26
Age

AMERICAN FEMALES

IRAQI FEMALES (BAGHDAD)

Mean Number of Orgasms Per Week

2.4
2.1
1.8
1.5
1.2
.9
.6
.3
.00

10 12 14 16 18 20 22 24 26 28 30
Age

10 12 14 16 18 20 22 24 26
Age

Petting

Intercourse with Prostitutes

Spontaneous Orgasms

Masturbation

Intercourse with Companions

TABLE 9. SPONTANEOUS ORGASMS AMONG IRAQI FEMALES (BAGHDAD)

N	AGE	ACCUMULATIVE INCIDENCE PERCENTAGE	FREQUENCY TOTAL POPULATION	STANDARD DEVIATION	ACTIVE POPULATION PERCENTAGE	FREQUENCY ACTIVE	STANDARD DEVIATION	PERCENTAGE OF TOTAL OUTLET
19	11	10.5	.18	.66	10.5	1.75	1.12	78.3
19	12	10.5	.18	.66	10.5	1.75	1.12	81.8
19	13	15.8	.15	.45	15.8	1.00	1.96	78.9
19	14	42.1	.63	.30	42.1	1.50	2.93	75.0
19	15	52.6	.52	1.20	47.4	1.11	.62	71.2
19	16	57.9	.36	1.34	47.1	.85	3.92	75.0
15	17	66.7	.50	1.34	60.0	.83	.48	87.7
14	18	78.6	.51	.93	71.4	.72	.78	86.4
13	19	69.2	.54	.91	61.5	.88	.67	83.0
10	20	80.0	.64	.86	70.0	.91	.68	79.0
8	21	75.0	.42	.22	62.5	.68	1.41	65.6
6	22	66.7	.42	.22	50.0	.85	1.08	60.0
4	23	50.0	.26	.49	50.0	.52	.67	32.1

periencing spontaneous orgasm in a given year and about three-quarters are doing so by late adolescence. The frequency of the active females drops from a little over once a week during adolescence to a little less than once a week by the early twenties. Spontaneous orgasms account for most of the orgasms reported by Iraqi females during the entire period. For the entire population of females an average of about four out of five orgasms come without any mechanical stimulation.

In Kinsey's sample less than a quarter of the American women had experienced spontaneous orgasm by age 25. These did not experience it more than three or four times a year. Spontaneous orgasms never accounted for more than an insignificant part of their total outlet.

Summary

Comparing the accompanying graphs for Iraqi males and females with the graphs for the American males and females, we see that the total outlet for American and Iraqi males is about the same. Iraqi females experience more orgasms than do American females. In both cases there is a considerable difference in pattern. For the Iraqi males the solitary activities of spontaneous orgasm and masturbation account for most of the orgasms during late adolescence but become less important thereafter. This move from the solitary to the social is slower among American males. Most of the

Iraqi's social sexual behavior is accounted for by visits to prostitutes.

The Iraqi female experiences a remarkably higher number of spontaneous orgasms than does her American sister. Intercourse is completely absent and petting relatively negligible. Almost all of the sexual activity of the unmarried Iraqi female is solitary.

The sharp difference between males and females in Iraq points up the radically divergent cultures in which each lives. In the educational and economic level studied, there is almost no sexual contact between the males and females before marriage. What petting and intercourse with companions the males have is experienced with lower-class females; on occasion, with servants in their houses. These data are consistent with the descriptive material on the isolation of the sexes and the role of prostitution in the urban centers presented in the first part of this article.

References

Bailes, Sylvia, Slavery in Arabia. Unpublished term paper. Philadelphia: Dropsie College for Hebrew and Cognate Learning, 1952.

Bliss, Frederick Jones, The Religions of Modern Syria and Palestine. New York: Charles Scribner's Sons, 1917.

Campbell, C. G., Tales from the Arab Tribes. London: Lindsay Drummond Ltd., 1949.

Coon, Carleton S., Caravan. New York: Henry Holt & Co., 1951.

Dickson, H. R. P., The Arab of the Desert: A Glimpse

Into Badawin Life in Kuwait and Saudi Arabia. London: George Allen & Unwin Ltd., 1951.

Glubb, J. B., *The Sulubbi and Other Ignoble Tribes of Southwestern Asia, General Series in Anthropology No. 10.* Menasha, Wisc.: George Banta Pub. Co., 1943, pp. 14-17.

Granqvist, Hilma, *Marriage Conditions in a Palestinian Village, II.* Helsingfors: Societas Scientarum Fennica, Commentationes Humanarum Litterarum, Vol. VI, No. 8, 1935.

Granqvist, Hilma, *Birth and Childhood Among the Arabs: Studies in a Mohammedan Village in Palestine.* Helsingfors: Söderström & Co., 1947.

Granqvist, Hilma, *Child Problems Among the Arabs.* Helsingfors: Söderström & Co., 1950.

Great Britain, Geographical Section of the Naval Intelligence Division Naval Staff, Admiralty, *A Handbook of Arabia, Vol. 1.* London: His Majesty's Stationery Office, 1920.

Gulick, John, *Social Structure and Cultural Change in a Lebanese Village.* New York: Wenner-Gren Foundation for Anthropological Research, Inc., 1955.

Harrison, Paul W., *The Arab at Home.* New York: Thomas Y. Crowell Co., 1924.

Khadduri, Majid, and Liebesny, Herbert J. (eds.), *Law in the Middle East, Origin and Development of Islamic Law, Vol. 1.* Washington: The Middle East Institute, 1955.

Kinsey, Alfred C. *et al., Sexual Behavior in the Human Male.* Philadelphia: W. B. Saunders Co., 1948.

Kinsey, Alfred C. *et al., Sexual Behavior in the Human Female.* Philadelphia: W. B. Saunders Co., 1953.

Marett, William C., "Some Medical Problems Met in Saudi Arabia." *United States Armed Forces M. J. 4;* 31-38, 1953.

Musil, Alois, *The Manners and Customs of the Rwala Bedouins.* New York: The American Geographical Society, Oriental Explorations and Studies, No. 6, 1928.

Philby, H. St. John B., *Arabian Highlands.* Ithaca, N.Y.: Cornell University Press, 1952.

Sinderson, Harry, "Some Health Problems of the Middle East." *The Royal Central Asian J. 34;* 131-143, 1947.

Tannous, Afif I., "Missionary Education in Lebanon." *Social Forces 21;* 338-343, 1943.

The Quran, Lahore, 1937.

Thomas, Bertram, "Anthropological Observations in South Arabia." *J. Royal Anthropol. Inst. Great Britain and Ireland 62;* 83-103, 1932.

Twitchell, K. S., *Saudi Arabia.* Princeton, N.J.: Princeton University Press, 1953.

United Nations, "Social Conditions in the Middle East." *Preliminary Report on the World Situation.* New York: United Nations, 1952.

Worthington, E. B., *Middle East Science.* London: His Majesty's Stationery Office, 1946.

SAMUEL Z. KLAUSNER

Israel,
Sex Life in*

ISRAELI patterns of sexual behavior are as divergent as the ethnic composition of the Israeli population. Sharp differences in attitudes and behaviors exist among immigrants from various European countries, immigrants from Middle Eastern lands, and native-born Jews as well as native-born and immigrant Arabs. Patterned differences according to ethnic origin are superimposed upon variations deriving from economic and educational differences and urban versus agricultural and Bedouin rural populations.

The author has assembled systematic quantitative data from a narrow segment of the population. In 1954, 101 interviews on sexual behavior were carried out. All the interviewees were from the middle and upper economic strata and had at least a high-school education. They were about equally divided between native-born Israelis of Eastern European parentage and recent immigrants from Baghdad. Most of the subjects were in their twenties and thirties at the time of the interview. The sample was not random, but it was highly homogeneous. The results are not, in general, applicable to the whole population but are suggestive of the patterns found in these sectors. This article will report on the unmarried portion of the native-born sample. (Data from the Baghdad

sample are included in the article, "Sex Life in Islam.")

The Interviews

In interviewing, it was necessary to establish a rapport that would allay the subjects' anxiety. All interviews were carried out verbally in a face-to-face situation. Interviewing in a closed room and with no one else present assured the respondent of privacy and promised secrecy. The protocols were recorded in a code in the presence of the interviewee. This was intended to add to the subject's assurance that no one else could read his sex history. A professional atmosphere was maintained by asking the questions in a matter-of-fact way. Slang references to sexual behavior were avoided.

It was discovered that anxiety could be kept at a minimum if the interview was begun with questions that provoked the least anxiety, slowly leading into more disturbing questions. Thus, the interview opened with questions about education and military experience. Then the question of source of sexual knowledge was broached. Subsequently, the age of first ejaculation, first menstruation, and first orgasm were requested. This led naturally to a question about the source of this first orgasm; and then this behavior was followed year by year through to the present. Interrogation about other sources of orgasm followed.

For males, questions were usually asked, in order, about nocturnal emissions, intercourse with prostitutes, intercourse with companions,

* This research was made possible by funds granted by the Ford Foundation. That Foundation is not, however, the author, owner, publisher, or proprietor of this research and is not to be understood as approving by virtue of its grant any of the statements or views expressed therein.

petting to orgasm, masturbation, and homosexuality. For females, the usual order was spontaneous orgasm, petting to orgasm, masturbation, intercourse with companions, and homosexuality. This "order of anxiety" was empirically determined and was the same for the native-born Israeli and Iraqi samples. Questions were asked in the format established by Kinsey (1948, 1953) so as to produce comparable results.

From prior information on the personality and culture of Middle Eastern women, difficulties were anticipated in interviewing Iraqi females. This did not prove to be the case. The relative ease with which it was possible to interview the Iraqi females may have been due to three factors. First, they were passing through a cultural transition. They had already left the society of Baghdad and had not yet been fully integrated into the new society. The old normative structure had been shattered and not yet replaced. Second, there was some generalization from the situation of a medical interview, since the interviewer was called doctor (of psychology). Finally, the females interviewed were rather sophisticated and were eager to become part of Western society. It appeared to some that providing information on sexual life was a normal way to behave in European society.

In the entire sample, there were only two failures to complete the interview. Both were late adolescent females; one from Baghdad and one native-born Israeli.

Validity

Several measures were taken to maximize the validity of the responses, *i.e.*, the accuracy with which responses reflected actual behavior. Respondents were not asked if they had engaged in a given behavior; rather, they were asked about the first time they had experienced it. The burden was on the respondent to deny having had the experience. When a respondent had difficulty in recall, it was found useful to begin with current behavior and work back to previous years. The interviewer constantly watched the emerging pattern of responses for its internal consistency.

A strong assurance of validity was the degree of involvement of the subjects. It was found that respondents became emotionally involved regarding the accuracy of their own responses and tended to become apologetic if they had difficulty in recalling the frequency of a given behavior at a given age. However, despite these safeguards, there is no doubt some invalidity in the responses because of the unintentional perceptual distortions to which all recall of past material is subject. This includes distortions deriving from deeper motivational forces that press toward minimization or exaggeration of various types of behavior. Among a small number of married couples interviewed, the males showed a tendency to report higher frequencies of marital intercourse than the females.

Definitions

The unit of reporting is the average number of orgasms per week at a given age from a given source.

Orgasm: A building up and sudden spasmodic release of muscular tension associated with clearly sexual activity. Sexual arousal without spasmodic release was not counted. For males, only ejaculations were counted.

Total outlet: The mean number of orgasms per week at a given age from all sources together.

Accumulative incidence: The proportion of the population ever having experienced orgasm from a given source up to a given age. For example, a 20-year-old who had intercourse at age 17 is counted in the accumulative incidence as having had the experience, although he may not have had any intercourse at age 20.

Active incidence: The proportion experiencing orgasm from a given source during a given year.

Spontaneous orgasm: An orgasm coming without any intentional mechanical stimulation of the body. This includes orgasms occurring spontaneously during exercise, and from sexual stimulation from reading or dreaming. This category covers nocturnal emissions among males.

Masturbation: Mechanical self-stimulation of the genitals or other erogenous zones, leading to orgasm. Stimulation may be manual or by bringing the erogenous zone into contact with an inanimate object.

Intercourse with prostitutes: Heterosexual intercourse in which the partner participates in consideration of a direct money payment.

Intercourse with companions: Heterosexual intercourse in which no direct money payment is involved.

Petting to orgasm: Heterosexual stimulation of genitals or other erogenous zones, leading to orgasm and without intromission of the penis. This varies from mere stroking of one by the other to actually placing the genitals in apposition without penetration.

Homosexual experiences were too infrequent in the samples to be reported quantitatively. None of the subjects admitted to intercourse with animals.

Results

Comparative data are based on the findings of Kinsey as reported for the highest educational group among single white males and females.

Age of Maturity

Native-born Israeli males report their first ejaculation at a mean age of 13.50 years. This compares with a mean age for first orgasm for the native-born Israeli females of 12.87 years. Their first menstrual period came at a mean age of 13.03 years. In all of these cases, the ages are slightly, but not significantly, below those reported by Kinsey for a comparable sample of American males and females.

Total Outlet

Males of 15 experience an average of two orgasms per week from all sources together. During the early twenties, the figure rises to about two and a third a week, or about twelve a month. The females at 15 have about three orgasms a month and increase to slightly over two a week by their early twenties. The males in the Kinsey sample had about the same order of activity as the Israeli males. However, the females in this sample have about five times the number of orgasms in their twenties as those studied by Kinsey. In the Kinsey sample

the males were about six times as active as the females, but it appears that the Israeli female has almost the same frequency of sexual activity as the Israeli male (Table 1).

TABLE 1. TOTAL OUTLET

AGE	ISRAELI-BORN MALES	ISRAELI-BORN FEMALES
11	.23	.01
12	.06	.01
13	1.72	.19
14	1.81	.50
15	1.93	.76
16	2.23	.88
17	2.57	1.47
18	2.08	1.80
19	1.99	2.19
20	1.85	2.01
21	2.37	3.67
22	2.36	2.31
23	2.12	2.18
24	2.39	1.91
25	1.52	—

Masturbation

By age 13, 40 per cent of the males have had experience in masturbating (Table 2). Over 75 per cent masturbated by age 16, and by the early twenties almost all have at one time or another tried this outlet. The proportion active in any given year rises to almost two-thirds by age 16 and then drops to about a fourth during the early twenties. Those who were masturbating did so on the average of twice a week during adolescence and somewhat less than once a week after 20. The decreasing importance of masturbation as a source of orgasm is reflected in the decreasing proportion of the total outlet of the whole population which it accounts for. At age 16, about two-thirds of all orgasms are self-stimulated; by age 21 only one in six orgasms is so accounted for.

Kinsey found that American males, in the same social and educational category, show about the same accumulative incidence of masturbation. They have a mean frequency of 2.22 per week at age 15, dropping to 1.31 between 21 and 25. Masturbation accounts for almost four-fifths of the total outlet at 15, and by age 21 over half of the orgasms are still from this source. The picture of higher adolescent and lower adult masturbatory frequency of the

TABLE 2. MASTURBATION AMONG ISRAELI-BORN MALES

N	AGE	ACCUMU-LATIVE INCIDENCE PERCENT-AGE	FREQUENCY TOTAL POPULATION	STANDARD DEVIATION	ACTIVE POPULATION PERCENT-AGE	FREQUENCY ACTIVE	STANDARD DEVIATION	PERCENTAGE OF TOTAL OUTLET
22	11	9.1	.23	1.07	4.5	5.00	—	100.0
22	12	9.5	—	—	—	—	—	0.0
22	13	40.9	1.16	2.09	40.9	2.83	2.48	67.4
22	14	63.6	1.22	1.89	35.8	2.06	2.10	67.4
22	15	72.7	1.31	1.91	27.3	2.06	2.05	68.0
22	16	77.3	1.18	1.93	63.6	1.86	2.16	52.9
22	17	81.8	1.26	2.51	59.1	2.14	3.00	49.0
22	18	81.8	.72	1.53	54.5	1.31	1.90	34.6
20	19	80.0	.46	.62	60.0	.76	.66	23.1
19	20	78.9	.57	1.58	47.4	1.21	2.18	30.8
14	21	85.7	.34	.71	43.0	.79	.95	14.3
11	22	90.9	.15	.32	27.3	.54	1.77	6.3
8	23	100.0	.05	.04	37.5	.13	—	2.4
7	24	100.0	.02	.04	28.6	.12	.07	.8
4	25	100.0	.05	.02	50.0	.11		3.3

TABLE 3. MASTURBATION AMONG ISRAELI-BORN FEMALES

N	AGE	ACCUMU-LATIVE INCIDENCE PERCENT-AGE	FREQUENCY TOTAL POPULATION	STANDARD DEVIATION	ACTIVE POPULATION PERCENT-AGE	FREQUENCY ACTIVE	STANDARD DEVIATION	PERCENTAGE OF TOTAL OUTLET
19	11	15.8	.01	.05	5.3	.25	—	100.0
19	12	15.8	.01	.05	5.3	.25	—	100.0
19	13	26.3	.13	.28	21.1	.63	.32	68.4
19	14	52.6	.28	.48	47.5	.59	.56	56.0
19	15	63.2	.49	.78	60.0	.85	.88	64.5
19	16	63.2	.54	.97	58.0	.94	1.13	61.4
19	17	73.8	.65	1.07	63.2	1.03	1.20	44.2
18	18	77.8	.62	.87	66.7	.93	.93	34.4
15	19	80.0	.89	1.27	66.7	1.33	1.36	40.6
13	20	84.6	.86	1.11	69.2	1.24	1.15	42.8
11	21	81.8	1.71	8.81	72.7	2.39	3.29	46.6
8	22	87.5	1.59	3.44	75.0	2.19	3.89	68.8
7	23	100.0	.96	1.44	85.8	1.12	1.50	44.0
3	24	100.0	.67	.76	66.7	1.00	.71	35.1

Israeli sample is closer to the pattern that Kinsey found in the lower educational and economic groups in America.

The data on masturbation for the females are roughly similar in accumulative incidence to those of the males (Table 3). Again about two-thirds of the females have begun masturbating by age 16, and by age 22 almost all have had the experience. However, unlike the males, the proportion of females active in each year shows a steady rise from 60 per cent at age 15 to 75 per cent at age 22. The active females are masturbating about once a week during

adolescence. The frequency increases to between one and a half and two times a week during the early twenties. At mid-adolescence, masturbation accounts for one-half to two-thirds of all orgasms for the females. Unlike the males, it still accounts for an average of 40 per cent of all orgasms during the early twenties.

Kinsey found much less frequent masturbation among American females in this same educational group, but what masturbation was found formed a larger proportion of their total outlet. The mean frequency tends to be between .3 and .4 per week. By age 20 not more than a third had experienced masturbation and not more than half had tried this outlet by age 25. The relative importance of masturbation in the total outlet was greater for American females. At age 15, it accounts for 93 per cent of the total outlet and for about half of the weekly orgasms at age 25. The pattern of masturbation among Israeli females is closer to that of the American males than to that of American females.

Petting to Orgasm

Petting to orgasm is a universal experience among the males of the sample (Table 4). By age 16 over half have already achieved orgasm through petting, and by 21 over 90 per cent have done so. During high-school years about half of the males are actively engaged in petting to orgasm to the extent of about once in two weeks. By the early twenties the active proportion declines slightly. Those who continue achieve orgasm in this manner about once a week. Throughout adolescence and early adulthood petting accounts for about one out of eight of the orgasms experienced in the sample.

The males in Kinsey's sample were less active in petting. By their early twenties slightly more than half have had experience. Those active

TABLE 4. PETTING TO ORGASM AMONG ISRAELI-BORN MALES

N	AGE	ACCUMU-LATIVE INCIDENCE PERCENT-AGE	FREQUENCY TOTAL POPULATION	STANDARD DEVIATION	ACTIVE POPULATION PERCENT-AGE	FREQUENCY ACTIVE	STANDARD DEVIATION	PERCENTAGE OF TOTAL OUTLET
22	11	—	—	—	—	—	—	0.0
22	12	—	—	—	—	—	—	0.0
22	13	—	—	—	—	—	—	0.0
22	14	4.5	.01	.01	4.5	.33	—	.6
22	15	27.3	.10	.32	27.3	.35	.57	5.2
22	16	54.5	.27	.45	50.0	.55	.50	12.1
22	17	68.2	.32	.45	54.5	.58	.46	12.5
22	18	77.3	.31	.44	54.5	.56	.47	14.9
20	19	80.0	.24	.40	50.0	.49	.45	12.1
19	20	84.2	.33	.57	47.4	.69	.67	17.8
14	21	92.9	.66	1.18	43.0	1.53	2.25	27.9
11	22	90.9	.34	.90	36.4	.92	1.39	10.2
8	23	100.0	.05	.08	37.5	.14	.10	23.6
7	24	100.0	.27	.41	57.1	.46	.45	11.3
4	25	100.0	.19	.24	50.0	.38	.18	12.5

TABLE 5. PETTING TO ORGASM AMONG ISRAELI-BORN FEMALES

N	AGE	ACCUMU-LATIVE INCIDENCE PERCENT-AGE	FREQUENCY TOTAL POPULATION	STANDARD DEVIATION	ACTIVE POPULATION PERCENT-AGE	FREQUENCY ACTIVE	STANDARD DEVIATION	PERCENTAGE OF TOTAL OUTLET
19	11	5.3	—	—	—	—	—	0.0
19	12	5.3	—	—	—	—	—	0.0
19	13	5.3	—	—	—	—	—	0.0
19	14	5.3	—	—	—	—	—	0.0
19	15	5.3	—	—	—	—	—	0.0
19	16	10.5	.01	.02	5.3	.12	—	1.1
19	17	31.6	.30	.65	26.3	1.16	.83	20.4
18	18	44.4	.52	2.52	44.4	1.16	.83	28.9
15	19	60.0	.55	.69	60.0	.91	.76	25.1
13	20	69.2	.47	.81	61.5	.76	.94	23.4
11	21	81.8	.64	1.14	63.6	1.02	1.31	17.4
8	22	75.0	.16	.35	37.5	.46	.48	6.9
7	23	85.8	.27	.41	57.1	.47	.60	12.4
3	24	100.0	.24	.37	66.7	.36	.43	12.6

TABLE 6. INTERCOURSE WITH COMPANIONS AMONG ISRAELI-BORN MALES

N	AGE	ACCUMU-LATIVE INCIDENCE PERCENT-AGE	FREQUENCY TOTAL POPULATION	STANDARD DEVIATION	ACTIVE POPULATION PERCENT-AGE	FREQUENCY ACTIVE	STANDARD DEVIATION	PERCENTAGE OF TOTAL OUTLET
22	11	4.5	—	—	—	—	—	0.0
22	12	4.5	—	—	—	—	—	0.0
22	13	4.5	—	—	—	—	—	0.0
22	14	4.5	—	—	—	—	—	0.0
22	15	9.1	.05	.21	4.5	1.00	—	2.6
22	16	27.3	.24	.60	22.7	1.05	.91	10.8
22	17	45.5	.51	.79	40.9	1.25	.78	19.8
22	18	59.1	.45	.71	54.5	.83	.80	21.6
20	19	65.0	.56	.91	65.0	.85	1.01	28.1
19	20	71.6	.40	.73	52.6	.75	.87	21.6
14	21	85.7	1.11	1.37	78.6	1.41	1.41	46.8
11	22	100.0	1.59	1.31	100.0	1.58	1.08	69.9
8	23	100.0	1.89	2.37	100.0	1.89	2.37	89.2
7	24	100.0	1.87	1.41	100.0	1.87	1.41	78.2
4	25	100.0	.88	1.44	50.0	1.75	1.74	57.9

TABLE 7. INTERCOURSE WITH COMPANIONS AMONG ISRAELI-BORN FEMALES

N	AGE	ACCUMU-LATIVE INCIDENCE PERCENT-AGE	FREQUENCY TOTAL POPULATION	STANDARD DEVIATION	ACTIVE POPULATION PERCENT-AGE	FREQUENCY ACTIVE	STANDARD DEVIATION	PERCENTAGE OF TOTAL OUTLET
19	11	—	—	—	—	—	—	0.0
19	12	—	—	—	—	—	—	0.0
19	13	—	—	—	—	—	—	0.0
19	14	—	—	—	—	—	—	0.0
19	15	—	—	—	—	—	—	0.0
19	16	—	—	—	—	—	—	0.0
19	17	5.3	.18	.80	5.3	—	—	12.2
18	18	11.1	.39	1.44	11.1	3.50	3.53	21.7
15	19	13.3	.38	1.29	13.3	2.84	3.06	12.8
13	20	7.7	.31	1.11	7.7	—	—	14.9
11	21	27.3	1.00	1.95	27.3	3.67	1.53	27.2
8	22	37.5	.16	.29	25.0	.61	.17	6.9
7	23	42.9	.60	.81	42.9	1.39	.61	27.5
3	24	33.3	—	—	—	—	—	0.0

have the experience about once in three weeks. At no time did this outlet account for more than 7.5 per cent of the total orgasms.

The females begin a bit later than the males (Table 5). Only one in three females has experienced orgasm through petting by age 17. About three-fourths have by age 21. At age 17 only one in four is active, while at 21 two in three females engage in petting to orgasm. Those who are active average about one experience a week during late adolescence. At this time it accounts for about a quarter of all orgasms experienced by the females in the sample. Petting becomes proportionally less important in the total picture after this.

Again the females in the Kinsey report are considerably less active, with only about one in three having had the experience by age 25. Their frequency is about one such experience in three months. Petting accounts for less than a fifth of the total orgasms.

Intercourse with Companions

By late adolescence, intercourse with companions accounts for a major share of orgasms experienced by Israeli native-born males (Table 6). Almost half have had intercourse by age 17, and the entire sample reported experience by age 22. At age 16, intercourse accounts for 11 per cent of all the orgasms of the male sample, and for one out of five of their orgasms at age 18. During their early twenties about three of four orgasms are achieved in intercourse. Those active are having intercourse about once a week during high school. The frequency increases to slightly under twice a week by their twenties.

The comparable males in Kinsey's study have an accumulative incidence of 44 per cent by age 20 and 64 per cent by age 25. Those active are having intercourse about three times a month. Intercourse with companions accounts for about 9 per cent of the orgasms at age 20 and for about 19 per cent at age 25. The difference between the two populations is striking. Intercourse with companions has from five to seven times the importance as an outlet for Israeli males during their early twenties as it does for American males. The active Israeli males have intercourse about three times as often as the active American males during this period.

Native-born Israeli females begin having intercourse somewhat later than the males (Table 7). By late adolescence only about 10 per cent have achieved orgasm in this way. About one-third have had the experience by age 22. However, once initiated into intercourse, they tend to maintain the practice. This is evidenced by the fact that the active incidence parallels the accumulative incidence. Those females active are considerably more active than the males.

They have intercourse two to three times a week during late adolescence. In the immediate post-high school years, intercourse accounts for over 10 per cent of all orgasms for the female population, and by the early twenties for over 20 per cent.

In the American sample only 10 per cent of the females have had intercourse by age 20, and 24 per cent by age 25. Their frequency is roughly three times a month.

Spontaneous Orgasm

Three out of four 16-year-old native-born Israeli males have experienced spontaneous orgasm, usually in the form of a nocturnal emission (Table 8). By the age of 18, 90 per cent have had ejaculation with neither social nor mechanical contact. However, there is a steadily decreasing frequency of the occurrence. During the high-school period a nocturnal emission seems to be an almost weekly happening for the three out of four experiencing it at all. After the age of 20 there is a rather sharp drop in frequency. For the active population, spontaneous orgasm occurs about twice a month at age 21 and about once a month after age 23. This outlet also decreases in relative importance as a source of orgasms. During adolescence one in four orgasms are spontaneous, while in the early twenties only about one in ten is so.

TABLE 8. SPONTANEOUS ORGASM AMONG ISRAELI-BORN MALES

N	AGE	ACCUMU-LATIVE INCIDENCE PERCENTAGE	FREQUENCY TOTAL POPULATION	STANDARD DEVIATION	ACTIVE POPULATION PERCENTAGE	FREQUENCY ACTIVE	STANDARD DEVIATION	PERCENTAGE OF TOTAL OUTLET
22	11	–	–	–	–	–	–	0.0
22	12	9.1	.06	.22	9.1	.63	.52	100.0
22	13	54.5	.56	1.51	54.5	1.03	1.96	20.9
22	14	63.3	.58	1.14	54.5	1.06	1.40	32.0
22	15	77.3	.47	.60	63.6	.74	.60	24.4
22	16	77.3	.54	.68	68.2	.80	.69	24.2
22	17	86.4	.48	.69	68.2	.70	.74	18.7
22	18	90.9	.51	.71	68.2	.75	.75	24.5
20	19	85.0	.57	.76	70.0	.82	.79	28.6
19	20	89.6	.39	.68	71.6	.61	.77	21.1
14	21	92.9	.26	.29	64.5	.41	.27	11.0
11	22	90.9	.28	.74	45.5	.61	1.06	11.9
8	23	87.5	.13	.17	62.5	.21	.18	6.1
7	24	85.7	.23	.35	71.4	.33	.38	9.6
4	25	100.0	.40	.45	75.0	.53	.45	26.2

TABLE 9. SPONTANEOUS ORGASM AMONG ISRAELI-BORN FEMALES

N	AGE	ACCUMU- LATIVE INCIDENCE PERCENT- AGE	FREQUENCY TOTAL POPULATION	STANDARD DEVIATION	ACTIVE POPULATION PERCENT- AGE	FREQUENCY ACTIVE	STANDARD DEVIATION	PERCENTAGE OF TOTAL OUTLET
19	11	—	—	—	—	—	—	0.0
19	12	10.5	.00	.00	10.5	.02	—	0.0
19	13	31.6	.06	.15	15.8	.37	.22	31.6
19	14	52.6	.22	.35	47.5	.47	.39	44.0
19	15	58.0	.27	.39	47.5	.59	.36	35.5
19	16	68.5	.33	.40	58.0	.57	.36	37.5
19	17	68.5	.34	.46	58.0	.59	.46	23.1
18	18	77.8	.27	.37	55.6	.49	.38	15.0
15	19	86.7	.37	.40	66.7	.55	.38	16.9
13	20	84.6	.37	.42	69.2	.53	.40	18.4
11	21	90.9	.32	.38	72.7	.44	.39	8.7
8	22	87.5	.40	.45	62.5	.64	.40	17.3
7	23	100.0	.35	.41	71.4	.49	.37	16.1
3	24	100.0	1.00	.50	100.0	1.00	.71	52.4

The accumulative incidences for the males in the Kinsey report are about the same as those for the Israeli males. However, nocturnal emissions occur in this sample only about once in three weeks. The relative importance of this outlet does not differ much from that for the Israeli males. In the Kinsey study, nocturnal emissions account for about a sixth of the orgasms experienced during the entire period.

The experience of Israeli females with spontaneous orgasms parallels that of the males (Table 9). By the end of high school about three out of four native-born Israeli females have had spontaneous orgasms, and about 90 per cent have had them by the early twenties. For those experiencing this outlet, frequencies are about once in two weeks during the entire period. As with the males, the relative importance of this outlet shows a steady decline with age but the drop is not so radical. During adolescence, about one orgasm in three for the entire native-born Israeli female population is accounted for by this outlet. By their early twenties only about one in six orgasms comes spontaneously.

The picture of the Israeli females differs sharply from that discovered by Kinsey in the United States. By age 25, less than a quarter have experienced this outlet. The women interviewed by Kinsey did not experience spontaneous orgasm more than three or four times a year. Throughout, this never accounted for more than an insignificant proportion of their total outlet.

Summary

During most of the period studied, the total outlet of native-born Israeli males was about the same as that of the American males. They differed, however, in the sources of their orgasms. For the Israeli male, spontaneous orgasm and masturbation account for most of the sexual activity in adolescence. As he approaches his twenties, this solitary sexuality is replaced by the social sexuality of petting and especially intercourse. The unmarried American male essentially maintains his solitary pattern through his early twenties. Petting and intercourse begin to assume a place of greater importance by the late twenties.

The total outlet of the native-born Israeli female is about the same as for the Israeli and American males. However, masturbation increases in importance with age, as does petting. Intercourse seems to have a greater relative importance during late adolescence than during the early twenties, when it is replaced by petting. It regains its importance by the late twenties. The American female has only a fraction of the total outlet of the Israeli female. However, the pattern varies. During late adolescence, most of the American female's activity is solitary, while about half of that of the Israeli female is social. By the mid-twenties, both patterns become similar in being about equally divided between solitary and social sources of orgasm.

These differences are probably not accounted for by physiological variations or by the influence of nutrition or climate. Rather, they may be accounted for by differences in society and culture. The fact that the total activity of the Israeli male and female is about the same hints that the usually discovered lower activity of the female may not be due to inherent physiological or psychological characteristics.

The Israeli youth studied were adolescent members of youth movements. Males and females mixed freely and most activities could be carried on by either. The higher proportion of intercourse on the part of the males reflects two facts. First, those females who do have intercourse are doing so with more than one male. Second, and more important, the middle- and upper-class males in the sample are having intercourse with lower-class females not appearing in this study.

The general fact that intercourse is more common among these unmarried Israelis is partly understandable in terms of early Zionist utopian ideology, which viewed intercourse as incidental. It may also be related to the youth culture's independence of the adult culture in Israel. Thus, adult values, or the attempts by the adult community to restrict the sexuality of the youth, are less effective in Israel than in America.

The observer of the Israeli scene will be puzzled. The general impression is that the social life of Israeli youth takes place in small cliques within the youth movements. These cliques include both boys and girls, and pairing off seems rare before the twenties. There is no "dating" culture. Yet the petting and intercourse data reflect some pairing off. It is likely that this pairing off for sexual activity is a rather transient affair.

References

Baratz, Joseph, A Village by the Jordan: The Story of Degania. New York: Roy Pub., 1955.

Irvine, Elizabeth E., "Observations on the Aims and Methods of Childrearing in Communal Settlements in Israel." Human Relations 5; 247-275, 1952.

Kinsey, Alfred C. et al., Sexual Behavior in the Human Male. Philadelphia: W. B. Saunders Co., 1948.

Kinsey, Alfred C. et al., Sexual Behavior in the Human Female. Philadelphia: W. B. Saunders Co., 1953.

Maletz, David, Young Hearts. New York: Schocken Books, Inc., 1950.

Reifen, D., "Sexual Offenses Against Children: A New Method of Investigation in Israel." Megamot 7; 339-405, October, 1956. (Hebrew with English summary.)

Shumsky, Abraham, The Clash of Cultures in Israel, a Problem for Education. (Teachers College Studies in Education.) New York: Columbia University Press, 1955.

Spiro, Melford E., Kibbutz, Venture in Utopia. Cambridge, Mass.: Harvard University Press, 1955.

Spiro, Melford E., Children of the Kibbutz. Cambridge, Mass.: Harvard University Press, 1958.

Wolman, Benjamin, "Sexual Development of Israeli Adolescents." A. J. Psychother. 5; 531-559, 1951.

SAMUEL Z. KLAUSNER

Jealousy

JEALOUSY may be defined as a feeling of displeasure accompanied by an urge for release which expresses itself either as fear of imminent loss of the love-object or as displeasure over a real or imagined erotic union that the love-object has with someone else. The feeling can be directed toward the love-object, toward the rival, or toward both.

In this definition no differentiation is made between jealousy when there is actually a "third party" and when there is merely the possibility of a "third party." The definition is purely descriptive. It says nothing of motive or of the inner structure of the feeling itself. We shall soon see, for example, that jealousy is not a *pure* feeling of displeasure. There are also some other important aspects of the problem, which are not taken into consideration in this preliminary definition.

Many attempts have been made to differentiate various types of jealousy: for example, masculine and feminine, primitive and social, normal and abnormal, sexual and nonsexual; but all these categories tend to merge into one another. By *primitive* jealousy is understood the rivalry felt by the loser in the courtship battles of animals. *Social* jealousy refers particularly to the concept of man's right to possess his wife. We will distinguish here, for practical reasons, between *sexual* and *nonsexual* jealousy, but it must be understood that this distinction only makes sense when the word sexual is used in its old and narrow meaning. Once the word sexual is used in its psychoanalytical meaning, the distinction disappears.

So-called Nonsexual Jealousy

Ludwig Klages (1928) has pointed out that jealousy is not limited to "feelings of sexual affection," but extends over the whole area of affectionate feeling.

The Oedipus Situation as a Pattern

From a psychoanalytical point of view, jealousy is rooted mainly in the Oedipus situation of the child. According to Freud, "normal" jealousy arises "from the Oedipus, or from the sibling, complex of the first sexual period." Flugel adds, "With the first establishment of object love toward the parent of the opposite sex, the conditions are present for the arousal of jealousy toward the parent of the same sex." This is the negative aspect of the Oedipus complex.

The Dutch psychologist Rita Vuyk (1959) distinguishes between jealousy, envy, and rivalry in the relations of children. Jealousy is the negative feeling occasioned by "the fear of losing something one has to a competitor." Envy is the negative feeling that arises when "someone else has something we want, or is allowed to do something forbidden to us." Rivalry is the "desire and effort to do better than others or another." "Jealousy arises when the child feels his sole possession of his mother is threatened, envy when he thinks another child is the sole possessor, rivalry when he believes achievement is a means to sole possession of the mother."

Parents show an unconscious jealousy in their relations with their children, a factor that can strengthen the irritation caused by the children, due, for example, to restricted living space. This apparent jealousy can also lead children to feel fear of retaliation and this fear is the most common cause of the child's overcoming the incest tendency (Flugel).

Where there are brothers and sisters, they naturally become rivals for the parents' favor.

Experience shows that this particular hate aspect within the family group appears strongest in the attitude of older toward younger children, but it is unlikely ever to be entirely lacking.

Situations Deriving from the Oedipus Complex

Negative feelings deriving from this impulse to jealousy within the family are often transferred to other aspects of social life. In the opinion of Flugel, a renewal of jealousy toward the parent of the same sex is normal when the child acquires a stepparent of the other sex. Thus, a boy acquiring a stepmother will be jealous of his own father.

Negative feelings toward a parent can later develop into a social attitude toward authority and be transferred to persons placed in authority. It is often very apparent in the attitude of individuals toward their church authorities, their teachers or physicians, their schools, city authority, state, or king. Flugel adds that the Christian doctrine of the Annunciation is based, at least in part, on a desire to avoid sexual jealousy of the Father, together with the envy, hostility, or contempt that would inevitably—especially in view of the general Christian attitude toward sex—accompany the notion of the Father as a sexually active being.

Jealousy of the mother, arising from the negative Oedipus complex, can later be transferred by the man to his wife as the mother of his children. The custom of male pseudopregnancy or couvade apparently derives from this.

It is further generally assumed that the hostile attitude of the older generation toward the younger, as expressed in the initiation rites of primitive peoples, is also partly due to jealousy.

Jealousy of and hostile feelings toward children on the part of parents also play their part in later life, especially when the child "in certain of the more important aspects of life" achieves superiority. This tendency, however, is nearly always mitigated by an impulse to identify with the child. When children marry, their parents often reveal a jealous attitude toward the son-in-law or daughter-in-law.

Jealousy between parents and children is always present in some degree. According to Flugel (1950),

"It is therefore not surprising that we find evidence of sexual jealousy between parents and children in many early myths and customs and in the legends and beliefs of many peoples, both cultivated and uncivilized. There is good ground for supposing that parent hatred based on jeaousy has been called into existence in innumerable successive generations and has thus had ample opportunity to impress itself on the forms, traditions, and institutions of human society." These impulses are particularly noticeable in monogamous families because here "the hatred bred of jealousy would necessarily be directed on to a single individual," while in more flexible polygamous marriages it "might lose in intensity through diffusion over a number of different persons."

Whereas many "savages" appear to exhibit a very considerable degree of affection toward their children, parents in civilized communities have often shown themselves, under a veneer of kindness or consideration, to be singularly brutal and selfish in their treatment.

Jealousy and the form of the family group are always closely connected. At one extreme is the proverbial primitive possession-jealousy of the lord of the harem and at the other the friendly group marriages, as found, for exampel, in Hawaii and Tibet. Here, with polygyny and polyandry, jealousy among partners of the same sex is rare.

The importance for culture development of the impulse to revolt against parents must not be forgotten, however. Many examples of outstanding cultural achievement are directly attributable to the father-son conflict. Flugel correctly points out that "the 'good' son or daughter frequently becomes a bad husband or wife, an inferior individual, and an unsatisfactory member of society."

True Sexual Jealousy

In the Animal Kingdom

Jealousy in the wider social sense is not unusual among the higher animals. Wolfgang Köhler reports jealousy among chimpanzees, another finds jealousy among parrots. Jealousy appears to be by no means an alien emotion to many domesticated animals. The courtship battles of animals are generally regarded as expressions of sexual jealousy in the narrow sense. Theodore Zell (1919) holds that observing the battles of stags first induced man to fight duels.

The attitude of the animal derives from the social organization of its species and from its mating habits. The fiercest courtship battles thus appear among the males of polygynous mammals. Such polygyny may be seasonal, as among the harem-acquiring solitary animals, stags, antelopes, wild pigs, and goats, and among the harem-acquiring herd animals, such as seals and kangaroos. It may also be perennial, as, for example, among howler monkeys. The courtship battles appear either as trials of strength during rut or as a defense of the harem by the "Pasha" against intruders. Wild pigs adopt an unusual arrangement, for sometimes the boar is not strong enough to drive away all rivals and we find equally strong boars joining a group of sows during the rutting season in a sort of seasonal group marriage.

One would expect similar courtship battles to appear among females of species that practice polyandry. This is, however, not the case; in the few instances of polyandry that occur in the animal kingdom, the males are very much smaller than the females and can even attach themselves to their mates. In this way, three to twelve dwarf males will attach themselves to the female Cirriped alcippe, a kind of crayfish, and will remain with her during life. On another cirriped, *Scapellum stearnsi*, over one hundred such dwarf males have been observed.

Among Humans

It has been recognized for some time that jealousy among humans is not particularly a sign of ardent love, but rather that it denotes the opposite, a narcissistic complex. In 1665, François de La Rochefoucauld wrote, "There is more self-love than love in jealousy." The eighteenth-century philosopher Marquis de Vauvenargues called jealousy a "sickness of self-love." Among more recent authors, Ludwig Klages regards "capacity to love" and "the egoistic will to possess" as the two mainsprings of jealousy, the latter being the stronger. Wilhelm Stekel (1917) writes, "Jealousy is the projection of a bad adjustment on to the environment. It is an atavistic flare-up of brutish ego-feeling, such as occurred in primitive man when defending his property. All children are jealous.

Jealousy takes us back to the springs of human instincts."

What does modern science have to say about this problem of jealousy? Apart from certain apt observations in the literature of character analysis, the problem seems to be primarily the concern of psychoanalysis and of social psychology.

Psychoanalysis regards jealousy as closely connected with narcissism. The degree of jealousy is generally proportionate to the narcissistic and not to the object-directed libido. The source of jealousy is a lack of capacity for love. According to Fenichel (1955), "The most jealous persons are those who are not able to love, but who need the feeling of being loved." Jones (1930) sees this overdeveloped self-love as compensation for an unconscious guilt complex.

Chronically jealous persons change the object of their emotion frequently. This restless, constant change of love-object arises from the fear that all the narcissistic demands that bind the jealous person to his love-object may finally be satisfied (Peine). Such a person is trying to satisfy his urge to be loved, his quest for reassurance, domination, and lack of frustration. This is what is meant by "possessing" a woman. Loss of the love-object means loss of one's own self-esteem. The jealous person shows pronounced inability to face the loss of love. When the love partner is regarded as personal property, the possibility arises that jealousy may become nothing but a support for self-esteem (Fenichel).

Especially prone to jealousy are those persons whose need for self-esteem is in the form of self-love. Demanding acceptance to compensate for an inferiority complex (the Othello type) may become a symptom of a neurosis. Such an inferiority complex is often linked to sexual impotence.

Sexual jealousy does not arise from frustration. If it did, defense against it would not be so difficult. The fact that it grows stronger and even becomes an obsession shows that it is in itself a defense mechanism. But what is jealousy a defense against? In Freud's opinion it is a defense against (1) the impulse to be unfaithful, and (2) the impulse to function as a homosexual. This applies to both normal and abnormal jealousy. An interesting theory of jealousy from a psychoanalytical standpoint is expressed by Fenichel, who maintains that "jealousies develop wherever the need to repress impulses toward unfaithfulness and homosexuality meet with the characteristic intolerance of a loss of love."

Pathological jealousy can lead to emotional outbursts and even to suicide or murder. The reaction to extreme consequences of jealousy depends on the attitude of the environment toward "understandable" emotional outbursts. For example, the almost routine acquittal handed down by French courts in crimes involving jealousy is usually regarded as a demonstration of the French national character and the general attitude of the French toward love.

Freud's attitude was, that women are more inclined to be jealous and envious than men, specifically because of penis envy and a greater narcissistic libido. Before Freud, Immanuel Kant recognized this when he said, "Men are jealous when in love, women even when not in love; for every lover won by other women reduces the number of lovers available to herself." But although the disposition to jealousy is generally more pronounced in women, we shall soon see that in specific sexual aspects the opposite is true.

In addition to psychoanalytical studies, there have also been sociological and social psychological studies on this subject. Helmuth Gottschalk (1936) investigated the problem of jealousy by interviewing 52 "normal, average persons," of whom 25 were men and 27 women. They were northern Germans and Danes, of various social strata and rural or urban surroundings, and belonged to three different religious denominations. The material should thus afford a fairly reliable insight into the world of modern northern Europeans.

In every sexual relationship there is a conflict that arises from the incompatible urges for close personal union and for variety. The urge for sexual variety is probably neurotic, but sometimes psychoanalysts appear to place too little value on the social relativity of our sexual behavior. In any case, an investigation of fidelity and infidelity in 93 marriages has shown that jealousy was not so insurmountable an obstacle to the solution of the problems of the marriage partners as is usually believed. The sexual history of mankind, moreover, shows that jealousy has varied so greatly in different places and at different times that one can easily conclude that social factors play an important part.

Gottschalk's investigation showed the prominent role played by sadism and masochism in the jealousy complex, and also the existence of certain differences in the jealousy shown by men and by women. Whereas 21 out of 25 men displayed a primarily sexual feeling of jealousy, for 21 out of 27 women sexual jealousy was not a primary factor.

In men, jealousy manifests itself in the first place as a shock of feeling either sexually inadequate or sexually repulsive, resulting in a simultaneous and sudden release of rivalry feelings, similar to those that occur in the animal world. The usual inquisitorial interrogation of the partner betrays a masochistic trait. Jealous males again and again demand a detailed reconstruction of the circumstance of and reasons for the acts of infidelity. In this way, jealousy serves as a form of self-punishment, and persons with masochistic tendencies are quite capable of creating situations that may give rise to jealousy. This aspect has been popularized in Schleiermacher's classic pun, "Die Eifersucht ist eine Leidenschaft, die mit Eifer sucht, was Leiden schafft" (jealousy is a passion which seeks with zeal what creates suffering).

Sexual jealousy also contains an element of direct lust. It may actually be sexually exciting. Sexual gratification may be obtained by the identification with the rival who has given reasons for jealousy. Combined with sadistic feelings, the act responsible for jealousy may be identified as a rape situation. This identification with a rapist may be extended on to subsequent sexual relations with the partner who has given reasons for jealousy. Jealousy in men is therefore a feeling that may contain gratification and pleasure as well as rejection and displeasure. Many previous researchers have not recognized this ambivalence of the jealousy complex. The unconscious provocation of situations leading to jealousy is motivated equally by the need for self-punishment and by the pleasure drive for sexual excitement.

Although the feeling of sexual rivalry may arise during a trivial flirtation or conversation, the specific shock of sexual displeasure related to jealousy becomes apparent only when there exists a closer relationship or union with a partner or, at least, the desire for it ("my" wife, "my" fiancé, "my" girl friend). A certain *drive for power* and an *urge for domination and possession* are therefore basic prerequisites for this shock of displeasure, with vanity, ambition, and imperiousness as close seconds. Gottschalk has expressed it thus: "The displeasure of jealousy does not arise because of a limitation of the sex-drive, but because of an injury to the possessive urge."

Women, according to Gottschalk, generally lack both these reactions of sexual rivalry and of injury to the right of sexual possession, and also the pleasure-displeasure ambivalence. In sexually free and natural women the *pleasure element* of sexually exciting images in the case of infidelity breaks through much more readily than in men. On the other hand, men often experience, as a result of social and moral notions, a suppression of the pleasure component, which amplifies the displeasure of sexual jealousy. Women are on the whole less jealous of the sexual union of the male with the rival than of the *spiritual union based on common interests;* the male asks *"What did you do?"*; the female, *"What did you discuss?"*

Sometimes *esthetic* feelings play a part in both sexes. The sense of the "esthetic" and the "unesthetic," however, is not relevant to the problem, being determined by external factors and also being differently constituted in different individuals.

The violation of the *possessive* feeling and the injury to self-esteem are *secondary, socially conditioned motives of jealousy.* Jealousy, therefore, according to Gottschalk, is "a natural, original, instinctive, sexual reaction which nevertheless is capable simultaneously of adapting itself to a large extent to the needs of society and of changing with them."

The element of the *injured self-esteem* (a kind of narcissistic injury) is a feeling of being scorned and is thus conditioned by social convention, which determines what is to awaken jealousy. Some people (as, for example, the Eskimos) who still practice wife-lending to guests show no trace of this injured self-esteem. In our society, on the other hand, the sex-denying philosophy of life influences the social basis underlying this narcissistic injury. If the sexual life is generally looked upon as "impure" and is overrated as something attainable only with great difficulty, then there naturally arises an injury to self-esteem when the partner takes up a new relationship.

The different valuation of the two sexes through the double standard is also a factor. For most men, women decline in "worth" if they engage in sexual relations that transgress convention. These men make an exception to this rule only as far as their own sexual acts are concerned. When, however, their partner is involved in a sexual act with another, they consider themselves "deceived." Thus, in our society the wife suffers less "social degradation" through the infidelity of her husband than the man does through the infidelity of his wife. Furthermore, a wife (particularly a happy one) is often proud of the erotic escapades of her husband, provided the desire to maintain the union with her remains unimpaired. This preference for social as opposed to sexual fidelity has been confirmed in an investigation of 250 Danish families by Gottschalk. An important reason why women generally show less real sexual jealousy than men thus lies in the double standard.

The socially conditioned injury to self-esteem occupies an important part in the jealousy complex. This fact may be noted in the not infrequent swapping of marriage partners with an almost complete lack of jealousy. The socially conditioned narcissistic injuries neutralize each other, as does also the overvaluation of the "sexual prerogatives."

Conversely, *insecure* persons are especially jealous, as are the vain and haughty ones. Here jealousy takes on the special form of a permanent fear of narcissistic injury. It expresses itself in those men who constantly supervise their wives, because to them even the thought of an eventual act of infidelity on the part of the "possessed object" is a most painful experience.

We must still deal with some fringe elements of jealousy. The displeasure over the loss of satisfaction of certain material, sexual, or spiritual needs is added as a fortifying factor to jealousy proper.

The sense of injury to the "feeling of solidarity" (perhaps a remnant of the herd instinct) plays an equally important role. This is exactly the opposite of external pressure, the "common necessity," a compensatory reaction to the feeling that one must always assert oneself in the struggle for existence. One wishes to be left "in peace." One does not want to feel threatened by external forces in one's own home. The injury to this feeling of solidarity, however, is felt more as pain, resignation, and disappointment than as jealousy. The feeling of solidarity, moreover, is not dependent on the exclusiveness of the union ("only we two"), but may be found also in "triangular" relationships, provided that the two partners of the same sex are good friends.

Is Jealousy Controllable?

The question still remains whether jealousy is controllable. Its variation according to time and place already gives food for thought in this connection. The aggressive reaction to injury in the form of rivalry feeling alone appears to be "naturally given." Here apparently lies (as comparison with animal psychology shows) a "normal" instinctive root. Every invasion of a sphere of instinctive interest, every impairment to satisfaction of an impulse causes aggression, and somewhere this aggression must be discharged. A complete suppression of such aggression would be ill advised from the point of view of mental hygiene. In other fields, however, we are daily exposed to numerous situations that provoke aggressive impulses, and yet we do not feel their direct satisfaction to be necessary. Aggressions can be diverted into neutral channels. If someone steps on my foot I must not immediately strike him, even though I may feel inclined to do so.

Here, therefore, we may discern a difference between the two situations, which we have placed at first in the same category. There is a natural kernel of jealousy in any sexual relation which is precisely the aggressive impulse springing from a release of the rivalry feeling. It is obvious, however, in normal individuals only when the partner has committed a serious sexual infidelity and only then when a "third partner" is involved. In other words, in the relationship of mutual love a "normal" kernel of

jealousy is not manifest, so long as an "outside" sexual relation of one of the partners does not occur.

Another component of jealousy is not "naturally necessary." We have seen that the violent "shock of sexual displeasure," in man in particular, has as its deeper cause the possessive attitude toward the love-object. This possessive attitude is not "natural"; it is in a large measure socially conditioned. We shall not err if we associate this attitude, which treats human beings like inanimate objects belonging to us, with the *anal* phase. As a result of the utterly inadequate sexual education that is still common, the sexual experience is intermixed for many adults with anal components. This fact is attested to by the wide and colloquial use of the expression "sexual purity." This idea of "sexual purity" unquestionably strongly fortifies the *aggressiveness* of jealousy.

The third main component of jealousy, injured self-esteem, which forms the *narcissistic* portion, owes its beginning to an increased need for a feeling of superiority. It is especially strongly marked in the "duelling mentality," still existing in certain countries. Surely no one since the days of Alfred Adler has challenged the thesis that in turn this need for superiority stems from feelings of inferiority. It is in this respect that insecure persons reveal themselves as the most jealous.

It is known that the stronger the narcissism, the weaker is the object-libido. (Adler has expressed this by saying that as the need for superiority increases the feeling of solidarity diminishes.) Thus the chronically jealous, insecure narcissist shows a still immature, incomplete relation to the object. Therefore, at least so far as this chronic form of jealousy is involved, *love and jealousy exclude one another*. The true object-love includes a desire for the good of the partner and can even, within certain limits, assent to his love for another.

From the viewpoint of psychological development, jealousy contains a large element of *infantilism* because of its anal and narcissistic components. It is a discharge of aggressive energy unadapted to reality, like a fit of rage and childish defiance. Indeed, all education is directed toward changing the pleasure-principle of the child into the reality-principle of the adult. In the jealous individual this development has been either unsuccessful or at least only partly successful. A consideration of available data will show that the behavior of a jealous person is not only inappropriate but barely adapted to reality. In case of a conflict with a third partner, jealousy usually does not prove an effective means to gain—or regain—the love of the partner. Jealousy neither breaks the spouse's union with a third partner nor brings together two persons who do not love each other, unless exceptional neurotic mechanisms are involved. In addition, the chronically jealous person, contrary to his conscious intention, runs the danger of losing his partner merely because of this continual jealous supervision.

August Forel (1931) has expressed similar ideas in his usual outspoken way. He maintains that there is no such thing as "justified jealousy." He writes, "People talk of justified jealousy, but I dispute its existence. There is a congenital atavistic jealousy and a pathological jealousy, but apart from certain neurotic conditions, any other form of this passion is crass stupidity." He goes on to say that a man who suspects his wife of infidelity has a right to discover the facts. But there is no sense in his being jealous. If he is wrong, his jealousy may hurt his wife. If he is right, he is faced with a choice: either to forgive or, if his wife stands revealed as unworthy and treacherous, to get a divorce. Men who are chronically jealous ought not to marry.

Jealousy and Marriage

There are in marriage three possibilities in this respect, if we disregard any question of legality.

1. The "third party" displaces the spouse, and the partner is happy and contented in this new love. Neither jealousy nor laws are of use against such buffets of fate. The painful loss of the "feeling of solidarity" must be borne.

2. The "third party" remains a secondary and less important phenomenon. In such cases—and they are the most common—jealousy is superfluous. In fact, in such a situation the "third party" can even enrich the marriage.

3. The rare situation may arise in which an equal love develops among the three individuals involved. Whoever believes in the infinite variety of human destiny will not shun such a possible solution. Should one stand in the way of love even when the direction it takes is not that prescribed by society? Even where rational considerations are useless, jealousy will accomplish little. The Russian poet Michael Arzybashev writes in his novel *Sanine* (1907):

Love imposes on us onerous duties only on account of jealousy, and jealousy was produced through slavery. Every kind of slavery produces evil. . . . Men shall have the use of love without fear or renunciation, and without barriers. . . . The forms of love will then also turn out infinitely richer through the concatenation of surprise and fortune.

In the face of love there can be only understanding and tolerance or love in return. Because these are the only mental attitudes that do justice to love, jealousy is unrealistic. Jealousy is an escape mechanism, a flight away from an outer conflict in relation to the "third party," and from an inner conflict (in the jealousy of suspicion) in relation to the spouse. Jealousy attempts to force a solution on the conflict, and because ineffective means are used, the conflict remains.

How then can one control jealousy if it is only in a minor degree—and that because of the kernel of the rivalry-feeling—"naturally necessary"? The social factors that have contributed to the growth of this feeling will change only slowly, but the forms of faulty individual development can be influenced through education. The whole matter is thus a question of education. If one succeeds in avoiding strong anal and narcissistic fixations in youth and in achieving a positive and tolerant attitude toward love life, thus adapting oneself to reality, then the agitations of sexual jealousy can be reduced to a minimum.

We cannot conclude such considerations without some statements of Bertrand Russell, who has also dealt with the problem of jealousy. Russell says:

Jealousy must not be regarded as a justifiable insistence upon rights, but as a misfortune to the one who feels it and a wrong toward its object. Where possessive elements intrude upon love, it loses its vivifying power and eats up personality; where they are absent, it fulfills personality and brings a greater intensity of life. In former days parents ruined their relations with their children by preaching love as a duty; husbands and wives still too often ruin their relations to each other by the same mistake. Love cannot be a duty, because it is not subject to the will. It is a gift from heaven, the best that heaven has to bestow. Those who shut it up in a cage destroy the beauty and joy which it can only display while it is free and spontaneous. Here, again, fear is the enemy. He who fears to lose what makes the happiness of his life has already lost it. In this, as in other things, fearlessness is the essence of wisdom.

References

Almquist, Johan, *Sexuallivet (Sex Life)*. Stockholm: Tidens Förlag, 1942.

Alverdes, Friedrich, *Tiersoziologie*. Leipzig: C. L. Hirschfeld, 1925.

Birnbaum, Karl, "Knankhafte Eifersucht und Eifersuchtswahn." *Sexualprobleme*, 1911.

Bohm, Ewald, "Is Jealousy Controllable?" *Internat. J. Sexology*, Feb., 1952.

Ellis, Albert, *The American Sexual Tragedy*. New York: Twayne Pub., 1954.

Fenichel, Otto, *The Psychoanalytic Theory of Neurosis*. London: Routledge & Kegan Paul, Ltd., 1955.

Flugel, J. C., *Människan, Moralen och Samhället (Man, Morals and Society)*. Stockholm: Natur och Kultur, 1946.

Flugel, J. C., *The Psycho-Analytic Study of the Family*. London: The Hogarth Press, 1950.

Forel, August, *Die Sexuelle Frage*. München: Ernst Reinhardt, 1931.

Foster, Sybil, "A Study of the Personality Make-up and Social Setting of Fifty Jealous Children." *Ment. Hyg.* 11; 53, 1927.

Freud, Sigmund, "Neue Folge der Vorlesungen zur Einführung in die Psychoanalyse." *Ges. Werke* (Bd. 15). London: Imago Pub. Co., 1940.

Freud, Sigmund, "Ueber einige neurotische Mechanismen bei Eifersucht, Paranoia und Homosexualität." *Ges. Werke* (Bd. 13). London: Imago Pub. Co., 1940.

Freud, Sigmund, "Psychoanalytische Bemerkungen über einen autobiographisch beschriebenen Fall von Paranoia (Dementia paranoides)." *Ges. Werke* (Bd. 8). London: Imago Pub. Co., 1943.

Gottschalk, Helmuth, *Skinsygens Problemer (Problems of Jealousy)*. Copenhagen: Fremad, 1936.

Hirschfeld, Magnus, *Geschlechtskunde*, II. Stuttgart: Julius Putmann, 1928.

Jones, Ernest, "Die Eifersucht." *Die Psychoanalytische Bewegung 2*; 1930.

Klages, Ludwig, *Die Grundlagen der Charakterkunde*. Leipzig: Johann Ambrosius Barth, 1928.

Laignel-Levastine, P., and Johannais, J., "Syndrome passionel de jalousie." *Ann. Med. Psychol. 100*; 329, 1942.

Meisenheimer, Johannes, *Geschlecht und Geschlechter im Tierreich*. Jena: Gustav Fischer, 1921.

Peine, Siegfried, "Von den neurotischen Wurzeln des gesteigerten Variationsbedürfnisses, insbesondere in der Vita sexualis." *Internat. Ztschr. f. Psychoanalyse*, 1922.

Russell, Bertrand, *On Education*. London: 1926.

Sokoloff, Boris, *Jealousy, a Psychiatric Study*. New York: Howell, Soskin, 1947.

Stekel, Wilhelm, *Onanie und Homosexualität*. Berlin: Urban & Schwarzenberg, 1917.

Sterba, Richard, "Eifersüchtig auf?" *Die Psychoanalytische Bewegung 2*; 1930.

Vuyk, Rita, *Das Kind in der Zweikinderfamille*. Bern: Hans Huber, 1959.

Zell, Theodor, *Die Diktatur der Liebe*. Berlin: Hoffman & Campe, 1919.

E W A L D   B O H M
Translated by Albert Abarbanel

Judaism and Sex

IN CONSIDERING Judaism's attitudes and teachings on any subject, one must constantly bear in mind that one is not dealing with any sort of monolithic Organized Church or even with a "religion" or a "Faith" in the sense of an established creed or formal set of beliefs. Rather must we understand Judaism as a religious civilization, a religiously oriented culture, the traditional way of life of a particular ethnic group. As such, Judaism is organic and dynamic, the product of an organic evolutionary development that has taken place over more than four thousand years, in most parts of the globe, and in dynamic interaction with many different cultures. One will therefore find official and authoritative statements and practices in traditional Jewish sources which are often mutually contradictory. Thus, Dr. Abraham Cronbach, in a brilliant paper on "Jewish Attitudes Towards War and Peace," which he presented before the Central Conference of American Rabbis just prior to the outbreak of World War II, demonstrated that if one assumed a five-point attitude scale, ranging from the most enthusiastic glorification of war at one extreme to the complete rejection of war for any cause at the other extreme, one could find good traditional Jewish sanction for any given position along this continuum. And substantially the same is true in the area of sex attitudes and practices.

General Attitudes

Let us, for example, posit such a five-point scale of attitudes toward sex, ranging from pansexualism and the complete absence of all social controls or inhibitions at one end to compulsive sexual abstinence and the complete rejection of sexuality at the other. The mid-point would probably then be represented by a rational, scientific attitude toward sex and an ethical type of self-control. About halfway between this mid-point and the first extreme we might define the compulsive sort of sexual freedom that is to be found in certain cultures where social pressures are exerted toward certain stereotyped forms of sexual expression. And about halfway between the mid-point and the other extreme of sexual abstinence and the rejection of sexuality, we might find an equally compulsive sexual moderation, where social pressures have been exerted to inhibit the sexual drive and channelize it narrowly into certain approved and equally stereotyped patterns, with a negative rather than a positive valence. We shall then find some Jewish authorities favoring each one of these points.

But the preponderance of Jewish authority and practice would lean somewhat toward the right of center, in the direction of greater social control and a negative valuation of most forms of sexual behavior outside of marital coitus. Without implying any actual statistical formulation of such data, we may represent the Jewish position by something like the skewed curve in Fig. 1.

True enough, one would not find any endorsement of unbridled sexual freedom. But one does find a pansexual statement such as that in the Talmud: "Were it not for the Evil Impulse [a term that usually carries the connotation of sex drive or libido] no man would build a house or marry a woman or engage in any occupation" (*Midrash Rabbah*, Genesis, chapter 9 and elsewhere). Similarly, the Zohar

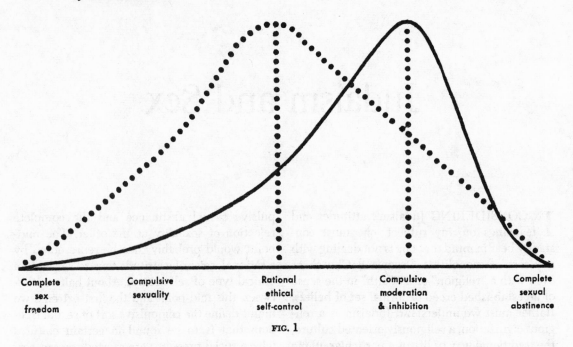

| Complete sex freedom | Compulsive sexuality | Rational ethical self-control | Compulsive moderation & inhibition | Complete sexual abstinence |

FIG. 1

proclaimed that wisdom will not come to the virgin.

What we have termed "compulsive sexuality" is at least to some extent implied in the rabbinic observation that the first commandment in the Bible is: "Be fruitful and multiply" (Genesis 1:28). At the same time, one must needs search far in traditional Jewish sources for anything resembling the completely negative attitude toward sex expressed by Paul in the New Testament: "It is well for a man not to touch a woman" and then his grudging concession: "It is better to marry than to burn" (I Corinthians 7). Nor would Jewish tradition anywhere support St. Augustine's statement: "The act of generation is sin itself and determines the transmission *ipso facto* of the sin to the new creature." But nevertheless, a widely accepted Jewish principle is: "Sanctify thyself through that which is permitted you," which is usually interpreted to mean that the good Jew will set himself a higher (super-halachic) ethical standard than the Jewish religious law itself would impose upon him, going "beyond the letter of the law."

Further demonstrating the contradictory character of much of the material with which we are dealing is the statement by the great physician, philosopher, and Talmudist, Moses

Maimonides: "We ought to limit sexual intercourse altogether, hold it in contempt, and desire it only rarely. . . . The act is too base to be performed except when needed" (*Guide for the Perplexed*, III, 49). And against this we have the statement by the almost equally renowned Nachmanides: "It is not true, as our rabbi and master [Maimonides] asserted in his *Guide for the Perplexed*, praising Aristotle for teaching that the sexual urge is a source of shame to us. God forbid that the truth should be in accordance with the teachings of the Greek! . . . The act of sexual union is holy and pure. . . . The Lord created all things in accordance with His wisdom, and whatever He created cannot possibly be shameful or ugly. . . . When a man is in union with his wife in a spirit of holiness and purity, the Divine Presence is with them."

We have already indicated that, generally speaking, the traditional Jewish attitude toward sex has been more positive than negative. True enough, peripheral and extremist Jewish sects, such as the Essenes, may at times have preached asceticism and practiced continence. And the apocryphal *Wisdom of Solomon* (3:13-14) similarly extolled the denial of sex: "Happy is the barren that is undefiled, she who hath not conceived in transgression. . . . And happy is the eunuch who hath . . . [not] imagined wicked things. . . ." But *per contra*, the equally extremist Sabbataians and Frankists endorsed all sorts of sexual excesses as divinely ordained measures for hastening the advent of the Messiah. And the cabalistic *Zohar* adopted the sexual relationship as the paradigm for the relationship between God and Man. Generally speaking, normative Judaism frankly accepted sexuality as a normal aspect of healthy life and, even more, as an endowment of the Creator, which it is a virtue to enjoy and a sin to deny oneself. Typical of the Jewish opposition to such asceticism is the teaching that "in the World-to-Come every man will be called to account for all the legitimate pleasures which he has not enjoyed."

As regards the direct control of sexual conduct, the late Dr. Louis Epstein, probably the outstanding authority on Jewish sex law and custom, pointed out that "there is a distinct lack of preaching on sex matters among the Hebrews of the pre-exilic period." The very earliest material in the Bible presents us with a very simple code of sex behavior. In the Second Commonwealth, after the return from the Babylonian Exile, this changed radically. There developed a considerable body of moralistic preachments. Sex mores became extremely restrictive, although there is some evidence suggesting that the actual conduct of large segments of the population did not at all accord with the ideals held forth by the authorities.

The Talmud, however, is again somewhat more accepting of sex and more permissive in regard to sex practices. In the Middle Ages, standards became more strict again, although one wonders once more whether this applies as much to the behavior of the masses of the people as it does to the preachments of the moralists, whose fulminations are likely to be vigorous in direct proportion to the laxity of behavior. At any rate, in our own time there would seem to be a somewhat opposite reaction, in that the sex attitudes of Jewish laymen and rabbis alike would appear to be extremely liberal, although there is some ground for surmising that sex morality among Jews may be more stable than among the population in general.

Sexuality of Women

It is interesting to note that Jewish tradition has always given full recognition to the sexuality of women. In fact, there has been a tendency from the Bible down through the later Jewish literature to regard the sexual drive in women as greater, more constant, and more aggressive than that in men. One frequently finds it asserted that it is women who lead men into sexual misconduct. And one provision in the Talmud, for instance, would permit a woman to be alone with two men (who would chaperone one another), but would prohibit a man from being alone with two women (because they might seduce him into lewdness). As Dr. David Mace indicates in his magnificent study of *Hebrew Marriage* (1953), the Bible cites numerous examples of women who took the initiative in sexual misdemeanors.

Thus, Lot's daughters plied him with liquor and then went to bed with him in turn, in order that they might have children (Genesis 19: 30-38). Potiphar's wife was the aggressor in the unfortunate episode with Joseph (Genesis 39: 7-18). And, for that matter, it was Eve who led Adam astray in regard to the eating of the "forbidden fruit," which is usually interpreted as symbolic of sexual knowledge. And her "curse" as a consequence was that she would be possessed by sexual craving for her husband (Genesis 3). Not related to any misconduct, but similarly representing frank sexuality on the part of both women involved is the story of the bargaining between Rachel and Leah for sex rights to their husband, Jacob (Genesis 30: 14-16). Also, as Mace points out, a wife might be punished for wrongdoing by being excluded from sexual relations with her husband, as David punished Michal (II Samuel 6:30-23).

Both Biblical and later Talmudic law make specific provisions for adequate satisfaction of a wife's (and even a concubine's) sexual "needs." For example, a husband was cautioned against embarking on a long journey without first having intercourse with his wife. And, similarly, he was required to have relations with her again as soon as possible after his return. The Talmud also provided that, given polygamy, a man should not marry more than four wives, so that he might distribute weekly sex relations equally among them and give each of them sexual satisfaction at least once a month. This rule was later taken over into Islam.

In several places the Talmud offers as a prescription for the begetting of sons the suggestion that the husband might earn this much-coveted reward by seeing to it that his wife was fully satisfied in intercourse before he himself reached his own climax. Said one of the rabbis: "Any man whose wife asks him for sexual relations will have sons like whom there were none [ever before]."

Nudity and Dress

The ambivalent attitude in sex matters is evidenced in the area of nudity and dress. Looking at the Bible objectively, one would gather that there was considerable freedom of dress, and that nudity and partial exposure of the human body were not infrequent. Something of this sort was involved in the quarrel between David and Michal, to which we have already alluded. Michal, having been brought up as a princess, was more finicky in these matters than her plebeian husband, David. But many other passages in the Bible also refer to nakedness as shameful. However, as Epstein suggests, it was apparently not so much obscene as humiliating, a nice distinction but quite probably a valid one.

In Mishnaic times, men and women sometimes bathed together in the nude. In Talmudic times, however, this was unknown, although male slaves sometimes attended women and female slaves sometimes attended men in the bathhouses. Both men and women also permitted themselves to be partially or completely naked when working or relaxing indoors. On the other hand, the wife of one of the rabbis of the Talmud reports as especially commendable on her husband's part: "When he has relations with me, he uncovers a handsbreadth and immediately covers it again." But then again, the Talmud also cites an opinion that a man may divorce his wife if she insists on wearing night clothes while they are having sex relations. However, during the Middle Ages, emphasis on modesty became extremely rigorous, and this continued until modern times.

Segregation of Sexes

Similarly, when we consider the segregation of the sexes, which has been marked among Jews in recent centuries, including our own, we find that men and women in early Biblical times mingled freely with one another. After the Babylonian Exile, women were required to stay out of sight, but this isolation of women was apparently alleviated in Talmudic times. However, in almost modern times (in the eighteenth century), the famous Elijah Gaon of Vilna held, in a notable "ethical will" addressed to his children, that it is better for women to pray at home rather than to appear publicly in the synagogue. During the Middle Ages, the authorities expressed their disapproval of mixed dancing and singing, but the masses apparently persisted in these practices. Even today, however, rigidly Orthodox Jews will not participate in mixed dancing. And the Chassidim, who emphasize the joyous element in worship and have cultivated singing and dancing as religious expressions, restrict this to the men.

Generally speaking, intimacies between the two sexes seem to have been discouraged throughout Jewish history, particularly in post-Biblical times. The *Ethics of the Fathers*, in the Mishna, prohibited "small talk" between men and women. And other contemporary writings went so far as to prohibit even touching a woman other than one's wife—an avoidance that is still today strictly observed by many pious Jews. Maimonides held that winking at a woman or gesturing to her playfully or admiring her beauty or smelling her perfume were all sinful acts, punishable by flogging. There were restrictions on kissing even one's close relatives, such as one's daughter or sister.

On the other hand, at various times in Jewish history these restrictions were considerably relaxed for engaged couples. Thus, it is reported that in Mishnaic times in Judea engaged couples might actually cohabit, although in Galilee during the same period they might not. Later Jewish practice, particularly in Babylonia, generally followed the stricter pattern. But in some parts of Europe—especially in Roumania, for example—during the Middle Ages, the more lenient pattern prevailed. And there are reports that in Sicily and southern Italy "most brides came to the nuptials in the full bloom of pregnancy."

Sexual Deviations

One might think that such rigid segregation of the sexes would have led to widespread homosexuality and other sexual aberrations. These seem to have been singularly absent from Jewish life, however. True enough, they are frequently referred to in the Bible. But they are usually attributed to other, neighboring peoples or are referred to as "foreign" importations, which are to be eradicated. The very name "sodomy," which is even today applied both to male homosexuality and to sexual intercourse with animals, is derived from the Biblical city of Sodom, which was destroyed in Abraham's time, according to the Bible story, because of these and other immoral practices (Genesis 18-19). And in the Book of Judges (chapters 19-20) it is reported that the other Israelite tribes made war upon the tribe of Benjamin and destroyed the city of Gibeah because the Gibeonites had attempted a homosexual assault on a traveling Levite and had murdered his concubine in a multiple rape.

Furthermore, we know from the Book of Kings and from the denunciations of the prophets that both male and female prostitutes were at times attached to the Temple in Jerusalem and to various local shrines. And we may assume from the stringent Biblical laws against homosexuality and bestiality, which were capital offenses, that these practices were certainly not unknown to the Hebrews in Bible times. Nevertheless, the repression of these practices was apparently so effective that we find the Talmud asserting: "A Jew is not to be suspected of pederasty or bestiality" (Kiddushin 82a). On the other hand, the Talmud prohibits a widow's keeping a pet dog, for fear of the suspicion of sexual abuse (Abodah Zarah 22b; Baba Metziah 71a), and in later times both Maimonides and Karo advised against unchaperoned asso-

ciation between young males (Yad I.B. 22, 2; Eben Ha-Ezer 24, 1). The law was much less strict, however, regarding females, placing it on the level of decency rather than of actual legality.

Masturbation

Masturbation is not referred to in the Bible. The term "Onanism," which has sometimes been applied to it, refers to a misinterpretation of Genesis 38:9, which actually referred to the practice of withdrawal as a contraceptive technique. Masturbation was rigidly interdicted throughout the later Jewish tradition, however.

In view of the modern recognition that this is a well-nigh universal practice, especially among young males, one wonders how effective the prohibition could have been in actual fact. And the detailed precautions against the practice that are prescribed in the Talmud and elsewhere lead one to suspect that it must have represented a very difficult problem of social control. But one Talmudic authority, at least, regarded masturbation as a capital crime (Niddah 13a). And the Zohar, in the Middle Ages, judged it to be the most reprehensible sin. As a precaution against masturbation, it was forbidden for a man to hold his penis even while urinating, except in the case of a married man whose wife was readily available for intercourse. Even an involuntary seminal emission rendered the individual ritually unclean and required a ritual bath for purification (Leviticus 15:16-17; Deuteronomy 23:10-12). However, according to the Bible the same apparently applied to normal sex relations (Leviticus 15:18), and even sexual thoughts were generally regarded as impure, although probably unavoidable.

Sexual Morality

Modesty and reticence are highly regarded virtues in Jewish tradition. The Talmud states: "Gehenna is made deep for the man who speaks lewdly and for him who listens to it and is silent" (Shabbat 33a). Nevertheless, none of this was considered incompatible with considerable frankness in discussion of sex matters. Girls were introduced early to the phenomenon of birth in the home. Very young boys were taught the Biblical passages dealing with the levitical laws of sex purity, and as they grew up they studied the many passages in the Talmud and in the *Shulchan Aruch* that deal with laws of marriage, divorce, and all aspects of sex relations.

Religious rituals such as circumcision could not but convey an attitude of the acceptance of sexuality as a normal part of life, even if we disregard the modern psychoanalytical interpretation of such rites as primarily functioning to legitimize sexual performance (the price having been paid) and decontaminate it of the guilt and anxiety with which it is primitively associated. And a religious observance such as the reading of the "Song of Songs" on Passover, even though it was interpreted allegorically, made sexual passion very clear and vivid to the young hearer.

It is interesting to note, however, that there has apparently never been any Jewish pornography. Although "the absence of evidence cannot be taken as evidence of absence," there seems to be no mention of the subject at all in Jewish law or literature. Possibly, the frank acceptance of sex and its essential healthiness left little room for prurience or the "return of the repressed" which pornography represents.

On the other hand, this high standard of sexual morality almost never went to the extreme of endorsing celibacy. Even the Jewish mystics and ascetics of the Middle Ages, although profoundly influenced by prevailing Christian patterns, did not discontinue regular marital relations. Nor has Jewish law ever actually interdicted sexual relations between unmarried persons.

Virginity in a bride was highly prized, of course. And numerous Jewish ethical teachings extolled premarital chastity for both young women and young men. But no penalty was imposed for violation of this ideal, and we must again clearly differentiate, as is so often necessary in the study of Jewish law and teaching, between moral precepts and legal prohibitions. Generally speaking, Judaism has maintained social control far more effectively by moral admonition and persuasion than by actual laws, which have usually been rather liberal and

which have further been interpreted and applied very leniently.

By the same token, children born either in or out of wedlock were fully legitimate in every respect. Bastardy referred only to the offspring of unions that would not have been permissible in marriage, such as incestuous or adulterous relations, or relations between a member of the priestly caste and a divorcee.

Incest and Adultery

Various degrees of consanguinity are described as incestuous in the Bible and in later Jewish law, and incest was considered one of the few sins or crimes that a Jew might not commit even under threat of death. Adultery was another such offense. But adultery, in Jewish law, applied only to the sex relations of a married woman with a man other than her husband. It was only in the late Middle Ages that it became possible for a wife to sue for a divorce because of her husband's infidelity. In earlier times, of course, polygamy was accepted, although it was probably never widespread among Jews. But it is related of at least two of the rabbis of the Talmud that, on visits to new communities in the performance of their duties, they would contract new marriages, which they would terminate by divorce before returning to their permanent wives at home. The system of concubinage was also well known in Biblical times and continued down even into the Middle Ages. Also, the less formal, legally unsecured status of "mistress" was not unknown in Jewish life to almost modern times.

Prostitution

Prostitution has been recognized in Jewish tradition from very earliest times. Although generally not approved and frequently condemned, it has perhaps, at times, actually been officially sanctioned by certain Jewish communities. Epstein, for example, reports on a number of rabbinic *responsa* of the Middle Ages in which some of the Jewish communities, especially in Italy, were considering setting up their own brothels to prevent young Jewish men from risking the death penalty that the Church had prescribed for any Jew who visited a brothel of Christian women. It should be noted, however, that the rabbinic authorities rejected this expedient. The Bible, of course, has many allusions to prostitution,—as in the story of Judah and Tamar, where it is treated quite matter-of-factly (Genesis 38)—and in the Talmud one of the rabbis is described as having habitually frequented prostitutes (Abodah Zarah 17a). On the other hand, the Talmud also tells the story of one young scholar who committed suicide out of shame because a courtesan happened to pick up and display to his companions a pair of phylacteries he had mislaid (Berachot 23a).

Rape and Seduction

Rape and seduction are likewise mentioned in both Biblical and later Jewish law. One thinks immediately, for example, of the cases of Dinah, the daughter of Jacob (Genesis 34), and of Tamar, the daughter of King David (II Samuel 13). Less aggravated—in fact, semilegal —but involving many more persons, of course, is the incident (described in Judges 21:16 ff.) of the Benjaminites and the maidens of Shiloh, which parallels closely the Roman legend of the Rape of the Sabine Women.

That the Hebrews engaged in the general practice of ravishing women captured in war is quite probable. But some attempt to meliorate this barbaric practice, without actually abolishing it, is found in Deuteronomy 22:10-14: "It shall be, if thou have no [further] delight in her, that thou shalt let her go whither she will; but thou shalt not sell her for money, nor reduce her to servitude, because thou hast humbled her."

Although it would appear that originally no distinction was made between seduction and rape, since emphasis was placed on the destruction of the girl's virginity, later Biblical law does set up such a distinction, apparently—although Epstein questions this. At any rate, the Talmud does clearly distinguish between the two. But the Talmud leans in the direction of leniency, pointing out that even in the case of rape the initial moral resentment on the part of the woman may gradually turn into an inward, instinctual consent (Ketuboth 51b). Similarly,

even artificial defloration seems to have been practiced on occasion in Talmudic times, although not officially approved.

Marriage

The chief safeguard of sexual morality, practiced almost throughout Jewish history, was that of early marriage. Eighteen was considered a maximal age for young men, and one who delayed marriage much beyond that age might be called to account before the elders of the community. Dowries and other provisions for parental support of the young couple made early marriage financially feasible. And the organized Jewish community frequently took over this responsibility when the parents themselves could not meet it.

Within marriage, there was apparently considerable sexual freedom, although not without numerous attempts at regulation. Leaning in the direction of what we have termed "compulsive sexuality" are the injunctions regarding frequency of intercourse. Thus, basing itself on the Biblical injunction (in Exodus 21:10), "her conjugal rights he shall not diminish," the law proceeds to specify that "each man is obliged to perform his marital duty according to his strength and according to his occupation. Gentlemen of leisure should perform their marital obligation every night. Laborers who are employed in the city where they reside should perform their duty twice weekly, but if they are employed in another city, once a week. Donkey-drivers [should have marital relations] once a week; camel-drivers, once in thirty days; sailors, once in six months. As for scholars, it is obligatory for them to have intercourse once a week, and it is customary for this to be on Friday nights" (*Shulchan Aruch,* Eben Ha-Ezer, 76:1).

It is worth noting that Jewish law prescribed the continuance of normal sexual relations throughout the duration of pregnancy and during the nursing period. In regard to the former, the rabbis said: "During the first three months of pregnancy, intercourse is harmful both to the woman and to the foetus; during the three middle months, it is harmful for the mother but beneficial to the child; and during the last three months, it is good for both the mother and the child, for because of this the child will come out clean and fast" (Niddah 31a).

Although some rabbinical authorities at various times recommended that coitus should be performed rapidly and with a minimum of byplay, others were much more liberal in their attitude in this regard. Certainly the "Song of Songs" in the Bible, the "Book of Proverbs," and other Biblical references are extremely frank and free in their sexual expressions. And in the Talmud we find a most interesting story involving two of the rabbis: "Rav Kahana once went in and hid under Rab's bed. He heard him chatting [with his wife] and joking and doing as he required. He said to him: 'One would think that [you] had never tasted of this dish before!' [Rab] said to him: 'Kahana, is that you there? Get out! It's rude!' Then [Kahana] replied: 'It is a matter of Torah, and I need to learn'" (Berachoroth 62a). Apparently, there was to be no false modesty when it came to a matter of scientific inquiry.

The Talmud also recommends that a couple should not separate too quickly after coitus. And going even further, another interesting Talmudic story tells of a woman who came to the famous Rabbi Judah ha-Nassi, the editor of the Mishna, with the complaint that her husband insisted upon certain irregular sex practices in his relations with her. The Rabbi declared that this was perfectly proper. And a parallel story is told of Rab.

True enough, one of the rabbis asserted that children are born lame because their parents use various positions in intercourse; that they are born dumb because their parents practice the genital kiss; that they are born deaf because the parents converse during intercourse; that they are born blind because the parents look upon one another's nakedness (Nedarim 20b). But the other rabbis participating in that particular discussion stoutly maintained that this was just one man's opinion and that "a man may do whatever he pleases with his wife."

Similarly, in the sixteenth century, Rabbi Joseph Karo, the author of the *Shulchan Aruch*, recommended great restraint during intercourse (Eben Ha-Ezer 25:2).

But Rabbi Moses Isserles, representing contemporary northern European opinion and practice, in commenting on this passage, asserted: "It is permissible for a man to do with his wife whatever he wishes. He may have intercourse at any time that he wishes, and he may kiss any part of her body that he wishes, and he may mount her in the usual manner or in an unusual manner.... But although all these things are permissible, one who sanctifies himself by [avoiding] that which is permitted him is considered holy." Here again we encounter that "super-halachic" (extralegal) standard of morality that may actually have characterized Jewish practice to a far greater extent than the legal permissiveness.

Contraception and Sterilization

Some of the variations of coital position were resorted to as attempts at contraception. Here again different Jewish authorities at different times in Jewish history have differed in their opinions. We have already seen in the Bible that the "sin of Onan" was his practice of withdrawal as an attempt at contraception (Genesis 38:9). And some later authorities used this as a paradigm for their condemnation of contraception.

More likely, however, Onan's offense was his refusal to beget offspring who would bear his brother's name in accordance with the law of the levirate, rather than the mere attempt to prevent conception. True enough, the rabbis interpreted any attempt at contraception on the part of the man as a violation of the Biblical commandment, "Be fruitful and multiply" (Genesis 1:28). But in contrast with the Roman Catholic position, even abstinence would constitute a sin from this standpoint.

During the Middle Ages, perhaps as a consequence of the decimation of the Jewish population, any attempt at contraception, by man or woman, was considered sinful, and is still so considered by many Orthodox Jewish authorities. But the Talmud and certain later authorities apparently did permit contraception by the woman, who was not considered to be bound by the Biblical commandment. And contraception (such as by use of a sponge) was even made mandatory in certain cases where the health of the mother or the welfare of a previous child might be involved. In fact, even the man was permitted to practice coitus interruptus (which was usually forbidden) to avoid impregnating a nursing mother. And in the latter part of the eighteenth century a Turkish rabbi permitted contraception (or perhaps demanded it) in the case of a woman who became extremely nervous or almost insane during pregnancy. (The reason that one frequently finds oneself in doubt as to whether a particular Jewish authority intended to demand a certain procedure or merely to declare it permissible is that the imperfect tense in Hebrew is used to convey either meaning, so that only the context may indicate whether the translation ought to be "may" or "should.")

On the other hand, the Jewish attitude never considered the function of intercourse to be for procreation only. It was obligatory even after the woman's menopause or in case the wife was congenitally sterile or wombless.

Artificial sterilization of the male was considered a sin punishable by flogging. But the Talmud reports that the wife of one of the rabbis drank a potion which was believed to produce sterility because she suffered great pain in childbirth, and this was apparently considered quite acceptable. One of the medieval Jewish authorities justified sterilization of a woman whose previous children had become moral delinquents.

Abortion

As regards induced abortion, there is a paucity of data available. The Bible itself does not mention it at all, although Mace suggests (following Gray) that the drinking of "Sotah-water" by the woman suspected of adultery may have been intended to produce abortion rather than immediate death. One might argue that therapeutic abortion, at least, would not be considered objectionable, since the embryo was considered a part of the mother (like a limb), and not a separate entity. Even a child that does not survive as long as a month after birth is considered by Jewish law for some purposes to be an abortus, and not a legal personality. Although Josephus reported that Jewish women who induced abortions were severely punished, this may have represented only the Sadducean position, when they were in power, not that of the Pharisees, whose teachings eventually became dominant in Jewish tradition. At any rate, Maimonides (in the twelfth century) specifically stated that, if a woman cannot give birth,

the fetus may be destroyed by medicine or by hand. But he limited this permission to cases where the infant's head had not already emerged. In this, Maimonides was following Talmudic law, and his statement was in turn incorporated into the *Shulchan Aruch*. The only point at issue was clearly at what time the fetus might be considered to represent an independent human being.

Later authorities varied greatly in their opinions, from a strongly negative stand to an extremely permissive one. In modern times, for example, the late Sephardic Chief Rabbi in Palestine permitted an abortion in the case of a woman who was threatened with permanent deafness if she went through with the pregnancy. And a great authority of the eighteenth century permitted an abortion even in the case of a woman who had become pregnant as the result of an adulterous relationship. Again, therefore, we are confronted with a variety of attitudes along the linear continuum we postulated, ranging from the extremely negative to something just short of a completely permissive stand, with the majority opinion somewhat to the right of center.

Eugenics

Jewish tradition was also acutely conscious of the concept of eugenics. For instance, the Midrash, attempting to justify Abraham's apparent parochialism in insisting that a wife for his son Isaac be brought from his own native land (Genesis 34:3-4), comments: "Even if the wheat of your own clime does not appear to be of the best, its seeds will prove more productive than others not suitable to that particular soil" (*Midrash Rabbah*, Genesis 59, 8). And the Talmud advised that an extremely tall man should not marry an extremely tall woman, lest the children be gawky; nor should an extremely short man marry an extremely short woman, lest their children be midgets (Bechoroth 45b).

Another of the rabbis advised that a young man should never marry a girl before he knows all about her immediate family, especially about her brothers, for "sons usually inherit the traits of their mother's brothers" (Baba Bathra 110a). Jewish law actually forbade one to marry into a family with hereditary taints (Yebamoth 64a). Such restrictions applied not only to physical traits, but to mental and spiritual traits as well. Thus, a scholar was cautioned against marriage with the daughter of an illiterate, and the daughter of a scholar was not to marry an illiterate man (Kiddushin 49b).

In summary, then, it is extremely difficult to generalize about Jewish sex attitudes and sex practices. The picture that emerges, however, seems to lean in the direction of a frank, non-puritanical attitude of acceptance of sex, accompanied by a rather rigid, self-imposed discipline of sexual restraint.

References

Brav, Stanley R. (ed.), *Marriage and the Jewish Tradition*. New York: Philosophical Library, Inc., 1951.

Cohen, Armond E., "A Jewish View toward Therapeutic Abortion and the Related Problems of Artificial Insemination and Contraception." In Harold Rosen (ed.), *Therapeutic Abortion*. New York: Julian Press, Inc., 1954.

Cole, William Graham, *Sex and Love in the Bible*. New York: Association Press, 1959.

Epstein, Louis M., *Marriage Laws in the Bible and the Talmud*. Cambridge, Mass.: Harvard University Press, 1942.

Epstein, Louis M., *Sex Laws and Customs in Judaism*. New York: Bloch Publishing Co., Inc., 1948.

Mace, David R., *Hebrew Marriage: A Sociological Study*. New York: Philosophical Library, Inc., 1953.

Patai, Raphael, *Sex and Family in the Bible*. New York: Doubleday & Co., Inc., 1959.

Zborowski, Mark, and Herzog, Elizabeth, *Life Is with People*. New York: International Universities Press, Inc., 1952.

RABBI SAMUEL GLASNER

Language and Sex

IN SPITE of the fact that there have been many studies of the two topics of language and sex, there has been, apparently, no single treatment of the linguistic aspects of sex as a whole. Indeed, neither the tremendous card index in the reference division of The New York Public Library, which contains more than 10,500,000 cards, nor the library of the Institute for Sex Research at Indiana University, founded by the late Dr. Alfred C. Kinsey, which is acquiring the largest collection of books in the world dealing with sex, has any entry under either "Language and Sex" or "Sex and Language."

The present study attempts to fill that lacuna. In preparing it, I was often asked such questions as, "But what *is* the connection between 'language and sex'—I don't know what you mean. . . ." In theory this relationship (with the exception of such obvious concepts as masculine, feminine, and neuter, which are omitted from the present study as they are dealt with in the standard linguistic reference works) is a very intangible one, and as such is practically unknown. How can the language we speak have anything to do with physical love? Strange as it may seem, sex, which enters into and/or dominates to such an astonishing degree so many aspects of the woof and warp of life, is also intimately connected with language.

The Ear as a Sex Symbol

For many centuries there has been an established relationship between the ear and the female sex organs. Thus, analysts—especially those of the early German-speaking school—have written about "*das Ohr als Vulvasymbol*," particularly in dream interpretation. Subsequently, cases were noted in which the ear was substituted for the vagina in masturbation (Gugitz, 1931).

This connection between the ear and the female sex organs is much more widespread and historical than is generally realized. As early as four thousand years ago the Egyptians cut the ears off adulteresses as punishment. In Burma young girls in the 12-to-14-year-old group were initiated into puberty rites in which their ears were bored—a symbol that they were entering the period of (latent) womanhood. Certain famous cultural and religious heroes were either conceived through or born from the ear (hence the medieval Latin hymn, "*Virgo Maria, Mater Christi, quae per aurum concepisti*"). Also to be noted is the fact that such divergent figures as Gargantua and Buddha were both said to have been born from the ear. A further indication of this symbolic relationship is found in the Jugoslav folk tale entitled "*Usi meggu nogama*," which literally means "The Ears Between the Legs," referring to the vulva. As is well known in psychoanalytical literature, the analogue of this symbolism is the tongue, which has a definite penile significance.

Sex and the Alphabet

Noting Sperber's (1912) interesting but now little-discussed essay on "The Influence of Sex-

585

ual Motives on the Origin and Development of Language," let us examine two examples of the relationship between sex and the alphabet. Scholars are at odds as to which culture "invented" writing—the Sumerians or the Egyptians; in any case this monumental step took place some five thousands of years ago among these people. In Sumerian (Kramer, 1944), the cuneiform designation (Fig. 1, below) is read *munus*, "woman." It is directly derived in three stages (from Fig. 2, Fig. 3, Fig. 4), from *sal*, "pudenda," (Fig. 5, below).

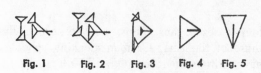

Fig. 1   Fig. 2   Fig. 3   Fig. 4   Fig. 5

Etymology of the English Word "Sex"

For a word whose meaning has caused such an infinity of pleasure, grief, trouble, pain, ecstasy, and suffering, it is remarkable that so little is known about the etymology of "sex." It apparently first appeared in English in 1382 in Wyclif's translation of the Bible—"Of alle thingis hauynge sowle of ony flehs, two thow shalt brynge into the ark, that maal sex and femaal lyuen with thee." The present sense of "sex," as it is understood in this *Encyclopedia*, was first used, interestingly enough, by John Donne, who also wrote, incidentally, "For Godsake hold your tongue and let me love" in "The Primrose" from his "Songs and Sonnets" (1631): "Be more than woman, shee should she would get above/All thought of sexe. . . ."

The *Oxford English Dictionary* derives "sex" from the Latin *sexus*, which means little more than the distinction between male and female: *sexus virilis, sexus muliebris*. Beyond that, nothing else seems to be known about the original meaning(s) of the term; according to Ernout-Meillet (1951), "la formation de *sexus* n'est pas claire."

Etymology and Phonology of a Familiar Word

Speaking of cuneiform writing, it is interesting to note that the first part of the word,

cuneus, ("wedge") is not related to the popular term of "powerful sexuality" (Partridge, 1951) for the female organ.

The etymology of this word is obscure: Middle English *queynte* ("Full privily he caught her by the queynte," Chaucer, *The Miller's Tale*, A 3276, 1383); also Middle English *cunte*, from Old Norse *kunta*, whence modern French *con*; Italian *conno* (*cunno*)—not used as often, however, as *fica*; and Spanish *cono*, *cona* are all derived from the Latin *cunnus*, cognate with Greek κυσοσ, *kusos* and κυσθοσ, *kusthos*, Welsh *cwthr* (recturm, vulva), Persian *kūn* (buttocks), Sanskrit *cushi* (ditch), etc.

According to the most authoritative dictionaries (Ernout and Meillet, 1951; Walde and Hofmann, 1938–1954), there appears to be no etymological relationship between *cunnus* and *cuneus*. In spite of the fact that the leading authorities (Grose and Partridge, 1931; Read, 1935, etc.) equate the Latin *cunnus* with the Greek *connos*, this author has found no etymological connection. The well-known work by Liddell and Scott (1953), the standard scholarly works by Boisacq (1938) and Hofmann (1949), and the technical studies by Vorberg (1932) do not mention it under "*k*," although Liddell and Scott do list κοννος, *konnos* ("a kind of trinket," "the beard") and cite the phrase κοννομ θριον, *konnou thrion* ("pebble of a trinket," "something worthless.") (Cf., incidentally, *connerie*, discussed later.) Vorberg concludes (pp. 130-131) that the etymology of *cunnus* is obscure and "*das Wort bietet also Gelegenheiten zu Haarspaltereien und Streitigkeiten der Sprachgelehrten.*" It must thus be stated that any κοννος, *konnos*, in ancient Greek cannot scientifically be shown to be related to the Latin *cunnus*, whence the European words and our own English-American term are derived.

The appearance of the final unvoiced alveolar-dental stop, "t," has not been recorded historically. Its presence is interesting and brings up again the *sehr, sehr heikle Frage* of whether there can be, actually, any meaningful emotional validity in the phonics of the words in a language. In five of the basic sexual terms in the English language in the middle of the twentieth century there is an unvoiced velar stop—in other words, a "k" sound.

Proponents of the "genius of the language" theory argue that there must be something significant in the fact that there is present in every one of these words this striking homophony—a phenomenon that is almost surely caused by analogy or coincidence. Furthermore, they might base their argument upon the theory that the presence of this plosive "k" in these terms can be equated with the vocalized dynamics of intercourse. It would be interesting to study comparable terms from hundreds, if not thousands, of languages and dialects and attempt to correlate the phonetics of sex terms with aspects of sexual activity.

The Condum Mystery

One of the most absurd manifestations of linguistic taboos imaginable has to do with the word "condom," or "condum," as it is also written. It has none of the stigma of the four-letter words nor is it in any way "obscene," "low," or "immoral." No one seems to know its etymon. Ostensibly there was a certain Colonel Condom in an English regiment in the 1660's who is said to have invented or somehow created this prophylactic device, which received much praise from such leading rakes of the day as the Earls of Dorset, Rochester, and Roscommon. It first seems to have appeared in Daniel Turner's *Syphilis*, London, 1717; apparently at that time it was a respectable word. Subsequently in the eighteenth century it fell into ill-reputation and was written with asterisks—"c****ms."

It has since remained in more or less ill-repute. Neither Webster's unabridged *New International Dictionary* nor Funk & Wagnalls' *New Standard Dictionary* even mention it. Most remarkable of all is that the *Oxford English Dictionary*, which admits a number of the tabooed terms in its twelve volumes, does not refer to it at all.

The history of these devices, which have been both extolled and condemned, is narrated in detail by Himes (1936), who reproduces a number of the handbills that played such an important part in the "condum squabbles" of those days. Interestingly enough, the term is not used in England as frequently as the expression "French letter," while the French designate these objects as *redingotes anglaises*.

Erotic Vocabularies

A fundamental aspect of language and sex is erotic vocabularies. Apparently all languages have certain specific terms that are socially taboo. How these particular expressions have acquired their unique place in the various languages is a curious and illogical phenomenon that has not been well studied.

It is not known which language has the largest erotic vocabulary. Bloch (1933) reported that in sixteenth-century French "there were more than three hundred words" for sexual activity. He also observed that "English is said to be first" regarding such lexicons, followed by German. This is a guess, however; Bloch did not pretend to be a philologist, and besides, the subject is little known in general. All told, the references at the end of this article, which are based on three of the largest and most important collections of sex literature in the United States—the Institute for Sex Research, the New York Academy of Medicine, and the New York Public Library—include only fourteen book-length studies in five languages—Classical Greek, Latin, English, French, and German (Bavarian).

Whether English has the largest erotic vocabulary or not, it has been the most extensively studied, specifically in the nine-volume work of Farmer and Henley (1890–1904) and the even more exhaustive investigation of Cary (1900–1920), which is, literally, unique. Henry N. Cary was a member of the Chicago College of Physicians and Surgeons, which was later incorporated into the University of Chicago. His hobby, in the first decades of the century, was collecting philological erotica. Eventually his unrivaled collection found its way into the Institute for Sex Research, where it was typewritten in 1947–1948. Only two copies exist (the original was insured for $1200.00) and the verbal lengths to which the English-speaking mind has gone to describe what is designated by the three unimpressive phonemes of "sex" stagger the imagination. Among the memorabilia of Cary's study is a list of synonyms for copulation—a total of twenty-nine pages, ranging, alphabetically, from "acme of delight" to "work," and including "fadoodle," "feather bed jig," "rootle," and "rumbusticate."

In English there is an expression "to cream off"; in French it is, neatly reversed—*écremer*, meaning "to milk," "to cause ejaculation." Although English is one of the most expressive of all languages, it does remain, from a creative viewpoint, more or less static. One cannot play with the English language as one can with other languages—German, for example, or Italian and French.

Erotolalia

One of the most singular aspects of the entire language-and-sex relationship concerns the use of tabooed sexual terms during, or in connection with, intercourse. The range of this verbalized eroticism may be said to have three stages: (1) an instinctive distaste—even disgust—over such "vulgar" words that tends to negate the erotic effects desired; (2) a neutral reaction, according to which the terms are neither stimulative nor unpleasant; and (3) a definite craving to hear, use, and generally experience such terms as an important aspect of sexual excitement and gratification.

The literature on this subject is scant, scattered, and probably tendentious. For some fifty years psychiatrists, analysts, and others concerned have been using the term "coprolalia" and its analogues *Koprolalia, coprolalie, coprolalia*, etc., to refer to "obscene language." But what does "obscene" really mean? Etymologically, obscene comes from the Latin *ob*—"over" and *caenum*—"filth, dirt." Since it appears that the concept of "filth" is first material, then moral, such terms as "coprolalia," including as they do, by extension, purely sexual matters as opposed to excretory terminology (the stem κοπρος, *copros*—"dung" refers exclusively to excretory matters), it would appear that this term is too broad.

Accordingly, I would like to propose a much more pertinent expression: "erotolalia" from the Greek *eroto*—pertaining to lovemaking"—plus *lalia*—"talk, chatter." In addition to being philologically scientific, it might be said to have a certain onomatopoetic aptness with its two alveolar-dental lateral *l* sounds, which followers of such philologists as Karl Vossler and Hugo Schuchardt would probably regard, without scientific proof, as significant through association—*lewd, lustful, lascivious, lecherous, lickerish, libidinous, voluptuous*, etc.

In this connection an interesting linguistic phenomenon is noted regarding the terms *fellatio* and *cunnilinctus*. As will be seen, both incorporate an alveolar-dental lateral *l*. In these two forms of sexual activity licking plays an important part. And we find that the sound this word begins with—*l*—is present in almost all of its Indo-European analogues. Thus: Sanskrit *lih*, Greek λειχω *leicho*, modern Greek γλειχω, *gleicho*, Gothic *-laigōn*, Old High German *leccōn*, Middle High German and Modern German *lecken* (the term *"auflecken"* is the vernacular for this kind of oral eroticism), Dutch *likken*, Old English *liccian*, Middle English *licke*, Old Norse *sleikja*, Swedish *slicka*, Danish *slikke*, Latin *lingere*, French *lécher*, Italian *leccare*, Spanish *lamer*, Portuguese *lamber*, Rumanian *linge*, Lithuanian *laizyti*, Lettish *laizit*, Old Church Slavic *lizati*, Serbo-Croatian *lizati*, Polish *lizác*, Russian *lizat*, Old Irish *ligim*, Modern Irish *lighim*, Welsh *llyfu*, and Modern Breton *lipat*. The implications would appear to be obvious.

Not only did the older German-speaking specialists designate "vulgar, obscene language" as an out-and-out form of "coprolalia," they also designated its users as *Wordsadisten* and *verbale Exhibitionisten*. This would seem to be an unthinking overgeneralization. Had they perhaps been more particular in specifying the more important categories, so to speak, in this complicated semasiologico-sexual differentiation, they would probably have, as I have done, equated "erotolalia" with *verbalisierte Wollüstigkeiten*—the pertinent German equivalent of the English—or perhaps *verbale Wollust* which also well describe this form of vocal loveplay. In French it is known as *foutre par l'oreille*.

Although neither of the Kinsey studies made

any mention of erotolalia, it appears to be a much more widespread—and thus, more important—sexual phenomenon than is generally realized. In one of the erotic classics, *The Lives of Gallant Ladies* by Pierre de Brantôme, there is a special chapter devoted to "Of Lovers' Speech," containing such observations as:

I have heard it said by many great knights and gallant gentlemen who have lain with great ladies, that they have found them a hundred times more dissolute and lewd in speech than common women and such. Wherein they use much art, inasmuch as it is impossible for a man, however vigorous, forever to druge and labour; but when he comes to repose and relaxation, it will please him and prick his desire when his lady diverts him with wanton tales and lewd and merry words so much that, though Venus sleep the soundest sleep in the world she will abruptly awake. Even as some ladies, discoursing with their lovers in public, whether in the chambers of Queens and Princesses and the like, will of a truth bewitch them with their dainty selective talk, till they are as wrought-up as if a-bed together; while we who look on imagine their conversation to be quite other.

For this reason Mark Anthony so loved Cleopatra, preferring her before his own wife Octavia, who was a past mistress of graceful phrases and elegant conversation, with her wanton and alluring ways, that Anthony forgot all else in his love of her. . . .

For when she, i.e., the mistress of M. du Bellay, is once alone with her lover, every gallant dame is willing enough to be free-spoken and to say what she pleases, so much the better to excite his desires.

I have heard many a tale told of those who have been favoured of fair ladies of high birth, or who have been curious to overhear them in talk a-bed with others, wherein they were said to be no less free and wanton in their speech than any courtesan of their acquaintance; but one may indeed wonder that since these ladies were so well accustomed to entertain their husbands with wanton words and phrases, and dissolute talk, even to making freely their most secret parts without any glossing over, yet when they are conversing in company with others they never once forget themselves nor let slip even one of these loose words. It must therefore be conceded that they are well skilled in the arts of self-command and dissimulation, since there

is naught for prancing and curvetting [the frisky leaping motion of a horse] like the tongue of a fine lady or a whore. . . .

In short, wanton speech has great efficacy in the game of love, and where it is not the pleasure is not complete. . . . For certain it is that a fair lady endowed with fair speech has a double joy to bestow.

The literature, especially as cited by Mencken (1938–1948) and Read (1934, 1935), is quite extensive, but there seems to be little specific agreement regarding the etiology of such desires. What is it in one person's background that makes her, and sometimes him, reject with varying degrees of emotion the use of such terms, while another person with a similar cultural background finds them sexually very stimulating? True, they are "forbidden," as Mencken calls them; true, too, that taboos in themselves, no matter whether they are or are not actually valid and appealing, automatically offer a challenge. Also, what is it about these words that is distasteful or stimulating? Is it their sounds? The way they look on the printed page? Their primordial meaning—the sheer earthiness of them? The entire subject is indeed obscure and irrational in the extreme.

Gilles de la Tourette's Syndrome

This is a neuropsychiatric condition characterized by two and sometimes three principal features: (1) multiple or generalized motor tics (during which, at onset, the *orbicularis oculi* or some other part of the facial muscle is alone affected, then the neck and upper extremities, and sometimes subsequently the entire body musculature); (2) compulsive vocal sounds (including various respiratory noises through the buccal and/or nasal orifice, uncontrollable explosive utterances of a meaningless, coprolalic, and erotolalic nature); and in some cases (3) various echo-phenomena (echolalia, echokinesis, echominia, and, less frequently, echopraxia). Despite the fact that many kinds of therapy have been employed, this syndrome appears to be virtually incurable (Mazur, 1953).

The Arbitrary Phonology of "Obscenity"

It is interesting to note the cogent observations of Helen Brown Norden, who in the thirties achieved a certain fame and/or notoriety with her article in *Esquire* Magazine, "Latins are Lousy Lovers":

I have never been able to understand why you can use some words and not others, because after all, words are nothing but a collection of vowels and consonants, and it seems sort of silly that you can use one set and it is considered polite, but if you use another set which means exactly the same as the first and which brings the same picture to mind you are considered a bum.

From the purist point of view, the Legman edition of *The Limerick* is certainly one of the most "obscene" books ever compiled, as practically every limerick is characterized by hypervivid "vulgar" and scatological concepts and expressions. To a person who could read English, but who did not know the "forbidden" words, the book would probably seem to be merely a collection of quaint, interestingly rhyming verses with a number of "nonsense-words." Yet, to the native speaker of English, the material is exceedingly graphic, often very witty, and to some, at least, erotically exciting. Why?

Erotic Sounds

Considering the importance of the aural organs in arousal and sexual play, one is not surprised to find that this phenomenon is extensively treated in the erotological—one is tempted to use the word—cosmologies, with their fantastic astrological, chronological, and physiological computations which are the *Anangaranga*—"The Stage of Bodyless One" of Kalyānamalla, and the *Kāmasūtra*—"The Rule of Love" by Vātsyāyana. Chapter VII of the latter catalogues the various kinds of sounds appropriate to the striking which is a part of Indian love-making:

> The sound Hin
> The thundering sound
> The cooing sound
> The weeping sound
> The sound Phut
> The sound Phat
> The sound Sut
> The sound Plat.

This incredible "phonology" is elaborated as follows:

While the woman is engaged in congress, the space between the breasts should be struck with the back of the hand, slowly, at first, and then proportionately to the increasing excitement until the end.

At this time the sound Hin and others may be made, alternately or optionally, according to habit. The man, making the sound Phat, strikes the woman on the head, with the fingers of the hand a little contracted. In this case, the appropriate sounds are the cooing sound, the sound Phat, and the sound Phut in the interior of the mouth, and at the end of congress the sighing and weeping sounds. The sound Phat is an imitation of the sound of a bamboo being split, while the sound Phut is like the sound made by something falling into water. At all times when kissing and such like things are begun, the woman should give a reply with a hissing sound. During the excitement when the woman is not accustomed to striking, she continually utters words of prohibition, sufficiency, or desire of liberation, as well as the words "father," "mother," intermingled with the sighing, weeping and thundering sounds.

Vātsyāyana adds this very pertinent footnote:

Men who are well acquainted with the art of love are well aware how often one woman differs from another in her sighs and sounds during the time of congress. Some like to be talked to in the most loving way, others in the most lustful way. Some women enjoy themselves with closed eyes in silence, others make a great noise over it, and some almost faint away. The great art is to ascertain what gives them the greatest pleasure and what specialties they like best.

Erotic Articulations

Surprisingly enough, there is almost no literature on the various sounds, as opposed to erotolalia, which occur during intercourse with the exception of the following somewhat fanciful remarks by Dutt, who comments:

Erotic articulations are the results either of the strikes or of the quick advance of the sexual pleasures reaching its climax in the *orgasm*. These articulations are of many kinds. But the articulations which follow the feeling of extreme joy due to the sexual union are of eight kinds and they are known as *viruta* or *murmurs*. Besides these there are seven kinds of interjectory sounds which are naturally expressed during *coitus*. These sounds resemble sometimes the nasal sound *"hing"* or the rumbling sound *"hong"* or the cooing of a dove or the moaning or weeping or the sound of high and deep breathing or the clicking sound of the tongue or such other noises which express feelings of extreme pleasure though outwardly denoting pain or annoyance. . . .

The love-cries of certain birds, such as the quail, the wild goose, the duck, the snipe, the turtle-dove, the cockatoo and the cuckoo, are well-known and such cries, when they are imitated by the partners in sexual communion, have a great psychological and physiological effect upon them. Of course such cries of the birds naturally come to the throat of the partners engaged in sexual congress, but even if they are executed deliberately during *coitus,* they have the desired effect of stimulating the sexual desire and pleasure of both the partners.

However whimsical this may be, it does raise an interesting question to the comparative linguist, especially the phonologist and/or the phonemicist: Is there any constant pattern of "erotic articulation" in the world's languages and dialects? Among English-American speakers it seems that the front-rounded vowel "O" is the most typical and perhaps the most eloquent articulation of sexual ecstasy, followed by the open-front vowel "Ah." It would be interesting to know what are the usual articulations during orgasm of speakers of languages characterized by consonantal clusters such as Aranta, a central Australian tongue, Avar in the Caucasus, Samoyedic, and Hungarian.

Even more interesting would be to listen to the erotalalia and erotic articulations of speakers of the Khoin languages—those of the Hottentots and Bushmen of southwest Africa. These languages are characterized by a series of "clicks"—dental, alveolar, cerebral, or alveolar-lateral and lateral; furthermore, each of the "clicks" can be uttered voiced, unvoiced, or nasal. To the non-Khoin listener these "clicks" are unusual in the extreme and sound like some fantastic tongue-clicking game during even a calm discussion.

Erotographomania

In addition to erotolalia there is also a sexual-linguistic phenomenon known as "erotographomania," a morbid desire to see written words of the four-letter type. This appears especially to be true in sexual relations between two lovers, in which one or both of the partners, usually the male, derives intense delight in reading such personal erotic writings. Also in this category come sexual diaries that provide excitement both for the person who writes one of them and the one to whom it is written.

Erotic Onomatology

Among the innumerable books written about physical love certainly one of the most perfervidly enthusiastic is the world-famous *Perfumed Garden* by Sheik Nafzawi, written around 1550 at the court of the Bey of Tunis. In it the Muslim erotologist presents an elaborate onomatological catalog of designations for the genitalia which is fanciful in its wry humor. Thus for the male:

> *al-tannān*—"The Bell-Ringer"
> *al-khayyāt*—"The Tailor"
> *al-'awwām*—"The Swimmer"
> *al-bakkā'ī*—"The Weeper"
> *al-makshūf*—"The Revealed One"
> *abu lu'āb*—"The Father of Spit"
> *al-shalbak*—"The Splasher"
> *al-hammāsh*—"The Exciter"

For the female:

> *abu turtūr* (hood, pointed cap)—
>   "The Crowned One"
> *al-qunfud*—"The Hedge Hog"
> *al-fashfāsh*—"The Watering Pot"

al-*ghurbal*—"The Sieve"
al-*mulki*—"The Duellist"
al-'*addad*—"The Biter"
al-*zunbūr*—"The Wasp"
al-*naffākh*—"The Pufferess"

Shakespeare and Sex

Any discussion of language and sex would have to include the observations on this subject made by the person who, if he did really write the works attributed to him, is considered the greatest of all writers—William Shakespeare.

In a singularly perceptive analysis of the interrelationship of the sexual drive and the (literary) creative urge, Eric Partridge has presented a detailed analysis of "Shakespeare's Bawdy"—in other words, an account of Shakespeare's descriptions of sex. To Partridge, Shakespeare's portrayal of sex is overwhelmingly great. The reader's attention is called to the following remarks, and he is asked to form his own opinion.

In contrast to, say, such writers as the ancient Greeks Athenaeus and Alciphron, who appreciated the beauty of the female buttocks and wrote appealingly about them (cf., respectively, *The Deipnosophists* [xii. 554 C-E] and *Letters of Courtesans* [iv, 14.3–5]), Shakespeare gives us merely "bum," "buttocks," "ass," and "posterior." Since, according to Partridge, the female organ represents to Shakespeare a kind of ineffable suprasexual, mystical adytum, one would certainly expect some of the Bard's noted imagery regarding this fundamental aspect of womanhood. However, one is greatly disappointed, for what is inspired about the terms that Shakespeare uses, such as "cliff," "corner," "crack," "den," "eye," "gate," "hole," "the lock," "plum," "pond," "ring," "secret parts," and "tail"?

Regarding the male organ, Shakespeare is equally unprovocative—"carrot," "instrument," "organ," "stump," "thing," "tool," and "yard." Concerning the act of coitus itself we may again be disappointed, for what is eloquent about such terms as "act," "action," "amorous rite," "bout," "business," "conversation," "copulation," "deed," "encounter," and "fornication,"—words known to all the groundlings who witnessed his plays?

Despite the fact that Partridge seems vastly impressed by Shakespeare's sexual language, is there really any mark of genius in the use of such terms as "attempt," "come to one's bed," "entice," "above (someone's) bed," "corrupt," "get a maidenhead," "seduce," "undertake," "woo," and "wrong"? Indeed, one searches vainly for some of the Bard's usual matchless imagery when one reads his allusions to lovemaking. Despite the fact that there are here and there a few imaginative terms—"fill a bottle with a tin-dish," whatever that may really mean, and "hang one's bugle in an invisible baldric," Shakespeare's vocabulary describing the love act, which should, it would seem, have provoked the poet to sublime efforts, is disappointingly limited and uninspired, as witness such dull, everyday expressions as "fit," "go," "have," "hit it," "jump," "know," "lay down," "make," "mount," "possess," "ride," "sink in," "take."

Indeed, despite Partridge's enthusiastic book, one is forced to conclude that the language-straining imagery that is so characteristic of Shakespeare in regard to practically every human emotion is, oddly enough, singularly lacking in his descriptions of physical love.

An English Linguistic-Sexual Phenomenon—the Limerick

The particular genre of humorous verse represented by the limerick is said to have had its origin in the barrack songs of soldiers in Limerick, Ireland, around 1700. The most famous writer of limericks was, of course, Edward Lear, who made this verse of five anapaest lines popular with his *Book of Nonsense* in 1846. Although his verses were witty poems suitable for any drawing-room conversation, the great popularity of the limerick was acquired toward the end of the nineteenth century by its use as a medium for expressing the most fundamental urges and concepts, in the most "obscene" fashion possible.

An interesting aspect of these verses is that they are principally written in English—as Douglas (1928) says: "A self-respecting Englishman would consider his life ill-spent had he not tried to add at least one limerick of his own personal composition to the national stock." The novelist also comments upon the fact that limericks are virtually meaningless to the Frenchman and the Spaniard. Because of the fundamental "obscenity" of limericks they have mostly been issued in fugitive, privately printed collections. Finally, however, the most celebrated were published by Legman (1953) in a stately, scholarly edition complete with seventeen hundred examples, notes, variants, and an index.

The Linguistic Artistry of John Cleland

In contrast to the "direct" obscenity of limericks or the Henry Miller school, which makes a point of bombarding the reader with countless "four-letter words," is the manner of presentation found in the *Memoirs of Fanny Hill* (1747 or 1748) by John Cleland.

This book is a minor literary masterpiece. The *Memoirs of Fanny Hill* are remarkable for their lack of anything resembling "obscenities." Yet, in spite of all its artlessness, Cleland has accomplished his purpose in writing a book that is "sexier" than many other attempts in the same genre which make a specialty of their outspoken sexuality. For the record, the author of *Fanny Hill* was hauled before the Privy Council after its publication. The Council decided, it is said, not to arrest the author but to bestow a pension of £100 a year on him, on the conditon that he gave up writing similar material. This he did and lived on amid his large library of philological books, dying at the stately age of eighty-two.

Ausonius and His Brilliant "Cento Nuptualis"

Another linguistic tour de force is the "Cento Nuptualis" by the Latin poet Ausonius. In the days when Ausonius lived (310–395 A.D.), Virgil was considered to be one of the greatest of all authors and as such was more or less sacrosanct. What Ausonius did—he says, at the command of the *"sanctus imperator Valentianus"*— was to go through the entire corpus of Virgil's

writings and select enough familiar phrases to make up a poem which he called "Cento Nuptualis"–"A Nuptial Patchwork." He stitched this linguistic patchwork together with such extraordinary wit that the reader who is accustomed to the majestic, plangent lines of Virgil is startled—and charmed—to see these phrases, which in context were so dignified, incorporated very much *out* of context into a very "obscene" poem describing what is frequently known as "connubial bliss."

The Sexuality of Lunar Terminology

Superficially considered, there would hardly seem to be any connection, linguistically speaking, between sex and the moon other than that of the usual folklore imagery. Actually, however, there is a very significant relationship, in Indo-European languages at least, as will be seen from the following words for "moon" and "month": Old Church Slavic *měsęci* ("moon," principally "month"); Old Persian *māh* ("month"); Tocharian B *mem* ("moon") and *meñe* ("month"); Gothic *měna* ("moon"), *měnōms* ("month"); English "moon" from Middle English "mone," from Old English *mōna*, akin to Greek μηνη, *mene* ("moon"), *men* ("month") and Latin *mensis* ("month"). The word "moon," accordingly, is derived from an assumed Proto-Indo-European form *měnes-*, *měn(n)s-* ("moon" and "month"), presumably from *mě-* ("measure"). Thus the three concepts, "moon," "month," and "measure" are related, with the sexual connection being seen in the etymon of "menses" (Latin *mensis*– "month," with the moon's orbital circumnavigation of the earth in twenty-seven and one-third days corresponding almost exactly to the menstrual cycle of some twenty-eight days).

The Erotic Terminology of Gastronomy

The influence that sex has exerted over the vocabulary of foods and eating in general is far greater than is generally realized. Thus, and interestingly enough, there are at least two words in the English vocabulary of cooking terms whose semantic history has a definite sexual connotation. These are *"stew"* with an earlier meaning of "brothel," and *"vanilla,"* which is derived from the Latin word *"vagina."* Whereas in these words, the sexual meaning appeared before the term was used in connection with food, the semantic background of the word "tart" (with the meaning of "loose woman") is the opposite. Just as we have transferred the term "honey" from the table delicacy into a term of affection, "tart," referring of course to a small pie or pastry, was first applied to a young woman as a term of endearment, next to young women who were sexually desirable, then to women who were careless in their morals, and finally—more recently—to women of the street.

In practically every language, including both the famous "cultural" languages of great nations and the lesser-known tongues of primitive races and tribes, there are many terms for food —often fruit—that are used with a definite sexual reference. Needless to say, these words appear more often in folk usage than among more sophisticated groups. Thus, as representative examples in American English we have *nuts, banana,* and *wiener* or "hot dog"—all with obvious meanings.

Oral eroticism also finds frequent expression in references to the loved one's lips in terms of food, as in Demetrius' words to Helen in *A Midsummer Night's Dream* (III. 2, 139):

O how ripe in show
Thy lips, these kissing cherries, tempting grow!

or as in this passage from Philip Massinger's *The Picture* (I, 1), in which Corsica addresses Hilario:

Love, how he melts! I cannot blame my lady's
Unwillingness to part with such *marmalade* lips.

or, again, as in Molière's farce, *Le mariage forcé,* in this compliment by the aging Sganarelle to the young Dorimène: *Vos lèvres appetizsantes*—"your appetizing lips." And finally, as in these lines of profound food-sex identification from Robert Herrick's "Kisses":

Give me the food that satisfies a Guest:
Kisses are but dry banquets to a Feast.

As an interesting example of how words come and go at different periods in the development of the language, I would like to cite the first three verses of a poem originally published in 1683 entitled "From Twelve Years Old I Oft Have Been Told" (Farmer [1893], Vol. ii, 91):

From twelve years old, I oft have been told,
A Pudding it was a delicate bit;
I can Remember my Mother has said,
What a Delight she had to be fed
    With a Pudding.

Thirteen being past, I longed for to taste,
What Nature or Art could make it so sweet;
For many gay Lasses, about my age,
Perpetually speak on't, that puts me in a rage
    For a Pudding.

Now at Fifteen, I often have seen,
Most Maids to admire it so;
That their Humor and Pride is to say,
O what a Delight they Have for to play
    With a Pudding.

The word "Pudding" here obviously refers to the male organ, and one might wonder why this term was used, as a pudding seems a very strange symbol for the penis. The explanation lies in the fact that the word pudding was first used to refer to the stomach or entrails of a sheep or ox stuffed with suet, meat, oatmeal, etc., very much like the Scotch haggis today. Later it was used in reference to certain kinds of sausages, and still later to the male organ.

In "A New Year Gift," a poem that appeared in 1661, sent to a "Fair Lady" accompanying some fruit and vegetables, it is the potato that appears as the male organ:

The next in order you shall have
A large Potato, and a brave:
It must be roasted in the fire
That Cupid kindled with desire.
The roasting it will mickle [a lot] cost;
It will bast itself when it is roast,
It needs no sugar, nor no spice
'T will please a Stomach n'er so nice.

While some form of the sausage appears to be the most popular synonym for the penis, it is names of fruits that are most commonly used in folk parlance to designate the female organs. In many cultures the apple is a symbol of the female breasts—as, for example, with the jocular Greek poet, Paulus Silentarius: "If, my pet, you gave me these two apples as tokens of your breasts, I bless you for your great kindness. But if your gift does not go beyond the apples, you wrong me by refusing to quench the fierce fire you lit."

In the "Hill Song" of the early Portuguese dramatist, Gil Vicente, "Hum amigo que eu havia,/Mancanas d'ouro m'envia"—"I had a friend who sent me golden apples," it again appears, this time as a token of love.

In Classical Arabic literature we find many similar references to the so-called forbidden fruit, as in these lines by an unknown ninth-century poet:

The apple, which I received from the hand
Of the most charming, gazelle-like maiden,
Which she had plucked herself from a branch
That was as supple as her own body.
And sweet it was to place my hand upon it
As though it was the breast of the one who gave it.
Pure was the fragrance of the apple,
Like the breath of the giver.
One could see the color of her cheek on it,
And I thought I was tasting her lips
When I began to eat the apple.

In English literature too, the apple is often used in a sexual connection. One of the earliest passages is buried away in the *Ancren Riwle*, the famous handbook for nuns written around 1200, in which the prioress sternly admonishes three prim young anchoresses venturing forth into the wicked world against the dire evils of the fruit.

"thes eppel, leove sustren, bitocneth
alle the thing lust falleth to
delit of sunne."
(*This apple, dear Sisters, is a token
of everything that arouses lust and
sensual delights.*)

The Italians use the word *fica* ("fig") for the vulva, an appellation which is also present in the French *figue* (in Old French *abricot* was used especially in reference to young girls) and

in Classical Sanskrit, as for example in the line, "A fig of delight," from a tribute to a woman by the great poet Amaru. The Greeks used *sukon* ("fig") to refer to both male and female organs, as in *The Peace* of Aristophanes (11.1344-1349):

Now live splendidly together
Free from adversity.
Pick [your] figs
May his be large and hard,
May hers be sweet!

Other food terms that were transferred to the feminine pudenda were κογχη—*kogche* ("mussel") and, with unusual imagination for the Greeks, κλιβανος—*klibanos* ("baking pot"). An entire book could be written on the many and sometimes astonishing designations for the vulva, but we should note that in Japanese it is called *momo* ("peach"), in German, *Pflaume* ("plum"), and in English, with a contrasting dearth of terms, *cherry*, which of course refers specifically to the hymen. There are, in addition, other terms in low English usage, as, for example, "bearded oyster."

In addition to "Honey" and "Honey Chile," there are a number of other endearing terms in English that originally referred to foods but have subsequently come to be used in speaking affectionately of persons of the opposite sex. Among them are "Sugar," "Sweetie Pie," "cookie"—usually in reference to attractive young girls—and even "dish," as in "She's a mighty nice dish." The current use of the word "cookie" as a term of endearment corresponds exactly to the first transference of reference of the word "tart," and it would be interesting to follow the future semantic development of the term to see if it too will acquire a definite sexual meaning.

In other languages, of course, this same process takes place. It might be noted that in contrast to most other Indo-European languages, the Slavic tongues show a lack of affectionate terms based on foods. Their expressions of endearment, usually formed by the addition of a diminutive suffix, stem rather from the animal and mineral kingdoms. In French, for example, there is *ma petite crotte*—"my little candy." In

Spanish affectionate expressions are *almiyar* ("sugar syrup") and *melocotón* ("peach"—but cf. its more specific connotation in Japanese above).

In Cuban Spanish an interesting semantic development has taken place in connection with the word *papaya*. Originally it referred to the fruit and was the only term employed. In the course of its history it also came to be applied to the female organ.

It was not long, however, before the Cubans became so intrigued with this second meaning that the word took on exclusively sexual connotations. Thus today *papaya* in Cuba has become synonymous with the female organs, and is a "low" term unpermissible in society. Accordingly another term for the fruit had to be created, and one now speaks decorously of the *fruta bomba*—the "bomb-fruit"!

Still another linguistic aspect of the relationship between food and sex is to be found in the transference of oral terms to the female sex organs. These include: (1) scientific expressions as *labia* ("lip") and *vagina dentata* ("toothed vagina"), a psychiatric term used in reference to masculine castration fantasies, and (2) folk-parlance, as in the Walloon expression *boque sin dints* ("toothless mouth"), which forms an interesting corollary to *vagina dentata*.

Although two technical articles (Blau, 1943; Kenner, 1945) have been devoted to popular terms for the clitoris, or rather to an apparent lack of folk designations, neither includes any designations having an oral reference. In view of the similarity, both physiological and symbolic, between the female oral and sex organs, it is surprising that there are so few known Indo-European nicknames for the clitoris—the "little tongue": the Walloon *linwette*, the German *Schamzünglein* ("little shame-tongue"), and the Danish *skamtunge*, with the same meaning, without, however, the diminutive connotation.

In conclusion, let us note that our word "appetite" (German *Appetit*, French *appetit*, Italian *appetito*, Spanish *apetito*, etc.) probably had originally a sexual connotation. It comes from Old French *apetit*, from Latin *appetitus* ("desire toward"), from *appetere*, from *ad*—

"to" plus *petere* (cognate with *im-petus*—"impetus")—"seek," "hunt," in other words "to direct oneself toward a place." In its early history, the word also had the meaning of "attack" or "approach with violence" (cf. the Greek term for appetite, ορεχις—*orexis*, cognate with the infinitive ορεγειν—*oregein*, "to stretch out toward something"), terms which would of course be an apt description of violent sexual passion, both in the initial "attack" and also in the orgasmic climax.

References

Alciphron, *The Letters of Alciphron, Aelian and Philostratus*. Translated by Allen Rogers Benner and Francis H. Robes. Cambridge: The Harvard University Press, 1949, p. 297.

Anthropophyteia (ed. by Friedrich S. Krauss). 10 vols. Leipzig: Deutsche Verlagsactiengesellschaft, 1904-1913.

Athenaeus, *The Deipnosophists*. Translated by Charles Burton Gulick. 7 vols. London: William Heinemann; New York: G. P. Putnam's Sons, 1927, Vol. 5, pp. 518-521.

Ausonius. Translated by Hugh G. White. 2 vols. London: William Heinemann; New York: G. P. Putnam's Sons, 1919, Vol. 1, pp. 387-391.

Blau, A., "A Philological Note on a Defect in Sex Organ Nomenclature." *Psychoanalyt. Quart.* 12; 481-485, 1943.

Bloch, Iwan, *Anthropological Studies in the Strange Sexual Practices of All Races in All Ages*. New York: privately printed, Anthropological Press, 1933, pp. 114-119.

Blondeau, Nicolas, and Noel, François, *Dictionarium Eroticum Latino-Gallicum*. Paris: Isidore Liseux, 1885.

Boisacq, Emile, *Dictionnaire etymologique de la langue grecque*. Heidelberg: Carl Winter's Universitätsbibliothek; Paris: Librairie C. Klincksieck, 1938.

Bourdeille, Pierre de (Seigneur and Abbot of Brantôme), *The Lives of Gallant Ladies*. 2 vols. Waltham Saint Lawrence, Berkshire: printed privately at the Golden Cockerel Press, 1924, pp. 169-173.

Buck, Carl Darling, *A Dictionary of Selected Synonyms in the Principal Indo-European Languages*. Chicago: The University of Chicago Press, 1949, pp. 54-55; 267-268.

Cary, Henry N., *Introduction to Sexual Vocabulary*. 2 vols. Originally compiled circa 1900-1920; transcribed onto typescript at the Institute for Sex Research, Bloomington, 1947-48.

Cary, Henry N., *Sexual Vocabulary*. 5 vols. Transcribed onto typescript at the Institute for Sex Research, Bloomington, 1947-48.

Cleland, John, *Memoirs of Fanny Hill*. Paris: Isidore Liseux, 1888.

Delvau, Alfred, *Dictionnaire érotique moderne*. "Freetown: Imprimerie de la Bibliomaniac Societé." Bruxelles: J. Gay, 1864.

Douglas, Norman, *Some Limericks*. Firenze: G. Orioli, 1928.

Dufay, P., *L'enfer des classiques*. Paris: Les oeuvres representatives, 1933, pp. 18-19.

Dutt, T. K., *Vātsyāyana's Kamasutra, the Hindu Art of Love*. Lucknow: The Upper India Publishing House, Ltd., pp. 86-88.

Ellis, Albert, Krassner, Paul, and Wilson, Robert Anton, "An Impolite Interview with Albert Ellis." *The Realist*, March, 1960.

Ernout, Alfred, and Meillet, Antoine, *Dictionnaire etymologique de la langue latine*. 2 vols. Paris: Librairie C. Klincksieck, 1951.

Farmer, John S., *Merry Songs and Ballads*. 5 vols. London: privately printed, 1893.

Farmer, John S., and Henley, William E., *Slang and Its Analogues*. 9 vols. London: Harrison & Sons, 1890-1904.

Farmer, John S., and Henley, W. E., *Vocabularia Amatoria*. London: privately printed, 1896.

Fuchs, Eduard, *Sittengeschichte*. 6 vols. München: Albert Langen, 1909-1912, Vol. 2, p. 246.

Grose, Francis (ed. by Eric Partridge), *A Classical Dictionary of the Vulgar Tongue*. London: Scholartis Press, 1931.

Gugitz, G., "Die Erotische Dichtung als Sinnesreiz." In Ernst Decsey *et al.*, *Das Gehör*. Wien: Verlag für Kulturforschung, 1931, pp. 69-109.

Himes, Norman E., *Medical History of Contraception*. Baltimore: The Williams & Wilkins Co., 1936, pp. 186-200.

Hirschfeld, Magnus, *Geschlechtskunde*. 5 vols. Stuttgart: Julius Püttmann, Verlagsbuchhandlung, 1930, Vol. 2, pp. 201-206.

Hofmann, Johann B., *Etymologisches Wörterbuch des Griechischen*. München: Verlag von R. Oldenbourg, 1949.

Jacobs, Noah Jonathan, *Naming-Day in Eden*. New York: The Macmillan Co., 1958, pp. 87-96.

Joffe, Natalie F., "The Vernacular of Menstruation." *Word 4*; 181-186, Dec., 1948.

Justinian (pseudonym), *Americana Sexualis*. Chicago: privately printed, 1939.

The Kāma Sūtra of Vātsyāyana. Benares, The Hindoo Kama Shastra Society; New York: The Society of the Friends of India, 1883-1925, p. 54.

Kenner, L., "A Philological Note on Sex Organ Nomenclature." *Psychoanalyt. Quart. 14*; 228-232, 1945.

Kramer, Samuel Noah, *Sumerian Mythology*. Philadelphia: The American Philosophical Society, 1944, p. 110.

Kryptadia. Vols. 1-11. Heilbronn: Henninger Frères, Éditeurs, 1884-1911.

LaCroix, Paul (Pierre Dufour), *History of Prostitution*. 3 vols. Chicago: Pascal Covici, 1926, Vol. 3, pp. 77-90.

Lecau, Pierre, "Les signes et." *Sphinx, revue critique embrassant le domaine entier de l'egyptologie 16;* 69-80, 1912.

Legman, Gershon, "Glossary." In George W. Henry *Sex Variants: A Study of Homosexual Patterns* (1st ed.). New York: Paul B. Hoeber, Inc., 1941, pp. 1149-1179.

Legman, Gershon, *The Limerick*. Paris: Les Hautes Études, 1953.

Lehmann, Friedrich R., *Kulturgeschichte und Rezepte der Liebesmittel*. Heidenheim: Erich Hoffmann Verlag, 1955, pp. 63-68.

Licht, Hans (Paul Brandt), *Sexual Life in Ancient Greece*. New York: E. P. Dutton & Co., 1934, p. 338.

Liddell, Henry George, and Scott, Robert, *A Greek-English Lexicon*. Oxford: The Clarendon Press, 1953.

Mazur, W. P., "Gilles de la Tourette's Syndrome." *Canadian M. A. J. 69*; 520-522, Nov., 1953.

Mencken, Henry L., *The American Language*. Vol. 1 New York: Alfred A. Knopf, 1938, pp. 300-311; Supplement I, New York, 1945, pp. 639-661; Supplement II, New York, 1948, pp. 143-144.

Michael, Richard P., "Treatment of a Case of Compulsive Swearing." *Brit. M. J.* 1506-1508, June 29, 1957.

Nefzawī, Sheik, *Der duftende Garten*. Wien-Leipzig: Verlag Schneider & Co., 1929, pp. 86-88; 94-96.

O'Meara, Donn, "Imaginary Diseases in Army and Navy Parlance." *Am. Speech 22*; 304-305, Dec., 1947.

Partridge, Eric H., *A Dictionary of Slang and Unconventional English* (4th ed.). New York: The Macmillan Co., 1952.

Partridge, Eric H., *Shakespeare's Bawdy*. London: Routledge, 1947; 2nd rev. ed., Routledge and Kegan Paul, 1955.

Pierrugues, Paul, *Glossarium Eroticum Linguae Latinae*. Paris: Hermann Barsdorf Verlag, 1826.

Pyles, Thomas, "Innocuous Linguistic Indecorum: A Semantic Byway." *Modern Lang. Notes 64*; 1, 1-8, Jan., 1949.

Queri, Georg, *Kraftbayrisch*. München: R. Piper & Co., 1912.

Rambach, Carolus, *Thesaurus Eroticus Linguae Latinae*. Stuttgart: privately printed, 1883.

Read, Allen Walker, "An Obscenity Symbol." *Am. Speech* 264-278, Dec., 1934.

Read, Allen Walker, *Lexical Evidence from Folk Epigraphy in Western North America*. Paris: privately printed, 1935.

Robertson, David M., and Fluck, Edward J., *Greek Love-Names*. Baltimore: The Johns Hopkins Press, 1937.

Sperber, Hans, "Über den Einfluss sexueller Motive auf Entstehung und Entwicklung der Sprache." *Imago* 1; 5, 405-453, 1912.

Stamatakos, Ioannos, *Lexikon tes neas Hellenikes Glosses*. Athenai: Ekdotikos Oikos Petrou Demetrakon, 1953.

Steward, Samuel, *French Sexual Argot*. Typescript, Bloomington: Institute for Sex Research, 1952.

Thornton, Henry, and Thornton, Freda (De Fremery), *How to Achieve Sex Happiness in Marriage*. New York: The Vanguard Press, 1939, pp. 20-30.

Vorberg, Gaston, *Glossarium Eroticum*. Stuttgart: Julius Püttmann, Verlagsbuchhandlung, 1932.

Vorwahl, H., "Sprache und Sexualleben." In Ernst Decsey *et al., Das Gehör*. Wien: Verlag für Kulturforschung, 1931, pp. 69-104.

Walde, Alois, and Hofmann, Johann B., *Lateinisches Etymologisches Wörterbuch*. 3 vols. Heidelberg: Carl Winter's Universitätsbuchhandlung, 1938-1954

DUNCAN MACDOUGALD, JR.

Latin America, Sex Life in

THE romantic sex symbol for Latin America is the dark-eyed señorita and guitar-playing caballero. Although balcony courtship was formerly practiced by Mexican middle-class groups, it has vanished—except in Hollywood.

The sex pattern is as varied as the climate: from the tropical to the deep-freeze of Antarctica and the high Andes, with the paradises in between. Climate and altitude have much to do with dress, metabolism, and sex habits, and the patterns vary in all twenty republics. City life, rural life, religion, social status—all are factors. In innumerable ways, too, the European, Indian, African, and Oriental races have contributed to sex mores. The mixed races (mestizos, mulattoes), with pure Indians and Negroes, comprising three-fourths of the population and dominating most of the continent politically, have, during the five centuries of New World occupation, developed their own peculiar sex customs.

Indian

Of a population of 180,000,000 (1956 estimate), probably 20,000,000 Indians still speak their native tongues—nearly a hundred—and 5,000 dialects. Guaraní prevails in Paraguay, not the official Spanish. In the Andes Quechua, Aimará, and Coya tongues prevail, except in cities. Maya and Nahuatl (Aztec) are spoken by millions in México and Central America. Primitive nomads, seafaring Alcalufs, headhunter Jíbaros of inner Ecuador, and urbanized and civilized Indians speak varied languages. Individual Indians, incidentally, have scaled the highest ranks of local society.

The complexities of Indian sex life have been extensively studied by anthropologists and are revealed by regional novelists: Heriberto Frías and Manuel A Azuela (México); Manuel Chavarría Flores and Carlos Samoya Chinchilla (Guatemala); Jorge Icaza and Humberto Salvador (Ecuador); Clorinda Matto and López Albújar (Perú). Numerous Chilean novelists have written about Araucanos.

Special Aztec deities looked after sex activities: diseases, orgies, continence, love, matrimony. Love prayers were addressed to Xochiquetzal, goddess of love and flowers. Xocotín (Sour Foot) was the goddess of the four sexual perversions. During religious fasts, all sex intercourse was forbidden; punishment could be death. No stigma was attached to homosexuals, lesbians, or nymphomaniacs; or to recognized "wantons," sometimes taken along on hunting trips (as among present-day Sherantes and other South Americans). The Aztecs made gold statuettes of various forms of copulation, including male sodomy.

Premarital Sex Life

Among modern Nahuas, premarital promiscuity is prevalent but in more isolated communities taboos are rigid and virginity is prized.

In some Zapotec villages in the Oaxaca sierras, all women except old ladies are kept inside the house whenever a stranger enters the community. Among other Zapotecs, unmarried girls —and even married women—are offered as hospitality to overnight guests, as they are among South American peoples (the Urubamba River Machiguengas). Girls of the Tehuantepec area (southeast México) are scarcely marriageable until they have had sex experience and are more desired if they have had illegitimate children, thereby proving their fecundity.

In the Quechua (Perú) harvest festivals, the boys are sparrow hawks, the girls, doves. Any babies that result are due to the *ñuapos*, ancestral spirits, always present in human form. In Cajamarca there is much horseplay between the sexes. A boy lifts up a girl's skirt, slaps her leg, and says, "Give me that leg." A girl lifts up a boy's shirt, slaps his kidneys, and says, "Give me that rump."

Among Chaco Indians, premarital promiscuity is the rule and is unusually prevalent among the Mato Grosso Bororos. Young girls are abducted into the men's clubs for mass orgies. Small naked girls approach strangers with their fingers in their sexual organs. Among Pilcomayos and Bermejos of the upper Chaco, the girl always takes the initiative. She grabs the belt of a boy or dances intimately behind him, and they go off to a nearby field for intercourse. Among the Brazilian Tupinambas, girls are promiscuous, but must be virgins to marry a chief. Boys can have sexual intercourse only after they have captured and killed two prisoners.

The Achaguas and Pirichús of Venezuela maintain houses of vestal virgins who are used sexually by the priests. In Cuzco, the Ñustas, the cloistered virgins of the old Inca Empire, had to be of noble blood; elsewhere, the most beautiful girls were chosen. Only the Inca and high nobles had sexual access to them. Sometimes girls were removed for concubinage.

Sherante and Apinayé girls of the Amazon are carefully guarded by a female relative until married. A Sherante youth who indulges in premarital relations is expelled from the bachelor's house and cut off from community activities. A boy can marry only after he has been initiated into the sixth (full adult) bachelor house. The Brazilian Gés have numerous bachelor houses: prepuberty, puberty, adult. When a boy has

his first intercourse, all the boys of his house are given new ornate penis sheaths and taken into an adult club.

Puberty Rites

Most groups (rarely in México, except for the primitive Lacandones) have intricate puberty rites for both sexes, the girls at first menstruation. Isolation may last only a few weeks, although wealthier parents maintain it for years. Frequently the girl's head is shaved. She is considered ripe for matrimony when her hair has grown back to chin length. But among the Warraú of the Orinoco delta, girls' heads are shaved at each menstruation, beads and white feathers are pasted to their scalps, and they are used by older men during the period. Older women initiate young boys. Also, among Colombian Capagas and Icas, older men initiate the girls. In many places the chief, medicine man, or priest has the right of first night with the bride.

Some puberty rites, celebrated by prolonged dance fiestas with feasting, drinking, dancing, and sometimes mock battles, involve terrible ordeals. In many instances all pubic hair is yanked out. In some Amazón tribes, some form of these ordeals begin at the age of 2. Among the Paraguayan Gayaqui and the Brazilian Tupinamba, at the first menses the girl is gouged in the back, breasts, and stomach with a sharp animal tooth or fish tooth and ash is rubbed into the wounds for a permanent tattooing. Both boys and girls are often subjected to fire-ant stings. Among the Amazón Piros, the girl is whipped, naked, with stinging nettles in front of boys to whet their desires.

Male and female circumcision or subincision, widely practiced, calls for feasting and dancing, sometimes lasting a whole month. When a girl reaches 9 or 10, a skilled old woman gets her drunk, then cuts off the clitoris and labia. Hemorrhage is stopped by herbs and clay. The women performing the operation must eat no meat, only broth and bananas, for two months previous to the operation. Among the Peruvian Iquitos, the operation is performed in the presence of the men in full war regalia: feathers, paint, and spears.

Upper Ucayali River tribes in Perú (the

Pishta, and many Quechuas) practice premarital deflowering at the first menses or shortly before marriage. The bloodied sharp-edged bamboo or glass knife (among Amazón Panóans, a clay penis) is sometimes given to the groom. Often he, or witnesses for him, observes the operation.

Courtship and Betrothal

Forms of courtship, bride-asking (*warmitapacoy* in Quechua), and betrothal are varied. Often marriage is arranged by parents at birth or in early childhood with exchanges of gifts, as among Chaco groups. Among the Zorcas (Cauca Valley, Colombia), betrothed infants sleep together in the girl's home. First intercourse takes place at first menstruation. A house is built for the couple, and in due time the wedding feast is celebrated. Among Pebans (Amazón), a man often raises a girl-child until she is ready for marriage. When parents arrange marriage after puberty, few tribes require the girl to marry a man distasteful to her. Today, for the most part, girls have free choice, although the families enter into negotiations for bride purchase, or dowry (a rarity). Among some Nahuas and South Americans, arrangements may be made by professional matchmakers, head man, or the priest (Catholic).

The Arecima girls (and those of other groups) do all the courting. In Pisac (Perú) girls go to the hills, pick *panti* flowers, and prepare food. The boys show up at about ten at night, playing flutes. The girl gives her bouquet to the boy she likes best. They sing and dance huaynos, and the girls whip the boys on the calves, hips, and buttocks as they dance. At dawn they dance and sing their way back to their ayllus, or clans. In other Andean communities, the boy hides near the girl's house and plays a charango, or flute. Either the dogs are set on him or the girl sings back. In later, intimate moments, they do not kiss but rub chins.

Among Nahuas, Talpanecs, and other Mexican groups, as well as in Central and South America, pretended or actual rape is part of courtship. Near the river, the boy jumps out of the bushes, smashes the water jar on the girl's head, drenching her, and tries to tear off her clothes. Her companions defend her with sticks, stones, hair-pulling and nail-scratching. If he is driven off, he is a chicken-hearted no-good. If he succeeds in stealing her clothes, her father and brothers go after him armed, threatening to kill him on sight. The boy sneaks a load of wood to their door, or ties a goat, sheep, or burro at the gate. If the gift is taken in, his family (parents, grandparents, aunts, uncles, in-laws) call en masse on the girl's parents, who pretend to be furious but who finally consider the family honor restored by payment of a marriage purchase.

Among Chilean Araucanos (as in many places), even if marriage arrangements have been made, the bridegroom must abduct the bride. All her relatives, male and female, put up a rough-and-tumble resistance. He gallops off with her to a hut in the woods. After some days, the couple take her mother a propitiary meal. The bride-price is paid and a four- to six-day wedding feast is celebrated, with specially composed ballads, the sacrifice of a young llama, dancing, feasting, and drinking of chicha (beer) and brandy.

Flight before or at the wedding, by either the bride or the groom, or both, is frequent. The guests bring them back forcibly amid much hilarity. Bride flight is typical of Amazon Ipurima marriages.

Bargaining for the bride is not always smooth. Each side utters bitter criticisms of the other's candidate. Although such remarks are expected, sometimes tempers grow short and a free-for-all brawl may break out.

The Peruvian anthropologist, J. G. Samanez, gives a detailed account of marriage bargaining, *yacapacuey* (*La Crónica*, Lima, October 30, 1916): The boy goes with his entire family in the early hours of the morning to the girl's house. The mother, already prepared, sings out:

"Who looks over my fence at such an ungodly hour?"

The boy: "The exhausted lover, no longer able to sleep, seeks the pigeon of his dreams."

Q. What merit does he have to ask for her?

A. He is young, hard-working, courageous.

Q. What does he own?

A. Land, cattle, and strong arms for work.

Q. What does he bring?

A. His family is here with the burro laden with food and amber chicha.

After further song, toward daybreak the visitors are welcomed in, food is laid out, drinking begins, and negotiations start.

In other villages, as Hildebrando Castro relates, the boy alone first calls on the father with a bottle of sugar-cane brandy, a *huatrchuco* (bright wool sash), and *llicla* (woolen scarf) in a concealed package. Pretending to be very embarrassed (as he probably is), he stammers and plucks shakily at his poncho, and finally hands over the bottle. This is the critical moment. If the father accepts it and launches into a tirade about his evil conduct and all he must do to be worthy, he is accepted. The mother comes in, and sometimes neighbors, and they drink up the bottle. Otherwise, the father leaves the room without a word or calls in neighbors and insults the boy as "a big-hoofed low-caste Indian who should find animals with which to reproduce himself."

Trial marriage (*sirvancuey*, Quechua; *amaño*, Colombian Pasto) is practiced nearly everywhere, from México to the Straits of Magellan. Depending on whether marriage residence is patrilocal or matrilocal, the girl or boy is virtually a slave during that period. Among Amazonians, the boy must show his worth by doing hard work in the fields, hunting, and fishing. More often the girl lives with the boy's family. If she proves adept at weaving, planting, household duties, caring for animals, and is obedient and humble to her mother-in-law and satisfactory on the love-mat, formal marriage is celebrated by tribal elders or the priest, or both, but often not until the birth of several children has proved she is fertile. If she is sent back to her family, they must return the marriage gifts. Sometimes under these circumstances she commits suicide. Anthropologist Bernard Mishkin estimates that less than 5 per cent of such trial marriages are unsuccessful.

The great Chibcha empire of Colombia and Panamá, divided into two powerful federations, the Zipe and Zaque, has provided many legends, doubtless often apocryphal. A Zaque ruler, without heir apparent, lined up likely candidates naked before a naked girl. The one who displayed no sexual alteration was chosen as crown-prince.

The Wedding

Among Colombian Patagoras, on the first day of the wedding feast the bride paints her husband's body and they sleep together, but without intercourse, in the company of other boys and girls. On the seventh night, he is led to the nuptial bed by an old man; she, by her brother. Painted sticks and weapons are piled beside it, and corn kernels are placed at the head which they throw at each other, a fertility symbol as well as a playful means of breaking down constraint.

Among Venezuelan Arawaks, the women cut the bride's hair off; the men shear the groom. She is then delivered to him, but must sleep the first night with the shaman. According to chronicler López de Gamarra, among early West Indian Caribs, "If the bridegroom is a cacique [chief], all the caciques invited to the wedding try out the bride before he does. If he is a marchant, the marchants; if he is a worker, the lord or some priest, and she is then considered very desirable." Among the Ecuadorian Cayapas and Colorados, the chief marries the couple, lectures them lengthily on their duties, and whips them.

The Onas and Yahgáns (Straits of Magellan), the Jíbaro head-hunters, and other tribes give extensive instructions, both at puberty and marriage. Engagements are usually brief, but the Colombian Amañi impose a four-months' ban. The couple is married in the communal house and must live there for a month with a teacher who instructs them on all domestic duties.

Among Venezuelan Guayquerí, an engaged girl must fast alone for forty days before marriage on a daily diet of six ounces of casava and fruit "to prevent her body being poisonous." At Amazón weddings, a turkey, tapir, or other animal is often sacrificed. At the marriage feast, Andean couples often do the "baby-doll" dance with a dressed-up stick or bread shape, then hand it over to those desired as godparents.

In one Mexican Oaxaca village, the guests scramble to snatch cigarettes tied to the feathers of a squawking turkey. When the poor bird has been stripped naked, they snatch at cigarettes tied to the clothing of the "squawking" bride. Before all her clothes are torn off, the groom carries her off to the marriage hut, where, as in many places, they are locked in by his mother and are serenaded all night, with intervals of shouted advice, often bawdy.

In some Andean villages after the couple has been locked in, the guests dance a special quadrille, known as "pirhualla-pirhua" (referring to the sex act), with lascivious postures denoting copulation. "Now nose to nose . . . now ass to ass . . . now kisses on the neck." Those who refuse to carry out the instructions of the caller are obliged to drink a glass of brandy filled "four well-spread fingers full." The dancers sing:

> Pirhualla, pirhua,
> How they enjoy themselves!
> Pirhualla, pirhua. . . . [Obscenity]
> I don't like
> Pirhualla, Pirhua
> With a bloody handkerchief;
> But how I like
> Pirhualla, pirhua
> With you beside me!
>
> Now . . . in the ears,
> Pirhualla, pirhua;
> They have to kiss
> Like viscachas
> Dying of hunger—
> Pirhualla, pirhua—
> And bounce the straw-mat
> Violently again and again.

Young blades sometimes shout boasts they have already slept with the bride. The groom inside beats her, she screams for help, weeps, and sings:

> Why did I ever get married,
> Being only a baby still? . . .
> Better had I never been born . . .
> In my mother's womb,
> I would have lived much better,
> Without pain, without suffering. . . .

The padrinos then burst in and pacify the couple.

In the morning, his mother or some female relative enters the cabin and comes forth with a bloodied handkerchief (among Quechuas, the testing cloth is of fine wool, previously woven by the bride). In Tehuantepec, México, the cloth is kept in a carved gourd with dried rose and carnation petals as evidence should evil tongues ever question the girl's virginity.

Marriage

Every marriage form exists: monandry, deuterogamy, polygyny, polygamy, polyandry (including Tibetan, Nair, etc.). Numerous types of polygamous-polyandrous kinship marriages exist: free sexual relations with anybody of opposite sex within the confines of consanguinity. According to López de Gamarra, speaking of early Caribs, many husbands and wives sleep together "like chickens." Many peoples (Venezuelan *llan* Indians, the Caingang of São Paolo) consider that marriage includes sexual rights with all sisters and daughters. Among the Siriones of eastern Bolivia, a man has sex rights with the wives of anyone he calls brother; a woman, with the husband of anyone she calls sister.

Soral polygamy is common throughout both continents (e.g., Peruvian Pinchús). It is the preferred type of polygamy among the Onas and Tehuelches. The Araucanos say it "prevents quarrels and jealousy." Among the Chamococos of the Chaco, as well as the Otomacos of the Venezuelan *llanos*, no marriages between young people are allowed. Older women marry youths, and old men marry young girls.

The Huatecans of northeast Oaxaca take added wives as soon as means become available for their purchase. The price varies according to age and pulchritude. A girl over 20 is worth little more than one sheep or an ax. A separate house is built for each new wife, and she is given a staked-out lot to cultivate, as is the Venezuelan Achaguan wife. In most communities, all plural wives live under one roof.

On the Popayán River in Colombia, all men sleep in the temple and their wives and children have separate houses. The same sex dichotomy is followed on the man's land; he has his own house, sometimes shared by male children, but never by females. A few steps away each wife has a separate house, its door facing his. He is supposed never to cross the threshold of any wife's house, although it is reported that he sometimes breaks the taboo when he is drunk.

The usual number of wives is three or four, but the Guatos of the upper Paraguay have from four to twelve, and some Araucanos have thirty. Chieftains, particularly in Colombia and Venezuela, may have hundreds.

Among Quechuas the first wife has authority over all subsequent "little" wives. In case of her husband's death she may not marry again except with her deceased husband's brother (the levirate). All "little" wives without children are taken over by the eldest son, although some groups permit their families to buy their liberty. A frequent arrangement is for the man to sleep with a different wife each night. She does his cooking, and when he returns from the hunt she hands him corn beer, bathes him, and paints his body to her fancy. Coitus then occurs.

Many tribes have obligatory cross brother-sister or cross-cousin marriages. Among many Amazóns the youth must provide his bride's brother with a sister in marriage or else toil for years for his in-laws without recompense. In case of divorce, usually the other couple also must divorce.

In various Amazón tribes and elsewhere, when a wife visits her mother, the husband "out of respect" cannot have intercourse in her house, but whistles his wife into the fields for intercourse. When a widow has only daughters, they continue to live with her after marriage, and the husbands must take their wives to the fields for intercourse.

Contraception, Abortion, Sterility, Venereal Disease

Contraceptives (Araucanos, *Stenomessen varigatum;* Quechuas, *malinhua*) are universally available. Abortion is chiefly by mechanical means, although the Jíbaros (Ecuador), Iquitos (Perú), and others have abortive drugs. Few groups ostracize or punish a girl for a child born out of wedlock, but among Yahgáns unmarried girls usually practice abortion. In the Amazóns (the Tucimas) abortion is practiced when the father is a white man or someone not of the clan, for any such child, even if legitimate, can enjoy no clan privileges. The Venezuelan Achaguas perform female infanticide with great ceremony and elaborately ritualistic burial.

Against sterility, Puno women (Perú) use frog ash with wine; the Simbas, a forest people, use the juice of various lianas.

Suicide with barbasco or curare because of impotence is said to occur among the Napo River (Ecuador) Pebans.

Both legitimate and superstitious cures exist for gonorrhea: brew of horse manure, types of cooked worms, drink made of lettuce honey and eggshell (Ica), cooked ants (Ica), cricket legs, although they may cause sterility (Cuzco, Ancash), Chicha beer boiled with brown sugar (Arequipa), kitchen grease soot and suet (Arequipa), cooked corn tassels (Andahuelas, Apurimac), salt and chicken manure (Cuzco). Cures for syphilis, which may supposedly be caused by eating taboo tapir meat (Amazón), are zarzaparilla, covering patient in hot bath with fresh, bloody cow skins (Puno), snake broth and fish (Puno, Ancash, and cat meat and vulture meat (Cajamarca).

Aphrodisiacs and Love Magic

For an aphrodisiac the Araucanos use *Justicia Pectorales* and jaropha. Among Amazonians (the Capaporas), the penis bone of the coati (*nashua*) is ground up and put in food or drink. The dye from the bark of the chuchuasi is also used.

Love charms and amulets are common, such as clay or metal clasped hands, hearts, penises, etc. St. Anthony's image is puissant, and not merely among Indians, but in every class in Latin American society. Quechua charms often are pairs, such as the cuya-cuya, a rough-shelled double nut, and *huayrnos*, double red-spotted black beans. In both Perú and México dried hummingbirds are helpful. A man who wears one around his neck will be much sought-after by women. Shavings from the nail of the middle finger ("the finger of the heart") put in any food or drink—there are many such love-charm ingredients believed to be aphrodisiacal —will stimulate love. The Araucanos have half a dozen such ingredients, the names of which have no translation. Measuring a man's penis (México, Perú) with paper, or clipping a snip of hair from under his testicles and wearing it either in a locket or with a scapulary of St. Anthony will cause him to propose marriage. This belief is shared even by upper-class whites.

Araucanos consult two types of professional

love magicians, those dealing in "white magic" (*paqo*) and "black magic" (*laiqa*). They provide charms and spells to repel or attract, or to break up a happy union. They divine the best kind of spouse and act as "private eyes" when infidelity is suspected. Around Cuzco, the witch recites a charm while a girl smokes two cigarettes and thinks of the desired person. The girl spits on the ash three times, makes a cross on her leg, and puts the rest of the cigarette in a flat package in her shoe for twenty-four hours. She then burns it, repeating the witch's prayers. Within twenty-four hours the desired person will present himself humbly.

Love magic, says Frances Toor in *Mexican Folkways*, is rare among primitive groups [this may be questioned] but is openly practiced in or near cities. In Morelos villages, a woman abandoned by her husband lies on the ground surrounded by funeral candles, reciting prayers. She beats the floor with her fists and calls out his name, invoking "Soul of Tulimán, Thou who art in Rome."

Forms of dress, body paint, hairdos, tattooing, ornaments, even colored threads are love charms and may also indicate sexual status: prepuberty, postpuberty, virginity, loss of virginity, married, divorced, widowed. Tupinamba girls, who have complete sexual freedom, must break the strings placed about their waists and arms at the time of their first menses as soon as they cease to be virgins. The strict Amazon Sherantes take away the virginal necklace. The naked Witotan women of the upper Amazón jungles paint elaborate designs to draw attention to the breast, buttocks, and sex area. All through Marajó Island, Santarém province, and the Xingú river area, pottery fig leaves are worn in front and behind.

Masturbation

Masturbation is performed openly, even on public thoroughfares, by Tarascan children. But among the Quechuas it is discouraged by stories of loss of memory, possible insanity, danger of tuberculosis, or the drying up of the bone marrow (this last also supposedly happens to those who fornicate standing up). The practice has many names: "drawing on the straw," "five against one," "to have relations with Manuela [penis or seminal ejection] de la Palma [palm of the hand]," "left-handed

Manuelita." Female masturbators and child Lesbians are called Mimetera (Caresser), Linguista (tongue caresser), Little Pitcher-drinker, Those-who-think-they-are-babies, Breast-suckers, Little Calves, Those-who-go-down-to-the-well.

Homosexuality

Sexual deviates and hermaphrodites are recognized without stigma, although transvestites are ridiculed by the Goyiros. The supreme Aztec deity, Ometecutli, and the Quechua Earth-Mother, Mama-Pucha, were ambisexual. Homosexuals are called Mamón (the Castilian academy word), Mary, Sailor, Big Butterfly, Left-handed, Little Berry, Warmed-over, Playboy, Ass-mover, Neck-biter, Cheat. Lesbians are called Tortilla-makers, Pastry-lovers, Mary-males. The Quechuas have many words and expressions for sodomy, bestiality, and pederasty. Deviates are numerous in the Cauca Valley in Colombia. In the 'seventies scientist Antonio Bertonio found much lesbianism, homosexuality, bestiality, and sodomy among the Aimarás (Andes), but in this century Harry Tschopik found no similar evidence, although he did note much transvestism (males wearing female dress). Araucano hunters and fishermen often take a young boy along for sexual purposes. On their return they throw him into the sea or the river so he has to swim ashore, and they approach their wives with embarrassment. Among the Caracas Indians, north Venezuelan Arawaks, and Cuban Tainos, homosexuals (*berdaches*) dress as women, pretend to menstruation, do women's work, and serve as prostitutes. Among the Lache and Caquiteros, homosexuals are married in regular ceremonies. A woman with as many as five male children and no females, is permitted to raise one boy as a girl.

Incest

Most Indians have strong taboos against brother-sister, uncle-niece, and cousin-cousin relations. Brother-sister incest is more usual than father-daughter incest. Among the Quechuas, the Inca emperor's Coya (Queen) was a full-blooded sister. Nobles were supposed to marry half-sisters. Among commoners, incestuous marriage (also of cousins) was forbidden, but nonmarital incest was practiced with the belief that it imparted nobility. Since all marriages were, and mostly are, endogamous within the ayllu or clan, it is almost impossible to marry a nonrelative. In certain groups (Caingang, southeast Brazil) brothers and sisters often cohabit until marriage, establishing a tie so strong that it is often continued adulterously afterwards. In one tribe, when the husband is sick the wife goes back to her parents' house temporarily, and his sister moves in to care for him.

Sex Crimes, Prostitution

Sex crimes and punishments vary widely. Adultery is usually accepted, or not overly resented; but sometimes it is considered an offense against the community. Among the Iquitos and the Machiguengas of the Urubamba River (Perú), wife-theft is common and not punished. There is also frequent temporary or permanent exchange of wives. Elsewhere, punishments range up to death, especially for the male lover. The wife rarely incurs public punishment. Among Venezuelan Zorcas she is not punished if one of her brothers kills the lover. Among the Serni (Brazil), the woman is severely flogged and the wounds subjected to stinging fire-ants. The husband and her lover fight until one is killed. Among the Cauca Valley Pantagoros, the adulterous wife is put in a separate hut and every male of the community may have intercourse with her, after which she is starved to death. In Ancash, a traveler ties the limber branches of the *nunumasha*, or teat-plant, a juicy splurge, into knots. If the knotted branches are still green and growing on his return, his wife has been faithful. Bigamy is rarely punished except where Indians have been forced into line with modern civil or religious statutes.

Rape, except in accepted premarital forms, is usually punished, sometimes with death. Among Nicaraguans, the offender must pay ransom money to the family or endure perpetual enslavement. Among the Nicaros, if a slave has intercourse with a daughter of the house, both are buried alive.

Although Quechuas have scores of sayings about prostitutes (the daughter of a whore is called "Seven Beds"), little prostitution in a commercial sense exists, although in most countries pretty Indian girls are drawn in by urban vice rings. In bygone days, among Nicaraguans, prostitution was more akin to polyandry. When a girl tired of that state, she obliged her clients to erect a fine house for her, selected one as a husband, whereupon her other lovers committed suicide. The wedding feast was prolonged by banqueting on their flesh. This has savors of sex among insects.

Mestizo

The mestizo—Indian-Spanish, Indian-Portuguese—is the dominant ethnic and political element in all highland Latin America, from México to Chile and Paraguay (in Perú, *cholo;* in Guatemala, *ladino*). Even in white Costa Rica, Argentina, and Uruguay, few older aristocratic families lack Indian blood. Northern Argentina, much of Uruguay, and Brazil are definitely mestizan. Honduras is approximately a three-way mixture of white, Negro, and Indian. Although Lima is largely a white city, Perú's saying is, "Who hasn't a bit of Inga [Indian] has a bit of Mandinga [Negro]."

The first Portuguese and Spaniards came without women and, throughout the whole colonial period, relatively few European females came over. Sexual relations and marriages with native girls were inevitable. The process is symbolized by Cortés' taking the Aztec Marina as his interpreter and bed-companion and having a child by her. Many Europeans married rich, noble Indian girls, an easy way to obtain recognition of land titles. Spanish nobles married Ñustas from the Peruvian vestal convents.

Intermingling broke down sex standards on both sides, often to the point of riotous debauchery which was much bewailed by the monks and priests (although some of them were also engulfed), who asked the royal authorities to send over Spanish or Portuguese women, even prostitutes, for they would easily find husbands.

The sex breakup was even greater among early generations of mestizos. In some cases, mixed offspring were raised as part of the Spanish community; in other cases they reverted to tribal ways; but most were outcasts from both races. By law a mestizo could **not** rise in the government, the army, or the ecclesiastical hierarchy, unless he traveled to Spain and bribed his way into the army or church there. Hence, he had to survive by his wits, chiefly as a go-between of the ruling and subjugated ethnic elements. The mestizos became overseers, small farmers, free-traders, smugglers, muleteers, or gathered in marauding bands of explorers who penetrated into untamed areas. The Paulistas or bandeirantes, those fierce, bold groups that swept inland into Mato Grosso and rich Minas Gerais and south to the Paraná River, seeking slaves and gold, but sometimes establishing new settlements, were *mamalucos*, men of mixed blood. Often the mestizo was superior physically and mentally to either progenitor race, and certainly was more cunning and burning with malicious resentments. His sex habits were lawless, and it took centuries before new standards, compounded from the habits of the two races and his own pragmatic experience, evolved into social norms.

The greater sexual vitality of the mestizo has been universally recognized in Latin American literature. It is romantically symbolized by the fiery actress Perricholi, mistress of a Peruvian viceroy: the heroine of Ricardo Palma's legend, of one of Prosper Merimée's most delightful yarns, and a character in Thornton Wilder's *Bridge of San Luis Rey*. Bernardo O'Higgins, liberator of Chile, was the illegitimate son of Viceroy Ambrosio O'Higgins and Isabel Riquelme, probably a mestizan. Flora Tristán, grandmother of the painter Paul Gauguin, and writer of best-sellers, had the blood of Spanish and Inca nobility in her veins. Known as one of "the seven most beautiful women of France," she threw aside a brutal drunken husband to become the mistress of a portrait-painter, and helped to found the feminist and labor movements of France. Other mestizan women became daring leaders, especially during the wars for independence, often disguising themselves as men and sharing bivouac and battle. One of the most passionate creatures in history was the mestizan epileptic Pancha Gamarra, wife of an early Peruvian dictator. She rode into battle dressed in male uniform, wore gold spurs, slashed cabinet ministers and generals across the face with her riding crop, and enjoyed innumerable paramours. The New World mestiza had a provocative new type of beauty. With them sex was daring and romantic.

Since the mestizo has become the dominant social class in most of Latin America, fuller consideration of his sex mores is reserved for sections dealing with the general habits of classes, countries, and regions.

Negro and Mulatto

Negro sex patterns, and merged forms by mulattoes (Negroes and whites) and Zambas (Negroes and Indians; *cafusos* in Brazil) and the further mixtures of all three races, are prevalent in the West Indies, Central America, Panamá, Colombia, Venezuela, the coasts of Ecuador and Perú, and in Brazil. Cuba at the coming of independence was probably at least 70 per cent Negro and mulatto. Haiti, of course, is an all-Negro republic, where rule by the Creoles (French-Negro) has steadily been supplanted by that of pure-blooded blacks. (Everywhere else in Latin America, "Creole" means a pure-blooded white born in America of European ancestry.) Early French traveler Frézier estimated that Bahía, Brazil, had twenty Negroes to one white. The children were instructed in the Angolan languages. Many Argentine gauchos were escaped slaves or mulattoes.

Origins of Sexual Culture

Negro sex habits go back to the life of the African groups, of every level of culture. For many centuries northern groups had large admixtures of Hamitic and Semitic blood. Their leaders attended Arabic universities, then the finest in the world, and their societies were more advanced than those of northern Europe.

Early Spanish and Portuguese licenses to import slaves stipulated that at least one-third had to be females. This paucity of women, plus uprooting, meant the destruction of former sex standards and much polyandry or loose relations with Indian women. The Indian remained more conservative; he still had his clan, his nation, his *patria chica* or small fatherland. The Negro had these things only in his head and heart, hence became a greater sex marauder. However, earlier habits tended to be conserved in early New World Negro kingdoms. Runaway slaves (Cimarrones), mostly from Panamá, escaping lashings and hot-iron brandings, joined marauding bands that grew into armies and, in conjunction with the Indians, set up the long-lived Mosquito kingdom, which the Spaniards were never able to subdue and which was eventually taken over by the English. In Brazil the Negroes established many inland fortified colonies (*quilombos*) with streets and dwellings (*mocambos*). In Uruguay "*quilombo*" has come to mean a noisy whorehouse. The largest Negro settlement, Palmeras in Pernambuco, with 30,000 inhabitants, established an independent kingdom that lasted more than half a century (1630–1697). But in general, sex confusion was heightened, as were superstitions, mostly by adoption of those from the Indians and whites.

Anthropological studies of New World Negroes are few, except those by Brazilians. Fernando Ortiz, the great Cuban scholar, has written memorable books on the Ñáñigos (Negro cultists), such as his *Hampa Afro-Cubana, Los Negros Brujos* (three editions). Numbers of books of Negro tales and legends have been published. For Brazil, we have Donald Pierson's fine *Negroes in Brazil* and many Portuguese books, the best perhaps that of A. Ramos, *O Folklore Negro No Brazil*. Ildefonso Pereda Valdés has written about Rio de la Plata and Brazilian Negroes. Early Spanish dramatists, such as Lope de Rueda, found the New World Negro a great source of spectacular drama. Many novels and sketches in Cuba, Haiti, Panamá, and elsewhere take up race conflict, such as Cuba's greatest novel, *Cecilia Valdés* by Cirilio Villaverde (1833), Rómulo Gallegos' *Pobre Negro* (Caracas), Gerardo Gallegos' *El Embrujo de Haiti* (Havana), and the beautiful story by Bernardo Arias Trujillo, *Risaralda* (Manzinales, Colombia).

Most writers are impressed by the superior fecundity of Negroes and mulattoes. The Negro woman, also snatched from traditional family and clan life, tended to become more libertarian, bold, arrogant, often flamboyant in dress and adornments, despite arbitrary colonial restrictions on what she could wear. Da Cunha speaks of the "outlandish topknots" of Negro girls in Bahía as contrasted to the careless mops of white women or the straight black hair of the *caboclas*, or Indian women. A loose woman in Uruguay is known by the Bantu word *milonga*. A servant there is a *mucama* (Bantu adopted from the Kafir). Many whites, the poor, the rich, and the noble, took Negro wives legally in spite of sporadic laws against miscegenation, and by all accounts such unions were usually felicitous.

Dances

Most of the dances and music of Brazil and farther north, with their richly woven sex meanings, are of African origin. Even traditional Portuguese and Spanish dances have been revitalized by Negro interpretations. Some dances, such as the Cuban rumba, mambo, són, and Congo, are lascivious according to "Anglo-Saxon" standards, but a distorted and inhibited alien viewpoint is not necessarily valid. The dance expressions of the African immigrants and their descendants represent physical, sexual, esthetic, and psychological norms of a more virile race in warmer climes.

The Brazilian northerners, black and white, dance *lundús, cocos* (Pernambuco especially), *batuques, macumbas, sambas* (*chibas* in Rio de Janeiro), *caterets* (particularly liked in Minas Gerais), *choradinhos*, and *biianos*. Few Negroes lack aptitude with the drums, *machete* (banjo), and the guitar, and in fiestas have at their command twenty-five instruments, few of which have reached other lands (e.g., *cavaquihno, pandero, cuica, reco-reco*).

These and other dances are performed at the fiesta of São Benedicto, the Negro saint par excellence, at which the Congos always have an armed guard with swords for three chosen queens. In Rio de Janeiro they dance the ancestor worship rite, the *cuneba*. The most mystic passionate celebration is the *candomble*, a devil-banishment dance that lends itself to much sexual extravagance. It is of Bantu origin and is also danced in Uruguay. The *macumba*, also Bantu (called *malambo* in Uruguay), is also a devil-banishment dance. The music is accompanied by constant clapping of hands, causing a rise in hysteria that often ends in sexual excesses. Through all these pagan affairs runs a thin vein of Catholicism. Chango, god of lightning and storms, is St. Jerome (in Rio, San Michael).

The voodoo (vodum) or "God Dance" of Haiti, brought from Africa by the Dahomies, is celebrated in the New World under the aegis of St. Anthony (the supreme god Eshu) and St. Patrick (Danballo, the winged rainbow snake god). It is a religious brotherhood, often celebrated by rooster sacrifice, perhaps originally by infant sacrifice. The ceremonies are moving. The scarlet thread of sex intertwines with basic life forces. In the passion of the dance a girl may pantomime sex intimacy with a guayava, split it and rub it over her breasts, and present it to her partner. If he eats it, she is his woman, for the time of the fiesta or longer, sometimes for life.

Although girls in Haiti for the most part enjoy free sex relations, they are rarely promiscuous; few women have greater dignity or pride. Graceful and resolute, most of them make loyal wives and are fiercely dedicated to their families and duties in a land of harsh survival. "A black skin but a white soul," is a local saying, although more often, as in Cuba and Brazil, it is the devil who is always white. As Martín Fierro puts it in the great Argentine classic poem: "The White paints the devil black/The Black paints him white."

Most slaves brought to Cuba came from the culturally advanced peoples of Africa, such as the Lucumí and Mandinga. On the island, the various languages fused into a lingua franca, Ñáñigo, spoken by a fourth of the population. Ñáñigo is also the religion, a mixture of African worship and Catholicism. The dances are before Santa Barbara, who occupies the altar alongside pebble gods and more elaborately dressed figurines of gods (orishas), saints, and spirits. Stirring music is played continuously with drums (bombas), kitchen pans, maracas or gourd rattles, and sticks, the frenzied beating of which creates the most remarkable rhythms and tones from chair legs, dishes, table tops, posts, and rafters. Some rumbas are danced in the near-nude. The dangerous bottle and knife dances require great skill and agility; much rum is drunk and, as restraints break down, bloody machete fights occur and couples slip off into the brush. These affairs are attended by both respectable women and town prostitutes. Actually the Ñáñigo fraternities are noble associations, with blood-brother obligations that demand aid to a fellow blood-brother and his entire family to the point of poverty and death.

Legends

Old religious legends are still strong among Cuban Negroes, particularly those of the Yorubas (Lucumí). One of the most delightful collections of legends is that by the mulatto Rómulo Lachateneré, *Oh, mio Yemayá!*, which reflects current sex attitudes. Obalá is now the Virgin of Mercedes (sometimes Christ), a bestower of sex magic. Ochún, the beloved Virgin of Charity of Copper, is the goddess of water, love, and fecundity, the luxurious creature who attracts all men with her lascivious dancing, spicy grace, and aphrodisiacal *oñi*. The *oñi* charm and the spirit-invoking *ecuelé* are potent factors in Cuban love life. A variant of the same goddess is Yemayá, ruler over fertilizing rains and love, "the Lorelei of both Cuban and Brazilian Negroes," now absorbed as the Virgin of Regla, patroness of sailors in Havana, as once in Cádiz. In a tale as pungent as *Oedipus*, she has incestuous relations with her mighty son Chango (Santa Barbara). Here, too, are marvelous portraits of the faithful wife and companion, Obá, who sacrifices her beauty to save her reckless, arrogant husband. Chango is powerful, cunning, roistering, bellicose, a prodigious seducer of women. He is alternately rich, glorious, and arrogant and utterly poor and miserable. Often he is represented locally as the giant San Cristóbal "who carries the child of God," a pre-Christian African saint. Lachatenere's magnificent opening tale is the story of the boatman Ogún, subduer of rivers. When he demands fare for ferrying the haughty elegant goddess Ochún, she strips off her clothes disdainfully and offers herself on a grassy bank in a lusty scene of consummation. It symbolizes the union of sun and water, and their offspring is the ruler of fire. These tales run the gamut of Cuban sex conduct, from reckless abandon to passionate loyalty and self-sacrifice.

Árias Trujillo's pictures of Columbian Negroes with their dances and sex-life, particularly the Sunday *charanga* dance fiesta, are magnificent: how the men get their *prebas* (samples) of rum in each cantina, arriving drunk; how the girls in their best dresses, cheap cotton but very washed and starched, brightly adorned and bejeweled, their heads looking like those of brightly ornamented saints, come swaying their bodies "with aphrodisiacal *frufru*" (sex appeal) to indulge in the wild erotic *currulao* dance, with its advances and retreats, its twining of bodies and simulated copulation.

The Special Problems of the Mulattoes

The mulatto's problem has been similar to that of the mestizo: he is a man with broken ties, a lost spirit but fierce with vitality. Unlike the mestizo, he has no valid rooted group to tie him, so all his aspirations are directed, perhaps falsely, to rising in the white world. There is little race bigotry in Cuba, although the ruthless Batista dictatorship had created some, but much bigotry does exist among Cuban mulattoes themselves, who set up exclusive social clubs and are contemptuous of members of their own race who have slightly darker pigmentation.

The Brazilian Da Cunho, prejudiced against the Negro, states the mulatto's dilemma with some accuracy: The mulatto has "a brilliant mind . . . but [is] unstable, restless, inconsistent, flaring up one moment, extinguished the next, . . . the victim of biological law, weighed down to the lower plane of less-favored races. Impotent . . . [in] forming any bonds of solidarity between the opposing forebears, he can reflect only their various dominant attributes in a permanent play of antitheses." Hence, he has "a rudimentary morality . . . the imperative automation of the lower races." However, scientific studies by the anthropological division of the Brazilian army show that mulattoes, on the average, are superior physically and mentally to both parent stocks.

In both Haiti and Brazil, the Negro had a patria or nation; as Gilberto Freyre puts it, "Every Brazilian, even the light-skinned fair-haired one, carries in his soul, when not on soul and body alike . . . the shadow or at least the birthmark of the aborigine or the Negro." There was no stigma on further intermarriage between the races, and the mulatto has attained to the highest posts in government, church, and army; he has made his mark in music, literature, painting. Many early mulattoes, of course, came directly from Lisbon, which at the time of the Conquest had a population of 10,000 Negroes, and this Europeanized mulatto enjoyed a particularly superior status in the New World and frequently married into the highest social levels. All Brazilian writers have recognized the virility, fecundity, and bold initiative of the mulatto, whose lustiness has done so much to forge the great Brazilian nation.

Spanish and Portuguese

Conquerors of the New World imported the sex habits of Spanish feudal Catholic society, an outward fetish of monogamy that had little relation to actual sex habits. Furthermore, that Catholic society had been modified by centuries of Moorish occupation in the south, with North African concepts of the seraglio and the cloistered woman. All told, the freedom of the Spanish woman had been greatly curtailed since the earlier days of Iberic nationalism, when society had been more democratic. Northern Spain was, by the time of the Discovery, in the flower of knighthood, feudal and militaristic. But all sex standards were in a state of chaos owing to prolonged civil war. The adventurous men who went overseas soon lost nearly all restraints in their contacts with the conquered peoples. Crews were often recruited from jails. Only the presence of large numbers of priests and monks provided a checkrein, and the Christian elements, as urban colonial centers were established, gradually restored submerged Spanish moral attitudes.

But relatively few women accompanied these men, and the result was concubinage and marriage with Indian and Negro women. Thus, the wife was a semislave from a subjugated race; even white women had fewer rights than they had enjoyed in Spain. Until a generation ago, even in México, which is more influenced by the United States, it was not unusual for a man to lock his wife in the house whenever he left. She could not even go to market, to which she had to send her servants. She was allowed to go only to Mass, if properly chaperoned. Daughters were more closely guarded than in any Indian puberty rite period.

Double standards inevitably resulted. The white wife was considered a paragon of purity and was devoted entirely to her home and the Church. The husband had access to Indian and Negro women, or to the "saltier" mestizas and mulattoes, with whom he consorted promiscuously or as concubines and "little" wives. It would be possible to fill a book with accounts of the orgies and debaucheries that occurred from the earliest days to the present. In more dissolute periods they even engulfed some of the clergy. As late as this century, it was customary for Chilean and Argentine gold washers in the islands south of the Straits of Magellan to seize an Alcaluf, Ona, or Yahgán girl, chain her outside a hut, toss her food as to an animal, and use her jointly for sexual purposes.

On big feudal haciendas, the lord of the manor always had first-night privileges with any peon girl who was getting married, and still does in remoter areas.

Upper-Class Sex Life

Sex life has remained more traditional in the old aristocracy than it has among the newer middle class, the rich industrialists, or the new factory wage earners. This is especially true in provincial areas.

Yet their women have achieved more freedom of late, especially now that education for girls is no longer restricted to closely guarded elementary convent schools. Higher education has become the rule, providing wider horizons and allowing for more unchaperoned liberty and freer marriage choice. Within the past few decades, urban expansion has been phenomenal; it is estimated that in a few more years México City will have a population of eight million. This, the coming of industrial progress, and more economic freedom for women have altered the sex habits of centuries.

This has meant no diminution of the "little wife" practices, although more discretion is now exercised. If a mistress is discarded or dies, it is still customary for the man to bring the children home to his legitimate wife to be cared for and educated along with his legitimate children and on a footing of equality, except if the newcomers are patently of a much darker hue or are obviously from a lower class.

Customarily, the head of the house takes his wife, and often all the children as well, out to dine, or to the cafe or the theater every Thursday night. Sunday is also a family day, when he takes everybody to church, enjoys their company during the afternoons, and receives callers then and in the evening.

The older aristocracy, with close-knit marriages, has often become morally and physically effete. An undue amount of homosexuality exists, and since this is now legally frowned upon, some of the leading families of Perú and México have been hit by scandals as a result of police raids. Brother-sister incest has come to light, although brother-sister marriages never occur.

The military caste has always been supremely lawless in sex matters. In México, Perú, and some other countries, the *rabonas*, the common-law wives of ordinary soldiers, accompany the armies even in battle, do the cooking, the toting, the foraging, carry supplies to the front line, and bear their babies by the roadside, catching up again in a few hours. The armies are also serviced by hangers-on—looser women and prostitutes. Officers customarily discard wives and mistresses with each ascension. In revolutionary times, girls are often taken by force to be mistresses—even from "first" families.

Some mistresses have not been brief birds of passage. The sultry mestiza mistress and private secretary of a famous Mexican general managed to retain her post during his term as president, when she truly became a power in the land and was his guiding spirit until his death.

The flagrant sex conduct of the military caste is matched only by that of the politicians, particularly in Cuba, México, and Perú, although greater discretion, thanks to public opinion, is beginning to be exercised. It has been almost a prerequisite for a cabinet minister (there are many dignified exceptions) to be a sex exhibitionist, flaunting his mistresses, often actresses, nightly in cafes and public places and taking them on trips and, of course, to all party caucuses, which are usually held picnic-style. The wife appears only on occasions of official protocol, government fiestas, celebrations, and dedications, or when some foreign dignitary is accompanied by his wife.

Until lately, no divorce laws existed in Latin America, but it is now quite customary for leading politicians to divorce earlier wives and seek more glamorous helpmates from the aristocratic classes. Dictator Fulgencio Batista of Cuba, married to a charming countrified girl with whom he had numerous children, put her aside to marry an elegant creature from the ranks of the aristocracy, although that social group had repeatedly and openly snubbed him previously. The leading mistress of one Caribbean dictator was the daughter of a leading family. The father was told his daughter would become the dictator's mistress and he would receive a cabinet position—or he could go to jail.

Numerous Mexican and Peruvian writers have disclosed the sordid sexual side of local politics, the orgies participated in by the daughters and even wives of the first families for the sake of avoiding difficulties for their husbands, sons, and brothers, or in order to secure good posts for them in the bureaucracy.

Middle-Class Sex Life

Middle-class sex relations are more normal and respectable and are pointed toward monogamy. Only the wealthier members continue the "little" wife practice, but few are without some hideout bachelor's apartment where girls can be taken discreetly.

The old system of closely guarding daughters and the rigid system of chaperonage broke down only a few years ago, predominantly in the cities. In more provincial countries, such as Guatemala or Costa Rica, many restraints persist. In México City only a few years ago it was illegal for any unaccompanied girl to be on the streets after nine o'clock at night unless she had a prostitute's card. Now girls go with their sweethearts to the movies, dances, and parties unchaperoned, or with girl friends, and suffer little molestation on the streets. Sometimes the fiction of chaperonage is maintained by sending a small brother or sister along with the courting couple, but it is also the custom for the boy to bribe the "chaperone" to play somewhere else.

These freer sex relations have arisen partly because of the greater economic independence of women. The women of the lower classes always worked, but those of the middle and upper classes were barred from employment by long custom. In 1903, in all México City, only 300 such were employed. Today in government offices there are probably more women than men; and they work in stores, offices, and factories. To chaperone such girls to work and home again four times a day is too much of a chore even for the most fastidious families.

Lower-Class Sex Life

The lower classes everywhere live on a poverty level. They are predominantly Indians and mestizos; in the Caribbean, Negroes and mulattoes. Many Indian and Negro sex customs survive, but are broken down and distorted, particularly among the new urban proletariat. Sexual standards are generally low, and the girls are often promiscuous. Common-law marriages are the rule rather than the exception, although they may endure for a lifetime. A vast percentage are condemned to live in one room, and children from infancy are obliged to witness sexual acts. Alberto J. Pani, in his *La Higiene en México,* describes the "horrible animal promiscuity of sexes of all ages." Earlier, Julio Guerrero in his brilliant *La Génesis del Crimen en México* went into great detail into this subject and described some of the sexual distortions and criminality that derived from it.

Yet most lower-class families live a relatively normal life. Misery makes the woman a loyal helpmate and provider. More so than in any other social group, marriage is a system of close economic cooperation in all tasks.

Prostitution

Prostitution is widespread, although in most places it is considerably more discreet and hidden than it was a few years ago. Nowhere is it suppressed; the Latin countries follow the French system of regulation and medical supervision. In México City girls are medically checked every week and must have their cards properly stamped. These cards vary according to the medical fee paid and indicate the minimum price the girl may charge. The government also maintains a special hospital where girls with venereal diseases are treated free of charge.

Formerly, México had endless blocks of open cribs. Today these have been largely eliminated and the traffic is restricted to regular houses. The prevalence of streetwalkers has also declined. This change is also true of Guatemala City and Lima, Perú. In Santiago and Buenos Aires there are few overt signs of prostitution. The two most corrupt places on the continent are Havana and Panamá. Panamá, as the crossroads of all the nations, caters to the American army on the Canal Zone, sailors, and tourists. Havana has streetwalkers everywhere, blocks of cribs, scores of dance cantinas with B-girls, and many houses, some very elegant. Sexual shows are staged; pornographic movies, showing the most extreme sex perversions, are openly available; vendors of French postcards are at every elbow; homosexual prostitutes solicit. Under Fidel Castro's regime, much of this has been cleared up.

The Family

An over-all examination of sex habits, some abnormal, some of relatively minor importance, should not leave the impression that Latin American sex life is bizarre or immoral because certain aspects are different from our own. The fact is that the vast majority of the people to the south live a highly ordered family life, although some of the sex patterns may be unfamiliar to us. The family is far more stable, important, and sacred than it is in the United States. It plays a more basic part in economic and social life, and it has been a great bulwark for survival over many troubled centuries.

Except in certain Indian communities, the family is largely a patriarchal institution. It usually embraces numbers of generations and is flexible enough to absorb all fairly near relatives. Except among the very wealthy, there are no idlers in the Latin American family. All contribute, all work, from the smallest tots to grandmothers, and all have a reasonable voice in the management of household affairs or in other matters that may affect the family. The family is an integrated economic and spiritual unit. Except for the poor, homes are kept spot-less; children are admirably trained; politeness and a certain formal etiquette are maintained between the various members at all times. The pattern of family life is being altered by the stresses of modernity, but by and large it represents one of the most gracious and successful expressions of life in the countries to the south.

References

Castro Pozo, Hildebrando, *Nuestra Comunidad Indígina*. Lima, Perú: El Lucero, 1924.

Covarrubias, Miguel, *Mexico South. The Isthmus of Tehuantepec*. New York: Alfred A. Knopf, Inc., 1946.

Delgado, Julian A., "Folklore y Apuntes para la Sociología Indígena." *Revista de Educación*. Lima 2; (3), 132-222, 1931.

Guerrero, Julio, *La Génesis del Crimen en México*. México, 1901.

Juárez Muñoz, J. Fernando, *El Indio Guatemalteco* (2 vols.). Guatemala, 1931, 1945.

Lachataneré, Rómulo, *Oh, Mío Yemayá*. Manzanillo, Cuba: El Arte, 1938.

Marín, Juan, *Hacia la Nueva Moral. Educación sexual y sus nuevas fórmulas sociales*. Santiago de Chile: Andrés Bello Press, 1934.

Ortiz, Fernando, *Hampa Afro-Cubana. Los Negros Brujos*. Havana, 1916; Madrid, 1917.

Pani, Alberto J., *La Higiene en México*. México: J. Ballesca, 1916.

Pardo, Luis Lara, *La prostitución en México*. México, 1908.

Pereda Valdés, Ildefonso, *El Negro rioplatense*. Montevideo: Claudia García, 1937.

Pierson, Donald, *Negroes in Brazil*. Chicago: University of Chicago Press, 1943.

Ramos, A., *O Folklore Negro No Brasil*. São Paolo, 1932.

Rose, Arnold M. (ed.), *The Institutions of Advanced Societies*. Minneapolis: University of Minnesota Press, 1958.

Sánchez, Luis Alberto, *Vida y pasión de la cultura en América*. Santiago de Chile: Ercilla, 1935.

Soto, Pedro Juan, *50 milliones de mujeres esclavizadas*. México: Instituto de Investigaciones de Trabajo, 1956.

Stewart, Julian H. (ed.), *Handbook of South American Indians* (6 vols.). Washington, D.C.: Smithsonian Institution, 1946-1949.

Toor, Frances, *Mexican Folkways*. New York: Crown Publishers, Inc., 1947.

Toor, Frances, *Three Perus*. New York: Crown Publishers, Inc., 1949.

Valdizán, Hermilio, and Maldonado, Angel, *La Medicina Popular Peruana* (3 vols.). Lima: Imprenta Torres Aguirre, 1922.

CARLETON BEALS

Laws on
Marriage and Family

I T MAY be broadly stated that the laws* relating to marriage generally have one of two
purposes, sometimes both encompassed within
a single rule. These two purposes are (1) the
fixing of financial responsibility so as to ensure
that the state will not have to bear the burden
of supporting dependent women and children,
and (2) the encouragement of marital unions
likely to produce acceptable offspring and the
confinement of sexual activity within the
boundaries of such a marriage. It is true that
in some instances one can divine legal concern
for sexual satisfaction per se as a vital element
in marriage but by and large even these instances seem to be related to the basic concern
for legitimate offspring.

Restrictions on Marriage

There are four general types of restrictions on
the right to marry: age, relationship, race, and
mental and/or physical health.

Age

There are generally two separate sets of age
requirements for marriage, an age bracket below which people are not supposed to marry
at all and a higher bracket within which they
may marry only with parental consent. In one
state, for example, no male below the age of 17
or female below 14 may marry at all; males between the ages of 17 and 21 and females be-

tween the ages of 14 and 18 may, however,
marry with parental consent. The fixing of age
minima seems to be motivated primarily by
economic and social considerations rather than
by consistent convictions relating to the minimum desirable age for sexual intercourse. One
finds, for instance, no real correlation between
the age at which the state will recognize the
right of a girl to marry and the age of statutory
rape, i.e., the age below which she is assumed
to be incapable of consenting to intercourse. In
one state, for example, intercourse with a
female under the age of 18 may subject the
male to imprisonment for a period ranging from
one year to life. The same state permits a girl to
marry with parental consent at 16.

In some states the requirement of parental
consent or even the minimum age requirement
itself can be waived by a judge or by the licensing official if the girl is pregnant, has already
borne a child by the prospective husband, or if
they have been living together as husband and
wife. Where couples have managed to secure
a license and marry without parental consent
the marriage is not subject to annulment if the
parties were at least over the minimum age at
which they might legally have married with
parental consent. If they were below the age
when they could have married even with parental consent, the marriage is in most, but not all,
states subject to annulment. The courts usually
have wide discretion in granting annulments
in this type of situation and will not ordinarily
annul a marriage if a child has been born of
the marriage or if the wife is pregnant.

* Most of the data on which the material in this article
is based are derived from cases reported in various
official law reports.

Relationship

Although all states have some definition of familial relationships within which people may not marry, there is little legal uniformity. In no state can a parent marry his child, a grandparent his grandchild, a brother his sister, or an aunt or uncle marry a niece or nephew. Beyond this area, however, the states differ widely. Most prohibit the marriage of first cousins; a few prohibit marriage of second cousins. Some prohibit the marriage of people between whom there is a legal but no blood relationship, such as stepparents and stepchildren, or the marriage of a father-in-law with the widow or ex-wife of his son or of a mother-in-law with the former husband of her daughter. It would be difficult to find a eugenic basis for this type of prohibition, but the historical basis is more obvious. Aside from other anthropological sources for this type of incest taboo, it has a historical basis in the Judeo-Christian ethic. Chapter 18 of Leviticus prohibits a man from marrying his daughter-in-law, his mother-in-law, the daughter or granddaughter of his wife, or his aunt by marriage.

Incestuous marriages, that is, marriages between relatives that are considered illegal under the law of the particular state, are not merely subject to possible annulment (as is true of marriages that do not meet the state's minimum age requirement); they are absolutely void. This means that no court proceeding need be brought to invalidate the marriage and that under no circumstances is the existence of a child or the pregnancy of the wife a factor in deciding the validity of the marriage.

Race

In a number of our states the law prohibits marriages between people of different races. However, these statutes have recently been under heavy attack on constitutional grounds and even those still standing are likely to fall within the near future. As might be anticipated, the most common prohibition is that of marriage between white and Negro. Some states attempt to define a Negro in terms of the amount of "Negro blood," e.g., anyone having one-eighth or more Negro blood. There is no uniformity in the definition. In one state anyone

is considered a Negro who has any nonwhite ancestry; in others, less than a quarter Negro blood would take one out of the category of Negro. Marriages between whites and Indians, Mongolians, Chinese, Japanese, Malayans, and Hindus are also prohibited in some states. It is apparently the "purity" of only the white race that it of concern here. Marriages between members of different nonwhite races are nowhere prohibited.

Like incestuous marriages, marriages in violation of these miscegenation statutes are not merely voidable, i.e., subject to being set aside by court order; in most states they are absolutely void. It should be remembered, however, that generally every state must recognize the validity of a marriage that is valid in the state in which it was entered into. Thus, a Negro and white who marry in New York where there is no prohibition against intermarriage are legally married in Virginia if they should later move to that state. However, a state does have some leeway in determining whether to recognize a marriage between *its own residents* that takes place outside of the state. A few states refuse to issue licenses to nonresidents whose marriage would have been prohibited by the laws of their home state. Some states will not recognize an out-of-state marriage between residents who leave the state for the purpose of entering into a marriage that would not have been permitted under the laws of the home state. Other states will recognize out-of-state marriages of their residents only if they do not conflict with public policy or are not incestuous or miscegenetic by the home state's standards. Such statutes are irrelevant where the couple actually resides or takes up residence in the state in which the marriage took place; they only apply where the couple goes to the other state for the sole purpose of marrying and returns to the home state thereafter.

Mental and Physical Health

Requirements relating to fitness to marry are comparatively recent. The most common is the requirement of a premarital test for venereal disease, which has now been adopted in many states. In a few states the presence of disease does not bar the marriage provided both parties have been informed of the existence of the infection or the doctor or the state board of health certifies that the disease is not in a transmissible stage. The requirements of the test may be waived in most states under special circumstances, e.g., if the woman is pregnant or has already borne a child by the husband-to-be. Waivers during wartime for soldiers on short leave were extremely common, perhaps in part on the theory that intercourse without marriage would be likely to result if the requirement were not waived.

The blood test requirements can usually be avoided by going to a state that has no such requirements. Such a migratory marriage is valid but some states have attempted to close the loophole by requiring that proof of a test be filed in the home state or by requiring that every pregnant woman be given a test for syphilis.

Some states prohibit the marriage of mental defectives, alcoholics, drug addicts, epileptics, or persons suffering from tuberculosis. Enforcement of such laws is often a matter of chance. In small communities the licensing official is likely to know enough about the people with whom he deals to make an intelligent judgment as to whether or not a license should be issued. The license clerk in a large city, however, is hardly in a position to judge whether an applicant for a license has any of these defects. A few states have made an attempt at real enforcement of their laws by requiring an applicant for a license to present a medical certificate stating that he has been examined and that no symptoms of alcoholism, drug addiction, epilepsy, feeble-mindedness, etc., have been observed.

Common-Law Marriage

A common-law marriage is one that exists merely by reason of a man and woman living together without a license or a formal ceremony. It is less widely recognized today than it was during the earlier days of this country's history. When people tended to live in areas where licensing officials and clergymen were not easy to reach and suffered economic circumstances that might make the cost of a ceremonial marriage prohibitive, common-law marriage was recognized in order to prevent bastardization of children and termination of unions that might cast the burden of supporting women and children on the community.

Today neither the geographic nor economic justifications for this type of marriage exist. Moreover, social security and workmen's compensation laws have made it likely that the first attempt to prove the existence of a common-law marriage will come after the death of one party. For this reason many of the states that still recognize common-law marriage insist that it must be proved that the couple openly cohabited as husband and wife. In some states, however, proof of cohabitation is not absolutely necessary. Some require only that the parties agree to consider themselves married.

The Role of Sex in Marriage

The law does not affirmatively define the rights and obligations of husband and wife to each other. It is necessary to look to individual laws and cases dealing with divorce, annulment, and separation to determine those factors whose absence in the judgment of the legislatures and the courts makes a marriage untenable.

The personal rights, as distinguished from the property rights, of spouses may be summarized as the following: The right and obligation to live together in a home of their own, consistent with the husband's financial means; the right to enjoy the person, affection, society, and assistance of the other; and the right to "normal" and exclusive sexual relations with each other.

Impotence

The basic importance of the sex factor is recognized by the fact that impotence is generally recognized as a ground either for divorce or annulment. When impotence is a ground for annulment of a marriage, the law usually requires that the incapacity be total and that it existed at the time of the marriage. Some states require too that it be continuing and incurable. Although the laws speak of impotence without distinguishing between impotence of husband and sterility of wife, for obvious reasons the cases almost always deal with male impotence. Frigidity on the part of the wife is normally not a ground since intercourse would be at least physically possible.

Sterility

It is interesting to note that, notwithstanding the overwhelming concern of the law for a marital relationship likely to produce, and capable of producing, legitimate offspring, sterility is not generally recognized as a fatal defect, as is impotence. Sterility is a ground for annulment in many states if the sterility existed at the time of the marriage and was known to the sterile party and concealed from the other. However, it is the element of fraud here rather than the sterility itself that is the ground for the termination of the marriage.

There are a number of reasons why sterility is less widely recognized as a fatal defect in a marriage than impotence. To begin with, unless it is known at the time of the marriage, it is quite possible that the sterility of a spouse may not be established until many years after the marriage is consummated. In a case involving impotence, the condition should be suspected within a day, a week, or a month of the marriage and the parties put on notice, so to speak, very early that the problem exists. Where sterility is concerned, its discovery may come after the marriage has existed for such a long time that the circumstances of the parties have become irrevocably altered. Moreover, one suspects that the insistence on male potency as a basic requirement for marriage is not unrelated to the concern for legitimate offspring. It may well stem from a conviction that a woman married to an impotent man may look to other men for an escape from the frustration of virgin wifedom, and such escape carries with it the inherent possibility of illegitimate offspring being foisted on the husband and/or the community.

Physical Incapacity

Although complete physical incapacity is recognized as a cause for divorce or annulment, partial physical incapacity or psychological factors that make a sexual relationship possible but not satisfactory are not so recognized. The complete refusal of one spouse to participate in intercourse is, in some states, considered to be desertion and is ground for divorce or legal separation. (The insistence of one party on the use of contraceptives has also been termed "desertion" in some cases.) However, where the extreme situations of complete impotence or complete abstinence do not obtain, lesser degrees of sexual incompatibility or dissatisfaction give no grounds for legal relief.

Abnormal Sex Practices

The law recognizes, as indicated above, the right of a spouse to expect "normal" sexual intercourse from his mate. There is no obligation to submit to "abnormal" or "unnatural" sex, however, and the request or insistence of one party on activities such as fellation, cunnilinctus, mutual masturbation, etc., may be termed cruelty and justify a divorce or legal separation. Even when such practices are engaged in by a married couple with full consent, the act may be as clearly within the state's criminal statutes relating to such practices as if the couple were unmarried; however, the facts in such a situation are unlikely to come to the attention of the legal authorities. The acts are not made legal either by the fact that the parties are married to each other or by their mutual agreement to engage in the practices.

In view of the fact that reliable studies indicate that a large percentage of the population indulges in what the law regards as "unnatural" sex practice, the courts are sometimes in the position of terming "intolerable cruelty" practices that a substantial number of married people find mutually satisfying. In some cases "excessive" requests for intercourse on the part of one party have also been termed cruelty. What will be deemed "excessive" will depend in any case on the personal orientation of the judge as well as on objective factors such as the health of the complaining party.

Adultery:
The Right to Exclusivity

Although there is tremendous variation among the laws of the individual states relating to such grounds for divorce as desertion, non-support, alcoholism, etc., there is almost complete unanimity that a spouse is entitled to the exclusive right to intercourse with his mate. So deeply imbedded in the law is this proposition that in almost all states a single instance of extramarital intercourse is sufficient to enable the other spouse to secure a divorce. A very few states consider adultery a ground for divorce only if accompanied by cohabitation by the adulterous spouse and another party, but these states tend to employ a double standard. In one state, for example, a husband may secure a divorce for a single act of adultery by his wife, but a wife is only entitled to a divorce if her husband actually abandons her and lives with another woman.

An act of extramarital intercourse must be voluntary to be considered adulterous. Thus, the fact that his wife was raped would not give the husband grounds for divorce. In several states it has been held that no divorce will be granted for adultery if the accused spouse was insane or otherwise mentally irresponsible.

Adultery must usually be proven by circumstantial evidence since it is only in the rarest of circumstances that there is an eye witness to the act. The fact of adultery is deduced by the courts from a set of circumstances that make it probable, as one court put it, that a man and woman were not engaged in saying their "Pater Nosters." Thus if a man and woman occupied a single hotel room, registered at a hotel, or lived together representing themselves as a married couple, or (the classic, and usually fraudulent, circumstance) were found in their night or under clothes in a room by witnesses, the courts will usually assume that adultery has been committed.

divorce will not be granted even if adultery is proven. One such is the case in which it can be established that both spouses committed adultery. Marriage counselors might consider dual adultery an indication of a genuinely troubled marital situation, but the courts, which deal with marital problems in terms of "guilt" and "innocence," generally rule this to be a situation where neither "guilty" party has standing to sue the other for divorce.

Another type of situation in which no relief will be granted is one in which the nonadulterous spouse "condoned" the adultery, that is, he or she learned about the adultery and, instead of separating or bringing immediate suit, agreed to try to forgive the lapse and resume the marriage. In such a case the adultery is, in effect, wiped off the books and no subsequent

action for divorce may be based on it. The result is that lawyers must advise a client whose spouse has committed adultery that any attempt to resume the marriage, in order to try to correct whatever led to the adultery or to determine whether the adultery had any substantial deleterious effect on the relationship, is fraught with the hazard that, if the attempt at reconciliation is not completely successful, the non-adulterous spouse will find that he has waived his right to sue for divorce.

A divorce will not be granted if the adultery was committed with the connivance of the suing party or his agent. The usual case of this sort occurs when one spouse hires a detective to secure evidence of adultery on which a divorce action can be based and the detective speeds up the process of accumulating the evidence by hiring someone to entrap the other spouse into an adulterous or apparently adulterous situation. No divorce will be granted in this type of situation, even if the spouse who hired the detective did not request or even know about the entrapment. Some states go so far as to hold that if connivance has once been proven against a spouse, he or she can never thereafter sue for divorce for any subsequent adultery, no matter how genuine.

In addition to the right to sue an adulterous spouse for divorce, many states allow a spouse to bring a civil action for damages against the person who has participated in the mate's adultery. This is known as an action for criminal conversation. In some states such an action can only be brought by the husband on the ground that the husband might, as a result of his wife's adultery, have spurious offspring attributed to him. In other states the wife, too, can bring such an action on the theory that the essence of the wrong is the destruction of the exclusive sex relationship between husband and wife, as well as on the ground that the husband might, as a result of his adultery, become infected with a venereal disease that might affect the health of the wife and children.

Suit for alienation of affections may also be brought in some states against a third party who has "deliberately" or "maliciously" interfered in the marital relationship. Although adultery may be involved here, in most states it is not the *sine qua non* of this type of action. Such a suit may also be brought against relations or friends that are of the same sex as the spouse. It is no defense to this type of action that affection did not exist between the husband and wife prior to the acts complained of or even that they were already living in disharmony or were separated. Nor need the suing spouse prove that the acts of the third party resulted in the abandonment or termination of the marriage.

Suits for both criminal conversation and alienation of affections have in recent years been outlawed in many states.

Marital Status and Other Sex Statutes

Laws relating to "unnatural" sexual relationships, contraception, and sterilization may fall with equal impact on the wed and the unwed.

Statutes relating to the sale, prescription, and use of contraceptive devices do not generally distinguish between the married and the unmarried. As a practical matter, many clinics have an announced policy of treating only married women. Although as of 1967 both government and private programs are tending to drop the distinction. In any event, *proof* that the patient is married is not ordinarily required; her statement that she is married is usually accepted. Since 1964, all state laws prohibiting or narrowly restricting the distribution of contraceptives to married women (or men) have been repealed or liberalized. When an unmarried minor is involved, a physician or druggist who prescribed or sold a contraceptive with knowledge of the minority might in some states be considered guilty of contributing to the delinquency of a minor. The new New York law, however, prohibits sale of contraceptives only to minors under 16.

In the area of sterilization except in two states there is no requirement that the operation be necessary to the health of the patient. However, doctors are more timorous when asked to sterilize an unmarried minor, where clearly special consents should be obtained in addition to that of the minor.

Artificial Insemination

No specific legislation has thus far been passed, and very few judicial decisions have been made, regarding artificial insemination. It is not possible, therefore, to answer with any degree of assurance questions such as whether the child is the legitimate child of the husband or the donor and whether the insemination constitutes adultery on the part of the wife or the donor, if he is married. In one Canadian case, the judge indicated that the wife was guilty of adultery even though there was no physical contact, on the theory that the essence of the evil of adultery is the lending of the reproductive organs to one other than the spouse, with the consequent possible pollution of blood lines. If the husband had consented to the insemination of his wife, however, such consent might bring the case within the doctrine of connivance, discussed above, and bar him from seeking a divorce. In some states the very wording of the statute ("sexual intercourse," "fornication," "living together out of wedlock") has prevented artificial insemination from being construed as adultery in the few cases that have arisen.

References

Harper, Fowler V., *Problems of the Family*. Indianapolis: Bobbs-Merrill, 1952.

Jacobs, Albert C., and Goebel, Julius, *Cases and Materials on Domestic Relations*. New York: Foundation Press, 1952.

Pilpel, Harriet F., and Zavin, Theodora, *Your Marriage and the Law*. New York: Rinehart & Co., 1952.

Richmond, Mary E., and Hall, Fred S., *Marriage and the State*. New York: Russell Sage Foundation, 1929.

Selected Essays on Family Law. New York: Foundation Press, 1950.

Sherwin, Robert V., *Sex and the Statutory Law*. New York: Oceana Publications, 1949.

Vernier, Chester G., *American Family Law*. 5 vols. Stanford, California: Stanford University Press, 1931-1938.

HARRIET F. PILPEL AND
THEODORA ZAVIN

Laws on Sex Crimes

A FIRST quick glance at the maze of laws that concern sex and sexual behavior may well justify the conclusion that sex is not legal. A cursory examination of these laws will leave the examiner with two major impressions. The first is likely to be one of amazement at the enormous amount of minute detail concerning sex that is encompassed within each specifically designed statute. In spite of the vague wording of many sex statutes and their use of omnibus terms, such as "carnal abuse" or "sodomy," other statutes may include incisive legalities concerning the mating of cattle (and where such mating may or may not take place and under what conditions), and give details of sexual behavior equal in many ways to details included in the most complex laws covering such difficult subjects as bankruptcy and trusts. The second impression is the realization that the ratio of enforcement of these laws as compared to their violation is very low. This does not mean that these laws can therefore be ignored, for until a statute is repealed it can be enforced at any time.

Another peculiar factor is that, whereas laws in general are constantly being written, amended, or repealed, laws concerning sex are not. When one compares sex laws with other laws, it will be seen that the normal functions of amendment and repeal have not occurred to anywhere near the same extent as in other fields over the last fifty years or so—with perhaps a few exceptions.

One final observation must be made at this point: Each state of the United States has its own code of laws concerning sex—and indeed many cities have additional regulations—and there is an incredible lack of conformity as to

actual prohibitions included or omitted, as well as to penalties prescribed. A crime resulting in a fine of $50 to a violator in one state may result in a five-year prison term in a neighboring state—and the same act may not be a crime at all in yet a third state.

Legal Requirements Concerning Sexual Intercourse

Throughout this section the various *restrictions* concerning sexual intercourse will be discussed in detail, but a clearer picture of these restrictive, or negative, laws will be gained if the *affirmative* aspects of the legal requirements are summarized briefly. If the legislature were to pass a law specifically and affirmatively outlining the conditions and requirements that must be present before two persons may engage in sexual relations the law would contain, for the most part, the following elements:

In the first place, and perhaps the most essential element, the parties must be legally married to each other at the time they engage in sexual intercourse. If one of the parties is not of the proper age and therefore cannot legally consent to the marriage, the other party may find himself facing a charge of statutory rape.

Secondly, generally speaking it can be said that the *only* form of sexual relations clearly prescribed within the law for a legally married couple is the insertion of the penis within the vagina. Variations, despite the fact that such variation may be described and prescribed by the reputable sex authorities as a form of pre-coital behavior, are restricted in all states under one law or another.

The act of intercourse must be voluntary on the part of *both* parties. The fact that a man is legally married to his wife does not give him the right to "rape" her.

Sexual intercourse between a married couple must be performed in private; coitus performed even in the company of friends is a crime.

It is well to mention in passing that a sexually legal marriage requires that certain specified individuals (such as uncle-niece, cousin-cousin, etc.) refrain from having sexual intercourse with each other, whether married or not. In addition, sexual intercourse between a Negro and white married couple is not legal in certain states. In certain other states that have no prohibition of this kind, sexual intercourse would still be illegal if the interracial marriage had been performed in a state in which such marriages are illegal—even though the marriage would have been legal if it had been performed in the state where the parties now live.

Crimes Involving Sexual Intercourse

Fornication

Fornication is the act of sexual intercourse by an unmarried person. In other words, if the fornicator is unmarried to the person with whom he or she has sexual intercourse, and/or is not married to any one else, the sexual intercourse is illegal.

However, various state laws have complicated the definition of fornication. For example, in many states fornication is not listed as a crime as such, but if two people who are unmarried to each other engage in sexual intercourse, and one of these two people is married to a third person, *both* are guilty of adultery. In still other states, if the unmarried person is a woman she is guilty of fornication, whereas if the unmarried person is a man he is guilty of adultery.

There are other variations that center around the question of whether or not a single act of sexual intercourse took place. In some states a single act is a crime; in other states the act must be committed more than once and must be "open and notorious." In still other states, the single act is called "fornication" and when the act becomes open and repeated it becomes a crime of "lewd behavior," or an act of "vicious indecency." Sometimes the determination as to whether or not a crime has been committed

depends entirely on whether or not a child was conceived during the single act of sexual intercourse. In such a jurisdiction, if a child was not conceived the crime of fornication has not been committed.

A final variation in some states is that if fornication is committed with a person with whom marriage would be forbidden by law (such as marriage between a white person and a Negro), the penalty is much more severe.

Generally speaking, the penalty for the crime of fornication is comparatively light, although in some states the penalty for the third and fourth offense can be heavy. In several states the only punishment is a fine, ranging from $10 to $100. Most states impose a fine and imprisonment, and such imprisonment may only be for thirty days. However, in some states the offender may be incarcerated for as much as five years, and in addition be fined up to $500.

Adultery

Adultery is generally considered in a more serious light by the courts. As a matter of fact, one court's attitude was: "Adultery is an aggravated species of fornication." Many of the same elements described in connection with fornication are present in the statutes regarding adultery. For example, a single act of adultery, in many jurisdictions, is not a crime. In others, not only must the act be frequent but, in addition, it must be "open and notorious."

Despite the existence of many detailed statutes concerning the crime of adultery, the number of convictions has decreased in the last fifty years to the point of almost none at all. For example, in New York State there have been less than five convictions for adultery in this century, despite the fact that the only ground for divorce in New York is adultery and that thousands of divorces are being granted each year because adultery has been committed.

Punishment for adultery, as for fornication, varies widely, from $20 to as much as $2,000 plus five years' imprisonment.

Rape

The evolution of laws concerning the crime of rape is one of the most complex of all legal developments regarding sex. One reason for this complexity is the fact that two separate crimes are merged in this single crime. First, is the crime of engaging in sexual intercourse without the sanctity of marriage, as required by law. Second, is the crime of assault. (In addition, the element of fraud has been introduced into the modern version of the rape statute.)

Generally speaking, the crime of rape consists of accomplishing sexual intercourse with a woman against her will, either by force or by threat of force. It is important to note that the crime is committed when force or *threat* of force is used. A woman does not have to die or be severely injured for the sexual act to be considered "a fate worse than death." Through the years the definition of the crime has been considerably broadened. For example, it was once required that actual penetration of the penis into the vagina take place and that there be an emission. In the United States today, emission is not required, and only the *slightest* penetration of the outer labia is necessary for the act to be considered rape.

To fully understand the meaning of the phrase "against her will" the phrase should be reworded to read "without the *lawful* consent." A woman might very well consent to sexual intercourse, but such consent would not be considered lawful under certain conditions. Therefore, she was actually consenting *against her will*. She may have consented because of fear of death or bodily harm, even though no actual force was used. Or she may have consented because she was insane or an imbecile. Such consent would not be considered lawful, and the male involved could be convicted of rape if indicted. So important is this aspect of rape in certain states that special statutes, apart from the rape statutes, have been enacted to cover this situation specifically (and in many instances with even greater penalties).

Consent obtained through the use of drugs, anesthetics, alcoholic beverages, or any substance that would cause a stupor and/or an increased sexual desire would be considered unlawful consent and would subject the male to prosecution under the rape statute. Some jurisdictions have supplemented this part of the rape statute with an additional law requiring that all doctors and dentists who use a general anesthetic in connection with a female patient may do so only in the presence of a nurse or other third person.

One of the most curious types of unlawful consent spelled out by the law of rape in many jurisdictions is the consent a woman gives to a man she thinks is her husband but who in fact is impersonating her husband. Needless to say, although sexual intercourse was accomplished without force or plunder and with the obvious consent of the female, the impersonator would be guilty of rape because the consent was fraudulently obtained and therefore not lawful.

If the female consents, but it can be proven that she did not understand the nature of the act she consented to, this would again constitute unlawful consent. For example, if a physician had intercourse with a patient, having obtained her consent by telling her that such an act was a necessary part of the treatment, and if it can be shown that the patient believed this to be so because of youth, ignorance, or deficient mentality and thus consented, such consent would not be considered lawful and the doctor would be guilty of rape.

Perhaps the most important type of unlawful consent is the consent that is obtained from a female who is under the age of consent specified by state law. This type of unlawful consent places the crime in the category of "statutory" rape. Here again the rape has been consented to, and thus no force or threat of force has been used in accomplishing sexual intercourse. On the theory that the youthfulness of the female is her own worst enemy and that she therefore does not know to what she consents, the law declares that, since she does not have the *capacity* to consent, sexual intercourse was accomplished without her consent, and that the male is therefore guilty of rape.

Certain very serious defects in the law regarding statutory rape exist in most jurisdictions today. Only two defenses are possible for a person indicted for statutory rape: (1) to deny that sexual intercourse occurred; (2) to prove that the girl was of the legal age of consent. No other defense is legally acceptable in most jurisdictions. The girl may look 25 years of age or older (the boy may actually be younger than the girl), but if in fact the girl was under the legal age of consent, and if in fact intercourse occurred, the boy would stand trial for statutory rape. In some jurisdictions certain changes have been made in the law as a result of obvious injustices arising in its administration. For example, it hardly seems fair for a boy of 16 to spend 5 years in prison for having had intercourse with a girl who was older than he but nevertheless 3 months under 18 (the legal age of consent in many jurisdictions). Yet that is what has happened in countless numbers of cases, despite the fact that in many of these cases the girl has clearly been shown to be the seducer. As a result, in a few jurisdictions the accusing female must prove that she herself was chaste. However, if the defendant proves that the girl was not chaste he will not be acquitted; usually both will be convicted of disorderly conduct or some similar offense.

As in all laws concerning sex, the one consistent thing about laws on statutory rape is that they are all different. Although 18 is the most common legal age of consent, in many jurisdictions almost every age from 7 to 18 is so considered. In this era of psychology we know that chronological age does not necessarily coincide with emotional age, or degree of maturity. The use of an arbitrary legal age of consent, regardless of the facts of the case, can therefore result in a great many injustices to both the female and the male. Many authorities have been advocating changes in this aspect of the law, but to date not enough have been made.

Generally, the penalty for statutory rape is as severe as it is for all kinds of rape. At least eighteen states impose death as the maximum penalty for rape. In many of these, the only alternative to the death penalty is life imprisonment. In other states, penalties range from one to one hundred years.

Abduction

The crime of abduction is included in the code of every state in the United States, although many of these states make no distinction in their statutes between the *purposes* for which the victim was abducted. Some jurisdictions have set "abduction for the purpose of sexual intercourse" in a class by itself, the chief reason being to provide more severe penalties

for this kind of abduction. For example, in one jurisdiction the abduction of a female for purposes of sexual intercourse can bring a term of life imprisonment. In many other states, the maximum penalty ranges around ten, fifteen, or twenty-one years.

A few states have an additional abduction statute in which the specific purpose of prostitution is defined. Here, too, the penalties are generally higher than in those abduction statutes that concern lesser purposes.

Seduction

In Shakespeare's *King John,* an illegitimate son asks his mother who his father was, and in answering her son, the mother aptly, though poetically, describes the very essence of seduction:

> King Richard Coeur-de-Lion was thy father:
> By long and vehement suit I was seduc'd
> To make room for him in my husband's bed.

It is this "long and vehement suit" that makes the difference between rape and seduction. In the latter the woman is induced to consent to unlawful sexual intercourse by enticements "which overcome her scruples by means of persuasions, solicitations, promises, and/or bribes without the employment of force."

Although common law recognized no crime of seduction, all but twelve states have enacted statutes making seduction a crime. Most of these statutes recognize only one method of seduction: the promise to marry the woman in the immediate or near future, if she will submit now. But the promise of marriage must be a clearly *unconditional* promise of marriage. For example, a promise to marry *if* the woman becomes pregnant is not considered a sufficiently unconditional promise to warrant a conviction of seduction. In some jurisdictions, however, the definition of male culpability has been widened over and above that of a mere promise of marriage. Any artful scheme that persuades a woman to submit to sexual intercourse is sufficient for a conviction in these few jurisdictions. Of course, the court in these jurisdictions requires that the woman prove she submitted as a direct consequence of whatever promise was made.

In many jurisdictions, conviction is obtained

only if the woman proves that she herself was chaste until seduced by the defendant. If she fails to prove this, or if the defendant proves that she had had intercourse with others prior to the alleged seduction, he will be acquitted. In other jurisdictions, the girl need only prove that she has a "reputation" of chastity, regardless of whether or not she was a virgin when she arrived upon the seduction scene.

In a few states, if the girl is over a certain stated age it is somehow assumed that she could not be seduced, and therefore could not legally pursue such an action against the man involved. In some states this age is 25, in others 21, and in still others 18. In other words, the girl must be *under* these ages in order to bring action. In three states the male must be *over* 21 (or 18, or 16, depending on the state) before he can be indicted for seduction.

An interesting question is whether or not seduction of a married woman can bring a conviction. It goes without saying that a conviction for seduction could not be made in those states in which the crime of seduction hinges on a promise of marriage, for even if the man had promised to marry the woman, it would be on *condition* that she get a divorce from her present husband: thus, the promise of marriage would not have been unconditional. It also goes without saying that a married woman would not usually be a virgin (although there are such cases on record) and that those jurisdictions requiring the element of virginity would therefore refuse to entertain an indictment for the crime of seduction. However, convictions are on record for the seduction of a married woman in those jurisdictions that accept *any* artful promise as a means of seduction and do not require the woman to be a virgin.

In most jurisdictions, if the seducer marries the seduced the prosecution will cause the case against the defendant to be dismissed. Some of these jurisdictions, however, require that the marriage take place before the prosecution is started; in others, if at any time during the trial the defendant marries the seduced, the case is dismissed then and there.

The penalty for seduction is generally on the severe side. In some states, a person so convicted can be imprisoned for as long as ten years. In addition, many states impose a fine of as much as $5,000.

Prostitution

The element of prostitution that sets it apart, legally speaking, from fornication or adultery is the fact that the prostitute permits access to her sexual parts in return for a fee. Many states have statutes that say just this—that is, the accused woman cannot be convicted of the crime of prostitution unless there is proof that she was paid, or that payment will be forthcoming. But in at least sixteen states the definition of the crime of prostitution has been widened to include "the offering of the body for sexual intercourse for hire" and "the offering of the body for promiscuous and indiscriminate sexual intercourse without hire."

It would be well at this point to mention two myths connected with the crime of prostitution. The first, and the more widely disseminated of the two, is that prostitution is and has been legal in a few states in the United States. The second myth is that houses of prostitution are visited most frequently by unmarried men. Statutes prohibiting prostitution exist in all states, including the State of Nevada. One myth undoubtedly grew from the fact that for a while a city in Nevada passed its own law that attempted to legalize and regulate prostitution within the city limits. This was soon brought to an end by a State Supreme Court ruling, but not soon enough to prevent the birth of the myth. Concerning the second myth, available statistics indicate that the majority of men who use houses of prostitution with any degree of regularity are married.

In addition to defining the over-all illegality of prostitution, individual statutes spell out, in detail, the various aspects of prostitutional activity. In no other sex law is there the multiplicity (and duplicity) of statutes that exists in those dealing with the single activity of prostitution.

The fact that prostitution is "big business," for example, is reflected in the individual statutory treatment of the various members of the prostitution "ring." The operator "maintains or keeps a house, place, or any structure whatever where prostitution is carried on with his permission and/or knowledge." The procurer engages in the crime known generally as "pandering," in that he procures the inmates of the house of prostitution. In certain states the procurer is also called an "agent" or a "pimp," depending upon the extent of his crime—that is, depending on how many girls he has been able to supply to a house, or houses. The pimp is usually the least important of the three, at least judging from the severity of his penalty in most states. In addition, there are statutes concerned with persons who transport women for purposes of prostitution; employment agencies who, knowing of the activity, send personnel to clean a house of prostitution; cab drivers who tell passengers the location of a house of ill-repute; husbands who live off the proceeds of their prostitute-wives; persons who have information concerning prostitutes or a house of prostitution and fail to give such information to the police; and so on.

There are two types of statutes that deserve more than just passing mention. The first are those statutes that deal with the prostitute herself. There is little sense to most laws concerning sex, when viewed in the light of modern penal science as applied in other areas of crime. But at least there is some justice in the fact that the prostitute, who pays the most in a certain sense of the word, receives the least penalty (usually a moderate fine and/or a few months in jail) in comparison to the penalties listed in the statutes discussed thus far. In a few states, rehabilitation programs are being set in motion whereby, upon conviction, the prostitute may dissociate herself from the illicit organization she may have been a part of. However, if she is subsequently proved guilty of loitering for the purposes of prostitution, the penalty will be higher than she would otherwise receive.

The second type of statute still to be reviewed is notable because of its absence in the laws of most states—namely, the statute concerning the crime the customer commits when he uses a prostitute. Even in those states that make it illegal for any person to enter a house or a place for the purpose of prostitution, the customer has been ignored by the courts on the ground that the statute applies to only those who are engaged in making prostitution available to the customer, such as the pimps, the procurers, and the prostitutes. Only about eight states have laws that specifically define the customer's use of a prostitute as a crime, and in those states there are very few convictions. Many authorities believe that if the customer were prosecuted "big business" prostitution and the bribing of public officials by "ring" heads would come to a swift end, since the high-paying customers would become discouraged. Evidence that law-enforcement agencies seem to be protecting the customer, thus perpetuating "big business" prostitution, is strengthened by the fact that, in states that do not have specifically designed "customer" statutes, the customer could be indicted and convicted under other general statutes—such as the disorderly conduct statutes, lewd behavior statutes, the aiding-and-abetting-the-commission-of-a-crime type of statute, and many others—and yet, by and large, is not. The prostitute is continuously, and often unconstitutionally, arrested and convicted, while the customer, her partner in crime—at least as defined by our law—is rarely, if ever, even arrested.

Incest

Simply defined, incest is copulation of a man and a woman who are related to each other in any of the degrees within which marriage is prohibited by law. As simple a crime as incest seems to be, confusions, disparities, and unnecessary complexities exist within the incest statutes of the various states. For example, some states have a single statute to cover the acts of incestuous *sexual intercourse* and of *intermarriage* of prohibited relations. In other states statutes distinguish between the two acts to the extent of considering incestuous sexual intercourse a grave crime and the act of incestuous marriage a minor one. In one state the maximum penalty for incestuous marriage is a $500 fine and/or six months in prison, whereas the maximum penalty for incestuous sexual intercourse is ten years. In another state, which has the same differentiation, the maximum penalty for incestuous marriage is three years, and for incestuous sexual intercourse, twenty years. The highest penalty in any state for incest is fifty years' imprisonment.

Other Forms of Sexual Behavior

Thus far we have dealt with laws concerning various aspects of sexual intercourse. But other forms of sexual expression are also legally restricted.

Masturbation

There are no laws in any state that prohibit masturbation. But there are two very important qualifications to this statement. The first concerns mutual masturbation. A number of states include mutual masturbation in the sodomy or "crime-against-nature" statute by specifically mentioning it. Other statutes are so broad that by implication mutual masturbation—whether practiced by man and man, woman and woman, man and woman, single or married—would be illegal and therefore subject to the same penalty (which is severe) provided for the crime of sodomy.

The second exception to the apparent legality of masturbation is the requirement of privacy while practicing it. A person who masturbates in public, or in an area where someone might see him, would be convicted of indecent exposure and, in some jurisdictions, for the additional crime of masturbating in public.

The act of masturbation is indirectly represented in at least half of the statutes that are usually referred to as "obscenity" statutes. Any article that is specifically designed for masturbating is labeled under the law as an "indecent article" and to manufacture, sell, or offer it—or even to possess it for the purpose of using it—is deemed illegal.

Masturbation is nowhere directly listed as a ground for divorce, but there are cases on record in which forcing a wife to watch the husband masturbate has been considered as evidence of extreme cruelty on the part of the husband, thus, in those jurisdictions where extreme cruelty is a legal cause of divorce, granting the wife a divorce.

Sodomy and
Crime-against-Nature Statutes

Of all statute titles, those of "sodomy" and "crime-against-nature" are the most misleading. For contained within these statutes are forms of sexual expression that are described, condoned, and in fact in most instances prescribed by leading authorities on marriage. In spite of this, these activities still remain on the illegal side of the law books—with heavy penalties attached thereto.

Here again each state has its own way of alluding to the acts contained in the statute and covered by it. In some jurisdictions reference to the term sodomy or crime against nature is made, while in others each act included under these terms is spelled out in detail. Originally sodomy was defined as the connection of the penis with the rectum, as practiced by males with each other in the ancient town of Sodom. The act of sodomy at common law was considered an act against nature, so that crime against nature was considered synonymous with sodomy. But gradually the definition of crime against nature became more and more encompassing, until today we have a typical statute that, although it is entitled a sodomy statute, includes many acts that are technically not sodomy. For example, note the wording of a typical statute:

Every person who shall carnally know, or shall have sexual intercourse in any manner with any animal or bird, or shall carnally know any male or female by the anus (rectum) or with the mouth or tongue; or shall attempt intercourse with a dead body is guilty of Sodomy.

Thus we find that pederasty, bestiality, buggery, fellation, cunnilinctus, and several other practices such as mutual masturbation are combined under the term of sodomy or crime against nature, either by specific reference or by implication. So vague are the statutes in many jurisdictions that the decision of what is and is not a crime against nature is entirely within the judge's discretion. As yet there seems to be no reflection in the statutes of modern-day thought and attitudes in regard to sexual forms of expression. Leading sex authorities therefore find themselves in the position of committing a crime when they advise, even for therapeutic reasons, practices that are actually against the law. For to advise an illegal act is in and of itself a violation.

Two states would seem to have no sodomy statute, and yet in one is a statute labeled the "lascivious acts" statute, which declares in effect that whoever commits any unnatural or lascivious act is guilty of a felony and is subject to a maximum term of five years and/or a maximum fine of $1,000. The other state has a law described as an "act relating to sex perverts," which covers the same area. This would indeed indicate that "sodomy" by any other name is sodomy plus many other practices.

The penalties for sodomy run as high as imprisonment for from sixty years to life, and in one state the minimum punishment is life imprisonment at hard labor. (This state, which prescribes life at hard labor for a husband and wife who express themselves sexually in a way deemed by the law as "against nature," at the same time would punish one who has intercourse with an animal with a prison term of only five years.) In no state is a distinction made between sodomy committed by persons married to one another and sodomy committed by persons not married to each other.

It should be added by way of final note that attempts to revise these statutes have been made by all the important law-revision committees in the United States and England, with little or no success as yet. For the laws as they now read seriously interfere with and actually hamper those who work in the fields of psychiatry, marriage counseling, and law enforcement. Eminent jurists such as Judge Learned Hand have long urged the revision of these laws so that the realm of personal privacy can be protected from futile and fumbling attempts at needless law enforcement.

Homosexual Behavior

Being a homosexual is not in and of itself illegal, but the problem does not end there. For when the homosexual expresses himself sexually with another male, his methods violate one or more laws already described in previous sections of this article—those concerned with mutual masturbation, the connection of the penis with the mouth, and the connection of the penis with the rectum. He is therefore subject to the same pertinent laws previously described.

But something more should be said about the administration of these laws. In many large cities homosexuals are apprehended by means of entrapment, even though entrapment is generally held to be unconstitutional. Police officers, working in pairs and in plain clothes, frequent bars, parks, and other areas where homosexuals are known to congregate and make themselves available as homosexual pickups. The moment a homosexual makes an active move in the direction of a pickup he is arrested by the disguised police officers and charged with loitering for the purpose of picking up a partner for homosexual activity. In many cases the police officer, in an effort to improve his "arrest" record, does not wait for the homosexual to make the pickup, but instead picks up the homosexual himself and, when the homosexual responds or acquiesces, immediately arrests him, as if the homosexual had made the initial advance. In almost no jurisdiction is psychiatric treatment available to the convicted deviate. He is usually given a suspended sentence after the first conviction, and 30 or 90 days in prison after the second—then thrown back on the streets again in a much worse condition, psychologically speaking.

Although laws against the practice of homosexuality theoretically can be applied to Lesbian behavior as well as to practices between two males, there as yet seem to be no cases where Lesbians have actually been arrested and prosecuted for engaging in relations with members of their own sex. Perhaps because no actual coitus can take place between two females and because no seed is actually "wasted," society has almost invariably taken a more permissive attitude toward Lesbianism than it has toward male homosexuality.

Obscene and Lewd Behavior

There are all kinds of statutes concerned with behavior that is classified by law as obscene. A number of states find it necessary to create a special statute for "Peeping Toms," even though such activity could be amply covered by the disorderly-conduct statute. In most "Peeping Tom" statutes no distinction is made concerning the sex of the peeper and the one he peeps upon, but one state makes peeping a crime only if the person spied upon is a female.

Some states have statutes making it a crime if animals such as horses, donkeys, cattle, and goats are permitted to mate within a certain number of feet of or in view of a school, public street, church, private home, or tavern. In some jurisdictions the penalty for permitting such an offense can go as high as a fine of $1,000 or one year in prison, or both.

Obscene talk in a public place or over a telephone can bring arrest and imprisonment. One state has a statute making it a crime to talk in an obscene manner over the telephone to a female telephone operator. Writing lewd letters to females (in some states, to anyone) can bring the author a fine of as much as $1,000 and three years' imprisonment.

There are also statutes specifically designed for the wall-and-fence artist. In fact, in one state the penalty is up to five years in prison for drawing an obscene picture on a public fence or wall.

Writing, printing, publishing, distributing, lending, renting, and selling books, pictures, pamphlets, films, figures, or images of an obscene and lascivious nature are usually all lumped together in one huge and vague statute. Such laws, despite their vagueness (which is often a reason for a statute being declared unconstitutional), have been held constitutional and are considered as part of the police powers of each state.

The continuous struggle to keep freedom of thought and speech from being curtailed by censorship by police officials, private groups (as self-appointed censors), state licensing boards, and commissioners has resulted in countless numbers of court decisions. If anything, these have further complicated the legal conception of what is, and what is not, obscene. Despite certain important decisions that have somewhat narrowed the definition of obscenity, what will be considered obscene in any particular court decision is still as unpredictable as it ever was. A film made within the shadow of the Vatican and approved by the Pope was nevertheless held to be obscene and sacrilegious by a license commissioner in an American city. A book, long accepted as one of the greatest ever written, was suddenly deemed unmailable. Scientific material on a study of sex, destined for a world-renowned scientist, was held up for three years by the U.S. Customs authorities. It has been said by many authorities in the field of the law of censorship that,

had the Holy Bible been written today, the most we could hope for would be an expurgated edition—if it could be published and distributed at all.

In the more liberal decisions of late, the obscenity of a book is usually determined by whether or not, as a whole, it tends to excite lustful desires. In other words, if the book as a whole has artistic merit but certain portions are obscene, it will not be held to be obscene—at least not in those jurisdictions that subscribe to the more liberal type of decision.

The confiscation of obscene material is handled by federal, state, and city or town officials. Police departments, post office police, license boards, city and state censor boards, and self-appointed censorship groups determine whether films, books, or magazines are criminally obscene. The main issue is always whether freedom of the press and freedom of speech are being curtailed or whether the censoring group—private or public—is acting within the police powers of the particular jurisdiction.

Because of the vagueness of the definition of obscene, it is always difficult for a lawyer to predict for a writer, publisher, or producer what will be deemed obscene by a court. It is therefore equally difficult for writers, artists, and other creators of artistic and literary forms to know where the bounds of art and obscenity begin and end.

Many jurisdictions have statutes that are entitled, with variations, "lewd and obscene behavior." These statutes are vague and all-encompassing and in general read as follows: "Any person who shall be guilty of open lewdness, or any notorious act of public indecency tending to debauch the morals and manners of the people, or who shall in private be guilty of an act of lewdness or carnal indecency. . . ." In some jurisdictions having such a statute the penalty can go as high as five years' imprisonment with an additional fine of $2,500, and in a few jurisdictions a lewd defendant can be sentenced to ten years behind bars.

This type of statute is most often used in the "almost-but-not-quite" kind of crime: an unmarried couple live together, but there is insufficient evidence of sexual intercourse to bring a conviction for the crime of adultery; two males are arrested under suspicious circumstances, such as both being in the nude and intoxicated, but there is no ascertainable evidence that sodomy has been committed; a man and woman are apprehended in a parked automobile, but the crime of fornication has not yet been actually committed. The statute at times has been used in legal battles waged by husbands and wives against each other. For example, one spouse will cause the arrest of the other spouse under this statute, thereby trying to force a cash settlement in some pending civil action between the two.

The Lawless Area

Two major categories illustrate the "lawless" area of sex: artificial insemination and the changing of one's sex. The word "lawless" is used here in a very narrow sense, for in these categories certain laws are enforced. However, these laws are not appropriate to or written specifically for these areas of "sexual behavior." Rather, they consist of old laws applied to a new subject. For example, most authorities agree that artificial insemination has certain legal dangers that can be avoided by means of appropriate laws, and that it is ridiculous to hold (as several courts have done) that a woman who has been artificially inseminated by her doctor has committed adultery—to say nothing of the fact that this in no way makes the practice of artificial insemination legally safer.

The husband, the wife, the donor, the doctor, and the resulting child are all in need of the protection that only suitable legislation can bring them, for difficult legal questions are involved. For example: Could the child claim support from the donor? Could the husband of the wife impregnated by the semen of a donor refuse to be liable for the support of the child? To what extent can a doctor be held liable if a child resulting from artificial insemination is defective in mind or body? Since a birth certificate is supposed to state the name of the child's father, is it legal to place the husband's name on the certificate instead of the donor's? In a divorce situation, does the father have the right to claim visitation of a child resulting from artificial insemination? These are only a few of the more troublesome types of questions that arise.

Misapplication of the law can also be observed in those cases in which a person, by having the penis and testicles removed, assumes the sex of a female. There is still much to be learned regarding the desire to change one's sex, and there is a need for some kind of regulation for the protection of such a person, as well as of the doctors who perform such an operation. But at the present time there is no specifically designed form of regulation to apply to the psychiatric and medical requirements inherent in this situation.

Several jurisdictions, for example, will prosecute a doctor who performs such an operation under what is called the "maiming" statute. This statute dates back to Medieval England, when each lord of the manor had a private army of his own and fighting men were at a premium. It was therefore made a punishable offense for one person to injure a "fighting limb" of another, thereby incapacitating him as a soldier. The penis can hardly be regarded as a "fighting limb," and as a matter of fact there are cases on record holding that it is not to be so regarded. All this, none the less, has not prevented several district attorneys from using this law in the way described above.

Conclusion

The majority of authorities in the fields of sex and law recognize the need for a change in laws that apply to sex, but thus far little has been done toward this end. Instead of changing the laws, it has been the practice of courts and law-enforcement bodies simply to ignore them. It goes without saying that ignoring a law is not the same as amending it, or legally nullifying it. Failure to enforce existing laws in effect breaks down public respect both for the observed and for the ignored laws.

Many law-enforcement authorities and law-revision committees have taken the position that laws concerning sexual behavior should be confined to three major areas: (1) sexual acts that involve the use of force or the threat of force; (2) sexual acts performed in public; (3) sexual acts that involve minors. According to these authorities, all other laws concerning sexual behavior should be eliminated as being unenforceable, useless, antiquated, inapplicable, and generally not within the province of law enforcement in the first place. Although a number of important studies have been made on the subject, all of them coming to approximately the same conclusions as those just stated, to date they have had little effect on the state legislatures.

References

Cases and Readings on Law and Society. American Casebook Series. St. Paul: West Publishing Co., 1948-1949.

Chesser, Eustace, *Sexual Behavior, Normal and Abnormal.* New York: Roy Pub., 1949.

Corpus Juris, Vols. 1, 27, 50, 53, 67. New York: American Law Book Co., 1914-1937.

Drummond, Isabel, *The Sex Paradox.* New York: G. B. Putnam's Sons, 1953.

Ellis, Albert, and Brancale, Ralph, *The Psychology of Sex Offenders.* Springfield, Ill.: Charles C Thomas, Pub., 1956.

Ernst, Morris, and Lindey, Alexander, *The Censor Marches On.* New York: Doubleday, Doran, 1940.

Guttmacher, M. S., and Weihofen, H., *Psychiatry and the Law.* New York: W. W. Norton & Co., Inc., 1952.

Hall, Gladys M., *Prostitution in the Modern World.* New York: Emerson Books, Inc., 1936.

Karpman, Benjamin, *The Sexual Offender and His Offenses.* New York: Julian Press, Inc., 1954.

Plowscowe, Morris, *Sex and the Law.* Englewood Cliffs, N. J.: Prentice-Hall, Inc., 1951.

Reinhardt, James Melvin, *Sex Perversions and Sex Crimes.* Springfield, Ill.: Charles C Thomas, Pub., 1957.

Sherwin, Robert V., *Sex and the Statutory Law.* New York: Oceana Pub., 1949.

Sherwin, Robert V., "Some Legal Aspects of Homosexuality." *Internat. J. Sexology 4;* 22-26, 1950.

Sherwin, Robert V., "Sex Expression and the Law. I. The Law of Rape." *Internat. J. Sexology 4;* 206-210, 1951.

Sherwin, Robert V., "Sex Expression and the Law. II Sodomy: A Medico-Legal Enigma." *Internat. J. Sexology 5;* 3-13, 1951.

Sherwin, Robert V., "Prostitution: A Study of Law and Disorder." *Internat. J. Sexology 5;* 201-205, 1952.

Vollmer, August, *The Police and Modern Society.* Stanford, Calif.: Bureau of Public Administration, University of California, 1936.

Williams, Glanville, *The Sanctity of Life and the Criminal Law.* New York: Alfred A. Knopf, Inc., 1957.

ROBERT VEIT SHERWIN

Literature and Sex

FOR the purposes of this article we use the word "sex" to describe the whole range of instinctive responses, actions, and repressions that move from the erotic impulse. By "erotic" we mean all that is related to love, using the word in its pure Greek sense, ἐρωτικός, as covering all areas of experience over which Eros holds sway.

We use the word "literature" to describe the body of writing that has survived the test of time and is generally accepted as having universal appeal for its form, its content, and its genius.

We treat "contemporary writing" separately because, although none of us can confidently foretell which of it will take its place in literature, we seek enlightenment on its significance for us and our times through exploring its relationship to the ageless sources of literary expression.

Our discussion will proceed by way of four approaches: (1) Portrayal of sex in literature; (2) the erotic motive in literature; (3) sublimation of sex in literature; and (4) sex in contemporary writing.

Portrayal of Sex in Literature

Unveiled portrayal of sex has characterized the writing of some periods and places while evasion and disguise of direct sex references have been the marks of others.

The two ancient literatures that have exercised the greatest influence on our literary history differed radically from each other at one fundamental level. In Greece the erotic was almost entirely directed to homosexual affection; among the Hebrews it was almost entirely restricted to heterosexual affection. Their writings, however, have one characteristic in common. They both abound in the frank treatment of sex.

Treatment of sex in Greek literature takes its emphasis from the fact that homosexuality reached an unparalleled extension and intensity among the Greek peoples. This was probably one consequence of their fanatical cult of the body in gymnastics and athletics, but it was also doubtlessly encouraged by powerful influences from the East. Among the Dorians, in Sparta and Crete, pederasty was literally a part of public education. In Athens it was punished only if it involved assault and rape, that is, in circumstances where sex offenses would be punishable anywhere. Greek literature plainly glorifies homosexual love.

The most representative lyric poet of Greece is Pindar, from one of whose poems we take the typical lines:

Right it is to cull love's blossom in due season, in life's prime; but whosoever has seen the rays flashing from the eyes of Theoxenus and does not swell with longing, his black heart was forged of steel and iron at a frozen flame, and Aphrodite honors him not. Either he is busy with all his might about gold, or else, sacrificing his heart to a woman, is borne along every path. But I, for the goddess's sake, waste away like wax of holy bees under the heat of the sun when I look at the young blooming limbs of boys.

His feminine counterpart in Greek literature is Sappho. She, with no more restraint than his, wrote of her love for a girl, a passage that loses nothing by being presented by her as a contrast to the coolness of a bridegroom to the sweet voice and laughter of his bride: "My heart beats, my voice fails, fire runs beneath the skin, the eyes see not, the ears buzz, sweat flows off me, trembling seizes me, and, fading like withered grass, I am as one dead."

Homer, in spite of the fact that the siege of Troy was undertaken because of Helen's unfaithfulness, wrote little about sex, but the most powerful pathos of the *Iliad* is the account of Achilles' dream of Patroclus after this dear friend had been killed: "But stand closer to me," he says, "that embracing each other for a little while, we may indulge in sad lamentation."

The murder of the Athenian tyrant Hipparchus by the two lovers Harmodius and Aristogiton, Alexander's love for Hephaestion, and the Sacred Band of Thebes are familiar literary themes. The gods Apollo, Poseidon, Heracles, and Ganymede were sung as homosexuals. In a world overwhelming him with mystery and despair, Oedipus turns to Theseus in Sophocles' *Oedipus at Colonus* to say: "I have found piety nowhere in the world as with you, and mildness of heart and absence of lies." Everywhere in Greek literature male love is praised and glorified.

Hebrew writing presents a startling contrast. Here the love of a man and a woman is the glorified affection. But never far below the surface of its portrayal is the dark undertone of its potential tragedy.

The Bible begins with the beautiful pastoral of the man and the woman in the Garden— the simple imagination of perfect love in a world at peace throughout its whole creation. This is the vision that forever afterwards haunts the memory of all Hebrew writers about love. We see its rosy glow in the story of Jacob and Rachel and in the idyll of Ruth.

No sooner is the story of the beatific Garden told, however, than the serpent enters, and there comes into the writing a bitter consciousness of the mingling of lust with love that drove the man and woman from Eden and confounded sex with disobedience to God, making it all but synonymous with sin. From that point forward, love and sin move side by side in Hebrew literature, inseparable companions frankly and realistically described. The love of Abraham for Sarah is tenderly told, but her beauty leads him to lie to Pharaoh, and his

dynastic ambition, reinforced by his belief in its divine sanction, causes him to turn to Hagar's bed that he may have a son. David, Jehovah's favorite from his youth, handsome, heroic, and altogether kingly, lusts for Bathsheba and commits murder that he may have her.

The moral dualism of the "knowledge of good and evil" permeates Hebrew writing. Sex poses one of the dominating moral problems with which it deals, and it portrays sex with unrepressed candor. Nowhere in literature is there plainer speaking about a sexually perverse society than in the descriptions of the cities of the plain, Sodom and Gomorrah. Never was rivalry between brothers for a woman more vividly summed up than in the swift murder of his brother Adonijah by Solomon for making a bid for the Shunammite woman.

The symbols of love are frequently used to describe the bonds of God and man in Hebrew hymns. In The Song of Songs the lover hymns his beloved for her own sake. He finds the world in her—she is a vineyard; she is in the clefts of the rock and the hidden hollow of the cliff. Her breasts are as walls with towers, her eyes like doves, her hair like a flock of straying goats, her teeth like washed ewes, her lips like a scarlet thread, her temples like pomegranates, her neck like the tower of David, the curves of her thighs like links of a chain, her navel like a king's goblet, her belly like a heap of wheat set among lilies. The lover himself is described hardly less fulsomely. And the embrace of the lovers is like a tree which the lover climbs, taking hold of the branches and finding in her breasts clusters of the vine and in her breath the odor of apples. Readers of this love song needed no interpreter to explain its images.

The greatest of Hebrew dramas, the Book of Job, deals with a theological question and has no fundamental erotic undertones. Greek drama, on the other hand, although restrained in overt sexual references because it was written for presentation to huge mixed audiences, is such a profound comment on erotic motivation in human conduct that it served as a treasury from which Freud drew some of the most comprehensive of his psychoanalytical insights.

The candor of the Greek writers was matched

by the Roman, but since Rome was not as infested with homosexuality, Roman writers speak more emphatically of the love of man and woman. Virgil does not hesitate to portray sexual passion realistically, especially when he writes of Venus. The *Ars Amatoria* of Ovid, the Roman Pindar, went so far in its candor that it outraged the Emperor Augustus, then engaged in a program of moral reform, and the poet was banished from the city and sent in exile to the half-barbarian town of Tomi near the mouth of the Danube.

The Middle Ages, which were sex-ridden to an extraordinary degree, produced a frankly erotic literature. The Arthurian Cycle and the romance of Tristan and Iseult stand as the outstanding examples. Ecclesiastical records are full of stories of bishops disciplining clergy who were faithless to their vows of celibacy, and these faithless acts are told with unflinching candor. Out of this struggle between the flesh and celibacy emerged the beautiful love story of Héloïse and Abélard, the details of which were sung by many minstrels. When Andreas Capellanus attempted to bring some sort of discipline into the sex habits of the twelfth century with his *Rules of Courtly Love,* he described love as a "certain inborn suffering derived from the sight of and excessive meditation upon the beauty of the opposite sex," and told of the abuses of his time as he laid down the maxims for their cure. Medieval preoccupation with sex reached its most artistic expression in the *Decameron* of Boccaccio, which set the pattern both in form and content for much of the literature that followed it.

Chaucer led the way out of the Middle Ages in England with his *Canterbury Tales* and *Troilus and Cressida. Troilus and Cressida* is full of sex symbolism, but the Tale of the *Wife of Bath,* the *Miller's Tale,* and the *Reeve's Tale* in the *Canterbury Tales* go beyond symbolism to overt sexual expressions. Chaucer had as few inhibitions as Boccaccio.

In France, Montaigne started modern French literature on its way with essays that included some calculated, as he said, to drive his essays out of ladies' parlors into their boudoirs. He set the tone and largely established the conventionally accepted vocabulary with which French literature has uniquely treated matters of sex in the intervening four hundred years, with only the temporary lapse into conventionality that marked the reign of Louis XIV.

English literature has had a more varied experience. The immediate successors of Chaucer wrote freely of sex throughout the Elizabethan period, but the Puritan Commonwealth brought an inevitable taboo. The Restoration of the Stuarts under Charles II, in turn, brought a reaction that gave English writing its frankest sexual expression prior to our own times. With the Great Rebellion of 1688, which put the Whigs firmly in the saddle, a more sober mood prevailed, settling down to a conventionality that reached its all-pervading height in the Age of Victoria and from which English and American writing truly began to emerge in the last generation. Thus, England and the United States were "under wraps" in the area of sexual expression for a century and a half—from Fielding and Sterne to James Joyce and D. H. Lawrence.

These men found in English literature no such accepted and classically correct vocabulary for descriptions of sex as the French had worked out, and part of the effort of the past fifty years has been to escape coarseness while not evading candor. The nineteenth-century taboo on sex in English writing has now bowed to a freedom unprecedented in American and English literature.

The Erotic Motive in Literature

Every book is an autobiography in the sense that no writer can keep himself out of what he writes. His unconscious reveals itself, and by careful scrutiny of his works one is able to uncover his unconscious motivations. Among these, erotic motivations have always been present, and their perception can in many cases go far to explain the origin and form of the writing itself. A book is not an accident. It is determined by the nature and experience of its author.

The name Homer, for example, may stand for one or for many men, but the profile of a distinct human being confronts us from one famous passage of the *Iliad,* the dream of Achilles about Patroclus in the twenty-third book. The most powerful passion of Achilles was friendship, and here we have the story of his grief over the death of his dearest friend—his lover. The language is so poignant, the self-accusations so personal, and the grief so moving that there can be no doubt that here the poet is remembering a loss of his own. Of this poet hidden in antiquity we can say without a doubt that he once loved supremely and suffered the loss of his beloved.

More subtle is Ovid's self-revelation in the third book of his *Amores,* where he tells of a dream in which he saw a crow peck at the breast of a white cow standing beside a bull and carry off a white hair. The cow, black envy in her heart, left her mate and went over to some other bulls. The interpretation given of the dream is that the white cow was Ovid's mistress, the bull himself, and the crow a procuress who would tempt his mistress to desert him. The passage is interesting because it forecasts Freud's interpretations of dreams, but our point here is that the incident came into literature out of the erotic fears of the poet, fears that, we may say, were later justified when Ovid's mistress did indeed leave him.

A more familiar example of the erotic motive within a poet is Dante. He met Beatrice when they were both 9 years old in the year 1274. He saw her only once afterwards, and she died when she was 25 years old. Two years after her death he married. But all through his later years he cherished the memory of Beatrice as the ideal of perfect love, and this erotic image became the source as well as the symbol of his great imaginative work.

Petrarch, Dante's successor in Italian poetry, worked by much the same erotic symbolism. When he was 23 in 1327 he saw Laura for the first time. She died twenty-one years later. He continued to live twenty-six years more. Yet throughout his life he wrote his love poems to her. Must we say that for forty-seven years he continued in passionate love for her? The evidence is somewhat against it for he had two illegitimate children even before she died. Rather, we must say that, as Dante sang the ideal of perfect love, Petrarch sang the ideal of faithful love.

In La Rochefoucauld we get a revelation of that very deep level of the unconscious, self-love—the egotism that lies close to the root of all emotions. He is generally known as a cynic, but this is a tribute to his awareness that life is acceptable to most men only through a process of self-deception, the other side of this coin being that such deception becomes itself responsible for personal and social evils. We cannot but hear echoes of our own unconscious in such phrases as, "Men would not live long in society were they not dupes of each other," "Wit sometimes enables us to act rudely with impunity," and, "When our vices leave us we flatter ourselves with the idea we have left them." "It is well that we know not all our wishes," he said, a pre-Freudian recognition of the unconscious.

Another kind of erotic motivation in literature is shown in writing that takes on the character of confession. We are familiar with it in St. Augustine. It came into modern vogue with two influential novels of the second half of the eighteenth century, Rousseau's *Nouvelle Héloïse* (1760) and Goethe's *Sorrows of Werther* (1774). Rousseau sought in art what he had not known in reality, for he tells us in his *Confessions* that he had reached the age of 45 before he realized that he had never enjoyed true love. Goethe, on the other hand, made literature out of experience, so that we know his Charlotte, his Frederica, and his Frau von Stein as we also know himself as Werther, Faust, and Wilhelm Meister. Goethe found in his writing a catharsis, his comment on Werther being: "I felt as if I had made a general confession and was once more free and happy, and justified in beginning a new life."

Goethe's genius inspired a train of successors who owed much to him for their ways of recording their love troubles; among them were Byron, Madame de Staël, George Sand. Byron is perhaps the most typical. Like Schopenhauer, he had unhappy relations with his mother which flared into violent quarrels. His reaction was one of intense love for his sister, Mrs. Augusta Leigh, for whom his passion was so great that it became a matter of scandal, although the alleged incest was probably never consummated. His true love was for Mary Chaworth, whose marriage to another man was the heartbreak of his life. His marriage proved unhappy and, after separation, he sought consolation in his various mistresses, the most noted being Mariana Segati with whom he lived from November, 1816, to February, 1818. The influences of all these emotional complications sound throughout his work which, indeed, reveals symptoms of hysteria. His last lines conclude: "Love dwells not in our will/ Nor can I blame thee, though it be my lot/ To strongly, wrongly, love thee still." He carried his erotic wounds to the end.

Powerful love for a sister played its formative part in other writers. Shelley was brokenhearted when he realized that his sister had passed from under his influence, and we get an echo of his tragedy in the first edition of the *Revolt of Islam* in which he made Laon and Cynthia, brother and sister, lovers. In his preface he declared that he could not see why the innocent love of brother and sister should be distasteful. In *Rosalind and Helen* he tells of a spot where a sister and brother had loved and their child was born, only to be torn to pieces by a mob, their ghosts forever haunting the scene.

A gentler influence of brother-sister love worked upon the writings of Wordsworth, Lamb, and Renan. Wordsworth lived always with the memory of Marie-Anne Vallon, by whom he had an illegitimate daughter in his youth in France, but whom he could not marry for good reasons. He took refuge in his sister Dorothy's company, and in his life with her drew upon her quiet strength for much of his inspiration. She was his eyes and ears, as he himself says, in the observations of nature that mark his writing, and she undoubtedly influenced him toward the respectability that kept reference to sex out of his writing and later turned him back to a conservative view of men and affairs. Lamb's love and care for his sister is one of the beautiful stories of the literary world. He watched over her during her fits of insanity, even after she had killed their mother in one of them, and together they collaborated in the writing of plays and poems. Renan's devotion to his sister Henrietta had much of the quality of Wordsworth's to Dorothy. His love for her and his mother kept him a Christian although he was a freethinker, and his *Life of Christ* shows signs of feminine influence, if not

of femininity in himself, in its portrayal of this profound subject.

The Brontë family provides a rich example of sisters and a brother who mutually influence each other, but the prevailing erotic impulse in Charlotte's writing was her love for M. Heger, her married teacher in Brussels whom she was forced to renounce and leave. The echoes of this disappointment cry out from all her books in one place or another, with the whole story being most fully told in *Villette*. In the twenty-first chapter of *Jane Eyre* she recounts a dream that is undoubtedly an unconscious report of her own disappointment when she found herself married to a man she did not love, and without the children she so earnestly had hoped to have. Her characters take their place alongside Werther and Hedda Gabler among the sex sufferers of literature.

Balzac presents another side of the unconscious. Always hard up for money, he continually sought for schemes to make him rich and to rid himself of his debts. Unconsciously he undoubtedly entertained ideas for gaining fame, love, and riches by some swift means, even though immoral. He repressed them, but they emerged in some of his strongest characters—Eugene Rastignac, Vautrin, Jacques Collins, and others—who were either villains in themselves or felt themselves tempted greatly by their evil companions. Inner conflict bursts often through the writing of this greatest of French novelists, and Eugene gives it clear voice in his cry: "Silence, sir! I will not hear you any more; you make me doubt myself." It is a cry that we know might have come not only from the soul of Balzac, but also from that of Dostoevski, Stendhal, and D'Annunzio, as Raskolnikoff, Julian Sorel, and George Aurispa.

Of somewhat the same temperament as men such as these but with another kind of psychological drive was Edgar Allan Poe. His character is too complex for analysis here, but briefly, having lost his mother in infancy, he evidently identified the womb and the grave in his unconscious; thus was evolved his preoccupation with stories of burial alive, such as *The Cask of Amontillado, The Black Cat,* and *Tales of the Grotesque and Arabesque. The Fall of the House of Usher* is a morbid reaction against the libido, and the dead figure of the sister moving from her grave to drag her brother to death while the whole house collapses about them is the expression of a psychosis originating in repression and reacting with fear.

Baudelaire was Poe's most fervent admirer, and his *Les Fleurs du Mal* echo Poe in many ways, but they also introduce us to another erotic manifestation among the writers of the later nineteenth century. This was the cult of the Love of Little Girls. It originated at Oxford where professors entertained small girls at tea parties. Among its literary voices were W. E. Henley, Francis Thompson, Robert Louis Stevenson, and Algernon Swinburne. Ernest Dowson, at the age of 25, saw the 12-year-old daughter of the proprietor of a Soho restaurant as she passed among the tables, fell in love with her instantly, and, despite her refusal of him, loved her till his early death. His story reminds us of Spinoza who lived all his life with a frustrated love for a little Christian girl. In 1909 Björnstjerne Björnson wrote of an adult man's love for a little girl in *When the New Wine Blooms*. Robert Browning wrote of similar love in his *Evelyn Hope*.

Stevenson also uncovers other erotic impulses in his *A Chapter on Dreams*. He is one of many writers who more or less anticipated Freud with analyses of these phenomena. They include Locke, Hobbes, Browne, Addison, Hunt, Dickens, and Lafcadio Hearn. The one who came closest to the Freudian insight was William Hazlitt in his essay *On Dreams*, in which he speaks of repression and of how "in dreams when we are off our guard [our passions and imaginations] return securely and unbidden." Freud has given his own interpretation of the dream of Jensen's *Gradiva*. Similar dreams from which literature has grown are Gautier's *Arria Marcella*, Stevenson's account of a dream in his *Across the Plains*, Kipling's *The Brushwood Boy, They*, and *The Dream of Duncan Parrenness*. A complete account of the dreams of literature would compel us to begin with Homer and the Bible and to come through Apuleius and Cicero, all the medieval writings, and the confessions of the saints to the present time. Plato has an eloquent passage on dreams in the Ninth Book of *The Republic*.

Related to the dream experience and also opening a long and broad look into the motivations of writers is the revelation in literature of the Oedipus complex. Cowper's poem "On the Receipt of My Mother's Picture" is a good example, and we find it evident in many passages of Stendhal, Shelley, Schopenhauer, Keats, and Lafcadio Hearn. Little as we know of the personal life of Shakespeare, we can say with certainty that the intense love Hamlet held for his father's memory and its powerful reaction upon his love-hate for his mother could not have been so memorably portrayed by a man to whom these passions were totally foreign in his own life.

An interesting contrast is Dickens, upon whom his mother seems to have had little influence at all. His was a love for two women, Maria Bradnell, his boyhood sweetheart who rejected him, and Mary Hogarth, his wife's sister who died young. They are the prototypes of the female puppets who fill his books. He reacted against the weak women who touched his life by his presentation of the marvelous male characters whose uniqueness reveals his genius.

The two outstanding poets who were Dickens' contemporaries, Tennyson and Browning, were part of the Victorian era to which open expression of sex was denied. But with them sex symbolism is almost as revelatory as would be frank speech. Tennyson, for example, says that he would like to be the jewel in the miller's daughter's ear that he might touch her neck, the girdle round her waist to clasp it "so close and tight," and the necklace on her bosom where he would "lie so light, so light." Browning is more explicit, as when he talks in *The Ring and the Book* of "so white, so warm, so wonderful between the breasts." In *The Last Ride Together* he says: "We ride together and I see her bosom heave," and continually reverts to the symbolism of the ride: "I and she ride together," "Riding's a joy." This whole poem is an excellent example of the unconscious use of symbolism in literature. It has a long tradition. Ben Jonson finds his rose "smells not of itself but thee." Many passages of Milton have a clear symbolic overtone. Shakespeare avails himself of the pun to suggest the sexual reference. Dowson, later than Tennyson and Browning, and more decadent, suggests that he thinks only of his true love while loving others when he writes: "I have loved thee, Cynara, after my fashion."

Not as its sole inspiration but as a powerful creative impulse the erotic motive runs through all literature.

Sublimation of Sex in Literature

Sublimation is the substitution, often unconscious, of a socially acceptable, even laudable, act or expression for one considered morally or socially reprehensible.

The clearest examples of sublimation of the sex instinct in literature appear in religious writings in which the love of the believer is turned to God and his devotion expressed in sublimated erotic terms. Thomas à Kempis and other devotional writers express their lavish love for the object of their adoration in terms elsewhere reserved to carnal lovers. Many hymns carry the same tone, notable examples being Charles Wesley's "Wrestling Jacob" and "Jesus, Lover of My Soul." Pascal and Renan offer other examples. In the world of fiction Tolstoi has magnificently painted a scene of sublimation in his account of the meeting of Alexandrei Alexandrovich and Vronsky at the bedside of Anna Karenina. The interplay of sexual terms and religious expression can be seen throughout all devotional writing.

Specific erotic motivations are also sublimated in literature.

Homosexuality is sublimated in the *Symposium* of Plato, and fully explored in the same temper by Pater ("the lover has become lover of the invisible, but still a lover") in *Plato and Platonism*. The immortal elegies—*Lycidas, Thyrsis, In Memoriam, Adonais*—celebrate the love of man for man. Leonardo writes of his loves in sublime terms, and Shakespeare sings of his in his sonnets. Whitman sublimates his into songs of men and universal brotherhood. Pater portrays *Marius the Epicurean* and Wilde *Dorian Gray*.

Exhibitionism finds sublimation in the tales of Boccaccio and Rabelais, the stories of Sterne and Fielding, *The Droll Tales* of Balzac, and the papers of Boswell.

Egotism speaks in the *Orations* of Cicero, the *Essays* of Montaigne, and the *Confessions* of Rousseau.

Hate finds classic expression in Ovid, Dante, Pope, Swift, Poe, and William Butler.

Sadism receives literary sublimation not only from the Marquis of Sade but also from historic writings, with their accounts of persecutions and tortures, and from such masters as Poe and Hardy with their tortured souls.

Masochism moved the pen of Proust to some of his most unforgettable passages that tell of his suffering and despair. It is also present in Rousseau. Letters of writers abound in it, as the authors dwell upon their disappointments and despairs, the letters of Keats containing notable examples.

Narcissism rises to the level of poetry in Whitman. Plato puts it into the character of Alcibiades. There is much of it not far below the surface of much controversial and autobiographical writing. Men such as Gibbon and Thackeray give evidence of it in their footnotes and asides, in which they hold mirrors up to themselves.

Sex in Contemporary Writing

Since the French discarded the proprieties of the age of Louis XIV they have been writing directly about sex, and have developed a technique and vocabulary for doing so. English and American writing at the beginning of this century had neither, for sex had been taboo since the middle of the eighteenth century. It was about 1910 that writers in English began to respond to the impact of the avant-garde ideas and techniques which, during the next two decades, influenced them more than any similar European contact since the seventeenth century.

James Joyce and D. H. Lawrence were the first modern writers in English to use the language of the bar, the street, and the barnyard with the freedom that marked French realistic fiction. The resulting shock, particularly that caused by *Ulysses*, was great, and must have amazed Frenchmen familiar with Zola, Mirabeau, and Huysmans.

In *Lady Chatterley's Lover* Lawrence attempted two things, and largely succeeded in both. He demonstrated how varied and interesting erotic sensations can be and how important is the part they play in the emotional situations involving them. And he tried to solve the problem of how to use words that, although they might offend some people and be unintelligible to others, could yet develop into a conventional and classically abstract vocabulary that would serve English writing for the description of sex as the accepted French vocabulary served writers in that language.

Both *Ulysses* and *Lady Chatterley's Lover* suffered the inevitable condemnation of suppression by the authorities, but they emerged to become influential enough to make it possible for their successors to ignore the restraints the nineteenth century had imposed on sex in writing.

Lawrence proceeded to become a sort of prophet of what he called "the dark gods" and, in his essay on Benjamin Franklin, declared himself emancipated from all conventional inhibitions glorified by that worthy man. Lawrence became a cult. His more naive followers believed that love would become simple and idyllic as soon as man was freed from the artificially cultivated restrictions of the older generation. Lawrence suffered no such illusion. His books, and those of Aldous Huxley who was greatly influenced by him, demonstrate that the personal problems of those emancipated from the old taboos are no less acute than those of their predecessors. *The Plumed Serpent*, with its central erotic-mystical cry, "I am not with you till my serpent has coiled its circle of rest in your belly," is both a violent and tormented book. "Lord," cries Lawrence, "deliver us from this need which can be neither stilled nor satisfied." "The mystery greater than the individual," of which he writes, "the powerful relationship of man to man," is both incomplete and painful. Lawrence could face this. Few others have been able to.

Both Huxley and Joyce first struck a note of daring triumph, with humor interspersed, irony and cynicism being their instruments. Both moved away from this to something like despair, expressing their inability to find satisfaction for their spiritual needs in their animal heritage. Huxley's reaction has been to turn to drugs and other artificial means to heighten his consciousness and otherwise to escape from the harsh realities of inner discontent and frustration.

Upon a generation disillusioned about personal emancipation through sex freedom burst the climactic experience of World War II, revealing the collapse of the old world order and introducing the Nuclear Age with its universal threat against individuality and social permanence. The postwar artist has been forced to create new standards out of the chaos.

Sartre and the Existentialists have turned in one direction. In a world without God they say that all moral values must be developed by man himself. He is free, beyond certain limits, to choose what he shall be and do. His life has significance only in its relation to others. He must "engage himself." Sartre's *Age of Reason* and other novels set this forth. In a similar way Albert Camus has portrayed in his books the hero struggling with the problem of how to "reconcile negative thought and the possibility of affirmative action." In Existentialism is the erotic drive to identification with other men, in conflict with the rational rejection of the philosophic ideal of unity. Camus, in *Actuelles II*, says: "I shall certainly be wary of giving any universal value to an experience which is personal; and this book proposes neither a dogma nor a formal morality. It asserts only, once again, that a morality is possible, and that it costs a good deal."

On the other hand, the younger writers of the Beat Generation and the Angry Young Men seek their answer in "disengagement." "I will take no responsibility" is their repeated declaration. Veronica Hall, in the *Monkey Puzzle*, has her heroine say to a doctor who is driving her in his large, vulgar car: "You're just a lot of infantile masturbators, you car drivers. Eternally frustrated because orgasm is the crash and the crash means death. You're in love with death, an attitude I could never tolerate." This might stand as the criticism of these younger writers by somebody outside them. Norman Mailer, who shares much of their outlook, puts it more sympathetically. He says that man is searching for "love" as he defines it: "Not love as the search for a mate, but love as the search for an orgasm more apocalyptic than the one which preceded it. Orgasm is his therapy—he knows at the seed of his being that good orgasm opens his possibilities and bad orgasm imprisons him." Here is orgasm without "engagement."

Tennessee Williams has made this the theme of his plays, which are terrifying but identifiable tragedies of sex and failure. He writes of neurotics because the neurotic is the key to the normal—the neurotic being normal, only more so. His women cry out for defilement—Blanche, Maggie the Cat, Alma, and Baby Doll; yet they seek to destroy the man who defiles them. Williams is obviously a feminine writer out to revenge himself, but from his private vengeance he lights up the moral disintegration of the worlds of his generation.

The writers of the Beat Generation in the United States—Kerouac, Brossard, Mandel, Solomon, and their fellows—express their sense of this same disintegration. They reject the past and the future, rebel against organized authority, hate the man who plays it safe. They are as Clellon Holmes says, "at the bottom of your personality, looking up." To them the woman is the "chick," manipulatable by generic "man." Their erotic drive is egotistic in a world where they know themselves to be alone and their problem to be to learn to live with their own knowledge.

The Angry Young Men (not a good name for them) in England are in revolt against the Establishment and the elders such as T. S. Eliot who nest in it. Men such as Colin Wilson, Kingsley Amis, and John Osborne speak for a tough intellectualism that questions everything accepted by their society—Labor Party slogans as skeptically as Tory arrogance. They belong to no party, join no groups, serve no "causes." They live in the present, all they can believe in. Theirs is the drive against all in their society that brands them "inferior." They cry for self-realization. They aim their fire wherever conscience dictates, and in their protest against both class and social disintegration they speak for the sovereign individual.

This assertion of the ego against the total social threat is the distinguishing characteristic of the young artist in our time.

The two major intellectual forces that influence the current interpretation of individual human character are those generated by Karl Marx and Sigmund Freud. The one affecting our subject is Freud's view, which envisions the individual as a battleground of inner conflicts whose solutions lie in uncovering their erotic sources, these sources being duly typed and classified by psychoanalysis. Writers, therefore, have often resorted to two expedients: creation of Freudian archetypes and confession. But confession has taken a form different from that of Rousseau or Goethe in that the writer exposes himself as a case study in Freudian terms. He attempts an objective view of sex, examining it clinically within Freudian terms of reference. This is at once more realistic and less spontaneous than the approach of D. H. Lawrence and marks a stage in the absorption of a powerful new idea into works of the imagination. Once this idea has been thoroughly absorbed its techniques will be less obvious and a new literature will emerge in which it will be taken for granted without being so explicit.

In the resulting literature we may expect sex to be at once more liberally defined and more comprehensively portrayed. The exaggerations of the traditional concept of the romantic individual will be corrected by the scientific analysis of the true individual. A new grasp of the total individual will thus be achieved, offering the writer of tomorrow a hitherto impossible comprehension of the role of sex in experience —which he can then translate into sex in literature.

References

Basler, Roy P., *Sex, Symbolism and Psychology in Literature*. New Brunswick, N.J.: Rutgers University Press, 1948.

Calverton, V. F., and Schmalhausen, S. D. (eds.), *Sex in Civilization*. New York: Macaulay, 1929.

Decker, Clarence R., *The Victorian Conscience*. New York: Twayne Pub., 1952.

Feldman, Gene, and Gartenberg, Max, *The Beat Generation and the Angry Young Men*. New York: Citadel Press, 1958.

Freud, Sigmund, *Wit and Its Relation to the Unconscious*. New York: Dodd, Mead & Co., 1916.

Freud, Sigmund, *Delusion and Dream*. London: Allen & Unwin, 1921.

Freud, Sigmund, *Civilization and Its Discontents*. New York: Cape & Smith, 1930.

Freud, Sigmund, *Leonardo da Vinci*. New York: Dodd, Mead & Co., 1932.

Hoffman, Frederick, *Freudianism and the Literary Mind*. Baton Rouge, La.: Louisiana State University Press, 1957.

Jones, Ernest, *Hamlet and Oedipus*. London: Gollancz, 1953.

Kirchway, Freda (ed.), *Our Changing Morality*. New York: Boni, 1924.

Lawrence, D. H., *Sex, Literature and Censorship*. New York: Twayne Pub., 1953.

Mordell, Albert, *The Erotic Motive in Literature*. New York: Boni, 1919.

Mullahy, Patrick, *Oedipus, Myth and Complex*. New York: Hermitage, 1948.

Wilson, Edmund, *The Wound and the Bow*. Boston: Houghton Mifflin Co., 1941.

Wilson, Edmund, *Axel's Castle*. New York: Charles Scribner's Sons, 1954.

FRANK KINGDON

Love, Altruistic

Its Cosmic-Ontological Conception

IN ITS cosmic-ontological aspect, altruistic love or Goodness, side by side with Truth and Beauty, has been thought of as one of the three supreme forms of cosmic energy or reality or value operating not only in the human world but in the whole cosmos. It is conceived as the unifying, integrating, and harmonizing cosmic power that counteracts the disintegrating forces of chaos, unites what is separated by enmity, builds what is destroyed by discord; creates and maintains the grand order in the whole universe. The familiar formula of practically all great religions: "God is Love" and "Love is God," is one variation of this cosmic conception of unselfish love. The perennial cosmic struggle between Ahura-Mazda as the good cosmic creator, in contrast to Ahriman, as the wicked cosmic destroyer, in Zoroastrian religion; and, generally, good God as the benevolent Creator in contrast to evil Satan as the Destroyer in many religions are variations of another ontological conception of love. The Empedoclean theory that "all things coalesce into a unity in Love and they all separate in the enmity of Strife," developed by many subsequent thinkers including Dostoevski, Tolstoi, Soloviëv, and Gandhi, supplies a third variety of this ontological conception.

According to it, all *empirical* forms of unselfish love in physical, biological, and human worlds are but the manifestations of this mysterious cosmic love.

Empirical Biological Altruism

As an empirical phenomenon altruistic love means a specific behavior of living forms striving—instinctively or consciously—to be helpful to other organisms. In *the plant-and-animal world* it has a mainly instinctive-reflexological character. There it manifests itself in innumerable actions-reactions of cooperation and aid, at least as frequent and common as the actions-reactions of the struggle for existence. Beginning with the reproduction activities of the unicellular and the multicellular organisms, through parental care for the helpless newborn progeny, and ending with thousands of diverse forms of rendering help, "the instinctive-reflexological altruism" among animal and plant organisms proves itself to be at least as general and important a factor of their life and evolution as the factor of the struggle for existence.

Without a minimum of aid and cooperation the very survival and continuity of practically all species are hardly possible. In this sense the cooperative altruistic forces are biologically the more important and vital than the antagonizing forces. The balance between the (instinctive-reflexological) altruistic tendencies and those that are disoperative and egoistic is relatively close among the organisms. All in all, however, the group-centered, altruistic drives seem to be somewhat stronger than the drives of egoistic nature.

Psychological and Behavioral Characteristics of Altruistic Love in the Human World

In the human world altruistic love appears simultaneously as a specific psychological experience and an overt behavior. Despite the large variety of concrete forms of altruistic experience and behavior, all genuine altruistic experiences and actions have two common characteristics: first, *the ego or I of the loving individual tends to merge and to identify itself with the loved Thee;* second, all the loved individuals are regarded and treated as the *end-value and not as a mere means* for anything and anybody. The more genuine and pure the altruistic love the more conspicuous are these properties. In the experience and conduct of weak or pseudo-altruism, they tend to disappear.

Depending upon a different combination of emotional, volitional, and intellectual elements, altruistic love as a *psychological experience* has different "tonal qualities" or "colors." They are marked by such terms as empathy, sympathy, kindness, friendship, devotion, reverence, benevolence, admiration, and respect. All these forms are opposite to the forms of *inimical* psychological experience called by terms such as hate, enmity, dislike, antipathy, and envy.

If altruistic love remains in the state of a purely psychological experience and does not manifest itself in respective altruistic *overt actions,* then it becomes an "unfulfilled" or not "fully realized" love. Such a purely "psychological" or "ideological" or "speech-reactional" love often turns out to be a pseudo-love or even a "hypocritical altruism." The phenomena of this sort of an "unfulfilled" love seem to be much more frequent in the human world than those of the "fulfilled," that is, "psychological" *and* "behavioral" love. There are millions of "ideological" or "speech-reactional" altruists in the human population; and there are comparatively few genuine "fulfilled" altruists who practice the noble altruistic precepts they preach.

Altruistic and Sexual Love

If in sexual love the partners' egos are merged into one loving "we," and if the mates regard and treat each other as the end-value, then sexual love becomes one of the forms of altruistic love. When these characteristics are absent, and when sex mates consider and treat each other as a mere means for obtaining a pleasure or utility, then sexual love turns into a relationship devoid of altruistic love. If sexual relations involve an element of coercion of one partner by the other (as in the case of rape), or an element of buying and selling sex services (as in the case of prostitution and "commercial" marriages), then sex liaisons become a form of relations inimical to altruistic love.

Five Dimensions of Altruistic Love

In order to be adequately described, and now and then roughly measured, the enormous complexity, multidimensionality, and quantitative-qualitative diversity of concrete phenomena of altruistic love can be reduced to five basic "dimensions": intensity, extensity, duration, purity, and adequacy.

1. In *intensity,* psychological-behavioral love ranges from zero to infinity, from giving a few cents to the hungry by a rich person, or from a purely verbal highfalutin "love," up to a free sacrificing of one's life, "body and soul," for the well-being of the loved person.

2. In *extensity,* love ranges from the zero point of love of oneself only (egotism) up to the love of all mankind, of all living creatures, and of the whole universe.

3. In *duration,* altruistic love ranges from the shortest possible moment to years, decades, often the whole life of an individual or of a group.

4. In *purity,* love varies from the "soiled" love motivated by selfish expectations of advantage, utility, pleasure, or profit up to the pure love motivated exclusively by love for love's sake, or by the love of a person for the person's sake, regardless of any utilitarian or hedonistic motives. Pure love knows no bargain, no reward. It asks nothing in return. Jesus' *Sermon on the Mount* and St. Paul's *Epistle* (I Cor. 13) beautifully describe this sublime love. All forms of a "bargaining love," including the heterosexual love in which the sex partner is loved only because he or she gives pleasure or utility, are the examples of "impure" love. Sometimes such a love becomes devoid of altruistic elements and degenerates into a relationship of enmity and hate.

5. *Adequacy* of love fluctuates from the blind to the "wise" love. In the inadequate love there is always a discrepancy between the subjective motives and purposes of love and the objective consequences of the unwise or inadequate actions through which the love is expressed. A

mother may love her child madly and may be ready to sacrifice anything for the child's welfare but, by realizing her love through wrong actions and means, she may spoil the child and endanger his well-being. All forms of such a blind love are mainly due to a lack of scientific knowledge as to what actions and means can or cannot produce the intended effects in the loved persons. Even the purest and most intense love can be blind if it manifests itself in scientifically wrong actions.

Such are the five basic "dimensions" of unselfish love. The higher any empirical love is on each and all of these dimensions, the greater it is quantitatively and the sublimer qualitatively.

Altruistic Love as Eros and Agape

Some of the eminent religious, philosophical, and ethical thinkers conceive of altruistic love as the *ego-centered eros,* while some others view it as the *egoless or the ego-transcending agape.*

The eros-conception of love assumes that a person who does not love himself or his ego cannot love anyone else. Consequently, in order to be an altruist one does not need to transcend or annihilate one's ego and one's desire of good for the self. One needs only to be "enlightened" about one's real self-interests, to keep one's ego from excess of "unenlightened selfishness," and to cooperate with other individuals for their mutual benefit. The ego-centered eros is thus utilitarian, hedonistic, and "rational" in its nature. It follows the precepts: "live and let live," "help others in order to be helped by others," "do not harm others in order not to be harmed by others." Such an eros-love is discriminative: it is bestowed only upon those who deserve and reciprocate it.

In contrast to eros agape-love is the egoless, self-giving love that "seeketh not its own" and freely spends itself. It comes to the human world from above (from its Cosmic Source or God). Being inexhaustible in its richness, like the sun agape shines upon and redeems the sinners no less than the virtuous. In this sense it is nondiscriminative, inscrutable, and incomprehensible to the ego-centered "rational" mind.

The discriminative eros loves its objects or persons because of their virtue and value; the nondiscriminative agape creates, by its love, value and virtue even in a hitherto valueless object or person.

These two forms of unselfish love—plus their mixed form—have been operating throughout the history of mankind. The eros and the mixed form of love seem to have been more common than agape-love. On the other hand, almost all of the greatest apostles of love, from Buddha and Jesus up to Gandhi, have preached and practiced agape rather than eros. Perhaps this explains to some extent the tremendous influence of such apostles upon millions of people and upon the course of human history.

Power of Unselfish Love

Scientific knowledge concerning altruistic love is, so far, almost negligible. A systematic study of the energy of love is still in its infancy. Our "know-how" to produce it efficiently, to accumulate, circulate, and use it in the human world, is also very limited. In spite of this ignorance, the very little we know of altruistic love still warrants the hypothesis that (1) "the grace of love" is one of the three highest energies known to man (along with those of Truth and Beauty); (2) this energy is different from, and irreducible to, the scalar quantities of physical sciences called "energy," "power," "work," and "force"; and finally (3) the energy of unselfish love potentially represents a gigantic—creative, recreative, and therapeutic—power. When it is better understood, reverently treated, and wisely used it can substantially help to free mankind from its gravest ills: war, crime, and insanity.

For the last few decades, biology, psychology, sociology, and other branches of science have steadily converged toward these conclusions. Their rapidly increasing body of evidence convincingly demonstrates the creative and re-creative functions of love in the mental, moral, and social life of individuals, societies, and mankind. Here is a brief list of some of these creative and therapeutic functions of unselfish love.

1. The energy of love appears to be indis-

pensable for the generation, continuity, and growth of living forms, for survival and multiplication of species, and for the maintenance of health and integrity—especially of human beings.

2. Loving and being loved is the best antidote against "egoistic" and "anomique" suicide. Those who are not loved by anyone and who do not love anybody are the first candidates for these most frequent forms of suicide.

3. The combination in a person of too little love with too much hate is largely responsible for many cardiovascular, respiratory, gastrointestinal, endocrinological, genito-urinary, and skin diseases, plus some forms of epilepsy and headache. An increase in genuine altruism is one of the best preventive and curative remedies of these ailments.

4. A minimum of a warm, especially motherly, love is a necessary condition for the survival and healthy growth of babies.

5. Likewise, a minimum of the grace of love is necessary for the growth of infants into mentally and morally sound citizens. Children deprived of this minimum yield a much higher percentage of delinquents and psychoneurotics than do those who grow in the climate of a warm and wise love.

6. One of the principal healing agents of mental disorders is the establishment of "rapport of mutual sympathy and trust" between therapist and patient, thus placing the patient in a milieu free from enmity and conflict.

7. Love-energy also contributes to the prolongation of human life. Other conditions being equal, altruistic persons live longer than egoistic individuals.

8. Love-energy is possibly the best "extinguisher" of interhuman enmity and strife in interindividual as well as in intergroup relationships. Experimental studies and historical events show that the old motto, "love begets love and hate begets hate" is essentially correct. When competently applied, a genuine altruistic love transforms enemies into friends, prevents and tames wars and bloody intergroup conflicts. It is a more reliable and efficacious power for pacifying persons and groups than the powers of hate, coercion, intimidation, and (in international policies) the age-old policy of the

Romans, *si vis pacem para bellum* (if you want peace, prepare for war).

9. The pacifying power of love appears also to be the main agency that terminates long and mortally dangerous catastrophes in the lives of nations. A careful and systematic study of all such catastrophes in the history of Ancient Egypt, Babylon, China, India, Persia, Greece, Rome, and of the Western countries shows that all such catastrophes were finally overcome by an altruistic ennoblement of the people, culture, and social institutions of these nations.

10. Love-energy increases not only the longevity of individuals but also the life span of societies and organizations. Small and big social organizations, built mainly by hate, conquest, and coercion—including the empires of Alexander the Great, Caesar, Genghis Khan, Tamerlane, Napoleon, or Hitler—as a rule have been short-lived. On the other hand, the longest-living organizations have been the great ethicoreligious bodies, such as Taoism, Confucianism, Hinduism, Buddhism, Jainism, Judaism, Christianity, and Mohammedanism, which have been dedicated to the altruistic education of mankind and to the cultivation of love in the human universe.

11. Finally, the gigantic power of love is manifested in the undying influence of the greatest apostles of love on countless millions of human beings and on the course of human history. These apostles, such as Lao-Tze, Confucius, Buddha, Zoroaster, Mahavira, Moses, Jesus, St. Paul, St. Francis of Assisi, up to Gandhi and other creators and leaders of altruistic religions and morality, have possibly been the most influential individuals in human history. In contrast to the short-lived, and often destructive, influence of autocratic monarchs, military conquerors, revolutionary dictators, and potentates of wealth, the great apostles of love have most tangibly affected the lives, minds, and bodies of untold billions of human beings during the millennia of history, and still affect us. Not having armed forces, nor wealth, nor other worldly means of influencing the human world, but exclusively by the power of their pure and abundant love, they have transfigured millions of men and women, reshaped cultures and social institutions, and most

tangibly conditioned the course of history and destiny of nations.

With an increasing knowledge of "the mysterious" love-energy, its creative and curative powers can be increasingly used for the growth of man's constructive creativity and for the liberation of mankind from wars, bloody strife, diseases, misery, and other forms of evil.

References

Sublime formulation of the precepts of altruistic love is given in the *New Testament's Sermon on the Mount* and the *Beatitudes,* in St. Paul's epistle: *I Corinthians* 13, in the *Bhagavadgita,* the *Dhammapada,* and similar religious-ethical texts of practically all great religions.

Aristotle, *The Nicomachean Ethics.* Any good translation.

Cicero, *On Friendship.* Any good translation.

D'Arcy, Martin C., *The Mind and Heart of Love.* London, New York: Meridian, 1947.

James, William, *The Varieties of Religious Experience.* New York: Modern Library, 1903.

Kropotkin, Peter, *Mutual Aid, a Factor of Evolution.* Boston: Sargent, 1955.

Montagu, Ashley, *On Being Human.* New York: Abelard, 1950.

Nygren, A., *Agape and Eros.* London: Westminster, 1937.

Scheler, Max, *Das Wesen und die Formen der Sympathie.* Bonn, 1931.

Solovyev, V., *The Meaning of Love.* London, 1945.

Sorokin, P. (ed.), *A Symposium: Explorations in Altruistic Love and Behavior.* Boston, 1950.

Sorokin, P. (ed.), *A Symposium: Forms and Techniques of Altruistic and Spiritual Growth.* Boston: Beacon, 1954.

Sorokin, P., *The Ways and Power of Love.* Boston: Beacon, 1954. (This work gives a full bibliography on all main aspects of altruistic love.)

Suttie, Ian D., *The Origin of Love and Hatred.* London: Julian, 1935.

PITIRIM A. SOROKIN

Love, Sexual

Definition

BY SEXUAL love is meant an emotional relationship between man and woman that is distinctively *sexual*, in that it typically develops between persons of opposite sexes, yet is distinguishable from "sexual desire" or "sexual impulse." The latter terms usually refer to a motive whose goal is genital intercourse. Sexual *love*, although some of its expressions may closely resemble those of the sexual impulse, differs from it in several ways.

Sexual love is also to be distinguished from a kind of "love" that is benevolent in quality and concerned with the well-being of another person. This may develop between any persons, regardless of sex, but when it arises between man and woman it is often confused with sexual love, partly because, here again, some of the expressions are similar. Love between the sexes, in other words, need not be *sexual* love.

The sexual motive to be discussed will hereafter be called *amorous emotion*. It differs from sexual desire or impulse first of all in that the individuality of the attractive person is of much greater importance. This is best seen when the two motives are at high intensities. The sexual impulse, when strongly aroused, tends to become progressively less discriminating, while reference to a person as being "in love" is synonymous with saying that he is exclusively attracted to one person. Sexual desire may become strong without reference to a particular person as its object; its arousal may be more "organic" than social. The amorous emotion, on the other hand, is essentially social in that it *begins* with what amounts to a choice of object.

Although sexually attractive traits of the kind commonly regarded as esthetic (beauty, charm, etc.) have an important role in the arousal of the sexual impulse, the primary stimulus, the genital organs, have never been considered as esthetic in the same sense—that is, have never been regarded as beautiful. The amorous emotion, on the other hand, has always been associated with beauty or comeliness in some degree, more especially from the masculine viewpoint, and the traits that arouse it tend to be peripheral to the genital zones; for example, facial features, voice, qualities of movement, personal "style," etc. In short, the esthetic aspects of the two sexual motives, while they overlap, may be said to differ at the core.

The two motives may also be distinguished by way of the *quality* of the emotional states, although the difference is not easy to define. Such terms as "lust," "carnal desire," and "venereal voluptuousness" have been used in references to the genital impulse, while "adoration," "romantic feeling," and "amorous admiration" have been used to characterize sexual love, as here defined.

A feature of amorous emotion often stressed in the literature on the subject is its tendency to include the whole of the personality of its object, while genital desire is more narrowly focused on the body and on behavior more or less directly related to the excitement of the genital impulse. This may be related to the difference in discrimination, since the greater the number of traits included in sexual attractiveness, the greater the scope of individuality.

It seems fairly agreed that, apart from exceptional instances ("love at first sight"), the amorous emotion entails a growth process of some duration. *Attraction* may be an immediate experience, comparable to the arousal of genital desire, but a strong amorous emotion must develop, like a new sentiment or interest, by way of repeated contacts. Genital desire, on the other hand, may be much more rapidly aroused when a person is organically ready. In man, it appears to be fairly readily excitable much of the time.

Sexual impulse and amorous emotion differ, again, in their terminal phases. The impulse is "extinguished in an act; there is a tension, a spasm, and a release." The decline of the amorous emotion tends, like its development, to be typically gradual. It may even persist to some degree despite the emergence of strongly unfavorable traits in its object. Another difference is summarized by Symonds (1946): "Sensual pleasure becomes extinguished when satisfied, whereas love continues unabated, indeed, is enhanced the more satisfaction a person derives from another."

Sublimation

How are these two kinds of sex related? Two major answers have been given to this question by modern students.

One answer is that amorous emotion is a "sublimation" of genital sex desire. The emotion is a kind of transformation of the impulse, this transformation occurring when the impulse is inhibited. The experience of being "in love," according to Freud, depends on the blocking of the desire for intercourse. "Sublimation" may not be complete, however, and one's feeling for a person may be partly sensual and partly amorous. Since, typically, being "in love" means that both feelings are present, sublimation is usually partial in this sense.

Some who have thought of sexual love in this way make little distinction between the two motives as experiences. Thus Young (1943) states: ". . . in romantic love the lovers are at once aroused and inhibited sexually. This state of conflict evokes the disturbing emotion known as 'being in love,' . . . The more strongly an individual is excited by sexual stimulation and the more completely this biological urge is frustrated, the greater will be his emotional disturbance."

Allport (1924) writes that during courtship "the sexual drive of the wooer is not yet released; every detail about the beloved from head to toe is, therefore, a stimulus which helps to augment the tonus already present in the pelvic viscera. This is the condition of being blindly in love."

In these examples little distinction is implied between amorous emotion and genital desire, and the emphasis is on inhibition. More frequently, the idea of sublimation includes a change in the character of the motive, in recognition of the differences cited above. A more typical example, comparable to the statements given by Freud and by Havelock Ellis, is the following by Waller (1938): "The mating impulse encounters, in our culture, a number of obstacles; the patterning to which it is subjected sets up a number of difficult conditions and necessitates many delays and postponements. Because of this blocking, the impulse increases in intensity, and is long-circuited into other channels of emotion and ideation. The sentiment of love as we know it is compounded of the bare impulse plus these elements of emotion and ideation. . . ." In other words, when genital desire is inhibited, sexual love results, along with certain ways of thinking about the attractive person.

Two Kinds of Sex

The second answer to the question of the sources of amorous emotion regards it as essentially independent of the genital impulse. It is a sexual motive in its own right, rather than a by-product of inhibition. This view was most clearly stated by Albert Moll (1898), one of the founders of modern sex psychology and a contemporary of Freud.

Man's sexual make-up includes, Moll believed, two entirely distinct parts. One of these is the impulse toward genital pleasure. The usual expression of this is sexual intercourse, but another is masturbation. It is thus not necessarily a *social* motive.

The other part of our sexual make-up is seen in the *attraction* of the sexes. It is best illustrated in the mutual interest of a young boy and girl who are visually fascinated with each other. They may be quite without knowledge or experience of the genital relationship. Although such attractions may lead to embraces, they may be entirely free of genital excitement. Attractions of this kind may be quite strong long before puberty, Moll believed, and exhibit such familiar traits as marked preference for a particular person of the opposite sex, embraces, confessions of feeling, gifts, etc. Such attachments eventually come to include genital stimulation and desire, but the initial attraction and emotion may be free of any evidence of this kind of arousal.

Among those whose views or findings are in harmony with Moll's formulation are Emil Lucka (1915), Edward Spranger (1928), R. Müller-Freienfels (1940), J. Ortega y Gasset (1933), G. V. Hamilton (1929), Charlotte Bühler (1931), and Sanford Bell (1902).

Bell made extended observations of the amorous behavior of school children. He concluded that there is a kind of attraction during childhood and youth that exhibits several of the features of adult sexual love (visual interest, preference, jealousy, embraces) but in which there is no evidence of genital sex arousal. The attractions and attachments observed seemed clearly to be expressions of a "different kind of sex." Bell gave many examples of the behavior on which Moll had based his sex psychology, and offered, as Robert Sears (1943) observes, a "considerably more factual and realistic" account of the sex behavior of childhood than Freud ever provided. The case materials collected by Havelock Ellis (1949) gave many comparable examples, and the data assembled by G. V. Hamilton also indicate a tendency for amorous emotion to appear earlier in development than genital sex desire, and to be experienced independently of this desire after puberty.

An adequate sex psychology must offer an interpretation of marginal behavior as well as of behavior that is clearly related to physical intercourse. Is the response to an exceptionally attractive face, for example, simply a genital sex response to a nongenital area, is it a quick *change* ("sublimation") of such a response into an esthetic appreciation of "beauty," or is it, in *basic* reality, what it may appear to be as an experience, namely, a response altogether different in quality from that which prompts one toward physical intercourse? That there are great differences, moreover, in what is judged an attractive human face also calls, and very importantly, for interpretation.

Status of Sublimation

The hypothesis of sublimation has been offered as a means of deriving, from the genital sex impulse, such marginal varieties of sexual behavior. Although it long antedates Freud, its wide currency in sex psychology may be attributed in part to his influence. Its popularity may also be traced to its assumed ethical value: it supposedly offers a way by which the genital urge may be altered and elevated into "higher" forms of expression, such as tender solicitude and sex-esthetic appreciation. Parshley wrote (1933): "The reality of sublimation has been assumed from early times down to the present but never has it been so generously embraced as by a strangely assorted group of our own contemporaries. Psychoanalysts, Y. M. C. A. moral guides, Shaw, Jane Addams, and R. C. Cabot unite, for once, in their acceptance of the principle, though it must be admitted that Freud himself thinks it is 'for the few,' and some recalcitrant psychologists . . . take a seriously critical attitude."

Much doubt has been expressed regarding the value of this concept. Little is known about it, and its very reality appears never to have been demonstrated. It has moved, as Levey (1939) points out, with very little testing or examination, from the status of hypothesis to that of doctrine.

Ethnography provides some evidence here. If the amorous emotion is a sublimated form of inhibited sexual desire, it should be absent, or low in incidence, in societies placing little restriction on sexual behavior. At least one such society has been thoroughly studied. A high degree of sexual freedom is permitted among the Trobriand Island natives. Malinowski (1929) reported, nevertheless, the presence of amorous desire and of fixations that were not wholly sensual. He found evidence of "what we ourselves mean by love." His account suggests the presence of strongly individualized amorous emotion in a society where no one, at any age, lacks genital sex outlets. Comparable data are reported of the Baiga people (India) studied by Elwin (1939).

In broader terms, the general incidence of amorous behavior among the peoples of the world should show some kind of correspondence with sexual freedom if the two are related through checks upon the genital impulse. Complete sexual freedom among primitives appears to be the exception rather than the rule. Nearly everywhere there are restrictions of some kind and degree. One would expect, accordingly, comparable evidence of the presence of the amorous emotion. On the contrary, it seems fairly agreed that, although there are scattered exceptions, the phenomenon of highly individualized attractions associated with strong emotion is not characteristic of the lower cultures.

The concept of sublimation has been questioned from other points of view. In the region of sex esthetics it is particularly weak. Freudians have not seemed aware of the paradox in the assumption of an unknown transformation process whereby the response to the unesthetic genital organs is converted into one that has been regarded as the foundation of all esthetics (that is, the response to sexual beauty). Sublimation leaves unexplained the phenomenon of sex-esthetic *aversions,* which are as positive, as reactions, as are attractions.

Sexual Choice

Individualized attractions and aversions have been reported among the lower animals. Darwin collected some data of this kind, observing that among birds the females sometimes exhibit strong preferences for certain males. He saw evidence of choice, again, in the response of females to the courtship displays and maneuvers of the males, and to their vivid colorings. He noted also individual antipathies and preferences among domesticated quadrupeds. More recently, comparable selective behavior has been reported in studies of the chimpanzee. Not only are definite preferences exhibited, but some individuals are much more discriminating in their choices than others. The parallel comes closest to human behavior, perhaps, in instances in which choice is apparently based on individuality of facial expression.

The problem of the nature of amorous emotion is inseparable from the fact of sexual choice. As earlier noted, the importance of the individuality of the object of amorous desire is one of the marks by which this desire differs from the genital impulse. The latter, in response to organic rhythms, may "press" before a partner is encountered. The very existence of amorous emotion, on the other hand, implies some degree of fixation. Discovery of the factors in choice becomes essential, therefore, to an understanding of the nature of amorous emotion.

The most widely current doctrine of the origin of the "love choice" is that of Freud, which traces it to the parent-child relationship. Freud, as is well known, regarded the child not only as erotically responsive but as capable of fixations of sexual interest. The child's first "sexual love" is the first female with whom he has an extended association—his mother. This is the "Oedipus complex," and it may importantly influence the direction of later interest, that is, the boy may unconsciously seek a "mother-image" in his attractions to the other sex. (For the girl, as well, the mother is the first love choice but, by a rather involved theoretical process in which castration fear and envy of the penis play a role, this erotic interest is shifted to the father.)

A resemblance may often be found, according to the Freudian school, between the loved parent and the person selected as a mate. Such resemblances may be of many varieties, mental and physical. Because of them, and because other traits may be incompatible, unsuitable marriages occur. The taboos against incest show that pressure is needed against sexual attractions within the family. Little by little such attachments must be weaned away and transferred outside the family, but in many subtle ways the original emotional relationship may enter into the sexual choices of the adult.

The findings of several investigations, including those of Burgess and Cottrell (1939), Hamilton, and Terman (1938), have failed to support this theory of choice. It has been criticized on other grounds, such as that it assumes that the adult amorous experience of "falling in love" is comparable to the child's affection for its other-sexed parent. It has been suggested that those who believe this have been misled by the surface resemblances in expression (i.e., contacts, caresses, embraces) between childish affection and adult sexual love. It has been suggested that this resemblance does not mean that the emotional states must be the same. If they are *not* the same, then it may be questioned whether adult amorous attraction can be explained by similarities between parent and lover.

Such similarities, when present, may more logically be seen as evidence that adult attractions—usually assumed to express mainly *sexual* love—may actually contain strong dependent needs, thus leading to choices influenced by child-parent attachments in which dependent needs are also primary. Reports of amorous behavior in childhood have further bearing at this point in providing evidence that strong love attachments outside the family may be formed in very early life. Some doubt is suggested, therefore, regarding the universality of the Oedipus situation, and its influence upon later amorous preferences.

Ego Need as Basis of Choice

Freud suggested another type of sexual choice: the "narcissistic." A person may seek a mate who resembles him in certain ways. He may find himself drawn to one who is like himself.

This view of sexual love was expressed by Weininger (1906) in terms of a seeking of an "ideal self." What we truly seek in another of opposite sex, perhaps without being aware of it, is a personality embodying our own conception of an admirable self. This ideal image is projected upon another, so that to fall in love is really to become enamored of one's own self-image, that is, one's ideal self-image. In this projection the actual traits of the loved individual must often be excluded from consciousness. This is the familiar blindness of the lover who sees what he wishes to see, believes what he needs to believe.

This psychology of choice has more recently been developed by Theodor Reik (1944), who suggests that so-called sexual love is not only very different from physical desire but is actually an affair of the ego-needs; it is thus not really sexual at all.

To be in *condition* for falling in love, according to Reik, a person must be dissatisfied with himself, frustrated in his self-esteem. This kind of discontent arises out of a realization of the difference between what one wants to be and what one is. A person who feels that he has achieved his personal goal will not feel the need that is essential to seeking another; he is complacent, will not fall in love. Readiness for this emotional disturbance depends on a need of and a longing for another self.

What has hitherto been called sexual love begins when someone is encountered who embodies the traits of the ideal self. This individual is thus a kind of substitute fulfillment of the personal ideal. It is for this reason that love is so possessive. (There is also, Reik thinks, a touch of envy in the admiration inspired by the beloved.) In this possession, however, the self is enriched because it is now completed through a kind of ownership of the qualities it previously lacked.

The love choice is thus made by the recognition, in another, of what a person feels that he himself lacks. When a choice occurs that apparently fails to correspond with the ideal, it may be because we are not always fully aware of all the features of our ideal mate. Some of these features may be unconscious.

Probably no one would debate that "ego-needs" and considerations concerning self-esteem may enter importantly into the vicissitudes of sexual courtship, just as they are involved in so many other human relationships. To regard the entire psychology of sexual love in this way, however, appears to commit the common error of mistaking a part for the whole. In this instance the "part," unfortunately, is not even an essential one.

The account so far leads to the obvious question of why this kind of love usually affects people heterosexually. (The genital impulse is not the answer, since Reik concedes that this impulse is to be distinguished from the kind of love under discussion here; he thinks, in fact, that "sex" and sexual love are unlike in origin and in nature.) The attraction of the sexes is handled by supposing that each of us imagines having a counterpart, or other-self, in the other sex. "The desire to be like a person of the opposite sex gives place to the wish to have that other person as one's own." (The easy shift here between "to be" and "to have" is notable.) A boy's desire for a girl is an expression of his wishful phantasy of himself as a girl. On this crucial point the theory apparently requires us to believe that everyone desires to have traits of the other sex, and this is why the boy's admiration of the girl's beauty is tinctured with envy, according to Reik, and why the girl's admiration of the boy's courage contains some jealousy. Man's sexual love of woman arises out of his frustrated desire to *be* a woman.

Concerning the amorous attractions of young children observed by Bell and others, this view would suppose a child not only to be discontented with his personality, but to have a considerable appreciation of the individuality of others.

The Esthetic Theory

One of the oldest attempts to answer the question of the basis of sexual love is the view that amorous attraction is an esthetic phenomenon. That there is a link of some sort between sexuality and the appreciation of beauty has been a recurrent surmise in the literature of esthetics as well as of sex psychology. Freud regarded the attraction of personal beauty as traceable to sex. Edward Spranger (1928) proposed that the "spiritual relation of the two sexes is . . . insofar as physical sexuality does not take the upper hand, an esthetic one." Santayana (1896) felt that esthetic responsiveness in general is related to the sexual process.

There is, of course, an obvious difference between the response to an art form and the response to sexual beauty. Sexual attractiveness extends, moreover, far beyond what is commonly defined as beautiful. The person who is sexually attractive to one may have little or no charm for another. Personal beauty is not a simple trait, and is probably a highly complex one. Variability from person to person in sexual preference may be said to be very great.

This *individual* factor in sexual esthetics was made the basis of a psychology of sexual love by Alfred Binet (1891). Binet sought the key to sexual attraction in the study of abnormalities, in which in certain individuals a single specific trait or feature ("fetish") arouses an intense emotion. The trait might be the hair, for example, or the eyes, or the quality of the voice, or a distinctive grace of movement. In abnormal people such traits are the *exclusive* interest of the "fetishist" (who may say, e.g., "For me the girl is nothing, her hair is everything") and it is in this, largely, that the abnormality lies.

The behavior of the fetishist often resembles, in certain important features, that of a normally amorous person, as we have been using this term. What interested Binet was the possibility that a *less* exclusive kind of attraction might provide a basis for the understanding of sexual love. A small degree of this abnormality might, in other words, be quite common. Everyone, he suggested, is to some extent a fetishist; we all have our special susceptibilities, expressed in our preferences for a coloring of eyes or hair, for a certain profile, a contour of nose or mouth, or a certain "style" or mannerism. Each of us may be, to some degree, sensitized to traits or qualities of some kind, and for each this may be "beauty." The individual esthetic response to such traits or qualities is, according to Binet, the basis of the amorous emotion.

Magnus Hirschfeld (1935) and G. Stanley Hall (1904) made observations in line with Binet's view. The esthetic theory in the form in which Binet developed it, with its emphasis on specialized individual susceptibilities and preferences, enlightens some of the traditional features of amorous behavior. The irrational side of attractions becomes more understandable. The notorious apparent "blindness" of the lover may be seen rather as a reflection of the blindness of the bystander, who lacks the peculiar sensitivity that would enable him to react similarly to the same object.

One current interpretation of the amorous emotion is that it is induced when a person "projects" his own desires and phantasies upon the love-object, and thus clothes it with qualities that in reality it does not possess. This may be carried as far as the view (e.g., that of De Rougemont, 1940) that physical beauty itself is simply an "attribute bestowed by a lover" rather than a characteristic of the object. Such a notion leaves unexplained, of course, why one person rather than another is chosen at the outset as a basis of "projection." It fails also to consider the many instances in which love is *not* "blind," that is, in which many agree regarding the attractions of a given individual. Such agreements indicate common factors in sex-esthetic preferences or, otherwise expressed, that beauty may have an "objective" basis.

A salient feature of the esthetic theory is that it recognizes the basic fact of choice in amorous behavior; that is, that the emotion is a response to a *selected* object. Its approach is analytical in that it leads to a search for specifiable traits. It is in harmony with the formulated view that there are two unlike modes of sexual response. It removes amorous behavior from the realm of delusion and "blindness," and makes it more an affair of individuality, less of irrationality.

Sociology

Individuality

Without individuality sexual choice is of course meaningless. A society may cultivate individuality or it may suppress it. It may subordinate it to other things, such as status. A society may also *value* individuality, cultivating its appreciation. Strong amorous attachments tend on the whole to be associated with the higher levels of culture. To parallel this, Lowie (1940) has noted that "Modern civilized societies notably differ from primitive man's in their attitude toward the individual. . . . Earlier periods and primitive communities never ignored individuality, but they subordinated it to social status." The emphasis, in our own society, on the expression of individuality and the cultivation of "personality" may be related to the important role of amorous emotion in mating behavior.

Among the Samoans, as reported by Mead (1928), awareness and appreciation of personality are at a relatively low level. The growing child learns to think of others in terms of group membership and lines of social cleavage rather than in terms of individuality. Choice is governed more by class than by person. In consequence of the lesser awareness of differences between persons, there is a lesser development of personalized feelings and fixations. Personal relationships become more shallow and casual; deep feelings occur less often.

In the sex relationships, correspondingly,

emotional ties are less likely to grow. Sexual attraction does not have the meaning that it has or may have in our own culture. "Romantic love" as a strong and exclusive fixation is not found among the Samoans, according to Mead (though there were occasional misfits whose capacity for emotion was greater than that of others, and who developed fixations). The romantic sentiment, as has often been pointed out, values the person rather than the type; it glorifies individuality; the ideal, when found, is always "different." In contrast with the Samoans, Malinowski found marked appreciation of personal differences and of sex-esthetic individuality among the Melanesians, along with evidence of the presence of important elements of sexual preference and emotional fixation as we ourselves know them. Mead points out that the American family fosters awareness of personality in several ways, and that growing preferences provide the basis of attitudes, in which choice is an important factor.

Status of the Sexes

The Freudian school has stressed "overestimation" as a factor in, if not the origin of, the amorous state. By this term Freud meant that the love-object is idealized and exalted. This is one way of saying that the *value* element in the amorous experience is important; for example, the general esteem in which woman is held in a given society.

Much has been written of the relation between woman's social status and man's feeling toward her as an object of amorous feeling. Where she is seen as mainly a breeder, a drudge, or a sexual toy, the incidence of the "romantic emotion" is reportedly much lower than it is in cultures in which her status is relatively high. For an inferior one may feel affection, or sensual desire, but not the respect and adoration that is essential to amorous emotion as we know it in America, for example. Idealization requires a kind of minimum social valuation; woman as a sex must be acknowledged as *worthy* of strong feeling. (That status is not all-important, however, is attested by the occurrence of occasional extraordinary fixations even in cultures where woman's status is low, as among certain primitives.)

Social class membership is a nonsexual value that heightens sexual attractiveness. This has often been illustrated in the medieval cult of woman-worship, in which the social rank of the adored mistress was usually above that of the lover, so that in addition to her beauty and virtue, she was exalted by her high "social quality."

Status of the Emotion

To such factors affecting the character and intensity of amorous emotion as the appraisal of individuality and the status of the sexes may be added the social "rating" of the emotion itself. The way it is experienced will to some degree be a reflection of the judgments made by each society and each age as to how important it is and what it should mean as a part of life. An epoch in which calm serenity and freedom from emotional distraction and turbulence is idealized will not value the amorous state as will an age of "sensibility," in which the emotional life is considered as having a certain "natural virtue." The esthetic response to sexual charms and to the longings they arouse probably fluctuates much less from one century to another than does the *esteem* in which these feelings are held and the role they are seen as playing in a well-adjusted or proportioned life. (The Hellenic exaltation of the friendships between men, and between man and boy, has been cited to illustrate the cultural weighting of one kind of emotional relationship.) A social history of sexual love might be written, it has been suggested, in terms of changing emphases of modes, styles, and "periods." A variety of influences doubtless determines the appraisal of the emotion at a given time and place. According to this appraisal, the individual may perceive it, when it comes to him, as no more than a minor incident of his affective career, perhaps to be viewed with wariness lest he "overestimate" it; or he may be prepared by his culture to accept it as an experience that may reach far beyond the more staple meanings of "sex," and as potentially invested with extraordinary motivating power.

Summary of Major Views on the Amorous Emotion

A recent study by the writer (1957), which offers the first systematic modern discussion of the amorous emotion, presents and evaluates the major views of the last century. Some of its findings and conclusions may be summarized.

An impressive variety of ideas about the nature of the amorous emotion have been advanced. It has been seen as a complex of many emotional factors, and also as a single "elemental." It has been interpreted as a derivative sexual motive—a by-product of inhibition of the impulse to genital intercourse—and, again, it has been regarded as independent of this impulse in origin and in expression. Emphasis has been placed on spontaneous "love need" as the essential factor in arousal of the emotion, with the choice of object incidental, and, again, emphasis has been placed upon special qualities of the attractive object as the truly essential factor. By a few students the amorous state has been regarded as symptomatic of some kind of emotional maladjustment and even of "nerve pathology." Although in general it has been treated as an implicitly sexual phenomenon, a few have regarded it as an expression of non-sexual personality needs and strivings.

There is considerable agreement that human sexual experience is not all-of-a-kind in quality or in mode of expression; that it includes affects that are unlike those directly converging to genital intercourse. To account for these affects, the idea of some kind of transformative process ("sublimation," "irradiation") is widely current. Because of the basic inadequacies of these attempts to derive one motive from another, however, an independent *amorous* mode of sexuality must be recognized, differing from the genital impulse in quality, in expression, and in stimulus. The goal of this motive is complete and exclusive *possession* of a person of opposite sex. In biological origin the motive may be seen as a means of ensuring approach and contact, and possibly of sustaining the association for a period.

The traits that arouse the amorous response are *esthetic* (beauty, comeliness, "charm," etc.); their locale may be any part of the body excepting the genital zones. Their main focus is the facial features—the central and endlessly rich complex of human physical individuality. They include also characteristics of movement ("grace"); the quality of the voice; distinction of mannerism ("style").

These sex-esthetic traits are entirely *formal*

as the term is used in art; that is, patterns (and "gestalts") of line and color, of "plastic structure," of tone and of motion. They are essentially *surface* traits, empty of meaning, best illustrated, perhaps, in a very young boy's visual fascination on first encounter with an attractive girl contemporary. Responses to such traits become intimately blended, as the individual matures, with the perception of nonsexual traits and qualities that are also attractive (e.g., animation, cheerfulness, amiability, etc.). What is ordinarily called sexual attraction includes responses to a variety of nonsexual traits, or traits that do not differentiate the sexes but are regarded as favorable, or are socially approved.

Although the close fusion of the amorous emotion with positive responses to nonsexual personality characteristics may make it difficult to discriminate between them, the former may be seen most nearly unalloyed in occasional fixations—often called "infatuations"—that develop despite uncongenial and even repellent behavior in an otherwise attractive person (conflicts of this kind being expressed, for example, in such observations as "She was irritable, untruthful, and selfish, yet I fell in love, nevertheless"). The emotion may also be seen, perhaps, "in relief," when strong attractions cut across the heavy resistance of racial or religious boundaries. It may be seen, too, in youthful attachments formed through superficial contacts before the appreciation of personality has fully developed.

Amorous attachments that are aroused solely by sex-esthetic traits do not have a high status in our culture. They are also sometimes classed as "infatuations" and are viewed as unstable and lacking in a sustaining factor. They are regarded as differing importantly from "true" love, in which traits other than those of esthetic quality have a larger role; for example, traits of "character," or those favoring compatibilities of temperament.

It is proposed, nevertheless, that "true" *sexual* love is one in which esthetic traits are primary, and that what may be socially appraised as an infatuation is in reality the genuine *amorous* emotion. Attachments that develop on a basis of the various socially approved traits or "virtues," including also benevolent impulses, are commonly called "love" relationships. This label need not be debated, provided such attachments are not regarded as *sexual*. Obviously, people are attractive to each other in many nonsexual ways. Love between the sexes need not, in other words, always be sexual love.

Yet, since such traits do not differentiate the sexes, they cannot be seen as primary factors in sexual love, although they may reinforce it. The effect of *unfavorable* traits upon the amorous emotion depends on the phase of amorous growth in which they appear. During the early period of an attraction, when the emotion is relatively weak, such traits may effectively counteract it, or markedly retard its development. An illustration would be the fairly immediate loss of interest in an initially attractive person with the discovery of undesirable items of behavior. If all the traits that finally destroy a love affair were in evidence at its outset many would never begin. Once amorous fixation has become strong, however, the same traits may fail to do more than create occasional conflicts.

The frequent failure to distinguish between sexual and nonsexual emotional states is illustrated in the common view that "true love" must exclude jealousy, since the latter is not compatible with a wholly unselfish concern for another. For this reason, in part, jealousy has acquired an unfavorable reputation. But if the essential factor in sexual love is the pleasure-seeking, self-gratifying, intensely possessive amorous desire, then jealousy must be admitted as a necessary phase of the amorous experience when possession is threatened. By this logic the "unjealous lover" is, as has often been surmised, not sexually "in love" at all.

Sex-esthetic preferences may be highly individualized; a person attractive to one may be only slightly or not at all attractive to another. There is, on the other hand, a considerable measure of agreement in judgments of sexual beauty. Several factors may be seen as importantly affecting sexual preferences. Social standards as to what is attractive vary greatly from group to group and from age to age. A wealth of ethnographic data can be assembled to show that choice is to a large degree a function of the culture. From one society to another the focus of interest shifts from feature to feature; e.g., small eyes may be a charm among one people, large ones among another; the mouth may be of little or of great importance; slenderness may be preferred to obesity, or vice versa.

Sexual choice is evident early in life. That human beings are originally, apart from experience, identical in responsiveness to all esthetic "patterns" in the region of sexual sensibility seems as unlikely as that they are identical in any other respect. Finally, the experiences of individual growth may be assumed to have an important role in the development of preferences.

In addition to sensual and esthetic elements, sexual choice is influenced by the sex-role behavior termed masculine and feminine; for example, the "active" and "passive" attitudes in courtship. In most, although not all, societies the initiative is regarded as properly that of the male. When a society approves different courtship tactics for the sexes, the exhibition of these tactics will enter into choice; that is, this behavior will have sexual value, meaning, for example, that woman's attractiveness will be heightened by the "feminine" character of her courtship behavior.

The variety of views on sexual love summarized above may be related to the meagerness of scientific data in this region of experience and behavior. This in turn reflects its conspicuous neglect by psychologists. Despite the legitimacy of the problems of human amorous behavior, and the preoccupation of our culture with romantic themes, very few psychologists have been interested in it. One consequence of this is the current failure to realize the inadequacies of Freudian theory as applied to this aspect of sexual psychology. Another is that our literature on sexual behavior is heavily overweighted with genital-sexual emphasis. The amorous emotion still awaits its Kinsey.

References

Allport, F. H., *Social Psychology*. Boston: Houghton Mifflin Co., 1924.

Bell, Sanford, "A Preliminary Study of the Emotion of Love Between the Sexes." *Am. J. Psychol.* 13; 325-354, 1902.

Binet, Alfred, *Études de psychologie expérimentale*. Paris: Octave Doin, 1891.

Bühler, Charlotte, "Zum Probleme der Sexuellen Entwicklung." *Z. Kinderheilk.* 51; 612-642, 1931.

Burgess, E. W., and Cottrell, L. S., *Predicting Success or Failure in Marriage*. Englewood Cliffs, N.J.: Prentice-Hall, Inc., 1939.

Darwin, Charles, *The Descent of Man*. New York: A. L. Burt, 1874.

de Rougemont, D., *Love in the Western World*. New York: Harcourt, Brace & Co., 1940.

Ellis, Albert, "A Study of Human Love Relationships." *J. Genet. Psychol.* 75; 61-71, 1949.

Ellis, Albert, *The Art and Science of Love*. New York: Lyle Stuart, 1960.

Ellis, Havelock, *Studies in the Psychology of Sex*. New York: Random House, 1936.

Elwin, Verrier, *The Baiga*. London: John Murray, 1939.

Finck, H. T., *Primitive Love and Love Stories*. New York: Charles Scribner's Sons, 1899.

Flügel, J. C., *The Psycho-analytic Study of the Family*. London: The Hogarth Press and The Institute of Psycho-analysis, 1926.

Ford, C. S., and Beach, F. A., *Patterns of Sexual Behavior*. New York: Harper & Brothers, 1951.

Freud, Sigmund, *Group Psychology and the Analysis of the Ego*. London: International Psycho-analytic Press, 1922.

Grant, Vernon W., *The Psychology of Sexual Emotion*. New York: Longmans, Green & Co., Inc., 1957.

Gross, L., "A Belief Pattern Scale for Measuring Attitudes toward Romanticism." *Am. Sociol. Rev.* 9; 463-472, 1944.

Hall, G. S., *Adolescence*. New York: Appleton-Century-Crofts, 1904.

Hamilton, G. V., *A Research in Marriage*. New York: A. and C. Boni, 1929.

Hirschfeld, Magnus, *Sex in Human Relationships*. London: John Lane, 1935.

Levey, H. B., "A Critique of the Theory of Sublimation." *Psychiatry* 2; 239-270, 1939.

Lowie, R. H., *Introduction to Cultural Anthropology*. New York: Farrar and Rinehart, 1940.

Lucka, Emil, *Eros: The Development of the Sex Relation through the Ages*. New York: G. P. Putnam's Sons, 1915.

Malinowski, Bronislaw, *The Sexual Life of Savages in Northwestern Melanesia*. New York: Eugenics Publishing Co., 1929.

Mead, Margaret, *Coming of Age in Samoa*. New York: William Morrow & Co., Inc., 1928.

Moll, Albert, *Untersuchungen über die Libido Sexualis*. Berlin: Kornfeld, 1898.

Moll, Albert, *The Sexual Life of the Child*. New York: The Macmillan Co., 1924.

Müller-Freienfels, R., *Die Liebe zwischen Mann und Frau*. Bad Homburg, V. D. H.: Siemens-Verlags-Gesellschaft, 1940.

Ortega y Gasset, J., *Uber die Liebe*. Berlin: Deutsche Verlags-Anstalt, 1933.

Parshley, H. M., *The Science of Human Reproduction*. New York: W. W. Norton & Co., Inc., 1933.

Reik, Theodor, *A Psychologist Looks at Love.* New York: Rinehart & Co., Inc., 1944.

Santayana, George, *The Sense of Beauty.* New York: Charles Scribner's Sons, 1896.

Sapir, Edward, "Observations on the Sex Problem in America." *Am. J. Psychiat.* 8; 527, 1928.

Schopenhauer, Arthur, *The World as Will and Idea* (Vol. III). London: Kegan Paul, Trench, Trubner, Ltd., 1891.

Sears, Robert R., *Survey of Objective Studies of Psychoanalytic Concepts.* New York: Social Science Research Council, 1943.

Spranger, E., *Psychologie des Jugendalters.* Leipzig: Verlag Quelle und Meyer, 1928.

Stendhal (Marie-Henri Beyle), *On Love.* New York: Boni and Liveright, 1927.

Strauss, A., "The Influence of Parent-Image upon Marital Choice." *Am. Sociol. Rev. 11;* 554-559, 1946.

Symonds, P. M., *The Dynamics of Human Adjustment.* New York: Appleton-Century, 1946.

Taylor, W. S., "A Critique of Sublimation in Males." *Genet. Psychol. Monog. 13;* 1-115, 1933.

Terman, L. M., *Psychological Factors in Marital Happiness.* New York: McGraw-Hill Book Co., 1938.

Waller, W., *The Family: A Dynamic Interpretation.* New York: The Dryden Press, 1938.

Weininger, Otto, *Sex and Character.* New York: G. P. Putnam's Sons, 1906.

Young, P. T., *Emotion in Man and Animal.* New York: John Wiley & Sons, Inc., 1943.

VERNON W. GRANT

Loving,
The Art of

Definition

EVER since Ovid's *Ars Amatoria* was translated into English, the phrase "the art of love" has had a somewhat salty flavor. However, that is not why a slightly different title is used for this article. "The art of love" speaks of love as a thing, whereas "the art of loving" refers to an activity.

This is an important distinction. So long as love is treated as a thing, to be built up mechanically by the addition of this piece of social relationship to that piece of amatory technique, it can never really flourish. To make the most of the human capacity for loving, it is necessary to treat it as an activity of the whole person, in which body and mind and emotions are all actively involved. This is not to deny the importance of social factors or of sexual techniques, but merely to put them in their proper place as aids to an essentially out-giving activity.

What we call "love" is a very complex thing. It includes what the Greeks called *agape,* a highly refined love of the spirit, and it also includes *eros,* a sensual love of the body. It is compounded of deeply physiological sexual urges, of esthetic preferences for a particular person's form and face, of emotional stimulation by speech and smile and gesture, of feelings of tenderness and protectiveness, of the desire for companionship and reassurance, of admiration and of tender affection, of self-gratification, and of self-denial. At a deeper level there may even be contradictory elements of desire to degrade, of strangely submerged hate impulses, but of these most of us are quite unconscious.

This complexity is what makes really rich loving difficult to achieve. It is not impossible, and no one should be deterred from a determination to achieve it, but it rarely drops unaided like manna from heaven. It is true, of course, that all normal people receive unasked the capacity for coition, and there can be great thrills of pleasure in that alone, but loving is more than copulation. It is also true that most of us develop without conscious thought something of each of the other elements of which love is compounded, but loving is more than a compound. To fuse these components into an active outpouring of the whole personality requires intelligent thought and a certain degree of sophistication, together with a capacity to unloose primitive passion without any sense of shame.

Intelligent thinking, however, must not take the form of cold-blooded cerebration whilst making love. There are couples who have read innumerable marriage manuals and articles on the art of love, but who fail to achieve sexual satisfaction because they set about things in the manner of a mechanic trying to start a reluctant machine. The time to learn about the art of loving and the techniques that can be put to its service is while *not* engaged in making love, when it is possible to be introspective and self-critical without interfering with that delicate interplay of personalities that successful loving requires. While actually making love, one may mentally note the success or otherwise of particular practices, and there should be just sufficient self-awareness to permit the conscious control of activities, but in the main one should allow freedom to the spontaneous impulses of the moment. A man may consciously decide that his wife's clitoris needs a little more stimulation, and change his position to permit it, but undue attention to what the textbook said may satisfy both him and his wife less than if he simply surrendered to a desire for deeper penetration. A woman may indicate to her husband that she would welcome caressing here or there, but if she worries about methods of attaining orgasm she is less likely to attain it.

The Many Successes of Love-making

There seems to be a fairly widespread delusion that some sort of moral obligation exists to achieve vaginal orgasm on each occasion of love-making, and many a woman's love life suffers from a quite unnecessary feeling of failure when this does not happen. Of course, the greatest sensation comes when the two partners reach the climax simultaneously, but this is not to say that other outcomes of love are to be despised. There can be a quiet, rich pleasure even if things go no further than the gentle caressing of each other's bodies, or the tentative beginning of copulation without great excitement. At times love can be expressed by means of the mouth, perhaps with tender contact of the lips or perhaps with passionate pressure and use of the tongue. At other times either partner may bring the other to orgasm, or each may bring each, by manual stimulation of the sex organs. Or, if the one has reached the climax in copulation and the other is still urgent, matters may be brought to a conclusion by vigorous caressing of the clitoris or penis. On yet other occasions, when the incompleted partner is too tired to respond to such caressing, it may be wise to lie awhile in each other's arms, and to leave the completion until rest has brought new vigor. And, if at times one partner is too tired or too keyed-up to respond fully, a period of gentle, smooth caressing and whispering of sweet nothings may allow gradual sinking to satisfying sleep. There is no prescribed pattern for making love, and no sort of obligation to reach the tape together as if loving were nothing but a three-legged race.

Confidence

Successful loving requires confidence—confidence in each other and confidence in one's self. A woman who suspects that her husband is simply using her as a convenient corpus for copulation will naturally feel resentful if he ejaculates while she is still left tense. The woman confident of her husband's love and consideration will be happy that he is happy and content in the knowledge that he will in some way relieve her tension. Similarly, a man who is unsure of his wife (or of himself) may be resentful if she attains orgasm while he is still unsatisfied; but a man without doubts will either continue until he reaches the climax or welcome manual stimulation by his wife. Or, if occasionally one partner is so exhausted as to be almost incapable of completing the other, the one still unsatisfied may resort to self-stimulation. In the absence of self-confidence or of mutual confidence, each occasion that is less than perfect becomes a "failure" and eats away at whatever confidence remains. But for confident lovers there is no failure, only varying degrees of success, and neither partner has any qualms about using whatever methods may be best suited to bring satisfaction on each occasion. Sometimes it may happen that either or both will not gain satisfaction in the sense of achieving orgasm, but a confident couple will be content to lie sweetly together, without any recrimination or self-blame, and know that things will probably be better next time.

Unfortunately, there are many factors in our society that make it difficult to develop the sort of mature confidence which is needed for the most successful loving. In the first place, there are general factors such as economic insecurity, fear of war, and worries arising out of daily occupation. Then, in many cases, there are specifically sexual worries, perhaps about the possibility of pregnancy or about potency. Only ostriches could fail to notice the many very dreadful features of the modern world—and there is no evidence that their love life is any the better for their blindering—but every effort should be made to insulate one's most intimate activities from these external disturbances.

The more acute sexual worries cannot be shut out in this way and should be dealt with effectively so that they are no longer cause for concern. In particular, a method of family planning that is effective, esthetically unobjectionable, inconspicuous, and does not require attention during love-making is for most couples an invaluable aid to the achievement of spontaneity.

Another and more subtle obstacle to satisfactory love relations is the romantic nonsense propagated by popular magazines, sentimental songs, and other media of mass communication. To be sentimental is at times very desirable, but it is dangerous if it is implied that true love can be found only on South Sea islands under a blue sky and a scorching sun. After all, such conditions are rarely available for the great mass of mankind. Or, on the other hand, it is sometimes implied that burning passion is only to be expected outside marriage, and that voluptuousness is proper to a mistress but not to a wife. Far less damage is done by the erotic literature that customs officials confiscate than by the trash that is sold openly on every bookstand. The former, even when it offends the common taste, is at least about real human feelings and real human situations, while the latter has no reality at all.

Interaction of Minds and Emotions

Spontaneity in loving depends first of all upon an innate physiological sex urge, which varies a good deal in power from one individual to another but with which most adults are sufficiently endowed. This is not enough, however, for spontaneous loving is not the same thing as unrestrained copulation, which any healthy mammal may perform. Loving implies an interaction of minds and emotions as well as a congress of genitalia, and it is precisely this fusion of the fleshly with the spiritual that constitutes the peculiar distinction of human love. The operative phrase, be it noted, is "fusion . . . with," not "restraining . . . by." Much misery has come from the notion that the carnal instincts are in some way unworthy and better

restrained by the purer powers of the spirit. For the human desire for fleshly sexual intercourse is a magnificent thing, to be gloried in and enjoyed to the uttermost, and the reason it should be fused with the spiritual is not that it may thereby be "purified," for it needs no purification, but that it may become yet more magnificent and yield yet greater joy. There are, of course, many occasions when restraint is desirable or even essential, but this is because of particular circumstances and not because of any inherent evil in bodily pleasure.

The Importance of Self-esteem

It is impossible to give one's self unreservedly to another, either in body or in spirit, unless one is first in complete possession of one's self. This is a rare achievement in perfection, but we can all come a long way toward it. To be in complete possession of one's own body means to have no reservations about it, no distaste for its structure, no disgust at its functions. It means to glory in the body, to be conversant with its limitations and yet see that it is good. It means to be proud of its capacities and to take joy in its pleasures. It means, in a very special sense of the word, "loving" oneself. Not as Narcissus did, in uncritical self-admiration, for that way lies failure to develop the capacity for loving others; nor selfishly, for true love will never sacrifice the beloved to itself; but so far as is necessary for the building of proper self-esteem and fortifying self-confidence. It is inherent in loving that the lover should be willing, even anxious, to put the interests and happiness of the beloved before his own inclinations; and sometimes this will mean, in the specifically sexual sphere, that one will accept a lesser satisfaction for oneself in order to give greater satisfaction to the partner. But this is a principle of willingness to sacrifice, and not an injunction to set oneself up as a martyr. Self-denial that amounts to self-abasement can be distinctly damaging, sometimes as damaging as downright selfishness.

Certainly in the early days of a sexual relationship it is good for each partner to take very great care to concentrate on ensuring that the other gains maximum joy, but it is also important to ensure that this does not develop into a habit of almost sickly tentativeness. As a relationship matures and the couple become more completely adjusted, it becomes more possible (and more desirable) to pay less attention to conscious considerateness and to allow self-assertion greater freedom of expression. Always there will be a need for care and tenderness, but not to the detriment of spontaneous vigor.

It is the woman rather than the man who is more often thought of as being in need of consideration, but in a confident love relationship she will enjoy the sensation that her lover is so swept away that he has lost all self-control. On a particular occasion she may lose something of the delicious thrills that can come from carefully considered stimulation, but in general she will gain something of more permanent value—a pride in her power of sexual stimulation. She may at times even be slightly shaken or bruised, but this soon passes away and the increase in her confidence remains. And, of course, the man whose wife has joyfully withstood his vigor should be sure to follow it by an especially grateful tenderness.

Masturbation and Heterosexual Development

The uninhibited acceptance of sensuality depends very much on early upbringing (although this is not to say that one cannot overcome an unsatisfactory training). Infantile masturbation may lead to the discovery that one's body is capable of yielding richly satisfying sensations, and fortunate are those who are allowed to make this discovery without the accompaniment of guilt or fear. With the coming of maturity, and specifically of mature love for another person, masturbation eventually gives way to the even richer sensations of heterosexual love, but this does not make masturbation in itself sinful or even in all circumstances undesirable. For most adolescents and young unmarried adults in our society, full sexual intercourse is prohibited either by religious conviction or by social convention, and in such circumstances masturbation is likely to continue. If it is accompanied by images of the loved one, and if it is free from all fear, it may

within limits actually aid the eventual establishment of satisfactory heterosexual relations. And when a couple is unable for some reason to have normal intercourse, mutual masturbation with loving words and phantasies may serve to enrich them.

Phantasies and Verbalizations

This question of what goes on in the mind while making love is an important one. We humans are marked off from the rest of the animal world by immensely greater mental powers, and to fail to use these powers is to remain on the animal level. It is one thing to accept the animal nature of our sexual physiology, and quite another thing to be content with it and neglect our peculiarly human potentialities. The joy of loving can be made much richer, can become more fully human, by bringing into play all our powers of imagination and expression. Individuals vary greatly in the extent to which they like to talk about their love, but certainly the dumb brute is no ideal to aim at.

In the preliminary stages of love-making, exchanged reminiscences of previous outstandingly successful occasions can be very stimulating, and there is no reason why one should not be stimulated by memories as well as by movements. As passion rises, some couples may be further stimulated by more forthright sexual conversation, and the only necessary limits are those imposed by the couple's own sensitivities. Nor need the mind confine itself to verbalization: it is also capable of calling up thrilling visual and other images, of responding to the sight and movements of the loved one's body, of taking pleasure in observed or recalled sounds and other sensations. It is in these ways, as well as in certain delicacies and restraints and deliberately imposed self-sacrifices, that human loving may be immensely richer than animal copulation.

There are those who regard such mental sexual activities as the debauchery of decadence, but they confuse debauchery with sophistication and decadence with civilization. Naturally, this type of activity may, like all others, be carried to excess, so that loving ceases to be an expression of total personalities and shrinks to a sort of carnalized mental masturbation, but this is not likely when a couple are also confident in their animal sexuality. The possibility of excess is not an argument against the use of a power, but only for discretion in its use. And it seems likely that, at any rate in the Western world, most couples would find greater joy in their loving if they were not afraid to set free their powers of pleasure in sexual thoughts and words and sights and sounds, in unison with the thrills of bodily contact.

Compatibility

This unison of mind and body implies shared interests, activities, and occupations. There is no need for man and wife to think alike and do alike all the time—indeed, it is much better if each brings something distinctive to their relationship and feels free to pursue individual interests—but there must be sufficient community of interest and taste to permit mental as well as physical communion. This is the justification of monogamous marriage from the humanist point of view, for the transitory affair does not provide the long-continued opportunity for the partners to come to know each other intimately. The first few occasions of intercourse may be intensely exciting, and sensually satisfying, but it is only with the passage of time that a couple can hope to reach the heights of loving. In many cases it takes time to achieve even physiological harmony, and this is often the cause of deep disappointment. For this the overromanticization of love in our culture must bear some responsibility, but so must the individual who has accepted without thought the idea that all becomes perfect on the wedding night.

A moment's consideration should indicate how unrealistic it is to expect immediate perfection in such a richly varied activity as loving. In most cases a good deal of experimentation will be needed before a couple discovers what modes of loving give them the greatest satisfaction. That is why, leaving quite aside all pronouncements of dogmatic theology or all conventions of suburban respectability, the idea of a couple's occasionally "going the whole way" to decide whether or not they are sufficiently adapted to marry is quite futile. Adap-

tation is not a thing that already exists: it is a thing to be brought about.

The Possibilities of Variety in Sexual Expression

As a sexual union matures, more and more possibilities of variety emerge. Considering merely the relative bodily positions and movements of the partners, there is a vast range of choice. Some will prefer the movements that are possible with the man lying above the woman, others those possible lying side by side, others those possible with the woman above, and many will prefer to ring the changes on these and other positions. But to talk in terms of bodily position is to risk appearing as an advocate for a sort of mechanical engineering, and the situation is in fact much more complex and subtle than that. A couple confident of themselves, and of each other, and sensitive to their mutual reactions, will also explore the infinite possibilities of varied caresses, varied speed, varied vigor, varied rhythm, and varied mental accompaniments to bodily activity. This they will do not in the way of coldly calculated experimentation, for that withers spontaneity, but rather in the manner of artists, expressing their feelings freely through the medium of their bodies and yet retaining just sufficient awareness of technique to learn from experience.

A Loving Atmosphere and the "Proprieties" of Love-making

Because we humans are social animals, capable not only of expressing innate urges but also of modifying them by learned behavior and enriching them by the interaction of personalities, what happens during physical love-making is much affected by what has gone before. A couple who have spent the evening withdrawn from each other, perhaps preoccupied by their separate activities or perhaps even hostile, can scarcely expect that the moment they go up to bed they will be able to make love successfully. There is nothing magical about being between a pair of sheets, and the most that can be immediately achieved in such circumstances is mere sexual detumescence. Richer loving is possible only if, first, the hostility or isolation is dissolved away and the two personalities brought into some sort of unison, and this is often more easily done before going to bed than after. Ten minutes with books put away and all distractions discarded, ten minutes spent in relaxed and friendly conversation, with perhaps a few kisses and a tentative cuddle, can establish a relationship from which to proceed further by natural stages after going to bed.

For that matter, there is no need to go to bed. Many people seem to imagine that what is perfectly proper in the bedroom is somehow improper in the living room, that what is permissible in the dark is impermissible in the light, that what can be decently done indoors is indecent in the open. But this convention that sexual intercourse must be undertaken only in conventional circumstances can be most damaging to spontaneity, and many a caress started auspiciously in one room has gone cold by the time the partners have moved into another—especially if they first go through all the customary bedtime toilet procedures. Indeed, there is among certain social groups an altogether excessive preoccupation with the niceties of detergency, and perhaps a little less concern for bacteriological sterility in intercourse might result in less emotional sterility also.

If there is the necessary privacy, love-making may be delightful by the warm fireside in the lounge, with whatever cushions or rugs lie at hand in the service of comfort. There is no need for undressing to be effected in one determined operation in bedroom or bathroom, for it can proceed garment by garment wherever privacy permits. And, although it can be delightful to come together already naked, there is also a special pleasure in gradually undressing each other. It is only rarely that most couples can find opportunity, consistent with the requirements of public decency, for loving out of doors, but soft grass and warm sun are very tempting and if intercourse is possible in these circumstances it can have a peculiar beauty.

Summary

The art of loving, then, is like any other great art. It requires the inner urge and a certain urgency, but it also requires restraint and discipline. It requires sensitivity and tenderness, but it also requires confidence and vigor. It needs knowledge and patient practice and diligent application, but it needs also the courage to experiment and to take some risks. Since two personalities are directly involved, there is a special need for considerateness and for self-sacrifice, but it is also necessary to guard against any tendency to self-submergence or self-abasement. More than any other art, loving demands a delicate fusion of often conflicting separates, but in maturity it yields rich rewards that more than compensate for every difficulty.

References

American Association of Marriage Counselors, *Marriage Counseling Today: A Casebook.* New York: Association Press, 1958.

Berl, Emmanuel, *The Nature of Love.* New York: The Macmillan Co., 1924.

Bibby, Cyril, *Sex Education: A Guide for Parents, Teachers, and Youth Leaders.* London: The Macmillan Co., 1944; New York: Emerson Books, Inc., 1946.

Bridges, James W., *The Meaning and Varieties of Love.* Cambridge: Sci-Art Publishers, 1935.

Chesser, Eustace, *Love Without Fear.* New York: New American Library, 1949.

de Rougemont, Denis, *Love in the Western World.* New York: Harcourt, Brace & Co., 1940.

Ellis, Albert, *How to Live with a Neurotic.* New York: Crown Pub., Inc., 1957.

Ellis, Albert, *Sex Without Guilt.* New York: Lyle Stuart, 1958.

Ellis, Albert, *The Art and Science of Love.* New York: Lyle Stuart, 1960.

Ellis, Havelock, *On Life and Sex: Essays on Love and Virtue.* New York: Garden City Publishing Co., 1937.

Fromm, Erich, *The Art of Loving.* New York: Harper & Brothers, 1956.

Grant, Vernon W., *The Psychology of Sexual Emotion.* New York: Longmans, Green & Co., Inc., 1957.

Hamilton, G. V., *A Research in Marriage.* New York: Boni, 1929.

Landis, Paul H., *Making the Most of Marriage.* New York: Appleton-Century-Crofts, 1957.

Levy, John, and Munroe, Ruth, *The Happy Family.* New York: Alfred A. Knopf, Inc., 1938.

Lucka, Emil, *Eros.* New York: G. P. Putnam's Sons, 1915.

Montagu, Ashley, *The Meaning of Love.* New York: Julian Press, Inc., 1955.

Reik, Theodor, *A Psychologist Looks at Love.* New York: Rinehart & Co., Inc., 1944.

Vincent, Clark E., *Readings in Marriage Counseling.* New York: Thomas Y. Crowell Co., 1957.

CYRIL BIBBY

Marriage

Definition

MARRIAGE is a social status defining the rights and duties of persons of opposite sex living in a more or less durable union. Other comparable social statuses are those of the single, the widowed, and the divorced. Social status refers to one's position in the group, or the evaluation of one's position by the group. The group distinguishes the married person from the single or the widowed or the divorced person. In some societies a youth is not considered to be an adult until he or she marries. The group or society may require a marriage license and a ceremony or wedding of some sort, as in Western societies today. Or, as in many preliterate societies, a man and woman who agree to assume the social status of marriage simply establish a household together. Their living together is evidence of marriage and is so construed by the community. There is a presumption that the relationship will endure and that it will differ from the more episodic and discontinuous relationship between them which may have existed previously.

The term *marriage* is usually applied only to human beings. Other animals mate, and their unions may be quite durable; but we do not call these unions marriages, because the lower animals do not have a culture that defines marital status.

Meaning of Marriage

A key to marriage is the sexual factor. This is scarcely surprising, since marriage is a relationship between persons of opposite sex. In Western society, sex apart from marriage is frowned upon, a fact that strengthens the significance of sex for marriage. But in many preliterate societies sexual intercourse before marriage is sanctioned for both sexes. There is a period of experimentation among adolescents in these societies that eventuates in the pairing off of congenial couples. Sex in these circumstances is not such a crucial motive for marriage as it is in Western society today. Instead, the economic motive is more decisive. Marriage is an effective arrangement for personal and societal self-maintenance and survival. Husband and wife, through division of labor, can more advantageously feed and clothe and protect themselves than either can by living separately. If, for example, an Eskimo hunter, in addition to trapping animals, had—at the close of a long, bitter-cold day of hunting—to return to his igloo and prepare his food, as well as to take care of his frozen clothes, he would be hard put to it. Instead, his wife has fresh clothes and a hot meal waiting for him. Eskimo women spend such long hours chewing frozen leather skins in order to make them supple that eventually they wear their teeth down to the gums.

From the standpoint of society, cardinal functions of marriage are reproduction and socialization of offspring. The group cannot survive unless its numbers are replenished, and the culture cannot be maintained unless it is transmitted afresh to each new generation. Marriage is the socially approved agency for reproducing the race. In rural Scandinavia, and in other traditional rural societies as well, it was the custom to accord rights of privacy to engaged couples, including the right to sexual intercourse. In many cases marriage occurred only after the woman was pregnant. This indicates the high priority placed on reproduction as a function of marriage. It also indicates that marriage is highly valued in connection with the rearing of children. Mankind has discovered that two parents are better than one for the education and protection of the young. A child has difficulty learning the appropriate behavior of males and females without the example and tutelage of both parents.

The Incidence of Marriage

In view of the great utility of marriage to the individual and society, it is not surprising that marriage is a universal institution and that, next to birth and death, it is the most common major experience in all societies. In some societies, such as India, it is nearly universal. There the Hindu religion makes marriage a sacramental duty, since Hinduism teaches that the married state is one of the essential four stages in an individual's life. As a result, the spinster is practically nonexistent. An unmarried woman of advanced age also is a rarity in preliterate societies. Hunting and agricultural societies, which utilize effectively the labor of women as well as of men, provide conditions that encourage the marriage of women.

Industrial societies, on the contrary, provide less opportunity for women to make a comparable economic contribution in marriage. In industrial societies, moreover, women are less dependent on marriage for economic support, since they can obtain jobs. As a result, marriage is generally less prevalent in industrial than in agricultural societies. In the United States, for example, about one in ten of both sexes reaches the age of 45 without having married. Some agricultural societies, however, have a smaller percentage of their population married than some industrial nations. Rural Ireland has one of the lowest marriage rates of all nations.

Age at First Marriage

Among the simians, mating occurs at puberty. It would seem that mating would have also occurred at an early age among our earliest human ancestors; but of this we can, of course, have no knowledge. The biological age for marriage and the cultural age for marriage may not coincide for, as we have seen, marriage carries economic, educational, and protective responsibilities for which the youth may not be as ready as they are for the sexual function. In a survey of a small sample of preliterate societies, none was found where the females married under the age of 16 and the males under the age of 20. Yet the practice in Western agricultural society, in earlier centuries, was for females to marry at the age of 12 and males at the age of 14. At least these are the common-law ages for marriage, although we do not know how many youths married at these ages. In the United States at present, eighteen states still recognize common-law marriage. The trend, however, is away from such marriage. The most common statutory age for marriage in the United States is 16 for females and 18 for males, with parental consent; without parental consent, the corresponding ages are 18 and 21.

The early age at marriage in literate agricultural societies is explained in part by the occupational situation. Since most boys know that, when they grow up, they will be farmers, and nearly all girls know they will be farmers' wives, they can readily receive the requisite training. On the contrary, in an industrial society the job situation is complex and often uncertain, and preparation takes longer. Another reason for earlier marriage in agricultural societies is the practice of living with one's in-laws, which is more extensive than it is in industrial societies.

In some countries, especially those of the East, there is the custom of infant betrothal. Children may be pledged to each other by their parents, and they may be legally married even before puberty, although they usually do not live together as husband and wife until they are sexually mature. If, as in India, it is the belief that all should marry, and if, moreover, it is the custom for one's family to choose one's mate, then it is understandable that legal commitments be made as soon as possible. Under the circumstances, why delay? The Indian government has sought to curb child marriages, and the Child Marriage Restraint Act of 1929 forbids marriages of males under 18 and females under 14. According to the 1951 Census, however, there were 2,833,000 married males, 6,180,000 married females, 66,000 widowers, and 134,000 widows between the ages of 5 and 14. The great mass of Indians, more than four-fifths of the total population, live in the more than 500,000 villages, 70 per cent of which have a population of 500 or less. In these villages the old customs are very strong.

In the United States in recent decades (since 1890) the percentage of young people under 25 years of age who are married has increased, despite an increase in schooling. An indication of the trend toward earlier marriage in the United States is the figures for the median age at first marriage. In 1890 the figures were 26.1 for males and 22.0 for females, whereas in 1950 the corresponding data were 23.0 and 20.1. This trend occurred both in urban and in rural areas and for whites and Negroes. The United States has one of the highest marriage rates of Western industrial nations, and a relatively high proportion of the population is married. The principal reasons are thought to be increased income and the spread of the practice of birth control.

Choice of Mate

In large areas of the world, as in India, marriages are arranged by kin. The potential groom's mother is usually the one who takes the initiative in finding a mate for her son, although go-betweens may arrange the details. This seems odd to most Westerners, who are accustomed to considerable self-determination in the choice of a mate. But arranged marriages make sense in the agricultural societies where they occur, for in these societies the family as a unit is the powerful force, tied as it is to property in land and the transmission of the family holding from generation to generation. Title to the land belongs to the family and not to individual members.

In this kind of economy, sons work for the family, and there are few, if any, occupations for women apart from the family farm. It is also the responsibility of a son to marry and to produce a male heir to perpetuate the family name and perhaps to perform essential religious duties. In choosing a wife, sentiment is not the predominant consideration but rather practical matters such as good health, good stock, and skill as a worker. Usually the young people

are given some voice in the selection of a mate, and the parents do not insist if their choice is opposed; but there are instances where the youths are not consulted, and their first glimpse of each other is at their wedding.

In industrial societies, where young people are not dependent upon their families for jobs and economic support, the youth have considerable freedom in choosing a mate. The situation is reversed, and it is the parents who may be accorded the veto power. Parents, however, may still greatly influence their child's choice of mate by the kind of community in which they live, the kind of associates they encourage, the kind of schools they select, and so on.

Even where, as in the United States, young people have considerable freedom in the choice of a mate, the freedom is not absolute but is subject to a number of limitations. One of these, which is universal, is the incest taboo. In all societies marriage is prohibited within certain degrees of family affinity. The taboo against marriage within one's immediate family is universal or nearly so. Beyond this point the situation varies. In the United States, for example, the marriage of first cousins is usually illegal, whereas among Arabs cousin marriage is preferred, or at least common. In some places the marriage of brothers and sisters has been permitted and even favored; but the practice has usually been restricted to the royal family, as in the case of the Ptolemies. Cleopatra was the product of a number of generations of brother-sister intermarriages. The explanation here is the belief in the special divinity of the royal family and the consequent need to keep the blood pure.

Many volumes have been written in the effort to explain the incest taboo. It is not an instinct, since it does not occur among the primates. One theory to account for the incest taboo is that incest is biologically harmful. Marriage outside the family may have eugenic value, but only if there is some defect or taint in the family line. Inbreeding is eugenically beneficial if it intensifies good traits, and is so used in animal and plant husbandry. Of course, there have been cases of defects such as hemophilia being transmitted through a royal family that has practiced intermarriage, but there have also been cases (such as the Ptolemies) where inbreeding did not lead to physical weakness. Since members of the same family are more likely than are unrelated persons to have the same defects, intermarriage is more likely to produce a double dose of defective traits. There is thus, in terms of probabilities, some safety in marrying outside the family. In most small pre-literate societies, however, the members of the band are likely to be kin, and there is in reality considerable intermarriage. This may be the reason for the rule which is sometimes found, known as village exogamy, that a mate must be sought from another community.

Perhaps the most plausible explanation for the rule against incestuous union is that marriage within the family would tend to disorganize it. Father and son and mother and daughter might be pitted against each other. This is, of course, the basis of the Oedipus and Electra theories of Freud.

In addition to exogamous rules affecting marriage, there are also endogamous ones, that is, rules prescribing some of the traits to be sought in a mate. Thus, a Moslem woman may marry only a Moslem man, although the man is free to marry a woman of any faith. The Roman Catholic Church discourages marriage outside the faith and permits it only under certain conditions. The Orthodox Jewish faith is also opposed to intermarriage. Also there are legal barriers against the intermarriage of whites and certain other races in some states of the United States, as well as in other countries.

There are many studies to show that, with respect to social characteristics, marriages tend to be homogamous, that is, that like tends to marry like. Thus, persons of the same economic and social-class positions tend to pair off. In the United States this is not due to endogamous rules such as those pertaining to religion, or to laws such as those having to do with race, but is the result of contact and group pressure. Members of the same socioeconomic class tend to associate in an intimate manner with one another more than with members of other classes, and these contacts become the basis for marriage. Studies also show homogamy in age, formal education, previous marital status, intelligence test scores, interests, and values.

On the other hand, there is evidence that in emotional characteristics there is a good deal of heterogamy, or the mating of opposites. For example, the submissive type of woman may be attracted to the type of man who likes to dominate; and the man who craves nurturance may find attractive the woman who likes to mother him. In other words, persons are attracted to those who tend to satisfy their emotional needs. It would seem, offhand, that this would be a sensible factor to keep in mind in choosing a mate and would contribute toward compatibility.

Methods of Mate Choice

In addition to arranged marriages and marriages initiated by the couple themselves, there are other methods of obtaining a mate, such as capture. This is almost never the usual method for any society and is used only against the enemy, whose captured women subsequently are more likely to occupy the status of concubines or slaves, usually without the rights of legitimate wives.

There is also the method of bride purchase, although the meaning is different from, say, that of a horse trade, for although a wife may be bought, she is not customarily sold. Marriage nearly everywhere involves economic considerations, and bride purchase should be thought of in these terms. A groom or his family pays so many head of cattle for a wife, probably because her family has invested a good deal in rearing her; when she marries, she leaves her parental home, and her family is deprived of her services, especially if village exogamy is the rule and she goes to live with her husband in another village. The bride price is to compensate the family for their economic loss. Or, financial considerations are used to help give the marriage stability. A Moslem bridegroom may contract to give his bride a certain sum, half at marriage and the other half should the marriage break up. More often than not, there will be economic contributions to the newlyweds from both families, the one supplying, say, the house and the other the furnishings. In many European cultures it was customary for the bride to bring a dowry to her marriage. So the economic contribution is sometimes made by the male and sometimes by the female (or their respective families), or both. In general, a determining consideration as to who makes the contribution is the relative value attached by the society to the economic role of men and women. Ideological influences may also be operative.

Marriage Ceremony

In most societies, marriage is differentiated from mere mating by a ceremony of some sort, commonly called a wedding. The community aspect is evident in part in the fact that on this occasion there may be group festivities and an appreciable distribution of food. The wedding with witnesses present is, moreover, a public acknowledgment of the new status being conferred on the couple.

Marriage is a secular matter in most preliterate societies; but, very early, marriage took on religious significance. Some religions regard marriage as holy; some regard it as sacramental, so sacred that it may not be broken. In the United States and in England, the law recognizes both civil and religious marriages. In France, on the other hand, a civil ceremony is required; a religious wedding alone is not legal. This forces a couple to have two marriage ceremonies if they want a religious ceremony. In some countries the civil ceremony must come first. In the United States religious weddings predominate. For certain religious groups, such as the Quakers, no officiating individual is required to perform a marriage; the couple simply plight their troth in the presence of witnesses.

In some areas there is also a requirement of a marriage license prior to the wedding and, in certain places, a waiting period before marriage. A growing practice is to require medical tests before a license is issued, covering a blood test and sometimes a chest X-ray. However, these tests are given just for information in many places and may not be used to prevent a marriage.

In some places, formal permission is required for marriage; in other places, informal consent of the group is sufficient. When both systems exist in the same society, a problem may arise, as in the United States, where in some jurisdictions both statutory and common-law marriage are recognized, whereas in other states—now a majority—only statutory marriage is legal. Common-law marriage developed in earlier times when societies were relatively small, with a homogeneous membership, little physical mobility, and the presence of few strangers in the local group, which meant that the group could readily control the behavior of its members by informal methods. Today, in our complex, highly mobile society with many strangers, public opinion is less effective as a means of social control, and more formal means of control are required. This explains why common-law marriage is being abolished.

The conflict of the two systems of common-law and statutory marriage is particularly sharp in many Latin countries of the Caribbean area and South America. The very high illegitimacy rates, often more than 50 per cent, that are reported for these countries reflect the fact that only statutory marriages are recorded as legal. Usually the state recognizes Church marriages but some states do not, which means that for the religiously minded, two ceremonies are needed, a religious and a secular one. Because of poverty, or pre-Christian traditions, many of the natives in Central and South America marry without benefit of clergy or the law. Their children are listed as illegitimate, but their marriages may be just as durable as the legal marriages.

There are, especially in some neighborhoods of large cities, men and women who live together in a relationship which is not common-law marriage but rather what is sometimes referred to as "free love." Greenwich Village in New York is such a neighborhood. Some unions may be said to be "trial marriages" because they eventuate in formal marriage, but many do not. Bohemians in these Latin Quarters may be viewed as persons who see in marriage only the loss of freedom and self-expression. No union of the sexes is a marriage unless it is, either formally or informally, recognized by society as binding.

Forms of Marriage

The two sexes that are united in marriage can be combined in a limited number of ways. (1) One male may be married to one female.

When this system is binding, and no exceptions are permitted, the system is known as *monogamy*. (2) One male may be wedded to more than one female. The system that sanctions this arrangement is called *polygyny*. (3) More than one male may be married to one female, an arrangement designated *polyandry*. Polygyny and polyandry are forms of plural marriage, or *polygamy*. Theoretically it is possible for more than one male to be married to more than one female, a system called group marriage, but this form of marriage does not appear as a cultural norm in any society.

Monogamous marriage is the most common variety, even in societies that allow plural marriage. The Koran permits a Moslem to have as many as four wives if he can support them and if he is able to show them equal consideration. Since this is difficult to do, plural marriage is not encouraged, it is said. Studies of Moslem countries show less than 10 per cent of marriages to be plural. Economic factors (the cost of supporting a family) favor monogamy, as does also the number of men and women of marriageable ages in a society, which is usually in fair balance.

Polygyny is the result not so much of biological factors as of cultural ones. When the society permits it, a man takes more than one wife in order to show his wealth or his position of importance or leadership. If he is a man with high social status, say a chief, he may be required by custom to have several wives. Thus, in the period of Mormon history when polygyny was approved, great pressure was brought to bear on the church leaders to practice polygyny, whether as individuals they wished to do so or not.

In Christian nations, monogamy is the rule, and no other arrangement is permitted. Many preliterate societies also follow the same practice. Even in the Moslem countries, the trend is away from polygyny, which is better adapted to agricultural conditions than to the new industrial society that is developing.

Whereas monogamy is numerically by far the most common form of marriage, the majority of societies permit polygyny. In a sample of representative cultures, including historical and contemporary as well as primitive societies, it was found that 43 were strictly monogamous

and 195 allowed at least limited plural marriage. Polygyny has certain advantages. It utilizes the reproductive capacity of females more fully than does monogamy. Among hunters, the hazards of life often lead to a surplus of women, since the men and not the women are the hunters. Under the circumstances, polygyny increases the women's chances of marriage. In the farming culture, the sexes are likely to be in fair balance, and this reason for polygyny is not so important; but additional wives have economic utility.

Whatever the reasons for the practice, it must not be thought that polygyny works to the disadvantage of the women or that they view it with disfavor. On the contrary, in a polygynous society the women are its chief supporters. In their dealings with their husband, the several wives may have some advantage in collective bargaining. They also benefit by the division of labor the system permits. Among Mormon women who were in plural marriages there was considerable objection to the system; but this was because the converts to Mormonism were recruited from Protestant denominations espousing monogamy, and the Mormons were surrounded by a culture favorable to monogamy and hostile to polygyny. The situation is different in most preliterate societies.

Since multiple marriage is not, however, without its special tensions, various arrangements are often followed in an effort to minimize them. One is the provision of separate dwellings for the several wives and their offspring. A status system is also established, with one wife designated the chief wife. The husband must follow a system of rotation in visiting his wives; and departure from the system, except with good cause, is viewed with disfavor. An interesting variety of plural marriage is sororal polygyny, the marriage of a man to several sisters. The advantage here is that the sisters are already better adjusted to one another than strangers are likely to be.

Polyandry is highly infrequent, perhaps because it goes counter to the biological tendency of the male to demand exclusive possession of his mate, judging by the evidence from the simians. If so, culture counteracts biology when polyandry occurs. The explanation is complex;

but an important consideration seems to be the scarcity of women in societies where polyandry is practiced, a scarcity resulting from female infanticide. Among the Todas, for example, the sex ratio was 127-259 males to 100 females. But why the infanticide? The answer is probably the extreme poverty of the people, resulting from the inhospitable environment. That this is not the sole reason for polyandry is shown by the fact that other societies have as extreme poverty without infanticide, and still others practice infanticide when the poverty is not so great. In the remote Himalayas, where arable land is scarce, fraternal polyandry is practiced, a group of brothers sharing a wife. All the children are regarded as the offspring of the eldest brother. When the brothers die, the estate goes to the sons, who in turn marry one wife. Polyandry appears to be associated with a system of land tenure that prevents fragmentation of already small land holdings. There is also a nonfraternal variety of polyandry, such as that found among the Marquesan. However, polyandry is very rare and is incompatible with the surplus of women generally found in human societies.

Residence

When marriage occurs, one or both of the spouses must leave the parental roof. Who shall it be, and where shall the couple take up residence? A sample of 250 societies showed the following distribution: In 146 cases the residence was patrilocal, that is, the bride went to live with her husband in his father's home. In 38 societies the residence was matrilocal, the husband going to live with his bride in her mother's house. An arrangement permitting a shifting back and forth, or matri-patrilocal residence, occurred in 22 societies. The newlyweds were permitted to live near the parents of either spouse (bilocal residence). A system like that in the United States, with the married couple setting up an independent residence in a new location (neolocal residence), occurred in 17 societies; and in 8, avunculocal residence was the rule, the married couple living at the residence of the maternal uncle of the groom. In short, it is usually the woman who changes residence at marriage.

Status of Married Women

The fact that the bride is usually the one to shift her residence means that ordinarily the loss of her economic services to her family is regarded as less serious than the loss of a son's services to his family. Here we have the principal key to the status of women in a society: the evaluation of their contribution to economic production.

The status of women is generally lower than that of men in hunting cultures because survival depends more on the hunters of big game, the men, than it does on the food gatherers, the women. In general, women have the lowest status of all in pastoral societies, where the care of the flocks is a masculine pursuit. The status of women is highest as a rule in hoe culture, because women play a big part in the planting and care of the fields, as among the Hopi. Women are thought to have discovered the domestication of plants. In advanced agriculture using the plow, however, the more muscular male is favored, and the status of women is lower than in the hoe culture.

Where the husband or some older male member of his family, say his father or grandfather, has the decision-making power, the system is called patriarchal. It is matriarchal where the power lies with the women. Patriarchal societies are very numerous, but matriarchal societies are rare and may be nonexistent. What usually passes for matriarchal is in reality a matrilocal system. Thus, among the Hopis, when a man marries, he goes to live with his wife's family. The Hopi women own the land and the crops. Descent is traced through the female line. A man's first loyalty is to his mother's clan. But the chiefs of the Hopi are men. Serious discipline of children is administered by the mother's brother, that is, by the child's uncle, not by his mother. A society that is often referred to in the literature as matriarchal is the Iroquois. True, the women comprising the council that chose the chief exercised considerable power; but the chief was always a man. Still, it may be said that in the sphere of the family, the women in a matrilineal, matrilocal society exercise considerable power.

Probably the most significant development

in marriage in recent times is the equalitarian relationship between husband and wife. There have been equalitarian systems of marriage in the past, and even among preliterates such arrangements can be found; but they have not been common. The singular thing about the present situation is the trend toward equality of husband and wife, not merely in the United States, but in societies around the world.

When a woman married one hundred years ago in the United States, she lost her separate legal status and became as it were a ward of her husband. Her personal property, acquired before marriage, became her husband's. Real property owned before marriage she retained, but her husband controlled its management and received all revenues derived from it. She could not sue or be sued or make a contract without her husband's consent. He was the sole guardian of their children. The divorce laws favored the husband.

At the present time, the married woman has full control of separate property owned by her before her marriage or acquired by her after marriage. Twelve states are so-called community property states, in which each spouse has an equal share of all income and property acquired after the marriage by either spouse. A married woman now has full contractual rights. In thirty-four states she is the legal co-guardian of her children. The divorce laws now favor women, principally in the greater number of grounds for divorce available to them, at least in practice if not in principle. Thus, a wife may sue her husband for divorce on the ground of physical cruelty or nonsupport; but it is not as appropriate for a husband to do so.

Prominent among the causes of the change in the status of women are economic factors, especially the great increase in the number of jobs available to women. In the earlier agricultural society, a farmer's wife worked hard and made an important economic contribution both at home and in the fields, but her work was unpaid family labor. Today, in our industrial economy, she works, if she is employed, as an individual, not as a member of a family team; she does not work for her family; and she is paid in money. This makes her economically independent of her husband. The probabilities are very great that she will have

worked before marriage; and she may continue to work after marriage, at least until the first child comes. More and more women who drop out of the labor market to have their families return to work after the children reach school age. During the 1950's in the United States, the number of working wives over 35 years of age increased by about 50 per cent, whereas the number under 35 rose by only 10 per cent. Regardless of age, the increase in the percentage of married women in the labor force has been phenomenal since just before the turn of the century. In 1890, 4.6 per cent of married women were gainfully employed, whereas the percentage in 1950 was 26.8, and in 1957, 30.8. Some of these married women were separated from their husbands, although not divorced. If we consider only married women living with their husbands, 29.6 per cent were in the labor force in 1957. Seven out of ten husbands are still the sole support of their wives. But if one is interested in the shape of things to come, then one notes the sharp increase in working wives over the years, indicating the strong likelihood that even more wives will be employed in the future.

The greater job opportunities for married women are not the only reason for their equalitarian status. Important, too, are the greater educational opportunities open to them. These two factors of jobs and schooling are, of course, interrelated, for the schooling helps to prepare for jobs, and the increased income of American families makes it possible to educate more girls as well as boys. The democratic principle is also a leavening influence, but the democratic idea is an old one and needs favorable supporting influences for its growth.

The Evolution of Marriage

There have been various efforts to describe the evolution of marriage as a social institution, but without much success. Herbert Spencer propounded the theory that the family has evolved from the simple to the complex, from the homogeneous to the heterogeneous. The modern family, however, is more simple in terms of organization and the scope of its functions than was the earlier family of agricultural times. Again, Henry Morgan advanced the theory that marriage has evolved by stages from earliest times to the present. Finding monogamy in increasing vogue in the present, he postulated that mankind must have initially lived in hordes, in a state of promiscuity. Later, according to Morgan, the family organized around the mother and children. The female was supposed to consort with a varying number of males. Still later, Morgan wrote, the male mated with a varying number of females, establishing patriarchal rule. And finally monogamy evolved.

This theory was erroneous. As Edward A. Westermarck showed in his *History of Human Marriage* (1891), strict monogamy existed in some societies from the beginning. At least, monogamy as the required practice is found in some preliterate societies with very rudimentary material culture. There is no knowledge regarding the marriage practices of our earliest human forbears, since marriage customs, unlike chipped flints, do not survive.

In short, no grand unilinear and world-wide evolution of marriage can be described, unlike technology, which has evolved from the simple flints of the Paleolithic age to the elaborate steel tools of the present, and unlike government, which has evolved from simple leadership to the complex organization of the modern state. Instead, with regard to marriage, we have variations in form and function, depending on changes in the social situation, mainly the means of economic production. Some of these variations have been described.

Although no evolution in the structure of marriage is discernible from earliest human times to the present, some highly significant, broad changes can be noted in marriage during, let us say, approximately the past two hundred years, or the period since the Industrial Revolution. These changes are evident also in lesser degree in Eastern societies now in process of industrialization. These changes are reflected in the breakdown of the extended family, emphasizing kinship, which is characteristic of rural societies. The extended family is a complex of marital groups; its breakdown has resulted in the establishment of the separate, small, independent household of husband, wife, and offspring. The extended family arranged the marriages of its youth, but the young people in our urban civilization show a strong preference for self-determination in the choice of a mate. Affection and psychological compatibility replace utilitarian and status considerations as the basis for choice. A new institution, courtship, is required if young people are to meet freely and to make their own selection, an institution not needed when marriages were arranged.

Most significant of all, mass education for both sexes and expanding occupational opportunities for women in an industrial society have led to relations of equality between husband and wife, replacing the patriarchalism of the past. Moreover, if a husband has several wives, it is difficult to achieve equality between husband and wife. Hence, polygyny is disappearing in areas of the world where the prevailing religion allows it as these areas become increasingly industrialized. Polygyny has always been a validating device for high social status. With industrialization, other methods of validating status, particularly the acquisition of consumer goods, become available to more persons, and the need for polygyny diminishes.

References

Ellis, Albert, *The Origins and the Development of the Incest Taboo*. New York: Lyle Stuart, 1963.

Goodsell, W., *A History of Marriage and the Family*. New York: The Macmillan Co., 1934.

Hobhouse, L. T., Wheeler, G. C., and Ginsberg, M., *Material Culture and Social Institutions of the Simpler Peoples*. London: Chapman and Hall, 1930.

Howard, G. E., *A History of Matrimonial Institutions* 3 vols. Chicago: University of Chicago Press, 1904.

Linton, Ralph, *The Study of Man*. New York: D. Appleton-Century, 1936, Chs. 10-11.

Lowie, Robert H., *Primitive Society*. New York: Boni and Liveright, 1925, Chs. 2-8.

Murdock, George Peter, *Social Structure*. New York: The Macmillan Co., 1949.

Nimkoff, M. F., *Marriage and the Family*. Boston: Houghton Mifflin Co., 1947.

Ogburn, W. F., and Nimkoff, M. F., *Technology and the Changing Family*. Boston: Houghton Mifflin Co., 1955.

Stern, Bernhard J., *The Family: Past and Present*. New York: D. Appleton-Century, 1938.

Westermarck, E. A., *A History of Human Marriage* (3 vols.) New York: The Macmillan Co., 1921.

M. F. NIMKOFF

Marriage Conciliation

MARRIAGE terminations by legal action are a matter of public record in most countries of the world today. From these records, and from estimates by scholars, where comparable recorded figures are not available, we learn that during the past century throughout the civilized world actions initiated by partners and terminations granted by courts (divorce, annulment, and separate maintenance) have increased many fold in proportion to population increases and in proportion to fluctuating marriage rates. The largest increases have occurred during the past quarter century in those countries in which industrialization is advanced and in which secular standards tend to prevail over religious sanctions.

During this same quarter century, in these same countries, but developing at a lag, marriage education, guidance, counseling, and reconciliation services have developed. Information about these services is difficult to obtain and figures are not closely comparable. Agency reports and unpublished office summaries from the professions of welfare, education, medicine, and religion tell of increasing numbers of requests for counseling services from unhappy and estranged marriage partners. Similarly, marriage-guidance bureaus, government-sponsored and supported in Britain, South Africa, Indonesia, and other countries, report that requests for adjustment and reconciliation counseling have increased over requests for sex education, marriage preparation, and preparental guidance.

Since unabated discord sooner or later appeals to the law, leaders in this profession, as Bradway (1956) and Rheinstein (1956) have shown, are coming to think of reconciliation as one of their responsibilities with domestic relations and matrimonial cases. In general, the incidence and spread of conciliation services roughly parallels increases in termination rates. The states of the United States, with their variety of grounds for termination and of court procedures, present a variety of counseling and conciliation programs. In the United States there is no national pattern and no national organization.

The year 1957 bids fair to become a landmark in the development of conciliation services. In September of that year, at Chicago, the International Association of Legal Science, of which Professor Max Rheinstein, Professor of Comparative Law, University of Chicago Law School, is chairman, conducted an eight-day institute on laws and legal devices to promote marriage stability. Counseling and conciliation shared the spotlight with divorce-law reform. The 110 participants, in addition to invited specialists from all corners of the United States, numbered 37 professors of law, jurists, and social scientists from 18 other countries, including Israel, Egypt, Japan, and the Soviet Union.

This paper focuses upon established practices at courts of domestic relations and matrimonial action in the United States. Descriptions of counseling and conciliation in other countries may be found in the following papers of the Chicago Institute (Rheinstein, 1957):

"Marriage Stability and Laws on Divorce," Max Rheinstein, University of Chicago, U.S.A.

"A Survey of Marriage and Educational Counseling in the Federal Republic of Germany," Hans Ficker, Professor of Law at the University of Mayence, West Germany.

"Social Policies and Marriage Stability,"

George Karlsson, Professor of Social Research, University of Uppsala, Sweden.

"Marriage Counseling and Conciliation Proceedings in Finland," Ilmari Melander, Professor of Law, University of Helsinki, Finland.

Discord and Estrangement

It has often been observed that the processes of discord, estrangement, and termination are destructive to the partners who as lovers once belonged to each other and to their children, the fruit of their love. With rare exceptions, young people in Western culture marry for love. Between newlyweds there is warmth, mutual gratification, and a high tolerance for foibles. Discord is unanticipated, and unwelcome. It starts hardly noticed. Are not disagreements a normal part of married living? It undermines slowly. Earning a living and starting a family involve heavy stresses. Misunderstandings aggravate. One or the other protests or makes demands. Retorts carry sarcasm or resentment. The threshold of tolerance begins to sink. Sharp issues arise over previously unnoticed trifles. One or both begin to feel unjustly accused, unfairly judged. Periods of pouting and heavy silence lengthen. Then "unexpectedly" comes a sharp verbal thrust, or a slap or jab. Now one or both begin to seek solace elsewhere. Relatives and friends learn of their trouble, and offer sympathy, not always disinterested. At the same time guilt feelings arise to complicate behavior. Communication thins out, and then is shut off—to save nasty scenes. Hostilities begin to harden. Who were once lovers have become enemies. "Suddenly" a particularly unpleasant encounter triggers one or both into litigation.

During this journey from love to litigation many experiences supply pressure and direction. Such outer stresses as irregular and insufficient income, periods of separation required by state or employer, or chronic illness, and such inner disturbances as irrational fears, compulsions to hurt, or a crippling sense of inadequacy, separately or in combination, may prove too much for whatever tolerances, loyalties, and integrating forces the marriage partners possess. So it transpires that disillusionment, repulsion, bitterness, and even vindictiveness take over and tear apart the affection that once united them.

With some who travel this road, inhibition, inadequate performance, or discomfort in sexual play and coitus, relative to expectations, are among the causal factors. For others, these reactions are symptoms of an estrangement that is creeping upon them primarily for other reasons. To almost everyone, counselors report, sexual intimacy becomes distasteful as discord mounts.

That desertion or divorce is less destructive than continuing cohabitation in unabated discord, that sooner or later most divorcing spouses emerge from their tensing bitterness or their depressions, that some become wiser, that a few (very few, recent research seems to indicate) later contract happy and lasting marriages—these considerations and eventualities cannot obscure the facts: marital discord and estrangement always retard and often reverse the processes of personality fulfillment in partners, and always impose hazards upon the child's healthy development, as the Gluecks (1950) in particular have shown. Although some emerge less harmed than others, characteristically the children of these partners do poor work in school, bite their nails, revert to nocturnal enuresis, and get into neighborhood trouble. In their teens, ill-disciplined, defiant, and feeling unloved, they damage property, steal, misbehave sexually. It is the ever-mounting discord that brings on these destructive consequences, not the act of desertion or filing for legal termination or the divorce decree.

That is, divorce may be the lesser evil for children in homes of discord. Welfare workers at courts and clinics often note that the legal settlement of their parents' difficulties, and definitive custody orders, bring a sense of relief. A recent annual report of the Essex County, New Jersey, Child Guidance Clinic stated that of their disturbed child clients, ten times as many were living with two quarrelsome parents as were living with one divorced parent.

Along with high discord rates and high divorce rates are found other symptoms. Although precise causal relationships cannot be proved with present knowledge, court records indicate that families with histories of discord, desertion, and divorce produce more than their proportional number of children with school behavior problems, delinquencies, and out-of-wedlock pregnancies. And in marriages that end in divorce, as Christensen's (1953) studies have indicated, the following are found in proportionately larger numbers than in the totality of marriages: a history of divorce in the family, a history of delinquency, youthful marriage, runaway marriage, premarital pregnancy, marriage by a civil official. Observation adds another factor, perhaps crucial: inadequate performance of their guidance and training functions by insecure parents who were themselves ill-prepared for marriage and parenthood.

Marital discord, estrangement, and termination (by desertion, or by court decree of separate maintenance, annulment, or divorce) may be understood also as symptoms of the struggle to adjust to change in the structure of society and to the processes of value disintegration and reintegration.

Between 1890 and 1950, the proportion of United States families subsisting from farming decreased from 64 to 17 per cent. In the 1950's one family in four was changing its residence each year. The fluctuating labor market, the pressure to become organization men, commercialized amusements that exploit sex, administered wages and prices, and costly and inadequate housing constitute a baffling milieu in which to fashion stable marriages. In the agricultural economy of a century ago, with its prescribed and unchanging roles, intolerably unhappy marriages were dissolved by premature death and by disappearance. Nowadays, with frontiers and great open spaces less and less available to unhappy husbands, with medicine prolonging life, and with the ways of the city on the ascendency, legal termination has become for many a preferred solution.

Increases in marital discord and termination rates are also related to changes in prevailing ideas and values. "Cool" discussions in popular media concerning human sex behavior and questioning traditional values are avidly read by youth whose feelings are anything but cold and scientifically controlled. In most nations today prostitution is no longer government-licensed, and women on all social levels are claiming the same rights to freedom of behavior

as men. Except among the highly sophisticated and disciplined, the theory of "male necessity" continues to sanction a more or less irresponsible expression of "biological drives." Under these circumstances it is not surprising that values governing sex behavior and marriage are fluid and casual throughout a considerable segment of the younger population the world over.

From this fluidity and casualness, certain groups (and in some occupations, as in the amusement field, these add up to a majority) have derived a set of values: 1) confession of love feelings each for the other sanctions sexual union—on the occasion of the confession and as a matter of course for as long as it is practical and desired by both; 2) a marriage certificate is a social convenience; 3) when a partner falls out of love, or into more intense love with another, whatever legal contract that exists must be dissolved. On these values has been erected a marriage system that consists of a series of affairs, marriages, divorces, remarriages—a system of seriated monogamy. Its operation is often complicated by unplanned and unwanted pregnancies, the daily chores of married living, the responsibilities of child care and nurture, and by the unfulfilled love and security needs of the partners themselves. Transitions from marriage to divorce to remarriage, and then again to divorce and remarriage, are seldom free from destructive emotionality.

Thus the patterns of interpersonal relationship to which individuals are predisposed and nurtured, the stresses of socioeconomic structures and processes, and the prevailing climate of ideas and values operate interrelatedly to keep the rates of marital discord and divorce at relatively high levels. It is in response to this total situation that conciliation services have developed.

The Law, The Courts, and Conciliation

Long before an attorney is asked to file a petition at court, deteriorating relationships have overheated and slowed down the routines of daily family living, and have jammed normal communication. Nor does bringing their dispute to the law do away with the underlying problems: understanding and satisfying each other's needs, disciplining responses with good will, and tolerating each other's weaknesses. On the contrary, invocation of the law tends to exacerbate discord and ill-will. This is due partly to the requirements of the law and partly to the codes and customs of lawyers (Pilpel and Zavin, 1952; Ploscowe, 1955).

For example, except in the 20 states where a partner is eligible for divorce on a showing of noncohabitation lasting continuously for two to ten years, state laws in the United States require the plaintiff to prove wrongdoing and maintain his own innocence. In fact, however, human nature being what it is, both partners have committed offenses and both have been wronged; both have been on the defensive over their own wrongdoing and both have harbored bitter or punitive feelings. Yet in law one is alleged to be guilty by the other who claims innocence. This procedural insistence on guilt and innocence brews resentments.

Again, a good attorney attempts to win and hold positions of legal strength for his client. This means in practice that along with charges of wrongdoing and demands for relatively large shares of family property, or high support payments, there is a readiness to bargain. Such an attitude and such maneuvers fan ill will, in the children as well as the partners.

As a third example, the law, legal practice, and court procedure operate to penalize forgiveness and forestall reconciliation. After charges have been made, even to show interest in the spouse who has been publicly charged with wrongdoing can mean condoning the offense and so voiding the charge. For this reason some attorneys keep partners apart during litigation, thus making more difficult the very reconciliation which one or both may wish to explore. Happily, many couples disregard the advice of legal counsel on this point and some otherwise conscientious attorneys disregard this point of law.

These experiences with the law—making or being served with charges of cruelty, neglect, or worse, filing answers and denials, appearing with counsel (even though defendant's counsel is present only to protect parental rights and material interests), maneuvering for legal position, bringing witnesses into open court to try to prove or disprove charges, and finally reading the decree that asserts innocence in one and wrongdoing in the other—these experiences tend to have destructive effects on clients. The guilt-and-punishment philosophy and the adversary postures and procedures of divorce law provide the self-righteous and arrogant with "field days." They offer the embittered sanctions for revenge. And upon those whose roads to divorce are long and sad, who come to court burdened with a sense of failure, they open old wounds and inflict new pain. In short, they tend to perpetuate and deepen animosities, multiply misunderstandings, and so to propel participants toward the point of no return (Alexander, 1953).

Under the guilt-and-punishment philosophy that continues to hold sway in most divorce courts, and under the adversary system, these destructive effects occur in both contested and uncontested cases, especially in the former. Three to four out of every five termination actions begin with one partner pressing for the legal end against the preference or better judgment of the other. This pressure continues until the antidivorce partner is convinced—if need be, up to the eve of the final hearing. Nor does this reluctant acceptance of divorce automatically resolve all differences regarding custody, visitation, child support, alimony, and disposition of property. Even with the one to two out of five who at the onset mutually agreed upon divorce, resort to the law tends to reactivate conflicts. The law's adversary posture corrodes relationships between the parties in all types of cases.

Less destructive individually, but also negative or noncontributive to the reconciliation of the partners and the stability of their home, are the procedures that grant divorce simply on the showing of noncohabitation for a given period of years (in 20 states of the United States, in Scandinavian countries, in West Germany, and in France, Yugoslavia, and others). Unless geared into conciliation programs, such procedures by themselves do nothing to counteract the progress of discord through estrangement and separation into legal termination.

These destructive effects of the law and of court procedures on matrimonial litigants and their children, and the failure of the law and the courts positively to foster reconciliation and family stability, have become matters of concern the world over during the past quarter century. In the United States several religious bodies have passed resolutions calling for changes and offering cooperation. Welfare workers repeatedly direct attention to the marriage counseling that is offered at their family-service agencies, but they have been slow to invest their skills at divorce courts. This reluctance would seem to be due to the beliefs that courts are authoritarian (whereas caseworkers depend upon the voluntary cooperation of clients) and that they may be politically influenced (Fisher, 1956; Sheridan and Brewer, 1957).

Lawyers and jurists have been the most articulate on this subject. The chairman of the Legal Section, National Conference on Family Life, May, 1948, a Boston, Mass., attorney and civic leader, concluded his report with, "the cost of our present divorce system in terms of human tragedy has become too high to be tolerated any longer" (Alexander, 1948). In 1954, addressing an assembly of social scientists, the chairman of the Interprofessional Commission on Marriage and Divorce Laws, a Toledo, Ohio, judge summarized, "thoughtful members of the legal profession in virtually every part of this country have been increasingly appalled at the unspeakable ineptitude and downright disastrousness of our old-fashioned legalistic ways of handling family troubles" (Alexander, 1956).

The grounds for this indictment are now rarely challenged. Proposed remedies, however, vary widely in form, purpose, and effectiveness. They range from nationalizing and rewriting the divorce laws (a political impossibility in the United States of America) to making applicants "cool off" for sixty days before permitting them to file petitions, from training attorneys to be marriage counselors to packing squabbling litigants over to their pastors' studies or into the judge's chambers for advice and persuasion. Similarly wide is the range of stated purpose: from "effecting reconciliation and saving marriages" through "helping clients correct their faults and try again" to "providing professional counseling relationships within which each partner can gain understanding of his part in the erosion of their

marriage, and can develop will and skills for happier performance of marital roles and more effective coping with marital problems." Only the more practical and plausible of these proposals are examined here.

Proposal 1:
Divorce Lawyers
Should Be Marriage Counselors

That in matrimonial actions lawyers should serve clients both as legal counsel and as marriage counselors is a proposition that in the U.S. has several eloquent advocates and a few serious practitioners. It is readily understood as an adaptation to new knowledge and to contemporary marriage problems of the age-old obligation of lawyers to serve as personal counsel to clients. In its more naive form this proposition holds that attorneys should be persuasive advocates of reconciliation, and at the other extreme that they should train for and engage in therapeutic marriage counseling as a part of their professional practice (Mariano, 1954).

This proposal misconceives the relationship of the professional marriage counselor with his client. Sound knowledge from advancing behavioral science and psychotherapeutic practice is of course broadening the perspective and tempering the practice in all professions, including the law. And a few enthralled lawyers have put aside legal practice to become marriage counselors. Skill in applying knowledge of human nature to legal tasks, however, is quite different from engaging in professional marriage counseling. By tradition and by codes of professional practice, the counselor-at-law is a giver of advice, a protector of rights, an advocate. The marriage counselor on the other hand is accepting, nonjudging, impartial, supportive —a coach in the game of marital living, a guide to deeper self-understanding and better disciplined conduct. When, with his client, legal counsel charges wrongdoing and fights to se cure divorce and the custody of a child or lower support payments, or when he defends his client's legal rights and interests against queries from the bench and attacks by his opponent, he inescapably immobilizes in that client the processes of self-insight, self-acceptance, and self-correction. Efforts by the client to pursue deeper self-understanding and greater skill in the arts of married living at the same time that he is fighting for his interests and rights can result only in rationalization, or self-deception. Neither in purpose nor in method are legal advocacy and marriage counseling congruent. In the long run, therefore, this proposal will not win acceptance with knowledgeable lawyers.

Proposal 2:
Create Reconciliation Judges or Masters

This proposal would modify judicial functions and processes to include reconciliation, and it has been widely publicized. Supplementing their service on the bench with interviews in their chambers, certain conscientious judges persuasively urge reconciliation. In a few jurisdictions, statutes or court rules have established conciliation courts or reconciliation masters: The request from one litigant that *their* case be referred automatically suspends other legal proceedings for a given period, generally 60 days. During this period hearings are held before the reconciliation judge or master. The Los Angeles Conciliation Court uses signed 60-day reconciliation agreements, tailored to the tension areas of their clients, and the judge has the power, which he uses only occasionally, of jailing those who break these agreements. Whether persuaded to try again or not, litigants with problem personalities may be urged to become clients of family-casework or mental-hygiene agencies. At the close of the given period, if reconciliation has not taken place, divorce proceedings are resumed (Burke, 1958).

Such programs give support and aid to partners who are reconciliation-minded. Yet they are hardly adequate to the total situation. In the first place, they reach only a small proportion of all the matrimonial litigants in their jurisdictions. For instance, reporting for 1956, a year when 31,871 marriage termination petitions were filed in its county courts, the Conciliation Court of Los Angeles stated that 1,580 applications were received and serviced, and that of this group about 45 per cent, that is

2½ per cent of all petitions filed, were reconciled. As will be seen later, this is a very low proportion. Reports from the first two years of the New Jersey State program, which uses reconciliation masters, are even lower. In the second place, these formal reconciliation proceedings do not make counseling available while divorce is pending—a crisis period when most litigants and their children suffer shock, so need personal help, and are teachable. Third, they do not serve divorce-minded prelitgants referred by attorneys. Finally, such proceedings tend to become mere formalities, or to facilitate duplicity. This appears where applicants for divorce, as in Switzerland and Finland, must first have navigated the conciliation proceedings of a lower court. In Japan also, divorcing partners must first secure clearance from a conciliation court. In the United States conciliation is more "voluntary" for the partner who invokes it than for the one who wants divorce. Formal conciliation proceedings, if "successful," end with expression of good intentions and signed promises. Lasting reconciliation on the other hand requires loyal attitudes and considerate behavior, which are learned through disciplined effort and long practice. Formal proceedings therefore can be only feeble aids to lasting reconciliation.

In this connection it should be noted that a few courts have offices called "divorce counsel" or "friend of the court," whose responsibilities are to investigate and report on the home situations of litigants, to protest perjured testimony, to protect the interest of children (especially to see that reluctant fathers keep support payments up to date), and to encourage reconciliation. It has been noted that these offices concentrate variously on the particular duties that their personnel are equipped to perform. Their over-all function is to facilitate the execution of the court's decrees.

Proposal 3:
Enlist the Pastors and Family Caseworkers of the Community

Believing that marriage counseling is a specialized professional service for which they are not equipped, a few attorneys and judges enlist the cooperation of churches and social agencies.

Having learned that introduction cards in clients' hands often fade away, they forward names of divorce clients. Pastors and caseworkers then reach out and invite these persons to use their services.

No figures seem to be available on court-referred conciliation counseling by pastors. It has been observed by certain judges and court counselors that most pastors who try this type of service soon abandon it. Apparently, except for two or three nationally known church clinics in large cities, the pressure of parish work and the complexity of the problems encountered crowd it out of daily schedules.

More numerous are programs of referral to family casework. The best known of these, at San Bernardino, California, reports that during its first year, 1957, 78 or 1 in 8, of the 624 to whom they wrote (presumably letters were sent to all that year's divorce litigants with children) responded to their offer of counseling. Of these 78, 12 couples (that is, about 4 per cent of the 624 individuals, 15 per cent of the 78 respondents) were reconciled. A few others used the agency's counseling services while their divorces were pending, and afterwards. By contrast, in the Family Courts of Ohio during the five years ending 1958, divorce petitions that were dismissed and that lapsed totaled 35-45 per cent of the petitions filed. What proportion of this total was reconciled through the offices of the investigator-counselors on the staffs of these courts cannot be known exactly, but Toledo Family Court figures suggest at least half. Although the proportions reconciled through privately supported agencies may rise as court cooperation becomes better understood in their communities, it appears that such programs are not as economical or efficient as those in which counselors have routine daily contacts with bench and bar, and are in positions to talk with litigants at moments when they feel they need help.

In an over-all program of community effort for more stable marriages, family casework and marriage counseling in family-service agencies is important especially in the early stages of discord. After litigation begins, however, counseling at courts reaches more litigants at teachable moments, and is associated with proportionately larger numbers of reconciliations.

Each of these three types of marriage conciliation program has its advocates. To the more thoughtful and realistic members of the legal profession, however, none is acceptable except as a temporary expedient. For they provide only *ad hoc* and limited remedies. In objectives, qualifications of personnel, and relationships with clients, all fall short. The reason is clear. They fail to come to grips with the interrelated core problems: the continuance during litigation of pre-existing discord and estrangement, the destructive effects of adversary procedure upon already frayed family relationships, and so the need for therapeutic counseling (in addition to legal advice and guidance) during the period of personal crisis and litigation.

Proposal 4:
Operate a Program of Counseling at the Court

The better to cope with these core problems, having noted the emergence of marriage counseling as a specialty in the welfare field, certain attorneys and jurists are introducing it as an adjunct to legal service and judicial procedure at divorce courts. These realistic yet conservative experimenters start with the judgment that in our increasingly complex society the traditional lawyer-client relationship has become more and more inadequate, unaided by other resources, to handle clients threatened with marital breakdown. They hold with behavioral science and clinical practice that a marital problem is a problem of interpersonal relationship regardless of whether or when it becomes a legal problem. They protest when lawyers treat a marital conflict solely as a legal problem and assume that the solution of the legal problem will resolve the personal problem to the benefit of all concerned. This they dub dallying with fictions. They see the values of marriage counseling. They distinguish between practicing marriage counseling and practicing law. Hence they invite into their courts counselors who are certified or otherwise have status in the welfare professions. Hence they insist that counseling services be operated under welfare principles and standards *pari passu* judicial procedures, and also that they do not interfere with or compromise the law.

Four Purposes of
Divorce-Court Counseling

As court programs of marriage counseling have been put into operation, appraised, revised, and consolidated, four interrelated guiding purposes have been clarified and established:

1. To secure and develop for bench and attorneys (a) reliable "background information" regarding the history and state of interpersonal relationships in the families of clients, (b) considered professional judgments regarding the condition and prospects of the children, and (c) recommendations for their future welfare (such needed information and opinion being unavailable to the bench through advocacy of attorneys in court);

2. Through short-term counseling relationships, upon request from clients in marriage-termination crises, to provide a limited amount of guidance and support, and in some cases re-educative psychotherapy (reconstructive psychotherapy is not the responsibility of court counselors—Wolberg, 1954);

3. To soften and counteract the destructive impact of adversary procedure, but not to supplant or modify legal processes;

4. To effect referral of clients who are ready for more counseling or psychotherapy to community family-service agencies or mental-hygiene clinics, or to pastors or psychiatrists.

In some communities where such divorce-court counseling programs have been attempted, they have failed to secure the backing of welfare workers, the support of the bar, or the cooperation of the majority of the bench. In these centers, professional traditions and loyalties or jurisdictional considerations seem to outweigh grasp of the need. Relatively few as yet, therefore, are the courts of matrimonial action in which personnel, philosophy, administrative structure, professional understanding of the need, and community support have combined to provide conditions favorable for the unhampered operation of such adjunct programs of marriage counseling.

One court that does is the Toledo, Ohio, Family Court. Its judge, Paul W. Alexander, is a student of family life and welfare administration, as well as of marriage and divorce law. He is a specialist judge, that is, he sits only on cases involving family relationships, including divorce, juvenile delinquency, and crimes against children. His administrative assistants and the attorneys who practice at the bar of his court are informed and infused with his philosophy: that in every way possible the judicial process shall help clients—or at least not hinder them—in coping with the human relationship problems that existed before, and underlie, legal issues.

In this court judicial process and counseling services move forward concurrently, case by case. At any time at the request of a client and his attorney, or at the judge's request with the consent of the attorneys, judicial proceedings may be interrupted and continued to a later session in order that a client may consider his problems with a counselor. Counseling contacts distinguish legal charges from the behavior and feelings of the partners and their children. The counselor is impartial, identifying with both disputants and siding with neither. To judge and attorneys he brings factual summaries and professional judgments regarding the relationships and welfare of the clients and their children—never evidence on the charges. In this cooperation of the marriage counselor with the counselor-at-law and the judge, each defers to the specializations and respects the professional responsibilities of the other (Bridgman, 1959; Virtue, 1956).

Who Are the Clients?

Marriage partners become clients of the Family Service Department of the Toledo Family Court by three well-marked routes.

Under Ohio's 1951 Mandatory Divorce Investigation Law, all divorcing parents of children under 14 years of age must be "investigated." This group accounts for 85 per cent of the department's intake. Although the obligation of these 2,200 clients a year (1,100 marriages) is discharged in one or two investigation interviews, one in three returns voluntarily for additional consultations. If more counseling time and competence were available it is probable that this ratio would rise, for a sympathetically conducted investigation interview becomes for many clients an acceptable invitation to a longer and deeper counseling relationship.

The second group of clients, 9 per cent of the intake, is made up of parents of older children, or with no children, and of partners against whom criminal charges have been made. Referred by attorneys or judge, they reach counselors in a variety of moods. A grim and stubborn plaintiff or a rebellious defendant, outwardly complying but inwardly resisting, may have only one brief interview. Insisting that the judge had "sentenced him to counseling," one fear-ridden defendant whooped with glee as he finally understood and scuttled from the counselor's office. Some initially resistant referrals are curious or anxious enough to become willing clients. Others are so apathetic or ambivalent that only slowly will they get to work on their real problems. Those who come eager for help profit most.

The third group, prelitigants considering divorce, number 6 per cent of the intake. They are sent by attorneys, occasionally by pastors and doctors. After one exploratory interview, about 30 per cent are referred to other community services or practitioners. Another 20 per cent are referred after two to four interviews. Of the remaining 50 per cent, that is, those who engage in short-term marriage counseling with a court marriage counselor, two out of three move into reconciliation, and one out of three goes on to divorce.

(Incidentally, telephone inquirers with marriage troubles—these average about 500 per year—are given the names and telephone numbers of community family-service agencies, or are advised to turn to attorneys, pastors, or physicians in whom they have confidence.)

Considering all three groups of clients together, five is the average number of interviews per client and nine the average number of contacts per case (including counselor consultations with attorneys). When litigation drags on for 18 or more months, and the partners are anxious or compulsive or hostile, there may be up to 20 guidance and supportive interviews. At the other extreme, a few clients are able to secure all that they can use in two or three interviews, occasionally even in one. Not infrequently ex-clients will volunteer that their one or two interviews, several months or a year before, turned the tide of their marriage. In retrospect it can be seen that such clients were encountered during highly teachable moments in their lives.

Getting Prior Histories

As each new case is registered, records of all previous court contacts with the partners and immediate members of their families are made available to counselors. These include both public records in the Clerk of Court's office and "protected" juvenile and family records. Family folders with records of one or more previous court contacts are found for well over two out of five divorce petitioners, and juvenile court counselors in these cases are consulted routinely. Through social-service exchange clearances, it is learned that just under two out of five have previously been clients of one or another community welfare agency, and that about one out of six has received family-casework service. With the knowledge and permission of clients, counselors consult these agencies. And, when mutually agreeable, the court counselor helps the client to resume contacts.

Available also, for clarification of intrafamily dynamics and for guidance in conducting supportive and re-educative interviews, are consultations with the court's part-time psychiatrist. And in those few cases in which fuller diagnoses are needed, when clients and counselor make requests jointly, one of the five court psychologists may administer tests, or the partners will have diagnostic interviews with the psychiatrist. In these many ways the other services of the Family Court contribute to the effectiveness of the marriage counselors.

Investigation Interviews

Within this framework of family-court philosophy, administrative resources, and colleague contacts, the marriage counselors in the Family Service Department at the Toledo Family Court pursue the program's four basic purposes in the following manner.

Their first responsibility is to supply judge and attorneys with up-to-date and usable information and appraisals. Their reports describe the hostilities, fears, and hopes of the partners whose past behavior, that is, symptomatic difficulties stated in legal terms, is being dealt with legally by the judge and attorneys. They suggest motives and with some they offer predictions of future behavior. Such background material adds human dimensions to cases. It can be especially useful in custody contests (fortunately a small percentage of all cases) when, in a welter of legal evidence, charges and denials, claims and counterclaims, a judge must decide which of the two enemies standing before him is likely to be the better parent in the future to their children. It can be useful also in reaching decisions on visitation and companionship rights.

Counselors as a rule develop reports with their clients. Discussion of the family record (only with the deeply disturbed is this not done) and the feelings and behavior of the children provides new perspectives and induces second thoughts. When a client realizes that the counselor is not making judgments, that information which would compromise either partner is being omitted from the report, and indeed that to a degree he is participating in the decisions as to what shall be reported, he begins to relax and to feel confidence in the counselor and the court.

Investigating and reporting responsibilities are also the basis of useful two-way communication between counselors and lawyers. In brief consultations, the counselor keeps up to date with what is transpiring legally, and the lawyer with the progress of the counseling relationship. These exchanges are particularly pertinent when litigants have character disorders or disturbing neuroses or psychoses (about 20 per cent do), and so could all too readily do further harm to themselves and their children.

Typical Case

Counselor contacts with a disintegrating wartime partnership, both before and after filing, illustrate how counselor, attorney, and judge cooperate at the Toledo Family Court. On three weeks' acquaintance, a local 16-year-old playgirl, well endowed with bounce and charm, married a visiting serviceman of 21. Upon his discharge a few months later they moved to his home town, where he secured steady work and spent considerable time with his aging parents.

As he became progressively drab and dutiful, she grew increasingly restless. Three years, two babies, "two affairs," and one dismissed divorce petition later, their incompatibility had reached a point where by agreement she crossed the country with the two children for a three months' vacation with her parents. Returning bouncier and more charming than ever, she said that now she hoped to make her marriage a success. Her husband was delighted, but within a month it became evident that she was two to three months' pregnant. Feeling betrayed, he rushed to an attorney, who referred both to the court marriage counselor. Through three interviews apiece and two joint sessions this couple struggled to face the facts and to understand each other's feelings—and defenses. Painfully they hammered out an agreement (by this time she was talking realistically with the counselor about her intimacies with the father of her unborn child): that she would hurry back across country to her home town, taking with her the younger child, a girl of 10 months; that he would go with the 2-year-old boy to live with his parents; that for the expenses of the new baby she would use the family medical and hospital insurance; that he would pay $10 a week support; and that he would file divorce on grounds of neglect which she would not contest. One week later this solution was "tested" in separate interviews with each. The husband then returned to the attorney, who prepared a separation agreement and filed his divorce. After a final interview with the counselor the wife returned across country to her parents—and lover. A few weeks later attorney and counselor together briefed the judge. The counselor's report told the story. The attorney prepared the case. In due course an uncontested divorce was granted.

Short-Term Counseling

In addition to providing information for judge and attorneys, investigation interviews are a learning experience for a considerable majority of matrimonial clients. And for a few, they flower into supportive or re-educative counseling relationships. Feeling accepted by his counselor, many a client begins to handle his confusions and frustrations and misbehavior with fewer defenses, with less guilt. As his posture changes—from "litigant being investigated" to "troubled partner seeking help"—the counselor restructures his responses toward building a good working relationship. Referral at this point to a casework or mental-hygiene agency outside the court, Toledo counselors have learned, postpones the client's "taking hold." Many referrals are made to community agencies, but never at this point in counselor-client relationships. Short-term re-educative and supportive counseling, with that counselor and in that place where he is accepted and feels at home, and at the time when he begins to grow in self-insight and to want to handle himself better, can be a crucially useful service to a court client, as well as a prelude to acceptance of long-term help.

Typical Case

An example of short-term re-educative counseling that ended in referral is the story of counselor relationships with the efficient yet frustrated wife of an ego-centered, overdependent, and rebellious man, ten years her senior. At the first interview she said, "I don't really want a divorce—that's why I dismissed my former petition—but I can't live with him either." At the end of her second interview she said sadly, "I never believed my husband when he accused me of overriding him; now I guess I am a part of his trouble." In her third interview, she caught glimpses of the inner fears that impelled her to take control of situations. The fifth contact included her husband—at his initiative. During this hour they began to learn how to perceive and accept each other's fears and compulsions.

This exploration of each other's real personalities continued at home—not without frustrations and explosions. Two months later this wife dropped her divorce petition. Their final interview dealt briefly with some of the snags they had encountered in trying to communicate their real feelings, went on to consider their toughest problem (a workable system of financial management on a low income), and ended with their referral to the local mental-hygiene clinic, primarily for the sake of their disturbed 10-year-old son.

Neutralizing the Adversary Process

The third responsibility of the marriage counselors at the Toledo Family Court, helping clients to understand, accept, and remain unharmed by the adversary process, is discharged through investigation and counseling interviews and also through additional specific contacts. For example, if a bitter wife demands more support than her estranged husband living in a rented room is willing to provide, the counselor may bring them together in conference to face the facts and agree upon a figure acceptable to both. This is then communicated to the attorneys for such legal action as they may care to take. When large sums of money are involved, this procedure is followed less frequently. Again, when as a matter of routine the wife's attorney attaches the husband's wages until the court can fix support payments, the gap between the partners tends to widen. To minimize this, and to help keep meager income available, the counselor informs the husband of the legal situation and advises contact with the attorneys and speedy agreement upon support-payment figures.

Using Community Resources

The counselor's fourth responsibility, introducing clients to appropriate long-term help, is also interwoven with the other three. In the nature of the court counselor's work, his contacts are limited to crisis periods in the lives of his clients, and to a relatively small number of interviews. Many dismissing clients can make their marriages permanently successful only with additional help. An even greater proportion of the divorcing clients need additional help to live comfortably with themselves or to contract happy second marriages.

Available in the community are four kinds of help: library guidance to reading on marriage and family problems; pastoral counseling; family casework; and psychotherapy.

The first is suggested to clients who have used their counseling relationships for fuller understanding of themselves and who have no unusual emotional disturbances or defenses.

Those to whom religion has meaning are referred to pastors. As one nagging and self-righteous wife of an alcoholic husband dismissed her divorce, their pastor helped both to establish themselves in appropriate A.A. groups and then to build self-respect by performing needed services in the parish. Another pastor developed a constructive relationship with an ex-client of the court after a sex crime charge and a suit for divorce had both been dismissed. In personal contacts, by eliciting public appreciation for his skilled carpentry service to the church, and by encouraging him to pitch the church's team to first place in the interchurch softball league, this pastor was a strong rehabilitating influence.

More frequent are referrals to family-casework and mental-hygiene treatment. Partners under stress who need more help than the court marriage counselors can give may be referred during the course of litigation. Others are referred at the close of their short-term counseling relationships.

Typical Case

An example of a case referred during litigation: The plaintiff was the mother of nine children, aged 6 to 16, was living in a heavily mortgaged home, and was employed as a cashier in a supermarket. The father was living with another woman; he was an intermittent visitor to the home, and when he did appear, was generally drunk and frightening.

At the time of the first contact, he was skillfully using threats and legal technicalities to oust his wife and secure both the house and custody of the children. Financially pressed and ignorant of the law, the mother and children had decided tearfully that going along would be the lesser evil. Investigation interviews with both, and then with the attorneys, precipitated the recommendation that this mother be awarded custody during the course of her divorce action, with the understanding that she become a client of the family-service agency.

Seeing the caseworker regularly, she improved both financial management and care of the children. With agency help the children enjoyed day camp and other opportunities during school vacations. Caseworker and court counselor kept each other informed. The counselor's report at the final hearing included provisions suggested by the agency.

Summary

This article outlines the problem of devising and fitting conciliation services to the discord and estrangement that is rampant in contemporary industrial and urbanized society. Incipient discord is dealt with by pastors, physicians, and welfare workers according to interest and competence. Continuing deterioration leads to the courts.

Briefly described and appraised are three more or less widely advocated proposals for marriage conciliation by modifying legal and judicial procedures. In detail is described the structure and operation of a fourth type of program in which the law and the welfare professions work together at the court, *pari passu*, case by case. This program of court counseling for reconciliation deals with the predicaments and needs of clients in matrimonial crises. It operates under tested welfare principles, using only professional marriage counselors. Basic is the Ohio mandate that in marriage termination cases parents of children under 14 must be investigated and that reports must be made to judge and attorneys. Upon this statutory requirement has been created the Toledo Family Court program of conciliation counseling and agency cooperation. This program flourishes because it is founded upon a powerful idea: Marital discord and estrangement being what behavioral science and clinical practice now know them to be, the law by itself is not adequate to meet the needs of matrimonial litigants, but the professions of law and welfare working together at the courts can with documented effectiveness midwife reconciliations and teach parties how to perform marital roles more satisfactorily, thus fostering more stable family life.

References

Alexander, Paul W., "Family Life Conference Suggests New Judicial Procedures and Attitudes toward Marriage and Divorce." *J. Am. Judicature Soc. 32;* 38-39, 1948.

Alexander, Paul W., "Let's Get the Embattled Spouses

Out of the Trenches." In "Symposium on Divorce, a Reexamination of Basic Concepts." *J. Law & Contemp. Probs. 18;* 1-106, 1953.

Alexander, Paul W., "Legal Science and the Social Sciences: The Family Court." *Missouri Law Rev. 21;* 111, 1956.

Annual Reports of the Toledo Family Court.

Bradway, John S., "Divorce Litigation and the Welfare of the Family." In "Symposium on Domestic Relations." *Vanderbilt Law Rev. 9;* 593-846, 1956.

Bridgman, Ralph P., "Counseling with Matrimonial Clients in a Family Court." In "Symposium on the Family Court." *J. Nat. Prob. & Parole Assoc.* Vol. 5, 1959.

Burke, Louis H., *With This Ring.* New York: McGraw-Hill Book Co., 1958.

Christensen, Harold T., and Hanna, J., "Premarital Pregnancy as a Factor in Divorce." *Am. Sociol. Rev. 18;* 53-59, 1953.

Fisher, Bernard C., *For the Family in Court.* New York: Community Service Society, 1956.

Glueck, Sheldon, and Glueck, Eleanor, *Unraveling Juvenile Delinquency.* New York: Commonwealth Fund, 1950.

Mariano, John H., "Legal Therapy and Divorce." *Kansas Law Rev. 3;* 36-43, 1954.

Pilpel, Harriet F., and Zavin, Theodora, *Your Marriage and the Law.* New York: Rinehart & Co., Inc., 1952.

Ploscowe, Morris, *The Truth about Divorce.* New York: Hawthorn Books, Inc., 1955.

Reports of the Marriage Division, Office of the National Ministry of Religion. Jakarta, Indonesia.

Reports of the National Council for Marriage Guidance and Family Life. Johannesburg, South Africa.

Reports of the National Marriage Guidance Council. London.

Rheinstein, Max, "The Law of Divorce and the Problem of Marriage Stability." In "Symposium on Domestic Relations." *Vanderbilt Law Rev. 9;* 593-846, 1956.

Sheridan, William H., and Brewer, Edgar W., "The Family Court, an Examination of Socio-legal Problems Involved." *Children 4;* 67-73, 1957.

Standards for Professional Practice of Social Work: A Code of Ethics. New York: *Social Work J.,* 1952.

Symposium on Divorce, a Reexamination of Basic Concepts. Durham, N.C.: *J. Law & Contemp. Probs.,* 1953.

Symposium on Domestic Relations. Nashville, Tenn.: *Vanderbilt Law Rev.,* 1956.

Symposium on the Family Court. J. Nat. Prob. & Parole Assoc., 1959.

The Lawyer and the Social Worker. New York: Family Service Association of America, 1959.

Virtue, Maxine Boord, *Family Cases in Court.* Durham: Duke University Press, 1956.

Wolberg, Lewis R., *The Technique of Psychotherapy.* New York: Grune & Stratton, Inc., 1954.

RALPH P. BRIDGMAN

Marriage Counseling

"THERE is something in marriage so natural and inviting, that the step has an air of great simplicity and ease" (Robert Louis Stevenson). Throughout the ages, men and women have tended to move into marriage in this way, expecting that it would offer the love, affection, understanding, support, and companionship each desired. We all want and need love and affection. It makes life richer and more abundant and gives satisfaction not attainable in any other way. It is in marriage, sanctioned by and embedded in our culture, that a man and woman together can build a life within the community that offers opportunity for developing and experiencing a continuity of love, affection, and sexual expression without censure from society and without undue personal guilt and anxiety. Marriage is one of the human relationships in which mutual growth and enjoyment can be achieved; in which healthy friction does occur, can be resolved, and can add to the depth of the relationship and the understanding and respect of each for the other.

Marriage—An American Way of Life

Marriage is today, as it has always been, part of the social fabric, and its structure, strengths, weaknesses, and values arise out of the particular cultural and psychological climate in which we live. The majority of people in America look forward to marriage as one of their major life goals. Today, couples who marry in their early twenties have a possibility of forty-one years of married life together before the death of either spouse, and the last third of that time, in all probability, will find the couple living together with none of the children in the home. Approximately 150,000 couples celebrated their fiftieth wedding anniversary each year in the 1950's and close to three-quarters of a million surviving couples have been married fifty years or more. Thus, the importance of marriage, as the primary source of emotional satisfaction in adult life and as the longest and most enduring of all adult human relationships, cannot be minimized. Added to this is the fact that in 1950 there were 10.3 divorces per 1,000 married females, 15 years and over, and that within five years after divorce about 50 per cent of those divorced are remarried. Marriage counseling is concerned not only with the prevention of divorce and broken homes, when a constructive relationship can be worked out, but also with facilitating the abilities of couples to live together in a satisfying and fulfilling union.

Professional Counseling— An Expression of Our Times

Marriage counseling has probably existed in some form from time immemorial, but marriage counseling as an expression of our particular time and culture is unique in several ways: specifically, in (1) the type of help sought; (2) the resources utilized for help; (3) the training of the individual counselor; and (4) the attitudes of the individuals counseled concerning moving into marriage, living within it, and its termination.

Formerly, when difficulties arose, couples turned naturally to family, friends, and relatives for advice, or to the family doctor, the religious leader, the wise within the community. Although today, in this country, as earlier, help from the family physician, the religious leader, or the wise may be sought, it is the professional and scientific element in the individual discipline of the helping person, along with his personal warmth and support, that is the quality desired, rather than the informal assistance sought in previous generations. Furthermore, as Sattong (1955) points out, the older members of the family, or the older women in the community, who in many instances functioned as comparatively informal counselors, now often distrust their capacity to help the younger generation.

What is new in the twentieth century is the conscious application of our knowledge of human behavior and personality development, derived from the findings of psychoanalysis, clinical psychology, child development, and cultural anthropology, to the problems of living. Through popular literature, radio, television, screen, and stage, the average person is continually informed of the possibility and importance of obtaining "outside" or "objective professional" help with problems of personal and interpersonal adjustment, and it has become almost a cultural "imperative" that individuals or couples should seek this kind of assistance when trouble arises in a marriage or before applying for a divorce. There is only the beginning of interest evident in exploring, at the courtship and premarital stage, what might be done to promote more adequate and constructive selection of marital partners. There is apparent, however, a very considerable evidence of the application of knowledge of child development to attempt to promote emotional health in childhood and youth.

Changing Attitudes and Values Sought in Today's Marriage

Another element of difference between today's and yesterday's situation in marriage counseling lies in individual attitudes toward marriage and termination of marriage. The conscious values sought in marriage today—affectional response, companionship, equality, and opportunity for individual self-expression—are part of the fabric of modern life. Often, however, individuals move into marriage unaware of their conflicting values and assump-

tions about marriage. On the one hand they may be committed to believing in the traditional ideal of marriage—marriage to the partner of choice on the basis of romantic love with the expectation that marriages so made will be monogamous and endure throughout the life of the partners. Conversely, each partner may be equally committed to believing in his or her right to freedom for individual achievement and personal happiness and in the right to terminate the marriage if it fails to provide these values on the assumption that it is the choice of marital partner that is "wrong."

For modern couples, the idea that marriage is terminable has, with the exception of some religious groups, permeated the concept of marriage, and the threat of this may become a verbalized or unverbalized part of every serious quarrel. This contrasts sharply with the values and attitudes of twenty-five years ago when divorce was seldom considered, despite unhappiness, and moral and religious sanctions formed a supporting bulwark for marriage. Moral and religious sanctions have become relative rather than absolute for many couples and the use of these older sanctions no longer offers the same degree of outer control and stability to marriage; nor does economic dependence on the male any longer control the actions of large numbers of women.

As a result of these changes, many marriages depend for their stability and permanency upon the ability of the partners to harmonize their mutual wants and needs to a satisfactory degree. Thus, the emotional adjustment between the marital partners must bear a large part of the burden of holding the marriage together. It is when this marital interaction begins to beget chronic unhappiness or to break down that the present-day couple, recognizing that the continuance of a mutually comfortable and supportive marriage depends upon a satisfactory relationship to each other, turns to some outer source for help.

Formal Development of Marriage Counseling

As a result of the widely prevalent concern with the breakup of marriages and with evidences of unhappiness and disharmony in marriage and their repercussions on the children involved, a great many professional services offering marriage counseling have developed.

These services represent many different points of view and are offered by persons with varied experiences and training—religious leaders, physicians, psychologists, social workers, educators in university counseling centers, specialized agencies, and private persons. Differences within the professional groups offering marriage counseling are related to their specific disciplines, which determine to a large degree their conceptions of human relationships, their orientation to marriage, the aims or goals of marriage counseling, and the kind of help that is made available to the marital partners. All professions engaged in marriage counseling, despite their other commitments, have in common a sincere concern with helping people with emotional distress. The methods by which they hope to achieve this purpose may differ, but this basic concern remains constant.

In the United States, formalized marriage-counseling services whose chief focus is the promotion of partner adjustment before and after marriage began when two clinics opened in 1928. Today there are facilities for marriage counseling within many of the large urban areas. Specifically, marriage counseling in the United States has developed along a number of lines: As an adjunct to the daily practice of professionally trained individuals (doctors, ministers, social workers, psychologists, etc.); as a development of already-established community services, notably the family-service type of agencies, child-study and parent-education groups, Planned Parenthood centers, social hygiene programs, and university counseling services; and as a service specifically focused on marriage counseling.

More recently, professionally trained persons in a variety of disciplines, who specialize in marriage counseling, have entered into full- or part-time private practice. At present there is a tendency to recognize marriage counseling as a distinct service differing from other inclusive types of family-counseling or case-work services. However, although differing views are held, marriage counseling, as most authors see

it, is not a profession or discipline in its own right, but rather a field of specialization within the daily practice of certain other professionally trained individuals or service agencies.

Description of Marriage-Counseling Services

Nature of Problems

Individuals or partners seeking counseling fall into two main groups, the premarital and the postmarital. A fair number of agencies and individual practitioners have few or perhaps no premarital clients, but in at least one university service 90 per cent are in this group. The problems presented include many phases of personality immaturities and maladjustments. Both the premarital and postmarital groups come with a great variety of sexual difficulties. Fears, ignorance, and misinformation, varying degrees of heterosexual inadequacy, including impotence and frigidity, as well as homosexuality and many deviations are present in this area. There are, as Bossard and Mudd (1957) have shown, many conflicts resulting from breaking emotional ties with parents, parental disapproval, choice of mate, infidelity, separation or divorce, reconciliation, alcoholism, infertility, health, and interreligious or interracial marriage.

Sources of Support

Support of these services has come from the sponsoring groups. Where this group has membership in the local community fund, sums are allocated through this source. In some cases, sponsors raise funds through contributions. Medical, religious, and university sponsors allocate funds from their own budgets. In addition, many services charge a fee for individual and/or group counseling. In the fee-charging clinics a certain proportion of clients are accepted without charge on the basis of the recommendation of the referring service. Other clients are charged as little as 50 cents per interview, or up to as much as $25 or more, with the majority falling between $1 and $5. Fees seldom cover more than half of the cost of the service. A very few of the older services have obtained grants from government and private foundations for research and in-service training.

Sources of Referral

Friends, relatives, professional individuals, other organizations, and agencies refer clients to marriage-counseling services. Sometimes knowledge of the service occurs through attendance at courses in marriage and family relations in schools, colleges, churches, etc. Sometimes articles in journals or newspapers, or television and radio programs, may bring the client to the agency. In a few instances the client may find a listing in the phone book.

Services Offered

The functioning clinics offer one or more of the following services: (1) individual and group counseling, (2) lending libraries, (3) family-life education programs, (4) in-service training, and (5) research.

Staff Personnel

Except for physicians, the pioneers in marriage counseling in this country had little, if any, graduate academic background. This is not surprising, as marriage counseling as a professional specialization was new and no specific training was offered at that time. Requirements for trained personnel have increased as counseling has acquired professional recognition. Many of the pioneers have worked for their graduate degrees while continuing on the job, and recognized services initiated since 1950 report that all staff personnel have a minimum of a master's degree, and many hold a Ph.D. or an M.D. Almost all of the services operating now have physicians and psychiatrists in consultant or supervisory positions. To promote and maintain minimum standards in this work in the United States, the American Association of Marriage Counselors in 1956 appointed a special Committee on Standards for Training to explore existing facilities and to recommend minimum standards for training.

Areas of Special Training Necessary for Marriage Counselors

As marriage counseling has become more clearly defined through the shared experience of many marriage counselors and examination of the processes involved, it has become apparent that certain areas of knowledge and skill are necessary to perform this function adequately. Specialization in marriage counseling, as an adjunct to other disciplines, to quote from an unpublished report presented by the Committee on Standards for Training at the Annual Meeting of the American Association of Marriage Counselors held in Cleveland, May, 1958, necessitates that

. . . the counselor have a knowledge of human growth and development, and of the dynamics of human behavior and human motivations; a capacity to differentiate between normal and abnormal behavior mechanisms; and some understanding of the everyday give-and-take problems of family living and relationships within the family group. In addition, the marriage counselor needs to be skilled in the use of basic counseling techniques, and to have developed an awareness of and disciplined control of his own biases, prejudices, attitudes, and needs as these may affect his work with clients.

Marriage Counseling Defined: Its Goals and Principles

Marriage counseling is defined by the present authors as the process by which a professionally trained counselor assists a person or persons to resolve the problems that trouble them in their interpersonal relationships, as they move into marriage, live within it, or make a decision to terminate it. The focus is on the relationship between the two persons moving into marriage, or already in a marriage, rather than, as in psychiatric therapy, on the reorganization of the personality structure of the individual. The major emphasis is on helping the marital partners to learn how to cope more adequately with the problems that face them.

As indicated earlier, there are several different schools of thought concerning methods, theories, philosophies, and techniques of marriage counseling. However, certain basic principles underlie the actual practice of competently trained professional persons and there is an essential agreement on the goals of marriage counseling—to help individuals or partners to come to some resolution of their conflicts and difficulties in order that they may achieve more adequacy in dealing with their problems, a greater capacity for suitable mate selection, and increased competence in interpersonal relationships.

The fundamental principles on which there seems to be some general agreement are: (1) respect, on the part of the counselor, for the human personality, including recognition of the client's right to his own choices, his own goals, his own standards of behavior, and his own solution to his problems as long as these do not violate the welfare of society; (2) realization by the counselor that, for help to be effective, the client must be working actively and responsibly with the counselor in finding a solution to his problems; (3) recognition that behavior has basic emotional components, and that lasting change can occur only if there is a change of feeling or attitude on the part of the client; (4) acceptance of responsibility by the counselor for helping the client to appraise his reality, including community attitudes and standards, and understanding the client's involvement and feelings in antisocial behavior without, however, condoning it; and (5) awareness, and control, by the counselor of his own biases, attitudes, prejudices, and needs as they may affect the counseling relationship.

Process of Counseling

There is general agreement that the relationship between the client and the counselor is the important medium through which help is given and the process of problem-solving and change takes place. It is recognized that "change" for the client lies not in what is done to him or for him, but in the degree to which he can derive something from this new experience in relationship to enable him to widen his perspectives, resolve some of his conflicted and troubled feelings, and, through this, change his way of dealing with his marital relationship. "Relationship" as used here implies, as Perlman (1957) indicates, acceptance of the individual as he is, understanding, warmth, support, and an expectation that the client has strengths and can be assisted in learning how to do something to help himself.

By the time an individual has reached adulthood, his major personality structure and patterns have become formed, and the process of growth and change has been both slowed and confined within certain limits. However, the counseling relationship, which meets some of the needs of the troubled and anxious person for acceptance, for emotional nurture and support, and at the same time stimulates him to re-examine his ways of feeling, thinking, responding, and behaving in the marital relationship, may enable the client to begin to change the behavior and attitudes that have been destructive to the marriage relationship.

The counselor may use various techniques in his work. These include psychological support (encouragement, support of strengths, reassurance, and development of new perspectives); the draining off of excessive anger or hostile feelings; clarification of conflicted feelings and help in dealing with guilt and anxiety; at times direct advice, information, and guidance; and assistance in reopening or strengthening verbal and emotional communication between the partners. Occasionally the client's way of relating to his partner that occasions difficulty is interpreted to him with the expectation that he wants to change and may be able to do so. However, as contrasted with psychiatric therapy, unless the counselor is also a psychiatrist or trained psychotherapist, there is usually no attempt to work with marital partners on the basis of preconscious or unconscious material, nor is there an attempt to help the client achieve insight into his deeper sources of motivation.

Marriage counseling has as its primary concern an understanding of the way in which each partner projects his attitudes, feelings, wants, needs, and daily behavior into the marital relationship. It is not enough for the counselor to understand each marital partner as an individual only; a psychosocial understanding of a marital problem involves an understanding of the way in which each partner functions in the interacting relationship that is the marriage. As indicated in a study by Goodwin (1957), it is within this interaction, as each partner tries to gain satisfaction of his or her needs, that a balance is created to support and complement the other partner—or to produce a destructive and conflicting relationship.

Because this interacting relationship plays such an important role in marital adjustment, marriage counselors in many instances counsel both partners. In certain other professional approaches in which marriage problems may be a factor, as in psychiatric treatment, each partner is often seen by a separate therapist.

The Marriage Council of Philadelphia

As a specific example of how a marriage-counseling center operates, we would like to describe briefly the group in which the authors of this article have been active participants.

The Marriage Council of Philadelphia, organized in 1932, offers individual and group counseling to individuals and/or partners, prior to marriage and after marriage.

Our principles, goals, and processes of counseling are in essential agreement with those defined above. In addition, we have found, through tested experience, that certain techniques, or ways of offering our services, are more efficacious than others.

It has been our experience over the past twenty years at the Marriage Council that in the majority of cases there are definite advantages to having one counselor work concurrently with both partners. The counselor is thus enabled to gain a firsthand knowledge of the feelings, attitudes, behavior, expectations, and goals of each individual partner as he or she relates to the other and to the marriage. Working with both partners, the counselor is in a better position to understand the changes each needs to effect in his way of relating to the other and to the marriage, and can thereby work more effectively with each. He is also in a position to create mutual understanding of the partners and to ease communication between them.

The Marriage Council has also found that the framework within which an agency offers its counseling services may become an important and dynamic factor in the counseling. We refer to such factors as the joint interview, fees, the timing of appointments, the inclusion of both partners, the use of bibliotherapy, and the use of schedules or carefully selected questionnaires.

Joint Interviews

Counseling with the two partners together is an important part of our total counseling process. Although certain hazards are involved, we believe that there are definite advantages to utilizing joint interviews at certain times during the counseling process. Both individual and joint interviews are usual in the initial or "intake" period of counseling, the joint interview emphasizing any feeling of unity the partners may have at the outset and giving the counselor an opportunity to observe how they interact with each other. As counseling proceeds, more joint interviews may be indicated to clarify points on which there is disagreement, or to furnish the partners, by discussion and cooperation, some experience in problem-solving. This may be the first wedge in re-establishing constructive communication between them. A final interview with both partners tends to solidify gains and to enable them to be supportive of each other as they begin to function without the help of the counselor.

Schedules

The use of structured schedules, which are simply worded questions on sexual behavior with multiple-choice answers, may help the client to discuss his sexual behavior, as well as that of his partner, at an earlier period of counseling than would be possible otherwise. The schedules thus make it possible to explore each spouse's feelings toward this aspect of their relationship—and what each believes the other's attitude to be. Many clients lack a vocabulary with which to talk about their sexual behavior patterns, feelings, and attitudes. We have found, on the basis of ten years' experience, that the use of these schedules (which were developed initially for research purposes) helps to allay the clients' anxieties about sexual matters, places a vocabulary at their disposal, and enables them to realize that other men and women have had, with variations, similar experiences. (This schedule is copyrighted and, by permission of the United States Public Health Service under whose research grant it was developed, can be furnished at cost by the Marriage Council to professional persons for professional use.) Through this procedure, as Mudd and Goodwin (1958) show, clients begin to examine their feelings and emotionally laden attitudes regarding the place of sex in living, to question the reliability of their information, and thus to achieve a new way of relating to this aspect of their marriage.

Bibliotherapy

Suggested reading material may be used to supplement the content of the interview hour. It is our belief that when reading is utilized as an adjunct to counseling, the clients' feelings about and reaction to this suggested reading should be incorporated into subsequent interviews.

Premarital Counseling

Premarital counseling, although it utilizes all the processes and techniques discussed, presents in addition special opportunities and problems. It needs an especially sensitive and skilled approach on the part of the counselor to reach its full potentialities.

In the experience of marriage counselors, premarital clients fall into three general categories: (1) Those clients who desire what is called "general preparation for marriage." This group consists of the young person who simply wants to talk over feelings and attitudes about his marriage and to have the opportunity to personalize the information he has obtained elsewhere, but who, as he sees it, does not have a problem. (2) Young individuals or couples who have a specific or focused problem or problems. There may be a number of specifics, but the person is focused on his particular situation, knows what he wants, uses the service for that, and moves on. (3) The individual who may seek counseling within a few days of the marriage date, finding himself suddenly beset with anxiety and conflicted feelings to such a degree that moving into the marriage becomes difficult or impossible.

In the latter category the counselor, faced with time limits and imminent reality factors, must make decisions concerning the type of help needed and possible. He has to judge what can be accomplished in a relatively short time

and what his responsibility is in stirring up anxiety and worries that he may sense but of which the client himself may not be aware. The counselor must often decide, in the case of an imminent wedding, whether it would be preferable to coast along with plans for the wedding and try to make the client feel sufficiently comfortable to come back for counseling after marriage (at which time he or she may recognize the problem areas and be ready to work on them) or whether to suggest postponement of the wedding.

When in premarital counseling (or in postmarital counseling) the question of child-spacing or family planning is brought up, the counselor must be aware of the individual's religious background and of the moral and emotional conflicts that may be engendered by such a discussion. Referral should be made to the proper medical and/or religious source for further discussion of this problem.

Family-Life Education

Since the agency's inception in 1932, approximately one-quarter of staff time has been spent on family-life education with groups. In the year ending September, 1958, nearly 8,000 individuals attended lectures and discussion groups under the leadership of a trained staff provided by the Marriage Council. The initiative in forming these groups was taken by the schools, colleges, churches, and community organizations in the Philadelphia area that wished to give their membership an opportunity to discuss various aspects of marriage and family life in a series of weekly meetings. In addition to discussion groups, three colleges offer individual counseling interviews with the leader, and 15 to 20 per cent of these groups have availed themselves of this service.

According to Mudd (1950),

the goals of family life education groups may be defined as follows: 1) to increase the general understanding of preparation for and adjustment to marriage, 2) to develop sound attitudes in relation to mariage, 3) to release uncomfortable feelings and alleviate anxiety, 4) to make help available in specific or general problems through group participation or by referral to a specific agency or resource, and/or suggested reading, 5) to represent "those who help"—psychiatrists, counselors and so on—in general as warm, kindly persons to whom individuals may comfortably and hopefully take their problems.

The subject matter of the lectures and discussions varies with the age, background, and particular interests of the group. Every effort is made in group discussion, as in individual counseling, to recognize and accept human variation, difference, need, and potential. Emphasis is placed on developing participation within the group rather than on answering questions, since participation is believed to be an important dynamic in encouraging change and growth. The cost of these group meetings is defrayed by the organizations which ask for leadership, and which pay the Marriage Council a fee commensurate with the time and expense to the agency of the leader's time.

Training Programs

One of the more recent developments in the field of marriage counseling is that of specialized in-service training in marriage counseling, on the postgraduate level, for persons in disciplines dealing with troubled individuals, such as medicine, social work, psychology, the ministry, and educational counseling. There is a wide variety in the selection of candidates for training, procedures used, scope of training programs, and opportunity for academic credit, but the primary emphasis throughout is on higher professional standards. The in-service training program at the Marriage Council is an example of this type of program.

It was in 1955 that Marriage Council affiliated with the University of Pennsylvania's Department of Psychiatry of the School of Medicine, becoming the division of Family Study, and the operational unit of the Division. At the present time, two groups of trainees are accepted for a nine-month supervised experience in marriage counseling. One group, primarily interested in deepening their own counseling skills and knowledge for use within their own discipline, is registered for a training program of nine months with a minimum of

seventeen hours weekly in the agency. This group may be comprised of clinical psychologists, social workers, etc., all with graduate degrees in their own fields and some experience in face-to-face counseling. These "trainees" are not primarily interested in receiving academic credit for this training, but in furthering their own capacities for helping others.

A second group of professional persons consists of those interested in securing a doctoral degree and who may elect to take the in-service training course at the Division of Family Study as part of their academic doctoral program in the School of Education. They, too, are obliged to meet the standards required in terms of education and prior counseling experience. At present, the University of Pennsylvania is offering a major in Mental Health in their School of Education's doctoral program. This interdisciplinary program is worked out through the Division of Family Study. Courses in the Department of Psychiatry, in-service training at the Marriage Council, and courses in the Graduate School, the School of Social Work, and the School of Education are available for credit toward the degree.

Among other programs for in-service training at present in operation are those at Merrill-Palmer School, Detroit, Michigan, at the Marriage Counseling Service, Menninger Clinic, Topeka, Kansas, and at a few universities.

Research

The question of the results of marriage counseling (in what percentage of cases was the situation improved and what factors make for success) is the subject of research within the marriage-counseling field. Research in recent decades by sociologists and psychologists is exploring and occasionally modifying our concepts of the family and its individual members. Social work and psychiatric research have dealt primarily with clinical problems focused on the pathology of the individual, with little emphasis on these disturbed individuals as interacting members of a family group. As Mudd (1957) has emphasized, little has been done in marriage-counseling research in terms of concentrating on the intricacies and specific patterns of interaction between marital partners, the dynamics of marital interaction, the effect of troubled marriages on the children or family group, and the processes or techniques that might be most helpful in these situations.

Looking toward the Future

The American Association of Marriage Counselors, in their book (1958) edited by Mudd, Stone, Karpf, and Nelson, emphasized several areas in which additional work is needed as part of a program to prevent marriage disorganization. Among these were: (1) an increased emphasis on family-life education that begins in the home and continues throughout school days; (2) development of counseling associations and medical services for all stages of family need; (3) development of more adequate training facilities for the counselor of tomorrow who would be "well grounded in the psychology and sociology of marriage and human relations, in the anatomy and physiology of sex, as well as in the skills and tools of counseling"; (4) additional research geared to "development of a theory of marital interaction and family living that would be cultural in perspective and from which a more adequate philosophy of the practice of marriage counseling might develop."

In an unpublished memorandum on Strengthening Family Life, prepared in 1956 for the Social Security Administration of the Department of Health, Education, and Welfare by Drs. Emily Mudd and Reuben Hill, the authors point out the highly favorable climate of opinion in the United States at present for the support of marriage and family life, and the widespread affirmation of the values associated with both marriage and parenthood. They comment:

If the family thus remains the basic unit of our society, any social or professional practice which helps to maintain competent marriages should in itself contribute to the strengthening of family life and indirectly of society. Long ago Confucius pointed out that good families are essential to good communities, and good communities to a good national life.

Marriage Counseling Outside the United States*

In the period between the two world wars something like marriage counseling was offered in a number of European centers, mainly in Germany. The emphasis was heavily in the direction of offering help to those with sexual problems and to giving legal advice. Because the leadership of these services was predominantly Jewish, they were suppressed when Hitler came to power.

In 1938, The Marriage Guidance Council was set up in England, concentrating at first on education for marriage, but later establishing centers for counseling in marital and premarital difficulties. In time some 80 centers united to form the National Marriage Guidance Council, and soon afterwards a similar council was formed to supervise the work of the half-dozen centers in Scotland.

This new service came to the attention of the British government, which had set up a committee to investigate the rapidly rising divorce rate, and modest grants were made available to support and extend the work of the Marriage Guidance Centers. These are staffed by both professional and lay counselors, all of whom have to undergo a searching selection process before being given a basic training and put to work under supervision. Because financial resources are inadequate to employ more than a few full-time workers, most of these British marriage counselors serve their agencies on a voluntary part-time basis. Careful selection, close supervision, and the ready cooperation of more specialized consultants enables a high standard of counseling practice to be offered without charge to the public. The number of counselors serving in this way in Britain is now close to a thousand.

The British pattern has, with minor modifications, been taken over by several of the Commonwealth countries—South Africa, New Zealand, and Australia in particular. There is a Marriage Guidance Council in Lagos, Nigeria, where a team of African counselors deals with the marital troubles (often polygamous marriages are involved) of their own people.

* This section was written by David R. Mace.

In Continental Europe a variety of experiments have been made in setting up marriage-counseling services, and standards have varied considerably. In 1952 the International Union of Family Organizations set up in Paris a permanent Commission on Marriage Guidance, which has brought leaders together each year for the exchange of ideas and experiences. Initiative in developing marriage counseling has been taken by various agencies—medical centers (as in Finland), citizens' advice centers (as in Holland), family organizations (as in France), churches (as in Italy). As experience is gained and better communication established from country to country, standards are steadily improving.

Social workers have until recently been less ready to move into the marriage-counseling field in Continental Europe than in the United States; but they are now doing so at an accelerated pace.

The development of private practice in marriage counseling outside the United States has been negligible. Payment of fees for counseling services is not in keeping with the European tradition, although there are exceptions to this general rule.

At the time of writing, some interest in the development of marriage-counseling services is being shown at government levels in India, in Ceylon, and in Indonesia. The domestic-relations courts in Japan make use of persons who offer a simple form of marriage counseling.

Present indications suggest that in the next few years developments in this field may be rapid throughout the world. It is important that, in the effort to provide new services quickly, high standards should be maintained.

References

Ackerman, Nathan W., *The Psychodynamics of Family Life.* New York: Basic Books, Inc., 1958.

Bernard, Jessie, *Remarriage.* New York: The Dryden Press, 1956.

Bossard, James H. S., "Divorce, Some Selected Repercussions." In Emily H. Mudd and Aron Krich (eds.), *Man and Wife.* New York: W. W. Norton & Co., Inc., 1957.

Bridgman, Ralph, "Marriage Counseling as an Emergent Professional Function." In *The American Family, Its Strengths and Problems* (to be published).

Cuber, John F., *Marriage Counseling Practice.* New York: Appleton-Century-Crofts, Inc., 1948.

Ellis, Albert, "Marriage Counseling with Couples Indicating Sexual Incompatibility." *Marr. & Fam. Living 15;* 53-59, 1953.

Ellis, Albert, "New Approaches to Psychotherapy Techniques." *J. Clin. Psychol.,* Monograph Supplement, July, 1955.

Ellis, Albert, "Neurotic Interaction between Marital Partners." *J. Counseling Psychol.* 5; 24-28, 1958.

Erickson, Eric, *Childhood and Society.* New York: W. W. Norton & Co., 1950.

Glick, Paul C., *American Families.* New York: John Wiley & Sons, Inc., 1959.

Goode, William J., *After Divorce.* Glencoe, Ill.: The Free Press, 1956.

Goodwin, Hilda M., "The Nature and Use of the Tri-dimensional Relationship in the Process of Marriage Counseling." Unpublished doctoral dissertation, University of Pennsylvania, 1957.

Harper, Robert A., "Should Marriage Counseling Become a Full-fledged Specialty?" *Marr. & Fam. Living 15;* 338-340, 1953.

Herbert, W. L., and Jervis, F. V., *A Modern Approach to Marriage Counseling.* London: Methuen, 1959.

Hollis, Florence, "Personality Diagnosis in Casework." In *Ego Psychology & Dynamic Casework.* New York: Family Service Assn. of America, 1958.

Laidlaw, Robert W., "Marriage Counseling." In Samuel Liebman (ed.), *Understanding Your Patient.* Philadelphia: J. B. Lippincott Co., 1957.

Mace, David R., "What Is Marriage Counseling?" *Public Affairs Pamphlet,* 250. New York: Public Affairs Committee, Inc., 1957.

Mudd, Emily H., "The Premarital Interview, an Interpretation of Professional Attitudes and Procedures." In *The Cyclopedia of Medicine, Surgery and Specialties.* Philadelphia: F. A. Davis Co., 1939. Pp. 812-820.

Mudd, Emily H., "Marriage Counseling." In *The Cyclopedia of Medicine, Surgery and Specialties.* Philadelphia: F. A. Davis Co. 21; 449-460, 1950.

Mudd, Emily H., *The Practice of Marriage Counseling.* New York: Association Press, 1951.

Mudd, Emily H., "Psychiatry and Marital Problems." *Eugen. Quart. 2;* 2, 110-117, June, 1955.

Mudd, Emily H., "Knowns and Unknowns in Marriage Counseling Research." *Marr. & Fam. Living 19;* 1, 75-78, 1957.

Mudd, Emily H., "Premarital Counseling." In Samuel Liebman (ed.), *Understanding Your Patient.* Philadelphia: J. B. Lippincott Co., 1957.

Mudd, Emily H., "The Special Task of Premarital Counseling." In Emily H. Mudd and Aron Krich (eds.), *Man and Wife.* New York: W. W. Norton & Co., Inc., 1957.

Mudd, Emily H., and Goodwin, Hilda M., "Marriage Counseling." In J. L. Moreno (ed.), *Psychotherapy.* New York: Grune & Stratton 3; 171-175, 1958.

Mudd, Emily H., and Krich, Aron (eds.), *Man and Wife*. New York: W. W. Norton & Co., Inc., 1957.

Mudd, Emily H., Stone, Abraham, Karpf, Maurice, and Nelson, Janet (eds.), *Marriage Counseling: A Casebook*. New York: Association Press, 1958.

Neubeck, Gerhard, "Factors Affecting Group Psychotherapy with Married Couples." *Marr. & Fam. Living* 216, August, 1954.

Perlman, Helen H., *Social Casework*. Chicago: University of Chicago Press, 1957.

Sattong, Phillip C., "The Dilemma of the Parent as Culture Bearer." *Social Casework 36;* 302-306, 1955.

Skidmore, Rex A., Garret, Hulda Van Steeter, and Skidmore, C. Jay, *Marriage Consulting*. New York: Harper & Brothers, 1956.

Stevenson, Robert Louis, *Virginibus Puerisque*. London: J. M. Dent and Sons, Ltd., 1925.

Stone, Abraham, and Levine, Lena, *The Premarital Consultation*. New York and London: Grune & Stratton, 1956.

Vincent, Clark E., *Readings in Marriage Counseling*. New York: Thos. Y. Crowell Co., 1957.

Wallis, J. H., and Booker, H. S., *Marriage Counseling*. London: Routledge, Kegan Paul, 1958.

Winch, Robert F., *Mate Selection*. New York: Harper & Brothers, 1958.

HILDA M. GOODWIN AND
EMILY H. MUDD

Marriage and Family Living, Education for

Development of Family Education Programs

IN ALL countries of the world, as industrialization proceeds and as more and more people live in congested urban areas, strains and tensions arise that tend to disrupt family living. These stresses reveal families that are structurally weak, and family instability and breakdown become a social problem.

Certain family difficulties commonly arise in countries that are becoming increasingly industrial and urban in character. For example, a rise in the divorce rate is common. Sexual irregularities also increase; role-shifting occurs, which disturbs the traditional relationship between the sexes; there is more strife between parents and children; juvenile delinquency rates rise. The traditional authoritarian religion loses its force; secularized influences become more powerful.

These circumstances in turn give rise to attempts to strengthen family life. Efforts are directed toward ensuring a greater measure of family stability or improving the chances for family survival. Among the various suggestions and plans, experiments with some type of education for marriage and family living are common.

Education for marriage and family living in some form is nothing new. Preparing young people for entering marriage and meeting the responsibilities of family life has always been done by society. The wisdom of the elders was passed along in informal conversations or, more formally, through puberty rites and initiations. Girls have always learned some of the skills and techniques of homemaking and child-rearing in their own families. In many countries, since the establishment of public schools, some of this instruction has been incorporated into the curriculum, particularly through departments of domestic science or, as they are now known, home economics. As this occurred, education for marriage and family living entered upon a process of formalization. Outside agencies began to supplement and eventually to supersede the family in the task of preparing the young for family life.

In the last several decades in all parts of the world concepts of family-life education have broadened markedly. Psychiatric and psychological insights have deepened; studies have revealed the close association between many personal and social ills and defects in family interaction and relationships. Bigotry, chronic alcoholism, sexual promiscuity, abnormal lust for power, juvenile delinquency, and similar maladies appear to be rooted in disrupted or unwholesome family life. The result is an increasing interest in programs of family-life education that will help individuals to prove their understanding of and capacity for forming and maintaining effective human interrelationships. Much instruction, particularly in the United States and in Western Europe, has come to center about the many interactions between individuals and within the family, and the characteristics in individuals that influence the quality of interpersonal relationships.

This article deals with the interpersonal-relationships aspect of education for marriage and family living. The value of learning the skills and techniques of homemaking is recognized and accepted. Indeed, as science and technology advance, this phase of education becomes increasingly complicated. The extent to which family-life education programs now focus on human interaction and relationships, however, makes an examination of this approach to the subject highly important.

Family-Life Education in the United States

Education for marriage and family living has probably gone further in the United States than in any other country of the world. Here the public-school system has borne a heavy part of the burden of family-life education. Still, there are many other organizations, some with local or state programs, and others which reach out nationally, that regard the promotion and improvement of family living as one of their major functions.

Organizations

The following are some of the organizations in the United States that achieve a kind of national coverage with their particular approach to family-life education. The American Institute of Family Relations in Los Angeles concentrates most of its direct educational activities in California, but it has reached communities throughout the nation with its family-life literature, and through speakers. The Association for Family Living in Chicago, and the Child Study Association of America in New York City, even though they concentrate most of their efforts on local programs, have also made significant contributions to the national picture. The American Social Health Association in New York City has promoted regional programs of family-life education in several sections of the United States. This has been done primarily through the schools, although increasing attention is being given to community family-life education. The National Congress of Parents and Teachers in Chicago, although seeking primarily to improve relations between school and home, still supports an extensive program of family-life education through adult education for parents. The National Council on Family Relations in Minneapolis, Minnesota, is a professional organization deeply interested in education for marriage and family living. The Planned Parenthood Federation of America in New York specializes in materials relating to family planning, fertility, and contraception.

The national organizations of the major religions have displayed a deep interest in education for marriage and family living. This is reflected particularly in the Cana Conference movement of the Catholic Church and the family-life education program of the National Council of Churches of Christ in the United States of America.

The Cana Conference movement has grown rapidly and is now a well-established feature in the family-life education program of the Catholic Church. The form of the conference varies somewhat from one part of the country to another. A typical program consists of a half-day or an all-day meeting held annually, or semiannually. Married couples attend to discuss problems and experiences, and to receive help in making their marriage and family life a success. The conferences deal with such subjects as the sacramental nature of marriage, the physical, psychological, and spiritual aspects of the marriage relationship, husband-wife roles and responsibilities, the nature and principles of marriage and family life, family finance, parenthood, and child-rearing.

Experience gained in the Cana movement indicated a need for preparing Catholic engaged couples for marriage and family life. The result was the development of the Pre-Cana Conference. The typical Pre-Cana Conference usually consists of three or four conferences given on several days. Each day's program features an authority from a different area of specialization. A common arrangement is for a priest to be the director, assisted by a doctor and an experienced married couple. All participate in the program. So popular have these Pre-Cana Conferences become that they are now considered an integral part of the Cana Conference movement.

The Protestant effort to promote family-life education stems mainly from the Department of Family Life of the National Council of Churches of Christ in the United States of America. The parent organization itself is the clearinghouse for forty cooperating denominations and forty-two state councils of churches. The Department of Family Life facilitates and encourages the exchange of information between its member units and seeks to keep them informed of new trends and research findings in the family field. It also prepares certain materials cooperatively on behalf of its members.

Family-Life Education in the Schools

In the United States the most systematic and extensively organized program of education for marriage and family life is found in the schools (American Association of School Administrators, 1941; Brown, 1953; Kirkendall, 1953; and Strain and Eggert, 1955). Ordinarily the initiative and insight of the local school authorities determine what kind of a family-life education program the schools of a particular community develop. These programs assume no standard form, their nature and scope depending upon the local situation. The interest of the educational leaders may be stimulated and help may be provided by certain of the organizations mentioned above, or more likely by local individuals or organizations interested in family-life education.

COLLEGES AND UNIVERSITIES

Programs for marriage and family-life education that have interrelationships as their focus originated at the college level. Credit for developing the first college course in marriage is usually given to Dr. Ernest Groves. In the middle 1920's at Boston University he organized instruction in preparation for marriage. In 1927, at the University of North Carolina, Dr. Groves established a course that had a strong influence upon the instructional programs in other colleges and universities. Subsequently, many other colleges and universities established similar courses.

In 1956 Dr. Judson Landis (1959) sent questionnaires to 1,600 junior colleges, four-year colleges and universities, teachers' colleges, and Catholic institutions to find how many offered courses in marriage and family relations. He also asked what proportion of the courses in marriage and family relations were functional, i.e., designed to help the student understand the place of the family in society. Whereas functional courses are personal in approach, the institutional course is impersonal—generally historical and sociological—in approach.

A total of 768 colleges responded to the query. Of this group 630 were offering a total of 1,027 courses with an enrollment of 77,000 students. Some 46,455 students, or over 60 per cent, were enrolled in functional courses. More than half of these courses were added to the curricula of the colleges between 1945 to 1955. The functional courses had increased more rapidly than the institutional courses.

Since some of the nonresponding colleges and universities doubtless had courses, it is estimated that over 100,000 United States students now register annually for marriage and family courses.

There has also been a rapid growth in the last ten years in the number of specialized courses. These courses are intended to train research workers and other specialists for organizing and teaching family-life education in schools and communities, or for some particular work with families. They include courses in marriage counseling, child and adolescent development, methods in family research, problems of aging, and methods of teaching.

A few colleges and universities have broadened their approach to the point of organizing departments of family life. Usually these departments are within schools of home economics, although Brigham Young University, at Provo, Utah, and Teachers College, Columbia University, New York City (and perhaps others), have organized Departments of Family Life that incorporate within them the traditional home-economics offerings. Florida State University, Tallahassee, Florida, has an interdivisional family-life program that utilizes appropriate offerings from the schools of education, psychology, and social welfare in its curriculum. The purpose of such arrangements is to provide the students with a realistic preparation for marriage and family life. Consequently, in addition to courses in preparation for marriage and the usual home-economics offerings, they may provide courses in family relations, child development and child rearing, family finances, and marital adjustments. Such schools, in addition to offering courses designed to help young people prepare for marriage, also provide offerings for persons who will teach education for marriage and family living, or who will deal with families in some other professional capacity.

High-School Family-Life Programs

Education for marriage and family living that focuses on interrelationships has now moved primarily into the lower schools, particularly the high schools that enroll students from ages 14 to 18. Many schools incorporate materials relating to family living in various common courses, particularly social studies and home economics. Many of the high schools have arranged their courses for both boys and girls. They attend classes together and participate in discussions in nonsegregated groups.

Most of these pupils are in their middle teens, and the courses ordinarily treat such topics as dating problems, getting along with parents, improving self-understanding, premarital sex standards, masculine-feminine roles, interfaith marriages, mate selection, and distinguishing love from infatuation. Some courses, depending on the time given, go beyond this and include materials relating to parent-child relations, child rearing, and such marital adjustments as budgeting, developing companionship, in-law relations, and older persons in the home. Materials relating to sexual adjustments in marriage, contraception, or abortion are practically never included.

One of the most comprehensive high-school programs of education for marriage and family living is found at Hayward, California. Here the program is located in the social studies department. In the ninth grade (for pupils about 14 years of age) a general personal-orientation course is provided. This course is designed to increase the self-understanding of individuals, and to assist with problems the pupils face in beginning dating and other boy-girl relationships. At the twelfth-grade level (for pupils about 17 to 18 years of age) a course

in family living is offered with the emphases mentioned in the paragraph above. Besides this the school has the usual home-economics offerings.

Beyond this each pupil has a counselor, who is also his social studies teacher and who serves as his personal advisor throughout his high-school career. This counselor is responsible for helping each pupil with his educational and personal problems (including family and inter-sex associations) in whatever way he can. Thus, the pupils have a program in education for marriage and family life that encompasses their total high-school program.

Unfortunately, throughout the country, most youths from the lower economic class drop out of high school before they can take these courses. The higher divorce rate in the lower economic class indicates that these pupils are more in need of education for marriage and family life than children from middle and upper economic class families.

Family-Life Education
in Elementary Schools

Less family-life education is provided at the elementary-school level than at the high-school or college level. This is because the pupils are still immature and very dependent upon their parents. As a result, most of what is done is designed to help the pupils appreciate their own families and to find their proper roles and places within the family. Ordinarily, considerable attention is given to the social adjustment of the pupil. The reasoning is that when a pupil is helped to improve his capacity for personal relationships with his parents, teachers, and friends he is indirectly being prepared for marriage and family life.

Sex Education

A few elementary schools and a fair number of high schools provide some sex education or, more accurately, reproduction education, for their pupils. The family-life movement is seemingly in the process of engulfing the movement for sex education. Sex education has been accepted as an integral part of a family-life education program, and most family-life teachers recognize an obligation to provide some instruction on this topic. This engulfing process seems all to the good. It has undoubtedly resulted in more rather than less sex education. When discussions on sex can be set in a context of concern for relationships they are less threatening for everyone concerned, particularly parents and teachers, and they have the advantage of moving sex education toward a realistic recognition of the problems of human sex behavior rather than focusing only on sterile knowledge, unrelated to the conduct of relationships.

This very realism raises another problem, however. A re-evaluation and a clarification of thinking about sexual standards is urgently needed in the United States. Unquestionably the uncertainty about how to handle issues involving sex and sexual conduct does more than any other single factor to retard the acceptance of family-life education. Teachers are uncertain about how to approach the subject, and some parents are unwilling for teachers to deal with the subject. The crux of the issue rests in the realm of ethics. What behavioral practices shall be regarded as right, and why? What standards shall be used for making such judgments? Unless some satisfactory and acceptable decision can be reached on these points, the sex-instruction phase of family-life education will probably remain a stumbling block for a long time to come.

PARENT EDUCATION

Children, obviously, are unable to do much directly to improve the quality of their total family environment. The parents are the only ones who can do this; therefore, generally speaking, the younger the children the greater the need for parent education. Educational leaders in elementary schools are among the staunchest proponents of parent education. These programs ordinarily feature discussion groups and utilize films and printed materials especially designed for parents. The programs themselves are usually under some sponsorship other than that of the schools.

NURSERY-SCHOOL PROGRAMS

The concern of nursery-school educators for parent education is likely to be still deeper and more direct. In fact, modern nursery-school philosophy emphasizes the importance of parent education, and the nursery-school situation is used as a vehicle for it. In Baltimore, Maryland, and Seattle, Washington, as examples, the participation of parents in the conduct of the nursery schools is used as a method for promoting and extending parent education.

Special Problems in Family-Life Education

Even though family-life programs in the United States have made much progress, some problems remain to be solved. One is the question of securing enough adequately trained teachers. In general, the demand that a family-life teacher be all-knowing and a paragon of virtue has died away. But it is still demanded that such a teacher be a mature individual, personally well adjusted and able to work effectively with people. Coupled with this is the recognition that a family-life teacher needs to be so prepared academically that his knowledge cuts across the lines of several of the traditional disciplines. Even though the demands are still rigorous, progress is being made in the effort to secure well-prepared teachers.

Reference has already been made to college-university level programs designed for the training of teachers of family life. Until a few years ago a person who taught marriage and family-life courses had to enter this work from some other field of specialization. Now, however, interested individuals can find teacher-preparatory programs designed specifically to qualify them for family-life education. The programs at Florida State University and at Teachers College, Columbia University, are the best known.

Still another problem is that of maintaining the educational advances made thus far against the encroachments of other demands on the time and energies of the school. There are mounting demands for an increased amount of instruction in the sciences and mathematics. Heavier and heavier demands are being made upon students as they prepare for their occupational careers. All this means pressure to find a place for new instructional materials in the school program. The effort to expand, or even to maintain, programs of family-life education in the curriculum may become increasingly difficult.

This points to still another problem: the need to find ways to evaluate the worth of family-life education programs. The very nature and purpose of the instruction makes evaluation most difficult. Effective evaluation information would, however, serve as a basis for curriculum revision. Ultimately, it would be useful in public-relations programs that are needed to maintain a public opinion favorable to family-life education.

Community Programs

Community programs of education for marriage and family living are becoming increasingly common in the United States. Again there is no standard pattern; in fact, many communities have no programs of this sort at all. Ordinarily, a community program of family-life education is sponsored by some particular organization for its own members or for such persons as can be attracted. For example, a church may organize parent discussion groups or plan a series of discussions or lectures for those about to be married. A radio station may plan a series of programs on some aspect of marriage and family living, or the library may assemble literature dealing with family life. Many local parent-teacher associations organize community discussion groups and provide leadership for a parent-education program. Many public-school systems in the larger cities now have divisions of adult education, and these divisions often sponsor some kind of family life programs.

In the United States there has been a tremendous outpouring of material on family life through the press, radio, and television. These materials range in quality from excellent to very poor. There are, however, many books and pamphlets and innumerable articles in popular magazines that deal with marriage and family relations. Many radio and television programs, as has already been indicated, have been built around this popular subject. Many films, textbooks, and pamphlets have been developed for use in the public schools.

Support for programs of family-life education is readily forthcoming. Inexperienced educators are likely to fear opposition, particularly from parents, but that almost never occurs if the programs are carefully planned and are promoted in accordance with sound educational principles.

Research

Programs of education for marriage and family living in the United States are now being given a scientific grounding through research. Research in family interrelationships and family interaction has progressed until there is a respectable amount of data upon which to base instruction.

Reliance upon traditional views and the dispensation of "common knowledge" are easy in this field. But the last twenty years has seen a marked expansion in research that throws new light and new insights on family adjustments. A compilation of titles of research published between 1945 through 1954 was made by Foote and Cottrell (1955). They listed 1,031 such publications. The amount of family research has continued to increase since then, and all indications are that it will continue to do so. This should put instruction concerning marriage and family life on an even firmer basis.

Reference to a few of the studies that have been made will provide some awareness of the scope and nature of the research that has been done. Goode (1956) has studied the post-divorce adjustments and problems of women; Winch (1958) has been testing theories of the basis for mate selection; Hill (1949) studied the impact of war separations and reunions on families; Peterson (1956) analyzed the relationship of religious affiliation to marital happiness; Burgess and Wallin (1953) have been concerned with factors affecting engagement success and failure; Landis and Landis (1953) studied the length of time it took couples to achieve certain kinds of marital adjustment; Johannis (1958) studied division of labor within the family; Bernard (1956) has analyzed remarriages; Christensen (1958) has studied the relationship of premarital pregnancy to marital success; Kirkendall (1961) has been interested in the impact of premarital sexual intercourse on interpersonal relationships; Burgess and Cottrell (1939) attempted to determine factors useful in predicting marital success; Eliot (1955) has studied the impact of bereavement on families. Rainwater (1965), Komorovsky (1964) and Bernard (1966) studied low income and minority group families; Reiss (1960) has analyzed premarital sexual standards.

Two pioneering studies that are widely quoted and deserve special mention are Terman's (1938) study of psychological factors influencing marital happiness and Kinsey's (1948, 1953) studies in human sexual behavior.

There are many other studies and other research workers who deserve mention but who must be excluded because of space limitations.

Family-Life Education in Canada

Family-life education programs are moving forward in Canada also, although more slowly than in the United States due to a more conservative, traditional point of view. This is particularly true in the schools, although advances are being made there. In 1950 the province of British Columbia published curriculum guides, or courses of study, that encompassed a program designated as "Effective Living." This was quite a comprehensive program and provided for the inclusion of family-life education instruction in grades 7 through 12. The province of Saskatchewan has also included family-life education in its curriculum.

A good deal of family-life education is carried out in Canada by the churches. The United Church of Canada, the Anglican Church, and the Catholic Church each has its program.

Programs in Other Countries

Although the most extensive and advanced programs of marriage and family-life education are found on the North American continent, other countries on all the continents are moving forward. Progress has perhaps been most rapid in the countries of Western Europe.

England

England, in particular, has manifested a keen interest in education for marriage and family living. This interest has grown out of the work of the National Marriage Guidance Council (see Wallis and Booker, 1958). This Council operates through local councils, which are organized to provide counseling facilities for couples whose marriages are threatened by disharmony. The main work of the Council and affiliates is still devoted to extending facilities for marriage counseling, but their experience in attempting to salvage ailing marriages has also created an interest in preventive measures. The result is that there is an awakening interest in England, as elsewhere, in the possibility of developing programs of education for marriage and family living.

The Council's present position is that the most important future developments lie in providing help for engaged couples and for young people prior to marriage. Already local councils provide talks and discussion groups for interested persons on such subjects as differences in religious beliefs, sexual standards and conduct, family financial problems, in-law relationships, wives working outside the home, and aspects of marital adjustment. Since these groups are not under the auspices of the school, enrollment is by personal decision and attendance is voluntary.

Attention is now turning toward the public schools, and interest in using this medium of education is growing. The first effort to provide in-service training for teachers who might instruct classes in marriage and family life was made in the summer of 1958, when the National Marriage Guidance Council set up a workshop at Reading University that was attended by 36 teachers.

Since this phase of the program is just getting under way, there is nothing to report as far as actual school instruction is concerned. The outstanding success of the past efforts of the National Marriage Guidance Council gives reason to believe that England is fertile ground for the development of education for marriage and family-life programs, and perhaps the next few years will see great advances in this field.

Sweden

Sweden, over a period of years, has developed an outstanding program of sex education. The National League for Sex Education, under the leadership of Dr. Elise Ottensen-Jensen, has been a powerful force in this effort. The Swedish government has now made sex education in the schools compulsory (Royal Board of Education in Sweden, 1956). Instruction is based upon a genuine concern for marriage stability and family welfare. For the latest information see Linnér (1967).

Netherlands and Belgium

The pressure of a rapidly increasing population on a limited land area has called forth the Netherlands Society for Sexual Reform. The society has as its first objective the promotion of birth control. However, experience with this program has led to the addition of still another objective, that of providing some kind of general broad education for marriage.

The result has been the organization of "Marriage Schools" in a number of the larger cities in Holland. These schools are sponsored by local branches of the Netherlands Society for Sexual Reform. As in England, enrollment in these schools is by personal decision and attendance is voluntary. The school is designed for engaged or about-to-be-engaged couples. A pattern has been established providing that the program consist of a series of eight lectures, each given by an acknowledged authority in his field. The usual plan is to include three meetings on the physical aspects of marriage, one on the legal aspects, one on eugenics, and three on sociological and psychological aspects.

Belgium has now organized a society that is patterned along lines very similar to those of the Netherlands organization.

India and Pakistan

Major strides toward family-life education in Asia have been taken in India and Pakistan. The movement in both of these countries had its origin in the tremendous pressures resulting from an already large, and continuously growing, population. In both countries conferences have been held on population policies and planned parenthood. The effort to educate the people of Pakistan and India to the need and value of family planning has had the financial support of the central governments and the strong support of governmental leaders.

As the leaders have proceeded with their educational efforts in these countries, an increasingly strong emphasis on family-life education has emerged. The following quotation (Fazalbhoy, 1958) is typical of the viewpoints that develop from experiences in working families:

If family planning is to plan the family in all aspects calculated to its welfare, services such as sterility service, marriage counselling, and sex education also come in as an inherent part of the whole programme. . . . The very mention of marriage counselling and sex education used to come as a shock to even the people working in the family planning movement till very recently. Of late, we are hearing a good bit about these new phrases. . . . We can ill-afford to neglect these services if we aim at human welfare as a whole. Immediate efforts are necessary to train a contingent of suitable workers to handle these very much needed services efficiently, for the greatest good of the greatest number.

The breadth that family-planning movements assume is well illustrated by the *Journal of Family Welfare,* published in India. This magazine is strongly devoted to the support and promotion of the family-planning movement, but it regularly features articles on sex education, marriage counseling, social and economic welfare of families, family-life education programs in schools and communities, family physical and mental health, and family interrelationships.

The World Family-Life Education Movement

Family-planning movements have been initiated and are being advanced in Egypt, Japan, Ceylon, China, Thailand, and doubtless many other places as well. The logic of prior experience would lead us to expect these efforts to advance to the point where broad family-life education programs are included as an integral part of the total plan.

The movement into family-life education programs from family-planning efforts seems to be concentrated in densely populated countries that lack a religious group strongly opposed to birth control. In predominantly Catholic countries family-life education has been developed mainly within the Church and in accordance with the teachings of the Church. France is one of the countries in which the Church-sponsored program has taken considerable root. In the 1930's young French couples wanting help with their approaching marriages established the Family Renewal Association. The purpose of this organization was to make possible week-end meetings during which couples, under the leadership of priests, could discuss the issues and questions of marriage. This movement was the inspiration for the Cana movement that developed later in the United States.

Exploratory efforts at family-life education are being made in other parts of the world: Peru, New Zealand, Germany, Australia, the Philippines, to mention a few. The indications are that this kind of education is becoming firmly established in many countries. It is also probable that family-life education will advance considerably in many other countries all around the globe within the next decade.

References—Books and Articles

American Association of School Administrators, *Education for Family Life*. Washington, D.C.: National Education Association, 1941.

Bernard, Jesse, *Marriage and Family Among Negroes*. Englewood Cliffs, N. J.: Prentice-Hall, Inc., 1966.

Bernard, Jessie, *Remarriage*. New York: The Dryden Press, 1956.

Brown, Muriel W., *With Focus on Family Living*. Vocation division bulletin, No. 249, Home economics education series, No. 28. Washington, D.C.: U.S. Office of Education, 1953.

Burgess, Ernest W., and Cottrell, Leonard S., *Predicting Success or Failure in Marriage*. Englewood Cliffs, N.J.: Prentice-Hall, Inc., 1939.

Burgess, Ernest W., and Wallin, Paul, *Engagement and Marriage*. Philadelphia: J. B. Lippincott Co., 1953.

Christensen, Harold T., *Marriage Analysis*. New York: The Ronald Press Co., 1958, Ch. 9.

Eliot, Thomas D., "Bereavement: Inevitable but Not Insurmountable." In Howard Becker and Reuben Hill, *Family, Marriage and Parenthood*. Boston: D. C. Heath & Co., 1955.

Ellis, Albert, and Harper, Robert A. *Creative Marriage*. New York: Lyle Stuart, 1960.

Fazalbhoy, Zarina A., "Organisation and Administration of Family Planning Clinics." *Journal of Family Welfare 4;* 93-98, 1958.

Foote, Nelson N., and Cottrell, Leonard S., *Identity and Interpersonal Competence*. Chicago: University of Chicago Press, 1955.

Goode, William J., *After Divorce*. Glencoe, Ill.: The Free Press, 1956.

Johannis, Theodore B., Jr., "Participation by Fathers, Mothers and Teenage Sons and Daughters in Selected Household Tasks." *The Coordinator 6;* 61-62, June 1958.

Kirkendall, Lester A., "Education for Marriage and Family Living." In Franklin Zeran (ed.), *Life Adjustment Education in Action*. New York: Chartwell House, Inc., 1953.

Kirkendall, Lester A., *Premarital Intercourse and Interpersonal Relationships*. New York: Julian Press, 1961.

Komorovsky, Mirra, *Blue-Collar Marriage*. New York: Random House, 1964.

Landis, Judson T., "The Teaching of Marriage and Family Courses in Colleges." In *Marriage and Family Living 21;* 36-40, February, 1959.

Landis, Judson T., and Landis, Mary G., *Building a Successful Marriage* (2nd ed.). Englewood Cliffs, N.J.: Prentice-Hall, Inc., 1953.

Linnér, Brigitta, *Sex and Society in Sweden*. New York: Random House, 1967.

Peterson, James A., *Education for Marriage*. New York: Charles Scribner's Sons, 1956.

Rainwater, Lee, *Family Design: Marital Sexuality, Family Size and Contraception*. Chicago: Aldine Press, 1965.

Reiss, Ira, *Premarital Sex Standards in America*. New York: Free Press of Glencoe, 1960.

Royal Board of Education in Sweden, *Handbook on Sex Instruction in Swedish Schools*. Board of Education Series No. 28. Stockholm 8, Sweden: The Royal Board of Education, 1956.

Strain, Francis B., and Eggert, Chester L., "Framework for Family Life Education." *Bulletin of the National Association of Secondary School Principals*. Washington, D.C.: The Association, December, 1955.

Terman, Lewis M., *Psychological Factors in Marital Happiness*. New York: McGraw-Hill Book Co., 1938.

Wallis, J. H., and Booker, H. S., *Marriage Counseling*. London: Routledge, Kegan Paul, 1958.

Winch, Robert F., *Mate-selection*. New York: Harper & Brothers, 1958.

Organizations

Three organizations of importance to this field are:

International Union of Family Organizations, 28, Place Saint-Georges—Paris (IXe). I.U.F.O. serves family organizations of the world in various ways, principally through governmental channels.

National Council on Family Relations, 1219 University Avenue S.E., Minneapolis, Minn. 55414. Especially important are its journals: *Journal of Marriage and Family* and *Family Life Coordinator*.

Sex Information and Education Council of the United States, 1855 Broadway, New York, New York 10023. Devoted to developing sex education programs and more modern concepts of sexuality.

LESTER A. KIRKENDALL

Marriage, Plural

THE forms of marriage have, traditionally, been classified as monogamy, polygyny, polyandry, and group marriage. It is generally agreed that monogamy is the basic and universal form of mating. And although polygyny is relatively widespread, there is no society in which polygyny is the only form of marriage. For the most part, it is to be regarded as a permissive rather than a mandatory matter. Polyandry, in the strictest sense, has been found in but few societies. Group marriage is extremely rare, though it had a prominent place in early anthropological theory. The concept was certainly misapplied to certain native customs in parts of Africa and Australia, in which a group of men of a certain age range had sexual access to a group of women of like age range. These relations were, however, not regarded as group marriages in the technical sense of the term.

Polygyny

The incidence of polygyny is reflected—in a rough way—by a count of the frequency of various forms of marriage found in the Human Relations Area File at Yale University. Murdock (1949) reports that of the 238 societies for which they have data on marriage forms, 81 per cent permitted some kind of polygynous mating. Eighteen per cent were strictly monogamous. Only two of the total were polyandrous.

Sororal polygyny is the pattern in which the preferred union is that of a husband with two or more sisters. In Murdock's sample of 132 societies that had some form of polygyny, 53 per cent either required or permitted the sororal

form. Some writers maintain that sororal polygyny tends, on the whole, to reduce the threat of friction among the wives since the sisters have already learned to adjust to each other. The present writer is inclined to question this generalization. In his study of Mormon polygyny he found that although wives who were sisters often got along reasonably well, there was a solid fraction of instances where they did not.

Household Arrangements

The household arrangements in plural families show certain variation. In some instances the wives and their families lived together in one household; in other cases each wife had a separate establishment. Then, too, there were situations where some wives had separate households while other wives resided together in one household. Mormon polygyny was an example of the latter pattern. According to Murdock's data, sororal polygyny was particularly well suited to the single-dwelling type of residence. Of his identifiable cases of sororal plural families, 85 per cent of the co-wives lived in the same dwelling. In contrast, for his sample, 50 per cent of the nonsororal families occupied separate domiciles.

Household arrangements are further complicated by the fact that residence may be patrilocal or matrilocal, depending largely on the systems of descent in vogue in particular tribes or societies. There is some pull and haul in working out a satisfactory correlation of the forms of marriage with the rules of residence. Yet sororal polygyny, says Murdock, seems particularly well "adapted to matrilocal residence." He believes that, on the whole, in the matter of residential locus "the relative efficacy of the marriage forms is greater than that of residence rules."

Economic Arrangements

Not only is place and form of household arrangement important, so too is the division of economic tasks among the wives. There is no uniform pattern of such division of labor, but some differential assumption of work is found everywhere, whether the families have a common household or separate ones.

For example, among the Cuna, in the Caribbean, one wife was put in charge of the housekeeping operations, another in charge of the cultivation of bananas and maize, and a third had charge of the cocoa trees. In the Mormon plural family system a wide variety of patterns of work arose. Sometimes the division was similar to that of the Cuna—particularly where there was a single dwelling. In other cases the household tasks were divided so that one wife was responsible for the cooking and serving of meals, another for the washing and ironing, another for the house cleaning, and still another for the garden and poultry.

Status of Wives

The status of the various wives differed considerably from one tribe or society to another. The relation of status to economic obligation is close. In a canvass of the Human Relations Area File by the present writer it was found that in three-fifths of the tribes the first wife clearly had the highest status. This did not mean, however, that she had complete dominance over the other wives. However, in one-fifth of these groups, the first wife did have considerable control over the assignment of economic tasks to the other wives.

The first wife did not always have the highest status, since a younger and more attractive wife might be the husband's favorite. Yet, if one is to judge from the author's Mormon data, the introduction of a younger wife into the family ménage often led to conflict. Moreover, it must not be forgotten that with few exceptions women have held a distinctly inferior place to menfolk, and this is true of both nonliterate and more advanced societies.

Despite the generally inferior position of women, it is worth noting that not infrequently a wife or the wives would act together to advise or suggest that a husband take an additional wife or wives, in order to lighten the burden of their economic or household duties. Such conjoint action is reported from many primitive tribes, and it was not uncommon in ancient China or among the Mormons. So, too, on occasion the wives might act in common to protect what they regarded as their rights.

Although data regarding the husband's distribution of time among the wives are scanty, the available evidence clearly indicates that some more or less regular schedule was the general rule. This might be a night-by-night rotation, a two- or three-day plan, or some longer cycle. The author's Mormon data show clearly that some regular and equalitarian rotation of time among the wives was an important factor making for more harmonious relations among the plural families.

Property and Inheritance

Ownership of property varies so greatly in tribal societies that no generalization as to pattern is possible. Sometimes the husband and father controlled the agricultural land, in other circumstances it might be an uncle or the oldest patrilineal or matrilineal member of the extended family. Often new marriages facilitated the accumulation of additional wealth. The whole matter, however, is complicated by the fact that among many nonliterate tribes all the property a wife brought from her own family remained under her control. Moreover, it was a common practice for the wife who had her own garden and poultry to keep for her own use and disposal whatever she made from the sale of the products.

An equitable distribution of income by the husband tended to make for harmony among the plural families. This was certainly the case among the Mormons: failure to treat all the families fairly as to property and income often made for conflict.

Systems of inheritance also differed considerably depending on the patterns of descent, on the systems of ownership, and on the rights of the wives. Among the Mormons special provision had to be made for the plural wives, since legally they were not married. Hence, unless a husband made special arrangements for them through a will or by gift, they had no claim on his property. Their children, of course, had claims, although under the law they were regarded as illegitimate.

Discipline

Discipline and control of polygynous families ultimately rested with the husband and father. Certainly this tradition obtained in Mormon plural families, deriving not only from the general cultural pattern of patriarchal control but also from the ecclesiastical system under which only men could hold the sacred priesthood. However, within this larger framework, in some instances the first wife had some control over the other wives, especially in the assignment of economic duties. Then, too, each wife more or less disciplined her own children, particularly the younger ones. The right of one wife to exercise any control over the children of another wife varied from tribe to tribe. With the Mormons, the extension of such rights varied from family to family. There was no formal rule on the matter.

Child Training

Whiting and Child (1953) contend that under sororal polygyny, where the co-wives usually reside in one house, early child training is likely to be more indulgent and "less severe in subsequent socialization" than in either non-sororal polygyny or monogamy. In nonsororal polygyny the wives usually occupy separate dwellings; moreover, rivalry among the wives—not so likely in sororal polygyny—easily prevents cooperation and sharing in child care.

The status of children will vary according to the relative status of their mothers. Where the first wife has top status and some control over the other wives, her children may then assume positions of superiority toward the children of other wives. There is considerable evidence of this kind of differential status among the Mormons, and this sometimes made for conflict. Again, since the first wife was the only legal spouse, her children were quite aware that they were the only legitimate children and in con-

flictive situations among the families often traded on this fact.

Conflict and Divorce

One common problem in polygynous families was rivalry and attendant jealousy among the wives, although some anthropologists believe that sororal polygyny made for toleration among the wives. Again there was considerable variability in this matter.

In some societies rivalry, jealousy, suspicion, and paranoidal tendencies become culturalized and all members carry on feuding as a routine matter. Regarding the Azande, Evans-Pritchard (1937) writes: "Within the household there is often bitter, though it may be concealed, jealousy between the wives, between brothers, between sisters. In a family itself a wife often hates and tricks her husband, and the husband is unceasingly jealous of his wife and bullies her. Children fear and sometimes hate their father...."

Every society develops some institutional means of terminating conflict between the spouses. In most tribes divorce is relatively easy, although it often involves some return of property, such as the bride price. This was as true of polygynous as of monogamous marriages. Conflict among the plural wives was doubtless the most common cause of divorce. If there was a good degree of cooperation, as in sororal polygyny, there should be less incidence of divorce than in the nonsororal form. Another reason for divorce was sterility of a wife. Among the Mormons—aside from the central one of infidelity—other causes of divorce were continuous conflict among the wives or conflict between the husband and a given wife.

Justifications for Polygyny

In concluding our section on polygyny we may examine the justifications put forth in defense of this form of plural marriage. The chief "reasons" seem to be, in order of importance: economic value of plural wives; status and prestige of the husband and father; provision for more children; and an excess of women. Religious sanctions were noted in some societies and this is definitely the core of justification among the Mormons, as it was among the ancient Hebrews. In addition, where tribal inter-marriage was permitted, it might be a device to maintain peaceable relations with neighboring tribes.

Polyandry

Polyandry, Murdock says, is a form of marriage "socially sanctioned and culturally patterned" involving "residential cohabitation as well as sexual rights." However, it occurs so infrequently that it may be regarded as an ethnological curiosity. Although some cultural anthropologists have described the occurrence of polyandry in certain North American Indian tribes, this is, strictly speaking, not the case. What has been mistaken for polyandry, Opler (1943) notes, was usually an example of extra-marital sex relations of a woman with a number of men, sometimes the brothers of her husband. Sexual rights with the siblings-in-law of the opposite sex were not infrequently granted to either spouse. But this does not constitute marriage.

There are but two tribes where polyandry is stable, preferred, and regarded as the normative form of marriage. These are the Todas of Southern India and the Marquesans of Polynesia.

The Todas

Among the Todas the preferred form of polyandry is fraternal, that is, the wife marries a series of brothers. Only occasionally is the nonfraternal type to be found. Among the Marquesans the nonfraternal form is common. In Toda polyandry several brothers establish a common household with one woman. Paternity of the children is determined by a ritual in which one brother presents the wife with a toy bow and arrow and all the offspring following this rite are credited to the husband who executed the ritual. Only when another husband carries out the bow-and-arrow ceremony does the paternity go to him, but again all the children are ascribed to the last husband to carry out the rite, even though he has been dead for years.

Among the Todas polyandry is definitely associated with low economic status. In fact the nobility not infrequently practices polygyny.

When the co-husbands are brothers they occupy one house, but in the occasional examples of nonfraternal polyandry they have separate dwellings and the wife rotates her visits among them.

The Marquesans

In the Marquesas polyandrous marriage is as stable as any other. There is usually a main husband who acts as an agent for the wife in the management of family affairs. The other husbands are not his brothers but the younger sons of families of lower rank. They are accorded considerable latitude and may leave one household to join another. Here, too, economic conditions are severe. Cultivation is difficult and the islands are subject to periodic droughts leading to crop failures, water shortages, and severe epidemics. Fishing is difficult and dangerous in the deep waters off the mountainous islands.

Group Marriage

Group marriage is sporadic and is never found as a societal norm. In the Human Relations Area File, the most frequent occurrence is among the Kaingang of Brazil. Yet even here only 8 per cent of recorded unions are group marriages, whereas 14 per cent are polyandrous, 18 per cent polygynous, and the balance monogamous. In some tribes, as the Chukchee of Siberia and the Dieri of Australia, sexual privileges may be practiced by a group of men and women of a given age range. But the economic responsibilities upon which genuine marriage must rest are not required. There is no evidence that group marriage exists or ever did exist as the prevailing type of marriage.

The form of marriage developed by John Humphey Noyes and put into effect in the Oneida Community was not really group marriage. Rather, it was a system, known as stirpiculture, of selecting mates in terms of certain physical and mental criteria.

References

Evans-Pritchard, E., *Witchcraft, Oracles and Magic Among the Azande*. London: Oxford University Press, 1937.

Ford, Clellan S., and Beach, Frank A., *Patterns of*

Sexual Behavior. New York: Harper & Brothers, 1951.

Hobhouse, L. T., Wheeler, G. C., and Ginzberg, M., *Material Culture and Social Institutions of the Simpler Peoples.* London: Chapman & Hall, 1930.

Murdock, George Peter, *Social Structure.* New York: The Macmillan Co., 1949.

Opler, Marvin K., "Woman's Social Status and the Forms of Marriage." *Am. J. Sociol. 49;* 125-146, 1943.

Westermarck, Edward, *History of Human Marriage.* New York: The Macmillan Co., 1921 (3 vols.).

Whiting, John W. M., and Child, Irvin L., *Child Training and Personality: A Cross-Cultural Study.* New Haven: Yale University Press, 1953.

Young, Kimball, *Isn't One Wife Enough?* New York: Henry Holt and Co., Inc., 1954.

KIMBALL YOUNG

Marriage,
Sexual Adjustment in

GIVEN adequate information and a mature emotional attitude, adjustment of the physical side of sexual activity is achieved with relative ease.

There has been some change, fortunately, in the last fifty years since the end of the Victorian Era, but not nearly enough change. Most young people still marry burdened with distressing questions. What will their first sexual experience be like? Will they be well mated sexually? Will there be great disparity in sexual desire? If there is, is it an insurmountable obstacle? Will the one suffer great pain, and must the other inflict such pain to consummate the marriage? May the vagina of the one or the penis of the other be too small or too large to make it possible to have intercourse and to give and receive the unique type of pleasurable experience that should be a part of sexual intercourse? If one overindulged in intercourse would it undermine the health?

The Basis of Adjustment

Real emotional adjustment in marriage comes to those couples who are brought up to, or come to, accept wholeheartedly the fact that basically marriage is an institution to provide sexual satisfaction. No one denies the joys of parenthood. But the basis of a real marriage is a completely satisfactory adjustment of the sexual side of marriage.

The mere fact that we are human makes the achievement of such adjustment difficult. We have all the desire, all the will, all the capacity of our most primitive mammalian ancestors. The difficulty is that we have a much larger cerebrum. This gives us the capacity to remember and to foresee.

Some ten to twenty-five thousand years ago man discovered the connection between sexual intercourse and childbirth. From that moment it could never be quite the same. He could no longer indulge in intercourse just for the instinctive pleasure it gave him. Either he was afraid of having more children or, as was frequently the case, he was most interested in having more children (witness the fertility rites of many primitive peoples), and must have wondered if this time it would succeed, and his wife would become pregnant. Intercourse became something to be concerned about, not to be practiced merely for pleasure. This changed its whole aspect.

And of course some women died in childbirth. Thoughtful males certainly could not laugh off their responsibility in the matter. That they could fall back upon the thought that it was "God's will" was poor comfort, at best.

The "Rights" of Marriage

During the Victorian Era it was accepted that sex could mean nothing to a "lady." She might submit to the desires of her husband, but that she would take an active part, or gain any pleasure from it, was unthinkable. Although we are no longer the prisoners of that attitude, we have still made only a partial escape.

Then along came another factor to further complicate the situation—women's rights. Women became entitled to a voice and a vote. Unfortunately, too many women interpreted that to mean that if they did not want sexual intercourse, married or not, they did not have to have it. That there are anatomical and physiological differences that need to be considered was never pointed out to them.

In our culture, as it is organized today, when a man marries he presumably gives up his right to pursue other females for the purpose of sexual pleasure. By the same token, when a woman marries, she undertakes to satisfy the sexual needs of her husband, and renounces her right arbitrarily to say no, women's rights to the contrary notwithstanding.

A young woman, lying on the examining table for her six weeks' postpartum check-up, recently replied to my question about refitting her with a diaphragm that it would not be necessary—her husband was suing for divorce. Under further questioning she stated that he accused her of never having been a real wife to him. Married only a few weeks before she became pregnant, she had had no desire for intercourse after that, and since she did not want it, she did not see why she had to submit to it!

Marriage is a sexual relationship. Whatever else it may be—culturally, socially, economically, financially—it is still basically a sexual relationship. The pleasure of sexual intercourse, the satisfaction it brings, the release from tension it confers upon the individual is all the reason that anyone needs for indulgence in it, and each member of a married pair has the responsibility of seeing that the other is sexually satisfied.

Reasons for Intercourse

Love, the strange human emotion that fixates our sexual attention upon one of the opposite sex, certainly contributes to the intensity of the sensations incident to intercourse. And just as the intensity of the sensation is greater with a desired and desirable partner, so the satisfaction achieved is more complete. But certainly, if we could be freed from our inhibitions, intercourse with any physically acceptable partner should be at least minimally pleasurable, as Havelock Ellis pointed out many years ago.

Thus, within the framework of marriage intercourse may be undertaken for a variety of reasons. In its most desirable form, it is the expression of a deep and abiding love and affection. Under these circumstances it may be preceded by a considerable period of affectionate display, leading only slowly up to the climax of the whole process, actual intercourse and the attainment of release from tension through orgasm.

But on other occasions, for no assignable reason, it may be what might be termed merely physically desirable. Affectionate display may be reduced to a minimum, with the purely physical aspects of sexual contact leading to almost immediate orgasm. The whole process may take a matter of a very few minutes, and still be a very satisfactory experience.

Each member of a married pair must be able to accept both types of experience—and various intermediate stages—if they are to work out the most satisfactory adjustment in marriage.

Approaches to Courtship

Being human is complicated! We remember and we foresee.

The male is the seeking partner in the majority of marriages.

These two propositions need to be appreciated and accepted. Why it is so we do not really know. But something in the male sex hormone does condition the nervous system so that it makes the individual more conscious of sex desire. This applies to both sexes. A woman, given male sex hormone as a therapeutic measure for any cause, may find herself with a well-nigh uncomfortable increase in sex desire.

It is well known that mental imagery, imagination, affects the male more than the female. Thus a man may sit looking at his wife through a comfortable evening of reading, listening to the radio, or watching television, and be quite ready to carry her off to bed, emotionally excited to the point of imperative sex desire. His wife may be quite unprepared for it. Here a little information makes possible a satisfactory adjustment. He must be willing to give her an opportunity of warming up to a consciousness of desire. But for her part, she must accept his advances and not try to avoid them.

A bride should train herself from the day she is married to accept her husband's affectional demonstrations. But being human is complicated. We remember and foresee. She will be married only a very short time before she learns that these demonstrations may lead to intercourse. She thinks she is too busy, or does not have time, or just does not feel like it. So she seeks to avoid it physically, by pushing him away, or refuses to accept it emotionally, even though she may, very virtuously, say to him, in effect, "Oh! All right. Go ahead if you want to. I'll be a good wife and let you." But she has tightened up and rejected his advances emotionally if not physically.

In either case she handicaps herself by so doing. One must move through a period of time and space, or experience, from the beginning of love-making to the achievement of its climax and the release from tension that it brings. The woman who consciously or unconsciously tightens up and rejects her husband's advances must move through a considerable space of negative feeling before she even gets to the starting point, as it were.

The common experience, then, is that if her husband does desire intercourse enough to go on with it, by the time he has achieved orgasm and release from tension she has moved only through her negative feelings and has just become interested. If now he would start all over again, she would be very happy to accept his advances.

The solution is simple. A woman can train herself to accept her husband's advances. She simply remains neutral—passive, if you will. She does not push him away, she does not tighten up emotionally; she lets herself literally melt back into his arms. She lets his hands roam over her body and accepts them, happily, as a demonstration of his desire for her and his satisfaction in possessing her. And when she does this she will almost invariably find that, within a matter of minutes, being carried off to bed will become a very satisfactory experience, and complete release from tension will be achieved relatively easily.

Many wives have no idea of their own sexual capacity simply because they have never given it a chance to develop. When each experience of sexual intercourse comes as the result of a contest between her and her husband, with him finally overcoming her reluctance or her grudgingly permitting the relationship, her chances of finding anything approximating the maximum in emotional pleasure is very slight.

Occasionally a wife will want intercourse more often than her husband. Where this is true it is something of a special case. If a woman makes a man feel inadequate sexually, she may literally emasculate him and render him impotent.

One husband seemed content with intercourse once a month, which, said his wife, simply left her "climbing the walls." Fortunately, each was mature enough to accept the situation. About once a week she would ask him to take her to bed. When she did this he accepted it with good grace and they invariably ended the evening with complete satisfaction for both.

The Channels of Communication

This brings us to another all-important proposition that needs be dealt with before considering specific instances. The channels of communication must be kept open! A wife would think nothing of it if her husband asked to have the morning coffee a little stronger or a little weaker, his shirt cuffs starched a little stiffer or a little softer, his steak cooked a little more or a little less. But how would she react to his suggestion that she tip her pelvis this way or that, or that she change position in intercourse, or that she caress him in a certain manner or a certain place? Will she accept it in the same spirit and respond in the same way by trying to do what pleases him? Or will she take it as an insulting criticism?

And what of him? If she dares suggest that he continue petting a little longer, will he do so gracefully or be insulted because it implies a shortcoming in his love-making technique? Does she dare indulge in some sexual experiments of her own, or would he be shocked by it?

One 30-year-old woman admitted that she only enjoyed intercourse about twice a year, when she dared to let herself go. When asked why she did not let herself go more often she replied with some vigor that if she did, her husband would think she was crazy!

Another 29-year-old appeared at the office, the most utterly crushed young woman I believe I have ever seen. She had just been divorced after a year of marriage. She had married a successful public accountant, 33 years old, who had waited to marry until he was secure in his profession and could afford a real honeymoon. They had started upon a two-month tour of the United States. Ten or twelve days after the wedding she had begun to menstruate. They thought, as many young people do, that they could not indulge in intercourse during this time. Two or three days later it was apparent from the turgidity of his erection that he was actually uncomfortable. Indulging in what Kinsey *et al.*, have appropriately termed "good mammalian behavior," and, as she said, for no reason she could explain, but merely because she had the impulse to do it, she curled herself down in bed and kissed his penis. From that moment he remained cold to her, and within the year they were divorced.

A 50-year-old woman, wife of a successful Methodist minister and mother of two grown children, came to the office with a problem, centered around the sexual impulse, that she was willing to discuss with no resentment or antagonism. Her trouble lay in the fact that she was sure she was going insane. It was this fear, and the knowledge that it centered around sex, that made her seek help.

To the question, "Do you enjoy sexual intercourse?" she replied in lukewarm fashion, "Oh —yes." But to the next question, "Do you reach orgasm?" she replied crisply, "Oh, yes." If she reached orgasm—and she did every time—what was the matter? What did she want? From her reply to the first question she was obviously lukewarm in her enthusiasm for it.

When asked a question that implied that the fault might be her husband's she would have none of it. She delivered a panegyric, describing him as a most kind, thoughtful, patient, and loving husband. He had always done every-

thing he could to see that she enjoyed intercourse and reached orgasm.

When asked, "Do you ever reach orgasm more than once?" she jumped as though she had been stuck with a pin. Words tumbled out in a torrent, to the effect that that was exactly the problem. She had been married for thirty years to a kindly, considerate, thoughtful, patient man. He had always seen to it that she enjoyed intercourse enough to reach orgasm—once! And she had never been satisfied! She had wanted to have the experience more than once. She was a thankless ingrate. And the Lord was going to punish her by making her insane!

Think of it! Married for thirty years to a kindly man—yet not once in that time had the channels of communication opened sufficiently for her to suggest that he continue love-making long enough to grant her the experience of reaching orgasm enough times to give her complete relief from all sexual tension!

Professional Advice

Patients will go to a physician readily for any and every complaint *except* those connected with the primary sex organs. Then they will go only when the distress is so acute that they are driven to it. If it concerns discomfort in sexual relations they are ordinarily even more reluctant to seek help.

The patients themselves are not always or perhaps even primarily to blame. Just as a child learns very quickly not to ask his mother questions that distress her, so patients learn not to ask doctors questions they cannot handle easily. And, of course, doctors were children long before they were doctors. Despite knowledge of the anatomy and physiology of the primary sex organs, not infrequently physicians are little better equipped, emotionally, to handle sexual problems than their patients. However, with the growth in knowledge and the change in attitude today, one should be able to find help with relatively little effort, from psychologists, marriage counselors, psychiatrists, or physicians.

The Differences of Sex

Men and women are very different people, and there is no reason why we should not rejoice over that fact. But it makes it much easier to live together if each sex appreciates that there are differences and makes allowances for them. A woman's sense of smell is usually keener than a man's. Men commonly indulge in heavier work or more vigorous exercise than do women and perspire more freely. Fresh perspiration has no offensive odor, but it is quickly affected by bacterial action. Men, therefore, must be willing to bathe often.

The vulvo-vaginal glands of a woman secrete a great deal of mucus. That in the vagina is affected by Doederlein's bacillus and is broken down into lactic acid, the component of sour milk that gives it its characteristic odor. For a woman, therefore, bathing frequently is also essential. And adequate care must be taken to cleanse the vulvo-vaginal area. One does not use the flat of the hand to wash around, in, and behind an ear; one uses one's finger. The same technique must be used around the vulva and the vaginal introitus. When little girls are brought up to believe it a sin to touch themselves in that area it may mean that they have to go through a whole emotional revolution to be able to do it. But in marriage it is essential.

Nowhere in the ordinary course of activity will one be as close to another as in bed at night. A bath before going to bed is therefore far more important than a bath in the morning. If a cold shower gives you a sense of invigoration and serves as a quick stimulant to get you into the day's work, fine, but the really important bathing rite, a bath before getting into bed with your spouse, should not be neglected.

Pain in Intercourse

Pain in intercourse is uncommon for a man. Occasionally, of course, there may be irritation of the skin or mucous membrane of the penis or glans that will be sensitive. When this is the case he should feel as free to consult a doctor as if he had a painful ear.

The mucus of the vagina is a perfect culture medium for bacteria. Hence the vagina may harbor pathogenic organisms as well as the harmless kind. These may set up irritation, even inflammation. Intercourse, instead of being a pleasurable experience, may actually be painful. If this occurs, a physician should be con-

sulted. Forty-nine times out of fifty it will be something easily amenable to medical care.

The clitoris is the primary seat of sexual sensation in the female. It is located about an inch anterior to the opening of the vagina where the labia minora (small lips) of the vulva come together. The fold thus formed is called the prepuce and commonly covers the clitoris. In a considerable majority of women it is adherent to the clitoris and frequently almost completely covers it. This greatly lessens normal sensation. To make the situation worse, small, pinpoint to pinhead-sized clumps of epithelial cells collect under the adherent prepuce. When this is so, stimulation of the clitoris, far from being a pleasant experience, may feel like having one's eye rubbed when there is a grain of sand in it. To free the adhesions is a matter of three minutes' work with a blunt probe by a competent physician.

Can a vagina be too small to permit intercourse? Or can a penis be so small as to fail to give the female partner sexual satisfaction? The answer to both questions is the same: only in the extreme case. True, some women have rudimentary vaginas and some men have pathologically small penises. But in the great majority of cases the individual would have been aware of this before reaching the age of marriage.

If a man is capable of having an erection, it is still possible even though the penis is smaller than average, to have satisfactory intercourse. If the penis is unusually large it is still possible. The vagina is capable of being contracted by voluntary control of the sphincter muscles until it can firmly grasp something no larger than a little finger, and it can be dilated or stretched to permit the entrance of something as large as one's wrist with no serious discomfort.

Occasionally the vagina may be foreshortened—because of a retroverted uterus or for some other reason. Deep penetration may be uncomfortable, even to the point of actual pain. This problem may be solved by varying the position. The wife may be above the husband, or, with the wife beneath, the husband may put his legs outside her slightly separated ones. He can then get all the satisfaction of pushing as hard as he wishes, but will not need to have any fear that he will penetrate deeply enough to cause pain.

Relaxation

Real sexual adjustment can come about in marriage only when a couple feel free to work toward such an end. They must free themselves from all sense of sin and guilt regarding sexual actions and activity. They must be willing to take time out to enjoy it. They must not put off attempts at intercourse until they are under such tension that they cannot take time to get the greatest amount of pleasurable experience from it.

One young couple with three children had a very practical solution to the problems of occasionally having a very good time together. Rather than spending money on night clubs or drinking bouts they spent an evening alone together. They hired a baby-sitter, bought a bottle of champagne, and went to a hotel room. There was no danger of interruption, no phone to ring, since only the baby sitter knew where they were. And emotionally it took them back to their first night together and the thrill that such a memory can bring.

Sexual intercourse is not exhausting. It is relaxing. But it does take some nervous energy to generate the spark of desire. Late, late, *late* TV shows, keeping one or both up until all hours, leave little in the way of the necessary spark to beget a pleasant sexual experience. If desire is present it is felt that the sooner it is over the better, because then each can roll over and go to sleep. Taking time to see that each benefits by the greatest amount of pleasant tension, ultimately relieved through the achievement of orgasm, just consumes too much time. Hurried through, it gives some physical relief, but a minimum of the emotional satisfaction that can be a part of intercourse.

From my conversations with hundreds of young couples I am convinced that one of the great hindrances to normal sexual adjustment in this central-heating-electric-light-radio-television age are all the benefits these confer. In the day of the fireplace, the pot-bellied base-burner, and the kerosene lamp, it was much more comfortable during much of the year to be in bed than out, and with all the emotional handicaps incident to the Victorian age, the comfort of being "early to bed" undoubtedly helped achieve some significant degree of sexual relaxation.

Sexual Technique

Enough has been said in many other places about positions in intercourse so that any detailed discussion here seems unnecessary. Any position that is mutually pleasurable is completely permissible. And any position that is desired by one should, if not difficult or uncomfortable for the other, certainly be tried, if for no other reason than the pleasure of variety. Whether or not a position will work is a matter far more of mental than of physical adjustment.

One young man was unable to persuade his wife to try any other position than face to face with him above. By a fortunate chance, for him, he met and had intercourse with a completely uninhibited young woman. To his surprise almost every position attempted worked very well, with little or no difficulty in achieving perfect union. His problem was to get his wife to attempt the positions and to yield sufficiently mentally and emotionally to let them work. It took two or three years of effort, but she finally found out that it was possible to do many of the things she was certain could never be done. And she finally came to enjoy the variety of experience which she had previously objected to most bitterly.

Havelock Ellis pointed out, many years ago, that when engaged in amative actions and reactions the ordinary criteria of esthetics simply no longer apply. Kinsey and his colleagues expressed the same thought in a somewhat different manner when they referred to many of the most intimate types of caresses as "good mammalian behavior."

The purpose of sexual intercourse, as far as the individual is concerned (and in this discussion we are not interested in the perpetuation of the race or any other consideration), is the pleasurable experience of a very intimate human relationship that has its climax in the achievement of orgasm (or orgasms), bringing release from the peculiar type of emotional tension known as sexual desire.

It does not matter how this is brought about. The all-important thing is that complete release from tension should be achieved. But it should be remembered that orgasm is not necessary in every case to bring about this release from tension. Certainly there will be occasions in everyone's experience when the mere act of love-making and caressing and the enjoyment of intimate bodily contact will yield complete satisfaction. Although acknowledging that this is true—in some instances—the really satisfactory experiences in the great majority of all instances end in orgasm.

Recent studies have explained the why of habit formation. They have shown that when nerve pathways are used it becomes progressively easier for stimuli to traverse these pathways because of actual anatomical changes. This applies especially to the achievement of orgasm in intercourse. The pathway must be formed by experience, and, with experience, becomes more and more firmly established. Although age—physiological and psychological—and hormonal components play a part, the establishment of the pathway of sexual experience undoubtedly contributes to the fact mentioned by Havelock Ellis sixty years or more ago and confirmed by the Kinsey studies: that women, as they grow older, achieve orgasm in a greater proportion of experiences of intercourse.

The Mutuality of Sexual Experience

Sexual adjustment in marriage is easy when a couple will throw away most if not all of their preconceived ideas about it and strive only to make it a mutually pleasurable experience. A husband need not feel called upon to demonstrate that he is the "great lover." What he ought to do is to try to find out what tactile sexual stimulation his wife, individually and particularly, enjoys. Are her breasts, buttocks, thighs, small of the back—or any part of her body—pleasantly sensitive to gentle—or firm—caresses with fingertips, lips, or tongue? And she should not hesitate to let him know what is pleasurable to her. One good rule to follow is that whatever caress one spouse has tried should be returned by the other, since the one

who initiated it probably thinks that it would be pleasant. If this rule is followed rapid progress may be made with very little vocal communication. But vocal communication should not be avoided when it may help.

The idea that orgasm must be attained simultaneously has great vogue. When it can be achieved easily there is certainly no objection to it, and it very possibly may add some emotional thrill to the experience. But a large part of the satisfaction of sexual intimacy is the feeling that one has conferred pleasure upon the other. As Dr. W. F. Robie pointed out years ago, to watch the other enjoy the experience of orgasm is in itself a very pleasant experience. Since a man usually loses his erection more or less promptly after orgasm and is then incapable, at least for a time, of further intercourse, it is usually better for him to see that his wife achieves sufficient satisfaction in one or more orgasms and to enjoy the knowledge that she has been satisfied. Then let her have the pleasure of knowing that she gives to him a similar experience.

It not only confers satisfaction to know that the other enjoys being petted and caressed, it also gives pleasure to know that the one doing the caressing enjoys doing it. The motions should not be gone through mechanically, with obvious signs that it is being done from a sense of duty. Let your imagination run riot if it wants to, and let yourself enjoy it and act as if you do.

Frequency

How frequently should a couple have intercourse? As often as they wish. As often as it is pleasant and satisfactory. They cannot do it too often, in the sense that they can do themselves any physical or physiological harm. They may become so relaxed that they will spend twenty-four hours in bed, but long before they could possibly be in any danger of starvation the "mortal pangs of hunger" would rouse them to the need for something in the way of sustenance other than love.

Some people have intercourse upon a more or less regular schedule; others prefer to go without for several days and then have intercourse several times during one evening or a weekend. Frequencies as well as positions, conditions, methods, and attitudes may be the subject of experimentation.

The greater the tension leading to the explosion of orgasm, the greater the release from tension, and the greater the real benefit to the individual. The greatest philosophers have failed to solve the question of the "why" of sexual desire. The continuance of the race depends upon it, and it was bred into us a million years ago. But sexual intercourse can—and should—be thoroughly enjoyed, be a mutually delightful experience.

It should be a mutual effort as well. It is not a question of a great lover or a great coquette striving only to please the other. It is a coordinated investigation of the mysteries of lovemaking with two people trying to achieve the maximum total of mutual pleasure. To do this they must be willing and able to laugh at some of their failures and to avoid taking offense at the seeming indifference of the other under certain circumstances.

References

Clark, LeMon, *Emotional Adjustment in Marriage.* St. Louis: C. V. Mosby Co., 1937.

Clark, LeMon, *Sex and You.* Indianapolis: The Bobbs-Merrill Co., Inc., 1949.

Dickinson, Robert L., *Human Sex Anatomy.* Baltimore: The Williams & Wilkins Co., 1949.

Dickinson, Robert L., and Beam, Lura, *A Thousand Marriages.* Baltimore: The Williams & Wilkins Co., 1931.

Ditzion, Sidney, *Marriage, Morals and Sex in America.* New York: Bookman Associates, Inc., 1953.

Ford, Clellan S., and Beach, Frank A., *Patterns of Sexual Behavior.* New York: Harper & Brothers, 1951.

Ellis, Albert, *The Folklore of Sex.* New York: Boni, 1951.

Ellis, Albert, *The American Sexual Tragedy.* New York: Twayne Pub., 1954.

Ellis, Albert (ed.), *Sex Life of the American Woman and the Kinsey Report.* New York: Greenberg Pub., 1954.

Ellis, Albert, *Sex Without Guilt.* New York: Lyle Stuart, 1958.

Ellis, Albert, *The Art and Science of Love.* New York: Lyle Stuart, 1960.

Ellis, Havelock, *Studies in the Psychology of Sex.* Philadelphia: F. A. Davis Co., 1925.

Geddes, Donald Porter (ed.), *An Analysis of the Kinsey Reports.* New York: E. P. Dutton & Co., Inc., 1954.

Grotjahn, Martin, *Beyond Laughter.* New York: The Blakiston Co., 1957.

Hamilton, G. V., *A Research in Marriage.* New York: Boni, 1929.

Kinsey, A. C. *et al., Sexual Behavior in the Human Male.* Philadelphia: W. B. Saunders Co., 1948.

Kinsey, A. C. *et al., Sexual Behavior in the Human Female.* Philadelphia: W. B. Saunders Co., 1953.

Kraines, S. H., and Thetford, E. S., *Managing Your Mind.* New York: The Macmillan Co., 1947.

Mead, Margaret, *Male and Female.* New York: Wm. Morrow & Co., Inc., 1949.

Murtagh, John M., and Harris, Sarah, *Cast the First Stone.* New York: McGraw-Hill Book Co., 1957.

Riddle, Oscar, *The Unleashing of Evolutionary Thought.* New York: Vantage Press, 1954.

Robie, W. F., *Rational Sex Ethics.* Ithaca, N.Y.: Rational Life Publishing Co., 1925.

Robie, W. F., *The Art of Love.* Ithaca, N.Y.: Rational Life Publishing Co., 1925.

Russell, W. Ritchie, "The Physiology of Memory." *Proc. Roy. Soc. Med. 51;* No. 1, 1958.

Stokes, Walter R., *Modern Patterns for Marriage.* New York: Rinehart & Co., Inc., 1948.

LE MON CLARK

Menopause

WHAT a source of fearful apprehension was the old concept of the "change of life!" Even as an adolescent male this writer vividly recalls the uneasy attitudes on this supposedly painful and dangerous period of transition. The impression at the time was that every woman had to pass through four or five years of suffering and anguish—and that she might not even pass through it alive.

A marvelous alteration of these false ideas has taken place in recent decades. Fearful misgivings about this time of transition in a woman's life may still linger among those who even now listen to "granny tales," but among the great majority of womankind there is far less fear of the approaching "change" than there is of approaching middle age or of the middle-age "spread." There are many reasons for this wholesome new attitude. First, the majority of women, about four-fifths in fact, pass through this period without any ill effects whatever and, as far as their health is concerned, without even being aware of it. In most of the other 20 per cent the symptoms are mild, and in the few who really do have untoward effects medical science offers assurance of easy alleviation. Of course, the more nervous a woman is the more likely is she to undergo the discomforts she expects—or to imagine she is undergoing them.

Some important changes do take place in the reproductive organs of the female during this time. As a result, the ability to produce offspring comes to an end: the ovaries cease to produce and liberate the eggs (ova) and the womb gradually abandons its monthly cycle of shedding the old lining and regenerating the new one. But otherwise a woman is still very much what she always was, and she can enjoy freedom from two previous worries: the possible fear of becoming pregnant and the periodic need of pads or tampons.

This does not mean that the change itself is the choicest time of life or that it leads to the most satisfying period in the life of a woman. Each period of life, from childhood to old age, has its joys and trials, but it must be emphasized that the transition period between the years of childbearing and those that follow is not to be dreaded. Indeed, it has its compensations, and can become an era of great fulfillment leading to years of happiness and calm.

Nothing to Fear

It is true that a small percentage of women can expect to have some nervous symptoms and mild disorders during the change, but these are easily abated under the care of a physician. One's physician must be consulted in those rare cases where symptoms are pronounced enough to cause fear, worry, or discomfort. Certainly it is reassuring for every woman to know that change of life is a physiological alteration that terminates the childbearing era and that it is not in any sense an abnormality or a disease or an illness.

(Certainly it is possible that women may become ill from other causes during the course of the change, but these are the coincidences that may have given apparent support to the gloomy forecasts of the pessimists.)

The slowing down and final cessation of certain functions of the ovaries are the immediate cause of the alterations in the reproductive lives of women during this period. The ovaries themselves are not independent glands, however: they are constantly receiving stimuli from the anterior lobe of the hypophysis or pituitary gland, which is located at the base of the brain. These relationships and the anatomy and physiology of the ovary will be described and illustrated later.

During the menopause the ovaries stop "laying eggs," the production of female sex hormones lessens, and the womb ceases its periodic changes and the resultant bleeding. Many women may "flood" during a portion of the change. but there is no reason to become alarmed about it. If hemorrhaging should become too severe it is best to see one's physician, as it may not have any connection with the menopause. It may be due to polyps inside the womb, in which case a dilatation of the neck of the womb and a scraping of its lining will be indicated.

No one should associate the time of the change with old age. In the modern era there is a great difference between middle life and aging. Nowadays women during and after the menopause may look years younger than they really are and live the kinds of lives they have always wanted to live but did not have the time to while rearing and caring for children. After the change a woman can really blossom out in many ways, spending more time than ever in creative endeavors and in the fulfillment of long-postponed dreams. Women may hope to live more healthful and more satisfying lives after release from the functions and duties related to the reproductive years.

If a woman thinks the change of life means a marked change in her sex life, she is probably right—a change for the better. After the reproductive years are over there is no need to worry about the onset of the next menstrual period or to be bothered with the urgent hygienic necessities of the four to six days. Nor is there any longer that excuse for postponing affectionate proposals of her husband—on the contrary, there is more likely no desire for postponement.

During the months or short years of change the sympathy and loving understanding of the husband will greatly lessen any unusual degree of symptoms. The children, with the possible exception of nearly grown daughters, will not be aware of what is going on—and, fortunately

in most cases, neither will the mother. If there are other grown women in the family it is wise that they, as well as the man of the house, be sympathetic and understanding; and the less said the better. There is always the family physician to turn to in those unusual cases in which definite symptoms of discomfort arise. The whole period may be over in less than two years even in the most severely affected; in many in far less time; and in the vast majority the change will hardly be noticed.

Onset and Duration of the Menopause

Any woman, after having reached the age of 35, may wonder from time to time whether or not some symptom or other means that she is beginning the change. Most probably at that age she is not, and it may be even ten years or more before positive proof of the menopause exists—cessation of the menses. The menses do not always cease all at once. A month or two may be missed, or there may be prolonged periods, or very short periods, or other variations until finally there is no show at all.

At what age does the menopause begin? There is a wide variation in the ages of women when the change actually begins. It is not too unusual for it to start as early as 35. However, it is much more apt to begin at 45 to 47, although it may not occur until the early or even the middle fifties.

Statistics show that in women in whom the menarche, or start of menstruation, occurred early (age 10 to 12) the menopause begins late, whereas in those in whom the onset was late, the pause begins early. These tendencies appear to run in families.

Early cessation of monthly flow may be caused by disease, especially when anemia occurs, as in tuberculosis. This cessation serves to protect the patient, for it conserves strength when it is vitally needed. A hormonal dysfunction, amenorrhea, also results in consecutive missed periods. If a woman is 40 or older she should not be surprised at such an event, and even less so if she is 45 or older. In any case it is a fine time for that annual physical examination.

Besides hormonal dysfunctions and disease, particularly those affecting the circulatory system, and in addition protracted emotional strain, there are several factors that appear to be related to early onset of the change. Some of these are a hypothyroid state with obesity, nursing babies too long, having babies too close together, frequent abortions or miscarriages, very cold climates, hard manual labor, and excessive output of energy.

On the other hand, the opposites of the foregoing conditions will in the majority of cases ensure a later onset of the menopause. These are good health with an excellent circulatory system along with equanimity (peace of mind), a euthyroid state with a lean body and an acute mentality, shorter periods of nursing offspring, proper spacing of children, avoiding abortions and miscarriages, a warm or temperate climate, and a normal output of energy.

One of the questions most frequently asked by women who have begun the change or who feel they are about to start it concerns the relationship between lack of menstruation and pregnancy. As long as there are any periods at all, there is some possibility of ovulation, and as long as eggs leave the ovary there is a possibility of becoming pregnant. The consensus seems to be that a woman who has entirely stopped menstruating for six consecutive months can be assured that ovulation has finally ceased and that there is no chance of conceiving. A pregnancy that occurs in a woman whose menses have been absent for six months or more is caused by an unusual and untimely ovulation. Normally, after the menopause no conception is to be expected, but to be absolutely certain some authorities advise waiting for a full year.

Some women can tell when they ovulate by a slight pain in the region of the ovary; on one side one month and on the other side the next. This is called *Mittelschmerz*, or middle-pain, because it occurs in the middle of the cycle during the childbearing years.

Pseudocyesis, or false pregnancy, is most apt to occur during the menopause. A neurotic woman with false pregnancy can even feel fetal movements and have imaginary breast changes. Some appear to have tumors in their abdomens —and a few may have, but the "tumors" are not pregnant wombs. The most prolonged case of

pseudocyesis this writer has known was that of a woman in her seventies who wrote letter after letter insisting she was pregnant; and as long as the correspondence lasted (for months), she still expected the "blessed event." This occurred long after tests for pregnancy had been discovered, but the woman persistently refused to have one done.

The duration of menopausal changes in women who have various symptoms of the menopause is usually from less than a year to two or three years, but somewhat longer periods of change have occurred. It is comforting, as we have emphasized before, to know that three-fourths to four-fifths of women pass through this period of life with no discomforts that can be called symptoms. When some of the usual signs and symptoms of the change, such as hot flushes or nervousness, do occur, modern medicines in the hands of well-trained physicians can remove or at least greatly ameliorate them.

Importance of the Glands

The various glands of the body have the function of preparing certain secretions which have specific functions. Exocrine glands pour their secretions through ducts to their destinations, whereas endocrine glands turn their secretions, or hormones, into the circulating blood. The first are called glands of external secretion because their products reach either the exterior of the body as perspiration, or the cavity of some internal organ as saliva in the mouth or gastric juice in the stomach. The second are called glands of internal secretion because their products remain in the circulating blood within the body proper until their functions have been served. Then they are broken down by chemical action and excreted.

In a sense the ovary is a gland of both external and internal secretion. In it develop the ova, one of which during the reproductive period of a woman's life is cast off each month, alternating on right and left sides. Each egg passes into the uterine tube and, if fertilized by a spermatozoon, enters the womb and starts a new life there. In addition, the ovary manufactures certain female sex hormones that pass into the blood stream and then to organs, such as the womb, the vagina, or the breasts, where they stimulate or inhibit function.

If one or more of these glands becomes overactive or underactive, harm is almost certain to result to the general health. This is particularly true of the glands of internal secretion, all of which are more or less dependent upon the normal function of the others.

The hypophysis (called the pituitary gland in the old anatomical nomenclature) is one of the endocrine glands whose functions are related to the reproductive processes in a direct manner. This little gland, located just beneath the brain, is about the size of a shelled hazelnut and is divided into three parts, or lobes. The anterior lobe is of primary importance in the development of the reproductive organs. In the female, hormones from the anterior lobe of the hypophysis stimulate the proper development of the female organs of reproduction, both internal and external, as well as of the secondary sex characteristics, such as feminine voice, hair distribution, and so on. Without these stimulating hormones the ovaries, the tubes, the vagina, and the external female parts would not form fully or, if formed prior to deprivation, would cease to function.

Ovaries: Focal Point of the Change

The internal organs of generation of woman are the ovaries, the Fallopian tubes, the womb (uterus), and the vagina. The ovary has two essential functions: to elaborate hormones and to develop ova. The act of conception is the fertilization of the ovum and its attachment to the wall of the womb, where it continues its development.

One ovary lies on each side of the upper portion of the pelvis near the upper end of the womb. These glands are of solid consistency and have an oval shape like an almond. They are about one to one and a half inches long and a quarter to a half inch in thickness. Until the onset of menstruation, at the average age of 12 to 14, the surface of the organ is smooth. With each ovulation a small protrusion known as the follicle stands up from the surface of the ovary. It grows larger and larger, although only

a small fraction of an inch in diameter, and on about the twelfth or fourteenth day of the average menstrual cycle it ruptures so that the ripe egg within may escape.

As this is repeated over the years little scars form and eventually the ovarian surface develops an uneven appearance. Toward the end of the reproductive years, usually around the age of 45 or 50, the gland becomes a mass of scar tissue. Eventually no more follicles develop and only the tissue that secretes hormones is active —and its activity continues to diminish. These changes are gradual and the body adjusts itself to them by compensations of one kind or another. The chief compensation is the increased activity of the outer or cortical portions of the adrenal glands, which are capable of elaborating sex-stimulating hormones.

As long as the ovary is actively performing its reproductive functions in a normal manner, one ovum each month may be expected to be expelled from one of the follicles. It is sucked into the upper end of the Fallopian tube by the action of thousands of tiny hairlike processes, or cilia, that line the upper extremities of the tube. This suction is exceedingly strong: instances of pregnancy have occurred following the removal of the ovary on one side and the tube on the other. This means that the ovum had to be drawn across a space of several inches, from one side of the pelvis to the other.

After the egg enters the tube it begins its descent toward the womb, which requires about four days. It has already been fertilized if pregnancy is to result, for the spermatozoa pass from the vagina, through the womb, and up the two tubes, where, at the upper ends, they lie waiting. As soon as the newly escaped egg cell is drawn into the upper end of one tube, one of these sperm cells pierces its coating and fertilization occurs. The fertilized egg passes down the tube into the womb, where it nests at some point on its wall. When the nesting of the fertilized ovum has taken place the earliest stage of pregnancy has begun.

The principal function of the womb is to nourish and retain the developing embryo, later called the fetus, until the pregnancy is over, and then to aid in its expulsion, which is the act of birth. During the childbearing years, the lining of the womb undergoes certain changes that around the middle of the cycle result in complete preparation for the reception of the fertilized egg. If a fertilized egg is not available the womb passes through another cycle and, following menstruation, gets ready for the fertilized egg again. Unless pregnancy occurs this repetition continues month after month throughout the years of normal activity of the ovary. If pregnancy does occur menstruation terminates because the lining of the womb has received what it was being prepared for and an ovarian hormone inhibits this cycle until well after the baby is born, sometimes as long as six months if the new offspring is breast-fed.

The ovaries are put in action by the hypophysis, which pours into the circulating blood hormones that regulate the cycles that take place each month. One of these, the follicle-stimulating hormone, brings about the development of the egg in its follicle up to the point of its rupture and the liberation of the egg.

After the rupture of the follicle a secondary structure is formed that lines the crater or interior of the follicle from which the egg escaped. This is known as the yellow body, and its formation and growth are stimulated by another hormone from the hypophysis. Its function is to secrete still another hormone, progesterone, which prepares the lining of the womb (the endometrium) for the reception of the fertilized egg. If conception occurs, the yellow body continues to develop and becomes a *true* yellow body, persisting until the end of pregnancy. As the end of pregnancy approaches this true yellow body begins to degenerate, the follicle-stimulating hormone regains the ascendency, and birth takes place.

After the follicle ruptures and the egg escapes a yellow body always develops, whether the egg is fertilized or not. If the egg is not fertilized, however, it will last only about two weeks and as it disappears the follicle-stimulating hormone will again become active. When the yellow body decreases in quantity menstruation takes place.

The ovaries have another important function. They have tiny cells within their substance which produce the female sex hormone, or estrogen. One of the principal functions of this hormone is to produce the estrus or sex desire, known also as libido. It also tones up the lining of the vagina and prevents soreness and irritation in that organ.

The entire mechanism of the female reproductive system is therefore a very complicated one that runs smoothly when all of its parts are healthy and working harmoniously together. In the childbearing years in healthy women that is the picture. As time goes on there is a gradual lessening in the activities of the hypophysis, which turns out smaller and smaller quantities of hormones that stimulate the ovary, so that menstruation becomes more or less irregular and then stops entirely. No longer is a yellow body formed and no longer does the lining of the womb undergo the monthly changes. Gradually the hormone cells of the ovaries become less active. There follows a period of readjustment that is more or less noticeable: most women scarcely observe anything more than the cessation of the menses; some have minor symptoms of discomfort; a very few have more distressing symptoms.

What we have been describing is the natural menopause. Artificial menopause is the cessation of menses that follows destruction of the ovaries by disease or by loss through surgery. The younger the woman the more severe will be the results of the loss of hormones of the ovaries; the nearer the menopause the loss takes place the less is she apt to suffer. In either case, early or late in the childbearing years of life, substitution hormone treatment will relieve the symptoms of the change.

Physical Symptoms of the Menopause

Only a very small percentage of women suffer to any marked degree from any of the discomforts that may accompany the menopause.

Hot flushes would seem to head the list of these discomforts. The basic cause is the same as that for all of the discomforts during the change: the slowing down of the functions of the ovaries with a resultant lessening of the hormones that have been keeping the body in equilibrium. In this instance it is the tone of the small blood vessels in the skin that is affected. There are tiny muscles in the walls of these little arteries and tiny nerves that supply them. Some of the nerves are constrictors and carry impulses that make the vessels smaller, forcing the blood elsewhere and blanching the skin. The other nerves are dilators and their function is to carry impulses that relax the tiny muscles in the walls of the arteries and make them larger, so that more blood enters the skin. This suffuses the areas with blood, particularly the areas of the face, head, and neck, and results in a reddening of the skin and a feeling of heat—commonly known as blushing.

These attacks may be light or severe. If they are severe they can be uncomfortable or even embarrassing. In extremely severe attacks the whole body may be affected. Occurring during sleep, they may bring about marked perspiration, wetting sleeping garments and even bedclothing, both of which may have to be changed. Fortunately, this degree of flushing is most unusual and even when so marked can be treated readily and successfully.

Nervousness, irritability, and anxiety stand high on the lists of menopausal symptoms. Nervousness, of course, can cause irritability, anxiety, and other discomforting states of mind. Women who have been inclined to be nervous for ten or twenty years before the change will suffer more from an intensification of anxieties and worries than women who have been of calm temperament. It is not unlikely that many symptoms can be laid at the doorstep of nervousness, for this state of mind can easily take on varied manifestations that resemble a wide variety of discomforts.

Every woman is familiar with the variations of moods that can affect her sex, ranging from mild upsets to severe emotionalism, and in rare cases even to hysteria. It would be superfluous to try to catalog them here. If they are truly a part of the picture during the change, one's physician can allay the cause by appropriate treatment.

The symptom that appears to be third on the list is *fatigue,* or a sense of listlessness—even exhaustion. Some authorities think this condition causes more patients to visit their doctors' offices than any others, as it may be among the first symptoms to indicate what is happening and it may outlast all others, or tend to. It must be remembered that the basic cause of any feeling of tiredness, fatigue, or lassitude is the same as that of all these discomforts—failure of the ovaries to perform as they used to. This results in temporary alterations in the nerves and blood vessels that deprive the body of the required tone for energy and alertness. As with the symptoms discussed above, this tone can be restored by substitution treatment.

It would be unwise to lay the blame for fatigue automatically on the menopause, as fatigue may be a symptom of many diseases, which must first be ruled out by careful physical and laboratory examinations. Only after a clean bill of health has been established can the menopause be positively determined as the causative factor of the fatigue. Then the course of treatment is clear. If this course of treatment were instituted at the onset and it was found later that the fatigue was symptomatic of some disease, valuable time would have been lost. Some of the diseased states that can cause tiredness are lack of proper vitamins, insufficient hemoglobin in the blood (anemia), hardening of the arteries, heart disease, tuberculosis, diabetes, and failure of the adrenal glands. There are many others.

This sense of lassitude may not be consistent. It may alternate every other day; there may be days of abounding energy and days of extreme fatigue. This is because the ovaries do not simply stop functioning all of a sudden—there may be little spurts of renewed activity from time to time. This is shown by the usual lessening of the menstrual flow, or by spotting from time to time, before the menses cease entirely.

The next condition attributed to the menopause is *sleeplessness,* or varying degrees of *insomnia.* It may consist of an inability to fall asleep as easily and naturally as one has been accustomed to do, waking during the night and lying awake, or waking early in the morning and not being able to go back to sleep. These three manifestations of insomnia are not common to the period of the menopause. Sleeplessness is a very frequent complaint among humans, even among those in moderately good health. In some women, however, in whom insomnia appears to be related to the time of the change it may in fact be caused by other symptoms, such as sweats occurring from severe hot flushes during the night. In other words, sleeplessness occurring during the menopause can be caused by various hormonal and other changes. If so, it will respond to the appropriate treatment. Patients suffering from menopausal insomnia should not take hypnotics or sleeping pills for this condition; they should consult their physician, who will direct the treatment at the cause.

The next alleged symptom that women have during the menopause is *general aches and pains*. Sometimes the type or location of the pains may be clear, as in the back part of the skull, in the neck, or at the back of the neck, but often they consist of vague, transient aches in the joints, pains in the chest that may be misinterpreted as heart disease, and so on. It must always be borne in mind that aches and pains are the symptoms of many different kinds of diseases and that it is necessary to rule out such possibilities before blaming them on the change. If the general health is found to be good, specific substitution treatment to compensate for waning ovarian hormones should remove all such discomforts.

The sixth and last of the alleged discomforts are *simple headaches* and *sick headaches* (migraine). All kinds of headaches occur in individuals of nearly all ages, although not as often in young children. It may appear to many women that during the change they have more and worse headaches, and perhaps some of them do. If other causes are ruled out the standard treatment for the various discomforts of the menopause will in all probability give relief to all types of headaches that may accompany the glandular alterations of this period.

Although this writer does not take too seriously the menopausal role of cause and effect in the following conditions, they may be mentioned as symptoms that are reported by some authors to be occasionally related to the change:

Abnormal rapidity of heart action and difficulty in breathing; sighing breath; decreased memory and concentration; blind spots in the visual field; a crawling-ant sensation in the skin; digestive disturbances with nausea, mild indigestion, and loss of appetite; needles-and-pins tingling of the skin; hands and feet falling asleep; cold hands and feet; numbness and tingling; forgetting of small things; frequency of urination; and last, but not least, psychoses (insanity). The less said about the allegation that the menopause is a causative factor of insanity the better!

In summary, approximately four-fifths of women will not suffer any serious discomforts during the change—and the one-fifth who do can receive medication that will alleviate those discomforts that really are related to the menopause. This applies to those symptoms caused by the slowing down of the glandular functions. The many types of aches, pains, and discomforts that may affect anyone at any time require a different kind of therapy.

Endometriosis (Misplaced Womb Lining)

Endometriosis, a condition that is terminated by the menopause, is caused by the passage of bits of womb lining (endometrium) upward through the uterine tubes and into the cavity of the abdomen. Here they become attached to various organs such as the ovary, the outer surface of the womb, the intestines, and so on.

These attached areas of womb lining are so-called chocolate cysts, and they may cause pain, especially during the menstrual period, for they respond to the monthly changes just as the lining of the womb does. Some cases are painless or almost so, depending upon the locations of the chocolate cysts, while others are severely painful. Another important symptom of this condition is dyspareunia, or pain during marital relations. Treatment alleviates this unfortunate disease; the menopause cures it.

How to Avoid Cancer

Since the change usually occurs in the middle or late forties it coincides with the time at which the so-called "cancer age" begins. Every one at this time of life, male and female, should be more alert than ever to detect early signs of cancer. Cancer, of course, occurs at any age, but is far more apt to affect the middle-aged and the old than it is the young, and if the beginning cancer is discovered early enough, it can be completely removed or irradiated.

Some conditions, termed precancerous conditions, may lead to subsequent cancer. Examples of this are dry, scaly, brown patches frequently seen on the temples, forehead, ears, and back of the hand during or after middle life, although more often in elderly persons.

The origin of cancer involves so many factors that a single or universal cause is unlikely. There is a wide variety of types of cancer and of the conditions that lead to them. Some of the theories concerning factors that contribute to the development of cancer are: (1) inherited susceptibility, (2) embryonic rests, (3) viruses, (4) biochemical agents, such as hormones, and (5) agents that may cause cancer by irritation (carcinogens).

1. That susceptibility to cancer occurs is borne out by the fact that in some families cancer has occurred in the same part of the body in more than one member. This is particularly significant when identical twins have the same type of cancer in the same organ. There seems to be an inherited susceptibility for some types of malignant tumors in the human, and in small experimental animals it has been proved that susceptibility to cancer can be transmitted to the offspring.

2. In embryonic life misplaced cells (embryonic rests) may eventually develop into cysts, benign (harmless) tumors, or even into malignant tumors (cancer).

3. Some tumors that have been produced experimentally in chickens are believed to be caused by viruses, and the virus theory of human cancer is now being widely investigated.

4. Although it is true that large doses of male hormone can alleviate suffering in some cases of cancer of the breast in women and that large doses of female hormone seem to do the same in cancer of the prostate in men, the opposite has not been shown to occur: that is, small (therapeutic) doses of male and female sex hormones have not been shown to cause cancer. If sex hormones are a causative factor in cancer, malignant tumors should occur much more frequently when the sex hormones are more abundant in the body. How, then, can one explain the fact that the so-called cancer age (after 45) has its onset when the sex hormones are decreasing in quantity, whereas when the sex hormones are quite plentiful (up to 45), cancer is much less prevalent?

5. Any substance that may irritate to the point of inciting cancer is known as a carcino-

gen. The substances number in the hundreds. Some are coal-tar products such as soot, pitch, creosote, crude paraffin oils, and anthracene oil. Others are products of petroleum, shale oils, chromates, arsenicals, and exposure to X-ray, radium, and the actinic rays of strong sunshine. The presence of carcinogens in tobacco smoke is borne out by the much higher rate of cancer of the lungs of male smokers, by the increasing rate of lung cancer in women since they have become heavy smokers, and by the efforts of tobacco companies to prove that their filters are better than others.

What are the danger signals of cancer? In an excellent book entitled *The Truth About Cancer,* Cameron gives the following sound advice:

LEARN THE DANGER SIGNALS

First, learn the early warning signs of cancer. Here they are summarized as "Cancer's Seven Danger Signals":

1. Any sore that does not heal.
2. A lump or thickening in the breast or elsewhere.
3. Unusual bleeding or discharge.
4. Any change in a wart or mole.
5. Persistent indigestion or difficulty in swallowing.
6. Persistent hoarseness or cough.
7. Any change in normal bowel habits.

These seven signs are your life-savers. They are easier to memorize than a simple multiplication table.

Take a few minutes, *now,* and fix them in your mind.

During and after the change every woman should go to her physician twice a year for a thorough physical checkup, with particular reference to the breasts and womb. A Papanicolaou smear, taken in a minute or less while a speculum is in place in the vagina, is absolutely painless and is strongly indicated at this time of life. The smear is sent to a cytology laboratory, where it is stained and examined under the microscope. An experienced cytologist can distinguish abnormal (precancerous or cancerous) cells from those that are normal, and if there is marked abnormality a biopsy of the womb is indicated. This consists of the excision of some small pieces of tissue, which are examined by a pathologist to determine whether precancer or cancer is present.

Speed is of the essence in dealing with cancer. If the affected organ can be removed before cancer cells have spread through lymphatic channels to lymph nodes and to other organs, that is the end of the cancer. But if the tumor continues to grow and invades surrounding tissues, the chances of such spread (metastasis) are greatly increased.

Sex at the Menopause

What about sex life during the change? There is no reason why a woman should not continue her sex life as usual; for if she has enjoyed it before, she should continue to do so. Her libido or sex desire will not undergo any change just because she is passing through the change—at least not for quite some time, or even then.

It is difficult for a woman who has always enjoyed sex to understand what is meant by frigidity. Sexual fulfillment comes so easily and naturally to her that aversion to sexual intercourse or failure to reach a climax is foreign to her. Unfortunately, there are many married women who have no strong urge for intimacies and are glad when it is all over. According to Kinsey (1953), 75 per cent of women attained orgasm during the first year of marriage, with fair percentages in the first, second, or third month. After the first year the percentage increased each year, and fifteen years after marriage was up to 90, but there was no increase after fifteen years, even up to the thirtieth year. There were, however, 11 women who attained their first orgasm between the fifteenth and twenty-eighth years of marriage.

During the change is a good time for a woman to take stock of her sexual self and to ascertain if she has really reached the pinnacle of marital bliss with her husband. Even if she has missed this pleasure all these years, it is not too late for appropriate treatment to change the picture. Certainly, if some women achieve orgasm between the fifteenth and twenty-eighth years of marriage (at age 50 in a patient of this writer), there is no reason why the usual methods of treatment should not be tried.

It must be emphasized that women who have always or nearly always enjoyed marital relations to the fullest may expect to continue to do so for many years to come. Those who have never achieved sexual fulfillment now have a wonderful opportunity to explore and find the paradise of married love.

In so far as this writer can ascertain, there is no opposition to the consummation of their love by a man and wife during or after the menopause. Even the rhythm method of contraception under certain conditions is not banned. A special encyclical issued by Pope Pius XI in 1936 entitled "On Chaste and Christian Marriage" states:

Nor are those considered as acting against nature who use their marital rights in the proper manner, although on account of natural reasons either of time or of certain defects new life cannot be brought forth. For in matrimony as well as the use of matrimonial rights there are also secondary ends, such as mutual aid [and] the cultivating of mutual love.

It is necessary at this point to call attention to one condition that will prevent a woman from having pleasure during or after the menopause; it may even cause very severe pain. This is dyspareunia, or painful intercourse. The cause is entirely different from the dyspareunia of endometriosis. During or after the menopause (and in some women approaching this time of life), an insufficient quantity of female sex hormone (estrogen) causes the lining of the vagina to thin out and to become raw and painful. The administration of estrogen by injection, by mouth, and/or by suppositories in the vagina will thicken the epithelium lining of the vagina.

Sex after the Menopause (Second Honeymoon)

Once the change has definitely arrived and the reproductive capacity is finally a privilege of the past, a couple should take stock of the future of their marriage with the idea of correcting any errors and of perfecting the partnership. Possibly there were faults on the part of one or both, and these may have caused bickering, fear, or criticism. Now is the time to discuss them in a quiet and cooperative spirit with the purpose of working together to remove all deficiencies that can be remedied.

What are some of the reasons couples do not

fully enjoy the most intimate of human relations? Has the wife been more or less on the frigid side? Or was she desirous enough but disappointed because her husband was always too quick for her? Was the husband too ardent or not ardent enough? Has the wife been dissatisfied because she was one of those fortunate women who needed multiple orgasms while the husband could not pace himself and give her the complete relief she required and longed for? Or were husband and wife perfectly suited and every union perfect bliss for both, with simultaneous climax (even if he had to wait to arrive with her on her final one)? Unfortunately, this type of couple is not average. If it were there would be far less dissatisfaction with the marriage relationship on the part of both men and women.

If everything was not as it should have been, what was done about it? Many women, sad to say, still think frigidity is just "their lot" and take it for granted. Yet only the most resistant cases of so-called frigidity are refractive to adequate treatment nowadays. The type of treatment will depend upon the underlying causes, and if the woman will accept treatment in a hopeful and cooperative spirit it is not likely that she will be disappointed.

It is just as likely that sexual maladjustment may have been due to failure on the husband's part. Unfortunately, many men assume that the sexual act is the same for women as it is for men—that they can become aroused just as readily and that they can be satisfied just as quickly. It is quite true that a small percentage of women can, but most women are like the bride who spoke for many when she said it was all over before she knew it had started. This may be due to premature or rapid ejaculation: the former before entry, the latter just afterward. Or it may simply be due to ignorance on the part of the husband. Sexual intercourse is an art, and some men do not understand that. They think they must start out at a fast rate and keep it up, instead of beginning slowly and occasionally slowing down or even stopping if necessary, in order to keep a pace with the wife and to reach a climax with her.

Again it may not be excessive speed on the part of the male; it may be impotence—inability to start at all. This unfortunate situation may occur in men of all ages and the cause is nearly always some sort of fear. One of the most common fears is fear of failure, especially in men who have had this happen. Fear of any kind is one of the greatest enemies of successful marital relations. It is generally conceded that in over 90 per cent of cases the impotence is psychogenic, and according to Kinsey (1948), it is "in actuality a relatively rare phenomenon."

All of this indicates that there should yet be a long period of normal sex relations between the husband and wife who reach the age of the wife's menopause together. Even if there are some difficulties there is much that can be done if proper help is sought. The statistics are reassuring.

In couples otherwise incompatible even complete sexual harmony will not make for happiness and often it will not even prevent divorce. It is an axiom that marriage based only on physical attraction is not likely to endure. Love is based on the finer and deeper things of life, including sex in its right place, and similar tastes and interests will make for a spiritual union in marriage that sex alone can never bring about.

The time of the change brings a real opportunity for a couple to achieve a stronger union through development of an improved sense of teamwork and through mutual interests, of whatever kind; it also brings an opportunity to correct any sexual inadequacies that may exist.

The Best Years Ahead

Although the menopausal woman is far from growing old she has reached at least the midpoint of life. It is a good time to take stock of life with her husband and plan ahead for the good things of life—children, grandchildren, nephews, nieces, relatives, and friends; new activities; long-postponed associations that time and circumstances will now permit. There is no end of possible worthwhile and engrossing activities, including charity and civic enterprises, P.T.A. or girl-scout activities, writing, painting, sewing, entering business.

It is a time to participate with one's mate in sports such as hunting, fishing, golf, or to have him participate in the things that interest oneself, such as landscape gardening, growing flowers, and cooking.

And it is a time for reading. A world of fine literature is available: history, biography, poetry, fiction, science. Truly, now one should have leisure to live!

If three-score and ten represents the age that men and women aspire to, it is also close to the number of years that one who has reached middle life may expect to live. It has been said that everyone begins to grow old from the moment of birth, but it is closer to the truth to say that one begins to grow old from middle age. In that sense we can understand what Robert Browning meant when he wrote:

> Grow old along with me!
> The best is yet to be,
> The last of life, for
>   which the first was made.

The change can indeed lead to wonderful new vistas. For a fair percentage of women in former times this period of life was a trying one, but the modern woman can live with added zest in "The best is yet to be."

The menopausal woman is a mature woman. From her forty or fifty years of living she has acquired much from observation and experience and is able to adjust to whatever requirements life may set before her. The experiences of her adult life, whether she has borne and reared children or not, has rounded her personality and taught her the niceties of human relationships. She is therefore thoroughly equipped to cope with the ordinary problems of living and to enjoy the activities and leisure time in the years ahead.

Truly the best years are ahead because of the learning that has gone on before. Now she can really live.

References

Cameron, C. S., *The Truth About Cancer*. Englewood Cliffs, N.J.: Prentice-Hall, Inc., 1956.

Davis, M., *Facts About the Menopause*. New York: McGraw-Hill Book Co., 1951.

Gray, M., *Changing Years*. New York: Doubleday & Co., Inc., 1958.

Kelly, G. Lombard, *The Doctor Talks on the Menopause*. Chicago: The Budlong Press, 1959.

Kinsey, A. C. *et al.*, *Sexual Behavior in the Human Male*. Philadelphia: W. B. Saunders Co., 1948.

Kinsey, A. C. *et al.*, *Sexual Behavior in the Human Female*. Philadelphia: W. B. Saunders Co., 1953.

Landau, M. E., *Women of Forty*. New York: Philosophical Library, 1957.

Levine, Lena, and Doherty, B., *Women Needn't Worry*. New York: Random House, 1952.

Lincoln, M., *You'll Live Through It*. New York: Harper & Brothers, 1950.

Malleson, J. G., *Change of Life, Facts and Fancies of Middle Age*. London: Delisle, 1957.

Special Encyclical Issued by Pope Pius XI, 1936. New York: Sheed & Ward, 1936.

Trevitt, F. B., and White, F. B., *How to Face the Change of Life with Confidence*. New York: Exposition Press, 1955.

G. LOMBARD KELLY

Menstrual Cycle

THE commonly used term *menstrual cycle* identifies the female sexual cycle of the higher primates by its most overt sign, menstruation. This recurrent phenomenon results from the thwarting of the reproductive purpose of the sexual cycle. During the menstrual cycle the endometrium, the mucous membrane of the uterus, is prepared for implantation of the fertilized egg, or ovum. If fertilization and implantation does not occur, the especially prepared endometrium regresses and is cast off along with blood from the vessels within the endometrium. While the endometrium is being cast off, the process of preparing for implantation begins again. Each menstrual cycle is considered to begin on the first day of menstruation and to end on the first day of the succeeding menstruation.

The female sexual cycle is controlled by the interplay of physiological and psychological forces established in the course of psychobiological maturation. The physiological rhythms of the cycle are basic to the development of sexual behavior. Thus, the dynamics of the female sexual cycle cannot be understood without a thorough knowledge of these rhythms.

First Menstruation

The first menstrual cycle terminating in the first menstruation, the menarche, heralds the onset of sexual maturity. In the human female the menarche usually occurs between the ages of 9 and 16, but younger or older ages have been reported in apparently physiologically normal women. The average age at the menarche in North America is 12.5 years. The first menstrual cycles are often irregular in occurrence and variable in rhythm. Variations of from 2 to 6 weeks between menses and even absence of cyclic phenomena for as long as 6 months or so have been reported. Furthermore, some cycles may manifest all of the physiological phenomena except discharge of an ovum from the ovary. Such anovulatory cycles presumably explain the relative sterility of adolescence.

Irregularity of Menstruation

After the first few years of sexual maturity ovulation is the general rule and the menstrual cycles become fairly regular. Absolute regularity, however, is almost certainly a myth. Eighty per cent of women have cycles averaging 28.6 days, with a span between 26 and 34 days. The remaining 20 per cent have either shorter or longer cycles, or exhibit considerable variation in cycle length. Variations of between 21 and 90 days occur in women who appear to be physiologically normal. Occasionally even longer intervals are encountered but these are apparently due to infrequent ovulations rather than to excessively long cycles. A few women in whom no physiological abnormality can be found ovulate only once or twice a year.

Toward the end of reproductive life the menstrual cycles again tend to become irregular in length and occurrence, and anovulatory cycles are frequent. At an age between 40 and 52 (the North American average being 48) the menstrual cycles cease. This is known as the menopause. It may occur between 35 and 40 or not until the late fifties. In general, the younger the age at menarche the older the age at menopause will be and vice versa.

Morphological and Physiological Processes

The menstrual cycle involves morphological and physiological processes occurring periodically and simultaneously in the uterus and ovary. The alterations in the endometrium of the uterus are governed entirely by the hormones produced in the ovary. The processes going on in the ovary, on the other hand, are independent of the endometrium and are under the control of the secretions of the pituitary gland.

The ovaries at birth contain, among other structures, several hundred thousand round clear cells with large nuclei, each cell surrounded by a layer of small spindle-shaped cells. The central cell in each of these cell clusters is the primordial ovum, and the whole cell cluster is referred to as a primordial follicle. Apparently the number of primordial follicles present at birth represents the entire supply for reproductive life. It has been suggested that new ova are formed continuously during reproductive life, as is the case with the sperm cells. However, no one has ever been able to present incontrovertible evidence for new ovum formation after birth. Before puberty, most of the primordial follicles have disappeared, so that at the onset of the menstrual cycles only about 30,000 remain. During reproductive life about 500 mature ova at the most are ovulated, but large numbers degenerate during each menstrual cycle so that after the menopause there are usually no remaining primordial follicles.

As puberty approaches the anterior lobe of the pituitary gland begins to elaborate at least three ovary-stimulating or gonadotropic hormones. Apparently a fine balance between two of these hormones (the follicle-stimulating hormone and the interstitial-cell-stimulating hormone) is necessary to produce an orderly sequence of events within the ovary. Under the influence of the follicle-stimulating hormone several primordial follicles begin to grow and under the influence of the interstitial-cell-stimulating hormone the cells of the growing follicles begin to secrete estrogen.

The increase in estrogen secretion produces progressive growth of the endometrium. The uterine mucous membrane increases in thickness and its blood vessels become more numerous and begin to grow toward the surface. The glands of the endometrium become more branching and show signs of preparing for secretory activity. Shortly before ovulation the endometrium appears to be slightly swollen due to the presence of extracellular fluid. Often early secretory activity occurs in the glands at this time.

Ovulation

As the growth of the primordial follicles continues, usually one begins to outstrip all others and also begins to move toward the surface of the ovary. It is from this largest of the growing follicles that the discharge of the ovum, or ovulation, will occur. The remainder of the stimulated follicles cease to grow at various stages in their development and degenerate. Occasionally, and more commonly in the later years of reproductive life, more than one follicle will achieve maturity. Two out of every three sets of twins is the result of such a double ovulation. Six out of every ten sets of triplets result from double ovulations; and three out of every ten are the result of a triple ovulation. Data on quadruplets and quintuplets also indicate the existence of multiple ovulations in these circumstances. However, quadruple and quintuple ovulations must be exceedingly rare.

The mature follicle is usually known as the Graafian follicle after the seventeenth-century Dutch anatomist, Regner de Graaf, who first described it in mammals. At full maturity the Graafian follicle is about one-half inch in diameter, and its cavity is filled with fluid rich in estrogen. Within the follicle are two important layers of cells. The inner layer, the granulosa, is made up of tiny cells and is extremely thin in the area at the ovarian surface. Opposite the ovarian surface the granulosa forms a pyramid many layers thick, in the center of which lies the largest known human cell, the mature ovum. This is a large clear cell with a good-sized nucleus, and is barely large enough (0.004" in diameter) to be visible to the naked eye. The layer just beneath the granulosa, the theca interna, is composed of large clear cells and is richly endowed with blood vessels. This layer is the principal source of estrogen, which it is by now producing in large amounts.

The high preovulatory peak of estrogen secretion produces an alteration in the balance of the pituitary gonadotropic hormones. The secretion of follicle-stimulating hormone is partially suppressed, while secretion of the interstitial-cell-stimulating hormone is enhanced. Current opinion holds that this altered ratio of pituitary gonadotropins induces rupture of the Graafian follicle and hence discharge of the ovum.

As the hour of ovulation approaches, the expanding follicle thins out the surface of the ovary causing destruction of ovarian cells until the follicle bulges out from the ovary. At the same time the pyramid of granulosa cells begins to loosen about the ovum so that the ovum and a few surrounding cells almost if not actually float free within the follicle. The outer wall of the follicle becomes thinner and thinner until it gradually begins to break open, and discharges the ovum. Thus, actual rupture of the follicle is a gradual and gentle process.

Postovulatory Phase

Ovulation signals the end of the first portion of the menstrual cycle. For obvious reasons this first portion can be referred to as the preovulatory, the proliferative, or the follicular phase of the cycle. It can be of various durations. On the other hand, the second portion of the cycle, which is referred to as the postovulatory, the secretory, or the luteal phase, is of rather fixed duration. It has been fairly clearly established that the occurrence of ovulation is generally 12 to 16 days before the menstrual flow begins. Thus, the duration of the preovulatory phase may be as short as 5 to 9 days if the total cycle length is 21 days, or as long as 44 to 48 days in cycles of 60 days' duration. In the average cycle of 28.6 days, the two major phases of the cycle will be about equal in length. Accordingly, most ovulations would be expected to take place on the fourteenth day of the cycle. Many careful studies of the time of ovulation indicate this to be so, but all such studies report a few ovulations as early as day 8 or as late as day 20, presumably in shorter or longer menstrual cycles respectively.

Although discharge of the ovum is a relatively gentle and gradual process, many women have noted on occasion a sudden sharp lower abdominal pain in mid-cycle, which can easily be correlated with the time of ovulation. On occasion this ovulatory pain is quite severe and may be followed by several days of dull aching lower abdominal discomfort. These ovulatory pains have been variously attributed to the breaking of the ovarian surface or to the discharge of small to moderate amounts of blood from the ruptured follicle. Indeed, infrequently there may be a minor degree of vaginal bleeding at ovulation time, which may last for several days. Even though vaginal bleeding is only rarely seen at ovulation, vaginal washings obtained at this time (when examined under the microscope) almost invariably contain a large number of red blood cells. The origin of this blood is not clearly understood. It may come either from the ruptured follicle through the Fallopian tubes and the uterus, or from blood vessels in the endometrium which shrinks, with loss of its extracellular fluid, due to the sudden decrease of estrogen support at ovulation time.

After ovulation the follicle wall partially collapses but the follicular cavity becomes filled with blood. The cells of the granulosa layer rapidly increase in size and probably also in number, compressing the central blood-filled cavity. Within a few days they are surrounded by blood vessels and show signs of considerable secretory activity. The follicle has thus been replaced by a new structure which has a bright orange-yellow color and has, therefore, been known since the Middle Ages as the corpus luteum, or yellow body. The corpus luteum is obviously from its appearance an endocrine gland. It is formed under the stimulus of a third gonadotropic hormone of the anterior lobe of the pituitary gland, luteotropin, which makes its appearance at the time of ovulation. Furthermore, luteotropin stimulates the corpus luteum to secrete progesterone, which prepares the endometrium for implantation and early maintenance of the fertilized ovum. There is evidence that the interstitial-cell-stimulating hormone influences the granulosa cells to store up precursor substances for progesterone production and that a little progesterone is actually manufactured before ovulation. However, no appreciable quantity of progesterone is secreted until after ovulation.

Hormonal Influences

Under the influence of progesterone a more or less orderly progression of changes occurs in the endometrium. These changes are sufficiently progressive for an experienced observer to be able to estimate the length of time since ovulation within a day or so from a portion of endometrium obtained at any time during the luteal phase. Similarly, the progressive changes in the corpus luteum as it waxes and wanes have been shown to be subject to dating within a day or so.

The progesterone-induced changes in the endometrium involve a gradual increase in its thickness. Also the endometrial glands become more complex and begin vigorous secretion. Blood vessels reach the upper layers of the endometrium. Special small coiled arteries or arterioles make their appearance. These vessels are essential for the blood supply of the ovum if pregnancy occurs. About the coiled arterioles the endometrial cells take on a swollen appearance, which gradually involves all the cells of the upper layers. These upper layers also show evidence of considerable extracellular fluid accumulation.

At this stage of the cycle, about 10 to 12 days after ovulation, estrogen, progesterone, and luteotropin secretion are at their peak, while interstitial-cell-stimulating hormone secretion is declining and follicle-stimulating hormone secretion is on the rise. Apparently, progesterone suppresses interstitial-cell-stimulating hormone and allows follicle-stimulating hormone secretion to increase, for at this time a new crop of follicles begins to grow in preparation for the next menstrual cycle.

If implantation of a fertilized ovum, which takes place on the sixth day after ovulation, has not occurred, estrogen and progesterone secretion soon wane. The mechanism by which further hormone production on the part of the corpus luteum is curtailed is not clear. It may be that the increasing estrogen secreted by the theca cells of the corpus luteum inhibits production of luteotropin, thus causing regression of the corpus luteum due to withdrawal of the stimulus for secretory activity. On the other hand, progesterone secretion may decrease simply because the supply of precursor substances is exhausted. The first suggestion is the more likely since, if implantation occurs, the implanted ovum secretes a gonadotropic substance that is capable of prolonging the life of the corpus luteum and the production of progesterone.

As hormone secretion wanes, the cells of the corpus luteum and of the endometrial glands show signs of secretory exhaustion, and the endometrium decreases in thickness due to loss of extracellular fluid. This endometrial collapse is associated with intermittent constrictions of the coiled arterioles. This intermittent shutting off of blood supply (ischemia) causes tissue damage both to the endometrial cells and to the walls of the blood vessels so that blood leaks into the tissues from both arterioles and veins. Tissue destruction releases toxic substances which promote further tissue destruction. White blood cells, scavenging destroyed tissue, are present in large numbers. This process does not occur simultaneously in all areas of the endometrium. However, within 24 to 48 hours sufficient areas have been involved that vaginal bleeding begins. The upper layers of the endometrium are eventually completely cast off.

The corpus luteum also shows rather marked changes during the menstrual flow. Intracellular and extracellular fluids are lost so that there is usually a considerable decrease in the thickness of the corpus luteum. Granulosa cells can be seen in all stages of death and destruction. Scavenging white blood cells are present in large numbers. Often the collapse of the corpus luteum leads to bleeding into the substance of the organ.

Menstrual Phase

From one-half to three-fourths of the menstrual discharge is blood. This blood is almost entirely venous in origin since at about the time menstruation begins the arterioles have constricted completely. The remainder of the discharge is composed of mucus, fragments of endometrium, and desquamated vaginal cells. The quantity of blood lost during menstruation varies from individual to individual and also from month to month in the same individual, the average total blood loss being from 1 to 6 ounces. The duration of the menstrual discharge also varies considerably. The average duration is 5 days, but the range is from 1 to 10 days. For most women, however, the length of menstrual flow remains fairly constant from month to month.

Even as menstruation begins the repair process is under way from the most basal layer of the endometrium, which is never cast off. Epithelium to cover the surface grows out from the bases of the glands and new blood vessels begin to make their appearance. In the ovary the new follicles are in active growth. The old corpus luteum is gradually shrinking and eventually, by the time several more menstrual cycles have taken place, will be replaced by scar tissue.

For purposes of descriptive convenience the ovarian and uterine cyclical morphology and physiology have been divided into phases. However, since this is a continuous biological system involving the influence of a fine balance of hormone production upon variable target organs, it must be realized that the menstrual cycle does not proceed with the precision of machinery. The characteristic picture of the follicular phase may persist up to the time of ovulation, or early luteal phase changes may take place before ovulation. The preovulatory, postovulatory, and menstrual states may vary in duration. Furthermore, the premenstrual ischemia largely responsible for the menstrual bleeding is usually preceded by the luteal phase, but bleeding may appear at the expected time even though there has been no ovulation and no corpus luteum formation. This bleeding, or anovulatory menstruation, occurs from a proliferative estrogen-dominated endometrium when estrogen secretion wanes. Similar bleeding from a proliferative endometrium occurs when estrogen administration to a woman whose ovaries have been removed is abruptly stopped. In the ovary in anovulatory menstruation complete follicular maturation does not occur, presumably due to an improper balance between follicle-stimulating hormone and interstitial-cell-stimulating hormone. A number of follicles may all reach the same stage of development and then simultaneously cease development and degenerate or become cystic. This arrest of development may occur early in follicle maturation so that all the follicles will be small, or may occur late so that a number of large cystic follicles are produced. In other instances a single large follicle may almost reach complete maturity, only to collapse and become filled with blood, producing an appearance quite similar to ovulation.

Since menstruation can occur without ovulation, it is obvious that menstrual bleeding cannot be explained on the basis of progesterone deprivation alone but must be related to waning of both estrogen and progesterone secretion. Therefore, the convenient hypothesis that menstruation represents the destruction of a prepared nest is not completely tenable. In early pregnancy, about the time after ovulation that menstruation would occur if there had been no pregnancy, vasoconstriction and bleeding take place about the developing ovum when progesterone and estrogen secretion wane temporarily. Menstruation can thus be regarded as an exaggeration of a physiological process for pregnancy. In pregnancy, when hormone secretion is higher, the changes are localized to the implantation site, and this localized injury facilitates maintenance of the embryo by providing blood and tissue substances for its nourishment until its own blood supply or placenta can be established.

Menstrual cycle changes occur not only in the ovary and endometrium, but also in the other tissues of the generative tract, in the breasts, and in mucous membranes throughout the body. These extraovarian and extrauterine changes are not as marked but the cyclic changes are sufficient to permit a rough correlation with the phases of the ovarian and uterine cycles. For example, definite follicular, luteal, and menstrual phase changes have been described in the Fallopian tubes. The immediate preovulatory changes favor transport and nourishment of the ovum during its four-day passage down the tubes.

In the early follicular phase the uterine cervical glands are uncomplicated and show little secretory action. What secretion there is has been shown to be inimical to the passage of sperm. As the follicular phase proceeds these cervical glands become more complex and actively secretory. At the time of ovulation the cervical secretion is abundant, full of glucose, thin, watery, and highly permeable to sperm. Indeed, cervical secretion at ovulation is so abundant that many women have considerable thin clear vaginal discharge at this time. After ovulation, secretory activity in the cervical glands rapidly disappears, and the cervical secretions again become inimical to sperm.

Changes in Vaginal Epithelium

The cyclical changes in the vaginal epithelium can also be correlated with the ovarian and endometrial cycles. Vaginal smears or washings can, therefore, be used to evaluate the degree of estrogen and progesterone production during the cycle. The change from estrogen domination of the cycle to progesterone domination is not, however, so clear-cut in the vaginal epithelium that the time of ovulation can be determined therefrom. Estrogen causes the vaginal epithelium to thicken and its superficial cells to cornify and desquamate in large numbers. These cornified cells are free of granules and their nuclei are small, fragmented, or entirely absent. White blood cells and bacteria are uncommon. In the luteal phase, on the other hand, white blood cells and bacteria are present in large numbers. Mucus and fragments of cornified epithelial cells are also in evidence. Most of the epithelial cells, however, have large nuclei and a granular cytoplasm. During menstruation the upper layers of the vaginal epithelium are shed, so that the smears show many more cells along with large numbers of red and white blood cells, much mucus, and many bacteria.

Changes in Breasts and Body Tissue

Whereas the cyclic changes in the Fallopian tubes, endometrium, cervix, and vagina are entirely due to estrogen and progesterone, the cyclic changes in the glandular apparatus of the breasts are under the influence of luteotropin as well as of the two ovarian hormones.

Apparently all three hormones are necessary for development of the secretory apparatus, for it is only during the luteal phase of the cycle or in pregnancy that secretory elements develop from the ducts which are the only glandular elements present in the mammary gland tissue during the follicular phase. The amount of extracellular and intracellular fluid in the breasts also increases during the luteal phase of the cycle. Thus, premenstrual enlargement and sensitivity of the breasts is a fairly common occurrence in women.

Premenstrual congestion and swelling of mucous membranes and other epithelia of the body are noted to some degree in all women, for all body tissues take part more or less in the luteal phase accumulation of intracellular and extracellular fluid that is so evident in the tissues of the genital apparatus. Premenstrual weight gain due to fluid accumulation averages at least five pounds. In some women severe generalized edema is a regular accompaniment of the luteal phase of the cycle. The arteriolar spasm seen in the endometrium during the 48 hours before the menstrual flow also affects arterioles throughout the body. In rare instances this generalized vasospasm is sufficient to evoke extragenital bleeding during the menstrual flow. The nasal mucous membrane is the most sensitive of all the extragenital mucous membranes to estrogen and progesterone. Accordingly, most of the cases of extragenital bleeding during the menstrual flow involve bleeding from the nose, but such "vicarious menstruation" has also been reported from the gastrointestinal tract, the lungs, the retina of the eye, and even from the skin.

Other Factors
Controlling the Menstrual Cycle

The pituitary-ovarian mechanisms initiating and controlling the menstrual cycle have been outlined above. There are, however, a number of other factors involved in the basic control of the menstrual cycle. The mechanisms by which these factors influence the phenomena of the cycle are very poorly understood. It is obvious, for instance, that adequate nutrition is necessary for normal function, since cessation of menstrual function is extremely common whenever women are subjected to a diet inadequate in calories and nutritional elements. It is not clear whether inadequacy of calories or inadequacy of some basic constituent of the diet is the principal factor. Recent evidence however, suggests that certain protein elements are essential to pituitary gonadotropin formation. Similarly, it is known that normal liver and kidney function for excretion and degradation of hormones is essential to menstrual rhythmicity.

Furthermore, it is recognized that well-balanced endocrine interrelations are necessary for normal menstrual cycles. Inadequate thyroid function, for instance, is associated with irregular and infrequent menstrual cycles, sterility, and even absence of cycles (amenorrhea). There is some evidence to suggest that adequate thyroid hormone production is essential for adequate luteotropin secretion by the anterior lobe of the pituitary. Similarly, the occurrence of menstrual cycle disturbances in certain types of endocrine malfunctions of the pancreas and adrenals suggests that proper function of these glands is necessary for menstrual rhythmicity.

The relationship between the central nervous system and the reproductive cycle is basic to an understanding of all these processes. An intact nervous system has long been known to be essential to the regulation of all aspects of the reproductive cycle. Transection of the spinal cord or interruption of the principal autonomic nervous system pathways to the ovaries and the uterus, for example, is always promptly followed by menstrual-like flow from the uterus. Indeed, neurological abnormalities at all levels of the nervous system from the cerebral cortex to the nerve endings in the ovary and uterus have been reported to be responsible for deviations from normal function.

It is only recently, however, that we have begun to understand the mechanisms by which the nervous system and the endocrine glands interact to integrate the reproductive cycle. There is now a large body of evidence, especially from subprimate forms of animal life, that the endocrine glands must be considered to be specialized end-organs of the central nervous system. As end-organs they are acted upon by the autonomic nerve centers in the hypothalamus and related nerve structures and,

in turn, as end-organs they act upon these so-called "visceral brain" centers. In other words, both nerve pathways and hormonal mechanisms function in neuroendocrine systems. Furthermore, there is evidence that "visceral brain" control of the endocrine glands is partially mediated by neurohumoral mechanisms, whereby these nerve centers elaborate chemical substances having specific effects upon endocrine glands and discharge these substances into the blood stream for transport to the glands upon which they have action.

From studies of the neuroendocrine mechanisms for integration of the reproductive cycle in lower animals it appears that certain hypothalamic centers control pituitary gonadotropic secretion under the influence of stimuli from the rhinencephalon and the brain stem reticular formation. These centers in turn are influenced by the effect of the ovarian steroids and possibly by the pituitary hormones. In other words, regulation of the pituitary-ovarian cycle is a function of an intrinsic "visceral brain" rhythm, which is in turn affected by the pituitary-ovarian hormones. It is within this area of the brain that the interplay of hormonal and psychological forces influencing the female sexual cycle takes place.

It must be realized that both hormonal and psychological forces serve only to modify the reactivity of the sexual apparatus. In psychologically mature and well-adjusted women, in whom sexual behavior is more or less subservient to the well-being of the total individual, fluctuations in sexual reactivity may be so subtle as to be unrecognized by either the individual or her environment. On the other hand, cyclic fluctuations will be exaggerated in neurotic individuals. For this reason, Theresa Benedek's (1952) studies of many sexual cycles in a group of neurotic women undergoing psychonalysis are particularly valuable in elucidating the influence of hormonal forces upon sexual reactivity. The psychoanalytic method is particularly useful because it focuses on unconscious attitudes that otherwise might escape attention. Benedek's view of the underlying cyclic pattern of emotional responses to hormonal activity has been substantiated by others and also closely parallels the impressions of observant gynecologists concerning the cyclic nature of the behavior patterns of less disturbed women.

Menstruation and Sexual Arousal

The follicular phase of the cycle, with its rising estrogen production, is associated with a sense of well-being and an integrated effective alertness leading to well-coordinated activity at all levels of the personality. In the more specific sexual sphere, active heterosexual activities can be recognized in overt and disguised sexual behavior as well as in dreams and phantasies. Unconscious destructive tendencies toward men can be recognized, but an extroverted positive orientation toward the male predominates. Sexual gratification will relieve the increasing sexual tension to some extent and hasten the ovulatory phase of well-integrated psychosexuality, in which the biological and emotional readiness for conception is expressed by the desire to be loved and possessed.

Whether or not the sexual tension of the follicular phase is relieved by sexual gratification, the early postovulatory phase is marked by a relaxation of tension. Psychosexual energy becomes concentrated upon introverted concerns of the body and personal welfare. The woman becomes more interested in her own bodily appearance. Readiness to receive the sexual partner gradually gives way to sexual passivity as progesterone production increases. Biologically, this outward passivity may be regarded as a sign of preoccupation with the nurturing of the ovum. The unconscious psychological material of the early luteal phase is concerned with the positive and negative aspects of motherhood. When pregnancy does not occur this period of introspective passivity is short-lived.

Psychological Effects of Menstruation

In the late luteal phase, as progesterone and estrogen secretion wane, feelings of anxiety and depression become apparent. Psychobiologically, this premenstrual state represents recognition of the frustration of the reproductive urge. The hormonal deficiency of the premenstrual phase leads basically to less well integrated sexual activity and to resigned passivity.

However, the emotional import of the preparation for menstruation is so fundamental to the personality structure that marked variations in behavior are to be expected. The low levels of hormone secretion allow psychic forces more related to the psychosexual development of the personality than to hormone levels to dominate. Accordingly, it is not surprising that the premenstrual phase is characterized by marked variations in behavior such as depressive reactions, apprehension, irascibility, resigned passivity, compulsive overactivity, and even hypomanic states.

Premenstrual tension of some degree is present in all women. In addition to the factors cited above, it appears that the physiological stimuli arising from tissue edema, and possibly from the changing hormone levels, either energize basic psychic forces or depress controlling forces within the personality. Thus the degree to which premenstrual tension manifests itself overtly might be considered a measure of the maturity of the personality structure. The importance of tissue edema in initiating the emotional changes of the premenstrual phase is indicated by the fact that administration of agents which reduce the edema usually improves or abolishes the overt manifestations of tension. Similarly, factors in the external environment of the individual can reduce or enhance premenstrual tension depending upon their significance to the personality structure. On the other hand, the virtual absence of premenstrual tension in anovulatory cycles indicates that progesterone secretion has an important role in the establishment of premenstrual tension.

Just before menstruation, when hormone levels are at a low ebb, there is often a recrudescence of sexual drive. The emotional import of this return of sexual libido may be due to hormonal influences, to factors basic to the personality structure, or simply to the multiplicity of physiological stimuli from the ischemic tissues of the generative tract.

The onset of menstrual flow is followed, once the flow is well established, by a decrease in tension and excitability, and hence a feeling of relief. While the hormonal levels remain low the predominant attitude is one of mild depression and depreciation of femininity. After a few days, normally still during the flow, the influence of the early follicular development of the new cycle reawakens the interest in sexual activity. This immediate postmenstrual peak of sexual interest suggests a drive to reassert the positive aspects of femininity. Thus, the primitive emotions liberated during the premenstrual and menstrual phases can be brought under control. Then, as estrogen secretion rises, the emotional content of the follicular phase reasserts itself.

During the follicular, ovulatory, and early luteal phases hormonal influences are dominant and usually in control of the basic psychological determinants of sexual behavior. However, it is possible for psychological forces to overwhelm the fundamental rhythmicity of the cycle. Gross disturbances, especially anemorrhea, occur in association with the psychoses. Suppression of the menses or even false pregnancy (pseudocyesis) occur in some women who are either extremely fearful or extremely desirous of pregnancy. Similarly, psychic shock, worry, fear, and even sudden changes in environment may produce profound disturbances of menstrual rhythmicity. Indeed, both gynecologists and psychiatrists report that all types of menstrual disturbances may result at times from purely psychological forces. Considering what dramatic events the menarche and the menopause are in the life of women, it is quite possible that the irregularities of early and late cyclic function are due more to psychological forces than to neuroendocrine influences.

On the other hand, during the premenstrual and menstrual phases of the cycle, when hormone levels are low, psychological forces largely determine the pattern of behavior. These psychological forces are primarily concerned with the many meanings of menstruation. Many of these meanings are centered around the conflicts encountered in early psychosexual development. Whether or not these conflicts have been settled, the menarche reawakens them. Thus the achievement of sexual maturity and reproductive capacity constitutes both a threat and a promise to the pubertal girl. Her physiology demands womanhood, but the old conflicts have opposing imports, and regression to the prepubertal state offers protection from both the new and the old conflicts. Each succeeding menstruation will recapitulate to some extent this same struggle between feminine sexuality and antisexuality.

Of course, the menstrual cycle is significant emotionally not only because of its relationship to sexual maturity and reproduction, but also because it manifests itself as bleeding. From the beginning of time menstruation has been associated with ideas of horror, with danger and fear of contamination in the mind of others, and with fear, shame, and guilt in the mind of the woman herself. To the pubertal girl the first sight of her own menstrual blood fills her with terror and shame connected with her unconscious castration fears, and with her unconscious conflict over excretory functions. She fears, on the one hand, that she has injured herself, has some horrible disease, or is being punished for forbidden sexual activities and phantasies, and, on the other hand, she is shamed by her inability to control something that bears a strong resemblance to a "dirty" excretory function.

Primitive Menstrual Beliefs

In primitive cultures the menstruating woman has always been regarded not only as dirty, but also as dangerous. She is believed to be particularly dangerous to all other manifestations of reproductive functions. Thus, her influence is especially damaging to crops, to domestic animals, and even more devastating to men. It is usually imperative, therefore, that menstruating women withdraw from the household, if not from the community itself. Menstruation is, accordingly, surrounded by many strict taboos, rituals, and strange superstitions. Elaborate rituals for purification following menstruation are common in some cultures, especially in the Hebrew and Mohammedan religions. In virtually all of the older cultures coitus during menstruation is specifically interdicted.

All of these primitive ideas represent basic human feelings that find overt expression among semienlightened people, but are more or less repressed into the unconscious among the more sophisticated. Thus, the primitive prohibition of coitus during menstruation is probably the most widely accepted of all restrictions upon human sexual behavior. Many sophisticated and sexually liberal individuals may rationalize their avoidance of coitus during the menstrual flow in terms of its "unesthetic" or "unhygienic" aspects, and indeed, this attitude may be related to the concept of menstrual blood as an excrement. However, the real attitude is more likely the unconscious fear of danger.

Conclusion

Thus, the premenstrual and menstrual phases of the cycle, the phases of little or no hormonal influence, are periods when basic emotions operate. The material presented accounts for the usual menstrual emotional content of depression and depreciation of femininity. Moreover, the wide range of unconscious concepts possible makes the range of behavior patterns encountered at this critical time in the female sexual cycle comprehensible. Similarly, it is understandable that suicides, deaths, illnesses, and crimes among women should be most common during menstruation and the premenstruum. It should be pointed out, however, that the attitudes depicted are by no means inevitable. They represent implicit rather than explicit orientations, not so much overt as potentially ready to seek expression at the first opportunity. The extent to which any of these attitudes may be apparent will be modified by individual differences in endowment, environment, and experience. Thus, most studies show that the time of ovulation does not represent the time of greatest sexual desire in the conscious minds of many women. There seems little doubt, however, that at the unconscious level ovulation is the time of greatest desire for heterosexual activity.

In this presentation of the female sexual cycle we have followed the historical pattern of developing twentieth-century scientific knowledge. Attention was first focussed on basic generative tract physiology. Recently we have begun to understand that other physiological mechanisms are intimately related to the establishment of cyclic phenomena. Finally, we have sought to integrate the emotional life of women into our understanding of the female sexual cycle as a function of the psychobiological unit. Although considerable information has already been accumulated, we are far from having an adequately clarified or coordinated view of the rhythms of female sexual behavior.

References

Benedek, Theresa, *Psychosexual Functions in Women.* New York: The Ronald Press Co., 1952.

Chadwick, Mary, *The Psychological Effects of Menstruation.* New York and Washington: Nervous and Mental Disease Publishing Co., 1932.

Corner, George W., Sr., *The Hormones in Human Reproduction.* Princeton: Princeton University Press, 1942.

Corner, George W., Sr., "Our Knowledge of the Menstrual Cycle, 1910-1950." *Lancet 1;* 919-923, 1951.

Corner, George W., Jr., "The Histological Dating of the Human Corpus Luteum of Menstruation." *Am. J. Anat. 98;* 377-401, 1956.

Deutsch, Helene, *The Psychology of Women.* New York: Grune & Stratton, 1944.

Israel, S. Leon, *Diagnosis and Treatment of Menstrual Disorders and Sterility.* (5th ed.), New York: Hoeber Medical Division, Harper and Row, 1967.

Kroger, William S. (ed.), *Psychosomatic Obstetrics, Gynecology, and Endocrinology.* Springfield, Ill.: Charles C. Thomas, 1962.

Lloyd, Charles W. (ed.), *Human Reproduction and Sexual Behavior.* Philadelphia: Lea and Fehiger, 1964.

Mazer, Charles, and Israel, S. Leon, *Menstrual Disorders and Sterility* (4th ed). New York: Paul B. Hoeber, Inc., 1959.

Noyes, R. W., Hertig, A. T., and Rock, J., "Dating the Endometrial Biopsy." *Fertil. and Steril. 1;* 3-25, 1959.

Rosenzweig, Saul, "Psychology of the Menstrual Cycle." *J. Clin. Endocrinol. 3;* 296-300, 1943.

GEORGE W. CORNER, JR.

Movement and Feeling in Sex

THE act of sexual intercourse, unlike other human activities, is shrouded in mystery. We know truly only that which we personally experience.

One's body sensations cannot be adequately expressed in words. It is even more difficult to describe the qualities of body movement. In the face of these handicaps, standards of response and reaction are very difficult to determine.

Sexologists have two sources of information about sexual behavior. The first is accumulated clinical experience. The second is the result of surveys and statistical studies. Kinsey's monumental work in the latter area is well known. Its evaluation as well as that of clinical observation depends, however, upon the framework of thinking that assigns to the sexual act its specific meaning and purpose. In the following study of the feeling and movement in the sexual act, some of the meanings in the total experience will be indicated.

Healthy sexual intercourse combines intense feelings and strong, active movements. To the best of my knowledge, this is as true of the woman as of the man. In the act of coitus itself, the feelings and movements are so fused and blended that the total act is a unity of emotional expression. For purposes of study and in dealing with cases of disturbance in the sexual function, much can be gained by a consideration and discussion of each component separately. It must be emphasized, however, that in the experience itself of sexual intercourse these two are not so easily separated.

Feeling

Like all other biological functions, the sexual act depends upon the build-up and release of tension. In bioenergetic analysis, we also speak of this process as one of charge and discharge. A feeling arises through a change in the bioenergetic charge, either locally or in the total organism, if the variation is of sufficient intensity to impress itself upon consciousness. We can add the observation that the perception of the feeling coincides with the arrival of the charge at the surface of the body (and of the cerebrum).

Although as yet no one has determined exactly what creates the attraction that draws two people of opposite sexes together, we are aware of the excitement, the tension, and the feelings it arouses. This attraction, or the force that creates it, can be equated with Freud's Eros. We also call it love. Love is our name for the drive that draws us to another person, unites us with them in spirit, and urges to physical closeness or intimacy. We cannot in this article elaborate upon other aspects of love, such as the love of God, but even here the concept of closeness or nearness is important.

Love is not sex, but contrary to what some psychologists believe (if the above definition of love is accepted), there can be no sex without love. To the degree that love or tender feelings are present in sex, to that degree will the sexual contact be experienced as pleasurable. It is questionable if one can voluntarily engage in sexual activity with a total absence of feeling. It is hardly likely that one can do so without any movement. The absence of pleasure in the sexual experience must be explained, therefore, by the presence of conflicting impulses.

The pleasure of contact, whether social or sexual, with a loved person is related to the amount of tender feelings or heart feelings evoked by and invested in the relationship.

This holds true for the relationships between mother and child, between friends, and between lovers. The feelings that are aroused by the attraction, or which grow out of the relationship, excite and charge the parties to it. They also tense them. They are pleasurable per se, and they are also pleasurable because one anticipates the pleasure of the release and discharge of the feelings by appropriate action. A person is not happy unless he can do something for a friend; a mother is frustrated unless she can take care of her child.

We must not assume that tension is necessarily unpleasant or harmful. Life itself depends on the maintenance of a certain tension or tone. The pleasure of appetite depends upon the tension of hunger; the satisfaction of sleep results from the tension of fatigue. One could multiply these examples manifold. We recognize the corollary, too. Nothing is so deadly as boredom, ennui, or the lack of excitement. A tension becomes painful only when the possibility of its release is too long delayed, or is obstructed. One calls to mind, as examples, hunger, the need to urinate, the holding in of strong anger and, certainly, a strongly aroused sexual desire.

The excitation resulting from the attraction between two individuals increases in intensity as the two individuals draw closer to each other. With the first physical contact, in kiss or embrace, this may be experienced as a streaming or melting along the front of the body from the heart region to the genitals. In the sexual relationship, the heightening of feeling through physical contact prior to the commencement of the act itself is called forepleasure. It is engaged in for that purpose. It is the pleasure of excitement and charge, and it also anticipates the end-pleasure of satisfaction. When the feelings reach a certain high intensity, the closest possible physical union of the two individuals is sought. This is arrived at by penetration of the penis into the vagina. In the course of penetration the pleasure of contact increases sharply until penetration is full and complete. When this is accomplished, there is a subsidence of the excitatory state, a change in the feeling tone. Love has achieved its object; the two are as close together as possible.

When one inquires into the feelings of the man at this point, one is told that he feels in, at home, or where he belongs. It is a contented feeling, one of relaxation. Ferenczi (1938) pointed out that the act of sex was, for the man, a symbolic return to the womb, to his original home. It is literally true for the male germ cells. The woman does not feel the same. She has no identification with the man in this return to the womb. Several whom I questioned reported that they felt full, complete. Others said that they felt that now they had the man in themselves, that he was part of them. And this, too, was a contented feeling. If the man symbolically returns to the womb, the woman, symbolically, is the womb that receives him.

The feeling of rest and contentment, as after a journey finished, does not last. New tensions arise, new needs make themselves felt. The new situation calls forth the specific movements of the sexual act which create new sensations and feelings. These we will study as part of our analysis of the sexual movements. Before we do so, however, let us examine some typical disturbances of feeling in this first stage of the sexual function.

What common disturbances are found in these feelings? Broadly speaking, the most important is the fear of falling in love. That is, the individual is afraid to experience an intense and overwhelming desire for another person. We may ask why anyone should be afraid of something that promises so much pleasure. The answers patients give all indicate earlier disappointments, the fear of rejection, the lack of hope, etc. One hears such remarks as: "What's the use." "There is no one." "I feel too vulnerable when I open up." "I don't want to be hurt again."

Analytic investigation of these reactions can generally trace them back to traumatic experiences in the relation of the individual to his parents. The mother who lets the child cry himself out, or cry himself to sleep, is creating future difficulties for that child in his adult love life. Such an experience can easily create deep-seated feelings of "what's the use, no one responds." The father who ignores the femininity of his daughter, because he had hoped for a son, handicaps the girl in her ability to relate as a woman to a man. Parents who pervert the parental relationship to satisfy their own emotional needs, the father who sleeps with his pre-adolescent daughter, or the mother who turns her sexuality toward her son, create such doubt, distrust, and confusion in their children that, later, adult patterns of give and take become almost impossible. The analytic and psychiatric literature is full of case histories that illustrate these points.

Another problem that patients present is that their love is of an infantile quality. The attraction and desire for the other person are strong, but are determined more by the need to be loved, to be held, and to receive pleasure than they are by the adult feeling of give and take, charge and discharge. In these individuals there is an unconscious conflict between the need to be excited and the need to release the excitement. They never seem to get enough love, to fill up. Their demands upon their partners are excessive. Their disappointment turns into reproach and the relationship suffers. Such individuals find that end-pleasure and satisfaction frequently escape them.

In our culture, men face a special problem in respect to love. Too frequently love is regarded as a commitment which the man feels will bind him to a permanent relationship. Love is equated with marriage, responsibility, and the loss of freedom. This may make a man hesitate to express his feelings, and this in turn reduces the feeling and the pleasure of the relationship.

If we have spoken of the feeling as separate from the movement, we have not meant to imply a lack of movement. Approach, contact, play, and penetration require movements that are appropriate to each stage and situation. In the fear of heightened feeling, the emotionally disturbed individual manifests an important aspect of his disorder by an inability to make the appropriate movements. The prolongation of forepleasure reveals the neurotic's fear of deeper intimacy and love. More seriously disturbed, the pervert avoids the closeness and unity possible only in the normal sexual act.

Movement

A distinction must be made between pleasure, which we have equated with love feelings, and satisfaction, which results from the expression of feeling and consists in the discharge of tension and energy.

The excitement of love has a different quality from the satisfaction of consummation. Whereas the first is stimulating, the second is calming and soothing. Love takes one out of the self. The satisfaction of discharge returns one to the self. Each has its place in the scheme of life.

When a person complains of a lack of *pleasure* in the sexual act, this should be interpreted as the denial of love or tender feelings. It may be a temporary condition, it may be limited to the one partner, or it may be due to factors external to the relationship. Feelings are not permanent fixtures. When a person complains of a lack of *satisfaction*, this must be interpreted as a failure to discharge the feeling or tension. Further, the amount of satisfaction depends upon the fullness of the discharge and also upon the intensity of the charge or feeling.

We said earlier that the act of coitus has two stages. The first stage is characterized by the drive for increased closeness and intimacy. It leads to complete penetration, which is followed by a momentary lull in the excitatory process. Symbolically, the man has returned to his original home, the womb; the woman receives the wanderer and is now full. Very soon new tensions appear. Let us pick up our study of the sexual movements at this point.

It must be emphasized again that movements do not occur apart from feeling. Feeling determines movement, but the movement may enhance or diminish the feeling. As early as 1872 Darwin observed that the expression of an emotion tends to increase the feeling.

The position and rhythm that the sexual partners adopt should be whatever suits their individual needs and mood at the time. The amount of thrust is dependent on the man's feelings, and the woman's receptivity. Normally, the movements of the man are more aggressive and forceful than those of the woman, but this pattern may be reversed to suit the mood. It is rare that both parties will move with equal vigor. Ordinarily, one partner dominates and the other takes a more passive role. Movements need not be continuous during this phase. They may be interrupted by short periods of rest or for adjustment of position. But the prolongation of the sexual act is functional only if its aim is to achieve a higher peak of excitation through a slower buildup.

For our discussion it is important to recognize that there are two phases in the rhythm of sexual movements: a first phase of voluntary movement and a second in which the movements are involuntary. These phases relate directly to charge and discharge. During the voluntary movements, the excitation increases. Discharge occurs only through the involuntary movements. If the involuntary movements fail to occur, the feeling fades away or "peters out" and the person is left with a sense of dissatisfaction.

The early movements in the act of coitus are slow and relaxed. The healthy male feels no desire to pierce the woman; on the contrary he has a sensation of "being sucked in," corresponding to a feeling in the woman of "sucking the man in." W. Reich, in his book *The Function of the Orgasm,* points out that in this period the body is less excited than the genitals. Consciousness of both parties is directed toward the perception of pleasure, and all movements are ego-controlled to heighten sensation.

In the second stage of the sexual act, the pleasure of contact becomes secondary to the pleasure of movement in relation to the sexual object. It is a change from pleasure based on sensory sensations to pleasure derived from kinesthetic sensations. The change-over is gradual and depends upon the rhythm of the pelvic movements. This rhythm increases to the climax. In the orgasm one loses sight of the specific quality of sensation in the overwhelming flood of feeling.

The kinesthetic pleasure depends upon the motility of the pelvis. Civilized human beings are ordinarily restrained in their daily movements. Their hips are not so free and their pelves are more bound than those of people who live under more primitive conditions. This restraint of pelvic movement must be overcome if the act of coitus is to be fully satisfactory.

During the first phase of movement this restraint is released. With increasing body sensation, the pelvic movements tend to become looser and freer. The pelvis regains a motility that enables it to move as if it were an independent segment. Slowly the pelvis begins to

swing, like the free swing of a dangling leg. As the pelvic movements in both partners take on this free-swinging quality, the tempo of movement increases. New and strong sensations of excitation appear in the pelvis and gradually spread through more of the body. The excitation in the genitals, meanwhile, tends to stay at the same level.

This first phase of the sexual movements occupies the longest time period of the sexual act. Its function seems to be to involve as much as possible of the body in the sexual movement. It prepares the way for passage of control of the movements from the head to the genitals and pelvis. It smoothes the transition from ego function to id function, which dominates the second phase. This phase should end when these functions have been accomplished. It terminates earlier in premature ejaculation because of the fear of the transition.

The second phase begins with a sudden increase in genital excitation. One experiences it as the opening of a dam with the release downward of a flood of feeling. Now the excitation rapidly mounts to a peak and is discharged. Any attempt to control or restrain the mounting genital excitation at this time is unpleasant and may be painful. Such a procedure frequently results in a shock to the body. For that reason the practice of coitus interruptus is bioenergetically harmful.

At the peak or acme the pelvic movements are definitely involuntary. These movements are the same thrust and withdrawal as before, but now they occur by themselves without conscious effort. Concomitant with the release of the dam, another series of muscular contractions occur in the man, leading to the ejaculation of the semen. The ejaculation is produced by the contraction of the smooth involuntary musculature of the prostate and seminal vesicles and consists of pulsatory squirts of the semen.

The orgasm in the man ordinarily combines the two involuntary responses. It is a matter of record that one can have an orgastic discharge without the ejaculation of semen (Kinsey). It is also known that one can ejaculate without the involuntary body reaction we have described above (Reich). Each in itself would be only part of a total orgasm. If neither involuntary reaction takes place and the semen is discharged as a flow without any pulsatory or ejaculatory contractions, it must be regarded as a failure on the part of the man to achieve orgasm.

In the woman, the counterpart of the ejaculation is the contraction of the smooth musculature surrounding the vagina. This action is felt by the man as a "pumping" of the penis. In addition, the woman also experiences the rhythmic involuntary movement of the pelvis exactly as the man does. This is a total body phenomenon in contrast to the limited response that involves only the genital apparatus. If the woman reaches her climax at the same time as the man, both responses are intensified.

Let us proceed with our analysis of the movements on the assumption that each partner has a total response, i.e., a full orgasm. After that we can decide how to evaluate partial responses, or incomplete orgasms.

The ejaculation in the man is accompanied by a sensation of heat in the penis. As the discharge occurs, in waves, the feeling of heat spreads through the pelvis and through the rest of the body. It is as if the body became on fire. When this occurs, the phenomenon of glow results, which may last long after the fire has died away. The experience of "glowing" must be regarded as the true ecstatic experience of the sexual act. The woman experiences her heat in a similar fashion, and she is also capable of experiencing the glow.

A total orgasm means that the total body is involved in the involuntary movements. This happens when the pelvic movements become strongly involuntary. Each forward swing of the pelvis is accompanied by an expiratory grunt and a wave of contraction that envelops the entire body. In this phenomenon, and only in this phenomenon, the organism pulsates as if it were one big cell in a convulsive reaction.

At the acme, there tends to occur a loss of ego-consciousness. This is a temporary eclipse of the ego and is not to be confused with a feeling of abandonment. Perhaps it would be more correct to say that the organism tends to lose consciousness of the self. Not only is there a perception of complete unity and identity with the partner, one also feels part of the total pulsating universe.

With the subsidence of the excitation following the discharge, consciousness of self returns. However, it is still somewhat clouded, and frequently it is dimmed by a strong desire for sleep. Reich believed that the discharge of tension was the result of a "flowing back of the excitation from the genital to the body." I should like to offer another interpretation.

The orgasm is a convulsion. It ends in the complete withdrawal of the man from the woman's body. If the first stage of coitus can be regarded symbolically as an attempt on the part of the man to return to the womb, the second stage must be considered as an emergence from the womb. In its very intensity it makes one think of the birth process. Man is reborn through orgasm. The whole act of sexual intercourse can be understood for the man as a symbolic return to the womb and rebirth. What of the woman's role? Since her first stage is a filling up, her second stage is an emptying. Where the man is reborn, the woman has given birth to him, symbolically of course. This may explain why some women have an orgastic experience when they do give birth. Others relate that they found the capacity to have an orgasm only after having given birth to a child.

Orgasms in the man and in the woman are identical bioenergetic processes and they are similarly experienced. We face the problem, however, of a lack of definition of orgasm. Because of this, there is widespread disagreement among sexologists in the evaluation of individual responses. I have attempted to show that the total or complete orgasm is an involuntary convulsion of the entire body concomitant in the man with the ejaculation of semen. The experience leaves one with a feeling of deep satisfaction and glow. Since discharge as an energetic phenomenon is a function of the involuntary movements, the complete absence of such movements, either of the smooth musculature or the striped musculature, would preclude any orgastic experience. Between these extremes there are all degrees and kinds of involuntary response, some pleasurable and some painful. The latter reactions must be regarded as defenses against the surrender to orgasm, and as such they reduce or prevent the achievement of satisfaction. We shall now discuss a few of the disturbances of sexual movement.

Every neurotic disability acts as a hindrance to the full orgastic experience. Every insistent pressure of reality impedes one's surrender to pleasure and to the id. These principles are elucidated in my book, *The Physical Dynamics of Character Structure*.

We have said before that the natural movement in the sexual act is based on a free-swinging pelvis. One of the most common distortions of this movement is the action of "pushing" the pelvis forward instead of allowing the natural thrust of a free swing. Let us see how the push works.

To make a forward movement with the pelvis when it is not swinging freely, many individuals tense the anterior muscles of the thighs, draw up the pelvic floor, and then contract and squeeze the buttocks together. This type of movement pushes or squeezes the genitals forward. In the man it concentrates feeling in the penis at the expense of pelvic sensation. One frequent result of this maneuver is premature ejaculation. Pushing and squeezing are typically found in patients with masochistic tendencies. In contrast, the natural swing of the pelvis is like the swinging of a dangling leg, neither pushed nor forced. The impulse for the natural movement comes from the legs; in pushing, the impulse comes from the buttocks.

An obstacle to full movement occurs when the muscles that unite the pelvis to the thighs below and to the lumbar spine above are chronically tense. Particularly in the rigid type of character structure one finds that these muscles are severely contracted as a part of general body rigidity. Since full movement of the pelvis is seriously impeded, the person substitutes a body sway for a pelvic swing. The body moves as a rigid tube and the whole sex experience tends to take on a mechanical quality. It is the "doing" of sex, not the experience of sex.

Another mechanism used to effectuate forward motion of the pelvis when free swing is impossible is the contraction of the abdominal muscles. By sucking in the belly, the pelvis can be brought forward. However, this procedure, which is *pulling* the pelvis forward as opposed to *pushing* it forward, stops the flow of feeling along the front of the body. Its consequence is the reduction of pleasure.

For all that the pelvic swing in a healthy individual is free, it is also the expression of body unity in movement. Even a leg in a dangling position cannot swing freely if the total body is not part of the motion and feeling. The head, too, must partake of this total movement and flow. If it is held stiffly, aloof, indifferent, the totality of the motion is destroyed. In the more severe emotional disturbances, this totality of body response is frequently absent. In schizophrenia, for example, the fragmentation that characterizes the personality also marks the body movements. The split between ego and sexuality that underlies the psychopathic condition is represented on the somatic level by a split between the feelings of the upper and lower halves of the body. This split destroys body unity and the natural sex movements.

The disturbances that occur in the involuntary movements parallel those that are found in the voluntary movements. The descriptions of orgasm in the man that are found in Kinsey's report show that the ability to surrender fully to the sexual release is most rare. Either there is little or no involuntary body reaction, or the involuntary movements are spasmodic, jerky, or hysterical. Instead of the release of body tension, many individuals experience increased muscular tension and rigidity. No one reported a feeling of glow and few had any marked pleasurable aftereffects.

When it is considered that every emotional problem and conflict has its counterpart in a somatic tension or spasticity, it becomes more understandable why full and complete orgasms are so rare. If the sexual experience is regarded as the emotional flower of one's love life, it will reflect in every way the plant that gives it sustenance and meaning.

References

Darwin, Charles, *The Expression of Emotions in Man and Animals*. London: John Murray, 1872.

Ferenczi, Sandos, *Thalassa, a Theory of Genitality*. New York: The Psychoanalytic Quarterly, Inc., 1938.

Freud, Sigmund, *Beyond the Pleasure Principle*. New York: Liveright Pub. Corp., 1950.

Freud, Sigmund, "Three Contributions to the Theory of Sexuality." In *Basic Writings of Sigmund Freud*. New York: Random House, 1938.

Kinsey, A. C., *et al.*, *Sexual Behavior in the Human Male.* Philadelphia: W. B. Saunders Co., 1948.

LaBarre, Weston, *The Human Animal.* Chicago: University of Chicago Press, 1955.

Lowen, Alexander, *The Physical Dynamics of Character Structure.* New York: Grune & Stratton, 1958.

Neumann, Erich, *The Origins and History of Consciousness.* New York: Bollinger Foundation XLII by Pantheon Books, Inc., 1954.

Reich, Wilhelm, *The Function of the Orgasm.* New York: Orgone Institute Press, 1942.

Reik, Theodore, *Of Love and Lust.* New York: Grove Press, Inc., 1958.

Szent-Györgyi, Albert, *Bioenergetics.* New York: Academic Press, 1957.

ALEXANDER LOWEN

Music and Sex

THIS article is written from a subjective point of view because of the very nature of music, surely the most expressive and least tangible of the arts. Not only does music differ greatly from continent to continent (and only the music of the Western world will be treated in this discussion) but it also varies from nation to nation. Little is known, scientifically, about the interrelationship of music and sex (only some eight studies have been made on the subject and none of them is definitive) so that it is impossible to dogmatize about it. Accordingly, the principal purpose of this article is to offer a generalized exploration of the subject.

Of the eight writings on sex and music, all but one were devoted exclusively to classical music.

An attempt will be made to discuss, at least *en passant,* the four genres of classical, popular, Latin-American, and jazz music.

Main Difficulties

In dealing with music-and-sex, three principal difficulties are encountered at once which may be designated as negative aspects of the topic: (1) confusions of definition, (2) cultural-emotional differences, and (3) factors of association.

Definition

The theme music-and-sex encompasses the entire spectrum of the emotional aspects of love from the apotheosis of idealized love as found in many famous operatic arias, notably *Fidelio* and in various *lieder,* to the depiction of savage, sensual lust as in Richard Strauss and

especially *Salome,* and including the mystic-romantic (Schoenberg's *Verklaerte Nacht* and perhaps his *Gurrelieder*), the amorous-flirtatious (*Der Rosenkavalier*), and the voluptuous-erotic (*L'Après-midi d'un Faune*). Admittedly these are arbitrary, subjective "classifications" to which not all listeners would agree. At least, however, they are fairly accurate generalizations.

Cultural-Emotional

The degree of cultural-emotional difference in the response pattern of listeners is very great. From observations of the bodily—and vocal—antics of younger listeners, for example, it is clear that they are "sent," both emotionally and —in varying degrees—erotically by popular singers, jazz artists, and rock 'n' roll musicians. Generally speaking, their over-all musical education is negligible; consequently, their emotive reactions to some of what is usually considered to be the (Western) world's most moving music—the Bach Chorales, the Verdi ensembles, and certain "symphonic" compositions of Wagner—would be atypical if contrasted with those of more "sophisticated" listeners.

Association

Association, or rather the cumulative effects of a variety of associations, plays a much more important part in creating an amorous mood than is usually realized.

According to the general public, "Star Dust" (music by Hoagy Carmichael, words by Michael Parrish) is recognized as perhaps "the most romantic American popular song ever written." But would it still be thus designated if it were not named "Star Dust" and if its lyrics did not personify the more or less abstract, self-identificatory romanticism that it does?

This is also the case with jazz—especially the blues—a music whose repertoire has a large number of compositions frankly sexual in theme, as for example: "My Daddy Rocks Me," "Gimme a Pig's Foot," "Cherry Red," etc. Although it is true that there is much in the music of jazz that is sexual, such selections as these do not necessarily and automatically fall into the sex-and-music category since a great deal of the erotic implications are derived from the title and the lyrics.

Sex and Music Instruments

Music has been identified with sex for a much longer period than is usually assumed. As a matter of fact, many kinds of musical instruments have had their origin in sexual symbols, or rather as representations of the genitalia. To primitive man one of the principal uses of musical instruments if not the chief use, was to celebrate life's primordial functions of sex and/or fertility.

Thus, in New Guinea the natives used a trough of stone, representing the vulva, which they pounded with a pestle, representing the penis of a spirit. One of the most important early instruments was the split drum, found in the Pacific Islands, Africa, and in certain areas of Asia, which was symbolic of the female sex. It was frequently in the form of a large tree trunk with a slit in the middle and was played by ramming it with a stick. When women played the drums—especially in East Africa—the drumstick was a phallic symbol. In other areas the drum was utilized at such sexual ceremonies as circumcision. In the Malayo-Polynesian area, such slit drums were an important form of sexual symbolism.

Later developments included the friction drums which, with their suggestive to-and-fro movement, indicated sexual intercourse. Among the Ba-ila of Northern Rhodesia young women were initiated into sex rites by a maternal aunt who placed a drumlike object made of an earthenware pot covered by a piece of hide between her legs and played it, with obvious gestures, with a reed. Sachs (1940) says:

The connection of friction drums with fertility and initiation rites is preserved in European traditions. Martinmas and the days before Christmas and Epiphany—the festivals which the Christians substituted for the rites of winter solstice—are the seasons in which boys go from house to house to sing old verses and rub the *rommelpot,* as the Dutch say, which often is artlessly made of a kitchen pot or a flowerpot and a bladder.

There are other "primitive" instruments associated with sex, including the so-called bullroarer from Brazil with its elliptical fish shape that signifies procreation and the "scrapers," especially the bone scrapers of the North and Central American Indians.

An instrument that has long been identified with sex in general, and with life and rebirth, is the flute, which is discussed at considerable length by Sachs (1940). Although this symbolic identification might seem naive to us, it has had great significance in many sexual manifestations—circumcision, menstruation, ceremonies, dances, rituals, etc.—around the world. In a number of European languages the word "flute" has definite sexual connotations, cf. the English expressions "the living flute," "the silent flute," "the one-eyed flute," etc., as in "The Cupid" (1736) Farmer:

> The flute is good that's made of wood
> And is, I own, the neatest;
> Yet none the less I must confess
> The *silent flute's* the sweetest.

Among certain ethnic groups magic sexual influences were attributed to this instrument. Thus, again according to Sachs (1940), young braves of the Cheyenne Indians played the flute:

. . . in order to help them in their courtship. Some flutes had a special power to influence girls. A young man might go to a medicine man and ask him to exercise his power on a flute, so that the girl he wanted would come out of the lodge when she heard it. The young man began to play the flute when he was at a distance from the lodge, but gradually approached it, and when he had come near to the lodge he found the girl outside waiting for him.

The connection between Eros and music instruments has not been limited to so-called "primitive" tribes. The most famous of European instruments in this category is the *viola d'amore*, which was used fairly extensively in the baroque and post-baroque periods, especially by Antonio Vivaldi (*Concerto in D Minor, Concerto in A Minor*). A second such instrument is the *oboe d'amore*, which appeared around 1720. Bach admired it for its ingratiating tone (*Cantata 37: Wer da glaubet*, 1725) and it was also used by Richard Strauss (*Sinfonia Domestica*, 1904) and Ravel (*Bolero*, 1927). Another "love-instrument" should also be mentioned—the *clarinette d'amour*, which appeared briefly in the last decades of the eighteenth century and was used by Johann Christian Bach (*Temistocle*, 1772). And finally, the cittern, a flat, pear-shaped (usually), nine-stringed instrument, was very popular in England, especially in the seventeenth century. These citterns were used in barbershops much as we read magazines to while away the time while waiting for a haircut. Citterns were also "associated with immorality, a cittern-girl being synonymous with a person of doubtful character" (Welch, 1911). Thus, in Morose's furious words (Ben Jonson, "The Silent Women," iii.5): "That accursed barber! . . . I have married his cittern that's common to all men."

Catholic Religious Music Versus Secular Music

When the music lover of today thinks of the heritage of European music, the glorious instrumental and/or operatic tradition of Western music usually comes to mind.

However, this is a popular conception and one that rarely takes into consideration the fact that up to a certain undefinable point in the period 1450-1550 the European musical tradition did not consist of instrumental and operatic works. The music of the Middle Ages and an important part of the Renaissance was created by the Church principally as a kind of theological *Gebrauchsmusik* to glorify that autocratic institution. As such it was predominantly vocal. In this connection these observations of Wooldridge are pertinent:

But it is not until the recognition of the triad, i.e., a chord of three tones—a particular note and its third and fifth—(about 1500) as a musical factor of importance and the consequent discovery of modal harmony, which before had not been in the least perceived, that the true distinction between sacred and secular composition becomes obvious in music.

Here, indeed, was a conditioned situation without parallel in the history of mankind. In each of the great preceding civilizations there had been no autocratic force to dictate musical tastes; accordingly, many kinds of music, including love songs, had been composed, depending of course on the civilization's musical culture. But during the Dark Ages Christianity effectively stifled the composition of secular "emotional" music, resulting in a thousand long years in which virtually no love songs, certainly one of the fundamental urges of the human heart, were composed! Although the musical dictatorship of the Church was ironclad for centuries, it could not restrain the natural, inherent desire of man to sing of nonchurchly things. Consequently, secular influences began some time toward the end of the first millennium of the Christian era to creep into sacred music.

Thus, two religious songs, O *Filii* and *Orientis partibus*, of the tenth century, are based on secular melodies. However, such compositions lie outside of the great tradition of European "classical" music, and it was not before the sixteenth century that woman or love entered into the music of the most outstanding composers. Although the great "Prince of Music" (Giovanni Pierluigi da Palestrina, 1525?-1594) did write secular songs that were fundamentally spiritual in essence, he is best known as a composer of religious music. Love in his madrigals is an abstraction. In none of the titles of his works does he give the name of a specific woman, in spite of the fact that he was married twice. This is additional evidence of the control of the Church, for what composer in love can refrain from writing music to, for, and of his beloved? During the sixteenth and seventeenth centuries the madrigal was the most popular form of musical expression that dealt with love.

The First European Vernacular Love Songs

Even before the madrigal, the theme of love, which had been repressed by the Church for more than ten centuries, made its appearance in European music, at first among the troubadours in southern France (Provence) and the *trouvères* in the north of the country in the period 1100-1300. Mention should be made of Guillaume duc d'Aquitaine (1070-1127), who is credited with writing the oldest lyrics in a modern European vernacular yet discovered. By any standards, this "Goliath of Prostitution," as he was admiringly known—van Bolen (1951) also called him "der groesste Wuestling des elften Jahrhunderts," freely, "the sexiest man of the eleventh century"—was remarkable. His two great pastimes were song-writing and whoring. He was a dedicated enemy of the Church, and, when he was not lusting after moon-breasted wenches, enjoying them, satyr-like, in the sun-soaked meadows of Provence and singing of them with ribaldry drenched with wine, delighted in constructing bordellos built exactly like abbeys.

This new genre of love poetry (and music) spread from Provence into Spain, somewhat into Italy, and especially into Germany where the Minnesingers (1150-1325), chivalrous love-singers, developed another distinctive school of lyric-musical expression. The German poems were less formal, less distant (cf. the famous Provençal concept of *"amor lontanha"*—"far-away love"), and less neurotic. Under any circumstances, the writings of the troubadours and the minnesingers during the period 1100-1325 were of great importance in the history of music-and-sex in Europe, as they presented a completely new concept of woman: a feminine creature to be loved and to love.

The Development of Opera and the Depiction of Woman in Music

Around the turn of the seventeenth century in Florence a new kind of musical expression was being formulated—the opera—with such works as *Dafne* (Giulio Caccini and Jacopo Peri, text by Ottavio Rinuccini, 1594), *Euridice*

(Peri-Rinuccini, 1600), *Orfeo* (Claudio Monteverdi-Alessandro Striggio, 1607). This was to introduce more and more the concept of sex, or rather of woman, into European music. To the majority of the great "presecularized" composers of the sixteenth century—Adriaan Willaert, Palestrina, Orlando di Lasso, etc.—the thought of dedicating a work to a woman, especially with romantic implications, was practically unheard of. Three hundred years later Romantic composers such as Chopin and Liszt were dedicating a sizeable number of their works to women to whom they were attracted. In the case of Chopin, who wrote about 225 compositions, some 54 of them fall in this category, while of the 701 works of Liszt, approximately 69 are dedicated to his feminine friends.

Obviously a great change had taken place in the concept of the role of love in music. As late as the latter part of the sixteenth century, woman as an active, motivating force in music was, generally speaking, nonexistent; by the end of the eighteenth century—thanks chiefly to the incomparable Mozart—she was a vital part of the classic operatic tradition. Although Gluck's *Orfeo ed Euridice* is earlier (1762) than Mozart's *Le Nozze di Figaro* (1786), Susanna, the Countess, and Cherubino (although the latter is a masculine page whose role is sung by a soprano) are the first really human women in opera, as Euridice is more a symbol of femininity than a living female. From that time on women continued to play a greater role in music and in the lives of its creators. Naturally the concept of women varied from one composer to another, and it is interesting to see how different musicians interpreted love.

To Paul Rosenfeld (1932), the late critic, Mozart's concept of woman is a "tender, warm, smiling divinity" in whom desire and gratification are equally matched. Beethoven, ever concerned with moral ideas and ideals, composed *Fidelio* as an impressive tribute to woman—and matrimony—in their loftiest estates. Because Rosenfeld's description of love in music is so felicitous, he will be quoted below, as it is no mean accomplishment to describe the emotions evoked by the most intangible of arts. To Brahms, woman was "a benign queen, steadfast," who represented "endurance and courage." In Chopin's intensely personal compositions she stood for "infinite grace, capriciousness, delicacy, pride, sensuous delights, suavity of bodily lines, intoxications and icy torments." The conception of love of Richard Strauss is "romantic irony: infatuation into disgust—*Don Juan* (1888), idealization into disillusionment—*Don Quixote* (1897), concordance into opposition—*Sinfonia domestica* (1903), passion into sadism—*Salome* (1905), and childlike love into demoniac hate—*Elektra* (1909)." And he might have added the suggestive orchestral machinations during the off-stage seduction of the virgin Diemut by the young sorcerer Kunrad in Strauss' satirical opera *Feuersnot* (1901).

The following list of compositions that woman has inspired or in which she plays a major role is purely random and arbitrary. Although Liszt dedicated a tenth of his works to women, he did not compose an excessive number of works devoted to that theme. His masterpiece, probably, the *Faust Symphony* (1854-1857), with its intriguing themes including the Gretchen motif (oboe playing against an *arpeggio* movement), is a beguiling portrayal of artless love. The pianist-composer's *Dante Symphony* (1855-1856), the inspiration for which Liszt had read together with Countess Marie d'-Agoult, his mistress and mother of his three children, is also a depiction in tone of the love of Paolo and Francesca. This theme of incestuous love was also the basis of a composition by Tchaikovsky in which a moving picture of the pathetic Francesca is painted by the tender melody of the clarinet playing over strings.

Hector Berlioz' *Symphonie Fantastique* (1830), which was composed for his adored Harriet Smithson, is a musical study of obsessive compulsive passion in which the melodic *idée fixe* (first expressed in C major, in the *allegro*) represents the ubiquitous Beloved One.

Anyone who was as expressive with the orchestral palette as Rimsky-Korsakov would quite naturally be expected to glorify Eros. This he has done more than once, perhaps most eloquently in the third section—"The Young Prince and the Young Princess"—of *Scheherazade*

(1888). There is of course little need to mention the sex-infused *Carmen* (1875) of Bizet, perhaps the most popular opera ever written, whose sensual beauty seemed to bewitch Nietzsche, as, indeed, it has many others.

Of all the great composers, Achille Claude Debussy occupies a unique position. For he, perhaps to a greater degree than anyone else, had the ability to recapture in luminous sound the wondrous workings of Nature, as in *Nuages* (1893) and *La Mer* (1903-1905). His concept of woman and love is also uniquely Debussyian, as witness the intangible, never-never atmosphere of his mystique-tinged opera, *Pelléas et Mélisande* (1892-1902). The famous *Prélude à l'Après-midi d'un Faun* (1892-1894), with its nymphs, pagans, and lovers, fairly sighs with sensuality, as does his *Sirènes* (1899) with the languorous loveliness of its choir of women. To quote Rosenfeld's words again, woman was, to Debussy, "divine, incommunicable, mysterious, unknown."

Other compositions of this century that have been inspired by the theme of love and/or woman are the following: The corrosive, barbaric force of woman as portrayed in the mimodrama, i.e., a musical pantomime that resembles the ballet but does not have the usual formal stylization of its dance elements, such as *La Tragédie de Salome* (1907-1910) by the French composer Florent Schmitt; the hyper-French erotic romance of Gustav Charpentier's opera *Louise* (1900), whose title role was so vividly created by Mary Garden; the tragic love of the legendary King Waldemar IV for the Princess Tove, as depicted in Arnold Schönberg's gigantic and poignant orchestral cantata *Gurrelieder* (1913), his "monodrama" *Erwartung* (1909), in which love is an enticing disillusion, and his musical drama *Die glückliche Hand* (1913), in which love lures its victims to delusional rapture; the enchanted folklore of love in Stravinsky's "conte dansé," *L'Oiseau de Feu* (1910), the violence of sex in his frenzied *Le Sacre du Printemps* (1913), and the pathetic frustration of love in his *Petrouchka* (1919).

Of all the composers who sang of physical desire, Richard Wagner is by far the most famous in the realm of musical eroticism, and his

Tristan und Isolde (1865) is a deliberately conceived, soul-moving apotheosis of carnal love. Despite its flamboyant and exaggerated prose, the description of this work by Charles O'Connell (1935) conveys to a remarkable degree the delirious rapture and agonizing beauty of Wagner's masterwork:

The ultimate, and the only complete meeting and union of man and woman is in the embrace of love. . . . It is no disembodied love, immaterial, spiritualized and denatured, that Wagner celebrates here. No such incandescent ecstasies were ever born of meetings of the spirit. Here is love that is fierce and exigent and consuming and insatiable; love which at a look, a word, a touch, races through the blood like flames; love which laughs at barriers, forgets enemies, and knows no loyalty but to itself; love which is normal and carnal and human. . . .

Now through the long night that passes, Tristan, all dour scruples done away, all knightly vows forgotten under the magic and the spells of love, holds the white loveliness of Isolde in his arms. Now the young girl, the innocent, the beautiful princess of Ireland, becomes heiress overnight to the ageless stratagems and arts of womankind. Now are celebrated the immemorial rites of love, the lovers heedless, careless, forgetful of all but the night, and their own hearts beating close, one upon the other. . . .

Now with the esurient senses appeased, come interludes of exquisite lethargy, sweet warm magical languors, mystical moments when the heart eases itself of burdens and confidences, of secret hopes and longings. Now as the lovers reflect upon their plight, they despair and long for death; now remembered ecstasy again besieges them. The handmaiden Brangaene warns in vain of approaching day; the henchman Kurneval bursts into the bower but a step before envious Melot and outraged King Tristan, his heart in Isolde's body, defends himself without hope or despair or fury, and takes a not unwelcome mortal wound.

Only music, vibrating in the invisible air, could dramatize such a moment. And what shall we say of such music as this? What magic is there, in wood and wind and brass, that can make this deathless song? What man is this who in his music evokes so surely and so terribly the longings and the sorrows and passion of all the lovers in the world? Answer there is none, for music speaks from heart to heart; to reason with it is to slay it.

In his intriguing book of musical memories, *The Other Side of the Record*, Charles O'Con-nell comments upon Stokowski's "Symphonic Synthesis" of the music that he arranged from *Tristan und Isolde* and defends the conductor's alleged emphasis upon the "sensual and erotic." Stokowski is of course keenly conscious of the role that sexual desire plays in music—particularly in the *Tristan* score. O'Connell narrates engagingly of an incident in a broadcast of the Love Music from the second act of *Tristan*—"music the erotic content of which he emphasized to the point of indecent emotional exposure." The denouement of this episode is quite unexpected and readers are referred to O'Connell's own version of what he called a "twenty-two minute orgasm."

The Perverse-Atypical Emotional Responses of Certain Types of Music

One of the most interesting aspects about music-and-sex is the singular fact that certain compositions that were specifically written to portray love or romance or woman are *not* particularly erotic. In this category are, oddly enough, many operatic arias and any number of the most famous *lieder*—including some of the greatest love songs in the Western musical tradition.

Conversely, a number of compositions have been written whose nature is in no way connected with sex—indeed whose subject matter is far removed from the erotic—which nevertheless tend to evoke an emotional-susceptible reaction. Among such works are certain of Chopin's Etudes and Nocturnes. It is remarkable that such stylized forms should have, for certain people at least, a definite emotional appeal—as do some of Bach's religion- and heaven-soaring chorale preludes and, oddly enough, Wagner's *Parsifal*, probably the most "religious" opera ever composed. It is of course not to be inferred here that there is anything intentionally erotic in this masterwork of religious mysticism — specifically redemption through, in Wagner's own words, "Love—Faith, Hope?" but its sheer, almost painful beauty cannot but affect the interested listener emotionally. This is especially true in such parts of the opera as the "Vorspiel" and the "Char-Freitags-Zauber," when the massed chorus of strings, all a-shimmer and luminous with celestial sound, actually seems to sigh forth in poignant loveliness—particularly in the Promise Theme (or the Guileless Fool theme as it is also known—*Parsifal* being an inversion of the Arabic "Fal parsi," "guileless fool") and the ethereal Nature Redeemed motive when the aging knight of the Grail, Gurnemanz, exclaims to Parsifal that the beauty of vernal nature is a tribute to Jesus Christ: "Das ist Char-Freitags-Zauber, Herr!" ("That is the spell of Good Friday, my lord!") Thus affected, i.e., thus put in a receptive, emotionally conditioned mood, as it were, many females find that their standards of resistance are emotive rather than "empirical," and as such are very susceptible to the allure of Eros.

The Castrati

Mention might be made here of a singular development in music history—the famous *castrati,* or eunuch singers, who might, wryly, fall into the "Music *without* Sex" section of this investigation. In the seventeenth and especially in the eighteenth century in Italy it was common practice to castrate gifted boy singers before their voice changed at puberty. Thus male singers remained contraltos and sopranos during their entire careers and maintained their characteristic high pitch as long as they were active.

Due to certain physiological changes as a result of this operation, the bodies of such eunuchs exhibit a greater development than is found in ordinary men, and often the voice was very powerful. Thus, one witnessed and heard the unusual spectacle of men of striking physique singing in some of the highest ranges of the human voice. Through this combination the *castrati* achieved enormous popularity and the most gifted—Caffarelli, Farinelli, Senesino, and Carestini—were the vocal idols of the day. Outside of Italy they were perhaps most in demand in London, where Handel wrote a number of operas featuring this kind of singing. An interesting aspect of their art, which *The Spectator* caustically designated "the shrill celestial whine of eunuchs," is the fact that in at least three famous more recent operatic roles female vocalists sing male parts (Cherubino in Mo-

zart's *Le Nozze di Figaro*—soprano, Prince Orlovsky in *Die Fledermaus*—mezzo-soprano, and Octavian in Strauss' *Der Rosenkavalier*—mezzo-soprano).

The Dance and Sex

The interrelationship between dancing and sex is well known (see Sachs, 1937). That it is a profound relationship is obvious—from the wildest "orgiastic" dances of "primitive" tribes to the effete tea dances of the present day. Erotic themes in one way or another have also been portrayed in ballet, as for example in such representative works, again selected at random, as Ravel's *Daphnis et Chloe* (1912), as well as *Le Sacre du Printemps* (1913), *Scheherazade* (1888), and *La Tragédie de Salome* (1907–1910)—which three have been noted above—*Sylvia* (1876) by Léo Delibes, and Ravel's *Bolero* (1928).

This last-named remarkable orchestral feat, which Ravel himself called "une danse lascive," is actually not a true Spanish *bolero*—the two-centuries-old folk dance characterized in varying degrees by the use of a triplet, usually in the second half of the bar—but an instrumental tour de force based on this dance form. In the preparation of this article, a number of women were questioned in regard to music that aroused them; a large percentage responded with conviction that the *Bolero* was one of "the sexiest." This almost goes without saying, for it appears to be a very accurate tonal depiction of the act of love-making.

First, are the drums, marking the rhythm, definite and suggestive of sexual movements—more specifically of "pelvic thrusts" (in psychiatrist Sandor Rado's terminology). Then comes the gentle presentation of the theme—although *Bolero* is technically a monothematic work. This motive really consists of two different "subthematical" developments, the first consisting of the suggestive flute-*motiv,* and the second (marked *solo bassoon* in the score but actually played by clarinet), which gradually develops into the relentless pounding "crescendo orchestral" (Ravel's words) that characterizes this breathtakingly controlled rhythmic spasm. It is of course this rhythm, inexorable, implacable, that makes *Bolero the* "sexy" composition that it is.

Popular Music and Sex

When the subject of sex and popular music arises, one automatically thinks of that genius, Cole Porter, whose *oeuvre* is a kind of musical erotikon, to use an apt word. The lyrics that Porter writes are admittedly the "sexiest" of any writer and it is contended that he likewise composes "sexy music." It is undeniable that his songs, with their long, sweeping lines ("I Concentrate on You"), their swelling crescendoes ("Night and Day"), their use of minor keys ("You'd Be So Nice To Come Home To"), and their emphasis on pulsating rhythmic effects ("Begin the Beguine") do possess a haunting appeal that induces an erotic mood. None of the other composers in this same category (Broadway musicals), such as Gershwin, Rodgers, and Berlin, has this uniquely Porteresque quality.

Another outstanding representative of popular music and sex is Francis Albert Sinatra, whose voice has probably aroused more erotic feelings among women than any other vocal organ in history. "The Voice" is reported to have similar effects upon countless males. The squealing teen-agers who rioted over him in his theater performances in the late 1940's may have been musically and intellectually immature; still, in many ways Sinatra remains the most outstanding of popular singers. His concept of songs is as remarkable as his vocal equipment, which enables him to interpret them almost as he desires. One of the explanations, perhaps, of his "sexy" and/or romantic appeal is the lullabylike quality, the almost motherlike tenderness, that he can impart to a Tin Pan Alley ballad—"Where Are You?" for example. One could also see erotic allure in his skilled use of such technical devices as *vibrato, appoggiatura,* and *rubato*—all of which he exploits to wring the utmost expression, both lyrical and musical, out of each selection. Thus it might be said that Frank Sinatra is maximally endowed vocally to eroticize the majority of responsive females who are interested in this kind of music.

Latin-American Music and Sex

Despite the universal popularity of several Latin-American dance forms, the popular music (in a none-too-authentic form) of this area has not been extensively studied by foreign musicologists, and material by native specialists is difficult to come by.

There are, as is to be expected, hundreds of different kinds of dances and songs on the continent and in the nearby Caribbean Islands of which a goodly part are of definite erotic nature. Perhaps the most famous of all is the *rumba,* an outspokenly sexual creation of Cuban Negroes. Although officially a carnival dance, the Afro-Cuban *conga* often falls into the erotic category, as do the Hispano-Cuban *guaracha* in 6/8 time and the rhythmically complicated *son.*

From "drum-mad" Haiti comes: (1) the Hispano-Negro *meringue,* with its gyrating thighs and hips (the French, i.e., Haitian, equivalent, frequently in the minor keys, of the Spanish *merengue*—which is, as a rule, in the major—the most popular and perhaps most characteristic dance in the Dominican Republic); and (2) the Afro-French mixture of drivingly rhythmic songs that form such an important part of the voodoo ritual. Jamaica is represented by the torso-twisting *mento,* not unlike a slower version of the *rumba,* fundamentally an expression of sex. Similarly, one could include the *bambula* from Haiti and the Virgin Islands and the "lascivious" (so designated by churchly observers) *tambou* from the latter locale. Finally, from this area, the pulsing rhythms of the *béguin* from Martinique, immortalized in Cole Porter's masterpiece, "Begin the Beguine," which might well be the greatest popular song ever composed. This is another erotic dance whose very name in argot means "infatuation" and/or "flirtation."

Jazz and Sex

Of all the interrelationships between music-and-sex, that which exists between jazz and sex is perhaps the most obvious. Although the etymon of jazz is uncertain, it is apparently an orthographic variant of *jass*—a vernacular expression with strong copulatory connotations. The attitude of the serious chroniclers of jazz—Stearns, Panassie, Ulanov, Shapiro and Hentoff, Smith, Russell, Ramsey, Hodier, Blesh, Finkelstein, Berendt, Feather, and Cerri (whose latest book, Luigi Cerri, *Antologia del jazz*, Milano, Nistri-Lischi, 1955, I would like to recommend as especially interesting and informative)—is a strange one: They describe vividly and in great detail the brothels of Storyville—the one-time center of prostitution in New Orleans, with its forty to fifty blocks of sex-and-music—yet there is no discussion of the relationship between sex and music. Longstreet is perhaps the most explicit regarding the "sinful" background and character of jazz and seems to delight in emphasizing, even glorifying it.

On the other hand, Farrell and Grossman, in their quaint tractate, which purports to present jazz as a sect of Christianity-four-to-the-bar, naturally take a very dim view of this relationship and stoutly maintain that it is overrated. However, a glance at such important works as *Hear Me Talkin' to Ya* (Shapiro and Hentoff), which is a collection of reminiscences of famous jazz figures, and *Mister Jelly Roll* (Lomax, 1955), a biography of the flamboyant pianist-composer Ferdinand Joseph Morton, whose business cards bore the legend "Originator of Jazz—Stomp—Swing," reveals the tremendous and inevitable role that sex has played in the development of "America's only original art form." The pages of such and many other studies are sprinkled with references to "pimps and hustlers," "some of the biggest prostitutes in the world" (Louis Armstrong, in Shapiro and Hentoff), "whorehouse, brothel, sporting house, cribs, house of assignation" (Danny Barber, in Shapiro and Hentoff), and "If a naked dance was desired . . . one of the girls would dance on a narrow stage. Yes, they danced absolutely stripped" (Jelly Roll Morton, in Lomax).

It was principally in such establishments as Miss Lulu White's "Mahogany Hall Stomp" (significantly enough, one of Armstrong's "classic" records was entitled "Mahogany Hall Stomp) and that of the Countess Willie Piazza that jazz came into being, and however intangi-ble and unprovable it might be, it seems hardly possible that there was not a considerable amount of mutual influence between the prostitutes and their dancing and the music, or, between the music and the prostitutes and their dancing. Since much of the musical material, the words, is outspokenly sexual, as any number of compositions in this idiom reveal ("How Do You Do It That Way?" "Worn-out Papa Blues," "Cherry Red," "My Daddy Rocks Me"), it is natural to assume that—given the Negro's fundamental, if not primordial, drive toward sexual expression and the particular atmosphere of Storyville (the purpose of which was, after all, the glorification of the most primitive aspects of sex)—a very close interrelationship would inevitably develop, and subsequently did develop. As Hugues Panassie, the Grand Panjandrum of jazz, states, "Le jazz est une musique de danse," and he goes on to elaborate upon the supreme importance of "la pulsation rhythmique."

Thus, for more than one-third of its approximately sixty-year-old history (roughly from 1900 to Benny Goodman, who in the mid-thirties reawakened the nation to "Swing Music" and the audience's emphasis upon listening to and appreciating its instrumental virtuosity), jazz developed and was developed as primarily *dance* music whose emphasis was, and generally still is, upon its *rhythm*. Given the innate connection between sex and rhythm, the relation between jazz and sex may be considered to be a profound and inherent one.

Because of space limitations there is much omitted here: the attitude of the Greeks toward the subject—especially the views of Aristotle, Plato, Aristoxenus, and Athenaeus and their views about the "lascivious" Lydian mode; the use of certain harmonic constructions to denote tension; the question of tension (and dissonance) in music and its erotic effects; the psychophysiological dynamics of erection brought about by music; the role of music in Casanova's life; the sex drives and sexual expression in Wagner, Liszt, and Richard Strauss; some of the rhapsodic sequences that occur in certain sections of the *Third Piano Concerto* of Rachmaninoff; the anomalous fact that Tchaikovsky, the harassed homosexual, wrote some of the most sheerly romantic melodies ever composed; the homosexual and the ballet, and the question of whether there can be such a thing as "homosexual music"; the strange appeal of prostitutes for Brahms; the psychodynamics of the sexual attraction of certain types of voices (cf. Mae West's "Come up and see me some time," an ordinary phrase sexualized into a national-cultural symbol); the realistic portrayal of intercourse which occurs as an orchestral interlude in Shostakovitch's brutal opera, *Lady Macbeth of Mtsensk* ("disgusting," the Soviet officials called it), with its back-and-forth *glissando* passages for trombones; the abnormally sensitive reaction of certain critics to "erotic music" ("Shostakovitch is without a doubt the foremost composer of pornographic music in the field of art"—the famous critic, W. J. Henderson, in Slonimsky, 1955, "Listening to this screaming music, i.e., jazz, for a minute or two one conjures up an orchestra of madmen, sexual maniacs, led by a man-stallion beating time with an enormous phallos"—Maxim Gorky, "Here [*Johnny Spielt auf*] love is perverted into an animal, cattlelike concupiscience; there is nothing in it but . . . sticky, froglike sexuality"—V. Gorodinsky, "die erotische Flagellanten Musik der Liszt-Wagnerischen Schule"—Eduard Hanslick, some of the leading popular female singers whose voices are considered "sexy," such as Sarah Vaughan, rich and purling, Peggy Lee, an amorous, meaningful pout, Lena Horne, and Doris Day, and with special recognition of Helen O'Connell's version of "Green Eyes" with the Jimmy Dorsey Orchestra (1939) for the way in which she turned six words, "Those cool and limpid Green Eyes!" into a veritable vocal orgasm; the romantic operettas of Victor Herbert, Franz Lehar, Oscar Straus, Rudolf Friml, Sigmund Romberg, and other apotheosizers of musical sensuality; and many others.

References

Blesh, Rudi, *Shining Trumpets: A History of Jazz.* New York: Alfred A. Knopf, Inc., 1958.

Bloch, Iwan, *The Sexual Life of Our Time.* New York: Falstaff Press, Inc., 1937, pp. 35-36.

Bloch, Iwan, *Sexual Life in England Past and Present.* London: Arco Publications Ltd., 1958, pp. 600-617.

Clarke, Cyril, *The Composer in Love.* London-New York: Peter Nevill Ltd., 1951.

Chase, Gilbert, *The Music of Spain.* New York: W. W. Norton & Co., Inc., 1941, pp. 257-272.

Decsey, Ernst *et al., Das Gehör.* Wien: Verlag für Kulturforschung, 1931.

Duncan, Isadora, "Dancing in Relation to Religion and Love." *Theatre Arts,* Aug., 1927, pp. 584-585.

Ellis, Havelock, *Studies in the Psychology of Sex* (4 vols.). New York: Random House, 1936, Vol. 2, pp. 112-135.

Elster, Alexander, *Musik und Erotik.* Bonn: A. Markus & E. Weber, 1925.

Feather, Leonard, *Encyclopedia of Jazz.* New York: Horizon Press, Inc., 1955.

Finkelstein, Sidney, *How Music Expresses Ideas.* New York: International Publishers Co., Inc., 1952.

Frings, Theodor, *Minnesinger und Troubadours.* Berlin: Akademie Verlag, 1949.

Grove's Dictionary of Music and Musicians (9 vols., 5th ed.). Edited by Eric Bloom. New York: St. Martin's Press, Inc., 1954.

Hirschfeld, Magnus, *Geschlechtskunde* (5 vols.). Stuttgart: Julius Püttmann, Verlagsbuchhandlung, 1930, Vol. 2, pp. 196-201.

Howard, Walter, and Auras, Imgard, *Musique et Sexualité.* Paris: Presses Universitaires, 1955.

Kierkegaard, Søren Aabye, "De umidelbare erotiske Stadier eller det musicalsk-erotiske." *Enten-eller,* Søren Kierkegaard's Samlede Vaerker (14 vols.). Kjøbenhavn: Gyldendalske Boghandels Forlag, 1901-1936, Vol. 1, pp. 30-95.

Lafitte-Houssat, *Troubadours et cours d'amour.* Paris: Presses Universitaires, 1950.

Laurent, Emile, and Nagour, Paul, *Magica Sexualis.* New York: Anthropological Press, 1934, pp. 201-211.

Leaf, Earl, *Isles of Rhythm.* New York: A. S. Barnes & Co., 1948.

Lehmann, Friedrich R., *Kulturgeschichte und Rezepte der Liebesmittel.* Heidenheim: Erich Hoffmann Verlag, 1955, pp. 66-68.

Lomax, Alan, *Mister Jelly Roll* (3rd ed.). London: Cassell & Co., Ltd., 1955, p. 50.

Longstreet, Stephen, *The Real Jazz Old and New.* Baton Rouge: Louisiana State University Press, 1956, pp. 53-68.

Mottini, G. Edoardo, *La donna e la musica.* Milano: Antonio Vallardi, 1931.

O'Connell, Charles, *The Victor Book of the Symphony.* New York: Simon and Schuster, Inc., 1935, pp. 499-500.

O'Connell, Charles, *The Other Side of the Record.* New York: Alfred A. Knopf, Inc., 1949, pp. 291, 296-297.

The Oxford History of Music (rev. ed., 7 vols.). Oxford: Oxford University Press, 1929-1932, Vol. 2 (by H. E. Wooldridge), pp. 114-116, 217-220.

Pan American Union, *Music in Latin America.* Washington, D.C., 1945, pp. 25-65.

Panassie, Hugues, *Jazz Panorama*. Paris: Editions des Deux-Rives, 1950, pp. 47-48.

Rosenfeld, Paul, *Modern Music, in Sex in the Arts*. New York, London: Harper & Brothers, 1932, pp. 146-166.

Sachs, Curt, *Geist und Werden der Musikinstrumente*. Berlin: D. Reimer, 1929.

Sachs, Curt, *The History of Musical Instruments*. New York: W. W. Norton & Co., Inc., 1940, pp. 25-59.

Sachs, Curt, *World History of the Dance*. New York: W. W. Norton & Co, Inc., 1937.

Saunders, Richard Drake, "Sex in Music." *Sexology 25;* No. 9, 574-579, April, 1959.

Shapiro, Nat, and Hentoff, Nat, *Hear Me Talkin' to Ya*. New York: Rinehart & Co., Inc., 1955, pp. 4, 5, 10.

Sheean, Vincent, *Oscar Hammerstein I*. New York: Simon and Schuster, Inc., 1956, pp. 267-270.

Slonimsky, Nicolas, *Music of Latin America*. New York: Thomas Y. Crowell Co., 1945.

Slonimsky, Nicolas, *Lexicon of Musical Invective*. New York: Coleman-Ross, 1955, pp. 23-26.

Sonnemann, Ulrich, "Erotic Roots of the Dance." *Dance*, Oct., 1946, *12;* 32-33.

Stearns, Marshall W., *Story of Jazz*. New York: Oxford University Press, Inc., 1956.

Stoll, Otto, *Das Geschlechtsleben in der Völkerpsychologie*. Leipzig: Verlag von Veit & Comp., 1908, pp. 732-736.

Ulanov, Barry, *History of Jazz in America*. New York: The Viking Press, Inc., 1952.

van Bolen, Carl, *Geschichte der Erotik*. Wien: Verlag Willy Verkauf, 1951, p. 119.

Weissmann, Adolf, *Der Klingende Garten*. Berlin: Verlag Neue Kunsthandlung, 1920.

Welch, Christopher, *Six Lectures on the Recorder*. Oxford: Henry Frowde, 1911, p. 205.

DUNCAN MACDOUGALD, JR.

Nature of Sex

MERE recognition of sex, by both animals and man, is an old and ingrained capacity requiring remarkably little effort. It long antedates the origin of language. As written into the laws of earlier and modern nations, however, the words male and female, man and woman, have proved to be something less than definitive and unchallengeable. In other words, whenever numerous individuals of our species are involved or examined some persons unaccommodated by those two categories are readily found. On the other hand, the popular concept of the term "sex" is only superficially and terminally related to the immense area of intensely biological accomplishment and invention that should be discussed in this article.

Sex is somewhat less than a universal attribute of living things. Its absence comes nearest to being usual only in the lowest forms of life. It further differs from truly universal organismal properties such as irritability, metabolism, and self-duplication in that it requires two individuals for its full expression. Although distinct from reproduction, its several manifestations are oriented or associated with that universal attribute and with conjugation.

The distinction between sexual differentiation and sexual reproduction is important. Not all lower organisms that have sexual reproduction have (now discernible) sexual differentiation, although some of them may have lost it. Phages, for example, give no evidence of sexual differentiation even though they certainly perform a sexual recombination of genes as a result of the conjugation of single haploid chromosomes from different sources, which is followed by a process analogous to but not identical with crossing over. In some algae and fungi any cell may, apparently, conjugate with any other, although in the bacterium *Escherichia coli*, Lederberg found that this is not true; there the cells are of two types, which he calls male and female, the latter being the recipient and the former the donor of genes at conjugation. Thus it seems that sexual reproduction must have preceded sexual differentiation even though some forms now lacking the latter may have lost it while retaining sexuality. We do not know whether any present-day lower forms that lack sexual reproduction represent a persistence of the asexual evolution from earliest times; we do know that sexual reproduction has been lost by some now living groups whose ancestors possessed it.

The dimorphism observable at or toward the end of development of the body parts of two organisms of a species usually reflects the unequal influence on development processes of two genetically unlike zygotes. This is to say that the species prepares two kinds of zygotes in which the assortment of genes is such as will provide every offspring with one or the other of two rather regularly unequal impulses to sex differentiation. Each zygote (i.e., each completed union of two gametes) obtains its assortment of genes through the union (syngamy, amphimixis) of gametes, a sperm and an ovum.

In some large groups of organisms it is only the sperms that bring to zygotes the dissimilar genes that predispose to two unlike impulses to sex differentiation; in still other groups this inequality is carried in two forms of ova. In either case, within the species, every normal union of a sperm and ovum starts the organism —from its very beginning—with one or the other endowment that is ultimately expressed as a male or a female type or form. It remains to remark that an intricate series of "maturation" events or processes, collectively called meiosis, commonly occurs in sperms and ova and prepares them for sexual union. Those processes consist of chromosome conjugation and two cell divisions, in the course of which the diploid chromosome number becomes reduced to the haploid.

The usually persuasive role of genes, as thus described, is both vastly illuminating and much hedged or conditioned. The neatly established genetic mechanism that automatically produces fairly equal numbers of zygotes hereditarily predisposed to maleness and to femaleness provides the key to a comprehension of the existing distribution of sex in living things. Nevertheless, during the past half century it has also become clear that in widely different organisms, lower and higher, this "genic predisposition" to either of the two forms of sex can be overcome or reversed by some elements of the environment. Clearly, therefore, these facts require a substantial addition to what was stated concerning the form in which sex is represented in the zygote. Those foundations are indeed established in all unions of normal sperms and eggs, and in the quite simple manner partly noted above.

Presumably the preceding remarks make it evident that the *nature* of sex is an elusive topic —one that offers uncertainties and difficulties of approach. Its further pursuit requires an examination of several distinct areas of observation and inquiry.

Origin of Sexual and Sex-Related Processes

One naturally looks first to microorganisms of obviously lower and higher orders for evidence of stages through which the complex processes of syngamy and meiosis have been or could be attained. That search has proved both rewarding and confusing. At best it is an unfinished task. Simpler elements are indeed found, but how to read what is observed in the uneven record is often unclear. Though the viruses fail to exhibit sex differentiation (Visconti), there is good evidence that mating followed by genetic recombination occurs in

some of these simplest of living particles (Levinthal, 1956). When different strains were mixed, bacteria yielded genetic evidence of recombination of genes that resembles syngamy and meiosis (Lederberg and Tatum, in Wenrich, 1954). In the blue-green algae, in which organized chromosomes apparently are absent, no similar "sexual" phenomena have been found. Are these forms degenerate, despite recent evidence (Dodson, 1953) that they represent the ancestral type from which all other algae—some of them sexual—are derived? In fungi the array of both asexual and sexual states extends practically from conditions commonly found in bacteria to those typical of animals.

Protozoa also exhibit both asexuality and sexuality in wide variety. Here it is evident that the groups in which syngamy is most commonly found are those that are most highly evolved. In some species of groups, such as Sporozoa and Foraminifera, diploid-haploid sequences are well established. In Ciliates, however, the better known conditions are so different and unusual as to require more extended description. In *Paramecium aurelia,* "mating types" were discovered and later subjected to a genetic study of the consequences of nuclear reorganization of the type exhibited there. This led to the significant result that, in each case, autogamy, or conjugation of sister cells or nuclei, occurred instead of true "endomixis" (Sonneborn, 1941). It is therefore still unknown how many of the earlier described but genetically untested cases of protozoan "endomixis" may prove to be autogamy or parthenogenesis.

The conditions attending and governing *conjugation* in several species of Ciliates were further analyzed by Sonneborn (1957) and that aspect of sexuality was much clarified in this group of Protozoa. It was found that every clone of every strain has a definitely assignable "mating type." Conjugation does not ordinarily occur between individuals of the same physiological class or mating type; it occurs between individuals of complementary mating types. Commonly the mating type is inherited by its asexually produced descendants. Clones of the same strain are either of the same or of complementary mating types. When complementary they conjugate, but they do not conjugate when they are of the same type. As a rule, there are two and only two interbreeding types within a variety.

In all these major divisions of microorganisms, asexual nuclear processes, various but simpler than those that deal with fertilization and meiosis, have proved their capacity to *maintain* the species—or a close derivative of itself—during millions of years. Such simpler processes, moreover, have partly replaced or succeeded the full expression of sexuality in several orders of higher Metazoa. Such considerations now lead one and another observer to ask: Is it profitable to suppose that "sex" arose only once in some ancestral group and has been handed down to all descendants? Or is it more probable that it has arisen sporadically in many different groups? The course actually taken in the evolution of sexual from asexual reproduction remains as unclear as that of many groups of microorganisms themselves (Wenrich, 1954).

The reasons for the existence of the function of sexuality and sex became known through studies in genetics. We know no basic biological reason why reproduction, variation, adaptation, and evolution cannot proceed indefinitely without sexuality or sex. We may rightly regard sex as a premium, a luxury. An adequate statement of the precise ways in which this function brings advantages to the species possessing it must be sought elsewhere (Muller, 1932, Altenburg; Wright). It is useful in long-term competition with an asexual species. Its advantages are sometimes conferred through providing a favorable amount of heterosis (by which is meant the increased vigor of hybrids as compared with their pure-breed parents). Of greater significance is the fact that along with the mechanism of sex determination there arose the mechanism of Mendelian heredity itself, involving segregation of homologous chromosomes, independent assortment of non-homologous chromosomes, and crossing over.

Occasional or common reversion to the asexual condition, as this is expressed by budding, has occurred in willow and fern, in sponges, in coelenterates, worms, and tunicates—where it ends. Again, hermaphrodite groups (e.g., parasitic worms) apparently have arisen from a dioecious state. This functional hermaphrodit-

ism can be accounted for in terms of "reproductive economy" (Altenburg). Finally, the various aspects of parthenogenesis, although rare in plants, are not uncommon in lower animals. Parthenogenesis is regarded as a degeneration from the ordinary sexual process, and in some forms the unfertilized cells that thus reproduce the organism are regarded as ova in which the division that halves the number of chromosomes is omitted; in such forms as rotifers and hymenoptera, haploid males are produced. Artificial, pathological, occasional, seasonal, juvenile, partial, and total parthenogenesis are to be distinguished. The first-named type has let us observe a few "fatherless frogs." Crustaceans, insects, and especially rotifers display most aspects of parthenogenesis to their fullest extent. Within the plant world one meets the observation that in parasitic fungi sexual reproduction tends to disappear; there the stimulation to cell division, which is usually provided by the sperm, is apparently replaced by the stimulating action of waste products of the host.

In the animal world behavior patterns arise in relation to the act of mating and even to the period or season of mating. Because the rewards were vast, some guidance and assurance of suitably related *behavior* eventually became recorded in the ever-evolving nucleus. Higher animal forms thus acquired a sex drive or instinct, and also the parental instinct whose activities cluster around the care, defense, and feeding of young. Thus the earliest of these finer and socially pointed activities emerge only in association with the sexual mode of reproduction.

In retrospect, it is clear that asexual reproduction has populated the soil, waters, and atmosphere of earth with many thousands of species, each represented by countless individuals. Mainly, however, that product consists of relatively simple organisms; none, apparently, has reached extremely high animal organization under continuous asexuality. On the other hand, it is equally clear that sexuality presides within the several peaks of animal organization, and has proved itself the fount of those animal attainments and values which make earth and man a meaningful place and being. Thus, within a very few *animal* groups, it has furthered or fathered the emergence of qualities such as sociality, love, ethics, purpose, and civilization. The older and bulkier plant world, although often and liberally touched with sexuality, was never mated to *neural* development. Its much more modest offerings—apart from a seductive variety of species—are found to relate to the exposure of a maximum amount of surface, to immense and well-scattered storehouses of sugar and starch, and to an ever-greening blanket for aged continents.

The Genetic Basis and Interpretation of Sex

Those species that consist of two distinct types, males and females, were early observed (Correns, 1907, among others) to be strikingly analogous with Mendelian genotypes—one being the homozygote and the other a heterozygote. But where the species is of one type that functions as both male and female, another and different mode of appraising the unlike sex determination, within two localized areas, had to be sought. In maize, for example, only the genotype is present; and there the female functions are localized in the ear-shoot and the male functions are in the terminal tassel. Presumably, both the chromosomes and the genes are identical in these two sexual regions. Hence this localized difference in sex must be put on the same basis as that of any other *organ differentiation*, for example, the difference between legs and wings in birds—both of which are modifications of ancestral limbs.

In a few animal species visible distinctions between the chromosome groups of the two sexes were known for some decades before the genic interpretation of sex assumed its present form. During that period "sex-chromatin" was assigned a quite rigid qualitative value in sex determination; and this period was one of sharp controversy over the rigid or the plastic nature of sexual difference. The outcome of this dispute is that everyone now grants the existence of a quantitative element, in one or another form, to sexuality. Nevertheless, the visible distinctions found in later cytological studies have proved to be extremely important. They have provided visual proofs of the location or even the translocation of numerous genes—in both

sex chromosomes and autosomes. They have so helped to mature firm knowledge of genetic processes that this visual evidence is now often wholly unnecessary for genetic analysis.

Two notable *types* of visible sex-chromosome arrangements exist in male and female animals and these will be briefly sketched. In one type the sex chromosomes are designated X and Y, the latter being smaller or (after further losses) completely absent. In this chromosome configuration, somatic cells of females contain two X's (XX); those of males, only one X and one Y (XY or XO). Here it is the heterozygous sex, the male, that produces gametes (sperms) of unlike sex potency and sex-determining ability. Species conforming to this type include most insects, some fishes, frogs, and mammals, including man. In the other type, the heterozygous sex is female producing eggs of two sex potencies and sperms of identical sex potency. The formula applicable here is ZZ for males and ZW (or ZO) for females. In some of these cases W has weakened through losses, as has Y in the former. Species having this type of sex determination include most separately sexed higher plants, moths, butterflies, toads, reptiles, and birds. Certain special items are immediately noted.

The sex ratio in the moth, *Talaeporia tubulosa*, has been modified at will (Seiler, 1920) both by "overripening" the eggs and by forcing them to undergo their maturation division under high or low temperature. This heterogametic (ZO) female more often retains the Z within eggs matured at 30°–37°C. and yields (with the Z found in all sperm) a 62 per cent excess of males. Matured at 12°–16°C., the Z is more often discarded into the polar body and only 39 per cent of offspring are males.

In the case of specific, generic, and wide varietal crosses it has been shown (Haldane, 1921) that if among the offspring one sex is absent, rare, or sterile, that sex is the digametic sex.

Some bisexual species of protozoa, fungi, and algae have produced strains in which only one sex appears. It seems that the mutation of a single gene here eliminates the missing sex.

For purposes of genetic analysis of sex, insects and plants are preferable to vertebrates. In insects the development of all sex characteristics is a direct expression of gene action and owes almost nothing to products of sex glands.

The fruit fly, *Drosophila melanogaster*, early became an extraordinary source of information on general genetic processes. Ultimately, studies conducted on this single species—an extremely complex higher organism—have perhaps had more influence in shaping current thought on "sex," as this quality exists in ourselves and higher Metazoa, than have studies made on any other organism. But this statement does not apply to microorganisms. There, partly in consequence of the more prevalent notion of sex that derives from higher animals, conditions have led Sonneborn (1941) to suggest that, "perhaps we should abandon the concepts of male and female in unicellular organisms and view sexual union as brought about by copulation-conditioning factors, some of which operate to bring together the cells, others the nuclei." The Drosophila studies do not illuminate those forces and "factors" most related to *conjugation*, although it is conceivable that such forces, tensions, and inequalities involve the whole of *basic* sexuality. Definitely, however, the Drosophila studies certify the existence and behavior of an array of genes and processes assignable to one or another order of relationship to sex in higher animals. Surely, too, those studies add a dimension to sex itself.

Much new light on the inheritance of sex was supplied by Morgan in 1913, and a clear understanding of cases of sex-linked inheritance was provided in 1910. Later, the occurrence of chromosomal nondisjunction, with resulting effects on sexual expression, was described. The nature of lethal factors associated with the sexuality there manifest was explored. Mutations, in great number, assisted all genetic interpretation. The "mapping" of gene locations on all of the four chromosomes became possible. Gynandromorphs and intersexes were met there after they had been given genetic study elsewhere (amphibia, birds, moths); but the Drosophila perspective outlined above proved useful to their more adequate interpretation wherever they are found. Among earlier associates who shared with Morgan the development of this genetic perspective were Sturtevant, Muller, and Bridges.

Of special concern here are the varied and numerous results which were utilized (Bridges, 1939; Muller, 1932, 1958) to frame the theory of "genic balance"—a theory involving sexual and nonsexual genes and applicable alike in the uniting gametes, in the entire normal organism, and in localized elements of the latter when these become sexually aberrant through loss or gain of chromosomal or genic elements. We quote Bridges (1939):

The central idea of the genic balance formulation is that each character or feature of the adult is produced by the joint action of all genes of the entire complement of chromosomes. Some of these genes are tending to drive the development in a particular direction or to increase it while others are tending to drive development in the opposite direction or to decrease it. Each of the genes is a producer in this joint effect, though for each particular feature some genes are much more directly concerned or more effective than others. The stage of development shown by each feature of the normal adult corresponds to the net effect of these opposed tendencies or a point of balance between the plus and minus modifiers.

Bridges described three principal ways in which the normal balance can be shifted to cause a new end-point in character development. Castle and Jennings provided early information on the relation of genes to sexuality.

Early and significant facts concerning quantitative aspects of sexuality were reported by Goldschmidt from an analysis of intersexes obtained from crosses of varieties of the gypsy moth. European specimens of *Lymantria dispar* are sexually unremarkable, as are those of a related Japanese variety, *Lymantria japonica*. If, however, a Japanese male is mated with a European female, normal male offspring and females showing a number of modifications in the direction of the male type are produced. When these female intersexes are mated with their brothers, half of the females thus produced are normal, half are intersexual. The reciprocal cross, European male and Japanese female, produces normal females and males in the first hybrid generation; but when these individuals are interbred they produce a certain proportion of males with female characters. Analyzing these and related data, Goldschmidt (1911, 1915, 1920, 1938) drew several important conclusions: The potentialities of each sex are possessed by the other, since either can become intersexual. The type of sexual differentiation that the fertilized egg will pursue, including that for an intersex, is determined at the time of, and by the mechanism of, fertilization. The normal determination of sex is bound up with the usual (female = the digametic sex) mechanism. It is not, however, the mere presence of these factors that is decisive, but rather their quantitative effect during development. The mode of inheritance in these forms (ZW = female, ZZ = male) is described variously in the earlier and later studies. Normal sexuality as well as the array of intersexual forms all result from the activity of unequal ("strong" and "weak") genes starting their functioning at variable times and proceeding at uneven rates. Winge (1937) and Bridges (1939) have notably criticized some of these conclusions.

Max Hartmann has noted that he was early (1909) convinced that a general theory of sexuality and fertilization can prove correct only if an assumed bisexuality could be confirmed as relative, not absolute. His extensive experimental evidence in support of this conclusion followed appreciably later. He observed (1923), for example, in three parallel filaments of Spirogyra, that any cell of the left-hand member functioned as a proper male in fusions with cells of the middle filament (female); still other cells of this middle filament, however, simultaneously functioned as male with the filament apposed to its other (right) side. Thus, at some points of the long middle filament certain cells of this simple organism were behaving as males while other of its equivalent cells were behaving as females. Similar results were later reported for other algae (Hartmann), for fungi (Blakeslee), and for a protozoan (Cleveland). Hartmann and others obtained proofs for the existence of two physiologically different sorts of gametes; some evidence for the presence of sex-specific substances (gamones) in gametes, even in those of algae; and some information on the chemical nature of those substances and their governing role in fertilization. From these materials he formulated three theses as a basis and content for a general theory of sexuality. These include: (a) general bipolar (+ or −; male or female) double sexuality; (b) general

bisexual potency; and (c) different relative strength of the male and female determination. Concerning the latter, it is conceived that this is attained either *hereditarily* through the relative strength of the male or female hereditary factors (genes) or *nonhereditarily* as modified by corresponding or matching action of outer and inner developmental conditions (Hartmann, 1943, 1956).

In vertebrates both differentiation and growth of several organs intimately concerned with reproduction, along with several other "decorative" characteristics, are *immediately* dependent upon a dominating presence of hormone of one or the other of two sex types produced, respectively, in (mainly) testis and ovary. For most of these, the genetic control rests on its initial determination of the gonad type, testis or ovary. The sex organs under this hormonal control include the sexual ducts (sperm; oviduct, uterus, vagina), prostate, penis, and mammary glands. The types of hormones involved include androgens (male), estrogens (female), and, in some forms, progesterone. From both types of gonad—from either aspect of the genetic determination—some or much hormone of the contrary type is often produced. A profusion of other and "secondary" characteristics—such as hair growth, voice, temperament, body size, and conformation—are all swayed by sex hormone, and some of them by a specific gene or genes in addition. In man and other mammals all male embryos are subjected to the often adverse influence of the estrogens produced by the mother.

The genetic interpretation of sex, in animals especially, has been concerned very largely with the numerous items that collectively give the species a very marked sex dimorphism. One may therefore well remember that many species high in the scale of animal organization show extremely little of such dimorphism, and in this they much resemble most of the plant world. Male and female starfish and sea urchins can be identified only by a biologist. In the gastropod, *Triton*, the sexes are practically identical. Many fishes and amphibians are dimorphic only in minimal degree. Crustaceans and insects provide examples of dimorphism far exceeding that observed in man—or any mammal. In view of this panorama one may ask whether, in which way, or to what extent, these occasional accompaniments of sex are actually related to *basic* sexuality—a nearly universal property of organisms?

Some years after Mendelian heredity had become well known and made much of its contribution to sexuality, a book by Doncaster (1914) stated: "It is a remarkable thing that apart from the fundamental attributes of living matter no single character is so widely distributed as sex . . . and yet of its true nature and meaning we have hardly a suspicion."

Sex Reversal

It is now established that, practically throughout the ladders of plant and animal organization, individuals provided with the full normal genetic endowment for either maleness or femaleness may and do develop into replicas —fair or complete—of the opposite sex. Some of these reversals occur "naturally," as responses to environmental *changes* normally encountered in the life cycle; other reversals result from rare or extraordinary but nevertheless naturally occurring conditions imposed during development or later life; still others occur only under experimentally planned changes in the conditions under which the organism is forced to develop or live. Examples will be cited.

Sonneborn (1957, 1958) observed that, in certain stocks of *Paramecium multimicronucleatum,* the "mating type" of each individual cell changes twice a day. For example, the animals of one stock are type A from about 4:00 P.M. to 9:00 A.M.; they are type B from about 10:00 A.M. to 3:00 P.M. This rhythmic changing persists in total darkness, the time of the changes being determined by when the animals last saw "dawn." That is, the rhythm is determined by an internal biological clock which is "set" by the transition from dark to light. Different stocks have different rhythms.

Females of some northern species of oyster become males soon after spawning; the male phase is of variable duration, apparently depending upon water temperature and time of the previous spawning; the next cycle of female and male phases then follows (Orton, 1924; Spärck, 1924; Coe). The crustacean *Angiostomum* functions as a male when young, as a female when older. In a large snail (*Limax maximus*) individuals undergo a much longer succession of sexual changes: female, hermaphrodite, male, hermaphrodite, female. The young larva of the worm, *Bonellia,* becomes a male if permitted to remain attached to the pharynx of a female but a female if denied that attachment (Baltzer, 1914). Sex reversal— ascribed to factors such as changed nutrition, length of day, etc.—has been observed in many plants. Schaffner (1921, 1929) induced reversal in hemp and hops and regarded change in "functional gradients, or metabolism" as mainly responsible.

Richard Hertwig (1906, 1912) and his students Kuschekewitch (1910) and Witschi (1914, 1924) "overripened" frog eggs before permitting fertilization and obtained almost or quite all male offspring. In these tests (also, Crew, 1921) the genetically female zygotes, one half the total, usually achieved sex reversal. Female frog larvae (*Rana sylvatica*), kept after the thirty-fourth day at or near the maximum temperature (32°C.) which they can permanently endure, were transformed to males; and reversals from male to female occurred under quite low temperatures (Witschi, 1929).

Forcing certain species of doves to rapid and continuous egg production (reproductive overwork) accented, in a seemingly progressive fashion, some feminine qualities in both males and females (Whitman, 1919; Riddle, 1912, 1914, 1917). In cattle the female co-twin of a male fetus is partially and variously masculinized (freemartin) following certain contacts of the two circulatory systems (Keller and Tandler, 1916; Lillie, 1919). The freemartin's own sterile testis seems to be the source of the male hormone that directs the development of accessory and secondary sex characteristics (Willier, 1921). In some fishes the physiological exhaustion of the ovary by egg production is later followed by the development of testicular tissue and the appearance of external male characters in females thus depleted. In suitably young specimens of common fowl the surgical removal of the solely functioning left ovary is often followed by the development of a functional *right* testis and other male characters (Benoit, 1923; Domm, 1924). Single parallel and more striking cases of sex reversal have been recorded for two adult birds. Both a fowl (Crew, 1923) and a ring dove (Riddle, 1924) that had laid eggs and reared young had their (single) left ovaries destroyed by localized and later restrained tuberculosis; after an interval they developed testes and the fowl fathered offspring.

This list of cases of sex reversal was not more narrowly restricted because there is a possibility that the "conditions" attending sex reversal permit a more intimate view of the "nature" of sex than does the full description given above of the genetic basis of sex determination. One must conclude that some impulse or feature of the "physiological state" imposed by the hereditary constitution can be overridden by one or another element of the environment. And one may assume that "genic balance" merely or mainly predisposes to one or the other of these two "physiological states" —also that these latter are and remain decisive both in normal sex determination and in its reversal.

The sex reversal, also its *next* re-reversal, may be provisionally regarded in various ways. Perhaps it can be considered an adaptive response to a changed environment. Perhaps one may find help in Crew's remark that, "the individual is a female when it may be and a male when it must." Perhaps, and more precisely, one may regard both of those changes as responses to and expressions of altered metabolic (respiratory; oxidative) rate or intensity—a view that is sketched in the next section. On that view the male-to-female reversals imply compulsion to a lower rate; female-to-male reversals, compulsion to a higher "metabolic" rate.

Metabolic Sexual Difference

To this point the term "sexual differentiation," when applied to higher forms, has been used in its commonly accepted sense, namely, to describe those sexual characteristics or acquisitions that *follow* zygote formation and become evident only still later as development proceeds; indeed, after sex hormones become active in the embryo or at adolescence. Certainly many and diverse characteristics do thus arise in some forms, although others are almost deprived of them; certainly, too, these items

"associated" with sex are under genetic control.

But the studies for review here relate to a more primitive sexual difference that already exists in conjugant or gamete, and thus *precedes* all zygote formation and embryonic development. This core or basic difference can be viewed as one *source* (or perhaps the only one) of conjugation and of cellular union; and, conceivably, it could serve as a primitive impulse or ingredient for the meiotic mechanism. Its very early existence, in this stripped and basic form, would be in good accord with the deduction that sexual reproduction preceded *visible* sexual differentiation in microorganisms, and also with the observation that sex (like reproduction or respiration) is an almost universal property of organisms; at least its kinship with universal properties is sufficient to place it in a category perhaps higher than that which includes ordinary genetic characters. In any case, the following studies require a consideration of "sex" not as a consequence of cellular unions, but rather as a precursor and attendant of such unions.

A book, *The Evolution of Sex,* by Geddes and Thomson (1889; revised 1901) provided a naturalist's survey of sex in plants and animals, and the first "metabolic" theory of sex. The authors were not concerned with sex determination. They were most impressed by the great extent to which, in unicellular organisms, a smaller and more motile individual (male) pairs with a larger more passive one (female); and with the persistence of these same distinctions in the sexual elements, sperm and ovum, of all Metazoa and the higher plant world.

They regarded sexuality primarily as an early cellular differentiation that prepares such cells for conjugation. Their main conclusion was that the sexes express divergent metabolic function: "Male and female are the results and expression of relatively predominant katabolism and anabolism, respectively." Another prophetic but much emphasized part of their view (1901) maintained that, theoretically, environmental or experimental means are capable of overriding other factors involved in sex difference.

From certain wild species of doves an unusual distribution of the sexes in offspring was obtained by Whitman (1919) and Riddle (1917) when the parents were forced throughout the long breeding season to rapid egg production with no "nesting" permitted. This unexpected distribution was emphasized when the "reproductive overwork" was combined with crossing, i.e., pairing birds belonging to different genera (or species) which, in the *Columbidae,* still permits almost full fertility. Combining the preferred type of cross (its reciprocal might show no such effect) with crowded egg production usually resulted in a definite excess of males at the beginning of the breeding season but a fair or considerable excess of females at or near its termination late in the year. In these particular wild species it was also found to be more common for the "first" egg of the clutch of two to yield a male and the "second" a female.

This situation led to gross chemical study of the eggs, especially the yolks (ova) that yielded those quite aberrant sex ratios. Such studies seemed particularly promising because the female bird is digametic—producing ova prospectively male and female—whereas the sperms are sexually alike. The ova (yolks) obtained at or near the season's beginning were found to differ from those obtained later under forced or crowded egg laying in the following ways: Egg size and yolk size were smaller; the percentage of water and lipoids in the yolks was smaller; total energy *stored* in ova was less. These same differences were found, on the average, also to distinguish groups of "first" yolks from "second" yolks of the clutch. Thus, a double correlation of the chemical findings with the prospective sexuality was reported. The higher "storage" value found for the female-producing ova was held to be the equivalent of lesser *oxidizing* capacity. Here a clearly "metabolic" sex difference could be expressed indirectly in terms of oxidation rate or intensity —that of males being at a higher and that of females at a lower level (Riddle, 1912, 1917, 1927).

The twofold change of the *sex ratio*, observed in the preceding tests, seems beyond satisfactory explanation at present. A large excess of males in hybrid birds is usual; but when this is coincident with full fertility its explanation becomes questionable. Even the appeal to sex reversal leaves some observations unexplained. The observed excess of females under "over-work" conditions raises some questions now unanswerable. Does this procedure—like low temperature in the digametic moth, *Talaeporia tubulosa,* cited earlier—usually cause the Z chromosome to be discarded into the polar body? Perhaps so, but that too fails to account for the more than two grades or degrees of sexuality and of metabolism observed in the several studies on doves. Thus, typical copulation behavior in the hybrid females was found in highest degree among the females hatched after the longest terms of crowded reproduction (Riddle, 1914). And, parallel to this, their normally atrophying right ovaries persisted more often and became larger under the reproductive overwork (Riddle, 1916).

Furthermore, the measurements on chemical and metabolic difference represent conditions attained in ova prior to polar-body formation. They exhibit graduated or progressive change which, in terms of sex ratio, becomes reduced to two grades, male and female; these two, however, still further reflected the underlying metabolic difference—each showing more than one grade of masculinity and of femininity.

Since a metabolic sex difference was present and established in these dove *gametes* it was concluded that an identical sex difference in any or all later life stages of birds can no longer be *solely* or confidently regarded as a "secondary" sex character. Here that difference preexists as a primary one; and although the sex hormones unquestionably intervene in later life stages of birds—and there provide substantial warrant for characters termed secondary—that fact gives no warrant for wholly dismissing this primary differential which conceivably may extend into or through the critical embryonic development.

Female sporozoa were found by Joyet-Lavergne (1925) to store greater relative amounts of lipoid granules than do males. He later measured the Rh in several species of plants and in sporozoa, interpreted their sex difference in terms of rate or intensity of oxidation, and compiled a useful summary of such studies (1931).

Whatever is involved in fertilization is probably related to or involved in the origin or the nature of sex. It now seems probable, therefore, that Warburg's (1908) demonstration of increased respiration following activation of the sea urchin egg was a most important step in the biochemical approach to both fertilization and sexuality. That observation clearly acquires further meaning in the light of facts supplied by Loomis (1957) which demonstrate that additional pCO_2 (the unhydrated gas, not including the three forms of dissolved CO_2)—doubtless incident to all increased respiration—serves, specifically, in Hydra to provoke the change from asexual reproduction (budding) to the formation of male and female gametes. This change "is controlled by the environmental conditions under which they are cultured." Others had suspected that CO_2 is not merely a waste product and observed that it accelerates development in frog eggs (Bellamy) and in chick embryos (Spratt). Loomis says: "The extensive work of Child has shown that differentiation and morphogenesis are intimately affected by respiratory and metabolic gradients. It need only be mentioned here that all such gradients are, *ipso facto*, gradients of pCO_2." This intimate nexus of the active molecular end-product of the respiratory function with asexuality-to-sexuality control in Hydra, and with speed of early *cellular* embryonic differentiation in general, invites thought concerning its relation to a differentiation—sexuality—that appeared early, perhaps repeatedly, and persists in nearly all dominant classes of both plants and animals.

Two of the roots—the premises—of any "metabolic" theory of sex reach into areas scarcely open to observation or test; thus, traces of the vague and inexplicit necessarily now attach to such theory. Nevertheless, one is permitted to regard sex difference as *primarily* the outcome—initially in very simple organisms—of a preferential clustering of the universal respiratory (oxidative; "metabolic") function around *two* unequal (quantitative) levels. Internal conditions and tensions thus established—within and between two related microorganisms—may or may not have led to one or more of the items now observed in conjugation; many of the closely relevant facts are not merely now unknown but must perhaps forever remain so. That occasional advantage would have resulted from the union of two such cells, thus

pitched or set at differing oxidation-reduction levels, can scarcely be doubted. That an advantageous difference of this type—a type that probably promotes the process of conjugation whose limits or domain so nearly coincide with those of sexuality itself—would fail to obtain or to *retain* a certain yet unique relationship with the genetic mechanism, seems quite improbable.

Sexual Drive or Sexual Instinct

In view of the nature of the volume of which this article is a part, few words on this topic belong here. By way of orientation, however, it is notable that many higher animals possessing a well-developed nervous system (insects), or this in addition to a sex-hormonal system (vertebrates), have acquired an innate and often compulsive sexual urge. The large role of neural, or of neurohumoral, mechanisms in this eroticism is unquestionable; but the inherited tie to sexuality requires further notice.

The *innate* aspect of this urge strongly indicates that a now unisolated gene (or genes) is involved; that, although not a "sex" gene, its inheritance and maintenance have depended upon the mechanism of sex determination; and that this "tie" to sexuality warrants the accrediting to sexuality—in contrast with asexuality—of certain biological patterns that have developed incidental to the existence of this urge or drive. In large groups of higher animals these patterns include the several activities of all or most members of the species—activities that give form to the social organization of brood, herd, flock, or troop. Presumptive evidence for the existence of a gene associated with this drive will be found in the description of the parental instinct that follows.

The Parental Drive or Instinct

Although this sex-related activity is evidently at least one step further removed from truly basic sexuality than is the sex drive, there is warrant for a brief reference to one of its chapters here. That chapter provides a rare paragraph on the identification and cooperation of a gene and a hormone. Moreover, the outcome of this cooperation, when framed and exercised in the nervous and muscular organization of vertebrate species, is both a form of love and ultimately an evident promoter and progenitor of love in general.

Weisner and Sheard (1933) showed that a substance contained in crude extracts of the anterior pituitary elicits this series of parental activities in young male and virgin female rats. The hormone actually involved was found to be prolactin, which was likewise responsible for inducing the onset of "broodiness" in actively reproducing fowl and doves (Riddle, Bates, and Lahr, 1934, 1935, 1942). In fowl an important and firm limitation on the hormone's effectiveness was verified. It induced these activities in all laying hens of races that carry a gene for "broodiness." It failed in all except one of several tests on White Leghorn hens—a race from which that gene has been almost entirely eliminated by selective breeding (1934).

Although certain hormones and other substances—progesterone, testosterone, desoxycorticosterone, intermedin, LH, and phenol—could also notably elicit the parental response in rats, it was made probable that they do so through release of prolactin from the rat's own pituitary gland. Pellets of each of the three substances heading the above list proved capable of causing a marked release of prolactin from the pituitaries of ring doves. Remaining substances could not be subjected to this test. (Riddle and Lahr, 1944).

The Abnormal Sexual Psyche

"Man not only loves, but he knows that he loves." Unlike his forbears, in man the sex impulses that he feels are subjected to repeated review by his reason, and also even to the haphazard ways in which his attitudes and impulses are regarded by his human associates. According to modern psychology, the imprints of this total experience are stored deeply in his unconscious self—in his developing personality. Thus, the equipment of adult man for a compulsory yet uniquely superior social role and for ethical choice is far greater than that observable in any of his still surviving ancestors. This socially built equipment becomes the actual and ultimate base for an explanation of parts, although of parts only, of the psychology commonly ascribed to human sexuality. For example, a part of the sexual psyche of pseudo-hermaphrodites is doubtless ascribable to genetic and hormonal sources, as are the urges of normal persons generally; but a residue of personal orientation, urge, and identification may arise from this nonbiological area. In general, this view places credence in the evidence that some psychological functions established after birth are of cultural origin, although nearly or quite ineradicable (H. H. Young, 1937; A. Ellis, 1945; Money, Hampson, and Hampson, 1957).

Much of the phenomenon of transvestism in man is probably also such a "native" psychic product. That is, in addition to the constitutional factor of sexual *ability*, parts of this powerful urge may be grounded so immediately and completely in a social and environmental substrate, in cognitive experience, that a deeper nexus with one or the other frame of sex genes or of sex hormones need not be sought. By definition, these cases lie outside one or both such frames, and investigation seems to have shown instances in which this anomalous urge was mismatched to both genetic endowment and prevailing type of hormone production. Some further support for this view is found in evidence that sex impulses, and associated ideas and preferences, are both "normal" and widespread during very early childhood (Freud; Moll; Kinsey, 1948). Opportunity for that complex to become integrated in man into a distinct personality factor—apart from his biology, and differentiated within his psychology—seems thus assured.

References

Bridges, C. B., "Cytological and Genetic Basis of Sex." In E. Allen (ed.), *Sex and Internal Secretions*. Baltimore: The Williams & Wilkins Co., 1939.

Castle, W. E., "The Quantitative Theory of Sex and the Genetic Character of Haploid Males." *Proc. Nat. Acad. Sci. 16;* 783-788, 1930.

Ellis, A., "The Sexual Psychology of Human Hermaphrodites." *Psychosom. Med. 7;* 108-125, 1945.

Geddes, P., and Thomson, J. A., *The Evolution of Sex* (2nd ed.). New York: Charles Scribner's Sons, 1901.

Goldschmidt, R. B., *Mechanismus und Physiologie der Geschlectsbestimmung*. Berlin: Borntraeger, 1920.

Goldschmidt, R. B., *Physiological Genetics*. New York: McGraw-Hill Book Co., 1938.

Hartmann, Max, *Die Sexualität*. Jena: Fischer, 1943; Stuttgart: Fischer, 1956.

Joyet-Lavergne, P., *La physico-chimie de la sexualité*. Berlin: Borntraeger, 1931.

Kinsey, A. C. et al., *Sexual Behavior in the Human Male*. Philadelphia: W. B. Saunders Co., 1948.

Loomis, W. F., "Sexual Differentiation in Hydra." *Science 126;* 735-739, 1957.

Money, J., Hampson, J. G., and Hampson, J. L., "Imprinting and the Establishment of Gender Role." *A.M.A. Arch. Neurol. & Psychiat. 77;* 333-336, 1957.

Muller, H. J., "Some Genetic Aspects of Sex." *Am. Nat. 66;* 118-138, 1932.

Muller, H. H., "Evolution by Mutation." *Bull. Am. Math. Soc. 64;* 137-160, 1958.

Riddle, O., "Proofs and Implications of Complete Sex-Transformation in Animals." In *Verhandlungen des I Internationalen Congresses für Sexualforschung*. Berlin: Marcus und Weber, 1927.

Riddle, O., "Metabolism and Sex." In E. Allen (ed.), *Sex and Internal Secretions*. Baltimore: The Williams & Wilkins Co., 1932.

Riddle, O., and Lahr, E. L., "On Broodiness of Ring Doves Following Implants of Certain Steroid Hormones." *Endocrinology 35;* 255-260, 1944.

Riddle, O., Lahr, E. L., and Bates, R. W., "The Role of Hormones in the Initiation of Maternal Behavior in Rats." *Am. J. Physiol. 137;* 299-317, 1942.

Sonneborn, T. M., "Sexuality in Unicellular Organisms." In G. N. Calkins and F. M. Summers (eds.), *Protozoa in Biological Research*. New York: Columbia University Press, 1941.

Sonneborn, T. M., "Breeding Systems, Reproductive Methods, and Species Problems of Protozoa." In *The Species Problem*. Washington: A.A.A.S., 1957, pp. 155-324.

Wenrich, D. B. (ed., Symposium), *Sex in Microorganisms*. Washington: A.A.A.S., 1954.

Young, H. H., *Genital Abnormalities, Hermaphroditism, and Related Adrenal Diseases*. Baltimore: The Williams & Wilkins Co., 1937.

OSCAR RIDDLE

Negro, Sex Life
of the African and American

THE sexual behavior of Negroes, like the sexual behavior of peoples all over the world, can only be understood when it is studied in relation to the social and cultural context in which attitudes and patterns of behavior in regard to sex are formed.

In all of Africa, sexual behavior is rigorously regulated by the customs or the mores of the different African societies. Although the sexual behavior of Africans may strike Westerners as "immoral" or bizarre, this does not indicate licentiousness on the part of Africans. As the result of European contacts, however, social disorganization has resulted, involving unregulated sex relations and what might be regarded as immoral conduct. However, such conduct is immoral only from the standpoint of the traditional African norms governing sexual behavior.

The sexual behavior of the American Negro presents a different problem because here we are dealing with a people who have been stripped of their traditional social and cultural heritage and have been in the process of assimilating European culture over a period of three centuries or more.

Africa

The diversity of peoples and cultures in Black Africa, or Africa south of the Sahara, makes it difficult to generalize about the sex life of Negroes. Nevertheless, there are certain basic features regarding the social organization and the mode of making a living in the area that make it possible to note the important determinants and elements in the sex life of the people.

The Family

The most important feature in regard to the social organization of the people of this area is the primary role of the family and the obligations of kinship. Although the ideal African family is polygamous, because of the sex ratio and differences in wealth, the number of men with more than one wife is limited. The polygamous families consist of one man with several wives and several sets of children, forming a joint family; since these joint families include several generations, they form what are known as extended families. These joint or extended families are a part of a larger kinship group or lineage. The sex life of the African can only be understood in relation to these lineage groups, which provide the basis of social obligations of people who are engaged in making a living and reproducing themselves.

Religion

The first fact of importance in understanding the sex behavior of Africans is that it is determined largely by their religious attitudes, which are associated with procreation. It is necessary to emphasize this basic fact because what follows in regards to the sex behavior of Africans is a logical consequence. To the African, the values associated with sex are a part of the religious values associated with reproduction and not with sex itself, which, in the

Western mind, has become largely divorced from procreation. For example, Africans do not believe that female chastity is a virtue, except within the restraints imposed by the society. In many African tribes or societies, sexual relations between unmarried persons are permitted, and under certain circumstances unmarried men are permitted to have sexual relations with married women. Then there are societies that regard conception before the puberty ceremonies, which involve religious rites, with greater disapproval than conception before marriage. Moreover, the idea of sexual exclusiveness in marriage ceases to have meaning where there is childlessness, and a sister may substitute for a barren wife or men may father children of their dead kinsmen.

Premarital and Extramarital Relations

Let us consider more specifically the attitudes of certain tribes towards premarital sexual relations. Among the Mohammedans in the Nupe kingdom in northern Nigeria, there is a deeply rooted traditional respect for chastity and the sanctity of matrimonial ties. But because of a system of class polygamy that permits men of the privileged stratum to enjoy women of a certain stratum, there is much extramarital sexual relations on the part of sex-starved women who are cast aside when their husbands take other wives.

This is not representative, however, of West Africa. Among the Hausa, unmarried boys and girls sleep together with the connivance of their parents. In northern Dahomey, among the Somba, if a girl is betrothed as a child she may take a lover other than her future husband. The children she may have by the lover will be counted as her husband's children. Among the Dogon the period of sexual freedom begins as soon as sexual relations are permitted between a betrothed couple. Each takes a lover and their relations with the lovers are controlled by certain rules. For example, when the girl becomes pregnant, the relationship with her lover ceases. In other parts of West Africa premarital sex relations may occur but often on the condition that conception does not occur before the puberty rites. Among some of the peoples of West Africa, a bride's virginity is tested and a Hausa husband may publicize her

failure by breaking a pot outside her house. Sometimes when the girl is found not to be a virgin the bride-price is reduced.

In East Africa among the warrior people, such as the Masai, premarital sex relations are institutionalized. The young warriors, who are organized to defend the cattle, carry on sex relations with girls who form a part of the village especially organized for that purpose. However, if a girl becomes pregnant, the man is required to pay for her initiation ceremonies. Among the Nuer, sex relations are regarded as a phase of the courtship behavior. But among another tribal group, the Luhya, when a man intends to marry a girl he makes no sexual advances, but behaves in a formal manner. Among the Hima, who have no institutionalized premarital sex relations, a married man is expected to let his brothers have sex relations with his wife. Among the peoples of Central Africa, many of whom trace their descent through their mothers rather than through their fathers, much emphasis is placed upon the puberty rites. This involves close supervision of the girls in their relations with males, and great emphasis is placed upon seeing that the girl does not become pregnant before initiation, which involves much instruction concerning sex. Among the Yao, for example, the initiation of girls is concluded with defloration. Among some of the peoples of this area, there was once a test of virginity at initiation. Some of the patrilineal tribes in Central Africa once attempted to supervise the girls before initiation, but it does not appear that much importance was attached to premarital virginity.

Turning to South Africa, one finds that among most of the peoples in this area sexual relations between boys and girls have been permitted. The warlike Zulus allowed freedom of sexual intercourse to couples who were planning to marry. But among other tribes there were various restrictions upon premarital sexual relations. For example, the Kgatla in the Bechuanaland Protectorate severely condemned prenuptial sex relations and if an unmarried girl became pregnant she was humiliated and publicly mocked and her child was generally killed.

It has already been noted that among the Mohammedanized peoples in the urban areas of Nupe the system of class polygamy has resulted in extramarital sex relations on the part of women. Here we are especially concerned with the general phenomenon of extramarital relations that occur in many parts of Africa. Among the Hausa people in Nigeria, where the women are subject to the Mohammedan rule of seclusion of wives, prostitution has been a long-established means by which women escape from marriages entered into against their will. Similarly, among many African peoples extramarital sex relations are permitted when the husband is impotent. There are tribes in Nigeria in which married women who have not borne children may have sex relations with other men because it is believed they may thus increase their chances of pregnancy.

But it should be emphasized that the freedom permitted in regard to premarital and extramarital relations does not mean that there are promiscuous sex relations. Where either occurs it is carried on according to established customary practices. Moreover, the general disapproval of sexual promiscuity in every part of Africa is indicated by the inability of promiscuous women to enter into marriage relations. Among the Luhya, to whom reference has been made, a girl who has had more than two or three love affairs will have little chance of marriage. Among the Nuer in the Sudan, a woman of easy virtue will have lovers but no offers of marriage, and if she has borne a child she will most likely become a prostitute. Once more it must be pointed out that, since sex is regarded as fundamental to procreation, the crucial factor in most parts of Africa is whether a girl has had sex relations before or after initiation.

Impact of Western Civilization

Important changes have occurred in Africa as the result of the impact of Western or European civilization, and it is necessary to indicate the nature of these changes in the sex behavior of Africans. The introduction of commercial crops has not only affected the system of subsistence agriculture but has also tended to uproot the basis of the traditional social life. By drawing males into the market economy it has created an imbalance in the sex ratio in rural communities. Men leave their wives and

children and unmarried men no longer grow up under the supervision of their fathers. As a result, the women are left to seek new sexual companions. Since the woman's economic function is disrupted or lost, she begins to regard sex as a personal pleasurable experience no longer associated with procreation.

Perhaps the most important direct effect of Western contacts upon sex behavior is due to the influence of Christianity. The Christian missionaries have generally regarded with disapproval the initiation rites and ceremonies, which in their eyes were immoral. A more objective view reveals that these rites were the means by which sex was socialized in that it was surrounded by religious attitudes that formed the basis of human solidarity. When these traditional sex behaviors were frowned upon or disallowed, the African girl and the boy grew up without any moralizing influence. The sex impulse became an individual biological matter to be satisfied in an adventitious manner.

The "freeing" of the sex impulse from the social control and moralizing influences of traditional African culture reached its extreme form in the towns and cities in Africa, which owe their existence to European industry and commerce. In the cities that had existed before European contacts, kinship had continued to form the basis of social life; in the new cities the old kinship basis has been undermined or destroyed. In its place has come, as in the West, a type of social existence that is based on a market economy, with money and wages. Social relations have thus become secularized. The traditional marriage payment, which often included cattle that had been carefully reared by the boy with a view to his betrothal and marriage, has become a simple financial transaction devoid of the sentiment and religious feeling that had bound the two families in the marriage payment or bride-price. With the migration of women, who have lost their traditional economic function, to towns and cities, illegitimacy and prostitution have become problems in the new cities of Africa. Sex is no longer associated with procreation and has lost its moral or religious significance. The purely hedonistic aspect of sex has become the chief value. It is in the new cities, with uprooted men and women, that sexual promiscuity flourishes.

In the modern cities, not only has social disorganization taken place, but life has been reorganized on a new basis, according to novel patterns and standards of behavior. New classes are coming into existence as the result of changed social distinctions and different sources of income and wealth. In the cities, where the most Westernized elements form the upper social strata, many have adopted the sex attitudes and patterns of behavior of their Christian teachers. Unfortunately, very often the so-called public sex morality of the West is not a true indication of their real sex behavior. Among the more sophisticated Westernized men and women are many who live according to what they find the most desirable in the sex attitudes of both Africans and Christians.

United States

What has been pointed out in regard to the sex life of the Negro in the new cities of Africa provides a convenient transition to a discussion of the sex life of the Negro in the United States.

Plantation Life

The Negroes who were brought to the English colonies and the United States were stripped almost completely of their cultural heritage. This was the result of the manner in which the Negro slaves were captured and sold on African slave markets, not to mention the manner in which they were "broken into" the plantations in the West Indies and in the United States. During the intertribal wars and the slave raids in Africa, the victims of the slave trade were torn from family and friends, and clan ties were broken. They were herded in barracoons or "concentration camps" on the coasts of Africa to await the slave ships that would transport them to the New World. In the New World, no respect was shown for kinship and other ties or for the African concept of what was normal or what was expected in sex behavior. The African Negro's sex appetite was not extinguished during this process. There are records of slaves in Louisiana who, being unable to find mates among the female Negro population, went into the woods and mated

with Indian women. This is indicative of an important fact, that the plantations demanded predominantly male Negroes and that it was not until 1840 that there were as many female Negroes as male Negroes in the United States.

Therefore, in considering the sex life of the American Negro, one must begin with the fundamental fact that at the beginning of his history in the United States his sexual behavior was determined by raw sex impulses and that these impulses were restrained by the discipline of the plantation regime. It was only gradually that the Negro's sexual behavior was socially and institutionally regularized, resulting from his acculturation and the development of the Negro community.

Under the plantation regime there was considerable variation in the sex behavior of Negroes. These variations were related to the extent to which the discipline of the plantation, and the consequent relations between Negroes and whites, enabled the Negroes to acquire the habits, attitudes, and sentiments of the whites. Under the most favorable conditions, the slaves acquired, through close association with whites, their ideas and attitudes concerning sex. This was achieved largely through moral and religious instruction, during which the slaves became a part of the white family group and participated in their religious life. This moral and religious discipline in sexual behavior was given a substantial basis in the opportunity to be "married," although not legally, according to some form, and to maintain a "conventional married" life. Such favorable conditions were the lot of a relatively small number of slaves: the house servants and the skilled mechanics. For the great body of slaves, the field hands, sexual relations between men and women were more or less casual and could be broken off at will or ended when the master sold his slaves or decided to break up sexual unions that displeased him.

Amalgamation of Races

An important aspect of the sex life of the Negroes during slavery and even since their emancipation has been the amalgamation of the races. From the beginning of the enslavement of Negroes there has been racial mixture, almost all of which has been outside of marriage or law. About one-twelfth of the slave population was comprised of mulattoes or mixed bloods, and three-eighths of the Negroes who were free before Emancipation were of racially mixed ancestry.

The conditions under which this racial mixture occurred have had a profound effect upon the attitudes of the Negro woman—but more especially of the mulatto woman—toward sex. The sexually seductive Negro or mulatto woman has been romanticized and all sorts of beliefs have grown up about the peculiar sexual attributes of the Negro, but more especially the mulatto, woman.

There has been, in addition, the influence of a racially mixed group who made up the backbone of the free Negro population because of their superior cultural and economic status. It was from this group that an intermediate caste was formed in some southern cities, such as in New Orleans. Institutional family life took root among these Negroes, and Western patterns of sex behavior and sex attitudes became a part of their traditions. These sex attitudes and patterns of behavior of the well-to-do free Negroes were practically the same as those of the slave-holding and propertied whites in the South, just as the sex life of the poor elements among the free Negroes did not differ from the free-and-easy sex behavior of the "poor whites."

Influence of Emancipation

The Civil War and Emancipation not only removed the discipline that the slave-holders had exercised over the sex life of the slaves but also tended to uproot their customary ways in sex relations. Thousands of Negroes became footloose and, wandering about the country, attempted to satisfy their sexual impulses whenever they had the opportunity. Many of them were especially attracted to the cities, where disorganization of Negro family life and sexual promiscuity have had a long history. Moreover, it was during this period that venereal diseases began to spread among the poor and illiterate Negroes.

After a period of much social disorganization the great mass of the Negro population in the South settled down to a way of life based on a modified form of the plantation system. It was among the rural Negro people that certain modes of sex behavior developed which may be fairly adequately described in a general way. Among the people the sexual impulse was regarded as a natural or human impulse that required satisfaction. There was no feeling of guilt about the desire to seek sexual satisfaction, except in those areas where the Protestant churches had introduced a puritanical attitude toward sex. Even in these circumstances they rationalized between the "natural" impulse to seek sexual satisfaction outside of marriage and the teachings of the Church. For example, following the Civil War in a number of localities in the South, there sprang up the quasi-theological doctrine that "two clean sheets cannot soil each other." According to this doctrine, premarital or even extramarital sexual intercourse between two Christians was not sinful, but such a relationship on the part of a Christian with a "sinner," or with a person who had not been converted, was sinful. It should not be inferred from this, however, that sex had only a hedonistic value. Although sex was natural and pleasurable for the masses of Negro folk, sexual freedom was a male prerogative; for women it was not so much a pleasurable experience as the means to reproduction, the means by which she fulfilled her destiny.

In the isolated rural areas of the plantation South where the Negroes were only slightly influenced by European ideas and sentiments regarding sex, there was considerable indulgence toward adolescents in their sexual contacts. When these sexual relations resulted in children, the children generally became members of the girl's family, even when the boy wanted to marry the girl, because her parents thought that she was too inexperienced to assume the responsibilities of motherhood or that the boy did not have sufficient economic means to support a family. Consequently, a Negro girl during a series of sexual contacts might have had three or four children by the time she was old enough or mature enough to marry. Her husband would accept her children as a part of the family, to which he might bring his children by other contacts and add children by his wife. Often, because of the mobility of males, one could come across Negro families with only females representing two or even three generations.

Such sexual behavior on the part of rural Negroes cannot be regarded as typical of all Negroes. It reflects a number of economic and more especially of social and cultural factors that have influenced the sex behavior of Negroes in the plantation South. In the areas outside of the cotton plantation areas, where Negroes have assimilated more of European sexual mores and have developed a community life based on land ownership, their sexual behavior approximates that of the whites. For example, the Negro church has exercised an effective control over premarital and extramarital sexual relations. It is regarded as a serious sin or social offense in some communities for a girl to become pregnant. In the areas in the upper South, especially among the Negro landowners who take pride in their social position and "purity of morals," for a girl to become pregnant before marriage has resulted in disgrace and expulsion from the community.

Urban and Northern Migration

The influence of these social and cultural factors upon the sexual behavior of Negroes has been greatly affected by the migration of Negroes to the cities, especially to the cities of the North. Rural folk who had maintained a relatively stable family life based upon habit and sentiments developed in the same household were unable to withstand the disintegrating effects of the urban environment.

All forms of social disorganization resulted from city life, and the most striking effects of this were on family life and the control of sex behavior. The most important effect upon sex life was the change in the attitudes of women. The males continued to seek sexual satisfaction wherever they could find it, and this continues to be reflected in the high illegitimacy rates among Negroes in cities. But the attitude of the urban Negro woman changed: sex became divorced from procreation and its pleasurable aspect was enhanced. The rural Negro woman might enjoy sex, but it was devoid of the romantic element that it acquired in the urban environment. Romanticization and even glorification of sex were stimulated by the songs and movies that are a part of the social world of Negroes in the slum areas of American cities.

Negro Middle Class

In the cities of the South as well as in the cities of the North, although more especially of the North, a new social stratification among Negroes resulted in a sharp differentiation of their sex behavior. In the older stratification of Negro society there was an upper class that formed what resembled a superior caste. It was differentiated from the great mass of the Negro population by lighter skin color, more education, and better income, although not entirely by occupation. In addition to their white ancestry, the most important factor was their standard of civilized behavior—which meant primarily that they maintained a conventional or puritanical code of sexual ethics. In the newer class structure that has emerged as the result of urbanization, the old puritanical sexual ethics have been lost, although they continue to influence the thinking and behavior of the new middle class which has become dominant in the Negro community.

The new middle class rejects anything associated with the Negro folk, and the free-and-easy sex life of the Negro folk is regarded as the most distinguishing characteristic of this class. But this respectable middle class, which represents on the one hand a pseudosophistication and on the other hand an absence of deeply rooted institutional controls of sex, cannot escape from its social origins; consequently, there is much hypocrisy about sex and much sexual irregularity. The importance of sex to this class is indicated by their extreme sensitivity to any charge that Negroes are freer or more easy in their sex behavior than whites. There is an element among this class whose behavior is more influenced by the churches and who inculcate in their children and maintain sexual conducts according to the accepted American standards. Among this stratum of the Negro middle class the tension between the sexual urge for gratification and the conventional standards is reduced to a minimum.

Psychosocial Aspects of Negro Sex Behavior

Here one should consider some of the psychosocial aspects of the sexual behavior of Negroes, which are closely related to their inferior status in American society. First, it should be noted that the Negro male has never been permitted to play the male role as defined by American culture. Second, white women have been taboo so far as Negro males are concerned. Third, the Negro woman has been defined mainly as a sexual object. All three of these facts have influenced the sex behavior of Negroes in the United States. For the Negro male, sex has often been the means by which he has asserted and attained his masculinity. Much of the sexual promiscuity of Negro males has been due to this rather than to any great sexual energy or powers that overrode social controls. Their sexual prowess has been a means of overcoming their inferior status not only in family relations but in relation to the white world. It is not without significance that the nicknames of some prominent Negroes indicate sexual prowess.

When the Negro male cannot attain his maleness through normal sex outlets, there is always the female role open to him. After all, the Negro woman was able to adjust to American society in a way that the Negro male could not do normally. Not only does the color line tend to disappear among homosexuals, but in the female role the Negro male no longer offers a challenge to white male dominance. Perhaps, and this is speculation, the Negro male homosexuals who publicly exhibit their deviation may represent the sexual adjustment of the Negro male to American society. Since the Negro woman's role has been defined largely as sexual, her emphasis of sex conforms to her position in American society.

The policy of the United States toward Negroes has only recently changed from one of separate development to one of integration. One can only speculate therefore upon the future sex behavior of the Negro. The lower classes in the Negro community will probably continue to lead a more or less free sex life. But as larger numbers rise to middle-class status they will adopt the conventional sexual patterns of Americans.

Whatever influence the Negro may have had on the sexual behavior of Americans has been through the subtle means of music rather than through any consciously formulated philosophy in regard to sex.

References

Ashton, Hugh, *The Basuto*. London: Oxford University Press, 1952.

Busia, K. A., *Report on a Social Survey of Sekondi-Takoradi*. London: Crown Agent for the Colonies, 1950.

Dollard, John, *Caste and Class in a Southern Town*. New Haven: Yale University Press, 1937.

Duvallon, Berquin, "Travels in Louisiana and the Floridas in the Year 1802." *J. Negro Hist. 2;* 172-181, 1917.

Evans-Pritchard, E. E., *The Nuer*. London: The Clarendon Press, 1941.

Frazier, E. Franklin, *The Negro Family in the United States*. Chicago: University of Chicago Press, 1939.

Herskovits, Melville, *The American Negro: a Study in Racial Crossing*. New York: Alfred A. Knopf, Inc., 1928.

Hollman, Ellen, *Rooiyard*. Capetown: Oxford University Press, 1949.

Kardiner, Abram, and Oversey, Lionel, *The Mark of Oppression*. New York: W. W. Norton & Co., Inc., 1951.

Labouret, Henri, *Les paysans d'Afrique occidentale*. Paris: Gallimard, 1941.

Nadel, S. F., *A Black Byzantium*. London: Oxford University Press, 1942.

Park, Robert E., "Negro Home Life and Standards of Living." *Ann. Am. Acad. Polit. Soc. Sci. 49;* 149-163, 1913.

Phillips, Arthur (ed.), *Survey of African Marriage and Family Life*. London: Oxford University Press, 1953.

Powdermaker, Hortense, *After Freedom: A Cultural Study in the Deep South*. New York: The Viking Press, Inc., 1939.

Radcliffe-Brown, A. R., and Forde, Daryl (eds.), *African Systems of Kinship and Marriage*. London: Oxford University Press, 1950.

Reuter, Edward Byron, *The Mulatto in the United States*. Boston: Badger, 1918.

Schapera, I. (ed.), *Western Civilization and the Natives of South Africa*. London: Routledge, 1934.

E. FRANKLIN FRAZIER

Nutrition, Health, and Sexuality

IT would be difficult to quarrel with the assertion that most creatures occupy themselves chiefly with obtaining food. It is also obvious that although organisms eat for individual survival, nourishment serves the purpose of species survival as well. In fact in some extreme cases—such as those of a few varieties of insects and spiders in which the female eats the male after copulation, or of the queen bee whose royal jelly makes her the sole procreator and sole long-living insect in the hive—nourishment may primarily be designed for reproduction. For some living organisms the procreational drive sometimes takes precedence over the nutritional drive. In one species of tropical fish, for example, the male carries the eggs and newly hatched young in his mouth for a period that may last as long as two months, during which time he is constrained by this task to fast. Aside from these cases, we cannot enumerate all the examples of nutritional preparations for procreation that take place among the astronomical variety of life forms on our planet.

Words such as *starved, hungry,* and *satiated* may serve both for food and for sex, and the frequency with which the term *sexual appetite* is heard should make us realize the connection between these drives in the consciousness of human beings. In addition, both drives in man are fraught with social and religious attitudes, which vary from culture to culture. In many regions food and sex are concomitants of a code of social behavior, a stranger being offered food and a bed companion in the course of normal hospitality.

In this article, however, we are primarily concerned with the ways in which nutrition affects sexuality. For civilized man the concept of sexuality requires the closest definitions and elucidations and must include fertility since even the earliest, prenatal nutritional experience prefigures the maturation of the sex organs, qualitatively as well as quantitatively.

Medical research indicates that under normal circumstances there is an equation between fertility and the libidinous drive. For example, the tendency for there to exist seasonal cycles in birth (the highest point in the cycle being February and March, the lowest September and October) may be related to the naturally larger number of foodstuffs available during the spring months and the consequent increased vitamin content in the average diet. The entire glandular system of the individual becomes activated by vitamins that are the chemical cousins of hormones and are vital to the proper functioning of the endocrine network in the body. Examples are the relation of vitamin E to pituitary-gland function, and the fact that the specific equivalences between vitamins A, C, and D and the various sex hormones are known to have expedited the treatment of cases of infertility and impotency.

Trace Elements

Even trace quantities of elements involved in co-enzyme systems with vitamins and hormones may, if inadequate in the diet, dictate the difference between fertility and infertility in the human animal, and between potency and impotency. The thyroid gland, which is closely bound with sexual vigor and successful gestation, is totally dependent upon the element, iodine. There was a time when goiter, a florid manifestation of iodine deficiency, was a common sight in landlocked areas where iodine could not be obtained through the eating of fish. Today in Europe and the United States, the incorporation of iodine in salt has all but eliminated this ailment, but not the suboptimal thyroid condition that still prevails among large numbers of persons whose daily intake of iodine is insufficient to maintain adequate thyroid function. Reduced fertility, libido, and potency is not the sole sequel to this insufficiency; it also leads to a general faulty metabolism of the cells of tissues, organs, and arteries with a resultant inefficiency of their function and a body-wide loss of vigor. The attribution of mild aphrodisiac capacities to shellfish may involve the relatively high quantity of iodine they contain and the sexually stimulating, though temporary, impact of elevated thyroid output it brings about.

This is true not only for iodine but for other trace elements as well; and the awareness of their importance in plant and animal vigor has led horticulturists and nutritionists into an arduous study of soils to determine the effect of minutely varying quantities of these elements on the vigor of plants and of the animals that eat them. Trace elements such as iron, copper, zinc, manganese, boron, molybdenum, cobalt, and others comprise less than 1 per cent of the weight of an average plant, but the presence or absence of these substances may influence the vitality of the entire organism and thus sexual vigor. The inability of organisms to resist deterioration and vital decline may rest in one or several cumulative nutritional "snubs" sustained prenatally or after birth. Stress caused by malnutrition may instigate biochemical "twisters," the involutional nature of which narrows to a base of ultimate decline in every area of function—of which infertility, depressed libido, and potency are but a few.

In a region in Florida, for example, 15 per cent of the children were anemic. In another region close by only 3 per cent suffered from this condition. Investigation of this anomaly revealed that the soil in the area of excessive anemia contained one-tenth the iron, one-half the copper, and one-fifth the phosphorus and calcium of the area where less anemia prevailed. Iron and copper are essential to the formation of hemoglobin, the compound in red blood corpuscles that carries oxygen to every cell of the body. A body whose cellular efficiency is impaired by anemia is on the way to subtle degenerative effects stemming from a metabolic lethargy on the cellular level that allows toxic products of incomplete oxidation to be formed, such as pyruvic acid, autoacetic acid, and lactic acids.

Metabolism is the sum total of chemical changes in the body. Adequate nutrition without adequate oxygen is akin to burning a candle in a partial vacuum. It will burn feebly, perhaps sputteringly. Even with adequate oxygen, efficient metabolism still depends on an army of additional agents, such as hormones, which serve as catalytic agents for cellular processes that could not take place otherwise. Thyroxin is thought to be the principal metabolic accelerator, although not the sole agent. Even with increased thyroid, increased food intake is necessary to provide adequate raw material for the accelerated processes.

This implies that the body has a biochemical "knowledge" not completely available to us and that vitamins and minerals are utilized by glands and other organs to fabricate biochemical substances in the quantity and balance required for health and in the amounts geared both to the productive capacity of the organ in question and to the capacity of the body at large to sustain them.

Nutrition of Prenatal and Early Childhood Periods

Thus, even a prenatal nutritional flaw might affect sexuality, because at that stage of development flaws may be built into an organism's structure. In such cases, although potency may be improved by treatment during maturity, fertility may be forever lost.

Dr. Jan Raboch, of the Karlovy University Sexological Department in Prague, found, on reviewing the histories of 1,000 cases of male sterility, that some of the patients not only were the last or penultimate children in large families but that their childhood nutrition had been deficient. Hypogonadism, resulting in inadequate development of the sexual organs and tissues, was as high as 43.3 per cent in this group. The deduction from this study was that each pregnancy reduces a mother's vitamin E and A supply, unless it is unusually high to begin with or adequately replaced.

Dr. Raboch cites research—published in *Virchow's Archives* of 1924—in which changes in human genitalia during starvation were observed. Under these conditions, before the pubertal age, germinal tissues disappear and are replaced by connective tissue. Testes before puberty are far more sensitive to malnutrition than are fully developed testes. During famine conditions the provision of vitamins A and E appears to be inadequate for the fetus and for the newborn child. The human infant, in fact, is born with very short reserves of vitamin E, which is assumed to be the antisterility vitamin. This shortage is usually compensated for by mother's milk, which contains—when the mother is adequately nourished—.940 mg. per 100 cc. compared to .060 mg. per 100 cc. in cow's milk. Vitamin E reserves allow for more efficient utilization of other vitamins in the body, particularly vitamin A in the gonadal sphere. Both vitamins A and E are fat-soluble, and are thus stored in the body instead of being excreted daily like water-soluble vitamins. In the case of both vitamin A and E, too, time may provoke an increment or a deficiency, depending on the diet. Vitamin A can attain a level where it may exert a toxic effect on the body, but so far no toxic limit has been established for vitamin E.

Swiss researchers found that the consumption of vitamin E in the newborn is very high, which confirms the belief that the quantity that passes from mother to child depends upon whether her store or replacement of the vitamin is adequate. When the mother has a small amount of vitamin E, less of the vitamin passes to the fetus via the placenta. Hence, the last children born in a family are furnished with smaller quantities of vitamins E and A than their earlier siblings. When, in addition, starvation aggravates this situation, the latecomer suffers an added nutritional shortcoming.

The depleted store of these fat-soluble vitamins (depleted by siblings) cannot be adequately compensated for postnatally. In France, for example, the vitamin E level in women was found to be very much lower in 1943 than in 1942 because of the shortage of nourishing food during the German occupation. In Holland, also, during the German occupation the level of vitamin E in the population suffered a comparable drop for the same reason.

Hence it would appear that the nutritional preparation for potency and fertility begins very early in life—in fact, prior to birth. The critical periods for the germinal glands are the first year of life, when the testes grow rapidly, and the pubertal period, when the germinal epithelium begins seminiferous activity. Dr. Raboch states that hypogonadism and degenerative changes in germinal tissue, brought about by a deficiency of A and E vitamins in the first year, are irremediable. He advocates that these vitamins be given prophylactically to pregnant mothers who have already given birth to several children. They should also be given to children who are bottle-fed right after birth, and especially to the last male descendants of large families. Symptoms of E and A hypovitaminosis do not usually appear in childhood but result in testicular changes that are not correctible by the later administration of these vitamins.

Vigor

It is regrettable that many infertility cases do not come to light until maturity, when impregnation is attempted. It is an uncontestable fact that amongst most people in Western society little conception takes place in proportion to sexual activity. A male may be fertile and impotent at the same time, or infertile and potent; and a woman may be analogously frigid and virile, or sexually responsive and barren. Although under normal circumstances, which rarely exist, fertility and potency parallel one another, these situations confront us with complexities in terms of the sexual apparatus in humans and confront us too with the need to define sexuality in humans as closely as possible by way of establishing a ground where it can meet with nutrition in a meaningful manner.

Castration obviously affects sexuality in a total way. The entire sexual mechanism is eliminated and there is nothing for psychological, nutritional, or any other factors to affect. But with subfertile and fertile individuals it is difficult to determine where vigor ends and interpersonal patterns, custom, training, trauma, cultural circumstances, intelligence, conditioning, and compensation take over in sexual capacities and activities. To deal as fully as possible with the influence of nutrition on sex, we must establish a qualitative as well as a relatively quantitative sexual norm and eliminate conditions that cannot be altered by nutrition. We can start by conceding influences of a psychological nature.

Vigor is the greatest single determinant of sexuality. It is the synergistic product of heredity, environment, age, and nutrition. It can be profoundly altered by psychic circumstances, which vary widely from person to person. Aside from these intangibles vigor is elusive, if not intricate, in its biological sense. It is not only the manifestation of energy in an organism. It may be the sign of the emergence of effective energy: energy that emerges as power and stamina after what is basically produced is drained off by inefficient patterns of behavior, external and internal stresses on the organism, idiosyncratic compensations or decompensations, or individual endocrinological orientations—which may little reflect on a person's essential vigor but which may charge his behavior up or down sexual avenues in parallel or paradoxical manifestations.

Observations made in Rochester, Minnesota, between 1939–1942 in an investigation of patients deprived of thiamine were summed up by Dr. Russell M. Wilder in the Milbank Memorial Fund's *The Biology of Mental Health.* Ten subjects who were well adjusted, congenial, industrious, and vigorous were subjected to a period of B₁ deficiency, the intake being about 450 micrograms. Their behavior pattern changed. They became forgetful, quarrelsome, apathetic, confused, depressed, restless, and anxious. These disturbances of attitude were aggravated by a loss of vigor and a disregard for morality in sex.

Dr. Morton S. Biskind, in a paper entitled "Nutritional Deficiency in the Etiology of Certain Sex-Endocrine Disorders," emphasizes the paradox in terms of the varying effects of B vitamin deficiency in the male and the female. While a B vitamin deficiency will decrease the libido of the male, the same deficiency will increase the female sex urge, because in B vitamin deficiency the liver continues to inactivate male androgens but not female estrogens, thus upsetting the androgen-estrogen balance in the body. A rise of the estrogen level in the male will depress his libidinous drives; in the female it will intensify it. Dr. Biskind points out that B vitamins are vital for hepatic inactivation of estrogens, and a husband and wife experiencing the same deficiency by sharing the same diet will be in comparable states of vigor in respect of the B vitamins but in opposite sexual states.

The effect of vitamin E is different. In 1928, Dr. H. M. Evans, one of its discoverers, found that animals receiving vitamin E showed better growth and vigor in addition to increased libidinous response, fertility, and potency. Practically all animals receiving only a small amount of wheat germ oil showed a daily improvement in constitutional state. Evans concluded that the loss of sexual interest resulted from a constitutional inferiority rather than specific testicular impairment.

Vigor probably represents—according to Dr. Evans—the total effective condition of the body, since the metabolic activities of the cell are not fundamentally energy-producing processes but chemical actions and reactions designed to rearrange the molecular constituents presented to the cell after alimentary breakdown. Were metabolism a matter of mere energy production, high-calorie foods such as fats and starches would constitute the maximum effective fare. But experiments carried out several years ago with radioactive tracers proved that only 2 per cent of the nutrients taken in by an organism emerges as energy. This means that 98 per cent may be utilized for other purposes: repair, regeneration, and replacement of tissues; enzymes, co-enzymes; hormones and other secretions needed to maintain the myriad processes essential to a state of physical well-being; and liquid requirements of blood, cells, and tissues. Since all chemical reactions, however, require heat for their instigation and give off heat during their interractions, energy may be the casual though vital by-product of biochemical cellular processes involved in the production of material fundamentally needed for the maintenance of the body at large. All body motions require not one but several preparatory and accompanying chemical reactions in order to occur. Motion produces heat but only by speeding up chemical reactions from the cellular to the tissue level. Vigor is then the total status of bone, muscle, tissue, cell, organ, nerve, and effective behavioral patterns.

Vigor is affected by nutrition even where organ and tissue are altered by age, but hardly in the clear and causologically simple way we may imagine.

The hunger experienced after coitus, for example, is often the sole result of muscular release. Nutritional-gonadal interractions are complex, often paradoxical, frequently proteal, and rarely without emotional and psychological entanglements, since both drives are highly charged and intricately bound up with early associative actions and reactions.

Fertility and Diet

Sometimes a rich diet will reduce spermatogenesis in men and fertility in women—probably by oxidizing the available vitamin E in the body and possibly because overnutrition may involve a preoccupation with the nutritional drive that partially occludes the reproductive one. Often sexuality will persist under conditions of nutritional deprivation that will impair other biologic reactions.

Dr. G. B. Leyton, himself a prisoner of war, describes in *Lancet* the effect of malnutrition on Russian prisoners of war in a German camp. On 1,350 calories a day, the Russians were required to work twelve hours a day, seven days a week, at hard labor in rock quarries and coal mines. Initially there was a loss of the feeling of well-being. Fat disappeared first, then muscle tissue. In three weeks the minds of the men were completely taken over by thoughts of food. Men normally quick-witted became dull. The capacity to concentrate vanished. Mental and physical lethargy set in. Several minutes were required to reply to a question. The prisoners slept twelve hours a day. They shuffled when they walked. As the deprivation went on, civilized behavior diminished. Moral standards and standards of personal cleanliness vanished. Interest in books and games disappeared. Curiously enough, however, sexual desire as well as the desire for alcohol and tobacco (oral substitutes) remained. Homosexual practices and

masturbation were common. Whether sexual longing persisted in those who contracted tuberculosis and hunger edema is not known.

Another study of the consequences of famine in German concentration camps by Per Helweg, Larsen H. Hoffmeyer, and others (1952) also found an increase in general inertia and apathy, making it practically impossible to arouse interest in anything. At the same time, moral standards were lost; the sense of responsibility for the welfare of others diminished. Active and passive sexual promiscuity was rampant.

A study by P. S. Vaishwanar of Nagpur, India, in the *International Journal of Sexology* may supply a partial explanation. Mr. Vaishwanar points up the paradoxical difference between nutrition and fertility in Eastern and Western populations. The birth rate of Dutch city dwellers, who were reduced to an energy and protein intake of 700–1,100 calories a day during World War II (between December, 1944, and April, 1954), experienced a two-thirds drop nine months later. However, it rose to unprecedented heights nine months after food supplies had become adequate. Yet India's birth rate, in spite of nutritional deficiencies of long standing, has remained persistently high, in the last decades dropping only from 46 to 45 per 1,000 population, a decrease ascribed to urbanization.

Mr. Vaishwanar makes the obvious deduction that in the East a high birth rate and expanding population are associated with undernourishment, while in the West the reverse is true. He suggests that factors other than nutrition are necessary to explain this paradox, since the fertility rate has been higher among ill-nourished communities than among better-nourished communities where contraception was not practiced. He assumes that, under normal conditions, instincts of reproduction and nutrition compete with each other. "When one retreats, the other advances," the psychological effect of hunger being to make sex compensate for nutritional appetites "shrunken" by deficiencies of protein. A loss of interest in food causes the sexual instinct to become dominant. Conversely, where a society has created conditions for good nutrition, it has also usually created higher standards of living generally, establishing a means by which members of that society can sublimate sex to intellectual and cultural attainments.

These explanations may or may not resolve the paradox entirely. Of course, in a society in which optimum nutrition goes hand in hand with an increased amount of goods, services, educational and cultural activities, and entertainment and recreational facilities, the increment of distractions may serve to divert attention from sex. However, the most diverting circumstance in such a society may be the very energy expended in obtaining this higher standard of living. Emile Zola, in *Germinal*, deals with life amongst the colliers of France whose threadbare economic circumstances left them with but one free and attainable pleasure, sex. Even at the asphyxial end of a mine catastrophe, a man and a woman collier abandon themselves in sexual embrace in a final, familiar sensuous experience that is not impelled by love or affection, or even by a desire to escape the imminence of death.

The fact that high fertility seems to be associated with the twilight zone of malnutrition, as shown by the steep rise in the birth rate immediately after a famine and by the high birth rate of poorly nourished people rather than of well-nourished people, might lead us to suspect that, in addition to cultural factors, those of a psychobiological and biological nature play a role. It may be that undernutrition is not a biological stimulus for sexuality but that overnutrition is a deterrent. A diet rich in animal fats in addition to a relatively high consumption of meats and dairy products, cheese, milk, eggs, etc., tends to oxidize vitamin E in the body. It may well be that during nutritional deficiencies, the vitamin E-sparing effect of decreased animal fat intake is great enough to compensate for the reduced replacement of the vitamin. This is more likely the case in Eastern countries, where a grain diet traditionally supplements the meager meat rations. The grains, however, are whole grains and contain some proteins, minerals, and vitamins, including not only vitamin E but mixed tocopherols—namely, this vitamin in all its varieties. In Western countries the grain supplements of a reduced meat diet or a diet lacking meat tend to be refined or are enriched with vitamins replaced by the producers, limited to a few of the B vitamins. Thus it may be that malnutrition in Eastern countries is not so severe, when it occurs, as in Western countries where refined grain foods—devoid of their natural vitamins and minerals—make for a more pronounced nutritional impoverishment.

The high amount of saturated fatty acids ingested in the average Western diet during periods of prosperity also predisposes the individual to vitamin E deficiency, as against the unsaturated fatty acids ingested in less developed areas in the form of vegetable fats (linoleic acid)—corn oil, linseed oil, sunflower seed oil, soy bean oil, and the like. Unsaturated fatty acids have a sparing effect on pyridoxine, one of the B vitamins, and probably on several other vitamins. They also affect the liver by reducing liver fat.

In the rat, the absence of the unsaturated fatty acid leads to scaly skin and caudal necrosis, growth retardation, kidney lesions, poor reproductive performance, and a high water consumption. The higher the fat consumption the greater the need for the unsaturated fatty acids.

Unsaturated fatty acids are synthesized to an extent from carbohydrates, the diet of the poor. But most important is the fact that an imbalance in the saturated-unsaturated fatty acid ratio in the body, implicit in the so-called rich diets that abound in Western nations, leads to vascular hardening, which slows down the passage of nutriments from the blood stream to the cells of the body and the passage of metabolic waste products from the cells to the blood vessels—and consequently to decreased vigor.

Thus we may have solved one important aspect of the paradox between the fertility of Eastern and Western populations on suboptimal nutritive fares. A comparably reduced caloric state in the West represents a greater condition of malnutrition than in the East, caused by the overconsumption of refined grain.

Fertility and the Psychological Impact of Hunger

There are, of course, several additional reasons for the relative disparity in fertility among populations under comparable conditions of nutritive deprivation, and without regard to the greater use of birth control in the Western countries. For one thing, the psychological impact of hunger on a people unaccustomed to hunger and on a people accustomed to it must be different.

Undernutrition does not induce so violent a reaction in those who are chronically hungry as in those who are well fed. A sustained vitamin shortage tends to decrease appetite, so that hunger does not create the degree of anxiety that is initially created in those unaccustomed to it. The fear sustained by well-nourished people in the face of food shortages compounds the nutritional drain incurred. Philosophies of life of the East have long adjusted the people to hunger, disease, and early death in chronically food-poor areas. The passivity of nature, encouraged by Oriental religions, is energy-conserving, permitting adaptations on lower metabolic levels to preserve vigor, just as the long sleeps in which starving people indulge tend to conserve energy and matter. Thus the greater calm with which the Eastern person meets the problem of nutritional deprivation enables him to nurse the internal nutrients he possesses more effectively than the Westerner.

In chronically deprived areas, people are used to obtaining maximum benefits from free or available pleasurable resources, such as human society, emotional exchange, sex, and children, since the other Westernized pleasures are relatively unknown and unattainable.

In normally secure societies, since external threat is diminished to the point where individuals no longer need to herd to create a factitious sense of security against overwhelming and destructive forces, the inclination is to detachment. The greater the security in a society, the greater the detachment in degree and number. The individual members of the society search for gratifications in the challenge of more refined and complicated intellectual activities.

Sweden, for example, a country with a high level of social and personal security, has the largest number of single-dwelling units per population in the world. This fact, plus casual, unresponsible, and detached sexual relationships, appears to be related to a rather high suicide rate. With cultural lags, such circumstances are never uniform for the population of any country, so that some individuals are always more adaptable to conditions of deprivation than others.

But a people with a high living standard, when confronted with nutritional deprivation, would be certain to suffer more intensely and chaotically from its effects than people in consistently deprived regions. Intellectual faculties and interests are among the first to vanish, and sexual desire persists until utter physical incapacity sets in. Here nutritional stress is raised to alarming proportions by psychological stress to produce the ultimate exhausting biological condition, formulated by Selye and confirmed by researchers all over the world, called the General Adaptation Syndrome. This is a condition that prefigures chronic and destructive disease conditions of the organism, and most certainly would be attended by a depression of sexual potency and constitutional vigor.

This fact was borne out in a study entitled "Experimental Induction of Psychoneuroses by Starvation." Dr. Ancel Keys, of the University of Minnesota, and his co-workers established that in a situation in which the bodily stores of fat and glycogen are depleted and the body consumes itself, the physical as well as mental consequences are far-reaching. Thirty-six normal young men were observed during six months of semistarvation—namely, a diet of the European famine type. There was no pronounced loss in the capacity of the special senses such as vision or hearing, but there were "marked tendencies for behavioral changes to follow uniform patterns."

As the stress of semistarvation progressed, the men became increasingly quiet, somber, apathetic, and slow in motion. Their irritability increased and stress brought on by internal rage was not outwardly expressed. Energy was conserved; effort was avoided. Former standards of morals and honesty diminished to a vanishing point. One man twice attempted sexual self-mutilation. Others increasingly engaged in daydreaming, often of the sexual sort, but there were marked signs of impotence and lack of vigor. Keys, in *The Biology of Human Starvation,* found just the opposite.

Stress

When the concept of stress is mentioned in this article it refers to an actual medical situation and implies physical reactions in which the nutritional status of an individual may be seriously undermined. The concept of stress was advanced by Dr. Hans Selye of the University of Montreal after close to two decades of research that involved hundreds of experimental animals and clinical work with human patients. The theory has since been widely verified by other scientific research.

Briefly, the theory postulates all threats such as infections, cold, heat, noxious chemicals, fatigue, injury, anxiety, obesity, and starvation as stresses to which the body responds at first with an alarm reaction set up by the adrenocorticotropic hormone secreted by the pituitary gland. This hormone, as its name implies, stimulates the cortex (outer bark of the adrenal glands concerned with body adaptation) to change internal and external conditions to produce mineral-regulating and other hormones to cope with the threat or threats in question. These hormones, in short, are body defenses called into action by a stress-producing condition.

If the body reacts too violently to the alarm, certain undesirable physical conditions—mainly allergy and collagen disorders—may ensue. But the next stage in the General Adaptation Syndrome is one of adaptation to the stress condition. The more reserve the organism has, the better its chances for adaptation. Continued or continual stress may exhaust the pituitary-adrenal axis, giving rise to a chain of physiological events that may incur derangements along the entire line of hormonal interrelationships, upsetting body biochemistry. They will be manifested in ailments ranging from defects in sexual function, infertility, and incapacitating chronic disorders to premature aging and even rapid death.

Endocrine Balance

It is one of the wonders of biology that the endocrine glands of many animals and humans operate in a harmony that is comparable to a symphony orchestra, with the conductor being a small gland the shape of a pea, located in a bony saddle at the base of the brain and called the pituitary gland. It is rightly referred to as the master gland of the body. It may be, for all we know, the master of the body. The pituitary gland controls the cycle of menstruation and gestation in the female and produces a number of hormones that stimulate the production of hormones from other vital ductless glands in the body, including thyrotropin, which orders the secretion of thyroxin from the thyroid gland; adrenocorticotropin, which biochemically commands the adrenal cortex to produce some fifty various hormones; gonadotropic hormones, which direct gonadal secretions; and an insulin-blocking hormone, to mention but a few. And all of these, plus the chemical products and processes in the body, require raw material that must be supplied by the food we eat, digest, assimilate into the blood, and circulate to all cells, tissues, and organs in the body.

To gain a small idea of what pituitary exhaustion would signify in human terms, Dr. Samuel Brody in his book, *Bioenergetics and Growth* (1945), states:

While hormones are named by their most spectacular effects, as "sex hormones," all hormones are in fact, general metabolic hormones; they are all involved in the transformation of energy matter. Thus, the thyroid is involved not merely in energy metabolism but in virtually every process in the body including mineral metabolism, sex activity, growth and development, and so on. The same is true for every hormone; they are all interrelated and exert widespread effects. However, the precise influence of a given endocrine depends on the age of the organism and on the scope of interrelation. . . . Some important endocrines, such as the gonads, may be removed with much less effect on general metabolism than others, such as thyroid, adrenal, pituitary. The extirpation of the pituitary is particularly serious, throwing out of gear practically all other endocrines and consequently all productive processes.

The anterior pituitary gland elaborates, among other secretions, two gonadotropic hormones. One is the follicle-stimulating hormone, which is involved in the maturation of egg or sperm and graafian follicles and in the secretion of estrogens. Another is the luteinizing hormone or the interstitial cell-stimulating hormone, which are involved, in the female, in the secretion of progesterone and the inhibition of estrogen secretion, and, in the male, in the stimulation of testicular interstitial cells and in androgen production. A lack of pituitary sex hormones arrests sexual development and results in abnormalities such as the Fröhlich syndrome.

In addition to the gonadotropic hormones, the thyrotropic hormone, and adrenotropic hormones, other hormones the pituitary gland is believed to secrete are the parathyrotropic, which stimulate secretions from the parathyroids, a cluster of little glands located atop the thyroid and involved in calcium metabolism in the body; a pancreatropic hormone, which stimulates insulin production; a glycotropic hormone, which is insulin-blocking; a diabetogenic hormone, which increases sugar production; a ketogenic hormone, which accelerates fat metabolism and ketone-body productions; a lactogenic hormone (prolactin); a mammogenic; somatropic or growth hormones; etc.

The anterior pituitary gland is also the central mediating station through which various environmental factors, such as climate, season, food supply, and psychic stimuli, control the sex cycle and other neuro-endocrine activities.

Brody describes a pendulum type of oscillation between the pituitary tropic hormones and the glands they control. Under stress the pituitary liberates excessive adrenotropic hormone, which induces the adrenal medulla to produce adrenalin. If adrenalin production is excessive, it reacts on the pituitary and depresses production of adrenotropic hormones. He describes periodic sex endocrine activity as an expression of this type of regulation. He surmises, too, that since animals whose gonads have been excised still continue to secrete estrogens and androgens, the adrenal cortex may also produce sex hormones since adrenal cortex hormones are chemically similar to sex hormones, a conjecture confirmed by an altered excretion of cortex hormones in various diseases of the adrenals.

It is indeed as W. T. Salter, in *Endocrine Function of Iodine,* says of the ductless glands:

The most important concept of endocrinology which emerges from the feverish activity of the past decade is the principle of endocrine balance. Discovered and rediscovered by several investigators of the past decade, the paradoxical truth has dawned finally that man or beast may suffer less from the loss of several glands than from losing a single one. For each of the precious juices the other secretions supply a partial antidote so that health and personality may be preserved delicately poised. . . .

Vitamins

All that hinges on the intricate maze of endocrine balance may not yet be fully known, but what is known is that endocrine function itself leans very heavily on nutrients—minerals, proteins, vitamins, and perhaps types and quantities of fats and starches.

Dr. Brody describes vitamins as exogenous catalysts and hormones as endogenous catalysts. He points to the similarity in chemical structure between vitamin D, for example, and sex hormone and to the similarity of vitamin D in some respects to parathyroid hormone, which regulates calcium metabolism, a process in which sex hormones also participate. Drs. Pillay and Kapadia discuss the similarity in effect between hormones and vitamins and point to the similar effects of vitamin C on urine excretion or retention. It is Pillay's impression that vitamin A is similar in therapeutic action on infertility to estradiol, vitamin C to progesterone, and vitamin D to testosterone because in premenstrual tension vitamin A as well as estradiol is prescribed; in threatened abortion vitamin C and progesterone; in dysmenorrhea vitamin D and testosterone.

Vitamins taken orally in food or otherwise are molecularly small enough to be absorbed through the small intestine into the blood stream, while hormones produced within the body itself are not as stable or molecularly as small as vitamins. In fact, they are usually proteins of high molecular weight that cannot pass into the blood without digestion. But they participate with vitamins and with other hormones in metabolic action. A case in point is carbohydrate metabolism, which involves the cooperation of B_1, B_2, nicotinic acid, insulin, anterior pituitary secretions, corticosterone (of the adrenal cortex), and adrenalin. A deficiency of merely one of these products can bring about serious and far-reaching disturbances of the body economy. All the enumerated vitamins and hormones are not sufficient to handle sugar utilization in the cell in the absence of insulin.

This disorder, called diabetes, is often characterized by diminished libido and sexual potency. Dr. Biskind, treating approximately 150 diabetics over a period of five years, noted that nutritional therapy not only improved the avitaminic defects but that there was almost without exception an improvement in general health and a remission of such disturbances as diminished libido and potency.

The roster of B complex vitamins is being extended continuously. Choline and inositol, two relatively recent additions to the B complex family, are specifically referred to as lipotropic factors. They may not only help arrest cirrhosis of the liver but also, via the liver, play an important role in the metabolism of fats. In the opinion of many medical men it is the shortage of B vitamins in conjunction with protein deficiency that causes the liver cirrhosis common among alcoholics, who are usually malnourished.

Degrees of B deficiency will induce comparable degrees of impaired liver function—not sufficiently severe perhaps to be clinically evident. The largest individual organ in the body, the liver, is charged with a horde of functions. It stores vitamins A and C, stores glycogen, iron, and copper for use in the red corpuscles of the blood, synthesizes protein, and produces a substance called bile which, metered through the gall bladder to the small intestine, helps to metabolize fats. The liver assists in inactivating and detoxifying a host of noxious chemicals taken into and produced by the body, including androgens and estrogens, which in excess quantities may ultimately create cancers, but in the more immediate course will decrease sexual urge in the male and increase it to unmanageable extents in the female.

One of the great hazards of obesity is that the starches ingested for the production of excess weight compete with the liver and the thyroid for vitamin B_1 specifically, impairing the function of both these organs, which have been shown to be important in sexual potency—the thyroid affecting fertility and gestation as well. Very likely the liver, if its function is impaired to a degree that permits toxic products to ruin the physiology, bears indirectly on fertility. Almost any adverse physiological condition will affect cases of marginal fertility, although the influence of toxic products of metabolism on health and disease has not been completely explored.

Nutrition and Sexual Aberrations

An investigation was made as to whether there was any correlation between nutritional deficiency and the occurrence of syndromes related to excess estrogen. A significant degree of correlation was found to exist—that is, patients with these syndromes had various signs of nutritional deficiency and hormonal disturbances, which responded promptly and often dramatically to complete and intensive nutritional treatment. Associated with these signs were other changes hardly designed to enhance any libido and potency left—excess nervous irritability, emotional instability, insomnia, headaches, impaired memory for recent events, "clouding" of consciousness, excessive tendency to tire, "restless legs," and peripheral neuritis —manifested in the early stages by a diminished vibratory sense and by spontaneous cramping of the muscles, and later by pain in the arms, legs, and lumbar area, loss of reflexes, and eventually actual muscle weakness.

Dr. Biskind makes it clear that the association of disorders brought about by nutritional deficiency with "aberrations" of the sexual function was no less common in the male than in the female. In more than 200 males studied, infertility with definite lowering of number and quality of spermatozoa was found, together with testicular atrophy, gynecomastia, and impaired libido and potency. These conditions were all improved with adequate nutritional therapy. The quantity and quality of sperm improved, and hence fertility, libido, and potency returned to normal. The size and texture of the testicles improved and gynecomastia subsided with vitamin regimen. Dr. Biskind also states:

> In the course of 7 years that these studies have been carried on, more than 900 cases involving pathologic uterine bleeding and the like were observed and treated with vitamin B complex in three independent series of cases in eastern, western and midwestern portions of the United States. The results were uniformly favorable, for not only did

the endocrine disturbances clear up but the indications of nutritional deficiency subsided simultaneously and vast improvement of the general health was the rule. In another series, administration of vitamin B complex during pregnancy led to striking reduction in the incidence of post-partum subinvolution of the uterus and its complications.

One complicating effect of a B vitamin deficiency in a married couple's diet (which they would be likely to incur because they share relatively the same diet) is that the woman would tend to develop, consequent to excess estrogens, an increased libidinous drive while the effect on her mate would be the reverse for the same estrogenic reason. In such a situation may lie the seeds of a serious marital conflict, one that marriage counselors might take into cognizance since simple nutritional therapy can restore libidinous equilibrium to the couple and rectify a problem that drawn-out, expensive psychological probing cannot adjust.

It must be mentioned however, that when psychogenic factors impair libido and potency, nutritional correction and androgen administration will have little effect on the sexual function. Therefore, the simultaneous treatment of nutritional and psychogenic defects must be advocated since, in Dr. Biskind's words, "physiologic recovery of testicular function will be of no avail in the presence of an inhibiting psychic disorder, while alleviation of the mental conflict alone will not permit normal tissue function in the presence of a physiologic defect."

Thus we return full circle to the separable, interacting influences of psychogenic and nutritional factors. We have traced the general line between fear and hostility of sexual impotence and frigidity and established both the cause and the effect as stress-creating conditions. In Western civilization even normal individuals may experience some omnipresent or recurrent anxiety that functions as a nutritional drain, which might lead to excess nervous irritability, memory impairment, clouding of consciousness, and emotional instability—not to mention impaired potency and libido, factors that are qualified as the features of B vitamin deficiency. The disturbances of interpersonal relationships likely to ensue under these conditions may spiral an initial trivial disturbance to

heights and may possibly require psychotherapy.

Obesity and Vitamin E

The normal depression of appetite consequent to B vitamin deficiency or psychogenic disturbances may actually produce the anomalous result of obesity in those people whose decrease of appetite represents a felt loss of an important source of pleasure and consolation. Or, in the curious reversal of natural reactions that takes place in highly developed cultures, where the primitive instinct has been obliterated by security, the person—whose desire for food should naturally diminish when he feels threatened—may escape from inner anxieties by the gastric route if food, as is often the case, is equated with security, safety, esteem, or love. This is reflected in the 25,000,000 obese citizens in the United States, 5,000,000 of whom are pathologically obese. These people have twice the normal chance of acquiring diabetes, high blood pressure, cardiovascular disorders, and (because of the rivalry between B vitamins and starches) diminished libido and potency.

Aside from B_1 deficiency, the chief danger of obesity is the tendency of the excess ingested fats to oxidize vitamin E, the endogenous catalyst utilized by the pituitary gland, whose effect on fertility and potency may be through its multifarious functions in the nutritional economy. Each one of the functions of vitamin E affects the over-all constitutional vigor and health of the individual, especially libido and sexual potency, through its role in muscle tonicity and capillary permeability.

Vitamin E is a fat-soluble vitamin and, unlike C and B vitamins (which being water-soluble can be flushed out of the system), is stored in the body. It is prone to decrease with time—often so insidiously that a deficiency can build up over a period of years. Dr. Raboch suggests that E vitamin should not be considered a specific antisterility vitamin but a substance very closely connected with the various biochemical processes and functions.

According to Hickman and Guggenheim, one of the most important functions of vitamin E is to guarantee the full utilization of vitamin A, although indications are that A is not the sole vitamin affected by E. French experimenters wrote in 1949 that testicular changes during starvation do not react to vitamin E but are improved by vitamin A, although the changes do not appear at all when both A and E are given simultaneously. This fact further bears on the reciprocity of both vitamins in their effect on germinal tissue. Another experimenter, Mason, claims that the histological picture of the testes in vitamin A deficiency differs from that in starving or E avitaminosis, and further claims that changes invoked by A avitaminosis regress after the administration of A. He noted also that, when there occurred a shortage of both A and E, the testes showed symptoms of E avitaminosis earlier than when only one of the two was deficient.

Raboch points out that therapy with vitamin E is more effective when whole wheat germ is used than when synthetic alfa-tocoferol is used. The reason may be that other tocoferols and vitamins of the B group are present in wheat germ, and may protect vitamin E from oxidation before it can be absorbed. He concludes that the effect of undernutrition on the development and activity of masculine germinal tissue cannot be explained by the absence of a few components in the food. The absence of certain amino acids, such as arginin, from the diet, unfavorably affects the formation and presence of spermatozoa, and he suggests that a series of factors, some of which are known to us and some of which are not, affect fertility.

Summary

To draw any tight and clear deductions from the work dealing with the impact of nutrition on sexuality would be difficult, although not unrewarding. Every problem of sexuality is an individual one as to nature, severity, and etiology. Psychological, sociological, cultural, and interpersonal factors crawl like indestructible ivy over the tangible biological structure, often occulting it and frequently altering it. But any sensible reflection should certainly convince one that the cultivation of wise nutritional practices, such as those implied in the material presented here, will—if other factors are not too severe—make for a healthier and more satisfactory sexual life.

References

Biskind, Morton, "Nutritional Deficiency in the Etiology of Certain Sex-Endocrine Disorders." *Internat. J. Sexology 2;* No. 1, 35-37.

Brody, Samuel, *Bioenergetics and Growth.* New York: Reinhold Pub. Co., 1945.

Guetzkow, Harold, and Bowman, Paul Hoover, *Men and Hunger.* Elgin, Ill.: Brethren Pub. House, 1946.

Helweg, Per, Hoffmeyer, Larsen Henrik, *et al.,* "Famine Disease in German Concentration Camps with Special Reference to Tuberculosis, Mental Disorders and Social Consequences." *Acta psychat. et neurol.* Copenhagen, 1952.

Keys, Ancel, *et al. The Biology of Human Starvation.* Minneapolis: Univ. of Minnesota Press, 1950.

Keys, Ancel, "Experimental Induction of Psychoneuroses by Starvation." *The Biology of Mental Health* (Milbank Memorial Fund). New York: Paul B. Hoeber, Inc., 1952.

Morgulis, Sergius, *Fasting and Undernutrition. A Biological and Sociological Study of Inanition.* New York: E. P. Dutton & Co., Inc., 1893.

Pillay, A. P., and Kapadia, R. M., "Vitamins in Male Infertility." *Internat. J. Sexology 7;* No. 1, 34-38.

Raboch, Jan, "The Importance of Nutrition in Masculine Fertility." *Internat. J. Sexology 4;* No. 4, 197-202.

Salter, W. T., *Endocrine Function of Iodine.* Cambridge, Mass.: Harvard Univ. Press, 1940.

Vaishwanar, P. S., "Nutrition and Fertility." *Internat. J. Sexology 7;* No. 1, 40-41.

ALBERT ABARBANEL

Orgasm,
Anatomy of the Female*

THE human female responds to successful sexual stimulation with all the physiological forces constrained within her body. Specific anatomical reactions to effective sexual stimulation, however, are confined to the breasts and the pelvic reproductive organs. The primary reaction within these organs of sexual response is one of marked congestion of the venous blood. Just as penile erection in the male is accomplished as the direct result of venous engorgement under the influence of mounting sexual tension so the breasts and the pelvic reproductive organs engorge with venous blood as sexual tension is successfully developed in the human female.

As opposed to the male's single primary genital response of penile erection the female exhibits multiple primary and secondary anatomical reactions during the various phases of her complete orgasmic response cycle. It is important that we understand the general terminology used to describe the female's sexual response cycle, so that the anatomy of the successive reactions of the breasts and the pelvic reproductive organs may be more effectively described.

Phases of Response

The human female's cycle of sexual response has been arbitrarily divided into four separate phases by the Washington University Sex Re-

* (This investigation was supported in part by Research Grant RG-5998, Division of General Medical Sciences, United States Public Health Service.)

search Project (Masters, 1959). These phases are, in order, (1) excitement, (2) plateau, (3) orgasm, and (4) resolution. The excitement phase may vary in length from a few minutes to as long as two or three hours, depending upon the intensity and the continuity of the patterns of sexual stimulation. This first phase of sexual response is measured from the human female's reception of any psychic or physical sexual stimulus to her entry upon the second or plateau phase of response. This is a somewhat shorter reaction sequence during which she gathers psychological and physiological strength from the mounting sexual tension, until her physical and mental forces are adequate for the leap into the third, or orgasmic, phase of sexual release. The entire orgasmic phase usually lasts from three to eight seconds. The length of the resolution, or fourth and final phase of the sexual response cycle, is roughly proportional to that of the first or excitement phase: the shorter the excitement phase, the shorter the resolution phase, and the more extended the excitement phase, the more the resolution phase is slowed.

Response of the Breasts

The most notable response of the breasts during the early excitement phase is that of nipple erection. It is important to realize, however, that erection of the nipples does not occur only as a response to sexual stimulation. The nipples may undergo erection in cold weather, or as a result of immersion in cold water, and the phenomenon has frequently been observed upon the removal of an excessively binding undergarment or after the continued pressure of sleeping in the prone position. There are many women who have inverted nipples incapable of erection; so that this reaction is not a constant finding, nor is it confined to the excitement phase of sexual response. It is present throughout the entire cycle.

As tension mounts under continued effective stimulation, the areolae (the pigmented areas of the breasts surrounding the nipples) become engorged and swollen partially obscuring the erection of the nipples and creating the false impression that this response has been lost.

The trapping or slowing of the venous blood flow in the breasts increases their size slowly, frequently until they are from a fifth to a quarter larger than normal by the time the excitement phase has reached its terminal stages. This congestive increase becomes more noticeable in large breasts. Early in the excitement phase the venous markings on the surface of the breasts become more noticeable as the blood vessels become engorged with the slowed venous blood flow.

After the excitement phase ends and the plateau phase is established, a measle-like rash sometimes spreads from the upper abdomen over the breasts, usually appearing first on the inferior surfaces of the breasts and being more noticeable in the blonde or redheaded female than in one of brunette coloring. It should be emphasized that the development and spread of this vasomotor phenomenon (sexual flush) during plateau and orgasmic phases is a characteristic reaction to effective sexual stimulation and will be produced only as a result of the development of severe sexual tension.

There is no particular breast response to the orgasmic phase of the sexual cycle. However, the sexual flush does reach its maximum spread as this phase of the cycle develops.

As the resolution phase is experienced, the breasts return to their normal size in a slow involution reaction that is the direct reversal of the changes during the excitement phase. First to disappear is the measlelike skin rash. Second to be lost is the swelling of the breasts. The areolae then begin to lose their engorged appearance. Finally, the nipples which have been almost hidden by the swollen areolar area appear to undergo a second erection response. This is actually a false erection reaction. The erect nipples are simply the last evidence of sexual tension to leave the involuting breasts, after an orgasmic experience has released the venous engorgement developed during the first two phases of the cycle.

We might emphasize here a point of telltale evidence of effective sexual stimulation. As the human female is responding to sexual stimulation, the appearance of a pink, granular rash may frequently be noted over the anterior chest wall and the breasts. A certainty of effectual sexual stimulation may be presumed, in the physiological response situation described. Unless the female is most adequately stimulated, she will not produce the measlelike rash (sexual flush) which is a true measure of the development of severe sexual tension.

The External Pelvic Anatomy

The response of the female pelvic reproductive anatomy to effective sexual stimulation also may be described in terms of the four phases of the sexual response cycle. The external sexual anatomy includes the clitoris, the major and minor labia, and the Bartholin glands, located on the inner aspect of the minor labia about two-thirds of the distance from the clitoris to the posterior vaginal wall. The anatomical reactions of these target organs to sexual tension will be described in detail.

The clitoris is a small, sensitive organ consisting primarily of erectile tissue. It varies considerably in size (usually about that of a green pea) and is located on the anteroinferior surface of the large pelvic bone (the symphysis pubis), which runs across the front of both male and female pelves. The clitoris is covered by the folds of the labia minora (the prepuce), which meet in the midline just above the urinary outlet (urethra). The prepuce protects the clitoris in the same manner that the foreskin protects the glans or head of the male penis. The clitoris and prepuce form the most sensitively erotogenic area of the female body.

As sexual tension mounts, the clitoris increases in size, but this response varies considerably from individual to individual. Occasionally, the increase may be minimal, but frequently a two- or threefold increase in size has been observed. This response is another result of the trapping of venous blood by a target organ as a result of sexual stimulation. The clitoris has a tremendous blood circulation for its size.

The increase in clitoral size is usually completed by the time the excitement phase has terminated. No particular plateau or orgasmic phase response has been described for the clitoris, and during the resolution phase the marked venous engorgement is lost very slowly. Frequently, the clitoris is the last of the pelvic sexual organs to return to normal after a period of sexual stimulation. Particularly is this true if the female does not attain relief of sexual tension by an orgasm after long excitement and frustrating plateau phases. The extended resolution phase of recession of the venous congestion frequently takes hours if orgasmic relief has not been achieved.

The pattern of response to sexual stimulation by the labia majora varies (as a general rule) with the number of children the individual female has produced. In the nulliparous female the labia major thin out and flatten upward and backward against the pelvic brim during later stages of the excitement phase, disappearing, for all clinical purposes, as the plateau phase is experienced. However, in the multiparous individual, particularly if significant labial varicosities are present, the labia increase in size from two to three times because of venous engorgement, hanging like the folds of a heavy curtain about the vaginal outlet. There is a tendency, even for markedly engorged, multiparous labia, to spread laterally as the plateau phase is neared, making the vaginal outlet more available to the male organ. As with the clitoris, there is no specific plateau or orgasmic phase response from the labia majora. Resolution, with return to normal anatomical position and size, occurs more rapidly in the nulliparous than in the engorged, multiparous labia.

The anatomical response of the minor labia to sexual stimulation has been of particular interest to investigators and has been dubbed the "sex-skin" reaction of the human female (Masters, 1959). This response has been compared to that of the labia of the monkey bitch in heat which is one of muted red discoloration of the entire vulval area (Zuckerman, 1930). During the human female's excitement phase, the labia minora increase in thickness from two to three times and extend laterally to provide additional support along the lateral axis of the vagina. This reaction develops an additional one to one centimeter and a half of effective coital length to the vagina. This additional support is, of course, missing along the immediate posterior vaginal wall.

After the plateau phase has been achieved, there is a marked color change in the minor labia. Again there is variation with the parity. The minor labia of the nulliparous female may turn a cardinal red, while the minor labia of the multiparous female (particularly if there are marked vulval varicosities) may turn almost burgundy red. These changes are always evidence of an impending orgasm.

If sexual stimulation of the female does not take her beyond the establishment of the plateau phase, the color changes just described for the minor labia do not occur. If, however, they do occur, and if the stimulation techniques that have caused them are maintained, the human female will always undergo an orgasmic experience. In other words, once the minor labia manifest the color changes of severe sexual tension, an orgasmic experience is not only imminent but inevitable, if the stimulation is maintained. Usually, the time from the onset of the color changes to the onset of the orgasm is only sixty to ninety seconds.

There is no particular anatomical reaction on the part of the minor labia to the actual orgasmic experience. The resolution phase is again the complete reversal in anatomical sequence of the excitement phase: first, the minor labia lose their sex-tension discoloration, they then lose their vascular tension (increased size), and finally they return slowly to normal anatomic positioning.

The Bartholin glands produce a mucoid secretion under the influence of sexual stimulation. It has been erroneously stated (Brown, 1950; Moll, 1912; Stone and Stone, 1953) that this is a response of the early excitement phase. The Bartholin glands do not secrete during the excitement phase of the sexual response cycle, unless it is maintained for a considerable time. The usual onset of glandular secretory activity is during the plateau phase, and material liberated is at most three or four drops from each gland. There is no particular orgasmic response, and the short resolution reaction consists simply of cessation of secretory activity.

The Internal Pelvic Anatomy

The internal organs of reproduction consist of vagina, cervix, uterus, Fallopian tubes, and ovaries. As yet, nothing is known of the response of the tubes and ovaries to sexual tension. The anatomical reactions of the vagina, cervix, and corpus will be described in detail.

Vagina

Probably the first definitive response of the entire female body to sexual stimulation develops within the vagina. Within ten to twenty seconds the organ begins its well-known process of lubrication. It was believed that lubrication of the vagina either came from the Bartholin glands or was the result of mucus secreted by glands within the cervical canal (Baver, 1927; Black, 1908; Dickinson, 1934). It is now well established that the lubrication comes from the walls of the vagina itself (Masters, 1959), despite the fact that there are no secretory glands within the walls of the vagina (Maximov and Bloom, 1930). The source of the lubricating material is still, therefore, in question, as are the biological properties of this material. However, the actual physical mechanism of vaginal lubrication has been repeatedly observed and may now be described in detail.

Almost immediately after the onset of sexual stimulation, the vagina develops what has been termed "the sweating phenomenon" (Masters, 1959). A glistening material appears on the vaginal wall, following in general the pattern of a transudate reaction. This material is of such consistency that it changes the normal acidity (pH) of the vagina (Masters, 1960). When it first appears on the walls of the vagina, one is reminded of a "sweat-beaded" forehead. Within short order, these droplets of lubricating material coalesce to form a well-lubricated vaginal barrel, which connotes advancing sexual tension. This phenomenon obviously develops very early in the excitement phase and is present in varying degree, whether or not the subject actually achieves orgasmic satisfaction.

The resolution phase is simply one of cessation of the secretory activity. However, the lubricating material has been demonstrated on vaginal wall surfaces two to three hours after termination of a complete response cycle.

During the later stages of the excitement phase, a consistent anatomical reaction develops within the inner two-thirds of the vagina. There is marked expansion not only in depth but in width of the lateral walls of the vagina, increasing the width of the inner two-thirds of the vagina from two to three times. The length of the vagina is increased from two to four centimeters depending upon previous childbearing experience. This increase of length and width occurs as the result of a jerky, arrhythmic display of expansive force and is independent of the basic vasocongestive reaction. It is essentially concluded by the time the plateau phase is reached. There are no further significant changes in the inner two-thirds of the vagina during the cycle.

During the plateau phase, the vaginal responses are confined to the external third of the organ. A marked vasocongestive reaction of the entire canal develops to such a degree that, as the plateau phase develops, the outer third of the vagina is constricted to a third or a half of its diameter during the excitement phase. This congested outer third of the vagina has been termed the orgasmic platform (Masters, 1959), and demonstrates the only significant vaginal reaction to the orgasm.

During the orgasmic experience, this platform contracts with a recordable rhythm, the timing essentially corresponding to the contraction of the penis during ejaculation (the male orgasmic experience). There are from four to ten regular contractions, with approximately eight-tenths of a second between contractions. The number of contractions varies with the intensity of the orgasm.

During the resolution phase, the orgasmic platform disappears first as a result of loss of target organ venous congestion. The engorged outer third of the vagina rapidly shrinks back to normal size. Although the detumescence is not quite as rapidly completed as is the loss of penile erection after the male ejaculation, the orgasmic platform disappears within sixty to ninety seconds after orgasmic relief of sexual tension. The increase of vaginal depth and width that developed during the advanced stages of the excitement phase slowly disappears. Frequently, it takes five to eight minutes for the vagina to return to normal size.

Cervix

The only remarkable cervical response to sexual stimulation is movement in conjunction with the reaction of the entire uterus. There is no secretory activity of the cervical glands at any time during the entire cycle of sexual response (Masters, 1959). The cervix is pulled back and away from the vaginal outlet and upward toward the false pelvis, as part of a total uterine movement during the latter part of the excitement phase. This observed withdrawal of the cervix from the vaginal axis occurs at the same time that the vagina expands in width and depth. There is no characteristic response of the cervix to the plateau or orgasmic phases. Immediately after orgasm, a slight patulousness (opening) of the external cervical os has been described (Masters, 1959). It is worth emphasizing again that no secretory activity of the cervical glands has been demonstrated.

With development of the resolution phase, the loss of vaginal wall vasocongestion and of the distension of the vaginal barrel causes the cervix to drop down into the depth of the vagina.

Uterus

The uterus is pulled upward into the false pelvis during the terminal stages of the excitement phase. This elevation of the uterus only occurs when it is in a normal anterior position, (resting anteriorly on the bladder rather than posteriorly on the bowel).

Although the mechanism of this elevation of the uterus—and of course of the concomitant withdrawal of the cervix from the vaginal floor —is not at present completely understood, it is obvious from the recent demonstration of muscle tissue in the sacrouterine ligaments (Krantz) that these ligaments may well play a part in the elevation of the cervix and corpus. The base of the broad ligaments (Mackenrodt's ligaments) is also suspected as playing a major part in the elevation of the lower uterine segment while the vagina expands in width and

length under the influence of increasing sexual tension.

No particular plateau phase response has been demonstrated for the uterus. However, during the orgasmic phase there are regular contractions of the uterine wall (Weisman, 1941) similar to the contractile reaction of the orgasmic platform. This anatomical indication of sexual release is particularly effective and easily demonstrated in the pregnant uterus. It may well be one of the causes of multiple pregnancy loss, particularly during the first three months after conception. Uterine activity during the resolution phase parallels the pelvic relaxation reaction. There is a return to normal uterine positioning as the vaginal walls collapse.

A clinical note of some interest may be inserted here: If a female who is capable of having regular orgasm is properly stimulated within a short period after her first climax, she will in most instances be capable of having a second, third, fourth, and even fifth and sixth orgasm before she is fully satiated. As contrasted with the male's usual inability to have more than one orgasm in a short period, many females, especially when clitorally stimulated, can regularly have five or six full orgasms within a matter of a few minutes.

Generalized Reactions

From the brief descriptions of the responses of the reproductive organs to effective sexual stimulation, it will be noted that the primary reaction is one of marked slowing and trapping of local venous blood flow. It should not be presumed, however, that the anatomical response to sexual stimulation is confined to the obvious target organs. The human female responds as a total body unit to effective physical and psychic sexual stimulation.

Although limitations of space do not permit detailed descriptions of these generalized body reactions, a few selected examples are in order. The measlelike rash (sexual flush) that appears over the surfaces of the breasts during the plateau phase of sexual tension response is by no means confined to those areas. As a matter of fact, this rash first appears over the upper abdomen and the diaphragm. The flush may also be noted over the arms, face, back, buttocks, and thighs as severe tension reactions develop during the terminal portions of the plateau phase. This generalized flush rapidly disappears early in the resolution phase, provided orgasmic release has been experienced. Without orgasm the flush disappears at a significantly slower rate.

The actual orgasmic experience is enhanced by generalized muscular contraction patterns far beyond the rhythmic contractions of the orgasmic platform and the uterus. The external rectal sphincter contracts in complete rhythm with the orgasmic platform during intense orgasmic responses. Many other muscle groupings throughout the entire pelvis and the lower abdomen, too numerous to mention here, develop spastic contractions as the individual reaches for orgasmic relief of her unendurable sexual tension. Even the musculature of the neck, hands, arms, feet, and legs have their own individual spastic contractile response to effective sexual stimulation.

The corded neck muscles, the swollen, flushed face, and the expanded rib cage are familiar aspects of total female response to sexual tension. In brief, the female target organs respond to the degree that the total female is sexually stimulated. The more effective this stimulation is, the more complete is her total body response to the physiological and psychological demands for sexual tension release.

References

Bauer, B. A., *Women and Love* (translated by E. S. Jerden and E. C. Paul). New York: Liveright Pub. Corp., 1927.

Bloch, I., *The Sexual Life of Our Time in its Relations to Modern Civilization.* London: Rebman, 1908.

Brown, Fredrich R., and Kempton, Rudolf T., *Sex Questions and Answers.* New York: McGraw-Hill Book Co., 1950.

Dickinson, R. L., *Human Sex Anatomy* (2nd ed. 1949). Baltimore: Williams & Wilkins Co., 1934.

Ellis, Havelock, *Studies in the Psychology of Sex* (4 vols.). New York: Random House, 1936.

von Hornstein, F. X., and Faller, A., *Gesundes Geschlechts Leben.* Otten, Switzerland: Otto Walter, 1950.

Kinsey, A. C., *et al.*, *Sexual Behavior in the Human Female.* Philadelphia: W. B. Saunders Co., 1953.

Krantz, Kermit, *Observations on the Gross and Microscopic Anatomy of the Vagina.* New York: New York Academy of Science (in press).

Masters, W. H., *The Sexual Response Cycle of the Human Female. I. Gross Anatomical Considerations.* Unpublished monograph, 1959.

Masters, W. H., *The Sexual Response Cycle of the Human Female. II. Vaginal Lubrication.* New York: New York Academy of Science, 1960.

Maximov, Alexander A., and Bloom, William. *A Text Book of Histology.* Philadelphia: W. B. Saunders Co., 1930.

Moll, A., *The Sexual Life of the Child.* New York: The Macmillan Co., 1912.

Negri, V., *Psychoanalysis of Sexual Life.* Los Angeles: Western Institute of Psychoanalysis, 1949.

Siegler, S. L., *Fertility in Women.* Philadelphia: J. B. Lippincott Co., 1944.

Stone, Hannah M., and Stone, Abraham. *A Marriage Manual.* New York: Simon and Schuster, 1953.

Weisman, Abner I., *Spermatozoa and Sterility.* New York: Paul B. Hoeber, Inc., 1941.

Zuckerman, S., "The Menstrual Cycle of the Primates." *Proc. Zool. Soc.* 691-754, 1930.

WILLIAM H. MASTERS
VIRGINIA E. JOHNSON

Orient, Sex Life in the

THIS article covers China, Korea, Japan, the Philippines, Indo-China, Indonesia (formerly Netherlands East Indies, now including the islands of Java, Sumatra, Celebes, Madura, Bali, etc.), Thailand, the Federation of Malaya, Singapore, Hong Kong, and Macao. In order to have a clearer idea of sex life in these various regions, it is necessary to give a short description of their history, geography, ethnology, customs, and religions.

History, Geography, and Ethnology

China

China has had a long history covering a period of over 5,000 years. Its literature is immense, and it has only been during the past century or so that Westerners have come to study it and understand China's contributions to the knowledge and advancement of the world.

The entire country covers 3½ million square miles and houses a population of over 450 million, now estimated by the People's Government to have risen to 600 million. The three main religions are Confucianism, Taoism, and Buddhism, with a sprinkling of one million acknowledging Christianity and Mohammedanism. Both the Chinese government and the people are tolerant in their religious beliefs and practices, and the people worship and pray in any way they like.

Japan

Before World War II, Japan included Korea, Formosa, and the three provinces of Manchuria. Since her defeat in 1945, the Japanese empire has been much reduced in size to her original four main islands of Hokkaido, Honshu, Shikoku, and Kyushu, which contain a total area of 147,000 square miles and a somewhat increased population of 87 million.

The Japanese are shorter than the Chinese and Koreans, but of similar build. There exists a physical difference between the social classes, the majority being descended from the Malay or Indonesian races, while the upper minority may be of Manchu-Korean origin. The aborigines, now confined to the northernmost island of Hokkaido, called Ainu, are a branch of the Caucasian race, and possess long hair and blue eyes. Chinese sources claim that the southern island of Kyushu, whose people are darker in color, stronger in physique, and often possess familiar Chinese surnames, are descended from the early youthful travelers of Fukien who were taken to the fairy "eastern isles" by pioneer Hsu Fu, a Chinese monk, by order of China's builder of the Great Wall, Emperor Chin Shih Huangti.

Korea

Korea was the bridge of eastern civilization over which the ancient Chinese civilization, culture, and Buddhism crossed from China to Japan during Han times (early Christian era). Her people still call themselves the Hans, and their capital city of Seoul is written with two Chinese characters meaning Han-city. Their national dress consists of a tall black straw hat, a flowing white gown, and long flowing hair, as handed down from the early Han period. Their women are very fair, gentle, and beautiful, and their sex life follows closely the Chinese pattern. The total area of Korea now covers 80,000 square miles, with a population of 20 million.

The language lies between the Chinese and Japanese.

Indonesia

Indonesia, until 1946 known as the Netherlands East Indies, is now entirely independent with a total area of 735,000 square miles and a population of 80 million. Its people are descended almost entirely from Melanesian and Malayan races, mixed occasionally with European and Chinese blood and showing their individual characteristics.

Indo-China

Indo-China, now divided into the separate republics of North Vietnam, South Vietnam, Cambodia, and Laos, covers a combined area of 284,000 square miles and contains a population of 27 million. The people have come from southern branches of the Mongolian race, including Lolos, Thais, and Yunnanese, whose individual traits may be recognized. The women as a rule possess delicate skin and features, comparable to those in Korea, and are said to have much charm.

Thailand

Thailand (also called Siam) occupies an area of 200,000 square miles and has a population of 17½ million, of whom 2½ million are of pure Chinese descent. There is much admixture of various branches of the Mongolian race and, as the religion is Buddhist, there is little difficulty in social and human contacts among the various communities.

The Philippines

The Philippines cover an area of 116,000 square miles and have a population of 17 million consisting of descendants of Spaniards, Malays, Tagalogs, Moros, Indonesians, negritoes, and Chinese. The religion is 80 per cent Roman Catholic, as a result of the early influence of the Spaniards, but the pure Chinese retain their own faiths and family manners and the Muslims of Mindanao enjoy their separate beliefs.

Federation of Malaya

Malaya, originally under British administration, is now separated into an independent Federation of Malaya and a limited self-governing Singapore. The Federation contains an area of 50,000 square miles and a mixed population of 6 million, of whom just over half are Malays who retain the religion and habits of Islam. The Chinese, Tamils, Europeans, and Eurasians retain their own beliefs and practices. The aborigines are very few in number and live in certain reserves adjoining the mountains.

Singapore

Singapore remains a British colony, with limited self-government in internal affairs. Being an important fortress of the Commonwealth, this island's defense and foreign relations are still entrusted to Great Britain. Singapore covers an area of 220 square miles, and the population, mostly descendants of and immigrants from the two southern provinces of Kwantung and Fukien, is rapidly reaching the 1½ million mark. They retain their homeland habits, although modern education has exerted a strong influence on the younger generation. In the early days, before their womenfolk came, the male Chinese found wives among local-born Siamese, Malays, and other natives.

Hong Kong and Macao

Hong Kong has been a British colony since 1841 and Macao has been under Portuguese occupation since 1558. They form interesting landmarks of British and Portuguese influence —one showing intense activity in progress and commercial development, the other still remaining a "Sleepy Hollow," whose income is mainly derived from the catering to sex, gambling, and opium. In Hong Kong, many of the leaders and progressive elements of the population are mixed descendants of early European and Arab pioneers who passed on their character and features to the present generation.

Courtship and Marriage Customs

China

In China, courtship and marriage customs have been handed down from ancient times, and with slight modifications have been followed by overseas Chinese wherever they have settled down. The latter have particularly adhered to the old traditions, irrespective of political changes in the home country.

Engagements are usually arranged by a female go-between. First, the family names (the father, mother, bridegroom, and bride) are exchanged on red paper and certain conditions (particularly financial in the case of poor families) are agreed upon. A wedding date is next fixed, when, according to the circumstances of the respective families, friends and relatives are invited to witness the rites. In the country districts, a special closed sedan chair is hired to convey the bride, who is dressed in a suitable red costume and is accompanied by a retinue carrying two big lanterns, two gongs, and a small orchestra, to the home of the bridegroom. The latter awaits at the door in formal wedding dress, lifts the curtain of the sedan, and invites the bride, whose head is covered by a red silk piece, to accompany him to the family altar for worship. Chairs are then placed side by side for the father and mother, and the newly-wed couple kneel before them and acknowledge their filial piety. After this, still kneeling, two cups of warm tea are held by the young couple and offered to the elders. The two parents return thanks by presenting each with a red packet containing some money.

Other close relatives receive similar obeisance, although not in a kneeling position. Next, the couple drink to each other's health, in silence. Lastly, they proceed to the bridal chamber. While the bride remains there, the groom leaves the room to attend to the guests and relatives. Alone, the bride allows an attendant to remove her ponderous red clothing and awaits the groom. While she is in isolation, the attendant (who is experienced and paid a regular fee) gives the bride lessons on the duties of a wife and the etiquette expected of her toward other members of the family. No doubt the techniques of sex are also explained to the inexperienced bride.

Malaya

In Malaya in the days before the Chinese Revolution in 1911, it was customary for the wedding celebration to last at least three days and nights. It involved a series of processions in double-horse carriages, one for the groom, who was accompanied by two youths of 10 called *kuya*, and the other for the bride, dressed in gorgeous colors, who had two little girls of 10 as companions.

Some preliminaries were also observed before the wedding day. Precisely at midnight the night before the wedding, both groom and bride-to-be, each in their own homes, were obliged to perform a strange *cheowthow* ritual: each would unwind his or her long hair (the men in those days still wore queues) before the altar and undergo a prolonged course of hairdressing so as to be assured that they had reached full maturity and were ready to procreate. No sleep was possible during this procedure, and on the day of the wedding both were often tired out. This peculiar ritual is probably a relic of an early anti-Manchu observance, when many patriots left the mainland to escape the orders of the ruling government to grow a pigtail as a sign of subservience. The ritual is now largely abandoned by modern families, especially as the obnoxious queue is gone.

The freshly made white starched pajamas worn by the bride and groom during the *cheowthow* ceremony are worn again on the night of the wedding. The parents are satisfied that the bride is a virgin if there is a red blot of blood on her trousers. Cases have been known where a new bride was ordered home and a divorce suit started because of the absence of this red spot.

In recent times, marriage ceremonies have been simplified with the disappearance of the queue and the suppression of the Manchu regime. The dark silk gauze gown, combined with an outer long satin robe and a yellow conical hat dressed with red cords, has now gone. Instead the groom wears a Western-cut suit with a carnation in his buttonhole, and the bride adopts a white European wedding dress, which can be rented for a few dollars, and carries in her right hand a bunch of artificial roses or lilies. On certain occasions mass weddings numbering twenty to forty couples are held. They dress in modern clothes and meet in a large guild hall, where the master of ceremonies conducts a joint ceremony, the couples sitting at a long table with each groom facing his bride. The entire celebration is finished within an hour and the total cost may be under $50 for each couple (as compared with the huge cost of the old-style ceremony).

There were no honeymoons in the old days,

and perhaps this was wise when all things are considered, as the newlyweds could pass their first days amid familiar surroundings with devoted servants at their call, instead of having to stay at strange places attended by complete strangers. In Penang and Singapore, the newlyweds, especially those of wealthy Hokien families, were invited to make their homes in the spacious premises of the bride's parents. In such cases, when the young man proved active and reliable, he could be well looked after by the father-in-law, encouraged in his profession or business, and later on become a partner. Quite a number of prosperous merchants now living received their first lift to success from their far-seeing fathers-in-law.

Among the Malays, who constitute more than half the present population of the independent Federation of Malaya, the Islamic code of life is strictly followed. Here the formal marriage rites known as *berstanding* are performed in the home of the groom's parents, and the guests call in order upon the bridal couple to convey their congratulations after being entertained at tea.

Theoretically, any Malay may marry four wives if he can support them, and can also divorce any one of them by appearing before his kathi (priest). Most marry young and beget many children, although through lack of care and proper nourishment a large proportion die during infancy.

Japan

This empire, once riddled with militarism from the time of the Tokugawa shoguns but now docile, industrious, and methodical in all things and exceedingly prosperous, has become a creditor nation after her severe defeat by the Allied Powers. The old family life based upon Confucian and Buddhist teachings still continues. Marriages are now conducted as in former times, when go-betweens helped to search for suitable candidates from respectable and upright families, and careful inquiries were made before any final settlement was fixed.

Japanese women have a tradition of good manners and docility, for they are taught from early childhood to obey their parents and their husbands, when married, and to bear and love his children. Wives are expected to stay up until the return of their spouses, however late,

and to wait demurely at the front door, smiling, patient, and subservient. Afterwards they must undress their masters and put them to bed with no complaint. In Japan, until after World War II, wives seldom if ever went out with their husbands. Female companionship for them consisted of paid geishas, who sang, danced, and drank with them and their men friends.

The wedding ceremonies are simple or complicated according to the financial status of the bridal couples. In any case, the Confucian rites, modified for Japanese usage, are followed. The groom wears a special kimono of rich satin, the bride's headdress is carefully done in ancient Han style with artificial pink flowers in abundance, and her gorgeous robes, supported by an attractive obi, are made from the best material available. Usually the bride enters the home of the groom and kneels on the tatami mat before the small family altar, after which the groom's parents kneel. The guests and relatives salute each other by falling on their knees and expressing good wishes. This Japanese ritual is, as a rule, simpler than that of the Chinese and follows a strict Japanese adaptation of Confucian teaching. The Japanese have been more fortunate than the Chinese, as their ceremonies have not been complicated by innovations introduced by the Manchu or by any invasion—until the war of 1941–1945.

During the past dozen years, marriage ceremonies have been much influenced by the five-year American rule of their country. The masses have become more liberal-minded and the women have won the vote as well as a considerable measure of freedom and independence.

The Philippines, Indonesia, and Indo-China

The marriage customs of these countries are influenced by early contacts with Spain, Netherlands, Britain, Portugal, China, and former Moslem invaders. The Philippines were much affected by three hundred years or more of Spanish rule from the time of Philip II, and the family customs followed those of their ancestors, whether they were Muslim or Spanish. There is a predominance of Roman Catholic thought in most of the islands, although in Mindanao Islam is the strongest religion. The natives have benefited immensely from American ideas of education, laws, and justice, as shown by their progressive ideas and commercial stability, as much as in their family relations.

Living among the Indonesians are at least two million Chinese, who stick rigidly to the customs and culture imported centuries ago from ancient Cathay. The new government respects their wishes in what they consider right and fair for their existence and welfare, so long as they obey the laws of the land and remain peaceful.

The three countries of Vietnam, Cambodia, and Laos have a cultural heritage from old China, although France has introduced much of her culture into these lands. The kings of Cambodia used to adorn themselves with the Ming official dress while France still exercised political domain.

Prostitution

No description of sex life in the Orient is complete without some reference to prostitution, which so frequently plays an important part in the daily life of the people. From ancient times, this oldest of female professions has been known and practiced among all classes in various degrees. Books such as the Chinese *Chin Ping Mei* and the Indian *Kamasutra* (with its reading text) and *Kama Kalpa* (with its innumerable illustrations gathered from abundant sculptural works scattered over the great peninsula) have given the most exhaustive accounts of prostitution and of the sex act, and the pictures, whether in the form of delicate paintings or of most intricate carvings, have for centuries been handed down from generation to generation.

China

In Peking, capital of the entire country during the Ming and Manchu periods as well as under the Republican governments, a large area of the southern portion of the city was once reserved for the brothel trade, which, however camouflaged, has never been discouraged by the authorities.

The singsong houses are situated among famous restaurants and theaters, and are patronized by young men as well as by staid officials. The lanes in this "red light" quarter, unlike the yoshiwara of Tokio and Yokohama,

are dimly lighted, but there is a brilliant lamp at the entrance to each house with small rectangular signboards indicating the names of the occupants and the districts from which they are supposed to come. As a visitor passes the entrance the gatekeeper announces in a stentorian voice, *lai k'o,* meaning "here comes guest." And indeed the visitor is treated to the utmost in hospitality. He is offered tea and fruit and entertained with songs and guitar playing. Alcoholic drinks are rarely provided. After choosing one among the ten or more members of the household, he may come at a later date and even invite friends to take simple meals there.

In Tientsin, one long street of singsong houses was divided into several sections controlled by the respective French, Japanese, German, Italian, and other foreign concessions. There was no other city in the world where such an assembly of Russian, Chinese (from numerous cities), and Japanese prostitutes could be seen. Each establishment had its own system and individual furnishings and menus.

In Shanghai, with its four million or more inhabitants, could be found perhaps the most luxurious houses of assignment for the entertainment of all kinds of visitors. French, Russian, American, and British women, as well as Chinese and Japanese girls, vied with one another to provide entertainment for their international clientele. Money flowed freely and any kind of drinks could be obtained. The Chinese had their own kind of enjoyment in the form of native music by their favorite songstresses, appetizing meals, and light *shaochiu* (warm rice wine) in the most select of quarters situated along Foochow Road. Before the arrival of automobiles, the singsong girls used to drive in their own rickshas fitted with as many as four to six acetylene lamps. They dressed in the latest fashion; in fact, manufacturing firms used these girls as models to advertise their wares. Although called singsong girls, most of them depended more upon their personal features than upon their singing abilities.

Canton, with a population of one and a half million inhabitants, provided its own kind of entertainment. Apart from the crowded quarter of Hsiakuan (Lower Gate), there existed a corner of the city adjoining the Pearl River from which one could approach a long row of twenty or more big stationary junks. These were held fast by iron chains in the center of the river, were brilliantly lighted, and were within a few steps of one another. Here were assembled vast singing halls that could be rented for an evening, and orchestral music provided the accompaniment to songstresses who could be selected from a list supplied by the management. The choicest food could be ordered at a moment's notice, for the river itself served as a floating market and emergency store. After the feasts bedrooms could be rented, but as air conditioning had not yet been introduced sound sleep could not be guaranteed in the cubicles. This exclusive spot of enjoyment was known as "Flower Boat Row," but its popularity died after a severe fire attacked all the fastened junks and caused some fatalities. The present government has not encouraged any reconstruction in this direction.

In Penang, Singapore, and Malacca, known together under the joint name of Straits Settlements before the end of World War II, promiscuous sex relations were indulged in extensively by the younger male generation, and more often than not they received their initiation in the attractive licensed brothels then in existence. In Singapore (Teluk Ayer district, comprising Temple, Sago, and Kokien Streets) and in Penang (Campbell Street), both streets and houses were well lighted at nighttime, and inside the houses were confined hundreds of *pipa chai* (guitar girls), corresponding to the singsong girls of Shanghai, who could be hired out at any time to entertain their male patrons in the numerous clubs, restaurants, and societies. Some of the large brothels had halls on the topmost story that could be hired for the evening (*hoiting*) for dinners, suppers, gambling, opium-smoking, singing, and business deals. Excellent food could be ordered, as well as drinks, and the bills at the end of each celebration could amount to hundreds of dollars.

Until the end of World War I and the functioning of the League of Nations, four common indulgences—women, gambling, drink, and opium—were almost synonymous. At that time, the smoking of opium could be seen everywhere, and many young men had their first experience in these halls in order to increase their sexual powers. Actually, opium is not an aphrodisiac, but it has the power to prolong sexual excitement and retard orgasm.

Japan

Japan is a paradise of enjoyment, known throughout the world for its beautifully cared-for gardens, fine hotels, clean habits, and entertaining geishas. There was a time when aggressive military officers armed with long swords and handy pistols spoiled the quiet scene, but since their defeat by the Allies in World War II and the foreign occupation of their proud land, the people have become more docile, and the normal gentle and winning manners of both men and women are more apparent.

Undoubtedly, Japanese women, with their intensive home training and educational background, make the best wives and also the best professional entertainers. Whether as geishas, in the guise of singers, samisen players, or dancers who live in Tokio's Nihonbashi area, or the more common juro women who ply their trade as cheap prostitutes in the Asakusa quarter, they have all received training in their several duties and may be classed as experts in the entertainment of men. There is order in everything they undertake (punctuality, courtesy, respect for preferences in food, music, and topics of conversation), and toward the end of the long meal one would indeed be a dullard not to appreciate such attentiveness.

Some geishas, like some ancient Chinese paramours, have risen high on the social ladder, such as the wife of the late Premier Hara.

In Yokohama and certain other localities, such as Nagasaki, Kobe, and Osaka, that are much frequented by European and American sailors, the prostitutes of the yoshiwara districts learn elementary phrases in English to accommodate their foreign patrons. Before World War I, the inmates of the brightly lighted pleasure houses were massed in the front windows adjoining the public lanes, so that they could be selected at will by the patrons. In later years, large photographs of the inmates have been on display and the guests have been able to make their choice from outside the houses.

Masturbation

There does not seem to be too much difference in the autoerotic practices of the young people, or at least the young males of the

Orient and of the West. Masturbation is a widespread habit among boys and is largely learned while they are at school, the older ones usually teaching the younger ones. It is perhaps less common among the people of those Oriental nations since the young marry early and can satisfy their sexual needs in heterosexual intercourse at a time when their desires are most intense. Oriental Moslems, for example, probably practice less masturbation than other Easterners because they frequently marry when they are in their teens and, if they can afford it, keep a harem of four wives.

Petting

In the past, petting has not been a common practice in the East; and even kissing was seldom indulged in before the advent of European and American movies. Formerly, it was considered exceptionally bad taste or immoral behavior for a couple to pet in public, and parents would not allow such behavior in the home. There used to be a saying among Chinese, Japanese, and Malays that couples did not rush into love at first sight or opportunity, but only learned to find each other and enjoy each other sexually after marriage. Love and sexual fulfillment were said to grow like plants. Since the two world wars, however, the younger generation of Orientals has learned the modern Western ways of seeking sex gratification prior to marriage. Kissing and petting have consequently become immensely more common than previously.

Premarital Sex Relations

Although old books give classical descriptions of free or forbidden love between the offspring of educated and official families, there is still a tendency for the morals of the children of the masses to be strictly supervised, especially in the case of young girls. Any deviation from family rules in this respect is frowned upon. The use of the purdah system among Mohammedans, including the wearing of veils outside the house, and the adoption of bound feet, once so common among the higher classes in China, are customs designed to enforce both premarital and postmarital chastity. In recent years, these customs have been breaking down,

and there has been a significant increase in premarital sex relations, at least on the part of females.

Adultery

However strict and harsh the official laws may be for preventing legally married couples from engaging in adultery, from time immemorial there have been many conspicuous examples of extramarital unions among the noblest people in the Orient. In Eastern countries, laws regarding adulterous relationships have been mostly man-made and therefore greater laxity is usually allowed for males than for females. The theatrical productions of most Eastern countries depict many adulterous alliances in which the male is responsible for the seduction of the female; yet the punishment is generally meted out to the female partner of these alliances. Although the double standard of sexual morality depicted in Oriental literature and art still largely exists, this, too, may be said to be breaking down to some extent among the more modern Easterners.

Conclusion

On the whole, sex life in the Orient has changed considerably, along with considerable modifications in the daily conduct of affairs and social matters. For example, the Chinese have for nearly half a century abolished the queue, which used to hang from the back of their heads and provided much laughter and derision from the more thoughtless and ignorant.

The Japanese, although wearing Western dress for office use, prefer their loose, long kimono in their private homes, and the women often discard their heavy hairdress in favor of a "perm," and wear slacks in the streets without undue self-consciousness.

Mohammedan women, who used to obey the laws of purdah by covering the entire face and showing only the bare eyes in the streets, now expose their full face and accompany their menfolk to shops and movies. Instead of confining women to the home to perform only household duties, the men now delight in showing them to their friends and relatives, and encourage them to exercise the political vote and to join them on the platform. Both men and their wives now visit dancing halls and restaurants, instead of the men seeking solace alone in geisha houses and spending beyond their means.

The effects of World War II may be a blessing for both victors and vanquished and lead to democracy, peace, and prosperity.

References

Anonymous, *Nightless City*. Tokio: Maruzen Bookseller, 1930.

Chin Ping Mei. New York: Privately printed, 1939.

de Mourant, George Souile, *Chinese Love Tales (Eastern Shame Girl)*. New York: Illustrated Editions Co., 1935.

The Dream of the Red Chamber (Hung Lou Meng). New York: Pantheon Books, Inc., 1958.

Edwardes, Allen, *The Jewel in the Lotus*. New York: Julian Press, Inc., 1959.

Ellis, Havelock, *Studies in the Psychology of Sex* New York: Random House, 1936.

Ford, C. S., and Beach, Frank A., *Patterns of Sexual Behavior*. New York: Harper & Brothers, 1951.

al Nefzawi, Sheikh, *The Perfumed Garden*. London and Benares: The Kama Shastra Society, 1886.

Shu-Chiung, *Yang Kuei-Fei, Most Famous Beauty of China*. New York: Appleton, 1921.

Shu-Chiung, *Hsi-Shih, Beauty of Beauties*. Shanghai: Kelly and Walsh, 1930.

Shu-Chiung, *Chao-Chun, Beauty in Exile*. Shanghai: Kelly and Walsh, 1931.

Takahashi, Tetsu, *Reports of Sexual Experience*. Tokio: Amatoria Co., 1953.

Thomas, P., *Kama Kalpa, the Hindu Ritual of Love*. Bombay: Privately printed, 1958.

Vatsyayana, *The Kama Sutra*. Paris: Librairie Astra, no date given.

Wu Lien-teh, *Plague Fighter*. New York and London: Oxford University Press, 1959.

WU LIEN-TEH

Perversions, Sexual

Definition

SEXUAL perversions (also called sex deviations, paraphilias, or psychosexual abnormalities) are ways in which sex gratification is obtained, mainly or exclusively, without penile-vaginal intercourse. Perversion may occur by the individual's selecting an abnormal sexual object or by engaging in abnormal relations with a usual sex object.

From a biological standpoint, the primary aims of sex are pleasure and reproduction, and include, at some stage, coitus between a man and a woman. When these aims are entirely sidetracked and, out of fear or fixation, the usual modes of heterosexual intercourse are completely omitted, then the individual's behavior is considered deviant.

The deviant's choice of sexual object may be someone of the same sex (homosexuality), an immature person (infanto-sexuality), or an animal (bestiality). Or, if his choice of object is heterosexual, his deviation may take the form of fetishistic attachment to, or injuring of another person (sadism), being injured (masochism), or to oral-genital or anal-genital relations used as an exclusive substitute for penile-vaginal coitus.

Causes of Perversion

The causes of perversion are difficult to unravel. The sexual instinct is similar to other basic human drives and is liable to distortion. Such distortion may occur through four main influences: (1) atavism, (2) mutations, (3) developmental anomalies, and (4) conditioning.

Atavism

By this is meant a return to ancestral behavior, as when a dog behaves like a wolf and attacks people. It is, however, not a satisfactory explanation for sexual perversions. Our ancestors, for example, did not habitually use the anus instead of the vagina (as the homosexual sometimes does); nor can atavism explain masochism, in which a man wishes to be injured. No one can believe that our ancestors wished to be hurt! Atavism, which was so enthusiastically exploited at the beginning of the century by Cesare Lombroso, the father of criminology, has been more or less abandoned as giving any sort of useful explanation for sexual perversions.

Mutations

It has been suggested by geneticists that perverse behavior may be due to disturbances in the inherited germ plasm, which are known as mutations. It is, of course, in such a way that new species arise. This would suggest that perversions are inherited anomalies that have arisen spontaneously, and would put sexual perverts on the same level as hemophiliacs ("bleeders"), who lack an essential element in their blood that stops bleeding. It is very improbable that perversions are inherited in that way, because, as we have pointed out, *they tend to prevent the man from fertilizing the woman.* If they are inherited they would tend to die out. Geneticists counter this by suggesting that the trait is a recessive one and not likely to appear in each individual. But the fact that some perversions are cured by psychological treatment refutes the theory that they are inherited.

Developmental Anomalies

This appears much more likely to be of importance than the two preceding theories. We know, for example, that the young ape obtains its sexual satisfaction in ways that would be regarded as perverse in a human being. It is only when the ape passes puberty and becomes an adult that it settles down to the normal pattern of having repeated intercourse with females and scaring off other male apes.

If an individual was for some reason prevented from passing through the proper stages of development and, as it were, stuck at one of the earlier stages, he would continue to obtain sexual pleasure in a way that, in the adult, would be regarded as perverse. Freud postulated that a human being passes through (1) oral stages, in which he obtains pleasure from his mouth, first by sucking and then by biting; (2) anal stages, first by extrusion and then by retention of excrement; (3) urethral stages, which are less easily defined; and (4) the stage at which sexual satisfaction is obtained from the primary sex organ. Eventually, enough emotion is directed to a sexual object and the adult capacity to love is developed.

There is a great deal of hate associated with the oral stage and it is suggested that if the individual becomes fixated there he will continue to derive pleasure from biting (sadism). Fixation at the anal stage produces homosexuality, and so on.

It is still not absolutely certain to what extent the individual develops spontaneously through these various stages and to what extent environment plays a part. This is probably insoluble because it is impossible to bring up a child normally without others in his environment.

Environmental Factors

Environment must be accepted as of great importance in the production of sexual abnormality. Pavlov discovered that it was possible to link almost anything to a reflex or instinct to form a stimulus. The classical one is a bell ringing to make a dog salivate, but any other stimulus, such as a light flashing, a noise, a puff of hot air, and so on, can be used. Obviously human beings can be conditioned by events that become attached to their sexual responses.

Thus, repeated sexual assaults can influence a child's sexuality, and it has been suggested that some forms of delinquency, such as stealing, can be conditioned in this way. The sadistic schoolmaster who beats his pupils on the buttocks may condition them to obtain sexual excitement from being beaten in later life, and so on.

The Sexual Instinct

We cannot estimate exactly how much the preceding factors influence the sexual instinct, but they may affect any one part of it. The instinct consists of four elements: (1) The stimulus, which is whatever "starts the machinery going." This varies in different people, so that one man may be excited by a blonde and another by a redhead, etc.; (2) The strength of the urge, which is dependent on both psychological and physical factors; (3) The mode of expression, which is what one does to the sexual object in order to obtain satisfaction; and (4) The sexual object itself, which may be a man, a woman, a child, an animal, or an inanimate object.

It is mainly in the mode of expression and the nature of the sexual object that something goes wrong in the sexual pervert: either he behaves wrongly to the right object, or he chooses the wrong object. We shall therefore discuss perversions under two headings—disorders of sexual expression and disorders of the instinctual object.

Disorders of Sexual Expression

Sexual Oralism

This is the obtaining of sexual pleasure exclusively from the application of the mouth to the sexual organs. When the female does it to the male it is known as fellation* and when the male does it to the female it is called cunnilinctus. It appears to be related to the sucking of the newborn baby, and Levy, for example, has shown that persistent sucking occurs when the child has not been allowed the breast sufficiently and soon sucks its fingers instead. Oralism is thus an attempt to deal with

---

* Often spelled *fellatio*.

sexuality in terms of breast-sucking. This explains why both the passive and active parties obtain pleasure from their behavior.

Oralism may be either homosexual or heterosexual, and it must be appreciated that it forms a perversion only when it completely replaces intercourse. As a form of stimulation leading to intercourse, or as a nonexclusive means to orgasm in its own right, it is a normal activity.

Sexual Analism

This is the use of the anus for sexual purposes. It is known legally as sodomy or buggery, and is against the law in many countries. It forms a common form of intercourse among a percentage—it is believed about 20 per cent —of male homosexuals but it must not be thought that they all indulge in it since many view such behavior with distaste. In any case, considerable experience (conditioning) is necessary before it becomes pleasurable and many homosexuals have told the writer that they avoid it because of the pain. Psychoanalytically it seems to be associated with the Oedipus complex and castration fears.

When used between males, the passive party can obtain full sexual satisfaction and ejaculation may occur at the height of the orgasm. This is probably due to the fact that the sexual organs and the anus have the same nerve supply.

This type of sexual conduct also occurs with members of the opposite sex, but in a very small percentage. The writer believes that less than 1 per cent of heterosexuals use anal intercourse regularly. This invalidates the theory that it is used as a substitute for vaginal intercourse and supports Freud's views. When heterosexual analism is used as an occasional variation from other forms of coitus, it is not a perversion, but is within the normal range of sex behavior.

Other Forms of
Abnormal Orificial Sexuality

The fissure beneath the breast, the armpit, and the folds between the thighs are sometimes used as main or exclusive sources of gratification. These may be used as ways of avoiding pregnancy and rarely give the passive party pleasure.

It must be emphasized that sexual oralism, analism, and other extravaginal forms of coitus are by no means perverted or neurotic under all or even most circumstances. Virtually all normal human beings have perfectly normal or subclinical tendencies to engage in these kinds of sex acts (as well as in mildly masochistic or sadistic activities). As Kinsey and his associates (1948, 1953) have pointed out, subclinical manifestations of oralism, analism, and extravaginalism are part of our mammalian heritage and it would be a rare, and in some sense an emotionally disturbed or perverted, individual who had no such tendencies.

It is only, therefore, when extravaginal forms of sex behavior become highly fetishistic, fixated, exclusive, obsessive-compulsive, or disorganized that we can correctly speak of a clinical manifestation of abnormality or perversion. The individual who under no circumstances other than engaging in oral-genital or anal-genital relations can come to orgasm; or who participates in these kinds of sex acts because he is irrationally afraid of penile-vaginal copulation; or who compulsively drives himself to these activities in a self-destructive manner—this individual is truly perverted. But his brother or sister who thoroughly enjoys extravaginal engagements, but enjoys them as a significant part, but not the whole, of his or her sex activity—this individual may not be in the least abnormal or perverted and may actually be more "normal" than a person who can only, under all circumstances, enjoy penile-vaginal intromission.

Coprophilia and Coprophagia

These terms mean an abnormal interest in excrements and a desire to eat secretions and excretions. For example, a man may be excited by consuming the saliva and food from the mouth of his lover. Similar interest is sometimes found regarding urine. Usually the act is confined to watching urination, but in some cases there is a desire to be urinated on or to urinate on the loved one. The use of "filthy" language during the sexual act is a related phenomenon. Possibly the desire to write pornographic letters and to inscribe obscene words on lavatory doors, etc., is connected.

This perversion has a number of deep-seated psychological roots. The consumption of secretions is most likely to be related to suckling, but writing obscenity is a crude form of sexual assault.

Sadism

Sadism and masochism do not appear in a pure form but are always mixed and interrelated. Sexual sadism is the obtaining of sexual pleasure from acts of cruelty. This seems to vary from frank sexual pleasure in cruel acts to a cruelty that seems unassociated with actual sexuality. It is of tremendous importance because of its social effects. Sadism results from some aberration of the aggressive instinct that does not undergo the usual modifications. Contrary to popular belief, the child is not a sweet little innocent but a ruthless savage and has very apparent death wishes. Psychoanalysts believe that sadism is associated particularly with the oral and anal stages of development. There seems no doubt that the sadist's aggressive emotion replaces what in others would be affection: he wishes to injure those parts of his "love object."

The original hate is probably directed against the mother, particularly toward her breasts. The following diagram (taken from the writer's book) shows two ways in which it may become transposed:

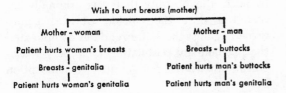

The "love object" may be a woman, a man, a child, or an animal, so that a similar transposition may occur in all these cases. It must be understood that this kind of sexual expression is compulsive and, although it can be satisfied for a time, the urge invariably recurs. Thus, although the sadist may be appeased by killing or injuring one person, he almost invariably repeats his behavior.

We can divide sadism into three groups.

1. Cruel Acts Unassociated with Appreciated Sexual Feeling

This has often been associated with religions: the burning of human beings during the Inquisition, sacrifices by Aztecs, witch hunts, and so on. Acts and interests unassociated with religion include the pleasure in much of animal hunting and a great deal of sadistic literature and "tough films." In fact, many detective novels have descriptions of torture and few Westerns are apparently complete without a brutal fight. It is not certain to what extent such literature and films are harmful by exciting sadistic feelings and to what extent they are healthy in that they suppress sadism by placing it in the realm of phantasy.

2. Cruel Acts Associated with Some Sexual Pleasure

In this case there is some sexual pleasure in cruel acts, but without a complete appreciation of its nature. Thus, in the past schoolmasters obviously enjoyed beating the unfortunate boys placed in their care, but would have been very indignant at the implication that this was homosexual sadism. The classic case of this type is the husband who beats his wife and the wife who patiently endures it. One is surprised that she does not leave him. The answer is that he is a sadist, obtaining pleasure from hurting her, and she is a masochist, unconsciously enjoying her misery. The only real sufferers are the children.

A great deal of this sort of sadism appears in phantasy—particularly in rumors of wartime: nuns invariably have their breasts cut off, men are castrated, and children violated by the enemy. Although such acts may occasionally occur, their frequency is infinitesimal compared with the rumor.

It is interesting to note that the Marquis de Sade, after whom sadism was named, was probably a sadist of this type, but although he was said once to have slightly injured a girl, he never killed anyone—although during the French Revolution he had ample opportunity to do so. Sadism of this type no doubt lay behind the persecution of the Jews in Germany and massacres that disfigure the past. It is probably the motive force behind senseless acts against girls, such as burning their clothes with cigarettes in the darkness of cinemas, cutting off parts of their hair when sitting behind them in buses, and so on.

This type of sadism is frequently associated with impotence, the phantasies draining off so much sexual energy that there is little left.

3. Acts of Cruelty Associated with Full Sexual Pleasure

These acts are accompanied or followed by erection, ejaculation, and orgastic pleasure, and are committed by men who put their sadism into action and emerge from the world of phantasy. They actually injure women. Alcohol will frequently release reactions which would otherwise have been kept in control, and the assaults on girls that occupy such a large space in the tabloid newspapers are often examples of this. The story seems to be that the young man goes to a dance, has too much to drink, and then follows a girl who is walking home alone. He may ask to accompany her or just follow behind. Once clear of others, he attacks her, punches her face, kicks her, and so on. That this is not due to disappointment at her refusing his advances is shown by the fact that frequently no advances are made and that he commences to at once attack.

In this group belongs the lust murderer, who probably kills the woman either by allowing his "love play" to get out of hand or for the deliberate evocation of sexual sensation. The lust murderer is frequently a quiet, well-behaved man, sometimes finicky in his personal cleanliness. Often psychopathic elements can be discovered in his life history.

The typical lust murder is characterized by periodic outbreaks. Cutting and stabbing, particularly of the breasts and genitalia, occur, as do sucking, licking, or mouthing the wounds. Biting the skin or drinking the blood may also occur. Erection and ejaculation may be followed by violation of the dying or injured victim. Karpman (1934) believes that there is an affective storm, but there is no evidence of this. The behavior is accompanied by intense sexual pleasure and excitement, and the pervert usually behaves normally until the next outbreak.

Like other perversions, sadism may be directed against any of the usual sexual objects: woman, man, child, or animal—or all of them, as in the case of Peter Kürten, who injured dogs, a squirrel, and sheep, and killed children, women, and men. In fact, he was a polymorphous sadist. Harmann, the homosexual mass murderer, killed boys and sold their flesh for food in the famine in Germany after World War I. Gilles de Rais, a companion of Joan of Arc, killed over two hundred young boys.

Sadism appears to be related to schizophrenia and to pyromania. Peter Kürten, for example, was a convicted pyromaniac before he started his career as a murderer. The curious lack of remorse which the sadist shows when confronted with his deeds is very schizophrenic. It would seem that the sadist has built up no prohibitions in his mind against exercising his cruelty either because he came from a home where there is no parental example, as did Kürten, or because he has rejected teachings instilled by his parents. The periodic behavior is merely related to the fact that all sexual behavior is periodic.

The writer pointed out eighteen years ago the seriousness of false murder confessions. These are frequently made by latent sadists, and if neglected the confessor may put his phantasies into action. It is important because it is a type of behavior that facilitates detection of a murder before it is committed. Similarly those who collect weapons—guns, revolvers, rifles, etc.—have latent sadism and are potential killers.

Masochism

This is the obtaining of sexual pleasure by being hurt, humiliated, dominated, bound, or degraded. Masochism is the reverse of the wish to hurt: the hostility that was originally directed against the outside world becomes turned against the self. Freud has complicated the problem by postulating a primary masochism, but we will not go into that conception here.

Male Masochism

In the male the mechanism appears to be as follows:

1. Wish to hurt mother
2. Wish to be hurt by mother
3. Wish to be hurt by women in general

The reversal is shown by the fact that some masochists wish to dress in female clothes (transvestism) and so resemble the mother. The patient identifies himself with her and therefore any hate he feels for her is turned back to himself. He then identifies all women with her and so wishes other women to hurt him.

In homosexual masochism this mechanism is carried one step further:

1. Wish to hurt mother
2. Wish to be hurt by mother
3. Mother equals a man
4. Wish to be hurt by a man

The double identification that occurs often escapes notice: Not only does the patient identify himself with his mother, but his persecutor also represents her.

FEMININE MASOCHISM

Masochism in women is more a way of life than a neurosis. From the psychoanalytical point of view, it is believed to be due to the child's discovery of the anatomical differences between boys and girls. The discovery that she has no penis turns the girl's aggression inwards rather than upon others. On the other hand, Horney believes that masochism is largely a conditioned reaction. She points out that the Russian woman in the time of the Czars believed that her husband did not love her unless he beat her, but under the Soviet rule she has become aggressive and self-assertive. Adler believes that the feminine wish for masculinity and her discovery of her lack of it is such a blow to her narcissism that her aggression is reversed. Deutsch believes that it is dependent on the father's inhibiting activity and that this is given a sexual tone. She thinks that when masochistic perversions appear in women they have as their basis a wish to be beaten. This they will allow for money, if they are prostitutes, or for love by sadistic lovers.

Freud's "moral masochism" is equivalent to the type of sadism in which cruelty (self-torture) is not appreciated to be sexually connected.

The history of every religion is filled with acts of masochism; fakirs who lie on beds of nails, Jesuits who practice flagellation, dervishes who thrust knives through their cheeks, and so on. The association of religion with self-torture is a complex one and not fully understood.

In general, masochism is of less social importance than sadism since others are not affected—except when so much sexual energy is drained off that the subject becomes impotent.

Frottage

Frottage is the sexual pleasure obtained by and seems to be due to a persistence of the infantile love of being cuddled and rubbed. It appears in young men who like to press against girls in crowded places, such as subways, assemblies at public festivals, and so on. Unless real annoyance is caused, their behavior is likely to pass unnoticed. Since such people rarely come for treatment, not a great deal is known of the psychopathology involved. Freud believed that *frottage* is a component instinct and that it probably has some biological basis: cats who like to rub against one's legs, animals who like to be stroked, and so on. *Frotteurs* are only truly perverted when they avoid coitus and other sex acts.

Scoptophilia* and Exhibitionism

Scoptophilia is the obtaining of sexual pleasure by looking at other people's genital organs. It occurs in one of two ways: observing unclothed people or watching people having sexual intercourse. Psychoanalysts believe that reversion to some primal scene, such as a wish to deny the lack of a penis in women (i.e., mother), or the wish to observe parental intercourse, lies behind this. However, there may be more to it than this since there seems to be considerable identification with the object observed and sexual excitement may occur.

Exhibitionism is exposing oneself to feel sexual pleasure. It is described by Fenichel and others as a denial of castration. He believes that it has two levels: (1) by revealing his penis the man is demanding that everyone admit that he has one; and (2) he wishes women to show themselves to prove that they have one also (i.e., deny castration). Thus, his exhibitionism is based on a denial of castration.

In men the desire is to show the genitals; in women the nipples as well as the genitals have sexual significance. Merely showing off the sexual parts is not sufficient; some reaction on the part of the onlooker must occur, such as shock, horror, or excitement. Exhibitionists frequently show themselves in a favorite spot such as a park, train, or alley. The writer once had a patient, a bus conductor, who exhibited his penis as the bus went along, thus obtaining the largest possible number of spectators.

Other psychiatrists believe that exhibitionism has different roots. Naville and Duboise-Ferrière suggest that it can be caused by

* Sometimes spelled *scopophilia*.

hypersexuality, hyposexuality, feeble-mindedness, chronic psychosis, epilepsy, constitutional psychopathy, delirium, nudism, or accidental factors. The suggestion by Rickles (1942) that it occurs mainly in timid men who are dominated by an assertive wife or mother accords most with the experience of the writer. In almost every case this element is found to be present. Exhibitionism is the seeking of love and resembles the love dances of savages and even the behavior of male animals to attract females. Arieff and Rotman believe that it is the most common sexual offense (35 per cent of all sexual offenses). In the writer's experience it usually responds well to psychotherapy and correction of the environment. Like most other so-called perversions or deviations, peeping and exhibitionism are abnormal only when they take extreme, fixated, or obsessive-compulsive forms.

Disorders of the Instinctual Object

Homosexuality

Homosexual behavior, or occasional sex acts between members of the same sex, is not unusual or abnormal. When a member of one sex is mainly or exclusively attracted to those of his own sex, he becomes a homosexual and is then perverted. Homosexuality, therefore, is fixated or primary or exclusive. In the past a large number of theories have been put forward: (1) It is a sin in which the homosexual turns voluntarily to "evil" behavior. This is disproved by the fact that a large number of homosexuals are unhappy with their condition and ask for help. (2) It is a degeneracy. This explains nothing and is disproved by those homosexuals who, far from being degenerate, are supremely intellectual, such Leonardo da Vinci. (3) It is an inherited disease. Kallmann's statement is usually put forward to prove this: that out of forty sets of identical twins in whom one showed homosexuality it was also discovered in the other. Yet other psychiatrists (Lange, West, 1955, and the writer) have seen identical twins in whom both were not affected in this way. Also, the fact that homosexuality can be cured by psychotherapy (the writer has published fourteen cases, Hadfield has reported four, and there are many solitary cases in the literature) shows that it cannot be of genetic origin.

(4) It is an endocrine illness. This was suggested by Glass, Deuel, and Wright twenty years ago and has been repeatedly disproved. Castration does not make a man homosexual, and the administration of male hormone does not cure a homosexual. Evident glandular disease appears in only about 5 per cent of homosexuals.

All the available evidence points to the fact that homosexuality is a psychological disease. It appears mainly in persons who have come from broken families, or where there are unsatisfactory parents, and is sometimes cured by psychotherapy. The writer has found it in young men where there has been (1) hostility to the mother; (2) excessive affection for the mother; (3) hostility to the father; (4) both (2) and (3), i.e., the Oedipus complex; and (5) affection for an insufficiently masculine father. No doubt there are many other possible factors. It can have narcissistic roots and may result from various forms of identification. In general, it seems to be caused by excessive identification with the parent of opposite sex; the boy molds himself after his mother and the girl after her father. This leads to behavior consonant with that of the opposite sex. The invert is immature and often timid with members of the opposite sex. Homosexuality may be associated with other perversions (such as exhibitionism, sadism), neurosis, insanity, or alcoholism.

Homosexuality is socially important because it may involve or lead to other offenses, such as blackmail and occasionally murder. Assaults on young boys by homosexual schoolmasters are common. Homosexual prostitution is found in large cities.

Inverts must never be told to marry in order to cure themselves. It does not cure them, they are often impotent, and it makes the wives unhappy and sometimes the children as well. The suggestion that they have intercourse with prostitutes may actually be a harmful one.

Homosexuals whose inversion stems from a neurosis almost always benefit from psychotherapy. Those whose personalities are too distorted (overtly feminine), as well as homosexuals who are also alcoholics or who are psychotic personalities do not respond. In these cases the alcoholism and the psychosis need treatment. Older homosexuals who are unresponsive to psychotherapy may benefit from treatment with estrogens, which diminish their libido.

Transvestism

Transvestism consists in deriving sexual gratification from dressing in the clothes of the opposite sex. Hirschfeld suggested that this may occur as various different perversions, and believed that there were four different types: (1) Heterosexual, (2) homosexual, (3) narcissistic, and (4) asexual. Others have suggested (5) bisexual.

We believe with Stekel that it is a manifestation of homosexuality: it is easy to see how homosexual behavior can shade off into transvestism. There also is an element of narcissism in transvestism (the patient likes "making himself beautiful") as well as of fetishism, since the clothes in themselves provide excitement. There are rarer types, such as the person who likes to dress as a baby.

Many male transvestites obtain sexual satisfaction from women but only when they are themselves dressed in feminine clothes. This does not mean that they are heterosexual but that they are homosexual only as far as the clothes are concerned. They have not molded themselves on their mother's whole personality, but merely accepted her clothes. Many authorities consider these transvestites heterosexual, but we cannot agree.

Transvestism is sometimes associated with suicide. The person dresses as a woman, makes up his face, puts on a wig, paints his fingernails and toenails, etc., and then kills himself.

Transsexualism

Transsexualism is a wish to change one's sex. Transvestism and homosexuality appear to be the basis of the desire to change to the opposite sex. It sometimes appears as a conscious desire for an operation, but occasionally the person believes that he is changing without consciously wanting to. The writer has seen a number of men who have castrated, or attempted to castrate, themselves, and have inflicted grave injury in the attempt. It is, of course, absolutely impossible to have one's sex changed (except in some instances of hermaphroditism). Sexual differences penetrate even to the bones, and one can tell the sex of a skeleton of someone who lived some seven thousand years ago. Trans-

sexualism is sometimes associated with psychosis (usually schizophrenia) and in any case is usually a severe psychosexual disease.

Infanto-Sexuality

This is the use of an immature person as a sexual object. Sexual assaults on children are not uncommon. The writer once gave evidence in the case of a schoolmaster who had interfered sexually with some twenty-five pupils. Freud suggested, probably correctly, that it is an attempt to overcome either internal or external prohibitions. The upbringing is often one that prevents a normal feeling to adult sexuality.

From the psychoanalytical point of view the selection of an immature object is the result of an unresolved Oedipus complex. Although one sexual assault may not be injurious to a child, it is possible that the child can be conditioned unfavorably by repeated interference. The suggestion, however, that all perversions are due to seduction in childhood is gross exaggeration.

Bestiality

Bestiality is the use of an animal as a sexual object. It is probably basically founded on two factors: opportunity (since it is common among farm workers, farmers' children, and so on) and an effort to overcome the same prohibitions we found in infanto-sexuality. It also occurs among the mentally defective but in their case it may be *faute de mieux* because they are unattractive to normal women. Many animals are unsuitable for other than sadistic sex acts. As with other perversions, alcohol is a common instigator. The writer once treated a farmer who obtained sexual pleasure from suckling ewes. This was easily traced back to a wish to suck the maternal breast and cleared up with analysis.

Autosexuality

These are perversions performed on oneself. Other perversions may have the mother as the sexual object (although she is disguised in some way) but in autosexuality the subject has failed to externalize his emotion, which is turned on to himself. He thus obtains satisfaction from his own body by masturbation or by self-fellation.

Masturbation is a stage in normal development and has no serious effects. It may even be beneficial since it exercises the sexual organs, but it falls within our definition of a perversion when it is exclusively practiced because of fear of heterosexual relations. Self-fellation appears to be rare and usually occurs in unloved children.

Necrophilia

Necrophilia consists in the use of a dead body as a sexual object. It would appear to be a fetish, sadism carried to the extreme, or a mixture of both (i.e., a perversion-fetish). Like all perversions, it is as old as mankind and is mentioned by Herodotus as having occurred in ancient Egypt.

Gerontosexuality

This is the use of an elderly person as a sexual object. Gerontosexuality is not easy to detect since it is not uncommon for young girls to marry old men, and vice versa (no doubt financial considerations often enter into this behavior). But when a young person *prefers* an elderly mate it is probably a perversion.

The assaults young men make on old women fall into the category of sadistic gerontosexuality. In such cases the old woman appears to be a substitute for the mother (as in other perversions).

Treatment

Sexual perversions are just as responsive to psychotherapy as any other neurosis. The only difficulty with this type of neurosis is that the patients find it difficult or even impossible to believe that they could find satisfaction from normal sexual relations. Thus, a very passive type of analysis is not always successful because the patient is inclined in such a case to expect the analyst to do all the work and does not try to help himself.

Throughout treatment of any form of perversion it is essential to continually reassure the patient that he can enjoy normal sexuality with more experience and that it will give him much greater sexual pleasure than he previously obtained by his deviant methods. The French say, "The appetite comes from eating" and this is as much true with sex as with food. Experience whets the appetite. Naturally one has a better chance with the young, the less experienced

in abnormality, the intelligent, and those who have a strong desire to get well. Older, blasé, cynical, and stupid patients, and those who do not believe that they can recover or do not wish to get well, are hopeless from the start.

There is a wearisome tendency to insist that perversions are not curable because there is no extensive list of cures in the literature. This is not true; there are innumerable scattered cases described in the literature. Only those who have never treated a case (or who have used incorrect therapy) have not had successes. Unfortunately, many psychiatrists will not publish their cases because of a regrettable fear that they may stigmatize themselves as specialists in perversions. But even the most perverse are fellow human beings and it is our duty to do what we can for them.

References

Allen, Clifford, *The Sexual Perversions and Abnormalities.* London: Oxford University Press, 1951.

Arieff, A. J., and Rotman, D. B., "Psychiatric Inventory of 100 Cases of Indecent Exposure." *Arch. Neurol. & Psychiat. 47;* 495-498, 1942.

Benjamin, Harry, "Transsexualism and Transvestism as Psychosomatic and Somato-Psychic Syndromes." *Am. J. Psychother. 8;* 219-230, 1954.

Berg, C., *The Sadist.* London: Acorn Press, 1938.

Berg, C., and Allen, Clifford, *The Problem of Homosexuality.* New York: Citadel Press, 1958.

Caprio, F., *Female Homosexuality.* London: Owen, 1957.

Cauldwell, D., *Transvestism.* New York: Sexology Corp., 1956.

Christoffel, H., "Exhibitionism and Exhibitionists." *Internat. J. Psychoanal. 17;* 321-345, 1935.

Deutsch, Helene, "On Some Aspects of Masochism." *Internat. J. Psychoanal. 25;* 150-155, 1944.

Ellis, Albert, and Sagarin, E., *Nymphomania.* New York: Macfadden-Bartell, 1965.

Ellis, Albert, *Sex Without Guilt.* New York: Lyle Stuart, 1958.

Ellis, Albert, *The Art and Science of Love.* New York: Lyle Stuart, 1960.

Ellis, Havelock, *Studies in the Psychology of Sex.* New York: Random House, 1935.

Fenichel, O., *Psychoanalytic Theory of Neurosis.* New York: W. W. Norton & Co., Inc., 1945.

Freud, Sigmund, *Basic Writings.* New York: Modern Library, 1938.

Glass, S. J., Deuel, H. J., and Wright, C. A., "Sex Hormone Studies in Male Homosexuality." *Endocrinology 26;* 590-594, 1940.

Hadfield, J. A., "The Cure of Homosexuality." *Brit. M. J. 1;* 1323-1326, June 7, 1958.

Hirschfeld, Magnus, *Sexual Anomalies*. New York: Emerson Books, Inc., 1948.

Horney, Karen, "The Problem of Masochism." *Psychoanalyt. Rev. 22;* 241-257, 1935.

Kallmann, Franz J., "Comparative Study on Genital Aspects of Male Homosexuality." *J. Nerv. & Mental Dis. 115;* 283-298, 1952.

Karpman, Benjamin, "Obsessive Paraphilias." *Arch. Neurol. & Psychiat. 32;* 577-589, 1934.

Kinsey, Alfred C. *et al., Sexual Behavior in the Human Male*. Philadelphia: W. B. Saunders Co., 1948.

Kinsey, Alfred C. *et al., Sexual Behavior in the Human Female*. Philadelphia: W. B. Saunders Co., 1953.

Lange, Theodore, "Studies in the Genetic Determination of Homosexuality." *J. Nerv. & Ment. Dis. 192;* 55, 1940.

Levy, David M., "Fingersucking and Accessory Movements in Early Infancy." *Am. J. Psychiat. 7;* 881-918, 1928.

London, Louis S., and Caprio, Frank S., *Sexual Deviations*. Washington: Linacre Press, 1950.

Naville, F., and Duboise-Ferrière, H., "Étude sur l'éxhibitionisme." *Schweiz. Arch. Neurol. u. Psychiat. 19;* 79-84 and 575, 1938.

Oliven, J. F., *Sexual Hygiene and Pathology*. Philadelphia: J. B. Lippincott Co., 1955.

Reik, Theodor, *Masochism in Modern Man*. New York: Rinehart & Co., 1945.

Rickles, N., "Exhibitionism." *J. Nerv. & Ment. Dis. 95;* 11-17, 1942.

Rubin, I., *The "Third Sex."* New York: New Book Co., 1961.

Stekel, Wilhelm, *The Homosexual Neurosis*. New York: Physicians and Surgeons Book Co., 1934.

von Krafft-Ebing, Richard, *Psychopathia Sexualis*. New York: Pioneer Publishers, 1944.

West, D. J., *Homosexuality*. London: Duckworth, 1955 (also published as *The Other Man*. New York: William Morrow & Co., Inc., 1955).

Westwood, Gordon, *Society and the Homosexual*. New York: E. P. Dutton & Co., Inc., 1953.

CLIFFORD ALLEN

Petting

Definition

PETTING has gradually come to be adopted as the generic term for physical contacts (other than the direct union of genitalia in coitus) designed to produce sexual arousal and/or satisfaction in interactions between postpubescent human beings. Although essentially the same activities are involved in the noncoital sexual relationships of children and of infrahuman species, these less consciously erotic pursuits are generally referred to as sex play.

Petting may be homosexual or heterosexual. We are confining our attention in this article to the latter. Petting may also be premarital, marital, and extramarital. It is to the premarital variety that we shall devote most of our space. And, finally, petting may be used as a prelude to sexual intercourse or as an end in itself, with or without orgasm.

Although petting is by no means confined to a particular postpubescent age group, it is most characteristically the heterosexual outlet of high-school and college youth. Sectional differences in definitions of types and degrees of petting are observable among such young people. In general, however, petting that is confined to lip kissing and mild embracing is referred to as necking. Differentiations from light to heavy petting are usually made on the basis of the degree of nudity and the degree of direct involvement of the genitalia in the manipulative processes.

History

As already implied, the overt behavior patterns designated as petting antedate the human species. Noncoital sex play appears to be a universal phenomenon among mammals and is, indeed, quite common among vertebrates of lower evolutionary classes, such as birds and reptiles. The living mammals most closely related to the human stock—namely, the anthropoids—are highly devoted to sex play.

It is quite evident, then, that petting is biologically rooted in a normal and natural way in the sensory satisfactions that derive from body-to-body apposition, stroking, biting, tongue-to-tongue contacts, caressing, scratching, mouth contacts with other parts of the body, and so on. Since the various techniques of petting even antecede the species *sapiens* and the genus *Homo*, obviously no rational case can be made that petting is a perverted and decadent invention of the present generation of youth.

When we examine the evidence available from other societies and from earlier periods in our own society, we are similarly impressed with the lack of specificity in time and place of human activities that are currently termed petting. All the petting techniques known to modern generations are found in the art and writings of ancient civilizations. In like manner, reports from anthropologists and other observers of preliterate peoples indicate the widespread presence of the same behavior patterns that we call petting. And, although the student of the early history of American society will not find references to petting under that name, he will find descriptions of such activities among our colonial ancestors under various designations like spooning, sparking, smooching, bundling, lolligagging, mugging, larking, flirtage, and courting.

Techniques

The techniques used in petting include almost every type of physical contact imaginable. We shall briefly describe some of the most common petting procedures in what is probably their decreasing order of frequency of use among contemporary youth.

Usually the initial and definitely the most frequently employed category of petting techniques is what we referred to earlier as necking —that is, kissing, hugging, and close, generalized body-to-body contacts. The relatively inexperienced individuals, or those who are blocked by moral or other considerations, may limit petting to this group of activities. Studies by Kinsey and others indicate, however, that all except a very small percentage of young people have engaged to some extent in at least this mild form of petting during their premarital period.

A second, somewhat heavier form of the necking stage of petting is what is variously termed deep kissing, soul kissing, tongue kissing, and French kissing. This deep kissing is often accompanied by a closer embrace and more manual activity (caressing), especially on the part of the male. The osculatory process itself involves mutual explorations of tongue, mouth, and lips.

Kinsey and his associates found that there were marked differences in the acceptance of deep kissing among the several generations in their female sample and among the socioeconomic and educational levels in their male group. The technique is more readily accepted among females of the most recent generation and among males of the higher economic and educational classifications. These same differences in acceptance among females by generation and among males by economic and educational groups tend to hold for the still heavier petting techniques that are discussed in the following paragraphs.

The various methods of petting that are focused primarily on other activities than mouth-to-mouth kissing are less widely accepted and practiced than necking and deep kissing. As brought out, some manual activity is generally involved in even the lightest of petting, but it tends to be generalized in the early stages. The traditional first point of specific focus of the manual aspects of petting for a majority of American young people seems to be the female breast. Many American males, especially of the high-school and college age groups, are more excited sexually by the sight or touch of female breasts than of female genitalia. We shall forego psychoanalytical or other speculation regarding the possible source of such erotic attachment to the breast, but it seems pertinent to observe that males of many other societies do not share this American enthusiasm.

In another sense, however, male stimulation of the female breast fits into the general petting patterns of other societies and of infrahuman sex play: namely, the preponderance of the action is undertaken by the male. It is noteworthy that the active participation of the female in petting is gradually increasing, so far as can be judged by studies that compare reports of younger and older generations. Still, the major conscious goal of petting seems to be the effort on the part of the male to arouse erotically his female partner. The specific technique of manual stimulation of the female breast conforms to this over-all aim. It is successful, however, so far as we can determine, with only a minority of females, but further arouses the vast majority of American males.

The incidence of the third technique of petting, male manipulation of the female breast, is greater than for any other method except those that focus primarily on mouth-to-mouth kissing. In Kinsey's sample, roughly three-fourths of the females who had not had premarital sexual intercourse had allowed males to manipulate their covered or uncovered breasts, and virtually all of the females who had had considerable coital experiences had permitted such activity.

Although some American youth consider male handling of the female breast an immoral practice, a much greater number connect tabooed feelings with mouth-breast contacts. Less than a third of the females in Kinsey's study who had not experienced premarital coitus permitted male manipulation of their breasts with tongue or lips. The fact that the percentage rises to close to 90 for females who had extensive premarital sexual intercourse would lead us to infer that perhaps this oral petting technique is considered almost as extreme a break from the moral traditions by the average unmarried American girl as is premarital coitus itself.

Slightly more than one-third of the Kinsey females without premarital coital experience had permitted the fifth petting technique: manual stimulation by the male of the female genitalia. The percentage rises close to 100 for females who had had extensive premarital sexual intercourse. The close correspondence of the statistics of incidence of mouth-to-breast petting and of manual stimulation of the female genitalia gives some support to the generalization that these activities are considered equivalents in "heaviness" and morality by many young people.

A petting activity that used to be considered quite indecent by large percentages of both males and females is the female manipulation of the male genitalia. Although some cultural change is in evidence regarding the moral evaluation of this technique, it is still apparently considered reprehensible by a majority of females who have not experienced sexual intercourse, and by some males, especially of the lower educational groups. Such petting is almost always initiated at the specific request of males, but some women come to find it a sexually exciting process for themselves.

A seventh petting technique is genital apposition. Roughly one-fifth of the females in Kinsey's study who had never had sexual intercourse had permitted males to place their genitalia directly against the genitalia of the females. The stimulation provided by such apposition is evidently similar to that of coitus, but it involves less risk of conception and is felt by some young people to be less immoral than actual penetration.

The last two techniques that we shall discuss are those that are most fully condemned in Western moral traditions. These are oral contacts with the genitalia of the male and of the female. We have already noted the strong taboo against mouth-breast petting for those women who have not experienced sexual intercourse. Oral-genital activities, however, have in many ways even stronger moral sanctions against them (even inside of marriage) than does sexual intercourse itself outside of marriage. Despite the evidence from infrahuman mammals of the biological normality of oral-genital contacts, there is a strong bias in the minds of many people that there is something peculiarly lewd and degenerate about the meeting of the mouth of one lover with the genitalia of the other. The Judeo-Christian codes have been firm in their labeling of mouth-genital contacts as abnormal and perverse in and out of marriage, but this attitude seems to be altering among some clergy of the more liberal Protestant and Jewish groups. In any case, the effectiveness of the moral sanctions against such behavior seems to be gradually decreasing. It is nevertheless true that the Kinsey study showed that only a relatively few females without coital experience had permitted males to stimulate their genitals orally and even fewer had undertaken to stimulate males correspondingly. The number of females who had premaritally participated in oral contacts jumped to about 20 per cent for each type for those with some premarital coitus and to roughly one-half of the group who had experienced more extensive premarital sexual intercourse.

The Case against Petting

Petting has frequently been attacked on a variety of physiological and sociopsychological grounds. The only evidence available of physiological disturbance concerns prolonged petting that stops short of orgasm. Some individuals, more predominantly males, report pains in the groin, headaches, and other forms of physical discomfort. Such accumulated tension may, of course, be quickly resolved by climax. When this happens, there is no evidence of even temporarily harmful physiological effects. For individuals who are afflicted with discomfort and who avoid, or are circumstantially prevented from having, an orgasm, the tension may last anywhere from a few moments to a few hours.

Although clear-cut instances are rare, some few individuals who habitually pet for prolonged periods to a point always short of orgasm may put their organisms to such great stress that they develop ailments of the genital tract, high blood pressure, ulcers, or some other affliction. Whether such conditions, if they do occur, can be properly laid at the door of petting or whether they can more appropriately be diagnosed as psychosomatic maladies of compulsive personality types is out of our scope to decide. Our point of concern is that the physiological case against petting only involves activity which falls short of orgasm and which results, in all except a few doubtful instances, in temporary discomfort.

The social and psychological arguments against petting tend to be considerably more involved. Many of the contentions about the harms to the individual and his society that ensue from petting can, when carefully and rationally analyzed, be traced to the Judeo-Christian moral traditions, which rigidly define the sex component of human behavior in terms of procreation. In its extreme applications in the orthodox religions (Roman Catholic, orthodox Jewish, and fundamentalist Protestant), the use of sex for pleasure not directly related to the aims of reproduction is, by this moral code, sinful. Hence, petting by even a married couple is immoral whenever it is not employed as a prelude to marital coitus which has pregnancy as its reasonable expectation. Premarital (and, of course, extramarital) petting is a much graver sin. Although some liberal Protestant and Jewish leaders have begun to support marital sex activity designed strictly for pleasure as an aid to sound marriage and, more specifically, have come to the defense of premarital petting as an emotional-educational device for young people who plan soon to be married, they are still in a distinct minority.

Sociopsychological arguments against premarital petting that at least allegedly do not stem from religious moral traditions seem to boil down to two main points: (1) such activity will interfere with future sexual functioning in marriage, and (2) it will lead young people to overemphasize the importance of sex in their choice of marital partners. Such data as are available fail to provide substantiation for the first of these two contentions. There is some clinical evidence to indicate that an individual who has consistently prevented himself or herself from reaching orgasm in petting *may* have some difficulty becoming reconditioned to reach climax in marital sexual activity. This would seem to be an argument against petting

short of orgasm, however, rather than against petting itself. Just as was true with the adverse physiological effects, this set of sociopsychological troubles appears in serious and more than transitory form only quite rarely and, even then, with a probably complicated causation.

The second contention of a nonreligious nature regarding the social and psychological undesirabilities of petting—namely, that it leads to an overemphasis on sex—is difficult to prove or disprove. Much importance in the consideration of evidence here must be attached to the judgment of what constitutes too much emphasis on sex. The general point often made, however, is that a couple that engages in constant premarital petting is not likely to spend sufficient time in determining nonsexual forms of compatibility or incompatibility. The case here would seem to be indisputable. It seems only fair to point out, however, that a couple that spends its time exclusively in *any* activity —whether it be watching television, going on bird hikes, or dancing in the moonlight—will unwisely limit the opportunities that each would have of coming to know the other one well enough to make a fairly intelligent judgment about the desirability of getting married.

When we caution about petting as a source of overemphasis on sex for couples who do not let the activity rigidly monopolize their time, our definition of what is "overemphasis" and of what amount of petting leads to such overstressing of sex becomes anything but clear. For some writers on the subject, *any* premarital petting is evidently defined as excessive and *any* emphasis on sex is automatically an overemphasis. Such an extreme form of the argument against petting patently takes root in the Judeo-Christian moral tradition that we have already mentioned: namely, the enjoyment of sex in any form other than that specifically directed toward procreation within the bonds of marriage is a sin.

A more moderate form of the case against petting on the grounds of overemphasis on sex goes something like this: It is generally wise for couples who are considering marriage to spend a good portion of their time together in situations that make romantic activity difficult. If courting couples spend most of their time making love, or most of their time in any other single-line pursuit, they are not likely to learn much about the kind of personality characteristics that are important in making for nonsexual compatibility or incompatibility in close day-by-day living. For couples (whether planning on marriage or not) who allow a considerable amount of their time for participation in a wide variety of social experiences to allot some time for petting—and especially for petting to orgasm—would not seem to constitute overemphasis on sex according to any rational definition.

A fact that is sometimes overlooked in the discussion of the relationship between petting and sexual motives for marriage is that overemphasis of a biological drive is more apt to occur among people who experience frequent frustration of that drive than among people who have regular satisfaction. A person who has suffered serious nutritional insufficiencies and deficiencies is much more likely to overstress the importance of food and to have his social judgments deleteriously affected by his search for food than an individual who has regularly partaken of an ample and well-balanced diet. Such evidence as we have would support the observation that such sex-starved couples as those who do not pet or those who do not pet to orgasm are more apt to overemphasize the significance of sex and to have their marital judgments adversely altered by the search for sex satisfaction than couples who regularly achieve orgastic satisfaction by petting or other means.

A correlative hypothesis often proposed along with the contention that premarital petting will lead a couple to place too much emphasis on sex is the assertion that marriage based primarily on sexual attraction is not likely to succeed. Few would deny that a marriage based on a rich variety of interests is superior to a marriage based on any single type of interest. Lurking behind this argument, however, is the supposition that a marriage based on nonsexual attractions is superior to a marriage based on sexual attractions. Evidence is lacking to support this supposition. Although *both* sexual and nonsexual compatibility are important in marriage, such data as are available would indicate that, under contemporary social circumstances, a marriage based primarily on sexual attraction is certainly superior to a

marriage based exclusively on nonsexual interests.

It is beyond dispute, however, that the various moral, irrationally founded arguments against petting are incorporated in the attitudes of many young people. Because some youth seriously believe various kinds of nonsense told them about petting, they have guilt feelings about proceeding with such activity. Such emotional conflicts are more common among females than among males, mainly because the pressure of moral responsibility is placed upon "nice" girls to set the limits short of petting of especially the heavy varieties.

The most formidable case against petting in our society today, then, may be succinctly stated as follows: Since many young people are conditioned to feel that petting is wrong, proceeding to do so causes serious emotional conflict for some of these persons. Should this be taken as a mandate, as some have assumed, for educators, parents, and other responsible adults to try to enforce more effective antipetting regulations among youth? Or should it be a challenge to our social leaders to effect changes in the attitudes about petting and other sexual matters which are inculcated in our young people? Perhaps the reader can better answer these questions after we have briefly dealt with the case for petting.

The Case for Petting

The chief constructive significance of petting would seem to lie in the opportunities it provides to youth to learn the art of heterosexual loving. It is not only the first source of sexual arousal and of orgasm for many girls in our society, but it is the main, broad sociosexual educative force for young people of both sexes. Such education and practical experiences in love expression are crucially needed by youth because of the tendency in Western society to induce drastic inhibition of erotic feelings in the period from infancy through puberty. Many boys and girls in America grow up not only with strong sanctions against the direct and intimate feelings of affection, but with outright distrust and hostility toward members of the other sex. Some type of permissive setting in which adolescents may learn literally and figuratively to "feel out" members of the other sex and to develop some degree of disinhibition of affection would seem to be a cultural necessity.

The taboos against premarital petting in American society are particularly unfortunate in the light of the even stronger moral sanctions against premarital coitus. In a cultural environment in which premarital sexual intercourse was not heavily condemned, sanctions against premarital petting would be of distinctly less significance. It certainly seems to be an absurd procedure for a society to instill strong sexual inhibitions in children and then to cut off both coital and noncoital avenues for adolescents to learn to overcome such inhibitions prior to sexual functioning in marriage. This is exactly what our society has officially attempted. The "success" of the official program, however, lies chiefly in its induction of guilt feelings in some young people who pet more than in the prevention of petting. The Kinsey reports indicate that premarital petting has steadily increased from older to younger generations. Since there has been no comparable increase in premarital sexual intercourse, we are led to infer that a growing number of young people have chosen to defy adult-inculcated guilt feelings and to take the noncoital route of sexual and affectional education.

To state the positive case for premarital petting more specifically, it offers the opportunity for young people to learn particular love-making techniques and responses to various types of persons of the other sex. In marriage, little chance is usually offered for the gradual acquisition of skill in, and unembarrassed ease in responding to, such activities as kissing, deep kissing, breast and genital fondling, mouth-genital contacts, etc., that youth can take their time in learning in the course of premarital relationships. Absence of a comfortable acceptance of such love-making procedures may be interpreted as rejection by the more experienced marital partner, or the quick introduction of such activities in marriage may frighten and induce sexual withdrawal on the part of a very inexperienced partner. Such feelings of rejection and withdrawal often permanently mar marital interactions.

As mentioned earlier, it is sometimes contended that premarital petting may lead to marriage on strictly sexual bases. Such petting, on the contrary, often seems to provide young people with an opportunity to respond over a considerable period of time to a fairly representative sample of persons of the other sex and thus come to know the kind of persons to whom they are more permanently attracted in both an erotic and broader affectional basis. A fairly expansive premarital sexual experience would appear to provide a background against which young people can make sounder marital choices. The sexually experienced would logically appear better prepared not to be misled by temporary erotic urges than the sexually inexperienced.

Marital and Extramarital Petting

Extramarital petting, like its premarital counterpart, may be understood chiefly in terms of moral compromise. Many married people, having sexual urges that are defined as illicit (that is, directed toward others than their spouses), consider their expression via petting less immoral than via coitus. In addition to the moral factor, extramarital petting is less likely to bring social and legal complications than is adultery and is a source of erotic satisfaction in situations where contraception is not available. Although adequate data are not procurable, extramarital petting, like premarital, would seem to be increasingly prevalent in recent generations. Any harm that ensues from extramarital petting is obviously not to be ascribed to the activity itself, but to guilt feelings in the participating individuals and to interactional disruptions that may develop in their respective marriages.

In marriage itself, petting is most often employed as precoital play. Such is not always the case, however. Just as in premarital and extramarital petting, the techniques may be employed as a substitute for coitus in order to avoid social (as in a public or semipublic situation) or conceptual consequences. More significantly, for many married women, petting activities, most specifically clitoral manipulation, are a more consistent and satisfying source of orgasm than coitus itself. Except in instances where coitus is compulsively avoided, there is no evidence that the use of petting as a major source of orgastic satisfaction in marriage is to be viewed as anything other than desirable.

Other Considerations

Although it is not too likely, petting couples can run afoul of the law in most jurisdictions in the United States and in certain other countries. Many of the so-called heavy-petting techniques, such as oral-genital activities, are in some places technically defined as criminal even in marital relationships. Also, when a minor is involved with an adult, the minor is subject to prosecution for juvenile delinquency and the adult for contributing to the delinquency of a minor. Where the minor is quite young, the adult is subject to severe penalties in many jurisdictions. Where the petting takes place in a public situation, the participants may be subject to prosecution for public indecency or disorderly conduct. Where two young people of approximately the same age level are involved, police in most jurisdictions are usually satisfied with "breaking it up" and "scaring them off" (with undesirable psychological, but not legal, consequences). The threat of legal action to support negative attitudes toward petting may nevertheless be viewed as an additional block to the sociosexual education of youth.

Some question is occasionally raised regarding habituation to petting as a form of sexual deviation. Where a person is irrationally afraid of sexual intercourse (such as attaching some strong significance to the technical maintenance of virginity) or is compulsively committed to certain noncoital sexual activities (such as breast manipulation), it is probably correct to view petting as perverted behavior. Where it is preferred to sexual intercourse as a pleasant variation (in or out of marriage), as a socially and/or legally less dangerous procedure in certain circumstances, as a means of avoiding pregnancy in situations where effective contraception is unavailable, as a gradual means of becoming familiar with the art of love-making in general or with some individual in particular, or where it is used as a regular supplement to sexual intercourse, petting may be considered "normal" in every psychological, social, and physiological sense.

In summary, heterosexual petting may be viewed as an intrinsically desirable and normal activity. Premaritally, its chief positive value is to provide training and experience in sociosexual adjustment to persons of the other sex. Maritally, it serves as enjoyable precoital play for most couples and as either an occasional or regular source of orgasm for some spouses, especially many wives. Extramaritally, petting functions for some couples as a less immoral activity than adultery, but may nevertheless be associated with personal guilt and marital conflict. Whatever may be a sound judgment regarding extramarital petting, there seem to be no serious counterindications for any type of premarital or marital petting other than those attached to irrational taboos and to neurotic fixations as a compulsive substitute for coitus.

References

Burgess, Ernest W., and Wallin, Paul, *Engagement and Marriage.* Philadelphia: J. B. Lippincott Co., 1953.

Comfort, Alex, *Sexual Behavior in Society.* New York: The Viking Press, Inc., 1950.

Daly, Maureen, *Profile of Youth.* Philadelphia: J. B. Lippincott Co., 1951.

Davis, Katherine B., *Factors in the Sex Life of 2,200 Women.* New York: Harper & Brothers, 1929.

Ehrmann, Winston W., "Influence of Comparative Social Class of Companion Upon Premarital Heterosexual Behavior." *Marr. & Fam. Living* 17; 48-57, 1955.

Ehrmann, Winston, *Premarital Dating Behavior.* New York: Henry Holt & Co., Inc., 1959.

Ellis, Albert, *The Folklore of Sex.* New York: Charles Boni, 1951.

Ellis, Albert, *The American Sexual Tragedy.* New York: Twayne Pub., 1954.

Ellis, Albert, *Sex Without Guilt.* New York: Lyle Stuart, 1958.

Ford, Clellan S., and Beach, Frank A., *Patterns of Sexual Behavior.* New York: Harper & Brothers, 1951.

Harper, Robert A., *Marriage.* New York: Appleton-Century-Crofts, Inc., 1949.

Kinsey, A. C. *et al., Sexual Behavior in the Human Male.* Philadelphia: W. B. Saunders Co., 1948.

Kinsey, A. C. *et al., Sexual Behavior in the Human Female.* Philadelphia: W. B. Saunders Co., 1953.

LeMasters, E. E., *Modern Courtship and Marriage.* New York: The Macmillan Co., 1957.

Sherwin, Robert V., *Sex and the Statutory Law.* New York: Oceana Pub., 1949.

Terman, Lewis M., *Psychological Factors in Marital Happiness.* New York: McGraw-Hill Book Co., 1938.

ROBERT A. HARPER

Phallicism
and Sexual Symbolism

PHALLICISM, or phallism, is the worship of the phallus or lingam, the male sex organ, and of the vulva, the female counterpart, also known as the yoni. The phallus is held holy as the giver of life and the vulva as its recipient. The term phallus is derived from the Greek φαλλος *phallos*, male organ. The phallic symbol is universal and has been revered in many cultures. It carries the connotation of "power," perhaps "magical power," and it is this that places it in the pantheon of nature worship, as a specific charm against sterility.

Origins of Phallicism

The adoration of sex is as old as mankind. Our earliest ancestors were awed by the wonder and mystery of creation and by their own power of reproduction, which, however hazily at first, they associated with the penis. What they could not understand they worshipped. There was, too, in their adoration an element of propitiation lest they be deprived of this supermortal and superlative gift if they did not value it as highly as it deserved. This worship developed dramatically into (or became an element of) the fertility rites so characteristic of primitive religion.

The all-important power of sex pervaded early man's whole outlook on the world. He saw the moon and water as female. The sun was the world's life-giving male and the earth the female welcoming his beneficence. The sowing of the seed, the vigor of the sun, and the response of the warm earth were all seen as expressions of sexual energy.

The earth became the mother goddess, personified by The Great Mother of God: in Asia Minor, the great womb of Nature. Fire and heat were male. Cold was female (a hint at a prehistoric idea of female frigidity?). They found sex symbols in mountains and valleys, trees, stones, serpents, birds, fruits, and flowers —wherever the shape of any object resembled the lingam or the yoni. Elements of this phase of sex worship survive in our times. The serpent and the swan are familiar contemporary erotic symbols.

The Androgynous (Bisexual) Gods

The earliest gods were believed to have both male and female powers and so to be independent and self-sufficient, able to create other gods as well as man. This was believed in all the lands of the ancient world.

Such beliefs gave rise to fantastic myths about the gods. To the Greeks, Apollo was a male-female god. The Roman Bacchus and Diana were often represented as bisexual. In Babylon it was believed that the first men created had one body and two heads, male and female, signifying that they had the organs of both sexes. The Egyptians held that some gods were male in front and female in the rear; sometimes they were human in front and animal in the rear. Siva, the Hindu half-goddess, half-woman, was a dual-sexed divinity. Occasionally Siva and her mate Devi were shown in one body. An ancient god might be pictured as male on the right side and female on the left side of the body.

Even Adam, the first man in Biblical history, was believed to have been bisexual. The Talmud says that Adam was a hermaphrodite—both male and female. In fact, the ancient idea of creation was that the first man combined both sexes and that in some mystic way the power that had wrought him split his body apart, thus creating Adam and Eve. As late as the twelfth century A.D., many philosophers and scholars believed that primeval men were androgynous.

Monuments to the Phallus

Proof that sex was worshipped among ancient and later civilizations is strikingly evidenced by excavations among the ruins of Babylonia, in India, China, and more recently in Egypt, Palestine, and especially in Corsica. Everywhere monumental stone and bronze phalli and amulets, crosses, and coins with obvious sex symbols plainly attest to the existence of phallicism.

The biggest find has been made in Corsica. In 1955, under the direction of Dr. Roger Grojean, a leading expert on the culture of the West Mediterranean, a team of distinguished archaeologists, members of the French Society for Prehistoric Studies, discovered prehistoric phallic monuments that are by far the largest yet found: stone statues, some six to ten feet high, representing the phallus in realistic detail and dating back to the Bronze Age. Previously they had come upon many lesser figures of the phallus scattered all over the island. But this last find revealed a whole group in the valley of the River Taravo, where an artistic civilization had apparently thrived some 3,500 years ago. About fifteen of the phallic statues have been set up where they were originally discovered, and the investigation continues today.

Among the Corsican finds are thirty-eight statues, one-half indisputably phallic in form. Ten of the statues differ from the other monuments: they have a human form on one side, with an artistically archaic face and a weapon on the chest. On the back only the nape has a definitely phallic shape. Other details may be interpreted as depicting shoulder blades and spinal column or as the anatomical complements of the phallus, the folds of the prepuce.

Closest to the statues in Corsica are those discovered in the Sudan. Human features are shown on one side and a phallus on the other. Similar figures of lesser size are to be seen in Brittany and in Argentina. The phallic statues found in most places, including those in Mexico and North and Central America, are usually small and crude, which is why the Corsican find is so spectacular.

Elsewhere phallic figures were erected on graves during the Bronze Age, not only in honor of the god of sexuality but as a symbolic connecting link between procreation (life) and destruction (death). A particularly striking example is an ex-voto to Dionysus on the island of Delas—a large stone phallus with a phallic bird carved on it.

Sexual Art in the Stone Age

In the Old Stone Age, 20,000 or 25,000 years ago, artists engraved, painted, or sculptured illustrations of unmistakable sexuality on cave walls. They pictured paired animals, pregnant buffalo cows, and other animals. Possibly they believed that by some magical influence this recognition given to reproduction would bring an ample supply for the hunt.

The male and female sex organs were often depicted; sometimes they were exaggerated to make them more impressive. Artists have marveled at the naturalism and accurate detail of this cave-wall art. It is obvious that prehistoric man was tremendously interested in procreation. His was a natural, healthy, and constructive preoccupation with fertility, particularly with the multiplication of animals he hunted and lived upon.

Later in the Stone Age ivory statuettes of nude women, obese or with greatly exaggerated buttocks, were carved. Vulvae, too, were engraved on cave walls, as were sketches of ithyphallic men (with the phallus in erection). Among the relics found in France are many carefully carved phalli made of reindeer horns.

Out of the Caves

The early art of the caves was succeeded by an art of a civilization more addicted to fresh air. Pictorial traces came out of the caves into protected mountain ledges, on cliffs and rocks. Panoramic pictures appeared, giving details of the mode of life led by primitive man. There were scenes of battles and dances. The women were no longer nude, but the men were covered with less clothing than the women. The phallus was still a feature, painted or drawn in various positions.

During the fifth and sixth centuries B.C., when metals and writing were discovered and civilization flowered in the Middle East, the phallus was no less valued and revered. This adoration continued into the Middle Ages and even to our own times, when simple country folk persist in showing veneration to the phallic statues still standing.

Forms of Sex Symbolism

The Language of the Hands

The Egyptians once considered the hand a symbol of the sun's life-giving power, and in the ancient world the hands and fingers were used to express a sex language. In different positions they had various meanings: The first finger extended sidewise, with the other fingers and thumb folded inward, was used as a phallic sign. The thumb and index fingers of the two hands meeting indicated the female sex organ, the sign used by Hindu dancers. Another symbol was the index finger bent to meet the thumb, a symbol still surviving in Latin countries. The palms of the hands pressed together, the index fingers extended upward, and the rest of the fingers of both hands intertwined expressed the union of the sexes. There were many other variations.

Crosses and Triangles

Crosses of different shapes and materials were worshipped by the ancients. In early Greece, Dionysus (Bacchus) and Apollo were represented by one form of cross; in other designs, Aphrodite. Prostitutes in India at one time wore a cross to signify the power to give life. The Egyptian cross, the *ankh,* signified the "key of life." This cross, T-shaped and surmounted by an oval addition typifying the matrix or womb, stood for immortality.

The swastika, adopted by the German Nazis, at one time had a sexual meaning. If the tails of the cross extended toward the left, it signified the female sex; if toward the right, the male sex. Many simple and crude forms of the swastika have been found in ancient ruins. It was used at one time as a symbol of Buddha. An ancient lead idol, excavated at Troy, has a swastika engraved over the likeness of the vulva.

Even the triangle was adopted as a sex symbol. The apex pointing downward was a symbol of the female; upward, of the male. When the two were superimposed, union was indicated. This latter form is the six-pointed "Star of David"—a sign still used in the Orient but without sexual significance. It has remained a mystic symbol, revered in certain religious rituals and in one of the degrees of the Masonic Lodge (The Royal Arch degree).

Phallic Amulets

Among the Romans the phallus was deified in the form of the god Priapus. The practice of carrying priapic figures as amulets against the evil eye and bad luck—that is, against loss of power—became common, thrived during the Middle Ages, and has not yet been entirely abandoned.

The Romans gave the phallic amulet the name of *fascinum,* in Old French *fesne,* when worn around the neck, and a great many of these amulets have been found, mostly in the River Seine. Some are prints, others medals made of lead—on one side the organs of the two sexes and on the other a cross.

Some Roman amulets are more elaborate. On one, a woman uses the phallus as a horse and rides on it; it has the two legs of a man on the phallus. Another represents an enormous phallus attached to the middle of the body of a little man.

The hand phallus, so called by historians, is also seen on amulets. Specimens of these amulets have been found that show two arms joined by a cord, one of them ending in the head of a phallus and the other having a hand. There are two forms of this type of symbol, both known and used since time immemorial. One, the more ancient, shows the middle finger extended with the thumb and other fingers lying on each other. The middle finger represents the virile member, and the two folded fingers on each side signify the testicles. The other has the hand closed but the thumb is stuck between the index finger and the middle finger. This form of the phallic hand, of which the meaning is clear from the rigid thumb, was well known among the Romans. It was considered an insult, much as it is today, to show a person a hand in this position. At that time it designated one who was addicted to unnatural sex practices.

This gesture seems to have been named *ficus* in the later Roman period; in French, *figue*; in English, fig. The fig was consecrated to Priapus as it was considered by the Romans to be the cause of his abundant production. The gesture *ficus*, sometimes known as *fica* since it was a word of feminine gender, persisted all during the Middle Ages, particularly in central Europe where the Roman customs were strong. The Italians called the gesture *fare la fica* (to make a fig at someone) perhaps because of the assumed resemblance of a fig to a vulva.

The phrase seems to have been introduced into the English language at the time of Queen Elizabeth. The translation was presumably "to give a fig." The English writers of the time are said to have called it *la figue d'Espagne,* the Spanish Fig. Thus, a character in *Henry V* says: "A fig for thy friendship, the fig of Spain." The phrase has been handed down to this day. We hear in English, "A fig for——" (anybody or anything).

Common Objects

In ancient civilizations, sex entered into the details of daily life, including various kinds of food. For example, it is believed today that the custom among Semitic peoples of eating fish on Friday originated from the ancient idea that a fish diet greatly increased sexual power. The arched mouth of the fish was compared to the vulva. In many old religious symbols this food item was given a sexual meaning.

The serpent, which plays such a prominent part in the story of creation in the Bible, also appeared in many sex symbols. Swallowing its own tail, it represented union of the sexes. It was considered hermaphroditic, as were the earliest gods and man. Live snakes were kept in the temples of the Early Greeks, where they were fed by nude priestesses. At the famous Oracle of Delphi, the priestesses were called pythonesses, the term carrying a double meaning of priestesses at Pytha and snake women. Snakes were in the shrine of Apollo and were fed in the same way. Many old Egyptian designs show the cobra. The serpent had various sexual meanings, chief of which was sexual desire.

Phallic Festivals

The history of phallicism reveals that sex and religion were intermingled in the ancient mind, and this relation persists to the present. Many of the symbols described could be called mixed symbols. An important role was played by the image of the phallus in ancient religious ceremonies in Egypt, China, and Japan, as well as in India. Featured was a giant phallus 360 feet high and covered with pure gold. Giant phallic statues nearly 200 feet in height guarded the temple of Venus at Hierapolis. The Eleusinian Mysteries of Athens, initiation into which all Athenians craved, linked rites of fertility (the buried seed) with hope of immortality.

The nude body was exposed in numerous ancient rituals. When a river had overflowed its banks and rains threatened, it was thought the rain could be dispersed if women exposed their naked bodies to the darkening sky. Today, in Africa, some tribal women practice a similar ritual to attract rain in time of drought.

During festivals of the goddess Ishtar in Babylonia, cakes resembling the male and female sex organs were baked and eaten. Similar cakes were prepared in honor of other gods, such as Baal and Astarte. Bread phalli were often seen in festivals and processions in early France.

The festival of Liber, an old Italian deity of fruitfulness later identified with Bacchus, the god of drunkenness and debauchery, took place at planting time. On this day the phallus, as the symbol of the god, was carried in procession through the fields and lanes around Rome to increase the crops. In Lavinium a phallus was taken to the public market place, where it was crowned with a garland of flowers by the most respectable and respected matrons of the city.

In rural districts the festival was characterized by the frankest symbolism and by unrestricted license; men and women cohabited along the roadside in honor of the marriage of Ariadne (Libera) and Bacchus (Liber). Cakes, phallic and yonic in shape, and honey and oil were offered to the gods.

Promiscuity and Prostitution

Phallicism began as a form of worship, a prehistoric, elemental form of religion. As time went on, the religious aspect faded, and the more sheerly sexual aspect was conveniently masked as adoration of the gods. Hindu phallicism was swathed in philosophy. In Greece, orgies were veiled as Orphic mysteries.

Considering the accepted mores of the ancient world, this degeneration of phallicism was almost inevitable. Permanent marriages, according to the custom of the Egyptians, were introduced in Greece by Cecrops in 2590 B.C. At the same time, no shame or blame was attached to casual or promiscuous cohabitation. The old tribal relationship was modeled on the habits of the mammal animals the primitive people prized. This was prevalent among the early Jews until Moses forbade it in the name of Jehovah. Incidentally, the power of procreation was revered to such an extent among the Hebrew tribes that oaths are said to have been taken on the phallus, much as they are on the Bible today.

Everywhere temptation and opportunity beckoned and there were no moral restraints. No disgrace was attached to being a prostitute. At one time girls followed the calling to earn a dowry. In Sparta, Lycurgus, the great lawgiver, ordered the maidens to exercise and to go naked in the processions as the young men did, and to dance that way, singing songs at solemn feasts. He intended to promote incitements to marriage but often the results were far different.

The countries were tropical or subtropical, clothing unnecessary, the bonds of matrimony not very binding, concubinage and prostitution freely permitted and even encouraged. Such were the conditions in Egypt, Greece, Rome, Syria, Irania, and other ancient lands where phallic worship was in vogue. In Rome, for example, there were twelve ranks of prostitutes, from the *Delicatae*, "kept women" or mistresses who corresponded to the *Hetaerae*

of the Greeks and who lived in luxury, to the wretched *Quadrantariae*, whose fee was the smallest copper coin made in Rome (about half a cent), a piece of fish or bread, or a drink. At that time every baker, tavern-keeper, bathhouse-keeper, barber, and perfumer kept attendant prostitutes to accommodate his customers.

Bakers' girls were sent out to sell little cakes in the shapes of phalli and yoni for sacrificial offerings in the temples of Priapus or Venus, and were prostitutes as a side line.

There were public and private *lupanaria*, or houses of prostitution, stocked with girl slaves who were at the service of the patrons at very small fees. During the persecution of the Christians the pretty girls and women were not killed in the arenas but were sent to the *lupanaria* as slaves.

The respectable, sheltered women were kept secluded in their homes, except on holidays or when they attended the public shows at the Colosseum or at the theaters. The shows were often grossly suggestive, the actors sometimes having monstrous property phalli fastened in front. These phalli were usually painted a brilliant red, from which may come our phrase, "painting the town red." Sanger, in his *History of Prostitution* (1899) writes: "At Rome, the walls of respectable houses were covered with paintings of which one hardly dares in our times to mention the subjects. Lascivious frescoes and lewd sculptures . . . filled the halls of the Roman citizens and nobles. . . . Such groups as satyrs and nymphs, Leda and the swan, satyrs and she-goats were abundant. All of these were daily exposed to the eyes of the children and young girls."

Contemporary Sex Symbolism

Use of sex symbolism in decoration was so frequent in classical art that it came to be accepted as conventional rather than as symbolic in the strict sense. This has led to its continuance through the ages. The cock, the serpent, and other such figures are now frequent in decoration, but without significance.

The same truth applies to architecture. In the Orient, temples and other such buildings are shaped in the form of a penis because of the association of their rites with procreation and fertility. But the West also has its buildings clearly showing a phallic influence, from the Empire State Building in New York and the Washington Monument in Washington, D.C., to the Y.M.C.A. Building in Jerusalem. In neither case is the form of the building functionally related to the activities for which it is designed. The esthetic value of the form has replaced its symbolic meaning, a process of conventionalizing which is equally apparent in festivals such as Easter, which have given to ancient fertility rites sublimations into more cultivated celebrations.

Psychoanalysis and Sexual Symbolism

Ever since the publication of Freud's *Interpretation of Dreams* in 1900 the term "sexual symbolism" has been almost synonymous with the existence of hidden or repressed sexual meanings in the free associations, dreams, literary productions, and other unconscious processes of human beings. Actually, Freud himself states that he merely rediscovered the existence of sexual symbolism in dreams, and that Scherner, in a largely unnoticed book (*Das Leben des Traumes*) published in 1861 was the real discoverer. Even earlier writers, such as Artemidorus of Daldus, seem to have had at least an inkling of the connection between sexual symbolism and dreams.

Following Freud's lead, a vast psychoanalytic literature on sexual symbolism has grown up, sparked by early contributions of Ferenczi and Rank (1924), Jones (1950), and Stekel (1943). At first, there was a tendency on the part of the psychoanalytic interpreters to produce a dictionary of dream interpretation that would authoritatively connect each symbol dreamed about with its sexual correlate—for example, to list *knife* as indicating a penis and *balcony* as representing breasts. It was soon noted, however, that the individual who uses dream or other unconscious symbols tends to employ them in his own unique manner—so that one person may use *knife* to represent a penis and another individual may use the same symbol to represent a hand, a tongue, or some other organ which may be used for sex purposes.

It was also observed, fairly early in psycho-analytic history, that the psychoanalyst or other would-be interpreter of unconscious sexual processes may himself attribute to symbols used by the dreamer meanings that are more often than not based on his own system of thought rather than on the underlying ideas and feelings of the subject. And the system of thought of the interpreter himself may be seriously in need of analysis.

The question of main importance in regard to unconscious symbolization of sexual thoughts and activities would seem to be: What specific symbols can be used to denote these sex acts? And the answer seems to be: Almost anything may be used by a given individual to symbolize his own sex urges and behavior, and the object he uses for this purpose at a certain time will depend on what is transpiring in his life at this time and what his general philosophy of life and sex may be.

A good case in point is daily speech. Reference to a slang dictionary will show that literally hundreds of different nonsexual objects have been used to denote sexual acts and organs. Thus, a penis has been called, in the English language, a prick, a yard, a cock, a pecker, etc.

Psychoanalysts have wrestled with the problem of sexual symbolism almost endlessly; and the definitive work on the subject, from a psychoanalytic point of view, has yet to be written. The factor of the symbolizer's defensiveness and resistance against seeing or naming the sexual object in its naked objectivity has been especially considered by psychoanalytic writers. Thus, as early as 1916 Ernest Jones published a paper in which he tried to show that the term "sexual symbolism" should be limited to the use of indirect representations of sexual images—to the use of metaphor, simile, analogy, allegory, metonymn, etc. Something was a symbol, Jones contended, if it referred to a repressed sexual wish—that is, if it were cathected by the affective impulse of this sexual wish. As Fenichel (1945) later stated, a serpent was a phallic symbol if it were cathected by phallic feelings.

It is surprising how little has been added to the psychoanalytic interpretation of sexual symbolism since Jones' original formulations. Jones, when he defined a sexual symbol as the use of a nonsexual object for a repressed sexual idea, was thinking in terms of the older psychoanalytic theory, which was occupied largely with the Id, rather than in terms of newer psychoanalytic formulations of the role of the Ego and its various defense mechanisms. So far as we know, no psychoanalyst has tried to define sexual symbolism in terms of the newer psychoanalytic formulations.

One can easily be too conventional, in a psychoanalytic sense, in interpreting sexual symbolism, and by being thus conventional miss the real point of an individual's symbolizing. Thus, in one clinical case an envious girl kept denying her anger and envy and attributing similar feelings to others. But one day when I (G.B.W.) supplied for her some words which she had unclearly heard on TV, she remarked that she had a sudden impulse to rip off my penis. I related this impulse to her jealousy of her young baby brother, when she was 19 months of age and he was just born, and to her impulse to rip off his penis, as something that had come between herself and her mother. As a result of my interpretation, she was able to accept and understand her own penis-envy, which she had previously talked about but not really accepted.

Further discussion and interpretation showed, however, that what this girl really wished for was not so much the penis as the ability to feel penis-envy—for that feeling would make her like other girls who were supposed to have such impulses, rather than being the unenvious, "good" nonentity her mother wanted her to be. Her basic anger at me and at others was not because we had deprived her of a penis but because we seemed to be forcing her to be overly "good"; and she was confused because, at one and the same time, she wanted to be "strong" and envious and wanted to be "good" and lovable. I cite this case mainly to show that human motivations are often most complex and cannot be unraveled by simple interpretation of obvious sexual symbolism (in this case, penis-envy).

As Stekel (1943) noted in his criticism of Freud, a dreamer may dream of a snake and really be thinking of a penis; but he may also be thinking of a woman or some other sexual or nonsexual object. Context, convention, custom, moralizing tendencies—all of these may be influential determiners of why an individual dreams of snakes or why a sculptor or a cake decorator uses snakes, cocks, or other symbols in a pictorial representation, particularly one that is made for a wedding or other ritual with sexual connotations.

Carl Jung (1952, 1953) and his followers have been particularly interested in sexual (and nonsexual) symbolism and its relationship to human personality. Where Freud implied that only what has once been consciously apprehended and then unconsciously repressed can be symbolized, Jung and his disciples hold that an individual can symbolize that which has never been conscious and which, as in the case of the so-called death instinct, never can be conscious. The Jungians solve some of the difficult problems in this area by positing not only an individual but a collective unconscious, in which supposedly resides archaic or archetypal ideas that have been handed down by individuals from generation to generation.

It is not within the scope of this article to trace the origins and development of symbolism in general and the attempts of numerous thinkers to solve the question of man and his relation to the universe by finding the hidden x that would explain the riddle and then symbolizing this x with some root-metaphor. We may merely quote Rank's (1929) view that "the real world itself, created by man, has proved to be a chain of symbol formations, uninterruptedly renewed, which represent not merely a substitute for the lost primal reality which they copy as faithfully as possible, but at the same time must remind us as little as possible of the primal trauma connected with it."

In any event, just because man has an almost infinite capacity to symbolize sex acts and thoughts by nonsexual representations, and because he is uniquely a symbolizing and language-creating animal, we must be careful not to give definitive, conclusive interpretations to any of his specific symbolizations. We can be fairly certain that imaginative and appropriate symbols for the genitals, for sex urges, and for every other aspect of human sexuality will continue to be made through the ages to come, and that these will tend, while having some general resemblance to the things they symbolize, to vary enormously from period to period, civilization to civilization, and individual to individual.

References

Barton, G. A., *A Sketch of Semitic Origins, Social and Religious.* New York: The Macmillan Co., 1902.

Breasted, James H., *The Dawn of Conscience.* New York: Charles Scribner's Sons, 1933.

Brown, Norman O., *Hermes the Thief.* Madison: University of Wisconsin Press, 1947.

Campbell, R. A., *Phallic Worship.* St. Louis: Campbell, 1887.

Cassirer, Ernst, *An Essay on Man.* New York: Doubleday Anchor Books, 1953.

Cassirer, Ernst, *The Philosophy of Symbolic Forms.* New Haven: Yale University Press, 1955.

Cutner, H., *A Short History of Sex Worship.* London: Watts, 1940.

Darwin, Charles, *The Expression of the Emotions in Man and Animals.* New York: Philosophical Library, 1955.

Dulaure, J. A., *Die Zeugung in Glauben, Sitten und Brauchen der Volker.* Leipzig: Deutsche Verlagsanstalt, 1909.

Dulaure, J. A., *The Gods of Generation.* New York: Panurge Press, 1923.

Fenichel, Otto, *Psychoanalytic Theory of the Neurosis.* New York: W. W. Norton & Co., 1945.

Ferdinant, Maximilian, *Sexualmystik der Vergangenheit.* Berlin: Privately printed, 1892.

Ferenczi, Sandor, and Rank, Otto, *Entwicklungziele der Psychoanalyse.* Vienna: International Psychoanalyse Verlag, 1924.

Fergusson, James, *Rude Stone Monuments.* London: J. Murray, 1872.

Goldberg, Isaac, *The Sacred Fire.* New York: Alfred A. Knopf, 1930.

Goodland, Roger, *Bibliography of Sex Rites and Customs.* London: George Routledge & Sons, 1931.

Gutheil, Emil, *The Handbook of Dream Analysis.* New York: Liveright, 1951.

Hannay, J. B., *The Rise, Decline and Fall of the Roman Religion.* London: Religious Evolution Research Society, 1925.

Hannay, J. B., *Symbolism in Relation to Religion or Christianity.* London: Trench, 1925.

Howard, Clifford, *Sex Worship.* Washington, D.C.: Privately printed, 1898.

Jones, Ernest, *Papers on Psychoanalysis.* Baltimore: The Williams & Wilkins Co., 1950.

Jung, Carl G., *Psychology and Alchemy.* New York: Pantheon Books, 1952.

Jung, Carl G., *Two Essays on Analytical Psychology.* New York: Pantheon Books, 1953.

Kerenyi, Karl, Commentary in Radin, Paul (ed.), *The Trickster.* New York: Philosophical Library, 1956.

Knight, Richard Payne, *Sexual Symbolism.* New York: Julian Press, 1947.

Pepper, S., *World Hypotheses.* Berkeley: University of California Press, 1942.

Piaget, Jean, *Growth of Logical Thinking from Childhood to Adolescence.* New York: Basic Books, 1958.

Rank, Otto, *Trauma of Birth.* New York: Harcourt, Brace & Co., 1929.

Rocco, Sha, *The Masculine Cross and Ancient Sex Worship.* New York: Butts, 1874.

Sanger, William, *History of Prostitution.* New York: Medical Publishing Co., 1899.

Schlesinger, A., *Geschichte des Symbols.* Berlin: Leonard Simon, 1912.

Scott, George R., *Phallic Worship.* New York: Mental Health Press, 1952.

Stark, Werner, *The Sociology of Knowledge.* Glencoe, Ill.: Free Press, 1958.

Stein, Leopold, "What Is a Symbol Supposed to Be?" *J. Analytical Psychol.,* 1957.

Stekel, Wilhelm, *Interpretation of Dreams.* New York: Liveright, 1943.

Strelitz, Paul, "Der Phalluskultus." *Geschlecht und Gessellschaft 6;* 10, 1911.

Tylor, E. G., *Primitive Culture.* New York: Henry Holt & Co., 1889.

Wake, C. S., and Westropp, M. H., *Ancient Symbol Worship.* New York: J. W. Bouton, 1875.

Wall, O. A., *Sex and Sex Worship.* St. Louis: C. V. Mosby Co., 1922.

Westropp, M. H., *Primitive Symbolism as Illustrated in Phallic Worship.* London: Ridway, 1886.

**ALBERT ABARBANEL AND
GEORGE B. WILBUR**

Planned Parenthood
around the World

PLANNED parenthood is not new. Long before the dawn of written history, primitive peoples in all parts of the world made some attempts to adjust the size of their families to the available means of subsistence. They did this, however, by wasteful and often cruel methods—by infanticide, abortion, killing the aged—by ritual taboos on the time of intercourse, or and by prolonging the nursing period. Only within the last century have scientific preventive measures been developed, and these are now beginning to play an important role in population and family planning.

In nearly every part of the world there is today a growing interest in planned parenthood. This interest stems from two major factors: First, there is an increased realization of the values of planned parenthood to individual and family welfare. It is being widely recognized that voluntary parenthood, the conscious regulation of reproduction, can contribute to the physical, emotional, and even spiritual stability of the family and the home. Second, there is a growing social awareness that population planning can contribute also to the social and economic stability of the family of nations and to the peace of the world. It is necessary today to bring about a better balance between populations and resources, between human fertility and soil fertility, between human production and human reproduction.

The widespread concern with population control at the present time is due in the main to the very rapid growth of the numbers of people throughout the world. In 1650, about 300 years ago, the total world population is estimated to have been about 500 million. Today it amounts to some two and three-quarter billion, or five times as many. These figures are significant. From the time when man first emerged upon the face of the earth, over a period of some hundreds of thousands of years, his numbers had been increasing very slowly. He was fruitful and he multiplied but the death rates from famine, from hunger, from wars nearly equaled the birth rate and populations remained fairly stable. Then quite suddenly, within a period of only 300 years, the global population increased fivefold, and at the present rate of growth it is likely to double every 40 years.

The reasons for this explosive rate of growth are many but the major cause has been the rapid conquest of disease. Fewer children die in infancy, fewer mothers die in childbirth, fewer men and women die from epidemic diseases. Everywhere the death rates have been declining and the population figures have been rapidly mounting.

This situation is leading many countries to concern themselves more intensively with the problem of population and to give greater thought to family planning as a partial solution to this problem. The following review presents the developments in planned parenthood in a number of the major countries in the world.

England

Malthusianism originated in England, and Great Britain was one of the first countries to accept family planning as a social practice. The first birth-control clinic was opened in London in 1922 by Dr. Marie Stopes. Since then, many other centers have been established by the English Family Planning Association, which is today an active and effective organization.

In 1944, a Royal Commission on Population was appointed especially to examine the population trends in Great Britain and to consider what measures, if any, should be taken in the national interest to influence future population growth. After a thorough and highly competent survey, the Commission brought in a comprehensive report and made a number of recommendations. On the question of voluntary parenthood, the Report stated:

We take the view that it is in the long run interests of the family that voluntary parenthood should become universal and that women should have the maximum freedom in the ordering of their lives . . . with the spread of effective knowledge of contraception, voluntary parenthood will become more or less universal. This will accelerate the fall in the numbers of the larger families except among those who deliberately decide to have them; but it will help to secure that children, whether in large or small families, are wanted children and are not the result of ignorance.

This enlightened and realistic approach has been a guiding principle in the family-planning movement in England. It places the emphasis upon the importance of the happy and well-integrated family, rather than on the large family.

Scandinavian Countries

Equally liberal is the attitude on family planning in Sweden, Norway, and Denmark. Sweden has no restrictive laws on contraception. A Swedish Population Commission report, published in 1935-1938, also stressed the importance of voluntary parenthood as a means toward a democratic family and population policy. The Swedish Association for Sex Education, organized 25 years ago by the Swedish pioneer in this field, Mrs. Elise Ottesen-Jensen, has been an effective force in the development of enlightened sex education in the schools and in the development of family-planning programs. Under its auspices a number of contraceptive centers have been established in Sweden. The clinic in Stockholm is located on one

of the main streets of the city and compares favorably with some of the best clinics in the United States. Family planning is widely recognized as an essential part of the country's social-welfare program. Clinics also exist in Norway and in Denmark, established by the Family Planning Associations in these countries.

Holland

Holland was among the first countries in the world to establish a contraceptive service. Under the leadership of Doctors John Rutgers and Aletta Jacobs, a center was organized in Amsterdam in 1890. Later several other centers were opened but these were staffed by trained midwives and nurses. In the 1930's, well-equipped clinics under medical direction were opened in Amsterdam, Rotterdam, The Hague, and other cities. Following the German invasion during World War II, all the clinics were closed and a number of the physicians associated with them were arrested. Since the end of the war, however, a new association has been organized and family-planning clinics have been reopened in many cities. In spite of considerable religious opposition, these services have been expanding rapidly.

Germany and Austria

Before the Hitler regime, Germany had a progressive and active planned-parenthood movement. During the Weimar Republic, after World War I, marriage-counseling centers and birth-control clinics were opened in many German and Austrian cities, and much progress was being made in the social and scientific aspects of planned parenthood. With the coming of the Nazi regime, however, the centers were closed and many of the active leaders of the movement were arrested and some of them executed. Medical education in the field of fertility control was stopped, and the publication of medical literature on the subject ceased. The German physicians who were educated under the Hitler regime, and with whom I had occasion to talk when I visited Germany soon after the war, had little knowledge of contraception. They had been taught in their medical schools that the use of contraceptive measures was physically dangerous and socially and racially harmful. "In this respect," an older physician, who had survived the Hitler era, said to me at that time, "the German doctors are now fifty years behind the stage we had reached before the war."

In recent years, however, there has been a reawakening of social and medical interest in planned parenthood. At present a new movement is emerging in West Germany in response to a growing public awareness of the social and medical needs. Dr. Anne Marie Durant-Wever and Dr. Hans Harmsen, both pioneers in this field, have organized a new Family Planning Association. In 1957 they conducted a European conference on family planning and sex education in West Berlin, and they are making a valiant effort to re-establish birth-control clinics and a wider planned-parenthood movement in West Germany.

France, Italy, Spain, Belgium

In western European countries where the Catholic religion is the predominant faith of the people—in France, Italy, Belgium, and Spain—there are no planned-parenthood services. The sale of contraceptive materials and the dissemination of planned-parenthood information is prohibited by law. Materials are not available in the open market, except prophylactic sheaths that can also be used for the prevention of venereal disease.

Within recent years, however, planned-parenthood organizations have been emerging even in some of the Catholic countries. In Italy an organization known as The Italian Association for the Study of Demography was established in 1953 by Dr. Vittoria Olivetti and her co-workers. The objective of this group is to promote family-planning ideas in Italy and to establish clinical services for this purpose. In France, Dr. Laguen Weill-Halle initiated a group—the Maternité Heureuse—with a similar goal in mind. In both these countries abortion is very widespread, but the planned-parenthood organizations emphasize especially the value of contraceptive measures as a means of eliminating the dangers of resorting to illegal and underground abortion.

What is the Catholic position on the subject of planned parenthood? In an address at the World Population Conference, held in Rome in 1954, a Jesuit priest, Father Stanislaus L'-Estapis, outlined the official Catholic attitude. According to the Catholic dogma, he said in effect: A couple should bring forth only the number of children they can adequately care for. Parenthood ought to be responsible. To achieve this purpose, however, Catholics can resort only to abstinence in marriage, or under certain conditions to periodic abstinence by following the rhythm method. The use of any mechanical or chemical preventive methods is considered to be against the moral law, against the law of nature, and hence prohibited by the Church. The major difference, then, is not on the basic idea of responsible or planned parenthood, but on the question of method and technique.

The Near East

In the Near East organized family-planning work has been established only in Egypt. Under the auspices of an official Population Committee, a number of centers have been established for teaching family-planning methods and for distribution of materials to that purpose. In the other Arabian countries—in Iran, Iraq, Syria, and Lebanon—there are no clinical contraceptive services in existence. A few individual physicians do provide contraceptive information but their services reach only a very small portion of the population in these areas.

The Moslem religion, in the main, is not opposed to the prevention of conception. In an article published in the *Journal of the Egyptian Medical Association* in July, 1937, the Grand Mufti of Egypt, in a comprehensive discussion of the question said, "It is permissible for either husband or wife, by mutual consent, to take any measures to prevent semen entering the uterus, in order to prevent conception." Other Moslem religious teachers, however, apparently hold a different view and oppose the dissemination of birth-control information.

Israel

In Israel, too, the strictly orthodox Jewish groups are averse to the use of contraceptive measures on religious grounds, and the government is opposed to population planning because the nation is eager to increase its numbers at present. Nevertheless, a Family Planning group and a few contraceptive services have been established in Israel. The hospitals and the medical departments of the health-insurance agencies, as well as the public-health authorities, are now giving consideration to the question of family planning, even if only on the basis of individual needs. Many of the physicians in Israel today have been trained in the West and are therefore well-acquainted with contraceptive techniques. Some contraceptive materials are now being manufactured in Israel, and they are used quite widely by couples in both rural and urban centers.

Japan

In the 1920's, Baroness Shidzue Ishimoto, now known as Mrs. Kato, organized a small family-planning group and established a birth-control center in Tokyo. After the onset of the Sino-Japanese War, the government disbanded the organization and the clinic was closed. During the last decade, however, there has been a marked reawakening to the urgency of the population question in Japan and a number of important developments have taken place.

In 1920 the population of Japan was 55 million. When the 1948 census showed that the population had reached over 80 million, official Japan became greatly alarmed. Early in April, 1949, the Japanese government appointed the Population Problem Council, which was composed of eighteen members who were experts in demography and sociology. In its report the Council dealt with ways of developing measures to improve Japan's economy and to extend its capacity to absorb and to feed its growing numbers, and with the need of readjusting population growth by popularizing the idea of contraception among all strata in the nation. The Council recommended, among other things, that the health centers and eugenic consultation offices throughout the country be mobilized to teach contraceptive practices and that the government furnish certain classes of the people with contraceptive drugs and materials free of charge.

In the same year, 1949, a so-called Eugenic Protection Law was adopted by the Japanese Diet. The law provided for the voluntary or, in some cases, compulsory sterilization of people with hereditary diseases or deformities, and also for the legal performance of artificial interruption of pregnancy when serious injury to the mother was feared for physical or economic reasons. This law was further amended in 1952 to give physicians even greater latitude in resorting to sterilizations and abortions, and thus abortion was practically legalized in Japan.

As a result of this new law, the number of pregnancy interruptions grew steadily. In 1950, some 500,000 official abortions were performed. By 1957 the number had reached over a million, not counting the number of unofficial and unreported abortions, which probably amounted to several hundred thousand. Although in the last three years there has been a slight decline in the incidence of official operations, the number of abortions still exceeds the number of live births in Japan.

India

India's present population is some 390 million people and it is growing at a rate of some 6 million annually. In 1946 a Health Survey and Development Committee, appointed by the Indian government, recommended that free contraceptives be supplied by the state whenever further pregnancy would be detrimental to the health of the mother. There are no legal or religious prohibitions against the use of contraceptives among the Hindus, although the teachings of Gandhi, who was opposed to contraception and advocated continence as the only method of family limitation, still have a very wide influence in India.

The Indian government, however, has recognized the vital importance of family planning for that country. In a discussion of the problem in April, 1951, Prime Minister Nehru said, "I am entirely in favor of limiting the growth of the population by institution of various methods, including birth control."

This attitude was later implemented by a practical plan. In 1951, the Health Ministry of India requested the World Health Organization to send a special consultant in family planning to advise the Indian government, and the writer was privileged to go on this mission. He remained in India for some ten weeks, traveling through the country and consulting with governmental, social, and public health leaders. As a result of the increased governmental interest, a considerable amount of progress is being made in the development of a family-planning program in India.

In 1952 the first Five-Year Plan was adopted by the Indian Parliament. The plan related to the social, economic, industrial, educational, medical, and health programs in India. One special chapter was devoted to family planning in India and read in part as follows:

Thee recent increase in the population of India and the pressure exercised on the limited resources of the country have brought to the forefront the urgency of the problem of family planning and population control. The application of medical knowledge and social care has lowered the death rate, while the birthrate remains fairly constant. This has led to the rapid increase in the growth of population. While a lowering of the birthrate may occur as a result of improvements in the standard of living, such improvements are not likely to materialize if there is a concurrent increase of population. It is, therefore, apparent that population control can be achieved only by the reduction of the birthrate to the extent necessary to stabilize the population at a level consistent with the requirements of national economy. This can be secured only by the realization of the need for family limitation on a wide scale by the people. The main appeal for family planning is based on considerations of health and welfare of the family. Family limitation or spacing of the children is necessary and desirable in order to secure better health for the mother and better care and upbringing of children. Measures directed to this end should, therefore, form part of the public health program.

To meet this need the government allocated over a million dollars to the Ministry of Health for the development of the family-planning program. Later, when the second Five-Year Plan was adopted in 1956, the amount was increased to 10 million dollars for a program of services, education, and research which is now under way. In India planned parenthood is no longer a matter of controversy; it is accepted as essential for family welfare and for national welfare.

References

Forslund, Kerstin, "Riksforbundet for sexuell upplysning." *J. Fam. Welfare 5;* No. 1, 52-55, 1958.

Levine, Lena, "Education for Family Life in Transition." *J. Fam. Welfare 5;* No. 3, 62-69, 1959.

Mukherjee, Radhakamal, "Population and Human Values." *J. Fam. Welfare 5;* No. 3, 28-37, 1959.

Nehru, Jawaharlal, Inaugural Address at the Sixth International Conference on Planned Parenthood. *J. Fam. Welfare 5;* No. 3, 4-10, 1959.

Reports of the Second and Third All-India Conferences on Family Planning. Bombay: Family Planning Association of India, 1956.

Reports of the Third, Fourth and Fifth International Conferences on Planned Parenthood. Bombay: Family Planning Association of India, 1955-1959.

Stone, Abraham, and Himes, Norman E., *Practical Birth Control Methods.* New York: The Viking Press, Inc., 1951.

Stone, Abraham, "Marital Maladjustments and Marriage Counseling." *J. Fam. Welfare 1;* No. 1, 5-9, 1954.

Stone, Abraham, and Levine, Lena, *The Premarital Consultation.* New York: Grune and Stratton, 1956.

Stone, Hannah M., and Stone, Abraham, *A Marriage Manual.* New York: Simon and Schuster, Inc., 1952.

Wadia, Avabai B., "Planned Parenthood in East Asia." *J. Fam. Welfare 2;* No. 2, 41-45, 1956.

ABRAHAM STONE

Polynesia,
Sex Life in

SINCE the first island within the huge Polynesian triangle delimited by Hawaii, New Zealand, and Easter Island was discovered in 1595 by the Spaniard Mendaña, who passed through and named the Marquesas group, the Polynesians have enjoyed an unrivaled reputation for their sexual freedom and hospitality.

Beginning with Quiros' chronicle of Mendaña's voyage, all accounts of the seventeenth- and eighteenth-century Pacific explorers are full of enthusiastic descriptions of the warm receptions given them at each landfall in Polynesia by crowds of beautiful and willing women. One of Bougainville's companions, the naturalist Commerson, even went as far as to assert (*Mercure de France,* November 1769) that the Tahitians "know no other god than love. Every day is consecrated to him. The whole island is his temple in which all the women are idols and all the men worshippers. And what women!" Knowing that Commerson was an eager reader of Rousseau, it is difficult to withhold the suspicion that he somewhat idealized the conditions. But Captain Cook, who was a very dispassionate and reliable observer, did not hesitate to make the following bold statement: "There is a scale in dissolute sensuality, which these peoples have ascended, wholly unknown to every other nation whose manners have been recorded from the beginning of the world to the present hour, and which no imagination could possibly conceive." Later visitors to Polynesia have told about their experiences in books with such alluring titles as *Isles of Eden, Island Daughters of Joy,* and

The Island of Desire and have contributed to create the now prevailing picture in Europe and America of Polynesia as the paradise of absolutely free, uninhibited love.

This is, however, a far from true picture. Sexual freedom undoubtedly was—and still is —much greater in Polynesia than in our Western Christian societies; it is even probable that if we could compile a list of all known societies and arrange them according to degree of social control of the sex instinct, putting the strictest first and the mildest last, our own society would come first and the Polynesian, as Cook suggested, somewhere near the bottom. (Murdock has made such an attempt in Chapter 9 of his book *Social Structure,* but unfortunately it is inconclusive due to inadequate information about many cultures.)

Sexual freedom in Polynesia was never complete. Not only were there many prohibitions but they seem to have been very strictly observed. The following general characteristics of these prohibitions, or moral norms, must be stressed:

1. They reflected very closely the aristocratic character of the Polynesian society, i.e., the chiefs and nobles had much greater sexual freedom than the commoners.

2. They were not always the same for the men and the women; as a rule the former had somewhat more sexual freedom than the latter.

3. Sexual sanctions became gradually more numerous and severe as the individual advanced in years.

The past tense has been used throughout this

article because its aim is first and foremost to reconstruct the pre-European conditions in Polynesia. The source material for this reconstruction is therefore mainly the printed and unprinted accounts of sea captains, missionaries, traders, and other early visitors and residents, whenever possible checked against later studies by professional anthropologists, including the author's own observation on islands where ancient customs still survive. It should also be pointed out here that interisland differences were so insignificant at the time of the discovery that Polynesia, at least for the present purpose, can be treated as an area of uniform culture.

General Attitude toward Sex

The Polynesian attitude toward sexual matters can best be described as appreciative, realistic, and frank. The sexual partner or the circumstances for intercourse might be considered wrong at some times, but sexual pleasure itself was never considered evil or repulsive to a Polynesian. Not even the gods and the priests regarded sex as sinful but themselves showed a hearty sexual appetite. Unknown also was the European romantic conception of love as a mysterious, almost supernatural force whose causes are undefinable. In Polynesia love was a game rather than a metaphysical entity, and the reasons that compelled a man or a woman to choose a particular partner in love or marriage were always entirely realistic.

To the Polynesians the sexual act was just as simple and natural as eating and drinking, and they could therefore talk of it in the same unembarrassed and direct manner. Likewise, all the parts of the body had names, which could be used at any time and anywhere, and it made no difference whether only one or both sexes were present.

Contrary to what one might suppose, Polynesians were comparatively well clothed, and only children under 5 went about quite naked. The older boys and men, when at work, wore a girdle of bark-cloth or plaited pandanus leaves and the older girls and women were clad in bark-cloth or leaf skirts reaching from the waist to the knees. The parts of the female body that Polynesians felt should be covered did not include the breasts, which therefore excited male interest very slightly. In sharp contrast to this, both men and women took great care to hide the genital organs, and it was especially unseemly for a woman to expose the lower part of the body. This may seem to accord but poorly with the numerous references in the literature to naked South Sea beauties. But the contradictions are only apparent, and it can in each case easily be shown that the narrator had witnessed a formal dance or a public exhibition in sexual technique, at which special occasions the Polynesian performers were allowed to diverge from the current rules of dress.

Means of Attraction

In Polynesia it was primarily physical qualities that made a man or woman desirable, and those most valued were beauty and sexual experience. The Polynesians resembled or even exceeded the Greeks in their intense worship of beauty; this is shown by the many stories of chiefs or nobles who made long and perilous sea voyages to distant islands to win famous beauties, whose bodily charms were described in a most detailed and realistic manner. Beauty competitions were also frequently held on all the islands, and the winners gained both honor and material advantages.

The Polynesian ideal of beauty was, however, very different from ours. To be regarded as perfect, a man or woman first had to be stout. An equally important requirement was to be white-skinned. This unexpected admiration for white skin in a people the overwhelming majority of whom were light brown is presumably due to the fact that the rulers who set the fashion were descendants of a light-skinned tribe; but whatever the origin of this preference, it explains to a large extent why European visitors always were so well received.

In order to improve on nature, Polynesian youths, especially those of noble birth, underwent protracted fattening and bleaching treatments. Men and women of all classes bathed several times a day and rubbed themselves regularly with oil to protect the skin and make it soft. It was also very important to have a pleasant smell, and those who were most bent on conquest used perfumes and decked themselves with sweet-scented wreaths of flowers. Clothes played a subordinate role as means of attraction, since all Polynesians dressed practically alike.

The Sexual Act

An excellent testimony to the value the Polynesians attached to sexual proficiency is Gifford's statement in his *Tongan Society*: "If a young man refrained from cohabiting with women previous to his marriage he was not highly desirable among the unmarried girls."

Intercourse between a married couple usually took place at night in their sleeping hut. Intercourse between occasional partners, either sanctioned or unsanctioned, more often than not took place during the day under the palm trees.

A prolonged foreplay seldom occurred, and at any rate the man seldom stroked the woman's breast. Kissing in the European sense was unknown and affection was instead shown through pressing noses together. To judge by present conditions (which give us our only clues in this case), little refinement in form of frequent changes of coital position was practiced, but men set great value on women who were able to make the kind of rotatory movement that was the basic element of their erotic dances. The ideal male partner showed great strength and endurance and was able to achieve and evoke several orgasms in rapid succession.

Because of the collectivistic character of Polynesian life, a loving couple had much less need to be alone and often had intercourse in the same house or in the same part of the wood as other couples.

Childhood

As might be expected of a people with so emphatic and appreciative an attitude toward sex as the Polynesians, they made no attempt to suppress sexuality in the younger generation. On the contrary, parents encouraged their children to indulge in free experimentation and realistic play.

To begin with, sexual instruction simply took the form of letting the children listen freely to the candid, outspoken conversations of their parents and relations. As all the members of the family slept in the same hut without partitions, the children often witnessed the sexual act in their own homes, and were also allowed, as the most natural thing in the world, to be present at deliveries, nude dancing, and demonstrations in the technique of sexual intercourse.

Masturbation was considered quite natural, and parents often urged their children to masturbate when they wanted peace and quiet, more or less as we give our children rubber teats. When the children grew older they had to learn various sex games. "Daddy, Mummy, and children," for example, was played much more realistically than our children play it. After a pretended cohabitation with a boy of the same age, the girl-mother, for example, often stuffed a coconut inside her dress and gave birth to her child, imitating labor pains very dramatically and letting the nut fall at the proper moment.

Dances of an erotic character were common. Cook wrote that in Tahiti, dances of this type were "performed by young girls, whenever eight or ten of them can be collected together," and added that they consisted of "motions and gestures beyond imagination wanton, in which they are brought up from their earliest childhood, accompanied by words, which, if it were possible, would more explicitly convey the same idea." Small children imitating sexual intercourse were a common sight on all islands. Only children of the same age, however, took part in these sexual games, and it was considered in the highest degree improper and abnormal for an adult person to show any interest in them. Any such offense was punished with extreme severity.

Puberty

No special puberty ceremonies or virility tests took place in Polynesia, but as soon as the children reached physical maturity their sexual education was completed with practical instruction in the technique of intercourse. This was done by letting the boys and girls have their first real intercourse with an older, experienced person. In most cases the instructors were older boys or girls who belonged to the same set, but often recourse was had to an aunt, uncle, or other relative of their parents' generation. Peter Buck gives a good description of this custom in his study, *Ethnology of Tongareva*: "The father appointed a woman of mature age to act as instructress and perform the ceremony of pressing back the foreskin of the penis. The purpose of this manipulation was to 'snap the tie,' *kia motu te sele*. The snapping of the tie was not the rupturing of the frenum as the wording might imply but the stretching of the opening of the foreskin so that it might pass the glans. For the custom the instructress and the victim retired to a hut where the coconut leaf wall sheets were lowered and only themselves were present. The ceremony of manipulation and instruction ended in coitus."

At the age of puberty the boys were also circumcised, except among the Maori people. The form of circumcision practiced by the Polynesians should perhaps be called incision or superincision, because instead of removing the foreskin, only a longitudinal slit was made in the upper side of it. The "operation" was quite painless and simple, and was usually performed with a bamboo knife by a priest-physician. Public opinion was so strongly in favor of superincision that practically all boys submitted to it; the few who eluded this obligation were made the butt of jeers and were unable to find any female partners.

Adolescence

The years immediately following puberty were the merriest, most carefree time of a Polynesian's life. Boys and girls of that age had as yet few duties toward their family and could therefore devote most of their time to dance, song, sport, and amusement. As a rule, they formed loosely organized "gangs" and roamed about from place to place. It must be stressed, however, that these gangs fulfilled an important social function, as they supplied their community with dancers, singers, entertainers, and workers any time a festival was celebrated—which puts them in a completely different category from our big-city youth gangs.

The parents thought it quite natural that the young people should give unrestrained expression to their *joie de vivre*, and sexual freedom was always unrestricted. A girl was definitely looked down upon if she remained at home,

and mothers boasted openly if their girls attracted an unusually large number of boys. On many islands the youths built special pleasure houses where they could entertain each other with song and dance and make love. These pleasure houses have often been compared to brothels but, despite certain outward similarities, the Polynesian pleasure houses were fundamentally unlike our establishments. They were visited only by unmarried young people, and the girls themselves chose their partners. Also, no sort of recompense was given; the very idea of payment would never have occurred to a Polynesian. Finally, the pleasure houses were not regarded as establishments of a socially or morally inferior nature, but were considered respectable in the highest degree.

If a girl happened to become pregnant, no particular significance was attached to it and no sanctions were imposed. As a matter of fact, a girl who had had a child before marriage was more sought after as a wife than one who had not, for she had thus shown that she was fertile, which was of great importance in the eyes of a Polynesian man.

There was one exception to the general rule that adolescence was a period of complete sexual freedom: the daughters of the most important chiefs had to be virgins. Tongan and Samoan chiefs were particularly strict about this, and high-born girls in these islands were never allowed to be alone, night or day. In Samoa such virgins acted as village hostesses, were given the best food, and were freed from all hard work, which shows the immense prestige they enjoyed. Although on other islands the number of such girls was smaller and the supervision more lax, the highest chiefs' daughters were urged to remain chaste. This rule was obviously due to a desire to keep the noble blood pure, for if the daughters of the nobility had been allowed the same freedom as ordinary girls, it would have been impossible to prevent them from occasionally having a child by a man of lower birth. To the class-conscious noble families such an event was considered an appalling disaster.

Marriage

Almost all Polynesian boys and girls married as soon as they became adults, and the only real obstacles to finding a life companion were deformity, extreme ugliness, or permanent disablement. This general preference for married life was, as is true among most other primitive peoples, mainly due to the fact that the family fulfilled important social and economic functions, and a married person fared much better in the struggle for existence than an unmarried person.

Numerous rules determined the choice of the marriage partner, their mutual rights, and the duties of a married couple. In all Polynesia marriages were prohibited not only between brothers and sisters but also between cousins and second cousins, and on many islands these taboos included even third cousins and great-grandchildren of cousins. A most remarkable and revealing exception occurred in Hawaii and Rarotonga, where sisters and brothers in the ruling families often married one another. In this case it was evidently due to the anxiety to preserve the purity of the noble blood.

A man or woman was not forbidden to seek a spouse outside his or her own tribe, but few seem to have done so. This is in accord with the Polynesians' strong feeling of kinship and need of family support. On the other hand, marriages outside the class barriers were generally regarded as almost criminal, and only if both parties belonged to the same class could somewhat lower birth be compensated for by personal advantages, primarily beauty and sexual accomplishment.

To prevent *mésalliances* it was chiefly the parents and not the young people themselves who decided whom they should marry. The higher the parents' social position, the more relatives had to be consulted, and when the heir to a really prominent ruler was to marry, the pros and cons of the contemplated union were generally discussed for several days at a meeting of hundreds of tribal members. How little regard high-born parents had for their children's feelings is seen by the fact that sons and daughters were often married off or betrothed while they were still children. Among the lower classes the young people had much greater freedom of choice, but in every case they had to have the parents' consent.

Only in the higher classes was a special marriage ceremony considered necessary; com-moners were regarded as married from the moment they began to live together with their parents' consent. In the islands where the chastity of the chiefs' daughters was most strictly guarded, public defloration took place in connection with the wedding feast.

Extramarital Relations

The Polynesians' ideal, like our own, was marital fidelity, but certain exceptions were made. As usual, the chiefs had greater liberty than their subjects, but the following three kinds of extramarital connections were allowed in all classes:

1. Between a married man and his sisters-in-law, and between a married woman and her brothers-in-law. As cousins were regarded as brothers and sisters, the number of permissible extramarital connections of this kind was quite considerable.

2. Between a married man and his name-brother's wife and sisters-in-law, and between a married woman and her husband's name-brother and his brothers. As in many other countries, it often happened that two men entered into a sworn brotherhood, which compact was sealed by an exchange of names. These name-brothers had the same sexual rights as real brothers.

3. Between a married woman and a male guest of the family, as determined by the husband.

In addition, high chiefs had the right to engage in all kinds of casual love affairs, the extent and number of which depended on each individual chief's power and diplomatic skill.

A divorce could easily be obtained, and it was considered quite natural and fully permissible for a man and woman to divorce simply because they considered themselves unsuited to each other. The divorce took place without any formalities whatsoever, and the practical and economic problems were easily solved by either the husband or wife—depending on whose parents the couple lived with—going back to his or her parents. The goods and chattels were divided between the parties, and if they had any children the wife usually took the girls and babies with her and the husband kept the older boys.

To the Polynesians it was quite unthinkable for an adult to live alone. Divorced men and women and widows and widowers married again quickly. As in ancient Israel, the levirate was an honored custom, which meant that a widow as a rule married a younger brother of the deceased husband. This was considered especially important if the widow had many children, because it was only in this way that the children could be kept in the family to which they belonged by blood. For the widow such a remarriage did not involve any great changes, as in most cases she already lived under the same roof as her brother-in-law and was accustomed to having sexual intercourse with him.

Polygamy

Although there was no formal obstacle to a commoner entering into a polygamous union, in reality polygamy was practiced almost exclusively among the nobility. Another and equally typical Polynesian limitation was that, on most of the islands, polygamy was mainly a privilege of the male sex. Thanks to the care with which the Polynesians have preserved their genealogies, it is possible to determine in a fairly satisfactory manner the extent to which polygamy occurred. The computations that have been made show that, at the most, 20 per cent of the total number of marriages were polygynous. However, large harems did not exist, and even very powerful chiefs rarely had more than two or three wives.

Polygyny was obviously not practiced out of a desire for change and new sexual experience, since Polynesian chiefs could satisfy this need with much less difficulties and responsibilities by the many extramarital liaisons to which they were entitled. There were other more compelling reasons. In the first place, all chiefs wanted a male heir and a great number of children in order to continue the family and increase its power. If the first wife was barren or produced only girls, the husband regarded it as his duty to the family and the community to take another wife. There were also economic reasons. A chief had a high standard of living to maintain, and was compelled to house and entertain guests of all kinds. The work involved was of

course facilitated by having several wives. Finally, there were many social and political considerations. As new and important political alliances had continually to be concluded and social connections established (and these objects were best attained by marriage), the chiefs found it only natural to remarry as the occasion demanded.

As in many other respects, the Marquesan Islands occupied a special position regarding the form of polygamy. Everywhere else in Polynesia the normal form of polygamy was polygyny, but the preferred form there was polyandry. The exception is at first sight all the more remarkable as polyandry is an extremely rare form of marriage, whereas about 80 per cent of the peoples of the world allow polygynous marriages. Opler (1943), for instance, who made a critical study of all alleged cases of polyandry, accepted the evidence regarding the Todas in southern India and the Marquesan Islanders as the only authentic instances of polyandry.

The main reason for the predominance of polygyny in Polynesia is the undeniable fact that it was a man-dominated society. In the Marquesas the men also dominated the social life, so there must have been strong factors working in the opposite direction. Contrary to a very widespread opinion for which Linton is mainly responsible, there existed no surplus of men. The most important reason for the frequent occurrence of polyandrous unions seems instead to have been the peculiar form that Polynesian prestige rivalry had taken in the Marquesas. The terrain was hillier than on other Polynesian islands, and to obtain a level foundation for a house the Marquesans always made a stone platform first. This platform-building had, with time, degenerated into a competition to possess the largest and finest platforms, and for a household to be able to maintain this prestige it was necessary for many men to belong in it.

Although prestige rivalry and economic factors combined to create a situation in which polyandry was the most advantageous form of marriage, no such marriages would probably have developed if a precedent had not been set: occasional cases of polyandry also occurred on other islands. Thus, far from being the completely isolated and unique phenomenon that it superficially seemed to be, the Marquesan form of marriage was only an adaptation of the Polynesian characteristic of adjusting to reality.

Like the polygynous marriages elsewhere in Polynesia, the Marquesan polyandrous marriages were restricted to the most high-ranking families. In yet another respect they were surprisingly similar to those prevailing in the rest of Polynesia, for a Marquesan woman who lived in a polyandrous union had very little power and authority, and it was always one of the husbands who was head of the family. The other husbands in the household were also subordinated to the chief husband, and not to the wife. The chief husband, moreover, was always regarded as father of all the children to which the wife gave birth. It might therefore be said that a Marquesan polyandrous family consisted not of a woman who was married to several men, but of a man married to a woman, and several other men.

There is no indication that there was any rivalry between the husbands. On the contrary, the first husband always tried to obtain as many ancillary husbands as possible for his wife. As the only factor that could induce a man to join a household was the sexual attraction of the woman, the Marquesans set an extraordinarily high value, even according to Polynesian standards, on beauty and sex appeal.

Homosexuality

Data on homosexual activities are very scarce, and the only thing we know for sure is that at least in the Society and Marquesan Islands a certain number of men freely indulged in such activities without suffering any social opprobrium. If we accept the hypothesis put forward by Kinsey and his collaborators that every human being has a physiological capacity to respond to sufficient stimuli originating in persons either of his own or of the other sex, and will do so unless culturally conditioned against making such responses, it is easy to understand why there were homosexual individuals in a society with such a liberal moral code as the Polynesian.

Considerably more difficult to explain is why, in the above-mentioned island groups, some of the homosexual men were also transvestites. But the statement by Wilson (1799) that the transvestites in Tahiti were always "kept by the principal chiefs" gives us a certain clue. All the servants in a chief's household were men, and to those who waited regularly on the noble women and performed female duties *the same taboos were applied as to women.* When a servant of this kind (who was thus, from the social standpoint, already regarded as a woman) was also homosexual, he might eventually take the logical step to identify himself completely with the other sex by assuming female dress. Another conceivable possibility is that a servant who was originally heterosexual might, simply from being continually identified with women, be tempted to play a woman's part in all respects.

Unwanted Children

The Polynesians knew of no contraceptive techniques, either chemical or mechanical, and had only the faintest idea of the female reproductive cycle. (Nor did any venereal diseases exist before the first contact with Europeans.) As a result of their intense sexual activity, many unwanted children were therefore born.

A device all women resorted to was to give away children, and adoption was a common Polynesian institution. Other ways of solving the problem, equally accepted and permitted by the society, were abortion and infanticide. In some cases the mother had to wait until after the birth of the child to dispose of it because attempts at abortion had failed. In other cases she evidently preferred to wait, either because she considered an abortion unpleasant and dangerous, or because she wanted to know if the child was a boy or a girl before making a decision regarding its fate.

Overpopulation was a serious problem on many islands in pre-European times and was without any doubt one of the main reasons for the frequent abortions and infanticides. The fact that these methods were employed more often among the lower classes than among the chiefs' families and the widespread custom of killing girls rather than boys point in the same direction. Egoistic motives also played a considerable part among both married and unmarried women, to which must be added the extremely important class considerations. The contempt of noblemen and noblewomen for people of low birth did not prevent all of them from having amorous liaisons with persons outside their class, but to allow a child of socially unequal persons to live was out of the question, as this would have diluted the noble blood and eventually wiped out class boundaries altogether. Since all these factors—overpopulation, pursuit of pleasure, and considerations of birth—were present to a much higher degree in Tahiti and Hawaii than in any other group, abortions and infanticide were much more frequent there than elsewhere in Polynesia.

The Arioi Society

The sexual practices of the members of the Tahitian *arioi* society have provoked more comments and curiosity than any other aspect of Polynesian sex life.

The most easily observable behavior of the men and women who belonged to the society was that they practiced absolutely free love and traveled about in the Society Islands, singing, dancing, and feasting. These pleasant activities were the only ones noticed by the earliest visitors. In reality, however, the society had another and much more serious purpose and was far from being as unique a phenomenon as it seemed when its existence first became known in Europe.

Like the polyandrous marriage form in the Marquesas Islands, the *arioi* society merely represented a further development of certain customs and ideas found everywhere in Polynesia but combined in a new and original manner. The prototype and embryo of the society were the loosely organized gangs of adolescents: on the neighboring Marquesas, Tuamotu, Austral, and Cook Islands the adolescents were called *karioi* or *ka'ioi*, according to the local dialect. Whereas a youth left these gangs to get married when he or she grew up, a member of the *arioi* society could remain as long as he liked. To become an *arioi*, therefore, was equivalent to obtaining the permission of the community to continue the merry, unrestrained life of a Polynesian boy or girl.

The most important difference, however, between the gangs of adolescents and the *arioi* society was that the latter had a religious object. Although no contradiction between religion and sex ever existed in Polynesia, the direct employment of sex in the service of religion, as was done by the *arioi* society, was different. The *arioi* members believed that their society had been founded by one of the gods, Oro, who had begun as a war god but had later taken over the role of god of fertility. The society was organized something like a masonic order with seven grades, and a man or woman who wished to be received into it had to go through a long period of probation. The society demanded of its members skill in dancing and singing, a profound knowledge of the religious myths and rites, and absolute obedience to their leaders. Another respect in which the society again resembled a masonic order was that it was divided into lodges on a geographical basis.

Sometimes the *arioi* members were sent for to provide entertainment at a marriage, the investiture of a new chief, or other ceremonial occasions, but they generally took the initiative themselves and required no pretext for a visit to a neighboring island beyond the fact that they were missionaries. The religious propaganda was, however, always very discreet, and the main part of their program consisted in dancing, singing, athletic contests, and sexual exhibitions. The numerous accounts in the literature of these Tahitian-style divine services have, since the time of Rousseau to the present day, contributed strongly to distort our ideas about Polynesian sex life.

References

Banks, Joseph, *The "Endeavour" Journal . . . 1768-71.* Sydney: 1961.

Bateson, Gregory, "Sex and Culture." *Annals of the New York Academy of Sciences, Volume XLVII;* 647-60, 1947.

Best, Elsdon, *The Maori.* Wellington: Government printer, 1924.

Biggs, Bruce, *Maori marriage.* Wellington: Polynesian Society Maori Monograph no. 1, 1960.

Bligh, William, *The Log of the Bounty.* London: 1937.

Buck, Peter, *Ethnology of Tongareva.* Honolulu, 1932.

Buck, Peter, *The Coming of the Maori.* 2nd ed. Wellington: 1958.

Collocott, E. E. V., "Marriage in Tonga." *J. Polynesian Soc. 4;* 221-228, 1923.

Cook, James, *The Journals of Captain James Cook on his First Voyage of Discovery.* Cambridge: 1955.

Cook, James, *The Voyage of the "Resolution" and "Adventure," 1772-1775.* Cambridge: 1961.

Crook, William Pascoe, *Journal.* Manuscript in Mitchell Library, Sydney, Australia.

Danielsson, Bengt, *Love in the South Seas.* New York: Reynal & Co., Inc., 1956.

Danielsson, Bengt, *Work and Life on Raroia.* New York: The Macmillan Co., 1957.

Deihl, Joseph, "The Position of Woman in Samoan Culture." *Primitive Man 2-3; 21-26,* 1932.

Firth, Raymond, *We, the Tikopia.* London: Allen & Unwin, 1936.

Fischer, H. Th., "Polyandry." *Internationales Archiv für Ethnologie, Volume 46;* 106-15, 1952.

Gifford, *Tongan Society.* Honolulu, 1929.

Handy, Craighill, "The Polynesian Family System in Ka'u, Hawaii." *J. Polynesian Soc. 4;* 187-222, 1951; *3;* 243-282, 1952.

Holmes, L. D., *Ta'u. Stability and Change in a Samoan Village.* Wellington: 1958.

Knoche, Walter, "Geschlectsleben auf der Osterinsel." *Ztschr. f. Ethnol.,* 1912.

Mead, Margaret, *Coming of Age in Samoa.* New York: William Morrow & Co., Inc., 1929.

Morrison, James, *The Journal of James Morrison.* London: Golden Cockerel Press, 1935.

Mühlmann, Wilhelm E., *Arioi und Mamaia.* Eisbaden: Franz Steiner, 1955.

Murdock, George Peter, *Social Structure.* New York: The Macmillan Co., 1949.

Opler, Marvin K., "Polyandry." *Am. J. Sociol.,* Sept., 1943.

Pukui, Mary Kawena, *Hawaiian Beliefs and Customs During Birth, Infancy and Childhood.* Honolulu: Bernice P. Bishop Museum Press, 1942.

Schidlof, B., *Das Sexualleben der Australier und Ozeanier.* Leipzig: Leipziger Verlag, 1908.

Shapiro, H. L., "The Practice of Incision in the Tuamotus." *Man,* 114, 1930.

Suggs, Robert, *Marquesan Sexual Behavior.* New York: 1966.

Suggs, Robert, "Love in Polynesian Atolls." *Man,* no. 293. London: 1962.

Tautain, L. F., "Étude sur le Marriage." *Anthropologie,* Vol. 6, 1895.

Vayda, A. P., "Love in Polynesian Atolls." *Man,* no. 242. London: 1961.

Williamson, Robert W., *Essays in Polynesian Ethnology.* Cambridge: Harvard University Press, 1939.

Wilson, *A Missionary Voyage.* London, 1799.

BENGT DANIELSSON

Population and Sex

Definition

THE word "population" refers to the number of people. The people concerned may be those who dwell in some area, such as a region or country, or those who make up a category (such as those who are above age 65), or both. The science of population, sometimes called "demography," deals with the accurate determination of the number of people and with the causes and consequences of changes in the number.

There are only three direct factors that can cause a change in population—the birth rate, the death rate, and migration. Any other factors must operate through one or more of these three. Accordingly, demographers deal with the statistical measurement and causal analysis of trends in fertility, mortality, and migration, and with the relation of these to the structure and size of human populations.

The consequences of population trends are economic, political, sociological, and genetic; and they may arise from the growth or decline in the number of people, from a change in the structure of the population (such as the age-sex composition), or directly from changes in birth, death, or migration rates.

Sex and Population

Obviously, the demographer's chief interest in sexual behavior arises from the role of sexual intercourse in reproduction and hence in the birth rate. The connection between sexual intercourse and the birth rate is, however, more complex and less direct than most physicians realize. When confronted with a change in the birth rate, or with a difference in the rate between one group and another, people often jump to the conclusion that the explanation lies either in a difference in the amount of sexual intercourse or in some change in the physical capacity to reproduce.

Thus, the high birth rates in underdeveloped countries are forever being "explained" by humorous references to an absence of recreational facilities that presumably raises the frequency of coitus, or else by reference to an alleged natural fecundity. Actually, no sound evidence has ever been adduced to show that there is any relation between either the frequency of intercourse or the inherent fertility and the level of the birth rate in any population.

Factors Affecting the Birth Rate

The exaggeration of the role of sexual intercourse and inherent fertility in birth-rate trends could be called the "biologistic fallacy" in popular reasoning about population. It overlooks the fact that the reproduction rate of any population, as Davis and Blake (1956) have shown, is determined by eleven specific variables, of which coital frequency per se is only one. These factors are classified into three groups: (1) those affecting exposure to intercourse, (2) those affecting exposure to conception, and (3) those affecting gestation and successful parturition.

The first group is divided into two subclasses: (a) factors governing the formation and dissolution of sexual unions, and (b) factors governing the exposure to intercourse within unions. The reason for this subdivision is that in every society there are customs and rules governing the age at which people may

841

get married (or start having sexual intercourse); there are social determinants of the proportion of women—large or small—who never marry (or start having intercourse) at all; and there are social customs or rules that determine how long the waiting period must be before a woman who is widowed or divorced can marry again, or whether she can remarry at all.

Unless the effect of these sociological factors governing the formation of unions is understood, we cannot see the behavior *within* unions in proper perspective. In other words, the second subclass—factors governing exposure to intercourse *within* unions—is limited in its effect by the first subclass. For example, there may be few limits to intercourse once people get married, but if a large proportion of women remain celibate, or if they enter reproductive unions at a late age, then the birth rate will nevertheless be low. Even within unions (or marriages), the restraints on intercourse may be of a ritualistic kind, calling for periods of voluntary abstinence, or of an accidental character (due to impotence, illness, unavoidable but temporary separations, etc.). Such restraints on intercourse differ in nature from coital frequency, which refers to how often intercourse is indulged in by a couple during periods when abstinence is neither enjoined nor forced on them by circumstances.

The second group of factors—those dealing with exposure to conception—illustrates further the danger of attributing reproductive performance to coital frequency. Sexual intercourse may or *may not* lead to conception, depending on two factors—whether contraception is used (and how successfully), and whether one of the parties is sterile or not. Since demographers are interested in the reproductive performance of groups of people, they distinguish carefully between the capacity to reproduce and the *actual* rate of reproduction. The former they refer to as "fecundity," the second, as "fertility"—a usage which is unfortunately different from that in medicine.

The "fecundity" of a population (its capacity to reproduce) has never been determined; it remains a theoretical concept, although it has been approximated statistically. Fertility (the actual rate of reproduction), on the other hand, is measurable by relating births to the population by age. A population that is perfectly capable of a very high birth rate may, as we know, have a low birth rate because it uses contraception successfully. It may also have a young age at marriage and a normal frequency of coitus within marriage; but, most of the time, it simply prevents intercourse from resulting in conception.

The third group of factors—those pertaining to gestation and parturition—means that even when coitus has occurred and has led to a conception, a live birth still may not result. A miscarriage, deliberate abortion, or stillbirth may have intervened. In some societies (e.g., Japan) voluntary abortion has been a principal means by which the birth rate is kept down. In other cases, notably among American Negroes, spontaneous abortion and stillbirths have been a significant factor.

In sum, any acceptable explanation of the birth rate must take into account all the kinds of factors mentioned. To pay attention only to some one factor, such as coital frequency or an assumed biological capacity or incapacity, is to give an erroneous interpretation. This point can be brought out more clearly, as we shall now attempt to do, by analyzing, for the sake of illustration, the differences in fertility between two countries and by reviewing the course of fertility in the entire world in modern times.

Fertility in Ireland and the United States

During the seven years 1950–1956, there was an average of 21.3 births per year for each 1,000 inhabitants in Ireland, and an average of 24.5 in the United States. If we look at these rates in comparison to a country such as Mexico, where the average birth rate during the same years was 45.5, they strike us as being quite similar. We might therefore assume that Ireland and the United States, demographically speaking, are much alike; but nothing could be further from the truth. Or, we might be puzzled by the fact that the Irish birth rate is lower than the American. We might, for example, say to ourselves that Ireland is strongly Roman Catholic and that therefore their birth rate should be higher; but this would be a non sequitur.

The first thing to bear in mind is that the birth rates used in the comparison are crude rates. Actually, most people (e.g. men, children, old women) are not capable of giving birth, so they should not be counted among the population at risk. Ireland has an older population than the United States (due to heavy emigration of young people), and this fact tends to push down her crude birth rate. Actually, the average number of births per 1,000 women aged 15–45 in the two countries is virtually identical, being 108 in Ireland on the average during 1950–1952, as against 106 in the United States. The similarity in level of fertility is thus greater than the crude rates imply.

The manner by which Ireland and the United States reach this common result is similar in only one respect: in both countries the births outside of wedlock are few. Other than that, the pattern is utterly different. The Irish control their birth rate primarily by marrying late, by not marrying at all, and by abstinence (for females) outside of marriage. The Americans control their birth rate primarily by practicing contraception within and outside of marriage. The following figures show the difference in pattern:

TABLE 1. PERCENTAGE OF FEMALES IN AGE GROUP WHO HAVE EVER MARRIED

| | AGE | | | | | |
	15–19	20–24	25–29	30–34	35–39	40–44
U.S., 1950	17.1	67.7	86.7	90.7	91.6	91.7
Ireland, 1951	1.1	17.7	45.6	63.6	71.5	73.3

More American girls aged 20–24 are, or have been, married than is the case with Irish women aged 30–34. More than a fourth of all Irish women never marry at all, and those who marry do so at about age 30 on the average. In the United States, only 8 per cent of the women fail to marry, and the rest get married for the first time at about age 20, as a rule. Normally a woman's reproductive span lasts about 30 years. If marriage is postponed until age 30 (assuming no illegitimacy), half of this span is lost to reproduction, and if this were the sole factor operating, the birth rate would be reduced by at least 50 per cent. If the age at marriage is 20, then only one-sixth of the

reproductive span is lost to reproduction. Furthermore, still assuming no illegitimacy, the reproduction of women who never marry at all is totally lost. Roughly speaking, more than 60 per cent of the potential birth rate in Ireland is reduced by marital postponement and nonmarriage among females, whereas in the United States less than 25 per cent is lost by these two factors.

If the marriage pattern were the sole difference between Ireland and the United States, the birth rate in the latter country would be twice that in Ireland. Since this is not the case, we must search for compensating factors in the Irish situation. This is to be found in the fact that the women of Ireland, once they get married, have more babies, doubtless principally because they practice contraception less. We find, for example, that the births per 1,000 married women under age 45 in Ireland during 1950–1952 were 254 per year, whereas in the United States the figure was only 155. Thus, married women in Ireland exhibit a birth rate about 65 per cent greater than do those in the United States. This compensates for the Irish postponement or abnegation of marriage and would give the two countries approximately the same crude birth rate if it were not for the difference in the age structure of their populations.

Demographic History

Ireland is unique in the world. Nowhere else do women marry so late in life or so frequently give up marriage altogether and yet have so little sexual life or reproduction outside marriage. Sweden has a relatively late age at marriage, but this is compensated for by a high rate of illegitimacy. If we look back over the last two centuries we find that the industrial peoples have tended to check their birth rates by the relatively simple means of abortion and birth control rather than by the drastic means of partial or total celibacy.

To understand the motives for checking the birth rate, we have to realize that mankind prior to the industrial revolution was normally subject to short-term (and sometimes violent), fluctuations in population, with virtual stability of numbers in the long run. The fluctuations were due to the death rate, which was almost uncontrollable and which came in spells with wars, epidemics, and famines. The birth rate tended to be high; only those communities could survive that had enough offspring to off-set the high mortality. The problem was how to get enough children, not how to stop them. Built into the social systems of the preindustrial societies, then, were strong incentives leading people to want to marry and to beget children. With the economic revolution that came to Europe in the period after 1500, death rates began gradually to decline, and this decline began to be fast and steady in the most advanced countries after 1850. The birth rate, however, remained comparatively high; there was thus a lag of the decline in birth rates behind the decline in death rates. This lag gave rise to the fastest population growth ever known until that time.

Actually, the greatest gains in saving lives were made at younger ages. The lowering of the death rate therefore was equivalent to a rise in the birth rate, since more of the children survived. The same birth rate that had previously prevailed would give rise to much larger families. Whereas in the old days a woman who had borne seven children might have only three of them living by a later time, the tendency was now for five or six of them to survive.

Thus, the nineteenth century came to be the century of big families. With the rise of cities, with the breakdown of class barriers and the consequent opportunity for social climbing, with the decline of the home as a place to work and of the family as a productive unit, and with the rising importance of education for social advancement, these abnormally large families became increasingly onerous to the parents. Under these conditions the age of marriage tended to come later and more people eschewed marriage altogether. But abortions also tended to increase, and above all the birth-control movement began.

Virtually all official bodies and guardians of traditional morality at first opposed contraception, and this is still true in many Western countries, but the desperation of couples faced with unlimited childbearing led them to seek whatever birth-control means they could find. The result was that in the early twentieth century the birth rate in industrial nations declined

faster than the death rate until, in the 1930's, the rate of population growth had been greatly reduced. The low point was mainly due, however, to the Depression. With the return of prosperity, with the increase in social security and state services to the family, there was a revival of the birth rate throughout the industrial world, especially after World War II. This revival, due mainly to a rise in marriage rates plus omission of contraception in order to have children, persisted in the newer industrial countries (Australia, New Zealand, Canada, and the United States), but it has already receded in most European countries.

World Population Growth

What has just been said applies to the industrial nations. They have gone through what has been called the "demographic transition"—a change from a regime of high birth and death rates to one of low birth and death rates, with an intervening phase of rapid population growth due to the lag of fertility decline behind death decline. But the fact is that only a small part of the world (less than one-third) lives in industrial nations. As a consequence, the world as a whole has not yet gone through the demographic transition; most of it is now in an early phase of the transition. Owing to the peculiar circumstances of the present time, the rapid growth phase of the cycle is now enormously increased, with the result that a veritable "population explosion" is currently being seen:

TABLE 2. ACCELERATION OF WORLD POPULATION GROWTH

	WORLD POPULATION (MILLIONS)	INCREASE IN 25 YEARS (PERCENTAGE)	YEARS TO DOUBLE AT THIS RATE
Past			
1900	1,550		
1925	1,907	23	84
1950	2,497	31	64
Future			
1975	3,830	53	41
2000	6,280	64	35

The populations shown for 1975 and 2000 are the United Nations medium estimates published in 1959. Although it is impossible to predict future populations with certainty, the U.N.

figures are conservative estimates of what the recent trends imply for the future. Only some world catastrophe or revolutionary change would cause the world total to diverge sharply from the estimate by the end of the century.

Reduced to the simplest terms, the reason for the continued acceleration of world population growth is that the two-thirds of the world still living in underdeveloped countries is experiencing, and will probably continue to experience, the most spectacular declines in the death rate ever known, while the birth rate remains at a high level. (A secondary reason is that the industrial countries have not only had a postwar recovery in births, as already noted, but have also had a continuation of their steady decline in death rates.)

The unprecedented and unforeseen drop in the death rate in underdeveloped countries results from bringing to them the most up-to-date public health techniques. In the industrializing nations of the nineteenth century, the fall in mortality was gradual because the new techniques had to be slowly invented; their invention and spread depended upon the slow process of economic development, public education, etc. The backward nations of today, however, can get the new health measures directly from the more advanced regions, with financial help and technical personnel supplied, often under international auspices. As a result, the death rate is being reduced at fantastic speed, regardless of whether or not local economic development is occurring. Since the lowering of the death rate in these areas does not depend upon public education or a rise in economic production, the institutional structure that supports a traditionally high birth rate is not destroyed. The result is a higher rate of population growth than anybody thought possible two decades ago. Many countries in Latin America and Asia are increasing their populations at around 3 per cent per year. At this rate the number will multiply 19 times within 100 years.

Consequences of Rapid Population Growth

The consequences of rapid population growth depend on the circumstances. In already densely settled peasant countries, the unprecedented growth currently being experienced is making economic development all the more difficult to achieve.

Egypt's population, for example, rose from 14 million in 1927 to approximately 25 million in 1958. The registered birth rate (known to be deficient) averaged 44 per 1,000 in 1950-1953, while the registered death rate, having fallen 30 per cent in ten years, was 19 per 1,000. The fact that the population has grown some three times faster than the area under cultivation would not be so deleterious if productivity in agriculture or if industrialization had risen faster; but neither of these things has happened. The proportion of the labor force engaged in manufacturing has hardly increased at all (being around 8 per cent in both 1927 and 1947), and half the male working force is still trying to make a living from farming, which means an astounding average of about 1,250 people dependent on farming for each square mile of cultivated area (as against about 35 in the United States). With Egypt's population growing so rapidly, any new lands that can be added to the cultivated area by new dams and irrigation works will be settled at the same old densities by the time the new works are completed.

Economic development, properly speaking, occurs only when the level of living is rising—that is, only when *per capita* real income is growing. Population growth in many underdeveloped countries is causing nearly all of the increase in national income to be used to support ever more people at much the same old *per capital* level. Since the aspirations of the people are rising, the result is political unrest and a willingness to try the most radical solutions.

In the industrial countries, particularly the newer ones like the United States, continued population growth is proving disadvantageous, not because of poverty but because of prosperity. As the goods and services used by each individual increase, and as the total number of individuals multiplies, the complications become formidable. For one thing, the demand on the rest of the world's resources becomes disproportionate. For another, the congestion of people and their possessions becomes so great that an increasing proportion of both are used simply to mitigate the effects of congestion. The population becomes increasingly urbanized, the urban agglomerations ever more huge. Already the New York metropolitan area contains about 15 million people, Chicago and Los Angeles around 7 million each.

These giant aggregates grow not only in people but in the material possessions for each person. Automobiles, radios, television sets, boats, houses, freezers and countless other possessions multiply much faster than the population. To accommodate these and at the same time live in urban areas, families move to the suburbs where a house, yard, and garage can be obtained. Since the family head often works in the central city, costly expressways and transportation networks have to be built. Each family has to own two or three cars. These automobiles, the industries that supply the material goods, the burning dumps that get rid of the mounting refuse—all combine to pollute the atmosphere, which is costly in terms of health and agriculture.

Ultimately, therefore, the rapid growth of both population and material wealth in industrial nations is self-defeating. The effort to escape the mounting congestion creates more congestion; the effort to escape nuisances creates more nuisances. Every economic activity wants more space. As the urban population grows, as each new space fills up, the quest for space takes the suburbs farther out, multiplies the connecting links, and increases the effort and cost. As time goes by, as the population doubles or triples and material possessions get more numerous, the additional costs will mount until they cancel the gains in wealth.

Population Policy

No matter where we look, it is difficult to find solid reasons why the world's population should increase at all, much less at an unprecedented rate. Are we, then, really destined to have the enormous future increases that present trends indicate? In the short run, probably so; but not in the long run.

One possible halt to population growth may be a third world war fought with weapons that can wipe out whole continents. It is precisely to avoid such catastrophic "solutions" that many observers suggest a policy of reducing births. Why not, one asks, provide the same international effort in behalf of birth control that has been provided in behalf of public health?

This view is frequently criticized. One hears this question: "Since economic development can keep ahead of population growth, why worry about the latter?" In this statement, the important word is "can." Certainly economic development *can* keep ahead of even rapid population growth for a time, but it does not always do so and there is no guarantee that it will do so in the future. Anyway, the two lines of action are not mutually exclusive. Use of birth control in industrial countries has not prevented economic advance. One of the purposes of controlling fertility is precisely to aid, not hinder, economic development. Furthermore, as we noted above, the sole problem is not that of getting enough to eat and wear. Population growth is causing great inconvenience in prosperous as well as in poor countries.

Another criticism is that birth-control devices are not perfect. True, but there are few things completely efficient. Polio vaccine is not invariably effective, nor are automobile brakes, but nobody suggests giving up these techniques for this reason.

A third criticism, that peasant people *love* children and therefore want as many as possible, is self-contradictory. If one loves children, one will not be so cruel as to have as many as possible. Children are loved in every society. Modern field studies show that peasant women, no matter how poor or uneducated, are not so stupid as to wish to bear, nurse, and care for an endless number of children.

Realizing that people cannot live in the second half of the twentieth century with respect to deaths and in the Middle Ages with respect to births, some governments are adopting policies designed to encourage birth control. Japan has been the most thorough and successful, Puerto Rico next, but India and several other countries are also pursuing such a policy.

Future population growth is thus not automatic. It is subject to human control. If the effort is made, the problem of exploding populations can be solved by lowering the rate of reproduction without waiting for war, starvation, epidemics, or grinding poverty to strike the balance.

One reason people have been so slow to control population by the simple means of birth control is doubtless the connection of reproduction with sex. Fortunately, it is not necessary, as we have seen, to prevent sex in order to prevent excessive population growth. Moralists, however, have tended to view children as a just punishment for sin (that is, for sexual enjoyment). They have felt that to release men and women from this punishment by making it possible for them to use birth control would encourage immorality (i.e., sexual enjoyment). Experience has shown, however, that if birth control is not used, other means will in time be found for limiting the birth rate. The case of Ireland shows that postponement of the age at marriage for women to age 30, and consignment of one-fourth of the female population to permanent celibacy, can be a substitute for contraception. Most human beings, other than professional moralists, consider such a solution to be extremely cruel.

References

Belshaw, Horace, *Population Growth and Levels of Consumption*. New York: Institute of Pacific Relations, 1956.

Brown, Harrison, *The Challenge of Man's Future*. New York: The Viking Press, Inc., 1954.

Davis, Kingsley (ed.), "A Crowding Hemisphere: Population Change in the Americas." *Ann. Am. Acad. Polit. & Social Sci. 316;* 1-136, 1958.

Davis, Kingsley, "The Sociology of Demographic Behavior." In Robert K. Merton *et al., Sociology Today*. New York: Basic Books, Inc., 1959.

Davis, Kingsley, and Blake, Judith, "Social Structure and Fertility." *Eco. Develop. & Cult. Change 4;* 211-235, 1956.

Glass, David V. (ed.), *Introduction to Malthus*. New York: John Wiley & Sons, Inc., 1953.

Grabill, Wilson H., Kiser, Clyde V., and Whelpton, Pascal K., *The Fertility of American Women*. New York: John Wiley & Sons, Inc., 1958.

Hauser, Philip M. (ed.), *Population and World Politics*. Glencoe, Ill.: The Free Press, 1958.

Meier, Richard L., *Modern Science and the Human Fertility Problem*. New York: John Wiley & Sons, Inc., 1959.

Milbank Memorial Fund *Current Research in Human Fertility*. New York: Milbank Fund, 1955.

Okun, Bernard, *Trends in Birth Rates in the United States since 1870*. Baltimore: The Johns Hopkins Press, 1958.

Petersen, William, *Planned Migration*. Berkeley: University of California Press, 1955.

Petersen, William, "John Maynard Keynes's Theories of Population and the Concept of 'Optimum.'" *Pop. Studies 8;* 228-246, 1955.

Roberts, George W., *The Population of Jamaica*. Cambridge: Cambridge University Press, 1957.

Russell, J. C., *Late Ancient and Medieval Population*. Philadelphia: American Philosophical Society, 1958.

Sulloway, Alvah W., *Birth Control and Catholic Doctrine*. Boston: Beacon Press, Inc., 1959.

Taeuber, Conrad, and Taeuber, Irene B., *The Changing Population of the United States*. New York: John Wiley & Sons, Inc., 1958.

Taeuber, Irene B., *The Population of Japan*. Princeton: Princeton University Press, 1958.

KINGSLEY DAVIS

Pornography, The Psychology of

"PORNOGRAPHY" is not a scientific term. It is an emotionally loaded word and means one thing to one person and quite another to somebody else. In the original Greek, it meant "letters of prostitutes," but that meaning has long been forgotten and no longer enters into the usage of the word as it appears in common speech, the press, and the literature.

In legal usage, pornography, particularly with the preamble "hard-core," has been used interchangeably with "obscenity." This has led to further confusions, but for all practical purposes, "hard-core" pornography and "obscenity" are used synonymously by the legal profession.

To the average person, "pornography" simply means "dirty pictures," "stag," "blue," or "French" movies, and beyond this—depending on the individual's degree of sophistication, attitudes, and beliefs—a variety of things from genuine pornographic writings (as will be defined) all the way to serious literature with erotic content or subject matter, and from so-called "girlie" or "cheese-cake" magazines to the "Venus of Milo," Michelangelo's "David," and Goya's "Nude Maja."

In order to give such a wide and loosely defined subject a more systematic treatment, we shall divide pornography into writings on the one hand and pictorial representations on the other. This will also aid in a more specific definition of pornography at which we feel we are able to arrive with regard to writings. Pictorial representations, however, have thus far eluded us in this respect.

Erotic Writings

In the case of writings, we have made a thorough analysis of hundreds of examples of "hard-core" pornography and have made a comparison with other types of literature with erotic content or subject matter that differ in certain essential qualities from pornography (narrowly defined). We have published the results of this analysis elsewhere in greater detail (Kronhausen and Kronhausen, 1959) but shall try to acquaint the reader with the basic issues involved in such a distinction.

For easier communication we have come to call all writings with erotic content or subject matter other than pornographic by the term *erotic realism*. By using this terminology we were able to include works both of fiction and of nonfiction in our differentiation.

In the case of *nonfiction* we are dealing, for example, with such publications as marriage manuals; psychological, anthropological, and sociological studies; anatomical, physiological, and biological texts; books covering family life problems; and a variety of similar publications. All of these, though communicating on various levels of sophistication, have in common the one factor that they are dealing primarily with *reality*. This reality may be of a psychological nature in one case, of a sociological nature in another, or of a medical nature in a third. But the fact remains that in every one of these cases, erotic subject matter is presented in the context of reality, regardless of the particular type of order of reality which the larger frame of reference demands.

With regard to nonpornographic *fiction,* we are dealing with still another type of reality, namely the "reality" presented by the inner world or psyche of the fictional characters and the interaction process between them. One has to put this kind of "reality" into quotation marks, because it does not refer to any event or series of events in history or to any processes that lend themselves to scientific verification. Yet even this kind of qualified "reality" represents an attempt by the author to communicate intrapsychic or social processes as he "sees" or experiences them to be with regard to the fictional situation he is attempting to describe and convey.

If this kind of creative effort results in the description or inclusion of erotic scenes or feelings and attitudes related to the sexual impulse in the context of a piece of fictional writing, say a novel or a play, we refer to this as an example of "erotic realism" as distinct from pornography.

We feel justified in doing so, because the *basic difference* between "erotic realism" and pornography lies in the different approach and handling of the problem of *reality* in pornographic writings as compared to literature of the erotically realistic type. In contrast to erotic realism, pornography is *not* concerned with reality at all, but sets aside all considerations of reality in favor of the wish-fulfilling phantasies of its (predominantly *male*) authors and the anticipated reactions of a predominantly male readership.

The aim of pornographic writings is to evoke erotic imagery in the reader in order to bring about sexual arousal. In other words, *pornographic writings are "meant" to function as psychological aphrodisiacs and are successful only to the extent that they accomplish this particular purpose.*

In keeping with these aims, pornographic writings follow a certain *general outline or organization* and employ a *number of specific mechanisms* which we believe can be isolated and demonstrated. In fact, we consider the presence or absence of these criteria, not in isolation, but *in relationship to each other* (that is, *as a cluster or configuration of factors*), as bona fide evidence as to whether any particular piece of writing is pornographic or not.

Before entering into a discussion of these criteria of pornography, it is important to keep in mind that any one, or even several of these characteristics may be present in other forms of literature. In pornography, however, the entire content is organized around these principles, and always with *emphasis on the physiological sex response,* in order to provide maximum erotic stimulation for the reader by appealing to his voyeurism. In addition, all disturbing reality elements are carefully avoided, so that one rarely hears of unwanted pregnancy, abortion, venereal disease, and similar unpleasant side-effects that occasionally accompany sexual relations.

Keeping these qualifications in mind, we are now ready to discuss the characteristic structure or organization of pornographic writings. After that, we shall examine the individual points which as a *configuration* constitute the most objective criterion of pornography.

The characteristic feature in the structure of pornographic writings is the buildup of *erotic excitement* in the course of the text. A pornographic book or story may start out with a scene which is only mildly erotic and not highly stimulating. In progression, it will then become "hotter" and "hotter," include an even larger variety of sexual activities and involve more and more people, until it culminates in the description of the most lascivious group scenes and mass orgies. This is in keeping with the over-all design of pornography and absolutely necessary if the writing is to act upon the reader as an erotic psychological stimulant ("aphrodisiac").

The major individual criteria or favorite sub-plots or sub-themes within this general framework are the following (in all these the emphasis is on the physiological sex response):

Seduction

Defloration

Incest

The permissive-seductive parent figure

Profanation of the sacred

Sexual vernacular

Supersexed males

Nymphomaniac females

Negroes, Asiatics, and "low-caste individuals" as sex symbols

Homosexuality (predominantly Lesbianism)

Flagellation

The list represents by no means all but merely the most outstanding, the most common, and the most easily recognizable sub-themes in pornographic writings. However, there are other minor, though no less fascinating and psychologically significant characteristics of pornographic literature, such as the recurrent mention of erotically stimulating odors of the body, especially of the sexual secretions; the frequent emphasis on pubic and/or axillary hair (depending on the geographic origin of the book); the frequency of human contacts with animals (especially with reference to the human female); female masturbation with phallic objects; and others.

Seduction

Characteristic of "pornographic" books is the fact that in seduction scenes the "victim" is, more often than not, a *willing collaborator*. In other words, the women who figure prominently in "obscene" books are generally as anxious to be seduced as the men are to seduce them. In fact, in some "obscene" stories the women are the aggressors and the men are the seduced, in which case the male "victims" are as easily "persuaded" as are the women.

Still another distinguishing feature of "obscene" seduction scenes is their *brevity*, due to the ease with which the seduction is accomplished. We will therefore not find page after page, or entire chapters, of a "pornographic" book devoted to the hero or heroine attempting the seduction of his or her lover, as is so frequently the case in ordinary fiction. In any "pornographic" story, the hero typically meets an individual to whom he is sexually attracted and in the next sentence or paragraph the couple are already in the midst of various sexual activities.

Defloration

In pornographic books, defloration scenes with strong sadistic elements play an important role; in fact, defloration is here almost synonymous with rape. These rapelike defloration scenes are psychologically significant in demonstrating the fusion of erotic and sadistic impulses.

The astonishing feature of the sometimes blood-curdling defloration scenes in pornographic writings is that the violated girl, no matter what degree of agony is inflicted upon her, invariably disclaims any concern over her pain and displays little, if any, resentment toward her violators.

Even though the defloration scenes in pornography are naturally concerned with *virgins*, the underlying philosophy seems to be that there is no need for actual rape, since the women in these wish-fulfilling pornographic phantasies are pictured as highly sexed, fiercely passionate creatures of impulse who do not need to be coerced once they have lost their virginity and experienced the pleasures of sexual relations.

Incest

The *overt* incest theme is as rare in modern literature as it was popular in antiquity. In contemporary literature it appears, with very few exceptions (as in Thomas Mann's novel *The Holy Sinners*, and his short story, *Blood of the Wolsungs*), only in *veiled* or *allegorical* form. Pornographic literature, however, can hardly do without open, frank, and undisguised incestuous relations. These relations between the closest of kin, say between brother and sister, father and daughter, or mother and son, are consummated without any, or with only minor qualms, guilt, and emotional conflict.

The psychological mechanism operating in this case is the presence of the social taboo which acts as a mental stimulant. Psychoanalytic experience indicates that latent incestuous leanings are present in most people in our culture. As these incestuous feelings are discouraged from early childhood, the culture succeeds in inhibiting their overt expression. Our moral training even succeeds in driving incestuous desires out of most people's conscious awareness. However, man's fascination with incestuous relationships prevails in spite of all the forces of repression, a fact to which not only clinical practice, but literature in general, and pornographic books in particular, give eloquent testimony.

The Permissive-Seductive Parent Figure

In keeping with the wish-fulfilling phantasy character of pornographic stories, they frequently include *super-permissive parent figures* who not only *condone*, but even *participate* in the sexual activities of the child, or who actually *seduce* and *initiate* the child into various sexual practices.

The use of permissive-seductive parent figures in pornographic literature makes some psychological sense. In the first place, it uses the Oedipal attraction of the child for the parent, or of the parent for the child, as well as the incest taboos of our society. It has, therefore the subconscious attraction of the extremely taboo.

Besides, the hyperpermissive parent figure may correspond to the child's phantasy of the "good" mother or father who would unequivocally accept his sexual and scatological interests, who does not scold when the child wets the bed, does not object when it plays with its feces, and who does not criticize or stop the child when it masturbates or engages in sexual play.

Profanation of the Sacred

Among the most obvious characteristics of pornographic books is the tendency of their writers to intermingle the sacred and the profane. Here again, the authors of pornographic books have intuitively built upon solid psychological ground. It has been clinically observed that there may be a special attraction in mixing that which is supposedly the most "holy" and that which is supposedly the most debased. Even the derivation of the word "sacred," coming from the Latin *sacer*, bears this out. In its original usage, the word could signify either sacred or profane, its meaning being completely interchangeable.

The special value which this strange mixture of opposites has for pornographic books probably lies in the heightening of erotic tension which it produces. By using profanity in the presence of the sacred, we are, so to speak, thumbing our nose at our own conscience and at the collective conscience or superego of society itself.

Many pornographic books include, among their central figures, persons connected with the clergy and religion, such as nuns, priests, and monks. These "holy" individuals are then depicted as engaging in highly tabooed sexual activities that are considered "mortal sins" by religious standards. In so doing, the objectionable character of the "crimes" is magnified and the sins are compounded.

The basic principle behind this pornographic usage is that, for many people in our culture, sex is still inextricably linked to sin. Now, if sex is sinful, then sexual acts, committed in sacred surroundings, or with the participation of representatives of religion, would constitute the ultimate in blasphemy. In this way it becomes possible for sexual acts to take on a special meaning as expressions of one's need to rebel, not only against social and religious institutions, but ultimately against those cultural inhibitions which have become part and parcel of one's own character structure. Since most of us are at least to some extent affected by these cultural frustrations, it is not difficult to see why the blasphemous element in pornographic books holds such a strong attraction for so many people, and especially for those who find their sexual needs in conflict with the moral and religious values of society, from which they have not been able to fully emancipate themselves.

Sexual Vernacular

The use of taboo words in pornographic books is closely related to the frequent mixture of the sacred and the profane that we discussed in the preceding section. Its chief attraction lies in the open defiance of the "superego," or conscience, the flagrant violation of the social conventions of polite discourse, the flaunting of one's independence, the throwing off of social responsibility, and the assertion of the instinctual primitive side of life against all the restraining and inhibiting forces of the environment.

Prostitutes the world over have always known the magic of pornographic words and have used this knowledge to their advantage. In fact, some individuals are not aroused unless their partner uses profane language. Since not many wives or "good" women in our culture are willing to accommodate such males in this respect, these men seek out prostitutes, some of whom specialize in this type of service. We know of cases where the man would phone a call girl or prostitute and ask her for nothing more than to "talk dirty" to him, often at fees surpassing those for sexual relations. In these cases, the prostitute engages her customer in vulgar sex talk and thus arouses him either in preparation for intercourse or for autoerotic purposes. But there are also some females who are very much aroused by the partner's use of sexual vernacular.

One may also find this kind of sex talk in erotically realistic fiction where it is used in character portrayal, but it is more characteristic of pornographic books. The reason for this lies, again, in the fact that pornographic books deliberately try to arouse the reader by the use of "dirty" language, just as in the cited cases the prostitutes use this technique to stimulate their customers.

Another characteristic feature of pornographic books is the *quantity* of taboo words used, which generally exceeds that of nonpornographic fiction by several hundred percent.

In contrast to works of erotic realism, pornographic books do not, as a rule, resort to swear words, probably because the necessity to express angry hostility seldom occurs in such books, whereas in realistic literature swearing is used to serve the same purpose that it does in actual life—the release of emotional tension and hostility. This, however, is not the aim of pornographic books.

Supersexed Males

In keeping with the unrealistic nature of pornographic books, one of their outstanding characteristics is the emphasis they place upon the exaggerated size of the male organ and of the testicles, and the copious amounts of seminal fluid ejaculated. It follows that all of these factors add up to the picture of men whose potency is almost limitless and whose sex drive is constantly at record strength.

Pornographic books go far beyond the biologically feasible or likely with regard to the large amounts of semen ejaculated by the hyperpotent heroes of these stories. Apparently, phantasies associated with the powerful ejaculation of semen act as an additional stimulant upon many individuals.

In any case, the overemphasis on male potency and male sex anatomy in pornographic books is psychologically understandable on the basis of man's pride in the penis and of the stimulating nature of phantasies concerning erection and ejaculation. It is also possible that

latent anxiety over potency has led some authors of pornographic writings to use reassuring and overcompensating exaggerations along these lines.

Nymphomaniac Females

In keeping with the wish-fulfilling nature of pornographic writings, the female characters in these stories are just as most men would wish women to be: passionate, sensuous, sexually highly responsive creatures.

The women in pornographic writings therefore lack the common traces of modesty, restraint, and sex-anxiety which are characteristic of the majority of women in our culture and with which nonpornographic fiction occupies itself at great length (here the novel *Lady Chatterley's Lover* is a cogent case in point, in that one of its central themes deals with the sexual liberation of Lady Constance Chatterley, which she finally achieves through a healthy physical and emotional relationship with her husband's gamekeeper).

Similarly to what we have seen to be the case with regard to the emphasis on male potency, pornographic books stress the physiological female sex response. Consequently, pornographic writings abound in references to the excitation of the clitoris, erection of the nipples, and copious female discharges (such as are rarely, if ever, found in the sexual behavior of the human female).

Negroes, Asiatics, and "Low-Caste" Individuals as Sex Symbols

In keeping with the popular notion that the colored races are extraordinarily virile, sensuous, and given to all kinds of "perversions," pornographic writings frequently feature one or more such persons to provide an added "exotic" element to their stories.

Common prejudice has it that Negro males possess larger genitals than Caucasians and pornography reflects this view. On the other hand, Asiatic women are often used as female sex symbols in pornographic writings, again in accordance with popular conceptions of Oriental sexuality.

Pornographic writings also emphasize the supposedly strong body odor of the Negro race, to which they attribute a sexually exciting quality.

In addition, pornographic writings make use of fictional characters (mostly males) from the lower social groups to portray uninhibited sexuality. Here again, pornography violates the actual facts of class-differentiated sexual behavior as they are known from large-scale statistical studies, such as the Kinsey reports.

Homosexuality

There are strong homosexual elements, if not direct references to homosexual acts and their detailed description, in nearly all pornographic writings. References to *Lesbian* activities and their descriptions by far outweigh incidents of male homosexuality in these stories.

The predominance of female homosexuality in pornography is most likely due to the fact that the male author and reader can more readily place himself in phantasy into a Lesbian scene because he experiences or visualizes these activities essentially as *heterosexual* situations. In addition, he can do so without the arousal of anxiety over his own possible latent homosexual impulses, as might be the case if he were to identify with a situation involving sexual acts between males.

Frequently, Lesbian scenes in pornographic books are supposedly narrated by females, but more often than not this female authorship is no more than a device to make the stories appear more "authentic."

While pornographic writings by and for Lesbians are extremely rare (as are pornographic writings by women in general), we have been able to study several pornographic manuscripts written by and for the enjoyment of male homosexuals. Manuscripts of this type are also not common, nor are they generally "professional," as is more frequently the case with regard to other types of pornography. Homosexual (amateur) pornography therefore consists usually of only a few typewritten or mimeographed pages and is somewhat more limited in the variety of sexual activities described.

It also appears that homosexual pornography has a decided sado-masochistic flavor. Repeatedly, one finds in them situations in which one or more aggressively dominant males lord it over one or more passive-submissive males, whom they subject to various sexual practices, often with the purpose of humiliating the weaker partner.

Flagellation

Flagellation, from its mildest to its most sadistic forms, is a frequent feature of pornographic writings. Many pornographic plots or dominant themes have been completely woven around flagellation, thus making a special appeal to those whose sex life is dominated by sado-masochistic phantasies or practices, and in some cases unmistakingly revealing the sexual predilection of the author.

Most of the pornographic flagellation literature in the English language dates from the Victorian era of the mid-1850's. At that time, England in particular was swept by a wave of flagellantism. Hundreds of so-called "massage-salons," houses of prostitution, and private clubs in London and elsewhere catered exclusively to this specialty, many of these establishments being equipped with complete torture chambers and huge arsenals of whips, spikes, wire brushes, and all the rest of the trade paraphernalia.

However, flagellation has always had its aficionados, not only in England, but also on the European continent and in the United States, and there has always been a literature catering to these tastes.

Generally, periods in which flagellation and flagellation literature flourished were times of severe sexual repression, as in the Middle Ages or during the Victorian era. However, recently in the United States there has come into vogue an "exotic" borderline literature, focusing on sado-masochism with strong elements of shoe-, corset-, underwear-, rubber-, leather-, and similar fetishisms which cannot be strictly classed as pornography.

With regard to all these criteria, pornographic writings are unique in that they differ from other types of literature in content, intent, and emphasis. The analysis of a piece of writing must consider the book under discussion as a whole and not take the presence or absence of one or several features common to pornographic literature as bona fide evidence on whether the writing is pornographic or not.

One must also keep in mind that in all these factors or sub-themes of pornography, the emphasis is on the *physiological sex response*. This is in accordance with the essentially *voyeuristic* nature of pornographic writings and with the aim to stimulate vivid erotic imagery in the reader. In fact, *the pervasive voyeurism in pornography* is one of its main and most obvious criteria which separate pornography from erotically realistic fiction. Erotic realism emphasizes the emotional, and not the physical, sex response, even though it sometimes includes some physiological description.

Erotic Pictorial Art

Turning our attention to erotic pictorial art, we find that we are unable to make as clear a distinction between pornographic and nonpornographic art as has been possible with regard to writings.

If we apply the same principles to erotic art, we immediately encounter certain theoretical difficulties which we were able to overcome in the case of literature, but which have thus far proven insurmountable obstacles when dealing with pictorial representations of erotic scenes, in paintings, sculpture, moving pictures, or any other art medium where nonverbal communication is employed.

We shall first have to consider the problem of *intent*. With respect to pornographic literature, we have tried to demonstrate by indirect evidence that the only or primary purpose of such writings (and by inference also the purpose of its authors) is to stimulate erotic imagery (phantasies) in the reader with the aim of promoting sexual arousal. Now, we are still relatively safe in assuming that such was indeed the intent with certain artists, such as Van Bayros or Zichy, who gave most of their time and talent to the portrayal of erotic scenes that they had been commissioned to do as illustrations for books which would come within our definition of pornography.

But this is also the outer limit within which we can speak with assurance about the "pornographic" intent of the artist. There are, of course, relatively few professional artists and amateurs who either by their own admission or by overwhelming clinical evidence can be said to have produced erotic art solely or mainly for the purpose of sexual arousal. On the other hand, there is no way of making such inferences with any degree of confidence in the vast majority of cases where more diversified artists have depicted similar or identical erotic scenes.

To illustrate: Are we to assume that artists such as Rembrandt or Picasso, to mention only two of the better known painters who have portrayed intercourse scenes, have done so *without* the intent to produce erotic arousal in the beholder, whereas other artists (such as the before-mentioned ones) have done so with that intent in mind?

And if we do speak about "intent," are we not obliged also to take into consideration the problem of conscious versus unconscious motivation? Clearly, the problem of distinguishing "pornographic" from nonpornographic art on the basis of "intent" cannot lead to definitive results.

Nor can we use the manner in which the problem of *reality* is handled by the artist as a valid criterion of "pornographic" art. Let us, for example, examine a painting from India, a reproduction of which we have in our files, showing a couple in intercourse while riding on the back of an elephant, with the male shooting a tiger with bow and arrow. Now, this kind of tiger hunt is very unlikely to have ever taken place, but is this picture therefore "pornographic," while a companion picture which we also have in our files, showing the same couple in a more common or probable intercourse position, is not pornographic? Obviously, we must reject this kind of reasoning and abandon the attempt to distinguish between "pornographic" art and "erotically realistic" art on the basis of whether the picture is to a greater or lesser degree in accord with reality.

It is even less possible to use the criterion of artistic *quality* or merit in the fine arts, just as we were unable to use it in our attempt to define pornographic literature. Obviously, whether a piece is well written or poorly written, or whether an art object is well executed or not, does not decide whether it is pornographic, nor is it a safe indication as to what motivated the writer or artist in producing it.

We may say that an erotic book or art object that shows little or no artistic merit may have as its sole object the sexual arousal of others and would therefore fall within our own psychological definition of pornography. However, whereas we have a number of supporting criteria and additional internal evidence for such judgments in the case of erotic literature, we do *not* have these advantages with respect to erotic art. We, on our part, would certainly not want to speculate on the motivation of a Rembrandt or Picasso in depicting various scenes of intercourse (including a self-portrait of Rembrandt during intercourse with his wife). The motives of these and many other acknowledged masters may have possibly been to express themselves artistically without special regard to the subject matter. But this is rather improbable. More likely, the erotic element played as much of a role for them as for the thousands of less talented artists and amateurs who have tried their hand on erotic pictures. The difference between erotic art and erotic writings is here again that in those cases where genuinely talented writers have produced writings within our psychological definition of pornography, these writings do contain a sufficient number of demonstrable internal "pornographic" criteria which are totally independent of the quality of the writing. Since this is not the case in erotic art, we cannot substitute the relative criterion of "quality" for the otherwise lacking criteria which could provide the needed additional evidence for such a distinction.

Having said this, it should be safe to point out that many of the specific criteria or subthemes of pornographic literature which we have enumerated and discussed also occur with amazing regularity in erotic art, including photographs and moving pictures. For example, one often finds in erotic art an exaggeration of the genitalia, especially of the penis. This is in evidence in the erotic art of the Greeks and Romans, where it is frequently connected with phallic worship, and in the erotic art of India.

On the other hand, the large genitalia on many of the Japanese woodblock prints and erotic scrolls cannot be said to reflect merely the phallic worship of the Shinto religion. There, the enlarged representation of the genitalia must be motivated by other factors. It is,

for example, known that these pictures were used by the Japanese and Chinese as a means of providing sex education (bride's "pillow-books"). This would, at least in part, explain the technique of focusing the viewer's attention on the genital area. However, there is little doubt in our minds that the emphasis on the genitalia is, in addition, motivated by the same factors that apply in the case of pornographic writings. (There are, for example, Chinese and Japanese erotica showing couples viewing such pictures with the obvious intent of sexual arousal.)

In keeping with the principles applicable to pornographic writings, the following favorite subjects are portrayed with some regularity in erotic art: sexual activities between Negroes and Caucasians, Lesbianism, activities involving animals, activities involving children, oral and anal contacts, group activities, mass-orgies, sexual activities involving nuns and priests, the presence of religious symbols in connection with sexual activities, female masturbation with phallic objects, and a large variety of sexual scenes involving sado-masochistic practices, flagellation, and fetishism.

If, in spite of all these parallel phenomena, we still desist from narrowly defining pornography in the arts, it is simply because there is no apparent way of ascertaining sufficient convincing evidence with regard to the motivation or intent of the artist, as we can, in the case of pornographic writings, obtain by deductive processes, at least with a greater degree of certainty.

Attempts have been made to define pornography in the arts by drawing the "limits" of the permissible in many different and completely arbitrary ways. In the arts, the illogicalness of doing so is even clearer than in the case of literature. Private or official censorship over the past twenty years has, for example, decreed that the female breast should not be portrayed, then retreated under pressure of changing community standards to say that the breast could be portrayed, so long as the nipples were not shown. The same kind of irrationality applies to the official attitude with regard to the genitalia and the pubic region. Pictures showing the genitalia are at present only permissible in nudist publications. "Girlie" magazines are allowed to show the pubic region, though not the genitals or the pubic hair. And so on, ad infinitum.

We have already indicated that even the portrayal of scenes of intercourse in the arts (as well as in photographic still and moving pictures) is no sure indication that such representations have been made, mainly or solely, for the purpose of erotic excitation—in other words, that they have been designed and produced as psychological aphrodisiacs. Even the most flagrant "stag" movie does not lend itself readily to such an investigation concerning the motivation for its production. Movies of sexual activities that have been produced by scientific researchers are, for example, frequently indistinguishable from professional or amateur sex movies made for the obvious purpose of erotic stimulation.

In brief: we have shown that literature may offer a sufficient number of valid criteria to allow for reasonable assumptions concerning its pornographic or nonpornographic nature. We have also pointed out that this cannot be done in the case of erotic art with the same degree of assurance and that any such attempts have thus far only led into various dead-ends of absurdity.

With this behind us, we must consider the psychological effects of erotic art and writings, because the social implications of the problem, especially the legal and extra-legal suppression of this material and the repeated attempts by the courts to arrive at a legally workable definition of pornography (or "obscenity"), are based on the assumed effects of erotica on the mind and the behavior of the individual.

There appears to be a differential response to erotica on the part of males and females. Kinsey *et al.* (1953) suggest that this differential sex response is the result of biological sex differences in the human male and female. These researchers suggest that the same differential sex response to visual stimuli as it applies to humans is noticeable in the subhuman animal kingdom. They refer, for example, to the fact that male animals are aroused by such visual stimuli as observing other animals in coitus, whereas female animals are not so stimulated. The Kinsey group of investigators marshal considerable and convincing biological evidence in support of their thesis that the human female is simply following in the pattern of subhuman mammals in her lack of, or greatly reduced, response to visual and auditory stimuli of an erotic nature. They stress that the female is more readily aroused by tactile stimuli—in other words, by direct physical contact of one form or another—than by the roundabout way of psychological stimuli which involve erotic imagery and phantasy.

In addition, women very rarely produce clearly erotic art and writings, despite the fact that many pornographic books are purportedly authored by women, for the vast majority of them have been written by men using female pseudonyms. This pretense is, so to speak, merely another "trick of the trade" in order to give the illusion that the supposedly female author was as sexually active and lascivious as the male author wishes us—or himself—to believe.

Women are, however, known to enjoy and to produce a literature and an art that is mildly "erotic," but which stresses general emotional relationships, love, and tenderness, and that is not erotically stimulating to most men, nor intensely stimulating to women either.

We shall therefore have to accept the fact that in our society a differential sex response to erotica exists. We do, however, reserve our opinion on whether the basis for this differential response is to be sought mainly on a biological or on a cultural and psychological basis. The predominantly male interest in erotica (psychological aphrodisiacs) may at least partly be due to the specific problem of the male with regard to his potency. The male, in order to effect genital intercourse, is dependent on the erectability of the penis. In other words, his need for psychological stimuli (aphrodisiacs) is greater in that respect than that of the female, who is able to initiate intercourse without the necessity of prior excitation.

The same problem, of course, holds true with regard to the threat of ultimate decline and loss of potency in the male, whereas the capacity for sexual intercourse on the part of the female is not impaired with advancing age. Just as the male is more interested in physiological aphrodisiacs than the female, in order to counteract the real or imagined threat of impotence, so would we expect him to be more interested in psychological aphrodisiacs.

Females in our society also have considerably less access to pornography than males and are consequently less familiar with it, which may account for some negative replies to inquiries about their response to such material. More important is the fact that girls in our culture receive a much more severe childhood training with regard to modesty and learn from an early age to conceal their sexual responses. This kind of cover-up is undoubtedly also involved in many of the seemingly neutral, "bored," or "disinterested" reactions of women to pornography.

From this point of view, younger individuals, particularly adolescent males at the peak of their biological sex drive, should theoretically be less interested in erotica as psychological aphrodisiacs than older males. However, in apparent contradiction to this, adolescents do show a strong interest in erotica. This interest may be due to the particularly strong sexual frustration of this group, for whom virtually all socio-sexual outlets are blocked by the arbitrary restrictions of society. In addition, at our present halfway mark in sex-education, erotica represent to this group (as well as to preadolescents) the only means of acquiring definite knowledge as to how sexual intercourse in its various manifestations is actually performed. Only if we could remove these factors would it be possible to assess the true extent of adolescent interest in psychological aphrodisiacs.

At any rate, further cross-cultural research on sexual behavior and particularly on the female sex response is needed before we can draw definitive conclusions on this point.

There also appears to be a differential response to erotica on the part of males from the lower social and educational levels as compared to those on the upper level. The higher we reach on the social and educational scale, the more interest one finds in erotica in general. For this phenomenon, the Kinsey group (1948) offer the following explanation: "The very fact that upper level males fail to get what they want in socio-sexual relations would provide a psychologic explanation of their high degree of responsiveness to stimuli which fall short of actual coitus." The Kinsey researchers feel that,

in addition, upper level males may have a greater capacity to visualize (erotic) situations. Such males are therefore said to be more affected by thinking about females, homosexual partners, and a variety of other erotic stimuli of a psychological nature.

Without necessary contradiction of all of this, there seems to be a considerable difference in the *type* of erotica which upper and lower level males prefer. Upper level males seem to prefer erotica of definite artistic merit, such as paintings and drawings by artists of superior skill and talent, as well as pornographic writings which show considerable imagination, fluency of style, and a plot which does not offend the intellectual integrity of these persons. The same principles apply for this upper level group of men with regard to photographs and moving pictures. In all these respects, they make, as may be expected, greater artistic and intellectual demands than "lower" level males; they frequently stipulate that they only prefer erotica with decided humorous, esoteric, or other elements added to the erotic subject matter. The lower level male seems to prefer photographs or movies showing erotic scenes to such representations in paintings, drawings, or statuary. These men apparently need a more direct type of stimulation and often remain totally indifferent to the "high-class" erotica which evoke a strong response from the upper level males.

Finally, we have to consider the objection against erotica raised by those who fear or are convinced that psychological aphrodisiacs have a "trigger-effect" in regard to acts of crime and violence. Most of our censorship laws are supposedly based on such assumptions and the problem of whether or not erotica do enter into the causation of crime, particularly of sex offenses, is therefore a serious one.

Most of the clinicians and researchers who have given the matter more than casual thought are inclined to believe that pornography is not a direct contributory cause of sex offenses. A delinquent or potential delinquent may conceivably pick up some information on *how* to perform an antisocial act through crime literature or movies, but he will not be able to acquire the *tendency* or inclination to commit antisocial acts in this manner. There is now considerable research evidence to that effect.

The effects of erotica other than writings have been no more subjected to scientific investigations than the effects of written pornography. This lack of research data is in itself a revealing cultural phenomenon. We have, however, sufficient experiental evidence to be certain that erotica do function as psychological aphrodisiacs and are capable of evoking physiological sex responses which may lead to sexual (*not antisocial*) behavior.

It is, of course, known that a good deal of sexual behavior has been arbitrarily declared illegal in our society. If erotica were able to encourage individuals to experiment with socially taboo forms of sexuality, this could be construed as leading to crime and delinquency. There is a possibility, though no evidence, that this may be the case in certain individual instances. General psychological experience, however, tends to support the thesis that most individuals will react to such stimuli according to a preconditioned pattern of behavior, regardless of the specific nature of the stimulus. To illustrate: an individual with no previous record of flagellatory or homosexual activities who is exposed to flagellatory or homosexual literature may be expected to react to such stimulation in accordance with his previous psychosexual disposition and sexual behavior pattern. In other words, if he becomes aroused by such specific psychological stimulation at all, he will most likely choose the same sex outlets (such as masturbation and heterosexual coitus) that he is accustomed to using, but will not be likely to engage in flagellatory or homosexual acts which are foreign to his psychosexual disposition and experience.

It is extremely doubtful whether even continued exposure to specific pornographic stimuli will result in behavioral changes, unless they are accompanied by actual contacts with individuals who are so predisposed. Such personal contacts are known to have the possibility of affecting behavior in nonsexual areas and may therefore be reasonably expected to have the same potential in the area of sexual behavior. In these cases, the role of erotica would remain a very minor one as compared to the effect of actual contacts with other individuals who may initiate the deviant sexual activity.

Ultimately, all of these problems concerning erotica cease to be purely matters of scientific concern and become issues involving moral convictions, religious beliefs, personal points of view, and social attitudes depending on the emotional climate of the community in which the problems arise. This, of course, is no longer the domain of the psychologist, but of the social philosopher who may or may not wish to take his cues from the social and behavioral sciences in arriving at the value judgments which are implicit in assessing this controversial area of human conduct.

One must also keep in mind that the effect of literature (in general) has been greatly overrated. The effects of literature with erotic subject matter have up to the present not been the object of controlled studies. The closest any studies come to our problem are those relatively few experiments with sex-educational literature. They seem to indicate shifts in *attitude* (in the liberal or more tolerant direction) do occur which are due to such reading, while behavioral changes are either not at all observable or are unpredictable as to the direction which they may take (individuals exposed to liberal sex-educational material may become more conservative in behavior).

One has to consider still another aspect of erotic art and literature, particularly of a scatological and sado-masochistic nature, namely, its possible therapeutic function as a harmless psychological release mechanism or "safety-valve" for certain individuals. While some scientists have expressed doubts concerning this function of erotica, others have cited rather convincing clinical cases in support of this theory (Ellis, 1961; Jahoda, 1954; Stekel, 1952).

References

Ashbee, H. W. (Pisanus Fraxi, pseudonym), *Index Librorum Prohibitorum*. London: privately printed, 1877.

English, Paul, *Geschichte der Erotischen Literatur*. Stuttgart: Julius Puettmann, 1927.

Fuchs, E., *Geschichte der Erotischen Kunst*. 2 vols. Munchen: Albert Langen, 1908, 1923.

Fuchs, E., *Illustrierte Sittengeschichte vom Mittelalter bis zur Gegenwart*. 3 vols. Munchen: Albert Langen, 1909-1912.

Gichner, L. E., *Erotic Aspects of Hindu Sculpture*. Washington: privately printed, 1949.

Gichner, L. E., *Erotic Aspects of Japanese Culture.* Washington: privately printed, 1953.

Gichner, L. E., *Erotic Aspects of Chinese Culture.* Washington: privately printed, 1957.

Giedt, F. H., "Changes in Sex Behavior and Attitudes Following Class Study of the Kinsey Report." *J. Soc. Psychol. 33;* 131-141, 1951.

Ginzburg, R., *An Unhurried View of Erotica.* New York: Helmsman Press, 1958.

Guyon, R., *The Ethics of Sexual Acts.* New York: Blue Ribbon Books, 1941.

Jahoda, Marie, *The Impact of Literature: A Psychological Discussion of Some Assumptions in the Censorship Debate.* New York: Research Center for Human Relations, 1954.

Kinsey, A. C. *et al., Sexual Behavior in the Human Male.* Philadelphia: W. B. Saunders Co., 1948.

Kinsey, A. C. *et al., Sexual Behavior in the Human Female.* Philadelphia: W. B. Saunders Co., 1953.

Kirkpatrick, C., Stryker, S., and Buell, P., "A Study of Attitudes Toward Male Sex Behavior with Reference to Kinsey's Findings." *Amer. Sociol. Rev. 17;* 480-487, 1952.

Kronhausen, E., and Kronhausen, Phyllis, *Pornography and the Law.* New York: Ballantine Books, 1959.

Lewinsohn, R., *A History of Sexual Customs.* New York: Harper & Brothers, 1958.

Mead, Margaret, "Sex and Censorship in Contemporary Society." *New World Writing,* 3rd Selection. New York: New American Library, 1953.

Reich, Wilhelm, *The Sexual Revolution.* New York: Orgone Institute Press, 1951.

Reik, Theodor, *Psychology of Sex Relations.* New York and Toronto: Holt, Rinehart and Winston, 1945.

Ross, R. T., "Measures of the Sex Behavior of College Males Compared with Kinsey's Results." *J. Abnorm. Soc. Psychol. 45;* 753-755, 1950.

Schidrowitz, L., ed., *Bilder-Lexikon.* Wien and Liepzig: Verlag für Sexual Forschung, 1928, 1929, 1930, 1931.

Scott, G. R., *Far Eastern Sex Life.* London: Gerald G. Swan, 1949.

Wulfen, Erich, *Sexualspiegel von Kunst und Verbrechen.* Dresden: Paul Aretz, 1928.

EBERHARD AND PHYLLIS
KRONHAUSEN

Premarital Sexual Intercourse

Definition

THE TERM *premarital sexual intercourse* is generally used to indicate the experience of coitus by an individual who is single and not previously married with a person of the other sex. Strictly speaking, it should be used to denote only the premarital coitus of persons who eventually marry. Since, however, more than nine-tenths of all people marry, most coitus of single persons is actually premarital. Nevertheless, this distinction should be kept in mind, especially with reference to specific research findings and inferences drawn from them.

Although the coitus of preadolescent children is "premarital," it is usually considered as a special case and is treated separately from that of postadolescent persons. A single act of coitus can be premarital for one partner, extramarital for the other, and adulterous for both, as in the case of a single person who has sexual intercourse with a married person. Most premarital coitus in our society, however, and apparently in many other cultures as well, involves partners who are both single. The sexual experiences of divorced and widowed persons, even though they are single in a social and legal sense, are usually referred to as "postmarital."

Cross-Cultural Comparisons

Although other animals, particularly the great apes, and man practice many of the same sexual activities (such as precoital foreplay, masturbation, homosexual activities, and of course, coitus), only man can engage in premarital, as well as in marital and postmarital, experiences because these involve the cultural concept of marriage, which is uniquely and universally human. All known groups of human beings, past and present, primitive and civilized, have had the institution of marriage; and all have dealt with the ubiquitous problem of premarital sexual intercourse by a great variety of means, including attempts to ignore completely its actual occurrence, forbid it with severe punishments, forbid it and forgive it with mild admonitions, and permit it under regulated conditions.

Contrary to the theories of some scholars of the past and to some folk beliefs among ourselves, complete sexual freedom as the socially sanctioned custom of a society is unknown. Under certain circumstances, however, and for specific classes of people, the sexual taboos and restrictions may be temporarily relaxed, but not abandoned. Examples of this in Western culture are the gaiety and romance connected with many European carnivals and festivals and our own Mardi Gras and the expected and accepted greater intimacy between an engaged than a nonengaged couple, wherein premarital coitus may or may not be forbidden. These occasions and similar ones among other peoples are not considered sexual license or promiscuity.

Most cultures have been more lenient than ours in permitting nonmarital intercourse. In fact, ours is one of the few that has had, during certain periods in our history, a blanket prohibition of all sexual intercourse outside the marriage relation. Murdock (1949), on the basis of evidence compiled from a world-wide sample of 250 societies, maintains that, except for a few societies, sex itself is not the focus of regulation, as might be assumed with the existence of a generalized sex taboo; the control of sex is in terms of sexual intercourse with respect to one or more other considerations to which sex is pertinent, such as marriage, kinship, social status, and reproduction. This seems particularly relevant to the subject of our discussion. Of the 158 societies in Murdock's sample for which there is sufficient information about these practices, premarital sexual intercourse is permitted in 70 per cent. In the other societies, the prohibition is directed mainly at the female and seems to be primarily concerned with preventing out-of-wedlock births.

In a minority of societies, adults attempt to prevent children from engaging in or observing any sexual activity. Some relax these restraints when the individual passes through puberty or reaches adulthood, whereas others maintain or even intensify their restrictive efforts. The prevention of premarital sexual intercourse and sometimes of other nonsanctioned sexual activities is accomplished by attempts either to instill in the individual the idea that these acts are wrong and to reinforce self-restraints by threats of adverse public opinion, ostracism, disgrace, or punishment, or to prevent males and females from being together by chaperonage of girls or segregation of the sexes. The latter methods, whereby the sexes are made sexually unavailable to one another through adult surveillance, are presumably more effective and probably more widespread than those whereby control rests upon inculcating self-restraint in the young. Even threats of disgrace and death have not always been effective in preventing young people from engaging in premarital coitus.

Among known societies, as Ford and Beach (1951) and other writers have indicated, there is at one extreme relative agreement and at the other considerable variance between actual behavior and the idealized standards of sex conduct. Among some people, sexual transgressions of the formal mores are invariably and summarily punished. There are many societies in which child sex play and postadolescent sexual intercourse are formally forbidden, but are tacitly accepted by the adults, who either ignore them or fail to punish those who are caught. A majority of societies tolerate or permit sex expression in childhood, such as masturbation and mutual fondling, and sometimes permit observance of adult sexual intercourse and premarital sexual intercourse in postadolescence.

Contrary to popular opinion, that premarital sexual relations are permitted does not mean invariably or even usually that adulterous relations are sanctioned after marriage. Although some societies allow the male, and even a very few the female as well, to have adulterous relations, the more usual combination is sexual permissiveness prior to marriage and sexual fidelity to the spouse after marriage. In fact, in some societies, the path leading to the selection of a lifelong marriage mate to which one is sexually faithful begins in youthful sexual liaisons which might be eventually guided by parental and familial, as well as by individual, considerations.

Western Culture

Within the stream of our own cultural heritage, the attitude toward sex and particularly toward premarital sexual intercourse has fluctuated considerably in time and place between a rigid adherence to a general sex taboo, as among some early Christians and more recently among the New England Yankees, and a liberal permissiveness, as among the Elizabethan English and contemporary northern Europeans. Furthermore, there has been considerable confusion about sexuality—not only because there has sometimes been a marked divergence between what people did and what they were supposed to do, but also because there has been a conflict among the ideals that people have held about sex, especially premarital coitus.

The religious tradition of our culture with respect to both Orthodox Jewish codes and Christian precepts, especially those of the Roman Catholic Church and some of the Protestant sects, has been a strict single standard that has consistently forbidden premarital coitus, or any sexual activity other than marital coitus, for both males and females. At the same time, however, there have existed slight to strong undertones of a double standard which, although formally prohibiting premarital intercourse for both sexes, have meant in reality the strong condemnation of female sexual transgressions but only the mild toleration, or even the encouragement, of male sexual exploits.

One of the marked trends in contemporary times is the development of a more permissive attitude toward adolescent and postadolescent sexual expression for both sexes, which might be termed a permissive, lenient, or liberal single code of sex conduct. In parts of northern Europe there has been a tendency to embrace this standard openly, particularly insofar as it applies to persons seriously in love or engaged. By contrast, in the United States, although a pronounced liberal attitude has developed toward petting, particularly in the lighter manifestations of it in the form of kissing and hugging without more intimate fondling, a strong formal taboo against premarital intercourse still exists. Within this formal frame of reference, however, a more permissive code toward premarital intercourse is tacitly or covertly becoming acceptable, especially within certain social groups.

In the history of Christendom, complete confusion and conflict regarding sex have occurred because of the coexistence of two contradictory ideals: one says that sex is evil and sinful, and the other that sex is wonderful and the full expression of life itself. This conflict has affected both the single person and the married, but it has probably been more acute, although less persistent, for the unmarried because sex in marriage is tolerated as a function of reproduction, whereas outside marriage it has no justification whatsoever. It might be said that the soul of Western man has been truly tormented and fascinated by the dilemma of sex.

Studies on Premarital Intercourse in the United States

Recently in the United States, particularly within the last century, a more tolerant, humanistic attitude has developed toward human sexuality which has tended to alleviate many of the old dilemmas about sex, but which has undoubtedly created new ones. This manifested and admitted greater interest in sex seems to stem primarily from two motives: the general curiosity of modern man to know himself, and the specific hope to find more satisfactory means of achieving sexual satisfaction in marriage.

These two considerations, when added to the age-old problem of Western man's guilt-provoking fascination with sex, may be viewed as a triumvirate that has stimulated the scientific study of sex and especially of the extent and significance of premarital sexual intercourse in the individual and his society. It seems no accident that the spectacular rise in the United States of interest in empirical research in the social and psychological fields in general has included also a scientific concern with the problem of sexual behavior.

Sources of Data

Although there have been literally thousands of clinical reports, anecdotal accounts, and scholarly commentaries about sexual behavior, there have been only about fifty systematic researches of actual human sexual behavior. By systematic research is meant the organized collection of data according to a prearranged scheme and their logical and statistical analyses.

Scientific interest in sexual behavior appeared first in anthropological and clinical studies of Europeans in the last half of the nineteenth century. To the Americans, however, belongs the honor of both initiating just four decades ago and producing since then most of the systematic research into human sexual behavior. A majority of these have been partly or wholly concerned with premarital sexual behavior. Although the total number of studies is small, the body of knowledge they represent seems scientifically substantial and respectable.

The pioneer studies were those of Max Exner in 1915 of 1,000 male college students and of Katharine Davis in 1929 of 2,200 women. The monumental studies of Kinsey and his associates (Kinsey, 1948 and 1953; and Gebhard, 1958) mark the current culmination of sex research. Other major studies of sexual behavior that include extensive data on premarital coitus are Hamilton (1929), Bromley and Britten (1938), Terman (1938), Landis (1940), Burgess and Wallin (1953), Ehrmann (1959). To these can be added almost thirty studies which, though of lesser scope, have made material contributions to our fund of knowledge. (See Kinsey, 1953, pages 94-96 for a list of published researches.)

These studies have generally attempted to determine the extent of premarital coitus, the relationship between it and other personal and social considerations, and the attitudes and values held about it. In a general way, there has been an attempt to answer these kinds of questions: How many people have intercourse before marriage? How often? Are religiously devout people less sexually active than the nondevout? What effect will premarital sexual intercourse have upon subsequent marital happiness? What do people think is right and proper about premarital sex conduct? Is their behavior consistent with these attitudes?

The sample populations in these studies have been mainly young people who were predominantly white, college-educated, urban, middle class, and Protestant. Substantial, though fewer, data have been collected on Jews, Roman Catholics, Negroes, and rural and noncollegiate parts of the population. The number of individuals in each study has ranged from 100 in Hamilton's study to several thousand in Kinsey's.

When allowances are made for the variations in research techniques and composition of the sample populations, these studies are more often in general agreement than they are contradictory. There is a growing confidence in the findings being obtained, but there is considerably less agreement on the *interpretation* of the significance of these findings. The American public apparently believes strongly in the scientific ethic which now seems to include cooperation in studies of sex. In this connection, it is pertinent to note that the extent of premarital coitus seems to be one of the best-substantiated "facts" of sexual behavior in American society.

The remainder of this article summarizes very briefly the principal findings of the systematic research into premarital sexual behavior in American society. The reader who wishes more detailed information is referred to the works cited in the references.

Incidence

The data indicate that probably a majority of Americans—a large majority of males and a substantial minority to one-half of females— have experienced coitus before marriage. The only accurate means of arriving at this finding is through the study of the premarital sexual histories of persons who are or have been married: the married, widowed, or divorced. Studies of single persons who have not been previously married are valuable for determining the extent of sexual activities in a given group up to that time; but they give only an incomplete picture of premarital sexual behavior because these subjects have not completed their premarital histories.

The incidence of premarital coitus among *married males* as reported by Hamilton (1929) is 54 per cent; by Terman (1938) 61 per cent; by Burgess and Wallin (1953) 68 per cent; and by Kinsey (1948) 67 per cent for college-level males, 84 per cent for high-school-level males, and 98 per cent for males who never went beyond grade school. Incidence of premarital coitus among *married females* as reported by Hamilton (1929) is 35 per cent; by Terman (1938) 37 per cent; by Landis (1940) 27 per cent; by Burgess and Wallin (1953) 47 per cent; and by Kinsey (1953) 50 per cent.

The incidence figures of premarital coitus obtained from sample populations of married persons (which would, of course, concern only their premarital histories) is usually higher than those obtained from sample populations of single persons. For example, the range in the incidence of nonvirgins in the six samples of *married males* cited above is between 54 and 98 per cent, and in twelve samples of *single males* (not given here) it is between 32 and 93 per cent. In the five samples of *married females* cited above the range is between 27 and 50 per cent, and in eight samples of *single females* (not given here) it is between 7 and 26 per cent.

Number of Partners

Women are somewhat more monogamous than men in their premarital sexual intercourse relationships. One-half or more of all women who are nonvirgins have coitus with their future spouse only, whereas a majority of men have this experience with both their future spouse and other women. A moderate minority of men (between 10 and 20 per cent) and a very small number of women (about 2 or 3 per cent) report having had premarital intercourse only with persons other than future spouses.

Evidence on the number of coital partners is supplied in several studies, including those by Davis (1929), Hamilton (1929), Bromley and Britten (1938), and especially by Terman (1938), Burgess and Wallin (1953) for both males and females, and by Kinsey (1953) for females only. Considering only those who were not virgins at marriage, the number of persons with premarital coitus with *future spouse only* is 66 per cent of the women and 27 per cent of the men in Terman (those born in 1910 or later), 72 per cent of the women and 40 per cent of the men in Burgess and Wallin, and 46 per cent of the women in Kinsey. Most of the remainder of the women stated they had premarital coitus with both future spouse and others, and most of the men that they had this experience with either future spouse and others or with others only.

Decade of Birth

The general supposition that the marked liberalization of premarital sex practices, the so-called "sexual revolution," occurred during the period of World War I and the Gay Twenties immediately following is substantiated in the research findings.

This change apparently had a more profound effect upon females than males. Whereas the males in the studies of Kinsey and his associates (1948 and 1953) showed only a small difference in this respect, the females born after 1900 (those who reached sexual maturity around World War I or later) showed an increase of two to three times as many nonvirgins at marriage as the females born before 1900. For example, the incidence of premarital coitus in females by age 20 is 8 per cent for females born before 1900 and 18 to 23 per cent for females born after 1900; by age 30 it is 26 per cent for females born before 1900 and 48 to 53 per cent for females born after 1900.

This same trend was also reported earlier by Hamilton (1929), Terman (1938), and Locke (1951), but only the sample of Terman contained enough females born before and after the turn of the century to form the basis for a generalization about this trend. The rise in the proportion of persons experiencing coitus prior

to marriage for each succeeding ten-year age group in Terman's sample, although marked for both sexes, was even more pronounced for females than males. The incidence of non-virgins at marriage among husbands is 49 per cent for those born before 1890 and 86 per cent for those born after 1910; among wives it is 14 per cent among the oldest group and 68 per cent among the youngest. These findings led Terman to draw the then astonishing conclusion that, should this trend continue at the same rate, "virginity at marriage would be close to the vanishing point for males born after 1930 and for females born after 1940." Subsequent studies, including those of Kinsey and associates, Burgess and Wallin, and others, indicate, however, that the trend did not continue and that there has been a leveling-off of the incidence of premarital intercourse: the proportion of males and females with this experience seems to have remained relatively constant in the last two decades.

Age at Marriage and Educational Level

Two of the major contributions of Kinsey and his associates are the findings that incidences of premarital coitus of males and females vary with their educational levels, although there is a pronounced sex difference, and that the female pattern is probably related more to nearness to marriage, whereas the male pattern seems to reflect other social class differences.

For example, 98 per cent of the males who had never gone beyond grade school and 84 per cent of those who had gone to high school but not beyond, but only 67 per cent of those who went to college, had had sexual intercourse prior to marriage. The findings of Hohman and Schaffner (1947) from a sample of Army inductees are comparable to those of Kinsey. A converse relationship is revealed in the figures for the female: 30 per cent of the grade-school females, 47 per cent of the high-school females, and over 60 per cent of the females who went to college had had premarital coitus.

When, however, the data of Kinsey (1953) for the female are analyzed in terms, first, of educational level and second, of nearness to marriage, a somewhat different picture emerges concerning their premarital sexual histories.

Girls in the grade-school groups began having premarital sexual intercourse in appreciable numbers before girls with more education did. By age 15, for instance, 18 per cent of the girls who never went beyond grade school, but only 5 per cent of the high-school group and 2 per cent of the college group, had experienced coitus.

The girls in the grade-school group, however, married earlier and their premarital histories were on the average shorter. The females with more education, although commencing their coital experiences at a later date, continued these activities for a proportionally longer period of time, and they eventually had more experience than the grade-school girl.

On the other hand, when these data are analyzed in terms of nearness to marriage, the apparent difference in terms of educational levels of the females tends to disappear, particularly for those married after the age of 16. The proportion of high-school, college, and graduate-school females with premarital coital experience who marry within the same five-year age range is relatively the same. This relation arises from the fact that a considerable portion of the coital activity of the female occurs within the year or two immediately preceding her marriage. In fact, of all the variables thus far studied, nearness to marriage seems to show the most marked correlation with premarital sexual intercourse among females.

Social Class

Some information on the comparative social class of companions is supplied by Hollingshead (1949) and Ehrmann (1955, 1959). Hollingshead observed, among high-school students, that boys of a higher social class exploit girls of a lower social class for sex purposes. In a sample college population, Ehrmann found that most males and females have their sexual experiences with persons of the same social class; but when class lines are crossed, the highest rate of premarital intercourse occurs between males of a higher and females of a lower social class.

Religion

With respect to religious considerations, the limited research findings indicate that the de-gree of religious devoutness as measured by regularity of church attendance or nonattendance is more uniformly related to patterns of premarital sexuality than is membership in any one of the three major religious groupings. According to Kinsey (1948 and 1953), the less devout males and females were sexually more active and had higher proportions of nonvirgins than the more devout. Furthermore, the difference among Protestants, Catholics, and Jews of the same degree of devoutness was generally less than the difference between the more and less devout of any one religious group.

One example of these findings concerns females who were married by age 25: 22 per cent of the devout and 44 per cent of the inactive Protestant, 21 per cent of the devout and 54 per cent of the inactive Catholic, and 23 per cent of the moderate and 42 per cent of the inactive Jewish females had experienced premarital coitus. Burgess and Wallin (1953) also found that, among the Protestants of college level, the religiously inactive couples were far more likely than the religiously active ones to have sexual intercourse frequently or occasionally, as compared to rarely or never before marriage. Their incidence figures for couples with the same, mixed, and no religious affiliations suggest that some of the difference might be associated more with formal participation in church activity than with religious identification. Premarital intercourse was lowest where both couple members were Catholic (29 per cent), highest where couple members had different religions (61 per cent) or none at all (56 per cent), and intermediate where both were Protestant (45 per cent) or Jewish (38 per cent).

Rural-Urban Residence

According to Kinsey (1948 and 1953), the urban male as compared to the rural male and the urban female after age 20 as compared to the rural female after age 20 have slightly higher incidences of premarital coitus.

Sex and Love

According to Ehrmann (1959) female premarital sexual expression, both petting and coitus, is primarily and profoundly related to being in love and to going steady, whereas male sexuality is more indirectly and less exclusively associated with romanticism and intimacy relationships. This conclusion receives confirmation from the findings of other investigators, particularly Terman (1938), Burgess and Wallin (1953), and Kinsey and associates (1953)—that a greater proportion of females than males have premarital coitus with the future spouse only.

Attitudes toward
Premarital Sexual Intercourse

The studies of attitudes about premarital sexual behavior have usually been either in terms of the extent to which persons approve or disapprove of this behavior as an abstract proposition (Do you think it all right for boys, for girls, to have sexual intercourse before marriage?) or in terms of the reasons people give for not engaging in this activity (What are the reasons for your not having had sexual intercourse?).

In general, studies of the first type have reflected the traditional mores even among young people, in that they have tended to condemn premarital coitus for both sexes and to expect girls to be more chaste than boys. These polls have also shown that romance and eventual marriage are justifications for greater sexual freedom in that greater sexual intimacies (through petting, however, rather than coitus) are approved for those who are going steady or engaged as opposed to those who are not.

Variations in the findings of research into the reasons for abstaining from premarital coitus suggest that, even though different techniques of investigation will produce different results, there may have been an actual shift in the attitudes of young people in recent years. For example, fear of pregnancy was cited as a much more important reason for not having premarital intercourse among the subjects in the studies of Bromley and Britten (1938) and of Rockwood and Ford (1945) than among those of Landis and Landis (1953), Burgess and Wallin (1953), and Kinsey (1948 and 1953). Morals, religious beliefs, family training, fears, and a desire to wait for marriage are the most important reasons given for restraints. In addition, Burgess and Wallin (1953) and Kinsey (1948 and 1953) point out that lack of opportunity, and Kinsey (1948 and 1953) that lack of desire, also are significant deterrents to sexual activity.

Even though youths in general formally condemn premarital coitus, as revealed in the studies of opinions and attitudes, a majority of those who have actually had this experience seem to condone, justify, or accept it. Several of the findings of Kinsey (1953) and one of Burgess and Wallin (1953) suggest this conclusion. According to Kinsey, among the unmarried females who had never had coitus, 80 per cent stated they did not intend to have it before marriage (the remainder said they would, considered it a possibility, or were undecided); but among those who had already had this experience, only 30 per cent said they did not intend to have more. Of this group, 69 per cent had no regrets, 13 per cent had minor regrets, and 18 per cent had definite regrets for having had this experience. An even larger proportion, 77 per cent, of the married women who were not virgins at the time of marriage expressed no regrets for their premarital coitus; 12 per cent had minor regrets and 11 per cent had definite regrets. An even more positive finding in this regard is cited by Burgess and Wallin (1953). Among their sample of engaged persons who admitted having this experience, 93 per cent of the men and 91 per cent of the women stated that sexual intercourse had strengthened their relationship.

Pregnancy

The Kinsey researchers are the only ones who have systematically collected and published findings on the relationship between premarital coitus and pregnancy. The estimate in Kinsey (1953), based on data supplied by over 2,000 single, white females with coital experience, is that 1 premarital pregnancy had resulted from each 1,000 copulations.

The percentage of single women who became pregnant, however, is relatively larger. As reported in Gebhard (1958), ultimately one-tenth of their sample of white, nonprison females had a premarital pregnancy. Of the premarital pregnancies that ended before marriage, almost nine-tenths were induced abortions and the other one-tenth were either spontaneous abortions or live births in about equal numbers. Among the women 36 years of age and older who had premarital coitus, about the same number of those who never married

(21 per cent) as compared to those who were married once and were still married (18 per cent), at the time they were interviewed had had a premarital induced abortion.

Marriage

The possible influence of premarital sexual intercourse upon subsequent marital sexual adjustment in particular and the marriage relationship in general has been a much-discussed topic in our society. Although the extent of the speculations upon this subject is still great, it is probably somewhat less now than it was a generation or two ago. The general public interest in this matter is reflected in the extensive discussion of this topic in textbooks on marriage and the family, and as a constant source of concern in novels, stories, and commentaries.

In spite of this great public and academic interest, there have been only a few systematic research studies on this question. Although they have been pioneering and exploratory, as are most studies in this area, they have been provocative and suggestive rather than definitive. The criteria that have been used by researchers to measure "marital happiness" have included such items as self-ratings of one's happiness, the desire to be married to another or not to be married at all, the desire for extramarital intercourse, complaints about one's spouse, amount of disagreement with spouse, the display of affection between spouses, and so on.

Generally speaking, the research findings do not confirm the old folk belief that premarital unchastity, particularly of the female, leads almost inevitably to marital conflict, unhappiness, and failure. Probably the outstanding fact about these findings to date is that premarital chastity shows only a slightly greater statistical relationship to subsequent general marital adjustment than does premarital unchastity. Furthermore, many other variables (such as childhood happiness, happiness of parents, lack of conflict with mother and father, attitude toward sex, parental discipline, and others) have been found to have a far greater relationship to marital adjustment than do premarital coitus or abstinence.

The three most important research-estab-lished relationships among premarital coitus, marital adjustment, and marital sexual adjustment (which include the one just discussed and two others) appear initially to be contradictory. Stated simply, they are: (1) premarital virginity is related to marital adjustment; (2) marital adjustment is related to marital sexual adjustment, particularly as indicated by the orgasm adequacy of the female; and (3) the marital orgasm adequacy of the female is related to her premarital sexual behavior. However, these findings are not contradictory for these simple reasons; first, each expresses a statistical probability relationship rather than an absolute cause-effect, or one-to-one, relation; and second, the variables in one set of considerations are not necessarily comparable to those in another (for example, virginity does not imply either presence or absence of potential orgasm adequacy).

Research findings on these questions with reference to premarital coitus are found in Davis (1929), Terman (1938), Locke (1951), Burgess and Wallin (1953), and Kinsey (1953), a few of which are briefly summarized here.

More of the unhappily married women (15 per cent) than of the happily married ones (6 per cent), in the study of Davis, reported that they had had premarital intercourse. Locke discovered that a significantly larger proportion of divorced men (85 per cent) than of happily married men (57 per cent) reported having had intercourse with a few or many women before marriage, but that there was no difference in this respect between the divorced and happily married women.

Terman found a small relation between men's and women's premarital sex histories and their marital happiness scores. The mean happiness scores of (1) husbands who had no premarital sexual intercourse experience was 70.9, (2) husbands who had intercourse with only the future wife was almost the same, 69.3, (3) husbands who had intercourse with "others only" was slightly lower, 67.1, and (4) husbands who had intercourse with both future wife and others was the lowest of all, 64.2. A similar distribution was found for wives. The mean happiness scores of (1) wives who were virgins at marriage was 69.6, (2) wives who had coitus with future spouse only was 67.0, (3) wives who had coitus with "others only" was 64.3, and (4) wives who had coitus with both future husband and others was 63.6. Burgess and Wallin report some association between premarital chastity or infrequency of premarital coitus and (1) love scores, (2) engagement success scores, and (3) marital success.

Three studies show a correlation between the wife's orgasm reaction in marital coitus and her premarital sexual behavior. Both Terman (1938) and Burgess and Wallin (1953) found that the wives who were most likely to experience orgasm usually or always, as compared to never or rarely, were those who had premarital intercourse with their future husbands and other men. The data of Kinsey (1953) indicate a correlation between premarital coitus, premarital coitus with orgasm, and premarital orgasm through other outlets, on the one hand, and marital orgasm on the other. These findings suggest that marital orgasm adequacy in coitus may be more directly connected with premarital orgasm experience, irrespective of the means through which it is achieved, rather than with premarital coitus per se.

References

Bromley, Dorothy D., and Britten, Florence H., *Youth and Sex*. New York and London: Harper & Brothers, 1938.

Burgess, Ernest W., and Wallin, Paul, *Engagement and Marriage*. Chicago, Philadelphia, New York: J. B. Lippincott Co., 1953.

Davis, Katharine B., *Factors in the Sex Life of Twenty-two Hundred Women*. New York: Harper & Brothers, 1929.

Ehrmann, Winston, "Influence of Comparative Social Class of Companions Upon Premarital Heterosexual Behavior." *Marr. & Fam. Living* 17; 48-53, 1955.

Ehrmann, Winston, "Some Knowns and Unknowns in Research Into Human Sex Behavior." *Marr. & Fam. Living* 19; 16-22, 1957.

Ehrmann, Winston, *Premarital Dating Behavior*. New York: Henry Holt & Co., Inc., 1959.

Ford, Clellan S., and Beach, Frank A., *Patterns of Sexual Behavior*. New York: Harper & Brothers and Paul B. Hoeber, Inc., 1951.

Gebhard, Paul H., Pomeroy, Wardell B., Martin, Clyde E., and Christenson, Cornelia V., *Pregnancy, Birth and Abortion*. New York: Harper & Brothers and Paul B. Hoeber, Inc., 1958.

Hamilton, G. V., *A Research in Marriage*. New York: Albert & Charles Boni, 1929.

Hohman, L. B., and Schaffner, B., "The Sex Lives of Unmarried Men." *Am. J. Sociol.* 52; 501-507, 1947.

Hollingshead, August B., *Elmtown's Youth*. New York: John Wiley & Sons, 1949.

Kinsey, Alfred C. *et al.*, *Sexual Behavior in the Human Male*. Philadelphia: W. B. Saunders Co., 1948.

Kinsey, Alfred C. *et al.*, *Sexual Behavior in the Human Female*. Philadelphia: W. B. Saunders Co., 1953.

Landis, Carney *et al.*, *Sex in Development*. New York and London: Paul B. Hoeber, Inc., 1940.

Landis, Judson T., and Landis, Mary G., *Building a Successful Marriage* (2nd ed.). Englewood Cliffs, N. J.: Prentice-Hall, Inc., 1953.

Locke, Harvey J., *Predicting Adjustment in Marriage*. New York: Henry Holt & Co., Inc., 1951.

Murdock, George P., *Social Structure*. New York: The Macmillan Co., 1949.

Rockwood, Lemo D., and Ford, Mary E. N., *Youth, Marriage and Parenthood*. New York: John Wiley & Sons; London: Chapman & Hall, 1945.

Terman, Lewis M., *Psychological Factors in Marital Happiness*. New York and London: McGraw-Hill Book Co., 1938.

WINSTON EHRMANN

Prostitution

PRACTICALLY all of the books, articles, and essays on the subject of the purchase and sale of sex services (usually and not too fortunately referred to as prostitution) fall into one of two categories: (1) those dealing with the subject impartially, scientifically, and objectively, examining it simply as an existing phenomenon in human society; and (2) those approaching it strictly within the atmosphere and confines of the Judeo-Christian (Western) civilization, therefore prejudging, disapproving, and—in most instances—more or less severely condemning all prostitutional relationships as objectionable, immoral, or "sinful." (In Anglo-Saxon countries, reformers often speak of the "social evil.")

The following article is meant to adhere as closely as possible to the first category.

Definition and Characterization

The word prostitution implies something bad, something derogatory. In using it here, concession is made to custom. It could best be replaced by a term that is less pharisaical, but more objectively descriptive. Such a term should not be charged with any emotional potential of a sanctimonious nature, leading to the usual righteous condemnation. "Sex service" may answer the purpose until a better term is invented.

The usual and rather narrow definition of prostitution is "promiscuous intercourse for hire," to which, however, can and should be added that such intercourse is largely indiscriminate, without affection, and frequently anonymous, payment being made in cash.

If honest affection on the part of the woman enters into the relationship, it ceases to be prostitution even if advantages are being gained. Likewise, the woman who gives her sexual favors unselfishly, without profit although without affection, should not be classed as a prostitute, some contrary opinions notwithstanding.

Types of Prostitutes and Prostitution

The *professional prostitute*, sometimes referred to as the *public prostitute*, derives her sole and only livelihood from her activity. It is her vocation. She may be a high-class "cocotte" or "courtesan" with relatively few lovers—one, for instance, paying her rent, another buying her clothes or luxuries, and others supplying ready cash. If she has only one lover at a time for whom she has no affection but to whom she is faithful in order not to lose him, she is a "kept woman," a mistress. It is a question of one's sensibilities whether to classify her as a professional prostitute or not. Whoever disapproves of her form of making a living is likely to use the derogatory term. The broad-minded and the impartial observer, however, will put her into a class by herself (that of a mistress), because the indiscriminate and promiscuous acts of prostitution are lacking.

The largest number of professional prostitutes and the most typical ones work in brothels. The number of brothels seems to be decreasing steadily in the Western part of the world but they are rather widespread in Eastern and Oriental countries. All types and classes can be found, from the most luxurious establishments to the cheapest "cribs" in slum areas. The girls working in the lower-class brothels are usually older and worn out. A similar type of girl is represented by many streetwalkers, who have relatively low remuneration. Those who find their clients in bars, hotel lobbies, or similar places receive much higher fees. Such more expensive girls may also be "call-girls." Either they live alone and have their own clients whom they serve by appointment, or they work for a madam with whom they split their earnings.

Most professional prostitutes are said to have "pimps." They are not necessarily procurers, but live on the girl's earnings and supply their emotional need for affection and companionship. Often they are married, not necessarily to each other. In the lower classes of prostitution, the pimp is usually also the "business manager," arranging for "bookings" in brothels, etc.

The *nonprofessional prostitute*, also known as the *clandestine* or *secret prostitute*, renders sex service as an avocation. She is usually gainfully employed or married but adds to her income by committing acts of prostitution. She may accept money or presents or derive other advantages. She is also referred to as the amateur. The number of such prostitutes is increasing as steadily as that of the professional prostitute is decreasing.

The amateur may work in a factory, store, or office, and is sometimes underpaid or out of a job. She may be a telephone operator, a waitress, or a manicurist. Chorus girls and models are considered to be particularly inclined toward part-time prostitution. But among nonprofessional prostitutes are also divorcees, housewives, students, and even schoolgirls. Whatever their vocation, they are unable to satisfy their desires for the better things in life with their allowances or salaries alone. In other instances, they accept occasional dates in order to meet immediate obligations (pressing debts, a sick husband or child, or needy parents). They illustrate the frequent transitory character of prostitution.

With minor variations, these definitions and examples apply to conditions in the larger cities of Europe and America, provided legal suppression has not succeeded in replacing the professionals almost completely by their clandestine competitors. Their number will largely be determined by the extent of the masculine demand at a given time or locality. Prostitution therefore is an effect, not a cause.

Prostitution usually refers to female prostitution, but there is also male prostitution—homosexual or heterosexual men offering themselves and their services to other men. This type of prostitution is widespread in large cities. Although both forms have much in common, homosexual prostitution constitutes a separate social, medical, and legal problem.

There is also heterosexual prostitution, in which females pay males (gigolos) for their sexual services, and a homosexual (Lesbian) form, in which females pay females. Their incidence is considerably lower than the first two, particularly when compared to the heterosexual female prostitution with which we are dealing here.

It is often difficult, if not impossible, to differentiate prostitution from ordinary fornication. Money may be given not to pay for sex services but to buy a present merely as a friendly gesture. The attitude of an observer, for instance a judge, and his evaluation of a particular incident, would be the decisive factors.

Very frequently females gain advantages by allowing sexual relations that they would otherwise refuse (procuring employment, for instance). Yet, in every-day language, this would not be considered prostitutional. Marriages exist in which wives demand payment for every act of intercourse with their husbands. Literally millions of American wives, having no love or sex desire for their husbands, continue to have sex relations with them in order to maintain the socioeconomic benefits of marriage.

One of the most common errors made in characterizing the activities of a prostitute is to say that she "sells her body." Havelock Ellis called this expression "crude and inexact." He felt that the prostitute should be classed with professional people who receive fees for services rendered. René Guyon, the pioneer French sexologist and a prominent legal expert, accuses the puritans of making a "deliberate mistake in bad faith" when they speak of a prostitute's "sale of her body." He calls such an interpretation "legal and social nonsense" because the prostitute merely hires herself for a "special and momentary use" and under a "legitimate contract," provided there is no violence or threat. Such a concept completely dispenses with moralistic and religious considerations and employs common sense and scientific detachment.

Another misconception that is based on a purely emotional reaction is the argument that prostitutional relationships are bad because "love cannot be bought." It is, of course, not "love" that a prostitute sells. She merely provides the opportunity for a man to find release from sexual tension in a manner physiologically more normal than, for instance, self-gratification.

There are enough valid reasons to criticize prostitution, at least in our day and age, without resorting to false, naive, and untenable arguments.

It would be logical and also scientifically sound to say, with Albert Ellis, that prostitution exists when a woman (or a man) engages in sexual relations for other than sexual or amative motives. With such a definition, much misunderstanding could be avoided. For the present discussion, however, the more narrow interpretation of prostitution as socially taboo and legally prohibited is the subject of description, examination, and evaluation here.

Some Historical Data

Throughout recorded history, prostitution has existed in one form or another. But even long before the dawn of civilization, acts of prostitution must have occurred when primitive man bought the woman he wanted, with a special morsel of food, clothing, or some other object, if he was not strong enough to take her by force.

There has always been and always will be a market for something men want and women have to sell. "The ever-raging animal in man," as Plato called it, has remained fundamentally the same throughout the centuries of culture and education.

The "marriage custom" is older than the human race. A "matrimonial" response in contrast to the sexual impulse exists in animals and in birds, as well as in mammals. Only as a by-product of marriage has prostitution come into being. In a state of true promiscuity, the extent of prostitution would be small indeed.

Religious Prostitution

One of the oldest known forms of prostitution was intimately connected with religion, and existed as "temple" or "sacred" prostitution. It originated in the Orient where, around 300 B.C., it was already highly developed and esteemed. The priestesses of the Babylonian temples rendered sex service for pay, and were always treated with great respect and dignity.

Herodotus describes the high form of temple prostitution that existed in the famous tower of Babel after its renovation. On the top floor was a sacred room with a large, richly adorned bed and a golden table. Every night a woman was chosen by her god to sleep there. We are not told whether she embraced the god only in her dreams or whether a mortal—a king, or a high priest—acted as "understudy."

Ancient Greece

In ancient Greece, men of all ages and classes favored prostitution, although marriage was held sacred, especially in Athens. There, as in Sparta and Corinth, visiting with hetaerae (companions), in or outside of temples, was an accepted custom by married as well as unmarried men. Hetaerae were not ordinary prostitutes but were mistresses of many men, as were the high-class courtesans of later days. They were not despised by other women; in fact, they were frequently envied. They served not only the sensuality of their clients but also their intellectual interests. Famous people, such as Pericles, Alexander, Plato, Socrates, Alcibiades, and Praxiteles, had intimate friendships with hetaerae, whose names they preserved for posterity.

The Athenian lawgiver Solon recognized prostitution. Although he described it as an "inevitable, if not necessary evil," he built a temple to Aphrodite Pandemos (which by that time had become identified with extramarital sexual practices). The Greeks appreciated business. The hetaerae paid taxes in accordance with the prices they charged. Not all of them "worked" in temples; most of them were in brothels and occasionally in what could be called a "maison de rendezvous," a form of call house but with a less commercial atmosphere. The state also provided for the poorer classes. In cheaper, tax-free brothels, customers paid no more than one obulus (about 3 cents in American money) for sex service.

In Corinth, the Temple of Aphrodite was usually thronged with beautiful women who charged high fees for their favors, part of which went to the State or to the Temple treasury. According to most Greek writers, organized prostitution performed a service for the State. It was not an instrument of licentiousness, but constituted a means to satisfy the natural wants of men. Homosexual prostitution was likewise recognized and flourished throughout the ancient world. Sacred prostitution was also bisexual, men offering themselves to other men as well as to women. In spite of the term "sacred," it was often a rather cold-blooded business proposition.

Rome and the Near East

In Rome, most prostitutes were slaves who had been captured in the wars. Brothels (lupanars) were numerous and were considered an aid to the purity of family life. The circus, the theaters, religious assemblies, and public gatherings all served prostitution. Courtesans were freely allowed everywhere. The Emperor Tacitus once attempted to abolish all brothels in Rome, but found it impossible. At one time in Rome prostitutes wore distinctive costumes, as richly and brilliantly dyed as they could afford. In the third century, all courtesans in the Roman Empire were taxed and the proceeds were devoted to popular amusements. Harlots received licenses and their names were registered. Legal attacks on Roman prostitution took place only in Christian times, never before.

In ancient Egypt, Arabia, and Israel, many courtesans were recruited from divorced and cast-off wives. The Hebrew code was extremely severe regarding Jewish maidens who became prostitutes, but condoned "strange women" as prostitutes. When Jesus protected a prostitute (but flogged the money-changers), he did not conform to the sexual intolerance of the Jews.

Did he do so because he saw a justification for prostitution?

Christianity

Later on, the leading fathers of the Christian Church were at times inclined to tolerate and even to sanction prostitution, and some Christian emperors derived taxes from brothels. On the other hand, the concept of original sin, and the condemnation of all sexual pleasure (even in the marriage bed, which was to serve procreation only), had its start in the same Christian Church that had adopted much of its antisexual philosophy from older Hebrew codes.

The Middle Ages saw many changes in the attitude of the authorities and of the public toward prostitution. Under Charlemagne and Frederick Barbarossa (twelfth century), laws against its practice were enacted, with severe punishments and the death penalty for (female) violators. In France in the thirteenth century, all courtesans were at one time driven out of the country after their possessions had been confiscated. Before the Crusades, brothels were destroyed but their inmates allowed to mingle freely with the population or to follow the armies. An unusual attitude is found in a paper read by a priest at the Council of Basel (1431), in which he argued that the sanctioning of prostitution was the only way to preserve good morals.

Venereal diseases were widespread in the Middle Ages. Although their cause was not known, it was somehow felt that brothels had something to do with their dissemination. When an epidemic of syphilis swept over Europe in the sixteenth century, the brothels were blamed and closed. Medical diagnosis had been preceded by shrewd medical observation. Gradually, prostitution became a public-health problem. Segregation and the red light districts came into existence. Toward the end of the seventeenth century, medical examinations of prostitutes were undertaken, and registration, distinctive dresses, and badges were required.

Probably the first attempt to approach prostitution from a social, philosophical, and scientific viewpoint "bereft of all hypocrisy and cant" was made in the early eighteenth century, when

Bernard Mandeville wrote the *Fable of the Bees,* preceding another Bernard by 100 years. In so many words, he anticipated Shaw's wisdom: "Any vice that cannot be suppressed should be made a virtue."

In England prostitution is not as old as it is on the European continent. Toward the end of the sixteenth century London was still a city about one quarter the size of Paris. The English "stew" and "ale" houses were centers of prostitution which, however, were (and still are) neither outlawed nor licensed. From time to time, puritan societies forced the police to close "bawdy houses" but the institution as such continued to flourish. Casanova, in his *Memoirs,* described the customs in London around 1750. We can gather that, knowing too little English, he was unable to use his art of seduction, but had no difficulty in buying what elsewhere was given to him so freely.

Up to the present time, England viewed prostitution with a measure of common sense. So did France, particularly under Napoleon the First, who, breaking with many of the older moralistic prejudices, established the system of the "maison de tolerance." These supervised brothels seemed to function well and were widely imitated in other countries. Yet, without taking advantage of the new medical discovery for preventing venereal diseases, French politicians, aided (or prodded) by the Church, succeeded only a few years ago in outlawing and closing all "houses." They did not do away with prostitutes nor with venereal infections (rather the opposite). But they did change the character of Parisian life, especially for tourists.

A reaction set in rather promptly. The police in Paris complained of a new "black market" in vice, impossible to control. Corruption increased and diseases spread, so much so that one of the originators of the repressive law (Mme. Richard) openly admitted in a book and in speeches that she had made a mistake and pleaded for the reopening of the brothels (the inmates were to be designated as "social workers" and not as prostitutes). So far she has had no success. It is always easier to have a new law passed than to have it repealed. Whenever something is suppressed for which there is a public demand, corruption and graft follow with large unearned incomes. In this way, new money and political powers are created that can successfuly preserve a *status quo* under which they profit.

The experiences in France did not deter Italy or Japan from following suit. They, too, closed their licensed or tolerated houses in 1958. Undoubtedly they will see a similar reaction. Japan, after only a few months under the new law, reported a significant increase in venereal diseases among prostitutes, who can now be found far outside the formerly restricted neighborhoods. Instead of the (at least partly) controlled brothels, Japanese cities are now said to have adopted the Western call-girl system.

China and Japan

The Orient has always had a more stable form of prostitution than has the Western world. For many centuries the cities of Japan had their "love quarters," the most famous being Tokio's Yoshiwara. China had its "Blue Houses" in urban areas, and its "Flower Boats" in coastal regions. Modern innovations must indeed resemble a true revolution. For a more detailed description of the history of prostitution in Oriental and other countries, the reader is referred to the books of Sanger (1921), Sorge (1920), Scott (1936), and McCabe (1932), and to the article on "Sex Life in the Orient" in this Encyclopedia.

The United States

Almost everywhere during the Middle Ages prostitution was treated with hypocrisy and violence. In modern times it changed to hypocrisy and confusion. Nowhere is this more evident than in the United States.

A. W. Calhoun, in his *Social History of the American Family* (1919), called the conditions in the South "rotten to the core." His rival from the South retorted that the North was "as bad as Rome in its worst years." The large American cities, until the turn of the century, had expensive "parlor houses," with inmates mostly of American birth, and houses of assignation, as well as cheap brothels and streetwalkers, many of whom were recruited from newly arrived emigrants. They were often shamefully exploited by the madams and the Capones of their day.

Attempts to regulate prostitution were generally similar to those made in England. Medical examinations of prostitutes at ten-day intervals were customary in various cities in the middle of the nineteenth century. Moralistic groups finally objected to this "licensing of vice" in spite of some success in checking venereal infections. Since then, examinations are only conducted when a woman is arrested as a suspected prostitute, usually under the obtuse "Vagrancy Act."

Typical of the American scene were and still are the "vice commissions," "vice crusaders" (usually self-appointed), "committees for the suppression of vice," a "social hygiene association," and others. The most notorious was the Committee of Fourteen. Around 1930 it was most active in "suppressing vice" in New York. Although its members gloried in the ever-increasing arrests of prostitutes, it was revealed during the so-called "Seabury Investigation," in one of the worst scandals of that sort, that a blackmailing ring of stool-pigeons, corrupt policemen, crooked judges, bondsmen, and lawyers were extorting money from women, whether they were guilty or not guilty. Thoroughly discredited, the Committee had to disband.

The American Social Hygiene Association, a "philanthropic" group existing on private donations, is of an entirely different nature. Under the guise of combating venereal diseases, it conducts a hysterical fight against prostitution and encourages its legal suppression. Rather than recommending, it strikingly ignores all prophylactic measures against venereal diseases, apparently believing that such infection is a punishment for sin.

Also typical of conditions in the United States in our days are the regularly recurring "clean-up campaigns," usually a political expedient on the part of a politically ambitious mayor, who appoints a fanatical police chief more concerned with vice than with crime. The latter uses his manpower to conduct raids on suspected call houses, individual prostitutes, and, incidentaly, bookmaking establishments, innocent card games, bookstores allegedly selling pornographic literature, etc. "Vice" is more

or less successfully driven underground or actually suppressed. The city (for example, San Francisco in 1957) is proudly proclaimed to be "clean," with an increase in crimes due to the preoccupation of the police and to other causes completely ignored, although factually admitted. Police corruption sometimes accompanies these tactics.

Most American cities undergo from time to time such eruptions of civic virtue, but sooner or later the former conditions return, the offenders merely having changed their tactics. Call houses and brothels, for example, become massage parlors or escort bureaus that, for a while, exist side by side with their legitimate competitors.

As this sketchy account has shown, the history of prostitution is, on the one hand, the history of unchanging human sexuality and, on the other, the history of human stupidity, avarice, and hypocrisy.

Sociological and Psychological Aspects

The Role of Prostitution

As we have seen, sex service on a commercial basis has existed throughout the ages. There have always been people who have made their living by supplying—either directly or as intermediaries—the means to satisfy the sex urge as a basic and irrepressible human instinct.

The human sex urge is fundamentally promiscuous. The establishment of marriage and the family with all their advantages—and the resulting promotion of monogamy—have only somewhat repressed and modified its basic character.

Monogamy is, after all, only an artifact of civilization. It is, no matter how desirable in this stage of evolution, by no means universally wanted nor individually and constitutionally attainable; nor is it, as an institution, uniformly successful. The man who does not care for variety in sex, or does not include it in his pursuit of happiness, is in the minority. He has either been rarely fortunate in finding a perfect mate, or nature has provided for him a "low-level" psychosexual constitution.

Whether it is admitted or not, the majority of men do desire novelty as well as variety in sex. This natural urge cannot be abolished, either by sermons or by laws. An intelligent society will therefore try to direct such urges into the least harmful channels. Tolerated but supervised sex services (prostitution) could provide such channels.

Our largely antisexual Western civilization insists on a different approach, no matter what the consequences may be. It outlaws prostitution, closes a possible safety valve, with the result that the polygamous man seeks non-prostitutional outlets for his libido. In this way we are likely to have more seduction with illegitimate pregnancies and abortions; more adultery and divorces; more rape and attacks on children; more homosexual activities for the bisexually inclined.

All these dangers have been pointed out again and again by thoughtful writers, by independent social scientists, and by sexologists. However, in our day and age, the views of the Church and of the sex-hostile puritan have invariably prevailed. The sociologist, Lecky, called the old-fashioned form of professional prostitution ("parlorhouses") a "bulwark for the home." Long before Lecky, the Roman Senator Cato remarked that he was always glad to see a man emerge from a brothel because "otherwise he may have gone to lie with his neighbor's wife." Even the Church has not always been opposed to prostitution. St. Augustine once warned: "Suppress prostitution and frivolous lust will ruin our society."

Returning to the present and to the American scene, it may be worthwhile to scan the statistical data that Kinsey and his group have been able to gather. They came to the conclusion that "the frequencies of coitus with females who were not prostitutes has increased to an extent which largely compensated for a decrease in contacts with prostitutes."

They also found that 69 per cent of white males in the United States had some experience with prostitutes. Of this group, 15 to 20 per cent have paid sex relations for "a five-year period." About 4 per cent of the total sex outlet of all American males is drawn from relations with prostitutes. (This is a "minimal" figure. The actual figure is undoubtedly higher. Kinsey once indicated to this writer that 10 per cent may be nearer to the truth.)

If one considers that 40 per cent of our population of 175 million (or 70 million) is composed of men in their prime, and if one further considers that such men have an average of three sex outlets weekly (210 million outlets), the total number of even this low 4 per cent prostitutional contacts (8,400,000 contacts a week) is truly staggering. The 10 per cent figure would swell the total weekly contacts with prostitutes in the United States to 21 million. To attempt their suppression by police methods appears almost childish in its uselessness. All that is ever accomplished is that prostitution is driven underground, that is to say, is diverted from a recognizable form that could be supervised into a system and into a section of society that is beyond any control.

The Social Position of the Prostitute

The social position of the prostitute has undergone constant changes. State and society have, with great regularity, alternately tolerated and combated the commercial service of sex.

Since the system itself, based on an unalterable demand of nature, cannot be abolished or prevented, the repressive efforts of the puritans were directed against the individual prostitutes. This resulted frequently in outright persecution, shameful methods of entrapment that are intolerable in any democratic society, in unjust punishment, and, on the part of the prostitute herself, in the adoption of an antisocial character and the finding of "protectors," in the form of pimps, racketeers, or corrupt officials. In this way, graft and venality arise out of efforts meant to promote morality. The parallel with the prohibition of alcoholic beverages easily suggests itself.

Arguments against the repression of prostitution invariably bring forth the counterargument that greater toleration would result in an increase of prostitution, in more temptation and more dissemination of venereal diseases. For an average intellect and for the average conformist's mentality this latter argument, together with the idea of "sin" attached to all nonmarital sex relations, has much appeal. Therefore attempts by scientists and more advanced thinkers to have sex service recognized morally, legally, and socially have been doomed to failure and the present unhealthy system of repression has been preserved, at least in many countries of the Western world.

An additional influence on the spread and character of prostitution is naturally exercised by economic conditions, depressions possibly increasing the supply, prosperity raising the demand (and the price).

The woman's approach to the entire question is too often ignored because of the more dominant masculine approach. To present the female attitude, Dr. Maude Glasgow (1945), an American woman physician, may be quoted. She claimed that prostitution is a man's business and is established and supported by men, who reap huge financial profits. The woman alone is the offender, whereas the man goes scot free. "Men," the doctor demands, "should be arrested, finger-printed, placed under police surveillance and perhaps imprisoned. . . . A register should be kept within a brothel of patrons, giving name, age, marital status and date of visit."

Although some of the charges made by the doctor are essentially true, it is not man's tyranny that is responsible for the injustices, but rather the biological differences between the sexes. The recommendation that the male customer be prosecuted together with the prostitute may appear militantly feministic, but is actually an emotional reaction rather than a logical analysis. To put such a proposition into practice would undoubtedly result either in an absurdly high number of arrests or in much more corruption. Furthermore, such repression of male sexuality could be highly dangerous. Explosions in the form of sex crimes, seductions, or diversion into homosexuality would be infinitely greater than they are under the present system, where they are certainly great enough. A more objective examination of the reasons women become prostitutes on a permanent or temporary basis would reveal a different and much more complex picture than the theory that they are merely victims of evil men.

It is obvious that prostitution must have distinct advantages for the woman, otherwise it would not continue to exist. The noted sociologist Kingsley Davis (1937) says that from a purely economic point of view the prostitute comes "perilously near the situation of getting something for nothing." He continues: "The woman may suffer no loss at all, yet receive a generous reward, resembling the artist who, paid for his work, loves it so well that he would paint anyway. Purely from the angle of economic return, the hard question is not why so many women become prostitutes, but why so few of them do." It is of course the limitation of the demand that would answer this question.

Some of the advantages that women derive through prostitution, at least within European and American cultures, seem to be as follows:

1. Prostitution, as previously noted, means the trading of sexual favors for a nonsexual advantage. But this employment of sex for nonsexual ends characterizes all our institutions (notably courtship and marriage) in which sex plays a part and which many women enter only for the economic and social status provided by men. As Davis says, this practice includes the employment of pretty girls in stores, cafes, charity drives, and advertisements which, while not generally involving actual intercourse, still contain and utilize erotic stimulation. Furthermore, engaging for profit in virtually any kind of nonsexual activity is also prostitution. Many girls, therefore, consciously or subconsciously, seem to realize that prostituting themselves sexually is no worse than prostituting themselves (usually for much less cash gain) vocationally, manually, or otherwise.

2. The economic rewards of prostitution are normally far higher than those of most other female occupations. This reward is not only for actual services rendered but also for the chance the woman is taking when engaging in an illegal occupation and for her loss of social standing in the community. An attractive girl, when working in large American cities as a call girl with good connections, may earn several hundred dollars a week for herself.

3. The call of adventure lures many girls to a life of prostitution. Prostitutes, especially when they are working for a "high-class" madam, call house, or brothel or are working for themselves in a good neighborhood, meet many intelligent, prominent, wealthy males whom they would never meet under ordinary circumstances. Their life is likely to be far more interesting and exciting than that of the average stenographer or shopgirl.

4. Not a few prostitutes find romantic attrac-

tions in their profession. Contrary to popular notion, a good many males become emotionally attached to and ultimately marry girls whom they first started to patronize as prostitutes. There have also been cases of a policeman marrying the girl he was sent to arrest as a harlot.

5. A small minority of prostitutes are so highly sexed that they actually enjoy many or most of their sex participations, and these women find a life of prostitution virtually ideal. Kinsey and his associates find that although most women are not as easily aroused or as highly sexed as are men, 2 or 3 per cent are far more interested in sex stimuli and sex relations than any man. It is likely that some prostitutes are in this group.

6. Many girls in our culture resort to a life of prostitution to satisfy some of their neurotic needs. There are those who are punishing themselves for some actual or imagined "sins." Others are neurotically tied to pimps or panderers who unscrupulously exploit them or virtually (though not physically) force them to work at their trade. Still others prostitute themselves to obtain narcotics. Some girls are rebels and become prostitutes to wreak (conscious or subconscious) revenge on their parents, broken homes, or society, or they enter prostitution on the rebound from an unhappy love affair.

7. Many girls who are too mentally deficient, psychologically inadequate, lazy, or physically weak to hold down regular employment in our culture find that they have to resort to prostitution in order to earn a living.

8. A large proportion of prostitutes, contrary to what the public often thinks, finds considerable expediency in temporary prostitution. Many of them work as call girls or in "houses" for a limited period of time, until a financial emergency in their families has been met, until a debt has been paid or certain luxuries have been acquired, or until other advantages have been gained. They may then return to a legitimate job or to being a housewife until a new emergency arises.

The Client

Several advantages of prostitution for the male have already been indicated by previous remarks. Aside from the necessity to relieve sexual tension when neither steady nor sporadic satisfaction is available through any other (nonprostitutional) contact, men visit prostitutes for the following reasons:

1. They need variety in order to satisfy their normal sex urges.

2. They are too shy emotionally, too handicapped mentally or physically, or too old to compete with other males in winning female sex partners on the basis of mutual enjoyment. The availability of a prostitute is actually a blessing to them.

3. Many men have deviated sex urges of a sadomasochistic or fetishistic nature that can only be satisfied in purchased sex relations. Frustration in this respect may be dangerous to society. Other men desire socially tabooed forms of sex relations that only paid-for sex service can provide for them. Others again have an active libido but are impotent, and could not satisfy a wife or sweetheart. To the prostitute their disability is immaterial.

4. A large number of men want to avoid obligations, are afraid of impregnating a girl, or want to escape emotional entanglements. Others do not have the time to court a girl until she may agree to sex relations on a nonmarital basis or they do not have the money for extended courtships. Still others do not want to take a chance to have their libido aroused by love-making and then perhaps be left frustrated by the girl's refusal to have intercourse. A visit to a prostitute may be, for all of them, simpler, safer, and even cheaper.

5. Some men merely want to relax in female company with ordinary conventions removed and, as Havelock Ellis noted, "add an element of gaiety and variety to the ordered complexity of modern life, a relief from its mechanical routine, a distraction from its dull and respectable monotony."

In connection with these advantages for individual males, prostitution, as mentioned previously, can have a salutary effect on society by preventing sex crimes or sexual neuroses that may develop under enforced sex starvation. This effect is, however, not generally admitted, in spite of the fact that studies have shown that sex crimes increase when prostitution is successfully suppressed. One should hardly need statistics to prove this connection. Common sense alone should tell us that it is true. It is impossible to estimate how many women and children have been raped so that our puritanical standards could be maintained. But many undoubtedly have.

Furthermore, it seems self-evident that the bisexual man who can be attracted and aroused by either sex will go the path of least resistance, choosing homosexual outlets with a possible permanent fixation, when the ("normal") avenue of heterosexual prostitution is blocked.

A final but by no means insignificant service that prostitution could render would be the prevention of hasty, ill-judged marriages, entered into almost solely as the result of sexual pressure. Utilization of the services of a prostitute could have diminished the imperious sex drive, making possible a more considered and therefore more hopeful union.

It can well be argued that, in a democratic society, there should be a place for all kinds of voluntarily entered, noncoercive sex relations, prostitutional or nonprostitutional. As long as prostitutes freely choose their profession and as long as some males harmlessly choose to enjoy their favors, rather than those of non-prostitutes (including their wives), two major modes of sex behavior instead of one are available for human satisfaction, and human existence can thereby be enriched.

Disadvantages

For both sexes the disadvantages of prostitution are evident. The worst aspect of this profession in large parts of the world is its illegality, which forces the girls of the demi-monde (half-world) into the underworld. Easy virtue, mental defects, or delinquency are made crimes. Stigmas remain for the girl as a former "social outcast" when she wants to enter or re-enter the so-called respectable society. Unless she can leave the profession relatively early in life, her prospects for the future are dim. One pimp may follow another, one exploiter be replaced by the next. Prisons and hospitals alternate. With every arrest and conviction a more hardened, resentful personality emerges. Increasing frustration easily leads to alcohol or dope, which in most instances means the end of the road.

The male customer of prostitutes runs his risks too wherever the profession is outlawed. He may be robbed, arrested, blackmailed, infected, or ruined by scandal. To most males, the honest, joyful cooperation of a sex partner is essential for their own enjoyment. Prostitutes rarely satisfy such hedonistic wishes, although many have learned to act the part and supply the illusion.

But, in spite of all, prostitution continues, merely changing its face with changing times and places.

Legal Aspects

The attitude of the law toward prostitution has always been one of confusion, contradiction, and change. The intention of the law is either to suppress prostitution as such, or to prevent its harmful consequences and by-products. An example for these two objectives is the situation in England as compared to that in the United States.

In England no prostitute can be punished for what she is. But if she does something in the interest of her profession, such as soliciting or advertising, she commits an offense. In that way she is different from those in other professions. Any working girl is allowed to flirt as much as she wants; let a known prostitute do the same thing and she can be arrested.

In the United States, prostitution is, for all practical purposes, illegal everywhere. Only in the state of Nevada is prostitution as such not unlawful by state law, but almost everything connected with it is illegal. A number of towns, however, in Nevada and in some other states, have red-light districts or allow brothels, but all of them operate illegally. They usually, although not always, buy immunity from law-enforcement agencies and politicians.

Naturally, it is often impossible to separate a prostitutional relationship from that of simple fornication. It is also impossible to decide how many sexual relationships for a monetary consideration a girl must have before she is classed as a professional prostitute. Furthermore, the prostitute, being a social outcast, is not likely to receive justice even in a court of law. In America it is even possible for a girl to be arrested and detained because a policeman merely suspects her of being a prostitute.

The laws dealing with prostitution, like most sex laws in Western countries, derive from the old Hittite and Hebrew moral codes that were taken over to a large extent by Christianity. Prostitution is therefore treated as a moral offense and a sin more than as a crime. Lawmakers act emotionally rather than scientifically when they formulate laws against sex service for a fee.

René Guyon (1934) calls prostitution "nothing more than one modality of sex-relations" and condemns "puritan-inspired" laws against it as "unjustifiable," a "scientific, social, and legal error." A woman's sexual attractiveness undoubtedly constitutes an economic asset comparable to an opera singer's larynx or a wrestler's muscular development. "The woman's sex value should be permitted to be used for her own benefit," continues Guyon, "and should be protected by law like any other value and asset of her personality." Dr. Edward Glover, of the Institute for the Scientific Treatment of Delinquency, of London, makes the following comments (1945):

We must remember that the definition of prostitution is for all practical purposes a legal one. Hence we must not neglect to consider how far our present legal procedures are responsible for aggravating the very condition they are intended to control. For example, to impose a fine is both irrational and absurd; it encourages the girl to repeat the offence in order to have the wherewithal to pay the fine. To imprison takes away her last chance to find "respectable" employment later on. In any case, the "moral" indignation so frequently expressed by magistrates dealing with prostitutes, although strictly speaking no part of their legal prerogative (which is to deal with infringements of law), is a positive encouragement to recidivism. Moralistic fulmination is never a very satisfactory form of therapy. Indeed, the authorities might well consider whether prostitution and other sexual irregularities might not be dealt with solely from the point of view of public decency, i.e. by summons and not by conviction, and even then only after due cautionings and warnings have been given and ignored. Appearance in Court would then be for acting in defiance of the warning. It is obviously idle to raise moral issues unless the Court is prepared to behave in a logical manner, to trace these moral problems to their innumerable sources, and to cooperate in removing or alleviating the causal factors.

The realization that brothels and prostitutes disseminated venereal diseases had a profound effect on the legal attitude. After ruthless persecution had run its course, laws of regulation and control came into existence, with enforced medical examinations and attempts to re-educate and reclaim the "fallen woman." Many European countries, particularly France, tried the system of regulation, and its actual value is still a debated issue.

For many years the struggle went on between those who favored "regulation" (with medical inspection) and those who wanted to abolish it (abolitionists). Both systems have their advantages and disadvantages, which are reflected in the ever-changing legal statutes. For the abolitionists, any "regulation" means "licensing vice" and is therefore objectionable. Those that favor regulation do so because they feel that even a superficial medical examination is better than none. They think of hygiene and the teaching of preventive measures first, while their opponents consider the moral issue before all others.

At present, the case for regulation appears to be losing ground. More and more countries are closing their medically inspected brothels. That, of course, does not mean that either they or the individual prostitutes cease to exist. Some of them merely continue as illegal enterprises and often pay for police "protection." Others change their outward appearance and function as "massage parlors," "dancing academies," or "Turkish baths," unless assignations go on in a tearoom or bar with an otherwise legitimate trade.

In order to procure evidence against such establishments or individuals and enforce the letter of the law, the police have to resort to methods of entrapment that are rather doubtful as to their "morality." Recently, John Murtagh, the Chief Magistrate of New York City, in a book written with Sara Harris, scathingly denounced these methods as contemptible, leading to corruption and degradation of police officers.

The English laws that are not directed against prostitution itself usually forbid the use of premises for illicit sexual intercourse, but only by more than one couple. A woman may entertain as many men as she wishes in her room or apartment without breaking a law. But if two girls live together and both entertain, the place becomes a brothel and is illegal.

In 1956, the British Wolfenden Report stirred the English-speaking countries. After long investigations, it recommended changes in the laws dealing with homosexuality as well as with prostitution. The latter, says the Report, "cannot be eradicated through the agency of the criminal law. It remains true that without a demand for her services, the prostitute could not exist, and that there are enough men who avail themselves of prostitutes to keep the trade alive. It also remains true that there are women who, even when there is no economic need to do so, choose this form of livelihood. For so long as these propositions continue to be true, there will be prostitution, and no amount of legislation directed toward its abolition will abolish it."

An agency in the United States that has fearlessly and with scientific detachment investigated the American sex laws and criticized most of them is the American Law Institute in Philadelphia. So far it has not yet dealt with prostitution. But even if it does and would make its recommendations as to changes in the law, it may take a generation or more until the lawmakers act and the present state of confusion and injustice is corrected in accordance with common sense and modern science.

Venereal Disease

"The professional prostitutes that come here for examination are generally very clean women. Some of them carry penicillin or terramycin tablets in their handbags." So spoke a health officer in charge of a medical clinic in an eastern prison of the United States. It is understood, of course, that this remark does not mean that all prostitutes are healthy and clean. Many are still infected and could spread the infection.

Routine examinations of prostitutes in the United States are carried out only on those that have been arrested. Drs. Rosenthal and Vandow (1958) report from the New York City Department of Health that in 1946 (one year before the introduction of penicillin) 23.6 per cent of arrested prostitutes had gonorrhea, as compared to 5.2 per cent in 1956. Syphilis was found in 21.3 per cent in 1946 and in only 8.5 per cent in 1956. "In 1946, 38.2 per cent of the arrested group of prostitutes had one or more venereal diseases; 10 years later, in 1956, this percentage had fallen to 13.2 per cent."

It is routine at this clinic, as in many others in the United States, that all prostitutes, infected or not, are given penicillin injections, either as a curative or as a preventive measure, because it is assumed that they have had frequent contacts with infection.

Naturally, prostitutes who are arrested do not represent prostitutes in general. It can be logically assumed that among those that never come in conflict with the law infections are rarer. The same higher intelligence that protected them against arrest has probably protected them against disease.

Modern Therapy and Prophylaxis

The previous quotation from a health officer illustrates two important facts that must be considered when the danger of veneral disease dissemination through prostitution is discussed.

First, even in the pre-penicillin days, the professional prostitute was a frequent, though not the principal, carrier of gonorrhea and syphilis. There are many statistics, including those gathered by the American Social Hygiene Association, especially in wartime, to prove this contention. The "amateur," the willing "pickup," and "friend" were much more dangerous. The professional, although more frequently exposed to infection, had, to some extent, learned to protect herself, and also her business and her clients. The "amateur," uncontrolled and uncontrollable, seeking pleasure for herself, often neglects the simplest hygienic measures.

Second, we are now well advanced in the understanding and use of antibiotic remedies. For the treatment and prevention of gonorrhea and syphilis the most effective antibiotic is still penicillin. When other so-called broad-spectrum antibiotics are used, it is for the treatment of gonorrhea only.

For the purpose of treatment or prophylaxis of gonorrhea, one single injection of an adequate dose of penicillin is effective in the vast majority of cases. For prevention, one or two tablets of 400,000 units of penicillin were found to be generally dependable when tested by the Navy. However, it is possible that strains of gonococci have developed that are resistant to penicillin, although possibly yielding to other antibiotics. This question is still being debated in scientific circles. In any event, gonorrhea continues to be a significant health problem, not to be ignored, although it can hardly be called "a menace to the nation's health," as it was twenty years ago. All these factors are to be considered in dealing with prostitution.

For syphilis, a single injection of an adequate dose of a slow-absorbing form of penicillin (for example, Benzathine Penicillin G) was established in 1954 "as a method of choice for the treatment of early syphilis." According to a two-year scientific study, it "yielded success rates of 96 to 100 per cent in the primary and secondary stages of the disease." In this way the time during which the Spirochaeta (responsible for syphilis) can be transmitted is greatly shortened. Yet syphilis has by no means been conquered, because public education as to prevention lags behind the advances in treatment.

Preventive methods, as practiced in non-marital sex relations and particularly in brothels and by individual prostitutes and their customers, have likewise undergone changes in the last decade. The once popular Sanitube and calomel ointment are largely outmoded. Antibiotic creams containing aureomycin or terramycin are being used, but their effectiveness is more than dubious. The liberal use of soap and water, with early urination after contact, is probably better than anything else, except, of course, the condom, which is still the best protective device.

Many professional prostitutes who visit private physicians regularly for inspection and smears insist upon a prophylactic penicillin injection at the same time, this method having proved to be more dependable than tablets.

The antibiotics, through their success in the prophylaxis and treatment of venereal diseases, have become a thorn in the side of the antisexual propagandists. They claim that by removing the fear of infection, immorality is encouraged. From their point of view, they are probably right. But what appears as "immoral" to them is not necessarily immoral to others, morality being not only a matter of time and geography, but also of individual conscience and conviction.

To summarize: Venereal diseases are more widely spread by nonprostitutes than by professionals, and medical science has advanced far toward their control and eventual eradication. Education of the public on preventive measures seems still to be urgently needed in order to remove what is left of the menace of these diseases.

Outlook

The future of prostitution is bound up with the future of society in general and the effect of wider and more effective sex education in particular. Professional prostitutes will continue to decrease in numbers as free love becomes freer and adultery more and more fashionable. "Sex service" for a fee will be rendered more on a part-time basis by otherwise employed women than as an exclusive occupation, except for a limited period of time.

Promiscuity on a nonprostitutional basis will increase but will be selective in form. Men, especially young men, will receive gratuitous sexual favors more readily, but some men will always have to pay for them. The demand will continue to produce a supply, less and less on a professional and more and more on an "amateur" basis.

"Heavy petting" as one form of sexual activity will probably become more popular and will be more easily procured than other forms, especially intercourse, from nonprostitutes. More and more prostitutes will begin to "specialize" in various forms of deviations.

So long as a society structure exists as we know it now, prostitution in some form must persist, not necessarily as a "problem" but rather as an established institution with all its advantages and disadvantages.

References

Adler, Polly, *A House Is not a Home.* New York: Rinehart & Co., Inc., 1950.

Benjamin, Harry, "Prostitution and Venereal Disease." *Med. Rev. of Reviews,* Sept., 1935 (revised and expanded, May, 1939).

Benjamin, Harry, "Prostitution Reassessed." *Internat. J. Sexology 4;* 54-60, 1954; *5;* 37-39, 1951.

Benjamin, Harry, and Ellis, Albert, "An Objective Examination of Prostitution." *Internat. J. Sexology 8;* 100-105, 1954.

Bloch, Ivan, *Die Prostitution.* Berlin: Markus, 1912.

Calhoun, Arthur W., *A Social History of the American Family.* Cleveland: A. H. Clark, 1919.

Davis, Kingsley, "The Sociology of Prostitution." *Am. Sociol. Rev. 2;* 744-755, 1937.

de Leeuw, Hendrik, *Sinful Cities of the Western World.* New York: Julian Messner, Inc., 1934.

Dufour, Pierre (Paul Lacroix), *Histoire de la Prostitution* (6 vols.). Paris, 1851-1861 (enlarged in German, Langenscheidt, 1924).

Ellis, Albert, "Prostitution Re-assessed." *Internat. J. Sexology 5;* 41-42, 1951.

Ellis, Albert, "A Study of 300 Sex Offenders." *Internat. J. Sexology 4;* 129-135, 1951.

Ellis, Albert, *The Folklore of Sex.* New York: Boni, 1951.

Ellis, Albert, "Why Married Men Visit Prostitutes." *Sexology 25;* 344-347, 1959.

Ellis, Havelock, *Studies in the Psychology of Sex.* New York: Random House, 1935.

Glasgow, Maude, "Prostitution—An Analysis." *Med. Woman's J. 50;* 25, 1945.

Glover, Edward, *The Psychopathology of Sex.* London: Inst. for the Study and Treatment of Delinquency, 1945.

Guyon, René, *The Ethics of Sexual Acts.* New York: Alfred A. Knopf, Inc., 1934.

Kinsey, A. C. *et al., Sexual Behavior in the Human Male.* Philadelphia: W. B. Saunders Co., 1948.

Kinsey, A. C. *et al., Sexual Behavior in the Human Female.* New York: W. B. Saunders Co., 1953.

McCabe, Joseph, *The Story of the World's Oldest Profession.* Girard, Kansas: Haldeman-Julius, 1932.

Murtagh, John M., and Harris, Sara B., *Cast the First Stone.* New York: McGraw-Hill Book Co., 1957.

Reitman, Ben L., *The Second Oldest Profession.* New York: Vanguard Press, 1931.

Robinson, W. J., *The Oldest Profession.* New York: Eugenics Pub. Co., 1929.

Rosenthal, T., and Vandow, I., "Prevalence of Venereal Disease in Prostitutes." *Brit. J. Ven. Dis. 34;* No. 2, 1958.

Sanger, W. W., *The History of Prostitution.* New York: Medical Publishing Co., 1921.

Scott, George Ryley, *The History of Prostitution.* New York: Greenberg Pub., 1936.

Sorge, Wolfgang, *Geschichte der Prostitution.* Berlin, 1920.

Wolbarst, Abraham, "The Suppression of Public Prostitution, a Factor in the Spread of Venereal Disease." *N.Y. Med. J. Rec.,* May 4, 1921, and June 6, 1921.

HARRY BENJAMIN

Protestantism
and Sex

THE attitude of the Reformers toward sex must be considered against the background of prevailing conditions in the late fourteenth and early fifteenth centuries. The clergy were forbidden to marry, yet substantial numbers of them were involved in sexual relations, some casual and clandestine, others open and more enduring, common-law marriages that were often blessed with offspring. Luther was convinced that "whoever does not marry must misconduct himself" and Calvin commented that "it is scarcely possible to find one convent in ten that is not rather a brothel than a sanctuary of chastity." One might suspect statements of this kind, considering their source, were they not substantiated by other historians of the period. Even Catholic writers admit that the conditions prior to the so-called Counter Reformation were deplorable. This state of affairs led Luther, already at odds with Rome over doctrinal questions, to question the whole institution of clerical celibacy. He came ultimately to strike at the very foundations of the traditional exaltation of virginity and celibacy on the twofold basis of his study of the Scriptures and his own experience.

Luther

Shortly after his move from the monastery at Erfurt to the faculty of the University of Wittenberg, Luther was given the responsibility of teaching Biblical theology. His growing familiarity with the Old and New Testaments (which was later increased still further by his translation of the Bible from Hebrew and Greek into German) resulted in his challenge to the accepted ecclesiastical doctrine and practice at many points. He found in the Catholic tradition already delivered to him a firm conviction that sex is a part of the divine creation and therefore to be affirmed by the Christian believer. Had there been sex between Adam and Eve in the Garden of Eden before the Fall, it would have been pure and holy. There would have been no uncontrollable lust, no shame over nudity, and no pain connected either with coitus or childbirth. The medieval tradition displays a remarkable unanimity in agreeing that Adam and Eve had not shared coitus before their expulsion from Paradise.

The original sin of the parents of the race, however, corrupted all facets of human life, sex among them. The first penalty and result of the Fall is what the Catholic theologians called concupiscence, the ravages of lust. This malady is by no means confined to man's sexual life; it pervades his entire existence. It makes him discontent with whatever he has, however much or little, and eager for more, be it money, power, knowledge, or sexual pleasure. The last is the most dramatic illustration of the predicament and therefore came into such frequent usage as an example as to become almost identical with concupiscence. But every major theologian of medieval Catholicism and the Reformation understood full well that sexual desire, awakening again each time it had been lulled to sleep, is only one facet of concupiscent lust. It is true that fallen man finds it difficult ever fully to satisfy his sexual urges, for the more he gets the more he wants. But the identical principle rules in all areas of life. Does he have money? He wants more. Is power, or fame, securely within his grasp, so that he says, "Enough"? Never. Always he reaches out so that he is never satisfied, but continually frustrated and restless.

This understanding of the human predicament led to the ascetic impulse in Christianity, even as it did in Buddhism. If man purges himself of what Gautama called *tanha,* or craving, and what St. Augustine called *concupiscientia,* or lust, then he takes the vows of poverty, chastity, and obedience, giving up his desire for possessions, for passion, and for power. This essentially monastic attitude led the Catholic church to distinguish between two orders: the higher, "more excellent way" of priest, monk, and nun, as opposed to the lower path taken by the weak and struggling laity. Luther's quarrel was not with the Catholic view of concupiscence and its tragic consequences in human life. He accepted that wholeheartedly and applied it with an even more rigorous consistency. He denied that any man or woman (save only a small and exceptional minority) could be free from lust, and he shattered the distinctions between the higher and lower ways.

His violent rejection of clerical celibacy was not, as his Roman Catholic detractors have sometimes suggested, motivated by his own inability to remain true to his monastic vows, by his uncontrollable passion for the nun who became his wife, Katherine von Bora. Chronology refutes such a canard. In 1521, four years before he had even met Katherine, he set forth his opposition to the whole institution in a letter to Melancthon:

The argument briefly is this: Whoever has taken a vow in spirit opposed to evangelical freedom must be set free and his vow be anathema. Such, however, are all those who have taken the vow in search of salvation, or justification. Since the greater number of those taking vows take them for this reason, it is clear that their vow is godless, sacrilegious, contrary to the Gospel, and hence to be dissolved and laid under a curse (*Briefwechsel,* 3, p. 224).

His argument, in other words, was theological and not personal. He married Katherine several years later out of a sense of duty, feeling that he ought to marry and finding Katherine on his hands in need of a husband. Theirs was no romance, in the modern sense of that term, although their marriage ripened into a mature affection and respect.

Luther's conviction was set against all those aspects of Roman Catholic piety that suggested a man could or ought to earn his own salvation by his good works. To Luther this was a blasphemous impossibility, since salvation was the absolutely free and unmerited gift of God. All men, including monks and priests, were sinners in the divine sight, deserving only damnation. All distinctions between higher and lower forms of life were therefore false and pernicious. The monk at his prayers in his cell was no less in need of divine mercy and grace than was the maid sweeping a room, and neither was the monk's "sacred" activity more pleasing in God's eyes than the maid's "secular" occupation. All work was sanctified, but none of it earned salvation. That came from God alone. Luther admitted that there may be those who by a special gift of God's grace are enabled to remain single, but to make a general rule binding on all religious orders seemed to him not only unwise but positively contrary to God's will. "There must be no general law and everyone shall be perfectly free. Any priest, monk or nun who cannot restrain the desires of the flesh should marry, and thus relieve the burden of conscience" (*Works,* Holman edition, Vol. 2, p. 401). Here Luther was simply following the Apostle Paul's advice to the Corinthians: "It is better to marry than to be consumed with passion" (I Cor. 7). In addition, he was concerned about the troubled consciences of the multitudes of the clergy involved in illicit sexual relations.

This, then, was the first consequence of the Protestant break with Rome, so far as the realm of sex is concerned: the destruction of clerical celibacy and the establishment of a married clergy. Note, however, that this did not spring from any higher valuation of the sexual impulse, from any conviction that sex is natural and good and therefore open to all. Rather,

Luther strikingly foreshadowed Freud in his insistence upon the irresistible power of the libido. Virtually no man is free of its imperious demand. Human beings must have a sex life of some kind or another and the least of all the evils possible is marriage, which God has provided as a remedy for concupiscence. Not that this was the original divine intention. Marriage as it was created was altogether pure and good and still retains vestiges of its original righteousness. But such is the wisdom of God that he provided the cure for the malady of sin even before the disease had put in its appearance!

Calvin

John Calvin, in most respects, followed the lead of his predecessor in reform, but he took a somewhat more positive view of the possibilities of marriage and sexuality. He agreed that the sexual life of man contains "an irregularity, which, I allow, is beyond others violent and next to brutish." But he insisted that

. . . whatever there is of vice or baseness is so covered over by the honorableness of marriage, that it ceases to be a vice, or at least is not reckoned a fault by God. . . . You may then take it briefly thus: conjugal intercourse is a thing that is pure and holy and honorable because it is a pure institution of God: the immodest desires with which persons burn is a fault arising from the corruption of nature; but in the case of believers marriage is a veil, by which the fault is covered over, so that it no longer appears in the sight of God (*Commentary on I Corinthians*, Ch. 7).

Calvin cautioned against two extremes: either to abhor sex and seek celibacy, regarding all forms of sexuality as evil and degrading, or to regard sex as self-justifying, arguing that "married persons might indulge themselves in whatever license they please." Sex in marriage, then, is no sin, but it must be proper and decorous, not immoderate or lustful. Medieval Catholic moral theology had seen sex as a two-lane highway, carrying the traffic of a double motivation. The first and most fundamental was procreation, the second, the quieting of lust. Any marital coitus entered with the purpose of begetting offspring was proper and correct, an

obedience to the divine command to "be fruitful and multiply." If reproduction were secondary to pleasure in motivation, then the spouse accepting intercourse on such grounds was free from sin, simply rendering what St. Thomas Aquinas called "the marriage debt," protecting the lusting partner from the worse sin of adultery. The initiating spouse, however, was guilty of venial sin, although the sacramental grace of matrimony covered the lapse from grace.

The Reformers scorned such nice distinctions and recognized the necessity and the validity of marital intercourse as a relief from libidinal tension. But this did not, in their eyes, justify utter license. Paul's "permission" to the Corinthians to engage in sexual relations in marriage was, according to Calvin, given "that they might not . . . loosen unduly the restraints of lust." Paul deliberately commented that he had written as he had on account of their infirmity—"that they may bear in mind that marriage is a remedy for unchastity, lest they should inordinately abuse the advantage of it, so as to gratify their desire by every means; nay more, without measure or modesty."

Classical Protestantism opened matrimony to all, clergy and laity alike, recognizing the power of the sexual drive over virtually every human being. But the Reformers were by no means emancipated moderns. They shared the suspicion of sexuality that had been the heritage of Western civilization since the Hellenistic Age in the third century B.C. The Calvinistic Puritans in England and the Anabaptists on the Continent laid considerable stress on the importance of companionship in marriage (see *What Christianity Says About Sex, Love, and Marriage*, by Roland H. Bainton, especially Ch. 5). But prudery and shame retained their sheltering position around human sexuality in Protestant circles generally throughout the modern period. Puritanism in the Reformed sector of Protestantism and pietism in the Lutheran combined to nurture the shadowy aura beneath which sex struggled to survive. The England of Queen Victoria led a proper existence, where all was modesty and decorum, approved alike by the Establishment and the Nonconformists. Continental Europe and the United States sought the same shelter and Protestantism led the way.

Twentieth-Century Protestantism

The long-overdue protest against the price paid by Western civilization for such repressions and against the hypocrisy that flourished in the darkness came in the late nineteenth century not from Protestant sources but from the secular world. Havelock Ellis in England and Sigmund Freud on the Continent shattered the complacency and the blindness of bourgeois society and stripped away the false front behind which hid powerful sexual drives and vigorous sexual activity. Neither of these pioneers nor their followers were libertines, either personally or theoretically. In fact, Freud was himself something of a proper Victorian. But both men insisted upon two things: first, that sex is a natural instinct to be accepted and enjoyed, and second, that sexual repression produces perversion and deceit.

The initial reaction to their protest from all quarters of polite society—and Protestant circles were no exception—was a storm of protest. The very foundations of sexual morality were threatened, so it seemed to Protestant divines on both sides of the Atlantic. Freud's religious scepticism was seized upon as evidence of his desire to attack the fortress of respectability and righteousness.

Twentieth-century Protestantism finds itself in a somewhat schizophrenic position with regard to sex. The supporters of traditional moralism, with all of its repressive restraints, still represent the majority. Sex is justified only within the bonds of matrimony; all else is sin. There are, of course, various gradations even within the ranks of the conservatives. Some would countenance mild premarital expressions of affection as comparatively harmless: holding hands, a chaste good-night kiss. Some would argue that the Kinsey studies should have been made but not published. Others would frown even on dancing as a dangerous arousal of the "lower" passions, eschew the cinema and most modern fiction, and persist in referring to a woman's legs as her "limbs." Probably the extreme reactionaries now find themselves outnumbered by the holders of a somewhat moderate position. But there is a growing company of liberal thinkers on the "left wing" of Protestantism. These men and women have not surrendered grudgingly to the advance of modern sexology but rather have embraced its findings with gratitude and enthusiasm, regarding all truth as coming from God.

It is perfectly clear to all contemporary Protestants that Western society is undergoing a sexual revolution of considerable magnitude. The relaxation of rigid codes of censorship in all forms of art and literature, the sexual emancipation of women, the high degree of deviation from the "accepted" moral standards, the apparent growth of male homosexuality—all of these things are so obvious as to be unavoidable.

Where Protestant schizophrenia appears is in the response to the revolution. The traditionalists call for a radical reform, a return to the old standards of decency and decorum. They argue that Freud and Ellis have been proven wrong. We have lifted the lid, talked about sex openly, written about it freely, raised children without repressions and fear. And the result? A healthier, more natural attitude toward human sexuality? On the contrary, a neurotic sex-saturated society that has lost all sense of balance. Beside the compulsive obsessions of twentieth-century culture, the Victorians were the emancipated ones. They were free to control themselves, whereas moderns are enslaved by their passions. Accordingly, the traditionalists seek a return to propriety, to morality, and to decency. They would censor art and literature, teach the young to discipline their desires and to channel their sexual drives into the place where they belong—matrimony. Their position represents essentially a return to the golden age of the pre-Freudian Era.

Against this company of conservatives in Protestant ranks is arrayed a minority of liberals who argue that it is impossible to reverse the clock, to go back. They agree that the situation is serious but they do not regard it as hopeless. What is called for is not a return to negative moralism but an advance to responsible freedom. Roman Catholicism appears to them, as it did to the sixteenth-century Reformers, to represent the path of legalism, of proscription, of the careful delineation of permitted and prohibited acts. This may well be not only an effective but the most effective way of dealing with the pitfalls and perils of the human libido. But it is not the Protestant way.

Classical Protestantism insisted upon what Luther called "the liberty of the Christian Man." The only absolute that this principle allows is the law of love, love of God and of neighbor. The specific application of that absolute in any concrete situation, however, must always be seen in context, in the light of the relativities of the individuals and the societies involved. Despite the so-called "emancipation" of modern society, there are still sizable walls of guilt, shame, and loathing surrounding sex.

The problems of twentieth-century society are not to be solved by applying greater restraints, by laying down more prohibitive laws, nor by seeking to enslave men to moral codes imposed upon them from outside themselves. Rather, those problems will be solved only by setting men free, by encouraging and enabling human beings to act with maturity and responsibility in adopting their own moral standards and to live by them because they spring spontaneously from within. In that enterprise, the assistance of modern psychotherapy and sexology are to be welcomed.

The split is essentially a question of strategy, of means rather than ends. No Protestant is complacent about the decay of family life, the breakdown of sexual responsibility, the anarchy of moral standards.

Two final words remain to be said. First of all, it should be pointed out that however divided Protestantism may be on many questions of sexual morality, it presents a well-nigh unanimous front on the question of birth control. Churches and individuals from the most diverse theological and historical traditions agree that planned parenthood is not only the right but the duty of the Christian family. Anglicans, Lutherans, Presbyterians, Methodists, Baptists, Congregationalists, Unitarians —all contend that marital coitus that is an expression of love is self-justifying. It does not require procreation to complete or sanctify it. Therefore, any method of spacing offspring that is compatible with the consciences of the individuals concerned is acceptable in Protestant eyes. No wrong is involved in the case of contraceptive devices or chemicals to assure the optimum economic and emotional environment for the arrival of a child. Official statements to that effect are appearing in increasing numbers from official Protestant bodies throughout the world.

The second word has to do with the problem Protestantism confronts as it seeks to minister to all sorts and conditions of men, especially the sexual deviant, of whatever magnitude. From the troubled boy or girl who suffers from guilt about masturbation, through those practicing premarital or extramarital intercourse, to the homosexual, Protestantism, with its traditional orientation toward conventional morality, has tended to cut itself off. The curious historical anomaly is that Luther's doctrine of the spiritual priesthood of all believers, which was supposed to bridge the gap between pulpit and pew, has in fact widened the gulf. The Protestant parson has become a paragon, a plaster saint, the guardian and the spokesman of all that is right and decent. His parishioners find it virtually impossible to turn to him for help with sexual problems, for they fear his shocked rejection of them as persons. Protestant seminaries are giving increasing training to future ministers in psychotherapy and counseling, but the problem remains. How can the church at one and the same time stand for stern moral codes and accept those who violate the codes? Roman Catholicism manages it with the anonymity of the sacrament of penance, which provides both personal protection and sacramental power. The Protestant pharmacopoeia possesses no such balm and therefore loses its wounded to the secular priesthood, the psychiatrist, and the psychoanalyst. In an age of sexual anarchy, such is a serious loss!

References

Bailey, D. Sherwin, *The Mystery of Love and Marriage.* New York: Harper & Brothers, 1952.

Bailey, D. Sherwin, *Sex Relations in Christian Thought.* New York: Harper & Brothers, 1959.

Bainton, Roland H., *What Christianity Says about Sex, Love and Marriage.* New York: The Association Press, 1957.

Calvin, John, *Commentary on I Corinthians.*

Cole, William Graham, *Sex in Christianity and Psychoanalysis.* New York: Oxford University Press, 1955.

Cole, William Graham, *Sex and Love in the Bible*. New York: The Association Press, 1959.

Doniger, Simon (ed.), *Sex and Religion Today*. New York: The Association Press, 1953.

Duvall, Sylvanus M., *Men, Women and Morals*. New York: The Association Press, 1952.

Hiltner, Seward, *Sex Ethics and the Kinsey Reports*. New York: The Association Press, 1953.

James, E. O., *Marriage and Society*. London: Hutchinsons, 1952.

Luther, Martin, *Works*. Holman edition.

Northcote, Hugh, *Christianity and Sex Problems*. Philadelphia: F. A. Davis Co., 1916.

Piper, Otto, *The Christian Interpretation of Sex*. New York: Charles Scribner's Sons, 1941.

Wylie, William P., *The Pattern of Love*. New York: Longmans, Green & Co., Inc., 1958.

WILLIAM GRAHAM COLE

Psychoanalysis and Sex

IN THE first years of this century psycho-analysis was considered almost synonymous with sex. In fact, Freud's monumental contribution to the understanding of the human psyche was repudiated as scandalous because of its emphasis on this unmentionable prime motive force, not only in neurosis but also in the lives of highly respectable people and in innocent babes. Far from being deterred by the bitter criticism of his work, Freud, with a handful of devoted helpers, concentrated more fiercely than ever on the nature and role of sexuality. He developed the concept of the sexual libido and eventually of Eros, a life-giving principle opposed to a Death instinct (aggression).

From the first, Freud observed that "something" opposed the free gratification of sexuality. This "something" he labeled the Censor and left it undifferentiated. By the nineteen twenties, however, he had proceeded to what he called the *structural* approach. The instinctual drives—the sexual instincts and aggression—were grouped together as the *id*. Controlling mechanisms were now seen as the *ego* (which is present in rudimentary form from birth but becomes elaborated and strengthened with experience) and the *superego* (roughly, conscience). The superego is not inborn, although it draws directly on instinctual forces. One might say that it is a part of the id which is normally precipitated out as a separate entity at about the fifth year of life and thereafter functions as a control if not an enemy of the primordial forces of the id.

In this article we shall first discuss Freud's views of the sexual instincts and the superego, and then review later developments of Freudian ego psychology. A third section will deal briefly with dissident schools which derive from Freud but deny the preponderant role he ascribed to the sexual instincts.

The Sexual Instincts and the Superego

Freud early broadened the concept of sexuality to include all the erogenous zones, notably the mouth, the anus, and the urethra. Other component instincts were tentatively mentioned. Primitive gratification from tactile sensations and from motility have been emphasized in recent years. Scoptophilia (pleasure in looking), masochism (pleasure in being hurt), and sadism (pleasure in hurting) were originally considered as component instincts, but were later reconsidered as derivatives.

Mature heterosexual genital satisfaction is achieved, if at all, only through a long process of development. The *focus* of the sexual drive is at first oral (first passive, a little later actively seeking and biting), then anal, then phallic. Freud felt that from about the sixth year until the approach of puberty the sexual drive went into a phase of relative abeyance, which he called the latency period. It re-emerges during adolescence, but at that time bears the mark of the special experiences of the infant and young child. Age demarcations for these phases of sexual development are not rigid. Furthermore they interact with each other in various ways depending on the constitution and experience of the individual child.

There is, nevertheless, a sort of consolidation of the emerging personality at each stage before it moves on to the next. If conditions surrounding a particular stage are especially difficult, the personality may remain essentially "fixated" at that stage. This means that the longings, the fears, and finally the techniques of coping with the problem of that stage of development tend to be built in as fundamental character traits. Overly abrupt weaning and premature or harsh toilet training are examples of common situations leading to profound modifications that tend to persist as deep-seated character traits, occasionally as neurosis or even psychosis. Interestingly enough, overindulgence and failure to encourage the child in his spontaneous impulse toward growth may produce similar results. Early experience of moderate delay in gratification seems important for the development of toleration of instinctual demands in later life which cannot be met immediately. Some mothers enjoy suckling the infant, but are lax about toilet training when the baby is ready for it, and perhaps fail to play with him in the usual way, which stimulates his spontaneous interest in objects and other people. There may be an unconscious wish for continuation of the symbiotic period of early infancy, a sort of jealousy of any personal autonomy that may infringe on the relationship. Often an oversolicitude develops that spares the baby many of the small tribulations of childhood but leaves him ill equipped for handling the inevitable difficulties of life independently. There are many variations, of course.

Stress has been laid here on overindulgence in early years because after a period of scientific advice to mothers concerning strictly regular feedings, regardless of howls, and toilet training at three months, the trend has gone rather too far in the other direction. The infant does indeed require gratification in the oral and excretory zones, but he must also be "hardened," like plants started in the hothouse which must be exposed to small doses of sun, wind, and dryness if they are to survive in the open garden. We shall return to this problem later.

During the phallic stage, the child's libido normally becomes centered on his phallus, or on its absence in the case of little girls. Partly the primal urge is gratified by masturbation, but also there seems to be a primal urge to find a sexual object. The object normally chosen by the little boy is the one he knows and loves the best—his mother. This "love" is the origin of the famous Oedipus complex. The early phallic urge is necessarily frustrated. The little boy is physiologically incapable of consummating the sexual act. The mother repels his fumbling sexual advances, sometimes with direct punishment, often with shock and anxiety which the child senses even though the psychologically informed mother may try to conceal them. He also observes that the father enjoys intimacies from which he is excluded. The father thus becomes his rival, bitterly resented and hated. On the other hand, the father as a person is also normally loved, respected, and taken as a model. Furthermore, he is so powerful that competition is futile. His commands, especially in the sexual area, may not be gainsaid.

In this complex dilemma, the little boy normally has recourse to a mechanism practiced since infancy—identification. Instead of fighting his parents, he "introjects" them. Their commands become his own commands. The policeman at the corner, external authority, is converted to the inner voice of conscience. In this fashion, according to Freud, the superego emerges as a separate entity. He called it the inheritor of the Oedipus complex.[1]

To understand Freud's concept of the superego adequately, one must realize that it is not the parental commands realistically considered as by the adult outsider, but the child's phantasy that is the determining factor. The father may never have spoken a harsh word to the child, but his very aloofness, often reinforced by the mother's subservience to him, may allow the child's phantasy to build up, unchecked by reality, to a harsh superego. The child projects his own hostility. Weak fathers and even those totally absent may produce the same result. Apparently the child *needs* controls of the early instinctual drives, once they

[1] The superego has been redefined even by analysts who call themselves Freudian. The opinion of this author is that Freud's definition is applicable, with minor modifications, to cultural conditions roughly similar to his Vienna. It is applicable to some primitive cultures but not, as Freud assumed, to all. Probably changes in our own family and social structure are gradually changing the predominant structure of the superego in our own society. For the nonce, however, deviations from Freud's essential model may still be considered more as the exception than the rule.

have found an object, and supplies them in phantasy when they are not forthcoming in reality.

Freud felt that the major fear leading to repression of sexual love for the mother—or rather, to its handling by the superego—was the loss of the penis. Many of his patients reported direct threats of cutting it off by the parents during the period of childhood masturbation. Probably such threats are rare nowadays, but strong disapproval persists, social as well as parental, which the little boy easily translates to the phantasy of direct bodily injury. Indeed, punishment for other misdoings tends to be assimilated to his main preoccupation at this period, and contributes to the *castration complex*. Freud considered this the nuclear complex in all neurosis, a point of difference with most other contemporary psychoanalytic schools.

The little girl's development is more complex. According to Freud, there is initially no psychological difference between male and female infants. The girl's interest must be transferred, however, from the clitoris—the female homologue of the penis—to the vagina. Her love object like the boy's, is at first the mother, but she soon learns that the clitoris is not a satisfactory organ of pleasure, and that boys are better equipped. She phantasies that the mother has done her this injury (she construes it as castration), or is at least an inferior being like herself. Hence female *penis envy* and attraction to the father develop. The penis of the male in the sex relationship and the conception and birth of a child normally become substitutes for the lack in herself. The normal psychological transition is from hatred of the mother (always mixed with the dependent love of infancy) to identification with her and introjection of her attitudes. This process is similar to the development of the superego in little boys, and this developing relationship with the parents is known as the Electra complex. Freud remarked, however, that this process is less abrupt for the little girl, that the superego is less intransigent, more personal, more directly related to the mother.

It has been observed that the infant who has *no* stable love object may actually die of emotional neglect despite good physical care.

Others may survive, but often seem incapable of abiding love for another person and deaf to the still, small voice of conscience. The technical term for this condition is psychopathy. It is thought to be caused by failure in the development of the superego along the lines indicated above. Under favorable circumstances, psychopaths are often charming, generous, talented, effective, with an undertone of irresponsibility and selfish whimsicality. They cannot stand monotonous routine or severe frustration. Theft and even murder come easier to them than to most of us. Although their actions are typically impulsive or foolish, they can cover up with a *sang-froid* impossible to the person encumbered with that troublesome item, the superego, rooted in the deep attachments of early childhood.

Thus, according to Freud, the Scylla of the difficult path toward maturity via the viscissitudes of the love (sexual) relationships with the parents is matched by the Charybdis of failure to establish such relationships at all. A middle road, charted by scientific study of the rocks and shoals, is our best hope for the future.

The Latency Period

Beyond noting the existence of latency, Freud himself was not much concerned with the psychodynamics of middle childhood. He thought that the sexual urge in humans was biologically diphasic—the early infantile drives reasserting themselves in puberty under pressure from the maturing gonads. Although no one doubts the pressure of direct sexual impulse in adolescence, Freudians themselves have carried further the study of what happens to the child during the latency period, and how adolescence differs from both infantile and senile sexuality, and from the mere re-emergence of the problems which have fallen under repression around the age of six. Such further study has involved investigation of the ego, a study which Freud always considered necessary and the next step he could not fully carry through.

Later Freudian Ego Psychology

It is significant that the first and still the most important name in this area is that of Freud's daughter, Anna. Her book, *The Ego and the*

Mechanisms of Defense (1936), remains a classic. In no way repudiating her father's position, she points out that the ego (Freud described it as being roughly the reality principle —not to be confused with the self of common parlance) operates from birth and develops its own defenses which must be clarified before one approaches the problems of the id. For example, a child may be destructive because he has insufficient control over his id impulses or because he has won release in therapy from inhibitions. But he may also be destructive because his very fear leads him to *identify with the aggressor.* There are many reasons for early aggressiveness. Anna Freud clearly saw how the defense mechanism of the emergent ego could simulate primary id impulses, although their dynamic background is quite different. "Reality" for the child is not the same as the objective reality viewed by the adult. We have already seen that identification with the person feared is a normal device of childhood in the formation of the superego. It may also be used in a neurotic setting.

Identification with the aggressor is only one example of the ego mechanisms Anna Freud studied in her work with children and adolescents. She cautions against an overly direct interpretation of sexual and aggressive behavior as a release of id impulses, whether spontaneous or appearing in the course of therapy. Very often they result from the adjustive maneuvers of the ego.

Heinz Hartmann has attempted a theoretical integration of the current emphasis on the ego with Freud's original position. (I repeat that Freud always said the ego should be studied, and was sympathetic toward the efforts of his daughter and others in this direction. What he could not tolerate was the repudiation of his basic tenets by the dissidents to be presented later.) Hartmann emphasizes that the ego has primary autonomy in some functions, notably those relating the organism to the outside world—for example, with the sense organs and their associated reflexes and such more generalized functions as speech and motility. In part these functions have an independent course of their own, which should not be ignored. They readily become tools of the instinctual drives, however, and attain an organization within this relationship which *becomes* relatively independent of its origin. Such organizations— there are many, with varying degrees of stability—are termed ego functions of secondary autonomy. For example, the development of speech has its own natural course with relatively small individual variations on the basis of constitutional endowment. If it becomes unduly linked with the emergent drives, exaggerations or impairments appear. One of the most familiar is chronic stammering. Its roots are usually psychological, but it does not yield easily to psychotherapy alone. Correction of speech *habits* is often a necessary secondary line of treatment. This observation suggests the secondary autonomy of the deviant speech pattern persisting beyond resolution of its emotional "cause." By the same token, however, the stammering cannot be cured by mere exercises so long as the "causative" drives are still in dynamic relationship to it.

The example from pathology serves to present with special clarity processes which are obscured by the complexities of normal growth. The autonomous subsystems of the ego, primary and secondary, are constantly integrated and reintegrated into broader units as the child matures. Ego institutions formed to meet the primitive instinctual problems of infancy are not abandoned, but are modified and included in the wider organizations by which the ego of the child and later the adult meets the assignments of living.

In general the ego has three important tasks, mediating: (1) among the instinctual drives themselves, (2) between id impulses and the superego, and (3) between the organism and reality. To these three, Hartmann adds a fourth —the synthetic function of the ego, that is, the general maintenance of the personality as an entity.

Among the Freudians, Erik Erikson has done most to study what he calls the search for identity. Space does not permit a detailed description of his views on earlier stages, which are essentially Freudian with special emphasis on how society influences the adaptation of the child at each stage. At all stages the child is building a "self," but during adolescence the business of establishing who and what he is becomes especially important, and may often supersede even the reactivation of the sexual drive. Talking about the meaning of life, about social problems, about one's personal vocational aspirations and sexual feelings is often more important to the adolescent than direct sexual activity. Some young girls grant sexual favors in a clumsy effort to be "popular," probably a larger number than those who are carried away by the sexual urge itself. Some invent scandalous affairs out of whole cloth in order to gain a sort of prestige among their age mates, or for other reasons. Even more frequently, young men find it necessary to prove their virility to their comrades or themselves. I know one idealistic young man who failed in his first essay with a prostitute and then felt it his *duty* to solve the problem by several transitory affairs before venturing upon marriage, which he considered as enduring and monogamous. It would not have been fair to his potential wife to marry without assurance of full masculinity.

Doubtless there are deeper reasons than those here mentioned for this "nonsexual" sexuality, but these examples will serve to suggest that the adolescent is influenced by more than lust or the unmodified return of attitudes repressed in childhood. Erikson's stress on the search for identity is clearly important. It has been emphasized here as one of the major *Freudian* approaches because it is closest to the position of the dissident schools of psychoanalysis about to be discussed. Erikson, however, like Anna Freud and Hartmann, retains and builds upon Freud's instinct theory, whereas the other schools repudiate the primary role of sexuality and aggression. For them these orientating instinctual drives are given short shrift as mere incidentals of the body's physiological equipment, important mainly because our culture has made them so. The key to understanding of the human personality lies in its sense of "self." Since the dissident schools disagree among themselves as to the nature and course of development for the "self," only three examples will be briefly presented.

Dissident Schools

Adler

Alfred Adler began his specialized work with a careful study of organ inferiority and soon came to the conclusion that it was not the organ that mattered, but the person's attitude toward it. Furthermore, *any* organ might produce a sense of *inferiority* against which the person might struggle in a variety of ways. A little later he observed that the child's position in the family was even more important than a defective organ in fostering an inferiority complex. Order of birth tends to set up a competitive situation with which the little child must cope. The first-born is dethroned by his successor; the second-born always has a pacemaker before him, more advanced in the years of early childhood, and so on. Adler then observed that the attitude of the parents played a crucial role in this drama. This role was not sexual as Freud had said. Instead the child was hated or spoiled, with characteristic reactions.

Adler believed that the infant has a native urge toward superiority. He is inevitably frustrated by his smallness and helplessness, and within the first five years develops modes of coping with this problem which tend to remain as his "life style" throughout life. If he has been loved and encouraged, he naturally approaches life with courage, social feeling, and common sense (that is to say, a grasp of reality). Otherwise he solves his problems "erroneously." He is selfish, lacking in true courage, and tries to satisfy himself by *phantasies* of superiority instead of by realistic efforts.

Sexuality as such plays no role in this scheme. However, since society calls women "the weaker sex" a *masculine protest* is a common compensation. Women may strive directly for power, or use their sex as a device for gaining power over men. Men with feminine trends may become exaggerated he-men, or as homosexuals try to dominate through weakness—a very common erroneous solution of the striving toward superiority.

Horney

Although Horney did not break from the Freudians until the late nineteen thirties, and at first repudiated any connection with Adler, she is discussed briefly here because eventually she came to acknowledge one aspect of Adler's theory—the extreme importance of the phantasy image of the self. She saw the major problem of the human personality at first as insecurity, and outlined the various "safety devices" employed in the effort to maintain self-esteem.

Her contribution toward understanding of what the Freudians call the defense mechanisms of the ego was great, but is not related to sexuality as such. She was more ready to acknowledge its importance in the individual case than Adler, as well as family constellation and wider cultural factors. The crux of neurotic development is, she believed, a *basic anxiety*, which springs from "the feeling a child has of being isolated and helpless in a potentially hostile world." This feeling arises more from the general attitude of the parents than from particular frustrations, although the latter determine the special form of the safety devices developed. Any pronounced development in one direction involves repression of other trends. For example, the overcompliant person must repress his natural self-assertiveness and above all the hostility consequent upon each surrender. Every act of assertion reinforces his neurotic fear of the consequences, not only from the outside world but from his own potential aggression. So his compliance is increased until it is no longer tolerable, and the psychic operation is continued in a vicious circle with increased conflict between overt compliance and repressed hostile aggression.

The human personality requires a sense of unity and self-esteem. Confronted with these serious inner conflicts, the person constructs an *idealized image* of himself which reconciles and justifies his neurotic expedients—and which eventually stifles his *real* self. In her last book, *Neurosis and Human Growth*, Horney presents the conflict between the idealized image and the real self as the central conflict in all neurosis. This position is a far cry from the castration complex as the nuclear cause of neurosis, but Horney herself recognizes the similarity of her position to Adler's concept of the self-aggrandizing phantasy versus realistic achievement with social feeling.

Jung

Jung broke from the Freudian coterie in 1912. He too felt that sexuality was overly stressed in Freud's theory, that the libido was not essentially sexual but a sort of general life energy taking many forms. His position is difficult to present briefly because, apart from an almost Hegelian emphasis on "opposites" in basic theory, any adequate discussion must take account of many dynamically important subdivisions which are thought of as relatively independent, although in constant interaction. Sex as such is important—as it is for Adler and Horney—only insofar as it is *made* important through the vagaries of individual experience—except in one respect. Jung thought that every person is essentially bisexual. The male frequently represses the female side of his nature, but it survives in the unconscious as the *anima,* a receptive, nurturing trend which normally softens the masculine logical, dominating, forming trend. In pathology this influence may be lost in a shriveled, ineffective, unconscious representative. Or the anima may predominate, as in the case of some homosexuals or excessively weak, tender men. The female counterpart of the anima is the *animus,* which may undergo similar transformations in the unconscious. The coquette who gathers male "scalps" without love and the virago may be controlled by their animus, whereas the oversubmissive woman who gives in to everyone may have in the unconscious a shriveled animus or a bottled up monster capable of extreme aggression.

Jung's position is that all aspects of the psyche are necessary to full development of the mature self, and that repression of any aspect leads to distortion in the unconscious, either as withering away or as pathological growth. It is a bit unfair to Jung to place the contra-sexual problem first. For him it is incidental to deeper dichotomies, especially the interplay between the basic attitudes of introversion and extraversion, and the four functions of sensation and intuition, feeling and thinking. Every personality, whether by constitution or by early experience, tends to be oriented toward one of these attitudes and functions. The fully healthy personality—so rare as to be considered the hero who has won through many obstacles—achieves an integration of these opposing trends, all necessary to full living. Most of us overemphasize one aspect to such a degree that its opposite becomes unconscious. Jung calls this personal opposite the *shadow*. The thinking type tends to repress the feeling aspect so that it grows monstrously in the unconscious without control and may burst forth with unexpected violence, or so far wither away as to leave the person with a miserable sense of emptiness and futility.

Another set of psychic constellations derives from the archaic experience of the race, renewed by each infant: the *collective unconscious*. These are represented by symbols called archetypes which are found the world over in art and also in psychosis. Examples are the compassionate mother and the mother as devouring witch, figures of power probably reflecting the primitive feeling of the father, geometrical images perhaps related to the early body image, actions such as crossing a river apparently associated with birth and rebirth. Some are beautiful, some hideous. In psychosis they have escaped control by ego-consciousness, the "I" of common parlance. In great art they express the profound experiences of humanity, and so have universal appeal to all who can accept the foundations of our common heritage.

Finally Jung introduced the concept of the *persona,* a term derived from the mask worn by the actors in Greek drama. This is the face which we present to the world and which most clearly reflects the social adaptations we have made from childhood on. Extraverts may have several faces chosen for their usefulness in different situations. Introverts, living more within themselves, tend to have only one. Sometimes the persona is almost consciously a mask which the person almost deliberately assumes, often with the uneasy feeling that he is not genuine, is never really "himself." Sometimes the person is so identified with his persona that he rarely feels that he is different from the front he shows the world. Unless this persona is deeply related to a mature Self, however, it may collapse in the face of any real challenge. Thus the perfect gentleman may become a whining cur in a concentration camp, or perhaps cling to a stiff formality under circumstances where a little human adaptability would actually save his life.

The persona reminds us of Horney's idealized image. Jung was less interested than Horney in tracing its origin and its dynamic relationship to the potential Self, which he considered a much more complex structure than her rather loose hypothesis of a "real self." For him the persona was one psychic construct among many. It might or might not play a crucial role in the dynamics of a particular personality.

Despite his emphasis on a monistic libido in contrast to Freud's dualistic approach to basic theory, Jung's contribution seems to this writer essentially pluralistic. Bisexuality has its repercussions in the contra-sexual form of the anima and animus. The primitive experiences of the infant (or race) are expressed in the archetypes. Broad personality trends appear as the attitudes of extraversion and introversion and in the four functions—and their unconscious shadow. And then there is the socially influenced development of the persona.

Jung believed that the therapist could understand the current dynamic interaction of these various constellations by the study of unconscious patterns—especially as revealed in dreams. Jung believed that he saw the constructive, forward-looking power of the unconscious better than Freud with his emphasis on the repression of sexual drives in early childhood. This criticism had some validity in 1912. It is less valid today after the development of Freudian ego psychology. But as Freudians have much to learn from Horney's investigation of the defense mechanisms of the ego, so they have much to learn from Jung's description of types and symbols of the archetypes and other representations of relatively durable aspects of the personality as it grows within the family and the social structure which reaches the young child first via the influence on the parents, but eventually quite directly in terms of the opportunities and frustrations offered to the child, the adolescent, and the adult.

The contribution of psychoanalysis is mainly an understanding of how a personality is formed and equipped to handle the circumstances of living. There are, of course, other dissident psychoanalytic schools of current importance, each with its own coherent theory of how the personality develops and functions. None of them rejects sex as a very significant factor because of the squeamishness shown by the medical profession as well as laymen when Freud first introduced his doctrine. What they reject is Freud's inclusive view of the sexual instincts, and their primary role in psychic development. Understanding of the subsidiary role played by sex in these schools depends upon understanding of the whole theoretical scheme, most of which is irrelevant to the special topic of this article. The three dissident schools presented in some detail serve as examples rather than as a full report of such schools.

The reader has doubtless noted many similarities among the differences described above. In conclusion, it may be remarked that by far the largest psychoanalytic group today is *Freudian*. It may be remarked further that *Freudians* are amending the limitations of Freud's early position in a manner Freud himself considered a necessary development of his theory. Freudian ego psychology seems on the way to correcting the one-sidedness against which the dissidents rightly protested, without the new limitations introduced by the new theories.

References

Abraham, Karl, *Collected Papers*. London: Hogarth Press, 1950.

Adler, Alfred, "The Homosexual Problem." *Alien. & Neurol. 38;* 285, 1917.

Adler, Alfred, *The Practice and Theory of Individual Psychology*. New York: Harcourt, Brace & Co., 1939.

Ansbacher, Heinz L., and Ansbacher, Rowena R., *The Individual Psychology of Alfred Adler*. New York: Basic Books, 1956.

Benedek, Therese, *Psychosexual Functions in Women*. New York: Ronald Press, 1952.

Bonaparte, Marie, *Female Sexuality*. London: Imago Pub., 1953.

Deutsch, Helene, *Psychology of Women*. 2 vols. New York: Grune & Stratton, 1944-1945.

Ellis, Albert, *An Introduction to the Principles of Scientific Psychoanalysis*. Provincetown, Mass.: Journal Press, 1950.

Erikson, Erik H., *Childhood and Society*. New York: W. W. Norton & Co., 1950.

Fenichel, Otto, *Psychoanalytic Theory of Neurosis*. New York: W. W. Norton & Co., 1945.

Ferenczi, Sandor, *Sex in Psychoanalysis*. New York: Basic Books, 1950.

Flugel, J. C., *Psychoanalytic Study of the Family*. London: Hogarth Press, 1950.

Freud, Anna, *The Ego and the Mechanisms of Defense*. London: Hogarth Press, 1937.

Freud, Sigmund, *Collected Papers*. London: Hogarth Press, 1924-1950.

Freud, Sigmund, *Basic Writings*. New York: Modern Library, 1938.

Freud, Sigmund, *Outline of Psychoanalysis*. New York: W. W. Norton & Co., 1939.

Glover, Edward, *Technique of Psychoanalysis*. New York: International Universities Press, 1955.

Hartmann, Heinz, and Kris, Ernst, "The Genetic Approach in Psychoanalysis." *Psychoanalyt. Stud. Child. 1;* 11-30, 1945.

Horney, Karen, *Neurotic Personality of Our Time*. New York: W. W. Norton & Co., 1937.

Horney, Karen, *Neurosis and Human Growth*. New York: W. W. Norton & Co., 1950.

Jones, Ernest, *The Life and Works of Sigmund Freud*. New York: Basic Books, 1955-1957.

Jung, C. G., *Two Essays on Analytical Psychology*. New York: Pantheon Books, 1953.

Menninger, Karl, *The Human Mind*. New York: Alfred A. Knopf, Inc., 1948.

Money-Kyrle, Roger E., *Development of the Sexual Impulses*. London: Kegan Paul, 1932.

Mullahy, Patrick, *Oedipus: Myth and Complex*. New York: Hermitage House, 1948.

Munroe, Ruth, *Schools of Psychoanalytic Thought*. New York: Holt, Rinehart and Winston, 1955.

Reich, Wilhelm, *The Function of the Orgasm*. New York: Orgone Institute Press, 1945.

Reik, Theodor, *Of Love and Lust*. New York: Farrar, Straus, 1958.

Spitz, René A., "Hospitalism. An Inquiry into the Genesis of Psychiatric Conditions in Early Childhood." *Psychoanalyt. Stud. Child. 1;* 53-74, 1945.

Stekel, Wilhelm, *Sexual Aberrations*. New York: Liveright, 1930.

Sullivan, Harry Stack, *Conceptions of Modern Psychiatry*. Washington: William Alanson White Foundation, 1947.

Suttie, Ian, *The Origins of Love and Hate*. New York: Julian Press, 1952.

Wittels, Fritz, *Critique of Love*. New York: Macauley, 1929.

RUTH L. MUNROE

Race and Sex

OF ALL the myths that beguile men, few are more powerful than the concept of "race." Yet it is a concept so confused that it is almost impossible to define.

From ancient times people of different colors and biological inheritance have mingled and married. Instances may be found recorded in such classical authors as Aristotle, Plutarch, Quintillian, Juvenal, and Martial.

The barriers against intermarriage have, over the years, been those of religion and class, rather than of the law.

H. G. Wells, taking the long view of history in *The World of William Clissold*, sums up his view in these words: "Everyone alive is, I am convinced, of mixed ancestry, but some of us are more white, some of us more Negro, and some of us more Chinese."

In the countries of the Caribbean and South America, 85 per cent of the people are non-white, Indian and Negro blood being so mixed in them that it is all but impossible to say which is preponderant.

Nature raises no barriers against the mingling of the races. In fact, wherever races meet, sexual interchange occurs. The offspring are not monsters or freaks of nature. They are average men and women experiencing whatever normal achievements their society allows them.

As early as 1757, for example, in Virginia, Peter Fontaine wrote in *Memoirs of a Huguenot Family*: "Many base wretches among us take up with Negro women by means of which the country swarms with mulatto bastards, and these mulattoes, if but three generations removed from the black father and mother, may, by the indulgence of the laws of the country, intermarry with white people, and actually do every day so marry."

Jefferson, watching the same events, went so far as to say: "The course of events will likewise inevitably lead to a mixture of whites and blacks, on the whole, a wise provision of Nature; and, as the former are about five times as numerous as the latter, the blacks will ultimately be merged in the whites." He then adds that this is "an ultimate issue, however remote, independent of the exertions of statesmen, which, notwithstanding its repugnance to our reason, as well as our prejudice, will arrive."

As long as slaves were kept in good supply by importation, any white man might be whipped for intimacy with a Negro woman. When importation of slaves was stopped, however, and the supply of slaves had to be maintained by natural processes, white men were paid bonuses up to $20 for each Negro woman they got with child.

Andrew Johnson, President of the United States, himself born a poor white, made this comment on his rich neighbors: "As you pass their dwellings, you'll see as many mulatto as Negro children, the former bearing an unmistakable resemblance to their aristocratic owners."

"Miscegenation, or the interbreeding of ethnic and racial groups is a universal phenomenon," wrote Dr. Franz Boas in 1922. It has been sometimes frowned upon, and at other times encouraged, according to the economy and mores prevailing; the same community, as we have seen, changed its attitude within a century according to changing circumstances.

Are There Laws of Race-Mixing?

Dr. Lester F. Ward, sometimes called the "Father of American Sociology," set forth four laws which, he thought, govern the mixing of races:

1. Women of any race freely accept the men of a race they consider superior. (Negro women will freely accept white men.)

2. Women of any race will vehemently reject men of a race they consider inferior. (White women will vehemently reject black men.)

3. Men of any race will prefer women of a race they consider higher. (Negro men prefer white women.)

4. Men of any race, in default of women of a higher race, will be content with women of a lower race. (Negro men unable to get white women will be content with Negro women.)

A close look at these "laws," however, brings out the fact that the emphasis is not on race as such, but upon "higher" and "lower," that is, on status rather than blood or color.

This is an interesting comment on the peculiar history of race discrimination in the United States.

It has its own story within the total history of slavery. Since time immemorial, wherever slavery or serfdom has existed, the law has recognized a lord's interest in the marriage of his villein, since his offspring add to the lord's wealth. It frowned on the marriage of the free and the unfree, since this threatened the lord's property rights in the offspring. Roman law, for instance, forbade the marriage of a free Roman citizen with a Greek slave, though, here, no question of white and black was involved. The decisive factor was *status*, involving, as it did, property rights.

This "common law" of slavery carried over into the laws of intermarriage in the American colonies. The master was forbidden to marry the slave. In the laws of Maryland of 1664, for example, the language is that of "free men" and "slaves," with no reference to color. Within thirty years they were changed. In the statutes of 1691, the law specified prohibition of intermarriage between white and Negro.

What had happened? Color had become a mark of status. Caste, on the basis of color, was established by law.

This brought with it not only the legal basis of caste, but the social patterns which everywhere follow caste. These comply very largely with the four "laws" of Dr. Ward.

One fundamental rule characterizes caste everywhere: the male of the lower class is excluded from sexual contact with the female of the upper class.

This does not carry over to forbidding the higher-class male from sexual contact with the lower-class female. He may consort with her. At least two Presidents of the United States are reported to have had children by Negro mistresses. It is also well known that the gentlemen of early American days gave their hospitality a flavor by providing a "wench" to entertain a guest, much after the fashion of Oriental princes who offered their visiting equals the favorites of their harems.

Southern convention still looks with a different eye upon a white man consorting with a Negro woman and a Negro man consorting with a white woman. The Negro is restricted to his own race. The white man may enjoy both races.

The Southern Lady

One consequence of this taboo against the Negro male was that it put the white woman in an especially protected position. She became the unassailable female. Thus grew the image of "the Southern Lady," an idealized figure around whom developed the exaggerated code of chivalry of "the Southern gentleman."

Under the pressure of this protective approach, laws governing defense of the lady grew stricter and stricter. Parallel with this, her image became more and more sentimentalized. She became a figure as idealized as the lady of Medieval chivalry. Caste reverted to feudalism for its prototype.

A natural corollary of this was that the Negro accumulated more hostility. Attitudes toward him became harsher as the ideal of "pure, white womanhood" became more dazzling. This has laid him open to easy attack on the basis of "rape" and other similar sex charges. Not only have these led, often on doubtful evidence, to mob violence and lynchings, but also to corruption of Court proceedings, in which a charge by one threatened lady has been enough to suspend the judicial weight of evidence. The presumption in such cases goes to guilt which has to be disproved rather than to innocence to be proved.

Punishments meted out to Negro men in such cases are frequently symbolic. Castration is obviously a sex revenge. Sex resentment is usually the passion which keeps lynching mobs at the emotional heat required for carrying out their violence, and reported comments from participators give ground for believing that the rope and the kicking figure hold sex symbolism for them.

In such acts of violence men are obviously motivated by neither rational nor logical, perhaps not even by conscious, drives. They are swept by emotional conditionings inflamed from infancy. They act in response to deeply imbedded folk imaginations and attitudes.

Folklore of Sex and Race

Race has developed its own folklore of sexual differences. Perhaps the most frequently recurring folk-idea is that the men of the inferior race have extraordinary virility. In particular, he is said to have larger genitals—an ascription which involves envy as well as hostility. This idea has been reinforced by some travelers, even so great a one as Sir Edward Johnson, who have returned from Africa with stories of individuals having enormous organs of sex. But it is by no means restricted to white-Negro comparisons. *Der Sturmer*, the Nazi's official newspaper, produced a whole gallery of cartoons picturing the Jews with exaggerated genital parts.

Almost as universal in race folklore is the attribution of inveterate sexuality to the female of the inferior race. In the South, for example, both among men in smoking rooms and among ladies in sewing circles, favorite stories find their point in some reference to the sexual intensity of Negro women. Stories like these, among all groups, reflect folk attitudes with peculiar clarity, so these stories in themselves testify to the folk-emphasis upon the Negro woman's sex resources. Again, this ascription carries over to sex attitudes toward other groups. The "red-haired Jewess," the Magdalen figure, and the Oriental seductress, the Mata Hari figure, carry the same idea.

Here we approach a third myth which, among the superior races particularly, has powerful influence. It is the idea that any move toward social equality is a move toward sexual equality. The fierceness with which this is propounded is perhaps the most vocal evidence of how sex fears enter into racial attitudes.

"Would you want your daughter to marry a Negro?" is a question presumed to stop all further discussion. The specter is calculated to enforce silence.

We note with interest that the caste pattern persists here. No one ever asks, "Would you like your son to sleep with a Negro woman?" As a matter of fact, young white men of the South often have their first sex experience with a Negro woman—and think that, by doing so, they maintain their chivalry by not using a white woman for premarital or experimental purposes. Older Southern men calculate to increase their reputations for virility by proving their power to consort with Negro women.

This folklore follows the patterns of folklore in all caste societies. It is caste not color which dominates, indistinguishable as they may be when color becomes the symbol of caste.

Eugenics

Caste, however, has been reinforced by eugenics, or, more accurately, by pseudo-eugenics.

It is worth recalling that the full title of Darwin's book was *The Descent of Man and Selection in Relation to Sex*. His cousin, Sir Francis Galton, extracted from this the study of eugenics, which he named, and which he defined as "the study of agencies under social control which may improve or impair the racial qualities of future generations either mentally or physically."

The idea that men can improve the quality of their progeny by sexual selection is one which exercises a peculiar fascination over men's minds. It may be difficult to define exactly what one means by "improving" men, but it is less difficult to make a fetish of so-called "pure blood," intermarriage confined to persons of the same race and color. This concept of "pure race" was seized upon by such pseudo-eugenists as Houston Stewart Chamberlain, in whose hands "pure Aryan" easily passed over into "Master Race"—inherently superior to others in intelligence and ingenuity, and thus foreordained to rule. The echoes of men such as Chamberlain sound clearly in the voice of Adolf Hitler, who carried "mastery" to its bitter conclusion in cosmic tragedy.

Eugenics is, to say the least, an incomplete science when applied to human generation. Its distinction between a "pure" and a "mongrel" race remains a doubtful category. Its influence on the study of sex and race has been rather to confuse than to clarify it.

Sociological Studies in Miscegenation

There is no comprehensive study of interracial marriages on a national scale in the United States. We have no exact figures on Negro-Caucasian, Caucasian-Oriental, or Negro-Oriental unions. There have been many studies on interreligious and international marriages, but these do not involve race.

The United States is cited as the country with strict taboos against racial mixtures, but figures do not show any high preponderance of interracial marriages, or of acceptance of them, elsewhere. Anthropological studies indicate that where such intermixture has taken place completely (as among the Moors and the Spaniards) it was accomplished relatively swiftly, and usually as a result of military conquest and entrance into the defeated country by invading armies.

In our present time, intermarriages have resulted from the invasion of armies, but both the conquered and the conquerors have tended to disapprove of them, as is illustrated in Japan. In general, assimilation has not been encouraged by such intermarriages.

Although we have no comprehensive national study of intermarriage in the United States, individual sociologists have made local studies. It must be confessed that these have employed relatively small samplings of from thirty-five to fifty families, but their findings are in general agreement and tend to confirm one another.

The sources will be found listed among the references. We can summarize the findings as follows:

Intermarriage and Group Attitudes

Those who tend to intermarriage are drawn from individuals who are rebellious against their own groups on both sides. Many of them feel rejected by their own group, and identify themselves with the rejected group. They modify their own norms to match those of the new group and idealize its way of life. This identification leads to dating and selection of a mate from the new group.

The social distance between the individual's original group and the one from which he selects his mate is a positive factor in the amount of hostility he has toward his own group.

Often, as an individual turns to the new group and accepts a new set of values, he is convinced that this action is a proof of his own "superiority," and he then returns to this to explain that his original rejection of, or by, his own group was itself due to this superior quality, rather than to any inadequacies in himself.

Frequently, as the individual assumes his place in the new group, he tends to go to extremes to emulate and defend its practices, as all new converts do. Observations in Hawaii indicates that American soldiers married to Japanese become more Japanese than their brides, who strive to become more Caucasian.

In Florida, a study showed no instance of a white spouse of a mixed marriage in any prominent community position. On the other hand, some Negro spouses were prominent in their communities. Most Negro leaders were of the opinion that a Negro spouse did lose some of his popularity. In Chicago disapproval was found to be more marked: "Negro professional men are likely to have fewer clients if they marry white women."

Inadequacy of Scientific Studies

Studies find their most specific data in marriage licenses issued by particular cities. But these are not always reliable. An investigation of such licenses in Washington, D. C., recorded thirty-six marriages of Negro and white; personal contact revealed that ten of these were not interracial marriages. In eight cases, both persons were obviously Negro. In two cases both were white.

Sister Annella (1956) attributes lack of accurate case studies to two reasons. First, it is difficult to locate the couples party to mixed marriages. Second, it is difficult to get such couples to talk about the subject.

Legal Status

In 1661 the Colony of Maryland passed a law declaring that all freeborn women who married slaves would thereupon serve their husband's master until the death of their husband, and that children born of such marriages would be slaves.

The first and only state to declare a law against miscegenation invalid was California in the case of *Perry et al.* vs. *Leppold etc.* Andre Perry, a white woman, and Sylvester Davis, a Negro, contended that the California statute forbidding intermarriage was unconstitutional because it denied free exercise of religious beliefs and participation in Church rites. Since both were Roman Catholics and the Church had no rule forbidding their marriage, they claimed they were entitled to receive the Sacrament of Matrimony. In October 1948, the Supreme Court ruled out a rehearing of the decision in their favor, and rendered a decision final except for possible reversal by the United States Supreme Court.

Twenty-nine States now have laws forbidding intermarriage: Alabama, Arizona, Arkansas, Colorado, Delaware, Florida, Georgia, Idaho, Indiana, Kentucky, Louisiana, Maryland, Mississippi, Missouri, Montana, Nebraska, Nevada, North Carolina, North Dakota, Oklahoma, Oregon, South Carolina, South Dakota, Tennessee, Texas, Utah, Virginia, West Virginia, and Wyoming.

Legislation prohibiting interracial marriages has been more common in Protestant countries and colonies than in those where Catholic opinion dominates; the Roman Catholic Church has no rule against such marriages, and secular law does not deny what the canon law sanctions.

Courtship and Family

Courtship is characteristically carried on *sub rosa*, except in instances where the couple involved relish shocking people or are openly defiant of conventions. This pattern continues in many cases after marriage. Such marriages are concealed from fellow-workers. In some cases investigated, parents were not notified; in others, they were told half-truths. (One Jewish girl simply told her father she was married to a Gentile.)

White families refuse to meet the spouse more frequently than Negro families. Negroes tend to accept the white spouse if he or she shows qualities Negroes find acceptable to them.

Where white families agree to meet the spouse, a warm relationship is likely to result. This is particularly likely to happen when the white family is foreign born.

None of the studies reports a situation where the mixed couple was ostracized by both groups.

Mixed couples are likely to live in areas where there is a small proportion of Negroes, that is, in peripheral areas between white and Negro communities.

Golden reports that his study showed that child production was small. The number of children averaged higher where the husband was Negro than where he was white. The children are considered to be Negro except when they are white enough to "pass." White parents find this hard to accept, but when they do accept it, the children's adjustment is easier.

Where couples prior to marriage had associated with radical or Bohemian groups, their popularity among such groups increased after marriage.

Of the white female partners examined among thirty-four couples averaging five years of marriage, most revealed attitudes of resentment against their mothers. Educational background averaged about two years of college. Original contact had come through common employment or common educational pursuits.

Security

Some sociologists have maintained that intermarriage and assimilation are so interrelated that they are functionally interdependent: intermarriage rises in proportion to the degree of assimilation. Some studies, however, indicate that mixed marriages are lower in rate among the oldest ethnic groups than among the younger ones. This would indicate that there are factors other than assimilation at work.

Dr. Simon Marcson of Queens College, in "A Theory of Intermarriage and Assimilation," comes to the conclusion that high education, middle-class status, middle income, professional and proprietary occupations, second and third generations, and rural farm areas are conditions facilitating intermarriage.

Dr. Risdon's conclusion is: "Interracially married couples must rely upon themselves and their power of determination to continue a marriage in the face of covert and, sometimes, overt social disapproval."

In general, the prognosis for interracial marriages already established, and the outlook for others, does not appear very favorable. The nature of society is such as to make difficult that security in orderly living which most people anticipate in matrimony.

References

Adams, P., *Interracial Marriage in Hawaii*. New York: The Macmillan Co., 1937.

Annella, Sister M., "Some Aspects of Interracial Marriage in Washington, D.C." *Journal of Negro Education 25;* 380-391, 1956.

Castle, E., Jr., "A Study of Negro-White Marriages in the Philadelphia Area." Thesis, Temple University.

Chang, C. K., "Assimilation in Hawaii and the Bid for Statehood." *Social Forces,* October, 1951.

Dollard, J., *Caste and Class in a Southern Town.* New Haven: Yale University Press, 1937.

Dubois, W. E. B., *Darkwater.* New York: Harcourt, Brace & Co., 1921.

Freeman, L., "Homogeny in Interethnic Mate Selection." *Sociology and Social Research,* July–August, 1955.

Golden, J., "Patterns of Negro-White Marriages." Thesis, Florida State University.

Handlin, O., *Race and Nationality in American Life* Boston: Little, Brown, 1948.

Kennedy, Ruby Jo Reeves, "Single or Triple Melting Pot: Intermarriage Trends in New Haven, 1870-1940." *American Journal of Sociology.*

Moton, R. R., *What the Negro Thinks.* New York: Doubleday, 1932.

Risdon, R., *A Study of Interracial Marriages Based on Data for Los Angeles County.* Indio, California.

Roberts, R. E. T., "Negro and White Intermarriage: A Study of Social Control." Thesis, University of Chicago.

Rogers, J. A., *Sex and Race* (3 vols.). New York: J. A. Rogers, 1942.

Seligman, E. R. A., and Johnson, A., "Miscegenation" in *Encyclopedia of the Social Sciences.* New York: The Macmillan Co., 1933.

Simpson, G. E., and Yinger, J. M., *Racial and Cultural Minorities* (rev. ed.). New York: Harper & Brothers, 1958.

Tannenbaum, F., *Darker Phases of the South.* New York: G. P. Putnam's Sons, 1924.

White, W., *Rape and Faggot.* New York: Alfred A. Knopf, Inc., 1929.

FRANK KINGDON

Reproduction, Human

Conception and Development of the Fetus

HUMAN reproduction starts with the introduction of the sperm into the vagina through intercourse. The sperm then travels through the cervix (neck of the womb) into the uterus, and from there to the Fallopian tube. In the tube it meets the ovum (egg), which has been expelled from the ovary and has found its way into the tube. Fertilization, or as it is known by the laity, conception, takes place in the tube. The fertilized ovum then divides into various stages and, after a three-day journey through the tube, finds it way into the uterus. After traveling around in the uterus for from two to four days, it imbeds itself in the previously prepared uterine lining.

At the time of implantation, the ovum "digests" its way under the cells lining the uterine wall and taps small blood vessels of the mother. It finds itself in a short time surrounded by a lake of the mother's blood, into which it dips its hungry cells. These cells grow out like streamers from the surface of the ovum, absorbing all the minerals, proteins, etc., that are essential to growth. With absorption of these nutrients, the ovum increases rapidly in size. Inside the ovum a thickened mass of cells now appears, called the inner-cell mass. It is from these cells that the embryo develops. The outer layer of the ball-like egg also continues to grow and from it the placenta, or afterbirth, is formed.

The development of the fetus in the next weeks and months is somewhat as follows: With the beginning of the fourth week, the egg is still barely visible to the naked eye. At the beginning of the fifth week, the embryo is a small piece of uniform, gray-white tissue. At the end of the fifth week, the backbone is beginning to form out of five to eight vertebrae, and the spinal canal is forming. The embryo at this time is ½₂ of an inch long and about ⅛ of of an inch wide. At the beginning of the sixth week the head is forming and the heart begins to be visible. At the end of the sixth week, all of the backbone is laid down, the spinal canal is closed over, and the tail end of the embryo is distinct. The beginnings of arms and legs are visible. Depressions appear beneath the skin where eyes are to be formed. The length at this time is ¼ inch.

At the seventh week, the chest and abdomen are completely formed and the beginnings of the fingers and toes appear. There are clearly perceptible eyes and the length of the fetus is about ½ inch. In the eighth week the face and features are beginning to form, the ears are forming, the length is now about ⅞ inch, and the fetus weighs about 1 gram. By the ninth week the face is completely formed and the arms, legs, hands, and feet are partially formed, including stubby toes and fingers. The length is 1⅕ inches and the weight about 2 grams. From this time on, the fetus looks very much like a miniature infant. At the end of the third month (thirteen weeks) the arms, legs, hands, feet, and toes are fully formed. The external genital organs begin to show differences, and at about the eleventh week a trained observer can determine sex. The eyelids are closed. If the fetus is removed and placed in a warm fluid, movements of arms and legs will occur. The head is extremely large in proportion to the body. The length of the fetus is 3 inches and it weighs about 1 ounce. At the end of the fourth month, the lay person can now distinguish sex. Fetal movements are felt and the heart can be heard. Fine hair is found along the skin, which is less transparent and pinker than previously. The eyebrows and eyelashes appear. It is now about 8½ inches long and weighs about 6 ounces.

At the end of the fifth month, hair begins to appear on the head and fat is deposited under the skin, although the fetus is still very lean. If it is born it might live for a few minutes, but it would never survive. The length is 12 inches and it weighs about 1 pound.

At the end of the sixth month, the fetus is covered with a cheeselike secretion, the skin is wrinkled, the hair on the head is fairly well developed, and the eyes are open. If it is born at this time, it might live for a few hours. Its length is 14 inches and it weighs just about 2 pounds.

By the end of the seventh month, the testicles in males descend into the scrotum. A child born during this month has a fair chance of survival. The age-old superstition that a baby born in the seventh month will do better than one born in the eighth month is wrong: each day that the baby comes nearer to term makes its chances for survival that much better. The length at this time is 16 inches and the weight is a little over 3 pounds.

At the end of the eighth month, the child is 18 inches long, weighs a little over 5 pounds, and of course is fully formed. If born now it will most likely survive.

At the end of the ninth month, or forty weeks from the day of the mother's last menstrual period, the baby is now what is called full term. The skin is smooth and is covered with the cheeselike secretion called vernix caseosa. The hair is about an inch long. The nails protrude a little beyond the finger and toe ends and the eyes are usually a slatish color. Circumference of the head equals the circumference of the shoulders. The length is about 20 inches and the weight is a little over 7 pounds on the average.

The amniotic fluid in which the fetus floats serves many purposes: (1) It prevents the walls of the uterus from cramping the fetus and allows its unhampered growth and movement. (2) It surrounds the fetus with a fluid of constant temperature. (3) It acts as an excellent shock absorber. A blow on the abdomen merely jolts the fetus and it floats away. For this reason, accidents to the mother that might be considered severe almost never injure the fetus.

During its existence in the uterus, the fetus automatically swallows the amniotic fluid that is manufactured by the cells lining the uterine cavity. The fetus excretes this as fetal urine. At the time of birth the amount of amniotic fluid is somewhere in the neighborhood of a quart. Amounts in considerable excess of this are considered pathological.

The fetus is attached to the placenta by the umbilical cord, which runs from the navel to the inner surface of the afterbirth. Extensions of fetal blood vessels run through the cord and then course through the placenta. The umbilical cord, a semitransparent jelly-like rope, averages 22 inches in length, although cords of a few inches to 50 inches in length have been recorded. Some are straight and some are twisted.

The placenta is a rather complex organ through which the fetus absorbs food and eliminates its waste products. The blood of the mother and the blood of the fetus come in close contact in the substance of the placenta and the materials pass over from one blood system to the other. If, for example, the mother's blood contains more sugar than that of the fetus, the excess comes over into the fetal blood until a relative equality of the two is reached. In this way, the sugar that the mother eats is fed to her baby. Similarly, the excess carbon dioxide of the fetal blood goes over into the mother's blood and is exhaled by her lungs. In this way, the mother breathes for her child. Other waste products of the fetus are likewise absorbed by the mother's blood and excreted by her kidneys. This delicate interchange between mother and fetus is further illustrated by the observation that cigarette smoking by a mother temporarily increases the rate of the fetal heart, although there is no proof that nicotine causes any ill-effects in the fetus. There are many other substances that pass through the placenta from the mother to the infant. Many antibodies, which later serve to prevent disease in the newborn infant, are passed over and in this way a child is born with an immunity, or at least a temporary immunity, to certain diseases.

The weight of the baby does not depend on the amount of weight the mother gains. It depends in some instances on the sex of the baby —boys being usually heavier than girls—and also on race. Other than this, little else is known about what causes one baby to be heavier than another.

Sex is determined by the chromosomes that are carried in both the sperm and the ovum. The study of genetics has advanced very rapidly in the last few years, many of our old ideas about the chromosomes having undergone a marked change, and it is probable that within the next year or two our theories on this subject will become more definitive.

Human reproduction depends on significant contributions of both parents, the male and the female, to the fertilized ovum and its development; and these contributions may be viewed from anatomical, physiological, pathological, and psychological frames of reference.

The Role of the Male

The male sexual apparatus may be divided into four parts: (1) organs for production of sperm, the testes; (2) organs for storage and conduction of sperm, the epididymides and ductus deferentes; (3) organs for mixing sperm with the vehicles to produce the semen, the prostate and the seminal vesicles; and (4) organs for delivery of the sperm, the penis and urethra with the accessory glands.

Spermatogenesis takes place in the testes and the adult spermatozoa are transferred through the epididymis and the ductus deferens, finally being ejaculated by the penis and deposited in the vagina at the time of intercourse. The sperm then migrates through the uterus into the Fallopian tube, where it meets the ovum, and fertilization takes place.

Spermatogenesis starts at puberty and may continue on into the ninetieth year. The normal sperm count is anywhere in the vicinity of 100 million per cubic centimeter. It was once thought that the minimum number required for pregnancy was approximately 60 million,

but it has been found that 20 million is considered capable of producing pregnancy.

The Role of the Female

The female anatomy consists of the vagina, the uterus, the tubes, and the ovaries. In the normal female, there are thousands of ova present in each ovary at birth. Each month, after puberty, ovulation takes place and an ovum is extruded from the ovary on about the fourteenth day of the cycle (in a 28-day cycle).

Hormonal factors influence this process. The pituitary gland produces follicle-stimulating hormone, the ovum is extruded, and the corpus luteum, which is formed in the area where the ovum was, produces both estrogenic hormone and progesterone. The egg then finds its way into the tube where, if sperm are present, it may be fertilized.

Ovulation usually takes place two weeks before menstruation. At the time of ovulation there is a sharp rise in the basal body temperature. The temperature remains elevated until menstruation, when there is a sharp drop. If fertilization takes place, the temperature remains elevated.

Factors in Fertility and Sterility

There are many factors in both the male and the female that may interfere with reproduction. Some are congenital and some acquired. Some of these can be corrected and some cannot.

In the male, undescended testicles, so immature that they can produce no sperm, can be the cause of sterility. The testes may be injured by trauma or by mumps, gonorrhea, or other infections. Gonorrhea is less likely nowadays to cause this, unless it is greatly neglected. Actually very little can be done to rehabilitate the testes once they have ceased to produce sperm, although some surgery has been successful. Also, production of sperm has followed successful therapy in cases of debilitation, other body illnesses, and obesity or low thyroid function. Psychological factors have also been known to influence not only the production but also the quality and quantity of sperm.

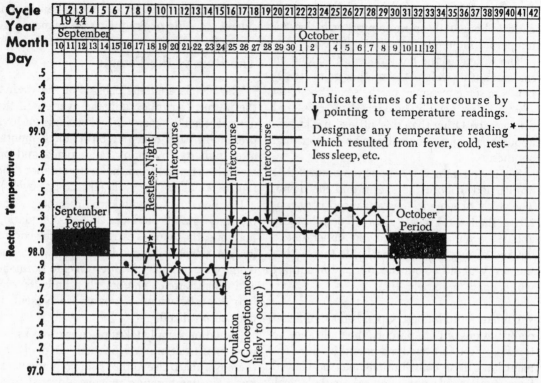

FIG. 1. Temperatures between periods

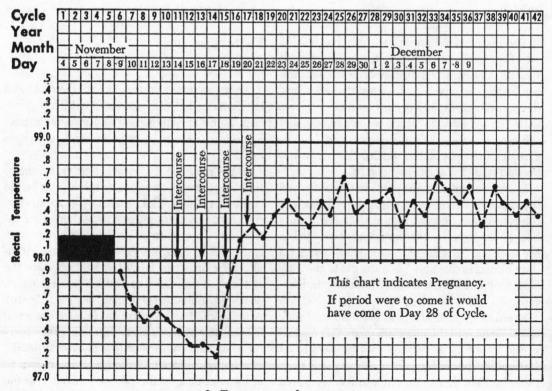

FIG. 2. Temperatures after conception

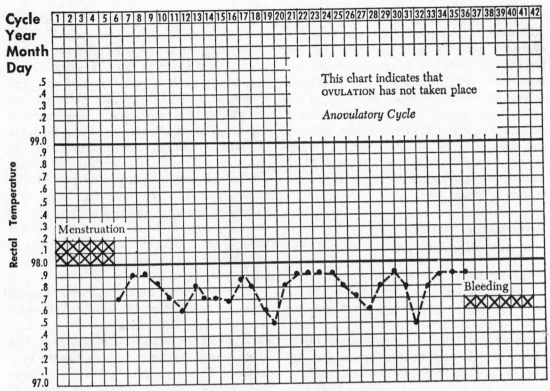

FIG. 3. Temperatures when ovulation has not taken place

A rare condition that produces sterility in the male is retrograde ejaculation, in which the semen is ejaculated into the bladder. It is possible to recover the semen from the urine by centrifuging the urine and then to inseminate the woman with the sediment (sperm), with successful results. Retrograde ejaculation may be congenital or acquired. It is acquired following operations on the prostate, transurethral resections, or fulguration of the verumontanum. Recently, some work has been done indicating that retrograde ejaculation may also be psychogenic in origin.

In the female there is a wide variety of conditions that may interfere with reproduction. As in the male, there are congenital and acquired conditions, and some that can be corrected and some that cannot. Among the congenital factors may be an absence of any or all the female organs, but this is rare. Malformations of the uterus that cause infertility, such as a double uterus, can often be corrected. Tubes that are partially closed can be surgically repaired and reimplanted into the uterus. Disturbances of menstruation due to ovarian

disfunction can be corrected. Acquired infections that cause sterility can be successfully treated.

Hormonal disturbances can cause infertility. The pituitary gland and the thyroid gland are the most important in this respect. Today, with potent natural and synthetic hormones, endocrine conditions can be corrected and pregnancy ensured.

Fibroid tumors of the uterus may interfere with fertility in two ways: (1) They may cause blockage of the tube, so preventing fertilization. (2) If fertilization does take place, they can cause the fetus to abort. These fibroid tumors can be removed, thus restoring fertility. As many as 150 tumors have been removed from a patient at one time; following such operations patients have succeeded in becoming pregnant and have delivered normal, healthy children. Some required Cesarean sections, but many delivered normally.

Another condition that causes sterility is azoospermia, in which the male has no sperm at all. In such cases of infertility artificial insemination has been used much more frequently in recent years than in previous years. It is difficult to estimate precisely the exact number of couples who are using this technique, but the number of babies so conceived that are born yearly in this country is estimated to be as high as 100,000. A large percentage of the patients who come for artificial insemination become pregnant. Case reports from different men engaged in this field show the success rate to vary from 60 to 90 per cent. That is, of all patients who are inseminated, 60 to 90 per cent become pregnant.

Psychogenic Factors in Reproduction

There is much evidence to support the premise that sterility can be psychogenic: We all know of many cases in which pregnancy has followed adoption or the decision to adopt. Successful psychotherapy in an infertile patient who has sought help for other reasons has also been followed by pregnancy. Pregnancies have resulted from a change of marriage, improved economic status, or the establishment of a home free from parental irritation. Excluding organic factors, how else can "one-child sterility" be explained?

Psychogenic sterility is not limited to the female. I believe that the male plays almost as important a role in this form of sterility, although he has been largely neglected by those interested in this approach to the subject. I have previously discussed (1953) the fact that the ejaculation and the quality and the quantity of the semen can be definitely influenced by psychogenic factors. In their book *Psychosomatic Gynecology*, Kroger and Freed state, "psychiatrists have shown that behind the conscious desire to have a child, there may be a deeper, unconscious wish not to have one." It must be emphasized that this can be equally true of both female and male.

The female personality types seen in patients with psychogenic sterility can be roughly divided into two fundamental groups: (1) the weak, emotionally immature, dependent, overprotected woman, and (2) the ambitious, masculine, aggressive, dominating, career type of woman. Group 1 can be subdivided further into (a) women who feel that their own upbringing

was inadequate and are afraid of motherhood, and (b) women who are not only afraid of motherhood but are afraid of pregnancy, labor, death, loss of figure, or loss of husband. Group 2 can also be subdivided further into (a) women who are motherly and tender but confine this attitude toward their weak husbands who need their motherliness, (b) career women, artists, scientists, woman suffragists who, although motherly, unconsciously avoid the conflict that might result in a split of their interests, and (c) the masculine, aggressive women who refuse to accept femininity. It must, of course, be borne in mind that none of these types is clear-cut and that there is an overlapping and merging of characteristics in all types.

In the first group, the overprotected females who were never allowed to make a decision for themselves, are the women who try to make a child-parent relationship out of their marriage. They have a repressed hostility toward their mothers. They feel that they would do unto their children as their mothers did unto them. They fear motherhood. Benedek (1952) states: "Functional sterility is a somatic defense against stresses of pregnancy and motherhood." It is in this group, however, that we find the women who become pregnant following adoption: they come to realize that the responsibility of caring for a baby is not as great as they had thought, and the unconscious mechanism responsible for their infertility is released. As Dunbar says, "The experience of a baby in the family may serve as a catalytic agent."

In subdivision *b* of this group, among women in whom fear of death, pregnancy, labor, etc., plays a role, we find no response of pregnancy to adoption. These women can adopt two, three, or more children and will not become pregnant.

In subdivision *a* of Group 2 we find the woman who has all the qualities of motherliness, is warm and tender, but who directs her motherliness to her husband, whose love for her is based on this quality. He needs a mother and she is it. If a child were born, this would threaten him. It could be said that a wife in such a marriage renounces motherhood out of love for her husband. However, in this type of case, the infertility may well be due to the husband's attitude. Deutsch (1945) has observed that "where men choose motherly women for their love partners, they become impotent when their wives are pregnant or after the children are born. Some flee their homes or become alcoholics."

Subdivisions *b* and *c* are not too difficult to understand. The career woman may be motherly enough, may have no fears of pregnancy, etc., and may have a good psychosexual development, but she is afraid that motherhood may interfere with her career. It is among this group that, following renunciation of career, pregnancy often results.

"One-child sterility," or secondary psychogenic sterility, is even more baffling than primary psychogenic sterility. The mechanism here is the reverse of what takes place in a pregnancy following adoption. The patient conceives without apparent difficulty, but then is overwhelmed by the responsibility of motherhood. Or, due to a complicated pregnancy or difficult labor or delivery, she may suffer enough psychic trauma to render her infertile. It is not uncommon to find women in this group whose infertility spontaneously resolves when the first child is 10 to 15 years old. During the interim she has matured somewhat, responsibilities have lessened, she does not believe she can get pregnant anyway, she is under less tension—and she becomes pregnant.

The response of the body to these psychic stimuli is probably through the hypothalamic tracts to the pituitary and adrenal glands and the ovaries. The uterus, tubes, and blood vessels can also be affected locally through the autonomic nervous system. Thus, through imbalance in the autonomic nervous system due to tension, a tubal spasm or interference with the peristalsis of the tube can occur, as well as irregular uterine motility, which may interfere with implantation. Through vascular changes, pelvic congestion may result, which may interfere with ovulation and thus produce infertility. Anxiety may produce changes in the vaginal and cervical secretions, just as it modifies salivary and gastric secretions, and this also may interfere with the patient's ability to conceive. Sperm count may also be altered by these mechanisms. All these phenomena are transitory and therefore, in most instances, defy

detection. When the stimuli are present long enough, actual somatic changes may take place, but these are nevertheless the result of emotional factors.

Summary

Human reproduction depends on male and female factors. Where there are abnormalities these can be corrected in many instances by medication or surgery. Artificial insemination is frequently resorted to. Until recently, those psychological factors that hinder human reproduction have not been considered. Today, these psychogenic factors are being studied in many large centers throughout the world, and more and more evidence indicates that a large percentage of infertility is due to psychosomatic factors.

References

Benedek, T., *Fertil. & Steril.* 3; 527, 1952.

Blakely, S. B., *Trans. Am. A. Obst. & Gynec.* 53; 151, 1940.

Bloss, J. R., *J. A. M. A.* 144; 1358, 1950.

Cary, W. H., in Engel, E. T., *Diagnosis of Sterility.* Springfield, Ill.: Charles C Thomas, 1946, pp. 168-185.

Cooke, W. R., *Am. J. Obst. & Gynec.* 49; 457, 1945.

Cosmack, G., *New York State J. Med.* 45; 2298, 1945.

Deutsch, H., *Psychology of Women* (Vol. 2). New York: Grune and Stratton, Inc., 1945.

Fischer, I. C., *Fertil. & Steril.* 4; 446, 1953.

Hirst, J. C., and Strousse, F., *Am. J. M. Sc.* 196; 95, 1935.

Hotchkiss, R. S., *Fertility in Men.* Philadelphia: J. B. Lippincott Co., 1944.

Kroger, W. S., *Fertil. & Steril.* 3; 543, 1952.

Kroger, W. S., and Freed, S. C., *Psychosomatic Gynecology.* Philadelphia: W. B. Saunders Co., 1951.

Lane-Roberts, C. *et al.*, *Sterility and Impaired Fertility.* New York: Paul B. Hoeber, Inc., 1948.

Margolin, S., and Kaufman, M. R., *M. Clin. North America* 32; 609, 1948.

Marsh, E. M., and Vollmer, A. M., *Fertil. & Steril.* 2; 70, 1951.

Mengert, W. F., *Ment. Hyg.* 15; 299, 1931.

Menninger, W. C., *Bull. Menninger Clin.* 7; 15, 1943.

Rock, J., and Loth, D., *Voluntary Parenthood.* New York: Random House, 1949.

Siegler, Samuel, *Fertility in Women.* Philadelphia: J. B. Lippincott Co., 1944.

Walser, H. C., *Am. J. Obst. & Gynec.* 55; 799, 1948.

IRVING C. FISCHER

Scandinavian Countries, Sex Life of

NORWAY, Sweden, and Denmark are all highly developed modern democracies, both politically and socially. In Sweden the feudal system took stronger hold and lasted longer than in Denmark and Norway, but at the present time the social contrasts also in Sweden have almost disappeared.

At the time of the Reformation, while the rest of Europe was wracked by religious wars, the Scandinavian countries quietly adopted a form of Lutheran protestantism, which avoided both the Roman and the Puritan extreme. The idea that sexuality is "sinful" is not so firmly implanted in the Scandinavian mind as it is in the official thinking of the Catholic countries or of England and the United States.

There has been, therefore, an almost perfect climate of opinion for reform in the three Scandinavian countries in the last few decades, and serious attempts have been made to bring laws and customs governing sexual behavior into line with modern thought. Since, however, each country has its own cultural background and its own current minority opposition, it has been found advisable here to treat each as a separate entity.

DENMARK

The Attitude of the Law

Civil Law

In Denmark, men under 21 and women under 18 require royal permission to marry. The insane, idiots, psychopaths, alcoholics, and epileptics must have a special license from the Ministry of Justice. A certificate under oath that they have not contracted a venereal disease is required from all persons intending to marry. Otherwise a physician shall inform both partners of the risks involved.

Each partner pledges support; both undertake to educate and care for the children. Property is in joint ownership, unless otherwise specified by marriage contract. Responsibility for legitimate children is shared and lasts until the child is 18. Responsibility for the child's property extends until the twenty-first year. Children have the right to inherit from both parents. In the case of illegitimate children whose father is unknown, the mother has sole responsibility. Where the father is known, rights and responsibilities are the same as for legitimate children.

Legal separation of marriage partners may be obtained by mutual consent or on demand by one partner. Divorce in the first case follows automatically after one and one-half years, in the second after two and one-half years. Other grounds for divorce are: four years' mutual estrangement, two years' desertion, legal disappearance, adultery, threat to life and limb, cruelty, imprisonment, danger of transmission of venereal disease and mental sickness of at least three years' duration without prospect of a cure. Where both parties request divorce, the decree can be given by a government board. If only one partner demands divorce, the case must come into court. The most usual form of divorce is that following automatically on legal separation.

Criminal Law

Adultery is not a crime. Bigamy, rape, pandering, white slavery, and the seduction of minors under 15 are crimes. The seduction of persons under 18 is also illegal, when the minor is in the care of the seducer.

The publishing and distribution of pornographic pictures, texts, or objects is only illegal if minors under 18 are involved. Dealing in contraceptive devices is only illegal if provocative advertising is used. Provision is made by the law for prosecuting offenses against public morals, but this is seldom used.

Brothels were abolished in 1901, registration of prostitutes in 1906. Prostitution as such is no longer illegal, but persons supporting themselves by this means can be compelled to take regular employment. Soliciting is punishable only if it takes the form of a public nuisance. Concubinage is not illegal; spreading infectious venereal diseases is.

Voluntary sterilization is permitted on medical or eugenic grounds. Involuntary sterilization is permitted only in cases of extreme mental weakness or following a criminal act. Castration is permitted as a means of forestalling criminal action and as a rule is only performed with permission of the individual. In cases of habitual criminals, however, it may be ordered by the courts.

Induced abortion is legal in the following cases: (1) where pregnancy endangers the life or health of the mother, (2) where pregnancy results from a criminal act, (3) where the child is likely to be born with mental or physical disabilities. Induced abortions are legal only if undertaken in public hospitals and if two physicians have pronounced them necessary or advisable. Since 1936 the regulations have been interpreted so that endangering the life or health of the mother includes possible damage to her fullest living or well-being; but decisions in this respect must be made not by two physicians but by a board consisting of a surgeon or gynecologist, a psychiatrist, and a representative of the Mothers' Aid Center.

Social Regulations

Excellent provision is made for the welfare of pregnant women and others. All pregnant women, rich or poor, married or unmarried, have the right to three free medical consultations with the physician of their choice. The physician is reimbursed by the government. They also have a right to seven consultations with a midwife, six before and one after confinement. In addition, a half liter of milk a day is provided during the first six months of pregnancy to all mothers within the scope of the Sick Fund, about 80 per cent of the population. Every mother has also the right to free consultation with her physician three times in the first year, twice in the second year, and once a year until the child goes to school, when health control becomes the business of the school medical officer.

The Gynecological University Clinics of Copenhagen and Aarhus offer a free delivery service to both married and unmarried mothers. The City Maternity Home in Copenhagen admits members of the Health Service for less than twelve dollars, all doctors' fees for confinement and after-treatment being borne by the government. After discharge from the hospital, a home visiting nurse calls on the mother and, where requested (that is, in about 95 per cent of cases), returns once every ten days until the baby is six months old and, thereafter, once a month until the child is one year old. Nurses check weight and nourishment and are trained to give advice to the mother on all problems of baby care.

Every mother has access to the Mothers' Aid Centers, which offer economic and legal help and also medical and social advice. There are approximately 77,500 babies born each year in Denmark. The Mothers' Aid Centers are consulted by some 50,000 mothers annually. The centers also offer help, where necessary, to mothers seeking legal abortion and arrange for legal adoptions. About 40 per cent of the 1,600 annual adoptions in Denmark are handled in this way. The centers, often with the aid of the University Institute for Human Eugenics, make a thorough check of the hereditary backgrounds of both the child and the adopting parents.

Many social workers, lawyers, psychologists, and physicians give their services to the Mothers' Aid Centers and assist in giving family counsel. All statements made to the staff of the center are regarded by law to be confidential and staff members may not be compelled to divulge information received at interviews.

Needy mothers are provided with baby linen, and house help is provided where needed. In extreme cases, convalescence in suitable surroundings is provided. Unmarried mothers are advised on legal problems. Mothers who have to support themselves are given vocational guidance.

Each center has a discretionary fund for providing immediate help where required. There are also three Holiday Homes, where mothers and children can be accommodated in special circumstances.

Sex instruction must, by law, be given as part of the normal biology course and, in Copenhagen, this is done. In the provinces, however, the situation is not so satisfactory. In country districts especially there is still considerable reluctance to comply with the law.

Venereal diseases must be reported and sufferers are given free treatment. This has been law in Denmark since 1773. In 1947, however, an amendment required sufferers not merely to report the infection, but also to reveal any possible source.

Sociological Aspects

The population of Denmark is approximately 4,500,000. There are approximately 35,000 marriages a year and 6,500 divorces. It has been estimated that 27 per cent of marriages end in divorce, but that as divorced and separated persons together amount to only 5 per cent of married persons, most divorced persons must remarry. Of women, 67 per cent marry while still under 25; 72 per cent of men marry while still under 30.

Premarital Sexual Experience

A recent survey showed that, of 284 women questioned, 80 per cent saw nothing immoral in premarital experience. Only four of them (1.4 per cent) reported loss of virginity at marriage; of those with premarital sex experience, about half had been virgins at the time of engagement. Loss of virginity under alcoholic stimulus was reported by 12 per cent. Half the women questioned reported two premarital affairs, 20 per cent reported three or more. The 284 women had had a total of 850 premarital affairs, of which some 400 were accounted for by one group of 22 women. The average age for loss of virginity was 19.1 years; for those with only one affair 19.9, for those with more than one affair 18.3. The older the girl when embarking on her first affair, the more permanent appeared the relationship. In 1960 55 per cent of all first-born babies were born less than nine months after the wedding.

Extramarital Affairs

No scientific surveys have been published, but Henrik Hoffmeyer, the principal physician of the Mothers' Aid Centers, has estimated that 80 per cent of men, and 30–45 per cent of women have at least one extramarital affair. Other observations seem to bear out these figures.

Abortions

With so many premarital and extramarital affairs and with continuing inadequacy of contraceptive knowledge, there is bound to be a great number of unwanted pregnancies, premarital pregnancies, and births out of wedlock. Surveys have shown that as many as one pregnancy in every two is unwanted, in the sense of being unplanned. Only 9 per cent of premarital pregnancies, 68 per cent of married pregnancies, and 42 per cent of third pregnancies were planned. It is therefore not surprising to find estimates of a figure as high as 50 per cent for pregnant brides. This is by no means a recent development. Figures drawn from records indicate that 46.9 per cent of the mothers of women examined had given birth to children early enough to indicate pregnancy at marriage. An inquiry held in country districts in 1890 indicated that two-thirds of all brides were pregnant.

A breakdown of 40,000 self-supporting mothers in Copenhagen, published by the Mothers' Aid Centers, shows that 40 per cent were divorced, 23 per cent legally separated, 10 per cent widowed, and only 17 per cent unmarried. In country districts the proportions might be somewhat different.

Legal abortions totaled 5,031 in 1952; in 1955, 5,434; in 1957, 3,775. The figure was stabilized at 4,000 the next years. Estimates of the number of illegal abortions vary from 12,000 to 15,000 per year. Most legal abortions are performed on married women, most illegal abortions on single women.

A survey of 423 pregnancies with 354 resultant births, of which 8 were twin births, showed the following breakdown: 6 legal abortions, 4 (out of 49 attempts) successful self-induced abortions, 5 illegal abortions, and 40 spontaneous abortions. From this it would appear that a considerable proportion of the estimated illegal abortions may in fact be spontaneous.

Masturbation

Masturbation among boys and men has not been scientifically studied in Denmark. Of 307 women recently questioned, 74 reported masturbation. Of these, 29 were unmarried, 37 married, and 8 divorced. Only 69 of these 307 were available for further questioning. Of these, 13 started masturbation before the age of 11, 33 started at puberty, and 23 when over 18. The adult women reported that masturbation was practiced most commonly when a sexual relationship had ended in death or divorce, or between two relationships.

Sexual Offenses and Prostitution

Sexual offenses are obviously comparatively rare in a land where the legal attitude towards sexual behavior is permissive.

Prostitution exists mostly in the bigger towns and ports and is centered either on the streets or the restaurants. There are also a number of part-time prostitutes. However, the number arrested for vagrancy total only a few hundred annually. Social legislation has removed most of the economic necessity for prostitution, and a progressive attitude to sexual morality has lessened the demand. The clients of prostitutes are mostly sailors, men in enforced separation from their families, tourists, and members of the upper classes. Middle- and working-class men prefer affairs to relationships with prostitutes. In Copenhagen there are also a few male prostitutes. For the most part they are not active homosexuals but make use of the needs of homosexuals and are often blackmailers.

Homosexuality

Active homosexuals may be assessed at perhaps 3–6 per cent among males and slightly more among females. There are no reliable figures available. Adolescent homosexuality, especially in schools where the sexes are segregated, probably runs somewhat higher. A survey of 315 women showed results startlingly smaller than those published by Kinsey, but this may be due to strong taboos against premarital heterosexuality in the United States, which may drive more Americans to homosexual contacts. The social position of homosexuals is relatively better in Denmark than in many other lands. However, there is still considerable prejudice, especially among those without benefit of higher education.

Venereal Disease

Venereal disease is not a major problem. In 1956 there were only 129 cases of gonorrhea, 7 cases of soft sores, 119 cases of contracted syphilis, and 8 cases of congenital syphilis treated.

Sexual Education

The sexual education of adults has not yet reached even the barely satisfactory standards of required education for children. Although, as stated, some education is given in schools, children must also be able to learn from their parents, which is not at present the case. There is no organization devoted specifically to sexual education, nor any scientifically edited periodical, but many individuals have tried to improve this state of affairs.

Population Growth

The population has increased fourfold in the last 150 years and continues to increase at a rate of 1.25 per cent per year. The excess of women over men is slight and unimportant. There is a considerable flow of population from the country to the towns, indicating a development from an agricultural to an industrial society. There has been no official attempt to foster a population increase, but the tax structure and some recent social legislation tend to favor the larger family.

Organizations

There is in Denmark a branch of the International Planned Parenthood Federation, which supports a clinic for family planning. The Mothers' Aid Centers run two clinics for marriage and family counseling in Aarhus and Copenhagen. The Society for Mental Hygiene maintains four offices for family counseling and for mental hygiene. Their Copenhagen office was used last year by 120 women and 80 men. Three marriage schools, two under the auspices of the church, were opened in Copenhagen ten years ago. Their courses include instruction in sexual problems, legal and social problems, family economy, housekeeping, and child care. Since October, 1958, child-guidance clinics have become an integral part of the child-welfare committees.

The active homosexuals have sought to protect their interests by forming a society. This has several hundred members, arranges social evenings, dances, etc., and, in collaboration with similar organizations in Norway and Sweden, publishes a little magazine.

Morals

Sexual relationships before marriage are not generally regarded as immoral, possibly because sexual behavior has developed slowly over a period of centuries, without any of the religious fanaticism engendered in other European countries at the time of the Reformation. No nationwide survey, however, has investigated this problem and it is difficult to be specific about a general attitude. In one limited survey of active church members, one in every five stated that they did not consider sexual relations even before formal engagement as immoral.

Surveys and Investigations

When the Kinsey report was published in Europe, it was immediately clear that many of its findings referred to a local cultural climate, and many similar investigations were undertaken in Europe to establish parallel or control investigations. In Denmark there has so far been no survey of male behavior, and only one excellent investigation of female behavior. This was undertaken by Dr. Kirsten Auken and its results have been referred to several times here. Her report was published in 1953. Professor Tage Kemp, a specialist in human genetics, made a study of 530 prostitutes in Copenhagen during the years 1931–1935. The girls ranged in age from 15 to 46 years and most had been employed as general servants. Only 29.4 per cent were mentally normal and of average intelligence. Most came from homes with too little money and too many children. Only a very few came from good homes.

References

Auken, Kirsten, *Undersøgelser over unge, kvinders sexuelle ad færd* (with an English summary). Copenhagen: Rosenkilde & Bagger, 1953.

Denmarks Statistik. Statistical Yearbook, Vol. 62, Copenhagen, 1957.

Fabricius-Moller, J., *Om samlivet* (Folkeudgave af kønslivet"). Copenhagen: Arnold Busck, 1955.

Geiger, Theodor, *Fortidens moral og fremtidens.* Copenhagen: Hans Reitzel, 1952.

Gottschalk, Helmuth, *Skinsygens Problemer.* Copenhagen: Fremad, 1936.

Gottschalk, Helmuth, *Moderne aegteskabs-problemer; om aegteskab, Familie og Konvention.* Copenhagen: Thaning & Appel, 1947.

Hartmann, Grethe, *Kønssygdomme,* in: *samliv og samfund.* Copenhagen: Hassing.

Hoffmeyer, Henrik, *Svangerskabsafbrydelser,* in: *samliv og samfund.* Copenhagen: Hassing, ohne Jahr.

Kemp, Tage, *Prostitution. An Investigation of Its Causes, Especially with Regard to Hereditary Factors.* Copenhagen: Levin & Munksgaard, 1936.

Lund, Troels, *Dagligt liv i norden. 9. Bog: Trolovelse.* Copenhagen: Gyldendal, 1903.

Mødrehjaelpen i Kobenhavn 1905–1955. (Official information booklet.)

Ranulf, Svend, *Moral Indignation and Middle Class Psychology. A Sociological Study.* Copenhagen: Levin & Munksgaard, 1938.

Saunte, Edel, *Aegteskabets jura,* in: *samliv og samfund.* Copenhagen: Hassing.

The Danish Mothers' Aid Centres: Review of Their History and Activities. Copenhagen: Det Danske Selskab, 1957.

EWALD BOHM
Translated by Albert Abarbanel

N O R W A Y

The Attitude of the Law

Civil Law

Men under 20 and women under 18 require royal permission to marry. The insane may not marry, nor may sufferers from active syphilis; but epileptics and sufferers from other venereal diseases may marry if the illness is revealed and both partners have seen a doctor for instruction.

Both partners pledge mutual support according to their means. Property is in joint ownership, unless otherwise stipulated by marriage contract. Responsibility for legitimate children is shared. A child of 12 or over must be consulted by the parents before certain decisions are made regarding his or her person. A child of 15 must be consulted in somewhat wider circumstances. Where the father is known the illegitimate child is in a similar position to the legitimate one.

Divorce follows one year of legal separation, or may be obtained by decree on the following grounds: 2 years' desertion, 3 years' disappearance, bigamy, adultery, threat to partner's health through venereal disease, cruelty to partner or children, 3 years' imprisonment or habitual imprisonment for vagrancy, drunkenness, or begging, certain moral offenses, or mental disease lasting at least 3 years without prospect of cure.

Criminal Law

The letter of Norwegian criminal law does not always reflect the spirit in which it is administered. For instance, homosexuality is a punishable offense, but is seldom prosecuted unless a minor is involved. Concubinage and the sale of contraceptives are other offenses that very seldom lead to prosecution.

Proceedings will normally be instituted by the authorities only when the public interest is involved, so that instances of homosexuality or bestiality that are unostentatiously practiced will not be brought into the light of day by court action. It is believed that the offense is less harmful to the public at large than the resulting notoriety.

In general, all sexual relations that are not mutually agreed to by both parties, or where one party is tricked into agreement, or where one party is a minor and not to be held responsible are illegal. Crimes such as homosexuality or incest are held to be contrary to the public interest. Because the minimum sentences for moral offenses are very high there is a tendency to avoid bringing cases into court, and it is even claimed that there have been some resultant unjustifiable acquittals. However, these high minimum sentences, which have been in effect since 1927, have greatly reduced the number of offenses handled.

Adultery is not a punishable offense; bigamy is, but not on moral grounds. Incest, which occurs more often in country districts than in the towns, is illegal. Pandering and pimping are both offenses, but prostitution as such is not, unless engaged in publicly.

Castration is not a punishable offense. It is also not used as a punishment, although it is often performed on convicted moral offenders, at their own request, to increase their chances of freedom.

Induced abortion is illegal, except on grounds stated in the law. The law was revised in 1964 and gives three types of indications for legal abortion: a combined medical and social one, a eugenic one, and a humanitarian one—in case the woman has been misused. Of special importance is the decentralized administration that makes possible quick resolutions in each case.

Social Legislation

The social services are greatly concerned with the mother-child relationship and are well organized. The laws that more or less directly protect the mother and child include:

1. Health Law of 1860, which provides, among other things, for health stations for mothers and children.

2. Midwifery Law of 1898, which restricts the practice of midwifery to graduates of state schools or to persons practicing by royal license.

3. A law of 1912 ensuring that there will be physicians available in all districts.

4. The Children's Laws of 1915, which clarify the position of legitimate and illegitimate

children and under which mothers' aid centers were opened to care for self-supporting mothers and their children to the age of 1 year.

5. Laws of 1930 covering the care of the sick, which also cover economic help for women giving birth. Having a child is totally without cost to the family. Even the taxi to the hospital is paid for by the state. Women living too far from a hospital are given suitable help by physician and midwife without cost, even where the journey involves a boat or reindeer sleigh ride. A cash allowance is also allowed each mother for subsidiary expenses connected with lying-in.

6. The Workman's Protection Law, 1936, which gives a pregnant woman six weeks' vacation without fear of dismissal, both before and after her time, and also other advantages.

7. The Child Care Law of 1946, which provides an allowance for all second and later children under 16, and also, in some cases, an allowance for the first child.

Among the many institutions directed toward the care of mother and child, the health stations for mother and child have helped most to give Norway its very satisfactory record in keeping down infant mortality. Mortality in the first year for children born alive is 2 per cent, and deaths attributable to pregnancy or lying-in are only 0.5 per cent. The number of health stations is constantly being increased, as they are popular and much utilized. Hygiene centers for mothers have also proved their worth. They perform a similar function to the health stations, but also offer instruction in sexual hygiene. Self-supporting mothers are liberally aided by the state. A woman with five children under 15, or under 20 if they attend school, receives an annual grant of 8,460 crowns compared to an average national income of 10,000-11,000 crowns.

Sterilization is permitted to avoid the transfer of congenital disease or deformity, both physical and mental. It is also permissible where the individual concerned is unlikely ever to be able to care for eventual children. The law does not define circumstances, and decisions are made either by the physician concerned or by the Ministry of Health. Consent of the individual must be obtained. The number of sterilizations has risen from 541 women and 112 men in the period 1934-1942 to 2,338 women and 231 men in 1945-1954. The increase was chiefly among normal women and the grounds were either bad health or inability to support further children. Families of these women averaged 4.1 children.

Sex education was almost nonexistent until 1932, when a group of physicians and medical students headed by the current President of the Health Ministry started a magazine that continued publication for three years, or until the group considered it had said all that needed to be said. This publication met with strong opposition. However, it proved extremely popular, and the articles, slightly rewritten, were published in book form in 1951. It is now the standard work on the subject. Some fifty other works have been published since the last war, but half of them are from religious houses, which in Norway means that they are both romanticized and prejudiced.

In the schools, since 1939, sex education has been part of the normal curriculum, but this does not mean that it is always taught. Questionnaires sent to some school districts on the extent of current sex education still remain unanswered. It would seem, however, that in most schools some such education is given. The official textbooks contain factual information, together with moral warnings. The teaching lays definite stress on the relationship between sexuality and responsibility.

Sexual Sociology

Marriage and Divorce

For the last 25 years, marriages performed have remained constant at 8 per 1,000 inhabitants, an increase of 2 per 1,000 over the previous 25 years. In the last ten years the average age of men and women married has dropped by 1 year to approximately 28 for men and 25 for women.

Births average 18.5 per 1,000 inhabitants nationally, with about 20 per 1,000 in country districts and 15 in the towns. There are some 63,000 live births per year in a population of 3,500,000. Population increase averages 1 per cent per year. On the average, marriages lasting 2 years have one child; 3–7 years, two children; 8–13 years, three children; 14–18 years, four children. Marriages with more children are uncommon, but families as large as 16 children are reported.

Divorces total some 2,000 annually, or 7.5 per cent. The figure for country districts is 4.5 per cent, for towns 11.5. Most divorces occur between the fifth and tenth year of marriage, with a minor peak at five years. Some 90 per cent of families that end in divorce have two children or less.

Illegitimacy

Illegitimate births are decreasing. Twenty years ago the published figure was 7 per cent compared with 3.5 per cent today, or 1 in 1,000. The three most northern provinces, due to special local conditions, have the high figure of 9 per cent illegitimate births per all births. Population in these provinces is sparse and distances great, and it is not unusual for a man and woman to have two or three children before marrying.

There are a few definite figures obtainable of children born in wedlock but conceived prior to marriage. These are drawn from certain specialized inquiries undertaken recently in Oslo. The over-all figure is approximately 35 per cent, but this varies with the age and social position of the mother. For mothers under 25, the figure is 60 per cent. For mothers of all ages in better social circumstances, the figure is 8.75 per cent; for those of low social status, 33.6 per cent.

Premarital and Extramarital Affairs

Premarital affairs have not been the subject of exact study, but the general attitude is known to have changed. It is no longer considered wrong for young people to stay together in mountain huts. The most common practice among the unmarried is to go to bed together after three or four dates. Most boys and girls have three or four affairs before marrying. The affairs may be of long or short duration. Students are, in general, less inclined to have affairs than working-class boys and girls, but this is largely due to the fact that their work is more time-consuming.

Extramarital affairs are difficult to estimate from the divorce figures or from any other statistics available. It may be assumed, however, that the average man and the average woman are both unfaithful once, or even twice, during a marriage that lasts more than three years.

Abortion

Both legal and illegal abortions are on the increase. In 1954, the last year for which figures are available, induced abortions undertaken or treated in hospitals totaled 16.5 per cent of births. Illegal abortions totaled 11.6 per cent of births. The estimated figures are: 5,000 for married mothers and 2,000 for unmarried. It is estimated that only 1 per cent of illegal abortions were followed by criminal proceedings.

Prostitution and Homosexuality

Prostitution is not a problem and exists only to serve sailors and tourists. Professional prostitutes are few and usually so demoralized or alcoholic that they must be regarded as unemployable. There is some part-time prostitution, where the favor granted is acknowledged by a gift of clothing, or perhaps simply an evening out.

There are a number of youths in Oslo, perhaps 20–30, who offer themselves to homosexuals. They are mostly from the criminal element and often attempt blackmail. Although homosexuality is a punishable offense, prosecutions average only two per year. It is estimated that homosexuals form 2–4 per cent of the population, but as the active homosexuals fear social rejection, it is difficult to obtain figures.

Population Growth

The population is well distributed among the various age groups, particularly from 5–50 years. Only 2 per cent of the population is over 80. Men over 65 account for 9 per cent of the total, women over 65, 11 per cent. This group increases yearly both in number and in proportion to the whole. The number of women in the child-bearing years has decreased of late.

Social legislation and the tax structure both favor families with children. Advice on birth control can be obtained from the mothers' aid centers, etc., and also, in the case of married women, from physicians. Some physicians still decline, on religious grounds, to give advice on birth control to single persons.

Organizations

Norway is not a member of the International Planned Parenthood Federation and there is no organization in the country specializing in sex education. A small group, mainly left-wing, existed between the two world wars, but was not revived after the occupation. Lately, a number of family and marriage counseling offices have been opened, mostly under church auspices. Christian ministers and doctors together run these offices. There are also some places where sound mental-hygiene advice is available and with it some advice on sexual matters.

Active homosexuals have their own society, which naturally operates under great difficulties and in the face of strong public opposition. The society has recently hired its own psychologist.

Morals

Only 3 per cent of Norwegians are regular churchgoers, but the church still seems to exercise considerable influence on the official attitude to sexual problems. During the recent prosecution of the writer Agnar Mykle on the charge that his novel *The Song of the Red Ruby* was indecent, considerable public debate occurred. Both the book and the trial received much publicity in newspapers and periodicals, and there were many eloquent arguments offered by the defense, which collected an imposing array of cultural leaders to speak on their behalf. The wealth of material provided by this affair leads to the belief that, although there is still a hard core of narrow-minded opposition, the majority opinion of the people today tends toward a mature and responsible attitude in sexual matters.

Sexuality seems to be accepted, especially by the young, as a normal and natural experience. There is still a tendency to prudery in country districts and there may be a tendency toward a too flippant attitude among young townspeople, but on the whole the position seems to be healthy. There is a movement to restore school texts of the classic authors—for example, Knut Hamsun—which were previously banned. Sex is no longer regarded as something sinful and dangerous, nor is there any evidence of a widespread movement to sweep away all moral rules. There seems, in fact, to be a general quiet determination to deepen our insight into the forces governing sexuality.

Research

Recent research has concentrated mainly on sexual biology, but there are also some excellent recent works on sexual sociological themes. A brief list of relevant works is given below.

References

Andenaes, Johannes, *Almindelig strafferet* (General Criminal Law). Oslo: Akademisk forlag, 1956.

Brun-Gulbrandsen, Sverre, *Kjonnsrölle og ungdomskriminalitet* (*Sex Role and Delinquency of Youth*). Oslo: Universitetsforlaget, 1958.

Diverse official documents. Vorschläge von Stortingsausschussen und Gesetzesvorschlage in einer Reihe sozialpolitischer Fragen.

Evang, Karl, *Health Services in Norway.* Published by the Norwegian Joint Committee on International Social Policy, Oslo, 1957.

Nissen, Ingjald, *Det absolutte monogami (Absolute Monogamy).* Oslo: Aschehoug, 1957.

Norges lover 1682-1957 (Norwegian Laws 1682-1957). Oslo, 1958.

Norges offisielle statistisk (Official Statistics of Norway). Statistisk Sentralbyra, Oslo.

Norsk Gallup institutt A/S. Kjonnssykdommer (*Venereal Disease*). Oslo, 1946.

Raknes, Ola, *Fri vokster (Free Growth).* Oslo, 1949.

Rasmussen, E. Wulff, "The Shock Method as a Measure of Hunger and of the Intensity of Conflict." *Acta psychol. 5;* 63-78, 1940.

Rasmussen, E. Wulff, *Alkoholens inflytelse på den seksuelle energi hos albinorotter. Utgitt av Landrodet for Edruelighetsund-ervisning.* Oslo, 1943. (The data will soon be published in English under the title, "The Influence of Alcohol on the Copulatory Ability, Libido Sexualis and Ejaculatory Capacity of the Albino Rat.")

Rasmussen, E. Wulff, "The Relation Between Strength of Sexual Drive and Fertility in Rats, Mice and Cocks." *Proc. Fifteenth Internat. Veterinary Congr.* Stockholm, 1953.

Rasmussen, E. Wulff, "Experimental Homosexual Behavior in Male Albino Rats." *Acta psychol.,* 1955.

Rasmussen, E. Wulff, *Some Experimental Methods in Psychobiological Research.* Oslo: Oslo University Press, 1957.

Rasmussen, E. Wulff, L'hypersexualité expérimentale chez le rat blanc après excitation et obstruction de la fonction sexuelle. (Publication in preparation.)

Waal, Nic *et al., Forhold mellom ektefeller i 75 ekteskap med vanskelige barn.* (Das Verhaltnis zwischen den Ehegatten in 75 Ehen mit schwierigen Kindern.) Unfinished manuscript.

TRYGVE JOHNSTAD
Translated by Albert Abarbanel

SWEDEN

The Legal Position

Civil Law

The marriage laws of 1924 provide that men may marry at 21, girls at 18. Exceptions require permission from the Provincial Government. The mentally ill, epileptics, and sufferers from contagious venereal diseases must obtain a special license from the Ministry of Health.

The law provides for a modified form of separate ownership of property. Each partner's property remains in his or her control, as does any property acquired during the marriage. However, each partner becomes entitled to a share of the property of the other—the so-called *giftoratt*—when the marriage ends through death or divorce. Certain provisions are made to protect this *giftoratt*. Neither partner may dispose of land without consent of the other. Other property arrangements may be made by marriage contract.

Parents have joint responsibility for, and control of, legitimate children till the children are 18. Either or both parents can be declared by the courts to be unfit, on grounds of gross neglect, alcoholism, improper behavior, or sickness, and be deprived of control.

Mothers have responsibility for, and control of, illegitimate children. Illegitimate children have no inheritance rights from the father, unless conceived during the engagement, or by declaration of the father that he wishes the child to inherit. There is no provision for collective responsibility for all of several possible fathers in Swedish law.

Divorce is governed by a law of 1920. An immediate divorce can be obtained on certain grounds. When this is not granted, the first stage of the divorce must be a separation recognized by a court of law. The separation can be granted on mutual request or when the court finds evidence of incompatibility. In all cases an attempt at mediation must first be made.

Grounds for an immediate divorce are three years' interruption of the marriage without legal separation, two years' deliberate desertion, three years' disappearance, bigamy, adultery, danger of contagion of venereal disease, threat to life, a long prison sentence, alcoholism, and a mental sickness that has lasted three years without prospect of cure.

Criminal Law

Adultery with abduction is regarded in Sweden as an offence dealt with only at the request of the injured party. Bigamy, incest, rape, and violation are considered crimes.

Seduction of girls under 12 years old is punishable with four to eight years in a house of correction; seduction of girls 12 to 15 years old with from six months to four years.

Pandering and dealing in women and children are punishable offenses.

Since 1944, homosexual activities are only punishable when children under 15 are involved, when they occur among institution internees, or when they are of such a nature as to cause public offense.

The publishing of pornographic literature is punishable with fine or prison sentence.

Contraceptives may be freely bought and sold and druggists are required to stock them.

Prostitution as such is not illegal, but vagrancy may be punished by forced labor.

Voluntary sterilization is permitted only by permission of the Ministry of Health, on eugenic grounds, or when the life or health of the woman is endangered.

Castration is permitted to men over 23, by agreement of the Ministry of Health, when there is a danger of criminal sexual activities.

Abortion is legal when sickness or physical weakness threatens the life or health of the mother, the pregnancy originated in a criminal act, there is danger of congenital idiocy, and the birth of the child would cause the mother serious psychological harm. A pregnancy may not normally be interrupted after the twentieth week, but in special cases this may be extended to include the twenty-fourth week.

Social Legislation

Pregnant women and mothers are well provided for in Sweden. Every woman, regardless of financial standing, has the right to free medical examination and treatment at the child welfare stations. Almost 70 per cent of mothers make use of this facility. The cost of the actual delivery is borne by the Health Fund, which also makes a cash provision for the mother and pays an allowance for the first three months of the child's life (in total 600–800 kronen). Women who have been on a job for one year may not be dismissed on account of pregnancy. They are entitled to six months' leave of absence. Payment for this leave is a matter of contract or collective bargaining.

Every child has a right to free care till he or she is 7 years old. This is provided by the prophylactic child welfare organization, which employs doctors and visiting nurses, who are, however, available only for advice, not for the treatment of diseases. Almost 90 per cent of parents take advantage of this service, with the result that Sweden's infant mortality rate—2 per cent—is the lowest in the world.

Every child is entitled to a hot free lunch at school. Some 60 per cent of all children use this facility. Children whose parents are not in the highest 25 per cent income level have the right to a free vacation journey on the railroads. The mother also receives a free pass. During their absence, the household is cared for by municipal home assistants.

Sex Instruction in Schools

Since 1955, sex education has been compulsory in all schools. The quality of the instruction is, however, not uniform. The official handbook suggests that it would be preferable if parents gave their children the necessary instruction, but that, since this is often not done, the school must take over the responsibility. The instruction is given by the classroom teachers, who receive instruction in methods. The 7- and 8-year-olds are given a brief and cursory explanation of sexual differences, insemination, development, and birth. The 11- to 13-year-olds are taught about menstruation, anatomy of the sexual organs, masturbation, development, and birth. The 14- to 16-year-olds go into these subjects more deeply and also learn about abortion, illegitimate births, unmarried mothers, venereal diseases, and perversion. Contraceptives are mentioned and ethical and social problems touched on. For the 17- to 19-year-olds all these subjects are dealt with more thoroughly. At this stage contraception is explained more concretely and heredity is discussed.

Sexual Sociology
Marriage and Divorce

In 1955 there were 52,250 marriages and 8,785 divorces. Of the adult total population in 1956 (7,290,112), 3,336,869 were bachelors, 3,422,973 were married, 402,310 were widowed, and 127,960 divorced. The divorced represent therefore about 3.7 per cent of the married. It must be remembered that most divorced persons remarry.

Of 52,250 brides in 1955, 7,126 were under 20; 22,430 were 20–24; 11,346 were 25–29; 4,980 were 30–34. The rest were older. Of the same number of bridegrooms, 1,161 were under 20; 16,119 were 20–24; 16,874 were 24–29; 8,431 were 30–34; the rest older. Of women, 57 per cent marry when under 25; 65 per cent of men under 30. The average age for marrying in Sweden is very high. For 100 years it was around 29 for men and 26 for women, though it may have fallen slightly in the last two decades.

Premarital Affairs

Premarital affairs are considered perfectly normal in Sweden, which is not surprising in view of the late age for marrying. In a recent survey, 95 per cent of the men aged 40 reported premarital affairs and 80 per cent of 20-year-old unmarried men reported sexual relations. Among male students the percentage was only 40 per cent, a figure related less to the social background than to the education and family conditions of members of this group.

Among men the average age for first intercourse lies between 17 and 19 years. Younger men are more likely to report having begun at 17, older men at 19. This reflects an observation made in other surveys, that in the last few years puberty has begun somewhat earlier. Town or country background seems to have little influence on the age of first intercourse, but whereas the older men report first intercourse mainly as a result of a chance encounter, the younger men more often report it as planned, though slightly more than 50 per cent still report chance. It is interesting to note that first intercourse is now more often reported with women of equal age, whereas earlier it was more likely to occur with older women.

In general it would appear that, in spite of

frequent outcries against the degenerating morals of youth, younger men seem to be increasingly inclined toward more stable sexual relationships following first sexual intercourse.

In the same survey, 80 per cent of married women reported sexual intercourse prior to marriage. In most cases first intercourse occurred between the ages of 18 and 21. There was no appreciable difference between women of town and of country backgrounds: but women of the upper classes appear to make their sexual debut somewhat later than those of the lower classes. Though no figures are available, it appears from various inquiries that the age of women at first sexual intercourse is somewhat lower than previously, which corresponds with a reportedly lower age for the start of menstruation.

For 95 per cent of the women, first intercourse was followed by a stable sexual relationship, but in only 14 per cent of the cases did this lead to marriage, and in a further 28 per cent to official engagement. The discrepancy between the male and female reports on the stability of the relationship following first intercourse would lead one to assume that either the women dressed up their answers or that a greater number of men had their first intercourse with a smaller number of promiscuous women. The masculine partner was in 65 per cent of cases older than the woman, and in 25 per cent of the same age. A special survey among those attending lectures on sex showed that two-thirds of the unmarried women and half of the married women had not experienced orgasm.

Unplanned Pregnancies, Premarital Pregnancies, and Illegitimate Births

In 1944, 30 per cent of first-born children were born within the first eight months of marriage. This figure has sunk somewhat since. In 1955, 10 per cent of all live births were illegitimate.

This indicates that the number of unplanned and undesired pregnancies in Sweden is very high indeed, especially when the 5,000 annual legal and 10,000 annual illegal abortions are taken into account. A survey in 1954 of contraceptive methods showed for Stockholm: 30.9 per cent coitus interruptus, 18.8 per cent condom, 13 per cent diaphragm, 0.83 per cent chemical products, and 15.95 per cent no means. Figures varied slightly between town and country districts, but coitus interruptus seems everywhere the most widely favored method.

Abortion

Legal abortions rose from 439 in 1939 to 6,328 in 1951 and fell to 3,869 in 1956. Illegal abortions are estimated at between 10,000 and 20,000. It is estimated that 46 per cent of pregnancies among unmarried women are terminated by legal or illegal abortion, but only 5 per cent of pregnancies among married women are similarly ended. Of the balance of 54 per cent of unmarried women becoming pregnant, about half marry, while the other half bear an illegitimate child.

Sex Offenses

In 1955 there were 234,539 offenses recorded by the police, of which only 2,825 were offenses against morals, a mere 1.2 per cent.

Prostitution

The improved standard of living in Sweden appears to have reduced prostitution to a negligible few hundred teen-age prostitutes, most of whom later find other trades. The general permissiveness of sexual mores has also helped reduce prostitution.

Since World War II, however, male prostitution has become a problem, especially in the two major cities.

Homosexuality

Since the easing of regulations concerning homosexuality in 1944, there are no figures available. There is a society for the furtherance of the needs of homosexuals, which has aims similar to its brother-societies of Norway and Denmark.

Venereal Disease

In 1955 there were 177 cases of syphilis, 13,852 cases of gonorrhea, and 16 cases of soft chancres. While the number of cases of syphilis is falling, the figures for gonorrhea are fairly constant.

Population Trends and Policies

The total population of Sweden has risen from 6,842,046 in 1948 to 7,341,122 in 1957. The present density is approximately 18 to the square kilometer and the yearly increase over the last ten years is only 0.73 per cent. The sexes are almost equally divided, with 1,005 women for every 1,000 men.

Sweden has no problem of overpopulation. From 1880 to 1934 the birth rate had been steadily sinking and, even when the distinguished social scientists Gunnar and Ivar Myrdal drew attention to what they called the Repopulation Crisis, a government committee came up with surprising findings. In spite of the falling birth rate, they considered that birth control was sound, for unmarried as well as for married couples. Abstinence was decried as entailing risks for those with emotional instability. The committee recommended compulsory sex education for doctors, district nurses, and midwives, and opened the first birth-control clinic in Sweden for the fitting of diaphragms, but it closed on account of insufficient public interest.

However, to encourage earlier marriage, a system of marriage loans was introduced. Loans up to 3,000 kronen are available for founding a family. The loans are repayable, with interest, over eight years. Approximately 20 per cent of the newly married take advantage of these loans. There is also provision for a housing allowance for the lower-income groups, which starts at 500 kronen and increases by 150 kronen for each additional child.

In addition, each child is granted a yearly allowance by the state, which can be drawn by the mother each quarter. This allowance is also available to children of unmarried mothers and to children with foster parents. The allowance, of 400 kronen, is deemed sufficient to buy clothing and shoes for a school child.

Education

The struggle for sex education for adults and in the schools dates well back into the nineteenth century, but it was only in 1945 that sex instruction became compulsory in the schools.

Organizations

The National League for Sex Education was founded in 1933 by Elise Ottesen-Jensen, currently President of the International Planned Parenthood Federation, who brought very

great talents to her chosen work. With the aid of the trades unions and the adult-education movement, she increased the membership of her organization to a quarter of a million in 1958.

The aims of the League include:

1. Sex education in all schools, teachers' colleges, and universities.
2. Consultation centers to give guidance and information on all questions relating to sex.
3. Repeal of anticontraceptive laws.
4. Legalization of abortion on eugenic, medical, and social grounds.
5. Revision of all legislation in this field in accordance with scientific opinion.
6. A thorough change of social and economic conditions in order to utilize research in the field of sex science.

So successful was the League in influencing the government toward a liberalizing of attitude that a whole new range of aims was undertaken along the same lines. The League has consultation centers in a dozen major cities, over 100 associated physicians, and a number of allied staff members. The consultation center in Stockholm was consulted by 838 persons in 1936. In 1956, more than 24,000 persons consulted the various centers.

In 1957 in Stockholm advice was given to 17,211 persons. Of these, 13,596 requested information about birth control. The others asked about pregnancy, menstruation difficulties, orgastic problems, frigidity, interruptions of potency, sterility, and masturbation conflicts.

The League also answers questions by mail—some 2,000 in 1956—and has produced several films. It arranges lectures and courses for adults and especially for school teachers. There are also courses for medical students.

The League has its own laboratory and manufactures diaphragms and chemical contraceptives. Condoms, which are imported from America, are tested by a machine specially designed for this purpose. The League has 25 distribution centers for its domestic and imported contraceptives.

In 1941, the League opened its own mother's home with beds for 27 mothers. Two workers are assigned to handling and investigating requests for legal abortion. Adoptions are also arranged. The League also publishes its own brochures, which have proved very popular, and a periodical.

It would not be an exaggeration to say that most of the forward steps in sex and family hygiene taken in Sweden in the past few years have been aided either by the League or the Population Committee. It also appears that their efforts have given an impetus to both local and national councils in the area of mother and child welfare.

The Mothers' Aid Centers, in 1956, received 17,558 visits and paid out assistance of 5,635,000 kronen. Since 1945, Child Welfare Stations, which give free advice to parents, have been established in all areas. There are 63 such stations in Stockholm alone, including the famous Children's village at Skå. There is also a family counseling office in Stockholm, supported by the city, and in several other cities similar offices are supported by the Society for Mental Health.

Morals

Today Sweden is highly industrialized, but it grew out of a peasant society. The division of labor between the sexes gave the men the fieldwork, the women the care of the stock. The young girls had their sleeping quarters outside the family rooms and close to the stalls. On Saturdays, it was usual to gather to spin wool, which afforded the young men a chance to visit. In some localities these visits were extended and occasionally, when the weather was inclement or the distance too large, they lasted through the night. On special occasions, as after dances, birthday parties, weddings, etc., collective sleeping quarters were arranged for the young people. But the fact that the men and girls slept in close quarters through the night did not result in inevitable sexual activity or promiscuity.

The consequence of such "social evenings" was the custom of "night courtship," which flourished in the dairy districts. Young men got together in the village and jointly called on one girl in her dairy-maid's hut. Strict rules of behavior, based on custom and tradition, governed these visits. While the girl had little choice as far as the callers were concerned, she had the right to send them away at will after she had selected one favorite to spend the night with her. During the first few night courtships with favored lads—and sometimes even for long periods—sexual restraint was obligatory and only on rare occasions was this traditional code of behavior broken.

Then, after a suitable number of nights spent by the girl with one preferred lad, a more or less durable sexual relationship was formed; and when the prescribed amenities had been followed, it was sanctioned as moral by the social group. But only after this social approval of an enduring affair was the male permitted to call on his girl alone on any night. At this point there would be an exchange of gifts.

In general then, ancient tradition gave social sanction to premarital sexual relationships. The legal responsibilities of marriage, however, began with the promise to marry. Such forms of "trial marriage" have persisted in some rural regions of Sweden from the ancient past. As the church authorities later opposed them, a cleavage developed between the moral principles of the church in regard to marriage and those which sprang from traditional Swedish folk custom. While the church emphasized the "consensus-principle" of marriage and thus based its sanctity on individual agreement, traditional concepts regarded the formation of a family as a function of the social group. (The custom of "night courting" is not peculiar to Sweden. It has flourished since ancient times also in some regions of Finland, the Baltic sea provinces, and other parts of the European continent, especially Austria and Bavaria. Immigrants have brought this traditional folk custom to America as "bundling.")

The gradual change of Sweden's economic structure, hastened by a growing industrialization of the country, affected not only the collective life of farm communities but also the traditional folk customs. The enduring premarital relationships of predominately rural society, however, survived in the more progressive industrial society, and their present acceptance has been aided by various tendencies toward sexual emancipation, including the popularity of birth control, more liberal attitudes about premarital relations and free love, and a greater interest in psychoanalysis. The relatively unrestrained sexual behavior now existing in Sweden has these origins.

Disregarding a small puritanical minority

among the middle classes, there is little sexual repression among the Swedish people today. On the other hand, aggressive tendencies have been repressed in Sweden, while they have been subject to growth in more puritanical countries.

In North American society for instance, competitiveness invites considerable expression of aggressiveness, but in Sweden this expression is more repressed because of social conventions, over-politeness, widespread bureaucracy, etc.

A brief analysis of a peculiar difference in the way of life of Danes and Swedes may be in order. We are concerned here with two forms of alcoholism. While the consumption of wine and beer is large in Denmark, it is overshadowed by that of hard liquor in Sweden. The figures per head of population in Sweden in 1954 are: 5 liters hard liquor, 1.9 liters wine, 27.6 liters beer. The corresponding figures for Denmark are 1.1 liters hard liquor, 2.8 liters wine, 66.6 liters beer. The average Swede, therefore, consumes five times as much hard liquor and only half as much beer and wine as the Dane. Hard liquor is the quickest means of releasing aggressive tendencies, and for that reason it has been found necessary in Sweden to post a policeman in every saloon from Friday evening to Monday morning. This is not necessary in Denmark where the lighter form of alcoholism—even in its chronic form—leads to less aggression and more feelings of well-being. In Sweden, relatively weak sexual repression and strong repression of aggression can be discerned in contrast to Denmark where weak sexual repressions go hand in hand with weak repression of aggression. In the United States, however, strong sexual repressions exist with relatively weak repressions of aggression.

Special Surveys

The most important sexual-sociological survey which has been made in Sweden in recent times is Dr. Gustav Jonsson's *Sexual Behavior of Swedish Youth,* issued by the Ministry of Justice in 1951. Dr. Jonsson's subjects were 500 draftees in their twenties, 500 men aged around 40, 314 women aged from 15-45, and 1,000 women who answered a questionnaire circulated by the League. In 1943, Dr. Gunnar Nycander published his *Personality and Morals,*

in which he, as a psychoanalyst, polemicized against morals that were based on religious opinions.

There have been a number of inquiries following the pattern of the Kinsey report, though on a smaller scale. Brattgard, of the Sahlgren Hospital in Gothenburg, investigated the relationship of personal attitudes to sexual behavior, a subject not covered by the Kinsey report. Lindberg, also from the Sahlgren Hospital in Gothenburg, made two separate investigations of homosexuality, using 100 men for each study. Both investigations gave similar findings. The first showed 5 per cent occasional homosexual behavior and 0.5 per cent genuine homosexuality. The second showed 4 per cent and 1 per cent respectively. The subjects were, in both investigations, suffering from mild neuroses and were all in the terminal stages of treatment.

References

Björkberg, Roland, "Pojkprostitutionen i Göteborg" (Boy prostitution in Gothenburg). *Populär Tidskrift för psykologi och sexualkunskap,* 1958, 1.

Brattgård, Sven-Olof, "Personalighetsattityd och sexuellt beteende" (Personal attitude and sexual behavior). *Svenska Lakärtidning* 47; 1677-1682, 1950.

Handbook on Sex Instruction in Swedish Schools. The Royal Board of Education, Series No. 28, Stockholm, 1956.

Herlitz, C. W., *Sex Instruction in Swedish Schools.* (Mimeographed information.)

Jonsson, Gustav, "Sexualvanor hos svensk ungdom" (Sex behavior of Swedish youth.) In *Ungdom möter samhället (Youth and Society).* Ungdomsvårdskommitténs slutbetänkande. Statens offentliga utredningar 1951; 41, Justitiedepartmentet. Stockholm, 1951. 1951.

Kälvesten, Anna-Lisa, "Family Policy in Sweden." *Marr. & Fam. Living* 17; 250-254, 1955.

Lennér, Anders, *Das Menarchealter.* Helsingfors, 1944.

Lindberg, Bengt J., "Fortsatta homosexualitetsundersökningar" (Continued investigations on homosexuality). *Svenska Lakärtidning* 49; 2358-2362, 1952.

Lindberg, Bengt J., and Tessing-Ericsson, Greta, "Homosexualit beteende hos mannen" (Homosexual behavior of men). *Svenska Lakärtidning* 48; 1997 ff., 1951.

Myrdal, Alva, *Folk och familj (People and Family).* Stockholm, 1944.

Myrdal, Alva, and Myrdal, Gunnar, *Kris i Befolkningsfrågan (The Repopulation Crisis).* Stockholm, 1934.

Nycander, Gunnar, *Personlighet och Moral (Personality and Morals).* Stockholm, 1943.

Riksförbundet för sexuell Upplysning 1933–1958. (Booklet), Stockholm, 1958.

Statistisk Årsbok för Sverige (Statistic Abstract of Sweden), 44, Stockholm, 1957.

Takman, John, "Prostituerade flickår i Stockholm" (Prostituted girls in Stockholm). *Populär Tidskrift for psykologi och sexualkunskap 1;* 1958.

The National League for Sex Education. (Booklet). Stockholm, 1949.

Wikman, Robert, *Die Einleitung der Ehe, eine vergleichende ethno-soziologische Untersuchung über die Vorstufe der Ehe in den Sitten des schwedischen Volkstums.* Åbo, 1937.

E W A L D   B O H M
Translated by Albert Abarbanel

Separation

Definition

SEPARATION as a legal term refers to a marital status in which husband and wife are no longer living with one another although neither has the right to remarry. In popular usage it usually refers to a status that serves as a substitute for, or precursor to, divorce. Psychologically, it is the converse of proximity, with effects that may be traumatic or salutary according to the circumstances. Sociologically, it affects family interaction by truncating role relationships; often it is the disturbance of role patterns or "habits" that constitutes the major trauma of separation. In order to include the legal, popular, psychological, and sociological conceptions, separation may be defined as any marital status that limits or cuts off the effects of proximity and reduces the intensity of intimacy.

Separation should be distinguished from alienation. Separation is to some extent, however minor, physical as well as psychological. It need not, however, be accompanied by alienation; letters or telephone messages may keep the relationship intact. Alienation is a growing-apart of the spouses, whether accompanied by separation or not. The spouses become estranged; that is, they become strangers to one another. They no longer share common interests, have common goals. The feeling of intimacy, of knowing one another, disappears. In the concept "alienation of affection" there is a third party involved; but alienation may occur without such personal intervention; it may be brought on by any conflicting interest.

Benefits of Separation in the Marriage Relationship

The conception of marriage in our culture is that the marital partners are united; marriage is a union. And in the first flush of ecstatic love, the partners may feel that they want never to be separated; they want to be together always, forever, to share every moment. Every hour they are not together seems an hour lost. They want to be one.

There is some question about how much of this intense intimacy human beings can stand. Almost inevitably the time comes when at least a brief letup in this "togetherness" is welcomed. Some respite in the form of a temporary separation is desired.

Every successful marriage probably develops its own "tension." An orbit of activities emerges that alternates union and separation in the most congenial rhythm. Most wives do not want their husbands home all the time. They welcome the daily separation that takes the husband out of the home. Among the many traumas of unemployment, and in many instances of retirement, is that of having the husband around all day. Wives sometimes speak with relief of the absence of their husbands even for several days. It gives them a vacation from certain responsibilities with respect to cooking, marketing, and the like. Folk humor refers to the husband who similarly anticipates with pleasure the absence of his wife for a short time. The pros and cons of separate vacations are discussed from time to time in the press.

The fact that brief, voluntary separations are

welcomed by so many and even advocated by some is suggestive with respect to the nature of the marital bond. Separation may be as intrinsically necessary a part of marriage as intimacy, although the degree varies from couple to couple. At one extreme there is the couple who brag that they have never been separated for even one night in all the years of their marriage; at the other, the couple who brag that they look forward to vacations from marriage every so often. Is one any more "normal" than the other? Is extreme dependence "better" than moderate independence?

Separation is, in effect, a test of a relationship. Absence may make the heart grow fonder, but it may also have the opposite effect. If it heightens awareness of a relationship grown routine and even stale, it may strengthen the relationship. The partners come to value one another more because of the temporary deprivation. If it offers an opportunity to regain perspective it is salutary. This is the kind of separation Anne Morrow Lindbergh advocated in her best-selling book *Gift from the Sea*. If, however, the separation points up the frictions of daily accommodations, separation may give the partners a sense of release that they welcome and may make them reluctant to resume daily contacts.

Classification of Separation

Separations may be classified on the basis of several kinds of criteria, namely: (1) degree, (2) duration, (3) voluntary-involuntary nature, and (4) intent.

Degree

Physical separation may be relatively minor or it may be complete. It may take the form of simply moving over to the edge of the bed. A further step is getting out of the common bed into a separate bed. Separate bedrooms constitute a further step. Some people advocate such separations as therapeutic; others deprecate them as nullifying the effects of proximity. It is harder to go to sleep in anger when sleeping together than in separate beds or in separate rooms. Contrariwise, it is argued that it is easier to live with others when it is possible to retreat

into the privacy of one's own room to regain composure and protection from too much stimulation.

Separation may take the form of moving out of the house entirely, or to a different part of town or, indeed, to a different city entirely. The significance of these degrees of physical separation lies in the effect they have on propinquity. There is much truth in the folk adage "Out of sight out of mind."

Separation may also be thought of as segmental or integral in degree. The wife may feel that she is separated or "shut out" from her husband's work life; or a husband may feel "walled off" from his wife by her exclusive preoccupation with the house or child care.

Duration

Separation may be very brief, as when the husband must be gone on an overnight trip; or it may last for many years. It may be a routine daily separation of several hours, as when the husband is at work. It may be recurrent but brief, as when one or the other partner goes on a visit or vacation or business trip.

Voluntary-Involuntary Nature

With respect to this criterion, separations may be (a) involuntary for both, (b) quasi-voluntary, (c) voluntary for one but involuntary for the other, or (d) voluntary for both.

Involuntary separations result from incarceration in prisons, commitment to mental hospitals, or military obligations. A study of separated persons as of 1940 showed that about 300,000 resulted from imprisonment or hospitalization for mental illness. At that time only a negligible number of separations were attributable to military service.

In some countries, notably in Latin America, wives are permitted to visit their husbands in prison. This practice is not permitted in the United States; but some people argue that since a prisoner's marriage is his most important tie with the outside world, every effort should be made to prevent the separation from ending in divorce. Similar arguments are made in the case of mental patients.

Separations may be said to be quasi-voluntary when they result from occupational necessity. Seamen, fishermen, and traveling salesmen fall in this category. They are called quasi-voluntary because if the persons involved valued marriage and family life more highly than their work they would not pursue occupations that rendered so much separation inevitable. Also quasi-voluntary are separations such as those resulting from the necessity to take care of relatives or to perform other duties. Those associated with work tend to be of fairly long duration and are recurrent. They are built into the relationship and need not be inimical to the marriage. The chief hazard lies in the danger of succumbing to the temptation of extramarital sex relations during separation.

In many cases only one of the spouses wants the separation. Whether it is the husband or the wife who is more likely to want the separation is not known. It is probably easier for a husband to stay away from home than it is for a wife to pick herself up and leave. But it may be easier for a wife to make a long "visit" to her parents' home. The data on divorce do not help much here. We know that more wives than husbands sue for divorce; but there is some evidence that men are more likely to initiate the process that ends in divorce. We do not have even this much information about the separations that do not lead to divorce.

Desertion is a special category of voluntary-involuntary separation. It occurs primarily in the lower socioeconomic classes; and it is overwhelmingly a male pattern of behavior. It tends to be chronic and repetitive and is usually identical with nonsupport. Children are more likely to be involved in desertions than in divorce; in fact, because of the class and family composition of the deserting population, it has been stated that desertion is a far greater cause of human suffering than divorce. The desertion rate may be even higher than the divorce rate. Social agencies have developed a cooperative system for locating deserting husbands and returning them or holding them responsible for the support of their families. Casework is usually tried before resorting to legal coercion.

Even if the separation is wanted by only one of the partners, it is usually possible for that partner to make the other one so miserable that ultimately both accept it.

Voluntary separation varies all the way from the salutary vacation from marital responsibilities referred to above to legal separation, which is like formal divorce. By far the largest number of couples who reported themselves to be in the separated status in 1940 (1,200,000 at that time) were separated for the same kinds of reasons as divorced persons; indeed, most of these separations were probably preludes to divorce, annulment, or permanent legal separation.

Separation is a well-defined phase of the divorcing process; in fact, divorce is usually the legitimization and official recognition of the *fait accompli* of separation. The separation may occur at almost any phase of the alienation process. In one study it was found that the separation had occurred one or more years before the decree in 40 per cent of the cases; contrariwise, in 6 per cent of the cases the separation did not occur until after the decree. By and large, persons in higher socioeconomic classes tend to separate later in the alienation process than do those in the lower; and separations are likely to occur earlier when it is the husband who first suggests divorce than when it is the wife. Traumas reach a maximum at the time of separation when such separation leads to divorce.

Five main types of separation as related to divorce have been distinguished by Goode (1956): (1) separation as a divorce preliminary, in which separation comes after a decision to divorce and is a step toward implementing that decision; (2) separation of short or long duration as a substitute for divorce and sometimes ending in desertion; (3) one-sided separation, in which one mate leaves without even serious joint consideration of divorce; (4) drifting separation, in which the mates have built separate and individual lives for themselves, have never actually given much thought to divorce, and may never divorce unless some new factor precipitates such a decision; and (5) the delayed separation that does not occur until after the divorce decree.

Intent

The problem of intent is important only in separations that are voluntary on the part of at least one partner. In some cases the intent may be a temporary relief from an intolerable conflict situation. In extreme cases it might even be a matter of self-preservation. It might be a tactic of revenge: "I'll show him (her)." It might be a rest from the tensions of propinquity, an escape from the rigors of prolonged intimacy. It might be a method of renewing zest in a relationship. It might be a bargaining tactic: "I'll come back if you will promise me this or that." The results may sometimes be surprising. A separation that began as a bargaining tactic on the part of one spouse might prove so congenial to the other that it becomes a liability rather than an asset. Or a separation that began as a temporary escape may become so pleasant that resumption of the relationship is no longer appealing. Or a separation that began as a tactic of revenge may reveal to both partners the depth of their relationship and the impossibility of breaking it.

Sexual and Social Adjustment

Whatever the nature of the separation, some kind of sexual adjustment must be made. In the case of women, this is less likely to be serious since they appear to be able to tolerate long periods of deprivation with relative ease. In the case of men, Kinsey found that separated men fell between single and married men in their patterns of sexual behavior. In the years before 30, the amount of sexual outlet in men in a postmarital status (widowed, divorced, separated) was roughly 90 per cent of that of men in a married status; thereafter the amount fell to about two-thirds. Most (about 80 per cent) of this outlet is in the form of heterosexual experience.

Aside from problems of sexual adjustment, there are social adjustments to make. If the partners are not ready to admit to the world that they are having marital difficulties, the problems may be compounded by the necessity of putting up a conventional façade or of finding good reasons to cover up the real reasons for the separation. If the world knows the nature of the separation, there is likely to be a good deal of pressure from family and/or friends in the direction of either reconciliation or definitive divorce. The partners are themselves likely to be in a state of emotional disturbance if for no other reason than the disorganization of regular and habitual patterns of living.

Statistical Data on Separation

Precise statistical data on separated persons are difficult to secure. There is no way of knowing the incidence or, except for a particular day on which a census study is made, the prevalence of the several types of separation. In the United States, in April 1955, there were 746,000 men and 1,400,000 women reported as separated, including those with legal separations, those living apart with intentions of obtaining a divorce, and other permanently or temporarily estranged persons. There were 414,000 women whose husbands were in the armed forces. In addition, there were 809,000 men and 943,000 women with spouses whose place of residence was different from theirs. These included immigrants whose spouses remained in another location as well as spouses of inmates of institutions.

The average age at which women had become separated was 28.9 years; the average duration of their marriages was 4.1 years. The separation rates for women were found to be inversely related to education, being about three times greater among white women with elementary education than among those with four or more years of college education. Separation rates were much higher for nonwhite than for white women. Separated women were least likely to have any income, and among those who did have incomes, the amount was likely to be smallest, as compared with women in other marital statuses. In one study, about half of all persons reported as separated had obtained legal separations.

In general, separated persons resemble divorced persons with respect to employment status of wives, presence or absence of children, nativity, urban-rural residence, and occupation; but in practically every respect they are on a lower rung.

Statistical records, valuable as they are, tell us nothing about the unknown number of persons who separate and return to one another in any one year. One estimate for Chicago gave the number of separated but nondivorced persons as twice the number of divorced persons.

Because of the absence of accurate records there is little on which to base a study of trends. In the past, casual separation was extremely difficult. Where was the separating spouse to go? In a rural area there was no place except back to parents, or to friends. In cities there were no living quarters except in boarding houses or hotels, and here separated persons, especially women, would be looked upon with suspicion. Such factors kept people living together despite alienation. The sheer mechanics of separation today are simple. The woman who wants a vacation from marriage can move freely. She can vacation by herself, travel by herself, get a job, run an apartment. The simple logistics of separation have been transformed by technology, whether the motivations have changed or not.

No unequivocal advice can be given with respect to separation. If it is planned as a brief therapeutic "breather" or vacation from marriage it may be salutary and preserve a sound relationship. If it is planned as a prolonged escape from marriage or if it is a substitute or precursor for divorce, it may destroy a salvageable relationship. In such cases it would be well to consult a counselor before extending the separation.

References

Beale, Calvin, "Increased Divorce Rates Among Separated Persons as a Factor in Divorce Since 1940." *Social Forces 29;* 72-74, 1950-51.

Folsom, Joseph K., *The Family and Democratic Society.* New York: John Wiley & Sons, Inc., 1943 (Chap. 15).

Glick, Paul C., *American Families. A Demographic Analysis of Census Data on American Families at Mid-Century.* New York: John Wiley & Sons, Inc., 1957.

Goode, William J., *After Divorce.* Glencoe, Ill.: The Free Press, 1956 (Chap. 11).

Ogburn, William Fielding, "Marital Separations." *Am. J. Sociology 49;* 316-323, 1949.

JESSIE BERNARD

Sex Differences

THE literature on sex differences is enormous and has been ably covered by such authorities as H. Ellis (1929), Scheinfeld (1943), and Zimmerman and Cervantes (1956). It includes experimental findings relating to differences between the male and female sexes on numerous anatomical, physiological, mental, and emotional traits. The present article, because of space limitations, will largely be concerned with differences in the sexual behavior of men and women and will make no attempt to survey the many other kinds of sex differences which have been and still are being theorized about and experimentally tested.

In the discussion that follows there will be an attempt to show male-female differences in sexual behavior that, according to empirical investigations, presently exist. It is possible, as Kinsey and his associates (1948, 1953) imply, that many of these differences exist because they are biologically determined, and that they therefore tend to hold for men and women in almost any place or period. It is also possible, however, that existing differences in sexual behavior are strongly influenced by the social-cultural environment of the communities in which they are observed, and that under other social-cultural circumstances, these observed differences would not occur or would be minimal.

The facts about male-female differences in sexual behavior that are presented in this article are to be viewed as "true," in the sense that they presently seem to exist; but they are not necessarily to be seen as immutable or necessary. Although it may *now* be true that females tend to have considerably less sex drive than males when they are in their teens, and that they do not tend to catch up with males in this respect until they are in their late twenties (Kinsey, 1953), it is possible, as A. Ellis (1954) points out, that as our attitudes toward female sex participation become more liberalized, teenage girls may move closer to male norms of sex drive. In any event, social-cultural influences on sex differences must be constantly kept in mind (Seward, 1946), and existing differences, however solidly they may be established by empirical observation, must not be taken as being of purely biological origin.

Male or female—the sex of the human being is determined at the instant of conception. The genes that decide the sex of the embryo are also the architects of its future, for male and female differ in every cell of their bodies from the moment life begins, and these differences influence every sphere of their lives. They range from the microscopic (the special mass of sex chromatin found in the nuclei of normal females but not males) to the macroscopic (the genitalia and other anatomical features). Some, such as the grosser muscular structure of the male, are obvious to even the least perceptive observer. Others, such as the subtle nuances in emotional attitudes, are not so easily discernible and may become apparent only during psychological testing. Some are rooted in their different reproductive roles; still others arise from the pressures and demands of the society into which they are born. Generally, however, masculine and feminine character traits result from the combined interaction of both biological and cultural factors.

Biological Differences

Biologically, man is the weaker sex. Approximately 120 males are conceived for every 100 females, but only 105 of them live to be born. Not only is the prenatal miscarriage rate higher for males; during the first year of life their death rate exceeds that for females by about 25 per cent. The average life expectancy of white females today is 73 years; that for males, 67 years. This has been attributed to the pressures modern life puts upon men as contrasted to the greater leisure women enjoy. But a study of American Catholic religious brothers and sisters, whose lives are subject to similar pressures, revealed that the nuns had an average life expectancy that was 10 per cent longer than that of their male counterparts—about what it is for American women generally. This greater longevity of the female is also true of most animal species studied. Apparently, the explanation lies in sex-linked hereditary factors.

Biologically the weaker, the male is, in every known society, bigger and stronger than the female. On the average, he is 6 per cent taller and 20 per cent heavier than she, his bones are larger and heavier, his muscles larger, thicker, and stronger. He has a higher metabolism rate: he produces more physical energy than she, and requires more food. His heart pumps more forcibly than hers—a sexual characteristic that is common among all mammals, so far as we know. His blood contains some 300,000 more red corpuscles per cubic millimeter than does hers, giving him a more favorable oxygen supply for the physical exertion for which his body is obviously designed. The woman's body, equipped with an insulating layer of fat under the skin and a greater adaptability to respond with reduced metabolism when exposed to heat and with increased metabolism when exposed to cold, is better able to adjust to extreme changes in temperature and to withstand the radical physical changes—menstruation, pregnancy, menopause—that her reproductive role imposes.

Given superior muscular strength and energy, the male is more active and assertive than the female. According to authorities such as Gesell (1946), very early in childhood girls show less physical strength (but finer muscular coordination) than boys, have a greater preference for indoor and more sedentary activities, and, even in infancy, sleep more.

By the age of 2, boys are more aggressive, pugnacious, and unruly than girls, who tend to be more timid, inhibited, and eager to please and conform. To some extent, this may be because girls are suppressed more; on the other hand, girls are more amenable to restrictions than their brothers. This is true in the animal kingdom too, where it is the male who rebels most when restrained.

The greater aggressiveness of the male is reflected in suicide and crime statistics. Approximately five times more men than women commit suicide, which is an act of aggression directed toward the self. More men than women commit crimes of violence, and there is some evidence to indicate a relationship between the commission of such crimes by women and their menstrual periods, when there may be hormonal upsets and metabolic disturbances.

Sexual Behavior

The physiological and psychological differences between men and women are revealed most clearly in their sexual behavior. Here each seeks the same goal—sexual gratification; they differ in the means by which they attain it. In both sexes, sexual arousal is accompanied by tumescence—the stiffening of the penis in the male and of the clitoris and vulva in the female, caused by an influx of blood into the erectile tissues. This tumescence of the male is necessary to the sexual act; unless his organ is in a state of erection he cannot penetrate the vagina of the female. Although tumescence in the woman is necessary to her sexual satisfaction, it is not necessary at all to her sexual function. She can receive the male even though she is not physically prepared for coitus, and even when she does not desire it.

Both men and women achieve sexual gratification through orgasm, the explosive discharge of nerve-muscle tensions at the peak of arousal, followed by relaxation. But only in the man is this release of sexual tension accompanied by ejaculation. What is sometimes mistaken for ejaculation in the female is merely the secretion of those glands that lubricate the vagina and facilitate entry of the penis, and in no way is comparable to the emission of semen by the male. In both sexes, orgasm involves the whole body, but in the woman it is not located in the genitals to the degree that it is in man, but is a more diffuse sensation. Many women can attain some pleasure from intercourse in which they do not reach orgasm, which would be unusual for men.

Once she is stimulated, the woman is capable of experiencing more orgasms in a single intercourse than the man. Orgasm in the male is limited by the amount of seminal fluid, and once a climax has been reached it is impossible for most men to maintain erection. Younger males are capable of multiple orgasms, but this is characteristic of only a small number. The capacity to have repeated orgasms in a limited period of time decreases with age; by the time they have reached their fortieth birthday, most men have lost this ability.

In her capacity to experience frequent orgasms, the human female is unique among mammals. But, like tumescence, this response is necessary only to her gratification, not to her biological function. For the man, charged with delivery of the sperm, each ejaculation is a reproductive act. The woman's reproductive role, which requires her to make radical physical and emotional adjustments, begins when she receives the sperm. Whether she has experienced orgasm or not is not significant.

Thus the sexual act, dependent upon the male's willingness and capacity to perform, demands that he play the more aggressive, and the female, the more passive, role. Rooted in their different biological functions, the male and female sexual characters develop: Dr. Helene Deutsch (1944) has described that of man, the impregnator, as centrifugal in nature —directed outwards, away from himself; that of woman, centripedal—directed inwards, toward herself.

Sex Drive

Because the behavior of human beings is governed to a large extent by their previous experiences in living, there are great variations in the sexual impulse between persons of the same sex, and the sexual drive in any one individual fluctuates markedly throughout a lifetime, influenced by many factors such as age, health, and environment. We have no means of accurately measuring and comparing sexual drive, but it is not usually as strong in the woman as it is in the man. During childhood, boys show more awareness of sex, as indicated in interest in animal intercourse and erotic stories, than girls do, and the male shows a need for overt sexual experiences much earlier than the female. The Kinsey reports indicate that by the age of 17 almost all males have had orgasms, but only 35 per cent of the females have experienced climax by this age. There are some women who never have an orgasm in their entire lives; it is doubtful if there exists a normal man who has not had orgasm.

The sex play of the preadolescent years is more often initiated by the boy than by the girl. Girls between the ages of 5 and 7 are most inclined to engage in such activity, but few girls participate in heterosexual sex play at the time they reach adolescence. The number of boys who engage in such activities, on the contrary, increases steadily throughout the years preceding adolescence, and the Kinsey researchers estimate that near puberty there are about seven boys involved in such activity for every girl. Whereas approximately the same number of girls who engage in sex play with boys also have at least one experience with a member of their own sex, a far greater number of boys participate in childhood homosexual activities, and in preadolescent years more boys have sex play with other boys than with girls. This may be attributable to the segregated play of the sexes, which makes companions of his own sex more easily available to the boy.

The male usually becomes aware of his sex much earlier than does the girl. As every parent knows, erections occur spontaneously in infant boys, and in many young boys they occur daily. This spontaneous reaction, which may be provoked by completely nonsexual physical or emotional situations, presents the boy with dramatic evidence of the relationship between erotic sensation and genital response. By the time he reaches adolescence he cannot ignore it; there is a sudden upsurge of sexual excitability, there are erections brought on by specifically sexual situations, there are automatic emissions of seminal fluid during sleep accompanied by sexual dreams—the "wet dreams."

Sexual dreams usually begin about a year after puberty and are a common experience for nearly all men. The Kinsey researchers found that 75 per cent of women ultimately may have such dreams—some to the point of orgasm—but women do not have these dreams as frequently as men. For the male, the greatest number occurs during the mid-adolescent years, and by the time they are 30 most men have few, if any, such dreams. Among women, this pattern is reversed. Fewer younger women have sex dreams, and the greatest number of women have such dreams between the ages of 40 and 50. There is a slight increase in the sexual response of girls at adolescence, but it is not so marked as that of boys. With less exposed genitals, the girl may remain unaware for a long time that any relationship exists between her sex organs and the sensations coursing through her body.

The sexual activity of women is more sporadic than that of men. Once he has become sexually active in his early teens, the man usually maintains a fairly regular pattern. There are some women who participate in sexual activity only a few times during their lives, and many women have great gaps of time between their experiences. The married woman who is separated from her husband through distance, divorce, or death reduces her sexual activity considerably, whereas the man in similar circumstances usually succeeds in continuing his sexual activity without reducing its frequency.

Masturbation

Masturbation, the self-stimulation of the genitals to induce sexual response, exists in the animal kingdom and in every known human society. Without any knowledge of its sexual implications, very young children of both sexes masturbate, with girls usually being more successful in achieving physical pleasure than the boys, perhaps because the boys do not yet have the muscular coordination necessary for the proper manipulation. Among human beings, as among the other mammals, masturbation with specific sexual intent occurs more frequently among males than among females. Most American boys experience their first ejaculation through manual stimulation of their own genitals, and during adolescence it is their major sexual outlet. Well over 90 per cent of men masturbate to orgasm at some time in their lives, the largest number of them with the greatest frequency during the mid-teens, after which the number of men who do begins to decrease steadily. Few men masturbate after marriage, although a man may do so when circumstances make regular intercourse unobtainable—such as separation from his wife, her illness, pregnancy, or unwillingness to permit intercourse.

The pattern of female masturbation is strikingly different. Fewer women ever engage in such activity—58 per cent of those interviewed for the Kinsey report having masturbated to orgasm at some time in their lives—and unlike the male, whose masturbation begins just before or just after puberty, more older women than younger ones masturbate. From the age of 13 (the average age of the first menstruation) until the age of 40, the number of women who masturbate continues to rise. Kinsey attributes this to an actual increase in the erotic responsiveness of the older women, the fewer sociosexual outlets available to them, a reduction in inhibitions, and greater sexual experience.

Again unlike the male, the female does not stop masturbating when she marries; numbers of married women continue to obtain sexual gratification in this way although they are having coitus regularly. There are women who have been married for many years and borne several children who have never experienced orgasm in coitus. But in 95 per cent of her masturbatory experiences the female reaches climax. This apparently is a question of technique. The masturbatory activity of most women consists of some stimulation of the clitoris (the small homologue of the male penis located near the outer surface at the upper end of her genitalia) or of the labia minora (the inner lips of the genitalia). Both are well supplied with nerve endings, which the inner walls of the vagina almost completely lack, and are the portions of the genitals first discovered by the young girl when she begins to explore her body. Because it is not so accessible, the vagina plays an unimportant part in the early sexual activity of most girls, many of whom reach adolescence ignorant of their true sex organ. Many women take five times as long to reach orgasm in intercourse as they do in masturbation; stimulation of the clitoris by the male partner would probably induce a quicker response. There is some question as to whether clitoral manipulation would be as necessary as it is to so many women had they not been conditioned to it. The sexually healthy woman derives greatest pleasure from intercourse in which there is deep penetration by the male, but this may be due in part to the psychological satisfaction such penetration gives her.

Psychosexual Stimuli

The male responds more readily, and to a greater variety of psychosexual stimuli, than does the female, who is most responsive to physical stimulation. Since the effect of such stimuli depends upon the associations they evoke, the male's previous experiences condition his sexual behavior more than hers do the female. In the foreplay which precedes coitus, and which is identical in many respects with "petting" behavior, the man stimulates the woman's body to a greater degree than she stimulates his. The male is most sensitive to pressure applied to the glans of the penis, and tactile stimulation of his organ usually brings direct, immediate response. Most women, however, prefer stimulation of other parts of their bodies before desiring genital contact, and often fail to understand the man's concentration on genital manipulation. It is a common situation in the marriage counselor's office to hear wives protest that their husbands employ only genital techniques or employ them too soon, while the husbands complain that their wives do not manipulate the male organ sufficiently.

The oral and manual stimulation of the female breast by the man is commonly employed, and may be more stimulating to the man than to the woman because of his greater capacity for psychological arousal. Also dependent upon the man's capacity for psychological response may be the oral stimulation of the female genitalia by the man. Oral stimulation of the male genitalia by the woman occurs less often, and many times only because the man requests it, although some women also are aroused by it.

Some women may have sexual phantasies while masturbating, but almost all men do. On the other hand, some women can have phantasies that lead to orgasm without masturbation, yet it is the rare man who can reach a climax by phantasy unaccompanied by physical stimulation. Reik (1957) has found that women are more apt to phantasy while having intercourse than men are, usually imagining that they are being made love to by their "ideal" man, or that they are the most beautiful and desirable of women. This probably reflects the woman's greater tendency to romanticize sex.

The huge business transacted in pornography, almost all of which is produced for men, is further evidence of the male's capacity to be stimulated by material that has sexual associations for him. Many men are aroused by seeing portrayals of the nude or near-nude female form; very few women are aroused by pictures of the nude male figure. The female body—especially the genitalia and to a lesser degree the breasts, legs, and buttocks—similarly arouses most men. Most women are not aroused by the sight of the male genitalia. Interestingly enough, the same situation pertains to the infra-human species of mammals in which the male, grooming the female, will become interested in her genitals, whereas a female busy grooming the male will completely ignore his genitalia.

A great many males are aroused by seeing their own genitalia, whereas very few women receive any stimulation from the sight of their own genitals. Since he receives stimulation from observing his genitals, the male finds it difficult to understand that the woman does not, and may be keenly disappointed when she is not aroused by the sight of his organ. This difference is perhaps best illustrated by the homosexual activities of men and of women. Most male homosexual relationships begin with genital exposure, and the relationship itself is most likely to consist of genital stimulation. Female homosexuals, on the other hand, may engage in the stimulation of all parts of the body for a long time before attempting genital stimulation, and there are cases of women who have had homosexual relationships for a decade or more before beginning genital activity. Exhibitionism, an aberration in which sexual gratification is attained through the public exposure of one's genitals, is an exclusively male phenomenon. The only females who customarily expose their genitals publicly are those employed in certain types of entertainment that cater to male audiences. The performing woman receives no stimulation from her actions.

Given the opportunity to observe others in sexual activity, most men are aroused; most females are not. Portrayals of such activity in moving pictures and photographs are erotically stimulating to the majority of men. The man's capacity for greater arousal by what he sees is also reflected in the fact that many more men than women prefer intercourse in the light, which furnishes opportunity for him to view his own and the woman's body, and something of his sexual action as well. Like the exhibitionist, the voyeur ("Peeping Tom") is exclusively male. Obscene stories, too, are more stimulating to the men than to the women who hear them.

Men are aroused by thinking of women, of past sexual relationships, of the relationships they will have in the future. Women are less often stimulated by thoughts of sexual activity, although some females are more "erotically minded" than is the average male. The male usually enters into intercourse already sexually excited, whereas the female may require a great deal of physical stimulation to bring her to the level from which he started. Once aroused, the male is less easily distracted than the female. Any discontinuance of physical stimulation interrupts her response. The crying of a baby, the creaking of the bed, the thought of ironing to be done—such things as these divert women from the sexual act. This is true of other mammals, too; food placed before a copulating pair will distract the female, but not the male.

Women are more inclined to spiritualize their sexual reactions. Unlike the male, whose erect penis provides evidence of his genital involvement in sexual sensations, the female does not discover the connection between her genitals and emotions so easily. It is more difficult for her to localize her sexual tensions, and at the same time easier for her to repress any excitation she feels in the genital area. With her weaker sex drive and more passive biological role, she is better able than he to idealize her sexual feelings and to sublimate them into emotional values. This may help explain the fact that the only psychological stimuli that arouse women equally as much as men are moving pictures and love stories with strong romantic elements.

Needs of Sexual Relationship

The male's greater need for a variety of sexual partners is accepted in all human societies, which accordingly permit him more sexual freedom than the female is allowed. In American society twice as many husbands are unfaithful as wives. Women are more tolerant of the extramarital affairs of their mates; infidelity is given as the prime reason for divorce by men much more often than it is by women. The woman's capacity for fidelity may be based upon her feebler sexual impulse—she is not so often aroused, nor with such ease, nor by so many different things, as the male; her greater dependence upon the continuance of the marriage; and the risks of pregnancy and severe social censure.

However, much more than the man, the woman seeks emotional involvement in her sex life. For many men, ejaculation becomes the actual goal of the sexual relationship; for women, the goal is more likely to be the tender relationship with the man. This may be seen in their very different attitudes when intercourse is completed. The man, sexual tension relieved, wants to withdraw, to sleep. The sexually satisfied woman is reluctant to release him; she wants the penis to remain inside her, to keep him with her a longer time. Reik suggests that this is because the woman identifies the penis with the child the man can give her, the portion of himself that will live within her.

The existence of the world's oldest profession, prostitution, is in recognition of the greater sexual needs of the male. The prostitute is usually a woman who has sexual relations with men for pay, but there are male prostitutes, too. However, they usually serve the desires of homosexual men, not of women. Whereas the female prostitute in most cases does not respond sexually to her customer and does not experience orgasm, the male prostitute usually does. In fact, his capacity to achieve ejaculation is often part of the arrangement. Very infrequently do male prostitutes have professional contact with women seeking heterosexual intercourse.

Age and Sexual Capacity

There is an enormous difference between the sexes in the effect age has upon their biologic capacity. The man is at his peak of sexual activity in the mid-teens, the woman not at hers until the late twenties. But from the time he reaches his peak, the capacity of the man begins a steady decline, whereas once she has attained her maximum level the woman remains there until she is 60 years of age. Thus the man's sexual interest is greatest at the time the woman's is not; she becomes most responsive at the time his sexual capacity is beginning its decline. A recognizable proportion of the male population becomes impotent with age—about 5 per cent by the age of 60, and 30 per cent by the age of 70—and most men probably would if they lived long enough. However, the male retains his fertility. Many older men could father children but for the fact that they can no longer deliver the sperm. The female, on the other hand, loses her fertility with age, but not her potency. Many older men, whose sexual activity has diminished, do become more active when they find new sex partners, adopt new techniques, or participate in some other form of sexual activity. This may be further evidence of the male's reliance upon psychological stimuli.

The sex life of the man is not subject to the reproductive cycle, as is that of women. Most female mammals will copulate with the male only when they are in estrus and conception is most likely to occur. The human female will receive the male at any time, but in most women sexual desire does follow a regular cycle, dependent upon the secretion of ovarian hormone. Unlike the lower mammals, however, women experience greatest desire immediately before and immediately after the menstrual period, when they are least likely to conceive.

The males of some rodents and fur-bearing mammals produce sperm and hormonal secretions only during the mating season, but the sex glands of most other mammals and of human males secrete hormones at a fairly steady rate.

Nor is there anything in the male to compare with the menopause in women. The menopause, which marks the end of ovarian function and reproductive capacity, occurs in all women sometime after the age of 40. It may come on quite abruptly, or it may be a gradual process. Although it marks the end of her child-bearing years, it is not accompanied by any decrease in her sexual desire. On the contrary, many women, freed from the fear of an unwanted pregnancy, experience an increase in sexual desire. There are some who believe that the man undergoes a "change of life" in his middle years. With age, the secretion of testicular hormone does decrease, but this is in no way comparable to the female menopause. It is, however, accompanied by the diminution of sexual capacity, whereas the menopause in women is not.

Homosexuality

Among the primates and the vast majority of human societies in which it is known to occur, homosexuality is far more common among males than females. In American society, twice as many men as women become involved in homosexual relationships, and most men probably have at least one such experience sometime during their lives. Such activity among women is sporadic, which is typical of female sexual activity generally, except for marital intercourse, which is usually regulated by the desire of the husband.

Women are less promiscuous in such relationships than men. Often two women will live together in a homosexual relationship for many years; similar long-term liaisons are practically unknown among men. To some extent this reflects the male's desire for variety in his sex life and the psychological stimulation he derives in anticipating the activity with a new partner, but it also reflects society's greater condemnation of such affairs among men. Women are permitted, even expected, to display their affection and admiration for each other, and unmarried women may share a household without raising any eyebrows. Men who behaved in like fashion would be suspect. The Lesbian's ability to find repeated gratification with a single partner probably also reflects the woman's need for an emotional attachment to the partner with whom she finds sexual satisfaction.

Sexual Aberrations

Sexual contact with animals is rare in the population as a whole, but it occurs more frequently among men than women. Boys are more aroused by observing animals in intercourse than girls are, and Kinsey estimates that 17 per cent of those raised on farms experience orgasm as a result of animal contacts. Only 8 per cent of males ever have experience with animals, usually during adolescence, and approximately 3 per cent of women are similarly involved.

Fetishism, an aberration in which the individual can become sexually aroused and satisfied only in the presence of certain objects, is an almost exclusively male phenomenon; if it exists among women at all it is very rare. Some fetishists require the object in addition to the sexual partner; in the most complete form of the perversion the object alone is sufficient. Since the articles fetishists value bear some connection to their early sexual experiences, its prevalence among men probably depends upon their ability to become conditioned by sexual experiences.

The Kinsey researchers found that more men than women responded sexually to sadomasochistic stories, and conjectured that this was due to the male's capacity for phantasy. However, as many women as men found erotic stimulation in being bitten. Masochism, the securing of sexual satisfaction through pain inflicted on one's self, has been regarded as essentially feminine in character, whereas sadism, the securing of sexual satisfaction through inflicting pain on others, has been considered essentially masculine. It has been suggested that the greater natural passivity of women makes it easier for them to adopt masochistic perversions, and sadism in men is an extension of the normally male aggressive qualities. Some psychiatrists have held that the woman's willingness to be penetrated by the male and to suffer in bearing and protecting her children is masochistic in nature. Helene Deutsch asserts that a certain amount of masochism as a psychological preparation for adjustment to the sexual functions is necessary in woman, and cautions that the danger of pathological distortion arises from this situation.

References

Bonaparte, Marie, *Female Sexuality*. New York: International Universities Press, Inc., 1953.

Deutsch, Helene, *Psychology of Women* (Vol. 1, Girlhood). New York: Grune & Stratton, Inc., 1944.

Ellis, Albert (ed.), *Sex Life of the American Woman and the Kinsey Report*. New York: Greenberg, 1954.

Ellis, Albert, *The Art and Science of Love*. New York: Lyle Stuart, 1960.

Ellis, Havelock, *Man and Woman*. Boston: Houghton Mifflin Co., 1929.

Ford, Clellan S., and Beach, Frank A., *Patterns of Sexual Behavior*. New York: Harper & Brothers, 1951.

Gesell, Arnold, and Ilg, Frances L., *The Child from Five to Ten*. New York: Harper & Brothers, 1946.

Gesell, Arnold, Ilg, Frances L., and Ames, Louise B., *Youth, the Years from Ten to Sixteen*. New York: Harper & Brothers, 1956.

Kinsey, A. C. *et al.*, *Sexual Behavior in the Human Male*. Philadelphia: W. B. Saunders Co., 1948.

Kinsey, A. C. *et al.*, *Sexual Behavior in the Human Female*. Philadelphia: W. B. Saunders Co., 1953.

Mead, Margaret, *Male and Female*. New York: William Morrow & Co., Inc., 1949.

Pollak, Otto, *The Criminality of Women*. Philadelphia: University of Pennsylvania Press, 1950.

Reik, Theodor, *Of Love and Lust*. New York: Farrar, Straus and Cudahy, Inc., 1957.

Scheinfeld, Amram, *Women and Men*. New York: Harcourt, Brace & Co., 1943.

Seward, Georgene, *Sex and the Social Order*. New York: McGraw-Hill Book Co., 1946.

Zimmerman, Carle C., and Cervantes, Lucius F., *Marriage and the Family*. Chicago: Henry Regnery Co., 1956.

EDWARD DENGROVE

Sex Drive

THE literature on human sexual behavior contains many references to "sex drive." Sex drive is used as an explanation for the occurrence of various kinds of sexual behavior, or as a description of the nature of sex itself. Yet when we attempt to find precisely what is being discussed, or what elements are included in sex drive we are baffled. The term is very loosely used by most speakers and writers. They proceed upon the assumption that the phrase "sex drive" will convey an equivalent meaning to all.

The Nature of Sex Drive

Actually, there are widely contrasting views concerning the real nature of the sex drive and whether its strength is determined mainly by physiological or by psychological components, or by both. Our knowledge of the characteristics and nature of the human sex drive is in the process of clarification, and this process is unlikely to be completed for some time to come. One reason our knowledge is so uncertain is that it is difficult to know how and where to begin with the needed research. The kinds of data needed to confirm or disprove hypotheses are by nature most difficult to obtain from human subjects.

Conditions being what they are, however, theories and decisions concerning the nature of the sex drive have not awaited elaborate research. The pressures of life have made some assumptions immediately necessary.

Physiological Explanations

A very common assumption has been that the sex drive is "physiological" or "biological" in nature. Individual differences in sexual strivings have been explained on the basis of differences in biological endowments. This assumption has seemed reasonable, for certainly at puberty there is an increased interest in sex and sexual experiences in both male and female. Reproductive capacities mature at this time and maturation is accompanied by obvious physiological developments. Glandular activity and the secretion of certain hormones accompany the pubertal processes, and they are certainly associated in some way with an increasing interest in and concern with sex.

Numerous writers have given very explicit expression to the assumption that the strength of the sex drive is physiologically generated, and that it is directly determined by chemical and hormonal secretions. The quotation that follows clearly exemplifies this point of view. Theodor Reik (1945) writes:

> . . . the crude sex-drive is a biological need which represents the instinct and is conditioned by chemical changes within the organism. The urge is dependent on inner secretions, and its aim is the relieving of a physical tension. . . .
>
> The crude sex-urge is easily satisfied and is entirely incapable of being sublimated. If it is strongly excited, it needs, in its urgency, an immediate release. It cannot be deflected from its one aim to different aims, or at most can be as little diverted as the need to urinate or as hunger and thirst. It insists on gratification in its original realm. The satisfaction of this particular urge cannot be fulfilled by the substitution of another goal.

Other writers who present very similar points of view include Brown and Kempton (1950), Kardiner (1954), Reich (1945), and Walker (1954).

Knowledge regarding the hormones—their

chemical composition, the nature of their interactions, and their effect upon various bodily functions, including sexual functions—has come slowly. It has advanced much more rapidly in recent years, but even yet is incomplete.

Most ancient and primitive peoples linked the male testes with the processes of reproduction and physical maturation. This association commonly included both human males and males in subhuman species. The capacity for, and the interest in, sexual activities by the males of various species was recognized as being dependent upon the possession of testes. Although the specific explanations for the observable effects of the loss of the testes were unscientific, it was clear that their early loss affected physical development and made reproduction impossible.

Several hormones, or chemical substances, which, created within the body, have significant effects upon various bodily functions were isolated during the nineteenth century. Important among these are the hormones secreted by the testes in the male and the ovaries in the female, commonly referred to as the gonadal, or sex, hormones. These hormones, in combination with others, have important effects upon various sexual and reproductive processes. They are associated with the processes that result in reproductive maturity, with the appearance of secondary sexual characteristics, and with psychic changes. It has also been believed that these hormones determine the degree of intensity of the sex drive.

Much doubt is now being cast upon the validity of the presumed relationship between castration and the intensity of the sex drive. In Chapter 18, "Hormonal Factors in Sexual Response," of *Sexual Behavior in the Human Female,* Kinsey and his associates bring together research data relating to the effect of hormones on the sexual behavior of both men and women. The primary purpose was to relate the effects of the injection of hormones, or of castration, and the consequent alteration of the hormonal balance in the body to possible alterations in sex behavior and, by inference, to changes in intensity of the sex drive.

Evidence indicates that the administration of male hormones (androgens) to either humans or animals may increase the general level of sexual response. Reports concerning the effects of the administration of the female hormones (estrogens) on sexual behavior and responsiveness are confused and contradictory. Some reports indicate that the level of sexual responsiveness is raised; others indicate no such consequence.

Neither does any clear picture emerge when the effects of castration on humans are studied. In some instances the amount of sexual activity is somewhat or markedly decreased, in others it is apparently either little changed or not affected at all. The picture is further confused by other factors, including (1) the inability to isolate the effect on sexual performance of such factors as aging, or the psychic effects of castration; (2) uncertainty concerning the physiological compensations the body may make to the loss of certain hormones through castration, or the effect that other hormones may have on the sexual processes; (3) uncertainty concerning the accuracy of the reports from castrated persons as to the effect of castration on their sexual performance; and (4) inadequate or poorly controlled comparisons between the sexual performance of castrates and noncastrates.

Beach (1948), after surveying studies of male castration, concludes:

Despite the frequency and possibly the accuracy of generalization regarding the depressing consequences of human castration, the literature is replete with references of complete retention of sexual function in individuals who have been castrated for many years.

After marshaling the evidence that is surveyed in Chapter 18, Kinsey and his associates conclude:

While hormonal levels may affect the levels of sexual response—the intensity of response, the frequency of response, the frequency of overt sexual activity—there is no demonstrated relationship between any of the hormones and an individual's response to particular sorts of psychologic stimuli, an individual's interest in partners of a particular sex, or an individual's utilization of particular techniques in his or her sexual activity. Within limits, the levels of sexual response may be modified by reducing or increasing the amount of available hormone, but there seems to be no reason for believing that the patterns of sexual behavior may be modified by hormonal therapy.

NEED FOR ELIMINATION

One of the earlier explanations of the adolescent sex drive was a strictly physiological one. The idea was that prolonged sexual abstinence resulted in the accumulation of secretions that were stored in certain glands of the reproductive system. These glands became engorged and this condition gave rise to nerve impulses, which in turn resulted in sex urges. Eventually, if no other outlet was provided, these secretions were discharged as nocturnal seminal emissions. This view resulted in the advice proffered the adolescent boy that he set up "controls" and endure his discomfort, i.e., avoid masturbation. In time he would be provided a natural release. Although current evidence indicates this explanation to be in error, it is still found in some writings.

Thus, Dr. Ernest Harms (1957) ties the sex urge very specifically to physiological functioning and eliminative needs. He comments, with his own emphases:

Throughout our social world there is a basic sex urge which is *not*, as we have pointed out before, identical with an urge to create offspring, or, as commonly expressed, "to raise a family." *The sex urge is caused rather by a physiological need for elimination.*

Dr. Harms, however, evidently sees the possibility of psychological or cultural forces influencing the sex urge, for immediately before writing the sentences just quoted he said, "Male and female in our society live under the influence of constant sexual stimulation with naturally induced hormonic and spermatic activity."

DRIVE RELATED TO AGE AND VIGOR

Kinsey's work, whether or not he intended it to have that effect, has done a great deal to fix the idea that the sex drive is very markedly a function of age and physical vigor. This relationship is regarded as applying particularly to males. The data that have contributed to this view are those concerned with total sexual outlet, and with age and sexual outlet. These data are found in Chapters 6 and 7 of *Sexual Be-*

havior in the Human Male. In these chapters Dr. Kinsey is concerned with the frequency of "sexual outlets." He finds that, quantitatively speaking, the highest frequency of experiencing orgasm is between the ages of 16 and 20. These data have been interpreted by many persons to mean that the male sex drive is strongest during the teen years. Thus, Kardiner (1954), in speaking of Kinsey's data, writes, "We learn that the peak of the sexual power of the male is in adolescence and from that time on gradually declines."

SEX AND HUNGER AS ANALOGUES

The belief that the sex drive is dependent upon and conditioned by physiological factors has led some writers to draw an analogy between the desire for sexual expression and the need for satisfying pangs of hunger and thirst. Blood (1955), for example, makes this comparison:

As another biological drive, sex is similar to hunger in many respects. Under the influence of hormonal secretions, sexual tension is felt. This tension sometimes assumes a compelling force, preoccupying the mind, making the individual restless and tense. Aroused by the sexual drive, the individual may engage in what he would normally consider reckless behavior. . . . The biological nature of the sex drive is reflected in the changes that occur as people grow older. Just as growing children at certain ages have ravenous appetites for food, so the sex drive is stronger at some ages than others.

Beach (1956), who is a physiological psychologist of note and a student of animal sexual behavior, questions the validity of this analogy. He points to certain differences, which to him mean possibly that "the two categories of drives have different evolutionary histories and will be found to obey different kinds of laws."

Beach notes that, whereas the lack of food and drink may cause death, the lack of sex has never killed anyone. He points out that when the organism is deprived of food and water a serious state of tissue need arises, and that if these needs are not met death eventually results. As food and water are supplied, the deprived organism moves toward a condition of tissue satisfaction and a state of satiation and well-being ensues.

The sexual appetite operates in reverse fashion. No serious tissue or biological need results from prolonged sexual abstinence. Indulgence in unlimited sexual activity results in a depletion of energy and, if continued long enough, the organism reaches a state of exhaustion. This condition is relieved by refraining from further sex activity for a period of time.

There are two other differences between sex and hunger as physiological states, according to Beach. The first is that the satisfaction of hunger is essential for the preservation of individual life, whereas sexual satisfaction is essential for the preservation of the species rather than the individual. The second is that sexual desires are aroused by external stimuli to "a much greater extent than is true of hunger or thirst."

With the latter observation Beach allies himself with those who give much weight to the belief that psychological factors are strongly influential in determining the degree of sex urgency or drive. Thus, Beach comments:

The adolescent boy's periodic preoccupation with sexual matters is traceable to psychological stimuli, external or phantasied, and is not dependent upon his recently matured reproductive glands. His erotic urges stem more from socio-cultural factors than from those of a strictly physiological nature.

Psychological Explanations

No one seems disposed to deny a physiological basis for sexuality, or to argue that sex drive has no relationship to physiology. An increasing number of persons, however, are coming to regard psychological components as very important, and probably of considerably more significance than the physiological component, in determining the urgency of the sex drive in the normal person.

In the following quotation Dr. Robert L. Dickinson (1940) went beyond those references which imply that the sex drive is a unitary physical force. He spoke of "endowment, capacity, and drive," and he tied the three very closely to physiological conditions. In his last sentence, however, Dr. Dickinson indicated his awareness that other than physical factors may have a bearing on the intensity of the sex drive.

The strain upon emotional balance (of the unmarried) probably is primarily in proportion to the functional vigor of the particular pair of glands, male or female, and its resistance to suppression. . . . The new knowledge of our internal chemistry and of the hormones or "excitants" makes it quite clear why there may be enormous differences in sex endowment, capacity and drive in different people. This reveals a status that is based upon physical factors instead of representing, as we had supposed, a matter of morals in resisting or in yielding to temptation. Here again a new orientation is in order.

Only an ample series of case histories and physical examinations will enable us to determine what part of a sex urge or excessive stress is the result of regular or seasonal cycles of hormone production, and what part is activated by mental preoccupations with stimulative ideas or by exposure to influences calculated to render alert and active the function of the sex organs.

Some anthropological studies have reported that the urgency of sexual needs in some societies seems to be no match for the urgency in most of our modern civilizations. The anthropologists refer in particular to societies that have allowed and accepted a free-and-easy access of the sexes to each other from puberty on.

Papers by psychologists and psychiatrists, reflecting both psychiatric research and clinical experience, emphasize that compulsive or obsessive use of sex (which by many would be regarded as evidence of a strong sex drive) is the result of emotional instability and immaturity in personality.

Between 1943 and 1947 the Psychiatric Service of the San Francisco (California) City Clinic made a study of 287 promiscuous and 78 potentially promsicuous girls and 255 promiscuous men. The writers who reported these studies drew conclusions supporting the view that the urge which led to a promiscuous use of sex arose from psychological causes. In reporting the results of a two-year study on promiscuous women, Lion and his co-authors (1945) wrote:

Some personality characteristics were common to the patients as a group. Noteworthy among these was the uneven development in the areas of physical, intellectual, emotional, and social maturity for individual patients. . . . Before they left home, group experiences through recreational, club, and extracurricular school activities, which are helpful to the individual in learning his place in an adult society, had been at a minimum. As a result, ability to accept organized group experiences was lacking or limited. Usually their associates were men and women, who like themselves, had not reached maturity although they attempted to fulfill the adult role. . . . Immaturity in characterological development was prevalent and was expressed especially in the patients' inability and unwillingness to assume responsibility for their behavior. Allocation of blame upon parents, husbands, and others to account for their own shortcomings was common. . . .

Contrary to popular belief, no evidence was revealed to indicate that this problem is produced by above average sex drive. In fact, *the majority of habitually promiscuous patients used promiscuity in an attempt to meet other problems rather than in an attempt to secure direct sexual satisfaction.* . . . (Italics in the original.)

Safier and co-authors (1949), reporting the results of an investigation at the same clinic for promiscuous men, said:

Promiscuity . . . was revealed to be a problem in interpersonal relationships. The degree of (sexual) satisfaction experienced by the promiscuous men was greater than that experienced by the promiscuous women; however, it appeared that in many cases, as with the women, promiscuity was engaged in an attempt to solve other problems. In nearly all cases this behavior appeared to be the result of conflicts, inadequacies, or disorganization within the personality. Incapacity for sustained love relationships or impairment of that capacity was revealed by almost every patient. Active hostility toward women was present in varying degrees among some of the men. . . .

. . . no evidence could be secured that promiscuity was the result of greater than average sex drive. With the exception of two patients the men did not themselves offer this explanation, and in those two cases it appeared that this explanation was a rationalization offered to cover up difficulties in relationship to women and sexual conflicts. Neither clinical data nor Rorschach studies revealed greater than average sensuality.

Although the authors quoted above did not discuss their assumptions concerning the origin or nature of sex drive, they were apparently assuming a "biologically" or "physiologically" induced drive.

Maslow (1954), who has made extensive studies of self-actualizing (exceptionally mature) people, discussed the place of sexual needs in the lives of these people. He wrote that for these people an orgasm

. . . is often a profound and almost mystical experience, and yet the absence of sexuality is more easily tolerated by these people. This is not a paradox or a contradiction. It follows from dynamic motivation theory. Loving at a higher need level makes the lower needs and their frustrations and satisfactions less important, less central, more easily neglected. But it also makes them more wholeheartedly enjoyed when gratified.

The excerpts just quoted, then, support the view that the use made of sex, and inferentially the strength of the sex drive, is markedly conditioned by the personal adjustment and emotional stability of the individual. The strength of the sex drive is determined much more by psychological needs than by physiological factors.

Sexual offenders are sometimes regarded as persons who have an intense physical sex drive. In the past decade several states of the United States, notably Oregon, California, Michigan, and New Jersey, have established commissions to investigate the cause and treatment of sexual offenses. The opinion that always emerges from these investigations is, to quote a report from an Oregon legislative committee (1956),

. . . [the fact] that sexual deviation is so regularly associated with inadequate families leads to the assumption that disorganization within the family may be the primary cause.

. . . although disorganization within the family is probably the primary cause, scientists generally are in agreement that the sex deviate is produced by a combination of all early childhood experiences, relationships and environment over a considerable period of time.

When discussing sexual deviates the influence of the sex drive is not always considered directly. When it is, it seems usually to be regarded as physiologically determined, and conclusions such as the one made by Avery (1953) result:

... it is difficult to evaluate the intensity of sex drives and the degree of preoccupation with sex for any group of persons, but, insofar as studies have been possible, they indicate that deviated sex offenders are *undersexed* rather than oversexed. (Emphasis by Avery.)

The nature of the sex drive, then, has not been fully established, but the importance of psychological factors seems to be increasingly emphasized. More and more, individual differences in sexual strivings and in the strength of the sexual urge are being explained in terms of personal and social experiences.

The Components of Sexual Responsiveness

This writer has suggested in another article (1958) still another approach to an understanding of sex drive—that of subdividing it into three components, sexual performance, sexual capacity, and sexual drive. A clear distinction between what one can do (capacity), what one does do (performance), and how strongly one desires or strives to do (drive) would be extremely helpful.

Sexual capacity is determined by the ability of the nervous and muscular systems to respond to sexual stimuli by orgasm and to recuperate from that experience to the point where orgasm can again be experienced. This capacity varies from person to person and probably represents the actual physical sex difference between individuals.

Performance, although limited at its upper extreme by capacity, will ordinarily vary according to physical and psychological factors. Performance is not an accurate measure of capacity because few, if any, persons perform to full capacity.

Drive is the strength or the intensity with which the individual wishes to perform. Drive seems to be very largely a psychologically conditioned component and may vary considerably from individual to individual and from time to time in the same individual.

A breakdown of this sort was seemingly in Dr. Dickinson's mind when he used the terms "endowment, capacity and drive" in the paragraph previously quoted.

Dr. Kinsey (1948) also seemed to recognize

that certain distinctions were needed. Thus, in *Sexual Behavior in the Human Male*, he differentiated between sexual capacity and sexual performance:

... It is probable that in a population which married at an earlier age, the highest frequency on the curve would come in the earlier adolescent group; but, in our society as it is, the high point of sexual performance is, in actuality, somewhere around 16 or 17 years of age. It is not later. The data which have already been given on the sexual capacity of the pre-adolescent boy (Chapter 5) indicate that the peak of *capacity* occurs in the fast-growing years prior to adolescence; but the peak of *actual performance* is in the middle or late teens. (Emphases by Kinsey.)

Only two pages further on, however, Kinsey seemed to confuse capacity and performance:

The identification of the sexually most active period as late adolescence will come as a surprise to most persons. General opinion would probably have placed it in the middle twenties or later. Certainly the average college student and the town boy of corresponding age will be startled to learn that their younger brothers who are still in high school surpass them in capacity and ofttimes in performance.

It is reasonable to expect that sexual performance in males will reach a peak in adolescence, for this is the period at which sexual curiosity is at its peak. According to Dr. Kinsey's data, on the average the peak of male performance comes only a year or so after sexual maturity. Curiosity and the novelty of having developed a new, exciting, and exhilarating capacity results in a high frequency of masturbation. At this age sexual functioning often has the same meaning as a new toy. It is something to try out, to experiment with, and to enjoy. Also, boys experience an immediate and highly localized pleasure as a result of handling their genital organs.

Adolescence is the period at which in certain respects the nervous system is very responsive to hormonal secretions. It is this responsiveness that determines sexual capacity. And, because the adolescent boy's neural mechanism responds readily to many kinds of stimulation, he experiences many erections. This may be the result of an incapacity of the newly activated neural mechanism to assort stimuli and channel them to the appropriate affectors—an ability that is developed later. The result is that the boy has erections at times when he is not excited by specifically sexual stimuli, probably because the tensions produced by various worries, fears, or frustrations are communicated to the nervous system, which in turn produces erections—and a desire for release. Thus, a boy may have an erection while sitting tensely in class at school or during the excitement of fast auto driving. Adolescent boys very frequently find themselves with erections upon awakening, and at other times during the day when they have not been excited by the usual sexual stimuli.

These circumstances easily explain sexual experimentation and the spontaneous discovery of masturbation. Erections and sexual tensions direct the boy's attention toward his genitals. He engages in genital play, discovers masturbation, and accepts it as a quick, pleasurable way of releasing tensions.

Another factor conditioning the level of performance at any age is opportunity. Opportunity will affect any kind of sexual behavior. Certainly no one can have heterosexual intercourse or a homosexual experience if no partner is available.

One of the reasons for the higher rate of orgasm frequency of adolescent boys as compared with that of adolescent girls is probably the physical formation and availability of the genital organs of the two sexes. A boy's attention is drawn to his genitals more easily than is a girl's. The penis is often erect and tense. It is easy to manipulate, and pleasure from manipulation comes quickly and easily. It seems natural that boys should masturbate more than girls.

Sexually "high-performers," assuming that they have a very responsive nervous system, may receive more pleasure from sexual activity and may therefore strive for more orgasms than "low-performers." Even so, they may still fall short of performing up to their full sexual capacity.

Several case histories will illustrate how the components of drive, capacity, and performance are related. Data involving two young men, A and B, will be compared. A was 20 years, 7 months of age, and B was 20 years, 6

months of age at the time the writer knew them.

A was very active sexually. He had masturbated during adolescence from 7 to 10 times a week. He had had intercourse with twenty partners, several of them with high frequencies and over a fairly long period of time. He still masturbated, sometimes daily, although not as frequently as before. A talked considerably about the strength of his sex drive, which he felt was much above the average.

B had used masturbation since he was about 13, but with a frequency of no more than 3 or 4 times a week. His capacity for multiple orgasms, however, increased the total number of outlets. He had had intercourse with four persons, but with three on a single occasion only. The fourth one was his partner on three occasions, all within a two-week period. At the time of interviewing masturbatory activity had dropped to a frequency of about twice a month. His comment was that his sex drive was not particularly strong, and his sex pattern bore this out.

B, however, had a marked capacity for sexual response. During his twentieth year he said he was able to reach 10 orgasms in 30 minutes, and he had a verified performance of 13 orgasms in one hour during that same year. These were attained by masturbation rather than by intercourse.

A, apprised of B's performance, commented, "I couldn't begin to touch it." This has been the reaction of several other high-performers.

Here, then, we have a situation in which B, who probably has a much higher sexual capacity than A, definitely seems to have a lower sex drive than A.

Still another boy, aged 22, rated his sex drive as not pressing and easily manageable. He reported that he had achieved 10 orgasms in 1 hour by masturbation, but his performance record was considerably below that of many other boys who considered that their sex drive was much stronger than he considered his.

Another boy, aged 22, reported 9 orgasms with one erection over a period of 45 minutes, this in masturbation. The report was unverified but apparently reliable. In this instance capacity was accompanied by a relatively strong sex drive.

Beach (1956) has been interested in the

processes involved in the operation of the sex drive. His studies on the sexual behavior of male rats have led him to postulate two partially independent physiological and neural mechanisms which function in sexual arousal and release. One is a sexual arousal mechanism (SAM), which operates to increase the male's sexual excitement to the point that copulation is possible (the copulatory threshold). The second is the intromission-ejaculation mechanism (IEM), which makes intromission possible and provides a source of sensory impulses. These sensory impulses increase in intensity until eventually the male arrives at the ejaculatory threshold. The chief difference between man and the lower animals is the greater tendency in man for the sexual arousal mechanism to be influenced by symbolic factors.

Male and Female Contrasted

Most of the literature on the human sex drive relates to the male. There has, however, been speculation about the relative strength of the sex drive in men and women. In the Western culture it is common to regard the male sex drive as stronger and more imperious than that of the female. This has not always been so. At other times and in other cultures the sex drive of the female has been regarded as the stronger. This view concerning the feminine sex drive was expressed by many European writers from 1500 to 1800.

Havelock Ellis believed that women seldom showed a complete absence of sexual emotion. He regarded sexual coldness and unresponsiveness in women as the result of faulty education and the inculcation of social inhibitions. He felt that there was no biological incapacity for sexual response.

The data collected by investigators such as G. V. Hamilton (1929), R. L. Dickinson and Laura Beam (1934), and Katherine B. Davis (1929) seemed to point to the same conclusion: they found that the achievement of orgasm through masturbation was common among the women participating in their studies. Dr. Kinsey (1953), after surveying the data previously collected and analyzing his own, concluded that in 95 per cent or more of all

her masturbatory experiences the female reaches an orgasm.

As scientific investigations are extended, more and more similarities between males and females are identified. Sexual feelings, reactions, and responses arise from physical structures that are practically identical in the two sexes. Orgasmic response is very similar in male and female, and little or no difference is found in their capacity to respond quickly to sexual stimuli. The two sexes do respond to different sexual stimuli, however. The male responds to a wider range of visual and psychological stimuli than does the female. Since in heterosexual association the stimuli that produce excitation in the male ordinarily come into consciousness first, this gives rise to the impression that men are more quickly excited than women.

After extensive comparisons of male and female sexual manifestations, Dr. Kinsey and his colleagues (1953) conclude:

In spite of the widespread and oft-repeated emphasis on the supposed differences between female and male sexuality, we fail to find any anatomic or physiologic basis for such differences. Although we . . . find differences in the psychologic and hormonal factors which affect the responses of the two sexes . . . males would be better prepared to understand females, and females to understand males, if they realized that they are alike in their basic anatomy and physiology.

Dr. Kinsey (1953) also attempts to dispose of certain erroneous or misconceived explanations for observed differences between the sexual responses of females and males. He writes that it "has been suggested that there are differences in the levels of 'sex drive' or 'libido' or innate moral capacities of the two sexes." The context of his discussion makes it clear that he does not support this point of view.

He does feel that "hormonal levels may affect levels of sexual response." The paragraph expressing this viewpoint has already been quoted.

Comparison of the data on sexual performance of males and of females has introduced a concept of differential response which is important. These data, Dr. Kinsey concludes, indicate the

. . . early development of sexual responsiveness in the human male and its later development in the female, the location of the period of maximum responsiveness for the male in the late teens and early twenties and for the female in the late twenties, the subsequent decline of the male's sexual capacities from that peak into old age, and the maintenance of female responsiveness on something of a level throughout most of her life.

Throughout the above quotation Dr. Kinsey used "response" and "responsiveness" frequently. He has not used the expression "drive" or "power." But if Dr. Kinsey avoided the use of these words others have not, and these performance data have been interpreted as showing that "the female sex drive reaches its peak several years after the male drive has begun to decline, and that this disparity in drive may lead to difficulties in marital sex adjustment." Here is another situation in which a distinction between performance, capacity, and drive might bring us nearer the truth.

The study made in England by Dr. Eustace Chesser (1956) contains data corroborating the idea that differences in male-female drive may well be due to environmental factors. He found that nine-tenths of married women who never achieved orgasm in their marital intercourse felt that men had stronger sexual desires than women. Of those who always or frequently attained an orgasm in marital intercourse, only three-fifths felt that the sexual needs of men were greater than those of women. Dr. Chesser thought that these differences might be construed, for the unresponsive group, as an expression of marital and sexual discord, and for the responsive group as a reflection of their own satisfactory sex lives. In other words, the more women were able to find satisfaction and pleasure in their sexual relationships, the more nearly they regarded their sexual needs and desires as equal to the males.

Conclusion

The data that are available would seem to warrant certain conclusions.

1. In their essential features the sex drives of men and women are very much alike. Such points of difference as do exist are due to environmental and psychological factors rather than to innate, biological characteristics.

2. The trend has been toward breaking the concept of sex drive into components. There is not yet agreement on what these components are, or just how they are interrelated.

3. More and more, variations in sex drive are being attributed to psychological rather than physical or biological factors.

If and as these points of view are substantiated, they will influence thinking about sex education and sexual conduct. Some of the unrealistic distinctions between the sexes may disappear. The validity of the double standard of sexual conduct will be further challenged. Sex behavior will be recognized as subject to modification, and will therefore be increasingly the object of attention among educators. In counseling, sexual problems will be clearly recognized as a part of the total behavior pattern.

References

Avery, Curtis E., *An Introduction to the Problem of the Sexual Deviate.* Portland, Oregon: E. C. Brown Trust, 1953.

Beach, Frank A., *Hormones and Behavior.* New York: Paul B. Hoeber, Inc., 1948.

Beach, Frank A., "Characteristics of Masculine Sex Drive." *Nebraska Symposium on Motivation.* Lincoln, Neb.: University of Nebraska Press, 1956, pp. 1-32.

Blood, Robert O., *Anticipating Your Marriage.* Glencoe, Ill.: Free Press, 1955, pp. 113-15.

Brown, Fred, and Kempton, Rudolph T., *Sex Questions and Answers.* New York: McGraw-Hill Book Co., 1950, pp. 130-31.

Chesser, Eustace, *The Sexual, Marital, and Family Relationship of the English Woman.* London: Hutchinson's Medical Publications, 1956, p. 450.

Davis, Katherine B., *Factors in the Sex Life of 2,200 Women.* New York and London: Harper & Brothers, 1929.

Dickinson, Robert L., "Medical Reflections upon Some Life Histories." In Ira S. Wile, *The Sex Life of the Unmarried Adult.* New York: The Vanguard Press, 1940, pp. 201-202.

Dickinson, R. L., and Beam, L., *The Single Woman.* Baltimore: The Williams & Wilkins Co., 1934.

Ellis, Albert, *The Art and Science of Love.* New York: Lyle Stuart, 1960.

Ellis, Havelock, *Man and Woman.* Boston and New York: Houghton Mifflin Co., 1929.

Ford, C. S., and Beach, F. A., *Patterns of Sexual Behavior.* New York: Harper & Brothers, 1951.

Hamilton, G. V., *A Research in Marriage*. New York: Albert & Charles Boni, 1929.

Harms, Ernest, "Elimination as a Major Basic Factor in the Total Human Sex Life." *J. Fam. Welfare 3;* 158-167, July, 1957.

Kardiner, Abram, *Sex and Morality*. Indianapolis: The Bobbs-Merrill Co., 1954, pp. 30, 64.

Kinsey, Alfred C. *et al., Sexual Behavior in the Human Male*. Philadelphia: W. B. Saunders Co., 1948.

Kinsey, Alfred C. *et al., Sexual Behavior in the Human Female*. Philadelphia: W. B. Saunders Co., 1953.

Kirkendall, Lester A., "Toward a Clarification of the Concept of Male Sex Drive." *Marr. & Fam. Living, 20;* 367-72, November, 1958.

Lion, Ernest G. *et al., An Experiment in the Psychiatric Treatment of Promiscuous Girls*. San Francisco, Calif.: City and County of San Francisco, Department of Public Health, 1945.

Maslow, A. H., *Motivation and Personality*. New York: Harper & Brothers, 1954, pp. 242-43.

Reich, Wilhelm, *The Sexual Revolution*. New York: Orgone Institute Press, 1945, p. 80.

Reik, Theodor, *Psychology of Sex Relations*. New York: Rinehart & Co., Inc., 1945, p. 90.

Safier, Benno, *A Psychiatric Approach to the Treatment of Promiscuity*. New York: American Social Hygiene Association, 1949.

State of Oregon, *Report of the Legislative Interim Committee to Study Sex Crime Prevention*. Portland, Oregon: State Office Building, 1956.

Walker, Kenneth, "The Celibate Male." *Practitioner, 172;* 412-13, April, 1954.

LESTER A. KIRKENDALL

Sex Offenders, The Psychology of

Definition

A SEX offense is any sex act which, in a given jurisdiction, is legally prohibited and penalized. A sex offender is an individual who commits a legally banned and punishable sex act. Most sex offenders (like most nonsex offenders) are never arrested or convicted for the acts they commit; consequently, the term "sex offender" is commonly used only in connection with convicted offenders—that is, those who have actually been apprehended and convicted of committing a legally banned sex act.

Classification of Sex Offenses

Many statutes listing sex offenses are vaguely worded and include such terms as "carnal abuse," "open lewdness," "sodomy," and "unnatural practices." These terms might—and often do—mean almost anything and vary widely in meaning from one legislative jurisdiction to another (Ellis and Brancale, 1956). If we look behind this semantic confusion we find that the actual sex acts that are commonly prohibited and penalized are as follows:

Forcible sexual assault—forcing a female to submit to sexual advances but stopping short of coitus. Mild sexual assault includes such acts as intent to kiss, embrace, or look under a woman's skirt; serious assault includes intent to rape, to force oral-genital contacts, etc.

Forcible rape—coitus with a female engaged in as a result of actual force or duress. Rape is often held to have been committed if the man's penis touched the woman's vulva, even though complete penetration did not take place.

Statutory rape—coitus with a female under the legal age of consent (which is usually 16 to 18 years) even though it is engaged in voluntarily, without the use of force or duress.

Incest—coitus with a close relative, such as copulation between a father and daughter, mother and stepson, brother and sister, etc.

Noncoital sex relations with a minor—noncoital contacts with an individual under the legal age of consent; or verbal sex acts with an individual under the legal age of consent (for example, talking about sex to children, impairing the morals of a minor, etc.).

Exhibitory sex acts—exhibiting the genitals to another individual in an active, aggressive manner; masturbating in public; urinating or defecating in public; appearing without sufficient clothing in public.

Obscenity—making indecent or offensive proposals to a member of the other sex; using improper language in public; disseminating "obscene" material.

Homosexuality—having sex relations with a member of the same sex.

Transvestism—dressing in the clothing of a member of the other sex and appearing in public so dressed (except for purposes of public entertainment).

Voyeurism—spying on nude people or on the sex activities of others.

Sex murder—finding sex arousal or satisfaction in the course of killing another.

Bestiality—having sex relations with animals.

Sodomy—having any kind of "unnatural" sex act, which, according to many statutes, includes homosexuality, bestiality, or oral-genital relations between consenting men and women.

Adultery—coitus between individuals at least one of whom is married to another person.

Fornication—coitus, or at least habitual coitus, between two unmarried individuals.

Prostitution—engaging in coitus or other sex relations for monetary gains.

Pimping or pandering—soliciting males to patronize a prostitute; soliciting girls to work as prostitutes.

Brothel-keeping—managing a house of prostitution.

Psychological Classification of Sex Offenders

Sex offenders need not necessarily be sex deviates or perverts and they may or may not be psychologically disturbed. Statutory rape, for example, or intercourse between underage individuals, is an exceptionally common occurrence in most parts of the world and is usually psychologically normal. However, if an adult male *mainly* or *only* has coitus with underage females and if he continues to do so in spite of the real danger of his being detected and legally penalized, he is to be strongly suspected of being an emotionally disturbed individual.

It is useful to differentiate between *sexually* and *psychologically* (or *psychiatrically*) deviated offenders. A sexually deviated offender is one who commits an offense because he is fearfully or obsessively-compulsively driven to a kind of sex behavior (such as homosexuality) that happens to be legally banned in his community. The fear or hostility that drives him to his offense is specifically *sexual* or linked to *sex* behavior (he may be afraid of failing in heterosexual affairs or may be hostile toward women and therefore may become exclusively homosexual).

A *psychologically* deviated offender is an individual who commits *any* offense, sexual or nonsexual, because he is driven fearfully or rebelliously to defying some public ordinance. Thus, a psychologically deviated offender may be afraid that he is weak and "unmanly" or may be generally hostile to people and he may

therefore resort to stealing or arson—or to some sex offense, such as rape.

A given offender, therefore, may be either sexually or psychologically deviated; or he may be both. Virtually all consistent delinquents or criminals are either mentally deficient or seriously emotionally disturbed—otherwise they would not keep committing offenses that usually place themselves in serious jeopardy. Many sex criminals are disturbed in exactly the same manner as are nonsex criminals, except that their crime happens to be a sex offense. Many of them, in fact, commit a considerable number of nonsexual in addition to sexual offenses.

Sex offenders may be divided, then, into four main categories: (1) Normal sex offenders who are not sex deviates or psychologically disturbed (e.g., many fornicators or adulterers); (2) Sexually but not psychologically deviated offenders (e.g., voyeurs who may be sexually overshy but who may not be *generally* disturbed); (3) Sexually as well as psychologically deviated offenders (e.g., compulsive exhibitionists who have a specific sex problem and who also are generally hostile and reckless and keep getting themselves into trouble); and (4) Psychologically but not sexually deviated offenders (e.g., psychotic individuals who masturbate in public or walk naked in the streets not because they have a specific sexual deviation but because they are generally emotionally ill).

Incidence of Sex Offenses

No highly reliable reports of the incidence of sex offenses have ever been published because of the inherent difficulties of gathering statistics in this field. Most actual offenders, as pointed out previously, are never arrested; many of those who are arrested are not convicted in spite of the fact that they clearly committed a statutory offense; many of those who are convicted are allowed to plead guilty to lesser charges (such as loitering, assault and battery, or disorderly conduct). Consequently, individuals who are finally convicted of a specific sex offense (and on whom we do have some statistics) represent only a relatively small percentage of actual offenders. Technically, as Kinsey and his associates (1948) validly point out, so many sex acts are legally banned in our society that some 95 per cent of the male population and a high percentage of the female at some time or other commit a sex crime.

Perhaps the best and most detailed study of sex offenses made to date is that by Radzinowicz and his associates (1957), who made a thoroughgoing investigation of offenses known to the police in England and Wales and estimated that in 1954 about 16,000 such offenses occurred. Of the known sexual offenses, the distribution of indictable offenses was found to be as follows: Indecent assault on females, 50 per cent; attempts to commit unnatural offenses and indecent assaults on males, 21 per cent; indecency with males, 13 per cent; defilement of girls between 13 and 16, 9 per cent; unnatural offenses, 7 per cent; rape, etc., 2 per cent; incest, 2 per cent; and defilement of girls under 12, 1 per cent.

In the United States there are about 40,000 arrests a year for major sex offenses and doubtlessly many more for minor offenses. The New Jersey State Police add about 800 to 1,000 individuals a year to their file of known sex offenders. They classify these offenders and their offenses as follows: Exhibitionism, 18 per cent; rape (including statutory rape), 45 per cent; perversion, 14 per cent; commercial sex, 7 per cent; unclassified, 16 per cent (Tappan, 1950).

Characteristics of Sex Offenders

As virtually all modern authorities on sex offenders have stressed, many myths exist about the overimpulsivity, aggressiveness, and recidivism of convicted offenders (Abrahamsen, 1950; Ellis and Brancale, 1956; Karpman, 1956; Radzinowicz, 1957; Tappan, 1950). Some of the truths in this connection are as follows:

1. The majority of convicted offenders are found to be rather harmless, "minor" deviates rather than dangerous "sex fiends."

2. Only a relatively small number (about 20 per cent) use force or duress upon their victims.

3. When they are not psychologically treated, convicted offenders are found to be frequent repeaters of both sexual and nonsexual offenses, even though their rates of recidivism may be lower than those of nonsex offenders.

4. Very few offenders may be designated as true "sexual psychopaths" since most of them, when intensively examined with modern psychological and psychiatric techniques of investigation, are found to be severely neurotic, borderline psychotic, or psychotic, or to have organic brain impairment. Studies at Sing Sing Prison in New York and at the New Jersey State Diagnostic Center show that the majority of convicted offenders suffer from some type of mental or emotional disorder, although it is not usually so pronounced as to meet the legal definition of mental illness.

5. Aside from those convicted of statutory rape and incestuous relations, most offenders tend to be sexually inhibited and constricted rather than overimpulsive and oversexed. The great majority of them are distinctly immature emotionally.

6. Convicted offenders tend to show subnormal intelligence in a higher percentage of the cases and bright normal or superior intelligence in a smaller percentage of the cases than does the general population. Subnormal intelligence is more likely to be found among offenders convicted of statutory rape, incestuous relations, and bestiality and less frequently found among those convicted of forcible rape, exhibitory acts, and disseminating "obscene" material.

7. The majority of offenders are quite young, being in their teens and early twenties. From 50 to 60 per cent of the convicted offenders are unmarried. Most of the offenders come from relatively poor educational and socioeconomic backgrounds.

Sexual Offenders and Sexual Deviates

There is considerable confusion in the public mind, and sometimes in the professional literature as well, between sexual offenders and sex deviates or perverts. Often the terms "offender" and "deviate" are used as if they were synonymous. As pointed out previously in this article, this is erroneous usage: since an individual may be a grave sex offender (for example, a brutal rapist) and yet be completely unperverted; or he may be extremely deviated (for example, may be a masochist who comes only to orgasm when his partner whips him) and may never commit a statutory sex offense.

Sexual deviation or perversion is an exceptionally difficult term to define accurately and does not (as is often erroneously stated) consist of behavior which is statistically rare, or unconventional or unethical in a given region, or "unnatural" or "unbiological" in the sense that it does not lead to human procreation. Psychologically, as I have pointed out in detail in *The American Sexual Tragedy* (1954) and *The Art and Science of Love* (1960), an individual may be considered sexually perverted if he can *only*, under *all* circumstances, enjoy one special form of sexual activity; or if he is obsessively-compulsively fixated on a given mode of sex behavior; or if he is fearfully and rigidly bound to one or two forms of sexual participation; or if he persists, in a disorganized and self-defeating manner, in engaging in sex acts which destroy his own well-being.

A sex pervert, then, either inappropriately overinhibits himself and fearfully confines his activities to unusually limited modes of expression; or else he self-destructively underinhibits himself and (often with considerable hostility) engages in behavior which literally carries with it serious legal or personal penalties. Most sexual perverts are unusually fetishistic or anti-fetishistic—that is to say, they are attracted only to a very narrow range of sex objects (as sadists are only attracted to those who will submit to them or pedophiles are drawn only to young boys); or they are repulsed by a certain type of sex participation (as fixed homosexuals are revolted by the thought of having sex relations with females). A minority of perverts are not fetishists or anti-fetishists but impulsively and/or compulsively engage in several kinds of sex acts (such as exhibitionism, peeping, and sex relations with minors) which are socially banned and self-destructive.

It is most important that we distinguish between sexual deviation and so-called "unnatural" sex practices, by which is often meant noncoital heterosexual relations between consenting adults. Although it is true that any person who *only* or *exclusively* enjoys fellation, cunnilinctus, or heterosexual mutual masturbation and virtually never desires penile-vaginal copulation even when it is freely available is fetishistically fixated on such a noncoital act and is therefore perverted, it is by no means true that anyone who enjoys oral-genital, anal-genital, and other extracoital acts as well as regular intercourse is similarly perverted. In fact, from a psychological standpoint, it may justifiably be said that some individuals who *only* engage in penile-vaginal intercourse and under no circumstances even try noncoital methods of heterosexual relations are extremely fetishistic and fearful and hence tend, in a minor sort of way, to be deviated.

It is also most important that we distinguish accurately between subclinical *tendencies* toward deviated behavior, which actually fall well within the normal range, and clear-cut overt manifestations of perversions. Thus, almost all normal human beings have some masochistic and sadistic tendencies; and many of these perfectly healthy men and women have some difficulty in coming to orgasm unless they are reasonably aggressive on certain occasions or unless they, in phantasy or fact, experience some degree of painful stimulation on other occasions. Particularly in the case of many individuals who at times have difficulty achieving climax, sadistic or masochistic tendencies are well within the range of normal sex behavior.

At the same time, when an individual can only reach his or her acme of sex satisfaction by resorting to extremely sadistic or masochistic acts—for example, by beating or being beaten by his or her sex partner up to and including the point where blood flows or physical injury results—there is little doubt that normal sex tendencies are then being taken to excessive extremes; and the result may justifiably be labeled "sex deviation." Similarly, although most human beings normally have some degree of attraction to members of their own sex, and may even occasionally engage in homosexual acts with members of this same sex, when such attraction continually, exclusively, and compulsively leads to overt homosexuality sex perversion may accurately be deemed to exist.

Tendencies toward plurisexual participations (including heterosexuality, homosexuality, masturbation, nocturnal and diurnal emissions without specific sex contact, and sex relations with animals) are the normal biological inheritance of virtually all human beings. It is only when these tendencies become over-channeled into specialized outlets or when they give way to disorganized and self-defeating pansexuality that we can correctly speak of the existence of sexual deviation or perversion.

Although most convicted sex offenders are distinctly perverted, in the sense just defined, many of them, such as those convicted of statutory rape, are not deviates; and of these non-deviated offenders, as noted above, some are psychologically normal, though perhaps at times more than a little rash in their activities, and others are psychiatrically deviated in general or nonsexual ways. In any event, although sex offenses and sexual deviation significantly overlap, they are by no means the same thing and should not be cavalierly lumped together.

Treatment of Sex Offenders

Convicted sex offenders are usually severely disturbed persons who cannot or will not confine their activities to legally accepted practices or who (perhaps more importantly) refuse to be sufficiently discreet and private about their legally proscribed activities. The mere fact that they are caught, and often frequently caught, in their acts puts them in a distinctly different category from other technical offenders, such as adulterers and fornicators, who are very rarely apprehended and convicted of any offense. In addition, many offenders (such as confirmed homosexuals) are, quite apart from the illegal nature of their offense, psychologically deviated because of their own groundless fears and hostilities, and would require psychological treatment even if their acts were not legally banned.

The psychological treatment of sex offenders is consequently quite difficult in most instances. It requires a tackling and an undermining of the offender's general and sexual disturbances; and it involves, in the final analysis if not in the beginning of psychotherapeutic treatment, a strong willingness on the part of the offender to work at his own improvement. However, sex deviates and sex offenders are notoriously uncooperative in this respect, and often receive so many neurotic gains or satisfactions from their aberrations that they have little or no incentive to work for basic changes in themselves.

Nonetheless, a defeatist attitude toward the treatment of sex offenders is not scientifically warranted. Several investigators, including the present writer, have found that sex deviates and offenders can be successfully treated both in institutions and in private practice. Unusually good results can often be obtained if the therapist employs a highly directive, rational psychotherapeutic approach that shows the offender his basic fear- and hostility-creating philosophies of living, how they originated, how he is continually sustaining them in the present, and how he can examine, question, and challenge them so that they significantly change (Ellis, 1956, 1958, 1959, 1965, 1966).

On a social level, the prevention and treatment of sex offenses would be distinctly abetted if the people of any community and its duly appointed and elected police, judicial, and legislative officials would take an objective and scientific rather than a traditional biased and punitive attitude toward sex offenders. Individuals commit offenses not because they are blackguards or degenerates but because (1) they are ignorant, mentally subnormal, or emotionally disturbed, or because (2) they are often following entirely normal psychophysical urges or drives that are wrongly and cruelly limited and banned in many jurisdictions. If society would see to it that all or most of its citizens were raised so that they were minimally ignorant and disturbed and maximally permitted to engage in harmless sex acts, there would be a sharp decrease in the existing high number of sex offenders.

More specifically, for the best kind of prevention of and treatment for sex offenses, the following general program is suggested:

1. Only those sex acts should be legally proscribed that involve (a) the use of force or duress; (b) an adult's taking sexual advantage of a minor; or (c) public acts that are distasteful to the majority of those in whose presence they are committed. Sex acts other than these, engaged in privately between two competent adults, should not be subject to legal processes or penalties.

2. All sex laws should be rewritten so that offenses are specifically and scientifically designated and defined in meaningful, consistent, nonoverlapping terms.

3. When individuals commit any sex offense that would still exist under the two preceding rules they should be given a complete psycho-

logical examination, after conviction but before being sentenced, to determine whether they are sexually and/or psychologically deviated.

4. All sex offenders, and particularly those who are diagnosed as being sexually or psychologically deviated, should be enabled to receive psychological treatment either (a) in their own community, while they are placed on probation, or (b) in a mental hospital or other institution that affords specialized psychotherapeutic care for sex offenders. If institutionalization is required, the convicted offender should remain in protective custody as long as he is so psychiatrically deviated as to be considered a menace to the rights and safety of his fellow citizens.

5. Under no circumstances should sex offenders (or, for that matter, nonsex offenders) be viewed as horrible, villainous criminals to be harshly punished to atone for their sins. Rather, they should be viewed either as relatively normal individuals who are rash enough to get into occasional difficulty or as seriously disturbed persons who are sufficiently disordered to keep getting into legal difficulties because of their sexual behavior. In either case, education and treatment, rather than excoriation and punishment, should be the lot of these already sufficiently unfortunate individuals.

6. It is most necessary, for the prevention and treatment of sex offenders, that every community favor the increase and improvement of general sex education. In this way children at an early age would be provided with scientific, objectively stated sex information, and a more liberal, socially sanctioned heterosexual participation on the part of young people would be encouraged.

References

Abrahamsen, David, *Report on Study of 102 Sex Offenders at Sing Sing Prison.* Utica, N.Y.: State Hospitals Press, 1950.

Allen, Clifford, *The Sexual Perversions and Abnormalities.* London: Oxford University Press, 1949.

Bailey, Derrick S. (ed.), *Sexual Offenders and Social Punishment.* Westminster: Church of England Moral Welfare Council and Church Information Board, 1956.

Bowman, Karl M., *Sexual Deviation Research.* Sacramento, Calif.: Assembly of the State of California, 1952.

Bowman, Karl M., "Too Many Sex Laws." *Nation,* pp. 286-289, 1958.

Buckle, Donald, "The Treatment of Sex Offenders." *Internat. J. Sexology 3;* 1-8, 1949.

California Sexual Deviation Research, January, 1953. Sacramento, Calif.: Assembly of the State of California, 1953.

California Sexual Deviation Research, March, 1954. Sacramento, Calif.: Assembly of the State of California, 1954.

de River, Paul, *The Sexual Criminal.* Springfield, Ill.: Charles C Thomas, Pub., 1949.

Drummond, Isabel, *The Sex Paradox.* New York: G. P. Putnam's Sons, 1953.

Ellis, Albert, *The American Sexual Tragedy.* New York: Twayne Pub., 1954.

Ellis, Albert, *The Art and Science of Love.* New York: Lyle Stuart, 1960.

Ellis, Albert, "The Effectiveness of Psychotherapy with Individuals Who Have Severe Homosexual Problems." *J. Consult. Psychol. 20;* 191-195, 1956.

Ellis, Albert, *Homosexuality: Its Causes and Cure.* New York: Lyle Stuart, 1965.

Ellis, Albert, *If This Be Sexual Heresy...* New York: Lyle Stuart, 1963; New York: Tower Publications, 1966.

Ellis, Albert, "Interrogation of Sex Offenders." *J. Crim. Law 45;* 41-47, 1954.

Ellis, Albert, "Rational Psychotherapy." *J. Gen. Psychol. 59;* 35-49, 1958.

Ellis, Albert, "Treatment of a Homosexual with Rational Psychotherapy." *J. Clin. Psychol. 15;* 338-343, 1959.

Ellis, Albert, and Brancale, Ralph, *The Psychology of Sex Offenders.* Springfield, Ill.: Charles C Thomas, Pub., 1956.

Ellis, Albert, Doorbar, Ruth R., and Johnston, Robert III, "Characteristics of Convicted Sex Offenders." *J. Sociol. Psychol. 40;* 3-15, 1954.

Foster, A. W., "Treatment of Sexual Offenders." *Marriage Hyg. 1;* 77-80, 1947.

Gebhard, Paul H., *et al., Sex Offenders.* New York: Harper & Row, 1965.

Glueck, Bernard C., "Psychodynamic Patterns in the Homosexual Sex Offender." *Am. J. Psychiat. 112;* 584-590, 1956.

Group for the Advancement of Psychiatry, Committee on Forensic Psychiatry, *Psychiatrically Deviated Sex Offenders.* Report No. 9, Revised, 1950.

Gurvitz, Milton, "Sex Offenders in Private Practice: Treatment and Outcome." Paper delivered at American Psychological Association Annual Meeting, Sept. 3, 1957.

Guttmacher, Manfred S., *Sex Offenses.* New York: W. W. Norton & Co., Inc., 1951.

Guttmacher, Manfred S., and Weihofen, H., "Sex Offenses." *J. Crim. Law 43;* 153-175, 1952.

Karpman, Benjamin, *The Sexual Offender and His Offenses.* New York: Julian Press, Inc., 1956.

Kinsey, Alfred C. *et al.*, *Sexual Behavior in the Human Male*. Philadelphia: W. B. Saunders Co., 1948.

London, Louis S., and Caprio, Frank S., *Sexual Deviation*. Washington: Linacre, 1950.

Pollens, Bertram, *The Sex Criminal*. New York: Macaulay, 1938.

Radzinowicz, L. (ed.), *Sexual Offences*. London: The Macmillan Co., 1957.

Report of the Committee on Homosexual Offences and Prostitution. (Wolfenden Report). London: Her Majesty's Stationery Office, 1957.

Report of the Governor's Study Commission on the Deviated Criminal Sex Offender. Lansing: State of Michigan, 1951.

Rickles, N. K., *Exhibitionism*. Philadelphia: J. B. Lippincott Co., 1950.

Sherwin, Robert V., *Sex and the Statutory Law*. New York: Oceana Pub., 1949.

Tappan, Paul W., *The Habitual Sex Offender*. Trenton, N.J.: State of New Jersey, 1950.

ALBERT ELLIS

Sex Reform Movement

THE demand for sexual reform arose in large measure out of modern pioneer work on the physiology and psychology of the sexual functions. Theories advocating different "unconventional" patterns of sexual behavior were, of course, not new. However, these were mainly literary or philosophical theories advanced by isolated thinkers and not scientific theories grounded on factual information or research. The modern demand for sexual reform is a new attitude born, for the most part, out of the new science of sexology.

The first task to be accomplished before sexual reform could become a practical possibility was to destroy what has been called "the conspiracy of silence." The right to study and to discuss the sexual functions in all their aspects, and to publish freely the outcome of such studies, had to be established. Even within the memory of those still living, the whole question was surrounded by a degree of secrecy that now seems to us almost incredible. A leading nineteenth-century physician expressed the considered opinion that even the ascription of sexual feelings to woman was "a vile aspersion," and many anatomical charts of that time omitted the sexual system completely. Both in Europe and in America there was a negative mythology of sex that provided the foundation of a repressive and antibiological morality. The sanction of this code was a system of taboos, and to undermine the authority of this morality was the first step in sexual education. The socialized control of the sexual functions, guided by scientific knowledge and based upon the needs of the individual and the community, must replace the old system which tried to handle the sexual problem by means of restric-

tions of an incredibly primitive, infantile, and superstitious nature. Havelock Ellis' monumental *Studies in the Psychology of Sex* presented an appalling picture of the sexual conflict, misery, and waste that occurred under the old dispensation.

The resistance to the new approach was both bitter and sustained. Some works that touched on the sexual function were, of course, tolerated. Early works on masturbation, with their horrifying phantasies in which the unfortunate victims were likened to "withered roses and walking corpses," were approved because they gave support to the dominant mythology of sex. When dispassionate scientific investigation began, however, powerful resistance was immediately mobilized against it.

In spite of intense hostility, and, in some cases, of actual persecution, the new science made headway steadily. The work of such men as Krafft-Ebing, August Forel, Albert Moll, Iwan Bloch, Sigmund Freud, Havelock Ellis, and Magnus Hirschfeld, to name only a few, could not be ignored indefinitely. The first volume of Havelock Ellis' great work might be prosecuted in England, but it was successfully published in America. Freud and Hirschfeld might be condemned to die in exile from their own countries, their books might be prosecuted in democratic lands and burnt in totalitarian ones, but history has proved how ineffective these methods are in dealing with new knowledge and ideas.

This alarming new science was aided by profound changes that were taking place in society. Evolutionary biology had taken a firm grip on men's minds, and science was generally becoming more important. Revolt against patriarchal and puritanical systems was gathering force. In literature the works of Ibsen and Wedekind, of Flaubert and Zola, among others, exerted considerable influence, and in addition to this the power of organized religious bodies was on the wane. A new climate of opinion, much more sympathetic to sexological investigation, was in process of formation.

Scientific research into the phenomena of sex and proposals for sexual reform were closely associated, together with early projects connected with sex education. The sexual reformers were interested in the whole range of sexual phenomena, healthy and pathological, individual and collective. Among the topics that arose for study were eugenics, prostitution, venereal disease, homosexuality, birth control, marriage, divorce, and sex education.

Homosexuality

At a relatively early date the important but heavily repressed question of homosexuality occupied considerable attention on the part of the Reformers, especially in Germany. This was greatly influenced by the publication of Albert Moll's *Conträre Sexual-Empfindung* (*Contrary Sexual Feeling*), which appeared in 1891, with a preface by Krafft-Ebing. In 1897 Magnus Hirschfeld founded the *Wissenschaftlich-Humanitäres Komittee* (Scientific Humanitarian Committee) for the promotion of the scientific study of homosexuality. The organization was to use the knowledge so gained for the education of public opinion on this subject, with a view to effecting ultimately the repeal of Paragraph 175 of the German Penal Code, which made homosexuality a criminal offense. In 1900 Hirschfeld founded the *Jahrbuch Für Sexuelle Zwischenstufen* (*Yearbook for Intermediate Types*). The scientific study of homosexuality had begun in earnest.

Consultation Centers

An important item in the field of sex reform was the establishment of consultation centers that dealt with sexual and marital problems. These centers were originally inspired by biological research, and were founded with the intention of forwarding a eugenic program for the betterment of the race. In 1908 a plea was addressed to the German Reichstag suggesting that no couple should be permitted to marry unless they could produce health certificates. Breitfeld, the author of this appeal, was supported, according to Max Hodann, by a scientific organization called the *Monistenbund* (Monistic Alliance). Although the request was ignored, the episode led to the foundation in 1911 of the first Eugenic Marriage Bureau at Dresden. In actual fact it was found quite impracticable to limit the activities of the Bureau to purely eugenic questions. The alarming incidence of unsuccessful marriages indicated that the offering of scientific help in this connection was a matter of great social urgency.

Prostitution and Venereal Disease

The problems associated with prostitution and venereal disease had also been occupying the attention of thoughtful people for some time past. These problems were made far more urgent by World War I. During and after the war a great increase occurred both in syphilitic infection and in gonorrhea. By that time much work had been done on these diseases. The gonococcus had been discovered in 1879 by Neisser, and Schaudinn and Hoffmann had conducted research on syphilis. Wassermann's work had been carried out in 1906, and Ehrlich and Hata had discovered Salvarsan in 1910. The main difficulties in dealing with these problems lay in making this new knowledge effective and in sufficiently overcoming the sharp divisions of opinion to allow for efficient collective action. The traditionalists believed that prostitution should be rigidly suppressed and the prostitute driven out and persecuted. Venereal disease, they maintained, was a just punishment for wrongdoing. This had been the view adopted by Florence Nightingale.

Those who took a more rational view of the problems believed that, whether we like it or not, prostitution in some form or another was probably as permanent a feature of life in the modern world as it was in ancient civilizations, and that at least some of its evils were created or intensified by the traditional attitude adopted toward it.

Some members of the reformist group advocated the registration and medical inspection of prostitutes; others claimed that such methods were unsuccessful in checking the spread of venereal disease. Still others, basing their objections on moral or feminist grounds, felt that such a solution was unacceptable to the modern conscience. Special bodies came into existence to deal with these specific problems, amongst which the American Hygiene Association and the British Social Hygiene Council are, perhaps, the most important.

Unfortunately, even today there is strong opposition to the dissemination of prophylactic information, especially to younger members of the community. In England, for example, no chemist can sell any device or chemical substance for the specific purpose of preventing the contraction of syphilis or gonorrhea, in spite of the fact that a government committee recommended such a procedure many years ago. The British Society for the Prevention of Venereal Disease issued a simply worded pamphlet that had a considerable circulation some years ago.

It was, however, the enormous casualties suffered during wartime that led to some modification of the older attitude. Much work has also been done on these problems by various committees of the League of Nations and the United Nations, although the value of much of this work has been impaired by the predominance of a moralistic rather than of a scientific attitude. The insistence on associating the problem of venereal disease too exclusively with prostitution, the attempts to close brothels and suppress the prostitute, and the failure to advocate the teaching of prophylactic methods as a normal part of sex education have come in for much criticism. The need for extramarital sexual outlets in "monogamous" societies has never been realistically faced, and, as the late Dr. Kinsey has pointed out, the prostitute has been assigned a special place among sex offenders "because she is forced to exist, either as a part of the criminal underworld, or as a protegée and partner of officialdom."

Birth Control

A question that has touched intimately the lives of millions of people has been that of birth control. The control of conception is, of course,

no new thing. Malthus had written his famous essay on population in 1789. He himself refused to recognize the mechanical or chemical control of conception, but with his followers after his death the history of birth control began anew.

Here again bitter opposition was encountered. In 1867 the famous indictment of Charles Bradlaugh and Annie Besant occurred as a result of the publication of a pamphlet entitled *The Fruits of Philosophy*, which contained practical advice on birth control. Powerful champions of the cause of family limitation, however, soon arose. In New York, Robert Dale Owen supported it. Dr. George Drysdale wrote in its favor, and in 1877 the Malthusian League was formed.

Opposition to the employment of anticonception techniques came from many of the religious bodies but, with the exception of the Roman Catholic Church, this opposition has very largely ceased and religious approval is generally given to family planning within marriage. Some countries, however, have enacted laws against the dissemination of contraceptive information and appliances. Margaret Sanger, the originator of the expression "Birth Control," was imprisoned in 1917, and the United States, France, Italy, and Germany were amongst the countries to write laws on their statute books against birth control. In spite of these measures, the use of contraception, or family planning, has continued to increase until, in the words of Havelock Ellis, it has become an essential part of the morality of civilized man. There seems little doubt that a sound knowledge of contraception is necessary both to deal with the urgent problem of world population and to reduce the high abortion rate.

Divorce

Another problem connected with making the sexual life of man happier and more rational has been that of divorce. Throughout history, marriage and divorce customs have shown a bewildering diversity, ranging from extremely simple and easy divorce arrangements to the complete denial of divorce under any circumstances. The religious bodies are divided on this question also, some accepting divorce in certain circumstances, and others, such as the

Roman Catholic Church, refusing, at least in theory, to allow divorce for any reason at all. Most of those who desired reform in this field were also concerned with providing as adequate a preparation as possible for marriage, in addition to reasonable divorce facilities for those whose marriages had broken down.

The trend in most countries in recent years has been to extend divorce facilities, making men and women equal in this matter before the law and recognizing that other offenses are perhaps even more disruptive of marriage than the time-honored one of adultery. In England, for example, in addition to adultery, divorce is granted for desertion of 3 years or more, for cruelty, for incurable unsoundness of mind for at least 5 years, for rape, for sodomy, and for bestiality. These new grounds became law in 1937 and were the result of a bill sponsored by Mr. A. P. Herbert in Parliament. The reforms follow very largely those recommended by the Royal Commission appointed after World War I.

The report of the latest Royal Commission is extremely disappointing. Although representatives of a number of liberal societies gave evidence, including the Progressive League, the Ethical Union, the Divorce Reform Union, and the Marriage Law Reform Society, the recommendations of the Commission are singularly out of step with progressive opinion, and it would seem that for a long time to come little further can be expected in the field of divorce-law reform. Professor O. R. McGregor (1957) rightly remarks that "The Report contributes nothing to our knowledge, and fails even to define and clarify opposing viewpoints, or to facilitate public discussion."

Many reformers would like to see the concept of "Matrimonial Offense" replaced by one of "Matrimonial Breakdown," and would like to abolish the conception of "collusion" and allow, with certain safeguards, divorce by mutual consent. It is also widely held that divorce should be granted after a long separation.

Most reformers contend that in these situations the welfare of the children should be of paramount importance, and that the law should concern itself more with suitable provisions for their physical and psychological health after divorce decrees have been granted. Divorce reform must be accompanied by an emphasis on the need for a sound sexual education for children, more marriage counseling work, and the promotion of a better understanding of the nature of marriage. Such a program should have great social value by decreasing the number of couples resorting to the drastic surgery of divorce.

Revaluation of Human Sexuality—Freud

In addition to the work of the medical sexologists in changing public opinion and promoting sex reform, we must also include the profound effect produced by the work of Sigmund Freud and his followers in the revaluation of human sexuality. As Havelock Ellis has reminded us, Freud preserved the detachment of the conventional physician. He did not attack the traditional sexual code directly, although he was engaged in attempting to remedy some of the evils that flowed from it and was personally deeply conscious of its defects. He once caustically remarked that the traditional education of the young was as realistic as sending people on a polar expedition dressed in summer clothing and equipped with maps of the Italian lakes.

It was not, however, through his advocacy of any radical change in sexual conventions that he broke with the traditions of his time, but rather through his attitude to the sexual functions as a whole. What had been surmised Freud investigated, and what had been whispered Freud said openly. For the first time in medical literature sexual phenomena were described precisely, with a wealth of detail, without apology, and as a matter of course. His stress on the sexual nature of the child, his extension of the whole concept of sexuality, and his study of the ramifications of sex in human life, of the sexual complexes within the family, and of the overwhelming importance of sex in the etiology of neuroses made it impossible to continue the traditional attitude of denigration and silence.

Companionate Marriage

Among the proposals for the reform of the institution of marriage, none provoked more alarm and resentment than the quite reasonable and moderate proposals of Judge Ben Lindsey. Lindsey was at that time Judge at the Denver Juvenile Court and had a very extensive experience with the behavior and problems of modern youth. It was his considered opinion that drastic reforms were needed, and in 1925 he and Wainwright Evans published their book, *The Revolt of Modern Youth.*

The suggestion with which Lindsey's name is usually associated is the recommendation of "companionate marriage" for the young. This was intended to give social recognition to practices that were already widespread and to provide as satisfactory a framework as possible for youthful sexual experiences that now occurred in a furtive, unsatisfactory, and often socially dangerous way. Such companionate marriages were to be accompanied by birth control and the right for childless couples who found themselves incompatible to divorce by mutual consent.

A storm of bitter opposition and misrepresentation broke on Lindsey's head. His suggestions were called "encouragements to promiscuity," "advocacy of free-love." Lindsey expounded his views again in a later book, *Companionate Marriage.*

Among those who viewed Lindsey's proposals sympathetically were Bertrand and Dora Russell. The former expressed his own views on marriage and divorce in his book, *Marriage and Morals,* which appeared in 1940. Havelock Ellis also reacted to Lindsey's suggestions with sympathetic approval.

Law and Sex—René Guyon

Perhaps the most radical, systematic, and extensive proposals for the reform of laws and conventions relating to the sexual functions have been made by Dr. René Guyon, traveler, philosopher, jurist, and legislative advisor to the Ministry of Justice, Bangkok, Siam. Guyon's basic contention is that the sexual organs and functions are just as amoral as are any other physiological manifestation of living beings. Thus the exercise of these functions is an inalienable right of the individual so long as such exercise occurs without violence, fraud, or constraint. The Judeo-Christian system, with its prohibitions and sex-negations, is both artificial and eccentric. What is called "sexual morality" is in direct conflict with reason and healthy life.

Dr. Guyon has been naturally concerned with the legislative side of the sexual question, and has criticized the "Universal Declaration of Human Rights" proclaimed by the Assembly of the United Nations in 1948, implying as it does the existence of one moral standard in the interests of which the freedom of the subject can be restricted. Guyon believes that, so long as the rights of others are not infringed, "Everyone has the right to sexual freedom and the free disposal of his or her body to that end; and no person shall be molested, persecuted, or condemned by the law for having voluntarily engaged in sexual acts or activities of any kind whatever."

The two concluding volumes of Dr. Guyon's massive work have not been published. The last volume is devoted to the organization of a pro-sexual society. Dr. Guyon's work, although commended in certain quarters, has not received the attention it deserves.

Magnus Hirschfeld and the World League for Sexual Reform

It became abundantly clear as time went on that the sexual reform movement must be organized and focused if it was to exert its maximum influence on public opinion and existing institutions. With this in view Dr. Magnus Hirschfeld of Berlin founded, in 1921, the International Congress for Sexual Reform. The purpose of this organization was to promote reforms in the sexual institutions under which men and women lived. At the second meeting in Copenhagen in 1928, what came to be known as the World League for Sexual Reform was founded. Further meetings were held in London in 1929, Vienna in 1930, and at Brno in 1932. Many distinguished men and women from all walks of life became members of the League or supported its work. Havelock Ellis, August Forel, and Magnus Hirschfeld were its first presidents. Later, Dr. Norman Haire and Dr. J. H. Leunbach occupied this position. Among the members of the League were Sigmund Freud, Bertrand and Dora Russell, Professor J. C. Flügel, Dr. William J. Robinson, Dr.

Harry Benjamin, Dr. Abraham Stone, Dr. G. V. Hamilton, Judge Ben Lindsey, and many other distinguished men and women, including Professor Pasche-Oserki, representative of the then sexually progressive Soviet Union. As Wilhelm Reich observed, the League "comprised the most progressive sexologists and sex reformers in the world."

As has already been pointed out, the League was not a purely academic body engaged in promoting sexual research. It was primarily a reformist organization interested in sponsoring a definite program and in working out what Hirschfeld called "a sexual sociology." Under this concept are subsumed sexual ethics, sexual criminal law, and sexual statesmanship. This last, in Hirschfeld's words, "involves the provision of a sexual code dealing not only with marriage and divorce but all sexual relations including those of unmarried persons, the difficult problem of prostitution, and above all the scientific regulation of birth" (Presidential Address at the Third Congress). It was the intention of the League to promote reform by appeals to the legislatures, the press, and the peoples of all countries and to help to create a new legal and social attitude toward the sexual life of men and women, based on the knowledge that had been acquired by scientific research in sexual biology, psychology, and sociology. The approach was to be objective and scientific, acknowledging the truth of Forel's declaration, that "there must be no conflict between sexual hygiene and sexual ethics." The laws of man must be brought into harmony with the laws of nature.

The program of the League may be summarized as follows:

1. The political, economic, and sexual equality of men and women.

2. The liberation of marriage, and especially of divorce, from the tyranny of Church and State. Legislation in such matters was to be concerned primarily with the protection of children. Free sexual education centers were to be provided.

3. Control of conception so that procreation may be undertaken only deliberately and with a due sense of responsibility. The repeal of all laws against birth control, and the provision of contraceptive facilities by public health authorities. Sterilization to be effected in suitable cases.

4. Reform in the abortion laws to enable pregnancies to be terminated by qualified doctors on economic, social, and eugenic grounds in addition to the existing medical indications.

5. Systematic and scientific sexual education for both the young and adults.

6. Race betterment by the application of the knowledge of eugenics.

7. Protection of the unmarried mother and of the illegitimate child.

8. A rational attitude toward sexually abnormal persons and especially toward homosexuals, both male and female.

9. The prevention of prostitution and venereal disease. No persecution of the prostitute was to be recommended, and no attempts at forcible repression were to be made. Economic and other changes that would permit adults to find reasonable sexual satisfaction in more acceptable ways were to be encouraged.

10. Disturbances of the sexual impulses to be regarded as more or less pathological phenomena and not, as in the past, as crimes, vices, or sins.

11. Only those sexual acts to be regarded as criminal that infringe the sexual rights of another person. Sexual acts between responsible adults, undertaken by mutual consent in private, to be regarded as the private concern of the participants.

12. A more rational attitude toward venereal diseases. The encouragement of treatment, which should be freely provided, and the avoidance of penalties and coercion. Prophylactic information to be freely provided.

The League pledged itself to strive for these reforms by serving as a link between organizations and individuals in all countries who shared its point of view, by disseminating the scientific knowledge of sex, and by combatting all forces and prejudices that stood in the way of a rational attitude toward sex.

The chief methods to be used to further these objectives were as follows:

1. The publication or the encouraging of the publication of both technical and popular scientific works that aimed at sexual reform on a scientific basis.

2. The production of an *International Journal of Sexual Reform*.

3. The holding of international congresses.

4. Propaganda by lectures.

5. Analysis of laws and collection of statistics relating to sex in all countries.

6. The drafting of sex statutes and general assistance in sexual legislation.

7. The provision of information to the legislatures of all countries.

When the League held its final meeting at Brno in 1932 the twilight of liberal thought was well advanced. In 1933 Hitler came into power, and for more than a decade Germany was in the grip of a totalitarian government implacably hostile to liberal and scientific thought.

One of the first victims in the scientific world of the new terror was Magnus Hirschfeld. In 1918 Hirschfeld had founded the Institute for Sexual Science in Berlin. This had been taken over by the Prussian government as an institution of great public importance, and Hirschfeld had presented his unrivaled collection of sexual material to the State. This Institute had become internationally famous. Public lectures of a popular and informative kind were given, questions were answered, and various types of advice and help were at the disposal of anyone who cared to apply. In addition, there were a sexological museum and a library of more than 20,000 volumes.

In May, 1933, the Institute was raided by Nazi students, and books, manuscripts, dossiers, and medical charts were removed and destroyed. Some of the property belonging to the League was also carried away. Hirschfeld was abroad at the time, and died at Nice two years later.

Sex Reform in England—Norman Haire

After the death of Hirschfeld, Dr. Norman Haire and Dr. Leunbach, the two surviving presidents of the World League for Sexual Reform, published a declaration which they sent to all members. They pointed out that existing political conditions made it impossible for the League to hold further international congresses or even to continue its work in many countries. "As far as we can establish the English section

is the only one which continues to function actively." The continuation of the League as an international organization was no longer feasible. Haire and Leunbach, therefore, declared the League dissolved. The individual sections, of course, had the right to decide whether they would continue to function independently or not.

Dr. Haire and Dr. Leunbach were sharply at variance on the question of the relation of the League to current political movements. Haire believed that all revolutionary activity should be kept out of the League's program, whereas Leunbach was of the opinion that the League had failed because it had not joined the revolutionary workers' movement. It was a disappointing ending to an organization that might have achieved so much in the field of sexual reform. Haire claimed, however, that the League's discussions had resulted in important changes in public opinion and in actual institutions.

It was not until after World War II that the Sex Education Society began its work in England with Dr. Norman Haire as its founder and president. With Dr. Haire were associated Dr. Harold Avery, Professor J. C. Flügel, Miss Barbara Low, and others. A little later, in August, 1948, Dr. Haire began the publication of *The Journal of Sex Education*. This was a popular scientific journal intended for the sexual enlightenment of intelligent laymen. It contained original articles on topics connected with the sexual functions, news from various parts of the world, book reviews, and a section dealing with readers' questions. The Society held lectures in London, many of these being given by Dr. Haire himself.

In common with many other members of the defunct League, Dr. Haire believed in the gradual education of the public, and that sexual institutions could be remodeled if a sufficient number of people became dissatisfied with existing conditions. The best way of ensuring sound reforms was, therefore, the patient elimination of misapprehensions and misinformation. Education and reform were thus organically related to each other. The life of the new Society and its journal was, unfortunately, not a long one. Dr. Haire was already a very sick man when he began this last phase of his work, and on his return from America, where he had planned a lecture tour, he was obviously a dying man. His death occurred on September 11, 1952, just after he had passed his sixtieth birthday.

Modern Sex-Reform and Sex-Education Movements

In spite of severe losses and the existence of powerful reactionary forces, the cause of sex reform and sex education has made considerable progress in many countries. Topics can be discussed and books published with far greater freedom than would have been possible at the beginning of the century. The fight for birth control has virtually been won. Many religious bodies now accept the practice as a normal part of modern marriage, and the family planning movement, which publishes a liberal and well-informed journal of its own, is well on the way to becoming a respectable institution in England. In Japan a good deal of work on sex education has been done by the Japanese Sexological Society. Its director, Tetsu Takahashi, has published some useful reports on its work. Progress has also been made in India, where the late Dr. Pillay founded the Society for the Promotion and Study of Family Hygiene Including Sex Hygiene. Although sex-reform movements were active in the United States in the nineteenth century, there has recently been no large organized group in this area. More in keeping with the American interest in sexual research, the Society for the Scientific Study of Sex has been started and is nonpartisanly devoting itself to fostering scientific discussion and research. Its main officers have been Drs. Hugo Beigel, Albert Ellis, Henry Guze, and Hans Lehfeldt, and its Executive Secretary is Robert Veit Sherwin.

Small societies are at work in most countries, each concerned with promoting some particular type of reform. In England the Abortion Law Reform Association has been active for many years, and there is very much support for its campaign to widen the grounds for therapeutic termination of pregnancy. It is widely realized that existing laws tend to drive such practices underground and lead large numbers of unfortunate women to seek help from unscrupulous, rapacious, and unqualified abortionists.

A good deal of dissatisfaction has been felt in connection with the way in which the problems of homosexuality and prostitution have been handled in England. A number of cases of homosexuality involving well-known people have come before the English courts during the last few years. A reform of the cruel and antiquated laws relating to homosexual practices between males is long overdue.

In 1954 a Departmental Committee was set up under the chairmanship of Sir John Wolfenden. The purpose of this Committee was to investigate the existing laws and their application to homosexuality and prostitution. The Committee published its report in 1957. The first part dealt with the problems of homosexuality. (It must be remembered that it has only been since 1885 that all sexual acts carried out between males have been criminal offenses, irrespective of the ages of the participants and the circumstances under which the acts occurred.) The most important recommendation made by the Committee on this subject was that the law should concern itself only with the protection of minors and those suffering from mental defects, and also with the preservation of public order and decency. Sexual acts carried by consenting adult males in private should, however, cease to be regarded as criminal offenses. The age of consent for such acts should be fixed at 21. "Sodomy," or pedication, should, the Committee thought, be redefined as a "misdemeanour" and cease to be classed as a "felony," and thus not be regarded as an exceptionally depraved act deserving exceptionally severe punishment.

The second part of the report, that dealing with prostitution, is both confused and reactionary. The Committee recommends increasing the fines for prostitutes, with imprisonment for a third conviction, and also suggests that the police should have the power to arrest a prostitute for soliciting without having to establish "annoyance" caused to any person by her behavior. This seems a most regrettable recommendation. It is, however, realized that any attempt to make prostitution "illegal" is doomed to fail, and the latter part of the second section is concerned more with administrative problems than with reform.

It seems likely that some of the recommendations contained in the report will be adopted by the government in the near future, especially those contained in the section devoted to the problem of prostitution. The recommendations on homosexuality and the proposed changes in the law seemed destined to collect dust in another government pigeonhole. The fear that the opportunity for making an important and much overdue reform will be lost has led to the formation of the Homosexual Law Reform Society, which includes among its members a former prime minister, Anglican bishops, and many distinguished scientific and literary people. This Society will press the government for legislation to give effect to the proposed reform of the law in connection with homosexual acts performed by consenting adult males in private.

Another area in which reform is urgently needed is in connection with the banning of books and plays. Ever since the attack on Flaubert's *Madame Bovary* in France, and the prosecution of Havelock Ellis' study of sexual inversion at the close of the last century, it has been clear that important literary and scientific works might be dealt with as pornography by ignorant officials. This impression was strengthened by the banning of James Joyce's *Ulysses* and of many other serious novels and plays. Not long ago three serious plays dealing with the question of homosexuality were being performed at private theater clubs in London because of the Lord Chamberlain's ban. Reformers have long been trying to bring about a more liberal and discriminating attitude regarding this matter. The World League for Sexual Reform was opposed to censorship, and held that people should be educated to meet all kinds of knowledge and to decide for themselves what they will accept or reject. The first step, it believed, was to remove the whole matter from the jurisdiction of magistrates, and to establish the right to present medical, psychological, sociological, and artistic testimony together with the right to appeal to a higher court.

In 1954 a Select Committee on Obscene Publications was set up. This Committee issued its recommendations in 1955. The published report makes it clear how much the definition of obscenity has changed during the last decades. Only the representative of the Public Morality Council still considered *Ulysses* obscene. In spite of some progress, however, the position is still extremely unsatisfactory in England. As Mr. Alec Craig remarked some years ago, "the law of obscene libel not only impedes the work of sex educators and hinders nudist propaganda, but constitutes an arbitrary threat to the novelist, the scholar and the bibliophile." In many cases fraud is practiced on the unsuspecting reader. Deletions from the text of some American novels are made in the English editions, and translations from the French are bowdlerized, without in either case informing the reader that this procedure has been adopted.

Unfortunately, at this time the government introduced a bill of its own to deal with horror comics, and this has hopelessly confused the whole issue. A full, comprehensive bill was necessary to deal with the matter as a whole. The Committee, originally under the chairmanship of A. P. Herbert, proposed that the state of mind of the accused should be taken into account. In other words, that "intention" should be an essential element in the offense. No attempt was made to define "obscenity," but literary and artistic merit were to be taken into account. Authors, publishers, and printers were given a locus standi in the courts in order to enable them to give and call evidence. Destruction of allegedly obscene publications by Customs authorities could take place only after a destruction order had been issued by a magistrate. The administration of the law should be made uniform by subjecting all proceedings to the consent of the Attorney General. This report of the Herbert Committee received an excellent reception, both press and public opinion supporting its recommendations. Supporters of the bill embodying its recommendations still await an opportunity of introducing it into the House of Commons as a Private Member's Bill.

In both the United States and England the question of artificial insemination is being widely discussed. It has been estimated that in 1941 this technique was used in over 10,000 cases in America. A recent symposium devoted to this subject has been published by the *New York University Law Review*. A good deal of artificial insemination is also being carried out in England. Existing laws are obviously not pertinent to the problems created by this practice. As far as public opinion can be ascertained, there seems to be widespread approval of the practice as long as the semen is obtained from the husband (A.I.H.). A great deal of opposition, however, exists when the semen is obtained from a donor (A.I.D.). The Archbishop of Canterbury has recently suggested that this latter practice should be made a criminal offense, and much sophistry has been employed to equate A.I.D. with adultery—to which, of course, it bears no resemblance. In England a committee has been appointed with the Earl of Feversham as chairman to inquire into the existing practice and legal implications of artificial insemination, and to consider whether any changes should be made in existing laws.

In reviewing the history of the sexual reform movement, it would seem that, although the impact of sexological research on legislation has not been spectacular in most countries, the impact of such research on public opinion has been very considerable. Sex morality is far less taboo-ridden than it was, for people know much more about the sexual functions. The Kinsey reports have been widely read and have made it abundantly clear that there exists an enormous range of sexual behavior, from the point of view of both extent and variety, among normal and healthy men and women. These reports also make clear the enormous gulf between current conventions and laws and actual sexual practice. It is good news to hear that these studies will go on despite Dr. Kinsey's death. They should have a most valuable effect on legislation. It will be remembered that the first of Dr. Kinsey's reports on sexual behavior in the human male (1948) revealed that 95 per cent of the males studied had engaged at some time or another in sexual activities which would, had they been detected, have involved detention in some penal institution. Nothing could exhibit more dramatically the utterly unrealistic nature of the sexual laws and conventions under which we still live. The recent English Chesser report on "The Sexual, Marital and Family Relationships of the English Woman" suggests that a considerable gulf exists between female profession and practice in that country.

Such studies are important in informing public opinion and in bringing home the need for making our laws and institutions more realistic and more in line with biological drives and psychological needs. The sex reformer must remember, however, that constant vigilance is needed to preserve educational reforms already won. It has been suggested, for instance, by a writer in the Los Angeles *Times* that the recent increase in venereal disease may be connected with the fact that lectures formerly given at the schools on sexual hygiene were quietly discontinued in 1953. In spite, however, of disappointments, setbacks, and the slowness of progress, the sex reformer should be encouraged by the thought that the laws and institutions in democratic societies cannot indefinitely resist the pressure of "ideas that have arrived."

References

Ditzion, Sidney, *Marriage, Morals and Sex in America*. New York: Bookman Associates, Inc., 1953.

Editorial, *Sexology 24;* 139, 1957.

Ellis, Albert, *Sex Without Guilt*. New York: Lyle Stuart, 1958.

Ellis, Havelock, *Studies in the Psychology of Sex*. New York: Random House, 1936.

Guyon, René, *Etudes d'ethique sexuelle*. Paris: Dardaillon, 1929–1938.

Guyon, René, *Human Rights and the Denial of Sexual Freedom*. Bangkok: Author, 1951.

Hirschfeld, Magnus, *Die Weltreise eines Sexualforschers*. Brugg: Bozberg-Verlag, 1933.

Hirschfield, Magnus,, *Sex in Human Relationships*. London: John Lane, 1935.

Hodann, Max, *History of Modern Morals*. London: Heinemann, 1937.

Kinsey, A. C. et al., *Sexual Behavior in the Human Male*. Philadelphia: W. B. Saunders Co., 1948.

Kinsey, A. C. et al., *Sexual Behavior in the Human Female*. Philadelphia: W. B. Saunders Co., 1953.

Lindsey, Ben B., and Evans, Wainwright, *The Revolt of Modern Youth*. New York: Boni & Liveright, 1925.

Lindsey, Ben B., and Evans, Wainwright, *The Companionate Marriage*. New York: Boni & Liveright, 1927.

McGregor, O. R., *Divorce in England*. London: Heinemann, 1957.

Minutes of Evidence Taken Before the Select Committee on the Obscene Publications Bill. London: Her Majesty's Stationery Office, 1958.

Reich, Wilhelm, *The Sexual Revolution*. New York: Orgone Institute Press, 1945.

Report of the Committee on Homosexual Offences and Prostitution. (Wolfenden Report). London: Her Majesty's Stationery Office, 1957.

Report from the Select Committee on Obscene Publications. London: Her Majesty's Stationery Office, 1958.

Rolph, C. H. (ed.), *Women of the Streets*. London: Secker & Warburg, 1955.

Russell, Bertrand, *Marriage and Morals*. New York: Liveright, 1929.

St. John-Stevas, Norman, *Obscenity and the Law*. London: Secker & Warburg, 1956.

Sherwin, Robert Veit, *Sex and the Statutory Law*. New York: Oceana Pub., 1949.

World League for Sexual Reform, *Report of the First International Congress in Berlin*, 1921. Leipzig: Georg Thieme, 1922.

World League for Sexual Reform, *Report of the Second International Congress in Copenhagen*, 1928. Leipzig: Georg Thieme, 1929.

World League for Sexual Reform, *Report of the Third International Congress in London*, 1929. London: Kegan Paul, 1930.

World League for Sexual Reform, *Report of the Fourth International Congress in Vienna*, 1930. Vienna: Elbemuhl-Verlag, 1931.

ROBERT WOOD

Sex Research Institutes

IN THE entire history of mankind there have been only a few well-organized sex institutes devoted either to clinical problems or to sex research. The two outstanding institutes of this kind, the Hirschfeld Institute for Sexology and the Institute for Sex Research founded by Dr. Alfred C. Kinsey at Indiana University, will be discussed in this article.

THE HIRSCHFELD INSTITUTE FOR SEXOLOGY

Although Richard von Krafft-Ebing, Albert Moll, August Forel, Havelock Ellis, and others had published important books in the field of the science of sex, and thus laid the foundation for the study of sex deviations in spite of the open hostility of the medical profession and the general public, Dr. Magnus Hirschfeld represented the zenith of such studies in his day.

Born in 1868 at Kolberg on the Baltic Sea, the son of a popular physician, Magnus seemed predestined to follow his father's profession, having been taken as an assistant on sick calls and allowed to witness surgery. Yet he wanted to become a writer, and studied comparative philology and philosophy before eventually turning to medicine and receiving an M.D. in 1893. After military service and much traveling, he began practicing in Magdeburg but soon moved to Charlottenburg, where he worked as a general practitioner until 1910. After a prolonged sojourn in London and Paris, he hung out his shingle as a specialist "für seelische Sexualleiden" (for psychological sexual disorders). This clinical practice and Hirschfeld's scientific medical research strengthened his conviction that the social ostracism and legal persecution of the homosexual were inhuman, unjust, and without foundation. It was thus that he began his lifelong fight for the intelligent treatment of the sexually inverted.

The first battle included an attack on the German Criminal Code, Statute No. 175, which provided for a prison sentence of up to five years for the crime of sexual intercourse between men. In 1909, a draft for a new penal code included, in Statute No. 250, a serious increase in penalty for male prostitution, abuse of minors, and animal contacts. A petition to the Reichstag asked for the abolition or change of this statute. The document was signed by scientists, doctors, jurists, artists, and writers; in fact, the names of over 800 well-known Germans appeared on the list. That fight began in 1896 and is still going on.

The Scientific-Humanitarian Committee

In 1897, Hirschfeld founded and headed the Wissenschaftlich-Humanitäre Komitee (Scientific-Humanitarian Committee), out of which grew the Institute for Sexology, with headquarters in his home in Charlottenburg, Berliner Strasse 104. Here he practiced and, with one secretary, Georg Plock, did an incredible amount of correspondence, edited the *Jahrbuch für Sexuelle Zwischenstufen* (*Journal for Intermediate Sex Stages*), and wrote the books that still rank as classics in the field of the problems of sex.

One branch of the work of the Committee, he explained, was devoted to science; the other was humanitarian, i.e., to help those who suffered from ostracism, persecution, extortion, and self-doubts leading to neuroses. The office

967

in Charlottenburg became the Mecca of all who desired and needed his advice and help. Similar institutions were founded in Hamburg, Munich, Leipzig, Magdeburg, Hanover, and Amsterdam under the leadership of such men as Iwan Bloch, Ernst Burchart, and Carl Hoefft.

Jahrbuch für Sexuelle Zwischenstufen

The organ or mouthpiece of the Committee was the *Jahrbuch*, which had as its purpose the enlightenment of the public on the true nature of homosexuality and other sexual deviations. From 1899 until World War I it was published monthly; later, for lack of funds, it appeared only four times a year. This journal was edited with the cooperation of scientists, doctors, jurists, and literary scholars—408 individuals in all. Besides original articles, there were monthly reports of meetings, financial statements, bibliographies, and book reviews of all new works on the subject of sex, both scientific and fictional, most of them written by Hirschfeld himself. There were newspaper reports of blackmailing, sex crimes, and persecution of homosexuals, transvestites, and fetishists. The publication carried the complete story of the Oscar Wilde case (Vol. III, 1901). An appreciation of the personality and poetry of Walt Whitman by Edward Bertz appeared in Vol. VII, 1, 1905. There was, indeed, no lack in this journal of important works on sexology during the last years of the nineteenth century and far into the twentieth century. The journal is a treasure trove even for present-day researchers, for it contained writings by Havelock Ellis, August Forel, Max Hirsch, Hans Licht, Sigmund Freud, Paul Näcke, Iwan Bloch, Albert Moll, F. Krauss, and Numa Praetorius (Hirschfeld's pseudonym), to mention only the best known. Critical comments on Statute No. 175, and the proposed stiffening of the law through Statute No. 250, run through all the volumes of the *Jahrbuch*.

Inquiry of 1903

One of the outstanding pioneering activities of the Scientific-Humanitarian Committee was the famous Inquiry of 1903 on the incidence of homosexuality and bisexuality. Dr. A. von Römer in Amsterdam in 1901 had conducted an investigation on a sample of 595 university students with questions concerning homosexuality and masturbation. Hirschfeld, feeling the necessity of a larger sample, turned to the student body of the Charlottenburg Institute of Technology. A letter was sent to the 3,000 male students, appealing to them in the name of science and progress to answer this question: "Is your love (sex) instinct directed to women (W), men (M), or women and men (W & M)?" Enclosed in the letter was an open postal card, addressed to the Committee, showing W, M, W+M, and at the bottom the ages from 16 to 30. No name was to be signed; the proper letter and the figure showing the age were to be underlined. There were 1,756 answers; some letters could not be delivered, others could not be counted, and some individuals refused or neglected to answer. The net result of the inquiry showed: 94 per cent heterosexual, 1.5 per cent homosexual, 4.5 per cent bisexual. The reactionary press called it seduction of academic youth, molestation, and insult. Four students sued Hirschfeld, who was sentenced to a fine of 200 marks or ten days' imprisonment.

In 1904, the same kind of letter was sent to 5,721 Berlin metalworkers (addresses obtained from the German Union) with the additional request to underline twice the W or M in W+M, indicating which bisexual urge was the stronger. Ages were indicated from 18 to 60+. In all, 1,200 addressees were never reached; of the remaining, 41.6 per cent answered. No complaints were made. The result:

> 94.25 per cent heterosexual
> 1.15 per cent homosexual
> 0.73 per cent W + M
> 1.88 per cent W̲ + M
> 0.58 per cent W + M̲
> 1.41 per cent questionable

(The averages in the three investigations correspond; the von Römer average was 1.9 per cent homosexual).

The Institute for Sexology

Because of the literally thousands of patients who came to Hirschfeld's Institute for help and advice, in addition to the doctors and other men of science who wanted to conduct research with

Dr. Hirschfeld, it became necessary to move to larger quarters. Soon after 1900 Hirschfeld bought with his private means one of Berlin's most handsome buildings, the palace of Prince Hermann von Hatzfeld, German diplomat, and originally the home of the famous violinist, Joseph Joachim. This institution became known as the Institut für Sexualwissenschaft (Institute for Sexology). On July 6, 1919, Hirschfeld formally presented it to the German people, along with its collections, library, and laboratories. After one year it became evident that additional room was needed for the Institute, which included a Department of Eugenics, a good-sized lecture hall, a surgery, laboratories, library, and exhibits. There was also lack of space to accommodate medical men and research workers coming to the Institute temporarily, as well as for cases brought in for observation and treatment. In 1921, the building next door was bought and remodeled. A restaurant became a lecture hall; stables in the back became exhibition and library rooms. In 1923, the Institute was recognized by the Prussian government as an institution beneficial to the public, and was named the Magnus Hirschfeld Stiftung (Foundation). The following departments were created: (1) Department for mental or emotional disorders, (2) Department for physical ailments and disorders of potency, (3) Department for sexual-legal matters, (4) Department for gynecology and marriage counseling, (5) Archives and ethnology, (6) Department of sexual reform, (7) Library, and (8) Ernest Haeckel Lecture Hall.

The "Hirschfeld Scrapbook"

One of Hirschfeld's devoted disciples and co-workers, Carl Th. Hoefft, Ph.D., chairman of the Hamburg branch of the Committee, compiled a huge scrapbook with the intention of eventually having it published. The scrapbook contains letters, invitations to conferences, pamphlets, handbills, posters, complete legal documents, minutes of meetings, questionnaires, announcements of lectures, tickets, book jackets—in short, everything indicative of the work of the Committee and the Institute, which were chiefly concerned with what Hirschfeld called Die homosexuelle Frage in ihrem Werdegang (the homosexual question and its de-

velopment). Unfortunately, the "Hirschfeld Scrapbook" was never published, but it escaped destruction and is now at the Institute for Sex Research at Indiana University in Bloomington, Indiana.

Although the items are by no means arranged in chronological order, in leafing through the pages of the scrapbook one gets an idea of the wealth of activities carried on by the Institute. The clinical departments were accessible to anybody suffering from any kind of sex anomaly, real or imagined, with resulting nervous, social, or legal difficulties. Original letters from patients and some full case histories are included, as well as complete questionnaires, some with the patients' answers.

Consultation and treatment were free of charge for those unable to pay. The library, easily accessible to patients, scientists, and other visitors, contained a complete literature on sex pathology. On the occasion of the Fifth Congress for the Science of Heredity, September, 1927, a card of invitation to a reception for delegates and the press shows what the guests could expect to see: an exhibit of photographs; collections in the fields of anthropology, racial science, heredity, ethnology; the special library; and a presentation of selected cases. A number of original posters saved in the scrapbook announced lectures by doctors and scientists. Posters from as early as 1895 were preserved publicizing lectures on homosexuality. A pink handbill announced "the sensational lecture on the Dangers for Male Youth, for men above 18 only, in Altona," since no such lectures were permitted in Hamburg. Fifty years ago great care had to be taken to avoid difficulties with the police, offending people's sense of modesty, or misleading minors. The scrapbook contains a handbill for two lectures: "The Sex Life of the Male.—The Sex Life of the Female. For men in the main hall of a well-known Berlin brewery at 9:00 P.M. For women in a side hall at 8:00 P.M. Adults only. Nov. 1913." When Dr. Burchard was to give a series of lectures on homosexuality in Danzig in 1906, Hirschfeld thought it advisable to ask the chief of police for permission. In his letter of request he explained that such lectures had been given in five German cities, and that women and minors were, of course, excluded.

Hirschfeld's Contribution

In the volume *Sex Anomalies and Perversions*, Hirschfeld condensed his life's work shortly before his death in 1935. His disciples published it in 1938, summarizing his contributions as follows:

1. Discovery that the quantity and distribution of sex hormones (andrin and gynecin) exert a decisive influence on the sexual personality.
2. Demonstration that all sexual anomalies are caused by irregularities of physical development.
3. Application of the findings of the psychoanalytic school to sex anomalies of physiological origin.

There is no doubt that Hirschfeld's contributions in the field of sex research have been important and have influenced the thinking of most of the workers who have followed him.

The work of the Scientific-Humanitarian Committee and of the Institute, located together in Berlin, continued until 1933. In that year the Institute was closed by the Hitler government, its material destroyed, its library publicly burned, and its workers driven into exile or sent to concentration camps. Hirschfeld fled first to Paris and later to Nice, where he died at the home of a friend on his sixty-eighth birthday.

References

Hirschfeld, Magnus, *Die Homosexualität des Mannes und des Weibes.* Berlin: Louis Marcus Verlag, 1920.

Hirschfeld, Magnus, *Geschlechtsanomalien und Perversionen.* Frankfurt a/M. and Stockholm: Nordische Verlagsgesellschaft, 1938.

Hoefft, Carl Th. (comp.), The "Hirschfeld Scrapbook." Now at the Institute for Sex Research, Indiana University, Bloomington, Indiana.

Jahrbuch für Sexuelle Zwischenstufen, Vols. I-XXI, 1899-1921.

Lewandowski, Herbert, *Ferne Länder, fremde Sitten.* Stuttgart: Hans E. Günther Verlag, 1958.

HEDWIG LESER

THE INSTITUTE FOR SEX RESEARCH

Beginnings

In July of 1938, Dr. Alfred C. Kinsey, then a zoology professor at Indiana University, began his epochal studies on human sexual behavior. For over twenty-five years prior to this time he had been doing intensive research in taxonomy and evolution, and had established himself as an authority in these highly specialized fields. For these studies Dr. Kinsey used the genus *Cynipid* (gall wasp). Through extensive field work in both the United States and Mexico he had collected several million of these insects, which he had examined microscopically, classified, and mounted. The statistical analyses that were necessary to comprehend the range and distribution of individual variation, as well as the similarities and differences between various local populations, required the collection of very large numbers of individual insects. As we shall see, it was undoubtedly this same spirit of breadth of investigation that led him in the direction of a statistical analysis of human sexual behavior.

In 1938 a lecture course on marriage for Junior and Senior students at Indiana University was instituted, and Dr. Kinsey was asked to give the lectures concerning the biological aspects of sex and marriage, as well as to be in general charge of the series. When he turned to the literature in the field of sex, he found to his amazement that, although much had been written, there were very few statistical studies of sexual behavior based on adequate samples. The best of the studies had only a few hundred subjects and these were highly selective.

At this time he began to consider the possibility of a statistical study of human sexual behavior on a nonselective, statistically adequate sample. Also, following his lectures in the marriage course, students, both married and single, were coming to him with questions about their own sexual adjustment. Again Dr. Kinsey was surprised to learn that the answers to these questions were rarely available in published sources.

Finally, after giving a talk one evening at one of the fraternities at Indiana University, he was bombarded with questions such as, "Is masturbation harmful?" "What effect does petting have on subsequent marital adjustment?" "Is homosexuality abnormal?" He turned to his audience and stated flatly, "Neither I nor anyone else knows the answers to many of these questions because of our lack of knowledge, but if you, and many like you, will be willing to contribute your own sexual histories, I will be able eventually to discover enough about human sexual behavior to answer at least some of these questions." The response was enthusiastic, and it can be assumed that for him this was the turning point from a study of insect taxonomy to the most extensive study of human sexual behavior that has ever been undertaken.

The Interview

In scientific investigation information is secured primarily by direct observation. However, in human sex research this avenue is blocked by our mores. Hence, a more indirect approach must be made.

The personal interview has been the tool utilized by the Institute for this purpose. The written questionnaire has been found wanting because of the dangers of faulty communication between the subject and the researcher, and because of the greater ease of falsification that it affords.

Over 300 separate points of information are covered in the sex histories. Subjects' experiences from earliest memories to the immediate past are recorded, with many cross-checks built into the history to be sure that cover-up, exaggeration, and misremembering are held to a minimum. External cross-checks are utilized, such as securing histories from spouses and re-interviewing the same subjects after at least a two-year lapse.

The recording of data is done at the time of the interview by using a complex coding system on a single sheet of paper. This serves several functions: (1) the interview may progress at normal speed without having to pause while the data are being recorded; (2) the confidentialness of the record is maintained; (3) the subject is reassured as to this confidentialness; (4) it allows for completeness—the interviewer can determine at a glance whether all questions have been asked; (5) the coded information from the history sheet may be transferred easily and systematically to IBM cards for statistical analysis.

The Sample

At the beginning of the research, the sampling was confined to Indiana University students and faculty. By the end of the first six months, 60 histories had been obtained, and at the end of the first year 300 were in the files. Early in the research it was discovered that there was a statistically significant difference in the sexual histories of college students and of persons who had never gone to college. Hence, by the end of the first year Dr. Kinsey had realized the necessity of widening his sample to noncollege people. In 1939 he began working at the Indiana State Farm, a state jail, and he also began taking histories of persons in surrounding small Indiana towns.

Random sampling was not considered possible for a sex investigation at this time. Instead, a one-hundred per cent sampling system was used. To avoid sampling bias caused by using only volunteers, *all* the persons in a group (such as a classroom, fraternity, factory, Sunday school, or rooming house) were interviewed. About 30 per cent of *all* histories in the Institute files have come from these one-hundred per cent groups, and most of the remaining cases have come from groups in which over 75 per cent were interviewed. By 1959 the Institute had 18,000 case histories taken by direct interview from persons in every part of the United States. About half are from males and half from females, with ages ranging from 3 to 90, and they represent a broad cross-section of the population of the country.

Financial Support

After about two years of work in the new field of human sexual behavior it became evident to Dr. Kinsey that this was a lifetime project. Although there was some opposition to the research by various individual faculty members at the University, the President and the Board of Trustees stood firm on the principle of the right of a competent faculty member to do *bona fide* research regardless of the unpopularity or controversial nature of the subject. Up to this time the work had been done without any outside financial support. Dr. Kinsey had already, from his own funds, hired Clyde E. Martin to help him with the gathering of data and statistical analysis; it was clear that this was just a beginning, that a bigger research staff would be needed, and that additional funds must be secured.

With this in mind, Dr. Kinsey in 1941 applied for funds to the Committee for Studies on Problems of Sex of the National Research Council to extend the scope of his work. By this time 1,600 histories had been secured, and he requested $1,600 for the following year. Dr. Robert M. Yerkes, chairman of this committee, Dr. George W. Corner, and Dr. Lowell J. Reed made a visit to the Indiana campus and approved the request for support of the research. The committee granted $1,600 for that year (1941–1942), raised it to $7,500 for the next, and to $23,000 for the third year. As the amounts were gradually increased, the staff expanded. By 1947–1948 the grants were totaling $40,000 per year, and remained at that figure until 1953–1954. All book royalties and all lecture fees paid to staff members have always been added to Institute funds; these have made up about a third of the entire cost of the research. Indiana University has supplied approximately another third of the necessary amount; the remaining funds have come from foundations. In 1957 the National Institute of Mental Health granted approximately $50,000 per year for three years to the Institute.

Since that time further major support for new investigations totaling well over a half million dollars has been supplied largely from government, but in part from private, sources. Federal support has originated from the National Institute of Mental Health and the National Institute of Child Health and Human Development.

Later History

In April of 1947 the Institute for Sex Research was officially incorporated as a nonprofit corporation under the laws of the State of Indiana. This was done so that the Institute as a body could legally hold possession of its case histories, library, films, and other materials, and could officially receive royalties from its publications and other monies. The basic purposes of the Institute as set forth in its charter are:

(a) To conduct research on human sex behavior

including its biological, psychological, medical, physiological, sociological, anthropological, and all other aspects by continuing and enlarging the research project on said subject heretofore carried on at Indiana University under the direction of Alfred C. Kinsey.

(b) To accept, hold, use, administer, and expend income, gifts, and grants of funds whether in the form of cash, securities, royalties, or any other form of property or income for use in connection with such research project.

(c) To acquire, hold, own, and administer research material, libraries, case histories, and other materials relating to the subject matter of said research project.

(d) To acquire, own, hold, rent, lease, sell, and convey such real estate and personal property as may be reasonably necessary to the carrying out of the Corporation's general purposes.

(e) To do all things reasonably incidental to the Corporation's general purpose which are permitted by law.

In the beginning the Institute was housed in the Biology building on the Indiana University campus, and occupied two rooms adjoining Dr. Kinsey's office. In 1950 it was moved to larger quarters on the ground floor of Wylie Hall. By 1955 the Institute was moved to Jordan Hall, the new life science building. More ample space there permitted expansion of the staff, library, archives, and collections. For the first time space was available for visiting scholars. This permitted the institution of a monograph series. These comprise scholarly works encouraged and sponsored by the Institute, but written by specialists in such fields as literature, anthropology, and fine arts. A final move of the Institute to nearby Morrison Hall was made in the spring of 1967. The present staff of about thirty-five includes five trustees, trained primarily in anthropology, psychology, and sociology, as well as data analysts, statistical assistants, librarians, archivists, a photographer, secretarial staff, and graduate student assistants.

After ten years of research, the Institute in 1948 published its first major work, *Sexual Behavior in the Human Male*. In it are detailed statistics concerning sexual behavior of a sample of more than 5,000 American males divided into different groups, e.g., educational, occupational, marital, age, and religious. Although very little advance publicity surrounded this publication, the American public purchased it so widely that the book remained at the top of the best-seller list for several weeks, and ultimately sold more than 250,000 copies. It was translated into a dozen languages.

The second volume, *Sexual Behavior in the Human Female,* was published in another five years (1953). The Institute was unable to restrain the flood of prepublication publicity although the second volume was written as soberly and matter-of-factly as the first. This volume also sold about 250,000 copies and was translated as widely as the first.

The third volume, *Pregnancy, Birth and Abortion,* was published in 1958. It analyzed the fertility records of the women whose case histories were on file. In 1965 a fourth study entitled *Sex Offenders, An Analysis of Types* was completed. This study was based on interviews with over 1300 convicted sex offenders, subdivided into fourteen types. The sexual histories of these fourteen groups of offenders were compared to those of two control groups: a "normal" group consisting of men never convicted for any offense, and a prison group of men convicted for various nonsexual offenses.

Currently three new studies are under way. These investigations are in the areas of sexual patterns of college youth, coping behavior in the homosexual community and homosexual community structure, and measuring the success of sex education for personal adjustment. New forms of the original interview have been developed for these studies and some of the field interviewing is being done by trained commercial survey teams for the first time.

On August 25, 1956, Dr. Kinsey died. Although his death was a tremendous loss to the Institute and to the world of science, he had established the Institute on such a sound and stable footing that the necessary reorganization and readjustment were accomplished easily. The trustees of the Institute (Paul H. Gebhard, Wardell B. Pomeroy, Clyde E. Martin, Cornelia V. Christenson, Alice W. Field, and Theodore W. Torrey) elected Dr. Gebhard as the Executive Director and Dr. Pomeroy as the Director of Field Research. Clyde Martin left the staff to continue his graduate studies in 1960, and Dr. Pomeroy moved to New York in 1963 to open a private practice in clinical psychology. Meanwhile two senior staff members and trustees had been added, John Gagnon and Dr. William Simon, both in the field of sociology.

Resources

The case histories described earlier constitute the backbone of the research material at the Institute. However, they by no means comprise all the data available for study. In addition, a considerable amount of supplementary data has been gathered concerning many of the individuals represented in the case histories. For those persons who have spent time in an institution, such as a prison or mental hospital, the Institute has obtained much additional material to supplement the sex histories. This has been acquired through intake and progress reports, clinical evaluation, treatment reports, parole and probation reports, and psychological tests. Autobiographical accounts have frequently been sent in by subjects who wish to provide additional insight into their individual experiences. Very extensive, long-time diaries have been contributed by about sixty subjects. These consist of day-by-day running accounts of overt sexual behavior as well as attitudes and feelings concerning the behavior. These longitudinal studies have been invaluable in helping to understand the dynamics of sexual behavior, as well as in giving additional information on various aspects of sexual behavior of particular groups of individuals.

Nearly a thousand day-by-day sexual calendars, ranging from one to forty-five years in length, have been secured from both men and women. From these an analysis of sexual behavior by days of the week, months of the year, seasons of the year, and so forth, can be made. These individual calendars also permit a check on the accuracy of behavior reported in the case histories of the same individuals.

The Institute for Sex Research has become the primary repository for sexual artifacts from all over the world. Some 30,000 photographs of sexual action, as well as over 20,000 photographs of drawings and paintings, are in its archives. A collection of sexual objects from many different countries gives further insight into the sexual practices and interests of humans. All these collections are carefully catalogued as to source, subject matter, and period to facilitate subsequent analysis.

The phylogenetic aspects of human sexual behavior can be analyzed by the use of 120,000 feet of moving picture film showing sexual behavior in seventeen different species of mammals. From these films it appears that there is essentially no type of human sexual behavior for which a counterpart cannot be found in our mammalian heritage.

The library of the Institute consists of about 20,000 volumes, and is reputed to be second only to the Vatican Library in its scope in the field of sex. Its sections on biology, medicine, psychiatry, psychology, anthropology, sociology, religion, and the law include the scholarly contributions in these areas. Equally important, because they reflect public opinion on matters of sex and because they provide original data for study, are the sections on fiction, classical literature, Oriental literature, Islamic literature, poetry, erotic literature, sado-masochistic literature, marriage manuals, biography, art, and still other subjects.

The library of the Institute is open to trained research workers who have *bona fide* research projects under way, and to other specialists who have scholarly need for access to particular portions of the library. The Institute has neither the facilities nor the legal right to open the library to the general public.

In 1950 the United States Customs confiscated a shipment of erotic material that had been sent to the Institute from Europe. For the next seven years they continued to hold many (but not all) importations from abroad which they considered pornographic or obscene. In October 1957, the case was finally decided in a federal court in favor of the Institute. This means that the Institute now has the legal right to import, for purposes of scientific study, material that under ordinary circumstances would be considered pornographic, erotic, or obscene. However, the Institute holds this right only if it does not distribute these materials to others, and only if no one except the staff members of the Institute and other *bona fide* research scholars have access to them. The case histories and all other supplemental data gathered from persons who have been subjects for the Institute's research are maintained as confidential material and are not available to other workers in the field.

Contributions of the Institute

1. For the first time an over-all assessment of what people do sexually has been attempted. The sampling has been uneven, with the result that a much better understanding has been gained of the sexual behavior of the better-educated and younger sections of the population than of any other groups. To obtain sex histories from a sufficiently large number of persons in categories still to be adequately sampled will take many years. The present sample of cases has been subdivided by sex, age, marital status, completed education, occupational class of subject and parents, age at puberty, religion, degree of devotion to religion, rural-urban background, and decade of birth. These classifications make possible comparisons between these groups as to differences and similarities in sexual behavior.

2. New data on many aspects of sexual behavior have been published. An analysis has been made of incidence and frequency data, as well as of many other aspects, of masturbation, sex dreams, petting, premarital intercourse, marital intercourse, extramarital intercourse, prostitution, homosexuality, and sexual contacts with animals. The concept of total sexual outlet has been originated and developed. The relation of sexual response and orgasm to aging, social level, age at puberty, marital status, decade of birth, religion and degree of religious devotion, and rural-urban backgrounds has been presented in detail. The wide individual variation in sexual response has been documented and emphasized. The role that psychological factors play in sexual response has been explored. Specific data have been published on sublimation, clitoral versus vaginal orgasm, impotence, premature ejaculation, and frigidity. The relationship of prefrontal lobotomy to sexual response, concepts of normality and abnormality, and the use of induced abortion are included in a partial list of the subjects on which new light has been shed. On a few points the data from the Institute have tested some of the Freudian hypotheses, such as the sexuality of young children and the concept of levels of sexual development.

3. The Institute hopes that its work will encourage other scientists to initiate further re-

search in the area of human sexual behavior. The availability of certain basic statistics on sexual behavior as described above makes it possible for other investigators to use these as controls against which to compare various experimental groups.

4. The Institute for Sex Research is at present the only existing repository in the world for all types of material relating to sex. It is being increasingly visited by scholars from many different disciplines who are using its facilities and data for their own studies. The study of human sexual behavior is of sufficient importance to warrant the existence of at least one organization such as the Institute for Sex Research.

Future Publications

Enough data have already been collected by the Institute to fill many books, monographs, and journal articles. As each piece of research is readied for publication, supplementary data will be gathered in that particular area.

The following is a list of some of the projected publications for which data have already been collected:

1. *Clinical problems in sexual behavior:* a summary of the scientific data on which clinical policies may be based;

2. *Development of sexual patterns among children:* data on how early attitudes and information are acquired and how they affect patterns of sexual behavior among adults;

3. *Drugs and sexual behavior:* the effect of the use of narcotics, marijuana, and alcohol on sexual behavior;

4. *The erotic element in art:* the extent to which an artist's work depends upon his sexual background and behavior;

5. *Female and male prostitution:* a study of the overt activities of prostitutes, their personalities, the factors that account for their prostitution, and the social significance of their activities;

6. *The heterosexual-homosexual balance:* an analysis of factors that have contributed to the development of heterosexual, homosexual, or combined patterns of behavior;

7. *Institutional sexual adjustment:* a study of the sexual adjustment made by males and fe-

males in prisons, mental institutions, boarding schools, and the armed forces;

8. *Male genital anatomy:* extensive data from the male histories, supplemented with a series of observed data from some of the scientifically trained subjects;

9. *Sexual customs in ancient Peru:* an attempt to reconstruct the sexual life of the pre-Inca Indians of Peru, as reflected in their extensive art and pottery;

10. *Sexual factors in marital adjustment:* a manual for the use of clinicians and all married persons;

11. *Transvestism and transsexualism:* a study of persons who dress in the clothing of the opposite sex or who wish to change their sex.

References

Publications by the Institute

Christenson, C. V., and Gagnon, J. H., "Sexual Behavior in a Group of Older Women." *Journal of Gerontology. 20; 3;* 351-356, 1965.

Gagnon, J. H., "Sexuality and Sexual Learning in the Child." *Psychiatry. 28; 3;* 212-228, 1965.

Gebhard, P. H., and Gagnon, J. H., "Male Sex Offenders Against Very Young Children." *American Journal of Psychiatry. 121; 6;* 576-579, 1964.

Gebhard, P. H., Gagnon, J. H., Pomeroy, W. B., and Christenson, C. V., *Sex Offenders: An Analysis of Types.* New York: Harper-Hoeber, 1965.

Gebhard, Paul H., Pomeroy, Wardell B., Martin, Clyde E., and Christenson, Cornelia V., *Pregnancy, Birth and Abortion.* New York: Harper & Brothers, 1958.

Kinsey, Alfred C., Pomeroy, Wardell B., Martin, Clyde E., and Gebhard, Paul H., "Concepts of Normality and Abnormality in Sexual Behavior." In Paul H. Hoch and Joseph Zubin (eds.), *Psychosexual Development in Health and Disease.* New York: Grune & Stratton, Inc., 1949.

Kinsey, Alfred C., "Criteria for a Hormonal Explanation of the Homosexual." *J. Clin. Endocrinol. 1;* 424-428, 1941.

Kinsey, Alfred C., Pomeroy, Wardell B., Martin, Clyde E., Gebhard, Paul H. *Sexual Behavior in the Human Female.* Philadelphia and London: W. B. Saunders Co., 1953.

Kinsey, Alfred C., Pomeroy, Wardell B., and Martin, Clyde E., *Sexual Behavior in the Human Male.* Philadelphia and London: W. B. Saunders Co., 1948.

Pomeroy, Wardell B., "Psychosurgery and Sexual Behavior." In Nolan D. C. Lewis, Carney Landis, and H. E. King (eds.), *Studies in Topectomy.* New York: Grune & Stratton, Inc., 1956.

WARDELL B. POMEROY

Smell and Sex,
The Sense of

THE sense of smell as it relates to the sexual life of man has been given only scant treatment by researchers on sex or on olfaction. Probably the only serious sustained work of any length on the subject was that of Havelock Ellis, who devoted one section of his *Studies in the Psychology of Sex* to smell. Works of rather doubtful value have been written by Bloch (1934), Galopin (1896), Tardif (1899), and Fauconney (1903). There are occasional references to smell in Freud, and a psychoanalytic study of the sense of smell in neuroses and psychoses was made by Brill (1932). Most studies on sex (except those dealing with lower animals) have omitted smell, and philosophers of love (such as Stendhal) have devoted only a few sentences to this subject, although the poets, perhaps anxious to find imaginative figures of speech, have not failed to comment on the odors of their beloved. Researchers on olfaction are inclined to exaggerate the importance of odors in the sexual and amorous life of man, but offer little scientific evidence to validate their theories.

This scanty treatment of odor in relation to man's sex life is twofold in origin: first, the sense of smell plays a very minor, almost a negligible, role in the sex life of civilized man; and second, olfaction itself is a little-understood, little-studied phenomenon, the entire literature of which has failed to bring forth a single acceptable explanation of the nature of the olfactory stimulus and response. Systematic and scientifically valid studies on olfaction are rare. Inasmuch as sex also suffers from a lack of valid experimentation and from a myriad of ill-founded, unsubstantiated data, it is obvious that there would be a paucity of material that combines the two fields.

Man's sense of smell has diminished, although it has not disappeared. The infrahuman animal detects odors at far distances and discriminates between similar and seemingly similar odors. The dog is aroused by the smell of the bitch and uses his smelling apparatus exclusively, with no tactile contact, in presexual play. Ellis (1936) reports on a male dog who was aroused by another male dog after the latter has had intercourse with a bitch. The aroused male smelled the odor of the female in heat, and attempted sexual relations with the source of that smell.

Among a few animals in whom arousal by olfactory means is the major method of winning a mate, Darwin contended that the males in whom the scent glands were most highly developed were the most successful in winning mates. Hence, by the process of sexual selection, these scent glands became accentuated in the offspring. Thus, Darwin wrote:

The development of these [scent] organs is intelligible through sexual selection, as the most odoriferous males are the most successful in winning the females, and in leaving offspring to inherit their greatly perfected glands and odors. . . . As the males of most animals search for the females, these odoriferous glands probably serve to excite or charm the female, rather than to guide her to the spot where the male may be found.

It is interesting that musk, highly valued as a perfume material and considered an "aphrodisiacal" odor (Zwaardemaker, 1895), should be so highly developed in those animals in whom the scent gland is the sexual attractant.

Whether the sense of smell in man declined as he became a biped (when the nose is closer to the ground, it can detect and trace odors the better—as witness the bloodhound, as well as snakes and lizards, whose sense of smell is highly developed), or whether this sense declined because it had largely lost its *raison d'être*, it has become a minor, almost vestigial, characteristic of civilized man. Supplemented, and supplanted, by more refined and exacting methods of perception and communication, the sense of smell is unable to serve to locate, identify, arouse, woo, or win the partner, and offers the partner little in the way of enhanced gratification.

Scholars traveling to lands still largely untouched by civilization have commented on the role played by smell in the sex life of primitive peoples. Some of these people are said to identify by means of smell; others, in contempt, speak of a person who does not have a smell. These passages in the works of naturalists and anthropologists seem to be few in number and narrow in scope, and the body of anthropological work adds up to a convincing picture of aboriginal man as being microosmatic (although perhaps slightly less so than Western man). If odor plays a larger role in the sex life of primitive than it does in civilized man, it nevertheless has an acutely minor role in his total sexuality.

In modern Western man, the use of odors to arouse members of the other sex is limited to the minor element of perfume, except for pathological cases of individuals who are aroused by odors of a fecal nature or by smells that would be considered repulsive by most people. Such instances of olfactory arousal may be linked with scatological arousal and may indicate a severe childish fixation or a manifestation of olfactory masochism.

In the latter case, the need of the individual to undergo punishment at the hands of the sex partner during the sex act takes on the form of being subject to "painful" olfactory stimuli. Inasmuch as the "pain" is inflicted by a partner who reflects the contempt of civilization for those enjoying repulsive and scatological odors, the olfactory masochist seems to be seeking

humiliation and self-abnegation. This search for pain and punishment, rather than the search for gratification by odor arousal, may possibly offer a clue to analinctus. In fellatio and cunnilinctus the heightened odors that may arise from the sex partner are easily detectable; but the fellator or cunnilinguist is probably not seeking the odor and therefore finding the method of gratification; rather, he (or she) is enjoying the method of sexual activity and is aroused by all concomitant stimuli, of which smell is a minor one.

Although romantic literature (particularly poetry) has many references to fragrances, arousal because of a specific odor is rare in human beings. Actually, the ideal of civilized man is not the diminution but the disappearance of natural body odor, and its replacement, at least in the female and to a lesser degree in the male as well, by perfume.

Efforts to classify perfumes according to the degree of sexual arousal have been lacking in scientific validity; in fact, all efforts at odor classification have been challenged (Sagarin, 1950). However, perfumers generally regard odors of the musklike types as aphrodisiacal or ambrosiacal. These odors are not only found in the sex glands of several animals (musk deer, muskrat, and others), but are widely known in plant life and have been reproduced synthetically.

For most men and women, olfaction offers little sexual enticement and slight sexual excitement. Perfume advertising is almost entirely centered around the theme of sex, and although this may in part reflect the element of exaggeration characteristic of advertising generally, it is also a result of the difficulty of describing an odor except in imaginative evocation. Perfume is one attribute, albeit a minor one, in attracting and arousing a potential mate. In that respect, it is to be grouped with other cosmetics, general physical appearance, and the surrounding atmosphere conducive to a satisfactory sexual life.

If attraction and enticement by odor are rare, not so is repulsion. The advertisement of the lonely girl who has an unattractive odor emanating from her body is not entirely fanciful.

During precoital periods and during sexual intercourse, body odors are said to change, heighten, and intensify, possibly adding to total gratification; but this is on a secondary and not too conscious level and has been little explored to date, so far as published data are concerned.

References

Bieber, Irving, "Olfaction in Sexual Development and Adult Sexual Organization." *Amer. J. Psychother. 13;* 851-859, 1959.

Bloch, Iwan, *Odoratus Sexualis.* New York: Panurge, 1934.

Brill, A. A., "The Sense of Smell in the Neuroses and Psychoses." *Psychoanalyt. Quart. 1;* 7-42, 1932.

Darwin, Charles, *The Origin of Species.* Many editions.

Ellis, Havelock, *Studies in the Psychology of Sex* (Vol. 2, Part 1). New York: Random House, 1936.

Fauconney, J. (Dr. Caufeynon, pseud.), *La volupté et les parfums.* Paris: Offenstadt, 1903.

Freud, Sigmund. *Civilization and Its Discontents.* Many editions.

Galopin, A., *Le parfum de la femme et le sens olfactif dans l'amour.* Paris: Dentu, 1886.

Sagarin, E., *The Science and Art of Perfumery* (1st ed.). New York: McGraw-Hill Book Co., 1945.

Sagarin, E., "On the Inherent Invalidity of All Current Systems of Odor Classification." *J. Soc. Cosmetic Chem. 2;* 25-35, 1950.

Tardif, E., *Les odeurs et les parfums: leur influence sur le sens génésique.* Paris: Baillière, 1899.

Zwaardemaker, H., *Die Physiologie des Geruchs.* Leipzig: Engelmann, 1895.

EDWARD SAGARIN

Social Order, Sex and the*

Some Definitions

Sex

SINCE sex is basic to the social order—in fact, prerequisite to it—it may seem a bit like gilding the lily to define it. Yet the very fact of its ubiquity has led to such careless use of the term that a denotation of the meaning intended here is necessary for clear communication. As every layman knows, reproduction is one of the major organ systems, having the specific function of continuing the species. What every layman does not know is that the reproductive functions may be carried on in social contexts that place widely different values on them, thereby accounting for the divergent attitudes reported by anthropologists returning from the bush, and by the clinician working with members of different subcultures.

Complicating the picture still further is the fact that among various cultures the social roles of the two sexes bear variable relationships to the underlying reproductive functions, sometimes adhering closely to the biological *Anlage;* sometimes deviating to the point of reversal. In what follows we shall attempt to maintain a conceptual distinction between the biological and social roles of the sexes.

Social Order

Our introductory remarks have suggested that an adequate understanding of individual behavior may be attained only by reference to the social context in which it occurs. Far from representing an instinctive absolute, the dependence of sexual behavior on the surrounding social order is strikingly demonstrated by its relationship to position in the dominance hierarchy from fish to man. At the human level, social pressures are communicated to individual members by a system of symbols which constitute the culture. "Social order" is a term sufficiently broad to include animal organizations as well as human cultures. The principal focus of the present article, however, will be certain aspects of sexual behavior in contemporary American society.

Subhuman Societies

Birds and Lizards

Throughout the vertebrate array, basic reproductive patterns are influenced by the social orders in which they occur. In as low a species as the American chameleon, dominance status rather than the sex of the individual determines the kind of sexual behavior displayed on a given occasion. A male may express masculine behavior in the presence of a subordinate while acting like a female when confronted with a more dominant member of his own sex. Among birds, the pigeon—whose flock organization is very flexible—further demonstrates the dependency of mating on social status. It has been found that the bird with temporary dominance, whether male or female, usually displays characteristic components of the male mating pat-

* Copyrighted title of book by same author, published by McGraw-Hill, 1946.

tern. Without multiplying examples, we may be safe in concluding from the evidence at hand that, although reproductive activities among species below the mammals seem to be primarily dependent upon internal mechanisms, they are subject to regulation and change by external factors.

Mice and Monkeys

When we reach the mammals, we find biological mechanisms less rigid in their operation and social influences correspondingly more numerous and complicated in their effects. Even as low a mammal as the rodent demonstrates dramatically the effects of social experience on the maternal behavior of male rats and mice after being caged with young.

Among primates, the over-all social structure defines the sex roles. Thus, in the macaque monkey and the baboon, dominance is closely correlated with the masculine, and subordination with the feminine roles. In the higher apes, greater variability appears. In gibbon society, the only sex differences are in the procreative act, social status resulting from personal qualities rather than brute force. For the chimpanzee, either sex may command priority although the male by virtue of his superior size and strength assumes the responsibility of guarding and defending the weaker females and juveniles. During the early weeks of a baby's life, the father remains close to his family, ready to lend the mother a helping hand.

It would appear from the evidence that, among primates, personality begins to play an important role in the community and that sexual as well as other specific forms of behavior must be viewed in relationship to the social order.

Preliterate Cultures

When we reach man, we find that social pressures transmitted through an intricate system of symbols shape individual conduct in every area of living. The value placed on procreation differs from culture to culture. Moreover, the range of behavior permitted men and women is redefined by each society (Ford and Beach, 1951). Whenever the struggle for existence is with "nature-in-the-raw," whether in the South Seas, the Old West, or the Chicago slums, there is little question of the muscularly stronger male's assuming the more strenuous role of coping with the physical environment while to the female falls the more sedentary lot of baby-tending and keeping the home fires burning. Certain basic regularities along these lines have been reported as underlying cultures with markedly different surface patterning of sex roles. In all, achievement appears as the chief preoccupation of the men; nurturing, of the women (Mead, 1949).

Sex as Growth

Margaret Mead, in her studies of New Guinea societies (1930), described two peoples with contrasting orientations for whom sex and sex roles have different meanings. Among the Arapesh, whose life centers around the concept of growth in its various aspects, sex is subordinated to child-rearing and seen as a form of nurturing. According to native belief, the child is the joint product of father and mother. Frequent intercourse between them is believed necessary to nourish the egg, but after it is safely launched, sexual abstinence is demanded. Immediately after birth, both parents share equally in caring for the infant. Erotic interest as such is not admitted. Rather than a highly charged affair, the sex act is apparently a comfortable mutual expression of affection.

Sex as Sin

Among the Manus of a generation ago, a very different picture of sex is revealed in terms of the over-all value system (Mead, 1930). This culture, like our own, was focused on the accumulation of wealth and property. Economic success was the goal of life, and the means to that end was trade.

Marriages represented one of the most important opportunities for investment because they provided for a variety of economic exchanges. Such investments were protected by a religion conceived of in terms of ancestral spirits, whose business it was to supervise their descendants' economic and sexual lives. Infractions of the strict sex code were analogous to our concept of "sin" with all its religious implications.

The sexual relationship between man and

wife was reduced to crude biological function, stripped of warmth and strained by shame. There was no happy model of a close mother-tie to indicate what might be expected from the new relationship. On the contrary, the little Manus bride looked forward with dread to her first sexual experience. Frigidity and pain were her traditional lot, and every woman conveyed to her growing daughters her own aversion to the "humiliation" of coitus. Love as a rich, shared experience was not recognized. In Manus society at that time sex was not an end in itself but merely secondary to the predominant value of property ownership.

Revisiting Manus 25 years later, Mead (1956) reported a new attitude toward the feminine role. Whereas formerly women were expected to be docile and passive, now, following the American model, they are encouraged to become spontaneous and actively loving. The cultural discontinuity involved in the sudden change in this area is a source of conflict for those caught in it during the transitional period.

Sex as Art

In contrast to the bland interpretation of sex among the Arapesh and its devaluation among the Manus is the high saliency it possesses for the Marquesans. In this polyandrous society, sex may help to compensate for severe threats concerning the supplies of food and women. Erotic overvaluation helps to reduce the tensions associated with both these sources of anxiety. The sensual is woven tightly into the entire fabric of the society. Not only does it characterize adult relationships, but children are introduced to it in earliest infancy.

In the structuring of Marquesan personality, tenderness has been exchanged for sensuality at every stage of development. Masturbation is used by adults as a pacifier for infants. Sexual play is practiced in childhood and regular intercourse begun before puberty. Between puberty and marriage young people form a special group whose function it is to entertain at public ceremonies with singing, dancing, and sexual accommodation of male visitors.

Marriage is polyandrous, reflecting the disproportionate sex ratio. Her rarity lends glamour to the woman and enhances her value as a sex object. By the distribution of her sexual favors, she is able to control her husbands. It is she who takes the initiative in the sex act while the man plays up her erotic wishes by an elaborate ritual. In contrast to the Arapesh, the feeding function of the breasts is subordinated to their sensual uses. Since the woman's chief role is a sexual one, she is relieved of the burden of child care.

Although these few examples do not begin to cover the range of variation in sex evaluations among preliterate peoples, they all point to the necessity of viewing sexual behavior in the context of the culture as a whole.

American Core Culture

Middle-Class Sex Patterns

Within our culture, it would be a gross oversimplification to perceive sex in univalent terms. A glance at Ellis' *Folklore of Sex* (1951) is sufficient to dispel any illusion in that direction. Middle-class ideology is itself broad enough to permit conflicting evaluations of sex to exist side by side. Sex-as-sin, hardy survivor of a repressive age, can hardly fail to remind one of the old Manus society. The Puritan sex mores are gradually yielding to the new "fun compulsion," which tends to give sexual behavior a preciousness that would do credit to a Marquesan. At the same time, we should note the increasing emphasis on the importance of child development, with the new pressures on fathers to share in the nurturing of their offspring. This trend could lead to an understressing of the specifically erotic aspects of marital relationships that would do the Arapesh credit. While all these analogies are obviously overdrawn and oversimplified, the point is that in a culture representing a wide diversity of values, the mores as part of that culture are also bound to be characterized by a multiplicity of values.

The diversity of sex mores in the American core culture is revealed by an extensive study of letters and intimate conversations with a large sample of men and women from what Hirsch (1955) calls the "upper cultural" levels. It appears from this material that Victorian mores have actually if not officially given way to an era of greater sex freedom that permits wide variability in the interpretation of acceptable sexual behavior. Moreover, discrepancies be-tween biological and social sex roles are the order of the day in a cultural segment where symbols may substitute for direct action in the struggle for existence. In many American fam-ilies, sex typing still follows the European tradi-tion, with the father serving as the more potent frustrater. In others, the parents share in both domestic and economic areas, while in still others, the domineering mother has taken the place of the authoritarian father as the pivot of the home.

Sex and the Culture of Poverty

Further variations become apparent when we examine the subcultures that make up the American scene. Across the tracks certain value differences are reflected both in sexual behavior and in social sex roles. The more immediate im-pulse expression finds an outlet in direct hetero-sexual activity (Myers and Roberts, 1959). Children's peer groups may discuss sexual rela-tions freely before puberty, and status, as Davis (1944) has shown, is augmented by sexual ex-perience. Masturbation, on the other hand, is more apt to be disapproved of as a perversion among working-class people, who narrowly channel their sexual expression in coitus, with comparatively little variation in technique and foreplay. In this connection, Kinsey *et al.* (1948) reported that manual and oral stimulation of the male and female genitals and of the woman's breasts occur more frequently in mar-riages in which at least the husband has at-tended college. These precoital practices oc-curred much less often among men who had not gone as far as high school.

As for social sex roles, in the slums as in the bush the more immediate contact with the en-vironment demands a sharper division of labor between the sexes. Rabban's (1950) study of sex-role identification among young children showed that those from poverty backgrounds who were alerted earlier to the crude realities they would have to face made an earlier sex identification than did those from the suburbs. As a result of the greater parental stress on sex differences, these children became sensitized to sex-appropriate behavior in play, dress, and attitude as part of the sex-role pattern of their subculture and were able to internalize it earlier.

Color and Sex

In the South

Beyond the color barrier, social-class differ-ences still hold. Among rural lower-class south-ern Negroes, vestiges of the antebellum mother-based family may be traced in the easy sex mores, which put little emphasis on legal matrimony. Marriage more often follows than precedes maternity, motherhood serving to validate the woman's worthiness and maturity. In the cities of the South, the lower-class woman is still dominant over the man but Vic-torian sex mores have been adopted. As a con-sequence, illegitimacy has acquired an official stigma while natural motherhood has lost its folk meaning and dignity.

In the North

For the northern lower-class Negro, as for his white status peer, early heterosexual behavior is the rule, little boys often attempting inter-course as early as 7 or 8 years of age (Kardiner and Ovesey, 1951). Regular coitus with older women is the pattern followed by adolescents. In this group, masturbation is regarded as neither a necessary nor a desirable outlet. In the case of girls, first intercourse is earlier than for white girls of comparable background. Ves-tiges of the double standard, however, appear in the greater marital fidelity expected of wives than of their husbands. All trace of the naive value of motherhood as such has given way to a moralistic distinction between married and unmarried motherhood.

The Negro middle class has paralleled that of Caucasian society. Striving for upward mobil-ity is indicated by a pattern of child-training practices according to which the value of re-spectability is thoroughly bred into the devel-oping personalities through emphasis on impulse delay. The family, which has assumed the patriarchal monogamous form of the sur-rounding culture, is the model for a good marriage.

Sexual behavior that is not congruent with such a goal is regarded as dangerous and in-fractions are severely punished. In sexual purity, the middle-class Negro has no peer. Continence and constancy are presented to the girl as the Cardinal Virtues, and although more latitude is allowed boys, there seems to be a pervasive reaction formation against sex, much as there is against dirt. In their zeal to ensure following the Caucasian ideal on the one hand, and to avoid confusion with Negroes of a lower class on the other, they have apparently overshot the mark and have paid a heavy price in impotence and frigidity.

Although the Negro family is no longer reduced to the "uterine family" of slavery the mother has remained its mainstay. From the times when men were at an economic disadvantage in getting jobs, a tradition of the mother as protector and provider grew up that has lingered on in open conflict with the patriarchal ideology of the core culture. This partial sex-role reversal has had deleterious effects on the interaction between the sexes, lowering the woman's evaluation of the man and the man's evaluation of himself. With improving self-esteem, however, Negro-Americans should be increasingly able to find their own identities and move to more validly equalitarian positions with their Caucasian peers.

Sex Behavior in Acculturation

The myriad subcultures in contemporary United States provide a wide spectrum of values that color both biological and social sex roles. Here we find in purer form the various themes already noted in the core culture.

The Patriarchal "Latins"

To illustrate, the patriarchal structure of Italian- and Spanish-American groups predisposes them to a sharp dichotomy, associated with a double standard of sex behavior. Male dominance is highly valued as a power symbol epitomized by the Mexican *machismo*. Aside from certain taboos regarding family and friends' families, a man is free to "play the field" and to regard all unprotected women as fair game. Women falling in the broad mother-sister category, however, are beyond the pale since the preservation of their virginity until marriage is implemented by the strictest sanctions in the culture.

The Matriarchal Irish

The Irish-American presents a very different picture. With the mother as the central controlling figure, the father takes on a more shadowy form. According to Irish tradition, sex is intricately bound up with a complicated familism and defection from the accepted mores is perceived as sin. Because of the cultural power of the Church, offenders are automatically declassed. Under this system, sex is generally de-emphasized and limited to procreation in wedlock. Mild, protracted courtships are usual; marital infidelity, rare; and celibacy, widespread.

These two examples of divergent subcultural evaluations of sex, although far from exhaustive, may at least remind us of the need to keep in mind the social context when attempting an appraisal of patterns of sexual behavior. Our perspective will be further broadened by ongoing cross-national studies in Europe and the Americas of adolescent attitudes toward social sex roles (Havighurst, et al, 1965; Seward, et al[1]).

Some Implications

Role Discontinuity

Perhaps the most outstanding feature emerging from this brief survey is the variability in meaning given to sex by different social orders. Even in animals, sexual behavior is biosocial rather than purely biological. Among people, whether preliterate or members of our complex society, sex mores and the social roles of men and women are in continual flux.

The lack of specificity and constancy in sex typing is an undeniable source of confusion since there are no blueprints to guide the individual during the course of his socialization. Unlike many of the more homogeneous cultures, few precedents for the new generation are to be found in the previous ones. As we have noted, not even the simplest societies like the Manus of New Guinea are safe from the encroachments of "progress." In our own fluid culture, preparation of children for their future roles by the parent generation becomes worse than useless—it is definitely misleading, parents becoming negative models to be avoided rather than emulated. A girl of today, for example,

1. Seward, Georgene H., *et al.*, *Adolescent Concepts of Adult Social Sex Roles, a Cross-National Study.* (In preparation.)

brought up in the ways of her grandmother would lack the self-assertion needed to hold her own in the contemporary world. A boy in an analogous situation, on the other hand, might very well show too much self-assertion to make a good organization man.

Apart from the generation-long changes in sex-role patterning, there are the sudden discontinuities that arise from time to time while the individual is growing up. What is appropriate boy or girl behavior at one age may be altogether inappropriate a little later. For the boy, boisterousness gradually gives way to gentleness as an essential ingredient of the acceptable masculine pattern. For the girl, ideals of greater passivity or activity shift with bewildering swiftness at different stages. A feminine paradox that continues to plague the girl into adulthood is the repeated problem that arises in her relationships with men as to when to "play dumb" and when she can afford to "play it straight" in keeping with the intellectual and educational level she shares with them (Heilbrun, 1963; Komarovsky, 1953).

Sex-Identity Problems

The flexibility of social roles in a society that stresses the individual as the focus calls into question the Freudian assumptions concerning fixed role models. Although the very young child becomes aware that there are different social expectations for boys and girls and, as Brown (1958) has shown, early expresses his preferences for certain sex-typed objects and activities, unilateral identification with mother or father figures as preparation for a stereotyped sex role loses meaning in the varied domestic climate of the American home (Seward, 1964).

With authority between father and mother more evenly divided than in former times and far-off places, the respective sex roles may appear rather "fuzzy" from the child's perspective. Under the circumstances, however, a certain degree of ambiguity may be preferable to early fixity in order to make room for the modifications required to meet changing cultural demands. Where flexibility is the rule, the individual should not be forced into a specific pattern. He needs to be left free to choose and to integrate his various role experiences. If the

home provides an atmosphere of harmony and acceptance, the child will internalize a positive attitude and be able to accept his sexual status along with other values. He will be able confidently to affirm his sex identity among his peers in whatever behavioral terms are currently appropriate to his age and circumstance. The parents' satisfaction in their own sex roles is the best recommendation for membership in whichever sex group the child belongs to. It is not necessary for him to imitate his parent's particular interpretation of the appropriate role. By the same logic, as Henry (1955) seems to imply, inversion may be assumed to result not so much from specific cross-sex identification as from the internalization of a negative self-image that includes the sexual as well as other areas of personality and is derived from an unhappy and insecure family situation.

Multiplicity of Role Choices

The variability that we have found to be characteristic of the development of social sex roles continues into adulthood, when a number of choices are open to members of both sexes. For women, the old-fashioned housewife and the newer-fashioned career girl stand at the extremes. The domestic woman, traditional in Western culture, is extolled by such classical psychoanalysts as Helene Deutsch (1945) and Therese Benedek (1952). At the feminist extreme, Simone de Beauvoir (1953) perceives women as a "second sex" forced to occupy what in her opinion amounts to a separate caste in society. Conflict between marriage and career has been most acute for the middle-class college girl for whom the traditional domestic role has failed to provide an adequate sense of personal worth (Seward, 1945; Weiss and Samelson, 1958). There are social as well as personal repercussions in the conventionally restricted feminine role. As the Swedish sociologists (Dahlström et al., 1967) remind us, unless the married woman actively participates in the larger society, the family is in danger of becoming isolated from the mainstream of the culture. Women today are no longer faced with the simple alternative of working either inside or outside the home, but with the far more difficult task of combining the female biological role with whatever social role would best express her particular needs and abilities. It is up to each individual to work out her special compromise between the two poles.

For men, there have also been role changes in line with the trend toward greater status equality between the sexes. Overlapping of social roles within the home as well as outside it has put "father" on a more intimate basis with his family. No longer is he cast as the distant ogre whose punitive image is invoked whenever the child disobeys the mother. Nor need he be downgraded as a mere "mother's helper." Fathers increasingly see themselves as active participants in the daily care, teaching, and play of their children. "Fatherliness," with all its connotations of gentleness and warmth, is gaining respect and acceptance in the culture. A study by Josselyn (1956) indicates that it is only those who have been overcontrolled by women, and consequently try to escape into a pseudomasculine world of drinking, swearing, and derogation of women, who see fatherliness as threatening to their masculinity.

New Role Integrations

Throughout our discussion we have stressed the need to keep separate the biological and social aspects of sexual behavior, which may be variously combined according to individual preference. In so far as individual preference follows natural cleavages, however, we should expect greater comfort to result.

The consistency with which certain sex differences have been reported strongly suggests that anatomy, if not destiny, at least plays an important part in setting the initial direction of male and female interests. Boys of all ages tend to be oriented toward motion, daring, and power; girls toward serving and conserving. We have previously referred to a similar sex difference in ethnological material. Underlying surface variations in code and custom among a variety of preliterate peoples, Mead (1949) found that males were found to be consistently preoccupied with achievement, and women with nurturing.

Approaching the problem clinically yet without adopting the masculine bias of the classical Freudians, Erich Fromm (1949) points out the fallacy of equating difference with efficiency. For him, differences in biological role have certain personality overtones. In the sex act, the male is put on his mettle to demonstrate his potency, while the female must wait for him to satisfy her. This fundamental difference in biological function underlies a tendency toward domination and achievement in men, and toward dependency in women. According to Fromm, it accounts for the "masculine" traits of initiative, activity, and courage, and for the "feminine" traits of patience, reliability, and charm. But since such characteristics, even though biologically derived, blend with those directly produced by culture, they may be played up or down in a given society and would not justify a universal casting of men and women in different social roles.

In any case, there is too much overlapping between the sexes in contemporary American society to risk a forced dichotomy in the ascription of social roles. As Komarovsky (1953) has pointed out in a discussion of women's education, woman's "nature" would be just as much violated by being forced into a feminized curriculum as by what is called the "imitation" of men. In other words, since the chief differences are between individuals rather than between the sex groups, sufficient flexibility must be permitted to foster the talents of individuals irrespective of their sex membership. That difficult role integrations are gradually being achieved is suggested by recent work in which college students interpreted the feminine role as a blend of both nurturing and achieving functions (Steinmann, 1963).

In so far as there are strong biologically determined predilections, however, the modal activities of the two sexes may be expected to gravitate around them by choice. Although pressures toward narrow sex-typing would do violence to the individual, all lines of evidence suggest that close congruity between biological and social sex roles provides the richest emotional rewards.

References

Arensberg, C. M., and Kimball, S. T., *Family and Community in Ireland.* Cambridge: Harvard University Press, 1940.

Barrabee, P., "How Cultural Factors Affect Family Life." In National Conference of Social Work, *The Social Welfare Forum.* New York: Columbia University Press, 1954.

Benedek, T., *Psychosexual Functions in Women.* New York: The Ronald Press Co., 1952.

Brown, D. G., "Sex-role Development in a Changing Culture." *Psychol. Bull.* 55; 232-242, 1958.

Burma, J. H., *Spanish-speaking Groups in the United States.* Durham, N.C.: Duke University Press, 1954.

Dahlström, E. and Liljeström, Rita, "The family and married women at work." In E. Dahlström, et al., *The Changing Roles of Men and Women.* London: Gerald Duckworth & Co., 1967.

Davis, A., "Socialization and Adolescent Personality." *Yearbk. Nat. Social Stud. Educ.* 43; 198-216, 1944.

de Beauvoir, S., *The Second Sex.* New York: Alfred A. Knopf, Inc., 1953.

Deutsch, H., *The Psychology of Woman; a Psychoanalytic Interpretation.* New York: Grune & Stratton, Inc., 1945.

Ellis, A., *The Folklore of Sex.* New York: Boni, 1951.

Ford, C. S. and Beach, F. A., *Patterns of Sexual Behavior.* New York: Harper & Brothers, 1951.

Frazier, F., "Sociologic Factors in the Formation of Sex Attitudes." In P. H. Hoch and J. Zubin (eds.), *Psychosexual Development in Health and Disease.* New York: Grune & Stratton, Inc., 1949.

Fromm, E., "Sex and Character." In R. Anshen (ed.), *The Family: Its Function and Destiny.* New York: Harper & Brothers, 1949.

Havighurst, R. J., et al., *A Cross-national Study of Buenos Aires and Chicago Adolescents,* New York and Basel (Switzerland): S. Karger, 1965.

Heilbrun, A. B., Jr., "Sex Role Identity and Achievement Motivation." *Psychol. Rep.* 2; 483-490, 1963.

Henry, G. W., *All the Sexes.* New York: Rinehart & Co., Inc., 1955.

Hirsch, A. H., *Sexual Misbehavior of the Upper Cultured.* New York: Vantage Press, 1955.

Josselyn, I. M., "Cultural Forces, Motherliness and Fatherliness." *Am. J. Orthopsychiat.* 26; 264-271, 1956.

Kardiner, A., *The Individual and His Society.* New York: Columbia University Press, 1939.

Kardiner, A., and Ovesey, L., *The Mark of Oppression.* New York: W. W. Norton & Co., Inc., 1951.

Kinsey, A. C. *et al., Sexual Behavior in the Human Male.* Philadelphia: W. B. Saunders Co., 1948.

Komarovsky, M., *Women in the Modern World.* Boston: Little, Brown & Co., 1953.

Mead, M., *Growing Up in New Guinea.* London: Wm. Morrow & Co., Inc., 1930.

Mead, M., *Sex and Temperament in Three Primitive Societies.* New York: Wm. Morrow & Co., Inc., 1935.

Mead, M., *Male and Female.* New York: Wm. Morrow & Co., Inc., 1949.

Mead, M., *New Lives for Old: Cultural Transformation —Manus, 1928-1953.* New York: Wm. Morrow & Co., Inc., 1956.

Myers, J. K. and Roberts, B. H., *Family and Class Dynamics in Mental Illness.* New York: John Wiley & Sons, 1959.

Opler, M. K., and Singer, J. L., "Ethnic Differences in Behavior and Psychopathology: Italian and Irish." *Internat. J. Social Psychiat.* 2; 11-22, 1956.

Rabban, M., "Sex-role Identification in Young Children in Two Diverse Social Groups." *Genet. Psychol. Monogr.* 42; 81-158, 1950.

Seward, Georgene H., "Cultural Conflict and the Feminine Role." *J. Soc. Psychol.* 22; 177-194, 1945.

Seward, G., *Sex and the Social Order.* New York: McGraw-Hill Book Co., 1946.

Seward, G., *Psychotherapy and Culture Conflict.* New York: The Ronald Press Co., 1956.

Seward, Georgene H., "Sex Identity and the Social Order." *J. Nerv. Ment. Dis.* 139 (2); 126-136, 1964.

Steinmann, Anne, "A Study of the Concept of the Feminine Role of 51 Middle-class American Families." *Genet. Psychol. Monogr.* 67; 275-352, 1963.

Weiss, R. E. and Samelson, Nancy M., "Social Roles of American Women: Their Contribution to a Sense of Usefulness and Importance." *Marriage Fam. Living.* 20; 358-366, 1958.

GEORGENE SEWARD

Soviet Union, Sex in the

The Setting

THE Soviet Union is a multinational state, with the Great Russians and their Slavic cousins, the Ukrainians and Belorussians, constituting about 75 per cent of the population. This study shall confine itself to the Russians as the most articulate expression of the mores of that Slavic majority. Most Russians come from Greek Orthodox Christian families, although a large proportion of those born and educated since the 1917 revolution regard themselves as agnostics, "nonbelievers," or atheists. But the break with the church has not erased Orthodox Christianity's teachings and mystique with regard to right and wrong, good and evil, sin and confession.

Within the last thirty years, the Soviet Union has changed from a predominantly peasant land, with the specific sexual habits of the Russian village, dominated by the local priest (who in the Orthodox Church is permitted to marry and, among Russians, usually had children), to a country half village and half overcrowded city.

In the city, the largest external factor in sex life is the absence of privacy of bedroom, toilet, and bath. Until the post-Stalin regime launched a massive urban housing program, only "upper-crust" urban couples had enough private space to enjoy thoroughly, or become thoroughly satiated, with each other's sexual company. For the vast majority of urbanites, a private bedroom—occupied only by a male and female adult—is still the exception; a private room and bath for a couple is still the badge of the upper class. For most married couples and young people in Moscow, Leningrad, Kiev, Kharkov,

Odessa, etc., conditions of domestic sexual privacy, as they prevail in the West, are still a dream. Millions of couples still share their bedchamber with children, parents, grandparents, in-laws, or boarders. In the age of Soviet nuclear advances, there are still millions of men and women whose nuptial bed is still separated by a mere curtain or a screen from the lonely crowd of blood relatives, in-laws, and subtenants. Because man is an adaptable animal, unwritten rules help to create the illusion of sexual privacy where there is none. We can assume also that would-be love-makers welcome those interludes when grandma is at the movies, daughter at a dance, or the other tenants off to the country. Perhaps these adverse conditions create their own compensations and sense of sexual adventure. On the other hand, modern Soviet society is strewn with marriages that have been destroyed on the domestic battlefields of communal bedrooms, kitchens, and toilets.

These conditions in the cities do not, however, represent a complete break with the sex climate of the primitive peasant hut of prerevolutionary Russia. When peasants flocked into the new factories in the early thirties, few were exchanging idyllic country cottages for city slums. Peasant huts often crowded parents, children, and grandparents into a single room and common beds. Sexual privacy could be found under the open sky, in the fields, but in the home itself, children were born, bedded, and raised on the very field of love on which they were conceived.

Only in very recent years, as technology and industry have begun to give millions of citified peasant sons the tastes of the Western middle classes, has the idea of domestic privacy become a major social goal, spurring the regime to more housing construction and the production of more and more domestic comforts formerly decried as petit bourgeois.

Woman

The basic element in the Soviet sex picture is the unique role of women in Russian society. To this day, millions of Russian women still earn their livelihood, or help support their families, by heavy physical labor. Women constitute a major work force on the farms and in industry; more so than before the revolution, because two great wars (1914–1918; 1941–1945), the civil war (1918–1921), collectivization (1929–1933), and mass purges (1937–1939) have decimated the male population. Women also play a greater role in certain arduous professions than they do in the West: for example, the great majority of doctors in the Soviet Union are women. Moreover, Soviet women played an active role in the last war, tending the wounded under fire, fighting as partisans, digging antitank trenches, manning factories under artillery and air attack. Even the daughters of the "upper crust" and the coeds in Soviet high schools and colleges are mainly of hard-working peasant or worker stock. Only in very recent years has a small minority begun to enjoy leisure, cultivate their appearance, and eat the balanced food that makes for slim health.

Whether a largely carbohydrate diet, hard physical labor, drab clothes, and poor housing conditions have robbed the majority of Soviet women of their essential femininity is another question. If the test is external appearance, fashion-plate sleekness, provocative dress—or undress—then, by Western standards, most Soviet women are not particularly feminine. But femininity is a matter of definition. Note the common complaint of American men, particularly those with wartime sexual experiences abroad, about the lack of femininity of the American female, despite the fact that she is probably the most pampered, best dressed, best fed, and best housed girl in the world.

In prerevolutionary Russia, the daughters of the nobility, land-owning aristocracy, and edu-

cated middle class were among the most elegant women in Europe. Many of them learned foreign languages from childhood, spent holidays abroad, followed the latest Paris fashions. Through generations of selective breeding, the female élite of Russian society, notably in the salons of St. Petersburg, had as much grace and beauty as the women of any cultured caste society from ancient Greece to modern India. The pages of Russian classical literature are filled with glittering images of Russian feminine beauty, elegance, and passion. It is enough to evoke the heroines of Russian literature from Lermontov and Pushkin through Tolstoi, Turgenev, and Dostoevski to Chekhov and Bunin in the recent past to prove the power of feminine beauty and spirit in Russian society of the prerevolutionary age. But even in the backward villages of old Russia, where neither Paris gowns nor literary salons could be found, young peasant girls very often possessed the unique grace and beauty of primitive rustic society. These girls, with their fresh good looks and strong bodies, bloomed at 16, worked and loved in the fields, bred large families, calmly accepted good fortune and tragedy, often gave birth—or died in childbirth—in the fields without a midwife, saw half their children carried off by hunger or epidemics long since conquered by medicine, and were old at 40 through too much toil, privation, and child-bearing.

The tragedy of the Russian peasant girl is perhaps best epitomized in Tolstoi's *Resurrection*, whose heroine, seduced by a young nobleman who had once been her childhood playmate, emerges through tragedy and degradation as a fortress of new strength and moral courage. To this day, through the trials of war, revolution, civil war, collectivization, and mass purges, through Nazi occupation and the austere years of postwar reconstruction, such peasant girls remain the heart and backbone of the Soviet land. They remain much the same today in their essential inner toughness, sincerity of emotion, and capacity to endure suffering and enjoy life. Today they are bearing fewer children, electricity is beginning to reach their homes, and literacy is much more widespread among them. In the coming generation, they too will be increasingly exposed to the Western domestic comforts that are already reaching the cities. But, whether daughters of the upper caste or peasants, natural grace, passion, and toughness of spirit remain striking characteristics of Russian women.

The Russian woman of today—both the middle-aged mother and her teenage daughter—is the product not only of hard-working Soviet society; she is conditioned also by the heroines of widely read nineteenth-century Russian literature. These figures help to shape her being and her dreams. And the moral standards of that literature, whose hallmark is emotional sincerity, both reflect and shape the national character. Because in the Soviet Union the Hollywood type of mass entertainment is rigidly curbed by the state, because there are no slick and pulp magazines devoted to love, crime, adventure stories, cosmetics, and "true confessions," the national literature continues to play a role that is probably without counterpart in the West. Only recently has general hunger for Western culture, shoddy as well as substantial, begun seriously to challenge the formative monopoly of the Russian past and the Soviet present. Now, for the first time on a large scale, highly individualized and therefore —by traditional Russian and Soviet standards— "nihilistic," "bourgeois," and "decadent" values are competing with collective and national ideals. Most great Russian writers and critics of the nineteenth century, no less than Soviet ideologists today, regarded individual happiness, individual search, and individual fulfillment as subordinate to some national, social, or religious end. Genuine liberalism, which held individual freedom to be the basic prerequisite of the good life, remained a relatively weak force. Not only the harsh realities of Russian life but the values of Russia's great writers and thinkers led the strong woman to subordinate individual happiness to some greater good—or evil.

Of course, both in big cities and in provincial centers, there always were—and are again—the wives and daughters of the *nouveau riche,* greedy and half-educated, who are, as their sisters everywhere, interested mainly in social climbing and petty intrigue. Moreover, at the top of Soviet society, as in the pre-Soviet past, all the vices of indolent wealth can be found. And at the bottom, village poverty and urban slums remain breeding grounds for prostitution, incest, rape, and murder, as in any society where ignorance, squalor, and violent appetite meet. But the organization man's spouse, protected and coddled by her split-level house, retirement plan, and country club membership, spending a good share of the national income on cosmetics, clothes, and work-saving devices, has just begun to capture the attention of Soviet women. The vast majority remain, often reluctantly, in a world of great social goals, imbued by tradition and experience and spurred by a sense of destiny. Now the middle-class social revolution is beginning to invade this world of austerity, passion, and ideals that subordinates individual happiness to a collective goal. What this new revolution will do to the Russian woman remains to be seen.

For the present, as Admiral Stevens suggested in his perceptive book *Russian Assignment,* the contemporary Soviet Russian woman still seems close to the following picture found in Tolstoi's *Cossacks*:

The Cossack looks on woman as an instrument of his well-being; he permits young girls to gad about, but he compels his peasant woman to work for him from youth even to advanced old age, and he regards a woman with an Eastern demand for submission and labor. As the result of such a view, the woman who develops intensively both physically and morally even though she is externally submissive, obtains, as generally in the East, an influence and weight in domestic life that is beyond comparison greater than in the West.

. . . [The man] feels confusedly that everything he uses and calls his own is the product of this [woman's] work, and that it is in the power of the woman, mother or wife, whom he counts his serf, to deprive him of everything that is of any use to him. Moreover, the continual masculine, heavy work and the worries that are entrusted to her hands have given a particularly independent, masculine character to the . . . woman and to a surprising degree have developed in her physical strength, decisiveness and firmness of character.

Admiral Stevens remarks that "although in most countries it is probably true that women pursue men more than is commonly admitted, there seems to be something in the Russian man that demands this reversal of the usual relationship. The spirit of Tatiana's letter confessing her love to Eugen Onegin is repeated over and over again throughout Russian literature, sometimes subtly, as in Turgenev's women, sometimes baldly and directly as over and over again in [the Soviet novel] *Grim River*."

When Stevens asked whether Russian women swear at their husbands when they get drunk, the reply was: "That depends on who holds the power in the family. If a man does not seize the power when he first marries, he is apt to have a rough time of it."

Man

The Soviet male is—as is man in every society—a paradoxical figure. The "successful" Soviet male pays just as heavy a price to get ahead, in his way, as does his American brother. In prerevolutionary Russia, the idea of dedicating one's life to hard work was not held in high regard. The aristocracy despised toil, the intelligentsia found greater gratification in the interplay of ideas; the men of the villages spent as much time wallowing in sloth, drinking, gambling, love-making, and exploding into violence, arson, and insurrection as in tilling the fields. Nor did the pre-Soviet proletariat concentrate on a life goal of individual economic security through hard work. Instead, workers flocked to political parties that promised the end of "the exploitation of man by man," the classless society that would ultimately liberate man from unpleasant toil. The diligent peasant, who expanded his fields and his possessions and hired others to work for him, was often the object of envy and scorn. The relatively small class of industrialists and merchants, who worked hard and exploited others to amass fortunes, was held in rather low esteem by aristocrats, workers, and peasants alike.

In Russian eyes, conscientious and efficient work was the mark of the Englishman and the German; when combined with shrewdness, it was the sign of the Armenian or Jew. A "true" Russian had "better" things to do with his life than to waste it in the countinghouse, the business office, the factory, or the corner store. The battlefield, the hunt, the gambling den, the legalized house of prostitution (medically inspected and patronized by all classes), the pogrom, the peasant revolt, the political strike and mass demonstration, the religious orgy in

which prayer, song, and vodka often went together, and, finally, the terror and ecstasy of revolution—these were some of the things that filled the life of the Russian male with so much violence, excitement, tragedy, and chaos.

In the Soviet era, this easy male turbulence, with its cycles of animal vigor and lassitude, has been attacked by a Communist puritanism which measures a man by his services to society —as defined and rewarded by those in power— rather than by the fulfillment of his own unique capacity for self-expression, creation, and individual happiness.

The Soviet system has tried to put work on a pedestal. In its efforts to tame the Russian male, it created the title of "Hero of Socialist Labor" and rewarded pace-setters in factories and mines with bonuses, creating a privileged caste of workers whose marks of achievement were the tonnages of coal they mined per day. It published the names of inefficient workers on billboards; sent chronically absentee workers to forced labor camps; invaded lunch hours and evenings with tiresome lectures on the virtues of still more work; installed loudspeakers in public parks to hammer the state's production goals into the minds of workers even on their holidays and picnics. "He who does not toil shall not eat" became the supreme law of the land. All these devices, combined with long hours of work, low real wages, endless queues, and a multitude of supplementary collective work chores, called voluntary but in fact compulsory, left a minimum of energy and time for the joy of living.

Because work was pushed so far beyond its possible contribution to individual welfare and happiness, no Soviet penal sanction could prevent loafing on an even more grandiose scale than had existed under the most inefficient Czarist bureaucracy. Thus, even as production increased and cities rose under the whiplash of Stalinist discipline and premium payments to the diligent, as modern tools replaced hand labor and the wooden plow, millions of Russian men continued to prefer vodka, woman, and song to the bonuses, privileges, and medals of the state.

Since World War II, and especially since Stalin's death, the Soviet regime has been forced to recognize that in a modern industrial society, further economic growth, as well as military-technological might, depends on greater efficiency and less slave-driving. It has shortened work hours, increased real wages, and produced more consumer goods. But Soviet man is still far from liberated from the driving hand of the state. His basically emotional, impatient, moody, effusive, generous, and violent nature still finds relatively few spontaneous outlets compatible with material or career success. He can, of course, become an outlaw, and the admittedly high crime rate, including large-scale juvenile delinquency, is proof enough that many choose this path. But he cannot freely chart an individual life unless he has demonstrated exceptional scientific or artistic talents that the state needs for its power and prestige. The ordinary Russian cannot raise money to start a pioneering enterprise of his own, except in defiance of the law. He cannot quit the laboratory or assembly line to open a gas station or a bar and grill. He cannot mount a soapbox to express his personal views. He cannot pick up his savings and emigrate to France, or join the Foreign Legion, or campaign for public office on a program of "throw the rascals out," or start a stockholders' action to force a company in which he owns shares to distribute profits more equitably, or form a cooperative to force consumer prices down, or organize a youth club to fight the local Young Communist League, or print a school paper advocating the teaching of St. Thomas or the Talmud. He cannot freely sell the produce of his brain and hand or start a crusading newspaper. Nor can any but a tiny minority board a plane or tramp steamer for a vacation in Rome, or save up for a month of private fishing and reflection on some Siberian river. In other words, his life is surrounded with external inhibitions and restraints that would make the most pliant American organization man and status-seeker wince. The free battlefields for creative male activity, as democratic society knows them, with all their perils and opportunities, scarcely exist for the Soviet male. He remains an instrument of the needs, appetites, and aspirations of the society in which he lives, rather than the master of his fate and pilot of his individual capacity for either creative effort or pleasure.

If all civilization is, to some extent, a repressive force, curbing man's innate appetite (Boris Pasternak says every man has the capacity to be a Faust and experience all things), and if modern technological society further constricts the opportunities for male self-expression, then in the Soviet Union the taming and curbing features of modern civilization conspire with authoritarian state power against the Russian male's exercise of his birthright to be himself.

By the Renaissance definition of Man—if to be a man means to live by one's full individual capacity to love and to fight for one's convictions and ideals—every man in Soviet society is somewhat of a failure. But because every man in the Soviet Union is in approximately the same boat, there is perhaps less conscious feeling of individual failure and inadequacy. In this respect, the civilian life of man in the Soviet system bears some resemblance to that of a draftee in the army of a democratic society. To men born and educated in a relatively free society, the army appears as an institution in which every absurdity, senseless command, and demeaning chore, from latrine duty to the repetition of commands by rote, is to be expected. The private, whether a prizefighter, scientific genius, or grocery clerk, is necessarily reduced to a tamed common denominator of automatic obedience. Yet, for the "adjusted soldier," obedience involves no profound loss of self-respect, because all that is demeaning is accepted as partly sham, part of the army game. A good part of the surface servility of the Soviet male, of his dutiful response to the orders of those in command, has something of the same hollowness and detached irony as the American GI's response to command, while a large part of his inner life, and of his individuality as a male animal, remains aloof, resentful but substantially untrampled. This double existence, marked by lip-service obedience and repetition of the official line, is not inconsistent with a subterranean freedom of the spirit and, as in the army, with a robust capacity for life and love.

The revolt against authoritarian restraint found its most violent mass expression in the wholesale rape committed by the soldiers of the Soviet Army in their march across Central Europe during the closing phase of World War II. In the cities and villages of Austria, Hungary, and Germany, females of all ages, including women in their seventies, were raped on a scale unprecedented in modern history. Revenge for the monstrous slaughter and devastation inflicted by Hitler's armies on the Russian motherland was certainly one of the driving forces in this great orgy. Another factor was the release of emotion at the end of the bloody carnival of death on the battlefields, on which millions of Soviet soldiers saw their comrades die before their eyes. So was the pent-up desire for love, even in a degraded form, after four years of mass murder. The same Russian soldier who in his native town used to court his best girl with love poetry of Pushkin, took every female in his path by force. In the immediate postwar period, the backwash of this saturnalia hit the cities of the Soviet Union itself. Girls were attacked in the streets of Moscow by returning veterans, and special military patrols had to be called in to restore domestic tranquility.

The Family

On the eve of the 1917 revolution, the stability of the family had been severely shaken by nearly three years of war, which had killed several million soldiers and separated millions of Russian wives and sweethearts from their men. International war was followed by a savage civil war that took another heavy toll of able-bodied men and by the emigration of the better part of the surviving Russian intelligentsia and middle class. The early years of Communist rule thus saw the disappearance or destruction of cultured Russian society. In those early days of Soviet rule, the end of "bourgeois morality" was an avowed objective of the state. The Leninist charge that "bourgeois morality" was nothing more than a hypocritical code to justify human exploitation resulted in the frank disavowal of all morality that did not serve the interests of the state.

During the first years of Soviet rule, for example, not only bigamy and adultery, but even incest was dropped from the statutory list of crimes. Religious marriages were no longer recognized by law, and the civil registration of marriage was reduced to a speedy formality. Divorce could be obtained quickly and cheaply,

at the wish of either party. During this period, which anti-Soviet propaganda abroad called the era of "the nationalization of women"—a vast exaggeration during even the bloodiest days of the Russian civil war—a poll at Moscow University (1922) showed that 41.5 per cent of the students began their sex life before 16 and 7.5 per cent before they were 13 years old.

Abortion was legalized but was rigidly controlled because the state wanted a high birth rate to compensate for the losses of war and civil war. In the case of a first pregnancy, abortion was authorized only if supported by urgent medical considerations. Moscow statistics for 1927 showed that 40.8 per cent of abortions were for medical reasons, 57.1 per cent were permitted on economic grounds, and only 2.1 per cent for other reasons. Neither the unmarried status of the girl nor the desire of the couple to plan the size of their family was accepted as valid grounds for abortion.

By 1936, however, the restratification of Russian society and the re-emergence of a privileged élite resulted in a sharp swing back to "bourgeois" moral standards. In that year the law legalizing abortions was abrogated. Divorce laws were tightened. Each divorce was registered on the individual's internal passport; then substantial fees were introduced. Finally, under a 1944 law, no absolute ground for divorce was recognized, except the political disloyalty of the spouse. A couple seeking a divorce first had to face a tribunal that attempted reconciliation. If that failed, a superior court weighed the petition and decided on a discretionary basis.

The aim of the 1944 law was clear from its title: "Decree on increase of state aid to pregnant women, mothers with many children, and unmarried mothers; on strengthening measures for the protection of motherhood and childhood; on the establishment of the title 'Mother Heroine' and on the institution of the order of 'Motherhood Glory' and the 'Motherhood Medal.'"

Under this law, the distinction between legitimacy and illegitimacy was restored; unmarried persons and parents of only one or two children were subjected to special taxes, while mothers with a large brood received progressively larger subsidies. A woman who had borne and raised ten or more children was entitled to the "Mother Heroine" award, carrying a lump payment of 5,000 rubles, plus 300 rubles monthly for four years.

The primary reason for the 1944 law was the huge population losses of collectivization and World War II. According to Winston Churchill, Stalin's own estimate of the losses caused by collectivization was 10 million lives. Reports at the 20th Communist Party Congress in 1956 showed a war population loss, including the birth deficit, of 30 to 40 million. Hence, the total population depletion through collectivization and World War II totaled about 35 to 50 million—or roughly equivalent to the population of France.

Despite the 1944 breeding incentives, urbanization, universal education, and the general awakening of middle-class tastes and appetites continue to reduce the urban birth rate. The realities of Soviet urban life again forced the legalization of abortion in 1954. Advocates of birth control, however, are still denounced as "fascist man-hating cannibals." To encourage child-bearing, pregnant women are entitled to wages while on maternity leave (extended, by decree of April 1, 1956, from 77 to 112 calendar days). Divorce remains expensive and difficult to obtain.

Soviet Youth Today

Russian youth as a whole does not talk much about the psychopathology of sex; knows little about Kinsey, the neo-Freudians of the West, or the latest birth-control rituals; regards homosexuality as the preserve of the ballet, the prison, and the Moslem territories of Soviet Central Asia; does not make love in public (as some Western visitors have noted with satisfaction); and indulges in little hypocrisy about love. Here is how a pert young blonde at the Black Sea resort of Sochi described her attitude to an inquisitive American:

"What do we need night clubs for? There's the moon, there's the beach and there's boys."

As an afterthought, she added:

"The only trouble is, sometimes there aren't enough boys."

Another foreigner who talked with a group of boys and girls on a Moscow park bench quoted them as saying there was very little "going steady" among the youngsters they knew, although sometimes affairs did last for a while. The usual date started with several hours of strolling, even in winter, generally in groups of two or three couples. If one of them had a room with a radio, the evening often turned into a party with several couples making love in the same room. When asked whether this was not unusual, they said: "Look, it happens all the time. You've got to understand—this is our life."

Among the young people in the cities, interest in cosmetics, beauty parlors, and Western clothes increases steadily. During the war, the movie *One Hundred Men and a Girl* made Deanna Durbin a model for thousands of Soviet girls. Later, the showing of old Tarzan films started an epidemic of Tarzan and Jane haircuts for boys and girls. In 1957, a Western-style jazz band at Leningrad University was the rage until it was put out of business. But short-wave jazz broadcasts from America continue to enjoy great popularity. "Come up and listen to my tape-recording of the latest American hits" is one of the favorite ways to attract girls.

A visiting American professor describes the following evening scene in Leningrad: "Two thousand or so youngsters dancing to fox trots, waltzes and a Soviet form of jazz. Mostly the couples just swayed back and forth, but there was also some fancy jitterbugging, obviously modeled on American dancing, even whistling when the music seemed to call for it."

The Young Communist League wages an endless battle against Soviet youth's intense interest in Western music, clothes, films, art, and literature, on the ground that such influences are decadent and corrupting. But these sermons are self-defeating because often lectures against rock'n'roll and juvenile delinquency are combined with tirades against French impressionism, atonal modern music, Camus, James Joyce, the revival of religious weddings and baptismal services, and interest in the political heresies of Polish and Hungarian youth.

To compete with the esthetic and emotional appeal of the Orthodox wedding ceremony, the

Young Communist League has been forced to campaign for more colorful and solemn civil weddings and has bowed to youth's desire for smarter clothes and better housing—even to the extent of promising special housing projects for young honeymooners.

Moreover, even Soviet films have begun to reflect the new climate. In the Stalin era, when squalid living conditions went hand in hand with official prudery, the passionate love scene was taboo. In the past few years, love for love's own sake has returned to the Soviet screen. The film that broke the ice was Chekhov's *The Anna Cross*, starring a ravishing young blonde and featuring a betrayed old fool of a husband, a flock of lecherous suitors, gypsy songs, imperial balls, and predawn sleigh rides, all in brilliant color. Many recent love films have been more in keeping with Soviet official morality, but even in these, love rather than politics dominates. Thus, the international prize-winning film *The Cranes Are Flying* is the story of a girl driven by loneliness to betray her lover, who fights and dies at the front. And in the recent *The House I Live In* the wife of a dedicated Soviet scientist, who is too busy for love, is also unfaithful. Both women are, nonetheless, portrayed sympathetically. But in the Russian tradition, they are basically moral and passionately devoted to a single man. As in *Anna Karenina*, infidelity is the core of the tragedy.

As in the United States, youthful criminality is a serious postwar problem. A study on drink and delinquency in the Soviet Union concludes:

Young adults of today are part of the "war generation" brought up without parental supervision under conditions of severe deprivation and often forced to fend for themselves. . . . These young men and women may have found it difficult to adapt themselves to a more orderly life. They may prefer to keep on dodging work and living on the fringes of Soviet society.

In 1956, two sons of Soviet Minister of Foreign Trade Kabanov and another young man were arrested for robbing apartments to finance what the Soviet press called "sex orgies." Their accomplices were the daughters of an army general, an air force colonel, and a secret police colonel. In August, 1957, a Moscow paper reported that three postgraduate students of the Academy of Sciences tried to rape a 17-year-old girl, who broke her vertebrae and both legs in a four-story leap to escape. The victim of the attack had been picked up as she was strolling with a girl friend through the streets of the Soviet capital during the World Youth Festival. When the students introduced themselves as members of a foreign delegation, the girls accepted the invitation to the Academy hostel. Here one of them managed to flee when she discovered her mistake. The case attracted wide attention because one of the assailants, Shamo Ragimov, was the son of the chairman of the Writers Union of the Azerbaijan Soviet Republic. In July, 1958, a noted Soviet soccer star was sentenced to twelve years in prison for raping a girl during a drunken country-house party.

A foreign student recently at Leningrad University quoted a girl as saying that the frequency of sex crimes in that city, the most European in Russia, made all but the main thoroughfares unsafe after dark. How often such things occur in the Soviet Union remains an official secret because press accounts appear only sporadically, when they serve some specific campaign of the regime. That they constitute a major problem is evident, however, from the post-Stalin reintroduction of the death penalty for murder and other crimes of violence. (The death penalty for nonpolitical crimes had been abolished in Russia in the eighteenth century, during the reign of Empress Elizabeth.)

The government has long claimed that prostitution disappeared from the Soviet Union together with other evils of the prerevolutionary social order. In reality, it thrived illegally through all the years of widespread poverty, when Russian girls, not very different from Sonya in Dostoevski's *Crime and Punishment* could be had for a pound of black bread or a pair of stockings. And even in the relatively prosperous Moscow of the Khrushchev era, a foreign journalist reports:

Tonight on Gorky Street I watched a good deal of bartering for sex going on with young girls quite openly, but in the darker sections of the street. I was told there were no actual brothels, but all kinds of arrangements were made on the street to keep this flourishing business going.

At the top of the social ladder today are Russia's new generation of "gilded youth," the sons and daughters of the "upper crust" who travel in their parents' chauffeur-driven limousines, dine far into the night at expensive restaurants, fill the best seats at the opera and theater, throw lavish parties at the family country villa, and rarely marry outside their class. Yet, with their craze for fast living, they are as much an individualistic affront to authoritarian Soviet Victorianism as the Soviet "shook-up" generation, whose vocabulary is peppered with Americanisms, who call the main thoroughfare of Moscow "Broadway," and who write such heresy as this letter from a young Muscovite to his friend in Siberia (quoted with appropriate horror by the *Komsomolskaya Pravda*, official organ of the Young Communist League, in July, 1958): "We believe in freedom of morals and our slogan is 'live fast.' We have no political aims, only moral ones [*sic*]. Anyone who wishes may roll in wine or rave in rock 'n' roll or fall into love's delight."

A young American student of Soviet affairs, who shared a sleeping-car compartment with a Russian girl (the practice is commonplace and carries no necessary implication of sexual intimacy) leaves us with this:

It was almost 2 A.M. and both of us were fighting sleep.

"Would you mind leaving the compartment for a moment? I would like to change." As I waited outside, I thought back how different this girl was from the "girl back home"—and in so many ways. She was a peculiar combination of the bitter and the sweet, the tough and the soft, a confirmed opportunist who "was crazy" about love poetry, a hard product of the Soviet system who had to ask me to leave the compartment so she could undress and get into bed.

In the phrase "hard product of the Soviet system," there is perhaps the haunting aroma of the sour grape. For despite wars and revolutions, purges and rock 'n' roll, the Russian girl—who does not tease the man she desires—can still spend the night with an attractive American and leave him with only the memory of fascinating conversation and the strength of Russian women.

References

"A Foreign Student at Leningrad University." *Interview Report* No. 21. Dept. of State, External Research Division, March, 1959.

Baltimore *Sun,* June 15, 1958.

Bauer, Raymond A., Inkeles, Alex, and Kluckhohn, Clyde, *How the Soviet System Works.* Cambridge: Harvard University Press, 1956.

Dicks, Henry V., "Observations on Contemporary Russian Behavior." *Human Relations,* May, 1952.

Fainsod, Merle, "What Russian Students Think." *Atlantic Monthly,* Feb., 1957.

Field, Mark G., "Drink and Delinquency in the USSR." *Problems of Communism,* May–June, 1955.

Geiger, H. Kent, and Inkeles, Alex, "The Family in the USSR." *Marr. & Fam. Living,* Nov., 1954.

Gould, Bruce, and Gould, Beatrice, "We Saw How the Russians Live." *Ladies Home Journal,* Feb., 1957.

Gregg, Richard A., "Russia's Pampered Youths." *Harpers,* August, 1957.

Griscom, H., "Report on Russian Youth." *Ladies Home Journal,* Feb., 1957.

Gunther, John, *Inside Russia Today.* New York: Harper & Brothers, 1957.

Jordan, William J., "Youth of the World: Nine Capitals Report—Moscow: Inconspicuous, but a Problem." New York *Times* Magazine, Feb. 23, 1958.

Kalb, Marvin L., *Eastern Exposure.* New York: Farrar, Straus and Cudahy, Inc., 1958.

New York *Herald Tribune,* Nov. 13, 1955; Sept. 1, 1957; May 3, 1959.

New York *Times,* July 13, 1958; July 26, 1958.

Orme, Alexandra, *Comes the Comrade.* New York: William Morrow & Co., Inc., 1950.

Peterson, William, "The Evolution of Soviet Family Policy." *Problems of Communism,* Sept.–Oct., 1956.

Phillips, Joseph B., "The Postwar Moral Climate: U.S.S.R." *Newsweek,* Feb. 24, 1947; March 3, 1947.

Sandomirsky, Vera, "Sex in the Soviet Union." *Russian Rev.,* July, 1951.

Stevens, Leslie Clark, *Russian Assignment.* Boston: Little, Brown & Co., 1953.

Teitelbaum, Salomon M., "Romance Revives in the Soviet Union." *South Atlantic Quart.,* Oct., 1946.

"The Ferment Among Soviet Youth." *Soviet Survey,* Feb., 1957.

"This Is the New Soviet Elite." *Newsweek,* Feb. 2, 1959.

Whitney, Thomas P., "Sex in the Soviet Union." New York *Times* Magazine, Jan. 1, 1956.

Yershov, Vassily, "Confiscation and Plunder by the Army of Occupation." In *Soviet Economic Policy in Postwar Germany.* New York: Research Program on the USSR, 1953.

BORIS SHUB AND
HELENE ZWERDLING

Standards of Sexual Behavior

Available Evidence

SCIENTIFIC research into the sexual standards of different countries is extremely new. It has been in the last thirty years only that good researches into this area have been carried out. Indeed, even today the evidence is uneven and sparse. The majority of extensive research into sexual standards and behavior has been carried out in America. To be sure, there is evidence on other countries; for example, Anna-Lisa Kalveston has reported on sexual research in Sweden, and in England, Eustace Chesser and Michael Schofield have conducted some elaborate research. Mention should also be made here of the extensive anthropological evidence on nonliterate cultures.

Perhaps the greatest drawback of present-day research is the accent on sexual behavior rather than on the sexual standards that underlie that sexual behavior. The author published in 1960 a comprehensive study that tries to summarize all the evidence on sexual standards that can be deduced from the major American studies on sexual behavior. Elaboration of many of the points in this article can be found there. In addition the author in 1967 published a book on his own research using the first national probability sample of America. A drawback of much of the available research is the fact that, especially in America, it applies mostly to the upper segments of the white-urban population and not to all classes .

Despite these weaknesses, the evidence today is sufficient to make some key observations about sexual standards and their trends in America and in some other parts of the world. Science is a continuing process and one cannot give up the search because it does not give full information immediately. We must be content that what we have is surely better than any blind hunches.

Premarital Sexual Standards

The area of behavior involving kissing, petting, and coitus before marriage is the one about which most is known. In most cases previous to the author's work, the standards that underlie these behaviors had to be inferred from the behavior itself. For example, Kinsey found that 85 per cent of the females in his sample who had had premarital intercourse had no serious regrets about it. This is taken as evidence that many of these women did not have a belief in abstinence that they were violating but that, in part at least, they must have accepted another standard that was more permissive and did not make them feel guilty about their behavior.

In this area of premarital sexual behavior, there are, in America, four major standards that young people accept and that find support in the research evidence.

Standard of Abstinence

First, there is the formal standard of abstinence, which forbids coitus before marriage for both men and women. This standard has several subtypes, some of which allow petting, others of which allow only kissing. Petting is used here to refer to sexual stimulation short of full coitus, involving those parts of the body that are ordinarily clothed, such as the breast or genital area.

Double Standard

The second major premarital standard in America is the ancient double standard, which basically states that premarital intercourse is forbidden to women but not to men. Females who indulge are therefore considered immoral, but males who indulge are not. Under this standard, petting and kissing are not so severely restricted as coitus but here, too, the male is given much freer rights than the female.

Permissiveness without Affection

The third major standard in America, less widespread than preceding ones, may be called permissiveness without affection, which holds that if two people are attracted physically to each other and both desire to have coitus, they may do so. Petting and kissing are, of course, also allowed on the same basis under this standard.

Permissiveness with Affection

The fourth and final premarital sexual standard is called permissiveness with affection. This standard is also less prevalent than the first two. It allows coitus for both men and women, but it requires that a strong, stable, and affectionate relationship be present.

Although these four standards have been best demonstrated to exist in America, I believe they are common to Western society and are applicable to most all the South American and European countries. However, there is a difference in the popularity of each standard; for example, the permissive standards are probably not as widespread in South America, where abstinence and the double standard seem to be overwhelmingly present. The opposite type of situation seems to prevail in the Scandinavian countries, in particular in Sweden, where permissiveness with affection seems to be more prevalent than the other standards; in fact, many of the young people are taught that if they are in love it is permissible to engage in coitus. England appears to be the country whose sexual standards most closely approximate our own in terms of the relative strength of each of the four standards.

There is only scanty evidence on the Oriental countries, but it is known that the double standard is quite widespread there. This is particularly true of China. Of course, industrialization in China and also in India is probably having a slow but sharp effect on the Oriental way of life and we may soon see a noticeable weakening of the double standard because of this.

The Polynesian cultures of the South Pacific are distinguished by their strong emphasis on the two permissive standards. This is also true for many African societies. In several of these areas the virginal and sexually apathetic woman is scorned and thought to be abnormal. This situation is also true for several of our Indian tribes in the American Southwest. The studies of Murdock (1949) and Ford (1951) indicate that the majority of these nonliterate cultures take a permissive attitude toward premarital petting and coitus. These researchers have made use of the Yale University Human Relations Area Files, which contain information on almost 200 cultures—probably the best source for such information today.

Thus, there is a good deal of individuality among different cultures as to their sexual standards, even though there may be some general similarities; and each culture must be carefully studied in order to fully understand the relative power of each subtype of sexual standard. Nevertheless, it seems safe to say that most of the Western world *formally* favors a standard of abstinence and *informally* favors a double standard, although there are strong trends working in a more permissive direction.

Standards on Adultery, Homosexuality, and Masturbation

In addition to standards concerning premarital sexual relations, there are standards concerning adultery, homosexuality, masturbation, and other forms of sexual behavior. The formal norms in America forbid adultery, homosexuality, and masturbation. However, there is a sort of informal double standard for adultery and to a lesser extent for masturbation that frowns upon these behaviors in women much more so than in men. Homosexuality is largely rejected by all major sexual codes in America.

It should be noted that since much of the past sociological research focused on premarital sexual relations, we do not know as much about other standards, such as those regarding adultery, homosexuality, and masturbation. However, we do have evidence from Kinsey that all three of these types of behavior are quite common in American society; for example, Kinsey reports that in his sample of married people of 40 years or over, about one-fourth of the wives and one-half of the husbands had committed adultery. In most cases some sort of disturbance in the marital relationship was involved and adultery was the outcome, but in other cases adultery as such was accepted. Many double-standard husbands took such liberties without feeling they were harming their marriages and without being willing to grant equal rights to their wives.

Homosexual behavior was also found to be quite common by Kinsey. He found that 37 per cent of the males and 13 per cent of the females had engaged in such behavior to orgasm at least once. But here too we know too little about how these people felt about their behavior. One could assume that, since all major American standards reject such behavior, most of these people suffered guilt reactions.

Attitudes toward masturbation, although still negative, seem to have become liberalized in America. Thus, many more people who masturbate today probably do so without as strong a guilt reaction. However, here too we lack sufficient information. We do know that in Kinsey's sample of several thousand men and women, by age 20 about one-third of the females and about nine of every ten men had masturbated.

Standards in other Western cultures regarding these three areas should be somewhat similar but one cannot be sure of the full picture until more research is carried out. For information on nonliterate cultures, we turn again to the work of Ford and Beach and of Murdock. Their findings indicate that casual adultery is commonly forbidden, as it too often leads to complications that disrupt the social organization. When it is allowed, it is usually strictly regulated so that it can occur only between certain people such as a husband and his sister-in-law. However, these restrictions are not required in several societies, such as the Eskimo, where during the winter months young married couples play a game called "putting out the lamps." In this game the oil lamps are extinguished and all the individuals scramble for a partner other than their mate, spending the night with the one they find.

Ford and Beach give evidence on masturbation and homosexuality in nonliterate societies. Masturbation seems to be very common but is most frequent among nonadults; homosexuality is much less common but many societies permit it under certain conditions for both men and women. As can be seen, our own attitudes on almost all sexual practices in the Western world are much more restrictive than those of nonliterate cultures.

Trends in Premarital Sexual Standards

Since exact sociological evidence on sexual behavior goes back less than thirty years, there is much in the area of trends that must be qualified and investigated more thoroughly. However, the evidence we have on America is consistent and points strongly in one direction. Starting in the 1920's, the Victorian "sexual dams" were breached and increases occurred in almost all forms of sexual behavior.

It should be clear that much of the permissive behavior that began in the 1920's occurred more on impulse or for excitement than for purposes of abiding by any standard, whether old or new. In time, standards did develop and in premarital relations the two older standards were liberalized and the two newer permissive standards were greatly enlarged.

Abstinence formerly placed a strong emphasis on the "untouched" quality of virginity. This has been sharply altered and today we find many women who believe in abstinence yet feel it is quite proper to pet to orgasm or masturbate their date. Thus, the standard of abstinence has been liberalized, adapting itself to the more sexually permissive changes that have been going on.

During this same time period the double standard also seems to have been severely weakened. There are probably fewer people today who can fully accept an unequal standard of behavior for men and women. Many people who formerly believed in the double standard have begun to feel that if they accept coitus for men they must also accept it for women. Frequently, however, these people cannot bring themselves to give full equality to the female so they have merely liberalized the double standard and have said that men can have coitus whenever they want but women can have coitus only when they are in love and/or engaged. Here, as in the case of abstinence, we find a liberalization occurring in order to make the standard adjust to a more permissive society.

Those who have found the liberalization of the standard of abstinence and of the double standard to be too conservative have joined the ranks of those who accept the standards of permissiveness without affection and of permissiveness with affection. Social changes occur gradually, so most of the shift seems to have gone to the less radical of these two standards, namely, permissiveness with affection, which requires a stable, affectionate relationship as a prerequisite for sexual intercourse.

Research Evidence on Changing Trends

Some of the research evidence on trends in standards will be seen in the following tables. Table 1 shows the increase in incidence of petting to orgasm in females of various generations, starting with the generation born between 1900 and 1910, which reached maturity in the 1920's. One can also see how such behavior increases as they became older.

TABLE 1. ACCUMULATIVE INCIDENCE OF PETTING TO ORGASM AMONG FEMALES

AGE	BORN BEFORE 1900	BORN 1900–1909	BORN 1910–1919	BORN 1920–1929
	PERCENTAGE[a]			
14	1	1	1	1
16	3	5	6	6
18	6	10	13	18
20	10	17	22	28
25	15	30	34	43
30	24	39	45	
35	26	44	53	

Source: Kinsey, *Sexual Behavior in the Human Female*, p. 275. Present-day rates for males are quite similar but the increase over previous generations is much smaller and such petting makes up a smaller percentage of the total male sex outlet.

[a] Accumulative incidence is a rate figured by taking all those eligible for an experience and seeing what percentage actually have the experience. For a full explanation, see Kinsey (1948), pp. 114–119.

The decrease in the number of women who were virginal before marriage is clearly indicated in Tables 2 and 3, which are from the studies of Kinsey and Terman, respectively.

The weakening of the orthodox double standard is also supported by the data in Table 4, where the number of men who engage in coitus *only* with others besides their fiancées has been drastically reduced. This indicates that many more such men are now having coitus with their fiancées because they now accept such behavior as moral for engaged women. Finally, the increases in the "Spouse only" and the "Spouse and others" categories in Tables 2, 3, and 4 are also evidence that many more people accept permissiveness with affection, i.e., premarital coitus when love or engagement is present. Some of this increase may also be a further indication of the growth of a new subtype of the double standard, which allows coitus for women if they are in love and/or engaged. Thus Tables 1 through 4 tend to support my contentions regarding changes in premarital sexual standards. The majority of the men and women in the Kinsey study and the Burgess-Wallin study said they had no serious qualms about their behavior, thus further indicating acceptance of more liberal standards.

TABLE 2. PREMARITAL COITUS OF WOMEN BY DECADE OF BIRTH

AGE	BORN BEFORE 1900	BORN 1900–1909	BORN 1910–1919	BORN 1920–1929
None	73.4	48.7	43.9	48.8
Spouse only	10.4	24.4	23.3	27.3
Others only	5.5	5.4	7.0	6.5
Spouse and others	10.4	21.0	25.6	17.4

Source: These data are based on Kinsey (1953), but were especially prepared for this paper through the kindness of Drs. Gebhard and Martin, of the Institute for Sex Research. These were based on 2,479 women who either were or had been married by the time of interview.

TABLE 3. PREMARITAL COITUS OF WOMEN BY DECADE OF BIRTH

	BORN BEFORE 1890	BORN 1890–1899	BORN 1900–1909
	PERCENTAGE		
None	86.5	74.0	51.2
Spouse only	8.7	17.7	32.7
Others only	1.9	2.5	2.1
Spouse and others	2.9	5.8	14.0

Source: Terman, p. 321. Rates for the 1910–1920 generation are not included here as they were based on few cases. Such rates can be found in the Kinsey studies.

TABLE 4. PREMARITAL COITUS OF MEN BY DECADE OF BIRTH

	BORN BEFORE 1890	BORN 1890–1899	BORN 1900–1909
	PERCENTAGE		
None	50.6	41.9	32.6
Spouse only	4.6	7.6	17.2
Others only	35.6	27.5	16.5
Spouse and others	9.2	23.0	33.7

Source: Terman, p. 321. The high rates of male virginity evidenced above are due to the high proportion of college men in this group. Kinsey found much lower percentages of virginity among those of lower education (by age 25, 90 per cent of males whose education stopped in the eighth grade had premarital intercourse). The college-educated males exceed in petting to orgasm, where about 60 per cent of them are involved by age 30, as compared to only about 15 per cent of the low-education groups (Kinsey, 1948, pp. 536, 550).

England is one of the few other countries for which we have comparable premarital trend data based on extensive studies. A glance at Table 5 indicates that, for the sample Chesser used, premarital coitus has also greatly increased in England among people born after 1900 who came to their maturity in the 1920's and later.

TABLE 5. PREMARITAL COITUS FOR ENGLISH WOMEN BY DECADE OF BIRTH

	BORN BEFORE 1904	BORN 1904–1913	BORN 1914–1923	BORN 1924–1933
	PERCENTAGE			
Coitus	19	36	39	43
Petting	7	22	29	25

Source: Chesser, p. 311.

Reports regarding trends from other European countries are more difficult to obtain but basically they indicate that a more permissive sex code is in the making. Trend reports on nonliterate cultures are almost completely lacking since these cultures are often studies only at one point in time and rarely is good sexual trend data obtained.

Trends in Adultery, Homosexuality, and Masturbation Standards

Again, for data on America, the Kinsey studies can be taken as adequate, especially for the better-educated urban, white classes of our culture.

Table 6 indicates that there has been an increase in extramarital coitus. However, here it is more difficult to determine standards since these data are not broken down into different

TABLE 6. ACCUMULATIVE INCIDENCE OF EXTRAMARITAL COITUS FOR FEMALES

AGE	BORN BEFORE 1900	BORN 1900–1909	BORN 1910–1919	BORN 1920–1929
	PERCENTAGE			
18			10	9
19		4	7	10
20	2	3	5	9
25	4	8	10	12
30	10	16	19	
35	18	26	25	
40	22	30		
45	21	40		

Source: Kinsey, *Sexual Behavior in the Human Female*, p. 442. Men also increased in this area, except for the college-educated group. Data on men were not broken down as accurately by birth decades so these charts are for women only, with only summary statements for males given in the text.

types. The preponderance of men who commit adultery (by age 40, one-half of the men had committed adultery while only one-fourth of the women had done so) indicates that here too our culture is probably more liberal regarding men and that a sort of double standard exists in this area. However, it is unlikely that the increase in adultery is due to an increase in such double standard beliefs since there is strong evidence that the double standard is weakening. It is more likely that this increase is related to our present 1-in-4 divorce rate. Adultery may accompany the breakup of a marriage and with more divorces there may thus be more adultery. Of course, other reasons apply also; these are only a few possibly important factors.

TABLE 7. ACCUMULATIVE INCIDENCE OF MASTURBATION TO ORGASM FOR FEMALES

AGE	BORN BEFORE 1900	BORN 1900–1909	BORN 1910–1919	BORN 1920–1929
	PERCENTAGE			
5	3	3	2	1
10	12	12	10	6
15	25	25	24	17
20	33	34	36	30
25	38	43	46	47
30	44	51	53	
35	49	57	63	
40	52	63		

Source: Kinsey, *Sexual Behavior in the Human Female*, p. 180. For males there is only a slight increase in lower-education levels.

Although Kinsey's figures for masturbation among males are only slightly higher in recent generations, the figures for women show a somewhat higher rate of increase. Table 7 indicates about 11 percent increase at age 40 for women born after 1900. Our standards seem to be more tolerant of masturbation today and this seems to be the trend despite the lack of any great increase in behavior. Most of the change in masturbation rates refers to women since the percentage of men who masturbate has been over 90 for several generations.

Homosexuality is even more evenly distributed over the various birth decades and there is practically no increase. Females, as seen in Table 8, by age 45 average about 13 per cent homosexual experience to orgasm. The comparable rate for males is 37 per cent. Again, I caution the reader that Kinsey qualified his findings and fully realized that they are not representative of all segments of American society. There is little evidence of an exact nature on trends in standards concerning homosexual behavior, but I believe that just as the rates have remained stable so have the attitudes toward such behavior. By and large, there is a strong feeling against homosexual contact, despite its apparent frequency. As our premarital sex codes become more liberalized, perhaps this attitude too will change, but as of today there is no firm evidence of such a change.

TABLE 8. ACCUMULATIVE INCIDENCE OF HOMOSEXUAL CONTACTS TO ORGASM FOR FEMALES

AGE	BORN BEFORE 1900	BORN 1900–1910	BORN 1910–1920	BORN 1920–1930
		PERCENTAGE		
12				1
15	2	2	2	3
20	5	6	4	3
25	8	9	7	6
30	9	10	10	
35	11	11	13	
40	11	12		
45	12	17		

Source: Kinsey, *Sexual Behavior in the Human Female*, p. 495. The rate for men was 37 per cent and also showed no increase.

There is little evidence on trends in the above three areas (adultery, masturbation, and homosexuality) from other Western societies. As far as non-Western cultures are concerned, our evidence concerning trends is even more scanty. We do have some good information concerning standards at the time researchers visited the culture, but very few cultures have been investigated as to their trends in sexual behavior, and thus trend information is sorely lacking on most cultures of the world. There is little ques-

tion, however, that many countries such as India and China are undergoing changes in their sexual standards due to the effects of industrialization. But until more complete sociological researches are carried out in those areas, we can only put forth the speculation that as they industrialize their sexual codes will become more like those of other industrialized cultures.

Reasons for Recent Trends

What happened before 1920, particularly in America, to cause the sexual "explosion" of that decade?

The American and Western sexual standards of today have deep roots. They can be traced to the Hebrew, Greek, Roman, and early Christian cultures. Deuteronomy in the Old Testament gives us ample evidence of the source of our own male-dominant type of double standard. The Greeks had the hetaerae, an organization of highly cultured prostitutes, and they also had homosexuality; but both of these were for men only. The Romans followed the Greek example with their own, somewhat cruder, versions of male favoritism in the area of sexual permissiveness. Thus, the double standard had strong supports in Western society, so strong that the full force of Christianity and its demand for a single standard of abstinence failed to conquer it. The double standard is, of course, not "just natural"; witness the many cultures today that do not hold to the double standard. The double standard probably originally began due to man's physical superiority over woman, and it is difficult to change, for men are often unwilling to give up an "advantage" they have enjoyed for many centuries.

The nineteenth century dealt the double standard a serious blow. The urban industrial revolution had occurred by that time and the face of America, together with that of most of the Western world, was changing. For the first time, women were able to earn a living without entering prostitution. This new economic power meant that women could act, in general, more independently of men.

Particularly in America, young people increasingly chose their own mates on the basis of love, ...

and the feminist movement continued in its drive to grant women the vote and general equality before the law. This trend toward permissiveness and equality was strongly reinforced by the improved economic position of women and the general urban-industrial type of society that was developing. Within a century women had carved an empire of wealth and status surpassing all previous achievements. Choice of mate by the young people themselves and consequent dating became widespread; contraceptive measures were developed that removed some of the fear of venereal disease and pregnancy; young people were allowed to go out alone; and Henry Ford gave them a "moving parlor" with his "invention."

Given this over-all picture, it is no wonder that by the 1920's there were great numbers of American men and women who no longer accepted the highly restrictive sexual codes of the nineteenth century. These people could afford to be independent, for all the new social forces were in their favor. Americans have come to accept a more permissive sexual attitude in a way that would shock our Victorian ancestors and with a nonchalance that would surprise even the iconoclasts of the 1920's. Since the 1920's, instead of increasing the frequency of sexual behaviors, the changes made have been consolidated. This, naturally, does not mean that Americans have fully thrown over the past. The older standards (abstinence and the double standard) are still very much present. But Americans have moved further away from orthodox forms of both these standards than ever before. Many similar forces have effected changes in European countries, England most likely being the closest in this respect to America. It is possible that as India, China, and other countries industrialize, such changes in their sex codes will also occur.

The Future of Premarital Sexual Standards

The area of premarital sexual standards in America is the one most studied, and although full evidence is lacking, much of what is said about America applies to many other Western cultures.

The evidence points clearly to increased permissiveness. This permissiveness will probably take three directions. First, there will be an increase in abstinent-believers who accept heavy petting. This seems to be the case in past generations (see Table 1) and should become increasingly true. The evidence indicates that very often petting standards are only temporary standards that girls drop when they fall in love and/or become engaged. At such times these people come to accept permissiveness with affection. The freedom granted young people, the intimacy they have in their "steady" and "pinned" relationships, makes this permissive trend quite likely. People do not like to feel guilty about their behavior, so it is likely that when they violate old standards they will come to accept more permissive ones in their place.

The second major direction our sexual standards will take will be toward continued modification of the double standard so as to permit coitus for women when in love but still allowing men coitus at any time. Equalitarian pressures strongly push in this direction. However, this trend is also probably only a transitory solution for it still contains too much inequality and female restrictiveness for our type of society.

The third direction in which our sexual standards will likely head is also in line with past trends: toward permissiveness with affection. The more conservative interpretation of this standard, which only allows coitus when love and/or engagement is involved, will become increasingly accepted. This standard is much more in accord with the strong equalitarian and permissive pressures that have developed with our urban-industrial type of society and, as Tables 2, 3, and 4 indicate, its acceptance has already greatly increased. Of course, there are elements that conflict with this standard, such as our religious institutions, but by and large it seems to have become integrated into our society. This does not mean that it is the most moral standard; many immoral customs fit very nicely into a society.

The standard of abstinence and the double standard will probably continue for many centuries more, but possibly within a hundred years or so they will no longer be the dominant standards in America, permissiveness with affection taking precedence. The college-educated group has most clearly demonstrated its tendencies in this direction and will probably lead the move in this direction.

As far as the fourth standard is concerned, permissiveness without affection is too radical to obtain a large following at the present time. If such a standard ever takes root in America it will probably be many centuries from today. Our extended permissiveness has been largely in the direction of affectionate, "person-centered coitus" rather than "body-centered coitus" and it is likely to remain that way for some time to come due to our strong association of deep affection with sexual behavior.

The Future of Other Sexual Standards

The evidence previously cited shows that, in America at least, there has been an increase in adultery. Unlike the trend toward increased premarital relations, however, this trend will probably slow down. Although our urban-industrial society is conducive to increased permissiveness, most of this permissiveness in the future will probably grow in the area of premarital relations. My own research in this area indicates that the same young people who strongly favor being allowed to engage in premarital coitus will argue quite firmly against extramarital coitus. For example, permissiveness with affection is a standard that has increased in importance in recent decades and this standard is one that stresses a monagamous type of love affair. Even on this premarital basis it emphasizes that one must be faithful to one's premarital partner. Thus, although there has been an increase in adultery, the association of love and sexual monogamy has shown no sign of weakening.

In regard to masturbation and homosexuality in America attitudes toward masturbation seem to have been liberalized, and this should continue since it agrees with the over-all courtship permissiveness. It is difficult to speak of changes in behavior in this area for, with increased liberalism in petting and coitus, masturbation, although more accepted, may actually decrease. Homosexual attitudes seem the slowest to alter but there is evidence of liberalization of laws on homosexuality in line with the Wolfenden report.

Conclusions

There is one important distinctive characteristic of the premarital trends discussed above. For the first time in Western society's written history our young people are devising a sexual code of their own making. Abstinence and double standard codes were parentally devised codes, codes that were integrated into a male-dominant, parentally run, extended-family type of system. In this sort of society parents chose the mates and women were valued for their economic assets and their ability to bear children. With the advent of a new kind of society, an urban-industrial society, the pressures for this older sort of courtship system have sharply decreased.

A new sexual code was needed to fit into this new type of society. It has been in process of development since the nineteenth century and its significance is that this time the young people themselves, in their new social relationships, are unconsciously evolving it. It is this newer sexual code that has modified and in some cases replaced the older, parentally devised sexual codes. The clash between the old and new codes is felt internally by many people in Western society, who are partly attached to both. Evidence supporting this point and others in this article can be found in the author's 1967 book.

American society, together with most of the Western world, has had a severely restrictive sexual code. As time moves on this is becoming much less the case but there still is a strong general sexual taboo that is quite rare in non-Western societies. American and other Western cultures seem to be involved at present in a change in that over-all sexual taboo, and there will likely be much conflict involved. We are in a state of transition and those who cling to the past get hurt by the customs of the present and those who rush to the future are damaged by the traditions of the past.

References

Aberle, Sophie D., and Corner, George W., *Twenty-Five Years of Sex Research*. Philadelphia: W. B. Saunders Co., 1953.

Bell, Robert R., *Premarital Sex in a Changing Society.* New Jersey: Prentice-Hall, 1966.

Burgess, Ernest W., and Wallin, Paul, *Engagement and Marriage.* Philadelphia: J. B. Lippincott Co., 1953.

Chesser, Eustace, *The Sexual, Marital and Family Relationships of the English Woman.* New York: Roy Publishers, 1957.

Comfort, Alex, *Sexual Behavior in Society.* New York: The Viking Press, Inc., 1950.

Davis, Kingley, "Sexual Behavior." pp. 322-372 in Robert K. Merton and Robert A. Nisbet (eds.), *Contemporary Social Problems,* 2nd edition. New York: Harcourt, Brace, 1966.

Ditzion, Sidney, *Marriage, Morals, and Sex in America.* New York: Bookman Associates, Inc., 1953.

Ehrmann, Winston, "Some Knowns and Unknowns in Research into Human Sex Behavior." *Marr. & Fam. Living 17:* 16-22, 1955.

Ehrmann, Winston, *Premarital Dating Behavior.* New York: Henry Holt, 1959.

Ellis, Albert, *The American Sexual Tragedy.* New York: Twayne Pub., 1954.

Ellis, Albert, *Sex Without Guilt.* New York: Lyle Stuart, 1958.

Ford, Clellan S., and Beach, Frank A., *Patterns of Sexual Behavior.* New York: Harper & Brothers, 1951.

Gebhard, Paul *et al., Pregnancy, Birth and Abortion.* New York: Harper & Brothers, 1958.

Gebhard, Paul H., Gagnon, John H., Pomeroy, Wardell B., and Christenson, Cornelia V., *Sex Offenders: An Analysis of Types.* New York: Harper, 1965.

Gorer, Geoffrey, *Exploring English Character.* New York: Criterion Books, Inc., 1955.

Guyon, René, *The Ethics of Sexual Acts.* New York: Blue Ribbon, 1941.

Himelhoch, Jerome, and Fava, Silvia (eds.), *Sexual Behavior in American Society.* New York: W. W. Norton & Co., Inc., 1955.

Himes, Norman E., *Medical History of Contraception.* Baltimore: Williams & Wilkins, 1936.

Kalvesten, Anna-Lisa, *The Social Structure of Sweden.* Stockholm, Sweden: University of Stockholm, 1953.

Kinsey, Alfred C. *et al., Sexual Behavior in the Human Male.* Philadelphia: W. B. Saunders Co., 1948.

Kinsey, Alfred C. *et al., Sexual Behavior in the Human Female.* Philadelphia: W. B. Saunders Co., 1953.

Locke, Harvey J., *Predicting Adjustment in Marriage.* New York: Henry Holt & Co., 1951.

Murdock, George P., *Social Structure.* New York: The Macmillan Co., 1949.

Pillay, Alyappin, and Ellis, Albert (eds.), *Sex, Society and the Individual.* Bombay, India: *Internat. J. Sexology,* 1953.

Queen, Stuart, and Adams, John, *The Family in Various Cultures.* Philadelphia: J. B. Lippincott Co., 1952.

Reiss, Ira L., *Premarital Sexual Standards in America.* Glencoe, Ill.: The Free Press, 1960.

Reiss, Ira L., "Personal Values and the Scientific Study of Sex," in H. Beigel (ed.) *Advances in Sex Research.* New York: Harper and Row, 1963.

Reiss, Ira L., "Premarital Sexual Permissiveness Among Negroes and Whites." *American Sociological Review 29;* 598-688, 1964.

Reiss, Ira L., "Social Class and Premarital Sexual Permissiveness: A Re-Examination." *American Sociological Review 30;* 747-756, 1965.

Reiss, Ira L., (ed.), "The Sexual Renaissance in America." *Journal of Social Issues 22;* 1-140, 1966.

Reiss, Ira L., "The Social Context of Premarital Sexual Permissiveness. New York: Holt, Rinehart, & Winston, Inc., 1967.

Rose, Arnold M. (ed.), *The Institutions of Advanced Societies.* Minneapolis: University of Minnesota Press, 1958.

Schofield, Michael, *The Sexual Behavior of Young People.* Boston: Little, Brown, 1965.

Terman, Lewis M., *Psychological Factors in Marital Happiness.* New York: McGraw-Hill Book Co., 1938.

The Wolfenden Report. New York: Stein and Bay, 1963.

IRA L. REISS

Sterilization

STERILIZATION is the act of making a male or female infertile, or incapable of producing its kind. In the female, this is usually done by removing the ovaries (oophorectomy) or by preventing the passage of the ovum to the uterus so that it cannot be fertilized (salpingectomy). These are surgical procedures. However, sterilization can be carried out by irradiation of either the ovaries or the testes, although this method is not commonly used.

Salpingectomy involves the tying of the tubes and the resection of a portion so that the two ends cannot meet. When further pregnancies are not advisable and sterilization of the female is indicated in the opinion of obstetrical consultants, it is usually carried out at the time of Caesarean section, if such is the method of delivery. If natural delivery occurs, it is generally carried out as a separate procedure at a later date. Since it is a major surgical procedure, it is less preferable, at least in this country, to male sterilization, which can be done as an office procedure. Therefore, when prevention of further impregnation is necessary it is more commonplace to sterilize the husband than the wife.

Vasectomy

Indications

Vasectomy is a minor surgical procedure designed to prevent the male from impregnating the female, without interfering with his ability adequately to perform sexual intercourse. It may be indicated for three major reasons.

The first is the *eugenic sterilization* of the habitual (convicted) criminal, moral pervert, or an individual with an inheritable mental disease (twenty-eight states in the United States have specific statutes sanctioning the procedure for these eugenic purposes).

The second is the *therapeutic sterilization* that is indicated when the wife's life may be endangered by repeated pregnancies. These medical indications are tuberculosis, cancer, cardio-renal-vascular diseases complicated by high blood pressure or hypertension, kidney disorders, and Rh blood incompatibilities. These disease processes are frequently exacerbated by pregnancy and may prove fatal to the wife. The presence of similar illnesses in the husband, which might prevent him from being a responsible wage-earner, is also an indication for therapeutic sterilization.

The majority of sterilizations are performed for socioeconomic reasons. It is in this third category that the physician finds himself on extremely shaky legal grounds, owing to inadequate or conflicting legislation regarding indications for sterilization. This category is frequently called *nontherapeutic sterilization,* since there is no medical necessity for it—aside from the emotional anguish caused by repeated pregnancies.

Operative Procedure

Vasectomy is an operation that severs the tubes through which sperm flows from its origin in the testicles to the ejaculating mechanism deep in the penis. This interruption prevents sperm from flowing into the seminal fluid.

The tubes that are severed are called the vasa deferentia. They are approximately twenty inches long and about an eighth of an inch wide. Since they are so superficially located in the scrotum, it is extremely easy to expose and cut them. At least one half to one inch of each tube is excised and the cut ends then ligated. A vasoligation is a ligation of the vasa without resection. There are variations in the techniques of such surgery, but basically the severance and ligation should be sufficient to prevent any sperm flow. The procedure takes about twenty to thirty minutes and a physician competent in this operation can generally accomplish it under a local anesthetic in his office. It is attended by few complications.

Occasionally an infection of the epididymis (an organ adjacent to the testicle) occurs, which may incapacitate the patient for several weeks. However, in this era of effective prophylactic antibiotics, such as penicillin and the mycin drugs, the incidence of infection is negligible, and generally the patient is in perfect health about twenty-four to forty-eight hours following operation. It is customary to prescribe a longer period of postoperative convalescence for the man who is engaged in heavy physical labor than for one whose job is sedentary.

Frequently the operative area blows up into a little sac, or granuloma, of sperm. This creates a lumpiness in the scrotum, but generally does not cause any trouble. It may be a good-sized sac at the beginning, but as time goes on scarring will enable it to diminish in size. After the surgery has been performed, it is important to examine the seminal fluid in order to ascertain whether any sperm are present. It is a good practice to examine at least two specimens, the first three weeks following surgery and the second six weeks postoperatively. If no mobile sperm are found, the patient is permitted to indulge in sexual intercourse without contraceptives.

Effectiveness

One wonders whether this procedure produces an absolute sterility with no chance of recurrence. When a large enough segment is excised, it is theoretically unlikely that the two ends of the ducts would be able to reunite and permit recanalization. Perhaps, therefore, the earlier reports of this phenomenon occurring were based on the fact that more vasoligations rather than partial resection vasectomies were performed. Also, it is conceivable that a physician unfamiliar with this procedure might sever other structures that look like the vasa

deferentia without actually achieving sterilization.

However, there are specific reports in the medical literature of recanalization with the restoration of fertility and consequent pregnancies. O'Connor in 1948 sent a questionnaire to 750 physicians engaged in this field, and 55 proven cases of recanalization were reported. In 1959 Reiser reported that a questionnaire to 971 urological surgeons revealed 41 proved cases of recanalization. In extremely rare cases there may be an accessory or abnormal third vas deferens that was not discovered upon routine examination and was therefore not severed. In many operations performed, however, I did not find a proved instance of a third vas deferens. In my estimation, the persistence of sperm after vasectomy is due either to inadequate resection or to simple vasoligation.

Psychosexual Complications

What of psychosexual complications? Does vasectomy result in increased sexual vigor or can it produce sexual difficulties in the male? Where fear of multiple pregnancies has existed in the family, the sexual act may be frequently accompanied by difficulties. Anxiety may lead to premature ejaculation or, conversely, to total impotence. The female may become frigid and develop vaginismus and an inability to achieve orgasm—where previously she had been quite satiated with proper orgasm. There are, of course, various gradations of these sexual problems. It is not uncommon to find husbands who so dislike submitting to the constant use of artificial contraceptives that they do not enjoy the sexual act. A certain percentage of males therefore use coitus interruptus, which, in turn, creates an unhappy state of affairs.

Vasectomy, by eliminating the need for these artificialities, may lead to an improvement in the sexual appetite and vigor of males. Popenoe, Garrison, and Gamble (1959) found that, of 151 men who had undergone vasectomy, sexual appetite increased in 17.9 per cent, in 74.2 per cent it remained approximately the same as it had been before vasectomy, and in only 7.9 per cent was it slightly diminished. In addition, the removal of the fear of pregnancy on the part of the female, as well as the freedom from contraceptives, often results in allaying any sexual anxiety she may have felt prior to her husband's surgery, and may lead to better sexual performance on her part.

Many patients ask whether the procedure has any effect on bodily functions—such as a feminizing effect. The answer is emphatically no. Follow-up studies reveal no effect on any physiological mechanism, either genital or hormonal. The average individual confuses this procedure with castration, which does have a feminizing effect. Castration is rarely performed, except in specific conditions, such as cancer of the prostate.

Is vasectomy permanent? Is it possible for a man who has been previously sterilized to have another operation to restore his fertility? These are questions that are posed to the doctor from time to time by patients who think in terms of future alterations of family planning. In cases such as a couple who desire, after five or seven years of sterility, to increase the size of their families, or when a man suffers a total loss of his family by accident or divorce, a restoration of fertility may be desired.

The answer is that a "revamping" operation known as a vaso-vasotomy can be performed that has a variable degree of success. In my routine interviews with patients, prior to an agreement to perform vasectomy, I indicate that the technique is considered to be permanently effective. However, in the event of a catastrophe, as noted, there is a plastic operation that will restore the continuity of the vas. Although technically not difficult, it cannot be guaranteed to re-establish sperm flow. O'Connor states that of 420 such restorative operations, 229 failed and 191 succeeded. "Success" simply indicated that sperm were once again found in the ejaculate fluid. Pregnancy cannot always be assured, however, because the number of sperm may not be adequate or they may not be sufficiently healthy. In more recent years, Dorsey (1953) achieved 90 per cent success in a small series of cases. Under average circumstances a success rate of approximately 50 per cent is generally considered a laudable one.

This operation requires a general anesthesia and hospitalization. The two ends of the tube that had been previously resected are rejoined and held together with fine sutures, with or without internal splinting. Sperm may appear within weeks or months following this procedure, and it is customary to follow the patient for at least a year before deciding whether or not it was successful.

Medicolegal Aspects

What is the attitude of doctors toward performing vasectomies? Where eugenic sterilization is sanctioned, the doctor finds himself in a rather secure position. Generally, eugenic sterilizations are done in state institutions and the indications are clearly warranted. However, as previously indicated, most therapeutic and nontherapeutic sterilizations are performed outside state institutions by private practitioners who have no state laws to protect them in the event of a suit. In California, for instance, insurance companies that provide malpractice insurance for physicians and surgeons do not cover or protect the physician in the event he performs a vasectomy and is sued. Almost all accredited hospitals do not permit this operation unless it has been agreed upon as a medical necessity by several other competent consultants. It is also permitted as an adjunct procedure in the treatment of prostate disease by prostatectomy—provided adequate consent forms have been signed.

Reiser recently submitted a questionnaire to members of the American Urological Association regarding the number of vasectomies they performed. Of 971, 52 per cent performed vasectomies, 47 per cent did not, and 1 per cent did not reply. A large segment of the medical profession refuses to do either therapeutic or nontherapeutic vasectomy because of religious or moral objections as well as because of the legal confusion concerning it. Holman (1954) says that the absence of specific statutes and court decisions places a tremendous burden upon the physician, even when the patient gives valid written consent to this operation. He states, ". . . while consent is doubtless valid if the operation is necessary to relieve or cure some existing disease, or safeguard the life of the patient, the validity of consent to an operation not required for any therapeutic reason, nor performed in accord with statutes relating to eugenic sterilization would, at least, be open to question." He further states, "aside from the statutes in the few states (Connecticut, Kansas, Utah, and Montana) that have prohibited it, we find no judicial or legislative announcement of public policy against the practice of sterilization."

The law in Kansas states that anyone who performs a sterilization operation, whether vasectomy or salpingectomy, for the purpose of destroying the powers of procreation, unless it is a medical necessity, is guilty of a misdemeanor. In Utah, it is a felony. Indiana, Mississippi, and Virginia have prohibitory provisions regarding nontherapeutic vasectomies. Regan (1956) says that according to the California code it might be construed as being an act of mayhem, which, following the old English code, is interpreted as the unlawful and malicious removal of a "member" of a human being. Sterilization, however, does not maim in the same sense as does, for example, the loss of an eye, a hand, or a leg, and is not therefore considered as constituting mayhem. This decision was handed down by the Supreme Court of Minnesota in the case of Christiansen *vs.* Thornby in 1934. When universal legislation is spelled out loudly and clearly, physicians will not fear performing these operations.

The fear of increasing malpractice action, especially in the State of California, has become a concern to all physicians. Doctors are beginning to think in terms of the malpractice potentialities of treating a patient as soon as he steps into their office. They can at least take some comfort when they carry a large malpractice insurance coverage. But when they do not, helping a patient can often boomerang in their faces. Reiser, from the same questionnaire mentioned above, found that 87 per cent of the physicians who performed vasectomies have never been faced with legal action, whereas 8 per cent have and 5 per cent did not reply. These figures may afford solace to some doctors who perform vasectomies, but one never knows when one may find oneself included in the 8 per cent. Yet, in spite of the absence of legal protection, there are still many physicians who carry out this procedure when they feel it is advisable and therapeutic.

Socioeconomic Aspects

I basically disagree with Reiser when he states that "further pregnancies which might endanger the life of a wife do not constitute a medical authorization to perform vasectomy

on the husband." Many physicians realize the importance, sexually and mentally, of a well-balanced family that is free of emotional tensions and anxieties. In this inflationary period of our history, with ever-mounting costs of living, the average wage-earner finds it very difficult to provide adequately for a large family. Many families are finding that caring for more than three children involves a severe economic burden. As each year goes by, with the dollar buying less and less, parents become more and more apprehensive about their ability to provide properly for the future of their already existing children. This, added to the apprehension of further pregnancies because of failure of contraceptives or because of inability to use them intelligently—or because of simple laziness in not using them at all and depending upon luck—can considerably worsen relations between husband and wife. Their constant worry can, indeed, color their emotional attitudes toward their duties as parents. There is little doubt that these are causative factors in a large percentage of present-day divorces.

Many of the couples who seek sterilization are not well educated or well informed on sexual matters. They are frequently from the lower income group and have the usual economic problems of this group. These families, as they grow larger in size, often find themselves in a situation that requires financial support by charitable organizations, both public and private. In addition, these large-sized families, especially those in the slum areas of our cities, provide a spawning ground for delinquents of all types.

The problem of world-wide birth control is a vast and profound one. Many countries with large populations, such as Japan, China, and India, have in recent years begun to take specific action to limit population by control measures. Mrs. Ruth Smith has reported, in a paper in the *Human Betterment Association of America News* (1959), on the program that is being accepted throughout many of the Asian countries, where birth control measures, such as contraception, are endorsed and abortion and sterilization are accepted.

Although there was an initial reluctance upon the part of the average Oriental to have his genital organs surgically altered, recently there has been an increasing demand for vasectomies, according to Dr. Abraham Stone (1959). He states, "In Lucknow, India, for instance I found that of 750 patients that applied to the Planned Parenthood Center for advice, 240 women and 20 men, or nearly 35 per cent were sterilized at their own request." He also says that "groups of men are brought down from neighboring areas for vasectomies once a week." They are brought to a center in one of the larger cities where surgical facilities for this purpose are available. Men choose the operation because of its simplicity.

Summary

In summary, sterilization is a method of preventing either a female or a male from reproducing offspring. When the conducting mechanisms are severed by salpingectomy or by vasectomy, none of the normal body functions are interfered with, as may occur with the removal of the specific organs of egg-formation (ovaries) or sperm-formation (testes). The removal of either ovaries or testes is not a commonplace method of sterilization. Since sterilization is much easier to accomplish in the male, the operation known as vasectomy is the more commonly used technique.

Vasectomy is indicated when undesirable hereditary traits are present, such as epilepsy, chorea, and hemophilia. It may be called for in individuals who are criminally insane or morally perverted, and when pregnancy would be dangerous to the wife suffering from a serious disease such as cancer, tuberculosis, diabetes, or Rh blood incompatibilities. Lastly, it may be advisable as a permanent measure of contraception and birth control when, for psychological and socioeconomic reasons, a moderately sized family is of prime importance for the total welfare of the family.

References

Donnelly, R. C., and Ferber, W. L., "The Legal and Medical Aspects of Vasectomy." *J. Urol. 81;* 259-263, 1959.

Dorsey, J., "Anastomosis of Vas Deferens to Correct Post Vasectomy Sterility." *J. Urol. 73;* 515-519, 1953.

Hayt, E., Hayt, L. R., Groeschel, A. H., and McMullen, D., *Law of Hospital and Nurse.* New York: Hospital Textbook Co., 1958.

Holman, E. J., "Medicolegal Aspects of Sterilization, Artificial Insemination and Abortion." *J.A.M.A. 156;* 1309-1311, 1954.

O'Connor, V. D., "Anastomosis of the Vas Deferens after Purposeful Division for Surgery." *J. Urol. 59;* 229-233, 1948.

Pearse, H. A., and Ott, H. A., "Hospital Control of Sterilization and Therapeutic Abortion." *Am. J. Obst. & Gynec. 60;* 285-301, 1950.

Popenoe, P., Garrison, and Gamble. Quoted in Smith *et al.*

Powell, T. R., "Compulsory Vaccination and Sterilization: Constitutional Aspects." *Ann. Int. Med. 18;* 637-646, 1943.

Regan, L. J., *Doctor and Patient and the Law.* St. Louis: C. V. Mosby, 1956.

Reiser, C., "Vasectomy: Medical and Legal Aspects." *J. Urol. 79;* 138-143, 1958.

Smith, H. W. *et al.,* "Panel Discussion; Medico-legal Aspects of Urology." *J. Urol. 81;* 244-258, 1959.

Smith, Ruth, *Human Betterment of America Association News,* April, 1959.

Stone, A., *Sterilization.* New York: Human Betterment Association of America, 1959.

Wesson, M. B., "The Doctor and the Law." *Urol. & Cutan. Rev. 54;* 577-582, 1959.

MURRAY RUSSELL

Stress and Sex

Definition

THE simplest definition of stress is "the rate of wear and tear in the body." Like an inanimate machine, the living mechanism of the human body shows signs of wear and tear as a consequence of usage. The accumulated results of such wear and tear are what we call aging, but the rate at which the wear and tear progresses, at any one time, is stress. Such biological stress manifests itself by a set of symptoms and signs that are known as the General Adaptation Syndrome (G.A.S.). Unlike most inanimate machines, the living body has a built-in defense mechanism that tends to repair the damage caused by stress. This is accomplished largely through nervous and hormonal reactions. Among the latter, the increased production during stress of hormones such as ACTH and corticoids (cortisonelike substances) is especially important.

Causes of Stress

Anything that forces the body to perform work is a cause of stress, or a *stressor;* hence, as long as we are alive we are always under some degree of physiological stress. However, in common parlance the word stress usually denotes an excessive degree of biological wear and tear. Among the most common stressors of man are psychic and nervous stimuli, infections, trauma, hypersensitivity reactions, muscular work, hemorrhage, intoxication with various drugs, and nutritional deficiencies.

Stress as a Cause of Sexual Derangements

The adaptive reactions with which the body combats stress may entail severe derangement in sexual life. It is well known that physical or mental fatigue, as well as any other type of stressful experience (diseases, loss of blood, etc.), diminishes sexual desire and may induce temporary impotence or frigidity. The nervous mechanisms involved in this type of reaction are not yet well known, but it has been demonstrated that the production of sex hormones is definitely diminished at times when the body must produce an excessive amount of those pituitary and adrenal hormones (ACTH, corticoids) that are more immediately necessary for the maintenance of health and even of life. This change in the type of hormone produced during emergencies has been called the "stress-shift in hormone production." It is well known, for example, that a sudden stressful experience (e.g., fright) may diminish or suppress egg-laying in fowl; the so-called "stress amenorrhea," the cessation of menstrual cycles during periods of stress in women, is due to an essentially similar mechanism.

Milk secretion is governed by the pituitary hormone, prolactin, whose secretion is likewise diminished during stress; this explains the diminution of milk secretion that often occurs in farm animals and in nursing mothers as a consequence of stress.

In the male, both sex hormone and sperm production can be severely impeded as a result of stressful experiences.

Stress as a Consequence of Sexual Derangements

Conversely, various types of sexual anomalies may, as a result of their frustrating effect, induce stress. It is particularly important to be aware of this mechanism because the emotional disturbances resulting from sexual derangements often cause diseases that are rarely recognized as having any relationship to sexual life.

Diseases produced by any type of maladjustment to stress are known as the "diseases of adaptation." Most common among these are nervous and mental diseases, high blood pressure, cardiac diseases, various types of arthritis, and duodenal ulcers. In most of these maladies, hereditary predisposition and previous personal experiences are principally responsible for determining which organ system will break down first as a result of stress.

The unprecedented attention that has been given by physicians to the subject of stress and to diseases of adaptation during the last two decades has clarified many of the biochemical mechanisms that may become deranged as a consequence of stressful experiences. As a result, several of these maladies have now become amenable to prevention and treatment.

References

Galdston, Iago (ed.), *Beyond the Germ Theory.* New York: Health Education Council, 1954.

Gross, Nancy, *Living with Stress.* New York: McGraw-Hill Book Co., 1958.

Selye, Hans, *The Stress of Life.* New York: McGraw-Hill Book Co., 1956.

Selye, Hans, *The Chemical Prevention of Cardiac Necroses.* New York: The Ronald Press Co., 1958.

HANS SELYE

Transvestism and
Sex-Role Inversion

TRANSVESTISM and sex-role inversion are often misunderstood by the general public, and are sometimes confused even by professional workers in the behavioral sciences. Though there are superficial resemblances, these phenomena are fundamentally different and, in the interest of a clearer understanding of them, it is important to distinguish one from the other. The essential difference is that transvestism is limited to and refers only to the desire for and act of wearing the clothing of the other sex. Sex-role inversion is a much broader and more pervasive phenomenon, involving identification with, preference for, and adoption of the entire role of the other sex, of which dress is only one aspect. This distinction is a basic one and will be elaborated in the discussion of sex-role inversion. In view of popular notions to the contrary, it should be added that neither transvestism nor inversion involves a condition of depravity or moral degeneration.

Transvestism

The word *transvestism*, sometimes spelled transvestitism, was introduced into the literature by the German medical scientist, Magnus Hirschfeld, in 1910. The literal meaning of the term is an apt description of the condition to which it refers, *trans* meaning "across" or "opposite" and *vestis* meaning "dress" or "clothing." Another and less frequently used term, *eonism*, was first used by Havelock Ellis in 1928 to refer to this same condition, and was derived from Chevalier d'Eon de Beaumont, an eight-

eenth-century French nobleman and diplomat who dressed and lived as a woman for many years.

Historical and Cultural Survey

The occurrence of transvestism may be traced back to almost the beginning of recorded history. More than thirty centuries ago it was reported in the religious practices in the Orient. The early Hebrews were also familiar with transvestism, as seen in Deut. 22:5: "A woman shall not wear that which pertaineth unto a man, neither shall a man put on a woman's garment; for all that do are abomination unto the Lord thy God." It is evident from this passage that transvestism was looked upon as morally reprehensible behavior and, hence, subject to punishment and divine wrath. The ancient Germans considered transvestites liabilities from a military point of view and reportedly drowned them as burdens. While accepted at certain periods and by certain groups during the Middle Ages, at other times and by other groups transvestites were looked upon with scorn, condemned, and, in some cases, burned as followers of heathenism. Among some modern-day "moralists" and much of the general public, transvestites are considered degenerative perverts and affronts both to Providence and to nature.

Despite centuries of censure and condemnation, some rather eminent individuals of both sexes have been transvestites. Well-known examples include Elagabalus, Roman Emperor (A.D. 205-222); Prince Philippe, Duke of Orleans and brother of Louis XIV; François de Choisy, French lord, clergyman, and diplomat; King Henry III of France; and Lord Cornbury, who was Governor of New York before the Revolutionary War. Among female transvestites are the names of James Barry, Mary Walker, and Nicholas de Raylan.

James Barry, who became Senior Inspector General of the English Army Medical Department, passed through life as a man and was described as having a certain "effeminacy" in "his" manner which "he" always tried to overcome. Mary Walker was the first American woman to be commissioned an Army surgeon (during the Civil War) and the only woman expressly granted Congressional permission to wear men's clothing. Nicholas de Raylan, who described "himself" as the "son" of a Russian admiral, was a secretary of Baron von Schlippenbach of the Russian Consulate in Chicago at the beginning of the present century and enlisted as a soldier in the Spanish-American War. Living as a man all "his" life, "he" was discovered to be a woman after "his" death in 1906.

In recent and contemporary times transvestism has been reported from many different societies, literate and nonliterate, throughout the world. It may be considered universal in occurrence and, within a given society, appears to occur in all groups and classes. Among some of the "less civilized" peoples, transvestism is tolerated and, in some cases, fully accepted and integrated into cultural and religious practices. Examples include a number of North American Indian groups (e.g., Plains, Zuni, Mohave, and Dakotas), the Eskimos, the Melanesians of the Malay Archipelago, the Polynesians of Tahiti and other South Sea islands, and the Tanala and Hovas of Madagascar. Some of these groups hold ceremonies in which the male transvestite is introduced into the "world and ways of women" and the female transvestite into the "world of men." Such a person is thereafter considered exclusively a member of his or her adopted sex and is granted appropriate recognition as such. As will be pointed out in the section on sex-role inversion, cases such as these and others discussed above probably include a number of *inverted personalities* rather than simple transvestites.

Nature and Description

It is evident that one criterion for the existence of transvestism is dependent upon the prevailing pattern of a particular culture with regard to masculine and feminine dress. For example, in China and other parts of the Orient, as well as in certain other parts of the world, women often wear trousers while men wear robes.

Another criterion is the *desire* on the part of the transvestite to look like the other sex by wearing the clothing of that sex. American women, coeds, and bobby-soxers, who wear jeans or slacks as a matter of convenience or because of the particular social environment rather than out of desire to emulate the male, obviously are not manifesting transvestism. Neither, of course, is the Scotchman who wears a kilt. In short, the crux of transvestism is the desire for, act of, and emotional accompaniments of appearing in the apparel of the other sex.

Estimates of the incidence of transvestism in the general population vary from 3 per cent to less than 1 per cent. It is difficult to determine the precise frequency since undoubtedly the vast majority of transvestites live their entire lives without coming to the attention of the psychiatric-psychological professions or being apprehended by enforcement officials. It has been estimated that probably more than 90 per cent of male transvestites carry on their activities only in private, although some of them wear feminine items most of the time under their outer masculine clothes. Since a future volume in the Kinsey series on sexual behavior is scheduled to deal specifically with transvestism, perhaps it will provide an index of the prevalence of transvestism.

The majority of authorities agree that transvestism is much more common among males than among females, the estimates of the ratio running from 2:1 to 50:1. This is particularly interesting in view of the fact that, in our own culture at least, it is permissible for girls and women but not for boys and men to wear cross-sex clothes. Thus, although females are given much more opportunity and freedom than males to wear cross-sex clothing, the number of female transvestites presumably is far less than the number of male transvestites. The explanation of such a sex difference would present a major theoretical as well as practical challenge. In any event, most of the discussion to follow will necessarily be limited to male transvestism since little is known about female transvestism. In addition, most of what is known about male transvestism has come from cases reported by psychopathologists and hence cannot be assumed to be typical of transvestites as a group, many of whom no doubt are never seen by members of the medical and psychological professions.

The typical male transvestite has a rather complete wardrobe of feminine apparel and accessories, including all kinds of underwear, dresses, skirts, negligees, high-heeled shoes, nylons, etc., along with cosmetics, wigs, jewelry, and other items that accentuate femininity. The desire to wear these things varies in intensity and duration from a continual, compelling, insatiable urge to periodic desires and indulgences. Characteristic of most transvestites is a feeling of relaxation, pleasure, and naturalness when wearing the clothes of the other sex. The sensory experiences of wearing and feeling the clothes and of seeing oneself in them in a mirror are fundamental factors. It is interesting to note that many male transvestites complain about the "drab" and "oppressive" qualities of masculine apparel, while describing feminine clothes as "attractive" and "comfortable"; female transvestites apparently do just the opposite.

Determinants

What factors or conditions are responsible for the development of transvestism? Attempts to provide an answer to this question may be grouped under two broad headings: biogenetic, and psychosocial.

The view that transvestism is biologically determined has long been held by a number of authorities. It rests on the assumption that genetic-chromosomal anomalies, congenital maldevelopment, or acquired postnatal imbalances provide the underlying basis for its occurrence. In other words, the transvestite is driven to wear the clothes and appear like the opposite sex by a hereditary predisposition or developmental state that gives rise to some kind

of incomplete sexual differentiation. Transvestites, then, "instinctively" wear cross-sex apparel and are assumed to be "intersexed," even though just what it is about them that is "intersexed" has not been demonstrated.

One major reason for the biogenetic interpretation of transvestism has been the fact that transvestites almost invariably report that the desire to possess and wear the clothes of the opposite sex was present "from the very beginning," or "as far back as I can remember," or "from my earliest childhood." The appearance of transvestite behavior as early as the first two or three years of life has been interpreted as demonstrating its innate or congenital basis. This interpretation fails to consider that early emerging behavior patterns may actually stem from early conditioning experiences. The statements of transvestites that they feel "normal" and "natural" in the clothing of the other sex have been taken as indications of the constitutional nature of transvestism, but here again, such feelings are probably the result of learning rather than of constitutional endowment.

Little, if any, evidence has been established to support the biogenetic hypothesis. In fact, recent research studies on a large number of various types of human hermaphrodites point conclusively to the primary importance of assigned sex at birth, sex of rearing, and *learned* sex-role identity, rather than of biological predispositions. Thus, among individuals with overt sexual components of both sexes (such as ambiguous external genitalia or a contradiction between external genitalia and chromosomal, gonadal, hormonal, or internal sexual characteristics), the crucial determinants of their sex-role concept and identity as male and masculine or as female and feminine have been found to be their early conditioning experiences, social learnings, and psychological developments, rather than the natures of their biological-anatomical anomalies. A person may be very confused in terms of chromosomal-genital-anatomical-physiological sexuality but be quite normal in his psychosexual development and, for example, show no inclination whatsoever toward transvestism, inversion, homosexuality, or other sexual disturbances.

The biogenetic concept of transvestism, then,

appears to have little validity and, at least in the present state of knowledge, must be regarded as lacking substantiation. Furthermore, cultural diversity in dress makes it improbable that we will find a biogenetic mechanism to explain the fact that a male transvestite, reared in certain parts of the Orient, desires and prefers trousers, while a male transvestite reared in the Western world desires and prefers skirts and dresses.

The psychosocial explanation of transvestism is in terms of learning, i.e., transvestism is regarded as an *acquired* motivational and behavioral pattern, directly traceable to conditioning experiences, usually occurring in childhood. As such, a person's preference for or compelling desire to wear the clothes of the other sex is no more the result of inborn constitutional factors than is a vegetarian's strict preference for meatless food or a Mohammedan's preference for worshiping Allah. It is true, of course, that just as in other aspects of human behavior, the ease with which conditioning will develop a strong preference can vary from person to person. Wide differences in sensory threshold have been clearly demonstrated and are quite evident. Nevertheless, practically all individuals are conditionable, i.e., have the potentiality for acquiring particular motives, preferences, and emotional states of varying degrees of intensity.

Whatever may be the unique combination of childhood experiences and circumstances in a given case of transvestism, one factor almost invariably found to be of prime importance is that in the first two or three years of life the child was accidentally or intentionally exposed to the experience of wearing and fondling the clothes of the other sex, allowing an imprinting process to occur, in which, for example, the male child's formative sensory experiences may be conditioned to feminine articles of clothing. A frequent related finding in the histories is that the child's hair was kept long and/or curled like that of a girl. In addition, the boy is often given extra attention and praise by the parent for wearing feminine clothes and appearing feminine. Interestingly enough, in some instances a young boy may be punished by being forced to wear feminine clothes, such "discipline" being referred to as "pinafore punishment"; nevertheless, such a boy may

come to be conditioned to feminine items just as surely as one who is rewarded for wearing them. It is reasonable to wonder about the motivations of parents who choose such a form of "punishment" for male children. Some parents may be more or less unconsciously saying to the child, "I wanted you to be a girl in the first place and since you disappointed me, I'll make you look like one." Other parents might be expressing a very different attitude, one of "I'll force you into an inferior role, I'll deny your privileged, masculine status and make you into a girl."

What kind of parent-child relations allow a male child to wear feminine clothes and have hair like a girl? In the typical pattern the parents, most often the mother, especially wanted a girl rather than a boy child, or for some other reason were particularly disappointed in their male offspring. A feminization process is carried out by the mother, who provides the boy with feminine clothes and proceeds to rear him as though he were a girl insofar as dress and appearance are concerned. Little Lord Fauntleroy is a well-known example of how some boys acquire predominantly feminine characteristics under the deliberate influence of the mother. Parental approval and praise are often directly connected with cross-sex dress: "Oh, you look like a little angel," "You're so pretty," "You'd make such a darling girl," "You're mother's favorite when you are all dressed up in a pretty dress," etc.

It is important to note here that this process involves both conditioning and instrumental or operant forms of learning; that a considerable amount of it is an involuntary learning experience; and that it often occurs in the *earliest* period of life before the child can even verbalize his feelings and preferences. This probably explains the fact that many transvestites report not only that the clothes of the other sex feel "natural," but also that they "can't help" feeling the way they do about wearing such clothes. In this connection, it is possible that the much greater incidence of transvestism reported in males compared to females may be based in part on the more frequent occurrence of boys dressed as girls in the *first two or three years of life*. A 2-year-old girl with a "butch" hair style, dressed in a shirt and trousers, is certainly rarer than a 2-year-old boy with long or curled hair and still in a dress. Of course, *after* the first few years this pattern is reversed, and girls but not boys are allowed to wear clothes of the opposite sex.

In any event, evidence suggests that in many instances the basis for the development of transvestism occurs in the early years of childhood. Furthermore, the influence of the wider cultural pattern would appear to be quite secondary compared to the formative learning experiences of the child. The fact that transvestism is often rooted in the earlier life of an individual would in part account for its very strong resistance to extinction.

It seems quite clear that the mother exerts a decisive influence in the development of transvestism. In case after case of male transvestism, the mother is described as "delighting in dressing the boy as a girl," "encouraging girlishness in her son," "pretending the son was a daughter," or "forcing her boy to wear feminine attire." In many cases the mother feminizes her son without apology or concealment; in other instances, she is intent on feminizing her son but goes about it with some degree of pretense or disguise. One male transvestite, for example, was almost full-grown before his mother finally remarked, "I rather like you in feminine clothes." As a group, mothers of transvestites tend to fit the description of "mom," as defined by Philip Wylie, Edward Strecker, and other authorities: an immature, narcissistic, selfish, chronically unhappy woman whose maladjustment seriously affects and impedes the psychological development and emotional maturity of her children.

The father pattern is usually one or the other of two types: (1) father-absence pattern, in which for one reason or another the father has little or no contact with the son (and there is no father-substitute such as a big brother or grandfather); or (2) father-son disturbed pattern, in which the father-son relationship is negative and unsatisfactory because of rejection and intense dislike of the son by the father, or because of marked domination of the father by the mother, together with overprotection of the son, which prevents a close, emotional bond to develop between father and son. A less frequently reported pattern is that in which the male child identifies with the mother and at the same time competes with her in an effort to win the attention and acceptance of the father.

Presumably a converse pattern is found in the childhood of female transvestites, i. e., the little girl is provided with boys' clothing which she is allowed, encouraged, or forced to wear. It seems likely, however, that female transvestism per se (transvestism without inversion) is an extremely rare phenomenon. Most cases of females who dress in masculine clothing are probably female inverts and not merely transvestites.

The *psychoanalytical interpretation* of transvestism is in terms of the nature of the early mother-child relationship. Although Freud himself had little to say about transvestism, other psychoanalytical writers have emphasized the central role of castration anxiety and identification with a threatening "phallic type" mother in the development of male transvestism. The little boy deals with his own castration anxiety allegedly by convincing himself that the mother has a penis, and thereby identifies with her. The centering of attention on the mother's clothes rather than on her body is said to be adopted by the little boy as a means whereby he can avoid acknowledging the anatomical difference between males and females, and, hence, deny the threat of castration. "Being like mother" occurs primarily with reference to wearing clothes like those of mother.

Some writers have viewed transvestites as individuals whose longing for the genitals of the other sex is displaced to a desire for their clothing and, as such, is indicative of an urge to be identified with the other sex. Incest fixation also has been mentioned as a contributing factor in that the desire for clothes is a symbolic representation of desire for sexual gratification with a family member of the other sex. Female transvestism is viewed as involving a more "pretending" condition (i. e., the girl pretends she has a penis) than male transvestism, and is considered as a displacement of envy of the penis to an envy of masculine dress, appearance, and status.

Transvestism and
Other Sexual Disturbances

Although transvestism may occur along with or in addition to other forms of sexual disturbance, such as homosexuality, fetishism, or exhibitionism, it is important not to confuse or equate it with any of these other phenomena.

It is unfortunate that transvestism is often considered nothing more than a form of *homosexuality*. As a matter of fact, these two phenomena are separate and independent. Research and clinical studies indicate that the majority of male transvestites are predominantly or exclusively heterosexual throughout their lives. Despite this, some authorities automatically suspect or assume homosexuality in all cases of transvestism and attempt to "explain" the heterosexual majority as "latent," "masked," or "repressed" homosexuals. This is akin to saying that all persons are really murderers or arsonists, but that they are "unconscious" killers or "latent" firebugs. Perhaps the simplest way of summarizing this discussion is to state that among a large number of predominantly or exclusively homosexual males, a minority will be found to be transvestites, and among a large number of male transvestites, a minority will be found to be predominantly or exclusively homosexual. The relative incidence of homosexuality among female transvestites is not known. It was hypothesized previously that most women who, through choice, wear masculine clothes are probably *inverted* personalities and not merely transvestites, and there is some evidence that among these inverted females the majority are homosexual.

Another phenomenon often linked with transvestism is *fetishism*, which refers to sexual arousal and gratification mainly or exclusively associated with some specific item of clothing, "nongenital" part of the body, or inanimate object. Some cases of transvestism may involve sexual excitement leading to orgasm in connection with a certain item of cross-sex clothing. If masturbation is instigated by *wearing*, rather than by fondling or caressing, an article of dress belonging to the other sex, and if this is the most prominent feature of the case, it might best be considered fetishism associated with transvestism, rather than pure transvestism. It should be added, however, that perhaps the majority of transvestites desire cross-sex clothes in their own right, rather than for purposes of masturbation, and that such desire is not necessarily associated with sexual gratification per se. It is necessary to stress, as in the case of homosexuality, that many transvestites are not fetishists and many fetishists are not transvestites.

Exhibitionism is another disturbance sometimes confused with transvestism. The fact that the typical transvestite obtains satisfaction by having other people look at him while dressed in cross-sex clothing as well as by looking at himself in a mirror does not necessarily indicate exhibitionism in a strict sense. Exhibitionism is a sexual disturbance in which exposure of the genitals brings erotic excitement and gratification, and, as such, occurs independently of transvestism and vice versa.

Hermaphroditism (androgyny or gynandry) is an anatomical-physiological condition in which there is ambiguity in the external genitals and/or contradictions among the chromosomal, gonodal, or hormonal factors, the external genital structures, and the internal accessory sexual structures. As a biological anomaly, hermaphroditism stands in sharp contrast to transvestism, in which the person's biological structures and functions are normal but his psychological development involved intense conditioning to the clothes of the other sex. Hermaphroditism is the result of organic constitutional factors, whereas transvestism is the result of psychosocial factors. As pointed out previously, careful study of many hermaphrodites shows that the crucial variable that determines their sex-role identity is *not* the nature or extent of their hermaphroditism but rather the consistency of their being reared as a boy or a girl and the degree to which they have desired and accepted a masculine or feminine role. On the other hand, a person may be partially or predominantly inverted in his or her sex role but completely normal in sexual anatomy and physiology. In short, hermaphroditism and transvestism are entirely different and completely independent conditions.

Treatment and Prevention

Because the condition often becomes fixated during childhood, transvestism is highly resistant to modification or extinction. Psychotherapy has been largely unsuccessful in providing a means of eliminating transvestic behavior. Some therapists, however, hold out hope, believing that most failures are caused by the patient's lack of desire for cure and that if his motivational state could be altered, effective results would follow.

There is little disagreement that an ounce of prevention is worth more than a ton of cure as far as transvestism is concerned. A psychosocial immunization against transvestism exists and consists of two components: (1) making certain the infant-child is exposed to and wears *only* clothes that are culturally appropriate and in accordance with his biological sex; and (2) creating an accepting, close, affectionate relationship with the parent of the same sex. The very real danger of dressing a child in cross-sex clothes, either by encouragement or by force, especially during the first few years of life, should be realized by all prospective parents and, in particular, by mothers. It is unfortunate that there are not ways whereby young children can be protected from parents who distort and warp their psychological development just as they are protected from physical brutality, neglect, and cruelty. A widespread educational program stressing the permanent damage a parent can do to a child in the psychosexual area might at least make some mothers ponder the consequences of conditioning a child to patterns of the other sex.

Sex-Role Inversion

Superficially, a person is either male *or* female, masculine *or* feminine. Sexual and sex-role differentiation show, however, gradations similar to those found in other life classifications (e.g., animal-plant or mammal-bird) and human dimensions (intelligence, height, etc.). Thus, the degree to which a person is male and masculine or female and feminine is relative.

The phenomenon in which a person of one biological sex *thinks, feels,* and *acts* like the opposite sex is called inversion or, more accurately, sex-role inversion. Identification with, preference for, and adoption of the sex role of the other sex is the essential meaning of inversion. A man, for example, whose interests, motivational states, and behavioral patterns are typical of women, is a male invert. Inversion, then, involves a psychosomatic disharmony, in that the psychological characteristics of an individual are typical of one sex but the anatomical composition is that of the other sex. This condition has been reported from ancient times and observed in almost every social group.

The desire of the invert for the role and identity of the other sex is often compelling, insatiable, and life-long. Male inverts, for example, describe themselves in terms such as the following: "I'm really a female but I have a male body," "I'm physically a male but emotionally a female," "Nature made a mistake and gave me a male body," "I'm male in name only." A demonstration of how complete the adoption of the role of the other sex may be is provided by cultures that are tolerant or accepting of such individuals. Thus, among the Mohave Indians, the male invert typically has a feminine name, looks and dresses like a woman, calls his penis a "clitoris," imitates menstruation by scratching his thighs to produce blood, feigns pregnancy and childbirth, and in every way possible follows the role of a woman. The completeness with which inversion may be established even in our own society is shown by the case of a male invert who throughout childhood lived with his mother as a "daughter," attended a modeling school, became a "saleswoman" in an exclusive ladies' shop on the West Coast, and was "maid of honor" at the wedding of a close friend.

Inversion and Other Sexual Disturbances

It is important to emphasize that the criterion of inversion is *psychological* and *behavioral*, rather than anatomical and physical, similarity to the other sex. Traits that are primarily the result of environmental conditions and learning should not be confused with features that are the result of heredity and maturation. The terms *masculinity* and *femininity* should be used to refer to the former, and *male* and *female* to the latter.

Such components of personality and traits of a person as preferences, social motives, and feelings; gait, gestures, and other bodily movements; general demeanor; communicative qualities such as enunciation, word associations, and word choices; and various everyday habits and mannerisms—these are for the most part *acquired* patterns through which culturally defined masculine or feminine modes of behavior are expressed. On the other hand, such features as bodily dimensions and shape; pubic hair distribution and presence or absence of beard; muscle potential; voice depth; internal and external genital structures; and related characteristics are part of the unlearned, constitutional make-up of a person. Thus, when an individual's thinking, feeling, and acting are more characteristic of the other sex than his or her own biological sex, the result is *inversion*; on the other hand, when the individual's structural features and physiological functions are both male and female, the result is some degree of hermaphroditism. It can be seen that inversion bears a relationship to masculinity and femininity similar to that which hermaphroditism bears to maleness and femaleness. Failure to make this basic distinction leads to conceptual confusion and such contradictory terms as "constitutional masculinity," "biological femininity," "psychic hermaphroditism," "instinctive female impersonators," and "innately feminine." It leads also to erroneous interpretations of acquired behavior patterns (masculine and feminine traits) as hereditary and maturational. The terms "virility" and "effeminacy" are commonly used to imply *both* male and masculine or female and feminine characteristics, i.e., to unlearned and physiological as well as to learned and psychological features and traits.

It is not difficult to understand why inversion has often been confused with transvestism and homosexuality. Whereas transvestism will almost always be found in cases of inversion (since desiring to wear the clothes of the other sex is one of the many aspects of adopting the role of that sex), the converse is not true; inver-

sion is not necessarily found in cases of transvestism. In fact, evidence suggests that the majority of transvestites are neither inverts nor homosexuals. Apart from their life-long fixation on feminine clothes, many male transvestites are masculine in sex-role behavior, are married, have families, live normal lives, and in some cases distinguish themselves in masculine undertakings such as the armed forces and athletics.

Passive, feminine male homosexuality and *active, masculine* female homosexuality will often be found among male and female inverts respectively. The male invert, for example, perceives himself as a female and will be inclined to seek sexual gratification from the "other" sex, that is, from males. Not all homosexuals, however, are inverts, since there are a number of other determinants of homosexuality. Inversion is only *one* condition that may be related to *one* form of homosexuality.

If many inverts are homosexual why not *all* of them? Since, for example, the typical female invert thinks, feels, and acts like a man, and since the typical man is sexually oriented toward women, then why are not all female inverts homosexual—that is, sexually oriented toward women? The answer to this question would appear to be along the following lines: Just as some women, who are normal in the sense of having adopted the feminine role, may be incapable of heterosexual adjustment because of unfavorable developmental conditioning or experiences in psychosocial relations with the *other* sex, so some female inverts may not be capable of homosexual adjustment because of adverse experiences in psychosexual relations with the *same* sex. However, if a woman, otherwise normal in sex role, finds sensory gratification and affective satisfaction with other women while experiencing disgust with members of the other sex, the result is likely to be a feminine female homosexual. In the same way, the male invert may have no inclination toward sexual relations with other men even though he is feminine through and through.

There are actually three different, independently varying components in the psychosexual development of an individual: (1) the constitutional composition as male or female, which is determined by genetic and maturational processes; (2) the process whereby a child *learns* how to be masculine or feminine, i.e., acquires a sex role; and (3) the process whereby a child *learns* how to channelize the raw energy of sexual drive toward one type of outlet or another, i.e., make the choice of sex object. A child is *born* a male or female but *learns* to be masculine or feminine and *learns* to seek and experience sexual satisfaction with members of the other sex or of the same sex. In the normal individual, these processes are consistent and integrated; the boy, as a male, learns to be masculine *and* to perceive females as potential love objects. Among noninverted homosexuals, the sex-role is normal except for the sex-object choice, whereas among inverted homosexuals neither sex role nor sex-object choice is normal. Among those individuals who are inverts but not homosexual, some may be heterosexual and some autosexual-narcissistic in object choice, while others may be more or less asexual or relatively hyposexed.

A term related to inversion but with a more specific meaning is *transsexualism*. The male invert who undergoes surgery to remove his male genital organs is a transsexualist ("going over to the other sex"), i.e., one who desires and receives sexual transformation by means of medical and surgical procedures. The widely known case of George (Christine) Jorgensen is an example. Some indication that inversion involving transsexualism is not necessarily an isolated occurrence or desire is suggested by the fact that, following the revelation of the Jorgensen case in the newspapers, the Danish endocrinologist, Hamburger, who supervised the "change of sex" procedures, received hundreds of letters from all parts of the world from individuals expressing the desire to have their sex changed.

Transsexualism is evident in the male invert who abhors everything male and masculine about himself, who has an overwhelming desire to be a woman not only in the full psychological and social sense but also in an anatomical sense, and who seeks surgery that will remove his maleness. Such inverts look upon their genitals as "dreadful deformities" and have an overwhelming desire to be a "complete woman."

The medical procedures involved in cases of male transsexualism exemplified by Jorgensen include: (1) hormonal castration by means of estrogenics which inhibit testicular functions; (2) electrolysis for the removal of facial hair; (3) surgical removal of the testes; (4) amputation of the penis; and (5) transformation of the scrotum into labialike structures and the creation of an artificial vagina by plastic surgery.

The fact that the transsexualist-invert belongs biologically to one sex but psychologically to the other sex commonly creates a deep-rooted, underlying pattern of maladjustment among such individuals. A healthy integration of the personality is hardly possible in such cases. Some authorities are of the opinion, however, that these individuals do improve in their adjustment to life after they have undergone the "change-over" operative procedures.

There have been a few instances of male transsexualists who, prior to their "transformation," have fathered one or more children. It is not difficult to imagine how confusing such a state of affairs must be to children whose "father" becomes a "woman."

Determinants of Sex-Role Inversion

Some authorities hold that the underlying basis of inversion is a genetically intersexed condition involving an inborn "irrepressible pattern" that is independent of early learning. Such individuals are often referred to as the "intermediate sex." The evidence, however, is lacking for this interpretation. In fact, as mentioned in the section on transvestism, recent investigations of individuals who are physically intersexed (hermaphrodites) point *away from* rather than toward a constitutional explanation of both inversion and transvestism.

The basis of inversion appears rather to be in the earliest parent-child relationships and is probably established during the second or third year of life. The child who becomes an adult invert has usually established a primary and continuing identification with the parent (or parent-substitute) of the other sex, and has adopted the sex-role of this parent. For one reason or another the family pattern is such that the child forms an excessively close and strong attachment to the parent of the opposite sex, while experiencing little or no emotionally satisfying relationship with the parent of the same sex.

The background of male inverts, for example, is typically one in which the *mother* encourages and reinforces the development of femininity while discouraging masculinity in the boy. Not uncommonly the mother makes no secret of her wish that the son had been a daughter and, in the first few years, "pretends" he is a girl. During this time there is a prolonged feminization process going on in which the mother and other women in the life of the young boy (grandmother, sisters, or other female relatives) surround him with patterns of femininity, dress him in girls' clothes, encourage him to play with girls and learn their ways, and treat him as though he actually were a girl. Usually, such a boy idolizes the mother and remains attached to her not only during childhood but throughout his life. During childhood such a boy typically becomes girlish in his behavior, learns to prefer dolls and other feminine playthings, develops a liking for domestic tasks to the exclusion of activities more common to boys, and desires to dress, look, and talk as much like a girl as possible. Usually he does not try to conceal his compelling drive toward becoming more and more feminine and, as adolescence and adulthood are approached, his desire to be accepted by society as a "complete woman" becomes even stronger. In brief, this constitutes the development of inversion.

There are, of course, individual variations in cases of inversion as in any other behavioral phenomenon. Thus, while male inverts as a group will characteristically show a childhood pattern of preference for playing with girls rather than boys, with a liking for girls' rather than boys' activities, there are exceptions to this pattern. In a given case of male inversion, for example, there may be a seemingly incongruent combination of dislike for playing with girls, an interest in domestic activities such as cooking and housekeeping, and a liking for mechanical toys, electrical apparatus, building materials, etc.

In cases where the boy has a relatively positive attachment to the father, or at least a relationship that is not one of basic rejection or hostility, and at the same time has a mother who allows, encourages, or forces him to wear feminine dress and develop other feminine patterns, the result is likely to be some degree of confusion in sex role. He may either show uncertainty as to his sex role or may actually develop two relatively distinct selves, one masculine and one feminine. One such individual described himself as "ruggedly masculine and aggressive" when dressed in masculine clothes, but "passive, gentle, and submissive" when in feminine clothes. It is evident that in such a case two sex roles, masculine and feminine, exist in the same personality. A variation of this pattern is exemplified by another subject, who reported feeling "opposite at times," "like two people in one, male and female," and "never completely male and never completely female." The patient had, during childhood, shown a mixture of feminine and masculine interests. As an adult, he alternated between an interest in muscle-building exercises and efforts to be "more of a man," and an urge to wear feminine clothing, use cosmetics, and appear more like a woman. Still another individual reported that when he was in his feminine role he tried to approximate the feminine image that he admired when he was in his masculine role.

It is interesting to note that cases such as those just described bear some resemblance to the phenomenon of dual personality. Part of the time the person is masculine in appearance and behavior; at other times the same person is feminine in appearance and behavior. Instead of a Dr. Jekyll and Mr. Hyde or an Eve White and Eve Black, there is a "Mr." Doe and a "Miss" Doe. There is, however, an important difference between individuals with dual sex roles and those with dual personalities. In contrast to cases of dual personality, in which one of the two selves is amnesic to the other, individuals who develop two sex roles are aware of the existence of both roles.

Treatment and Prevention

So far as is known, there is not a single case of clearly established adult inversion that has been cured by psychotheraphy or any other form of treatment. Although this does not necessarily mean that a restructuring of personality is impossible, especially if the patient desires strongly to effect such a change, it does mean that an inverted individual is likely to remain so throughout his life. The extreme resistance of inversion to change is based at least in part on the fact that it is typically conditioned in the earliest years of life, before the child is able to verbalize his emotional and motivational states. Moreover, almost invariably the invert is so satisfied with his adoption of the role of the other sex that he will never want to change his sex-role inversion, and therefore either will not attempt or will consciously resist any basic therapeutic change.

The *prevention* of inversion is clearly indicated and consists of educating parents to accept, respect, and rear a child in accordance with his biological sex. It would, for example, appear to be almost impossible for a boy to grow into a male invert if in early life he had: (1) a father (or father-substitute) who accepts, respects, and loves him *as a male*, to whom the boy can and will want to look as a model upon whom to pattern his own personality; and (2) a mother (or mother-substitute) who accepts, respects, and loves him *as a male* and who encourages him to develop manliness, to be masculine, to become a man. The corresponding pattern in the case of girls will prevent the development of female inversion: parents who accept, respect, and love the little girl *as a girl*—a mother the little girl both wants, and learns, to imitate, and a father who gives the little girl love and admiration for her femaleness and her efforts to develop along feminine lines.

References

Barahal, H. S., "Female Transvestism and Homosexuality." *Psychiat. Quart.* 27; 390-438, 1953.

Benjamin, H., "Transsexualism and Transvestism as Psycho-somatic and Somato-psychic Syndromes." *Am. J. Psychother.* 8; 219-230, 1954.

Brown, D. G., "Inversion and Homosexuality." *Am. J. Orthopsychiat.* 28; 424-429, 1958.

Cappon, D., "Psychosexual Identification in the Somatic Pseudohermaphrodite." Paper read at Am. Psychiat. A., San Francisco, Calif., May, 1958.

Cauldwell, D. O. (ed.), *Transvestism.* New York: Sexology Corp., 1956.

de Savitsch, E., *Homosexuality, Transvestism and Change of Sex.* Springfield, Ill.: Charles C Thomas, 1958.

Devereux, G., "Institutionalized Homosexuality of the Mohave Indians." *Human Biol.* 9; 498-527, 1937.

Ellis, A., "The Sexual Psychology of Human Hermaphrodites." *Psychosom. Med.* 7; 108-125, 1945.

Ellis, H., *Studies in the Psychology of Sex* (Vols. I and II). New York: Random House, 1936.

Fenichel, O., "The Psychology of Transvestism." *Internat. J. Psychoanalyt.* 11; 211-227, 1930.

Friend, M. R., Schiddel, Louise, Klein, Betty, and Dunaeff, Dorothy, "Observations on the Development of Transvestism in Boys." *Am. J. Orthopsychiat.* 24; 563-575, 1954.

Gutheil, E. A., "The Psychologic Background of Transsexualism and Transvestism." *Am. J. Psychother.* 8; 231-239, 1954.

Hamburger, C., "The Desire for Change of Sex as Shown by Personal Letters from 465 Men and Women." *Acta Endocrinologica* 14; 361-375, 1953.

Hamburger, C., Sturup, G. K., and Dahl-Iversen, E., "Transvestism." *J. A. M. A.* 152; 391-396, 1953.

Hampson, Joan G., Money, J., and Hampson, J. L., "Hermaphrodism: Recommendations Concerning Case Management." *J. Clin. Endocrinol. Metab.* 16; 547-556, 1956.

Henry, G. W., *All the Sexes: A Study of Masculinity and Femininity.* New York: Rinehart & Co., Inc., 1955.

Hirschfeld, M., *Sexual Anomalies.* New York: Emerson Books, Inc., 1948.

Hora, T., "The Structural Analysis of Transvestitism." *Psychoanalyt. Rev.* 40; 268-274, 1953.

Karpman, B., "Dream Life in a Case of Transvestism." *J. Nerv. & Ment. Dis.* 106; 292-337, 1947.

Litin, E. M., Giffin, Mary E., and Johnson, Adelaide M., "Parental Influences in Unusual Sexual Behavior in Children." *Psychoanalyt. Quart.* 25; 37-55, 1956.

Lukianowicz, N., "Survey of Various Aspects of Transvestism in the Light of Our Present Knowledge." *J. Nerv. & Ment. Dis.* 128; 36-64, 1959.

Money, J., Hampson, Joan, and Hampson, J. L., "Imprinting and the Establishment of Gender Role." *Arch. Neurol. & Psychiat.* 77; 333-336, 1957.

Olkon, D. M., and Sherman, Irene C., "Eonism with Added Outstanding Psychopathic Features." *J. Nerv. & Ment. Dis.* 99; 159-167, 1944.

Prince, C. V., "Homosexuality, Transvestism and Transsexualism." *Am. J. Psychother.* 11; 80-85, 1957.

Redmount, R. S., "A Case of a Female Transvestite with Marital and Criminal Complications." *J. Clin. & Exper. Psychopath.* 14; 95-111, 1953.

Reinhardt, J. M., *Sex Perversions and Sex Crimes.* Springfield, Ill.: Charles C Thomas, 1957.

Worden, F. G., and Marsh, J. T., "Psychological Factors in Men Seeking Sex Transformation." *J. A. M. A.*, 157; 1292-1298, 1955.

Yawger, N. S., "Transvestism and Other Cross-sex Manifestations." *J. Nerv. & Ment. Dis.* 92; 41-48, 1940.

DANIEL G. BROWN

Venereal Diseases, The

GLOBAL in incidence, the venereal diseases (Latin *venus, vener* = the goddess of love) are among the major afflictions of mankind. Although many years of application of present knowledge are still required, the use of penicillin and other antibiotic drugs has made the control of these diseases a practical possibility. Their complete elimination is no longer a fantastic goal.

They represent those infections usually acquired as a result of heterosexual and homosexual intercourse and allied activities. Because the causative organisms usually dwell only in human beings and cannot thrive outside of the body, the venereal diseases are almost always contracted by the direct transfer from one person to another. The organisms multiply best in moist areas, hence the prevalence of initial signs of the infection on and around the genitals, anus, and mouth. This, too, explains the usual mode of transmission, since sexual activities tend to bring these sites into apposition.

In this article an attempt is made to present the main features of the modern diagnosis and treatment of five venereal diseases: syphilis, gonorrhea, chancroid, granuloma inguinale, and lymphogranuloma venereum. Brief mention will also be made of a related group of widespread conditions—nonvenereal syphilis or endemic syphilis.

Syphilis

The word "syphilis" was first used by the physician Fracastoro in a poem published in 1530. In the thirty-five years immediately preceding this, the disease, or other diseases mis-taken for it, had spread wildly over Europe; a concurrence that later led to the theory that Columbus and his men had imported syphilis from America during the historic voyage of 1492. The etymology of the term is uncertain, but it is probably derived from the Greek words meaning "swine" and "love." The hero of Fracastoro's poem was a swineherd or shepherd boy, whose name was Syphilis and who was affected with the disease.

The modern study of syphilis started rather late in the bacterial era, mainly because the organism eluded detection long after those causing other diseases had been discovered and means of combating them had been devised. In 1903, Metchnikoff and Roux demonstrated the transmissibility of syphilis to apes, and in 1905, Schaudinn and Hoffmann discovered the causative organism. During this time, indirect methods for diagnosis were being perfected and in 1906 to 1907, Wassermann, Neisser, and Brück applied the complement-fixation reaction of Bordet and Gengou to syphilis. This reaction has since been known simply as the Wassermann test (blood test—B. T.—or serological test for syphilis—S. T. S.).

Blood Tests

Since the introduction of the Wassermann test, many methods of testing the blood serum of patients suspected of having syphilis have been devised. The Eagle, Hinton, Kahn, Kline, VDRL, Mazzini, and Rein-Bossak tests are but a few of the American tests in use, and practically every country has its own modification.

All serological tests depend on the detection of an antibody produced in the blood serum by the syphilitic infection. It is now known that the above-listed classic tests are far from specific and have given erroneous results in a wide variety of unrelated diseases, such as respiratory infections, malaria, small-pox vaccination, leprosy, and others. This has often led to an unwarranted diagnosis of syphilis in a great many patients and to much unnecessary treatment. Fortunately, this confusion is now resolving with the introduction of the newer specific tests such as the Treponema Pallidum Immobilization (TPI) (Nelson and Mayer), Treponema Pallidum Complement-Fixation (TPCF), Reiter Protein Complement-Fixation (RPCF), and others. These newer tests reach such a degree of specificity that a negative result almost certainly will rule out a diagnosis of syphilis.

The combined use of a specific serological test and a specific curative drug, penicillin, has made for a more relaxed management and follow-up of the disease. Although it still is necessary to search out sources of infection, one can now avoid throwing patients into a constant state of apprehension with repeated blood tests, often for a lifetime, and a surveillance that has often compromised occupation, marriage, pregnancy, and social life. Now that standards of blood testing and treatment have been clarified, it is hoped that included in the benefits of disease eradication will be the erasure of stigma, shame, and syphilophobia which previously were fostered by uncertain diagnosis and treatment.

Etiology and Epidemiology

The etiological agent of syphilis is a corkscrew-shaped organism known as the *Treponema* (Greek, spiral thread) *pallidum* (Latin, pale). *T. pallidum* has a cylindrical body with eight to fourteen rigid spirals and is best seen with the aid of a dark-field microscope. The organism is difficult to stain and culture.

Far from being the great scourge, it has recently become apparent that syphilis can be a benign disease in 50 per cent of all infected persons. From the Boeck-Bruusgaard studies, begun in the 1890's and now nearing completion, several facts emerge. Among patients who acquire early syphilis and who receive no treatment, some 50 per cent will not experience any disability or inconvenience, some 25 per cent will be left with residual evidence of the disease but no disability or shortening of their life span, and some 25 per cent will experience serious disability from late manifestations or be killed by it.

After *T. pallida* have entered the body, they multiply and disseminate through the blood stream to all organs. In an untreated patient, the subsequent events have been divided by tradition into the following stages: early infectious syphilis, latent syphilis, and late syphilis.

Early Syphilis

Syphilis may be regarded as early at any time within two years after infection. During this period, all or almost all of the contagious skin and mucous membrane lesions will have occurred. This stage is subdivided into primary and secondary syphilis.

PRIMARY SYPHILIS

The primary lesion of acquired syphilis, the chancre, develops at the point of inoculation, usually within two to six weeks and most commonly on the anogenital organs. These lesions, however, have also been described on the lip, mouth, fingers, and breast. The chancre usually begins as a small red papule that becomes eroded and moist. Frequently, there is nothing characteristic about it and it may or may not be hard. There may be multiple chancres. The only other sign at this stage is a firm, painless, movable, swollen lymph gland at the site of regional lymph drainage; when the chancre is on the penis, the gland would appear in the groin.

The duration of the primary lesion varies considerably. In all cases, however, chancres are self-limited and heal without treatment. The secondary lesions of syphilis generally develop before the chancre disappears, but occasionally the primary lesion heals before other manifestations are noted. The primary and secondary stages may overlap or may be separated by variable periods of time.

During the early part of the primary stage or before it, the microorganisms leave the blood stream and invade the other tissues of the body. This generalized invasion of the body by treponemes usually results in the development of lesions that characterize the secondary stage of the disease.

SECONDARY SYPHILIS

The lesions of secondary syphilis develop anywhere from two to six months after infection and represent the initial reactions of various tissues, especially skin and mucous membrane, to the organisms carried to them by the blood and lymphatics. These lesions, as well as the chancre, contain treponemes in large numbers and their demonstration in the skin and mucous-membrane lesions by dark-field microscopic examination is diagnostic.

Cutaneous manifestations of syphilis show great variability in appearance. The more commonly seen are oval, scaly, and red areas; reddish-brown papular lesions; scaly, flat, discoid patches; moist, macerated, wartlike lesions in the body folds; flat, gray erosions on the mucous membranes of the mouth, anus, or vulva; and papules and nodules on the palms and soles. The lesions occur in such a wide variety that they may be confused with many nonsyphilitic skin conditions.

Constitutional reactions, ordinarily mild, are very common in early syphilis. These consist principally of headache, malaise, low-grade fever, sore throat, and occasional faint pains.

As a rule, the secondary lesions are not destructive and heal without scar formation in varying periods of time, even without treatment. Usually, they disappear within a few weeks or months but occasionally they persist for as long as a year. They are ordinarily painless and do not itch. The serological blood tests are always positive at this stage.

Latent Syphilis

In following the course of an untreated syphilis, we now enter the latent period. This is the phase of the disease, seen at least two years after the initial infection, in which there are no clinical signs and symptoms referable to syphilis. It is diagnosed solely by positive tests for syphilis in the blood serum and by a past history of the infection.

The diagnosis of latent syphilis is arrived at by exclusion and should be made with great care and only after thorough physical examination. It is in this group that unwarranted diagnoses were often made, since the old serological tests were nonspecific and not sensitive enough. Such "biologically false positive" reactors are much less frequently seen with the newer, more specific tests. In any case, the accurate diagnosis of latent syphilis has become in some respects an academic matter; the patient will probably receive antisyphilitic treatment eventually.

Late Benign Syphilis

As a general rule, overt manifestations of late syphilis do not appear until some ten years after infection. Many exceptions to this rule occur, but in the majority of patients, late syphilitic lesions are diagnosed between the tenth and thirteenth year after infection. They include an almost overwhelming multiplicity.

The skin lesions of late syphilis consist of gummas and grouped nodules. A gumma begins as a small tumor that breaks down to form an ulcer that may be single or multiple and can occur anywhere on the cutaneous surface. Gummas cause marked destruction and heal with scarring. The grouped nodules, reddish in color, can often be recognized by their arcuate and ringed configuration. The lesions of late syphilis are noninfectious and are devoid of treponemes.

Late lesions may occur in the mouth, tongue, and throat with the production of thickenings or ulcerative destruction. Bones, joints, eyes, and most other organs may be similarly involved in the chronic inflammatory process.

The term "cardiovascular syphilis" is used to describe syphilis of the aorta and heart, a most serious form of the disease. The inflammation of the aorta leads to a weakness of its wall and an outpocketing, known as a saccular aneurysm. The sac may progress to large dimensions and eventually rupture, with fatal results.

The term "neurosyphilis" is used to describe late syphilis of the brain and spinal cord. Because the syphilitic changes in the central nervous system may be diffuse or focal, there is no limit to the variety of clinical manifestations that can appear. General paresis and tabes dorsalis are the main forms of neurosyphilis, but the disease may take the form of meningitis, cerebral hemorrhage, brain tumor, deafness, blindness, mental disturbance, and epilepsy.

Syphilis in Pregnancy and Congenital Syphilis

Penicillin therapy is so effective in this regard that even if treatment is given late in pregnancy when the fetus is already infected, active congenital syphilis after birth may be completely prevented.

If infection with syphilis has taken place in the newborn, the earliest manifestations resemble those of the secondary stage and the lesions are heavily seeded with organisms. In addition, cartilage, bones, and brain may be involved. Later in childhood and in early adult life, congenital syphilis may cause involvement of any organ or system and produce clinical pictures similar to the acquired disease.

Treatment of Syphilis

The therapeutic agent of choice for all types of syphilis is penicillin. It is so far superior to any previous method of treatment as to supplant it completely. It is capable of producing biological cure of the disease in a proportion of cases that approaches 100 per cent. Since Mahoney introduced this therapy in 1942, no treponemes have been found to be resistant to the drug. Courses of treatment vary from one injection to a dozen, depending upon the stage of the disease and the form of the drug used.

When penicillin is contraindicated in the penicillin-sensitive patient, some of the other antibiotics, such as Aureomycin and Terramycin, may be given by mouth with equally felicitous results.

Nonvenereal Syphilis (Endemic Syphilis)

It has recently become clear that there exists a closely related group of infections, all caused by treponemal organisms, that under different environmental conditions can develop similar clinical syndromes. Hudson (1958) and others even think in terms of a single worldwide disease, "treponematoses," that had its ancient origin in Africa, gradually spread, and, in so doing, may have altered its character from nonvenereal to venereal.

It seems reasonable, therefore, to consider the treponemal diseases or treponematoses from the epidemiological point of view as (1) nonvenereal juvenile infections occurring in endemic form and contracted in childhood, and (2) venereal infections occurring in sporadic form, contracted during sexual activities and numerically far less frequent than the endemic form. Venereal syphilis as described in this article belongs to this group.

Nonvenereal or endemic syphilis affects masses of population in many countries and comprises similar or identical conditions with different local names:

Yaws	the endemic treponematosis of the tropics				
Pinta	"	"	"	"	Central America
Bejel	"	"	"	"	Iraq and Syria
Njovera	"	"	"	"	Southern Rhodesia
Dechuchwa	"	"	"	"	Bechuanaland
Siti	"	"	"	"	British West Africa

All these are basically endemic syphilitic infections that are acquired in infancy. They are at present being widely attacked with penicillin therapy in widespread eradication campaigns under the sponsorship of the World Health Organization. Besides sharing a close cross immunity, indistinguishable causative organisms, and similar host response with venereal syphilis, all of the above-listed treponemal diseases also show a uniformly excellent curative response to penicillin.

Gonorrhea (The Clap)

Gonorrhea (Greek, a flow of seed), the most prevalent of the venereal diseases, usually presents as an infective discharge of pus from the genitals. The causative organism is the gonococcus (*Neisseria gonorrhoeae*), and in the adult, nearly all cases are contracted during sexual intercourse with an infected person.

Unmistakable references to gonorrhea are contained in very early Chinese writings and in the Bible. Some medical historians consider that the Hebrew rite of circumcision may have been introduced as a preventive of balanitis, a frequent complication of gonorrhea. Galen, A.D. 130, first employed the term gonorrhea, translated as "flow of seed." During the late Middle Ages, gonorrhea was thought to be a manifestation of syphilis. This concept gained support from the classic error of John Hunter who, in 1767, misinterpreted the syphilis infection that resulted from self-inoculation with pus from the urethra of a patient supposedly infected only with gonorrhea. In 1830, Ricord properly delineated the two diseases. In 1879, Neisser identified the causative organism, which he called "gonococcus," and, several years later, it was cultivated on artificial media by Bumm. Interest in the disease attained special prominence in 1943, when the very striking susceptibility of the *N. gonorrhoeae* to penicillin was demonstrated.

The sites usually attacked are the urethra in the male and the urethra and cervix of the female. Spread then takes place to the surrounding regions, but the disease is usually restricted to the genitourinary locale. The rectum of both sexes may be infected either by direct extension from the genitals or by anal intercourse. Rarely, the organisms involve the skin and joints and, more rarely, the brain and blood. Accidental infection, although uncommon, may be acquired by children and from close contact with infected adults. The eyes of the newborn may be infected during delivery.

Gonorrhea in the Male

By far the most usual manifestation of gonorrhea in the male is an acute urethritis acquired during sexual intercourse with an infected woman. A rectal infection may be acquired by homosexuals, while other patients may be rare victims of an accidental gonococcal conjunctivitis. Dirty toilet seats, dirty towels, exercise, and strains have no part in causing the disease.

SIGNS AND SYMPTOMS

The most striking feature is a creamy, greenish-yellow discharge from the penis. This occurs after an incubation period of from two to seven days following sexual intercourse. At the onset, the discharge is thin and watery but becomes full-blown in 24 to 48 hours. The discharge is sometimes asymptomatic, but usually it is accompanied by burning on urination, most often felt at the tip of the penis, which is somewhat red and swollen. As the infection passes backward along the urethra, pain and burning on urination become more severe, and this is often combined with a distressing desire to pass urine continually. With much inflammation, painful erections may become quite a problem.

COMPLICATIONS OF GONORRHEA IN THE MALE

If untreated, the infection may gradually spread and extend itself to produce local and general complications. Local involvement is restricted to the genitourinary tract and includes lymphangitis, periurethral abscess, prostatitis, vesiculitis, epididymitis, cystitis, and urethral stricture. Of the acute complications, epididymitis is the most agonizing, with its attendant pain and marked swelling of the structures leading to the testis, the swellings often reaching the size of an orange. Occasionally, the organism breaks the bounds of the genitourinary area and becomes blood-borne to produce complications of a more generalized nature. The most important of these are arthritis, iritis, conjunctivitis, skin infections, and more rarely endocarditis or meningitis. Associated with fever, malaise, and marked debility, these complications, prior to the introduction of modern antibiotics, occasionally resulted in death.

DIAGNOSIS

The diagnosis of gonorrhea is made in the laboratory. The identification of the organism is made by microscopic and culture examination of a drop of urethral pus.

Gonorrhea in the Female

In acute gonorrhea, the patient will usually complain of a vaginal discharge. The vulva may be red, raw, and irritated and give a sensation of pain and burning. A certain amount of burning and frequency of urination may also be present.

COMPLICATIONS

Two distinct and specific complications arise in females: infection of the vulvovaginal glands (bartholinitis) and infection of the uterine tubes (salpingitis).

In bartholinitis, a large, tender, painful swelling appears on one or both sides of the vulva. This abscess may rupture spontaneously, discharging thick pus, or progress onward to a fixed, nontender, firm cyst that must be removed surgically.

Salpingitis is associated in its acute stage with severe lower abdominal pain on one or both sides, and with tenderness, malaise, and fever. Sometimes the acute attack does not entirely resolve, leading to tubal abscess on one or both sides. Such lesions cause a great deal of colicky abdominal pain, menstrual irregularity, sterility, and chronic invalidism. They frequently require surgical treatment.

Gonorrhea in Children

Gonorrhea in the child is usually the result of accidental nonvenereal infection, although sexual assault, mutual masturbation, or sexual exploration and experimentation may be involved in the etiology. It is very uncommon in male children and runs a course similar to that in the adult. Most frequently, it attacks female children, wherein it produces an inflammation of the vulva and vagina with little or no spread to other organs. The child complains of soreness of the vulva, and burning on urination may be present. The vulva is red and swollen and a purulent vaginal discharge swarming with organisms may be obvious. Then again, as in the adult female, the discharge may be watery and contain but few organisms. The anorectal region is frequently involved.

Gonococcal Ophthalmia

Gonococcal ophthalmia was at one time responsible for one-third of all cases of blindness in children. This incidence was drastically decreased upon the adoption of the Credé procedure of instilling a drop of a 1 per cent solution of silver nitrate into the eyes of the newborn immediately after birth. This procedure has since been replaced by the use of penicillin locally.

The conjunctiva of infants is very vulnerable to the gonococcus and infection is conveyed to the child during parturition, usually during passage through the infected cervix. When such invasion has occurred, symptoms are apparent within 48 hours. Clinical signs include edema of one or both eyelids, frequently bilateral, and a free discharge of pus. The conjunctivae will be red. In severe cases, clouding of the cornea, then ulceration and perforation that involves the complete eye takes place.

Prophylaxis just after birth with either silver nitrate or penicillin has largely eliminated gonorrheal ophthalmia in children. If it does occur, the prognosis is excellent with the early instillation of penicillin into the eye at frequent intervals. This may be combined with injections of penicillin. The prognosis is good in cases uncomplicated by ulceration and gross destruction. If the latter irreversible damage has occurred, scarring and blindness may result.

Treatment of Gonorrhea

The disease can now be cured easily with the newer antibiotics. Penicillin is the most commonly used, although the sulfonamides, the tetracyclines, streptomycin, chloramphenicol, and others are also effective. Complications such as urethral stricture, chronic salpingitis, and chronic arthritis may require special surgical or physical therapies.

Chancroid
(Ulcus Molle, Soft Chancre)

Chancroid is an acute auto-inoculable, genito-infectious disease caused by the streptobacillus of Ducrey (*Hemophilus ducreyi*), characterized by ulcerations at the sites of inoculation and frequently accompanied by swelling and suppuration of the local lymph glands.

Chancroid was differentiated from syphilis by Bassereau (1852) and Ducrey (1889), who described the causative organism. Nicolle (1899) reproduced the infection in monkeys and Greenblatt and Sanderson (1937) established the human disease. Ito (1913) prepared the first vaccine from cultures of *H. ducreyi* and Reenstierna (1920) used it for skin-testing. The test has since become known as the "Ito-Reenstierna test."

Clinical Characteristics

About 12 to 36 hours after sexual intercourse, the disease begins as an inflamed papule or pustule, which soon breaks down to form a ragged ulceration. The edges of the ulceration are irregular and the crater is partially filled with a dirty-gray slough. Chancroidal ulcers are always painful and usually bleed easily on manipulation. They vary in size from a few millimeters to two centimeters. On occasion, they can extend to gigantic proportions and destroy large areas of skin.

The ulcer may remain single but usually becomes multiple following auto-inoculation. These secondary lesions appear on areas in direct apposition or as small satellite ulcers.

The organism has a preference for the skin; rarely are the mucous membranes affected. In the male, the lesion is often on the prepuce, especially at its internal surface, and on the frenum and penile shaft. In women, it is located usually on the labia majora, vestibule, or clitoris. There may be extension to the perineum, thighs, abdomen, and anus.

In about one-third of the cases, the regional lymph glands of the groin may be involved. This inguinal adenitis or bubo (Greek, *boubon* —the groin, a swelling in the groin) is usually on one side but may be bilateral. A painful and tender swelling arises approximately two weeks postinoculation. The swelling increases, the overlying skin reddens, thins, and finally ruptures, leaving a ragged, purulent ulceration that may slowly extend up and down the groin area. If not treated, the ulcerations can last and drain for months.

Diagnosis

The demonstration of *Hemophilus ducreyi* in material from the ulcer or from the affected lymph gland is definite proof of the chancroidal nature of the lesion. However, the culture of Ducrey bacillus is difficult and requires special media, and, although diagnostically reliable, is seldom done in practice. A Ducrey vaccine skin test (Ito-Reenstierna test) is often of value in establishing a diagnosis: a positive reaction indicates that the patient has or has had a Ducrey infection.

Chancroid may be contracted simultaneously with other venereal diseases. Combinations with syphilis, lymphogranuloma venereum, granuloma inguinale, and gonorrhea present bizarre clinical pictures that require expert interpretation of clinical, laboratory, and serological findings.

Treatment

With proper treatment, an absolute cure of chancroid can be obtained in every instance. The most effective drugs are the sulfonamides, with sulfadiazine as the drug of choice. Certain of the other antibiotics have also been found effective: streptomycin, chlortetracycline, oxytetracycline, and tetracycline. Duration of treatment varies from three to eight days. Within 24 hours pain decreases, the lesions become drier, pus is no longer formed, and the ulcer commences to heal.

Lymphogranuloma Venereum (Lymphopathia Venerea, Climatic Bubo, Maladie de Nicolas et Favre)

Lymphogranuloma venereum is a systemic disease manifested by both constitutional symptoms and acute and chronic tissue changes in the inguinal and anorectal regions. It is caused by a virus similar to the virus that causes psittacosis.

In 1913, Durand, Nicolas, and Favre recognized lymphogranuloma venereum as an independent disease and reported the first clinical and pathological descriptions. Definite proof of its specificity was made by Frei with the skin test that bears his name. Hellerstrom and Wassen in 1930 transmitted the disease to monkeys, and Rake, McKee, and Shaffer cultured the virus on the yolk sac of a chick embryo.

Symptoms

The disease process usually includes the following stages: (1) invasion by the viral agent, usually unnoticed, (2) primary stage: genital or anorectal lesion, (3) invasion of lymph nodes, (4) late sequelae due to fibrotic changes in or around lymph nodes (Coutts, 1950).

Only a few days may elapse between sexual contact and the appearance of the primary lesion. This appears as a small blister that soon bursts, leaving a shallow, grayish ulcer with clear-cut edges, not hard, and surrounded by reddened skin. It is usually painless and heals rapidly without leaving a scar. These fleeting lesions appear on the glans and prepuce of the penis, the vulva, the vaginal walls, or the cervix. Initial lesions may also be found within the urethra or in the anal region. If picked up during cunnilinctus, the virus can produce blistering and swelling of the tongue, followed by enlarged glands in the neck. Conjunctivitis due to lymphogranulomatous infection has also been reported.

The secondary stage—enlargement of the local lymph glands—usually takes place seven to fourteen days later. Pain in the groin, followed by palpable and visible enlargement of the lymph nodes, may be the only symptoms. These buboes become adherent to the underlying tissues and soon form a large, single, tender inflammatory mass which, in the majority of patients, breaks down and suppurates. This inguinal adenitis may be unilateral but frequently it is bilateral. When the initial lesion is intra-urethral or anorectal, the infection spreads to the pelvic nodes, whereas an initial infection of the vagina spreads to the perianal and deep pelvic nodes.

The tertiary stage presents itself in well-defined syndromes or in isolated or associated manifestations in different organs or systems. The more easily recognized are elephantiasis of the penis, scrotum, or vulva; urethrogenito-perineal syndromes; rectal stenosis; and plastic induration of the penis. Left untreated, the disease may lead to broken-down infected communications between the rectum and vagina or between the rectum and bladder that can result in exhaustion and death from sepsis. The adenitis is accompanied by constitutional symptoms consisting of chills, sweats, fever, prostration, loss of weight, nausea, vomiting, headache, stiffness of the neck, and bronchitis. Acute systemic invasion by the virus may bring about enlargement of all lymphatic nodes, the spleen, and the liver. A fatal termination is very rare but may occur in patients with rectal strictures and other complications.

Diagnosis

The diagnosis of lymphogranuloma venereum is not readily made in the laboratory. The cultivation and identification of the virus in material taken from an infected patient is not a procedure easily available to the physician. Apart from the clinical picture, the Frei skin test has a high specificity and should be done in every suspected patient. This test consists of the intradermal injection of antigenic material prepared from ten-day chick embryos that have been injected with the virus. The test is positive if, after 72 hours, a papule of at least 7 mm. in diameter appears at the site of injection. A positive Frei test indicates that the patient has been at some time infected with the virus of lymphogranuloma venereum. A complement-fixation serum test should also be done since it gives results parallel with those of the skin test.

Treatment

The results obtained in the treatment of lymphogranuloma venereum are less satisfactory than are those in syphilis, gonorrhea, chancroid, and granuloma inguinale. The introduction of the sulfonamides, the tetracyclines, and chloramphenicol has improved the prognosis of the disease, but it cannot be said that the available medications are effective in every instance. In cases of inguinal adenitis, the outlook is good. Advanced rectal strictures and large masses may require extensive surgical and plastic repair. In many instances, in spite of available treatment, it is impossible to eradicate the disease.

Granuloma Inguinale (Granuloma Venereum, Donovanosis)

Granuloma inguinale is a chronic infectious disease that is characterized by extensive ulceration and scarring of the skin and subcutaneous tissues, particularly of the genitals but also involving extragenital sites. The condition is auto-inoculable and only slightly transmissible, as evidenced by the fact that the marital partner seldom becomes infected. The term "venereal" may not be appropriate because in many cases infection is probably not conveyed by sexual intercourse.

An early reference to the disease was made by MacLeod (1882). Donovan (1905) found organisms in the cells of infected tissue. Anderson (1943) was able successfully to cultivate these organisms on yolk sacs of chick embryos and thereupon named them *Donovania granulomatis* (*Klebsiella granulomatis*).

The disease is widely distributed in tropical and subtropical regions. It is also found in temperate zones and in the United States, mostly in the southern states.

Symptoms

The disease commences as a small red papule or nodule, most frequently on the penis or labia. Initial sites may also be the groins, anus, rectum, face, and neck. The lesions increase in size, break down, and, as ulcerations coalesce, spread. The spread is along the creases of the groins and down to the perineum and perianal regions. Usually the attack is limited to the skin and adjacent mucous membrane. A striking feature and a diagnostic one is the absence of lymph-node involvement. Extension is slow and relentless with no tendency to spontaneous healing. As the tissues are destroyed they are replaced by red, moist, fetid, and oozing granulation tissue that is friable and bleeding. The total process is capable of marked destruction of the genitalia, all being replaced by thick scar tissue. Systemic manifestations are usually minimal, rectal strictures being the most difficult to treat.

Diagnosis

This is by microscopic examination for the organism in stained smears. The material should be collected by scraping the edges of very active lesions, and the search for the organism should be prolonged and careful, for at times it is difficult to find. The organism is exceptionally difficult to cultivate, as it does not readily grow on any of the common laboratory media.

Treatment

It has definitely been proven that streptomycin, aureomycin, terramycin, erythromycin, chloramphenicol, and oleandomycin are of value. Within 48 hours after the start of treatment the lesions become drier and cleaner. Pain disappears, healthy granulation tissue develops, and in one to two weeks complete healing with scar formation takes place. Complete cure may be obtained in practically every case with judicious use of the available medications.

Prophylaxis of Venereal Diseases

Prophylactic kits containing ointments, tubes, gauze bags, and other paraphernalia have now been largely abandoned. Their use required such time and effort, often not available, that they were found to be impractical.

The simplest and best prophylactic, and one that should be routine for all males, is the use of a condom during intercourse and of soap-and-water washing after intercourse. For women, an antiseptic vaginal douche and a similar soap-and-water washing of the genitals are recommended.

During the war large groups of military personnel were given, on an experimental basis, oral antibiotics prior to sexual exposure. This was found to be an adequate venereal disease preventive. The adaptation of this method to civilian life, however, presents problems that so far have not been solved.

References

Canizares, O., *Modern Diagnosis and Treatment of the Minor Venereal Diseases.* Springfield, Ill.: Charles C Thomas, 1954.

Greenblatt, R. B., Barfield, W. E., Dienst, R. B., West, R. M., and Zises, M., "A Five-Year Study of Antibiotics in the Treatment of Granuloma Inguinale." *Am. J. Syph., Gon. & Ven. Dis. 36;* 182, 1952.

Grin, E. I., "Endemic Syphilis and Yaws." *Bull. World Health Org. 15;* 959, 1956.

Guthe, T., and Willcox, R. R., "Treponematoses: A World Problem." *Chron. World Health Org. 8;* 37, 1954.

Hudson, E. H., *Non-Venereal Syphilis.* Edinburgh: E. & S. Livingstone, 1958.

James, E. B., "Premarital Intercourse, Venereal Disease and Young People." *Public Health, LXIXX;* 258, 1965.

Kanof, N. B., Blau, S., and Rein, C. R., "Syphilis." In Wohl, M. (ed.), *Long-Term Illness.* Philadelphia: W. B. Saunders Co., 1959, p. 500.

King, A., *Recent Advances in Venereology.* Boston: Little, Brown and Co., 1964.

King, A. and Nicol, C., *Venereal Diseases.* Philadelphia: F. A. Davis and Co., 1964.

MacAlpine, I., "Syphilophobia." *Brit. J. Ven. Dis. 33;* 92, 1957.

Rein, C. R., and Kitchen, D. K., "Mass Eradication Treatment of Treponemal Diseases with Penicillin. Laboratory and Clinical Basis for Selection of Effective Schedules." *Am. J. Syph., Gon. & Ven. Dis. 37;* 37, 1953.

Sigal, M. Michael (ed.), *Lymphogranuloma Venereum.* Florida: University of Miami Press, 1962.

Stokes, J. H., Beerman, H., and Ingraham, N. R., *Modern Clinical Syphilology.* Philadelphia: W. B. Saunders Co., 1944.

Thomas, E., "Current Status of Therapy in Syphilis." *J. A. M. A. 162;* 1536, 1956.

Turner, T. B., and Hollander, D. H., "The Biology of the Treponematoses." *World Health Org. Monogr. Series No. 35,* Geneva, 1957.

Willcox, R. R., *Text-Book of Venereal Diseases and Treponematoses.* Springfield, Ill.: Charles C. Thomas, 2nd Edition, 1964.

Youmans, J. B. (ed.), *Syphilis and other Venereal Diseases.* The Medical Clinics of North America. Philadelphia: W. B. Saunders Co., Vol. 48, No. 3, May 1964.

SAUL BLAU

Index

Fragonard, Jean Honoré, 175
France
  aging in, 397
  censorship, 243–244
  contraception, 381
  divorce, 383
  education in family living,
    703–704
  homosexuality, 382
  literature, 243–244, 633
  marriage, 667
  marriage counseling, 694
  nudism, 276
  phallicism, 822
  planned parenthood, 829
  premarital coitus, 507
  prostitution in, 872, 873
  reform movements, 378–379, 958
  role of the sexes in, 396
  social dancing in, 327
Franklin, Benjamin, 83–84, 277,
    361, 638
Frazer, Sir James, 188, 189
Frazier, E. Franklin, 362
Frederick I, Emperor, 872
Free Enquirer, 84
Free Inquiries, 84–85
Free love, 85–86, 667
Freed, S. C., 908
Freedom (sexual), 439–449
  Arapesh, 443
  Comfort on, 446
  defined, 439–440
  A. Ellis on, 447
  H. Ellis on, 446–447
  Kinsey on, 447
  McDougall on, 445–446
  Mace on, 446
  Manus, 441
  Marquesans, 443
  Medieval English, 441–442
  modern Scandinavians, 444
  Mohler on, 446
  Oneida Community, 445
  Puritans, 442
  Shakers, 440–441
  Sorokin on, 446
  Stokes on, 447
  trends in, 447–448
  Trobrianders, 444–445
  twentieth-century Americans,
    442–443
  U.S.S.R., 443–444
  Victorians, 442
Freeman, Linton, 303
Frei, 1029
French, E., 787
French kissing, 813
French Revolution, 375
French Society for Prehistoric
    Studies, 820
Freud, Anna, 891–892, 893

Freud, Sigmund, 28, 33, 66, 154,
    188–189, 347, 364, 636,
    639, 647, 767, 824, 889–
    896, 956, 960, 968, 976
  Adler and, 893
  on the artist, 315, 320
  on beauty, 163
  on child sexuality, 285
  childhood theories, 258–260
  on frigidity, 451
  on homosexuality, 486, 487–488
  on jealousy, 567, 569, 570
  on masochism, 806, 807
  religious skepticism of, 886
  revaluation of, 959
  on sex symbolism, 824
  on sexual abstinence, 45, 46
  on sublimation and art, 164–
    169
Freyre, Gilberto, 610
Frías, Heriberto, 599
Frigidity, 190, 450–456
  defined, 450
  divorce and, 616–617
  organic causes, 450–451
  psychological causes, 451
    ignorance, 453
    sex shame, 451–453
  relationship causes, 451
  stress and, 1010
  treatment, 453–455
    medical, 454–455
    psychological, 454–455
    self-therapy, 453–454
Friml, Rudolf, 755
Fromm, Erich, 171, 985
Frottage, 807
Fruits of Philosophy, The
    (Bradlaugh and Besant),
    958
Fruits of Philosophy; or The
    Private Companion of Young
    Married People (Knowl-
    ton), 85, 87, 237, 460
Frumkin, Robert M., 363
Fuch, Edward, 175
Function of the Orgasm, The
    (Reich), 742
Functions and Disorders of the
    Reproductive Organs, The
    (Acton), 457

Gabor, Eva, 216
Gagnon, John, 973
Gainsborough, Thomas, 162
Galbraith, Anna M., 218–219
Galen, 1027
Galopin, A., 976
Galton, Sir Francis, 366–367,
    899
Gamarra, López de, 602
Gamble, 1006

Gandhi, Mahatma, 641, 830
Gaon, Elijah, 578
Garden, Mary, 750
Garland, Madge, 161, 163
Garrison, 106
Gastronomic terminology, 593–596
Gathings, E. C., 243
Gauguin, Paul, 172
Gautama Buddha, 884
Gautier, Théophile, 636
Gavotte (dance), 327
Gebhard, Paul H., 35, 205, 862,
    866, 973
Geddes, P., 764
Geiger, K., 444
Geishas, 799
Gender-role imprinting, 476–478
General Adaptation Syndrome
    (G.A.S.), 782, 1010
Genet, Jean, 238
Genetics, 760–763
  sexual perversions, 802
Gengou, 1023
Genius, The (Dreiser), 242
Geriatrics, 75
Germany
  abortion, 383
  artificial insemination, 381
  contemporary dance, 314, 323,
    324
  contraception, 381
  divorce, 383
  education in family living, 704
  homosexuality, 382
  marriage counseling, 693
  nudism, 274–276, 277
  planned parenthood, 828–829
  premarital coitus in, 507
  reform movements, 378, 957,
    958, 960–962
  role of the sexes in, 395
  youth revolt in, 397
Germinal (Zola), 781
Gerontological Society, 77
Gerontosexuality, 810
Gershwin, George, 753
Gesell, Arnold, 932
Gibbon, Edward, 637
Gide, André, 163
Giedt, F. H., 205
Gifford, 834
Gift from the Sea (Lindbergh), 927
Gilles de la Tourette's syndrome,
    589
Gillray, James, 162
Girdles, 222, 223
Glasgow, Maude, 876
Glass, S. J., 808
Glover, Edward, 157, 879
Gluck, Christoph Willibald, 749
Glückliche Hand, Die (Schöen-
    berg), 750